Brazil

THE ROUGH GUIDE

WITHDRAWN

There are more than one hundred Rough Guide titles
covering destinations from Amsterdam to Zimbabwe

Forthcoming titles include
Chile • Indonesia • Maya World • New England

Rough Guide Reference Series
Classical Music • European Football • The Internet • Jazz
Opera • Reggae • Rock Music • World Music

Rough Guide Phrasebooks
Czech • Egyptian Arabic • French • German • Greek
Hindi and Urdu • Hungarian • Indonesian • Italian • Japanese
Mandarin Chinese • Mexican Spanish • Polish • Portuguese
Russian • Spanish • Thai • Turkish • Vietnamese

ROUGH GUIDE CREDITS

Text editor: Paul Gray
Series editor: Mark Ellingham
Editorial: Martin Dunford, Jonathan Buckley, Samantha Cook, Jo Mead, Kate Berens, Amanda Tomlin, Ann-Marie Shaw, Sarah Dallas, Chris Schüler, Helena Smith, Julia Kelly, Caroline Osborne, Judith Bamber, Kieran Falconer, Olivia Eccleshall (UK); Andrew Rosenberg (US)

Production: Susanne Hillen, Andy Hilliard, Judy Pang, Link Hall, Nicola Williamson, Helen Ostick
Cartography: Melissa Flack, David Callier, Maxine Burke
Online Editors: Alan Spicer (UK); Geronimo Madrid (US)
Finance: John Fisher, Celia Crowley, Catherine Gillespie
Marketing & Publicity: Richard Trillo, Simon Carloss, Niki Smith (UK); Jean-Marie Kelly, SoRelle Braun (US)
Administration: Tania Hummel, Alexander Mark Rogers

ACKNOWLEDGEMENTS

As authors and updaters, we should jointly like to thank all the staff of state and municipal tourist offices who have helped us, as well as editor Paul Gray, cartographer Sam Kirby, proofreader Jennifer Speake, and Narrell Leffman and Andy Young for Oz and US updates. Individually, we would like to thank:

Oliver – Graça Salgado and Eduardo Silva in Rio, and Fabiana Migliari and Claudia Erthal in São Paulo.

David – Romario, still.

Jens – Andréa Martos of Sebrae in Campo Grande; Joel Souza in Cuiabá; Aldo Silva for buying my drinks in Cuiabá without telling me; Sonia Maria da Silva

Oliveira on the Rio Urubú for her *caipirinha* and doughnuts; Alcides dos Santos Filho in Pirenópolis and all at Aravinda; Luciana, Érico and Lilian in Brasília for great nights failing to see Hale-Bopp; and most of all to Jacinta da Braga and family in Belo Horizonte for their kindness and hospitality, and to Rosane in São João del Rei, for beautiful days and Hale-Bopp at last!

Stephen – Johan Frijns for invaluable help updating the Northeast; Graziella Vieira at the Tourism Secretariat in Maranhão; and everyone from the tourist office in Sergipe.

PUBLISHING INFORMATION

This third edition published January 1998 by Rough Guides Ltd, 62–70 Shorts Gardens, London WC2H 9AB.
Reprinted in February 1999.
Distributed by the Penguin Group:
Penguin Books Ltd, 27 Wrights Lane, London W8 5TZ
Penguin Books USA Inc., 375 Hudson Street, New York 10014, USA
Penguin Books Australia Ltd, 487 Maroondah Highway, PO Box 257, Ringwood, Victoria 3134, Australia
Penguin Books Canada Ltd, 10 Alcorn Avenue, Toronto, Ontario, Canada M4V 1E4
Penguin Books (NZ) Ltd, 182–190 Wairau Road, Auckland 10, New Zealand
Typeset in Linotron Univers and Century Old Style to an original design by Andrew Oliver.
Printed in England by Clays Ltd, St Ives PLC.
Illustrations in Part One & Part Three by Edward Briant; illustration on p.1 by Dilwyn Jenkins and on p.599 by Henry Iles.

Brazil

THE ROUGH GUIDE

written and researched by

David Cleary, Dilwyn Jenkins
and Oliver Marshall

with additional contributions by

Stephen Cviic, Jens Finke and Jim Hine

THE ROUGH GUIDES

THE ROUGH GUIDES

TRAVEL GUIDES • PHRASEBOOKS • MUSIC AND REFERENCE GUIDES

 We set out to do something different when the first Rough Guide was published in 1982. Mark Ellingham, just out of university, was travelling in Greece. He brought along the popular guides of the day, but found they were all lacking in some way. They were either strong on ruins and museums but went on for pages without mentioning a beach or taverna. Or they were so conscious of the need to save money that they lost sight of Greece's cultural and historical significance. Also, none of the books told him anything about Greece's contemporary life – its politics, its culture, its people, and how they lived.

So with no job in prospect, Mark decided to write his own guidebook, one which aimed to provide practical information that was second to none, detailing the best beaches and the hottest clubs and restaurants, while also giving hard-hitting accounts of every sight, both famous and obscure, and providing up-to-the-minute information on contemporary culture. It was a guide that encouraged independent travellers to find the best of Greece, and was a great success, getting shortlisted for the Thomas Cook travel guide award,

and encouraging Mark, along with three friends, to expand the series.

The Rough Guide list grew rapidly and the letters flooded in, indicating a much broader readership than had been anticipated, but one which uniformly appreciated the Rough Guide mix of practical detail and humour, irreverence and enthusiasm. Things haven't changed. The same four friends who began the series are still the caretakers of the Rough Guide mission today: to provide the most reliable, up-to-date and entertaining information to independent-minded travellers of all ages, on all budgets.

We now publish 100 titles and have offices in London and New York. The travel guides are written and researched by a dedicated team of more than 100 authors, based in Britain, Europe, the USA and Australia. We have also created a unique series of phrasebooks to accompany the travel series, along with an acclaimed series of music guides, and a best-selling pocket guide to the Internet and World Wide Web. We also publish comprehensive travel information on our web site:

http://www.roughguides.com/

THE AUTHORS

An anthropologist by trade, **David Cleary** first went to Brazil in 1984 and has lived there for six years, off and on. He began by writing a thesis about Amazonian gold-mining, and went on to do research and lecture all over the North and Northeast. He currently works as a consultant, setting up environmental projects in the Amazon with Brazilian and European partners. He has never regretted the decision to work in Brazil – despite originally knowing little about the country – because he liked the music and loved the football.

Dilwyn Jenkins headed for South America after leaving school at 18. Since then he has gained an MA in Social Anthropology, written *The*

Rough Guide to Peru and other travel books, made films and written endless articles, mostly about the Amazon. These days, Dilwyn lives in Wales with his wife and four children, and specializes in rainforest, renewable energy, travel and environmental issues.

Oliver Marshall first visited Brazil in 1982 and has regularly returned for work, study and, above all, pleasure. Subjects for research have included ethnicity and immigration history in the South and Southeast, as well as poultry and pig production in western Santa Catarina. He is currently a Visiting Research Fellow at the University of London's Institute of Latin American Studies.

READERS' LETTERS

Thanks to those who wrote in with comments on the last edition

Bonnie Bloch; Katrine Bohn; Peter Clarke; Jonathan Cotterill; Sharon Dexter; Margaret Eno & John Quinn; Tom Fleagle; Kate Gooding; Kate Gregson; Ian Griffiths; Xanthe Hall; Claire Hands; Herbert Klein; Jojan Kraaykamp; Gopi Krishnan; Odd Karsten Krogh; Joe MacFarland; Iain Mackay; Bart Manche; Josileide Manning; Jon Miles; Mike Milner; Peter Milton; Olivia Nickel & Devin Kelso; Philip Pennefather; D. J. Plug; Louise Rands; Maria Helena Riley; Claire Ritchie; David Scott; Chris Shaw; John Sirnister; Anne-Margrethe Sonneland; Meike Stepp; Joris Verbeelen; Michael Whitney & Andrew Whelan; Joanna Wilkinson; George Luke Xuereb.

CONTENTS

• CHAPTER 3: THE NORTHEAST 199–314

• CHAPTER 4: THE AMAZON 315–388

• CHAPTER 5: BRASÍLIA, GOIÁS AND TOCANTINS 389–419

• CHAPTER 6: THE MATO GROSSO 420–465

• CHAPTER 7: SÃO PAULO 466–508

• CHAPTER 8: THE SOUTH 509–598

PART THREE CONTEXTS 599

BRAZIL'S REGIONS AND STATES

For political and administrative reasons, Brazil's 25 states and one federal district are divided into five regions, terms that are used throughout this book and which you will hear widely referred to in Brazil itself.

NORTH (THE AMAZON)
Acre
Amapá
Amazonas
Pará
Rondônia

CENTRE-WEST
Brasília (Federal District)
Goiás
Mato Grosso
Mato Grosso do Sul
Tocantins

NORTHEAST
Alagoas
Bahia
Ceará
Maranhão
Paraíba
Pernambuco
Piauí
Rio Grande do Norte
Sergipe

SOUTHEAST
Espírito Santo
Minas Gerais
Rio de Janeiro
São Paulo

SOUTH
Paraná
Rio Grande do Sul
Santa Catarina

LIST OF MAPS

MAP SYMBOLS

═══	Major road	⌐ℓℓℓ	Cliffs
═══	Minor road	⍭	Lighthouse
▬▬	Railway	⁗	Steps
─Ⓜ─	Metro station & line	▲	Mountain peak
─ ─	Ferry route	ⓘ	Tourist office
⋯⋯	Waterway	⊠	Post office
▬ ▬ ▬	Chapter division boundary	◉	Hotel
▬▪▬▪▬	International border	▣	Restaurant/bar
▬ ▬	State border	▮	Building
✕	Airport	┼	Church
★	Bus stop	⁺₊⁺	Cemetery
◔	Cave		Park
⅏	Marsh		National park
♆	Castle		Beach
⅏	Viewpoint		Swamp

INTRODUCTION

B
razilians often say they live in a continent rather than a country, and that's an excusable exaggeration. The landmass is bigger than the United States if you exclude Alaska; the journey from Recife in the east to the western border with Peru is longer than that from London to Moscow, and the distance between the northern and southern borders is about the same as that between New York and Los Angeles. Brazil has no mountains to compare with its Andean neighbours, but in every other respect it has all the scenic – and cultural – variety you would expect from so vast a country.

Despite the immense expanses of the interior, roughly two-thirds of Brazil's **population** live on or near the coast; and well over half live in cities – even in the Amazon. In Rio and São Paulo, Brazil has two of the world's great metropolises, and nine other cities have over a million inhabitants. Yet Brazil still thinks of itself as a frontier country, and certainly the deeper into the interior you go, the thinner the population becomes. In reality, though, the frontiers have been rapidly disappearing since the construction of the highway network in the Amazon in the 1960s.

Other South Americans regard Brazilians as a **race** apart, and language has a lot to do with it – Brazilians understand Spanish, just about, but Spanish-speakers won't understand Portuguese. More importantly, though, Brazilians look different. They're one of the most ethnically diverse peoples in the world: in the extreme south, German and Italian immigration has left distinctive European features; São Paulo has the world's largest Japanese community outside Japan; there's a large black population concentrated in Rio, Salvador and São Luis; while the Indian influence is most visible in the people of Amazonia and the Northeastern interior.

Brazil is a land of profound **economic** contradictions. Rapid postwar industrialization made Brazil one of the world's ten largest economies and put it among the most developed of Third World countries. But this has not improved the lot of the vast majority of Brazilians. The cities are dotted with *favelas*, shanty towns which crowd around the skyscrapers, and the contrast between rich and poor is one of the most glaring anywhere. There are wide **regional differerences**, too: Brazilians talk of a "Switzerland" in the Southeast, centred along the Rio–São Paulo axis, and an "India" above it; and although this is a simplification, it's true that the level of economic development tends to fall the further north you go. This throws up facts which are hard to swallow. Brazil is the industrial powerhouse of South America, but cannot feed and educate its people. In a country almost the size of a continent, the extreme inequalities in land distribution have led to land shortages but not to agrarian reform. Brazil has enormous natural resources but their exploitation so far has benefited just a few. The IMF and the greed of First World banks must bear some of the blame for this situation, but institutionalized corruption and the reluctance of the country's large middle class to do anything that might jeopardize its comfortable lifestyle are also part of the problem.

These difficulties, however, rarely seem to overshadow everyday life in Brazil. It's fair to say that nowhere in the world do people know how to enjoy themselves more – most famously in the annual orgiastic celebrations of **Carnaval**, but reflected, too, in the lively year-round nightlife that you'll find in any decent-sized town. This national hedonism also manifests itself in Brazil's highly developed **beach culture**; the country's superb **music** and dancing; rich regional **cuisines**; and in the most relaxed and tolerant attitude to **sexuality** – gay and straight – that you'll find anywhere in South America. And if you needed more reason to visit, there's a strength and variety of

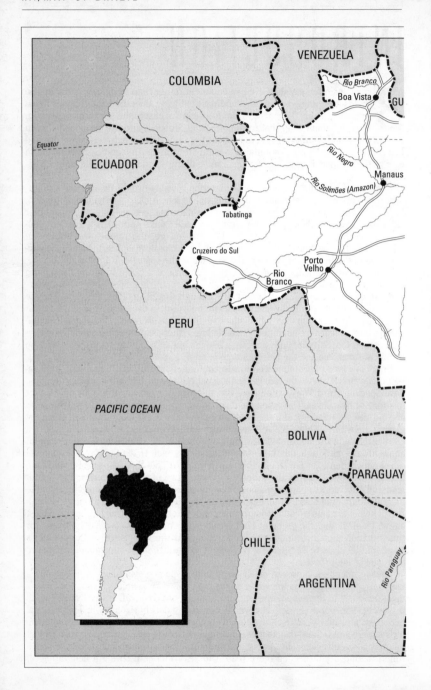

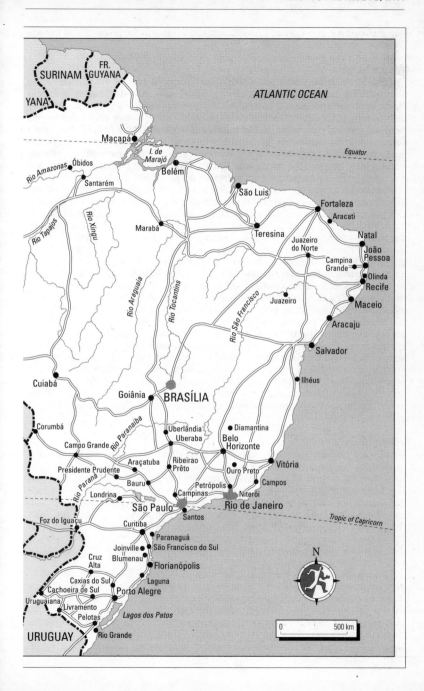

SURINAM FR. GUYANA

YANA

ATLANTIC OCEAN

Macapá

I. de Marajó

Equator

Rio Amazonas Óbidos

Santarém

Belém

São Luis

Fortaleza

Aracati

Natal

Marabá

Teresina

Juazeiro do Norte

João Pessoa

Campina Grande

Olinda

Recife

Juazeiro

Maceío

Aracaju

Salvador

Ilhéus

Cuiabá

Goiânia

BRASÍLIA

Corumbá

Rio Paranaíba

Uberlândia

Uberaba

Diamantina

Belo Horizonte

Campo Grande

Araçatuba

Ribeirao Prêto

Ouro Preto

Vitória

Présidente Prudente

Bauru

Campos

Londrina

Petrópolis

Campinas

Niterói

São Paulo

Rio de Janeiro

Foz do Iguaçu

Curitiba

Santos

Tropic of Capricorn

Paranaguá

Joinville

São Francisco do Sul

Cruz Alta

Blumenau

Florianópolis

Caxias do Sul

Laguna

Cachoeira de Sul

Porto Alegre

Uruguaiana

Livramento

Pelotas

Lagos dos Patos

URUGUAY

Rio Grande

Rio Tapajós

Rio Xingu

Rio Araguaia

Rio Tocantins

Rio São Francisco

Rio Paraná

N

0 500 km

popular culture, and a genuine friendliness and humour in the people that is tremendously welcoming and infectious.

Where to go

The most heavily populated and economically advanced part of the country is the Southeast, where the three largest cities – **São Paulo**, **Rio de Janeiro** and **Belo Horizonte** – form a triangle around which the economy pivots. All are worth visiting in their own right, though Rio, one of the world's most stupendously sited cities, stands head and shoulders above the lot. The **South**, encompassing the states of Paraná, Santa Catarina and Rio Grande do Sul, stretches down to the borders with Uruguay and northern Argentina, and westwards to Paraguay, and includes much of the enormous **Paraná** river system. The spectacular **Iguaçú Falls** (at the point where Brazil and Argentina meet) are one of the great natural wonders of South America.

The vast hinterland of the South and Southeast is often called the Centre-West and includes an enormous central plateau of savanna and rock escarpments, the **Planalto Central**. In the middle stands **Brasília**, the country's space-age capital, built from nothing in the late 1950s and still developing today. The capital is gateway to a vast interior, the **Mato Grosso**, only fully charted and settled over the last three decades; it includes the mighty **Pantanal** swampland, the richest wildlife reserve on the continent. North and west, the Mato Grosso shades into the **Amazon**, a mosaic of jungle, rivers, savanna and marshland that also contains two major cities – **Belém**, at the mouth of the Amazon itself, and **Manaus**, some 1600km upstream. The tributaries of the Amazon, rivers like the Tapajós, the Xingu, the Negro, the Araguaia or the Tocantins, are virtually unknown outside Brazil, but each is a huge river system in its own right.

The other major sub-region of Brazil is the **Northeast**, the part of the country that curves out into the Atlantic Ocean. This was the first part of Brazil to be settled by the Portuguese and colonial remains are thicker on the ground here than anywhere else in the country – notably in the cities of **Salvador** and **São Luis** and the lovely town of **Olinda**. It's a region of dramatic contrasts; a lush, tropical coastline with the best beaches in Brazil, slipping inland into the *sertão*, a semi-arid interior plagued by drought and appallingly unequal land distribution. All the major cities of the Northeast are on the coast – the two most famous are Salvador and **Recife**, both magical blends of Africa, Portugal and the Americas.

When to go

Brazil splits into four distinct **climatic** regions. The coldest part – in fact the only part of Brazil which ever gets really cold – is the **South and Southeast**, the region roughly from central Minas Gerais to Rio Grande do Sul, which includes Belo Horizonte, São Paulo and Porto Alegre. Here, there's a distinct winter between June and September, with occasional cold, wind and rain. However, although Brazilians complain, it's all fairly mild. Temperatures rarely hit freezing overnight, and when they do it's featured on the TV news. The coldest part is the interior of Rio Grande do Sul, in the extreme south of the country, but even here there are many warm, bright days in winter and the summer (Dec–March) is hot. Only in Santa Catarina's central highlands does it occasionally snow.

The **coastal climate** is exceptionally good. Brazil has been called a "crab civilization" because most of its population lives on or near the coast – with good reason. Seven thousand kilometres of coastline, from Paraná to near the equator, bask under a warm tropical climate. There is a "winter", when there are cloudy days and sometimes the temperature dips below 25°C (77°F), and a rainy season, when it can really pour. In Rio **the rains** last from October through to January, but they come much earlier in the Northeast, lasting about three months from April in Fortaleza and Salvador, and from May in Recife. Even in winter or the rainy season, the weather will be excellent much of the time.

The **Northeast** is too hot to have a winter. Nowhere is the average monthly temperature below 25°C (77°F) and the interior, semi-arid at the best of times, often soars beyond that – regularly to as much as 40°C (104°F). Rain is sparse and irregular, although violent. **Amazonia** is stereotyped as being steamy jungle with constant rainfall, but much of the region has a distinct dry season – apparently getting longer every year in the most deforested areas of east and west Amazonia. And in the large expanses of savanna in the northern and central Amazon basin, rainfall is far from constant. Belém is closest to the image of a steamy tropical city: it rains there an awful lot from January to May, and merely quite a lot for the rest of the year. Manaus and central Amazonia, in contrast, have a marked dry season from July to October.

AVERAGE TEMPERATURES (°C) AND RAINFALL

The first figure is the average **maximum** temperature; the second the average **minimum**; and the third the average number of rainy days per month

	Jan	Feb	Mar	Apr	May	Jun	Jul	Aug	Sep	Oct	Nov	Dec
Belém	31	30	30	31	31	32	32	32	32	32	32	32
	23	23	23	23	23	23	22	22	22	22	22	22
	24	26	25	22	24	15	14	15	13	10	11	14
Belo Horizonte	27	27	27	27	25	24	24	25	27	27	27	26
	18	18	17	16	12	10	10	12	14	16	17	18
	15	13	9	4	4	2	2	1	2	10	12	14
Brasília	27	28	28	28	27	26	26	28	30	29	27	27
	18	18	18	17	15	13	13	14	16	18	18	18
	19	16	15	9	3	1	0	2	4	11	15	20
Manaus	30	30	30	30	31	31	32	33	33	33	32	31
	23	23	23	23	24	23	23	24	24	24	24	24
	20	18	21	20	18	12	12	5	7	4	12	16
Porto Alegre	31	30	29	25	22	20	20	21	22	24	27	29
	20	20	19	16	13	11	10	11	13	15	17	18
	9	10	10	6	6	8	8	8	11	10	8	8
Recife	30	30	30	30	29	28	27	27	28	29	30	30
	25	25	24	23	23	22	21	22	22	23	24	24
	7	8	10	11	17	16	17	14	7	3	4	4
Rio de Janeiro	30	30	27	29	26	25	25	25	25	26	28	28
	23	23	23	21	20	18	18	18	19	20	20	22
	13	11	9	9	6	5	5	4	5	11	10	12
Salvador	29	29	29	28	27	26	26	26	27	28	28	29
	23	23	24	23	22	21	21	21	21	22	23	23
	6	9	17	19	22	23	18	15	10	8	9	11
São Paulo	28	28	27	25	23	22	21	23	25	25	25	26
	18	18	17	15	13	11	10	11	13	14	15	16
	15	13	12	6	3	4	4	3	5	12	11	14

GETTING THERE FROM BRITAIN

There are plenty of choices of carriers to Brazil, with Rio and São Paulo being the most usual destinations, although there are increasing numbers of flights to the Northeast. Direct flights are often fully booked well in advance and you may want to consider a flight via another European or South American country. You will almost always get the cheapest fares by booking through an agent rather than direct with the airlines. When buying your ticket to Brazil, you should consider the possibility of adding an air pass for travel within Brazil (see p.28).

To find the best deal, look in the travel classified pages of national newspapers such as the *Guardian* or *Observer*, or, for London departures, in the London listings magazine, *Time Out*. The **agents** and **operators** listed on p.4 also make a good start, all of which offer a wide range of flights at competitive prices. If you plan on purchasing some kind of air pass or want to book a hotel room for your first few days in Brazil, it is certainly easier to go through a specialist agent.

The independent travel specialist *STA Travel* offers some special discount flights, while **students** and anyone **under 26** can also try *Campus Travel*. Student union travel bureaux can usually fix you up with flights through one of these operators.

Depending on the airline, **children** pay between 50 and 67 percent of the discounted fares, while infants under the age of two generally pay 10 percent of the airline's cheapest official, non-discounted fare.

FLIGHTS AND FARES

Three airlines operate **direct flights** from Britain to Brazil, British Airways and the Brazilian carriers Varig (Brazilian Airlines) and Transbrasil. The official **APEX fares** of Varig and British Airways are generally identical, currently starting at £838 for a sixty-day return **to Rio or São Paulo** in low sea-

---

AIRLINES IN BRITAIN

Aerolíneas Argentinas 54 Conduit St, London W1 (☎0171/494 1001).

Air France 10 Warwick St, 1st Floor, London W1 (☎0181/742 6600).

Alitalia, 27–28 Piccadilly, London W1 (☎0171/602 7111).

Avianca Linen Hall, 162 Regent St, London W1 (☎0171/408 1889).

British Airways 156 Regent St, London W1 (☎0171/897 4000 or 0345/222 111).

Canadian Airlines International 15 Berkeley St, London W1(☎0181/667 0666 or 0345/616 767).

Iberia 29 Glasshouse St, London W1 (☎0171/830 0011).

KLM ☎0990/750900.

Lufthansa 10 Old Bond St, London W1; Phoenix House, 78 St Vincent St, Glasgow G2 (☎0345/737747).

TAP 19 Regent St, London SW1 (☎0171/839 1031).

Transbrasil Abbey House, Suite 311, 4 Abbey Orchard St, London SW1 (☎0171/976 7994).

United Airlines 193 Piccadilly, London W1 (☎0181/990 9900).

Varig Brazilian Airlines St George's House, 61 Conduit St, London W1 (☎0181/564 7555).

VASP ☎01293/523928.

AGENTS AND OPERATORS IN BRITAIN

Campus Travel, 52 Grosvenor Gardens, London SW1W 0AG (☎0171/730 8111); 541 Bristol Rd, Selly Oak, Birmingham B29 6AU (☎0121/414 1848); 61 Ditchling Rd, Brighton BN1 4SD (☎01273/570226); 37–39 Queen's Rd, Clifton, Bristol BS8 1QE (☎0117/929 2494); 5 Emmanuel St, Cambridge CB1 1NE (☎01223/324283); 53 Forest Rd, Edinburgh EH1 2QP (☎0131/225 6111); 166 Deansgate, Manchester M3 3FE (☎0161/833 2046); 105–106 St Aldates, Oxford OX1 1DD (☎01865/242067). Student/youth travel specialists, with branches also in YHA shops and on university campuses all over Britain.

The London Flight Centre, 131 Earls Court Rd, London SW5 9RH (☎0171/244 6411); 47 Notting Hill Gate, London W11 3JS (☎0171/727 4290); Shop 33, The Broadway Centre, Hammersmith, London W6 9YE (☎0181/748 6777). Long-established agent dealing in discount flights.

North South Travel, Moulsham Mill Centre, Parkway, Chelmsford, Essex CM2 7PX (☎01245/492882, fax 356612). Friendly, competitive travel agency, offering discounted fares worldwide – profits are used to support projects in the developing world, especially the promotion of sustainable tourism.

STA Travel, 86 Old Brompton Rd, London SW7 3LH, 117 Euston Rd, London NW1 2SX, 38 Store St, London WC1E 7BZ (☎0171/ 361 6262); 25 Queens Rd, Bristol BS8 1QE (☎0117/929 4399); 38 Sidney St, Cambridge CB2 3HX (☎01223/366966); 88 Vicar Lane, Leeds LS1 7JH (☎0113/244 9212); 75 Deansgate, Manchester M3 2BW (☎0161/834 0668); 36 George St, Oxford OX1 2OJ (☎01865/792800); and branches in Birmingham, Canterbury, Cardiff, Coventry, Durham, Glasgow, Loughborough, Nottingham, Sheffield and Warwick. Worldwide specialists in low-cost flights and tours for students and under-26s, though other customers welcome.

Trailfinders, 42–50 Earls Court Rd, London W8 6FT (☎0171/938 3366); 194 Kensington High St, London, W8 7RG (☎0171/938 3939); 58 Deansgate, Manchester M3 2FF (☎0161/839 6969); 254–284 Sauchiehall St, Glasgow G2 3EH (☎0141/353 2224); 22–24 The Priory, Queensway, Birmingham B4 6BS (☎0121/236 1234); and 48 Corn St, Bristol BS1 1HQ (☎0117/929 9000). One of the best-informed and most efficient agents for independent travellers; they produce a very useful quarterly magazine worth scrutinizing for round-the-world routes (for free copy call ☎0171/938 3366).

TOUR AND OVERLAND OPERATORS

Encounter Overland 267 Old Brompton Rd, London SW5 (☎0171/370 6845). Overland tours of South America including Brazil.

Exodus 9 Weir Rd, London SW12 (☎0181/675 7996). Overland tours of South America including Brazil.

Explore Worldwide 1 Frederick St, Aldershot, Hants GU11 (☎01252/319448). Overland tours of South America including Brazil.

Twickers World 23 Church St, Twickenham, Middx TW1(☎0181/892 8164). Wildlife and ecology tours.

LATIN AMERICAN FLIGHT AND TOUR SPECIALISTS

Adventure South America Top Deck House, 131–135 Earls Court Rd, London SW5 (☎0171/244 8641). Overland tours of South America including Brazil.

Journey Latin America 14–16 Devonshire Rd, London W4 (☎0181/747 8315); 2nd Floor, Barton Arcade, 51–63 Deansgate, Manchester M3 (☎0161/ 832 1441). Flight agents and tour operators for Brazil and Latin America.

Last Frontiers Swan House, High St, Long Crendon, Bucks HP18 9AF (☎01844/208 405).

Individual itineraries, flights and specialist photography and other tours to Brazil and Venezuela.

Passage to South America Fovant Mews, 12a Noyna Rd, London SW17 (☎0181/767 8989). Flight agents and individual itineraries to Brazil and elsewhere in South America.

Steamond Travel 23 Eccleston St, London SW1 (☎0171/730 8646). Flight agents and tour operators for Brazil and Latin America.

son, £995 high season (July and December). With these tickets return dates are in theory fixed, but once in Brazil both airlines will allow you to change the date (within the sixty days) for a fee of around £75. These fares are pretty notional and you will get the same tickets through travel agencies with substantial price reductions: to Rio on British Airways for around £650 low season, £900 high season, on Varig for around £600 low season or £775 high season. Transbrasil's official fares are comparable to anything that an agent can offer, with fares to Rio at around £540 low season and £627 high season.

The **cheapest fares** are often offered on TAP (Air Portugal), via Lisbon, VASP, via Brussels, or on Iberia, via Madrid. Other inexpensive options include Alitalia, via Rome, Air France, via Paris, KLM, via Amsterdam, and Lufthansa, via Frankfurt. As prices tend to be the same whether you begin your journey in London or at one of Britain's **regional airports**, you may find it better value and more convenient to use one of these airlines rather than fly out of Heathrow or Gatwick.

THE NORTHEAST AND THE AMAZON

There is an ever-increasing number of flights into Brazil's **Northeast** from Europe, bypassing São Paulo and Rio. The only airline with **direct flights** from London to the Northeast is Transbrasil, which serves Recife and Salvador, both officially at around £512 low season and £583 high season, but a little cheaper through specialist discount agencies. In addition, Air France, TAP and Brazil's VASP (from Brussels) fly to Recife, and TAP also operates a service to Salvador.

If you want the **Amazon** to be your point of entry into Brazil, the cheapest way is to fly to Miami where you can connect with the twice weekly Lloyd Aéreo Boliviano service to Manaus (around $600 return). An unusual, but fairly expensive and time-consuming route is with Air France from Paris to Cayenne in French Guyana (£702) and then onwards with Varig to Macapá (£220) or Belém (£350). Similar fares are obtainable with KLM on its route from Amsterdam to Paramaribo, from where Surinam Airways flies onwards to Macapá and Belém. If you want the western Amazon to be your point of arrival, you're best off flying with Avianca to Bogotá in Colombia and taking a connecting internal flight to Leticia (£550

London–Leticia low season, £700 high season), just a short taxi ride from the Brazilian town of Tabatinga.

OTHER TICKET OPTIONS

Several airlines offer **stopovers** to or from Brazil at no extra cost. Apart from the airlines with European transit points already mentioned, options include: United via New York or Miami (£580 low season, £750 high season); Avianca via Bogota (£717 low season, £836 high season); and Canadian via Toronto (£680 low season, £760 high season). A ticket with Aerolíneas Argentinas to Buenos Aires (£560 low season, £670 high season) allows a stopover in Rio, often the best choice if you want to see something of Brazil and Argentina.

Combining Brazil with a longer trip in the southern hemisphere, or putting together a **round-the-world ticket**, is possible but expensive. Aerolíneas Argentinas flies to Sydney (£925 low season, £1350 high season) with up to two stopovers in either direction permitted in Rio, Buenos Aires, Rio Gallegos and Auckland. Alternatively it's possible to fly one way to Australia with Aerolíneas Argentinas via Rio (£635 low season, £800 high season) and return via Asia or North America (prices vary according to the route chosen).

PACKAGES AND TOURS

If your trip is short, and if your plan is simply to visit Rio for two weeks, then **package holidays**, flight and accommodation included, can be very good value. A week in a three-star hotel in Copacabana can cost less than £700, and for an extra £400 you can add on a week's tour taking in three or four key places such as Manaus, Salvador and Iguaçu. These packages can be found in brochures at any travel agent, such as Kuoni and Thomas Cook, and through some of the specialists listed here. If you want to go for *Carnaval* you'll need to book months in advance and pay much more.

More varied **tours** are offered by many specialist operators and upmarket package companies. Journey Latin America has 22-day guided tours of Brazil (prices ranging between about £1500 and £2500), as well as larger-scale overland options which also take in Paraguay, Bolivia and Peru, or Chile and Argentina. If the ready-packaged tours don't appeal to you, Passage to South America specializes in planning itineraries to meet individual requirements, including hotels and transportation within Brazil. Last Frontiers prepares individual itineraries and occasional small groups to attend *rodeios* or to learn to play polo. Twickers World specializes in wildlife and ecology tours, but with prices starting at £1900 (including flights) for seventeen days, they're not cheap. Other overland trips are offered by Exodus, Explore Worldwide, Encounter Overland and Adventure South America, visiting Brazil along with one or more other South American countries from three weeks to three months for £1500–3000.

BY SHIP

It is still just about possible to get to Brazil from Europe **by ship**, though it's expensive and slow. You'll travel by cargo boat, most of which have room for around twelve passengers travelling in some luxury. They take about three weeks to cross the Atlantic, depending on where they call en route. A good first stop for information on seaborne options is the Strand Cruise Centre (see box).

Gdynia America Shipping Lines, a Polish company, departs Hamburg or Antwerp every month or so via the Canaries to Santos, Rio, Montevideo (Uruguay) and Buenos Aires, returning through Santos and on up the Brazilian coast

---

SHIPPING AGENTS AND COMPANIES

Strand Cruise Centre Charing Cross Shopping Concourse, The Strand, London WC2 (☎0171/836 6363).

Blue Star Line Albion House, 20 Queen Elizabeth St, London SE1 (☎0171/407 2345).

Gdynia America Shipping Lines 238 City Rd, London EC1 (☎0171/251 3389).

Grimaldi Lines Eagle House, 109–110 Jermyn St, London SW1 (☎0171/930 5683).

---

to Ilheus and Salvador. The cheapest one-way berth on this is about £1000, sharing a cabin. Blue Star has a departure from London approximately every seven weeks for a seven-week round trip, calling at Salvador, Santos and Recife. The round trip costs £2950 – and you can spend seven weeks in Brazil and catch the next ship back if you want – one-ways start at £1400 to Santos. Grimaldi Lines has two departures a month from Italy (Genoa and Livorno; from about $1200 one way) to the Brazilian ports of Rio, Santos and Paranagua, and just over once a month from London to Hamburg, Rotterdam, Antwerp, West Africa and Brazil (from about $4000 return). Finally, Peter Dohle Lines (book through Strand Cruise Centre) sails from London via Hamburg, Rotterdam and Antwerp to Santos and São Francisco do Sul for about $2500.

GETTING THERE FROM IRELAND

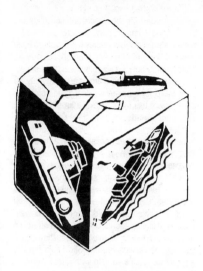

There are no direct flights from Ireland to Brazil, but there are good connections via London or other European capitals. The best deals are available from budget or student travel agents in Ireland, but it's also worth contacting specialist agents in England for cheap fares, an unusual route or a package.

Flying out of Dublin, the cheapest discount fare is with Iberia (IR£605) with an overnight stop in Madrid required, but this is included in the ticket price. Better connections are via London with British Airways (IR£800) or via Paris with Air France (IR£775).

In practice, these prices mean that you're often better off taking advantage of the cheap air fares between Ireland and Britain and picking up an onward flight from London with another airline (see "Getting there from Britain" above). Aer Lingus, British Midland or Ryanair fly from Dublin to London for around IR£69–89; from Belfast, there are British Airways or British Midland flights for around £80–100.

AIRLINES AND AGENTS IN IRELAND

AIRLINES

Aer Lingus 40–41 O'Connell St, Dublin 1, 13 St Stephen's Green, Dublin 2, and 12 Upper St George's St, Dun Laoghaire, all use centralized reservations at Dublin airport (☎01/844 4777); 2 Academy St, Cork (☎021/327 155); 136 O'Connell St, Limerick (☎061/474 239); Northern Ireland reservations ☎0645/737747.

Air France 2nd Floor, 29–30 Dawson St, Dublin 2 (☎01/844 5633).

Air Portugal 1st Floor, 54 Dawson St, Dublin 2 (☎01/679 8844).

British Airways 9 Fountain Centre, College St, Belfast BT1 6ET (☎01232/899 131 or 0345/222 111); reservations in the Republic ☎1800/626747. BA doesn't have a Dublin office; Aer Lingus acts as its agents.

British Midland Reservations in the Republic ☎01/283-8833; in Northern Ireland ☎0345/554554.

Iberia 2nd Floor, 54 Dawson St, Dublin 2 (☎01/677 9846).

Lufthansa Reservations in the Republic ☎01/844 5544.

Ryanair Reservations in the Republic ☎01/609 7800.

DISCOUNT AGENTS

Flight Finders International 13 Baggot St Lower, Dublin 2 (☎01/676 8326). Discounted flights.

Joe Walsh Tours 34 Grafton St, Dublin 2 (☎01/671 8751); 69 Upper O'Connell St , Dublin 2 (☎01/872 2555); 8–11 Baggot St, Dublin 2 (☎01/676 3053); 117 St Patrick St, Cork (☎021/277 959). General budget fares agent.

Trailfinders 4–5 Dawson St, Dublin 2 (☎01/677 7888). Competitive fares with connections out of all Irish airports.

USIT Fountain Centre, College St, Belfast BT1 6ET (☎01232/324073); 10–11 Market Parade, Patrick St, Cork (☎021/ 270900); 33 Ferryquay St, Derry (☎01504/371888); Aston Quay, Dublin 2 (☎01/602 1600); Victoria Place, Eyre Square, Galway (☎091/565177); Central Buildings, O'Connell St, Limerick (☎061/415064); 36–37 Georges St, Waterford (☎051/872601). Student and youth specialists for discounted flights.

GETTING THERE FROM NORTH AMERICA

The main gateways to Brazil in the US and Canada are Atlanta, LA, Miami, New York and Toronto, and it's possible to fly direct from these cities on a number of airlines to various destinations in Brazil. Varig is the main carrier and offers the most flights from the US, with the majority going to either Rio or São Paulo, though it is possible to fly into Brasília, Recife, Manaus and Belém from Miami. The other basic carriers serving Brazil are American, Canadian, Continental, Delta, Japan Airlines (JAL) and United, and the domestic airlines VASP and Transbrasil, which offer some of the lowest fares.

FROM THE US

Apart from discounted tickets, the cheapest way to travel is with an **Apex** (Advance Purchase Excursion) ticket, although these carry certain restrictions: you have to book, and pay, 21 days before departure, spend at least seven days abroad (maximum stay three months), and you tend to get penalized if you change your schedule.

However, discount outlets can usually do better than any Apex fare. They come in several forms. **Consolidators** buy up large blocks of tickets that airlines don't think they will be able to sell at their published fares, and sell them at a

discount. Besides being cheap, consolidators don't normally impose advance purchase requirements (although in busy times you'll want to book ahead to be sure of getting a ticket), but they do often charge very heavy fees for date changes. Also, these companies' margins are pretty tiny, so they make their money by dealing in volume – don't expect them to entertain a lot of questions. **Discount agents** such as STA, Council Travel and the others listed on p.10 also wheel and deal in blocks of tickets offloaded by the airlines, but they typically offer a range of other travel-related sevices such as travel insurance, youth and student ID cards, car rental, tours and the like. These agencies tend to be most worthwhile to students and under-26s who can often benefit from special fares and deals. You should bear in mind, however, that discount agents tend to concentrate on high-volume routes to major cities; they'll give you a good deal on Rio and São Paulo but are unlikely to be able to help with direct flights to the Amazon or cities in Northeastern Brazil.

Travel clubs are another option for those who travel a lot – most charge an annual membership fee which may be worth it for discounts on air tickets, car rental etc. You should also check the travel section in the Sunday *New York Times*, or your own major local newspaper, for current bargains, and consult a good travel agent. A further possibility is to see if you can arrange a **courier flight**, although the hit-or-miss nature of these makes them most suitable for the single traveller who travels light and has a very flexible schedule. In return for shepherding a parcel through customs and possibly giving up your baggage allowance, you can expect to get a deeply discounted ticket. You'll probably also be restricted in the duration of your stay.

If Brazil is only one stop on a longer journey, you might want to consider buying a **Round-the-World (RTW) ticket**. Some travel agents can sell you an "off-the-shelf" RTW ticket that will have you touching down in about half a dozen cities (Rio de Janeiro and São Paulo are on some itineraries); others will have to assemble one for you, which can be tailored to your needs but will probably be more expensive.

Regardless of where you buy your ticket, the fare will depend on the season. **High season** is June 21–August 7, then again December

10–January 10 and always during *Carnaval* (Feb–March). Low season is any other time.

DIRECT FLIGHTS

The greatest number of flights and destinations are offered by **Varig**, the Brazilian national airline, which flies regularly to **Rio** and **São Paulo** from New York, LA, Atlanta and Miami, as well as weekly to **Belém**, **Manaus**, **Fortaleza** and **Recife** via Miami. Excursion-fare ticket prices vary depending on your length of stay in Brazil: count on spending at least $200 more for a ticket for up to three months than a ticket for up to one month. Fares to Rio and São Paulo are almost always the same. Varig's one-month excursion fare from New York to São Paulo is $1060 high season, $910 low season, although unrestricted fares can go as high as $1750. From Miami to São Paulo, fares are $970 high season and $820 low season. Fares from Los Angeles to São Paulo are $1266 high season and $1163 low season.

The **other airlines** serving Brazil fly chiefly out of New York, LA or Miami to Rio and São Paulo, with JAL, for example, flying from LA to São Paulo for $1648 high season and $1448 low season. Two major domestic airlines within

Brazil, Transbrasil and VASP, run a limited amount of flights from the US to Brazil; both offer a high-season fare of $1111 from New York to Rio. Transbrasil also operate direct flights out of Orlando and Washington DC, in addition to the usual cities.

In a country the size of Brazil, **open-jaw tickets** can be very good value, allowing you to fly into one city and out from another. Varig's fares from LA to Rio and São Paulo, for example, are $1366 high season and $1266 low season for an open-jaw Apex ticket valid for a minimum of 21 days.

If you plan to include Brazil as a stop on a **Round-the-World ticket**, figure on $1800 for a ticket including New York, Paris, overland to Madrid, São Paulo, and a return to New York. Slightly more than $4000 will get you from London to Rio, South Africa, North Africa, Southeast Asia, Australia, Japan, the US and back to London.

When buying your ticket, it's a good idea to think about an **airpass** for travel within Brazil (see the box on p.28), as internal flights are expensive and you can only buy your pass outside South America.

AIRLINES IN NORTH AMERICA

Aerolíneas Argentinas ☎1-800/333-0276
Flies daily from New York, LA and Miami to Buenos Aires then on to Rio and São Paulo. Flights leave Montréal and Toronto twice a week.

American Airlines ☎1-800/433-7300
Flights daily from New York, Miami, Dallas and LA to Rio and São Paulo.

Canadian Airlines ☎1-800/426-7000
Flies direct out of Toronto five times a week to São Paulo, and every day from Toronto to São Paulo and Rio through Miami.

Continental Airlines ☎1-800/231-0856
Daily flights to Rio and São Paulo from Newark, NJ.

Delta Airlines ☎1-800/221-1212
Daily flights from Atlanta and Miami to Rio and São Paulo.

Japan Airlines ☎1-800/525-3663
Flights twice a week from LA to São Paulo.

TAM Airlines ☎1-888/235-9826
Daily flights from Miami to São Paulo, starting in 1998.

Transbrasil Airlines ☎1-800/872-3153
Daily flights from Orlando and Miami to São Paulo and Rio, four times a week through Brasília to Rio; six times a week from New York to Brasília, São Paulo or Rio, and three times a week out of Washington DC.

United ☎1-800/538-2929
Daily service from New York and Miami to São Paulo, and a daily service from Miami to Rio.

Varig ☎1-800/GO-VARIG
Daily service from New York, Atlanta and Miami, and four flights a week from LA, to Rio and São Paulo, with connections to other cities. From Miami you can fly weekly into Manaus, Belém, Recife and Fortaleza.

VASP ☎1-800/732-8277
Flies five times a week from LA, Miami, New York and Toronto to São Paulo and Rio, with connecting flights to other cities in Brazil.

FLIGHTS VIA OTHER SOUTH AMERICAN CITIES

If you're looking for slightly cheaper fares, and can put up with the longer flight times, it's worth checking out what the national airlines of Brazil's South American neighbours have to offer. Aerolíneas Argentinas, for instance, flies to Rio and São Paulo from Miami, New York and LA, via Buenos Aires. Others to try include AéroPeru, Avianca, Ladeco, TAM and Viasa.

If you plan on travelling in other South American countries besides Brazil, the **Mercosur Airpass**, which is available through Aerolíneas Argentinas, is well worth considering as it allows you to travel on eight different airlines covering Argentina, Brazil, Paraguay and Uruguay far cheaper than buying individual tickets (see p.28).

FROM CANADA

Direct flight choices from Canada are limited to **Canadian** and **VASP**, who fly from Toronto five times a week to São Paulo. Apex fares on Canadian and VASP are similar, CDN$1678 to São Paulo in high season and CDN$1444 in low season. Aerolíneas Argentinas offers an alternative, though the flight is longer, flying from Toronto to Miami to Buenos Aires and then Rio for CDN$1623 in high season and CDN$1483 low

season. They also fly from Montréal via New York and Buenos Aires to Rio.

For a wider choice of destinations and a more competitive deal, your best bet is to fly to Miami, New York or LA and make your connections from there. Discount travel agents will be able to offer good prices on routes via the US. Travel Cuts is the most reliable student/youth agency, and also offers some deals for non-students; or check the travel ads in your local newspaper and consult a good travel agent. For **Round-the-World** tickets, your best bet is to include a major US departure point, like New York or Los Angeles, in your itinerary.

PACKAGE TOURS

Package-deal vacations may not sound like your kind of travel, but don't dismiss the idea. Many agents can put together surprisingly flexible deals and they can be great for your peace of mind, if only to ensure a worry-free first week while you're finding your feet on a longer tour. If you've only a week or two, you could end up getting the best value and making the most of your time, particularly if you have special interests, by using one of the specialists listed in the tour operators box. For example, a simple airfare-plus-accommodation package for five nights in

DISCOUNT AGENTS AND TRAVEL CLUBS IN NORTH AMERICA

Brazilian American Cultural Center (BACC), 16 West 46th St, 2nd floor, New York, NY 10036 (☎212/730-1010). Travel club offering members discounted flights.

Council Travel, 205 E 42nd St, New York, NY 10017 (☎1-800/226-8624; www.ciee.org). Student/budget travel agency, with branches in many other US cities.

Moment's Notice, 7301 New Utrecht Ave, Brooklyn, NY 11204 (☎718/234-6295). Discount travel club.

Skylink, 265 Madison Ave, 5th Floor, New York, NY 10016 (☎1-800/AIR-ONLY or 212/573-8980), with branches in Chicago, LA, Montréal, Toronto and Washington DC. Consolidator.

STA Travel, 10 Downing St, New York, NY 10014 (☎1-800/781-4040 or 212/627-3111). Other branches in the Boston, Chicago, LA and San Francisco areas. Worldwide discount travel firm specializing in student/youth fares; also

student IDs, travel insurance, car rental and rail passes.

Travel Avenue, 10 S Riverside, Suite 1404, Chicago, IL 60606 (☎1-800/333-3335 or 312/876-6866; www.travelavenue.com). Full-service travel agent that offers discounts in the form of rebates.

Travel Cuts, 243 College St, Toronto, ON M5T 1P7 (☎1-800/667-2887 or 416/979-2406), and other branches all over Canada. Organization specializing in student fares, IDs and other travel services.

Unitravel, 1177 N Warson Rd, St Louis, MO 63132 (☎1-800/325-2222). US consolidator.

Voyages Cuts, 3480 rue McTavish, Montréal, PQ H3A 1X9 (☎514/398-0647); and Université de Laval, Pavillon Maurice Pollack, 1258 Ste.-Foy, Québec, G1K 7P4 (☎418/654-0224). Discount travel agent.

Worldtek Travel, 111 Water St, New Haven, CT 06511 (☎1-800/243-1723 or 203/772-0470). Discount travel agency.

TOUR OPERATORS AND PROJECT ORGANIZERS IN NORTH AMERICA

Abercrombie & Kent, 1520 Kensington Rd, Suite 212, Oak Brook, IL 60523-2141 (☎1-800/323-7308). Tours to the Amazon, multi-country tours, and individually customized tours.

Adventure Center, 1311 63rd St, Suite 200, Emeryville, CA 94608 (☎1-800/227-8747). Group tours of South America that include Brazil.

BET Tours, 13701 SW Candle Dr, Suite 300, Miami FL 33131 (☎1-800/438-4448). Individual and group tours in Brazil and Argentina.

Brazil Nuts, 1150 Post Rd, Fairfield, CT 06430 (☎1-800/553-9959). Tours that promise to take you off the beaten track to experience Brazil's cities, the Amazon basin and the Pantanal.

Brazilian Vacation Center, 16 West 46th St, 2nd floor, New York, NY 10036 (☎212/840-3733 or ☎1-800/848-2746). One of the largest tour operators specializing in tours to Brazil ranging from ecology tours to the Amazon to city tours, especially Rio, and a host of different *Carnaval* packages. Always competitively priced.

Brazilian Views, 201 E 66th St, Suite 21G, New York, NY 10021 (☎212/472-9539). Customized tours for those interested in arts and crafts, with workshops in needlework, weaving, horticulture, birdwatching and fishing in the Amazon and Pantanal.

City Tours, 26A Oak St, East Rutherford, NJ 07073 (☎1-800/238-2489). Individual and group travel throughout South America specializing in city tours and day excursions.

Conservation International, 2501 M St, Suite 200, Washington DC 20037 (☎1-800/429-5660). Offers the opportunity to work on environmental volunteer projects in Brazil.

Earthwatch, 680 Mt Auburn St, Watertown, MA 02272 (☎1-800/776-0188 or 617/926-8200). Organizes trips for volunteers to work overseas on scientific and cultural projects, with a strong emphasis on protection and preservation of the ecology and environment.

Explorers Travel Group, 1 Main St, Suite 304, Eatontown, NJ 07724 (☎1-800/631-5650 or 908/542-9006). A well-established company specializing in customized tours to the Amazon and other parts of South America.

EcoAdventures, 960 N San Antonio Rd, Suite 201, Los Altos, CA 94022 (☎1-800/969-4900).

Individually tailored packages, plus river cruises up the Amazon into Peru.

Festival Tours, 737 West Oak Ridge Rd, Orlando, FL 32809 (☎1-800/327-2838). An all-encompassing tour operator to Central and South America focusing on main tourist sights.

Focus Tours, 14821 Hillside Lane, Burnsville, MN 55306 (☎612/892-7830). Ecology-oriented tours, custom-designed to take groups or individuals to destinations such as the Amazon, the Pantanal and the Atlantic forest regions.

IST Cultural Tours, 225 W 34th St, Suite 913, New York, NY 10122 (☎212/563-1202 or 1-800/833-3804). Specializes in educational travel, working with Brazilian academics and naturalists to give an understanding of Brazil.

Ladatco Tours, 2220 Coral Way, Miami, FL 33145 (☎305/854-8422 or 1-800/327-6162). General tour operator to Central and South America offering special Rio tours.

Lost World Adventures, 220 Second Ave, Decatur, GA 30030 (☎1-800/999-0558). Four- and five-day expeditions to the Pantanal; groups travel overland and by boat along the Cuiabá River.

Nature Expeditions International, 6400 E El Dorado Circle, Suite 210, Tucson, AZ 85715 (☎1-800/869-0639). Concentrates on Amazon River cruises and camping, with extensions to the Peruvian Amazon and Machu Pichu.

Portuguese Tours, 321 Rahway Ave, Elizabeth, NJ 07202 (☎1-800/526-4047 or 908/352-6112). A big company offering escorted, individual and group tours customized to meet your needs; *Carnaval* packages; combined Brazil and Argentina tours; and any number of city package vacations with "add-on" options.

Safaricentre, 3201 N Sepulveda Blvd, Manhattan Beach, CA 90266 (☎1-800/223-6046). Offers nature and adventure tours of the Amazon and the Pantanal, and a cultural tour to Salvador.

Solar Tours, 1629 K St NW, Suite 502, Washington DC 2006 (☎202/861-5864). A big operator throughout Latin America, offering cruises, city tours, jungle trips and *Carnaval* specials.

Victor Emanuel Nature Tours, Box 33008, Austin, TX 78764 (☎1-800/328-8368). Birdwatching tours.

Copacabana in a four-star hotel can cost as little as $900. For a little more, Festival Tours offers a five-night package to a four-star beach hotel in Rio including Brazilian breakfast every morning, day excursions and transfers for $999.

Many operators can arrange add-on trips to a Rio-based package vacation or there are tours centred around two or three locations – Portuguese Tours offers the "Tale of Three Cities

Tour" to Rio, Iguaçu and Buenos Aires for ten days for $1819. **Carnaval** tours are big business, so expect to pay more at this time of year, between $2000 and $3000 for a five-night stay – Portuguese Tours, Solar Tours and the Brazilian Vacation Center are all specialists. The Brazilian Vacation Center is one of the largest tour operators to Brazil, offering comprehensive deals on Rio and the Amazon in particular.

GETTING THERE FROM AUSTRALIA AND NZ

Not surprisingly, the best deals to Brazil are offered by South American airlines. There are also plenty of flights via the USA, but they generally work out more expensive and time-consuming. Similarly, Round-the-World fares including South America are notoriously expensive, but can be worthwhile if you have the time to make the most of a few stopovers.

From Australia, all flights to Brazil leave from Sydney. The most direct routes are with Aerolíneas Argentinas, which flies to Rio and São Paulo via Auckland and Buenos Aires, or with Lan-Chile via Santiago. The other airlines that serve Brazil (Qantas in conjunction with Varig, and United) route via Los Angeles, and some touch down in Miami as well. **From New Zealand**, your best bet is the Aerolíneas Argentinas flights from Auckland to Rio or São Paulo via Rio Gallegos (Patagonia) and Buenos Aires.

If you plan to do a fair amount of travelling within Brazil (or to other South American countries), think about buying an **air pass** with your main ticket. These passes offer substantial savings, but can only be bought outside South America; see box on p.28 for details of the various options.

FARES

Whatever kind of ticket you're after, first call should be one of the **travel agents** listed in the box, who can fill you in on all the latest fares and any special offers. If you're a **student** or **under 26**, you may be able to undercut some of the prices given here; STA is a good place to start. In general, fares depend on the **duration of stay**, rather than the season: cut-off points are 21 days, 45 days, 3 months, 6 months and 1 year; but bear in mind that prices for flights (and everything else) soar during *Carnaval* (Feb–March).

AIRLINES

Aerolíneas Argentinas, 580 George St, Sydney (☎02/9283 3660); 15/135 Albert St, Auckland (☎09/379 3675).

Lan-Chile, 30 Clarence St, Sydney (☎02/9299 5599 & 1800/221 572).

Qantas, 70 Hunter St, Sydney (☎13 1211); 154 Queen St, Auckland (☎09/357 8900 & 0800/808 767).

United, 10 Barrack St, Sydney (☎13 1777); 7 City Rd, Auckland (☎09/379 3800).

Varig Brazilian, 64 York St, Sydney (☎02/9321 9179); 6/299 Queen St, Auckland (☎09/379 4455).

On the **more direct routes**, you should be able to get a return fare for A$2399 for visits of less than 21 days; if you want to stay longer than this, you'll be looking at fares around A$2600. Special offers with Aerolíneas Argentinas and Lan-Chile sometimes bring fares to Brazil down as low as A$1779 for stays of up to 45 days, though your plans will need to be fairly flexible to take advantage of these last-minute bargains. Flights **via the US** are all pretty similarly priced, costing A$2800 for a six-month ticket. **From New Zealand**, the cheapest return fare you're likely to find is around NZ$2599.

In a country the size of Brazil, **open-jaw tickets**, which allow you to fly into one city and out from another, can save valuable time that would otherwise be spent backtracking. For example, flying into Rio and out of São Paulo (or vice versa), will set you back around A$2770/NZ$2900.

RTW TICKETS

Given these fares and routings, **Round-the-World tickets** that take in South America are worth considering, though there are far fewer itineraries than for the more common Asian, North American and European routes; the limited choice also tends to make them more expensive than other RTW options. Ultimately, your choice of route will depend on where else you want to visit besides Brazil, but possible itineraries include starting from either **Melbourne**, **Sydney** or **Brisbane**, flying to Auckland, Papeete, Los Angeles and London, making your own way to Paris from there, then flying to Buenos Aires and taking a side-trip to São Paulo or Rio on the way back home (from A$2999); fares for a similar itinerary from **Auckland** start at NZ$2799.

TRAVEL AGENTS

Anywhere Travel, 345 Anzac Parade, Kingsford, Sydney (☎02/9663 0411).

Brisbane Discount Travel, 260 Queen St, Brisbane (☎07/3229 9211).

Budget Travel, 16 Fort St, Auckland, plus branches around the city (☎09/366 0061 & 0800/808 040).

Destinations Unlimited, 3 Milford Rd, Auckland (☎09/373 4033).

Flight Centres Australia: 82 Elizabeth St, Sydney, plus branches nationwide (☎13 1600). New Zealand: 205 Queen St, Auckland (☎09/309 6171), plus branches nationwide.

Northern Gateway, 22 Cavenagh St, Darwin (☎08/8941 1394).

STA Travel Australia: 702 Harris St, Ultimo, Sydney; 256 Flinders St, Melbourne; other offices in state capitals and major universities (nearest branch ☎13 1776, fastfare telesales ☎1300/360 960). New Zealand: 10 High St, Auckland (☎09/309 0458, fastfare telesales ☎09/366 6673), plus branches in Wellington, Christchurch, Dunedin, Palmerston North, Hamilton and at major universities.
Web site: *www.statravelaus.com.au*
email: *traveller@statravelaus.com.au*

Thomas Cook Australia: 175 Pitt St, Sydney; 257 Collins St, Melbourne; plus branches in other state capitals (local branch ☎13 1771, Thomas Cook Direct telesales ☎1800/063 913); New Zealand: 96 Anzac Ave, Auckland (☎09/379 3920).

SPECIALIST AGENTS

The following agents specialize in South American travel arrangements, and can help with flights, accommodation and car rental, as well as fully inclusive tours.

Adventure Specialists, 69 Liverpool St, Sydney (☎02/9261 2927).

Adventure World, 73 Walker St, North Sydney (☎02/9956 7766 & 1800/221 931), plus branches in Brisbane and Perth; 101 Great South Rd, Remuera, Auckland (☎09/524 5118). Agents for a vast array of international adventure travel companies.

Affordable South America, 288 Queen St, Melbourne (☎03/9600 1733).

South America Travel Centre, 104 Hardware St, Melbourne (☎03/9642 5353 & 1800/655 051).

South American Adventure Travel, 132 Wickham St, Fortitude Valley, Brisbane (☎07/3854 1022).

South American Experts, 82 Elizabeth St, Sydney (☎02/9235 3522).

South American Trekking Specialists, 4/49 Market St, Sydney (☎02/9283 2000).

PACKAGE TOURS

Package holidays from Australia and New Zealand to South America tend to be either expensive, reflecting the high cost of the flights, or of the extended overland variety. Specialist travel agents like Adventure World and the South America Travel Centre offer a range of Brazilian itineraries, such as a two-week trip starting in Rio and visiting Salvador, with a brief foray into the Amazon, for A$3010/NZ$3330 per person, not including flights from Australasia; or a basic ten-day city-based tour of Brazil and Argentina (from A$2640, including return flight from Sydney). If you baulk at the fully packaged experience, shorter **add-on tours** give you the flexibility of combining independent travel with say, an Amazon cruise (three days from Manaus starts at A$550 per person, including all meals); or, if you've got your heart set on *Carnaval*, **pre-booked accommodation** costs around A$700 per person for 4 nights.

    Adventure tours are worth considering if you want to cover a lot of ground or get to

places that could be difficult to reach independently. Peregrine offers seventeen days travelling between Rio and Buenos Aires (or vice versa) for A$1575 (not including flights), while Explore Worldwide's extended trip takes in the Iguaçu Falls, Rio and the Amazon, plus highlights of Peru and Bolivia, staying in hotels and on a riverboat (26 days, A$4885/NZ$5375, airfares extra).

RED TAPE AND VISAS

Citizens of most Western European nations, including the UK and Ireland, only need a valid passport and either a return or onward ticket, or evidence of funds to pay for one, to enter Brazil. You fill in an entry card on arrival and will get a tourist visa allowing you to stay for ninety days. Australian, New Zealand, US and Canadian citizens need visas in advance, available from the relevant embassies; a return or onward ticket is usually a requirement.

    Do not lose the **carbon copy of the entry card** the police staple into your passport on arrival, as you may be fined when you leave if you don't present it. A sensible precaution is to photocopy it and also keep a record of your passport number in case it is lost or stolen. If you do lose your passport, report to the *Polícia Federal* (see p.46) and then obtain a replacement travel document from your nearest consulate. You'll then have to return to the *Polícia Federal* who will put an endorsement in your passport giving you 72 hours either to return to your original point of entry into Brazil for a replacement entry card or to leave the country altogether. So, for example, if you lose your documents in Rio and entered Brazil here, the formalities don't present too much of a problem. However, you may be hundreds of kilometres from your point of entry and far from a land border, in which case you'll have to decide whether to remain in Brazil illegally or leave the country earlier than planned.

A **tourist visa** can be **extended** for another ninety days if you apply at least fifteen days before it expires, but it will only be extended once; if you want to stay longer you'll have to leave the country and re-enter. There's nothing in the rule book to stop you re-entering immediately, but it's advisable to wait at least a day. For anything to do with visas you deal with the federal police, the **Polícia Federal**. Every state capital has a federal police station with a visa section: ask for the *delegacia federal*. A $10 charge, payable in local currency, is made on tourist visa extensions.

CONSULATES

Foreign countries are represented at **embassy** level in Brasília and most also maintain **consulates** in Rio and São Paulo. Elsewhere in this vast country, consulates, vice-consulates or honorary consulates are found in many major cities, from Manaus to Porto Alegre. Levels of service will vary depending on the nature of the particular post, but at the very least you can count on

> **BRAZILIAN EMBASSIES AND CONSULATES ABROAD**
>
> **AUSTRALIA** Embassy: 19 Forster Crescent, Yarralumla, Canberra, ACT 2600 (☎02/6273 2372); Consulate: 31 Market St, Sydney (☎02/9267 4414).
>
> **BRITAIN** 32 Green St, London W1 (☎0171/499 0877).
>
> **CANADA** 450 Wilbroad St, Sandyhill, Ottawa, ON KIV 6M9 (☎613/237-1090); consulates also in Montréal (☎514/499-0968); Toronto (☎416/922-2503); Vancouver (☎604/687-4589).
>
> **IRELAND** Europa House, Harcourt Centre, Harcourt St, Dublin 2 (☎01/475 6000).
>
> **NEW ZEALAND** No representation – apply to Canberra through your travel agent.
>
> **USA** 3006 Massachusetts Ave NW, Washington DC 20008 (☎202/238-2700); consulates also in Atlanta (☎404/521-0061); Chicago (☎312/464-0244); Houston (☎713/961-3063); Miami (☎305/285-6200); Los Angeles (☎213/651-2664); New York (☎212/757-3080); San Francisco (☎415/981-8170).

some immediate help. Addresses and telephone numbers of embassies and consulates can be found in the "Listings" section of the cities in the *Guide*. Where their country doesn't have a representative, a Commonwealth national can seek help at a British mission, and a European Union citizen at an EU mission.

LONGER STAYS: ACADEMIC VISITS

Academic visitors and researchers making a short trip or attending a conference are best advised to enter on a tourist visa, which cuts down on the bureaucracy. If you're staying for a longer period, or intend to do research, you need to get a special visa, known as an "**Item IV**" before you leave home. To obtain this, you'll need to present a letter from a Brazilian Institute of Higher Education saying it knows about, and approves, your research, and you will be formally affiliated to the institution while you do it. Visas are issued either for six months, a year or two years; if in any doubt about exactly how long you're going to stay, apply for the two-year visa. One-year visas can be extended for a further year inside Brazil, but only after months of chasing up the police, and often involving a trip to the Ministry of Justice in Brasília.

On arrival on an "Item IV", you must **register** at the *seção dos estrangeiros* office in the nearest federal police station to where you are based. Take some passport photographs, and you will be issued with an identity card; you can expect registering and getting the card to take at least a day of mindless drudgery, sitting in lines and chasing around, but it has to be done. If your work involves taking samples out of Brazil, a whole new bureaucratic ballgame begins; you will need to get in touch well in advance with the Brazilian Embassy and with the Brazilian institution in question.

WORKING

Working in Brazil is illegal for people entering on a tourist visa, although many do, either clandestinely or leaving and re-entering every three months. It is possible to make a living in a city **teaching English**: scan the noticeboards of universities, where schools advertise for English teachers, no questions asked. You'll need to be able speak at least some Portuguese first. There are very few other possibilities.

INSURANCE

Most people will find it essential to take out a good travel insurance policy that covers not only medical expenses and emergency repatriation, but also loss or theft of baggage and expenses for delays or cancellations.

However, **credit and charge cards** (particularly American Express) often have certain levels of medical or other insurance included, especially if you use them to pay for your trip. It can be quite comprehensive, anticipating anything from lost or stolen baggage and missed connections to charter companies going bankrupt; however, certain policies (notably in North America) only cover medical costs. Note also that very few insurers will arrange on-the-spot payments in the event of a major expense or loss; you will usually be reimbursed only after going home. In all cases of **loss or theft of goods**, you will have to contact the local police to have a report made out so that your insurer can process the claim.

If you plan to participate in **watersports** or do some **hiking**, you may have to pay an extra premium; check carefully that any insurance policy you are considering will cover you in case of an accident.

BRITAIN AND IRELAND

In Britain and Ireland, travel insurance schemes (from around £50 a month) are sold by almost every travel agent and bank – or try a specialist insurance firm. Policies issued by Endsleigh Insurance (97–107 Southampton Row, London WC1; ☎0171/436 4451), Worldwide, Elm Lane, Tonbridge, Kent TN10 3XS (☎01732/773366), or Columbus Travel Insurance (17 Devonshire Square, London EC2; ☎0171/375 0011) are all good value.

NORTH AMERICA

Before buying an insurance policy, check that you're not already covered. **Canadian provincial health plans** typically provide some overseas medical coverage, although they are unlikely to pick up the full tab in the event of a mishap. Holders of official **student/teacher/youth cards** are entitled to accident coverage and hospital in-patient benefits – the annual membership is far less than the cost of comparable insurance. **Students** may also find that their student health coverage extends during the vacations and for

one term beyond the date of last enrolment. **Homeowners' or renters' insurance** often covers theft or loss of documents, money and valuables while overseas.

After exhausting the possibilities above, you might want to contact a specialist **travel insurance** company; your travel agent can usually recommend one, or see the box below. Travel insurance **policies** vary: some are comprehensive while others cover only certain risks (accidents, illnesses, delayed or lost luggage, cancelled flights, etc). In particular, ask whether the policy pays medical costs up front or reimburses you later, and whether it provides for medical evacuation to your home country.

The best **premiums** are usually to be had through student/youth travel agencies – ISIS policies, for example, cost $48–69 for fifteen days (depending on level of coverage), $80–105 for a month, $149–207 for two months, $510–700 for a year.

AUSTRALIA AND NZ

Travel insurance is available from most travel agents, or direct from **insurance companies** such as Cover More, 9/32 Walker St, North Sydney (☎02/9202 8000 & 1800/251881), or Ready Plan, 141 Walker St, Dandenong, Melbourne (☎03/9791 5077 & 1800/337 462), and 10/ 63 Albert St, Auckland (☎09/379 3208). A typical policy covering Brazil will **cost** A$130/NZ$145 for two weeks, A$190/NZ$210 for one month, A$280/NZ$310 for two months.

TRAVEL INSURANCE COMPANIES IN NORTH AMERICA

Access America ☎1-800/284-8300.

Carefree Travel Insurance ☎1-800/323-3149.

Desjardins Travel Insurance – Canada only ☎1-800/463-7830.

International Student Insurance Service (ISIS) – sold by STA Travel (☎1-800/777-0112).

Travel Guard ☎1-800/826-1300.

Travel Insurance Services ☎1-800/937-1387.

TRAVELLERS WITH DISABILITIES

Travelling in Brazil for people with disabilities is likely to be difficult if special facilities are required. For example, access even to recently constructed buildings may be impossible, as lifts are often too narrow to accept wheelchairs or there may be no lift at all. In general, though, you'll find that hotel staff are helpful and will bend over backwards to be of assistance to try to make up for the deficiencies in access and facilities.

Buses in cities are really only suitable for the agile and for those who don't mind being thrown about. **Taxis**, however, are plentiful but fairly expensive if you need to rely on them. Long-distance buses are generally quite comfortable, with the special *leito* services offering full reclining seats. Internal **airlines** are helpful, and wheelchairs available at most airports.

CONTACTS FOR TRAVELLERS WITH DISABILITIES

Centro de Vida Independente, Rua Marques de São Vicente 225, Gavea, Est. da PUC, Rio de Janeiro (☎021/257-0019). Campaigning organization for disabled rights and advice on travel in Brazil.

BRITAIN AND IRELAND

Disability Action Group, 2 Annadale Ave, Belfast BT7 3JH (☎01232/491011). Information about access for disabled travellers abroad.

Holiday Care Service, 2nd Floor, Imperial Building, Victoria Rd, Horley, Surrey RH6 7PZ (☎01293/774535). Provides free lists of accessible accommodation abroad, and information on financial help for holidays.

Irish Wheelchair Association, Blackheath Drive, Clontarf, Dublin 3 (☎01/833 8241). Information about access for disabled travellers abroad.

RADAR (Royal Association for Disability and Rehabilitation), 12 City Forum, 250 City Rd, London EC1V 8AF (☎0171/250 3222; Minicom ☎0171/250 4119). Produces a biennial holiday guide for long-haul destinations (£5 inc. p&p).

Tripscope, The Courtyard, Evelyn Rd, London W4 5JL (☎0181/994 9294). This registered charity provides a national telephone information service offering free advice on international transport and travel for those with a mobility problem.

NORTH AMERICA

Directions Unlimited, 720 N Bedford Rd, Bedford Hills, NY 10507 (☎914/241-1700). Travel agency specializing in custom tours for people with disabilities.

Jewish Rehabilitation Hospital, 3205 Place Alton Goldbloom, Chomedy Laval, Quebec H7V 1RT (☎514/688-9550, ext. 226). Guidebooks and travel information.

Mobility International USA, PO Box 10767, Eugene, OR 97440 (Voice and TDD: ☎541/343-1284). Information and referral services, access guides, tours and exchange programs. Annual membership $25 (includes quarterly newsletter).

Society for the Advancement of Travel for the Handicapped (SATH), 347 5th Ave, Suite 610, New York, NY 10016 (☎212/447-7284; http://www.sittravel.com/). Non-profit travel-industry referral service that passes queries on to its members as appropriate; allow plenty of time for a response.

Travel Information Service (☎215/456-9600). Telephone information and referral service.

Twin Peaks Press, Box 129, Vancouver, WA 98666 (☎360/694-2462 or 1-800/637-2256). Publisher of the *Directory of Travel Agencies for the Disabled* ($19.95), listing more than 370 agencies worldwide; *Travel for the Disabled* ($19.95); the *Directory of Accessible Van Rentals* ($9.95); and *Wheelchair Vagabond* ($14.95), loaded with personal tips.

AUSTRALIA AND NZ

ACROD (Australian Council for Rehabilitation of the Disabled), PO Box 60, Curtin, ACT 2605 (☎02/6282 4333).

Disabled Persons Assembly, 173–175 Victoria St, Wellington (☎04/811 9100).

HEALTH

Although there are no compulsory vaccinations required to enter the country, certain precautions should be taken, certainly if you're staying for any length of time or visiting the more remote regions. Taking out travel insurance is vital, and you should take all possible precautions to guard against AIDS, a major worry in Brazil. It's a good idea to take your own first-aid kit with you, including antiseptic cream, sealed bandages, a course of *Flagyl* antibiotics, *Imodium* (*Lomotil*) for emergency diarrhoea treatment, rehydration sachets and hypodermic syringe and needles as you cannot rely on needles being sterile in Brazil.

PHARMACIES AND MEDICAL TREATMENT

Most standard drugs are available in **pharmacies**, *farmácias*, which you'll find everywhere – no prescriptions are necessary. A pharmacy will also give injections (you need a tetanus jab if you get bitten by a dog) and free medical advice, and they're a good first line of defence if you fall ill.

If you are unlucky enough to need **medical treatment** in Brazil, forget about the public hospitals – as a foreigner you have virtually no chance of getting a bed unless you have an infectious disease, and the level of health care offered by most is appalling. You can get reasonably good medical and dental care privately: North Americans will think it fairly inexpensive, Europeans used to state-subsidized health care will not. A doctor's visit will cost on average about US$50; drugs are relatively cheap. Local tourist offices and smart hotels in big cities will have lists of English-, French- and German-speaking **doctors**; ask for a *médico*. Outside the larger centres, you will probably have to try out your Portuguese. If a medical emergency occurs in an out-of-the-way location, there's an excellent **air ambulance** service (☎011/5506-0606, fax 011/846-8689) that guarantees collection anywhere in the country within 24

hours of calling. If considering this option be sure to contact your travel insurance company before phoning for a plane.

FOOD AND WATER

Many diseases are directly or indirectly related to impure **water** (see box) and contaminated **food**, and care should be taken over what you eat and drink.

With a little common sense, it's quite easy to establish whether food is fresh or not, and always ensure that it's properly cooked. Special caution should be taken with seafood, especially **shellfish** – don't eat anything that's at all suspicious. Fruit and salad ingredients should be washed in bottled or purified water or, preferably, peeled. Ultimately you are going to run some risks with food, so if you're going to enjoy your stay to the full, there's no sense in being overly paranoid.

Even in the most remote towns and villages **mineral water** (*água mineral*), either sparkling (*com gás*) or still (*sem gás*), is easily available and cheap. To avoid dehydration be sure to drink plenty of non-alcoholic liquids, always carry a bottle of water on long trips and check that the seal on any bottled water you use is intact.

As with food, it's difficult to be on guard all the time; fruit juices are more often than not diluted, at best with only filtered water, and while it is wise to avoid ice in general, this is nigh on impossible.

YELLOW FEVER

It is highly recommended to be vaccinated against **yellow fever** if you're going to **Amazonia**. A viral disease transmitted to humans by mosquitoes, yellow fever can be fatal. Symptoms are headache, fever, abdominal pain and vomiting. Victims may appear to recover and, without medical help, bleeding, shock and symptoms of kidney and liver failure may develop. The only treatment is to keep the fever as low as possible and prevent dehydration. Fortunately a yellow fever vaccine is available which offers good protection for ten years. Cars, buses and boats en route to western Amazonia are regularly stopped and anyone who can't produce a **valid YF certificate** has to be vaccinated on the spot, often with a communal needle.

Emergency phone numbers vary from place to place, but you'll always find them listed in phone boxes – look for *Bombeiros* or *Polícia Civil*.

WATER PURIFICATION

Contaminated water is a major cause of sickness due to the presence of bacteria, viruses and cysts. These micro-organisms cause diseases such as diarrhoea, gastroenteritis, typhoid, cholera, dysentery, poliomyelitis, hepatitis A, giardiasis and bilharziasis and can be present even when water looks clean and safe to drink.

Bottled water is widely available in Brazil, but if you are considering trekking in remote regions or want to take all possible precautions, there are various methods of **treating water** whilst you are travelling. **Boiling** is the time-honoured method which will be effective in sterilizing water, although it will not remove unpleasant tastes. A minimum boiling time of five minutes (longer at higher altitudes) is sufficient to kill micro-organisms.

Chemical sterilization can be carried out using either chlorine or iodine tablets or a tincture of iodine liquid. When using tablets it is essential to follow the manufacturer's dosage and contact time, whilst, with tincture of iodine, you add a couple of drops to one litre of water and leave to stand for twenty minutes. Iodine tablets are preferred to chlorine as the latter leave an especially unpalatable taste in the water and also are not effective in preventing such diseases as amoebic dysentery and giardiasis. If you are using sterilizing tablets, a water filter is useful, not least to improve the taste.

Water filters alone will remove most bacteria and cysts, but not viruses, which, due to their microscopic size, pass through into the filtered water.

Purification, a two-stage process involving both filtration and sterilization, removes or destroys all waterborne disease-causing micro-organisms. Portable water purifiers range in size from units weighing as little as 60 grams which can be slipped into a pocket, to 800 grams for carrying in a backpack. A low-cost and highly recommended range made by Pre-Mac is available in the UK from British Airways Travel Clinics (see p.22) and specialist outdoor equipment retailers (call ☎01732/460333 for details of local stockists); in Ireland through All Water Systems Ltd, Unit 12, Western Parkway Business Centre, Lr Ballymount Rd, Dublin 12 (☎01/456 4933); in the USA and Canada, contact Outbound Products (☎1-800/663-9262; in Canada ☎604/321-5464).

MALARIA

Malaria is endemic in **northern Brazil**, and anyone intending to travel anywhere in Amazonia should take it very seriously. In recent years, rates have climbed as mosquitoes have become more resistant to insecticides, and a few unwary tourists die avoidably every year. With simple precautions you can minimize the chances of getting it even in highly malarial areas, and, properly treated, a dose of malaria should be no worse than a severe bout of flu. But make no mistake – unless you follow the **precautions** outlined here, and take malaria prophylaxis before, during and after you pass through Amazonia, malaria can kill.

There are two kinds of malaria in Brazil: **falciparum**, which is more serious but less common, and **vivax**. Both are transmitted by anopheles mosquitoes, which are most active at sunrise and for an hour or so before sunset. Even in very malarial areas, only around five percent of anopheles are infected with malarial parasites, so the more you minimize mosquito bites, the less likely you are to catch it. Use **insect repellent**: the most commonly used in Brazil is **Autan**, often in combination with Johnson's Baby Oil to minimize skin irritation. The most effective mosquito repellents – worth looking out for before you leave home – contain **DEET** (diethyl toluamide). Wear long-sleeved shirts and trousers, shoes and socks during the times of day when mosquitoes are most active. Sleep under a sheet and, crucially, use a **mosquito net**. Nets for hammocks (*mosqueteiro para rede*) cost around $15 and are easily available in Amazonian cities.

The use of **antimalarial drugs** in Brazil is complicated. They all have side-effects, and if your stay in the Amazon is limited to Belém or Manaus, where malaria has been eradicated, it is probably best not to take any. Outside the big cities it is best to stick to chloroquin-based drugs: don't forget to start taking them before you leave, and continue taking them for the prescribed period after you get back. Some doctors prescribe a more modern drug called mefloquin, which goes under the brand name of Lariam. This has very strong side-effects, and its use is controversial. You are strongly advised not to take it prophylatically, no matter what your doctor says: stick to chloroquin.

The only justification for taking Lariam along is if you know you will be spending an extended period of time in rural parts of the Amazon: in that case you could take Lariam, but only to treat yourself with in the event of catching chloroquin-resistant malaria. Short-term travellers should not take mefloquin under any circumstances.

Malaria has an incubation period of around two weeks. The first **symptoms** are generally muscle pains, weakness and pain in the joints, which will last for a day or two before the onset of malaria fever proper. You need immediate treatment and a blood test to identify the strain. **Malaria treatment** is the one public health area where Brazil can take some credit. Dotted everywhere around Amazonia are small malaria control posts and **clinics**, run by the anti-malaria agency SUCAM – ask for the *posto da SUCAM*. They may not look like much, but the people who staff them are very experienced and know their local strains better than any city specialist. Treatment in a *posto* is free, and if you do catch malaria you should get yourself taken to one as quickly as possible; don't shiver in your hammock and wait for it to pass. It often does, but it can also kill.

CHAGAS' DISEASE

Another serious disease you should guard against is **Chagas' disease**. This is endemic in parts of the **Northeast** and **Amazonia** and, although it is difficult to catch, it can be serious, leading to heart and kidney problems that appear up to twenty years after infection. The disease is carried in the faeces of beetles which live in the cracks of adobe walls, so if sleeping in an adobe hut, make sure nothing can crawl into your hammock; either use a mosquito net or sling the hammock as far from walls as you can. The beetle bites and then defecates next to the spot: it itches and you rub infected faeces in when you scratch it. So before scratching a bite you know wasn't caused by a mosquito, bathe it in alcohol. If you are infected, you will have fever for a few days which will then clear up, and though the disease can be treated in its early stages, it becomes incurable once established. If you travel through a Chagas area and get an undiagnosed fever, have a blood test as soon as possible afterwards.

DENGUE FEVER

Dengue fever, a viral disease transmitted by mosquito bites, is increasingly common in all Brazilian cities save the extreme south of the country. The symptoms are debilitating rather than dangerous: light but persistent fever, tiredness, muscle and joint pains, especially in the fingers, nausea and vomiting. It is easily treatable, but you will feel pretty grim for a week or so. It is much more widespread than any other disease in urban areas, and is currently the focus of much educational and preventive work by the Brazilian government – due, cynics might say, to the Minister of the Environment catching it in Rio in 1996. The same precautions against mosquito bites outlined in the section on malaria above apply here.

HEPATITIS

Wherever you go, protection against **hepatitis A** is a sensible precaution. Hepatitis A is transmitted through contaminated water and food, resulting in fever and diarrhoea and can cause liver damage. Gammaglobulin injections, one before you go and boosters every six months are the standard protection. If you plan to spend much time in Amazonia or the Northeast, or if you know that you will be travelling rough, it's well worth protecting yourself. If you have had jaundice, you may well have immunity and should have a blood test to see if you need the injections. A new vaccine – Havrix – is proving very effective and lasts for up to ten years, although it is still rather expensive.

DIARRHOEA, DYSENTERY AND GIARDIA

Diarrhoea is something everybody gets at some stage, and there's little to be done except drink a lot (but not alcohol) and bide your time. You should also replace salts either by taking oral rehydration salts or by mixing a teaspoon of salt and eight of sugar in a litre of purified water. You can minimize the risk by being sensible about what you eat, and by not drinking tapwater anywhere. This isn't difficult, given the extreme cheapness and universal availability of soft drinks and *água mineral*, while Brazilians are great believers in herbal teas, which often help alleviate cramps.

If your diarrhoea contains blood or mucus, the cause may be dysentery or giardia. With a fever, it could well be caused by **bacillic dysentery** and may clear up without treatment. If you're sure you need it, a course of antibiotics such as tetracyclin or ampicillin (travel with a supply if you are going off the beaten track for a while) should sort you, but they also destroy "gut flora" which help protect you. Similar symptoms without fever indicate **amoebic dysentery** which is much more serious, and can damage your gut if untreated. The usual cure is a course of metronidazole (*Flagyl*), an antibiotic which may itself make you feel ill, and should not be taken with alcohol. Similar symptoms, plus rotten-egg belches and farts, indicate **giardia**, for which the treatment is again metronidazole. If you suspect you have any of these, seek medical help, and only start on the metronidazole (750mg three times daily for a week for adults) if there is definitely blood in your diarrhoea and it is impossible to see a doctor.

CHOLERA

Cholera is a water-borne bacterial disease which has become endemic to many parts of Brazil, especially in the Northeast during the 1990s. It flourishes in a combination of hot climates and unsanitary conditions, and can be found anywhere in Brazil from Rio northwards. It is most common in the big cities of the Northeast, especially Fortaleza, and in the western Amazon in the border region with Peru. Rarely fatal for the young and fit if acted on immediately, in most cases the illness is no more severe than a sudden and nasty bout of diarrhoea, treated with standard rehydration methods, antibiotics and a saline drip. Left untreated, it can kill within 24 hours by dehydrating its victims. Providing you take sensible precautions with food (especially shellfish) and drinking water, you won't get it. If you are really concerned, vaccines are available with an effectiveness rate of between sixty and seventy percent.

HIV AND AIDS

Brazil has the world's third highest number of **AIDS** sufferers, surpassed only by the USA and Uganda. There are many reasons for this: a scandalous lack of screening of either blood donors or supplies; the level of gay sex between Brazilian men, amongst whom bisexuality is common; the popularity of anal sex, not least amongst heterosexual couples; and the sharing of needles, both amongst drug users in large cities and when giving injections. There are high-profile public education campaigns on TV and billboards, but there is still widespread ignorance of how the disease is transmitted, and fear and persecution of its victims. Things have not been helped by the Catholic Church, in Brazil usually so liberal on many issues,

which has taken a firmly conservative stance on the use of condoms.

A non-exaggerated knowledge of the disease and how it is transmitted is the best defence. It is especially important not to be stampeded by the hysteria which surrounds AIDS in Brazil. Firstly, AIDS is not evenly distributed throughout Brazil. A large majority of sufferers and HIV carriers are concentrated in **Rio** and **São Paulo**, where you should take extra care. Between them, these two cities have reported twice as many AIDS cases as the whole of Britain. Wherever you are, make sure that if you have an injection it is with a needle you see being removed from its packaging. (It is now possible to buy travellers' medical packs which contain sterile needles, attachments for intravenous drips and the like: they're available from immunization centres.) **Avoid blood transfusions unless absolutely neccessary**. Aid agencies in Brazil now provide their staff with bloodbanks, so worried are they about the lack of screening of blood used in both the private and the public hospital networks. In Rio state alone in 1996, 370 people acquired HIV through hospital blood transfusions – that's more than one a day. If you need blood, repatriate yourself or get your embassy to do it.

Finally, **use a condom**. Only a tiny minority of Brazilian men carry them as a matter of course. They are widely available in pharmacies, where you should ask for a *camisinha* or a *camiseta de Vênus*. There are often local shortages, however, and Brazilian condoms are not as durable nor as reliable as condoms in the developed world. Take a good supply along with you: you can always give them away if you don't use them.

It's worth stressing that the large Brazilian **gay community** is working hard to raise public awareness, lobbying for research money and fighting against prejudice. Even taking into account the ugly eruptions of homophobia, the level of popular acceptance and tolerance of gays is still much higher in Brazil than anywhere else in South America, in the major cities at least. The gay scene has certainly quietened over recent years, but it's still there and Rio is particularly popular with gay tourists.

THE AMAZON

Given the remoteness of many parts of the **Amazon** and the prevalence of insects and snakes, health care takes on a special significance. Despite the heat, you should wear long trousers all the time and use repellent to guard against disease-spreading insect bites. If you are trekking through forest or savanna, it is vital to wear good boots which protect your ankles from snake bites, chiggers and scorpions, and you should never trek alone.

Snakes are timid and only attack if you step on them, unless you are unlucky. Many of the

MEDICAL RESOURCES FOR TRAVELLERS

BRITAIN

British Airways Travel Clinic, 156 Regent St, London W1 7RA (☎0171/439 9584), no appointment necessary; there are also appointment-only branches at 101 Cheapside, London EC2 (☎0171/606 2977) and at the BA terminal in London's Victoria Station (☎01276/685040). BA also operates around forty regional clinics throughout the country (call ☎0171/831 5333 for the one nearest to you); airport locations at Gatwick and Heathrow.

Hospital for Tropical Diseases, St Pancras Hospital, 4 St Pancras Way, London NW1 0PE

(☎0171/388 9600). Travel clinic and recorded message service (☎0839/337733; 39–49p per minute) which gives hints on hygiene and illness prevention as well as listing appropriate immunizations.

MASTA (Medical Advisory Service for Travellers Abroad), London School of Hygiene and Tropical Medicine (☎0891/224100; 39–49p per minute). Operates a travellers' health line 24 hours a day, 7 days a week, giving written information tailored to your journey by return of post.

IRELAND

All of the following places offer medical advice before a trip and medical help afterwards in the event of a tropical disease.

Travel Medicine Services, PO Box 254, 16 College St, Belfast 1 (☎01232/315220).

Tropical Medical Bureau, Grafton St Medical Centre, 34 Grafton St, Dublin 2 (☎01/671 9200).

Tropical Medical Bureau, Dun Laoghaire Medical Centre, 5 Northumberland Ave, Dun Laoghaire, Co. Dublin (☎01/280 4996).

US AND CANADA

Canadian Society for International Health, 170 Laurier Ave W, Suite 902, Ottawa, ON K1P 5V5 (☎613/230-2654). Distributes a free pamphlet, "Health Information for Canadian Travellers", containing an extensive list of travel health centres in Canada.

Center for Disease Control, 1600 Clifton Rd NE, Atlanta, GA 30333 (☎404/639-3311; http://www.cdc.gov/travel/travel.html). Information on outbreak warnings and suggested inoculations, among other things. Web site is very useful.

International Association for Medical Assistance to Travellers (IAMAT), 417 Center St, Lewiston, NY 14092 (☎716/754-4883), and 40

Regal Rd, Guelph, ON N1K 1B5 (☎519/836-0102). A non-profit organization supported by donations, it can provide a list of English-speaking doctors in Brazil, climate charts and leaflets on various diseases and inoculations.

Travel Medicine, 351 Pleasant St, Suite 312, Northampton, MA 01060 (☎1-800/872-8633). Sells first-aid kits, mosquito netting, water filters and other health-related travel products.

Travelers Medical Center, 31 Washington Square, New York, NY 10011 (☎212/982-1600). Consultation service on immunizations and treatment of diseases for people travelling to developing countries.

AUSTRALIA AND NZ

Auckland Hospital, Park Rd, Grafton, Auckland (☎09/379 7440).

Travellers' Medical and Vaccination Centre, 7/428 George St, Sydney (☎02/9221 7133); 3/393 Little Bourke St, Melbourne (☎03/9602 5788);

6/29 Gilbert Place, Adelaide (☎08/8212 7522); 6/247 Adelaide St, Brisbane (☎07/3221 9066); 1 Mill St, Perth (☎08/9321 1977). Web site: http//:www.tmvc.com.au

most poisonous snakes are tiny, easily able to snuggle inside a shoe or a rucksack pocket. Always shake out your hammock and clothes, keep rucksack pockets tightly closed and take special care when it rains as snakes, scorpions and other nasty beasties quite sensibly head for shelter in huts. **If you do get bitten** by a snake, try to catch it for identification. Use a shoelace or a torn piece of shirt wound round the limb with a stick as a tourniquet, which you should repeatedly tighten for twenty seconds and then release for a minute, to slow down the action of the poison. Contrary to popular belief, cutting yourself and sucking out blood will do you more harm than

good. It goes without saying that you should get yourself to a doctor as soon as possible. If you are well off the beaten track, small pharmacies even in remote villages usually stock serum, but you must know the type of snake involved.

The humidity means that any cut or wound gets infected very easily. Always **clean cuts** or bites with alcohol or purified water before dressing. As a general rule, leave all insects alone and never handle them. Even the smallest ants, caterpillars and bees can give you nasty stings and bites, and scorpions, large soldier ants and some species of bee will give you fever for a day or two as well.

INFORMATION AND MAPS

You'll find tourist information fairly easy to come across once in Brazil, but you're unlikely to find much before you leave home. The Brazilian National Tourist Board (EMBRATUR) no longer maintains offices outside of Brazil and, instead, tourism promotion is usually assigned to a junior diplomat of the Trade Section of Brazil's embassies or larger consulates (see p.15) – but don't expect more than a few dated brochures.

TOURIST OFFICES

In Brazil, facilities vary greatly. Popular destinations like Rio, Salvador and towns throughout

the South have efficient and helpful **tourist offices**, but anywhere off the beaten track has nothing at all.

All **state capitals** have tourist information offices, which are open during office hours, announced by signs saying "**Informações Turísticas**". Most provide free city maps and booklets, but they are usually all in Portuguese, although you occasionally see atrociously mangled English. As a rule, only the airport tourist offices have **hotel booking services**, and none of them are very good on advising about budget accommodation. There are EMBRATUR offices in a few of the major centres, but the local tourist offices are usually more helpful; these are run by the different state and municipal governments, so you have to learn a new acronym every time you cross a state line. In Rio, for example, you'll find national (EMBRATUR), state (Turisrio) and city (Riotur) offices.

MAPS

We've provided **maps** of all the major towns and cities and various other regions. More detailed maps are surprisingly hard to get hold of outside Brazil, and are rarely very good: there are plenty of maps of South America, but the only widely available one that is specifically of Brazil is the *Bartholomew Brazil & Bolivia* (1:5,000,000) which is not very easy to read. Much better are the six regional maps in the *Mapa Rodoviário Touring* series (1:2,500,000), which clearly mark all the

MAP OUTLETS

BRITAIN

Aberdeen Map Shop, 74 Skene St, **Aberdeen**, AB10 1QE (☎01224/637999).

John Smith and Sons, 57–61 St Vincent St, **Glasgow**, G2 5TB (☎0141/221 7472).

James Thin Melven's Bookshop, 29 Union St, **Inverness**, IV1 1QA (☎01463/233500).

The Map Shop, 30a Belvoir St, **Leicester**, LE1 6QH (☎01162/471 4000).

London: Daunt Books, 83 Marylebone High St, W1M 3DE (☎0171/224 2295); 193 Haverstock Hill, NW3 4QL (☎0171/794 4006).

National Map Centre, 22–24 Caxton St, SW1 0QU (☎0171/222 2466).

Stanfords, 12–14 Long Acre, WC2E 9LP (☎0171/836 1321); 52 Grosvenor Gardens, SW1W 0AG (☎0171/730 1314); and 156 Regent St, W1R 5TA (☎0171/434 4744).

The Travel Bookshop, 13–15 Blenheim Crescent, W11 2EE (☎0171/229 5260).

Newcastle Map Centre, 55 Grey St, **Newcastle upon Tyne**, NE1 6EF (☎0191/261 5622).

Blackwell's Map and Travel Shop, 53 Broad St, **Oxford**, OX1 3BQ (☎01865/792792).

Latitude, 34 The Broadway, Darkes Lane, **Potters Bar**, Herts EN6 2HW (☎01707/663090).

The Map Shop, 15 High St, **Upton-upon-Severn**, Worcestershire WR8 0HJ (☎01684/593146).

IRELAND

Waterstone's, Queens Bldg, 8 Royal Ave, **Belfast**, BT1 1DA (☎01232/247355).

Waterstone's, 69 Patrick St, **Cork** (☎021/ 276 522).

Dublin: Easons Bookshop, 40 O'Connell St, Dublin 1 (☎01/873 3811).

Fred Hanna's Bookshop, 27–29 Nassau St, Dublin 2 (☎01/677 1255).

Hodges Figgis Bookshop, 56–58 Dawson St, Dublin 2 (☎01/677 4754).

Waterstone's, 7 Dawson St, Dublin 2 (☎01/679 1260).

USA

Travel Books & Language Center, 4931 Cordell Ave, **Bethesda**, MD 20814 (☎1-800/220-2665).

Rand McNally, 444 N Michigan Ave, **Chicago**, IL 60611 (☎312/321-1751).

New York: The Complete Traveller Bookstore, 199 Madison Ave, NY 10016 (☎212/685-9007); Rand McNally, 150 E 52nd St, NY 10022 (☎212/758-7488; call ☎1-800/333-0136 ext 2111 for other locations, or for maps by mail order); Traveler's Bookstore, 22 W 52nd St, New York, NY 10019 (☎212/664-0995).

Phileas Fogg's Books & Maps, #87 Stanford Shopping Center, **Palo Alto**, CA 94304 (☎1-800/533-FOGG).

Rand McNally, 595 Market St, **San Francisco**, CA 94105 (☎415/777-3131).

The Map Store Inc., 1636 1st St, **Washington DC** 20006 (☎202/628 2608).

Adventurous Traveler Bookstore, PO Box 1468, **Williston**, VT 05495 (☎1-800/282-3963; http://www.AdventurousTraveler.com).

Canada

Ulysses Travel Bookshop, 4176 St-Denis, **Montréal** (☎514/843-9447).

Open Air Books and Maps, 25 Toronto St, **Toronto**, ON M5R 2C1 (☎416/363-0719).

World Wide Books and Maps, 736 Granville St, **Vancouver**, BC V6Z 1E4 (☎604/687-3320).

AUSTRALIA AND NZ

The Map Shop, 16a Peel St, **Adelaide** (☎08/8231 2033).

Specialty Maps, 58 Albert St, **Auckland** (☎09/307 2217).

Bowyangs, 372 Little Bourke St, **Melbourne** (☎03/9670 4383).

Perth Map Centre, 891 Hay St, **Perth** (☎08/9322 5733).

Travel Bookshop, 20 Bridge St, **Sydney** (☎02/9241 3554).

major routes, although these, even in Brazil, are difficult to find.

In Brazil, a useful compendium of **city maps** and **main road networks** is published by Guias Quatro Rodas, a Brazilian motoring organization, which also has guides to Rio, São Paulo and other cities, states and regions. These are easy to find in bookstores, newsagents and magazine stalls.

Very clear maps of individual states are published by Polimapas, and are usually available on the spot. At 1:1,000,000 these are the largest scale of all, though they actually have less detail than some of the above mentioned. Topographical and hiking maps are difficult to find, though very occasionally they are available from municipal tourist offices or national parks in Brazil.

COSTS, MONEY AND BANKS

Until a short time ago, Brazilian inflation was astronomical, and the country was a very cheap destination for anyone who had hard currency like the dollar. Since 1994, however, Brazilian inflation has – at least officially – been less than ten percent annually, stabilized by the famous *Plano Real*. At a stroke this made Brazil no longer cheap to foreigners, since a tightly controlled exchange rate was central to the plan's success. Although the exchange rate has improved a little over the last couple of years, the cost of living in Brazil is now about the same as in most of Europe and the US.

Since the introduction of the *Plano Real*, US dollars are accepted as payment only in luxury hotels and souvenir shops in the big cities. However, given Brazil's chaotic economic history, we are continuing to quote prices in this book in **US dollars**: in the event of a sudden monetary crisis, as predicted by certain commentators, this should give a reliable idea of what you'll be paying on the spot.

At the time of writing, the Brazilian *real* is maintaining a rough parity with the dollar, ie approximately R$1=US$1 (it's allowed to float about fifteen percent in either direction).

MONEY AND PRICES

The Brazilian currency is the **real** (pronounced "hey-al"), plural *reais* (pronounced "hey-ice"). It's written as R$ and is made up of one hundred *centavos*, written ¢. **Notes**, all the same size but different colours, are for 1, 5, 10, 50 and 100 *reais*; **coins** are 1, 5, 10, 25, 50 *centavos* and 1 *real*. Coins are irritatingly similar, and have to be scrutinized closely to tell them apart.

The **cost of living** in Brazil is now rather high compared to its inflationary past, since prices ended up being stabilized at a relatively high level: just before the *Plano Real* came in everyone naturally put their prices up. Some things, fortunately, are still cheap: most foodstuffs, including eating out in most restaurants, clothes and bus travel. Other things are astronomically expensive: plane tickets (unless part of an air pass), film, sun cream and anything electrical. One hangover from hyperinflation is that prices are still not quite standardized from place to place, and you can still find bargains if you have the time and patience to shop around.

All the same, Brazil is still a viable destination for the budget traveller, especially in urban areas. The cheapness of food and budget hotels – and the fact that the best attractions, like the beaches, are free – still makes it possible to have a very good time for under $50 a day. Staying in good hotels, travelling by comfortable buses and not stinting on the extras will now cost you around $150 a day.

CHANGING MONEY

In large cities, only the head offices of major **banks** (Banco do Brasil, Banco Itaú, Banespa) will have an exchange department (ask for *câmbio*); whether changing cash or travellers' cheques, you'll need your passport. You can also change cash and travellers' cheques in smart hotels and in some large travel agencies. The best rates, however, are usually to be found in a **casa de câmbio**, but these only operate on any scale in Rio and São Paulo.

Exchange departments of banks often close early, sometimes at 1pm, although more often at 2pm or 3pm, and it can take up to two hours to complete all the necessary paperwork. Some banks will only change a minimum of $100 per transaction, and the Banco do Brasil imposes a commission fee of $20 regardless of the amount to be changed. Airport banks are open seven days a week, others only Monday to Friday. You'll find life much easier if you bring only **US dollar banknotes and travellers' cheques**. Only in *casas de câmbio* in Rio and São Paulo will you be able to change other currencies.

Outside large cities it can sometimes be difficult to change money at all, but an ever-increasing number of branches of the Banco do Brasil provide this service. If you get stuck, travel agents or smart hotels are worth a try, though most will only accept dollar banknotes; if they don't buy themselves, they will know who does.

The main **credit cards** are all now widely accepted in Brazil, even in rural areas. Mastercard and Visa are the most prevalent, with Diners Club and American Express also widespread. Even so, don't expect to rely entirely on cards, as some businesses – even ones you would expect to – don't accept them or accept only a very limited range. And when hotels offer low-season discounts, they may make a condition that the bill is paid with cash. If you do pay by card in a shop which doesn't have an automatic swipe register, the shop will have to use chronically overloaded phone lines to check the balance, which can take an inconvenient amount of time. Note also that Brazilians are quite fussy about your signature matching that on your card.

You can obtain **cash advances** on all major cards at most bank branches in big cities; in smaller towns only the main branch of Banco do Brasil will do it. Visa is much the easiest card to get a cash advance on. Don't join the queues for the tellers, but look for a sign saying *Cartão* or *Saques por Cartão*; if there aren't any, wave your card at one of the managers behind a desk, and they will point you in the right direction. Far easier and much faster is to use one of the ever increasing number of **ATMs**. Again, Visa cards are the most widely accepted.

To change Brazilian currency back into dollars when you leave, you need to show **bank exchange receipts** to the value of what you want to change. These receipts are called *comprovantes*, and banks will type one out for you on request when you buy Brazilian currency – *casas de câmbio* do not issue them.

EXCHANGE RATES

In the past, most visitors to Brazil would change all their dollars at the effectively legalized black market (*paralelo*) rate, which appeared daily on the finance pages of newspapers and which was sometimes as much as 50 percent higher than the rate offered by banks. However, the black market was another casualty of stabilization, and there is now little difference between official and other exchange rates. You will see two rates being quoted for cash: the *oficial*, which is what a bank will pay you, and the *turismo*, which is what you will get in a hotel or travel agency; travellers cheques have slightly lower rates, even in banks. The *turismo* is usually only two or three points less than the *oficial* and, unless you're changing large amounts of money, it's often worth living with this lower rate to avoid the inconvenience of changing your money in a bank.

GETTING AROUND

Local travel in Brazil is always easy. Public transport is generally by bus or plane, though there are a few passenger trains, too. However you travel, services will be crowded, plentiful and, apart from planes, cheap. Approximate journey times and frequencies can be found in the "travel details" at the end of each chapter, and local peculiarities are pointed out in the text of the *Guide*.

Car rental is also possible, but driving in Brazil is not for the faint-hearted. Most international car rental companies have local agencies and there are quite a few reliable Brazilian ones as well. Hitchhiking, over any distance, is not recommended.

BUSES

The **bus system** in Brazil is excellent, as good as anywhere in the Americas, and makes travelling around the country easy, comfortable and economical, despite the distances involved. Intercity buses leave from a station called a **Rodoviária**, usually built on city outskirts.

Buses are operated by hundreds of private companies, but **prices** are standardized, even when more than one firm plies the same route, and are very reasonable: Rio to São Paulo is around $20, Rio to Belo Horizonte $35, São Paulo to Brasília $50, Recife to Salvador $40 and Fortaleza to Belém $60. Long-distance buses are comfortable enough to sleep in, and have on-board toilets (which can get smelly on long journeys): the lower your seat number, the further

away from them you'll be. Buses stop every two or three hours at well-supplied *postos*, but as prices are high it's not a bad idea to bring along water and some food to last the journey.

There are luxury buses, too, called **leitos**, which do nocturnal runs between the major cities – worth taking once for the experience, with fully reclining seats in curtained partitions, freshly ironed sheets and an attendant plying insomniacs with coffee and conversation. They cost about a third of the price of an air ticket, and between two and three times as much as a normal long-distance bus; they're also less frequent and need to be booked a few days in advance. No matter what kind of bus, it's a good idea to have a light sweater or blanket during night journeys as the air conditioning is always uncomfortably cold.

TICKETS AND LUGGAGE

Going any distance, it's best to **buy your ticket** at least a day in advance, from the *Rodoviária*, or in some large cities, from travel agents. An exception is the Rio–São Paulo route, where a shuttle service means you can always just turn up without a ticket and never have to wait more than fifteen minutes. Numbered seats are provided on all routes: if you want a window ask for *janela*. If you cross a state line you will get a small form with the ticket, which asks for the number of your seat (*poltrona*), the number of your ticket (*passagem*), the number of your passport (*identidade*) and your destination (*destino*). You have to fill it in and give it to the driver before you'll be let on board. Buses have **luggage** compartments, which are safe: you check pieces at the side of the bus and get a ticket for them. Keep an eye on your hand luggage, and take anything valuable with you when you get off for a halt.

PLANES

It's hardly surprising that a country the size of Brazil relies on **air travel** a good deal; in some parts of Amazonia air links are more important than either the roads or rivers. Any town has at least an airstrip, and all cities have airports, usually some distance from the city but not always: Santos Dumont in Rio, Guarulhos in São Paulo and Guararapes in Recife are all pretty central. The main domestic carriers are **VASP**, **Varig** and

Transbrasil; important regional airlines include the Varig subsidiary RioSul, mainly serving the South, and TAM, which concentrates on the centre west and Amazon.

Flying to the Northeast or Amazonia from southern Brazil can be tiresome, as many of these long-distance routes are no more than glorified bus runs, stopping everywhere before heading north again. In planning your itinerary, it's a good idea to check carefully how many times a plane stops – for example, between São Paulo and Fortaleza a flight may stop as many as four times or as few as one. On scheduled domestic flights you should check in an hour before take-off, but expect delays if the plane you're catching is arriving from elsewhere.

A word of **warning**: in many parts of Amazonia air travel in small planes, or **aerotaxis**, is very common – the regional word for these flights is *teco-teco*. Before taking one, you should be aware that the airstrips are often dangerous, the planes routinely fly overloaded and are not reliably maintained, and no checks are made on the qualifications of pilots – some don't have any.

TICKETS AND FARES

Flights tend to be booked up in advance (with the exception of the Rio–São Paulo shuttle, though here the flights at the beginning and end of the working day get crowded) and you need to book a *passagem* as far ahead as you can. Prices, once reasonable, are now high: Rio–São Paulo costs $140, Rio–Salvador $300, Rio–Iguaçu $300, Rio–Manaus $770. Return fares are double the one-way fares. If you plan on flying a lot in a relatively short time, then consider buying an **air pass** before you leave for Brazil (see box).

For all internal flights you have to pay an **airport tax**: between $7 and $9 depending on the airport, payable in local currency at the airline desk of the company you're travelling with (not the check-in desk, except at Rio and São Paulo); airline desks are usually in the entrance hall of the airport. Departure tax for all international

---

AIR PASSES

When buying your international ticket, you should consider the possibility of adding an **air pass**: even if you plan on taking just a couple of flights, they can work out far cheaper than purchasing individual tickets. Brazil's three main airlines – Transbrasil, Varig (along with its regional subsidiaries RioSul and RioNordeste) and VASP – all offer passes, their basic conditions being virtually identical. Air passes can only be bought **outside Brazil** and only Transbrasil passes are available to anyone regardless of which airline they're travelling into the country on.

Varig's **Brazil Airpass** is still the most easily available of the three and gives access to the largest route network, but it can now only be purchased if you travel into Brazil with Varig or British Airways. The air pass fare is $490 low season, $540 high season, for adults and children (infants pay ten percent) and gives you five coupons for use within a period of 21 consecutive days. Coupons are not valid for the same route in the same direction more than once. Connecting flights count as only one coupon and you can buy a maximum of four additional coupons for $100 each. You can leave your route completely open, to be decided in Brazil, or you can specify it at the time of purchase, in which case changes of route are not permitted (but flight times and

dates can be altered). Bear in mind though that flights on some routes can be heavily booked long in advance. Less expensive regional Varig passes providing four coupons valid during a 21-day period are also available covering south and central Brazil ($350 low season, $400 high season) or the Northeast and the Amazon ($290 low season, $340 high season).

An even greater bargain is the **Mercosur Airpass**, an air pass covering eight airlines of Argentina, Brazil, Paraguay and Uruguay which can only be bought **outside South America**. The regulations are fairly complicated but basically allow two stopovers per country (plus point of origin) up to a maximum of eight coupons, although an extra coupon is allowed to give you use of both the Argentine and Brazilian airports at Iguaçu Falls. The route must include at least two countries and the price of a pass is based on the number of miles flown, always working out to cost far less than purchasing regular tickets. As examples of the kind of price to expect for a Mercosur Airpass, the route Rio–Iguaçu–Buenos Aires–Rio costs $225, while the route Rio–Recife–Salvador–São Paulo–Asunción–Buenos Aires–Montevideo–Rio works out at $545. Prices may be affected by the time of year that you travel.

flights is $18, payable in local currency or dollars when you check in.

It is always a good idea to **reconfirm** onward flights a day or two in advance: it can be done over the phone – airline offices always have someone who speaks English – and you can make seat reservations at the same time. Another point to remember is that if you have an air pass and change your flights, always remember to cancel the original flight. If you don't, the computer flags you as a no-show, and all your other air pass reservations will also be cancelled.

TRAINS, FERRIES AND BOATS

You probably won't be taking many **trains** in Brazil. Although there's an extensive rail network, much of it is for cargo only, and even where there are passenger trains they're almost invariably slower and less convenient than the buses. Exceptions are a few **tourist journeys** worth making for themselves – in the South and Minas Gerais especially – and one or two specific routes, such as the luxurious service between Rio and São Paulo.

Water travel and ferries are also important forms of transport in parts of Brazil. Specific details are included in the relevant parts of the *Guide*, but look out for the ferry to Niterói, without which no journey to **Rio** would be complete; **Salvador**, where there are regular services to islands and towns in the huge bay on which the city is built; in the **South** between the islands of the Bay of Paranaguá; and most of all in **Amazonia**.

AMAZON RIVERBOATS

In Amazonia, rivers have been the main highways for centuries, and the Amazon itself is navigable to ocean-going ships as far west as Iquitos in Peru, nearly 3000km upstream from Belém.

In all the large riverside cities of the Amazon – notably Belém, Manaus and Santarém – there are *hidroviárias*, ferry terminals for waterborne bus services. **Amazon river travel** is slow and can be tough going, but it's a fascinating experience. On longer journeys there are a number of classes; in general it's better to avoid *cabine*, where you swelter in a cabin, and choose *primeiro* (first class) instead, sleeping in a hammock on deck. *Segundo* (second class) is usually hammock space in the lower deck or engine room. Take plenty of provisions, and expect to practise your Portuguese.

The **range of boat transport** in the Amazon runs from luxury tourist boats and three-level large riverboats to one- or two-level smaller boats (the latter normally confining their routes to main tributaries and local runs) and covered launches operated by tour companies. As a rule, most local boats cost about $20 a day (including food), more for the tourist boats and tour-based launches. The most popular route is the **Belém–Manaus trip** which costs $65–90 (hammock space) and takes four to six days.

CITY TRANSPORT

Shoals of **local buses** clog city streets: you enter at the back – where route details are posted – and move through a turnstile as you pay your fare. **Fares** are all flat rate, and rarely more than 50¢. Buses often get unbelievably crowded, and in large cities are favourite targets for pickpockets. It's safer to go immediately through the turnstile even when there are seats at the rear, as *assaltantes* prefer the backs of buses where they can make a quick getaway through the rear door.

There are also good modern **metrô** systems in Rio, São Paulo, Belo Horizonte, Porto Alegre and Recife. Again, they're cheap and efficient, and they're also relatively safe – but since they weren't built with tourism in mind, their routes are not always the most useful.

TAXIS

There are enormous numbers of **taxis** in Brazilian cities, but they are now fairly expensive. City cabs are metered, but the meters always lag way behind inflation. On the windscreen you'll see a sticker for a *UT* (*unidade taxímetro*), showing by what fraction or multiple you should reduce or increase the meter figure. This gives you a rough idea of what you're paying, though the exact fare is determined by the *tabela*, the card with price readjustments to which the driver will refer at the end of the journey – ask to see it if you suspect you are being overcharged.

Taxis in small towns and rural areas do not have meters, and you need to agree the fare in advance – they'll be more expensive than in the cities. Most airports and some bus stations are covered by taxi co-operatives, with a slightly different system: attendants give you a coupon with fares to various destinations printed on it – you pay either at a kiosk in advance, or the driver. Tipping is not obligatory, but appreciated.

DRIVING AND CAR RENTAL

Driving standards in Brazil hover between the abysmal and the appalling: in 1996 over 50,000 people died on Brazilian roads, easily the highest toll in the world, and on any journey you can see why, with thundering trucks and drivers treating the road as if it were a Grand Prix racetrack. City driving would make even an Italian blanch, and takes a lot of getting used to. Fortunately, inter-city bus drivers are the exception to the rule: they are usually very good, and many buses have devices fitted that make it impossible for them to exceed the speed limit.

Road quality varies according to region: the South and Southeast have a good paved network; the Northeast has a good network on the coast but is poor in the interior; while roads in Amazonia are by far the worst, with even major highways closed for weeks or months at a time as they are washed away by the rains. Over half of Brazilian cars now run on *álcool* – a mixture of petroleum-based fuel and alcohol – which is half the price of *gasolina*, but which works less efficiently. Outside of the towns and cities, **service stations** can be few and far between, so keep a careful eye on the fuel gauge. Service stations do not accept international credit cards, so make sure you always have sufficient **cash**.

RENTING A CAR

Renting a car in Brazil is relatively straightforward, as long as you're confident that you can handle the drivers. Hertz, Avis and other big-name international companies operate here, and there are plenty of Brazilian alternatives, such as Interlocadora, Nobre and Localiza. Unidas are also represented throughout the country and are highly recommended, as their cars are always in excellent condition, service is efficient and – if you take out their comprehensive insurance policy – there is no excess payable if your car is stolen or damaged. Often, though, you'll find the lowest rates are offered by smaller, local companies, but this can be a risky proposition. Car rental offices (*locadoras*) can be found at every airport and in most towns of any size. Try to avoid renting an alcohol-powered car: they always take two or three tries before they start, whatever the weather, they accelerate more slowly, and have a maddening tendency to cut out in lower gear if you make the slightest mistake with the clutch.

Renting a car can be a useful way of seeing a small area which would take days to see on public transport, or of getting to places otherwise entirely inaccessible. Most cities are fairly well signposted so getting out of town shouldn't be too difficult; if city traffic is daunting, try to arrange to collect your car on a Sunday when traffic is light. If at all possible, avoid driving at night because potholes (even on main roads) and *lombardas* (speed bumps) may not be obvious, and breaking down after dark in a strange place could be dangerous. An **international driving licence** is useful: although foreign licences are accepted for short visits, you may have a hard time convincing a police officer or a rental company of this.

Rates start from around $60 a day for a Fiat Uno or similar; if reserved from outside Brazil you get 100 "free" km, thereafter it's 25¢ per km. If you arrange your car rental in Brazil, you usually get unlimited mileage included in the price. Four-wheel drive vehicles, such as Toyota Land Cruisers, are sometimes available, but are extremely expensive.

CAR RENTAL AGENCIES

BRITAIN
Avis ☎0990/900500.
Budget ☎0800/181181.
Hertz ☎0990/996699.

IRELAND
Avis ☎01/874 5844.
Budget ☎0800/973159.
Hertz ☎01/676747.

NORTH AMERICA
Avis ☎1-800/331-1084.
Budget ☎1-800/527-0700.

Hertz ☎1-800/654-3001,
    in Canada ☎1-800/263-0600.

AUSTRALIA
Avis ☎1800/225 533.
Budget ☎13 2727.
Hertz ☎13 3039.

NEW ZEALAND
Avis ☎09/526 2847.
Budget ☎09/375 2222.
Hertz ☎09/309 0989.

Only luxury vehicles are available with automatic transmission. When you're quoted a price, make sure that it includes **insurance** (which is compulsory) and that there are no other hidden "extras". Even when insurance is included, you could well be liable to pay twenty percent of the market value of the car (around $2000 for a small car) if it's stolen or damaged in an accident, though a few companies, such as Unidas, offer genuinely comprehensive policies. If you have a US or Canadian credit card, you may find that it can be used to cover the additional liability – check before leaving home. In any case, a credit card is essential as a deposit when renting a car.

As you would anywhere, carefully check the condition of the car before accepting it and pay special attention to the state of the tyres (including the spare), and make sure there's a jack, warning triangle and fire extinguisher. All cars have front and back seatbelts, three-point belts in the front and lap belts in the back. Their use is compulsory, and stiff on-the-spot fines are imposed on drivers and front-seat passengers found not to be wearing them.

Parking, especially in the cities, can be tricky, and it's worth paying extra for a hotel with some kind of lock-up garage – on the street you'll often be approached by someone offering to "guard" your car, and it's usually worth a few cents to prevent your self-appointed guardian from doing any damage. In any event, never leave anything visible inside the car if you don't want to lose it.

ACCOMMODATION

Accommodation in Brazil covers the full range from hostels and basic hotels clustered around bus stations to luxury resort hotels. You can sometimes succeed in finding places to sleep for as little as $5 a night, but more realistically, a clean double room in a one-star hotel will set you back upwards of $20. As is so often the case, single travellers get a bad deal, usually paying almost as much as the cost of a double room.

DORMITORIES AND HOSTELS

At the bottom end of the scale, in terms of both quality and price, are **dormitórios**, small and very basic (to put it mildly) hotels, situated close to bus stations and in the poorer parts of town. They are extremely cheap, just a few dollars a night, but usually unsavoury and sometimes positively dangerous.

You could stay for not much more, in far better conditions, in a **youth hostel**, an *albergue de juventude*, also sometimes called a *casa de estudante*. There's an extensive network of these, with at least one in every state capital, and they are very well maintained, often in restored buildings. It helps to have an IYHF card with a recent photograph – you're not usually asked for one, but every so often you'll find an *albergue* which refuses entry unless it's produced. The Federação Brasileira dos Albergues de Juventude in Rio produces an excellent illustrated guide to Brazil's hostels. The cost per person is between $10 and $14 a night.

Demand for places far outstrips supply at certain times of year – December to *Carnaval*, and July – but if you travel with a **hammock** you can often hook it up in a corridor or patio. A major advantage that hostels have is to throw you together with young Brazilians, the main users of the network: they are generally friendly and intensely curious about life abroad, as they don't meet many foreigners this close up.

PENSÕES, POSTOS AND POUSADAS

In a slightly higher price range are the small, family-run hotels, called either a **pensão** (*pensões* in the plural) or a *hotel familiar*. These vary a great

YOUTH HOSTEL ASSOCIATIONS

Australia Australian Youth Hostels Association, Level 3, 10 Mallett St, Camperdown, NSW (☎02/9565-1325).

Brazil Federação Brasileira dos Albergues de Juventude, Rua da Assembléia 10, Sala 1211, Centro, Rio de Janeiro (☎021/252-4829).

Canada Canadian Hostelling Association, Room 400, 205 Catherine St, Ottawa, ON K2P 1C3 (☎613/748-5638).

England and Wales Youth Hostel Association (YHA), Trevelyan House, 8 St Stephen's Hill, St Alban's, Herts AL1 2DY (☎01727/855 215).

London shop and information office: 14 Southampton St, London WC2 (☎0171/836 1036).

Ireland An Oige, 39 Mountjoy Square, Dublin 1 (☎01/830 4555).

New Zealand Youth Hostels Association of New Zealand, PO Box 436, Christchurch 1 (☎03/379-9970).

Northern Ireland Youth Hostel Association of Northern Ireland, 22 Donegall Rd, Belfast, BT12 5JN (☎01232/324 733).

Scotland Scottish Youth Hostel Association, 7 Glebe Crescent, Stirling, FK8 2JA (☎01786/451 181).

USA American Youth Hostels (AYH), 733 15th St NW 840, PO Box 37613, Washington DC 20005 (☎202/783-6161).

deal: some are no more appealing than a *dormitório*, while others are friendlier and better value than many hotels. They tend to be better in small towns than in large cities, but are also usefully thick on the ground in some of the main tourist towns, where hotels are generally more expensive: Olinda and Ouro Preto are two good examples. In southern Brazil, many of the *postos*, highway service stations on town outskirts, have cheap **rooms**, and showers, that are usually well kept and clean.

You will also come across the **pousada**. This can just be another name for a *pensão*, but can also be a small hotel, running up to luxury class but usually less expensive than a hotel proper. In the Amazon and Mato Grosso in particular, *pousadas* tend to be purpose-built *fazenda* lodges geared towards the growing eco-tourist markets and are not aimed at budget travellers.

HOTELS

Hotels proper run from dives to luxury apartments. There is a Brazilian classification system, from one to five stars, but the absence of stars doesn't necessarily mean a bad hotel: they depend on bureaucratic requirements like the width of liftshafts and kitchen floorspace as much as on the standard of accommodation – many perfectly good hotels don't have stars.

Hotels offer a range of different rooms, with significant price differences: a **quarto** is a room without a bathroom, an **apartamento** with (actually a shower – Brazilians don't use baths); an

apartamento de luxo is normally just an *apartamento* with a fridge full of (marked-up) drinks; a **casal** is a double room; and a **solteiro** a single. In a starred hotel, an *apartamento* upwards would normally come with telephone, air conditioning (*ar condicionado*) and a TV; a *ventilador* is a fan.

Rates for rooms vary tremendously between different parts of Brazil, but start at around $20 in a one-star hotel, around $30 in a two-star hotel, and around $45 in a three-star place. Anything above three stars and you'll pay "international" prices. Generally speaking, for $35–50 a night you could expect to stay in a reasonable mid-range hotel, with bathroom and air conditioning. Many hotels in this range in Brazil are excellent value for the standard of accommodation they offer. During the off-season most hotels in tourist areas offer hefty discounts, usually around 25–35 percent, but when discounts are offered, credit cards are not accepted.

Most hotels – although not all – will add a ten percent **service charge** to your bill, the *taxa de serviço*: those that don't will have a sign at the desk saying "*Nos não cobramos taxa de serviço*", and it's very bad form to leave the hotel without tipping the receptionist. The price will almost invariably include **breakfast** – gargantuan helpings of fruit, cheese, bread and coffee – but no other meals, although there will often be a restaurant. Hotels usually have a **safe deposit box**, a *caixa*, which it's advisable to ask about when you check in; they are free for you to use and, although they're not invulnerable, anything left in a *caixa* is safer than on your person or unguarded in your room. Many hotels also offer a safe deposit box in your room, which is the safest option of all.

Finally, a **motel**, as you'll gather from the various names and decor, is strictly for couples. This is not to say that it's not possible to stay in one if you can't find anything else – since they're used by locals they're rarely too expensive – but you should be aware that most of the other rooms will be rented by the hour.

CAMPING

There are a fair number of **campsites** in Brazil and almost all of them are on the coast near the bigger beaches – mostly they're near cities rather than in out-of-the-way places. They will usually have basic facilities – running water and toilets, perhaps a simple restaurant – and are popular with young Argentines and Brazilians. There are a few fancier sites designed for people with camper vans or big tents in the back of their cars. In all cases, however, the problem is **security**, partly of your person, but more significantly of your possessions, which can never really be made safe. Great caution should be exercised before **camping off-site** – only do so if you're part of a group and you've received assurances locally as to safety.

EATING AND DRINKING

It's hard to generalize about Brazilian food, largely because there is no single national cuisine but numerous very distinct regional ones. Nature dealt Brazil a full hand for these

varying cuisines: there's an abundant variety of fruit, vegetables and spices, as you can see for yourself walking through any food market.

There are four main **regional cuisines**: **comida mineira** from Minas Gerais, based on pork, vegetables (especially *couve*, a relative of spinach) and *tutu*, a kind of refried bean cooked with manioc flour and used as a thick sauce; **comida baiana** from the Salvador coast, the most exotic to gringo palates, using fish and shellfish, hot peppers, palm oil, coconut milk and fresh coriander; **comida do sertão** from the interior of the Northeast, which relies on rehydrated dried or salted meat and the fruit, beans and tubers of the interior of the Northeast; and **comida gaúcha** from Rio Grande do Sul, the most carnivorous diet in the world, revolving around every imaginable kind of meat grilled over charcoal. *Comida do sertão* is rarely served outside its homeland, but you'll find restaurants serving the others throughout Brazil, although – naturally – they're at their best in their region of origin.

Alongside the regional restaurants, there is a **standard fare** available everywhere that can soon get dull unless you cast around: steak (*bife*) or chicken (*frango*), served with *arroz e feijão*, rice and beans, and often with salad, fries and *farinha*, dried **manioc** (cassava) flour that you sprinkle over everything. *Farofa* is toasted *farinha*, and usually comes with onions and bits of bacon mixed in. In cheaper restaurants all this would come on a single large plate: look for the words *prato feito*, *prato comercial* or *refeição*

completa if you want to fill up without spending too much.

Feijoada is the closest Brazil comes to a national dish: a stew of pork, sausage and smoked meat cooked with black beans and garlic, garnished with slices of orange. Eating it is a national ritual at weekends, when restaurants serve *feijoada* all day.

Some of the **fruit** is familiar – *manga*, mango, *maracujá*, passion fruit, *limão*, lime – but most of it has only Brazilian names: *jaboticaba*, *fruta do conde*, *sapoti* and *jaca*. The most exotic fruits are Amazonian (see p.318): try *bacuri*, *açaí* and the

---

UNDERSTANDING BRAZILIAN MENUS

Food (*Comida*)

açúcar	sugar	legumes/		pão	bread
arroz	rice	verduras	vegetables	peixe	fish
azeite	olive oil	manteiga	butter	pimenta	pepper
carne	meat	mariscos	seafood	queijo	cheese
farinha	dried manioc	molho	sauce	sal	salt
	flour beans	ovos	eggs	sopa/caldo	soup

Seafood (*Frutos do Mar*)

agulha	needle fish	mariscos	mussels	pitu	crayfish
atum	tuna	moqueca	seafood stewed in	pirarucu	Amazon river fish
camarão	prawn, shrimp		palm oil and	polvo	octopus
caranguejo	large crab		coconut sauce	siri	small crab
filhote	Amazon river fish	ostra	oyster	sururu	a type of mussel
lagosta	lobster	pescada	seafood stew, or		
lula	squid		hake		

Meat and Poultry (*Carne e Aves*)

bife	steak	costeleta	chop	vitela	veal
bife a cavalo	steak with egg	fígado	liver	frango	chicken
	and *farinha*	leitão	sucking pig	pato	duck
cabrito	kid	linguiça	sausage	peru	turkey
carne de porco	pork	picadinha	stew	peito	breast
carneiro	lamb	salsicha	hot dog	perna	leg
costela	ribs	veado	venison		

Fruit (*Frutas*)

abacate	avocado	goiaba	guava	melão	melon
abacaxi	pineapple	graviola	cherimoya	morango	strawberry
ameixa	plum, prune	laranja	orange	pera	pear
caju	cashew fruit	limão	lime	pêssego	peach
carambola	star fruit	maçã	apple	uvas	grapes
cerejas	cherries	mamão	papaya		
côco	coconut	manga	mango		
fruta do conde	custard apple	maracujá	passion fruit		
	(also *ata*)	melancia	watermelon		

extraordinary *cupuaçu*, the most delicious of all. These all serve as the basis for juices and **ice cream**, *sorvete*, which can be excellent; keep an eye out for *sorvetarias*, ice-cream parlours.

SNACKS AND STREET FOOD

On every street corner in Brazil you will find a **lanchonete**, a mixture of café and bar. They sell beer and rum, snacks, cigarettes, soft drinks, coffee and sometimes small meals. **Bakeries** – *padarias* – often have a *lanchonete* attached, and they're good places for cheap snacks: an *empada*

or *empadinha* is a small pie, which has various fillings (*carne*, meat, *palmito*, palm heart and *camarão*, shrimp, the best); a *pastel* is a fried, filled pasty; an *esfiha* is a savoury pastry stuffed with spiced meat; and a *coxinha* is spiced chicken rolled in manioc dough and then fried. In central Brazil try *pão de queijo*, a savoury cheese snack that goes perfectly with coffee. All these savoury snacks go under the generic heading *salgados*.

If you haven't had **breakfast** (*café da manha*) at your hotel, then a bakery/*lanchonete* is a good place to head; and for a more substantial meal *lanchonetes* will generally serve a *prato comer-*

Vegetables and Spices (*Legumes e Temperos*)

alface	lettuce	coentro	parsley	mandioca	manioc/cassava
alho	garlic	cravo	clove	milho	corn
arroz e feijão	rice and beans	dendê	palm oil	palmito	palm heart
azeitonas	olives	ervilhas	peas	pepinho	cucumber
batatas	potatoes	espinafre	spinach	repolho	cabbage
canela	cinnamon	macaxeira	roasted manioc	tomate	tomato
cebola	onion	malagueta	very hot pepper,		
cenoura	carrot		looks like red or		
cheiro verde	fresh coriander		yellow cherry		

Useful Terms

acarajé	fried bean cake stuffed with vatapá (see below)	garrafa	bottle
		grelhado	grilled
alho e óleo	garlic and olive oil sauce	jantar	dinner, to have dinner
almoço	lunch	mal passado/	
assado	roasted	bem passado	rare/well done (meat)
bem gelado	well chilled	médio	medium grilled
café colonial	high tea	milanesa	breaded
café de manhã	breakfast	na chapa/na brasa	charcoal grilled
cardápio	menu	prato	plate
churrasco	barbecue	sobremesa	dessert
colher	spoon	sorvete	ice cream
copo	glass	taxa de serviço	service charge
conta/nota	bill	tucupi	fermented manioc and chicory sauce used in Amazonian cuisine
cozido	boiled, steamed		
cozinhar	to cook		
entrada	hors d'oeuvre	vatapá	Bahian shrimp dish, cooked with palm oil, skinned tomato and coconut milk, served with fresh coriander and hot peppers
faca	knife		
feijoada	black bean, pork and sausage stew		
garçom	waiter		
garfo	fork		

Drinks

água mineral	mineral water	chopp	draught beer
cachaça	sugar cane rum	com gás/sem gás	sparkling/still
caipirinha	rum and lime cocktail	suco	fruit juice
café com leite	coffe with hot milk	vinho	wine
cafézinho	black coffee	vitamina	fruit juice made with milk
cerveja	bottled beer		

cial, too. In both *lanchonetes* and *padarias* you usually pay first at the till, and then you take your ticket to the counter to get what you want.

You can get food at a growing number of **fast food** outlets in cities, which look garishly American but take the hamburger or hot dog and "Brazilianize" it, much improving it in the process. All sorts of things are added, and the menus are easy to understand because they are in mangled but recognizable English, albeit with Brazilian pronunciation. A hamburger is a *X-burger* (pronounced "sheezboorga"), a hot dog a *cachorro quente*; a *bauru* is a club sandwich with steak and egg; a *mixto quente* a toasted cheese and ham sandwich.

Food sold by **street vendors** in Brazil should be treated with caution, but not dismissed out of hand. You can practically see the hepatitis bugs and amoebas crawling over some of the food you see on sale in the streets, but plenty of vendors have proper stalls and can be very professional, with a loyal clientele of office workers and locals. Some of the food they sell has the advantage of being cooked a long time, which reduces the chance of picking anything up, and in some places – Salvador and Belém especially – you can get good food cheaply in the street; just choose your vendor sensibly. In Salvador try *acarajé,* only available from street vendors – a delicious fried bean mix with shrimp and hot pepper; and in Belém go for *maniçoba,* spiced sausage with chicory leaves, or *pato no tucupi,* duck stewed in manioc sauce.

RESTAURANTS

Restaurants – *restaurantes* – are ubiquitous, portions are very large and prices are extremely reasonable. A *prato comercial* is around $5, while a good full meal can usually be had for about $15, even in expensive-looking restaurants. Cheaper restaurants, though, tend only to be open for lunch. Specialist restaurants to look out for include a **rodízio,** where you pay a fixed charge and eat as much as you want; most **churrascarias** – restaurants specializing in charcoal-grilled meat of all kinds, especially beef – operate this system, too, bringing a constant supply of meat on huge spits to the tables.

In many restaurants you will be presented with unsolicited food the moment you sit down. This is the **couvert,** which can consist of anything from a couple of bits of raw carrot and an olive to quite an elaborate and substantial plate. Although the price is generally modest, it still has to be paid for. If you don't want it, ask the waiter to take it away.

Brazil also has a large variety of **ethnic restaurants,** thanks to the generations of Portuguese, Arabs, Italians and Japanese who have made the country their home. The widest selection is in São Paulo, with the best Italian, Arab and Japanese food in Brazil, but anywhere of any size will have good ethnic restaurants, often in surprising places: Belém, for example, has several excellent Japanese restaurants, thanks to a Japanese colony founded fifty years ago in the interior. Ethnic food may be marginally more expensive than Brazilian, but it's rarely exorbitant.

The bill normally comes with a ten percent service charge, but you should still **tip,** as waiters rely more on tips than on their very low wages.

VEGETARIAN FOOD

Being a **vegetarian** – or at least a strict one – is no easy matter in Brazil. Many Brazilians are unwilling vegetarians, of course, surviving on the staple diet of rice, beans and *farinha* – and there's wonderful fruit everywhere – but this is not food that you'll find in restaurants, except as side dishes.

If you eat fish there's no problem, especially in the Northeast and Amazonia where seafood forms the basis of many meals; and in the larger cities there are occasional **vegetarian restaurants** (usually described as *Restaurante Natural*), although they are often only open during the day. But elsewhere you're up against one of the world's most carnivorous cultures. In the south and centre west, *churrasco* rules – served at restaurants where you eat as many different cuts of meat as you can manage, and where requests for meals without meat are greeted with astonishment. At most restaurants – even *churrascarias* – huge salads are available but, if you're a vegan, always enquire whether eggs or cheese are included. If you get fed up with rice, beans and salad, there are always pizzerias around.

HOT DRINKS AND SOFT DRINKS

Coffee is the great national drink, served strong, hot and sweet in small cups and drunk quickly. However, coffee is often a great disappointment in Brazil: most of the good stuff goes for export, and it often comes so stiff with sugar that it's almost undrinkable. By far the best coffee is found in São Paulo and points south. You are never far from a **cafézinho** (as these small cups of coffee are known; *café* refers to coffee in its raw state). Coffee is sold from flasks in the street, in *lanchonetes* and bars, and in restaurants, where it comes free after the meal. The best way to start your day is with *café com leite*, hot milk with coffee added to taste.

Tea (*chá*) is surprisingly good. Try **chá mate**, a strong green tea with a noticeable caffeine hit, or one of the wide variety of herbal teas, most notably that made from *guaraná* (see below). One highly recommended way to take tea is using the **chimarrão**, very common in southern Brazil: a gourd filled with *chá mate* and boiling water, sucked through a silver straw. It needs some practice to avoid burning your lips, but once you get used to it is a wonderfully refreshing way to take tea.

The great variety of fruit in Brazil is put to excellent use in **sucos**: fruit is popped into a liquidizer with sugar and crushed ice to make a deliciously refreshing drink. Made with milk rather than water it becomes a **vitamina**. Most *lanchonetes* and bars sell *sucos* and *vitaminas*, but for the full variety you should visit a specialist **casa de sucos**, which are found in most town centres. Widely available, and the best option to quench a thirst, are *suco de maracujá*, passion fruit, and *suco de limão*, lime. In the North and Northeast, try *graviola*, *bacuri* and *cupuaçu*. Sugar will always be added to a *suco* unless you ask for it *sem açúcar;* some, notably *maracujá* and *limão*, are undrinkable without.

Soft drinks are the regular products of corporate capitalism and all the usual brands are available. Outshining them all, though, is a local variety, **guaraná**, a fizzy and very sweet drink made out of Amazonian berries. An energy-loaded powder is made from the same berries and sold in health stores in the developed world – basically, the effect is like a smooth release of caffeine without the jitters.

ALCOHOLIC DRINKS

Beer is mainly of the lager type and excellent. Brazilians drink it ice-cold and it comes mostly in 600ml bottles: ask for a *cerveja*. Many places only serve beer on draught – called *chopp*. Generally acknowledged as the best brands are the regional beers of Pará and Maranhão, *Cerma* and *Cerpa*, but the best nationally available beers are *Skol* and *Brahma*. *Antártica* is similar and more widely available, *Kaiser* is a little watery. However, all Brazilian beer is stuffed with anti-oxidants and preservatives, which contributes to thumping hangovers the next day even after only a few.

Wine, *vinho*, is mostly mediocre and sweet, though some of the wines produced in the South

aren't too bad. In the Italian areas of Rio Grande do Sul, try the small farmers' own wines – very different from European and US wines but excellent in their own right. Among the better commercial ones are Almaden, Chateau Chandon, Baron de Lantier and Cotes de Blancs (white – *branco*) and Forestier, Conde de Foucaud, Chateau Duvalier and Baron de Lentier (red – *tinto*). Best of all, though, are the wines of the Casa Valduga, occasionally available in Rio's and São Paulo's best hotels and restaurants. Perfectly drinkable wine is also produced in Santa Catarina and in Paraná, while the wine from Espirito Santo, Minas Gerais and São Paulo is pretty dreadful, produced purely for regional consumption. An up-and-coming area for the production of wine is the Bahia–Pernambuco border, despite the region's proximity to the equator. Imported wines from Chile and Argentina (or Europe) are generally better and often cheaper than even the best that Brazil produces.

As for spirits, you can buy **Scotch** (*uisque*), either *nacional*, made up from imported whisky essence and not worth drinking, or *internacional*, imported and extremely expensive. Far better to stick to what Brazilians drink, **cachaça** (also called *pinga* or in Rio, *paraty*), which is sugar cane rum. The best *cachaça* is produced in stills on country farms; it is called *cachaça da terra*, and has a smoothness and taste the commercially produced brands lack. You won't find it in stores, but it's often on sale in markets. There are scores of brands of commercially produced rum: some of the better ones are Velho Barreiro, Pitu and 51.

Brazilians drink *cachaça* either neat or mixed with fruit juice. Neat, it's very fiery, but in a cocktail it can be delicious. By far the best way to drink it is in a **caipirinha**, along with football and music one of Brazil's great gifts to world civilization. This is rum mixed with fresh lime, sugar and crushed ice: it may not sound like much, but it is the best cocktail you're ever likely to drink. You should stir it regularly while drinking, and treat it with healthy respect – it is much more powerful than it tastes. Variants are the *caipirosca* or *caipiríssima*, the same made with vodka. Waiters will often assume foreigners want vodka, so make sure you say *caipirinha de cachaça*. You can also get **batidas**, rum mixed with fruit juice and ice, which flow like water during *Carnaval*: they also pack quite a punch, despite tasting like a soft drink. A *cuba libre* is a rum and Coke.

There are no **licensing laws** in Brazil, so you can get a drink at any time of day or night.

TRAVELLING WITH KIDS

Travelling with kids is relatively easy in Brazil as they're made to feel welcome in hotels and restaurants in a way that's not always so in Europe or North America. Furthermore, travelling as a family will bring you into contact with people you might not otherwise meet, as well as saving you from hassle: the Latin stereotype of respect for the family holds good in Brazil.

Travelling around Brazil takes time so try not to be too ambitious in terms of how much you aim to cover. Because of frequent scheduled stops and unscheduled delays it can take all day to fly from one part of the country to another. Long bus journeys are scheduled overnight and can be exhausting. Children pay full **fare** on buses if they take up a seat, ten percent on planes if under two years old, half fare between two and twelve, and full fare thereafter. Newer **airports** have a **nursery** (*berçário*) where you can change or nurse your baby and where an attendant will run your baby a bath, great on a hot day or if your plane's delayed. If you plan on **renting a car**, bring your own child or **baby seat** as rental companies never supply them and they are very expensive in Brazil. Cars are fitted with three-point shoulder seatbelts in the front, but most only have lap seatbelts in the back.

In **hotels**, kids are generally free up to the age of five and rooms often include both a double and a single bed; a baby's cot may be available, but don't count on it. It's rare that a room will sleep more than three, but larger hotels sometimes have rooms with an interlinking door. If you're planning on staying more than a few days in a city you may find it cheaper and more convenient to stay in an **apartment-hotel** which will sleep several people and comes with basic cooking facilities. Baths are rare in Brazil, so get your kids used to **showers** before leaving home. Occasionally a hotel will provide a plastic baby bath, but bring along a travel plug as shower pans are often just about deep enough to create a bath.

Food shouldn't be a problem as, even if your kids aren't adventurous eaters, familiar dishes are always available. Portions do tend to be huge, often suitable for two large appetites, and it's perfectly acceptable to request additional plates and cutlery. Most hotels and restaurants provide high chairs (*cadeira alta*). Commercial **baby food** is sold in Brazilian supermarkets but is limited to a very small and expensive range of Nestlé products – bring your own. If your baby is on formula, bring enough with you as the Portuguese instructions on locally produced powdered varieties may be difficult to understand and, in any case, your baby may find a change unsettling. Pay special attention to **water** and either bring a water purifier (see p.19) or a travel kettle and boil mineral water rather than tap water. Washing out bottles can be awkward, so it makes sense to bring with you an ample supply of pre-sterilized disposable bottles (not available in Brazil). Medium-category hotels usually have a **minibar** (*frigobar*) in the rooms where you can store bottles and baby food, but where there isn't one you will be able to store things in the hotel's refrigerator. A small cooler box or insulated bag is a good idea and while ice compartments of *frigobars* are useless, you can always place your freezer blocks in the hotel's freezer (*congelador*).

In general, Brazilian infants don't use disposable **nappies/diapers** (*fraldas*), due to the high cost, around $15 for twenty. Brands such as Pampers are sold in pharmacies and supermarkets but it's worth bringing as many with you as possible.

Health shouldn't be a problem, but before planning your itinerary, make enquiries as to whether the **vaccines** recommended or required in some parts of Brazil (in particular the Amazon) are likely to have any unpleasant side-effects for babies or young children. For most of Brazil, the only likely problem will be the strength of the tropical sun and the viciousness of the mosquitoes: bring plenty of **sunscreen** (at least factor 20 for babies and factor 15 for young children) and an easy-to-apply **non-toxic insect repellent**.

COMMUNICATIONS: MAIL, PHONES AND MEDIA

Postal services within Brazil are cheap, though sending airmail abroad is expensive. The phone network, too, is impressive, especially considering the size of the country: public phones are everywhere, most places can be dialled direct and rates are low.

POST OFFICES AND LETTERS

A **post office** is called a *correio*: they have bright yellow postboxes and signs. An imposing *Correios e Telégrafos* building will always be found in the centre of a city of any size, and from here you can send telegrams as well; but there are also small offices and kiosks scattered around which only deal with mail. Because post offices in Brazil deal with other things besides post, queues are often a problem. Save time by using a franking machine for stamps; the lines move much more quickly. **Stamps** (*selos*) are most commonly simply available in two varieties – either for mailing within Brazil or abroad. A foreign postage stamp costs around $1 for either a postcard or a letter up to 10 grammes. It is very expensive to send parcels abroad – if you plan to cross into Paraguay consider sending packages from there, as it has much lower postal rates.

Mail within Brazil takes three or four days, longer in the North and Northeast, while airmail letters to Europe and North America usually take about a week or sometimes even less. **Surface mail** takes about a month to North America, and three to Europe. It is not advisable to send valuables through the mail.

TELEPHONES

Public telephones are called *orelhões*, "big ears", after their distinctive conch-shaped covers. They come in two varieties: red for local calls and blue for inter-urban. Phones are operated by **tokens** called *fichas*, which are on sale everywhere – from newspaper stands, streetsellers' trays and most cafés. For local calls you need a *ficha local*, which costs practically nothing, for long distance a *ficha interurbano*, costing about

---

DIALLING CODES AND USEFUL NUMBERS

If you're dialling from abroad, the international code for Brazil is ☎55.

Calling direct out of Brazil, dial ☎00 followed by the relevant country code, followed by the number.

Country codes: Argentina ☎54   Australia ☎61   Britain ☎44   Canada ☎1
                Ireland ☎353   New Zealand ☎64   Paraguay ☎595   USA ☎1

You can dial direct to operators in the following countries using these numbers:

        Australia ☎0008061   Britain: use BT charge card number below
        Canada ☎0008014   USA: use charge card numbers below

For unlisted countries use the international operator number.

International operator ☎000333   International operator from a public phone ☎000107
            Reverse-charge international calls ☎00080 plus country code.

Telephone charge cards: AT & T ☎0008010   BT ☎0008044   MCI ☎0008012   Sprint ☎0008016

25¢. Lift the phone from the hook and get a dialling tone before inserting the token. *Interurbano* tokens are more difficult to find, and are best bought at a public telephone exchange, a *posto telefônico;* however, you'll find over half the public inter-urban phones out of order. Calling from a *posto telefônico* (see below) is the best option for long-distance and international calls, although outside large cities they shut at 10pm. There are no cheap rates on local calls, but **long-distance calls** are cheaper after 8pm. Many phones, especially in places like hotels, bus stations and airports, now take **phone cards** (*cartao de telefone*), available everywhere tokens are sold. They come in 25, 50, 75 or 100 units, can be used for both local and inter-urban calls and cost around 5¢ per unit. It's always worth carrying one, as they're much more convenient than tokens. You need to insert the card first, then pick up the phone and wait for the dialling tone.

The **dialling tone** is a single continuous note, **engaged** is rapid pips, and the **ringing tone** is regular peals, as in the United States. The phone system in Brazil is continually overloaded. If you get an engaged tone, keep trying – nine times out of ten, the phone is not actually engaged and you get through after seven or eight attempts. The smaller the place, the more often you need to try: be patient.

USING A POSTO TELEFÔNICO

Although run by the various state phone companies, each **posto telefônico** works the same way: you ask at the counter for a *chave* and are given a numbered key. You go to the booth, insert the key and turn it to the right, and can then make up to three completed calls. You are billed when you return the key – around $2.50 a minute to the USA or Europe.

To make an inter-urban call you need to dial the trunk code, the *código DDD* (pronounced "dayday-day"), listed at the front of phone directories. For international calls, ask for *chamada internacional;* a reverse-charge call is a *chamada a cobrar.* Reversing the charges costs about twice as much as paying locally, and it is much cheaper to use a telephone charge card from home. Except in the most remote parts of Amazonia and the Northeast, everything from a small town upwards has a *posto.*

MEDIA

As in the USA, Brazil has a regional **press** rather than a national one. The best of Rio and São Paulo compares well with anywhere in the world; elsewhere newspapers are at best mediocre but are always valuable for listings of local events. Brazil also boasts a lurid, but enjoyable yellow press, specializing in gruesome murders, political scandals and football.

The best **newspapers** are the *Folha de São Paulo* and the Rio-based *Jornal do Brasil,* usually available, a day late, in large cities throughout the country. Both are independent, slightly left of centre, and have extensive international news, cultural coverage and entertainment listings. Stodgier but reasonable is the right-wing *Estado de São Paulo,* while the *Gazeta Mercantil* is a high-quality equivalent of the *Financial Times or Wall Street Journal.* Also widely available is *O Globo,* the mouthpiece of Roberto Marinho's Globo empire (see below), right of centre, but with the advantage of Caruso, the best of Brazil's political cartoonists. In Brazil, as in Argentina and Chile, the political cartoon is a widely respected art form and often screamingly funny. The most enjoyable of the yellow press is *Última Hora,* especially good for beginners in Portuguese: limited vocabulary and lots of pictures.

There are also two very good weekly current affairs **magazines**, both independent and left of centre, *Veja* and *Isto É.* They are expensive, however, around $5, since their readership is exclusively middle class. You will find Brazilian editions of most major fashion and women's magazines. The weekly *Placar* is essential for anyone wanting to get to serious grips with Brazilian football.

Apart from airports and five-star hotels, where you can find the *International Herald Tribune,* the *Economist* and the *Brazil Times,* an English-language Brazilian paper aimed largely at the business community, **English-language newspapers** and magazines are very difficult to find in Brazil.

TV AND RADIO

Brazilian TV is ghastly, the worst you are ever likely to see, and therefore compulsive viewing even if you don't understand a word of Portuguese. There are several national channels, of which the most dominant is **TV Globo**, the centrepiece of the Globo empire, Latin America's largest media conglomerate, now moving into Hispanic television in the USA and also expanding into Spain and Italy. It was built up by Brazil's answer to Rupert Murdoch, **Roberto Marinho**, now over eighty, one of the most powerful men in Brazil, and a sinister figure: very cosy with the military regime and prone to use his papers and TV channels as platforms for his ultra-conservative views. The other major national channels are Manchete, TV Bandeirantes and SBT.

The channels are dominated by **telenovelas**, glossy soap operas which have massive audiences in the evenings, especially in small towns and the countryside. Perhaps the most riveting programme is **Silvio Santos**, Sunday afternoons on SBT, whose trademark is shouting "Who wants the money?" and then throwing banknotes into the studio audience while the cameras record the confusion and the fights. **Football coverage** is also worth listening to, a gabbling and incomprehensible stream of commentary, punctuated by remarkably elongated shouts of "Gooooool" whenever anyone scores – which is often, Brazilian defences being what they are. However, there are a few genuine highlights, notably **Jô Soares**, the funniest and cleverest of Brazilian comedians, who hosts a very civilized late-night chat show on SBT every weekday.

Radio is always worth listening to if only for the music, so a cheap transistor radio is a good thing to take with you. FM stations abound everywhere and you should always be able to find a station that plays local music. Shortwave reception for the BBC World Service is good in Brazil.

OPENING HOURS AND PUBLIC HOLIDAYS

Basic hours for most stores and businesses are from 9am to 6pm, with an extended lunch hour from around noon to 2pm. Banks don't open until 10am, stay open all day, but usually stop changing money at either 2pm or 3pm; except for those at major airports, they're closed at weekends and on public holidays. Museums and monuments more or less follow office hours but many are closed on Monday.

Although plane and bus **timetables** are kept to whenever possible, in the less developed parts of the country – most notably Amazonia but also the interior of the Northeast – delays often happen. Brazilians are very Latin in their attitude to time, and if ever there was a country where patience will stand you in good stead it's Brazil. Turn up at the arranged time, but don't be surprised at all if you're kept waiting. Waiting times are especially long if you have to deal with any part of the state bureaucracy, like extending a visa. There is no way out of this; just take a good book.

BRAZILIAN PUBLIC HOLIDAYS

There are plenty of local and state holidays, but on the following national holidays just about everything in the country will be closed:

January 1

Carnaval – the five days leading up to Ash Wednesday

Good Friday

April 21 – Remembrance of Tiradentes

May 1 – Labour Day

Corpus Christi

September 7 – Independence Day

October 12 – Nossa Senhora Aparecida

November 2 – Dia dos Finados (the Day of the Dead)

November 15 – Proclamation of the Republic

December 25

FESTIVALS

Carnaval is the most important festival in Brazil, but there are other holidays, too, from saints' days to celebrations based around elections or the World Cup.

CARNAVAL

When **Carnaval** comes, the country gets down to some of the most serious partying in the world. A Caribbean carnival might prepare you a little, but what happens in Brazil goes on longer, is more spectacular and on a far larger scale. Everywhere in Brazil, large or small, has some form of *Carnaval*, and in three places especially – Rio, Salvador and Olinda – *Carnaval* has become a mass event, involving almost the entire populations of the cities and drawing visitors from all over the world.

When exactly *Carnaval* begins depends on the ecclesiastical calendar: it starts at midnight of the Friday before Ash Wednesday and ends on the Wednesday night, though effectively people start partying on Friday afternoon – over five days of

---

A CARNAVAL WARNING

Wherever you go at *Carnaval*, take care of your possessions: it is high season for **pickpockets and thefts**. Warnings about specific places are given in the text, but the basic advice is – if you don't need it, don't take it with you.

---

continuous, determined celebration. It usually happens in the middle of February, although very occasionally it can be early March. But in effect the entire period from Christmas is a kind of run-up to *Carnaval*. People start working on costumes, songs are composed and rehearsals staged in school playgrounds and back yards, so that *Carnaval* comes as a culmination rather than a sudden burst of excitement and colour.

During the couple of weekends immediately before *Carnaval* proper there are carnival balls, *bailes carnavalescos*, which get pretty wild. Don't expect to find many things open or to get much done in the week before *Carnaval*, or the week after it, when the country takes a few days off to shake off its enormous collective hangover. During *Carnaval* itself, stores open briefly on Monday and Tuesday mornings, but banks and offices stay closed. Domestic airlines, local and intercity buses run a Sunday service during the period.

Three Brazilian carnivals in particular have become famous, each with a very distinctive feel. The most familiar and most spectacular is in **Rio**, dominated by samba and the parade of samba schools down the enormous concrete expanse of the gloriously named *Sambódromo*. It is one of the world's great sights, a production beyond even Cecil B. De Mille, and is televised live to the whole country. However, it has its critics. It is certainly less participatory than Olinda or Salvador, with people crammed into grandstands watching, rather than down following the schools.

Salvador is, in many ways, the antithesis of Rio, with several focuses around the old city centre: the parade is only one of a number of things going on, and people follow parading schools and the *trio elétrico*, groups playing on top of trucks wired for sound. Samba is only one of several types of music being played, and if it's music you're interested in, Salvador is the best place to hear and see it.

Olinda, in a magical colonial setting just outside Recife, has a character all its own, less frantic than Rio and Salvador; musically it's dominated by *frevo*, the fast, whirling beat of Pernambuco.

Some places you would think are large enough to have an impressive *Carnaval* are in fact notoriously bad at it: cities in this category are São Paulo, Brasília and Belo Horizonte. On

<table>
<tr><td colspan="3">CARNAVAL DATES</td></tr>
<tr><td>1998 Feb 21</td><td>1999 Feb 13</td><td>2000 March 5</td></tr>
</table>

the other hand, there are also places which have much better *Carnavals* than you would expect: the one in **Belém** is very distinctive, with the Amazonian food and rhythms of the *carimbó*, and **Fortaleza** also has a good reputation. The South, usually written off by most people as far as *Carnaval* is concerned, has major events in Florianópolis primarily aimed at attracting Argentine and São Paulo tourists, and the smaller, but more distinctive *Carnaval* in Laguna. There are full details of the events, music and happenings at each of the main *Carnavals* under the relevant sections of the *Guide*.

OTHER FESTIVALS

The third week in June sees the **festas juninas**, mainly for children, who dress up in straw hats and checked shirts and release paper balloons with candles attached (to provide the hot air), causing anything from a fright to a major conflagration when they land.

Elections and the **World Cup** are usually excuses for impromptu celebrations, too, while

official celebrations, with military parades and patriotic speeches, take place on September 7 (Independence Day) and November 15, the anniversary of the declaration of the Republic.

In towns and rural areas you may well stumble across a **dia de festa**, the day of the local patron saint. It is all very simple: the image of the saint is paraded through the town, with a band and firecrackers, a thanksgiving mass is celebrated, and then everyone turns to the secular pleasures of the fair, the market and the bottle. In **Belém** this tradition reaches its fullest expression in the *Cirio* on the second Sunday of October, when crowds of over a million follow the procession of the image of Nossa Senhora de Nazaré, but most *festas* are small-scale, small town events.

In recent years many towns have created new festivals, usually glorified **industrial fairs** or **agricultural shows**. Often these events are named after the local areas' most important product such as the *Festa Nacional do Frango e do Peru* (chickens and turkeys). Occasionally these local government creations can be worth attending as some promote local popular culture as well as industry. One of the best is Pomerode's annual **Festa Pomerana** which takes place in the first half of January and has done much to encourage the promotion of local German traditions.

FOOTBALL

Brazilian football (*futebol*), currently revitalized by its 1994 World Cup win, is revered the world over and is a privilege to experience at first hand. Games are usually enthralling: the mixture of intoxicating attack and clumsy defence which has traditionally marked Brazilian international sides is to be found at all levels of the game in Brazil, which makes for plenty of goals and entertainment. The stadiums are often spectacular sights in their own right, and Brazilian crowds are fantastic: wildly enthusiastic, and bringing along their own excellent live music - a packed Maracanã has more drummers than the largest samba schools. The only downside is a recent upsurge of crowd violence, provoked by small but highly organized hooligan groups. It is not a good idea to wear
a local team shirt to a match, although foreign team shirts will guarantee you a friendly conversation with curious fans.

Football was introduced into Brazil by Scottish railway engineers round about the time of World War I, and Brazilians took to it like a duck to water. By the 1920s the Rio and São Paulo leagues which dominate Brazilian football had been founded, and Brazil became the first South American country to compete in the World Cup, sending a squad to Italy in 1938. Getúlio Vargas was the first in a long line of Brazilian presidents to make political capital out of the game, building the beautiful Pacaembu Stadium in São Paulo and then the world's largest stadium, the Maracanã in Rio, for the **1950 World Cup**, which Brazil hosted.

In that competition they had what many older Brazilians still think was the greatest Brazilian side ever, hammered everybody, and then in the final, with the whole country already celebrating, came up against Uruguay. Unfortunately the Uruguayans hadn't read the script and won 2–1, a national trauma that still haunts popular memory nearly fifty years on.

Yet success was not long in coming. A series of great teams, all with **Pelé** as playmaker, won the World Cup in Stockholm in 1958 (the only World Cup won by a South American team in Europe), Chile in 1962 and, most memorably of all, **1970 in Mexico**. Mexico saw the side that is now widely regarded as the greatest in football history, with Pelé playing alongside such great names as Jairzinho, Rivelino, Carlos Alberto, Gerson and Tostão. As three-time winners, Brazil also got to keep the Jules Rimet Trophy, the original World Cup.

It took Brazil until **1994** to reclaim the World Cup, deservedly beating Italy on penalties in a dramatic climax to what had been an occasionally dull final. It touched off enormous popular rejoicing, as Brazil became the first country to win the World Cup for the fourth time. This was a triumph built on such un-Brazilian virtues as a combative rather than a creative midfield, and a solid defence. Only in attack, where the genius of **Romário** found the perfect foil in Bebeto, was the 1994 side truly Brazilian.

Brazil look well placed to defend their crown in France in 1998. Their current manager, wily old fox **Zagalo**, who also managed the 1970 team, has built a side truer to their attacking traditions than the 1994 team, which was criticized even within Brazil for being too boring. The prodigy **Ronaldo**, who will be only 21, is their best prospect since Pelé, and they have two extraordinary attacking midfielders in **Juninho** and **Giovanni**. As ever, their problems are in defence, especially in goal, and in bearing up under the impossible pressures generated by the most demanding football public in the world.

GOING TO A MATCH

Going to a football match is something which even those bored by the game will enjoy purely as spectacle: the stadiums are sights in themselves, and a big match is watched behind a screen of tickertape and waving flags to the accompaniment of massed drums and thousands of roaring voices. The best grounds are the temple of Brazilian football, Maracanã in Rio and the Art Deco Pacaembu in São Paulo, one of the most beautiful football stadiums in the world. Tickets are cheap – less than a couple of dollars to stand on the terraces (*geral*), around $5 for stand seats (*arquibancada*); championship and international matches cost a little more. Grounds are large, and stadiums usually well below their enormous capacities except for important matches, which means that you can almost always turn up and pay at the turnstile rather than having to get a ticket in advance. Most stadiums are two-tier, with terracing at the bottom surrounding the pitch, and seats on the upper deck. Even the small cities have international-class stadiums: they're a municipal virility symbol.

The number of regional championships and national play-offs means there is football virtually all the year round in Brazil – the **national championship** is a complicated mix of state leagues and national sudden-death play-offs. Even though many major Brazilian stars play in Europe these days, there is still enough domestic talent to support very high quality football.

TEAMS AND SHIRTS

Good teams are thickest on the ground in Rio and São Paulo. In Rio, **Flamengo** and **Fluminense** annually play out the most intense rivalry in Brazilian club football, meeting several times a year in local derbies that are good fixtures to go for; together with **Botafogo** and **Vasco** they dominate *carioca* football. In São Paulo there is similar rivalry between **São Paulo** and **Coríntians**, whose pre-eminence is challenged by **Guaraní**, **Palmeiras**, **Portuguesa** and **Santos**, the latter now a shadow of the team that Pelé led to glory in the 1960s. The only clubs elsewhere that come up to the standards of the best of Rio and São Paulo are **Internacional** and **Grêmio** in Porto Alegre, **Atlético Mineiro** in Belo Horizonte, **Salvador** and **Bahia** in Bahia, and **Sport** in Recife.

Brazilian football **shirts**, true to national character, are stylish and much more colourful than their European equivalents. They make great souvenirs. Costs range from around $40 for an official repro shirt bought at a sports shop, to around $10 for unauthorized cotton copies available in any clothes shop. The most common ones you will see are the red and black hoops of Flamengo, the green and maroon stripes of Fluminense, the white with red and black hoop of São Paulo, and the blue and black stripes of Grêmio. The instantly recognizable national shirt, canary yellow and nicknamed *canarinho*, is also ubiquitous.

POLICE AND TROUBLE

Brazil has a reputation as a rather danger-ous place, both for people and their posses-sions. It's not entirely undeserved, but it's a subject that is often treated hysterically, and many visitors arrive with a wildly exagger-ated idea of the perils lying in wait for them. While you would be foolish to ignore them, don't allow worries about safety to interfere with your enjoyment of the country. Certainly, if you take the precautions out-lined below, you are extremely unlikely to come to any harm – although you might still have something stolen somewhere along the way.

ROBBERIES, HOLD-UPS AND THEFTS

Remember that while being a gringo can attract unwelcome attention, it can also provide an important measure of protection. The Brazilian police can be extremely violent, and law enforce-ment tends to take the form of periodic crack-downs. Therefore, criminals know that any injury to a foreign tourist is going to mean a heavy clampdown, which in turn means no pickings for a while. So unless you resist, nothing is likely to happen to you. That said, having a knife or a gun held on you, as anyone who's had the experience will know, is something of a shock: it's very diffi-cult to think rationally. But if you are unlucky enough to be the victim of an **assalto**, a hold-up, try to remember that it's your possessions rather than you that's the target. Your money and any-thing you're carrying will be snatched, your watch will get pulled off your wrist, but within a

couple of seconds it will be over. *On no account resist*: it isn't worth the risk.

TAKING PRECAUTIONS

As a rule, *assaltos* are most common in the larger cities, and are rare in the countryside and towns. Most *assaltos* take place at night, in back streets with few people around, so stick to busy, well-lit streets; in a city, it's always a lot safer to take a taxi than walk. Also, prepare for the worst by locking your money and passport in the hotel safe – if you must carry them, make sure they're in a **moneybelt** or a **concealed internal pocket**. Do not carry your valuables in a pouch hanging from your neck. Only take along as much money as you'll need for the day, but do take at least some money, as the average *assaltante* won't believe a gringo could be skint, and might cut up rough. Don't wear an expensive watch or jew-ellery: if you need a watch you can always buy a cheap plastic digital one on a street corner for a couple of dollars. And keep wallets and purses out of sight – pockets with button or zips are best.

More common than an *assalto* is a simple theft, a **furto**. Bags that look like they come from the First World are an obvious target, so go for the downmarket look. You're at your most vulnerable when travelling and though the luggage compart-ments of buses are pretty safe – remember to get a baggage check from the person putting them in and don't throw it away – the overhead racks inside are less safe; keep an eye on things you stash there, especially on night journeys. On a city beach, never leave things unattended while you take a dip: any beachside bar will stow things for you. Most hotels (even the cheaper ones) will have a safe, a *caixa*, and unless you have serious doubts about the place, you should lock away your most valuable things: the better the hotel, the more secure it's likely to be. In cheaper hotels, where rooms are shared, the risks are obviously greater – some people take along a small padlock for extra security and many wardrobes in cheaper hotels have latches fitted for this very purpose. Finally, take care at *Carnaval* as it's a notorious time for pickpockets and thieves.

Recently, a new form of crime has started at international **airports** in Rio and São Paulo. Well-dressed and official-looking men target tourists arriving off international flights in the arrivals lounge, identify themselves as police-men, often flashing a card, and tell the tourists to go with them. The tourists are then pushed into a car outside and robbed. If anyone, no mat-ter how polite or well-dressed they are, or how good their English is, identifies themself as a policeman to you, be instantly on your guard – real policemen generally leave foreigners well alone. They won't try anything actually inside a terminal building, so go to any airline desk or grab one of the security guards, and on no account leave the terminal building with them or leave any luggage in their hands.

THE POLICE

If you are robbed or held up, it's not necessarily a good idea to go to the **police**. Except with some-thing like a theft from a hotel room, they're very unlikely to be able to do anything, and reporting something can take hours even without the lan-guage barrier. You may have to do it for insurance purposes, when you'll need a local police report: this could take an entire, and very frustrating, day to get, so think first about how badly you want to be reimbursed. If your passport is stolen, go to your consulate first and they'll smooth the path (see p.14). Stolen travellers' cheques are the least hassle if they're American Express: in Rio and São Paulo they take your word they've been stolen, and don't make you go to the police.

If you have to deal with the police, there are various kinds. The best are usually the **tourist police**, the *polícia de turismo*, who are used to tourists and their problems and often speak some English or French, but they're thin on the ground outside Rio. In a city, their number should be dis-played on or near the desk of reasonable hotels. The most efficient by far are the **Polícia Federal**, the Brazilian equivalent of the American FBI, who deal with visas and their extension; they have offices at frontier posts, air-ports and ports and in state capitals. The ones you see on every street corner are the **Polícia Militar**, with green uniforms and caps. They look mean – and very often are – but they generally leave gringos alone. There is also a plain-clothes **Polícia Civil**, to whom thefts are reported if there is no tourist police post around – they are overworked, underpaid and extremely slow. If you decide to go to the police in a city where there is a consulate, get in touch with the con-sulate first and do as they tell you.

DRUGS

You should be very, very careful about **drugs**. **Marijuana** – *maconha* – is common, but you are in serious trouble if the police find any on you. You'll probably be able to bribe your way out of it, but it will be an expensive business. Foreigners sometimes get targeted for a shakedown and have drugs planted on them – the area around the Bolivian border has a bad reputation for this. The idea isn't to lock you up but to get a bribe out of you, so play it by ear. If the bite isn't too out-rageous it might be worth paying to save the has-sle, but the best way to put a stop to it would be to deny everything, refuse to pay and insist on seeing a superior officer and telephoning the nearest consulate – this approach is only for the patient. **Cocaine** is not as common as you might think as most of it passes through Brazil from Bolivia or Colombia for export. Nevertheless, the home market has grown in recent years, most worryingly for crack cocaine.

Be careful about taking anything illegal on buses: they are sometimes stopped and searched at state lines. The most stupid thing you could do would be to take anything illegal anywhere near Bolivia as buses heading in that direction get taken apart by the *federais*.

WOMEN TRAVELLERS

Despite the nation's ingrained *machismo*, sexual harassment is not the problem you might expect in Brazil. Wolf-whistles and horn-tooting are less common than they would be in Spain or Italy, and while you do see a lot of men cruising, more than you might think aren't looking for women, which spreads what hassle there is more evenly between the sexes for a change. The further north you go, blondes (men as well as women) bring out the stares, but attention which can seem threatening is often no more than curiosity combined with a language barrier.

Chances of trouble depend, to an extent, on where you are: the stereotype of free-and-easy cities and of small towns and rural areas that are formal to the point of prudishness often holds good – but not always. Many interior Amazon towns have a frontier feel and a bad, *machista* atmosphere. Also bear in mind that in any town of any size the area around the *Rodoviária* or train station is likely to be a red-light district at night – not somewhere to hang around. The transport terminals themselves, though, are usually policed and fairly safe at all hours.

Women travelling alone will arouse curiosity, especially outside the cities, but the fact that you're a crazy foreigner explains why you do it in most Brazilian eyes; it shouldn't make you a target.

There is no national **women's movement** in Brazil, but there are loosely linked organizations in big cities and some university campuses, and a growing awareness of the issues; the more important or accessible groups are listed in the Guide. *Mulherio* is a national feminist paper.

DIRECTORY

ADDRESSES Trying to find an address can be confusing: streets often have two names, numbers don't always follow a logical sequence, and parts of the address are often abbreviated (Brasília is a special case – see p.395). The street name and number will often have a floor, apartment or room number tacked on: thus R. Afonso Pena 111-3° s.234 means third floor, room 234. "R" is short for Rua, "s" for *sala*, and you may also come across *andar* (floor), *Ed.* (*edifício*, or building) or *s/n* (*sem número*, no number), very common in rural areas and small towns. All addresses in Brazil also have an eight-digit postcode, or *CEP*, often followed by two capital letters for the state; leaving it out causes delay in postage. So a full address might read:

Rua do Sol 132-3° andar, s.12
65000-100 São Luís – MA.

BARBERS For men, a visit to a barber is one of the cheaper luxuries Brazil affords. Wherever it says "Cabeleireiro" you can treat yourself to an old-fashioned, non-automated haircut and shave, invariably with hot towel and cut-throat razor, with Brylcreem and facial massage as optional extras, for no more than a dollar or two.

CINEMA Most films shown in Brazilian cinemas are American with subtitles. These all reach Brazil very soon after they're released in the US (and often before the UK) and entrance is very cheap. Both Rio and São Paulo have a good art-house cinema network; in Rio the Estação chain, with branches in Botafogo, Catete, Flamengo and Copacabana, is especially good. If you understand Portuguese, look out for movies by two great Brazilian directors, the modernist Glauber Rocha, and the more conservative Nelson Pereira dos Santos. Also try to see the definitive film of modern Brazil, *Bye bye Brasil*, even if you don't speak a word of Portuguese: it has a fabulous soundtrack by Chico Buarque.

ELECTRICITY Electricity supplies vary – sometimes 110V and sometimes 220V – so check before plugging anything in. It's a fair bet that you'll blow the fuses anyway. Plugs have two round pins.

GAY BRAZIL Gay life in Brazil still thrives in the large cities, despite the long shadow cast by the AIDS problem (see p.21). The scene benefits from a relaxed tolerance in attitudes towards sexuality. Gay life is highly visible: female impersonation and transvestism scale heights unseen in Britain or the United States. Attitudes do vary from region to region: rural areas and small towns, especially in Minas Gerais and the South, are deeply conservative; the medium-sized and larger cities are not. The two most popular gay destinations are Rio and Salvador. Pointers to gay life for specific places are given in the *Guide*. A refreshing point to bear in mind is that in Brazil the divide between gay and straight nightlife is very blurred: in the overlap you will find many places popular with both gays and straights. There is as yet no national gay organization in Brazil.

LAUNDRY There are hardly any laundries in Brazil, but even the humblest hotel has a *lavadeira* who will wash and iron your clothes. Agree a price beforehand, but don't be too hard – livelihoods are at stake. Larger hotels have set prices for laundry services – usually surprisingly expensive.

THINGS TO TAKE

A universal electric plug adaptor and a universal sink plug.

A sheet or two (if staying in youth hostels).

A small flashlight.

Earplugs (for street noise in hotel rooms).

High-factor sunscreen.

A pocket alarm clock (for those early morning departures).

An inflatable neck-rest, to help you sleep on long journeys.

A multi-purpose penknife.

A needle and some thread.

Plastic bags (to sort your baggage, make it easier to pack and unpack, and keep out damp and dust).

Items for a basic **first-aid kit** are listed on p.18, for travelling with children on p.38.

LEFT LUGGAGE Most bus stations will have a *guarda volume* where you can leave bags. In cities it's usually a locker system, open 24 hours – there's a booth where you buy a key, and a token for every day that you want to leave things; you leave the tokens inside the locker. In smaller places it will usually be a lock-up room operated by a bus company, so check the opening hours before you leave anything. They're safe enough to leave your bags for short periods while you look for a hotel, but don't check money or anything really valuable, especially if you are leaving them for longer periods.

MUSEUMS Many museums in Brazil do not charge for admission; when they do, entrance is almost always modest, $1–2 being typical, and as such, is unlikely to deter tourists. Brazil's few museums that have the international connections, financial means and security occasionally host special touring exhibitions from abroad and in these cases, entrance charges are somewhat higher than normal.

PHOTOGRAPHY Only regular 35mm 100 ASA Kodacolor film is easily available in Brazil and even this is likely to be poorly kept, expensive and past its "use by" date. If you use anything else, bring it with you. In the Amazon and other forests, 400 ASA film and possibly a flash and tripod will be necessary as it can be surprisingly dark. Small batteries are also hard to get hold of and will be very expensive if you find them. A polarizing filter is essential if you have an SLR camera. If possible try to keep the film at a constant temperature before and after use, and process it as soon as possible.

STUDENT CARDS An international student card, or a FIYTO youth card is well worth carrying. It will get you occasional reductions at museums and the like, but more importantly it serves as an extremely useful ID for bus drivers and hotels, saving you from having to keep your passport available at all times. Any official-looking card with a picture and number on it will serve almost as well.

TIME ZONES Brazil is large enough to have different time zones. Most of the country is three hours behind GMT, but the states of Amazonas, Acre, Rondônia, Mato Grosso and Mato Grosso do Sul are four hours behind – that includes the cities of Manaus, Corumbá, Rio Branco, Porto Velho, Cuiabá and Campo Grande.

TIPPING Bills usually come with ten percent *taxa de serviço* included, in which case you don't have to tip – ten percent is about right if it is not included. Waiters and some hotel employees depend on tips, so don't be too mean. You don't have to tip taxi drivers (though they won't say no), but you are expected to tip barbers, hairdressers, shoeshine kids, self-appointed guides and porters. It's useful to keep change handy for them and for beggars.

TOILETS Public toilets are not very common and often disgusting. The words to look for are *Banheiro* or *Sanitário*: where they're marked (less often than you might hope) *Cavalheiros* means men, *Senhoras* or *Damas* women. It's always a good idea to carry some toilet paper with you.

CHAPTER ONE

RIO

T he citizens of the ten-million-strong city of **Rio de Janeiro** call it the *Cidade Marvilhosa* – and there can't be much argument about that. Rio sits on the southern shore of a landlocked harbour within the magnificent natural setting of Guanabara Bay. Extending for twenty kilometres along an alluvial strip, between an azure sea and jungle-clad mountains, the city's streets and buildings have been moulded around the foothills of the mountain range which provides its backdrop; while out in the bay there are innumerable rocky islands fringed with white sand. The panoramic view over Rio is breathtaking, and even the concrete skyscrapers which dominate the city's skyline add to the attraction.

Although riven by inequality, Rio de Janeiro has great style. Its international renown is bolstered by a series of symbols that rank as some of the greatest landmarks in the world, the **Corcovado** ("hunchback") mountain supporting the great statue of Christ the Redeemer; the rounded incline of the **Sugar Loaf** mountain, standing at the entrance to the bay; and the famous sweep of **Copacabana beach**, probably the most notable length of sand on the planet. It's a setting enhanced by the annual, frenetic sensuality of **Carnaval**, an explosive celebration which – for many people – sums up Rio and her citizens, the **cariocas**. The major downside in a city given over to conspicuous consumption is the rapacious development which is engulfing Rio de Janeiro. As the rural poor, escaping drought and poverty in other regions of Brazil, flock to swell Rio's population, the city is being squeezed like a toothpaste tube between mountains and sea, pushing its human contents out along the coast in either direction. The city's rich architectural heritage is being whittled away and, if the present form of economic development is sustained, the natural environment will eventually be destroyed, too. It's a process unwittingly hastened by Rio's citizens who look forward optimistically to the future, most with the hope of relief from poverty, some with an eye to the main chance and greater wealth.

The **state of Rio de Janeiro**, surrounding the city, is a fairly recent phenomenon, established in 1975 as a result of the amalgamation of Guanabara State and Rio city. Fairly small by Brazilian standards, the state is both beautiful and accessible, with easy trips either east along the **Costa do Sol** or west along the **Costa Verde**, taking in unspoilt beaches, washed by a relatively unpolluted ocean. **Inland** routes make a welcome change from the sands, especially the trip to **Petrópolis**, the nineteenth-century mountain retreat of Rio's rich.

The best time to visit both city and state, as least as far as the **climate** goes, is between May and August, when the region is cooled by trade winds and the temperature remains at around 22–32°C. Between December and March, the rainy season, it's more humid, the temperature more like 40°C; but even then it's never as oppressive as it is in the north of Brazil. Nevertheless, you shouldn't underestimate the sun: drink plenty of liquid and don't try for a quick tan in the midday heat.

RIO DE JANEIRO CITY

Nearly five hundred years have seen **RIO DE JANEIRO** transformed from a fortified outpost on the rim of an unknown continent into one of the world's great cities. Its recorded past is tied exclusively to the legacy of the colonialism on which it was founded.

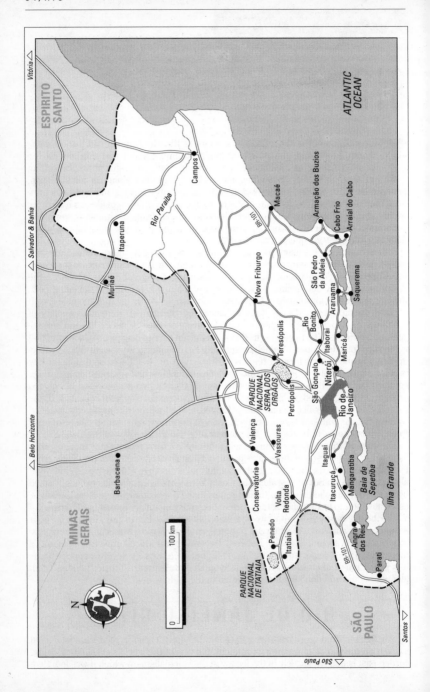

No lasting vestige survives of the civilization of the **Tamoios** people, who inhabited the land before the Portuguese arrived, and the city's history effectively begins on January 1, 1502, when a **Portuguese** captain, André Gonçalves, steered his craft into Guanabara Bay, thinking he was heading into the mouth of a great river. The city takes its name from this event – Rio de Janeiro means the "River of January". In 1555, the French, keen to stake a claim on the New World, established a garrison near the Sugar Loaf mountain, and the Governor General of Brazil, Mem de Sá, made an unsuccessful attempt to oust them. It was left to his son, Estácio de Sá, finally to defeat them in 1567, though he fell – mortally wounded – during the battle. The city then acquired its official name, São Sebastião de Rio de Janeiro, after the infant king of Portugal, and Rio began to develop on and around the Morro do Castelo – in front of where Santos Dumont airport now stands.

With Bahia the centre of the new Portuguese colony, initial progress in Rio was slow, and only in the 1690s, when **gold** was discovered in the neighbouring state of Minas Gerais, did the city's fortunes look up, as it became the control and taxation centre for the gold trade. During the seventeenth century the **sugar cane** economy brought new wealth to Rio, but despite being a prosperous entrepot, the city remained poorly developed. For the most part it comprised a collection of narrow streets and alleys, cramped and dirty, bordered by habitations built from lath and mud. However, Rio's strategic importance grew as a result of the struggle with the Spanish over territories to the south (which would become Uruguay), and in 1763 the city replaced Bahia (Salvador) as Brazil's capital city. By the eighteenth century, the majority of Rio's inhabitants were **African** slaves. Unlike other foreign colonies, in Brazil miscegenation became the rule rather than the exception: even the Catholic Church tolerated procreation between the races, on the grounds that it supplied more souls to be saved. As a result, virtually nothing in Rio remained untouched by African customs, beliefs and behaviour – a state of affairs that clearly influences today's city, too, with its mixture of Afro-Brazilian music, spiritualist cults and cuisine.

In March 1808, having fled before the advance of Napoleon Bonaparte's forces during the Peninsular War, **Dom João VI** of Portugal arrived in Rio, bringing with him some 1500 nobles of the Portuguese royal court. So enamoured of Brazil was he, that after Napoleon's defeat in 1815 he declined to return to Portugal and instead proclaimed "The United Kingdom of Portugal, Brazil and the Algarves, of this side and the far side of the sea, and the Guinea Coast of Africa" – the greatest **colonial empire** of the age, with Rio de Janeiro as its capital. During Dom João's reign the Enlightenment came to Rio, the city's streets were paved and lit, and Rio acquired a new prosperity based on **coffee**.

Royal patronage allowed the arts and sciences to flourish, and Rio was visited by many of the illustrious European names of the day. In their literary and artistic work they left a vivid account of contemporary Rio society – colonial, patriarchal and slave-based. Yet while conveying images of Rio's street-life, fashions and natural beauty, they don't give any hint of the heat, stench and squalor of life in a tropical city of over 100,000 inhabitants, without a sewerage system. Behind the imperial gloss, Rio was still mostly a slum of dark, airless habitations, intermittently scourged by outbreaks of yellow fever, its economy completely reliant upon human **slavery**.

However, by the late nineteenth century, Rio had lost much of its mercantilist colonial flavour and started to develop as a modern city: trams and trains replaced sedans, the first sewage system was inaugurated in 1864, a telegraph link was established between Rio and London, and a tunnel was excavated which opened the way to Copacabana, as people left the crowded centre and looked for new living space. Under the administration of the engineer **Francisco Pereira Passos**, Rio went through a period of urban reconstruction that all but destroyed the last vestiges of its colonial design. The city was torn apart by a period of frenzied building between 1900 and 1910,

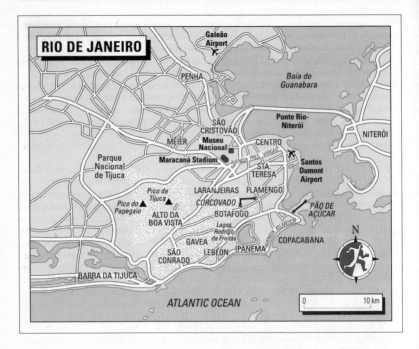

its monumental splendour modelled on the Paris of the Second Empire. Public buildings, grand avenues, libraries and parks were all built to embellish the city, lending it the dignity perceived as characteristic of the great capital cities of the Old World.

During the **1930s** Rio enjoyed international renown, buttressed by Hollywood images and the patronage of the first-generation jet set. Rio became the nation's commercial centre, too, and a new wave of modernization swept the city, leaving little more than the Catholic churches as monuments to the past. Even the removal of the country's political administration to the new federal capital of Brasília in 1960 did nothing to discourage the developers. Today, with the centre rebuilt many times since colonial days, most interest lies not in Rio's buildings and monuments but firmly in the **beaches** to the south of the city. For sixty years or so these have been Rio's heart and soul, providing a constant source of recreation and income for *cariocas*.

The favelas

There's another side to Rio that says much about the divisions within the city – the **favelas**. Although not exclusive to the capital, these slums are all the more stark in Rio because of the plenty and beauty that surround them. In a low-wage economy, and without even half-decent social services, life is extremely difficult for the majority of Brazilians. During the last thirty years the rural poor have descended on urban centres in search of a livelihood. Unable to find accommodation, or pay rent, they have established shanty towns on any available empty space, which in Rio usually means the slopes of the hills around which the city has grown.

They start off as huddles of cardboard boxes and plastic sheeting, and slowly expand and transform as metal sheeting and bricks provide more solid shelters. Clinging precariously to the sides of Rio's hills, and glistening in the sun, they can from a distance appear not unlike a medieval Spanish hamlet, perched secure atop a mountain. It is, however, a spurious beauty. The *favelas* are creations of need, and their inhabitants are engaged in an immense daily struggle for survival, worsened by the prospect of landslides caused by heavy rains, tearing their dwellings from their tenuous hold on precipitous inclines. The people who live there are denied public services, and are forced to live in conditions which promote ill-health – little better in fact than the squalor that typified Rio de Janeiro in the seventeenth century. Bound together by their shared poverty and exclusion from effective citizenship, within their communities the *favelados* display a great resourcefulness and co-operative strength in their struggle to force the authorities to meet their needs.

Orientation

Arriving in a big city can be a daunting experience, and many people come to Rio de Janeiro, scramble their way to Copacabana and go no further, except on an occasional foray by guided tour. The beaches, though, are only one facet of Rio. The city is divided into three parts – centre, north and south – and the various *bairros* (neighbourhoods) have retained their individuality and characteristic atmosphere. So, while you'll certainly want to get a good dose of the beaches, you may prefer to put up in a quieter quarter and explore the rich history of the centre as well. Rio's layout is straightforward and the transport system makes it easy to get around – just buy a **map** (*Planta do Rio*) from any city kiosk.

Centro

Centro is the commercial and historic centre of Rio, and though the elegance of its colonial and Neoclassical architecture has become overshadowed by the towering office buildings, it has by no means yet been swamped. It's an effective grid, cut by two main arteries at right angles to each other, **Avenida Presidente Vargas** and **Avenida Rio Branco**. Presidente Vargas runs west from the waterfront and the Candelária church to Dom Pedro II **train station** and on to the **Sambódromo**, where the *Carnaval* procession takes place. Rio Branco crosses it in front of the Candelária church, running from **Praça Mauá** in the dockland area, south through **Praça**

TROUBLE – A WARNING

Although it sometimes seems that one half of Rio is constantly being robbed by the other, don't let paranoia ruin your stay. It's true that there is a lot of petty theft in Rio: pockets are picked and bags and cameras swiped. But use a little common sense and you'll encounter few problems, certainly since none of the real, drug-industry-related violence will touch you. That said, there are certain areas that should be avoided.

In **Centro**, contrary to popular belief, Sunday is not the best time to stroll around – the streets are empty, which means you can be more easily identified, stalked and robbed. And with nobody about, there is little hope of immediate assistance. The area around **Praça Mauá**, just to the north of Centro, should be avoided after nightfall. Along the Avenida Atlântica in **Copacabana**, the areas in front of the *Help Discoteque* and the *Rio Othon Palace Hotel* are also likely places to encounter trouble. Copacabana's record, though, has been much improved since the authorities started to floodlight the beach at night. Around the **Praça do Lido** in Leme, a red-light district, gringos are fair game; nor is it advisable to wander unaccompanied around the darker corners of the **Parque do Flamengo** after nightfall. Finally, tourists who choose to walk between **Cosme Velho** and the **Corcovado** are increasingly being subjected to robbery and assault – something that can be best avoided by taking the train, which is more comfortable anyway.

Mahatma Ghandi to the **Avenida Beira Mar**. On the west side of Avenida Rio Branco is **Largo da Carioca**, which provides access to the hilly suburb of **Santa Teresa**, whose leafy streets wind their way upwards and westwards towards the Corcovado. At the foot of the slope on which Santa Teresa is built lies **Lapa**, just south of Centro, an inner-city residential and red-light district, its past grandeur reflected in the faded elegance of the **Passeio Público** park.

On the east side of Rio Branco, **Rua da Assembléia** contains the *Turisrio* **tourist office**, and runs into **Praça XV de Novembro**: the square near the water where you'll find the **ferry station** for boats and hydrofoils to Niterói (across the bay) and the Ilha de Paquetá (to the north).

Both Avenida Rio Branco and Praça XV de Novembro are good places to catch a **bus to the southern beaches**, an area known as the Zona Sul – any bus with the name of a distant beach, like Leblon, passes along the coastline, or parallel to it.

Zona Norte

The northernmost part of Rio, the **Zona Norte**, contains the city's industrial areas and the major working-class residential *bairros* with little in the way of historic interest or natural beauty. However, the **Museu Nacional** in the Quinta da Boa Vista park is a splendid collection well worth making time for. This apart, you're not likely to go much further north than Praça Mauá, exceptions being trips to and from the international airport, inter-city bus terminal and the **Maracanã Stadium**, Brazil's football Mecca.

Zona Sul

The **Zona Sul**, the name used to cover everything south of the city centre, though generally taken to mean just the *bairros* shouldering the coastline, has much more to attract you.

Following the Avenida Beira Mar south from Centro, the zone is heralded by the **Parque do Flamengo**, an extensive area of reclaimed land transformed into a public recreation area and beach. First up is the *bairro* of **Glória**, where the whitewashed church of Nossa Senhora da Glória do Outeiro, high on a wooded hill, makes an unmistakable landmark. Beyond, Beira Mar becomes Avenida Praia do Flamengo, which leads into the *bairros* of **Catete** and **Flamengo** – together with Glória, areas where you'll find innumerable cheap hotels. On the other side of Flamengo is the **Largo do Machado**, whose central position, between the centre and the beach areas, makes it a useful place to base yourself. From the square you can reach the *bairros* of **Laranjeiras** and **Cosme Velho**, to the west. The latter is the site of the **Corcovado** and the famous hilltop statue of Christ the Redeemer.

Further south, the bay of **Botafogo** is overshadowed by the **Sugar Loaf** mountain, looming above the *bairro* of **Urca**. From Botafogo, the **Pasmado Tunnel** leads to **Leme**, a small *bairro* whose three kilometres of beach, bordered by **Avenida Atlântica**, sweep around to **Copacabana**. Now one of the world's most densely populated areas, Copacabana is less classy than it once was, losing ground to its western neighbours, **Ipanema** and **Leblon**, which provide another four kilometres of sand and surf. These areas are the most chic of the residential *bairros*, with clubs and restaurants sitting amidst the stylish homes of Rio's more prosperous citizens.

Ipanema and Leblon are situated on a thin strip of land, only a few hundred metres wide, between the Atlantic Ocean and the **Lagoa Rodrigo de Freitas**, a lake tucked beneath the green hills of the **Tijuca National Park**. On the north side of the lake are the **Jardim Botânico** and **Jóquei Clube** racecourse and, just to the west, the *bairro* of **Gávea**. Further south, through Gávea, the *Auto-Estrada Lagoa-Barra* leads into **São Conrado** and its southern neighbour, **Barra de Tijuca**, the preserve of Rio's middle classes. São Conrado, in particular, shows up the great contradictions in Brazilian society: overlooking the elegant Gávea Golf Club and the prosperous residences that surround it is the **Favela Roçinha**, a shanty town clinging to the mountainside and reputedly home to 200,000 people.

Arrival and information

You're most likely to fly in to Rio or arrive by bus, though there is a train station, too. Be warned that opportunistic thieves are active at all points of arrival, so don't leave baggage unattended or valuables exposed; be especially careful of dangling cameras and wallets stuffed into back pockets.

By air

Rio de Janeiro is served by two airports. The one at **Santos Dumont** deals mainly with the shuttle services to and from São Paulo, Brasília and Belo Horizonte, and is at the north end of the Parque de Flamengo, immediately east of Centro. From here, every 40 minutes ($7) an air-conditioned *executivo* bus will take you through the Zona Sul, stopping wherever passengers want to get off along the beaches of Copacabana, Ipanema, Leblon and São Conrado. Taxis are readily available from outside the terminal but you're likely to be overcharged by drivers not willing to activate the meter – the fare should amount to around $20 to Copacabana. If it's your first visit to Rio or if your Portuguese is poor, a less stressful option is to purchase a voucher from one of the many radio-taxi stands within the terminal. You'll be directed to your cab and will be charged a flat rate of around $30 to Copacabana. Alternatively, cross the road and catch an ordinary bus from Avenida Marechal Câmara, which you can reach by crossing the pedestrian walkway in front of the airport terminal: #438 to Ipanema and Leblon via Botafogo; #442 to Urca; #472 to Leme. For Copacabana, #484 goes from Avenida General Justo, over which the walkway crosses.

The **international airport** at Galeão lies on the Ilha do Governador in Guanabara Bay, 14km north of the city. On arrival make sure that your passport is stamped and that you retain your immigration form, as failure to do so can cause problems come departure. **Customs** rarely give foreign visitors a second glance. If you have nothing to declare walk through the green channel and you'll be asked to press a button, a random selection method: if the light flashes green, you're home and dry; if it's red, be prepared to expose the contents of your bags to customs officials. In the arrivals hall, ignore the hotel and taxi touts and consult one of the official **tourist information** desks – RioTur, Turisrio or EMBRATUR. You'll get useful and relevant information here, but avoid the desks which represent private concerns, trying to pass themselves off as official agencies. The official desks will check hotels for vacancies for you, but not at the very cheapest places. **Changing money** is not a problem, as the airport has a *casa de câmbio*, as well as the only branch of the Banco do Brasil not to charge the flat-rate $20 commission.

To reach your hotel, catch one of the air-conditioned **executivo buses**, which run every half-hour between 5.20am and 11pm, either via Centro to Santos Dumont, or along the coast, via Centro, to Copacabana and on to São Conrado. Outside these hours, a **taxi** ride is the only alternative. Buy a ticket at either the Cootramo, Coopertramo or Transcoopass desks, near the arrivals gate, and give it to the driver at the taxi rank; to Flamengo costs about $22, Copacabana $30. Use the air-conditioned taxis operated by the airport; it's best not to take the ordinary taxis (yellow with a blue stripe), and don't

---

The **telephone code** for Rio is ☎021.

accept a lift from one of the unofficial drivers hanging about in the airport. There's a new highway out to the airport and the drive takes about fifteen minutes into the centre or around half an hour to Zona Sul, unless you meet the rush hour. The drive will take you through one of Rio's industrial sectors – so don't worry if it looks a bit grim at first; you're going the right way.

Heading out to the international airport, arrange for a fixed-fare taxi to pick you up from your hotel (get reception to do it or phone Transcoopass ☎270-4888, Coopertramo ☎260-2022 or Cootramo ☎270-1442), or take the air-conditioned bus which follows the Zona Sul coastline and can be picked up on Avenida Delfim Moreira (Leblon), Avenida Vieira Souto (Ipanema), Avenida Atlântica (Copacabana), Avenida Beira Mar (Flamengo), or on the Avenida Rio Branco in Centro. Inside Galeão, departure desks are split into three sections: internal Brazilian flights from Sector A; Sectors B and C for international flights. And remember that there's a **departure tax** of $8 for internal flights or $18 for international flights, payable in either US or Brazilian currency (but not a mix of the two).

By bus

All major inter-city bus services arrive at the **Novo Rio Rodoviária** (☎291-5151), 3km north of Centro in the São Cristovão *bairro*, close to the city's dockside at the corner of Avenida Rodrigues Alves and Avenida Franscisco Bicalho. International buses from Santiago, Buenos Aires, Montevideo and Asunción, among others, use this terminus, too. The *Rodoviária* has two sides, one for departures, the other for arrivals: once through the gate at arrivals, either grab a taxi ($7 to Centro, $15–30 to the Zona Sul), catch an *executivo* air-conditioned bus along the coast towards Copacabana and Leblon(every half-hour from directly outside the arrivals side of the station), or cross the road to the ordinary bus terminal in Praça Hermes. Alternatively, head first for the **tourist office** desk (daily 8am–8pm) at the bottom of the stairs, in the middle of the foyer in front of the main exit – they'll help with hotels, and advise which buses to catch.

A more central terminal, the **Menezes Cortes Rodoviária** in Rua São José (☎224-7577), handles services from some in-state towns such as Petrópolis and Teresópolis, but mainly operates buses to and from the suburbs and Zona Sul.

Leaving Rio by bus and travelling out of the state, it's best to book two days in advance. The same goes for services to popular in-state destinations, like Búzios or Paratí, which fill up at weekends; or for travelling anywhere immediately before or after *Carnaval*. Most **tickets** can be bought from travel agents all over the city, while inside the main *Rodoviária*, on both sides, upstairs and down, you'll find the ticket offices of the various bus companies. There are places to buy food and reading material inside the bus station, so you can stock up for the journey, though the buses stop for refreshments every couple of hours or so on long trips, anyway. You can reach the *Rodoviária* on bus #104 from Centro, #127 or #128 from Copacabana, and #456, #171 or #172 from Flamengo.

By train

The main **train station**, the Dom Pedro II Ferroviária, known to most people as the Central do Brasil, is halfway along Avenida Presidente Vargas in Centro, almost opposite the Campo de Santana park: easy to spot with its high clock tower. The few remaining services from São Paulo and Vitória stop here, as well as suburban trains running to and from the outlying northern districts of Rio.

There's a taxi rank outside the station and the journey to the Zona Sul costs around $20–30; if you want to get to Flamengo, Botafogo or Copacabana, the taxi will run through Centro and out along the coast; to reach Ipanema or Leblon, the driver may go via the *bairro* of Cosme Velho and through the Antônio Rebouças tunnel, emerging on the north side of the Lagoa Rodrigo de Freitas. Otherwise, the Estação Central metrô stop (see below for details of the metrô) is next to the station (in Praça Duque de Caxias), and the metrô will take you as far as Copacabana; or, on the other side of Avenida Presidente Vargas, there is no shortage of buses running down into Centro and beyond; #438 or #464 to Leblon; #474 or #475 to Ipanema; #455 or #456 to Copacabana; #442 to Urca; #472 to Leme; #498 to Largo do Machado.

Information

Apart from the information you pick up at your point of arrival, at some stage you'll probably want to make use of the **tourist offices** in the city. There are three official agencies, none of them particularly efficient.

Information about Rio itself is from Riotur, which distributes maps and brochures and has a helpful multilingual telephone information service; main offices are in Centro at Rua da Assembléia 10, ninth floor (Mon–Fri 9am–6pm; ☎297-7117), and in Copacabana at Av. Princesa Isabel 18 (Mon–Sat 9am–6pm). Most of Riotur's information can also be picked up at the *Rodoviária*, the international airport and the Sugar Loaf. Information about the state of Rio is from Turisrio, at Rua da Assembléia 10 on the seventh floor (☎531-1922); and the most basic information about the rest of Brazil from EMBRATUR, on the way to the Maracanã stadium at Rua Mariz e Barros 13, in Praça da Bandeira (☎273-2212).

Note that if you're going to stay in Brazil for over six months, you are obliged to **register** at the *Registro de Estrangeiros*, Polícia Federal, Av. Venezuela 2 (Mon–Fri 11am–4pm; ☎263-3747).

Getting around

Rio's **public transport** system is cheap and effective: most places can be reached by metrô, bus or taxi, or a combination of these; while for getting about the state you might want to rent a car – though driving in the city itself is not recommended unless you have nerves of steel.

The metrô

The safest and most comfortable way to travel is by using Rio's **metrô** system, in operation since 1979. At present it's limited to two lines, which run from Monday to Saturday, 6am to 11pm: **Line 1** runs from Copacabana (the newly opened Praça Cardeal Arcoverde station), north through Centro and then out to the Sãens Pena station in the *bairro* of Maracanã; **Line 2** comes in from Maria de Graça, to the north of the city, via the Maracanã stadium, and meets line 1 at Estação Central, by Dom Pedro II train station.

The system is well designed and efficient, the stations bright, cool, clean and secure. And the trains are air-conditioned, a relief if you've just descended from the scorching world above.

Tickets are bought as singles (*ida*; 60¢) or returns (*doplo*; $1.20), or are valid for ten journeys. The latter can save time, but it costs the same and you can't share a ten-journey ticket, as the electronic turnstiles only allow entrance at eight-minute intervals. You can also buy integrated bus/metrô tickets, useful to make the link between the metrô station at Botafogo and Ipanema or Leblon. You catch the buses directly outside the metrô station: they both run circular routes between Botafogo and Leblon, the #M21 going via the Jóquei Clube, the #M22 via Copacabana.

Buses

It's sometimes suggested that it's irresponsible to encourage tourists to use the **city buses** because they're badly driven, will probably end up getting you lost and are the scene of much petty theft. But, while it's true that some of Rio's bus drivers have a somewhat erratic driving style – to say the least – it's well worth mastering the system: with over three hundred routes and six thousand buses, you never have to wait more than a few moments for a bus, they run till midnight and it's not that easy to get lost.

Numbers and **destinations** are clearly marked on the front of buses, and there are plaques at the front and by the entrance detailing the route. You get on at the back, pay the seated conductor (the price is on a card behind his head) and then push through the turnstile and find yourself a seat. Buses are jam-packed at rush hour, so if your journey is short, start working your way to the front of the bus as soon as you're through the turnstile; you alight at the front. If the bus reaches the stop before you reach the front, haul on the bell and the driver will wait. This kind of confusion really only occurs during **rush hour**, which is 5pm to 7pm in the evening. In the beach areas of the Zona Sul, especially along the coast, **bus stops** are not always marked. Stick your arm out to flag the bus down, or look for groups of people by the roadside facing the oncoming traffic, as this indicates a bus stop.

To avoid **being robbed** on the bus, don't leave wallets or money in easily accessible pockets, or flash cameras around. If there's a crush, carry any bags close to your chest. Have your fare ready so that you can pass through the turnstile immediately, as pickpockets operate at the rear of the bus, by the entrance, so that they can make a quick escape, and don't let the turnstile come between you and anything you don't want to lose. Special care should be taken on buses known to carry mostly tourists (such as those to the Sugar Loaf) and which are consequently considered rich pickings by thieves.

RIO: SOME USEFUL BUS ROUTES

From Avenida Rio Branco: #119, #121, #123, #127, #173 and #177 to Copacabana; #128 (via Copacabana), #132 (via Flamengo) and #172 (via Jóquei Clube) to Leblon.

From Praça XV do Novembro: #119, #154, #413, #415 to Copacabana; #154 and #474 to Ipanema.

From Avenida Beira Mar, in Lapa, near the Praça Deodoro: #158 (via Jóquei Clube), #170, #172 (via Jardim Botânico), #174 (via Praia do Botafogo), #438, #464, #571 and #572 to Leblon; #472 to Leme; #104 to Jardim Botânico.

From Copacabana: #455 to Centro; #464 to Maracanã.

From Urca: #511 (via Jóquei Clube) and #512 (via Copacabana) to Leblon.

From the Menezes Cortes terminal, adjacent to Praça XV de Novembro: air-conditioned buses along the coast to Barra de Guaratiba, south of Rio; on the return journey, these buses are marked "Castelo", the name of the area near Praça XV.

To Novo Rio Rodoviária: #104 from Centro, #127 or #128 from Copacabana, and #456, #171 or #172 from Flamengo.

To the train station: any bus marked "E. Ferro".

Parque do Flamengo: any bus marked "via Aterro" passes along the length of the Parque do Flamengo without stopping.

Between Centro and the Zona Sul, most buses run along the coast as far as Botafogo; those for Copacabana continue around the bay, past the RioSul shopping centre, and through the Pasmado Tunnel; those for Leblon, via the Jóquei Clube, turn right at Botafogo and travel along Avenida São Clemente.

Taxis

Taxis in Rio come in two varieties: **yellow** ones with a blue stripe, often none too luxurious, which cruise the streets; or **radio cabs**, white and with a red and yellow stripe, ordered by phone. Both have meters and unless you have pre-paid at the airport, you should insist that it is activated. Also, when you get into a cab, make certain that the meter has been cleared after the last fare. The flag, or *bandeira*, over the meter denotes the tariff. Normally this will read "1", but after 10pm, and on Sundays, holidays and throughout December, you have to pay twenty percent more; then the *bandeira* will read "2".

Generally speaking, Rio's taxi service is reasonably priced and it is not in the cabbies' interest to alienate tourists by ripping them off. However, late at night, drivers often quote a fixed price that can be up to three times the normal fare. Whether you accept this depends on the availability of other cabs and how badly you need to travel. Radio cabs are thirty percent more expensive than the regular taxis, but they are reliable; companies include Coopertramo (☎260-2022), Cootramo (☎270-1442) and Transcoopass (☎270-4888).

Ferries and hydrofoils

From Praça XV de Novembro **ferries** transport passengers across Guanabara Bay to the city of Niterói (see p.111) and to Paquetá Island, a popular day-trip destination to the north of Guanabara Bay. The ferries are extremely cheap and the view of Rio they afford, especially at sunset, is well worth the effort, even if you don't set foot in Niterói. Crossings to Niterói are very frequent and cost about 50¢; just turn up and buy a ticket. The CONERJ company ferries (Companhia de Navegação do Estado de Rio de Janeiro; ☎231-0388) run Monday to Saturday, every fifteen minutes from 6am to 11pm; Sunday and public holidays, every thirty minutes from 7am to 11pm. To the island of Paquetá, there are eight departures a day from 5.30am to 10.30pm and tickets cost about $2. Also from Praça XV de Novembro, Transtur (☎231-0339) operates **hydrofoils** to Paquetá (departures every hour Mon–Fri from 10am to 4pm, Sat, Sun & holidays 8am to 3pm); Transtur also operates to Niterói every seven minutes from 6.15am to 8.15pm.

Trams

Rio's last remaining electric **trams**, the *bondes* (pronounced "bonjis"), climb from near Largo Carioca, across the eighteenth-century Aqueduto da Carioca, to the inner suburb of Santa Teresa and on to Dois Irmãos. An open tram, it still serves its original purpose of transporting locals, and hasn't yet become a tourist service. The views of Rio are excellent, but beware of the young chaps who jump onto the tram and attempt to relieve you of your possessions. It's not really a big deal, as there are guards on all the trams, but keep your wits about you. The tram station is adjacent to the Nova Catedral and waiting passengers stand in eight lines, one for every row of seats on the tram; the fare is just a few cents which you pay on board.

Driving in Rio

If you're renting a **car** then you must understand what you're letting yourself in for. Rio's road system is characterized by a confusion of one-way streets, tunnels, access roads and fly-overs, and **parking** is not easy. **Lane markings**, apart from lending a little colouring to the asphalt, serve no apparent practical purpose (though it seems to be regarded as bad luck to allow your vehicle to remain between the lines demarcating any lane for more than a second or two). **Overtaking** on the right appears to be mandatory and, after nightfall, obeying **traffic lights** is optional. (See p.108 for details of car rental in Rio.)

Accommodation

There's no shortage of choice of **accommodation** in Rio, but it's as well to bear in mind two things. From December to February (inclusive) is **high season**, so if you arrive then without an advance booking, either make one through a tourist office or leave your luggage in the *guarda volumes* (baggage offices) at the *Rodoviária* or at Santos Dumont airport while you look; there's no point lugging heavy bags around Rio's hot thoroughfares, and it makes you vulnerable to theft. One other period when prices tend to fluctuate wildly is at *Carnaval*, when accommodation becomes that much harder to find. During the low season, hotels usually lower their prices by around thirty percent but, when a discount is given, you may not be allowed to pay with a credit card (which budget hotels rarely accept anyway).

There is keen competition for tourists and you should be able to find a reasonable double room for $40–60. It is unusual for a hotel not to have air conditioners in each room; and, unless otherwise indicated, hotels serve some form of breakfast included in the price. The highest concentration of budget places is in Glória, Catete and Flamengo, but reasonably priced accommodation can be found just about anywhere. If you have any problems with unscrupulous hotel owners, call SUNAB (Mon–Sat 8am–6pm; ☎262-0198), the government's consumer affairs agency.

There are no **campsites** within easy reach of Rio, but there are a handful of **hostels** in Botafogo and Copacabana (listed below) for those with a youth hostel card; remember, however, that the universities are on holiday between December and March, when these places will be packed out. For **apartments**, try Rio Star Imóveis Ltda in Copacabana (☎275-8393; English and French spoken) or Rio Flat Service (☎274-7222), which has apartment buildings in Copacabana, Leblon and Lagoa – from $40 a day for a small apartment, with breakfast and swimming pool. If you want to be in Ipanema, call Ipanema Sweet (☎239-1819), who have one- and two-bedroom apartments near the beach from $50 per day.

If you're stopping in Rio for a while, check out the classified ads in the *Jornal do Brasil* for **rented rooms** – "*vaga*" (vacancy) and "*quarto*" (room) signify space in someone's home; "*conjugado*", abbreviated to "*conj*", means a bedsitter.

The city centre: Centro, Saúde and Lapa

Most of the cheap *pensões* are in the north of the city, or near Dom Pedro II train station, but they're mostly inhabited by full-time residents, usually single men, who are working in Rio. It's hard to find a vacancy, and you will be looking in areas that are not particularly safe. Lapa, in the southern corner of the city centre, is a far better bet. There are countless small hotels in this down-at-heel red-light area, and – surprisingly – most of them are clean and cheap enough.

Ambassador, Rua Senador Dantas 25 (☎297-7181). A safe and comfortable place to stay in the heart of Cinelândia, near the Biblioteca Nacional. ④.

Americano, Rua São Joaquim da Silva 69. A basic but friendly *pensão* near the Passeio Público park. ②.

Bragança, Av. Mem de Sá 115 (☎242-8116). Popular, well-equipped place with bar, telephones and TV. ②.

Guanabara Palace, Av. Presidente Vargas 392 (☎253-8622). The only luxury hotel in the centre – the haunt of expense account visitors doing business in Rio. ⑥.

Ipiranga, Rua São Joaquim da Silva 87. Cheap and friendly – well placed for walking to Centro and for buses to the Zona Sul. ②.

Marajó, Rua São Joaquim da Silva 99. Comfy beds and efficient showers, probably the best choice in the area. Also has some singles for around $18. ②.

Marialva, Av. Gomes Freire 430 (☎221-1187). A good hotel at the intersection with Mem de Sá across from the cathedral: singles start at around $10. ②.

Nelba, Rua Senador Dantas 46 (☎210-3235). Simple but clean, but its Cinelândia location means that street noise can be considerable. ③.

Glória

Glória, too, is not without its share of prostitution, but the *bairro* has a faded grandeur that's worth getting to know. It's not a dangerous area and is usefully located between Centro and the beaches and restaurants of Zona Sul.

Cândido Mendes, Rua Cândido Mendes 117. Located on the other side of the metrô station, to the left; clean and inexpensive. ②.

Casa da Hospedagem, Rua Catete 36. To the south of this area, this is a very basic, friendly place. ②.

Glória, Rua do Russel 632 (☎205-7272). This elegant hotel is something of a Rio landmark set amidst the cobbled roads of the Morro da Glória. Built in the Forties, the hotel is now a good distance from the sea, because of the landfill that created the Parque do Flamengo and allowed highways to be built linking Centro with Zona Sul. The *Glória* is a great place to stay if you can afford it – it's certainly Rio's best hotel within easy proximity of downtown. ⑥.

Monte Castelo, Rua Cândido Mendes 201. Reasonably priced and comfortable. ②.

Turístico, Ladeira da Glória 30 (☎225-9388). From opposite the Estação Glória, climb up round to the right of the Igreja de N.S. Outeiro da Glória and through the Lago da Glória. A highly recommended hotel; friendly, clean and cheap, with bath, breakfast and a place to leave valuables. It's a favourite budget traveller's haunt and consequently usually busy, so try and book ahead. ②.

Catete, Flamengo and Botafogo

Catete and Flamengo, centred around the Largo do Machado and once the chic residential *bairros* of the middle classes, are well served by hotels – all a good bit cheaper than the ones at Copacabana. It's a convenient place to stay, too, handily placed between the centre and the beach zone, with buses, taxis and the metrô providing easy access. For some reason, Botafogo offers few hotel possibilities, but if you want to stay in Rio's best eating-out district, there are a couple of options.

Chave do Rio Hostel, Rua General Dionísio 63 (☎286-0303). Comfortable and very friendly youth hostel in a beautiful renovated house just off Voluntarios da Patria in Botafogo. Beds, in small rooms, go for $12 per head and there are cooking and laundry facilities.

Ferreira Viana, Rua Ferreira Viana 58 (☎205-7396). Inexpensive, but a little cramped and with a communal shower room. ②.

Flórida, Rua Ferreira Viana 69–81 (☎245-8160). Highly recommended: spacious rooms, private showers, nice and clean and with a safety deposit box. ④.

Hispânico Brasileira, Rua Silveira Martins 135 (☎225-7537). Pleasant and airy, near the Catete metrô station. ②.

Imperial, Rua Catete 186 (☎205-0775). A good-value, very comfortable place. ③.

Lisboa, Rua Artur Bernardes 29 (☎265-9599). A basic place on the second street on the left up from Largo do Machado. ②.

Monte Blanco, Rua Catete 160 (☎225-0121). Very clean and friendly; around $14 a single. ②.

Monterrey, Rua Artur Bernardes 39 (☎265-9899). Cheap place with a great atmosphere – one of the city's best budget choices. ②.

Paysandú, Rua Paissandu 23 (☎225-7270). Rooms have bathroom and TV and there's a decent restaurant on the ground floor, too. The front doors close at midnight but there is a night porter on duty. ③.

Real, Rua Real Grandeza 122 (☎246-6221). Comfortable and good value with many of Botafogo's restaurants located in the surrounding streets. ③.

Regina, Rua Ferreira Viana 29 (☎225-7280). Excellent value for good-quality rooms. ③.

Rio Claro, Rua Catete 233 (☎225-5180). Good double rooms, but singles are without air conditioning. ②.

Venezuela, Rua Paissandu (☎205-2098). Opposite the *Hotel Paysandú*, it's clean and safe, but a bit poky. ③.

Copacabana, Leme and Ipanema

Although the bulk of Rio's high-class, expensive hotels are located by the beaches in the Zona Sul, it is possible to find reasonably priced accommodation here, too. If you're really on a tight budget, you're best off using one of the Copacabana youth hostels.

COPACABANA AND LEME

Acapulco, Rua Gustavo Sampaio 854 (☎275-0022). Very comfortable hotel in a quiet location in Leme behind *Le Meridien*. ④.

Angarense, Travessa Angarense 25 (☎255-3875). Just down a sidestreet off Avenida N.S. de Copacabana, this hotel offers safe, if cramped and gloomy rooms. ②.

Biarritz, Rua Aires Saldanha 54 (☎255-6552). Just down from Avenida Atlântica, this clean and friendly place is located in a quiet backstreet. ③.

Cánada, Av. N.S. de Copacabana 687 (☎257-1864). A good compromise deal for this area; the well-equipped and relatively spacious rooms would cost double were they facing the beach. ③.

Copa Linda, Av. N.S. de Copacabana 116 (☎255-0938). This hotel, on the second floor, provides good, basic accommodation, although many rooms are small. ③.

Copacabana Chalet Hostel, Rua Pompeu Loureiro 99 (☎236-0047). Just a short walk from the beach – popular but noisy. $12 per head.

Copacabana Paia Hostel, Rua Tenente Marones de Gusmão 85 (☎236-6472). Set several blocks back from the beach, off Rua Figueiredo Magalhães, this is probably the best of Rio's hostels. It charges $12 per head, but double rooms (including a private bathroom and basic cooking facilities) are also available. ②.

Copacabana Palace, Av. Atlântica 1702 (☎255-7070). A glorious Art Deco landmark where anyone who is anyone has stayed. Renovated to a high standard over the last few years, this is a great place to end a trip to Brazil if you can possibly afford it. ⑧.

Excelsior Copacabana, Av. Atlântica 1800 (☎257-1950). This is a reasonable mid-range choice in the middle of Copacobana's beachfront. One of the oldest buildings on the *avenida*, it tries to maintain the atmosphere of a bygone age. ⑥.

Le Meridien, Av. Atlântica 1020 (☎275-9922). A huge hotel in Leme with all the conveniences that are expected from this French-owned chain. There's a good pool on the beach in front of the hotel which is carefully watched by security patrols. With its cafés, restaurants and boutiques, for many guests this is their only experience of Rio. ⑧.

Martinique, Rua Sá Ferreira 30 (☎521-4552). A popular hotel quietly located near the western end of Copacabana, towards the fort. ④.

Ouro Verde, Av. Atlântica 1456 (☎542-1887). Discreetly elegant with excellent service, attracting guests who return year after year. The hotel also has a very good French restaurant (see p.98). ⑤.

Praia Leme, Av. Atlântica 866 (☎275-3322). This cosy hotel with only two floors offers the best value for a beachfront location. Its popularity means that an advance reservation is highly recommended. ④.

Predia Leme, Av. Princesa Isabel 7, Loja 14/15 (☎275-5449). A wide range of rooms; some have small kitchens and sea views. ③–⑤.

Santa Clara, Rua Décio Vilares 316 (☎256-2650). A budget-oriented hotel that's excellent value and very friendly. It's situated just past the cemetery, and close to the Túnel Velho leading to Botafogo's restaurants and museums.

Toledo, Rua Domingos Ferreira 71 (☎257-1990). Small but pleasant rooms halfway down Copacabana, just one block from the beach – excellent value. ④.

IPANEMA

Arpoador Inn, Rua Francisco Otaviano 177 (☎247-6090). In a quiet location away from the traffic, this is good value for the area. You'll pay more for a beachfront room but, in any case, it's the rear-facing rooms that allow you to see absolutely wonderful sunsets. ④.

Caesar Park, Av. Vieira Souto 460 (☎287-3122). Thought of, by many, as being Rio's finest hotel – certainly it's the city's most expensive and it features every luxury that its celebrity guests would expect. ⑧.

Carlton, Rua João Lira 68 (☎259-1932). A small and friendly place in a very classy area. ④.

Ipanema Inn, Rua Maria Quiteria 29 (☎287-6092). Excellent value, tucked in behind the five-star *Caesar Park Hotel*, so at least you'll have some nice neighbours. ④.

São Marco, Rua Visconde de Pirajá 524 (☎239-5032). A good deal for its location, just a few minutes from the beach, but rooms are small. ④.

Vermont, Rua Visconde de Pirajá 254 (☎247-6100). Simple rooms, but excellent location and good value. ⑤.

The city centre

Much of historical Rio is concentrated in **Centro**, with pockets of interest, too, in the neighbouring **Saúde** and **Lapa** quarters of the city. You'll find you can tour the centre fairly easily on foot. It's worth repeating, though, that the real interest of Rio lies elsewhere – at the beaches of the Zona Sul, and the heights of Urca and Corcovado – and it's not the most exciting city in Brazil to explore. Lots of the old historical squares, streets and buildings have disappeared this century under a torrent of redevelopment, and fighting your way through the traffic – the reason many of the streets were widened in the first place – can be quite a daunting prospect.

Nonetheless, if you have the time, there is still a lot to see, and a quite different side to Rio than that of the beaches and spectacular viewpoints. The cultural influences that shaped the city through its five centuries of existence – the austere Catholicism of the city's European founders, the squalor of colonialism and the grandiose design of the Enlightenment – are all reflected in the surviving churches, streets and squares. And although a lot of what remains is decidedly low key, there are enough churches and interesting museums to keep anybody happy for a day or two. Above all, a walk around Rio – old and new – gives you an idea of the wealth generated by the rich lands that the Portuguese conquerors appropriated five hundred years ago.

Praça XV de Novembro and around

Praça XV de Novembro is the obvious place to start. Once the hub of Rio's social and political life, it takes its name from the day (November 15) in 1899 when Marechal Deodoro de Fonseca, the first president, proclaimed the Republic of Brazil. One of Rio's oldest **markets** is held here on Thursday and Friday (8am–6pm). The stalls are packed

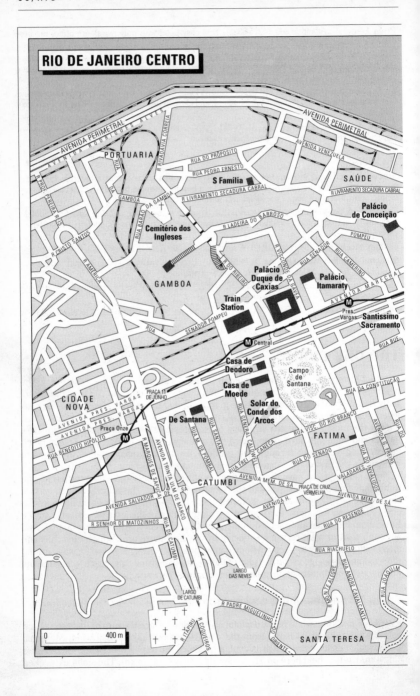

RIO DE JANEIRO CENTRO

AVENIDA PERIMETRAL

AVENIDA PERIMETRAL

AVENIDA RODRIGUES ALVES

AVENIDA VENEZUELA

PORTUARIA

RUA RIVADAVIA CORREIA

RUA DO PRÓPOSITO

RUA PEDRO ERNESTO

S Família

SAÚDE

R LIVRAMENTO SECADURA CABRAL

R LIVRAMENTO SECADURA CABRAL

RUA BARÃO DA GAMBOA

R PROF. PEREIRA RÊS

R CRISTO SANTOS

R AMÉRICA

RUA DA GAMBOA

Cemitério dos Ingleses

R LADEIRA DO BARROSO

Palácio de Conceição

POMPEU

RUA SENADOR

RUA CAMERINO

GAMBOA

RUA DO RIBEIRO

RUA VISCONDE DA GÁVEA

Palácio Duque de Caxias

Palácio Itamaraty

AVENIDA MARECHAL

RUA SENADOR POMPEU

RUA

Train Station

RUA S DO FIM

M Central

M Pres. Vargas Santissimo Sacramento

RUA RUE

Casa de Deodoro

Casa de Moede

CIDADE NOVA

Campo de Santana

RUA DA CONSTITUIÇÃO

PRAÇA 11 DE JUNHO

AVENIDA PRES. VARGAS

Solar do, Conde dos Arcos

AVENIDA PRES. VARGAS

De Santana

RUA GENERAL CALDWEL

RUA M. DE LIMA

RUA SANTANA

RUA VISC. DO RIO BRANCO

Praça Onze

M

RUA BENEDITO HIPÓLITO

AVENIDA TRINTA ULM DE MARÇO

RUA MARQUES DE SAPUCAÍ

FATIMA

RUA DO RIACHU

AVENIDA G. TRAVES

RUA FREI CANECA

RUA DO SENADO

VALADARES

AVENIDA MEM. DE SÁ

AVENIDA MEM. DE SÁ

CATUMBI

PRAÇA DE CRUZ VERMELHA

AVENIDA SALVADOR

AVENIDA H.

RUA DO CATUMBI

R SENHOR DE MATOZINHOS

RUA DO RESENDE

RUA RIACHUELO

LARGO DAS NEVES

RUA MON. TEALEGRE

RUA ANDR CAIALCANTE

RUA JOAQUIM

LARGO DE CATUMBI

R PADRE MIGUELINHO

R ITAPIRU

R COQUEIROS

ORIENTE

SANTA TERESA

0   400 m

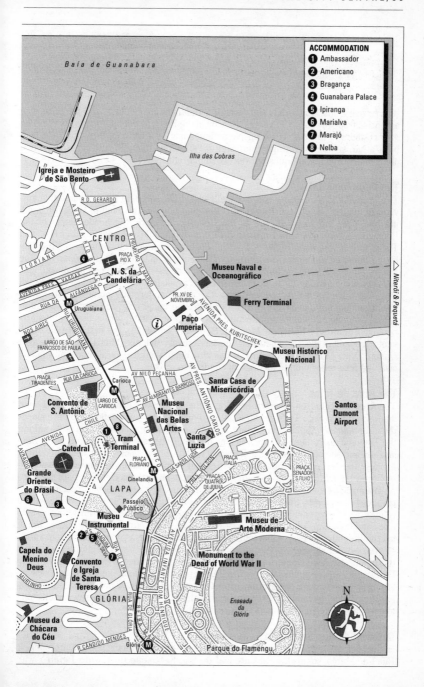

ACCOMMODATION
1. Ambassador
2. Americano
3. Bragança
4. Guanabara Palace
5. Ipiranga
6. Marialva
7. Marajó
8. Nelba

Baía de Guanabara

Ilha das Cobras

Niterói & Paquetá

Igreja e Mosteiro de São Bento

R.D. GERARDO

CENTRO

PRAÇA PIO X

N. S. da Candelária

Museu Naval e Oceanográfico

PR. XV DE NOVEMBRO

Ferry Terminal

Uruguaiana

Paço Imperial

Museu Histórico Nacional

LARGO DE SÃO FRANCISCO DE PAULA

AV NILO PEÇANHA

Carioca

Santa Casa de Misericórdia

PRAÇA TIRADENTES

RUA DA CARIOCA

Santos Dumont Airport

Convento de S. Antônio

LARGO DE CARIOCA

CHILE

Museu Nacional das Belas Artes

Santa Luzia

Catedral

Tram Terminal

PRAÇA FLORIANO

AVENIDA

Grande Oriente do Brasil

Cinelandia

LAPA

PRAÇA ITÁLIA

PRAÇA QUATRO DE JULHO

PRAÇA SENADOR S.FILHO

Passeio Público

Museu Instrumental

Museu de Arte Moderna

Capela do Menino Deus

Convento e Igreja de Santa Teresa

Monument to the Dead of World War II

GLÓRIA

Museu da Chácara do Céu

Enseada da Glória

B. CÂNDIDO MENDES

Glória

Parque do Flamengo

N

MUSEUM CHARGES IN RIO

Museum charges are negligible, generally less than $1, and are only given in the text where they are unusually high.

with typical foods, handicrafts and ceramics, and there are paintings and prints, as well as a brisk trade in stamps and coins. Nearby in the Praça Marechal Ancora, by the *Alba Mar* restaurant, there is an expensive antiques market (Saturday 8am–5pm) – a laid-back affair, selling everything from Melrose's tea tins to eighteenth-century French clocks; nearly all the antiques are European in origin.

The Paço Imperial
The Praça XV de Novembro was originally called the Largo do Paço, a name that survives in the imposing **Paço Imperial** (Tues–Sun 11am–6pm). Built in 1743, the building has, over the years, served as the Governor's Palace, the headquarters of the Portuguese government in Brazil until 1791 and, later, of the Department of Post and Telegraph. It was here, in 1808, that the Portuguese monarch, Dom João VI, established his court in Brazil (later shifting to the Palácio da Quinta da Boa Vista, now the Museu Nacional), and the building continued to be used for royal receptions and special occasions: on May 13, 1888, Princess Isabel proclaimed the end of slavery in Brazil from here. It's been tinkered with over the years, undergoing numerous structural modifications, but has lately been restored to its original state and provides an interesting example of colonial architecture. Right on the square, too, is the seventeenth-century **Faculdade Cândido Mendes** (Mon–Fri 8am–9pm), the first Carmelite convent to be built in Rio. Used between times as a royal residence (after 1808 the Dowager Queen, Dona Maria I, lived here), it has also been altered several times, and is still awaiting final renovation to its original condition.

The Arco de Teles
The **Arco de Teles**, on the northern side of the square, was named after the judge and landowner, Francisco Teles de Meneza, who ordered its construction upon the site of the old *pelourinho* (pillory) in around 1755. It's really an arcade rather an arch, linking the Travessa do Comércio to the Rua Ouvidor (this latter street was previously the *Beco do Peixe* and site of the first free fish market in Rio). The *arco* originally contained three houses; one of these was home to the Menezes family, but all were severely damaged by fire in 1790. More engaging than the building itself, is the social history of the Arco de Teles and its immediate vicinity. In the luxurious apartments above street level lived families belonging to Rio's wealthy classes, while the street below was traditionally a refuge for "beggars and rogues of the worst type; lepers, thieves, murderers, prostitutes and hoodlums" – according to Brasil Gerson in his *History of Rio's Streets*. In the late eighteenth and early nineteenth centuries, one of the leprous local inhabitants – **Bárbara dos Prazeres** – achieved notoriety as a folk devil: it was a common belief that the blood of a dead dog or cat applied to the body provided a cure for leprosy, and Bárbara is supposed to have earned her reputation around the Arco de Teles by attempting to enhance the efficacy of this cure by stealing new-born babies and sucking their blood. Behind the Arco de Teles is the Beco de Teles, a narrow cobblestone alley with some charming nineteenth-century buildings.

Catedral de São Sebastião
At the back of Praça XV de Novembro, on the corner where Rua VII de Setembro meets Rua I de Março, stands the old **Catedral de São Sebastião do Rio de Janeiro**, with

the image of St Sebastian, Rio's patron saint, high on the front of the church. Building started in 1749 and, to all intents and purposes, continued right into the twentieth century as structural collapse and financial difficulties necessitated several restorations and delays: the present tower, for example, was built as late as 1905 by the Italian architect Rebecchi. Inside, the high altar is detailed in silver and boasts a beautiful work by the painter Antônio Parreires, representing *Nossa Senhora do Carmo* seated amongst the clouds and surrounded by the sainted founders of the Carmelite Order. Below, in the **crypt**, are the supposed mortal remains of Pedro Alvares Cabral, Portuguese discoverer of Brazil. In actual fact, he was almost certainly laid to rest in Santarem in Portugal.

Museu Naval e Oceanográfico

Close to Praça XV de Novembro, down Rua Dom Manuel, is the **Museu Naval e Oceanográfico** (daily noon–4.30pm). Housed in what was originally the naval headquarters, the museum's excellent collection (laid out in ten rooms on two floors) shows the chronology of Brazil's naval history – from sixteenth-century nautical charts and scale replicas of European galleons, to paintings depicting scenes from the Brazil–Paraguay War and exhibits of twentieth-century naval hardware. It's all very well presented, the museum watched over by naval ratings in formal, starched white uniforms who hand out felt overshoes to protect the highly polished parquet floor. Above all, the collections provide an insight into the colonial nature of Brazilian history: the exhibits show that Brazilian naval engagements were determined by the interests of the Portuguese Empire until the nineteenth century; as a primarily slave-based plantation economy until 1888, Brazil's military hardware came from the foundries of industrialized Europe. The most impressive items are the handcrafted replicas of sixteenth-century galleons – the *São Felipe* complete with its 98 cannons – and the first map of the New World, drawn by Pedro Alvares Cabral between 1492 and 1500.

Along Rua I de Março to Praça Pio X

Heading up **Rua I de Março** from the *praça* you'll pass the museum and church of **Santa Cruz dos Militares** (Mon–Fri 8am–6pm, Sat 8am–2pm), its name giving a hint of its curious history. In 1628, a number of army officers organized the construction of the first church here, on the site of an early fort. It was used for the funerals of serving officers until, in 1703, the Catholic Church attempted to take over control of the building. The proposal met stiff resistance, and it was only in 1716 that the Fathers of the Church of São Sebastião, which had become severely dilapidated, succeeded in installing themselves in Santa Cruz. Sadly, they were no more successful in the maintenance of this church either, and by 1760 it had been reduced to a state of ruin – only reversed when army officers again took control of the reconstruction work in 1780, completing the building that survives today. It's built from granite and marble and, inside, the nave, with its stuccoed ceiling, has been skilfully decorated with plaster relief images from Portugal's imperial past. The two owners long since reconciled, there's a **museum**, with a collection of military and religious relics, on the ground floor.

Further along Rua I de Março is the late eighteenth-century **Igreja da Ordem Terceira do Monte do Carmo** (Mon–Fri 1–3pm), whose seven altars each bear an image symbolizing a moment from the Passion of Christ, from Calvary to the Crucifixion, sculpted by Pedro Luiz da Cunha. The high altar itself is beautifully worked in silver. The church and adjacent convent are linked by a small public chapel, dedicated to Our Lady of the Cape of Good Hope, and decorated in *azulejos*.

The Igreja de Nossa Senhora da Candelária

At the end of Rua I de Março you emerge onto **Praça Pio X**, dominated by the **Igreja de Nossa Senhora da Candelária** (Mon–Fri 7am–noon & 2–4.30pm, Sat 7am–noon), an interesting combination of Baroque and Renaissance features. It owes this variety of style to the financial difficulties which delayed the completion of the building for more than a century after its foundation in 1775. Inside, the altars, walls and supporting columns are sculpted from variously coloured marble – grey, white, green, yellow, red and black. Eight pictures in the dome represent the three theological virtues (Faith, Hope and Charity), the cardinal virtues (Prudence, Justice, Strength and Temperance) and the Virgin Mary – all the work of João Zeferino da Costa. There's more grand decoration in the two pulpits, luxuriously worked in bronze and supported by large white angels sculpted in marble.

The Avenida Presidente Vargas

Until 1943 the church was hemmed in by other buildings, but it was appointed its own space when the **Avenida Presidente Vargas** was constructed, opening up new vistas. The avenue runs west for almost three kilometres and has fourteen lanes of traffic, and when work started on it in 1941 there was considerable opposition from the owners of houses and businesses which were demolished in its path – not to mention clerical dissent at the destruction of a number of churches. The avenue was inaugurated with a military parade in 1944, watched by Vargas himself in the year before he was deposed by a quiet coup. Until the construction of the Sambódromo, the main *Carnaval* procession took place along here.

Back towards the waterfront, turn into Rua Visconde de Itaborai and you will pass the **Alfândega Antiga** (Tues–Fri 10am–8pm, Sat, Sun & holidays 10am–5pm), the old Customs House, which was constructed in 1820 by the French architect Grandjean de Montigny, in Neoclassical style. It's been home to a bizarre array of organizations in its time, from the English merchants who arrived after the opening of the port to free trade in 1808, through the Mauá Gas Company and the Brazilian Society for the Protection of Animals, to the Socialist organizers of Rio's 1918 general strike.

From São Bento to the Largo da Carioca

Heading north, on the continuation of Rua I de Março, the Ladeira de São Bento leads to the **Igreja e Mosteiro de São Bento** (daily 2.30–5pm, open also for mass with Gregorian chant Mon–Sat 7.15am, Sun 10am), in the *bairro* of **Saúde** overlooking the Ilha das Cobras. The monastery was founded by Benedictine monks who arrived in Rio in 1586 by way of Bahia. They had been offered a piece of ground in the corner of Praça XV de Novembro, by Rua VII de Septembro, which they declined because of the noise emanating from the adjacent fish market, and started building instead on the present site in 1633, finishing nine years later. The facade displays a pleasing architectural simplicity, its twin towers culminating in pyramid-shaped spires, while the interior is richly adorned. The altars and walls are covered by images of saints, and there are statues representing various popes and bishops, work executed by the deft hand of Mestre Valentim. The panels and paintings particularly, late seventeenth-century work, represent valuable examples of colonial art, while six lateral altars, illuminated by lamps fashioned from silver, add texture to the interior's atmosphere. There is not much else to grab your attention in the area. The monastery is next to **Praça Mauá** and the docklands, a seedy and run-down part of the city that you'd do best to avoid at night.

Largo Santa Rita

Heading along Rua Dom Gerardo from the monastery leads you to the north end of Avenida Rio Branco, on the far (west) side of which (off Visconde de Inhaúma) is **Largo**

Santa Rita and its church, the Igreja da Santa Rita (Mon–Sat 8am–noon & 2–5pm). Built on land previously used as a slaves' burial ground, the building dates from 1721, its bell tower tucked to one side giving it a lopsided look. It's not one of Rio's more attractive churches, but the interior stonework is a fine example of Rococo style, and it's magnificently decorated with a series of panels, three on the high altar and eight on the ceiling, painted by Ananias Correia do Amaral and depicting scenes from the life of Santa Rita.

Rua Uruguaiana: Saara and Largo de São Francisco de Paula

To return south, to the Largo da Carioca in Centro, cross Avenida Presidente Vargas and continue down Rua Uruguaiana. In the streets to your left (between Uruguaiana and I de Março) lies the most interesting concentration of shops in Rio, in the area known as Saara. Traditionally the cheapest place to shop, it was originally peopled by Jewish and Arab merchants, who moved into the area after a ban prohibiting their residence within the city limits was lifted in the eighteenth century. Curiously, a new wave of Jewish and Arab merchants – along with, most recently, Chinese and Koreans – have in recent years moved back into the area. In the maze of narrow streets you'll find everything from basic items of beachware and handicrafts to expensive jewellery. The streets are lined with stalls selling trinkets and are thronged with street traders and folk musicians, so it's always a lively place to visit: particularly good buys here include sports equipment, musical instruments and records and tapes.

Halfway down Rua Uruguaiana is Largo de São Francisco de Paula, whose church, the Igreja de São Francisco de Paula (Mon–Fri 10am–noon & 2–4pm), has hosted some significant moments in Brazil's history. Behind the monumental carved wooden entrance door the Te Deum was sung in 1816 to celebrate Brazil's promotion from colony to kingdom; in 1831, the mass celebrating the "Swearing-in" of the Brazilian Constitution was performed here. More tangibly, the chapel of Nossa Senhora da Vitória, on the right as you enter, was dedicated by Pope Pius X to the victory of the Christian forces over the Turkish in the naval battle of Lepanto in 1571. The meticulous decoration is attributed to Mestre Valentim, who spent thirty years working on the chapel, while the paintings on the walls were done by a slave who called himself Manoel da Cunha. With the consent of his owner, Manoel travelled to Europe as the assistant of the artist João de Souza, and on his return bought his own freedom with money earned from the sale of his artwork.

Across from the church is the Real Gabinete Português de Leitura (Mon–Fri 9am–5pm), a library dedicated to Portugal and Portuguese literature. The building was completed in 1887 and is immediately identifiable by its magnificent Manueline-style facade. The reading room is lit by a red, white and blue stained-glass skylight and contains many of the library's 350,000 volumes. Amongst the rarest is the 1572 first edition of Os Lusíados, the Portuguese national epic poem by Luis de Camões, based on Vasco da Gama's voyage of exploration, and there are usually small displays from the library's collection.

The Largo da Carioca

From Largo de São Francisco de Paula, Rua Ramalho Ortigão leads the short distance to Rua Carioca. On the way, you can stop for a well-earned beer in Rio's oldest cervejaria, the Bar Luiz at no. 39. It's been here since 1887, changing its original name – the Bar Adolfo – following World War II, for obvious reasons. The bar was once a favourite watering hole for Rio's Bohemian and intellectual groups and though it's a little faded these days, it's still a bustling, enjoyable place to be – the beer's cold and you can get wurst if you want it. The wonderful Art Nouveau Confeitaria Colombo is just one block from here at Rua Gonçalves Dias 32 (see p.95).

The Largo da Carioca itself has undergone considerable transformation since the turn of the century, many of its buildings demolished to allow widening of the square and the improving of nearby streets. Today street traders selling leather goods dominate the centre of the square, while a couple of things of interest remain, most notably the **Igreja e Convento de Santo Antônio** (Mon–Sat 7am–6pm), standing above the *largo*. It's known as St Anthony of the Rich (to differentiate it from St Anthony of the Poor, which is located elsewhere in the city). A tranquil, cloistered refuge, built between 1608 and 1620, it's the oldest church in Rio and was founded by Franciscan monks who had arrived in Brazil in 1592. A popular saint in Brazil, St Anthony's help was sought during the French invasion of 1710: he was made a captain in the Brazilian army and in a startling lack of progress through the ranks it was 1814 before he was promoted to lieutenant-colonel, retiring from service in 1914. More improbably still, the tomb of **Wild Jock of Skelater** lies in the crypt. A Scottish mercenary who entered the service of the Portuguese Crown during the Napoleonic Wars, he was later appointed commander-in-chief of the Portuguese army in Brazil.

This aside, the interior of the church boasts a beautiful sacristy, constructed from Portuguese marble and decorated in *azulejos* depicting the miracles performed by St Anthony. There is rich wooden ornamentation throughout, carved from jacaranda, including the great chest in the sacristy. The image of Christ, adorned with a crown of thorns, came from Portugal in 1678 – a remarkable piece of work of great skill and spiritual perception.

West from Praça Tiradentes

Leave Largo da Carioca by turning left along Rua Carioca, and you're soon in **Praça Tiradentes**, named after the leader of the so-called Minas Conspiracy of 1789, a plot hatched in the state of Minas Gerais to overthrow the Portuguese regime (see p.158). This nationalist struggle, which was partly inspired by the American War of Independence, came to nothing and Tiradentes was captured and executed as an example to other anti-imperialists. His resurrection as a national martyr came only with Brazilian independence in the nineteenth century.

In the square stands the **Teatro João Caetano**, after João Caetano dos Santos, who based his drama company in the theatre from 1840. He also notches up a bust which stands in the square, a reward for producing shows starring such theatrical luminaries as Sarah Bernhardt. In the second-floor hall of the theatre hang two large panels painted in 1930 by Emiliano di Cavalcanti, one of Brazil's great modernist artists, which, with his usual use of strong tropical colours, explore the themes of *Carnaval* and popular religion. The original theatre on this site, the Teatro Real, erected in 1813, had a much more political history: it was here in 1821 that Dom João VI swore obedience to the Constitution promulgated in Lisbon after the Porto Revolution. Three years later, at the end of the ceremony proclaiming Dom Pedro I Emperor of Brazil, a fire razed the old theatre to the ground.

Campo de Santana and around

Three blocks west of Praça Tiradentes, along Rua Visconde do Rio Branco, is the **Praça da República** in the **Campo de Santana**. Until the beginning of the seventeenth century this area was outside the city limits, which extended only as far as Rua Uruguaiana. Its sandy soils made it unsuitable for cultivation and the only building here was the chapel of St Domingo, sited in the area now covered by the asphalt of Avenida President Vargas, and used by the Fraternity of St Anne to celebrate the festivals of their patron saint – hence the name, Campo de Santana (field of St Anne).

By the end of the eighteenth century the city had spread to surround the Campo de Santana, and in 1811 a barracks was built to house the Second Regiment of the Line, who used the square as a parade ground. From here, Dom Pedro I proclaimed Brazil's independence from the Portuguese Crown in 1822, and after 1889 the lower half of the square became known as Praça da República. The first president of the new republic, Deodoro de Fonseca, lived at no. 197 Praça da República. At the start of this century, the square was landscaped, and today it's a pleasant place for a walk, with lots of trees and small lakes ruled by swans. In the centre lies the **João Furtado Park**, worth visiting in the evening, when small, furry shapes can be seen scuttling about in the gloom – gophers, happily, not rats.

Directly across Avenida Presidente Vargas is the Praça Duque de Caxias and the **National Pantheon**, on top of which stands the equestrian statue of the Duque de Caxias, military patron and general in the Paraguayan War – his remains lie below in the Pantheon. Nearby, the **Dom Pedro II train station** is an unmistakable landmark, its tower rising 110m into the sky and supporting clock faces measuring 7.5 by 5.5m, all linked to a central winding mechanism. In front of the station, at Av. Marechal Floriano 196 (running parallel to Avenida Presidente Vargas), the **Palácio do Itamaraty** is one of Rio's best examples of Neoclassical architecture. Completed in 1853, as the *pied-à-terre* of the great landowner Baron of Itamaraty, it was bought by the government and was home to a number of the republic's presidents. The *palácio* now houses the **Museu Histórico e Diplomático do Itamaraty** (Tues–Fri 10am–5.30pm, Sat & Sun 2–5.30pm), a repository of documents, books and maps relating to Brazil's diplomatic history, its collections primarily of interest to serious researchers (archives open for consultation Mon–Fri 1–5pm). Of perhaps wider interest, however, is the part of the building painstakingly restored to show how the upper classes lived in the nineteenth century.

North of Itamaraty is Gamboa, an extremely seedy port area and home to Rio's oldest *favelas*. The only reason to visit Gamboa is to go to the **English Cemetery** (*Cemitério dos Ingleses*), the oldest Protestant burial site in Brazil. In 1809 the British community was given permission to establish a cemetery and Anglican church in Rio, essential if English merchants were to be attracted to newly independent Brazil. Still in use today, the cemetery is set in a beautiful hillside location looking down to Guanabara Bay. The inscriptions on many of the stones make poignant reading, memories of the days when early death was almost expected. The cemetery (Mon–Fri 8am–4pm, Sat & Sun 8am–12.30pm) is at Rua da Gamboa 181. It's best to call the caretaker (☎233-4237) before visiting to confirm that the gates will be open. The area has a reputation for being dangerous and you'd be wise to go by taxi; under no circumstances walk alone along the approach road passing through the tunnel from the nearby central train station.

From the Nova Catedral to Cinelândia and Praça Floriano

Back behind the Largo da Carioca, the unmistakable shape of the **Nova Catedral** (Mon–Sat 7am–6pm, Sun 9am–6pm) rises up like some futuristic teepee. Built between 1964 and 1976, it's an impressive piece of modern architecture and a considerable engineering feat, whatever you think of the style: the Morro de Santo Antônio was levelled to make way for the cathedral's construction, and the thousands of tons of resulting soil were used for the land reclamation project that gave rise to the Parque de Flamengo. Similar in style to the blunt-topped Mayan pyramids found in the Yucatán region of Mexico, the cathedral is 83m high with a diameter of 104m and has a capacity of 25,000 people. Inside, it feels vast, a remarkable sense of space enhanced by the absence of supporting columns. Four huge stained-glass windows dominate, each measuring 20 by 60m and corresponding to a symbolic colour scheme – ecclesiastical green, saintly red, Catholic blue and apostolic yellow. From outside, you'll be able to see the **Aqueduto da Carioca**, which carries trams up to Santa Teresa, the *bairro* on the hill opposite; the tram terminal is between the cathedral and the Largo da Carioca.

Along Avenida República de Chile, and right down **Avenida Rio Branco**, you'll come to Praça Marechal Floriano and the area known as **Cinelândia**, named after long-gone movie houses built in the 1930s. Today it's a bustling location whose bars fill up with thirsty office workers at the end of the day. Rio Branco, originally named Avenida Central, must once have been Latin America's most impressive urban thoroughfare. Old photos show it bordered by Neoclassical-style buildings of no more than three storeys high, its pavements lined with trees, and with a promenade that ran right down the centre. Nowadays, however, the once graceful avenue has been swamped by ugly office buildings and traffic pollution.

Praça Floriano

The **Praça Floriano** is the one section of Avenida Rio Branco that still impresses. There are several sidewalk cafés on the western side of the *praça* which are popular central meeting points in the evening when the surrounding buildings are illuminated and at their most elegant. In the centre of the square is a bust of **Getúlio Vargas**, still anonymously decorated with flowers on the anniversary of the ex-dictator's birthday, March 19. At the north end of the square the **Teatro Municipal**, opened in 1909 and a dramatic example of Neoclassical architecture, was modelled on the Paris Opera – all granite, marble and bronze, with a foyer decorated in the white and gold characteristic of Louis XV style. Since opening, the theatre has been Brazil's most prestigious artistic venue, hosting visiting Brazilian and foreign orchestras, opera and theatre companies and singers. There has been talk of initiating English-language tours around the building, which is worth checking out; the theatre has its own fine restaurant and bar, the *Café do Teatro* (Mon–Fri 11am–4pm), which is richly adorned with Assyrian-inspired mosaics.

On the opposite side of the road, the **Museu Nacional das Belas Artes** (Tues–Fri 10am–6pm, Sat & Sun 2–6pm) is a grandiose construction built in 1908 to imitate the Louvre in Paris. The European collection includes Boudin, Tournay and Franz Post amongst many others, but it's the **Brazilian collection** which is really interesting. Organized in chronological order, each room shows the various stages in the development of Brazilian painting as a result of the influences imported from Europe: the years of diversification (1919–28); the movement into modernism and eclecticism (1921–49); and the consolidation of modern forms between 1928 and 1967, especially in the works of Cândido Portinari, Djanira and Francisco Rebolo.

The last building of note on the Praça Floriano is the **Biblioteca Nacional** (Mon–Fri 9am–8pm, Sat noon–6pm), whose stairway was decorated by some of the most important artistic names of the nineteenth century, including Modesto Brocas, Eliseu Visconti, Rodolfo Amoedo and Henrique Bernadelli. If you speak Portuguese and want to use the library, the staff are very obliging.

Lapa

Continuing south from Cinelândia, Avenida Rio Branco passes Praça Mahatma Ghandi which borders the **Passeio Público** park (daily 7.30am–9pm), well into Lapa *bairro*. A little past its best, and neglected by the authorities these days, the park is, nevertheless, a green oasis away from the hustle and bustle of the city. Opened in 1783, it was designed in part by Mestre Valentim, Brazil's most important late eighteenth-century sculptor, its trees providing shade for busts commemorating famous figures from the city's history, including Mestre Valentim de Fonseca e Silva himself. One of the most recent busts to be placed in the park is that of Chiquinha Gonzaga, who wrote the first recorded samba for *Carnaval – Pelo Telefone*. Other diversions include Valentim's fountain, the *Chafariz dos Jacarés*, fashioned as a group of alligators cast in bronze. Sunday morning is a good time to wander through the Passeio Público, when a stamp and coin market is held inside the park.

On the Rua do Passeio, which runs under the Teatro Mesbla, the **Museu Instrumental Delgado de Carvalho** at no. 98 (Mon–Fri 8am–5pm) is in the entrance to the Federal University's School of Music. The collection, initially organized by the composer Delgado de Carvalho in 1901, contains musical instruments from various parts of the world, combined with a more interesting selection of indigenous exhibits.

The rest of **Lapa** has much the same faded charm as the park, attractive enough to want to explore – though it would be wise not to wander the streets unaccompanied at night. It's an old *bairro*; Brasil Gerson, writing in his *History of Rio's Streets*, notes that it was traditionally known as an "area of 'cabarets' and bawdy houses, the haunt of scoundrels, of gamblers, swashbucklers and inverteds and the 'trottoir' of poor, fallen women" – evidently a place to rush to, or avoid, depending upon your taste in entertainment. Until the mid-seventeenth century, Lapa was a beach, known as the "Spanish Sands", but development and land reclamation have assisted its slide into shabby grandeur.

From Lapa you can walk down to the Avenida Beira Mar, where the **Monument to the Dead of World War II** is a clearly visible landmark. Next to the monument, at the north end of the Parque do Flamengo (see p.86) is the ugly **Museu de Arte Moderna** (Tues–Sun noon–6pm), designed by the Brazilian architect and urbanist Afonso Reidy, and inaugurated in 1958. The museum's collection was devastated by a fire in 1978 and only reopened in 1990 following restoration. The permanent collection is still extremely small but the museum hosts visiting exhibitions and it's worth checking what's on.

Northeast to the Museu Histórico Nacional

Heading northeast from the Passeio Público, along Rua Santa Luzia, you pass the **Igreja de Santa Luzia** in the Praça da Academia, an attractive eighteenth-century church whose predecessor stood on the seashore – hard to believe today, as it's overwhelmed by the surrounding office buildings. On December 13 every year, devotees enter the "room of miracles" at the back of the church and bathe their eyes in water from the white marble font – reputedly a miraculous cure for eye defects.

Rua Santa Luzia intersects with the busy Avenida Presidente Antônio Carlos, on which stands the imposing **Fazenda Federal**, the Federal Treasury. Directly across the road from here, the **Santa Casa de Misericórdia**, a large colonial structure dating from 1582, was built by the Sisterhood of Misericordia, a nursing order dedicated to the care of the sick, and the provision of asylum to orphans and invalids. It was here in 1849 that, for the first time in Rio, a case of yellow fever was diagnosed, and from 1856 to 1916 the building was used as the University's Faculty of Medicine.

The Santa Casa is not open to the public, but you can visit the attached church, the **Igreja de Nossa Senhora de Bonsucesso** (Mon–Sat 8am–noon & 1–3pm), which contains finely detailed altars, a collection of Bohemian crystal and an eighteenth-century organ.

Close by, in Praça Rui Barbosa, is the **Museu do Imagem e Som** (Mon–Fri 1–6pm), which explains Rio's social history using records, tape recordings, books and film. There's also a fascinating photographic collection (numbering some 10,000 prints, though sadly only a fraction are displayed), documenting the city's life from the turn of the century until the 1940s.

Museu Histórico Nacional

The nearby **Museu Histórico Nacional** (Tues–Fri 10am–5pm, Sat & Sun 2–5pm) is uncomfortably located in the shadow of the Presidente Kubitschek flyover that runs into the Parque do Flamengo. Built in 1762 as an arsenal, it later served as a military prison where escaped slaves were detained. In 1922 the building was converted into an exhibition centre for the centenary celebrations of Brazil's independence from Portugal; it has remained a museum ever since.

The large **collection** contains some pieces of great value – from furniture to nine-teenth-century firearms and locomotives – but it's not very well organized at present and awaits a much-needed restructuring. Nevertheless, the displays on the second floor, a documentation of Brazilian history since 1500, make this museum a must. Artefacts, charts and written explanations trace the country's development from the moment of discovery to the proclamation of the Republic in 1889 – a fascinating insight into the nature of imperial conquest and subsequent colonial society. Clearly demonstrated, for example, is the social structure of sixteenth-century Brazilian society, including the system of *sesmarias*, or royal land grants of enormous dimensions, which provided the basis for the highly unequal system of land tenure that endures today. Through the use of scale models and imaginatively arranged displays, the agrarian and cyclical nature of Brazil's economic history is explained, too, organized around a slave-labour plantation system which produced – at different times – sugar cane, cattle and cotton, rubber and coffee. The story continues into the eighteenth and nineteenth centuries, following the impact of the English industrial revolution, the spread of new ideas following the French Revolution, the transition from slavery to free labour and more recent twentieth-century developments.

Santa Teresa and the Corcovado

Before you hit the beaches of the Zona Sul, two of the most pleasant city excursions are to *bairros* to the southwest of Centro. **Santa Teresa** offers an excellent respite from the steamy hubbub of Rio's main thoroughfares, while visiting Rio without making the tourist pilgrimage up the **Corcovado** is unthinkable.

Santa Teresa

Santa Teresa, a leafy *bairro* composed of labyrinthine, cobbled streets and steps (*ladeiras*), and with stupendous vistas of the city and bay below, makes a refreshing contrast to the city centre. Although it clings to the side of a hill, Santa Teresa is no *favela*: it's a slightly dishevelled residential area dominated by the early nineteenth-century mansions and walled gardens of a prosperous community that still enjoys something of a Bohemian reputation. The attractions are enhanced by an absence of the kind of development that is turning the rest of Rio into a cracked, concrete nightmare. There is not a great deal of traffic on the roads up here, which are dominated instead by ageing trams hauling their human load up and down the hill.

Trams run from Centro, from the terminal behind the massive Petrobrás building, adjacent to the Nova Catedral and Largo do Carioca. Two lines run every fifteen minutes between 5am and midnight; the one for Dois Irmãos permits you to see more of Santa Teresa. Be warned that tourists on the tram are often targeted by thieves who find it easy to jump on and off. If you must carry a camera hold onto it securely and keep it out of sight. The best time of day to ride the tram is mid-morning and mid-afternoon when it's less crowded and, consequently, less chaotic. For added safety, hop on one of the trams carrying a police officer to watch over tourists.

The tram (*bonde*) takes you across the seventeenth-century **Arcos da Lapa**, a monumental Roman-style aqueduct, high over Lapa, and past the **Carmelite Convento de Santa Teresa**, which marks the spot where a French force was defeated by the city's inhabitants in 1710. As you climb, the panoramic view of Guanabara Bay drifts in and out of view between the trees which line the streets. On your right, you'll pass the **Bar do Arnaudo**, a traditional meeting place of artists and intellectuals (see p.95); when the tram reaches the terminus at the top, you can stay on (and pay again) to descend for something to eat here. One of the *bairro*'s more notorious residents is Ronnie Biggs, a member of the gang behind the Great

Train Robbery in 1963. He escaped from prison in the UK and now in exile in Rio. His latest business venture is hosting barbecues on Saturday afternoons at his house right by the *Bar do Arnaudo*. He charges over $100 a head for the food, his autograph and the opportunity to take photographs of him; if you're interested, ask for him at the bar.

From the bar, it's an enjoyable, well-signposted walk downhill to the **Museu Chácara do Céu** (Wed–Sun 1–5pm) at Rua Murtinho Nobre 93, in a modernist stone building set in its own grounds – one of Rio's better museums. It holds a good eclectic collection including Picasso's *Le Danse* and a grouping of 21 crayon sketches by Cândido Portinari, all scenes from Cervantes' *Don Quixote*. In the upper hall, two screens depict the life of Krishna and there are twin seventh-century iron-sculptured horses from the Imperial Palace in Beijing; on the second floor there's artwork from Brazilian painters Djanira and Heitor dos Prazeres.

The Corcovado

The most famous of all images of Rio de Janeiro is that of the vast statue of Christ the Redeemer gazing across the bay from the **Corcovado** (hunchback) hill, arms outstretched in welcome, or as if preparing for a dive into the waters below. The **statue** (daily 8.30am–6.30pm), 30m high and weighing over 1000 metric tons, was first planned to be completed in 1922 as part of Brazil's centenary independence celebrations. In fact, it wasn't finished until 1931. The French sculptor Paul Landowski was responsible for the head and hands, and the rest was erected by the engineers Heitor Silva Costa and Pedro Viana.

In clear weather, fear no anticlimax: climbing to the statue is a stunning experience by day, and nothing short of miraculous at night. In daylight the whole of Rio and Guanabara Bay is laid out before you; after dark the floodlit statue can be seen from everywhere in the Zona Sul, seemingly suspended in the darkness that surrounds it, and often shrouded in eerie cloud. Up on the platform at the base of the statue the effect of the clouds, driven by warm air currents, and the thousands of tiny winged insects clustering round the spotlights, help give the impression that the statue is careering through space out into the blackness that lies beyond the arc of the lights – dramatic, and not a little hypnotic.

The **view** from the statue of Christ the Redeemer can be very helpful for **orientation** if you've just arrived in Rio. On a clear day, you can see as far as the outlying districts of the Zona Norte, while on the south side of the viewing platform you're directly over the Lagoa Rodrigo de Freitas, with Ipanema on the left, Leblon on the right; on the near side of the lake, Rua São Clemente is clearly visible, curving its way through Botafogo, towards the Jardim Botânico and the racecourse; and on your left, the small *bairro* of Lagoa can be seen tucked in beneath the Morro dos Cabritos, on the other side of which is Copacabana.

It is, of course, a thoroughly exploited tourist experience. There are the usual facilities for eating, drinking and buying souvenirs. On the walk up to the statue, someone will probably take your photograph clandestinely and, when you descend, a saucer, complete with your photograph superimposed on it, will be thrust before you – if you don't want the saucer, no one is going to twist your arm.

Back down at the bottom, if you have the time and inclination, a five-minute walk uphill from the cog-train station on Rua Cosme Velho will take you to the **Museu Internacional de Arte Naïf** (Tues–Fri 10am–6pm, Sat & Sun noon–6pm),which boasts the world's largest naive art collection. Although most of the work displayed is by Brazilian artists, the museum features paintings from throughout the world, with work from hotbeds of naive art such as Haiti, the former Yugoslavia, France and Italy especially well presented. Across the road, a short distance further uphill, you'll reach the **Largo do Boticário**, named after the nineteenth-century apothecary to the royal family, Joaquim Luiz da Silva

Santo, who lived here. A picturesque little corner of Rio, the mid-nineteenth century houses here (some with fronts decorated with *azulejos*) are built in the colonial style, while round about are pebbled streets and a fountain in a small courtyard.

Getting to Corcovado

All major hotels organize **excursions** to the Corcovado. Alternatively, the easiest way to get there yourself is to take a **taxi** – about $15 from the Zona Sul, a little more from Centro. **Buses** run to the *bairro* of Cosme Velho – take the #422 or #497 from Largo do Machado, the #583 from Leblon or the #584 from Copacabana – and stop at the **Estação Cosme Velho**, at Rua Cosme Velho 513. From there you take a cog-train (every 20–30min between 8.30am & 6pm; $15 return), a thirty-minute ride to the top, where only 220 steps remain between you and the viewing platform. You can also **drive** up to a car park near the top if you wish, but if you want to **walk** go in a group, as reports of assaults and robberies are becoming ever more frequent. However you choose to get there, keep an eye on the weather before setting out: what ought to be one of Rio's highlights can turn into a great disappointment if the Corcovado is shrouded in cloud.

Zona Norte

The parts of the **Zona Norte** you'll have seen on the way in from the transport terminals aren't very enticing, and they're a fair reflection of the general tenor of northern Rio. But there are a couple of places well worth making the effort to come back out of the centre for – especially the **Museu Nacional** in the Quinta da Boa Vista, which you reach by metrô (get off at Estação São Cristovão) or by bus #472, #474 or #475 from Copacabana or Flamengo, or #262 from Praça Mauá.

The Quinta da Boa Vista

The area covered by the **Quinta da Boa Vista** (daily 7am–7pm) was once incorporated in a *sesmaria* held by the Society of Jesus in the sixteenth and seventeenth centuries. The Jesuits used the area as a sugar plantation, though it later became the *chácara* (country seat) of the royal family when the Portuguese merchant Elias Antônio Lopes presented the Palácio de São Cristovão (today the Museu Nacional) and surrounding lands to Dom João VI in 1808. The park, with its wide open expanses of greenery, tree-lined avenues, lakes, sports areas and games tables, is an excellent place for a stroll, best during the week as weekends can get very crowded. You may as well make a day of it, and see all the sights once you're here.

The Museu Nacional

In the centre of the park, on a small hill, stands the imposing Neoclassical structure of the **Museu Nacional** (Tues–Sun 10am–4pm), the oldest scientific institution in Brazil and certainly one of the most important, containing extensive archeological, zoological and botanic collections, an excellent ethnological section and a good display of artefacts dating from classical antiquity – altogether, an estimated one million pieces exhibited in twenty-two rooms.

The **archeological** section deals with the human history of Latin America, displaying Peruvian ceramics, the craftsmanship of the ancient Aztec, Mayan and Toltec civilizations of Mexico, and mummies excavated in the Chiu-Chiu region of Chile. In the Brazilian room, exhibits of Tupi-Guarani and Marajó ceramics lead on to the indigenous **ethnographical** section, uniting pieces collected from the numerous tribes that once

How do you like your coffee, sir? The Banda da Ipanema at the Rio *Carnaval*

Ipanema beach, Rio

Spot the ball gown

Copacabana sunset

Arriving at the Scala Gay, Rio

Rio by night from the Corcovado

The Museu da Inconfidência and Igreja do Carmo, Ouro Preto

Samba school *bateria*

populated Brazil. The genocidal policies of Brazil's European settlers, together with the ravages of disease, reduced the indigenous population from an estimated six million in 1500 to the present-day total of less than two hundred thousand. And while the destruction of Indian culture was once the result of the plundering greed of private adventurers, the Brazilian state must now shoulder the blame for the dispersal of the remnants of tribal society. Policies facilitating land speculation in the Amazon have led to the theft of the very source of the Indians' physical and spiritual sustenance – the land itself – and though Brazil was a signatory to the Geneva Convention of Human Rights, its politicians have apparently failed to read the text of the charter.

The ethnology section also has a room dedicated to Brazilian folklore, centred around an exhibition of the ancient Afro- and Indo-Brazilian **cults** that still play an important role in modern Brazilian society – *macumba, candomblé* and *umbanda*.

On a different tack, the mineral collection's star exhibit is the **Bendigo Meteorite**, which fell to earth in 1888 (for sign-seekers, the year slavery was abolished) in the state of Bahia. Its original weight of 5360kg makes it the heaviest metallic mass known to have fallen through the Earth's atmosphere. And beyond the rich native finds you'll also come across Etruscan pottery, Greco-Roman ceramics, Egyptian sarcophagi and prehistoric remains – all in all, a good half-day's worth.

Museu da Fauna, Jardim Zoológico and the Feira do Nordeste

Also in the Quinta da Boa Vista is the **Museu da Fauna** (Tues–Sun 9am–4.30pm), which has organized a collection of stuffed birds, mammals and reptiles from throughout Brazil, worth a look on the way to the **Jardim Zoológico** (Tues–Sun 9am–4.30pm), close by. What was once a run-down and dirty zoo has been transformed recently – the animals look happier and the grounds are now kept scrupulously clean by zealous functionaries – but it's still basically an old-fashioned place where animals are kept in small cages to be stared at.

The **Feira do Nordeste**, held every Sunday (6am–1pm) in the Campo de São Cristovão, close to the Quinta da Boa Vista, is probably the best of Rio's regular **outdoor markets**. A replica of the great Northeastern markets, with stalls run by people in traditional costume, there are typical handicrafts, food, caged birds, tropical fish – while music from the parched Northeastern backlands fills the air. Best buys are beautifully worked hammocks, leather bags and hats, folk medicines and spices. Go as early as you can, on any bus marked "São Cristovão" – #469 from Leblon, #461 from Ipanema, #462 or #463 from Copacabana.

Maracanã Stadium

To the west of Quinta da Boa Vista, a short walk across the rail line, over the Viaduto São Cristovão, stands the **Maracanã Stadium**, more formally known as the Mario Filho Stadium. Built in 1950 for the World Cup, it's the biggest stadium of its kind in the world, holding nearly 200,000 people – in the final match of the 1950 tournament, 199,854 spectators turned up here to watch Brazil lose to Uruguay (see pp.43–44). Well over 100,000 fans attend local derbies, like the Flamengo v Fluminense fixture, and during November and December games are played here three times a week, as many of Rio's teams have followings that exceed the capacity of their own stadiums; kick-off is at 5pm.

Attending a **game** is one of the most extraordinary experiences Rio has to offer, even if you don't like football, and it's worth going for the theatrical spectacle. The stadium looks like a futuristic colosseum, its upper stand (the *arquibancadas*) rising almost vertically from the playing surface. Great silken banners wave across the stand, shrouded by the smoke from fireworks, while support for each team is proclaimed by the insistent rhythm of massed samba drums which drive the game along. *Carioca* supporters are animated to say the least, often near hysterical, but their love of the game is infectious.

The Maracanã is open for **guided tours** too (Mon–Fri 9am–5pm; ☎264-9962). You'll be shown through an interesting **sports museum**, see the view from the presidential box, reached by lift, get to wander through the changing rooms and have a chance to tread on the hallowed turf itself.

Getting there and seeing a game

The Maracanã is an easy and inexpensive destination to reach by **taxi**, but if you come by **metrô** (line 2), get off at the Maracanã station and walk southeast, along Avenida Osvaldo Aranha. By **bus**, it's the #464 from Leblon (Ataúlfo Paiva) via Ipanema (on Visc. de Pirajá), Copacabana (Avenida N.S. de Copacabana) and Flamengo (Praia do Flamengo).

The **entrance** is on Rua Prof Eurico Rabelo, Gate 18. Arrive in plenty of time (at least a couple of hours before kick-off for big games) and buy your entrance card at any of the **ticket offices** set in the perimeter wall – a ticket for the *gerais* (lower terracing) costs about $4, the *arquibancadas* (all-seated upper terracing) about $8. Then go round to the entrance and pass your card through a machine at the turnstile. It gets frantic around the ticket offices before big games and if you're not there early enough you may get stranded outside, as the kiosk attendants leave their positions as soon as the starting whistle blows so as not to miss an early goal. After the game, it's a bit tedious getting back into town as transport is packed. Watch your belongings in the thick crowds.

Zona Sul

From Rio's Bay of Guanabara to the Bay of Sepetiba, to the west, there are approximately 90km of sandy **beaches**, including one of the world's most famous – Copacabana. Uniquely, Rio's identity is closely linked to its beaches, which shape the social life of all the city's inhabitants, who use them as a source of recreation and inspiration. For many, the beach provides a source of livelihood, and a sizeable service industry has developed, providing for the needs of those who regard the beach as a social environment – as significant, say, as the pub is in England.

Rio de Janeiro's sophisticated **beach culture** is entirely a product of the twentieth century. The 1930s saw Rio's international reputation emerge, as Hollywood started to incorporate images of the city in its productions, and film stars started to grace the Copacabana. Rio was one of the first destinations for the newly established jet set: "flying down to Rio" became an enduring cliché, celebrated in music, film and literature for the last fifty years.

The most renowned of the beaches, **Copacabana**, was originally an isolated area, cut off from the city by mountains, until 1892 when the Túnel Velho link with Botafogo was inaugurated. The open sea and strong waves soon attracted beachgoers, though Copacabana remained a quiet, sparsely populated *bairro* until the splendid Neoclassically styled *Copacabana Palace Hotel* opened its doors, its famous guests publicizing the beach and alerting enterprising souls to the commercial potential of the area. Rapid growth followed and a land-fill project was undertaken, along which the two-lane **Avenida Atlântica** now runs.

Prior to Copacabana's rise, it was the beaches of **Guanabara Bay** – Flamengo, Botafogo, Urca and Vermelha – that were the most sought after. Today, the most fashionable beaches are those of **Ipanema** and **Leblon**, residential areas where the young, wealthy and beautiful have only to cross the road to flaunt their tans.

BEACH BEHAVIOUR: SURVIVING IN STYLE

Sport, food and fashion

Maintaining an even tan and tight musculature is still the principal occupation for most of Rio's beachgoers. Joggers swarm up and down the pavements, bronzed types flex their muscles on parallel bars located at intervals along the beaches, while the tradition of **beach football** is as strong as legend would have it on the Copacabana – certainly, there's no problem getting a game, though playing on loose sand amidst highly skilled practitioners of Brazil's national sport has the potential for great humiliation. There's lots of volleyball, too, as well as the ubiquitous **batball**, a kind of table-tennis with a heavy ball, and without the table. It's extremely popular with the kind of people who wait till you've settled down on your towel, and then run past spraying sand in all directions – taking an electric cattle-prod to the beach is the only way to keep them off.

A lot of people make their living by plying **food** – fruit, sweets, ice cream – and beach equipment along the sea shore, while dotted along the beaches are makeshift canopies, from which you can buy cold drinks. Like bars, most of these have a regular clientele and deliver a very efficient service – remember to return your bottle when you've finished. Coconut milk, *côco verde*, is sold everywhere, and is a brilliant hangover cure. You don't need to be wary of the edibles either: if the traders were to start poisoning their customers, they'd soon lose their hard-won trading space on the beach and their livelihood.

Beach fashion is important, too, and you'll come across some pretty snappy seaside threads. Fashions change regularly, though, so if you're really desperate to make your mark, you should buy your swimming togs in Rio.

Beaches: the bad news

● Many of the beaches are **dangerous**. The seabed falls sharply away, the waves are strong, and currents can pull you down the beach. Mark your spot well before entering the water, or you'll find youself emerging from a paddle twenty or thirty metres from where you started – which, when the beaches are packed at weekends, can cause considerable problems when it comes to relocating your towel and coconut oil. Copacabana is particularly dangerous, even for strong swimmers. However, the beaches are well served by **lifeguards**, whose posts are marked by a white flag with a red cross; a **red flag** indicates that bathing is prohibited. Constant surveillance of the beach fronts from helicopters and support boats means that, if you do get into trouble, help should arrive quickly.

Pollution is another problem to bear in mind. Although much has been done in recent years to clean up Guanabara Bay, it is still not safe to swim in the water from Flamengo or Botafogo beaches. While usually the water beyond the Bay at Copacabana and Ipanema is clean, there are times when it isn't, especially following a prolonged period of heavy rain when the city's strained drainage system is unable to cope. Fortunately, these periods are rare.

● Giving your passport, money and **valuables** the chance of a sun tan, rather than leaving them in the hotel safe, is madness. Take only the clothes and money that you'll need; it's quite acceptable to use public transport while dressed for the beach. Don't be caught out either by the young lad who approaches you from one side, distracting your attention with some request, while his mate approaches from the other side and whips your bag: it's the most common and efficient method of relieving you of things you shouldn't have brought with you in the first place.

The beaches are described in the order you come across them as you head south out of the city – from Flamengo to Leblon and beyond. As well as full details of the sand and surf, you'll find coverage of the other sights in the Zona Sul, as most of the beach areas are backed by a *bairro*, with its own character and amenities.

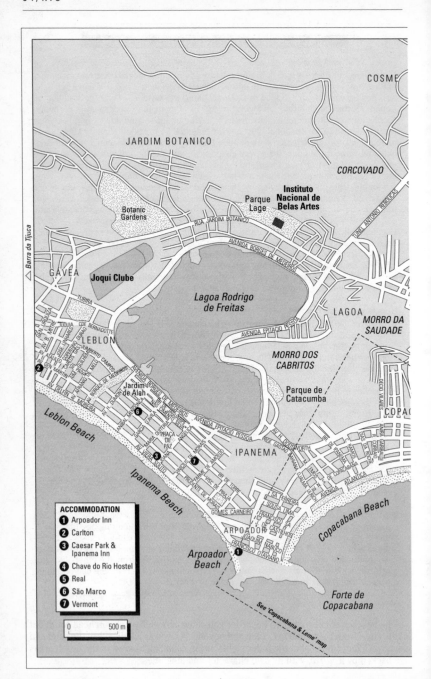

COSME

JARDIM BOTANICO

CORCOVADO

Parque Lage

Instituto Nacional de Belas Artes

Botanic Gardens

RUA JARDIM BOTANICO

AVENIDA BORGES DE MEDEIROS

◁ Barra da Tijuca

GÁVEA

Joqui Clube

TUBIRA

LEBLON

Lagoa Rodrigo de Freitas

LAGOA

MORRO DA SAUDADE

AVENIDA EPITACIO PESSOA

MORRO DOS CABRITOS

COPA

Jardim de Alah

⑥

Parque de Catacumba

AVENIDA BORGES DE MEDEIROS

AVENIDA EPITACIO PESSOA

PROF. GASTAO BAHIANA

Leblon Beach

PRAÇA DE PAZ

③

⑦

IPANEMA

Ipanema Beach

Copacabana Beach

GOMES CARNEIRO

ARPOADOR

Arpoador Beach

①

Forte de Copacabana

See 'Copacabana & Leme' map

ACCOMMODATION
① Arpoador Inn
② Carlton
③ Caesar Park & Ipanema Inn
④ Chave do Rio Hostel
⑤ Real
⑥ São Marco
⑦ Vermont

0   500 m

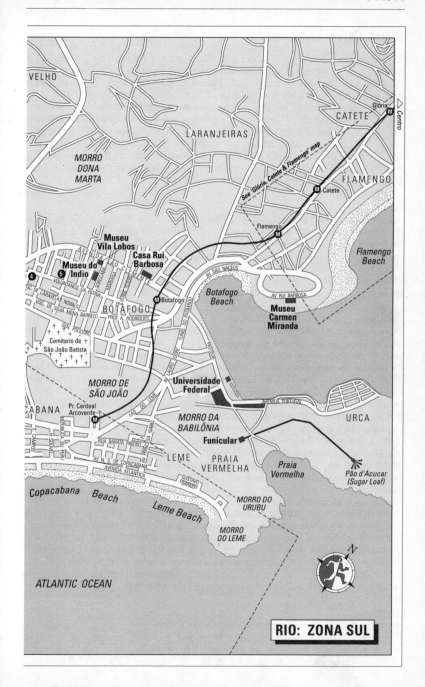

VELHO

LARANJEIRAS

*MORRO
DONA
MARTA*

Glória Ⓜ

△ Centro

CATETE

FLAMENGO

See 'Glória, Catete & Flamengo' map

Ⓜ Catete

Flamengo

Ⓜ

*Flamengo
Beach*

**Museu
Vila Lobos**

**Casa Rui
Barbosa**

**Museu do
Índio**

Ⓜ Botafogo

*Botafogo
Beach*

AV DAS NAÇÕES

AV RUI BARBOSA

**Museu
Carmen
Miranda**

AVENIDA SÃO CLEMENTE
VOLUNTÁRIOS DA PÁTRIA
SOROCABA
MARIANA
VISC. DE CARAVELAS
NOVAIS
VISC. DE SILVA MENA BARRETO
GEN. POLIDORO

Ⓠ

Ⓢ

BOTAFOGO

PROF. A. RODRIGUES

Cemitário de
São João Batista

LAURO DORE

TÚNEL DO PASMADO

PASTEUR

*MORRO DE
SÃO JOÃO*

**Universidade
Federal**

AVENIDA PASTEUR

URCA

CABANA

Pr. Cardeal
Arcoverde Ⓜ

LADO DO LEME

REPÚBLICA DO PERU
S. CAMPOS
SIQUEIRA
PRINCESA ISABEL

RUA BARATA RIBEIRO

AV N. S. DE COPACABANA

AVENIDA ATLÂNTICA

*MORRO DA
BABILÔNIA*

Funicular

*PRAIA
VERMELHA*

*Praia
Vermelha*

*Pão d'Açucar
(Sugar Loaf)*

LEME

Copacabana   Beach

GUSTAVO
SAMPAIO

Leme Beach

*MORRO DO
URUBU*

*MORRO
DO LEME*

N

ATLANTIC OCEAN

RIO: ZONA SUL

Glória, Catete and Flamengo

The nearest beach to the city centre is at Flamengo, and although it's not the best in Rio, you might end up using it more than you think since the neighbouring *bairros*, Catete and Glória, are useful and cheap **places to stay** (see p.65). The streets away from the beach – especially around Largo do Machado and along Rua do Catete – are full of inexpensive hotels, and there's a pleasant atmosphere to this part of town. Until the 1950s, Flamengo and Catete were the principal residential zones of Rio's wealthier middle classes, and although the mantle has now passed to Ipanema and Leblon, the *bairros* still have a pleasantly relaxed appeal. Busy during the day, the tree-lined streets are alive at night with residents eating in the local restaurants; and though the nightlife is nothing special, it's tranquil enough to encourage sitting out on the pavement at the bars, beneath the palm trees and apartment buildings.

Glória

Across from the **Glória** metrô station, on top of the Morro do Glória, stands the **Igreja de Nossa Senhora da Glória do Outeiro** (Mon–Fri 8am–noon & 1–5pm, Sat & Sun 8am–noon), decked with excellent seventeenth-century *azulejos* and nineteenth-century marble masonry. It's an attractive church, worth the twenty-minute detour, and behind it you'll find the **Museu da Imperial Irmandade de Nossa Senhora da Glória** (Mon–Fri 8am–noon & 1–4pm, Sat & Sun 8am–noon), which has a small collection of religious relics, *ex votos* and the personal possessions of Empress Tereza Cristina.

Catete

On the Rua do Catete, adjacent to the **Catete** metrô station, stands the Palácio do Catete, home to the **Museu do República** (Tues–Sun noon–5pm). The palace was used as the presidential residence from 1897 until 1960, and it was here, in 1954, that Getúlio Vargas turned his gun on himself and took his own life, believing he had been betrayed. The building was built between 1858 and 1866 as the Rio home of the Barão de Nova Friburgo, a wealthy coffee *fazenda* owner. As a historical museum, the *palácio* continues where the Museu Histórico Nacional leaves off, with the establishment of the first Republic in 1888. The collection features both period furnishings and presidential memorabilia, though it's the opulent marble and stained glass of the building itself that make a visit so worthwhile. The grounds include a new exhibition space, theatre and art gallery, which means there is often something happening here at night – the flood-lit gardens make it a magical venue. The restaurant, in a glassed-in turn-of-the-century terrace overlooking the gardens, is only open at lunchtime and boasts the best salad buffet in Rio.

Divided between two buildings, one inside the palace grounds and the other in an adjacent house, is the **Museu de Folclore Edison Cruz** (Tues–Fri 11am–6pm, Sat & Sun 3–6pm), a fascinating folkloric collection which unites pieces from all over Brazil – leatherwork, musical instruments, ceramics, toys, Afro-Brazilian cult paraphernalia, photographs and *ex votos*. Behind the palace lies the **Parque do Catete** (daily 9am–6pm), whose birdlife, towering palms and calm walks are good for a few moments' cool recuperation. It's a nice place to take small children as it has a pond with ducks and other water fowl, a playground and tricycles and other toys.

Flamengo

If you follow Avenida Beira Mar away from Centro you enter the **Parque do Flamengo**, the biggest land reclamation project in Brazil, designed by the great Brazilian landscape architect and gardener, Roberto Burle Marx, and completed in 1960. Sweeping round as far as Botafogo Bay, it comprises 1.2 square kilometres of

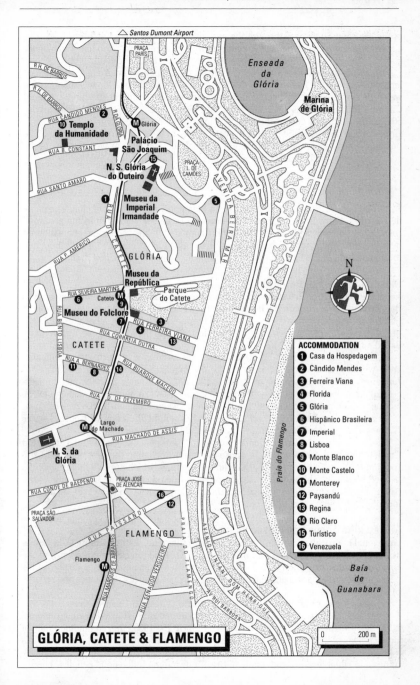

GLÓRIA, CATETE & FLAMENGO

0   200 m

ACCOMMODATION

1 Casa da Hospedagem
2 Cândido Mendes
3 Ferreira Viana
4 Florida
5 Glória
6 Hispânico Brasileira
7 Imperial
8 Lisboa
9 Monte Blanco
10 Monte Castelo
11 Monterey
12 Paysandú
13 Regina
14 Rio Claro
15 Turístico
16 Venezuela

prime seafront. You'll pass through the park many times by bus as you travel between Centro and the beach zone, and it's popular with local residents who use it mostly for sports – there are countless tennis courts (open 9am–11pm) and football pitches.

The **beach** at Flamengo runs along the park for about a kilometre and offers excellent views across the bay to Niterói. Unfortunately, it's not a place for swimming as the water here is polluted. Instead, you might want to take a look at the quirky **Museu Carmen Miranda** (Tues–Fri 11am–5pm, Sat 1–5pm), located in front of Av. Rui Barbosa 560, at the southern end of the park. Carmen was born in Portugal, made it big in Hollywood in the 1940s and become the patron saint of Rio's *Carnaval* transvestites. The museum contains a wonderful collection of kitsch memorabilia, as well as some of the star's costumes and personal possessions including fruit-laden hats and posters.

Botafogo

Botafogo curves around the 800m between Flamengo and Rio's yacht club. The name derives, reputedly, from the first white Portuguese settler who lived in the area, one João Pereira de Souza Botafogo. The bay is dominated by the yachts and boats moored near the club, and again the beach doesn't have much to recommend it to bathers due to the pollution of the bay. However, there's plenty to see in the *bairro* itself.

Museu Casa de Rui Barbosa
From the Botafogo metrô station, away from the ocean along Avenida São Clemente, is the **Museu Casa de Rui Barbosa** at no. 134 (Tues–Fri 1–4pm), set amidst the lush bowers of a garden with well-kept paths and borders. Built in 1849, it became the home of Rui Barbosa, jurist, statesman and author, in 1893, and the federal government established a museum here after his death.

Born in Bahia state, Barbosa (1849–1923) graduated as a lawyer in São Paulo and, later, working as a journalist and critic of the monarchy, founded the newspaper *A Imprensa*. He became senator of Bahia and in 1905, and again in 1909, made unsuccessful attempts to be elected as the country's president. A liberal, he made an excellent opposition politician, earning himself exile between 1893 and 1895, years he spent in Argentina and England – perhaps where he bought the copy of Courbey's *The Working Constitution of the United Kingdom*, found in the library.

The museum is basically a collection of his possessions – beautiful Dutch and English furniture, Chinese and Japanese porcelain (including the first plumbed bathroom in Rio), and a library of 35,000 volumes, amongst which are two hundred works penned by Barbosa himself. Barbosa conferred a title on each room in the house – the Sala Bahia, Sala Questão Religiosa, Sala Habeas Corpus, Sala Código Civil – all of them identified with some part of his life.

Museu Villa-Lobos and Museu do Índio
On Avenida Sorocaba, a turning off Avenida São Clemente, is the **Museu Villa-Lobos** at no. 200 (Mon–Fri 10am–5.30pm). Established in 1960 to celebrate the work of the Brazilian composer, Heitor Villa-Lobos (1887–1959), it's again largely a display of his personal possessions and original music scores, but you can also buy tapes and records of his music here.

Botafogo's other museum, the **Museu do Índio** (Tues–Fri 10am–5.30pm, Sat & Sun 1–5pm), lies in the next street along, at Rua das Palmeiras 55. Housed in an old colonial building, the museum was inaugurated on April 19, 1953, the commemoration of Brazil's "Day of the Indian" – not that there were many around by then to celebrate. It's a broad and interesting collection, containing utensils, musical instruments, tribal costumes and ritual devices from many of Brazil's dwindling indigenous peoples. There's a good photographic exhibition, too, and an accessible anthropological explanation of the rituals and institutions of some of the tribes. The attached shop is excellent, selling original artefacts at reasonable prices. The ethnographical section of the Museu Nacional (see p.80) probably provides you with more information, but this museum is still being developed and worth a look to check progress – certainly since they've started to build examples of indigenous housing in the grounds.

Urca and the Sugar Loaf

The best bet for swimming this close to the centre is around **Urca**. There are small beaches on each side of the promontory on which this wealthy *bairro* stands, its name an acronym of the company that undertook its construction – Urbanizador Construção. Facing Botafogo, the **Praia da Urca**, only 100m long, is frequented almost exclusively by the small *bairro*'s inhabitants; while in front of the cable car station (see below), beneath the Sugar Loaf mountain, **Praia Vermelha** is a cove sheltered from the South Atlantic, whose relatively gentle waters are popular with swimmers.

You should come to Urca at least once during your stay, anyway, to go to the **Pão de Açúcar**, which rises where Guanabara Bay meets the Atlantic Ocean. In Portuguese the name means "**Sugar Loaf**", referring to the ceramic or metal mould used during the refining of sugar cane. Liquid sugar cane juice was poured into the mould and removed when the sugar had set producing a shape reminiscent of the mountain. The name may also come from the Tupi-Guarani Indians' word *Pau-nh-Acuqua*, or "high hill" – a more apt description. The first recorded non-indigenous ascent to the summit was made in 1817 by an English nanny, Henrietta Carstairs. Today, mountaineers are a common sight scaling the smooth, precipitous slopes, but there is a cable car ride to the summit.

The **cable car** system has been in place since 1912; sixty years later the present Italian system, which can carry 1360 passengers every hour, was installed (daily 8am–10pm, every 30min; $12). It's in Praça General Tibúrcio, which can be reached by buses marked "Urca" or "Praia Vermelha" from Centro, #107 from Centro, Catete and Flamengo, or #511 and #512 from Zona Sul (returning to Copacabana takes 1hr 30min as the bus first passes through Botafogo, Leblon and Ipanema). The 1400-metre journey is made in two stages, first to the summit of **Morro da Urca** (215m), where there is a theatre, restaurant and shops, and then on to the top of Pão de Açúcar itself (394m). The cable cars have glass walls and once on top the view is as glorious as you could wish. Facing inland, you can see right over the city, from Centro and the Santos Dumont airport all the way through Flamengo and Botafogo; face Praia Vermelha and the cable car terminal, and to the left you'll see the sweep of Copacabana and on into Ipanema, while back from the coast the mountains around which Rio was built rise to the Tijuca National Park. Try and avoid the busy times between 10am and 3pm: it's best of all at sunset on a clear day, when the lights of the city are starting to twinkle. Leading down from the summit are a series of wooded trails, and it's easy – and safe – to get away from the crowds.

On the lower hill, the Beija Flor **samba school** performs every Monday at 10pm, a touristy affair that costs about $40 for dinner and the glitzy floor show (☎791-1353); on Thursday and Friday live music shows start at 10pm, and you can eat and drink till 2am – check in the *Jornal do Brasil* for what is going on. This hill is also the location of the expensive *Carnaval* ball (see p.105).

Leme and Copacabana

Leme and **Copacabana** are different stretches of the same four-kilometre beach. Avoid walking through the Túnel Novo that links Botafogo with Leme as it's a favourite place for tourists to be relieved of their wallets. The **Praia do Leme** extends for a kilometre, between the Morro do Leme and Avenida Princesa Isabel, by the *Meridien*

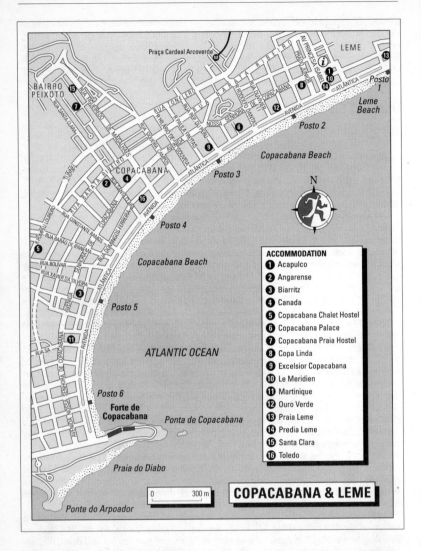

ACCOMMODATION

1 Acapulco
2 Angarense
3 Biarritz
4 Canada
5 Copacabana Chalet Hostel
6 Copacabana Palace
7 Copacabana Praia Hostel
8 Copa Linda
9 Excelsior Copacabana
10 Le Meridien
11 Martinique
12 Ouro Verde
13 Praia Leme
14 Predia Leme
15 Santa Clara
16 Toledo

0   300 m

COPACABANA & LEME

Hotel. From there, the **Praia de Copacabana** runs for a further 3km to the military-owned Copacabana Fort. Along the way, *postos* (concrete lifeguard stations with toilets and showers) have recently been installed.

Leme beach is slightly less packed than Copacabana and tends to attract families. The *Meridien* maintains a hawkish security watch on the part of the beach nearest the hotel and so it's a good place to park your towel.

Copacabana is amazing, the over-the-top atmosphere apparent even in the mosaic pavements, designed by Burle Marx to represent images of rolling waves. The seafront is backed by a line of prestigious, high-rise hotels and luxury apartments that have sprung up since the 1940s, while a steady stream of noisy traffic patrols the two-lane **Avenida Atlântica**. Scattered around the *bairro* are some fine examples of Art Deco architecture, none more impressive than the *Copacabana Palace Hotel* on Avenida Atlântica, built in 1923 and considered one of Rio's best hotels. Families, friends and lovers cover the palm-fringed sand – at weekends it's no easy matter to find space – the bars and restaurants along the avenue pulsate, while the busy **Avenida Nossa Senhora de Copacabana** is lined with assorted stores, which – like the *bairro* in general – are in a gradual state of decline, being pushed aside by the shopping malls of the Zona Sul.

Copacabana is dominated to the east by the Pão de Açúcar and circled by a line of hills that stretch out into the bay. A popular residential area, the *bairro*'s expansion has been restricted by the Morro de São João, which separates it from Botafogo, and the Morro dos Cabritos, which forms a natural barrier to the west. Consequently, it's one of the world's most densely populated areas, and a frenzy of sensual activity, most of which takes place in a thoroughly impressive setting. Some say that Copacabana is past its best and certainly it's not as exclusive as it once was. You'll be frequently accosted by a stream of the dispossessed young and old – who want money, or the scraps off your plate, while the street traders work into the night, selling T-shirts, lace tablecloths and plastic Rio car numberplates. It's still an enjoyable place to sit and watch the world go by, though, and at night on the floodlit beach football is played into the early hours.

Arpoador, Ipanema and Leblon

On the other side of the point from Copacabana Fort, the lively waters off the **Praia do Arpoador** are popular with families and the elderly as the ocean here is slightly calmer than at Ipanema. From here, as far as the unkempt and balding greenery of the Jardim de Allah, a couple of kilometres away, you're in **Ipanema**; while thereafter lies **Leblon**. There are few apartment buildings in either *bairro* that don't have their own pistol-toting guard, eyes alert to anyone who looks out of place in this rich person's hangout. Much calmer than Copacabana, the beaches here are stupendous, though there's not much in the way of bars and restaurants near the beach: in fact, the only bar/restaurant on the front is *Caneco*, at the far end of Leblon, a good spot to aim for anyway. As with Copacabana, Ipanema's beach is unofficially divided according to the supposed interest of the beach users. Thus the stretch of sand east from Rua Farme de Amoedo to Rua Teixeira de Melo is where gay men are concentrated, while *posto* 9 is where artists and intellectuals ponder life. On Sunday, the seafront roads – Avenida Vieira Souto in Ipanema, Avenida Delfim Moreira in Leblon – are closed to traffic, and much skateboarding and the like takes place.

Since the 1960s, Ipanema has developed a reputation as a fashion centre second to none in Latin America. It's hard to say whether in fact that's true, but certainly the place is packed with bijou little boutiques, flogging the very best names in fine threads. If you do go shopping here, go on Friday and take in the large **food and flower** market on the Praça de Paz. Most visitors are more likely to be able to afford something at the so-called **Hippy Market**, held between 9am and 6pm on Sunday in Praça General Osório. Once, the traders here hawked their wares in the streets of Copacabana, but now they gather together and wait for the tourists to come to them. Artisans from all over Brazil sell a variety of goods – leather, interesting jewellery, hammocks and crocheted table cloths, shawls and cushion covers.

Lagoa

Back from Ipanema's plush beaches is the Lagoa Rodrigo de Freitas, always referred to simply as Lagoa. A lagoon linked to the ocean by a narrow canal that passes through Ipanema's Jardim de Allah, Lagoa is fringed by apartment buildings where Rio's most seriously rich and status-conscious live. On Sundays this area comes alive as people walk, jog or cycle the 7.5km perimeter pathways around the lagoon, play or watch baseball (a popular meeting place for American residents), or just watch the passers by.

The steep hill slopes behind the apartment buildings are still well forested and, in 1979, the **Parque da Catacumba** (daily 7am–6pm) was developed on one of the more accessible hills, by the southeast corner of the lagoon on Avenida Epitácio Pessoa. It's a wonderful shaded place to relax, and the dense tropical vegetation forms an excellent backdrop for Brazil's only **sculpture park**.

Jardim Botânico and Gávea

To the northwest of the Lagoa lies **Jardim Botânico** *bairro*, whose **Parque Lage** (daily 9am–5pm), designed by the English landscape gardener, John Tyndale, in the early 1840s, consists of half a million square metres of forest, with a labyrinthine path network and seven small lakes – just the spot for a little shady relaxation. A little further along the Rua Jardim Botânico, is the **Jardim Botânico** itself (Tues–Sun 11am–6pm; $4), half of it natural jungle, half laid out in impressive avenues lined with immense imperial palms that date from the garden's inauguration in 1808. Dom João used the gardens to introduce foreign plants into Brazil – tea, cloves, cinnamon and pineapples among them – and there are now five thousand plant species, amongst which live monkeys, parrots and other assorted wildlife. There are also a number of sculptures to be seen throughout the garden, notably the *Ninfa do Eco* by Mestre Valentim. Above all, though, the garden offers you an insight into the nature of tropical rainforest (albeit a tame one as the garden is well patrolled by uniformed officers), and the feel and smell of the vegetation provide a welcome contrast to the exhaust fumes polluting the streets outside. The **entrance** is at Rua Jardim Botânico 1008, where there's a car park, a souvenir shop and the garden's library with English-language literature about the plants inside.

Gávea and the Jóquei Clube

On the **Gávea** side of Lagoa lies the **Jóquei Clube**, also known as the Hipódromo da Gávea, which can be reached on any bus marked "via Jóquei" – get off at Praça Santos Dumont at the end of Rua Jardim Botânico. Racing in Rio dates back to 1825 though the Hipódromo wasn't built until 1926. Today, **races** take place four times a week, every week of the year (Mon & Thurs night, Sat & Sun afternoon), with the international Grande Prêmio Brazil taking place on the first Sunday of August. A night at the races is great fun and foreigners can get into the palatial members' stand for just a few *reís*, but remember, no one in shorts is admitted. It's an entertaining place, especially during the midweek racing under floodlights, when the air is balmy and you can eat or sip a drink as you watch the action. You don't have to bet to enjoy the experience – it's not very easy to understand the betting system they use anyway.

Also in Gávea is the **Parque da Cidade** (daily 8am–5.30pm) and **Museu Histórico da Cidade** (Tues–Fri 1–5pm), at the end of Estrada de Santa Marinha: bus #591, #593 or #594 from Copacabana; #179 or #178 from Centro. The museum is contained within a two-storey nineteenth-century mansion once owned by the Marquis de São Vicente, and the collection is all related to the history of Rio from its foundation until the end of the Old Republic in 1930. The exhibits – paintings, weapons, porcelain, medals – are arranged in chronological order; the first salon deals with city's foundation, the rest with the colonial period.

West: Vidigal, São Conrado and Barra de Tijuca

Back on the coast, to the west of Leblon, lies kilometre after kilometre of white sand. **Praia do Vidigal**, tucked under the Morro Dois Irmãos, is only about 500m long, and used to be the preserve of the inhabitants of the **Favela do Vidigal**, one of the biggest shanty towns in Rio. They lost their beach with the construction of the *Rio Sheraton Hotel*, the sands appropriated for the use of hotel guests.

West again, the beach at **São Conrado**, dominated by high-rise hotels, is becoming ever trendier: frequented by the famous and packed with hang-gliders and surfers at weekends, its star is in the ascendant – and it's certainly a beautiful beach. **Bus** #500 from Urca will take you to São Conrado via Avenida Atlântica (Copacabana), Avenida Vieira Souto (Ipanema) and Avenida Delfim Moreira (Leblon).Before you get carried away, though, enormous inequality is close at hand. Above São Conrado, on the slopes between the Tijuca mountains and the peak of Pedra dos Dois Irmãos, sits **Favela Roçinha** – spuriously picturesque and glistening in the tropical sun. Here, over 200,000 Brazilians live, for whom a salary of around $100 a month is about as much as an entire family can expect.

The last area within the city limits is **Barra de Tijuca**, with clean waters and white sands that run for over 16km. The first four kilometres are hard by the residential area, where there's no shortage of facilities; after that, the beach is less developed and you'll need a car to reach the extreme stretches, though the whole length is popular at weekends with the beach party and barbecue set. You can reach Barra de Tijuca by **bus** from Copacabana (#553), or from Botafogo metrô station (#524).

Parque Nacional da Tijuca and Alta da Boa Vista

When the Portuguese arrived, the area which is now the city of Rio was covered by dense green tropical forest. As the city grew the trees were felled and the timber used in construction or for charcoal. However, if you look up from the streets of Zona Sul today, the mountains running southwest from the Corcovado are still covered with exuberant forest, the periphery of the **Parque Nacional da Tijuca** which covers an area of approximately 120 square kilometres, and is maintained by Brazil's State Institute of Forestry (IBDF).

In the seventeenth century the forests of Tijuca were cut down for their valuable hardwood and the trees replaced by sugar cane and, later, coffee plantations and small-scale agriculture. In the early nineteenth century the city authorities became alarmed by a shortage of pure water and by landslides from the Tijuca slopes. Eventually it was decided that a concerted effort was needed to restore Rio's watershed and, in 1857, a **reafforestation project** was initiated: by 1870 over 100,000 trees had been planted and the forest was reborn. Most of the seeds and cuttings that were planted were native to the region, and today the park serves as a remarkable example of the potential for the regeneration of the Atlantic forest.

Following on from the success of the forest, the IBDF has gradually been re-introducing fauna. The forest is once again the home of insects and reptiles, ocelots, howler monkeys, agoutis (a type of rodent), three-toed sloths and other animals. Most successful of all has been the return of **birdlife**, making Tijuca a paradise for birdwatchers. One problem that has recently arisen is that the over-stretched park rangers have a difficult time preventing residents of the eight neighbouring *favelas* from hunting wildlife to eat or to sell.

Routes into the park

The park offers lots of walks and some excellent views of Rio, and though areas of it have been burnt, it remains an appealing place to get away from the city for a few hours. Buses don't enter the park so a **car** is useful if you plan to do an extensive tour: you can go in via Cosme Velho *bairro*, near the **Entrada dos Caboclos**, and follow Estrada Heitor da Silva Costa. (Areas of the park are used as *terrenos*, places where *candomblé* and *umbanda* ritual ceremonies are performed: *caboclos* is the collective name for the spirits involved in these cults.) An alternative entrance is at Rua Leão Pacheco, which runs up the side of the Jardim Botânico (off Rua Jardim Botânico) and leads to the **Entrada dos Macacos** and on to the **Vista Chinesa**, above the Museu Histórico da Cidade in Gávea. From here there's a marvellous view of Guanabara Bay and the Zona Sul. Both of these entrances lead to different roads that run through the park, but they converge eventually in the *bairro* of **Alta da Boa Vista**. If you're intent upon **walking**, you should be warned that even the shorter trip from the Entrada dos Macacos will mean a hot, dehydrating climb for more than 20km.

If you don't have your own transport, it's much easier to aim for the area to the north of the park known as the **Floresta de Tijuca** (daily 7am–9pm). Take a bus to Alto da Boa Vista (#221 from Praça XV de Novembro; #233 or #234 from the *Rodoviária*; #133 or #334 from Rua Jardim Botânico) and get off at Praça Alfonso Viseu near the **Entrada da Floresta**, with its distinctive stone columns – where you'll notice an old British telephone booth next to the *Robin Hood* bar. A few hundred metres after the entrance (where you can buy a **map**) is a 35-metre-high waterfall and, further on, the **Capela do Mairynk**, built in 1860, but virtually completely rebuilt in the 1940s. The chapel's most interesting feature are the three altar panels painted by Candîdo Portinari, one of Brazil's greatest twentieth-century artists. In fact, the originals now form part of the much depleted collection of the Museu de Arte Moderna (see p.77) and those in the chapel are reproductions. The lush forest is full of secluded grottos and waterfalls, but do use the map as it's possible to wander off the beaten track. If you have the energy, you can climb all the way to the **Pico da Papagaio** (975m) or **Pico da Tijuca** (1021m) – peaks in the far north of the forest, above the popular picnic spot known as **Bon Retiro**. Alternatively, you can join a tour of the park; a very good one is run by Jeep Tour Ecologia, Rua Marechal Mascarenhas 93, Copacabana (daily 9am & 2pm; ☎256-8297). However you approach the park, wear a swimsuit under your shorts as there are plenty of waterfalls under which you can take reinvigorating showers.

The whole park is a good place for a picnic, but there are also two decent **restaurants** that serve lunch: *A Floresta*, offering rustic Brazilian food, and *Os Esquilos*, which is more expensive with a rather uninspired "international" menu.

Eating and drinking

As one of the world's most exotic tourist resorts and with (for Brazil) a relatively large middle-class population, Rio is well served by restaurants offering a wide variety of cuisines – from traditional Brazilian to French and Japanese. In general, however, eating out in Rio is not cheap – and it can be very expensive – but there's no shortage of low-priced places to grab a lunchtime meal, or just a snack and a drink: at a *galeto*, where you eat, diner-style, at the counter; or at a *lanchonete*, the ubiquitous Brazilian café, which serves very cheap combined plates of meat, beans and rice, as well as other snacks. *Cariocas* dine late, and restaurants don't start to fill up until after 9pm.

A NOTE ON DRINKING

The lists given below are for both eating and drinking. Many bars serve food and lots of restaurants allow a night's drinking, too, so you should be able to find somewhere that suits you. In most regions of Brazil, **beer** comes to your table in a bottle, but in Rio draught beer – or *chopp*, pronounced "shopee" – predominates. A good place to sample Brazil's national drink, **cachaça**, is at the *Academia da Cachaça*, Rua Cde. Bernadotte 26, Leblon, a small bar where there are three hundred available brands to sample – treat it with respect at all times.

Generally, last orders will be taken around midnight in most places, but there are others where you can get a meal well after 2am.

The suggestions below are listed alphabetically under the city *bairros*, with other self-explanatory sections on particular types of eating and drinking.

Fast food, snacks, cakes and ice cream

There's no shortage of **hamburger** joints in Rio, though it's worth bearing in mind that there's a good chance that the ground beef used comes from the Amazon, where immense ranches are displacing Indians, peasants and trees at a criminal rate. You'll get better, more authentic and cheaper food at any *galeto* or *lanchonete* – there are plenty in the Centro or at Copacabana, though most are closed at night. You won't really need any guidance to find these; the places given below deal in more specialized fare.

If you're just peckish, then it's nice to take **tea and cakes** at *Confeitaria Colombo*, which has two branches, in Copacabana at Av. N.S. de Copacabana 890 and in the Centro at Rua Gonçalves Dias 32 (closed Sat at 1pm and all day Sun). Founded in 1894, the *Colombo* recalls Rio's *belle époque*, with its ornate interior decoration and air of tradition; the branch in Copacabana has a decent restaurant upstairs, too. Also in Copacabana, and good for **sandwiches**, is *Cervantes*, Av. Prado Junior 335 (near Leme); at Leblon you'll get a fresh, crisp **salad** at *Gulla Gulla* in the *Hotel Marina Palace*, Avenida Delfim Moreira – a bit pricier than usual, but recommended. There are more cakes at the *Bonbon d'Or*, Rua Visc. de Pirajá 351 in Ipanema, or at any branch of *Kopenhagen*. For a choice of **ice cream**, aim especially for *Mr Ice*, Rua Ayres e Saldanha 98, Copacabana; *Babuska,* at Rua Aníbal de Mendonça 55, Ipanema, and Rua Rainha Guilhermina 90, Leblon; or – if you're visiting the Jardim Botânico – *Mil Frutas*, Rua Jardim Botânico 585. The *Polis* bar on Avenida Ataúlfo Paiva in Leblon is a particularly good place for a **suco** (fresh, iced fruit juice).

Check the **fruit markets** for something exotic and healthy: at Botafogo on Wednesday by Praça Canoinhas; Flamengo on Sunday in Largo do Machado; Copacabana on Thursday near Praça do Lido.

Centro and Santa Teresa

The restaurants in the city centre cater largely for people working in the area, and at lunchtime the service is rushed. Around the Praça Tiradentes, particularly, there are lots of cheap eating places, bakeries and bars, while Santa Teresa has a couple of specialist restaurants.

Adega do Pimenta, Rua Almirante Alexandrino 296, Santa Teresa. German cuisine – lots of sausage and sauerkraut, and very pleasant for lunch or dinner. The Santa Teresa tram passes the restaurant. Moderate.

Alba Mar, Praça Marechal Ancora 184, a short walk from Praça XV de Novembro (Mon–Sat 11.30am–4pm; ☎240-8378). Founded in 1933 and housed in the remaining tower of the old municipal market, this cool, green, octagonal building provides a superb view of Guanabara Bay. Stick with the seafood, served by serious-looking waiters in white uniforms. Moderate.

Bar do Arnaudo, Rua Almirante Alexandrino 316, Santa Teresa (Tues–Sat noon–10pm, Sun 11am–6pm). Just up from the *Adega do Pimenta*, an excellent place to sample traditional food from Brazil's northeast, such as *carne do sol* (sun-dried meat), *macaxeira* (sweet cassava) and *pirão de bode* (goat meat soup). Inexpensive.

Bar dos Estudantes, Praça Tiradentes. Basic food and friendly service for next to nothing.

Bar Luiz, Rua Carioca 39 (closed Sun). Near Largo da Carioca, this run-of-the-mill restaurant and bar, serving German-style food, is considered quite an institution and is still a popular meeting place for journalists and intellectuals (see p.73). Inexpensive.

VEGETARIAN FOOD

Vegetarians won't have any serious problems in Rio. While beans and rice are always available for basic sustenance, don't be shy of asking the waiter in any restaurant to have the kitchen prepare something a little more tasty: if nothing else, you'll get a plate of fresh vegetables. Specific recommendations are listed below, but in Centro you could also try *Health's*, Rua dos Beneditinos 18, *Greens*, Rua do Carmo 38, *Le Bon Menu*, Rua Araújo Porto Alegre 71, or *Zan*, Travessa do Ouvidor 25.

Associacão Macrobiótica, Rua Emb. Regis Oliveira 7, Centro (lunchtime only). An inexpensive macrobiotic restaurant – busy and, strangely enough, with some dishes which include fish.

Café Bohemia, Av. Santa Luzia, off Av. Rio Branco. A bit different: a decent vegetarian restaurant by day, and at night a mixture of comedy store and transvestite revue, with a bit of dancing thrown in; entry is about $4 and it starts after midnight.

Macro Nature, Travessa Cristiano Lacorte (Mon–Fri 9am–10.30pm, Sat & Sun 9am–6pm). An excellent healthfood shop and restaurant (though the menu is limited) in Copacabana.

Natural, with branches in Botafogo (Rua 19 de Fevereiro 118; lunch only) and in Ipanema (Rua Barão de Torre 171). Not strictly vegetarian restaurants as fish can be had, too, but the food is good and cheap.

Sabor Saúde, Rua Ataulfo de Paiva 630–A, Leblon. A better-than-average vegetarian restaurant claiming to serve only organically grown produce. Inexpensive.

Semente, Rua Joaquim Silva 138, Lapa (closed Sat, Sun & holidays). Basically vegetarian, but fish and even chicken sneak onto the East Asian-influenced menu. Inexpensive.

Bar Ocidental, Rua Miguel Couto 124. One of several bars on a small pedestrianized road near the Largo de São Francisco de Paulo. Sit at a table outside and enjoy an early evening *chopp* and a plate of fresh sardines. Inexpensive.

Caldeirão, Rua do Ouvidor 26. Open at lunchtime for good, cheap seafood, with a pleasant atmosphere. The raw materials land near Praça XV de Novembro and from there head towards your plate – try *badejo* (a type of fish) or *capixaba* (seafood stew).

Cosmopolita, Travessa do Mosqueira 4 (Mon–Fri 11am–midnight, Sat 11am–4pm). A long-established and excellent Portuguese establishment in Lapa with a loyal, rather Bohemian, clientele. Inexpensive.

Entrecote, Rua Gonçalves Dias 82, a block west of Av. Rio Branco. A steak house, popular and inexpensive, with a friendly atmosphere.

Miako, Rua do Ouvidor 45, north side of Praça XV (☎222-2397; closed Sat evening & Sun). One of the first Japanese restaurants in Rio. Sushi, sashimi, teppan-yaki and *filé na chapa*. Moderate to expensive.

Penafiel, Rua Senhor dos Passos 121 (Mon–Fri 11am–3.30pm). Superb – and amazingly inexpensive – Portuguese dishes have been served here since 1916.

Rio Minho, Rua do Ouvidor 10 (☎231-2338; lunch only, closed Sat & Sun). Tasty Brazilian food at fair prices in a restaurant that's been going for 100 years. The kitchen concentrates on seafood – try *badejo* fish, lobster in butter, prawn in coconut milk or the fried fish with red peppers, rice and broccoli. Moderate.

Sentaí (O Rei da Lagosta), Rua Barão de São Felix 75. A wonderful daytime-only Portuguese seafood restaurant full of local colour. Take care in this rather rough part of the centre, but it's a restaurant well worth taking a slight risk to get to. Inexpensive.

Flamengo

As well as the places listed below, there are numerous restaurants, *galetos* and *lanchonetes* around the Largo do Machado.

Adega Real, Rua Marques de Abrantes, a few doors along from the *Café Lamas*. No haughty nouvelle cuisine here, just piles of good basics – if you like decent-quality food in large quantities, this place is recommended as the friendly waiters serve up tasty portions sufficient for at least two people. The restaurant opens onto the street, and on Fridays you can hang on to the bar and swallow draught beer until 4am; the *bolinhas de bacalhau* (cod balls) are worth testing. Inexpensive.

Alho & Óleo, Rua Barque de Macedo 13, down at the bottom near Praia do Flamengo. Tasty home-made pasta and good food (try the salami flavoured with pepper and lemon) in an upmarket atmosphere, but reasonably priced.

Café Lamas, Rua Marques de Abrantes 18. This 120-year-old restaurant serves well-prepared food to members of the art and journalism worlds. Always busy, with a vibrant atmosphere, it's a good example of *carioca* middle-class tradition, and highly recommended. Open until 4am. Moderate.

Botafogo and Urca

Botafogo undoubtedly hosts some of Rio's most interesting restaurants, often overlooked by tourists because they lie a bit off the beaten track, hidden away in back streets. There are few places to eat in Urca, but it's a pleasant place for a relaxing meal.

Adega do Valentim, Rua da Passagem 178 (☎295-2748). A comfortable restaurant (especially the front salon) serving up good Portuguese food. Expect to pay around $20 per person for a satisfying munch through cod, onions, potatoes and smoked ham.

Botequim-184, Rua Visconde de Caravelas 184, at the Lagoa end. Good, varied food in a lively establishment; next door, the *Overnight Bar* is a friendly place for a few drinks afterwards. Moderate.

Cochranes, Rua das Palmeiras 66. Food and drink in a lively atmosphere reminiscent of an English wine bar. Live music, too, and the patronage of some of Rio's gay community. Moderate.

Comidinhas 46, Praça Joia Valansi, Rua Muniz Barreto. Brazilian cooking, with inexpensive dishes from the state of Minas Gerais. Not at all bad – and with some of the best cheese in Rio.

Garota da Urca. A small restaurant on the Urca seafront just after the old TV Tupi studios. The best views of any Rio restaurant, looking back towards Botafogo and the Corcovado, with good food, too; the *peixe a garota* is a delicious fish risotto that serves two for around $15.

La Mole, Praia de Botafogo 228. Inexpensive, palatable Italian food; nearby and similar are *Bella Blu*, Rua da Passagem 44, and *Bella Roma*, Rua General Gois Monteiro 18.

Macondo, Rua Conde de Irajá 85 (☎226-9485). Tasty northeastern food – *carne seca*, *carne do sol*, pumpkin stews – served in a lovely old Botafogo residence. Inexpensive.

Madrugadas, Rua Sorocabana 305. Inexpensive homemade pasta dishes, including a sauce made with figs and nuts, in a cosy place with friendly service.

Raajmahal, Rua General Polidoro 29 (☎541-6999; closed Mon). An Indian restaurant that is English-owned, and extends itself well beyond the basic curry. Let the waiter know how well seasoned you want your dish, as the restaurant tends to cater for the local preference for mild curries. Moderate.

Copacabana and Leme

It comes as no surprise that Copacabana is riddled with restaurants, but that doesn't mean that the choice is particularly good – unless you enjoy sitting in a restaurant swamped with holidaymakers being shuttled about by tour companies. For this reason, one to avoid is the *Palace*, Rua Rudolfo Dantas. Steer clear, too, of places like *Le Pre Catalan*, in the *Rio Palace Hotel*, or *Le Saint Honore*, in the *Hotel Meridien* – unless you're convinced that nouvelle cuisine supplies sufficient calories to sustain human life, and have desire to pay through the nose.

A Marisqueira, Rua Barata Ribeiro 232 (☎237-3920). A good spot for seafood. The restaurant has been around for over forty years, with a more recent branch in Ipanema, in Rua Gomes Carneiro. The food is well prepared, though perhaps a little unimaginative and a touch on the pricey side.

A Polonesa, Rua Hilário de Gouveia 116 (☎237-7378; Tues–Fri 6pm–1am, Sat & Sun noon–1am). Polish food in a tiny restaurant, presided over by Dona Josefa for the last four decades, with unusual dishes such as herring with apple and onion, shachlik kebab and goulash. Inexpensive to moderate.

Arataca, Rua Figueiredo Magalhaes 28, halfway along Copacabana (☎255-7448). Brazilian food dominates the menu, in particular traditional dishes from the Amazonian state of Pará: try *surubim*, *tucunaré* or *pirarucu*, fishes from the waters of the Amazon Basin, served grilled, in stews (*caldeirada*) or in coconut sauce; *pato no tucupi* is duck in *tucupi* sauce; and for dessert, have a go at the exotic *cupuaçu* fruit. Inexpensive.

La Trattoria, Av. Atlântica, by *Hotel Excelsior*. Cheap and cheerful, the best Italian food in Copacabana.

Mala e Cuia, Rua Raimundo Correria. Superb Minas Gerais cooking at very reasonable prices.

Ouro Verde, Av. Atlântica 1456, just after Praça de Lido (☎542-1887). Part of a hotel (go through the lobby and use the lift), the restaurant serves international cuisine featuring some snappy French cooking and a gracious maitre d'; don't go in shorts. It's quite expensive but well worth it for a treat, as the food is good and the dishes are creative; nice desserts too.

Shirley, Rua Gustavo Sampaio 610, Leme (☎287-0335). Stuffed away in a side street behind the *Hotel Meridien*, this is not one of Rio's classiest eateries, but the Spanish food served up is both good and inexpensive.

Traiteurs de France, Av. Nossa Senhora de Copacabana 386. Simple cooking, but one of the very few affordable and good French restaurants in Rio.

Lagoa

Most of the restaurants in Lagoa are on the Avenida Epitácio Pessoa, which runs along the east side of the lake: generally plush, pricey, air-conditioned and boastful of their views over the lake – which are usually obscured by trees.

Café Lagoa, Av. Epitácio Pessoa 1674, tucked into the southern corner of the lake by Ipanema. The cheapest and oldest of the lakeside restaurants, it's usually full of families from the adjacent neighbourhoods; white-coated waiters deliver beer, German sausage and smoked pork chops the size of football boots to your table. Arrive by 9pm and grab a seat on the patio, from where there's a good view of the lake. Inexpensive and definitely recommended.

Lagoa Charlie, Rua Maria Quitéria 136 (☎287-0335). Mexican food, eaten outside on the terrace, or inside where you'll be charmed or annoyed by serenading musicians who stroll between the tables. Moderate to expensive.

The Queen's Legs, Av. Epitácio Pessoa 5030. A facsimile Victorian pub, good for a beer and a game of darts downstairs – but don't bother with the upstairs restaurant, which is overpriced and over-regarded.

Ipanema

There are lots of expensive restaurants in Ipanema, but budget eating choices are fairly limited. There are, however, some great, late-opening **bars** where you can sample a taste of the high life.

Alô-Alô, Rua Barao de Torre 368. A piano bar with live jazz until 4am, this is a smart place to lounge on sofas and listen to faultlessly executed music. Cover charge. Expensive.

Baroni Fasoli, Rua Jangadeiras 14, near Praça General Osório. Reasonably priced Italian place in an area otherwise brimming with expensive choices.

Barril 1800, Av. Viera Souto 110. This and *Alberico's* at no. 236 – both more bars than restaurants – are well frequented by the young and beautiful, and good places to fill your face with cold beer after a hot day on the beach. Moderate.

Casa da Feijoada, Rua Prudente de Morais 10. *Feijoada* is served daily here, along with other traditional Brazillian dishes. Moderate.

Del Mare, Rua Paul Redfern. Seafood in comfortable surroundings, though some of the prawn dishes are more expensive than they should be. Moderate.

Doubiansky, Rua Gomes Carneiro 90. You're likely to suffer from culture shock here – Russian food (and rather good it is too) in the quintessential *carioca* suburb, Ipanema. Moderate.

Garota de Ipanema, Rua Vinícius de Morais 49. Always busy, this bar has entered the folk annals of Rio de Janeiro since the song of the same name (*The Girl from Ipanema*) was written in here one night when the muse came to Tom Jobim, the song's composer. Few better places in Rio for a beer, but the food is unexceptional and overpriced.

Lord Jim, Rua Paul Redfern. An English boozer serving steak and kidney pie, fish and chips and High Tea. Downstairs, there's a dart board amongst the horse brasses and fake half-timbering. It opens at 5pm and is busy with English expats bemoaning the number of "foreigners" in Brazil. Moderate.

Saideira, Rua Gomes Carneiro, near Praça General Osório. Eating and drinking through the night, until 8am. The term *saideira* means "one for the road" and it's a place that the night-people stop off at after strenuous entertainment in the clubs round about. Worth considering for a late – or early – snack. Inexpensive.

Sal e Pimenta, Rua Barão de Torre 368, above the *Alô-Alô* (☎521-1460). An American Express Goldcard joint; you'll need to make a reservation, and the fifteen-percent service charge is outrageous – but it's gracious international cuisine served in pleasant surroundings overlooking a courtyard. Expensive.

Satyricon, Rua Barão de Torre 192. Good Italian food, especially seafood, in pink surroundings. Expensive.

Leblon

Many of Leblon's restaurants are situated along the Avenida Ataulfo de Paiva, also where you'll find a lot of the late-opening bars. Another popular food and drink venue is Baixo Leblon, the area around Rua Dias Ferreira three or four blocks back from the beach, which is very lively at the weekend.

Alta Munchen, Av. Ataúlfo de Paiva 410 (☎294-4197). A varied menu of German and Swiss dishes; on a hot evening the veranda is a pleasant place to eat. Open until 3am and reasonably priced.

Antiquarius, Rua Aristides Espínola 19 (☎294-1049). Widely rated as the best Portuguese restaurant in Rio (and possibly Brazil), with seafood the thing to eat here. Definitely no shorts. Very expensive.

CHURRASCARIAS

A number of Rio's *churrascarias* (barbecue houses) serve their meats **rodízio** style. For a set price (approximately $10–15), a selection of salads, beans and potatoes is laid out before you, followed by the repeated arrival of the waiter bearing roast meats skewered on a sword. You choose the piece that takes your fancy, and the waiter deftly transfers it from skewer to plate – cuts of filet mignon, pork, chicken, ham, sausage, brisket of beef, and anything else that's had its head over a gate.

The following *churrascarias* are all recommended:

Estrela do Sul, Avenida Reporter Nestor Moreira, Botafogo. This place has a long history and a good reputation.

Gaúcha, Rua das Laranjeiras 114, near Largo do Machado. A bit of a barn, but with live music and a dance floor.

Majórica, Rua Senador Vergueiro 11–15, Flamengo. A long-established, better-than-average place to attack a T-bone. If you're not in the mood for beef, try the excellent trout from near Petrópolis.

Marius, Av. Atlântica 290, at the top end of Leme's beach. Probably the most popular *rodízio* in Rio, it seats over three hundred, and what it lacks in elegance it makes up for in service and atmosphere.

Plataforma, Rua Adalberto Ferreira 32, Leblon. Upstairs, tourists are entertained by a samba show, downstairs you mingle with *cariocas* – and afterwards you can always stagger to the *Academia de Cachaça* round the corner (see p.94), and sample a few with the benefit of a good lining in the stomach.

Caneco 70, Av. Delfim Moreira 1026, at the very end near the Praça Atahualpa (daily 10am–3am). The only restaurant serving the beach in Leblon; the terrace upstairs provides a nice view of the scenery. Moderate.

Degrau, Av. Ataúlfo de Paiva 517. Extensive international cuisine; it doesn't figure in Rio's gourmet guides, but it's always busy, and the food is satisfactory and affordable.

Le Coin, Avenida Ataúlfo de Paiva 658. Reasonable international cuisine; inexpensive and no complaints.

Le Tarot, Rua General Urquiza 104. Popular with young people, fairly standard international cuisine, and not expensive.

Pizzeria Guanabara, Av. Ataúlfo de Paiva 1228. Good if nothing special, and they keep serving pasta and pizza until 5am. Inexpensive.

Gávea

Not an obvious choice for restaurants but a night at the races and a dip into the food available there is fun.

Guima's, Rua José Roberto Macedo Soares 5, on the opposite side of Praça Santos Dumont from the *Jóquei Clube* (☎259-7996). A small, intimate restaurant with a happy atmosphere, catering for artists and intellectuals; the food is delicious, and even the *couvert* of wholemeal bread and paté is worth the price. Try steak in a mustard and pear sauce and one of the brilliant desserts. One of Rio's best and not too expensive.

Jóquei Clube, Praça Santos Dumont. There's racing on Monday and Thursday nights, and at the weekend, and you can enjoy the palatial surroundings and a decent meal in the restaurant overlooking the race track. Inexpensive.

Les Artistes, Rua de São Vicente 75 (☎239-4242). An unusual combination for Brazil: a decent, reasonably priced French restaurant. On Wednesday and Saturday, good cassoulet is served.

Nightlife and entertainment

The best way to find out what's on and where in Rio is to consult *Caderno B*, a separate section of the *Jornal do Brasil*, which lists cinema, arts events and concerts; *O Globo*, too, details sporting and cultural events in the city. *Veja*, Brazil's answer to *Newsweek*, includes a weekly Rio supplement with news of concerts, exhibitions and other events; the magazine reaches the news stands on Sunday. You shouldn't be stuck: there's no end of things to do come nightfall in the city whose name is synonymous with *Carnaval* (see p.104), samba and jazz.

Samba

Samba shows are inevitably tourist affairs, where members of Rio's more successful samba schools perform glitzy music and dance routines. Still, some are worth catching. Every Monday night at 10pm, the Beija Flor (☎791-1353) school performs at the Morro da Urca, halfway up Pão d'Açúcar; $20 entrance includes dinner from 8pm, a well-executed show and spectacular views, though it's a tad snooty. For a less touristy experience of a samba school, you can easily arrange to go and watch rehearsals held from August to February (see p.107), mainly at various points in the Zona Norte.

Of the **clubs**, try *Clube do Samba*, Estrada de Barra 65 in Barra de Tijuca, with lots of dancing and a nice open-air bar. Dedicated just to samba, Saturday often sees shows by big names like Beth Carvalho, Alcione, João and Giza Nogeuiral (check in the *Jornal do Brasil*); entrance costs about $10 which is typical for this type of set-up. More big names, too, at *Canecão*, Av. Wenceslas Bras 215, Botafogo, which can get pleasantly

GAY RIO

If you're expecting **gay nightlife** to rival San Francisco or Sydney, you may well be disappointed. There are few areas of concentration and, apart from transvestites who hang out on street corners and during *Carnaval*, the scene is unexpectedly discreet.

The best introduction to Rio's more traditional male gay society is *Le Ball* (formerly *The Club*), a bar in the Travessa Cristiano Lacorte, just off Rua Miguel Lemos, at the Ipanema end of Copacabana. Opposite this, the *Teatro Brigitte Blair* hosts a gay transvestite show from around 10pm, as does the now rather seedy *Teatro Alaska*, inside the Galeria Alaska at Av. Nossa Senhora de Copacabana 1241. In Centro, the *Café Bohemia*, Avenida Santa Luzia off Avenida Rio Branco, features now legendary transvestite shows that are considered a must-see for many gay tourists. A five-minute walk from here in Lapa, behind a pink façade under the Aqueduto da Carioca, is the *Casanova*, Rio's oldest and most interesting gay bar. In business since 1929, the *Casanova* features lambada and samba music, with large ceiling fans to cool down the frenetic dancers. In Botafogo the bar *Cochranes*, Rua das Palmeiras 66, is a civilized and relaxed venue favoured by gay society, though it's not exclusively gay; *Taminos* at Rua de Passagem is always busy, has relaxed good music and decent food; and in Copacabana, *Encontros*, on Praça do Lido set back from Avenida N.S. de Copacabana, is also popular, although mainly with tourists.

Tradition has it that some bars around Cinelândia in the city centre are popular meeting spots for gay men, though tradition doesn't indicate exactly which establishments are appropriate, while in Copacabana, the beach area in front of the *Copacabana Palace Hotel* is frequented by gay bathers, and the café, *Maxims*, next to the *Copacabana Palace* is a fun gay place to hang out. The strip of beach between Rua Farme de Amoedo and Rua Teixeira do Melo in Ipanema is another well-known gay meeting point.

See the "Carnaval" section, p.105, for information about Rio's gay balls.

---

rowdy of an evening. For cheaper, early evening entertainment there are the *Seis e Meia* **shows** (at 6.30pm, as the name suggests): in Centro try the *Teatro João Caetano*, Praça Tiradentes, or the *Paço Imperial*, Praça XV de Novembro.

Discos, live music and jazz

Although Rio's discos and piano bars attempt sophistication, the product is generally bland and unpalatable. Discos, particularly, too often pump out a steady stream of British and American hits, interspersed with examples from Brazil's own dreadful pop industry.

Most of the big **discos** are private clubs, but if you're staying in one of the five-star hotels, and promise to spend a minimum of $20 per person, you can usually arrange temporary membership. Soft options for the wealthy and unadventurous are *Hippopotamus*, Rua Barre de Torre 354, Ipanema, and *Studio C*, Rua Xavier da Silveira 7, under the *Hotel Rio Othon Palace* in Copacabana. Halfway along Avenida Atlântica, *Help* is a massive disco which gets mobbed at weekends; entrance is about $10. Other *boates* (disco clubs) are: *Caligula*, Rua Prudente de Morais 129, Ipanema, which costs $12 entrance and attracts some famous types; and the more tranquil *Biblos*, Av. Epitácio Pessoa 1484, Lagoa, with good popular home-grown music and jazz (Tues). *Peoples*, Av. Bartolemeu Mitre 370, Leblon (☎294-0547), is one of the trendiest spots in Rio: upstairs the city's fashion-conscious middle class listen to live music of varying quality; downstairs (invitation only) in the private club, chemically assisted rich-kids sustain a funky posture till dawn. All pretentious nonsense, but a bit of a laugh, though with a $20 cover charge, it's not a cheap night out.

For **live rock music**, give the *Crespúsculo de Cubatão*, Rua Barata Ribeiro 543, a whirl. Part-owned by Ronnie Biggs, its atmosphere, when busy, is curiously in keeping with the club's name, "Cubatão Twilight" – Cubatão being an industrial area near São Paulo which pollution has made virtually uninhabitable. Entrance is about $5. *Let It Be*, Rua Siqueira Campos 206, also has live rock combined with taped music that, not surprisingly, favours old stuff from the Fab Four.

Another option is for live **reggae** at *Casa Branca*, Rua do Catete 112, near Largo do Machado – sessions every Sunday until 4am, a lively crowd, lots of students, and cheap entrance.

Jazz

Rio de Janeiro has a tradition of **jazz music** that extends well beyond *The Girl from Ipanema* and which is celebrated in the **Free Jazz Festival**, usually in late August or early September, based in the theatre in the *Hotel Nacional* in São Conrado; for more information, contact Dueto Productions, Rua Visconde de Pirajá 146 in Ipanema. In past festivals, Brazilian musicians like Egberto Gismonti, Hermeto Pascoal, Airto Moreira and Flora Purim have combined with the likes of Art Blakey, Sarah Vaughan, Ray Charles and Stan Jordan – an important event on the international jazz circuit.

Amongst the clubs that specialize in **live jazz** and tend to have consistently good programmes are *Jazzmania*, Rua Rainha Elizabeth 769 (☎287-0085), on the corner between Copacabana and Ipanema, and *Peoples*, Av. Bartolomeu Mitre 370, Leblon (see p.101); both have cover charges of around $10–15. The latter is very trendy, but make sure you go on the right night and avoid the dreadful country-and-western band that has a regular Tuesday spot. In both cases, it's a good idea to call to find out who's playing; be prepared to be turned away if it's especially crowded on the evening that you choose and you're not dressed stylishly enough.

Brazilian dancing

Brazilians can dance, no question about that. The various regionally rooted traditions in folk music remain alive and popular, and if you'd like to get into a bit of Brazilian swing, go in search of the more traditional dance halls.

Gafieiras

Gafieiras originally sprang up in the 1920s as ballrooms for the poorer classes, and today they remain popular because they are places where *cariocas* can be assured of traditional dance music. The most famous – both highly recommended – are *Estudantina*, Praça Tiradentes 79 (1st floor; Thurs 10pm–3am, Fri & Sat 11pm–4am), and *Elite*, Rua Frei Caneca 4 (1st floor; Fri & Sat 11pm–4am, Sun 9pm–3am), both in Centro. *Estudantina's* decor recalls an earlier age, and with live bands on the stage busying the generally young dancers along, and a small veranda to cool off on, it's a good place to go; *Elite* is smaller, more traditional and has a famous ball during *Carnaval*. Both charge around $4 entrance.

Asa Branca, Av. Mem de Sá 17, in Lapa (Tues–Sun 10pm–3am; ☎252-4428), is another good option for a jig, principally Big Band-style samba; admission is around $15, depending on who's playing. Next door is *Arcos de Velha*, a dance hall where the band play *fundo do quintal* style – around a table rather than on the stage. For the most beautiful of surroundings and lively Brazilian music, try *Botanic Dancing Brazil* from Thursdays to Sundays after 10pm in the Jardim Botânico. Under the viaduct in Lapa, there's also *Circo Voador*, housed under a big top on some evenings, with open-air dancing and drinking on others. It puts on *forró* (see below), samba and *trio elétrico* music, is inexpensive and has some excellent Northeastern bands.

Forró

For some accordion-driven swing from Brazil's Northeast, look for a **forró** club. The term *forró* (pronounced "fawhaw") originates from the English "for all", a reference to the dances financed by English engineering companies for their manual labour forces, as opposed to the balls organized for the elite. As drought and poverty have forced the *nordestino* to migrate south in search of employment in Brazil's large urban centres, so the culture has followed. At Rua Catete 235, *Forró Forrado* (Fri–Sun 10pm–late) has an excellent band and a mixed clientele that spans Rio's social scale. On Saturday nights, there's also the *Forró da Praia*, on Avenida Nações Unidas near the Botafogo recreation ground. Also on Saturday nights in Zona Sul, *Forró do Leblon* at Rua Bartolomeu Mitre 630 in Leblon and *Forró do Copacabana* at Av. Nossa Senhora de Copacabana 435 in Copacabana are convenient places to check out.

Film, classical music and exhibitions

Rio is the home of the **Brazilian Symphony Orchestra**, and the orchestra of the *Teatro Municipal* – the theatre which is home to the city's **ballet** troupe and **opera** company. This is the venue for almost everything that happens in terms of "high culture", with four or five major productions a year. All kinds of events attract famous names, and prices are reasonable; again, check the *Jornal do Brasil*.

For musical, photographic and fine art **exhibitions**, it's worth checking at the headquarters of *Funarte*, around the corner from the Museu das Belas Artes in Rua Araújo de Porto Alegre; either go and get a copy of their programme, or keep an eye on the newspapers. Particularly good are the photographic exhibitions under the direction of Walter Firmo, and the musical **recitals** that take place in the Sidney Millar room on the first floor of *Funarte*.

It's always worth checking out what's on at the **Centro Cultural Banco do Brasil**, Rua Primeiro de Março 66, Centro (☎216-1426), which puts on an excellent programme of films, music and plays, usually free. Situated in a lovely, grand and cool building, it has several exhibition halls, two cinemas and two theatres.

Film

Brazil is one of the world's largest film markets. Most European and American films are quickly released in Brazil and play to large audiences on big screens with their original soundtracks. **Cinemas** are cheap ($4) and among the best are the *Largo do Machado I & II* and the *São Luiz I & II*, both in Largo do Machado; the *Ricamar* and the *Roxy*, along Avenida N.S. de Copacabana; and *Condor Copacabana* in Rua Figueiredo Magalhães. *Jornal do Brasil* lists what's on and where. There's an excellent chain of art-house cinemas, called *Estação*, showing the latest films on the international circuit. Check out the *Estação Paissandu*, near the corner of Rua Senador Vergueiro and Rua Paissandu, Centro, the *Estação Cinema 1* in Leme, the *Estação Botafogo*, Rua Voluntarios da Patria 88, and the latest *Estação* in the Museu da Republica, Palacio do Catete.

Since 1984 Rio de Janeiro has hosted **Rio-Cine**, an international festival of film that includes some TV and video productions as well, and ranks alongside those of Cannes, Montreal and Moscow. It takes place over ten days in November and is based in the Convention Centre of the *Hotel Nacional*: contact the organizers at Rua Paissandu 362 (☎285-7649), in Flamengo. *Cariocas* love the cinema, have very catholic tastes and their festival lacks the snobbery that has marred Cannes. Over three hundred films are shown during the festival, with parallel screenings in cinemas all over Rio. Obscure foreign films can play to packed houses that charge minimal entrance fees.

Rio's Carnaval

Carnaval is celebrated in all of Brazil's cities, but Rio's is the biggest and most flash. From the Friday before Ash Wednesday to the following Thursday, the city shuts up shop and throws itself into the world's most famous manifestation of unbridled hedonism. Its greatest quality is that Rio's *Carnaval* has never become stale, something to do with its status as the most important celebration on the Brazilian calendar, easily outstripping either Christmas or Easter. In a city riven by poverty, *Carnaval* represents a moment of freedom and release, when the aspirations of *cariocas* can be expressed in music and song.

The background

The direct origins of *Carnaval* in Rio can be traced back to a fifteenth-century tradition of Easter revelry in the Azores that caught on in Portugal and was exported to Brazil. Anarchy reigned in the streets for four days and nights, the festivities often so riotous that they were formally abolished in 1843 – although the street celebrations have remained the most accessible and widely enjoyed feature of *Carnaval* ever since. In the mid-nineteenth century, **masquerade balls** – *bailes* – were first held by members of the social elite, while processions, with carriages decorated in allegorical themes, also made an appearance, thus marking the ascendancy of the procession over the general street melee. Rio's masses, who were denied admission to the balls, had their own music – *jongo* – and they reinforced the tradition of street celebration by organizing in *Zé Pereira* bands, named after the Portuguese tambor which provided the basic musical beat. The organizational structure behind today's samba schools (*escolas da samba*) was partly a legacy of those bands sponsored by migrant Bahian port workers in the 1870s. Theirs was a more disciplined approach to the *Carnaval* procession: marching to stringed and wind instruments, using costumes and appointing people to co-ordinate different dimensions of the parade.

Music written specifically for *Carnaval* emerged in the early twentieth century, by composers like Chiquinho Gonzaga, who wrote the first recorded **samba** piece in 1917 (*Pelo Telefone*), and Mauro de Almeida e Donga. In the 1930s, radio and records began to spread the music of Rio's *Carnaval*, and competition between different samba schools became institutionalized: in 1932 the *Estação Primeira Mangueira* school won the first prize for its performance in the *Carnaval* parade. The format has remained virtually unchanged since then, except for the emergence – in the mid-1960s – of the **bandas**; street processions by the residents of various *bairros*, who eschew style, discipline and prizes and give themselves up to the most traditional element of *Carnaval* – street revelry, of which even the principal *Carnaval* procession in the Sambódromo is technically a part.

Carnaval – all the action

Rio's street celebrations centre around the **evening processions** that fill **Avenida Rio Branco** (metrô to Largo do Carioca or Cinelândia). Be prepared for the crowds and beware of pickpockets: even though the revellers are generally high-spirited and good-hearted, it's as well to keep the little cash you should take in inaccessible places (like your shoes), wear only light clothes and leave your valuables locked up at the hotel.

Most of what's good takes place down the Avenida Rio Branco. The processions include samba schools (though not the best), *Clubes de Frevo*, whose loudspeaker-laden floats blast out the frenetic dance music typical of the Recife *Carnaval*, and the *Blocos de Empolgacão*, including the *Bafo da Onça* and *Cacique de Ramos* clubs, between which exists a tremendous rivalry. There are also *rancho* bands, a traditional *carioca* carnival music that predates samba.

Bandas

In whatever *bairro* you're staying there will probably be a **banda** organized by the local residents; ask in your hotel. Starting in mid-afternoon, they'll continue well into the small hours, the popular ones accumulating thousands of followers as they wend their way through the neighbourhood. They all have a regular starting point, some have set routes, others wander freely; but they're easy to follow – there's always time to have a beer and catch up later.

Some of the best *bandas* are: the *Banda da Glória*, which sets off from near the Estação Glória metrô station; the *Banda da Ipanema* (the first to be formed, in 1965), which gathers behind Praça General Osório in Ipanema; and the *Banda da Vergonha do Posto 6*, starting in Rua Francisco Sá in Copacabana. There are dozens of others, including several in each *bairro* of the Zona Sul, each providing a mix of music, movement and none-too-serious cross-dressing – a tradition during *Carnaval* that even the most macho of men indulge in.

Carnaval balls

It's the **Carnaval balls** that really signal the start of the celebrations, warm-up sessions in clubs and hotels for rusty revellers, which are quite likely to get out of hand as inhibitions give way to a rampant eroticism. They all start late, normally after 10pm, and the continual samba beat supplied by live bands drives the festivities into the new day. At most of the balls, *fantasia* (fancy dress) is the order of the day, elaborate costumes brightening the already hectic proceedings – but don't worry if you haven't got one; just dress reasonably smartly.

You'll often have to pay an awful lot to get into these affairs, as some of the more fashionable balls attract the rich and famous. If you've got the money and the silly costume, then those worth checking out include the Pão de Açúcar, on the Friday before *Carnaval*, halfway up the famous landmark – spectacular views, exotic company, but well over $100 a head and a trifle snobby (☎541-3737 for details). The Hawaiian Ball, hosted by the Rio Yacht Club, opens the season on the Friday of the week before *Carnaval*: it takes place around the club's swimming pool, amid lavish decorations, and is popular and expensive (about $80); tickets from the Yacht Club, on Avenida Pasteur, a few hundred metres before the Sugar Loaf cable car terminus. The Friday immediately before *Carnaval* (which doesn't officially start until Monday) is a big occasion, too, with the Baile de Champagne and the Baile Vermelho e Preto taking place. The latter (the "Red and Black Ball") has developed a particular reputation as a no-holds-barred affair. Named after the colours of Rio's favourite football team, Flamengo, it's a media event with TV cameras scanning the crowds for famous faces – exhibitionism is an inadequate term for the immodest goings-on at the Red and Black celebrations. In Leblon the *Monte Libano* (☎239-0032 for details) hosts a number of "last days of Rome" festivities – the Baile das Gatas, Baile Fio Dental, even Bum Bum Night – sexually charged exercises all, though safe to attend and reasonable at around $35 a ticket.

There are a number of **gay balls**, too, which attract an international attendance. The Grande Gala G is an institution, usually held in the *Help* disco on Copacabana's Avenida Atlântica. Another is the Baile dos Enxutos, hosted by the *Hotel Itália* on Praça Tiradentes, Centro.

Over the last few years, the *Scala* club in Leblon has become an important centre for balls, and has hosted the Baille Vermelho e Preto amongst others. You can confirm venues by phoning the *Scala* (☎274-9148), or by asking at the box office, Av. Afriano de Melo Franco 292, Leblon.

Samba schools and the Desfile

The **samba schools**, each representing a different neighbourhood or social club, are divided into three leagues, each allowing promotion and relegation. Division 1 schools play in the Sambódromo, Division 2 on Avenida Rio Branco and Division 3 on Avenida 28 de Setembro, up in Aldeia Campista, near the Maracanã Stadium.

Until 1984, the main procession of Division 1 schools – the Desfile – took place along Avenida Presidente Vargas. It has since been shifted to the purpose-built **Sambódromo**, further along the avenue beyond the train station, a concrete structure 1700m long which can accommodate 90,000 spectators. On the Sunday and Monday nights of *Carnaval* week, some 50,000 others, divided up into the various samba schools, take part in a spectacular piece of theatre: no simple parade, but a competition between schools attempting to gain points from their presentation composed of song, story, dress, dance and rhythm.

It all starts in the year preceeding *Carnaval*, as each samba school mobilizes thousands of supporters who will create the various parts of the school's display. A theme is chosen, music written, costumes created, while the dances are choreographed by the **carnavelesco**, the school's director. By December, rehearsals have begun and, in time for Christmas, the sambas are recorded and released to record stores.

At the **Desfile** itself, the schools pass through the *Passarela do Samba*, the Sambódromo's parade ground, and the judges allocate points according to a number of criteria. Each school must parade for between 85 and 95 minutes, no more and no less. The **bateria**, the percussion section, has to sustain the cadence that drives the school's song and dance; the *samba enredo* is the music, the *enredo* the accompanying story or lyric. The **harmonia** refers to the degree of synchronicity between the *bateria* and the dance by the thousands of **passistas** (samba dancers); the dancers are conducted by the **pastoras**, who lead by example. The **evolução** refers to the quality of the dance, and the choreography is judged on its spontaneity, the skill of the *pastoras* and the excitement that the display generates. The costumes, too, are judged on their originality; their colours are always the traditional ones adopted by each school. The **carros alegóricos** (no more than ten metres high and eight wide) are the gigantic, richly decorated floats, which carry some of the **Figuras de Destaque** ("prominent figures"), amongst them the **Porta-Bandeira** ("flag bearer") – a woman who carries the school's symbol, a potentially big point scorer. The **Mestre-Sala** is the dance master, also an important symbolic figure, whose ability to sustain the rhythm of his dancers is of paramount importance.

The **Comissão da Frente**, traditionally a school's "board of directors", marches at the head of the procession, a role often filled these days by invited TV stars or sports teams. The bulk of the procession behind is formed by the **alas**, the wings or blocks consisting of hundreds of costumed individuals each linked to a part of the school's theme.

Traditionally, every school has in addition to parade an **Ala das Baianas** – hundreds of women dressed in the flowing white costumes typical of Salvador – in remembrance of the debt owed to the Bahian emigrants, who introduced many of the traditions of the Rio *Carnaval* procession.

The **parade** of schools starts at 7.30pm, with eight schools parading on each of the two nights, and goes on till noon the following day. Two stands (7 & 9) in the Sambódromo are reserved for foreign visitors and **seats** cost over $100 per night. Though much more

---

SAMBÓDROMO PARADES

The starting dates for the Sambódromo parades for the next few years are as follows:

1998 Feb 22	1999 Feb 14	2000 March 5

SAMBA SCHOOLS

If you can't make *Carnaval*, you can get a taste of the samba schools at the *ensaios* (rehearsals) below. They take place from August to February, Friday to Sunday at about 10pm.

Beija-Flor, Rua Pracinha Wallace Paes Leme 1652, Nilopolis (☎791-1353). Founded 1948; blue and white.

Estação Primeira de Mangueira, Rua Visconde de Niterói 1072, Mangueira (☎234-4129). Founded 1928; green and pink.

Portela, Rua Clara Nunes 81, Madureira (☎390-0471). Founded 1923; blue and white.

Mocidade Independente de Padre Miguel, Rua Cel. Tamarindo 38, Padre Miguel (☎332-5823). Founded 1952; green and white.

Império Serrano, Av. Ministro Edgar Romero 114, Madureira (☎359-4944). Founded 1947; green and white.

---

expensive than other areas, they are more comfortable and have good catering facilities. Other sections of the Sambódromo cost from $10 to $40 and the seating options are: the high stands (*arquibancadas*), lower stands (*geral*) and the ringside seats (*cadeiras de pista*; $25) – these last the best, consisting of a table, four chairs and full bar service.

Unless you have a very tough backside you will find sitting through a ten-hour show to be an intolerable test of endurance. Most people don't turn up until 11pm, by which time the show is well under way and hotting up considerably. **Tickets** are available principally from Turisrio, Rua da Assembléia 10 (☎297-7117), or through the Banco do Brasil, with offices in most major capital cities. Book well in advance if you can, or try local travel agents, who often have tickets available for a modest commission.

Listings

Airlines Aerolíneas Argentinas, Rua da Assembléia 100, 29th floor, Centro (☎292-4131), and Av. Nossa Senhora de Copacabana 312–313, Copacabana (☎255-7144); Aeroperu, Praça Mahatma Gandhi 2, Centro (☎210-3124); Air France, Av. Rio Branco 257a, Centro (☎398-5929 or 532-3642); Alitalia, Av. Presidente Wilson 231, 21st floor (☎240-7822); American Airlines, Av. Presidente Wilson 165, 5th floor, Centro (☎220-0603); Avianco, Av. Presidente Wilson 165, 8th floor (☎240-4413); British Airways, Av. Rio Branco 108, Centro (☎242-6020); Canadian Airlines, Rua da Ajuda 35, 29th floor, Centro (☎220-5343); Iberia, Av. Presidente Antônio Carlos 51, Centro (☎220-3059); KLM, Galeão Airport (☎398-3700); Lufthansa, Av. Rio Branco 156, Centro (☎282-1253); Pluna, Rua México 11, Centro (☎262-4466); SAS, Av. Presidente Wilson 261, 6th floor, Centro (☎210-1222); South African Airlines, Av. Rio Branco 245, 4th floor (☎262-6252); Swissair, Av. Rio Branco 108, 10th floor, Centro (☎297-5177); TAP, Av. Rio Branco 311, Centro (☎210-1277); Transbrasil, Av. Atlântica 1998, Copacabana (☎236-7475), and Rua Santa Luzia 651, Centro (☎297-4422); United Airlines, Av. Presidente Antônio Carlos 51, Centro (☎220-1550); Varig, Av. Rio Branco 277, Centro (☎220-3821), Rua Rodolfo Dantas 16, Copacabana (☎541-6343), and Rua Visc. de Pirajá 351, Ipanema (☎287-9440 or 287-9040); VASP, Rua Santa Luzia 735, Centro (☎292-2112), and Rua Visconde de Pirajá 444, Ipanema (also ☎292-2112).

Airport enquiries Galeão international airport: general enquiries ☎398-5050; international flights ☎398-4133; domestic flights ☎398-6060. Santos Dumont, for shuttle flights to São Paulo, Belo Horizonte and Brasília: ☎262-6311 for general enquiries; ☎262-6212 for flight information; ☎220-7728 for reservations.

American Express Av. Atlântica 1702, Copacabana (at the *Copacabana Palace Hotel*).

Banks and exchange You can get good rates for your dollars at the 24-hour bank at the airport on arrival; avoid the porters, whose rates are lower. Banks are listed in the Yellow Pages (*Lista Telefonica Classificada*) under "*Bancos*": main branches are concentrated in Avenida Rio Branco in Centro and Avenida N.S. de Copacabana in Copacabana. It's worth remembering that although most banks remain open until 4.30pm you can usually exchange money only until 3pm or 3.30pm. The Banco do Brasil and international banks have *câmbio* sections but you will be stung with the $20 flat-rate charge. You can do better at a branch of *Bradesco* or *Banespa* – which also have ATMs for cash advances on Visa cards – or (for cash only) at one of the *casas de câmbio* which are clustered on Avenida Rio Branco in Centro. Foreign banks in Rio include: Chase Manhattan, Rua Ouvidor 98, Centro (☎216-6112); Citibank, Rua da Assembléia 100, Centro (☎276-3636); Lloyds, Rua da Alfândega 33, Centro (☎211-2332); Royal Bank of Canada, Rua Ouvidor 90, Centro (☎231-2145); Standard Chartered, Av. Rio Branco 110, Centro (☎222-5090).

Books For English-language books, branches of Unilivros are all over Rio, including ones at the Largo do Machado (Flamengo), Av. Ataúlfo de Paiva 686 (Leblon) and Rua Visconde de Pirajá 207 (Ipanema). Branches, too, of Siciliano at Av. Rio Branco 158 (Centro), Av. N.S. de Copacabana 830 (Copacabana) and Rua Visconde de Pirajá 511 (Ipanema). The Livraria Susan Bach, Rua Visconde de Caravelas 17, Botafogo, has an unrivalled collection of Brazilian books, especially strong on history.

Car rental Avis, Av. Princ. Isabel 150, Copacabana (☎295-8041); Budget, Av. Princ. Isabel 350, Copacabana (☎295-0040); Delta, Rua Farme de Amoedo 76, Ipanema (☎287-0590); Hertz, Av. Princ. Isabel 334, Copacabana (☎275-3245); Interlocadora, Av. Princ. Isabel 186, Copacabana (☎275-6546); Localiza-National, Av. Princ. Isabel 214, Copacabana (☎275-3340); Nobre, Av. Princ. Isabel 150 (☎541-4646), and Rua da Passagem 29/47, Botafogo (☎295-9547); Unidas, Av. Princ. Isabel 350, Copacabana (☎275-8496). Prices start at about $60 per day (the Brazilian companies are often cheapest); you'll need a credit card and your car will be delivered to your hotel.

Consulates Argentina, Praia de Botafogo 228, Botafogo (☎551-5498); Australia, Rua Voluntários da Pátria 45, Botafogo (☎386-7922); Austria, Av. Atlântica 3804, Copacabana (☎227-0040); Belgium, Rua do Ouvidor 60, Centro (☎252-2967); Canada, Rua Lauro Müller 116, Botafogo (☎275-2039); Denmark, Av. das Américas 3333, Barra da Tijuca (☎325-4711); France, Av. Pres. Antônio Carlos 58, Centro (☎210-1272); Germany, Rua Pres. Carlos de Campos 417, Laranjeiras (☎553-6777); Ireland, Av. Princ. Isabel 323, Copacabana (☎275-0196); Netherlands, Praia de Botafogo 242, Botafogo (☎552-9028); Peru, Av. Rui Barbosa 314, Flamengo (☎551-6296); South Africa, Av. Pres. Antonio Carlos 607, Centro (☎533-0216); Sweden, Praia do Flamengo 344, 9th floor, Flamengo (☎242-8035); UK, Praia do Flamengo 284, 2nd floor, Flamengo (☎553-3223); USA, Av. Presidente Wilson 147, Centro (☎292-7117); Venezuela, Praia de Botafogo 242, Botafogo (☎551-5398).

Dentists Hellishly expensive in Brazil, but if the pain is too great to bear try one of the following clinics: Assistência Dentária, Av. das Américas 2300, Barra de Tijuca (☎399-1603); Dentário Rollin, Rua Cupertinho Durão 81, Leblon (☎259-2647); Clínica de Urgência, Rua Marquês de Abrantes 27, Botafogo (☎226-0083).

Festivals and events February: *Carnaval*; March: Brazilian Grand Prix; May: International Festival of Dance, Grande Prêmio Jóquei Clube Brasileiro, Festa de São Pedro and maritime procession in Guanabara Bay; August: Brazilian Sweepstake, Rio Marathon and Free Jazz Festival; November: Rio Cine Festival; December: Festival de Iemanjá.

Health matters For medical emergencies, English speakers should try a private clinic such as Sorocaba Clinic, Rua Sorocaba 464, Botafogo (☎286-0022); Centro Médico Ipanema, Rua Anibal Mendonça 135, Ipanema (☎239-4647). Normally, they'll send an ambulance, but if they haven't got one, phone Clinic Saviour (☎227-5099 or 227-6187) or Pullman (☎236-1011 or 257-4132). Best bet for any non-emergency problems is the Rio Health Collective, which has an information and referral system for physical and mental health problems. A non-profit-making organization, its phone-in service is free, and provides names of qualified professionals who speak foreign languages; ☎325-9300 ext. 44. There's an office, open during normal business hours, in the Banco Nacional building, next to the Barra Shopping, Av. das Américas 4430 (room 303), Barra de Tijuca. Or your consulate should have a list of professionals who speak an appropriate language. If you speak Portuguese, call Golden Cross – the national health insurance service – which operates a 24-hour referral service in Rio (☎286-0044; outside Rio ☎021/800-3070).

Laundry Laundromat, Av. N.S. de Copacabana, 1226, Copacabana; Rua Miguel Lemos 56, Copacabana; and Rua Marquês de Abrantes 82, Flamengo. All hotels have a laundry service, too, but these are always very expensive.

Maps Most kiosks (*bancas*) sell reasonable maps of Rio. *Guia Quatro Rodas* do a good one.

Music shops CDs and tapes are a bit cheaper in Rio than in Europe and similar to prices in the USA. Most stores still have old recordings available on vinyl at bargain prices. Try Bilboard, with branches in Copacabana (Rua Barata Ribeiro, 502) and Ipanema (Rua Visconde de Pirajá, 602), and Gabriela with several branches including one in the RioSul shopping centre and another at Av.

Ataúlfo de Paiva 467, Leblon. If you want to experiment with Brazilian music, ask one of the attendants for a selection to listen to. For secondhand records, go to Toc Discos, Rua Uruguaiana 18 and Rua Sete Setembro 139, both branches in the Centro. Buying tapes, the more expensive the recording, the more likely it is to last.

Newspapers and magazines There are several kiosks where foreign-language newspapers are available, including ones on Rua Lauro Muller, Botafogo, at junctions along Avenida N.S. de Copacabana, Copacabana, on Rua Visc. de Pirajá/Praça Gen. Osório, Ipanema, and along Avenida Rio Branco in Centro. The *Herald Tribune* and *Miami Herald* are the two most easily available English-language newspapers in Rio, and *Time, Newsweek* and the *Economist* are all readily available. The *Jornal do Brasil* and *O Globo* are Rio's two main newspapers, while the weekly news magazine *Veja* features a useful *Veja Rio* insert, listing and reviewing cultural events in the city.

Pharmacy 24-hour service from Farmácia do Leme, Av. Prado Junior 237, Leme (☎275-3847); and Farmácia Piauí, Av. Ataúlfo de Paiva 1283, Ipanema (☎274-7322).

Police Emergency number ☎190. The beach areas have police posts located at regular intervals, and there are police stations at Rua Hilário de Gouveia 102, Copacabana (☎257-1121); Rua Bambina 140, Botafogo (☎226-0227); Rua Humberto de Campos 315, Leblon (☎239-6049); Rua Maj. Rubens Vaz 170, Gávea (☎279-5096); Praça Mauá 5, Centro (☎263-6080); and Praça da República 24, Centro (☎242-5518). The special Tourist Police are located at Avenida Afrânio de Melo Franco (opposite the Teatro Casa Grande), Leblon (☎511-5112).

Post offices *Correios* are open Mon–Fri 8am–6pm, Sat 8am–noon. There's a *Central de Informações* at Av. Presidente Vargas 3077, Centro (☎293-0159). Main post offices are at Rua Primeiro do Março (corner of Rosario) in Centro; Av. N.S. de Copacabana 540 in Copacabana; Rua Visconde de Piraja 452, Ipanema; Av. Ataúlfo de Paiva 822, Leblon.

Public holidays Most places will close on the following days: Jan 1; Jan 20 (Dia de São Sebastião); *Carnaval* and Ash Wednesday; March 1 (Founding of the City); Good Friday; April 21 (Remembrance of Tiradentes); May 1 (Labour Day); early June (Corpus Christi); Sept 7 (Independence Day); Oct 12 (Nossa Senhora Aparecida); Nov 2 (Finados); Nov 15 (Proclamation of the Republic); Dec 25.

Shopping Purpose-built shopping centres – *Shoppings* – have mushroomed over Rio during the last decade. The best known and most central of them is RioSul, before the Pasmado Tunnel at the end of Botafogo. Apart from branches of department stores, like C&A, there are also supermarkets, fashion boutiques, record stores and lots of places to grab a snack; air-conditioned, too, which is a blessing. Others are at Gávea (Rua Marquês de São Vicente) and Leblon (Avenida Ataúlfo de Paiva), the latter specializing in those little items of interior decoration that turn a house into a gold-plated bordello.

Women's groups *Associação Brasileira de Mulheres Universitárias* (University Women's Group), Praça Mahatma Gandhi 2 (☎220-6085); Faculty of Women's Studies (Catholic University), Rua Mqe. de São Vicente 225, Gávea (☎274-9922 ext. 288); Black Women's Collective, Av. Mem de Sá 208, 2nd floor (☎252-7459); Rio Women's Collective (☎259-9226 or 266-7459); DAWN (Development Alternative with Women for a New Era), Neuma Aguiar, IUPERJ, Rua de Matriz 82 CEP 22260. Also, *Delegacias da Mulher*, women's police stations, are being established in various locations – Av. Pres. Vargas 1248, 5th floor, is the first fully operational one.

RIO DE JANEIRO STATE

It's easy to get out of Rio city, something you'll probably want to do at some stage during your stay. There are good **bus** services to all the places mentioned below, while the easiest trips are by ferry to the **Ilha de Paquetá** or **Niterói**, just over the bay. After that, the choice is a simple one: either head east along the **Costa do Sol** to Cabo Frio and Búzios, or west along the **Costa Verde** to Ilha Grande and Parati; both coasts offer endless good beaches and little holiday towns, developed to varying degrees. Or strike off **inland** to Petrópolis and Teresópolis, where the mountainous interior provides a welcome, cool relief from the frenetic goings-on back in Rio.

If you fancy **renting a car** (see p.108 for addresses in Rio), this is as good a state as any to brave the traffic: the coasts are an easy drive from the city and stopping off at more remote beaches is easy, while your own wheels would let you get to grips with the extraordinary scenery up in the mountains.

Ilha de Paquetá

The **ILHA DE PAQUETÁ** is an island of one square kilometre in the north of Guanabara Bay, an easy day trip that is very popular with *cariocas* at weekends. It was first occupied by the Portuguese in 1565 and later was a favourite resort of Dom João VI, who had the São Roque chapel built here in 1810. During the naval revolt of 1893 against the government of Floriano Peixoto, the island was the insurgents' principal base: their HQ, the Chácara dos Coqueiros, still stands, though it's not open to the public. Nowadays, however, the island is almost entirely given over to tourism. About 2000 people live here, but at weekends that number is multiplied several times by visitors from the city. They come for the tranquillity – the only motor vehicle is an ambulance – and for the beaches, which sadly are now heavily polluted. Still, it makes a pleasant day's excursion – with colonial-style buildings that retain a certain shabby charm – and the trip is an attraction in itself: if possible, time your return to catch the sunset over the city as you sail back. Weekdays are best if you want to avoid the crowds, or in August come for the wildly celebrated **Festival de São Roque**.

The best way to get around is by **bike**, thousands of which are available to rent very cheaply from near the ferry terminal; you can also take a ride in a small horse-drawn cart (*charrete*) or rent one by the hour if you want to take your time and stop off along the way. Not that there's a great deal to see. When you disembark, head along the road past the Yacht Club and you'll soon reach the first **beaches** – Praia da Ribeira and Praia dos Frades. **Praia da Guarda**, a few hundred metres on, has the added attraction of the *Lido* restaurant and the **Parque Duque de Mattos**, with exuberant vegetation and panoramic views from the top of the Morro da Cruz, a hill riddled with tunnels dug to extract china clay.

Practicalities

Ferries (see p.63) for Paquetá leave from near Rio's Praça XV de Novembro, Centro, take around an hour and cost about $1. The hydrofoil is three times as quick, costs around $7 on weekdays and $12 at weekends.

If you want to stay over, there are a few pleasant small **hotels**, the least expensive being the *Paquetá* at Praça Bom Jesus 15 (☎021/397-0052; ②). More expensive, but with air conditioning, are the *Lido*, Praia José Bonifácio 59 (☎021/397-0377; ③), and, the largest on the island, the *Flamboyant* at Praia Grossa 58 (☎021/397-0087; ③). There's a **tourist office** on Praia José Bonifacia, near the intersection with Rua Manuel de Macedo, on the opposite side of the island from the ferry landing.

East: Niterói and the Costa do Sol

Across the strait at the mouth of Guanabara Bay lies **Niterói**, founded in 1573 and until 1975 the capital of the old state of Guanabara. Though lacking the splendour of the city of Rio, Niterói, with a population of half a million, has a busy commercial centre and lively nightlife – well worth a visit, certainly, as it's the gateway to the **Costa do Sol** to the east.

Buses out of Niterói head east along the **Costa do Sol**, which is dominated by three large **lakes** – Maricá, Saquerema and Araruama, separated from the ocean by long, narrow stretches of white sandy beach – and flecked with small towns bearing the same names as the lakes. Approximately 10km directly south of Niterói are a number of smaller lakes, too, collectively known as the **Lagos Fluminenses**, though these aren't really worth the effort to get to as the water is polluted. However, the evil-smelling sludge which surrounds them is purported to have medicinal properties. The main lakes are also muddy, but at least the water here is clean and much used for water-sports of all kinds. The brush around the lakes is full of wildlife (none of it particularly ferocious), while the fresh, salty air makes a pleasing change from the city streets.

Niterói

You can reach **NITERÓI** either by car or **bus** across the 14km of the Ponte Costa e Silva, the Rio–Niterói bridge (bus #999 from the Menezes Cortes bus terminal), or, much more fun, by catching the extremely cheap **ferry**, every fifteen minutes from the CONERJ docks, close to Praça XV de Novembro. **Hydrofoils** leave from the same dock every few minutes, too. On arrival, pick up a copy of the free map of Niterói at the helpful **tourist office** (daily 9am–6pm) in the ferry terminal.

An historic city in its own right, Niterói has several buildings worth seeing, but they are in isolated spots throughout the city. A short distance southwest of the ferry terminal, the **Ilha da Boa Viagem** (April–Dec, 4th Sun of each month, 1–5pm), connected to the mainland by a causeway leading from Vermelha and Boa Viagem beaches, offers excellent views across the bay to Rio. On the island, guarding the entrance to the bay, are the ruins of a fort, built in 1663, and opposite, there's a small chapel dating from the seventeenth century.

Praia de Jurujuba, long and often crowded, is reached from the centre along the beautiful bayside road by bus #33 ("via Fróes"). On the way, it's worth taking a look at the church of **São Francisco Xavier**, a pretty colonial church said to have been built in 1572. The church is open rather irregularly, but the priest lives next door and will open it up on request.

A short distance southeast along the coast, through Jurujuba, is the **Fortaleza de Santa Cruz** dating from the sixteenth century. The largest fort guarding the bay, it's still in use as a military establishment, but you can visit daily between 9am and 4pm. Check out the archeology museum as well if you have time, the **Museu de Arqueologia de Itaipu** (Wed–Sun 1–5pm), in the ruined eighteenth-century Santa Teresa convent near Itaipu beach. Around here, to the east of Niterói, beyond the bay, there are loads of **restaurants, bars and hotels**, all of which fill up with *cariocas* at weekends. The only particularly distinctive place to eat in Itaipu – or, for that matter, anywhere in Niterói – is *Coelho á Caçarola* at Av. Central 20 (closed Mon–Wed) which has on its menu some 25 different rabbit dishes. **Tourist information** is available from a helpful office in São Francisco at Estrada Leopoldo Fróes 773 (Mon–Fri 9am–6pm).

Maricá and Saquerema

MARICÁ, 40km from Niterói, is the first stop on the Costa do Sol. A small fishing centre standing on the north bank of the lagoon, its peaceful waters are only narrowly separated from the ocean surf by the **Barra de Maricá** and **Ponta Negra** beaches. From Ponta Negra the view of the coast is breathtaking, while the atmosphere here is more laid-back than in Rio de Janeiro's Zona Sul. Nearby, in **UBATIBA**, the colonial farm of Rio Fundo has been turned into a museum exhibiting relics from the centuries of slavery.

SAQUEREMA, 100km to the east of Rio, is a larger town in a beautiful natural setting, squeezed between the sea and its 16-kilometre-long lagoon, retaining vestiges of its origins as a fishing village. Local anti-pollution legislation means that the environment still sustains much wildlife, including the *microleão* monkey which you may be able to glimpse on a walk into the nearby forests. Saquerema has a healthy agricultural sector, too, based on fruit cultivation, and orchards surround the town. The main business nowadays, though, is holidaymaking: you'll find holiday homes, art and craft shops and young surfers here in abundance. The **Praia de Itaúna**, 3km from town, is favourite with the surfers, who gather every year for the National Championship in mid-May. A strong undertow makes its waters potentially dangerous for the casual swimmer. If you want to swim without struggling against the currents head instead for the **Praia da Vila**, where the seventeenth-century church, Nossa Senhora de Nazaré (daily 8am–5pm), stands on the rocky promontory. For fishing, the **Praia de Jaconé** is a popular haunt, stretching 4km west of Saquerema.

All in all, if you're looking for a place to stop awhile, there's a lot to recommend Saquerema: a relaxed atmosphere, plenty of bars and restaurants, and lots of action at the weekend. **Places to stay** near the centre of town include the *Lagoa Azul*, Av. Saquerema 1580 (☎0246/51-1142; ④), which has a pool, and the *Pousada Berro d'Agua* at Av. Oceânica 165 (☎0246/51-1876; ③). Simpler, but friendly, is the Pousada da Mansão, Av. Oceânica 353 (no ☎; ②), which also permits camping.

Araruama and around

Fourteen kilometres further along the coast, **ARARUAMA** stands on the edge of one of the largest lakes in Brazil. The lake – of the same name as the town – covers an area of 192 square kilometres, its saline water fringed with sand that is said to be effective in treating rheumatic and dermatological conditions. The water is clean and the white, sandy banks shine as bright as snow under the tropical sun.

The town itself has started to sprawl a bit as holiday homes, campsites and hotels have been built to accommodate the growing numbers of *cariocas* who come here at the weekend. Nonetheless it's still relatively small-scale and there's no shortage of unpolluted beaches within walking distance – bathed most evenings in the warm glow of sunsets so beautiful that they evoke tranquillity in even the most boisterous of week-enders. While there are **beaches** all round the town, the most popular ones are located some distance away – **Praia Seca**, the nearest of these, with its impressive dunes, is some 16km away, part of the much larger **Maçambaba** beach, which continues all the way to Arraial do Cabo (see p.114). The road between Araruama and Cabo Frio passes alongside these beaches; there's an occasional bus, or you can take a taxi, though either way it can be hard to get transport back.

Accommodation choices in Araruama include the luxury beachside *Hotel Senzala* (☎0246/24-2230; ⑥), 10km from the centre in the district of Iguabinha, and the *Parque Hotel Aruarema* (☎0246/65-2129; ④), nearer the centre at Rua Argentina 502, both of which have pools. The *Hotel Carrateiro* (②), on the outskirts of town on the intersection of Rua Dom Pedro I and Rua Martin Alfonso, is your cheapest bet.

São Pedro da Aldeia

Around Araruama is one of Brazil's most important salt-producing regions, and the windmills that pull the saline solution up to the surface dominate the skyline. The salt-pans into which the solution emerges are of various sizes but are always square and arranged juxtaposed like a great patchwork quilt, speckled with small piles of salt brushed into heaps from the surface of the pans. At the north end of Araruama lake, the small town of **SÃO PEDRO DA ALDEIA**, a 22-kilometre bus ride east of Araruama on the way to Cabo Frio, is built around a Jesuit church and mission house (Mon–Fri 8am–noon & 2–5pm, Sat & Sun 8am–noon) which date back to 1617. Perched on a hill above the shores of the lake, the town provides a marvellous view over the salt-pans and surrounding area.

The cheapest **hotel** in town is the *Lobo* on Rua Dr. Antônio Alves 50 (☎0194/21-2411; ③), but if you're after a pool, try the *Pousada Sal e Sol*, a couple of kilometres from the centre of town at Alameida Geniho 60 (☎0194/21-2315; ⑤). Excellent fish dishes are served at the *Restaurante Vovó Chica* at Av. Getúlio Vargas 32.

To Araruama and Cabo Frio via Rio Bonito

Instead of reaching Araruama along the coast there's a **direct bus** from Rio's *Rodoviária*, useful if your final destination is either Cabo Frio or Búzios. Buses leave every hour and you can buy tickets from the 1001 bus company at their office in the *Rodoviária*.

The route leaves Niterói by the BR-101, heading inland towards São Gonçalo, then takes the BR-104 to Itaboraí, turning towards the coast again at Rio Bonito. After Itaboraí, the bus enters a wide valley, ringed by mountains rising either side in the distance. At **RIO BONITO**, the road rises into a tumbling mountain range, whose fertile, verdant slopes and valleys are taken up by **coffee** plantations; everywhere, thousands of coffee bushes stand in neat, well-tended rows. Once through the mountains, you descend to the sea, with the corrupt odour of the saltworks assaulting your nose as you speed between the saltpans into Araruama and on to Cabo Frio.

Cabo Frio

During the summer months, and especially at weekends, **CABO FRIO** is at a pitch of holiday excitement, generated by the out-of-towners who come here to relax in the fresh sea breezes. The town was founded in the late sixteenth century, but it's only really in the twentieth century that it's developed, thanks to the salt and tourist industries. Cabo Frio is built around sand dunes and there are **beaches** everywhere: indeed, this is the only attraction, since the town is neither attractive nor well planned, but it is a relaxed place and the bars are full of happy holidaymakers at night.

The closest beaches to town are the small **Praia do Forte**, near the centre, with its fort of **São Mateus** (daily 8am–6pm) built by the French in 1616 for protection against pirates, and the larger, more popular **Praia da Barra**. The best beaches, though, all lie outside Cabo Frio, a taxi ride or decent walk away on the route to Arraial do Cabo, another small town a few kilometres to the south (see p.114). Six kilometres north in the direction of Búzios, near Ogivas, lies **Praia Peró**, a good surfing spot, peaceful and deserted on weekdays, and further on lies the small **Praia das Conchas**, with its sand dunes and clear, calm, blue waters.

On arrival, it's a three-kilometre walk in from the **bus station** to the centre, along Avenida Júlia Kubitschek. There are excellent bus connections to and from Rio, São Paulo, Belo Horizonte and Petrópolis as well as up and down the coast. Praça Porto Rocha, the location of the very helpful **tourist office**, telephone office and Banco do Brasil, marks the centre of town. Alongside the square is one of the town's very few buildings of note, the church of **Nossa Senhora da Assunção**, built in 1615 by the Jesuits, which has been perfectly preserved. One block west of here, at Largo de Santo Antônio 55, is the *correiro*.

Practicalities

There are plenty of **hotels** and **pousadas** in and around Cabo Frio, though during summer weekends it can be difficult to find a room. The lowest priced *pousadas* are in the town centre on Rua Jorge Lóssio and Rua José Bonifácio; the best ones include *Porto Fino* on the former at no. 160 (☎0246/43-6230; ③), and *Cochicho do Xandico* at no. 224 (☎0246/43-2525; ③), and on the latter, *Atlântico* at no. 302 (☎0246/43-0996; ③). Most hotels and *pousadas*, however, are concentrated along the beaches. Praia do Peró boasts Cabo Frio's most expensive hotel, the small and very comfortable *La Plage* (☎0246/43-5690; ⑦). On the same beach is the more attractive *Quintais das Dunas* (☎0246/43-3894; ⑤) which also has a pool. The *Praia do Peró* (☎0246/43-2182; ④) is more basic. Closer to town, there are plenty of places on Praia do Forte at lower rates:

Porto Fino II (☎0246/43-3291; ③). There are also several good **youth hostels**, all charging around $12 per person: a short walk from the bus station (turn right when exiting it) is the *Pousada Suzy*, Av. Júlia Kubitschek 22 (☎0246/43-1742), and behind it is the *Albergue Muxarabi*. Best of all, about 1km from the bus station, is the *Praia da Palmeiras* at Rua das Palmeiras 1 (☎0246/43-2866).

Cabo Frio has no shortage of **restaurants** both in the town centre and on the beaches. In the centre, the *Picolino* at Rua Marechal Floriano 319 is noted for serving the town's best fish dishes, while at Praia do Forte, *La Carreta*, Av. Nilo Peçanha 443, is an excellent *churrascaria*.

Arraial do Cabo

Six kilometres south of Cabo Frio, **ARRAIAL DO CABO** nestles amongst more sand dunes, surrounded by hills. It's home to the Institute of Marine Research, based on Cabo Frio island (4km east of the town), whose object is to increase the level of marine life in the region. The aim is a laudable one, though it's uncertain whether the purpose is ecological or has to do with replenishing stocks for next season's marine sports. The **beaches** around Arraial do Cabo are good: the main ones – Grande, Prainha and Pontal – can be reached on foot, while Forno can only be reached by boat from the town. You can also go by boat to the **Ilha de Cabo Frio**, a large unspoilt island with excellent beaches, sand dunes and superb views from its 390-metre peak. You might be interested, too, in the **Manoel Camargo Centre for Popular Arts**, on Avenida Liberdade, which has an excellent collection of arts and crafts on display. It's a much more attractive place to stay than over-developed Cabo Frio, but there's little in the way of budget **accommodation**: try the *Porto dos Anjos* (☎0246/22-1629; ②), the *Pousada das Canoas* (☎0246/22-1212, ext. 277; ④) or the *Hotel Praia dos Anjo* (☎0246/22-1378; ④), all at Praia dos Anjos. There is, however, a **youth hostel** at Rua Joaquim Nabuco 23.

Búzios

Keep time free for **ARMAÇÃO DOS BÚZIOS**, or Búzios as it's more commonly known; direct buses run from Rio five times a day, or every thirty minutes from Cabo Frio, a bumpy fifty-minute ride along a cobbled road. A place of great natural beauty, it's a bit like taking a step out of Brazil and into some high-spending Mediterranean resort: built in the Portuguese colonial style, its narrow cobbled streets are lined with restaurants, bars and chic boutiques where you can buy beach gear at extortionate prices. Búzios has been nicknamed "Brazil's St Tropez", and it comes as little surprise to find that it was "discovered" by none other than Brigitte Bardot, who stumbled upon it by accident while touring the area in 1964. Despite being transformed overnight from humble fishing village to playground of the rich, Búzios didn't change much until, during the last decade, some serious property development took hold. Now, during the high season, the population swells from 8000 to 38,000, the fishing boats that once ferried the catch back to shore take pleasure-seekers island-hopping and scuba diving, and the roads connecting the town with the outlying beaches have been paved.

The town and its beaches

Búzios consists of three settlements, each with its own distinct character. **Manguinos**, on the isthmus, is the main commercial centre with a tourist office, Banco do Brasil and a 24-hour medical centre. Midway along the peninsula is **Armação** where many of Búzio's best restaurants are concentrated. Continuing from Armação, along the coast, you reach **Ossos**, the oldest settlement with a pretty harbour, a tourist information booth, bars, restaurants and hotels.

Within walking distance of all the settlements are 27 white-sand **beaches**, cradled between rocky cliffs and promontories, and bathed by crystal blue waters. It doesn't matter which you choose – Brava, Ossos, Ferradura, Geribá – as each is charming, the ocean offshore studded with little islands covered in luxuriant vegetation. The Brava, Ferradura and João Fernandes beaches all have *barracas*, which serve cold beer and fried fish. You can rent kayaks or pedalos, or indulge in a little windsurfing or diving. And in the evening, bars and restaurants fill up after 9pm and stay open till late, while the streets are the venue for some designer strolling – Ray Bans in hand and designer knitwear draped over shoulders.

Accommodation

Accommodation is expensive and in the high season, December to February, reservations are essential; if you can't find a room in Búzios, you could consider staying in Cabo Frio where rooms are always cheaper and easier to come by. Most of the lower-priced *pousadas* are in or near Armação.

Pousada do Arco Íris, Rua Manoel Turíbio de Faria 182, Armação (☎0246/23-1256). One of the cheaper *pousadas* in town. ④.

Pousadinha em Búzios, Rua Manoel Turíbio de Faria 202, Armação (☎0246/23-1448). Very pretty and worth trying if you're looking for something as inexpensive as possible. ③.

Pousada Byblos, Morro do Humaitá (☎0246/23-1162). Comfortable rooms and a pool set amidst beautiful surroundings. ⑥.

Estalagem, Rua de Pedra 156, Armação (☎0246/23-1243). This *pousada* has nice rooms opening on to a courtyard and a bar with live jazz in the evenings. ④.

Pousada Mediterrânea, Rua João Fernandes 58, Ossos (☎0246/23-2353). Small and friendly with a delightful view. ④.

Pousada Moana, Praça Eugênio Harold, usually referred to as Praça Ossos (☎0246/23-1355). A small *pousada* built round a lovely courtyard with a swimming pool. ⑤.

Hotel Nas Rocas (☎0246/29-1303). The most exclusive place to stay, a resort on its own private tropical island, the Ilha Rasa. Getting there is straightforward: you can either arrange to be met by one of the hotel's boats for the 10-minute crossing or, should you happen to have your own helicopter, there's a landing pad on the island. ⑧.

Pousada dos Sete Oecaods Capitais, Praça Eugênio Harold, Ossos (☎0246/23-1408). One of the more reasonable places in Búzios if you're trying to keep the costs down. ④.

Eating and drinking

Restaurants are, predictably, expensive, and in the off season many close. The greatest concentration is in Armação along Rua de Pedra, with *Le Streghe* at no. 201 serving fine Italian food and *La Poste Restante*, no. 222, and *Au Cheval Blanc*, no. 181, specializing in excellent French dishes. Cheaper options include the *barracas* on the beaches selling grilled fish or the numerous pizza places. Finally, there's always the Belgian-run *Chez Michou Crêperie* on Rua de Pedras, a popular evening hangout thanks to its open-air bar, cheap drinks and excellent crepes.

Northeast to Campos

If you're not yet tired of **beaches**, you'll find more beautiful examples around the pretty colonial village of Barra de São João and Rio das Ostras, an hour or so up the coast. Near the latter, the iodized waters of the **Lagoa da Coca Cola** (yes, really) boast more medicinal qualities – everyone must be very healthy in this neck of the woods. If you want to stay round here, you'll find *pousadas* in both these places.

The next town of any size is **MACAÉ**, on the edge of a large sugarcane-producing region. Again, you'll find excellent beaches here, but the city is more industrial than what has gone before, and the arrival of offshore oil drilling seems unlikely to increase its attractions. From here the main road heads northeast, inland around the Lagoa Feia, to **CAMPOS**, on the River Paraíba some 50km before it flows into the sea. Again it's predominantly a sugarcane-producing town, and its primarily agro-industrial nature makes it a less than attractive target, given the local alternatives.

West: the Costa Verde

The mountainous littoral and calm green waters of the aptly named **Costa Verde** ("Green Coast") provide a marked contrast to the sand and surf of the coastline east of Rio. One of Brazil's truly beautiful landscapes, the Costa Verde has been made much more accessible by the **Rio–Santos BR-101 Highway** – something, however, that has led to an increase in commercial penetration of this region. The fate of this 280-kilo-metre stretch of lush vegetation, rolling hills and tropical beaches hangs in the balance between rational development and ecological destruction, and so far the signs augur badly. Ecologists warn that fish stocks in the Bay of Sepetiba, which covers almost half the length of the Costa Verde, are in constant danger of destruction because of pollu-tion. Enjoy your trip; you may be amongst the last to have the privilege.

There are two ways to reach the Costa Verde from Rio. By **car**, drive through the Zona Sul by way of Barra de Tijuca, to Barra de Guaratiba. The road runs past kilome-tre after kilometre of white sand, but you'll need to be mobile to reach any of it. Alternatively, take one of the **buses** from Rio's *Rodoviária*, which leave the city by the Zona Norte and follow the BR-101 to Itacuruçá and beyond.

Itacuruçá

ITACURUÇÁ, around 90km from Rio, is a tranquil hamlet that attracts wealthy yacht-ing types. The attraction here is obvious: the village nestles between rolling hills and a malachite-coloured sea, its offshore **islands** – Jaguanum and Itacaruçú, with their pleasant walks and beaches – easily reached by boat. Tours of the islands can be arranged with the **tourist office** at Praça da Igreja 130, in Itacuruçá, or are operated direct from Rio (ask at *Passamar Turismo*, Rua Siqueira Campos 7; ☎021/233-8835).

Both islands have luxury **hotels**, the *Hotel Elias C* (☎021/287-5796; ⑨) and *Hotel Pierre* (☎021/247-8938; ⑦) on Itacuruçú, and *Hotel Jaguanum* (☎021/235-2893; ⑦) on the neighbouring island.

Mangaratiba

Muddy beaches and the incongruous industrial presence of the *Terminal de Sepetiba* put off many people stopping at **MANGARATIBA**, which lies 25km west of Itacuruçá along the BR-101. The town setting is attractive though, with a mountain backdrop, a beautiful bay in front with fishing boats at anchor and a late eighteenth-century church dominating the main square.

Ferries make the hour-and-forty-minute trip to Ilha Grande (see p.119), and there are also some very good **beaches** just about within walking distance of the town – to the north, da Ribeira (2km), Ibicuí (5km), Brava (6km) and Grande (14km) are the main ones, while to the south lie do Saco (3km), São Bras (9km) and Goiabal (16km), the site of a *Club Mediterranée* (☎021/789-1635). Anyone will tell you where to find them, but on the whole the initial impression is the correct one; there are better spots to stay further along the coast.

Five **buses** a day run from Rio to Mangaratiba – currently at 5.30am, 9am, 12.30pm, 3pm and 6.45pm – and if you catch the earliest bus you'll make the daily ferry to Ilha

Grande. Nevertheless, if you do need to stay, Mangaratiba is by no means an unpleasant place to spend a night. There are a couple of **hotels** in town, the very basic *Rio Branco* (②) on the main square and the *Pensão do Almir* (④) on the road leading to the hospital. Heading from the main square along the seashore, you'll find several good fish restaurants.

Angra dos Reis

From Mangaratiba, the road continues to hug the coast as it wends its way westwards, rising and falling between towering green-clad mountains and the ocean. Roughly 60km west of Mangaratiba lies **ANGRA DOS REIS**, a shabby little town, but nevertheless one with a history. The lands around here were "discovered" by the navigator André Gonçalves in 1502, though it wasn't until 1556 that a colonial settlement was established. The port first developed as an entrepot for the exportation of agricultural produce from São Paulo and Minas Gerais. Fifteen slave-worked sugar refineries dominated the local economy which, with the abolition of slavery at the end of the nineteenth century, suffered a dramatic collapse. The 1930s saw the economy regenerated, with the construction of a new port, and shipbuilding remains an important local trade – although the latest venture is Brazil's first nuclear power station, located nearby.

The main reason to come here is to get out to the thirty or so islands in the bay, but the town itself is worth a look on the way, and it's easy enough to tour on foot. There are guided tours (daily 10am–5pm) around the late sixteenth-century church and convent of

---

TIMEBOMBS IN PARADISE

There's no doubt that the Costa Verde is one of Brazil's most beautiful stretches of coast, so it's not surprising that so many hotel and holiday home complexes are appearing on the hillsides and in the picturesque coves. What is incredible, however, is that the coast has been chosen as the location of two of the potentially most environmentally destructive complexes – an oil terminal and a nuclear power plant.

The Petrobrás **oil terminal** is, at least, out of sight, located 25km east of Angra, so you only need contemplate the damage that an oil spill could wreak on this ecologically fragile stretch of coast when you pass the barrack-like housing complexes for the Petrobrás workers on the BR-101, the main coastal road towards Angra.

Perhaps more worrying are the **nuclear power plants**, Angra-1 and Angra-2, some 40km west of Angra. The project was directly managed by the Brazilian military and it's difficult to imagine a more insane place to put a nuclear reactor. Not only is it sited by a particularly pretty little bay, a few hundred metres from BR-101, but there would be enormous difficulties should an emergency evacuation be necessary, as the mountains here plunge directly into the sea. In addition, the plant is in an earthquake fault zone, in a cove that local Indians call *Itaorna*, the moving rock.

The plant's safety record is already in doubt, and since 1985 it has been shut down for unspecified repairs over twenty times. In 1993, an accident led officials to admit to a rise in radiation levels within the plant and it has been closed since. Officials insist that there has been no leak of radiation beyond the plant, but environmentalists say there may be cracks in the reactor's primary container system and want it shut down for good. No decision has been made about the plant's future but it would be humiliating for the military to abandon the project – Angra-1 can supply 20 percent of Brazil's electricity needs and Angra-2 is still being built and there would be huge problems to solve in decommissioning the plant.

If you want to visit the plant, the **Visitors' Centre** offers a predictably professional public relations show (Mon–Fri 8.30am–4.30pm, Sat & Sun 8.30am–3pm), but otherwise it's impossible not to see the enormous site from the road.

Nossa Senhora do Carmo, in Praça Osório, as well as around the mid-eighteenth-century church and convent of **São Bernardino de Sena** (Tues–Sun 8–11am & 1–5pm), on the Morro de Santo Antônio. Best use of time, though, is to take in the old **town hall** and jail, in Praça Nilo Peçanha, an interesting colonial building dating from the beginning of the seventeenth century and still in use today as the municipal seat of government. For all the historical interest, however, Angra dos Reis suffers from its rather unprepossessing aspect, and in the end most people usually can't wait to get out.

Boat trips and beaches

Boat and fishing trips are Angra's stock in trade, and a tour of the local islands – Cataguazes, Pitanguí, Duas Botinas, Senhor do Bonfim, Gipóia and Do Maia (amongst others) – is an absorbing experience. Numerous leisurely cruises around the bay are on offer, and most yachts have a bar at which you can fill the time between stops for swimming at beaches penned in between clear waters and tropical forest. Visiting **Gipóia** by boat, for instance, allows you a couple of hours to splash about and get something to eat in the *Luiz Rosa* bar – all very relaxing.

Various companies run trips, so it's best to ask at the **tourist information office** (daily 8am–6pm) in Largo do Lapa, right across from the bus station and next to the **Cais de Santa Luzia**, from where the boats depart. Trips can also be arranged on the quay with independent operators, but check on the noticeboard for those boat owners who have been authorized to carry tourists. Most trips leave around 10am and return in the late afternoon. Prices with independent boat operators vary, but on average you'll pay around $10 a head.

Beaches in the town are nothing special. Better ones are found by following the Estrada do Contorno (by car), or catching a **bus** from the bus terminal (Vila Velha line; buses leave hourly) to the beaches of Bonfim, Gordas, Grande, Tanguá, Tanguazinho, Ribeira or Retiro. There are other beaches within reach, too: along the main BR-101 highway, in the direction of Rio, good spots for bathing and free camping are Garatucaia and Monsuaba.

Practicalities

Back in Angra dos Reis, the bus terminal, tourist information and ferry for Ilha Grande (see p.119) are all located within a few steps of each other. There's no shortage of **hotels** if you're planning to stay around for the beaches and islands, but most are on the pricey side. Try the modest but comfortable *Hotel Londres*, Av. Raul Pompéia 75 (☎0243/65-0044; ④). At a similar price, but not as good, is the *Palace Hotel*, Rua Coronel Carvalho 275 (☎0243/65-0032; ④), while, for only slightly more, you'll get a pool at the *Acrópolis Marina* on Avenida das Caravelas (☎0243/65-2225; ④).

There'll be no trouble **eating and drinking** either, with lots of restaurants and bars: try *Cheiro Verde*, Rua Pereira Peixoto 53, which has Arab cuisine, and *Taberna 33* at Av. Raul Pompéia 110 which serves decent pizzas.

Serra do Mar

If you want to take a break from beaches, the forested **Serra do Mar** lies inland immediately behind Angra. By far the easiest and most enjoyable way to penetrate the forest is by **train**, on the line constructed a hundred years ago to export coffee from the once-rich coffee region of Rio Claro. Today the line is mainly used to take coal to the Volta Redonda steel mills, but on weekends and holidays, a train takes tourists 40km inland as far as Lídice. The single-track route is an impressive engineering feat, and the views along the entire route are impressive. The train stops from time to time, allowing passengers to take pictures of the coast below, waterfalls and forest. The train leaves Angra at 10.30am, arriving back at 4.30pm; tickets ($22 including lunch on the train) should be purchased at least a day in advance from Montmar Turismo, Rua do Comércio 11, Angra (☎0243/65-1705).

Some 22km beyond Angra, there's an excellent **youth hostel**, the *Hospedagem Rio Bracuí* (☎021/531-2234), a little way inland on the bank of the Rio Bracuí. This is an excellent spot from which to take walks into the Serra do Mar following any of the numerous forest trails. To get here, take any bus going along the coast and get off just after the bridge which crosses the Rio Bracuí. Turn right and head inland along the Estrada do Surubim, and the hostel is located 200m on your left.

Ilha Grande

ILHA GRANDE comprises 193 square kilometres of mountainous jungle, historic ruins and beautiful beaches (amongst which Praia Lopes Mendes is outstanding) – excellent for some scenic tropical rambling. The main drawback is the ferocity of the local insects, so come equipped with repellent.

Islands like this deserve a good pirate story, and Ilha Grande is no exception. According to legend, the pirate **Jorge Grego** was heading for the Straits of Magellan when his ship was sunk by a British fleet. He managed to escape with his two daughters to Ilha Grande, where he became a successful farmer and merchant. In a fit of jealousy he murdered the lover of one of his daughters and, shortly afterwards, a terrible storm destroyed all his farms and houses. From then on, Jorge Grego passed his time roaming the island, distraught, pausing only long enough to bury his treasure before his final demise. If there is any treasure, though, it's in the island's **wildlife**: parrots, exotic hummingbirds, butterflies and monkeys abound in the thick vegetation. To the west of the island there's an **ecological reserve** where it's all easily observed for free.

Ilha Grande offers lots of beautiful **walks**, but it's sensible to take some basic precautions. Even with a map the island's trails can be extremely confusing, so it's a good idea to go with a local guide; set out as early as possible and inform people at your *pousada* where you are going, if possible in writing. Carry plenty of water with you and remember to apply sunscreen and insect repellent at regular intervals. Darkness comes suddenly, and even on a night with a full moon, the trails are likely to be pitch-black due to the canopy formed by the overhanging foliage; if at all possible, carry a flashlight with you – most *pousadas* will be happy to lend you one. Whatever you do, avoid straying from the trail: in part this is because you could easily get hopelessly lost, and in part because of rumours of booby traps primed to fire bullets, left over from the days when the island hosted a high-security prison.

Around the island

As you approach the low-lying, whitewashed colonial port of **VILA DO ABRAÃO**, the mountains rise dramatically from the sea, and in the distance there's the curiously shaped summit of Bico do Papagaio ("Parrot's Beak"), which rises to a height of 980m and can be reached with the assistance of a local guide in about three hours. On the opposite side of the island from Vila Abraão are the ruins of the **Antigo Presídio**. Originally built as a hospital, it was converted to a prison for political prisoners in 1910 and was finally dynamited in the early 1960s. Among the ruins, you'll find the *cafofo*, the containment centre where prisoners who had failed in escape attempts were immersed in freezing water. The ruins can be reached in about two and a half hours from Abraão by following the island's only road – the walk there is not particularly enjoyable, but you'll be rewarded for your efforts by reaching a stunningly beautiful beach. Nearer to Vila do Abraão, and overgrown with vegetation, stands the **Antigo Aqueduto** which used to channel the island's water supply. There's a fine view of the aqueduct from the

Pedra Mirante, a hill near the centre of the island, and, close by, a waterfall provides the opportunity for a cool bathe on a hot day.

For the most part the **beaches** – Canto, Júlia, Comprida, Crena or Morcegoare, to name a few – are still wild and unspoilt. They can be reached either by **hiring a boat** ($10–12 per hour) and circumnavigating the island's coast or **on foot** across the many trails that network the interior. The hike from Abraão to **Praia da Parnaioca** will take about five hours, so it's no jaunt and a guide is absolutely essential. By the *praia* is a ghost town, an old fishing village abandoned by its inhabitants because of their fear of escaped prisoners from the former high-security prison on the island and only slowly coming back to life. The prison was closed in April 1994, not before earning the island something of a dangerous reputation as escapes were not infrequent. Today the only dangers come from *borachudos*, almost invisible but vicious gnats that bite without your feeling or hearing them.

Practicalities

There are **boats** from both Mangaratiba and Angra dos Reis to Abraão on Ilha Grande, each taking ninety minutes or so. From **Mangaratiba** to Abraão, the boat leaves at 8.30am daily and returns at 5.30pm Monday, Wednesday and Friday, 11am Tuesday and Thursday and 4pm Saturday and Sunday. From **Angra dos Reis**, boats leave for Abraão at 3pm on Monday, Wednesday and Friday, returning at 9pm Monday, Wednesday and Friday. Tickets cost $5; if you miss the ferry you might to be tempted to hire a small launch to do the crossing for around $40–50. If you have a car, you'll have to leave it behind on the mainland, but you can get advice at the ferry terminals on where to find a secure, lock-up parking spot.

Accommodation is mostly around Vila do Abraão, and when you arrive you'll probably be approached by youths intent on taking you to a room. One of the best places, though, is in Praia Grande (a 2hr walk or 20min boat ride) on the trail to Praia Lopes Mendes: the *Fazenda Paraíso do Sol*, the largest hotel on the island and the only one with its own pool (make reservations in Rio on ☎021/262-1226; ⑥). In Abraão, one of the nicest options is the *Pousada Mar da Tranquilidade* (☎0243/65-2833; ⑤ half-board), which is rather expensive but has excellent rooms with hot showers; otherwise try the *Tropicana* (Rio ☎021/331-8227; ⑤), *Holândes* (Rio ☎021/331-8227; ④), *Beto's* (Rio ☎021/780-1202; ③) and *Alpinos* (São Paulo ☎011/229-1073; ③). Reservations in the high season, especially at weekends, are essential. If you can cope with the bugs, **camping** is a possibility as there are several good, secure sites in Abraão, some of which are attached to *pousadas* – off-site camping is strictly forbidden. Finally, there's a **youth hostel** in Abraão, which charges $12 a night (☎021/264-6147).

Nightlife is reasonably lively with seafood restaurants and bars, while the *Calango da Jovina* bashes out some eminently danceable *forró* music. **Carnaval** is well celebrated here, much more relaxed and less intense than the Rio experience; and watch, too, for the festival of São João (Jan 20) and the Pirate Regatta, which takes place in February.

Tarituba

Back on the mainland, the road west rises amidst the most exhilarating scenery that the whole coast has to offer. About 60km from Angra, is **TARITUBA**, a charming little fishing village, still relatively untouched by tourism. Any bus going along the coast will let you off at the side road that leads to the village, or there are buses several times a day from Parati, 35km further west.

There's not much to the village – a pier along which fishing boats land their catches, a few *barracas* on the beach serving fried fish and cold drinks and a pretty church – it's simply a place to relax in, away from the often brash commercialism of Angra and Parati. There are a couple of decent **pousadas**, but it can be difficult to get a room in high season or even to make telephone reservations. The most comfortable is the *Tarituba* (☎0243/65-2401 or 021/987-3205; ④) which has large rooms with private verandas and hammocks overlooking the pool and beach beyond. Simple, but very friendly and right on the beach is the *Pousada de Carminha* (☎0243/71-1120; ③) whose large rooms do not have private bathrooms. Bear in mind that here, as right along the coast, the *borachudos* and mosquitoes are murder, so bring plenty of insect repellent and mosquito coils with you.

Parati

About 300km from Rio on the BR-101 is the Costa Verde's main attraction, the town of **PARATI**. Inhabited since 1650, Parati (or more correctly, Vila de Nossa Senhora dos Remédios de Paraty) has remained fundamentally unaltered since its heyday as a staging post for the eighteenth-century trade in Brazilian gold, passing from Minas Gerais to Portugal. Before white settlement, the land had been occupied by the **Guaianá Indians**, and the gold routes followed the old Indian trails down to Parati and its sheltered harbour. Inland raids and pirate attacks necessitated the establishment of a new route linking Minas Gerais directly with Rio de Janeiro, and as trade was diverted to

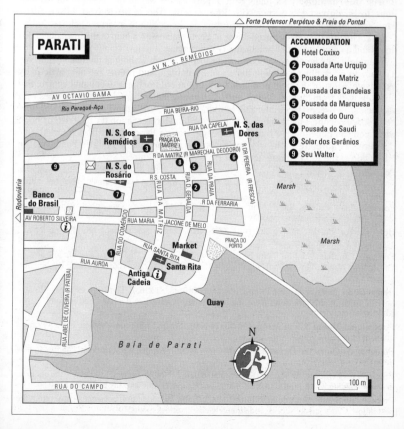

Rio, Parati's fortunes declined. Apart from a short-lived coffee-shipping boom in the nineteenth century, Parati remained hidden away off the beaten track, quietly stagnating but intact. Nowadays, though, UNESCO considers Parati to represent one of the world's most important examples of Portuguese colonial architecture, and the entire city has been elevated to the status of a national monument.

Today, Parati is very much alive, with its population of 15,000 involved in fishing, farming and tourism. The town centre was one of Brazil's first planned urban projects, and its narrow cobbled streets, out of bounds to motorized transport, are bordered by houses built around courtyards, adorned with brightly coloured flowers and alive with hummingbirds. The cobbles of the streets are arranged in channels to drain off storm water and allow the sea to enter and wash the streets at high tides and full moon. There's an air of prosperity in Parati, as there is in Búzios, yet it has a much more democratic feel to it, and by and large provides a more satisfying experience than its chic counterpart on the Costa do Sol.

Arrival, information and accommodation

The **bus station** is about half a kilometre from the old town; turn right out of the station and walk straight ahead. The best way to orientate yourself is to head for the **tourist information kiosk** (daily 8am–11pm), on the way to the old town on Avenida Roberto Silveiro at the corner with Rua Patitiba. The **main tourist office** (daily 8am–7pm; ☎0243/71-1266) is next to Igreja de Santa Rita in a former jail, the Antiga Cadeia. The office supplies a guidebook in Portuguese with a map of the town, local bus times and a complete list of hotels and restaurants.

You might well be offered **accommodation** by people waiting at the bus station, but it's easy to track down yourself; the standard is high, and rooms are not particularly expensive. Most of the best **pousadas** are in the old Portuguese colonial centre, five minutes' walk from the bus station, and often young lads will guide you to the ones with vacancies. Between December and March, however, this entire area is packed, and hotel space becomes hard to find: if you are without a reservation try to arrive by noon when you can hope to get a room from people leaving Parati earlier than planned.

There's a **campsite** on the way into town, and another on the Praia do Pontal, on the other side of the Rio Perequé-Açu river from the town centre.

Pousada Arte Urquijo, Rua Dona Geralda 79 (☎0243/71-1362). Somewhat pretentious with classical music at all times and lots of works of art on the walls, but very intimate. The pool is tiny, though. ⑤.

Pousada das Candeias, Rua da Matriz 13 (☎0243/71-1246). There's a very pretty patio here with small, simple but adequate rooms. ④.

Hotel Coxixo, Rua do Comercio 362 (☎0243/71-1460). Comfortable rooms, a beautiful garden and a good-size pool. Excellent value. ④.

Pousada Familiar, Rua José Vieira Ramos 262 (☎0243/71-1475).This simple *pousada* just outside the old town is owned by a friendly multilingual Belgian and has clean rooms and laundry facilities. $15 per person.

Pousada da Marquesa, Rua Dona Geralda 99 (☎0243/71-2163). The least expensive luxury hotel in town. Wonderful views from the bedrooms, an attractive pool and all the comfort you could need. ⑥.

Pousada da Matriz, Rua da Matriz (☎0243/71-1610). Small, basic rooms but one of the cheapest in the old town. ③.

Pousada do Ouro, Rua Dr Pereira 145 (☎0243/71-2033). Anyone who is anyone chooses to stay here; discreet luxury. ⑦.

Pousada do Príncipe, Av. Roberto Silveira 289 (☎0243/71-2266). Located just outside the old town in a new building which tries to look old. Good value if you're after a comfy bed and a large pool. ⑤.

Pousada do Sandi, Largo do Rosário (☎0243/71-2100). Vulgar luxury, but some people rate it the best in town. Very snooty service and strangely characterless rooms. ⑦.

Seu Walter, Rua Marechal Deodoro 489 (☎0243/71-2341). Just outside the old town, this is one of the cheapest *pousadas*. Simple but friendly. ②.

Solar dos Gerânios, Praça da Matriz (☎0243/71-1550). A beautiful Swiss-owned *pousada* with rustic furniture and curios. Most rooms have balconies, but try to get one overlooking the square. ③.

The Town

Parati is a perfect place simply to wander aimlessly, each turn of the corner bringing another picturesque view. The town's small enough that there's no danger of getting lost and, no matter what time of day or night, you can feel pretty confident that you won't be a victim of an assault. There are, however, several buildings worth seeking out if you don't happen to come across them anyway.

As with most small colonial towns in Brazil, Parati's churches traditionally each served a different sector of the population. Dating back to 1646, **Nossa Senhora dos Remédios** (daily 9am–5pm) on the Praça da Matriz is Parati's main church and the town's most imposing building. During the late eighteenth century, the church – built for Parati's bourgeoisie – underwent major structural reforms and the exterior, at least, has remained unchanged since then. Parati's aristocracy had their own church built in 1800, the particularly graceful **Igreja das Dores** (daily 1–5pm) with its own small cemetery, three blocks from the main church by the sea. Along Rua do Comércio is the smallest church, the **Igreja do Rosário** (Mon–Fri 9am–noon) built in 1725 and used by the slaves. Finally, at the southern edge of the town is the **Igreja de Santa Rita** (Wed–Sun 10am–noon & 2–5pm), the oldest and architecturally most significant of the town's churches. Built in 1722 for the freed mulatto population, the facade is the most elaborate, in Portuguese Baroque style. Attached to the church is the small Museu de Arte Sacra with a collection of religious artefacts from Parati's churches. Next to Santa Rita you'll find the late eighteenth-century jail, the **Antiga Cadeia**, now the main tourist information office (see p.122) and a handicraft centre. Opposite is the lively **fish market**.

To the north of the old town, across the Rio Perequé-Açu on the Morro de Vilha Velha, is the **Forte Defensor Perpétuo**, constructed in 1703 to defend Parati from pirates seeking to plunder gold ships leaving the port. The fort underwent restoration in 1822 and today the simple structure houses the Museu de Artes e Tradições Populares (Tues–Sun 10am–5pm), with a permanent display of fishing tools and basket ware, and handicrafts for sale.

Beaches and islands

Keeping yourself amused should be no problem, even if you quickly exhaust the possibilities of the town itself. From the **Praia do Pontal** on the other side of the Perequé-Açu River from town, and from the **port quay**, *baleiras* and *saveiros* (whaling and fishing boats) leave for the beaches of Paraty-Mirim, Jurumirim, Lula and Picinguaba. In fact, there are 65 islands and about 200 beaches to choose from, and anyone can tell you which are the current favourites. Hotels and travel agents sell tickets for trips out to the islands, typically at a cost of $15–20 per person, leaving Parati at noon, stopping at three or four islands for a swim and returning at 6pm. You can reach some of the mainland beaches by road – ask at the tourist office for details of bus times or, if you have a car, check the condition of the local roads which often get washed away after heavy rains. **Paraty-Mirim** is a popular choice, but the beaches are dirty, the sea very shallow and utterly calm. Better places to head for are **Trinidade**, where there are several beaches, some with calm seas and others with waves, or the fishing village of **Tarituba** (see p.120). If you're really feeling energetic, you can hire a **mountain bike** for $10 a day from Paraty Tours at Av. Roberto Silveira 11, who also supply maps marked with suggested itineraries covering beaches, mountains or forests. They can also arrange **car rental** for around $70 a day.

The **Boa Vista distillery** is worth a visit, too (boats from the quay). Home of the famous Quero Esse brand of *cachaça*, the old colonial house here was once the residence of Thomas Mann's grandfather, Johan Ludwig Brown, before he returned to Germany in around 1850. The caretaker, and master distiller, will give guided tours of the *alambique* before plying you with a liquor that has distinctly invigorating properties.

Eating, drinking and entertainment

The town has plenty of good **restaurants**, charging an average of $15 for a meal, but prices vary enormously, and often restaurants that look expensive prove to be surprisingly reasonable. Most restaurants make a point of letting you know that their dishes are suitable for two people. Predictably, fish is the local speciality, but there are quite a few pizzerias around, too. There are plenty of watering holes to keep you amused into the evening, but out of season the town is extremely quiet.

In May, June and July **festivals** celebrating local holidays are frequent occasions, and in the square the folk dances – *cerandis*, *congadas* and *xibas* – demonstrate the European and African influences on Brazilian culture.

Around Parati

Another good way to see a bit of the landscape is to catch a bus from the bus station, heading inland towards Cunha, and get off after about 8km at the **Cachoeira das Penhas**, a waterfall up in the mountains that offers a chance to bake on the sunscorched rocks of the river gully and then cool off in the river. From here you can descend from rock to rock for a few hundred metres before scrambling up to the road above you, which, after 2km, crosses a small bridge into **PONTE BRANCA**. At the end of the village, overlooking the river, is a restaurant, the *Ponte Branca*, where you can take a break and have a cold beer. The walk from the waterfall takes you amongst the hills, up and down dale, and past tropical fruit plantations, all very pleasant. You'll probably manage to get a lift back to Parati from the restaurant when you're sufficiently refreshed.

Inland: north to the mountains

Excellent bus services from Rio de Janeiro make the **interior** of the state easily accessible, and its mountainous wooded landscape and relatively cool climate are a pleasant contrast to the coastal heat. There's not a great deal in the way of historical interest, but the scenic beauty of the countryside, studded with small towns still bearing their colonial heritage, is an attraction in itself.

Volta Redonda

From Rio, the Cidade do Aço bus company runs a service along the BR-116 to **VOLTA REDONDA** and the heartland of Brazil's steel industry. Situated on the banks of the **River Paraíba**, the city is dominated by steel mills, and though it may once have been a picturesque little village, it's now an expanding industrial monster.

If you want to visit the **steel mill**, you can, but you need to arrange the guided tour about a week in advance, either with the headquarters of the Companhia Siderúrgica Nacional, Avenida XIII de Maio, Rio de Janeiro, or locally at the *Hotel Alta Bela Vista* (☎0243/48-2022; ⑤). Tour buses leave from Rio and travel direct to the mills; the journey takes about three hours and the price is negligible. If you want to **stay** in the town centre, apart from the *Bela Vista*, there's the *Sider Palace Hotel* at Av. Alberto

Pasqualini 10 (☎0243/48-1032; ⑤) and the *Embaixador* at Travessa Luís Augusto Félix 36 (☎0243/48-3665; ③).

Volta Redonda serves as a textbook example of the (often disastrous) way that Brazil is developing, economically and socially. To all intents and purposes, the city has been a company town since 1941, and the urban structure represents the priorities of the company – slums for the poor and nice neighbourhoods for the management sprawl on opposite sides of the river, the water so polluted by industrial and domestic effluence that its plant and animal life have been almost completely destroyed. Apart from industrial conflict and pollution, according to a report in the *Jornal do Brazil* the citizens of Volta Redonda also have to cope with the highest incidence of hypertension and deaths caused by cardiovascular disease in the country. All this in what four decades ago must have been one of the healthiest climates in Brazil.

If you're not remotely interested in steel production then don't waste your time in Volta Redonda, but press on along the BR-116 highway 40km to Itatiaia Park.

Parque Nacional do Itatiaia

Nestling in the northwest corner of the state, 165km from Rio, between the borders with São Paulo and Minas Gerais, the **Parque Nacional do Itatiaia** is the oldest national park in Brazil, founded in 1937 and covering 120 square kilometres of the Mantigueira mountain range. People come here to climb – favourites are the **Pico das Agulhas Negras** (2787m) and the **Pico de Prateleira** (2540m), and the park is also an important nature reserve.

The park comprises waterfalls, primary forest, wildlife and orchids – but tragically a fire in 1988 ravaged some twenty percent of the park's area. In the area affected by the fire, forest and pasture land were devastated, rare orchids and native conifers (*Podocarpus lamperti* and *Araucaria angustifolia*) destroyed; the fire reached areas of the Serra da Mantigueira, 2500m above sea level, wiping out forty kilometres of mountain pathways. In the areas most favoured by biologists, who come to study the rich fauna and flora, the once beautiful alpine scenery now resembles a lunar landscape. Also severely affected were the many natural springs and streams which combine to form the Bonito, Preto, Pirapitinga and Palmital rivers; these supply the massive hydrographic basin of the Paraíba plate, giving much needed oxygenation to the Paraíba watercourse in one of its most polluted stretches. Ecologists reckon that it will take more than twenty years to repair this environmental disaster. For the casual walker, however, there's still plenty of unaffected park to be seen.

Accommodation and information

The town of **ITATIAIA**, situated on the BR-116, is surrounded by beautiful scenery and makes a good base: it has plenty of **hotels**, mainly found along Via Dutra, the road that links the town and park – take the minibus marked "Hotel Simon" from Praça São José. The *Hotel Simon* itself (☎0243/52-1122; ⑥ full board) is extremely comfortable and in a beautiful setting, with a wonderful orchid garden attached (daily 9–11am). Nearby is the much cheaper *Pousada do Elefante* (④ full board), which is simple but also has a pool. Back in town, there's a **youth hostel** at Rua João Mauricio de Macedo Costa 352 (☎0243/52-1232). There's **cabin accommodation** in the park, but it has to be booked about two weeks in advance at the Administração do Parque Nacional de Itatiaia (☎0243/52-1461) in Itatiaia town. You can get **information** and maps at the park office located near the entrance; and before you come it's worth contacting the Clube Excursionista Brasileira, Av. Almirante Barroso 2, 8th floor, in Rio (☎021/220-3695). Tourist information is also available from the Secretaría de Turismo in Itatiaia, at Rua São José 210 (☎0243/52-1660 ext. 305).

Penedo

The other possible base for the park is the small town of **PENEDO**, which was settled in 1929 by Finnish immigrants. Today much is made of the town's Finnish heritage, despite the fact that only a tiny minority of the population are of Finnish origin. Nevertheless, Finnish dances are performed every Saturday night at the *Clube Finlandia* and it's also a good place if you like saunas. The **Museu Kahvila** – really little more than a snack bar, at Travessa da Fazenda 45 – has a small display relating to Finnish immigration in the region. It's usually easy to find a place to stay – there are dozens of hotels in and near Penedo, though few real budget places. Most people eat at their hotels, whose rates generally include full board, but in town it's worth trying the excellent Finnish-inspired open sandwiches at the *Restaurante Skandinávia*, Av. das Mangueiras 2631 (closed Wed). The town is popular with weekenders from São Paulo and Rio, who come for the horseriding and to buy the various jams, preserves and local liquors which are produced here.

Vassouras, Valença and Conservatória

Northeast of Volta Redonda are a few other small towns which make good targets if you have a car and a few spare days. All are notable for their eighteenth- and nineteenth-century architecture and attractive natural settings.

Vassouras and Valença

Vassouras and Valença are both university towns, and both considered as national historical monuments, key centres of Brazil's nineteenth-century coffee-based economy. Today, dairy farming has almost totally replaced coffee production, but relics from the days when the "coffee barons" reigned supreme locally and nationally are still visible.

VASSOURAS, on the main BR-393, is the smaller and more attractive of the two towns, with many late nineteenth-century buildings in the centre of town around the Campo Belo. However, it's the old **coffee fazenda houses** nearby that are the main attraction, but without your own car you won't be able to see much. The tourist information office is at Rua Barão de Capivari 20 (Mon–Fri 9am–6pm) and will give details of which of the privately owned houses are open for visits. The most impressive ones are located off the RJ-115 highway north of town, with **Santa Mônica** being the oldest, best preserved and generally the most interesting of the houses. Another beautifully preserved house that's often open to visitors is **São Fernando**, about 1km from Massambará, an outlying district in the *município* of Vassouras. If you want to **stay**, the *Mara Palace* at Rua Chanceler Raul Fernandes 121 (☎0244/71-2524; ④) and the *Santa Amelia*, Av. Rui Barbosa 526 (☎0244/71-1897; ⑤), are both central.

VALENÇA is less attractive, but the *fazenda* houses off RJ-145 and RJ-151 to the east merit a look: ask at the tourist office at Praça XV de Novembre 676 (Mon–Fri 9am–6pm). The **hotels** in Valença are simpler and less expensive than in Vassouras. The best is *Hotel dos Engenheiros*, Rua Teodorico Fonseca 525 (☎0244/52-0522; ③), while, near the *Rodoviária*, there's the more basic *Valenciano*, Praça Paulo de Frontin 360 (☎0244/52-0890; ③).

Conservatória

About 30km west of Valença on the BR-143, the little town of **CONSERVATÓRIA**, 518m above sea level, is much visited for its fresh climate. It's a very tranquil place, though perhaps a bit self-conscious of its status as a tourist attraction. There are numerous **hotels** in the town if you want to stay for a night – all much the same, starting at around ④. At night, one or two of the local citizens indulge in a spot of public serenading, maintaining an old and nowadays rare tradition; and the music combines well with the warm breezes, a pleasant background to an evening's relaxation. South of the town, just off RJ-137, are a number of colonial-style mansion houses – for directions and viewing details ask at the tourist office in Valença.

Petrópolis

Sixty-six kilometres directly to the north of Rio de Janeiro, high in the mountains, stands the imperial city of **PETRÓPOLIS**. The route there is a busy one, with Fácil and Única company buses leaving Rio every fifteen minutes, but even so you may have to wait a day or two for a bus with available seats. It's worth the hassle, for the journey there is a glorious one. On the way up, sit on the left-hand side of the bus and don't be too concerned with the driver's obsession with overtaking heavy goods vehicles on blind corners, bordered by naked rock on one side and a sheer drop on the other – it's a one-way road, and the return to Rio is made by a different route which also snakes its way through terrifying mountain passes. The scenery is dramatic, climbing among forested slopes which give way suddenly to ravines and gullies, while clouds shroud the surrounding mountains.

In 1720, Bernardo Soares de Proença opened a trade route between Rio and Minas Gerais, and in return was conceded the area around the present site of Petrópolis as a royal land grant. Surrounded by stunning scenery, and with a gentle, alpine summer climate, it had by the nineteenth century become a favourite retreat of Rio's elite. The arrival of German immigrants contributed to the development of Petrópolis as a town, and has much to do with the curious European Gothic feel to the place. Dom Pedro II took a fancy to Petrópolis and in 1843 designated it the summer seat of his government. He also established an agricultural colony, which failed because of the unsuitability of the soil, and then in 1849 – with an epidemic of yellow fever in Rio – the emperor and his court took refuge in the town, thus assuring Petrópolis' prosperity.

The Town

You can easily do a tour of Petrópolis in a day, returning to Rio in the evening (or continuing inland). Simply strolling around is as good a way to pass the time as any, with plenty of elegant mansions, particularly along **Avenida Koeller**, which has a tree-lined canal running up its centre, or on **Avenida Ipiranga**, where you'll also find the German Lutheran church.

The **Palacio Imperial** on Avenida VII de Setembro (Tues–Sun noon–5pm) is a fine structure, set in beautifully maintained gardens. Once a royal residence, it now houses a fascinating collection of the royal family's bits and pieces. On entry, you're given felt overshoes with which to slide around the polished floors, and inside there's everything from Dom Pedro II's crown (639 diamonds, 77 pearls, all set in finely wrought gold) to the regal commode.

The cathedral of **São Pedro de Alcântara** (Tues–Sun 8am–5pm) blends with the rest of the architecture around, but is much more recent than its rather overbearing neo-Gothic style suggests – it was only finished in 1939. Inside, on the walls, are ten relief sculptures depicting scenes from the Crucifixion; in the mausoleum lie the tombs of Dom Pedro himself, Princess Regent Dona Isabel and several other royal personages. If you need more direction to your strolling, then other grand buildings to track down are the **Palácio de Cristal**, Rua Alfredo Pacha (Tues–Sun 9am–5pm); **Casa Santos Dumont** on Rua do Encanto (Tues–Sun 9.30am–5.30pm), an alpine chalet built in 1918 and the home of the Brazilian aviator of that name; and **Quitandinha** on the Estrada de Quitandinha, just outside of town. Once the Quitandinha Casino, this last building stopped receiving the rich and famous when the Brazilian government prohibited gambling in 1946; today it serves as a sports club. Nearby, at Rua Cristóvão Colombo 1034, is the **Casa do Colono Alémão** (Tues–Sun 9am–1pm), which has a

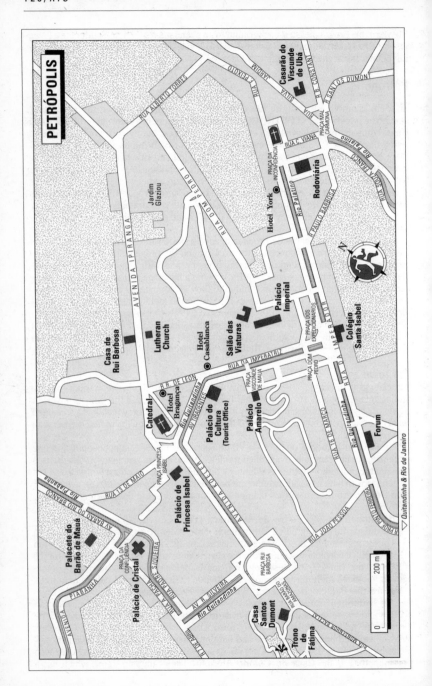

PETRÓPOLIS

Rua Alberto Torres

Casarão do Viscunde de Ubá

Rua Visc. de Itaboraí

Rua C. Viana

Praça da Inconfidência

Rodoviária

R. B. Constant

Praça Mal. Carmona

Hotel York

Rio Palatino

R. Paulo Barbosa

R. Souza Franco

R. Santos Dumont

Jardim Glaziou

Avenida Ipiranga

Rua Dom Pedro I

Palácio Imperial

Colégio Santa Isabel

Praça dos Expedicionários

Casa de Rui Barbosa

Lutheran Church

Hotel Casablanca

Salão das Viaturas

Rua da Imperatriz

Praça Dom Pedro

Praça Visconde de Mauá

Rua da Imperatriz

Catedral

R. R. de Leon

Hotel Bragança

Rio Quitandinha

Av. 7 de Setembro

Palácio de Cultura (Tourist Office)

Palácio Amarelo

Rua 16 de Março

Rio Quitandinha

Forum

Praça Princesa Isabel

Avenida Tiradentes

Palácio de Princesa Isabel

Rua 13 de Maio

Av. Barão do Rio Branco

Rio Piabanha

Rua Silveira

Palacete do Barão de Mauá

Praça da Confluência

Palácio de Cristal

Avenida Piabanha

Praça Rui Barbosa

Av. R. Quitandinha

Rio Quitandinha

Rua João Pessoa

R. Bar. Pinto Pinto Ferreira

Casa Santos Dumont

Trono de Fátima

Rua Amazonas

▽ Quitandinha & Rio de Janeiro

0   200 m

small collection relating to the German immigrants who settled in and around Petrópolis in the early nineteenth century. German-speaking visitors may also be interested in visiting the tomb of the Austrian-born writer **Stefan Zweig** who committed suicide with his wife in Petrópolis. You can take a look at the outside of his house at Rua Gonçalves Dias 34 in the suburb of Valparaiso, near the municipal cemetery.

Practicalities

There's a **tourist office** (Mon–Fri 8.30am–6.30pm, Sat 8.30am–1.30pm) at the Palácio da Cultura near the intersection of Rua da Imperatriz and Avenida Tiradentes. Petrópolis has easy access to some lovely climbing country, and if you're going to do any **hiking**, contact the Centro Alpinista, Rua Irmãos d'Angelo 28 – it's an amateur association, so go after 8pm.

There are some decent **hotels** in town, such as the *Hotel York* at Rua do Imperador 78 (☎0242/43-2662; ③), which is very convenient for the *Rodoviária*, but otherwise lacks atmosphere. A number of former mansions have been converted into hotels: the *Bragança*, behind the cathedral at Rua Raul de Leon 109 (☎0242/42-0434; ④), is very pleasant, as is the *Casablanca*, next to the Palacio Imperial at Rua da Imperatriz 286 (☎0242/42-6662; ④). **Restaurants** are surprisingly poor in Petrópolis, most of the best being some distance from town. However, there's a good and moderately priced Portuguese restaurant in the *Hotel Bragança*, and an excellent budget choice at *Ki-Mania*, Rua do Imperador 898, which has a buffet where you pay by the weight of the food you select. If you have a car, *Chico Verissimo* at Rua Agostino Goulão 632 (closed Mon) serves very good but pricey French food, with a wonderful view from the terrace.

If you're heading on to Teresópolis make sure you travel during the day, so as not to miss the scenery. If you're going to São Paulo or Belo Horizonte, there's no need to return to Rio as there are direct bus services from Petrópolis.

Teresópolis

While **TERESÓPOLIS** can be reached directly from Rio by bus, the best route is from Petrópolis. It's not a long journey, no more than 40km, but the road to this highest town in the state (872m) passes through the **Serra dos Órgãos**, much of which is a national park – dramatic rock formations here resemble rows of organ pipes (hence the range's name), dominated by the towering **Dedo de Deus** ("God's Finger") peak. Teresópolis, like Petrópolis, owed its initial development to the opening of a road between Minas Gerais and Rio during the eighteenth century. It, too, was a favoured summer retreat (for Empress Teresa Cristina, for whom the town was named) and though smaller than Petrópolis it also shares some of its Germanic characteristics, including a benevolent alpine climate. The town itself is extremely dull, built along one main street which changes its name every couple of blocks, and the interest lies entirely in the surrounding countryside. There are, however, magnificent views from almost anywhere in town – especially from **Soberbo**, where the Rio highway enters Teresópolis, with its panoramic view of Rio and the Baixada Fluminense.

Around Teresópolis

There's plenty to do in the surrounding countryside, so get your walking boots on. Lakes and waterfalls – the **Cascata dos Amores** and the **Cascata do Imbuí** – provide good swimming; there's the **Mulher de Pedra** rock formation; and good birdwatching around the **Granja Comary** (on the BR-495).

The main attraction, though, is the **Parque Nacional da Serra dos Órgãos**, where favourite peaks for those with mountain-goat tendencies are the Agulha do Diablo (2050m) and the Pedra do Sino (2263m); the latter has a path leading to the summit, a relatively easy three-hour trip (take refreshments). It costs about $1 to enter the park and the State Forestry Institute rents out basic **accommodation** for climbers in hostels (☎021/642-1070), for about $15 including full board. There are some campsites, too, but no equipment for rent, so you'll need to come prepared.

For more information about all these places, visit the **tourist office** (Mon–Fri 8am–5pm) on Avenida Lúcio Meira (one of the names of the main street in Teresópolis town centre). **Guidebooks and trail maps** can be purchased in front of the Igreja Matriz at the *Cupelo Banco de Jornais* – maps are a must because, while there are walks all over the place, they are not signposted. In the national park, you'll also be able to hire guides inexpensively.

Practicalities

Most of the many **hotels** in Teresópolis are located on hillside beauty spots, far from the town centre. The best of them is the *Rosa dos Ventos* (☎021/742-8833; ⑦) on the Nova Friburgo road, some 22km from town. Cheaper alternatives are the *Philips*, Rua Duval Fonseca 1333 (☎021/742-1636; ④), *Hotel Center*, Rua Sebastião Teixeira 245 (☎021/742-2970; ③), the *Flórida*, Av. Lúcio Meira 467 (③), and the *Várzea Palace*, Rua Sebastião Teixeira 41 (☎021/742-0878; ②), which is a beautiful white building offering amazing value. There is also a **youth hostel** at Rua Farjadi 171.

Only a couple of **restaurants** stand out, but both are expensive: *Dona Irene*, Rua Yeda 730 (☎021/742-2901; closed Mon & Tues), serves marvellous Russian food and reservations are essential; *Margô* at Rua Heitor de Moura Estevão 259 (closed Mon) specializes in German cuisine.

In January, Teresópolis hosts the **Curso Internacional PRO-ARTE**, with live classical music performances (information from the tourist office).

Nova Friburgo

NOVA FRIBURGO, to the northeast of Teresópolis, was founded by a hundred Swiss immigrant families from the canton of Friburg, transferred to the region by royal decree in 1818, and whose only other activity of note was that they introduced the first sauna into Brazil. The Germanic influence remains, principally in the architecture of the **Conego** area of this attractive town of 90,000 people, which lies in a valley surrounded by mountains. During the summer, Nova Friburgo's many hotels and campsites are brimming with city folk who come to enjoy the waterfalls and wooded trails or take on the local peaks – like **Caledonia**, a favourite with hang-gliders. Less of a hike, the dramatic rock formations of the **Furnos da Catete** forestry reserve on the road to Bom Jardim (23km north on the BR-492) offer an excellent walk; and for an easy view of the world a cable car (9am–5.30pm) from Praça dos Suspiros in town takes you to the summit of **Morro da Cruz**, some 1800m up.

You could easily stay awhile in this peaceful town, and there are a number of good **hotels**, many of which are surrounded by lovely gardens and feature pools and other recreational facilities. Some, like *Buksky* (☎0245/22-5052; ⑤), 4km along the Niterói road, lie a short distance outside of town; nearer the centre is the *Hotel São Paulo*, Rua Monsenhor Miranda 41 (☎0245/22-9135; ③). Budget options include *Hotel Montanus*, Rua Fernando Bizzotto 26 (☎0245/22-1235; ②), or the *Hotel Fabris* (☎0245/22-2852; ②), at Av. Alberto Braune 148 (the same street as the bus station).

For **eating**, try the *Oberland* delicatessen on Rua Fernando Bizzotto, which doubles as a restaurant with good, cheap Swiss and German food – veal sausage, sauerkraut and the like. The *Churrascaria Majórica*, Praça Getúlio Vargas 74, is good, too, and in the same square you can buy homemade preserves and liqueurs. For a major splurge, head out to the district of Amparo, 14km east of town on the RJ-150, and try the excellent French–Swiss restaurant the *Auberge Suisse,* located in a small and rather exclusive hotel with the same name.

To reach Nova Friburgo from Rio takes about three hours by **bus** (departures from *Novo Rio Rodoviária* every 30min). You'll head across the Rio–Niterói bridge, and out on Highways 101, 104 and 116. It's also possible to get a bus from Teresópolis.

travel details

Buses

Frequent departures from *Novo Rio Rodoviária* to all parts of Brazil. **International** departures daily to Asunción (30hr), Buenos Aíres (50hr), Montevideo (37hr) and Santiago (70hr).

Rio to: Angra dos Reis (hourly; 2hr 30min); Belém (1 daily; 52hr); Belo Horizonte (20 daily; 6hr); Brasília (8 daily; 18hr); Búzios (2 daily; 4hr); Cabo Frio (5 daily; 2hr 30min); Campo Grande (1 daily; 21hr); Fortaleza (1 daily; 43hr); Foz do Iguaçu (6 daily; 22hr); Ouro Preto (1 daily; 8hr); Parati (5 daily; 4hr 30min); Petrópolis (every 30min; 90min); Recife (4 daily; 38hr); Salvador (6 daily; 27hr); São Luis (1 daily; 50hr); São Paulo (every 15min; 6hr); Teresópolis (every 30min; 2hr); Vitória (9 daily; 8hr).

Planes

Frequent **domestic** flights from Sector A of Galeão airport on Ilha do Governador to all state capitals and other internal destinations. **Rio–São Paulo** shuttle from Santos Dumont, downtown, every 30min from 6.30am to 10.30pm (55min). The airport also has less frequent services to Brasília, Belo Horizonte and Curitiba.

MINAS GERAIS AND ESPÍRITO SANTO

T he French geologist Gorceix summed up **Minas Gerais** 150 years ago, when he wrote that the state had "a breast of iron and a heart of gold". Its hills and mountains contain the richest mineral deposits in Brazil, and led to the area being christened "General Mines" when gold and diamonds were found at the end of the seventeenth century. The gold strikes sparked a wave of migration from Rio and São Paulo, which lasted a century and shifted the centre of gravity of Brazil's economy and population from the northeast decisively to the south, where it has remained ever since. In the nineteenth century new metals, especially iron, steel and manganese, replaced gold in importance, while the uplands in the west and east proved ideal for coffee production. Land too steep for coffee bushes was converted to cattle pasture, and the luxuriant forests of southern Minas were destroyed and turned into charcoal for smelting. The bare hills are a foretaste of what parts of Amazônia might look like a century from now, and only their strange beauty – sea-like, as waves of them recede into the distance – saves them from seeming desolate.

Mineral wealth still flows from Minas' hills, but iron, bauxite, manganese and steel have superseded the precious metals of colonial times. The eighteenth-century mining settlements of Minas Gerais are now quiet and beautiful colonial towns, with a fraction of the population they had two hundred years ago. They're called *as cidades históricas*, "the historic cities", and are the only colonial survivals in southern Brazil that stand comparison with the Northeast. Most importantly, they're the repository of a great flowering of Baroque **religious art** that took place here in the eighteenth century: *arte sacra mineira* was the finest work of its time in the Americas, and Minas Gerais can lay claim to undisputably the greatest figure in Brazilian cultural history – the mulatto leper sculptor, **Aleijadinho**, whose magnificent work is scattered throughout the historic cities. The most important of the *cidades históricas* are **Ouro Preto**, **Mariana** and **Sabará**, all within easy striking distance of Belo Horizonte, and **Congonhas**, **São João del Rei**, **Tiradentes** and **Diamantina**, a little further afield.

In more recent times, too, Minas Gerais has been at the centre of Brazilian history. *Mineiros* have a well-deserved reputation for political cunning, and have produced the two greatest post-war Brazilian presidents: **Juscelino Kubitschek**, the builder of Brasília, and **Tancredo Neves**, midwife to the rebirth of Brazilian democracy in 1985. It was troops from Minas who put down the São Paulo revolt against Getúlio Vargas' populist regime in the brief civil war of 1932 and, less creditably, the army division in Minas which moved against Rio in 1964 and ensured the success of the military coup.

In keeping with this economic and political force, the capital of Minas, **Belo Horizonte**, is a thriving, modern metropolis of nearly three million people – the third largest city in Brazil and second only to São Paulo as an industrial centre, which, with its forest of skyscrapers and miles of industrial suburbs, it rather resembles. It lies in the centre of the rich mining and agricultural hinterland that has made the state one of the economic powerhouses of Brazil. This area is called the *Triângulo Mineiro*, and runs from the coffee estates of western Minas to the mines and cattle pastures of the valley of the **Rio Doce**, in the east of the state: a thickly populated and relatively prosperous region. You can read the area's history in its landscape, the jagged horizons a direct result of decades of mining. The largest cities of the *Triângulo* apart from Belo Horizonte are Juiz de Fora in the south, Governador Valadares to the east, and Uberaba and Uberlândia in the west – all modern and unprepossessing; only Belo Horizonte can honestly be recommended as worth visiting.

All *mineiros* would agree that the soul of the state lies in the rural areas, in the hill and mountain villages of its vast **interior**. North of Belo Horizonte, the grassy slopes and occasional patches of forest are swiftly replaced by the stubby trees and savanna of the Planalto Central (leading to Brasília and central Brazil proper); and in northeastern Minas, by the cactus, rock and perennial drought of the *sertão* – as desperately poor and economically backward as anywhere in the Northeast proper. The northern part of the state is physically dominated by the hills and highlands of the **Serra do Espinhaço**, a range which runs north–south through the state like a massive dorsal fin, before petering out south of Belo Horizonte. To its west is the flat river valley of the **Rio São Francisco**, which rises here before winding through the interior of the

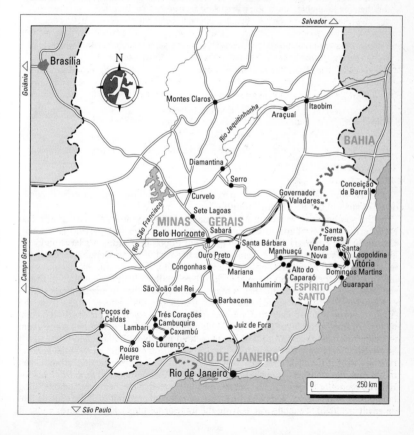

COMIDA MINEIRA

Minas Gerais' delicious **regional food**, *comida mineira*, is one of Brazil's most distinctive – based mainly on pork, the imaginative use of vegetables, *couve*, a green vegetable similar to spinach, and the famous *tutu*, a thick bean sauce made by grinding uncooked beans with manioc flour and cooking the mixture. Many of the dishes originate from the early mule trains and *bandeirante* expeditions of the eighteenth century, when food had to keep for long periods (hence the use of salted pork, now replaced by fresh) and be easily prepared without elaborate ingredients.

Comida mineira is not difficult to find: outside Belo Horizonte it is rare to find restaurants that serve anything else, and the capital itself has plenty of authentic establishments, provided you know where to look (see p.145). There are also small stores everywhere serving Minas Gerais' *doces* (cakes and sweetmeats), and you should seek out the local melt-in-the-mouth cheeses, made both from goats' and cows' milk. Among the **typical dishes** are:

Tutu a mineira Most typical of all dishes, found on every menu; roasted pork served with lashings of *tutu*, garnished with steamed *couve* and *torresmo* (an excellent salted pork crackling).

Feijão tropeiro ("Mule driver's beans") A close relative to *tutu a mineira*, with a name that betrays its eighteenth-century origins; it features everything that is in a *tutu* but also has beans fried with *farinha* (manioc flour) and egg, often with onion, thrown into the mix.

Frango com quiabo Chicken roasted with okra and served sizzling with a sideplate of *anju*, a corn porridge that *mineiros* eat with almost anything.

Carne picadinha A straightforward, rich stew of either beef or pork, cooked for hours until tender.

Costelinha Stewed ribs of ham.

Dobradinha Tripe stew cooked with sweet potatoes. The stews (including the two above) often include the excellent Minas sausages, smoked and peppery.

Doce de leite A rich caramel sludge.

Brigadeiro The ultimate in chocolate snacks, so rich it should come with a health warning.

Northeast. And to the east, life in the parched landscapes of the *sertão mineiro* depends on the waters of the **Rio Jequitinhonha**.

In the southwest of Minas, in fine mountainous scenery near the border with São Paulo, are a number of **spa towns** built around mineral water springs: **São Lourenço**, **Caxambu** and **Lambari** are small and quiet, but **Poços de Caldas** is a large and very lively resort. Perhaps the most scenically attractive part of Minas Gerais – certainly the least visited – is the **eastern** border with Espírito Santo. There's some spectacular walking country in the **Caparaó** national park, where the third highest mountain in Brazil, the 2890-metre **Pico da Bandeira**, is more easily climbed than its height suggests.

Espírito Santo, the small coastal state that separates eastern Minas from the Atlantic, is the kind of place that you rarely hear about, even within Brazil. It's completely off the tourist map. This is hard to understand, as the interior has some claim to being the most beautiful part of Brazil. Settled mostly by Italians and Germans, it has a disconcertingly European feel – Jersey cows graze in front of German-looking ranches, and if it weren't for the heat and the hummingbirds darting around, you might imagine yourself somewhere in Switzerland. Vast numbers of *mineiros* head for Espírito Santo for their holidays, but are only interested in the beaches, the one thing landlocked Minas lacks. This has the fortunate effect of cramming all the crowds into an easily avoidable coastal strip, leaving the interior free for you to explore.

The only place of any size is **Vitória**, a rather grimy city saved by a fine location, on an island surrounded by hills and granite outcrops. It was one of the few spots on the coast that could be easily defended, and the **Botocudo Indians** were able to restrict the Portuguese to scattered coastal settlements until the last century. This is one of the reasons the interior is relatively thinly settled; the other is the sheer difficulty of communications in the steep, thickly forested hills that rear up into mountains along the border with Minas. The semi-deciduous tropical forest that once carpeted much of the southern coast of Brazil still survives relatively unscathed here – and is what southern Minas would have looked like before the gold rushes. To a degree, the forest resembles Amazonian jungle, but if you look closely during autumn and winter (April to September) you'll see that many of the trees have shed their leaves. The best way to view the region is to make the round of the towns which began as German and Italian colonies: **Santa Teresa**, **Santa Leopoldina**, **Domingos Martins** and **Venda Nova** – the last near the remarkable sheer granite face of **Pedra Azul**, one of the least-known but most spectacular sights in the country.

BELO HORIZONTE

The best way to approach **BELO HORIZONTE** is from the south, over the magnificent hills of the Serra do Espinhaço, on a road that winds back and forth before finally cresting a ridge where the entire city is set out before you. It's a spectacular sight: Belo Horizonte sprawls in an enormous bowl surrounded by hills, a sea of skyscrapers, *favelas* and industrial suburbs. From the centre, the jagged rust-coloured skyline of the Serra do Espinhaço, which gave the city its name, is always visible on the horizon – still being transformed by the mines gnawing away at the "breast of iron".

Despite its size and importance, Belo Horizonte is less than a century old. It was the first of Brazil's planned cities, laid out in the 1890s on the site of the poor village of Curral del Rey, of which nothing remains. As late as 1945 it had only 100,000 inhabitants; now it has almost thirty times that number, an explosive rate of growth even by Latin American standards. It rapidly became the most important pole of economic development in the country, after São Paulo, thanks to the wealth of the *Triângulo Mineiro* and the energy of its inhabitants. And while it may not be as historic as the rest of the state – only a few public buildings survive from its early days – it's difficult not to be impressed by the city's scale and energy. Moreover, its central location and proximity to some of the most important *cidades históricas* (Sabará is only just outside the city, Ouro Preto and Mariana less than two hours away by road) make it a good base.

The **central zone** of Belo Horizonte consists of the large area within the inner ring road, the **Avenida do Contorno**; the centre is laid out in a grid pattern, crossed by diagonal *avenidas*, that makes it easy to find your way around. The spine of the city is the broad **Avenida Afonso Pena** and the *Rodoviária* is in the heart of the downtown area, on the corner of Afonso Pena and Contorno. Accommodation of all standards is nearby. Just down from the *Rodoviária* along Avenida Afonso Pena is the obelisk in the **Praça Sete**, the middle of the hotel and financial district and the city's busiest part; a few blocks further down Afonso Pena are the trees and shade of the **Parque Municipal**. A short city bus ride south lies the chic area of **Savassi**, with its nightlife, boutiques and art cinemas, and the **Praça da Liberdade**, Belo Horizonte's main square – dominated by a double row of Imperial palms and important public buildings.

The two places **outside the centre** you're most likely to visit are the artificial lake and Niemeyer buildings of **Pampulha**, to the north, and the rambling nature reserve of **Mangabeiras**, on the southern boundary of the city.

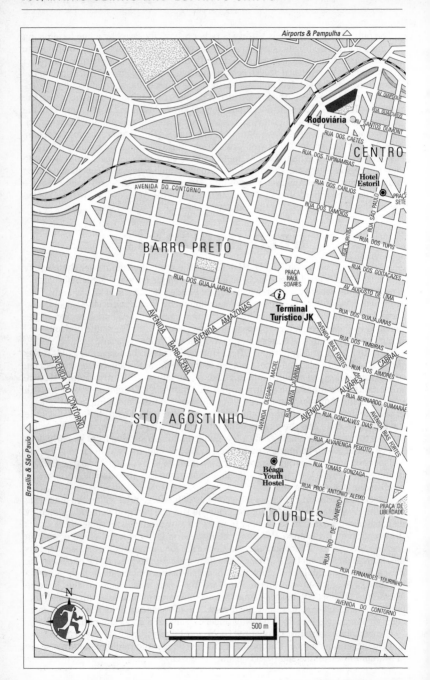

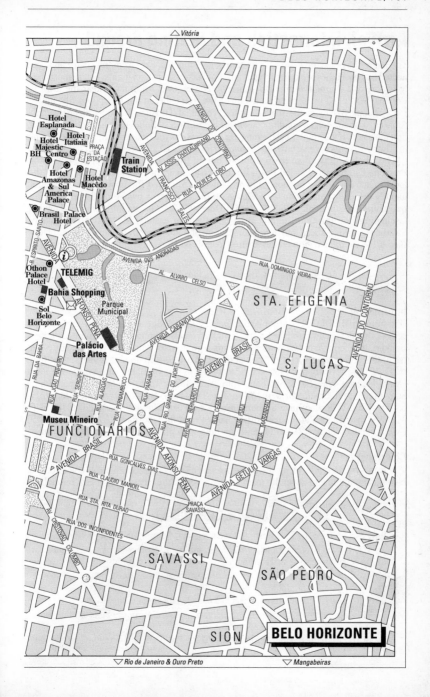

△ Vitória

Hotel
Esplanada
Hotel
Itatiaia
Hotel
Majestic
BH Centro
PRAÇA
DA
ESTAÇÃO
**Train
Station**
Hotel
Amazonas
& Sul
America
Palace
Hotel
Macêdo

Brasil Palace
Hotel

(i)
Othon
Palace
Hotel
TELEMIG
Bahia Shopping
Sol
Belo
Horizonte
Parque
Municipal
**Palácio
das Artes**

AVENIDA DOS ANDRADAS
AL. ALVARO CELSO
RUA DOMINGOS VIEIRA
STA. EFIGÉNIA

Museu Mineiro
FUNCIONÁRIOS

S. LUCAS

RUA GONÇALVES DIAS
RUA CLAUDIO MANOEL
RUA STA. RITA DURÃO
RUA DOS INCONFIDENTES
PRAÇA
SAVASSI

SAVASSI

SÃO PEDRO

SION

BELO HORIZONTE

▽ Rio de Janeiro & Ouro Preto   ▽ Mangabeiras

Arrival, information and getting around

The nearer of Belo Horizonte's two **airports** is Pampulha, 8km from the centre and connected by bus #1202 (see below), but it now only takes short-haul flights. You're more likely to arrive at the new Aeroporto Tancredo Neves, over 30km away near the town of Confins, but linked by **airport buses** that leave you either at the *Rodoviária* (the *ônibus convencional*; $1) or at the tourist centre, Terminal Turístico JK, west along Avenida Amazonas (the faster, air-conditioned *ônibus executivo*; $5). Both buses have rather erratic timetables (every 20min at best, every 2hr at worst); if you're departing by plane, phone in advance to check departure times (*convencional* ☎271-1335; *executivo* ☎271-4522).

The tropical Edwardian **train station**, one of the finest buildings in the city, is on Praça da Estação (also called Praça Rui Barbosa), near the *Rodoviária*. Apart from the local metrô commuter service, only one line has survived the post-privatization cuts, namely the daily connection with Vitória on the coast, now owned by the giant industrial combine Companhia do Vale do Rio Doce (CVRD). It's an interminably slow but fascinating ride through the industrial heartland of eastern Minas (via Governador Valadares), taking about fourteen hours, much of it following the valley of the Rio Doce (see p.148 for information on departures from Belo Horizonte and buying tickets).

> The **telephone code** for Belo Horizonte is ☎031.

Information

The municipal BELOTUR organization is very knowledgeable about the city and the rest of the state, and publishes a free and extremely comprehensive monthly guidebooklet, the *Guia Turística*, which contains a good map. You'll find it in the city's better hotels and in the **tourist offices** at Rua Tupis 149, 10th floor (Mon–Fri 9am–6pm; ☎277-7669); Mercado das Flores, at the corner of Rua da Bahia and Av. Afonso Pena (Mon–Fri 8am–8pm, Sat & Sun 8am–4pm; ☎222-4336); Tancredo Neves airport (daily 8am–6pm); and the *Rodoviária* (Mon–Fri 8am–8pm, Sat & Sun 8am–4pm; ☎277-6907). BELOTUR also have a phone number for specific queries: ☎220-1310. TUR-MINAS, the Minas state tourist office, is at Praça da Liberdade, Av. Bias Fortes 50 (Mon–Fri 9am–6pm; ☎212-2134) and can help with planning routes in the interior.

City transport

The **bus system** works along the same lines as elsewhere in Brazil but is colour-coded: blue buses run up and down the main *avenidas* within the city centre, yellow buses have

---

USEFUL BUS ROUTES

Yellow SCO2: from the *Rodoviária* to Praça Sete and Savassi, via Praça da Liberdade.

Blue 1001: from Avenida Afonso Pena (between Rua Espírito Santo and Rua Tupis) to Praça da Savassi via Praça da Liberdade.

Blue 1202: from Avenida Afonso Pena, down the tree-lined Avenida Amazonas and out to Pampulha airport.

Blue 4001: from Avenida Afonso Pena to Praça da Liberdade.

Blue 2001: from the Parque das Mangabeiras down Avenida Afonso Pena to Praça Sete and the *Rodoviária*.

Blue 6001: from the northern entrance of Parque das Mangabeiras to Savassi and the centre.

circular routes, white buses are "express", stopping only at selected points, and red buses are radial, connecting outlying suburbs and *favelas* with the centre. Virtually all routes include a stretch along Avenida Afonso Pena, usually the most convenient place to catch a bus if you are staying in the centre. Buses are very frequent; see the box for route details.

Otherwise, **taxis** are cheap, even by Brazilian standards, and there is a city **metrô system**. This, however, was built with workers rather than tourists in mind and serves only to link the industrial suburbs with the centre. It runs Monday to Friday (and holidays) 5.45am–11pm, Saturday 5.45am–5pm.

Accommodation

You don't need to stray far from the centre for **accommodation**, as there are scores of hotels, most fairly reasonable, within easy reach of the *Rodoviária*. The only alternative options are to stay in one of the smart hotels in Savassi, or to head for the two **youth hostels** – both are a short taxi ride from the *Rodoviária* and are very popular, so phone ahead to check that they have space. There are lots of *dormitórios* bunched around the *Rodoviária*, but they cater mainly for prostitutes and their clients.

Youth hostels

Albergue de Juventude Chalé Mineiro, Rua Santa Luzia 288 (☎467-1576). This hostel in the *bairro* of Santa Efigênia, 3km from the centre, has its own garden and very modern facilities. Breakfast available. Take bus #2701. ②.

Albergue de Juventude Pousada Beagá, Rua Santa Catarina 597 (☎275-3592 or 337-1845). This is the more central of the two youth hostels, located in the *bairro* of Lourdes, near Savassi. Again, breakfast is available. ②.

Hotels

Hotel Amazonas, Av. Amazonas 120 (☎201-4644, fax 212-4236). Almost next door to the *Sul America Palace*, a slightly overpriced mid-range choice (though discounts of up to 30 percent are usually offered). The staff are efficient, and the breakfasts generous; the best rooms face onto the palm-lined *avenida*. ⑥.

Brasil Palace Hotel, Rua Carijós 269 (☎ and fax 273-3811). A fine 1940s building overlooking Praça Sete, that still looks like the cinema it once was. The rooms are excellent and exceptional value for money, with baths as well as showers, TV, *frigobar* and air conditioning. ④.

Hotel Esplanada, Av. Santos Dumont 304 (☎273-5311, fax 222-7725). One of the few hotels (as opposed to *motels*) on this street, slightly fusty but friendly, and pretty good value given the TVs and fridges in the rooms. Cheaper *quartos* also available. ③–④.

Hotel Estoril, Rua Carijós 454 (☎ and fax 201-9322). A good central location, slightly more expensive than the *Brasil Palace* but not as nice, though still reasonable value. Private car parking available. ⑤.

ACCOMMODATION PRICE CODES

In this guide, accommodation has been categorized according to the price codes outlined below, based on US$. These categories represent the minimum you can expect to pay for a **double room in high season** – though note that many of the budget places will also have more expensive rooms. Rates for hostels and basic hotels where guests are charged **per person** are given in US$, instead of being indicated by price code. See p.31 for further information.

① under $20	③ $30–45	⑤ $60–80	⑦ $120–175
② $20–30	④ $45–60	⑥ $80–120	⑧ $175 and over

Hotel Itatiaia, Praça da Estação 187 (☎274-0003, fax 274-4576). In a distinctive 1940s Art Deco edifice facing the station, with a lobby resembling that of an old bank, this hotel (with its own parking) is friendly and convenient, though decidedly tatty in outward appearance. ④.

Hotel Macêdo, Praça da Estação 123 (☎222-9255). By far the best of the cheaper options, with good clean rooms (though some of the furniture has clearly seen better days), even cheaper *quartos*, and a basic breakfast. Some rooms have excellent views over the *praça* and the train station, but those overlooking Av. Amazonas can be noisy at night. ②.

Hotel Majestic BH Centro, Rua Espírito Santo 284 (☎222-3390, fax 222-3146). Though hardly majestic, this hotel has a wide range of large, clean, basic rooms – nothing special but well priced, and *quartos* are considerably cheaper. ③–④.

Othon Palace Hotel, Av. Afonso Pena 1050 (☎273-3844, fax 212-2318). This huge 1970s skyscraper is the city's only central hotel with five stars, but how it got them is anyone's guess. Staff are snooty, the rooms nothing special at all, and the only advantage over the *Brasil Palace* seems to be its pool and sauna, which hardly warrants the extra $150 you would pay for a double. ⑧.

Sol Belo Horizonte, Rua Bahia 1040 (☎ and fax 274-1344). A new four-star hotel, far better than the *Othon Palace*, with pleasant rooms, friendly and efficient service, a pool and sauna. At weekends (Fri–Sun), when the company executives go home, rates are considerably cheaper (⑥). ⑦.

Sul America Palace, Av. Amazonas 50 (☎201-1722, fax 212-7117). Popular two-star hotel with a municipal car park at the side and very friendly staff. Good value. ④.

The City

Even the most patriotic *mineiro* would make few claims for the architecture of Belo Horizonte, dominated as it is by nondescript 1960s and 1970s high-rises. Nonetheless, there are a few graceful exceptions, notably on **Praça da Liberdade**, which is lined with palm trees and grand government offices built at the time of the city's creation in the 1890s (the centrepiece, the beautiful Palácio do Governo, is open to visitors on Sundays 9am–6pm). And if you stand in the heart of the city, in **Praça Sete**, and look around you, it's hard to call it ugly: Avenida Afonso Pena is broad enough not to be dwarfed even by the huge skyscrapers that line it, the pavements are thronged with people, and the graceful lines of palms add a touch of elegance to Avenida Amazonas, stretching away downhill.

The Praça Sete and Parque Municipal

Something is always happening in the Praça Sete. It's the main venue of street draughts tournaments, when rows of hustlers set up boards on the pavement and play all comers for money. The bars and *lanchonetes* stay open until midnight, even later at weekends, and when the rest of the city has gone home to sleep, the square is the base for scores of homeless people, huddling around fires on deserted pavements, in front of the plush skyscrapers of international banks.

A few minutes' walk up Avenida Afonso Pena from Praça Sete brings you to the only relief from the traffic and noise that you'll find downtown: the green and shade of the **Parque Municipal** (Tues–Sun 6am-6pm). Other than this park, if you want greenery in Belo Horizonte, you have to leave the city boundaries at Mangabeiras (see p.142) or be content with views of distant hills. Beautifully laid out, the park encompasses a boating lake, two thousand species of tree, shaded walks much patronized by courting couples, aviaries, a permanent fairground and exercise yards where Brazilian men make their sweaty sacrifices to the national cult of the body beautiful. It also contains the main arts complex in the city, the Palácio das Artes.

The Palácio das Artes
The **Palácio das Artes** (entrance on Avenida Afonso Pena) is one of the few really fine modern buildings in the city, of which the citizens of Belo Horizonte are justifiably proud.

So much so that when parts of the *palácio* burned down in March 1997, reconstruction began barely a week later, and a mammoth benefit show was organized in the Mineirão football stadium to fund the repairs. Before the fire – and there is no reason why things should change much once the rebuilding is completed – the *palácio* was divided into a number of well laid-out **galleries** (daily 9am–9pm), with exhibitions concentrating on modern Brazilian art, a couple of small **theatres** and one big one, the **Grande Teatro**, on which no expense had been spared but which suffered most in the fire.

Though it's hard to believe in such a large city, the *palácio* is also the only place in Belo Horizonte where you'll come across a good display of the distinctive *artesanato* of the state, in the **Centro de Artesanato Mineiro** (closed during the rebuilding, but normal hours are Mon 1–6pm, Tues–Fri 9am–9pm, Sat 9am–1pm, Sun 10am–2pm). A large shop rather than a gallery proper, it's nevertheless a place you can wander around and look without being pressured to buy. Although there's a lot of dross here, there is also some excellent pottery – stubby figurines and realistic clay tableaux. Distinctive though it is, you wouldn't be wrong in thinking that the best work looks Northeastern: it comes from the valley of the Rio Jequitinhonha, in the *sertão mineiro*, and contains elements of both traditions. Hammocks, clothes, wall hangings and rugs, roughly woven from the cotton that grows in northern Minas, are also of a high quality, although the best work – the striking collage wall hangings, for example – is too bulky to be transported easily. Despite the sleek surroundings, the prices here are reasonable: not more than twice what you'd pay where the work comes from.

Feira de Arte e Artesanato

It's worth making an effort to be in Belo Horizonte on a Sunday morning for the **Feira de Arte e Artesanato** – a massive market that takes over the Avenida Afonso Pena bordering the Parque Municipal. It's always packed, and by mid-morning moving through the narrow avenues between rows of stalls gets difficult; by 2pm, stallholders are packing up and leaving, and by 4pm the city's efficient street cleaners will have removed all trace of the market.

An excellent place for bargains, the market is split into sections, with related stalls grouped together – jewellery, leather goods, cane furniture, clothes, food, paintings and drinks, to name but a few. Prices of more expensive items and clothes are fixed – a lot of things on view are labelled – but otherwise there is some scope for bargaining. Highlights are the truly awful fluffy toys and sentimental paintings; very good jewellery and reasonably priced precious and semi-precious stones, cut and uncut; good T-shirts; and the wide variety of inexpensive excellent food. There is no arts and crafts section as such: several of the stalls underneath the palms lining the centre of the square do have *artesanato*, but it's not as good as the stuff available outside Belo Horizonte.

As always with Brazilian markets, what's going on around you is just as interesting as what's for sale. If you can find a seat, set up camp at one of the **bars** at the corner with Rua da Bahia, and watch the stallholders hustling, buyers negotiating and people doing the same as you – just enjoying the action or listening to the buskers and serious musicians who play at the fringes of the crowds and sell tapes of their work.

The Museu Histórico Abílio Barreto

Although Minas Gerais has some of the best museums in Brazil, Belo Horizonte itself is poorly endowed in this respect. There's a sample – nothing more – of the tradition of religious art in Minas at the **Museu Mineiro** (Tues–Fri 11.30am–6.30pm, Sat & Sun 10am–4pm), near the Parque Municipal at Av. João Pinheiro 342, but the only museum in the city really worth a visit is the **Museu Histórico Abílio Barreto** – and that's currently closed for renovation (phone ☎277-4361 for information).

To get there when it's open, you need to take the #5901 bus (marked "Nova Floresta/Santa Lúcia"); the most convenient stop to catch the bus is along Avenida Amazonas between Rua Espírito Santo and Rua Caetés. If you ask the conductor for the *Museu Histórico*, you'll be dropped on Contorno, a block away, from where there are signs to the museum on Rua Bernardo Mascarenhas. The area is called Cidade Jardim, and is rapidly becoming one of the most fashionable, upper-class parts of the city, with new skyscrapers sprouting like weeds. It's an ironic location for the oldest building in the city, the only one that predates 1893 when construction of the new capital began.

The museum was once a *fazenda* (estate house), built in 1883, comfortable but not luxurious, and typical of the ranches of rural Minas. It has been perfectly preserved and, though now swamped by the burgeoning city, it once stood on its own, a few kilometres away from the church and hovels of the hamlet of Curral del Rey, which straggled along what is now the stretch of Avenida Afonso Pena opposite the Parque Municipal. There is the usual collection of old furniture and mediocre paintings, upstairs, and in the garden an old tram and turn-of-the-century train used in the construction of Belo Horizonte. Far better is the rustic wooden veranda at the front, where you can sit with your feet up and imagine yourself back in the 1880s.

By far the most interesting part of the museum is the **galeria de fotografias**, juxtaposing the sleepy village before it was obliterated – mules, mud huts and oxcarts – with views of the modern city through the decades; there are a couple of well-designed maps to help you get your bearings. The last remnant of Curral del Rey, the eighteenth-century Igreja Matriz, was flattened in 1932: these photographs, and carved bits of the church piled in a shed in the garden, are all that remain of the vanished community.

Equally remarkable is the series of photographs that record the building of Belo Horizonte and its early years: a trashed building site becomes the Parque Municipal; the train station stands in glorious isolation (it's now dwarfed by the surrounding buildings); and the Praça Sete is shown as it was in the 1930s, ringed by trees and fine Art Deco buildings, of which only the Cine Brasil (now the *Brasil Palace Hotel*) is still standing. Like Rio, urban architecture in Belo Horizonte was at its peak in the 1930s and 1940s, when the city was an elegant political capital, rather than an economic centre, and it has suffered since at the hands of the developers. A classic demonstration of this is the wonderful Art Deco market building, the Feira de Amostras Permanentes, which you can now only appreciate here in the museum. It was demolished in 1970 and replaced by the *Rodoviária*.

Parque das Mangabeiras

Unlikely as it may seem amid the skyscrapers of Avenida Afonso Pena, the city limits are only a short bus ride away to the south. Here, the urban sprawl is abruptly cut off by the steep hills of the **Serra do Curral**, a natural barrier that forces the city to expand in other directions. The views of the city from its slopes are spectacular, and it's also the site of a huge nature reserve, the 600-hectare **Parque das Mangabeiras** (Tues–Sun 8am–6pm), where you can walk along forest paths that open out now and again to reveal the city below. To get there, catch the blue #2001-C bus, marked "Aparecida", from Avenida Afonso Pena between Avenida Amazonas and Rua Tamóios: it's a fifteen-minute steep drive to the terminus above the park entrance. When returning to the city, you can avoid having to climb back up to the main entrance by leaving the park through the small northern gate, much lower down, and catching the #6001 bus just outside.

The park is so big it has its own **internal bus service**; buses leave every thirty minutes from the left of the entrance, and end up there again twenty minutes later after making a circuit of the park. Near the entrance is a well-kept leisure area, with fountains, rows of *lanchonetes* and an open-air amphitheatre, the **Teatro de Arena**, where something often happens on Sundays. The best view of the city is from the **Mirante da Mata** viewing platform, a twenty-minute walk from the entrance; the finest walks are along the nature trails and streams of the **Parque Florestal**, a little further along. **Maps** of the park are available from the park office near the main entrance.

Mirante da Cidade

The single most spectacular view of the city is from the **Mirante da Cidade**, outside the park, largely hidden by trees behind the palatial governor's residence. Take the #2001-C bus for Mangabeiras (or the #2001-A), but get off just before at Praça do Papa, where the Pope celebrated Mass in 1982, and walk east up the steep Rua Bady Salum for a short kilometre. The view is splendid: too high up for the grime and *favelas* to register (although pollution can obscure things on a bad day), it makes Belo Horizonte seem like Los Angeles, an impression reinforced if you go by night, when the carpet of lights below really is magnificent.

Pampulha

Some distance north of the centre is the luxurious district of **Pampulha**, built around an artificial lake which is overlooked by the finest modern buildings in the city – the Museu de Arte, the modernist Igreja de São Francisco and the Casa do Baile. They are instantly recognizable as the work of architect **Oscar Niemeyer**, creator of Brasília, and landscape designer **Burle Marx**, both Communists and presumably horrified by the subsequent development of the area: it's become a rich residential district, where cars do not so much drive as swish and rich kids don't know where the bus stops are.

The Igreja de São Francisco de Assis

The construction of the **Igreja de São Francisco de Assis** (Mon–Fri 8am–noon & 1.30–6pm, Sat 8.30am–6pm, Sun 9am–6pm), with its striking curves and *azulejo* frontage, provides a roll-call of the greatest names of Brazilian modernism: Burle Marx laid out its grounds, Niemeyer designed the church, Cândido Portinari did the tiles and murals and João Ceschiatti (best known for his gravity-defying angels in Brasília's cathedral) contributed the bronze baptismal font. It was decades ahead of its time and it's astonishing to realize that it dates from the 1940s. The best time to see it is on Sunday, when Mass is said at 10.30am and 6pm. To get there, take bus #2004 (marked "Bandeirantes/Olhos d'Água") from Avenida Afonso Pena, between Avenida Amazonas and Rua Tupinambás.

The Museu de Arte and Casa do Baile

The **Museu de Arte da Pampulha** (Tues–Sun 8am–6pm) is more difficult to reach: take the #2215 bus from Rua dos Caetés and get off when you see a sign for the *museu* to the left – you then have to walk down to the lakeside Avenida Otacílio Negrão de Lima, turn right, and the museum is on a small peninsula jutting out into the lake. It's worth the trip, although the small collection of modern art it holds isn't at all compelling in itself. The building, however, is a product of two geniuses at the height of their powers. Niemeyer constructed a virtuoso building, all straight lines and right angles at the front but melting into rippling curves at the back, with a marvellous use of glass. And Burle Marx set the whole thing off beautifully, with a sculpture garden out back and an exquisite garden framing the building in front.

Directly opposite, on the other side of the lake, the **Casa do Baile** (currently closed for renovations) is by the same duo. Once a concert hall, it has been turned into a restaurant serving *comida mineira* at very reasonable prices. Get there on the #1202 from Rua São Paulo between Avenida Amazonas and Rua Carijós.

Football in Pampulha

Belo Horizonte's main football stadium, the **Mineirão**, is also situated in prestigious Pampulha. With a capacity of 130,000, the Mineirão is a world-class stadium (in fact the world's second-largest covered stadium), but it's rarely more than half-full, and usually much less. One of Brazil's better teams, Atlético Mineiro, play here and they're worth catching if you're in Belo Horizonte on a Sunday when they are playing at home. Local derbies, especially against Cruzeiro, are torrid and very entertaining affairs, and often end with the destruction of a large number of the city's buses. The #2004 bus passes by, but like all bus journeys to Pampulha, you should allow an hour to travel from the centre. Entrance costs around $4, $5 for the *arquibancada* (stands).

Eating, drinking and nightlife

Outside the immediate downtown area, **restaurants** tend to be upmarket and expensive: this is especially so in Savassi, where the bars are fine but the restaurants are mostly mediocre and vastly overpriced. If air conditioning and servile waiters are what you want, you'll find them in abundance in places along the lower reaches of Rua Alagoas and Rua Sergipe. In general, it's best to head for *comida mineira* restaurants, or else take your pick from a vast array of Arab, Chinese, French, Italian, Japanese and even German places. The free monthly *Guia Turístico* published by BELOTUR contains up-to-date listings of Belo Horizonte's better restaurants.

People say that **nightlife** in Belo Horizonte is also concentrated in Savassi, but this is a little misleading: chic nightlife certainly is, but you'll find lively pockets of bars and clubs throughout the central area, as well as in the *bairros* of Barro Preto and Pampulha.

Snacks, street food and restaurants

The best area for **cheaper eating places** is downtown, around Praça Sete and towards the rail station, where some of the sandwich bars and *lanchonetes* serve better food than pricey restaurants in other parts of town. One block from Praça Sete on Rua Rio de Janeiro is the *Shopping Cidade* where you'll find the full range of international fast food in air-conditioned comfort. Flashier still, with a very decent range of upmarket *comida por kilo* restaurants (as well as an excellent ice cream parlour on the first floor), is the new *Bahia Shopping*, one block west from Avenida Afonso Pena on Rua da Bahia. **Juice bars** are also one of Belo Horizonte's delights: *Pastelândia* on the corner of Avenida Afonso Pena and Rua da Bahia has the full range.

Street food is worth trying, too. On Saturdays between 10am and 4pm, food stalls go up along Avenida Bernardo Monteiro on the corner with Avenida Brasil; the food can be good and is always cheap. Similar stalls crowd the busy Sunday market on Avenida Afonso Pena. Around Praça Sete you'll often find *doceiros* (sweetsellers) in the late afternoon and early evening, hoping to tempt homebound office workers.

For your own supplies, head for the modern and colourful **Mercado Central** (Mon–Sat 7am–6pm, Sun 7am–noon), between Avenida Augusto de Lima and Rua Curitiba, which, as well as basic foodstuffs, purveys a range of weird and wonderful local delicacies, such as salted tripe, dozens of types of smoked sausages and cheeses, strange nuts and preserves.

Restaurants

The highlight of eating out in Belo Horizonte is the excellent (though usually expensive) selection of **comida mineira restaurants** serving the state's regional specialities (see p.134), but there are also a large number of very decent Arab places.

A Bella Torta, Rua Rio Grande do Norte 1263, Savassi (☎281-8500). At the corner with Av. Getúlio Vargas, one of the few unpretentious places in Savassi and a good place to line the stomach before going clubbing, serving a varied menu at very reasonable prices. Try the *Torta de Galinha com Catupiri*, a chicken-and-cheese quiche. *Comida por kilo* ($7 per kg) at lunchtimes.

Bagdá Café, Rua Grão Mogol 271, Sion (☎225-7535). Upmarket Arabic cooking, with live music Wed–Fri, and belly-dancing Thurs–Sat. Take a taxi to find it (Sion is south of Savassi outside the central ring road).

Bem Natural, Av. Afonso Pena 941, Edifício Sulacap, 2 blocks east of Praça Sete. Belo Horizonte's best vegetarian restaurant, combined with a healthfood shop and alternative bookstore. Open Mon–Fri: full menu at lunchtime, soup only 5–8pm.

Bonsai Matsuri, Av. Brasil 1740, Savassi (☎261-0036). On the corner with Rua Alagoas, this good Japanese restaurant is the cheapest in Belo Horizonte, though à la carte sushi and sashimi with drinks will still put you back around $30 a head. The best deal is on Sundays when there's a *rodízio* system for sushi: eat as much as you want for $17.

Center Pizza, Av. Afonso Pena near Rua Tamóios. Cheap fast food and pizzas.

Chilis, Rua Rio Grande do Norte 1139, Savassi (☎261-7918). Mexican burritos, enchiladas, tequila, margaritas . . . bring your sombrero and mule. Around $15 a head.

Dona Lucinha, Rua Padre Odorico 38, São Pedro (☎227-0562). This and its sister restaurant (*Dona Lucinha II*, Rua Sergipe 811, Savassi; ☎261-5930) offer a superb *comida mineira* buffet for $12. The vegetables all come from Dona Lucinha's own farm, the waiters speak English and there is a selection of excellent homemade liqueurs to sample.

Dragon Center, Av. Afonso Pena 549, near the *Rodoviária* beside *Hotel Financial*. This Chinese restaurant is the nearest available good food if you have a couple of hours to kill while changing buses. À la carte in the evenings.

Emporium, Av. Afonso Pena 4034, Mangabeiras (☎281-1277). *Comida mineira* meets the Internet (they have their own website), with lashings of *cachaça* thrown in for good measure. The designer look that other *comida mineira* restaurants seem to be evolving towards. Daily 11am–1.30am. Take bus #5508 from Rua dos Caetés, or #2001 from Av. Afonso Pena in the centre.

Mala e Cuia, Av. Antônio Carlos 8305, Pampulha (☎441-2993). Situated by the lake near Aeroporto de Pampulha and decorated in typical *mineiro* style. You'll get a very filling meal of regional cuisine here from around $8 a head. Live music Thurs–Sun.

Osaka, Av. Getúlio Vargas, Savassi (☎281-2494). One of the cheaper Japanese restaurants in and around Savassi, though still expensive. Sushi *rodízio* on Tues and Wed.

Pier 32, Av. Afonso Pena 3328, 1km east from the Parque Municipal (☎225-0782). Excellent buffet for $15 (concentrating on seafood on Thurs) and a nice bar.

Quibelanches, corner of Rua dos Caetés and Av. Amazonas. One of the cheapest Lebanese restaurants in the city, simple but with a wide range of authentic dishes, both *por kilo* (lunchtimes) and à la carte.

Nightlife and entertainment

There are several areas in the central part of city where the **bars** spring to life once it gets dark. Most days of the week, the bottom end of **Rua da Bahia** between Avenida Afonso Pena and Praça da Estação is particularly lively: the bars put out tables under the palm trees and the action goes on until the small hours. The area around the intersection of **Rua Rio de Janeiro and Avenida Augusto Lima** is also good, but more student-like. There are a couple of small theatres and cinemas close by, and a group of bars and restaurants: *Mateus* on the corner is a good one. It's also worth checking out the bars along **Rua Guajajaras** between Rua Espírito Santo and Rua da Bahia. Much further out, with outlandish performance art "happenings" at 8.30pm and the rare knack of peacefully blending in the oddest of people, is the 24-hour *Bar do Lulu*, Rua Leopoldina 415, Bairro Santo Antônio (☎342-3185) – take a taxi.

The more sophisticated bars are in **Savassi** and neighbouring **Funcionários**, both pleasant places in which to spend an evening. Drinks are only marginally more expensive here than anywhere else, and the bars get very crowded at weekends. One of the few unpretentious places along Rua Alagoas is *Diário da Noite*, on the corner with Rua Cláudio Manoel, with infectiously danceable music (daily from 4pm). *Café*, around the corner at Rua Cláudio Manoel 583, is one of the places where the fashionable gather to be seen. *Chopperia Margherita Ville* and *Sausalito Point* at the intersection of *ruas* Tomé de Souza and Pernambuco are always busy, and most people end up drinking their beer on the street outside (both open till 4am).

Cachaça

If you want to be initiated into the wonderful world of **cachaça** (sugar cane rum), a trip out to the *Alambique Cachaçaria*, Av. Raja Gabáglia 3200, Chalé 1, Estoril, is a must, and also offers beautiful night views of Belo Horizonte from the top of the hill. Beside the live music, the main attraction here is the *cachaça Germana*, their own brew which comes mixed with herbs and honey. They also serve the traditional *caipirinhas – cachaça* with ice, lemon and sugar – as well as straight shots. A single shot costs 50¢ and a bottle, $11 – make sure you're not driving. The easiest way to get here is to take a taxi from the centre: a ten to fifteen-minute ride for about $4.

Discos and live music

The most popular current nightclub in swish **Savassi** is *Máscaras* at Rua Santa Rita Durão 667, with two dance floors, separate bars and video rooms, all kitted out in chic, modern style (open until 6am at weekends). It operates a similar system to many of Brazil's more upmarket nightclubs, where you pay for seats at a table, or *mesa*; if you are going in a group, it's best to book a table (☎261-6050). A similarly glitzy club in Savassi is *Parte Non*, popular with the scotch-drinking brat-pack, at Rua Rio Grande do Norte 1470 (☎221-9856). *Café com Letras*, Rua Antônio de Albuquerque 781 (☎225-9973), is much cheaper and more laid-back, and usually features good jazz, while the small *Terra Brasilis* bar at Rua Tomé de Souza 987 has excellent live samba. Further out at Av. Bandeirantes 1299 in Mangabeiras, the downbeat *Café Concerto* hosts some interesting local bands.

For a more raw clubbing feel, the up-and-coming *bairro* of **Barro Preto** is the place to be, stuffed with enough good live music venues to make a club-crawl possible. Quite the most outrageous is the gay club *Fashion*, Rua Tupis 1240 (11pm onwards; ☎271-3352), where you can sweat the night away to an eminently danceable pulse. Strong on Bahian sounds are *Circuito*, Rua Conquista 308 (☎271-3211), and the more rootsy and reggae-orientated *Bar Nacional*, Av. do Contorno 10076 (Thurs–Sun; ☎271-3211); *Alameida Jazz*, Av. Barbacena 823 (☎337-1930), oddly enough, features jazz. With its university, the *bairro* of **Pampulha** has a more studenty feel. Try *Quioske Deck*, Av. Portugal 3663 (☎441-3591), for samba and Bahian sounds, or *ICEX*, Campus da UFMG, which tends towards hard rock and Brazilian grunge.

In the **city centre**, live music is also easy to come across, though many of the venues are well-hidden and very local affairs. *Cantina do Adnan* at Rua Espírito Santo 291 (daily 5pm–sunrise; free entrance Sun–Thurs) is currently the best of a number of places on that road and on Rua dos Caetés, all of them raw, energetic and distinctly dodgy (take no valuables). Much mellower is the jazz in the *Bar da Estação*, an unusual and very pleasant venue in the train station's old ticket office. Another excellent place, with live bands Tuesday–Saturday, is *Jequitibar*, Av. Assis Chateaubriand 573, to the east of the train station (☎271-6522). On Thursdays, dance music and trampoline artists are followed by drag queens Yoko and Carlinhos Brasil, sashaying in the limelight of the *Café Belas Artes Liberdade*, Rua Gonçalves Dias 1581 (☎222-4924), to the southwest of the centre in Lourdes.

Big names in music play at *Minascentro*, Av. Augusto de Lima 785 (☎201-0122), and at the *Palácio das Artes* (☎237-7333; see p.140). Check the local papers to see who is playing, but expect to pay $25–60 for a ticket.

Cinema and theatre

One of the main attractions of Savassi is the **art cinema**, *Ciné Pathé* on Avenida Cristóvão Colombo, which combines an alluring location with imaginative and non-dubbed programming (there's another art cinema in the Palácio das Artes, but see p.141). For **theatre**, there are dozens of venues around town, though all productions are in Portuguese. In Lourdes, *Teatro na Cidade*, Rua da Bahia 1341 (☎273-1050), sometimes hosts musicals, while *Teatro do ICBEU*, Rua da Bahia 1723 (☎271-7255), occasionally shows opera. Contact BELOTUR (see p.138) for further addresses and for discounted tickets.

Listings

Airlines American Airlines, Rua Guajajaras 557, Centro (☎273-3622); British Airways, Rua São Paulo 1106, sala 305, Centro (☎274-6211); Lloyd Aéreo Boliviano, Rua Sergipe 1034, Funcionários (☎227-3390); Pantanal Linhas Aéreas, Rua Guajajaras 557, 2nd floor, Centro (☎238-7138); TAM, Pampulha airport (☎443-5500); Transbrasil, Rua Tamóios 86, Centro (☎274-3533); United Airlines, Rua Paraíba 1000, 10th floor (☎261-7777); Varig/Nordeste/Rio-Sul, Av. Olegário Maciel 2251 (☎291-9292); VASP, Av. Olegário Maciel 2221, Lourdes (☎330-5588 or 0800-998277).

Airports Apart from some Brasília, Rio and São Paulo commuter flights (Transbrasil, TAM and Rio-Sul), all destinations are served by Aeroporto Internacional Tancredo Neves; the airport is near the town of Confins, and is sometimes called after it. Flight enquiries on ☎689-2700 (Tancredo Neves) or ☎441-2000 (Pampulha). See p.138 for airport transport.

Air-taxis Sobel, Pampulha airport (☎441-8166); Viganó, Av. Raja Gabáglia 3601, loja 5, São Bento (☎984-5646).

Banks and exchange The following tend to have better rates than the Banco do Brasil: Banco Itaú, Av. João Pinheiro 195; Banco Sudameris, Av. João Pinheiro 214; MG Turismo & Câmbio, Rua Guajajaras 1353, loja 31, Terminal Turístico; Nascente Turismo, Rua Rio de Janeiro 1101, Centro.

Buses The *Rodoviária* (☎201-8111) is right at the end of Av. Afonso Pena by the Av. do Contorno. Bus companies are: Expresso União (☎201-5691) for Caldas Novas; Real Express (☎201-7287) for Goiânia and Anápolis; Setelagoano (☎201-5277) for Sete Lagoas; Viação Cometa (☎201-5611) for Campinas, Curitiba, Rio and São Paulo; Viação Gardênia (☎201-8117) for spa towns; Viação Gontijo (☎201-6130) for most main destinations in Minas, Espírito Santo, Goiás, São Paulo state and Paraná, as well as Curitiba and Salvador; Viação Itapemirim (☎271-1019) for Araguaina, Belém, Brasília and Vitória; Viação Motta (☎201-7332) for Campo Grande; Viação Pássaro Verde (☎421-1166) for *cidades históricos* and Tocantins; Viação Penha (☎271-1019) for Brasília and Cristalina; Viação Sandra (☎201-2927) for *cidades históricos*; Viação São Geraldo (☎201-9366) for Salvador; Viação Útil (☎201-1019) for Rio. See "travel details" at the end of this chapter for service frequencies.

Car rental Hertz, at the airports and Av. João Pinheiro 341 (☎224-5166 or 224-1279); Interlocadora, at the airports and Rua dos Timbiras 2229 (☎275-4090); Localiza, at the airports and Av. Bernardo Monteiro 1567 (☎0800-312121).

Carnaval Concerned at the lack of a proper *Carnaval* in Belo Horizonte, the *prefeitura* inaugurated the first annual *Carnabelo* in 1994. It takes places in June – contact BELOTUR (see p.138) for details.

Consulates Argentina, Rua Ceará 1566, 3rd floor, Funcionários (☎281-5288); Chile, Rua Gonçalves Dias 82, Funcionários (☎221-7230); France, Rua Pernambuco 712A, Funcionários (☎261-7805); Germany, Rua Timbiras 1200, 5th floor, Centro (☎222-6644); Italy, Av. Afonso Pena 3130, 12th floor, Serra (☎281-4211); Netherlands, Rua Sergipe 1179, Loja 5, Savassi (☎227-5275); Paraguay, Rua Guandaus 60, room 102, Santa Lúcia (☎344-6349); Portugal, Rua da Bahia 2140, cj. 200, Lourdes (☎291-8064); Sweden, Rua Dezenove 117, Cidade Industrial (☎333-4333 ext 120); Switzerland, Av. Getúlio Vargas 447, 6th floor, Funcionários (☎221-0333); UK, Av. Afonso Pena 952, sala 500, Centro (☎222-6318); Uruguay, Av. do Contorno 6777, 13th floor, salas 1301–4, Funcionários (☎296-8293); USA, Rua Timbiras 1200, 7th floor, Centro (☎213-1571).

Football See p.144 for details of the Mineirão stadium in Pampulha.

Hospitals For an ambulance, phone ☎192. Hospital das Clínicas da UFMG is attached to the university, Av. Alfredo Badalena 190, Santa Efigênia (☎239-7100).

Laundry *Laundromat*, Rua Timbiras 1264, beside the Igreja Boa Viagem (Mon–Sat 8am–8pm).

Police ☎190.

Post office The main post office is at Av. Afonso Pena 1270 (Mon–Fri 9am–7pm, Sat & Sun 9am–1pm). Collect poste restante round the back at Rua Goiás 77.

Shopping The main centre for *artesanato* in the city is the *Centro de Artesanato Mineiro* in the Palácio das Artes (see p.141). Other stores include *Codevale*, Av. do Contorno 4777, Serra (Mon–Fri 8am–7pm, Sat 8am–noon), which specializes in material from the Jequitinhonha valley, and *CENARTE*, Rua Tupinambás 956, Centro (Mon–Fri 11.30am–6pm, Sat 9am–1pm). Hippy gear can be found on Sundays around Praça Sete. Food, medicinal plants, *Umbanda* (voodoo) accessories and wickerwork can be found in the *Mercado Central* (see p.144).

Taxis ☎443-2288.

Telephone Trunk and international calls from TELEMIG offices at: Tancredo Neves airport; the *Rodoviária* (ground floor); Rua Paraíba 1441 in Savassi; and Av. Afonso Pena 1180 – all open daily until 10pm. The main branch, at Av. Afonso Pena 744, is open 24hr.

Trains Trains run daily to Vitória on the coast at 7am, taking just over 14hr. Tickets are sold in the pink building to the right of the station (☎201-8813) up to a month in advance (Mon–Sat 7.30am–6pm, Sun 7.30am–noon), or between 5.30am and 6.50am on the day of departure. Ticket prices are $8.50 (2nd class), $11.50 (1st class) and $17.50 (executive).

Travel and tour companies There are a number of specialist eco-tourism agencies dealing with trekking, hiking, caving, canoeing, rafting and cycling trips in Minas. Contact *Terra Nossa*, Rua Domingos Vieira 348, sala 1309, Santa Efigênia (☎241-6161); *Trilhas d'Água*, Rua Presidente Arthur Bernardes 409, Boa Esperança, Santa Luzia (☎641-3185); or *Primotur*, Rua Pium-í 364, loja 4, Cruzeiro (☎221-3118). *Trilhar*, Rua Osmário Soares 310, Dom Bosco (☎417-6746) organize day trips.

Around Belo Horizonte

The most popular trips out from the capital are to the *cidades históricas* (see p.149), but there are a couple of other less-frequented sites that also warrant a visit, one to the north, a convenient stop if you are heading for Brasília or Diamantina, and the other to the east beyond the nearest of the *cidades históricas*, Sabará.

Gruta Rei do Mato

One of the most astonishing underground attractions of Minas Gerais lies 60km north-west of Belo Horizonte on BR-040, opposite the junction for Sete Lagoas, and makes an excellent day out from the capital. Legend has it that a mysterious fugitive originally discovered this enormous **cave** and used it as a home. He became known as "Rei do Mato" (King of the Bush) and the name has stuck to the cave itself.

The series of caverns (guided tours daily 8am–5pm; $1 in summer; ☎031/773-0888) extends for over 2000m and is 300m deep in some parts, and includes some prehistoric cave art. The third room is particularly impressive, with two parallel columns formed by interlocking stalactites and stalagmites, and is regarded as the only equal in the world to the formations in the famous caves at Altamira in Spain.

Buses from Belo Horizonte to Sete Lagoas (run by Setelagoano; every 30min from 6.30am to 1pm), Diamantina (see p.172) or Brasília pass the cave; the journey takes about an hour. In the summer there is a **bar** open for refreshments at the site.

Parque do Caraça

A hundred and thirty kilometres east of Belo Horizonte lies the impressive **Parque do Caraça** (daily 7am–5pm, 9pm if you're staying in the park), named after the impression of a gigantic face in the surrounding mountains. The park is situated at 2400m above sea level; temperatures drop sharply on summer evenings and it can get very cold in winter. There are plenty of signed walks of varying difficulty on the tracks through the mountains – information is available from the hotel at the park entrance (see below). The park's imposing lake provides a good opportunity for swimming from its small beaches, and there are also several natural pools by the waterfalls within the park. **Buses** from Belo Horizonte to Santa Bárbara (about 4 daily, run by Viação Pássaro Verde) will drop you at the entrance to the park, and a trip here makes an excellent weekend break from the city.

Santuário do Caraça

Situated at the only entrance to the park is the **Santuário do Caraça**, formerly a seminary and a school, and now converted into a hotel. The **school**, famous in Brazil, was founded on the site of a hermitage and seminary in 1774, and for 150 years educated the upper classes of Minas Gerais, including generations of Brazilian politicians. In 1965 a fire destroyed much of the building, the theatre was burnt to the ground and the library lost twenty thousand of its thirty thousand books.

The building was restored in 1991 and transformed into a **hotel**, *Hospedaria do Caraça* (☎031/837-2698, reservations essential; ⑤), managed by the remaining members of the order. It's a comfortable, low-key place to spend a few relaxing days. Some parts still remain from the original religious life of the building including rooms for private prayer, a few bedrooms and the cellar. The neo-Gothic church of Nossa Senhora Mãe Dos Homens, added in 1883, was also spared by the fire, and has beautiful French stained-glass windows, marble and soapstone carvings and a seven-hundred-pipe organ built in the seminary itself.

There is a small **museum** attached to the church with exhibits rescued from the fire including English and Chinese porcelain, furniture and a sundial. One of the greatest attractions of the place are the **wolves** (*lobo-guará*) which live in the surrounding woods. One of them comes near the church almost every day to be fed by Brother Tobias.

THE CIDADES HISTÓRICAS

The **cidades históricas** of Minas Gerais – small enough really to be towns rather than cities – were founded within a couple of decades of each other in the early eighteenth century. Rough and violent mining camps in their early days, they were soon transformed by mineral wealth into treasure houses, not merely of gold, but also of Baroque art and architecture. Well preserved and carefully maintained, together the towns form one of the most impressive sets of colonial remains in the Americas, comparable only to the silver-mining towns that flourished in Mexico at roughly the same time. In Brazil, they are equalled only by the remnants of the plantation culture of the Northeast, to which they contributed much of the gold you see in the gilded churches of Olinda and Salvador.

Although some have acquired a modern urban fringe, all the historic cities have centres untouched by modern developers – and a couple, like **Tiradentes**, look very much as they did two centuries ago. All have colonial churches – **Ouro Preto** has thirteen – at least one good museum, steep cobbled streets, ornate mansions and the particular atmosphere of places soaked in history. It was in them that the **Inconfidência Mineira**, Brazil's first bungling attempt to throw off the Portuguese yoke, was played out in 1789. And here the great sculptor Antônio Francisco Lisboa, **Aleijadinho** or the "little cripple", spent all his life, leaving behind him a body of work unmatched by any other figure working in the contemporary Baroque tradition.

ALEIJADINHO (ANTÔNIO FRANCISCO LISBOA)

Although little is known of his life, we do know roughly what **Aleijadinho** looked like. In the Museu de Aleijadinho in Ouro Preto is a crude but vivid portrait showing an intense, aquiline man, clearly what Brazilians call *pardo* – of mixed race. His hands are under his jacket, which seems a trivial detail unless you know what makes his achievement truly astonishing: the great sculptor of the *barroco mineiro* was a leper, and produced much of his best work after he had lost the use of his hands.

Despite being recognized as a master sculptor during his lifetime, only the barest outline of the life of Antônio Francisco Lisboa is clear. He was born in Ouro Preto in 1738, the son of a Portuguese craftsman; his mother was probably a slave. For the first half of his exceptionally long life he was perfectly healthy, a womanizer and *bon viveur* despite his exclusively religious output. His prodigious talent, equally at home in wood as stone, human figures or abstract decoration, allowed him to set up a workshop with apprentices while still young, and he was much in demand. Although he always based himself in Ouro Preto, he spent long periods in all the major historic towns except Diamantina, working on commissions; but he never travelled beyond the state. Self-taught, he was an obsessive reader of the Bible and medical textbooks, the only two obvious influences in his work, one with its imagery, the other underlying the anatomical detail of his human figures.

In the late 1770s, his life changed utterly. He began to suffer from a progressively debilitating disease which seems to have been leprosy, although even this is not certain. As it got worse he became a recluse, only venturing outdoors in the dark, and increasingly obsessed with his work. His physical disabilities were terrible: he lost his fingers, toes and the use of his lower legs. Sometimes the pain was so bad his apprentices had to stop him hacking away at the offending part of his body with a chisel.

Yet despite all this he actually increased his output, working with hammer and chisel strapped to his wrists by his apprentices, who moved him about on a wooden trolley. It was under these impossible conditions that he sculpted his masterpiece, the 12 massive figures of the prophets and the 64 lifesize Passion figures for the **Basílica do Senhor Bom Jesus de Matosinhos** in Congonhas (see p.166), between 1796 and 1805. They were his swansong: failing eyesight finally forced him to stop work and he ended his life as a hermit in a hovel on the outskirts of Ouro Preto. The death he longed for finally came on November 18, 1814: he is buried in a simple grave in the church he attended all his life, Nossa Senhora da Conceição in Ouro Preto.

Aleijadinho's prolific output would have been remarkable under any circumstances: given his condition it was nothing short of miraculous, a triumph of the creative spirit. The bulk of his work is to be found in Ouro Preto, but there are also significant items in Sabará, São João del Rei, Mariana and Congonhas. His achievement was to stay within the Baroque tradition, yet bring to its ornate conventions a raw physicality and unmatched technical skill that gives his work unique power.

Practicalities

The nearest *cidade histórica* to Belo Horizonte is **Sabará**, only a local bus ride away; the furthest is **Diamantina**, six hours north by bus from the capital, in the wild scenery of the Serra do Espinhaço. Two hours southeast from Belo Horizonte, **Ouro Preto** is the ex-capital of the state and the largest of the historic cities, with **Mariana** a short distance away. And two hours to the south of Belo Horizonte is **Congonhas**, where the church of Bom Jesus do Matosinhos is considered to be Aleijadinho's masterpiece. A two-hour bus ride further south are **São João del Rei** and **Tiradentes**.

Only in Sabará is **accommodation** difficult. All the others are well supplied with places to stay, and are worth more than a quick day trip. If you only have a little time to spare, the best option from Belo Horizonte is probably Ouro Preto: you can easily get there and back in a day, and – though everyone has their own favourites – it is the most classically beautiful of all.

Sabará

SABARÁ lies strung out over a series of hills, wound around the Rio das Velhas. It was here that the first alluvial gold strikes in Minas were made, on the banks of the river; both Ouro Preto and Mariana are downstream. Many of the cobbled streets are so steep they have to be taken slowly, but ascents are rewarded with gorgeous churches, austere on the outside, choked with carving and ornamentation inside. The only drawback is the dearth of accommodation. Sabará's proximity to Belo Horizonte would make it the ideal base for seeing the metropolis, but for some mysterious reason there is only one hotel in the historic town, and one on the outskirts. Fortunately, the frequency of the **bus** link (every 15min from 4am to midnight) makes it an easy – and unmissable – day trip from the city: catch the red #5509 bus on Rua Caetés one block up from Avenida Afonso Pena. Start early; all the churches are open in the morning only.

The Town

Standing in **Praça Santa Rita**, you're in the centre not just of the oldest part of Sabará, but of the oldest inhabited streets in southern Brazil. Founded in 1674, Sabará is the most venerable of the *cidades históricas*, and was the first major centre of gold mining in the state, although attention shifted southwards to Ouro Preto and Mariana by the end of the seventeenth century. It was founded by Borba Gato, a typical Paulista cut-throat who combined Catholic fervour – the town's first name was Vila Real de Nossa Senhora da Conceição de Sabarabuçú, later thankfully shortened – with ruthlessness: his determined extermination of the local Indians made gold mining possible in Sabará.

Not until forty years after its foundation were the mud huts and stockades of the early adventurers replaced by stone buildings, and it wasn't until the second quarter of the eighteenth century, when gold production was at its peak, that serious church building began, and the village began to acquire an air of permanence. A fair proportion of the local gold ended up gilding the interiors of the town's churches, but by the turn of the nineteenth century, all the alluvial gold had been exhausted and the town entered a steep decline. Sophisticated deep mining techniques, introduced by Europeans in the nineteenth century, failed to stop the decline and Sabará became a small and grindingly poor place – today, the colonial zone is fringed by *favelas*.

Igreja de Nossa Senhora de Ó

The very early days of Sabará are represented by the tiny **Igreja de Nossa Senhora de Ó**, one of the oldest, and certainly one of the most unusual, colonial churches in Brazil. It's a couple of kilometres from Praça Santa Rita; a signposted walk, or you can take the local bus marked "Esplanada" from the square. It is extremely unusual since it doesn't look in the least Portuguese: an austere, irregularly shaped exterior is topped off by an unmistakably Chinese tower, complete with pagoda-like upturns at the corners. The cramped interior, dominated by a gilded arch over the altar, also shows distinct oriental influences, but the church is so old – it was started in 1698 – that nobody knows who was responsible for its unique design. The most likely explanation is that the Portuguese, despairing of the local talent, imported a group of Chinese craftsmen from Macau. There were certainly artisans from Macau in Diamantina, to the north, where streets are named after them, but here no other trace of them survives.

Matriz Nossa Senhora da Conceição

Sabará's main church, **Nossa Senhora da Conceição** (Wed–Fri 10am–noon and for Mass on Sun) is on Praça Getúlio Vargas, signposted from Praça Santa Rita. Started by

MINAS BAROQUE

There are three distinct phases of **Baroque church architecture** in Minas. The **first**, from the beginning of the eighteenth century to about 1730, was very ornate and often involved extravagant carving and gilding, but left exteriors plain; sculpture was formal, with stiff, rather crude statues. The **second phase** dominated the middle decades of the eighteenth century, with equally extravagant decorations inside, especially around the altar, and the wholesale plastering of everything with gold; the exteriors were now embellished with curlicues and panels in fine Minas soapstone, ceilings were painted and sculpture noticeably more natural, although still highly stylized. The peak was the period from 1760 to 1810 and this **third phase** of *barroco mineiro* can be stunning: the exterior decoration was more elaborate, but the interiors are less cluttered, with walls often left plain, and fine carving in both wood and stone. By now, too, the religious sculpture, with its flowing realism, had broken the stylistic bounds that confine most Baroque art.

the Jesuits in 1720, it's a fine example of the so-called first and second phases of Minas Baroque. Succeeding generations added features to the original layout and inside it's extremely impressive, with a double row of heavily carved and gilded arches, a beautifully decorated ceiling and, once again, Chinese influence in the gildings and painted panels of the door leading to the sacristy.

Nossa Senhora do Carmo

The church of **Nossa Senhora do Carmo** on Rua do Carmo, a vintage third-phase church, is a good contrast, while it's also a demonstration of the remarkable talents of Aleijadinho, who oversaw its construction and contributed much of the decoration between 1770 and 1783, a time when he was at the height of his powers. The interior manages to be elaborate and uncluttered at the same time, with graceful curves in the gallery, largely plain walls, comparatively little gilding and a beautifully painted ceiling. Aleijadinho left his mark everywhere: the imposing soapstone and painted wood pulpits, the banister in the nave, the flowing lines of the choir, and above all in the two statues of São João da Cruz and São Simão Stock. You can tell an Aleijadinho from the faces: the remarkably lifelike head of São Simão is complete with wrinkles and transfixed by religious ecstacy.

Nossa Senhora do Rosário dos Pretos da Barra

Despite being left half-built and open to the elements, the church of **Nossa Senhora do Rosário dos Pretos da Barra**, fifteen minutes' signposted walk from Praça Santa Rita on Praça Melo Viana, is just as fascinating as the more ornate buildings. It was built by slaves, who actually did the work in the gold mines: until the mines declined, a large majority of the population of all the historic cities was black. Organized into lay societies called *irmandades*, the slaves financed and built churches, but this one was begun late, in 1767, and with the decline of the mines the money ran out. Although sporadic restarts were made during the nineteenth century, it was never more than half-built and when slavery was abolished in 1888, it was left as a memorial.

The Museu do Ouro

The **Museu do Ouro** (Tues–Sun noon–5.30pm) is a short but steep signposted walk up from Praça Santa Rita on Rua da Intendência, but well worth the effort. Built in 1732, this is the only royal foundry house remaining in Brazil. When gold was discovered in Minas Gerais, the Portuguese Crown was entitled to a fifth of the output but had to collect it first. To do so, it put a military cordon around the gold mines, and then built several royal foundries, where gold from the surrounding area was melted down, franked and the royal fifth deducted. The functional building that now houses the museum easily reveals its origins: it is built around an interior courtyard, overlooked by a balcony on three sides, from where the officials could keep an eagle eye on gold being melted into bars and weighed. Along with the other royal foundry in Ouro Preto, it was Brazil's most heavily guarded building.

Most of the museum is devoted to gold-mining history. **Downstairs** are rooms full of colonial scales, weights, pans and other mining instruments, and a strongroom where until 1986 you could see genuine eighteenth-century gold bars and jewels in the safe. Unfortunately, that year two men walked in, put a pistol to the guard's head and walked off with the safe's contents, which have never been recovered: the bars on display now are plaster casts of the real thing, although they look authentic enough. **Upstairs** you'll find the usual collection of colonial furniture and some moderate *arte sacra*, but also some interesting prints and one very fine painted ceiling, representing the four continents known at the time it was built. In a room off the courtyard, to the right of the large wooden water-driven grinding mill, is a model of the **Morro Velho** mine in nearby Nova Lima, the deepest gold mine in the world outside South Africa. There's a commemorative photograph of the 44 Welsh mining engineers and single Brazilian lawyer who began it, all working for the wonderfully named St John del Rey Gold Mining Company.

The rest of the town

If you tire of colonial sightseeing, just wandering around the bars and cobbled streets near the Praça Santa Rita is very pleasant, too. There are lots of impressive buildings, notably the **Prefeitura** on Rua Dom Pedro II, and the nineteenth-century **theatre** on the same street: it was designed as an opera house and completed just as the gold ran out – the interior is open during the day from Tuesday to Friday. Before you leave the town, have some water from the **Chafariz do Rosário** on Praça Melo Viana, as it's believed that all those who drink from the fountain will one day come back to Sabará.

Practicalities

The nineteen-kilometre journey from Belo Horizonte takes roughly thirty minutes, though the bus station is at the far eastern end of town; ask the driver to show you the best stop for the colonial centre, from where you should easily find Praça Santa Rita. There is a rudimentary **tourist office** around the corner, but it doesn't stock maps and isn't really worth bothering with, and the colonial zone is small enough to manage without a street plan. If in doubt, any road going uphill will invariably lead you to a church, from where it's easy to get your bearings. **Buses back to Belo Horizonte** are best caught on the main road leading out of town at the bottom of the colonial zone by the river.

There are several **bars and restaurants**, which get lively at weekends: *Cê Qui Sabe* at Rua Mestre Caetano 56 (☎031/671-2906) and *314* at Rua Comendador Viana 304 (☎031/671-2313) both serve a reliable *comida mineira*. Cheaper places are clustered around Praça Santa Rita, and dotted throughout the old centre, often in people's front rooms. If you want to **stay** in the vicinity your only options are the *Solar dos Sepúlvedas*, Rua Intendência 371 (☎031/671-2705; ④), with five rooms and a small pool, and the very reasonable *Hotel do Ouro*, Rua Santa Cruz 237, Morro da Cruz (☎031/671-2082; ③), which is the brightly painted building you see hanging on the cliff-edge to the right as you come into town.

Ouro Preto

The drive to **OURO PRETO**, 100km southeast of Belo Horizonte, begins unpromisingly with endless industrial complexes and *favelas* spread over the hills, but in its later stretches becomes spectacular, winding around hill country 1000m above sea level and passing several valleys where patches of forest survive: imagine the entire landscape covered with it and you have an idea of what greeted the gold-seekers in the 1690s. On arrival, the first thing that strikes you is how small the town is, considering that until 1897 it was the capital of Minas – its population is still only around 65,000. That said, you can see at a glance why the capital had to be shifted to Belo Horizonte. The steep hills the town is built around, straddling a network of creeks, severely limit space for expansion: any larger than it is at present and you would need climbing gear to get around. Yet Ouro Preto's very existence is a sign of how rich the gold seams were, as you'd need a compelling reason to build on such irregular terrain. But the hills and vertiginous streets (some so steep they have steps rather than pavements) are vital ingredients in what is one of the loveliest towns in Brazil, an almost unspoilt eighteenth-century jewel.

Avoid coming on Monday if you want to see the sights, as all the churches and most of the museums close for the day. Also, buy your ticket back to Belo Horizonte as soon as you arrive (or the day before if you've stayed over) as buses fill up very quickly. Some people complain about Ouro Preto being touristy – and it is more commercialized than any other *cidade histórica* – but they miss the point: it's because there really is something to savour here that the visitors come. From the modern *Rodoviária* on the outskirts of town where you arrive, or, even better, coming into Ouro Preto from the other side on the road from Mariana, the town is spread out below you, every hill crowned with a church, a sea of tiled roofs and straggling lines of colonial buildings. At **Easter** time, the town becomes the focus of a spectacular series of plays and processions lasting for about a month before Easter Sunday, during which the last days of the life of Christ are played out in open-air theatres throughout the town. The tourist office can supply programmes and dates or you can get information from TURMINAS and BELOTUR in Belo Horizonte.

Some history

Less than a decade after gold was struck at Sabará, a Paulista adventurer called **Antônio Dias** pitched camp underneath a mountain the Indians called Itacolomi, with an unmistakable thumb-shaped rock on its summit. Panning the streams nearby, he found "black gold" – alluvial gold mixed with iron ore – and named his camp after it. It attracted a flood of people as it became clear the deposits were the richest yet found in Minas, and so many came that they outstripped the food supply. In 1700 there was a famine and legend has it that people died of hunger with gold nuggets in their hands.

The early years were hard, made worse by a war started in 1707 between the Portuguese and Paulista *bandeirantes*, who resisted the Crown's attempts to take over the area. The war, the **Guerra das Emboabas**, lasted for two years and was brutal, with ambushes and massacres the preferred tactics of both sides. Ouro Preto was the Portuguese base, and troops from here drove the Paulistas from their headquarters at Sabará and finally annihilated them near São João del Rei. From then on, Ouro Preto was the effective **capital** of the gold-producing area of Minas, although it wasn't officially named as such until 1823. Indeed, compared to places like nearby Mariana, Ouro Preto was a late developer; all but two of its churches date from the second half of the eighteenth century, and several of its finest buildings, like the school of mining and the town hall on Praça Tiradentes, were not finished until well into the nineteenth century.

The gold gave out about the time that Brazil finally became independent in 1822, but for decades the town survived as an administrative centre and university town; a school

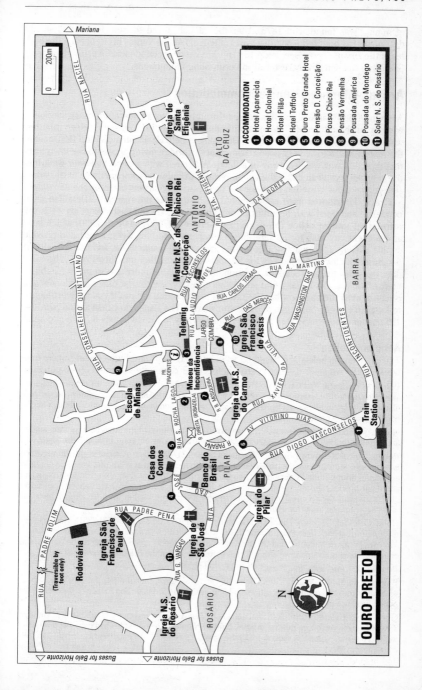

OURO PRETO

ACCOMMODATION
1 Hotel Aparecida
2 Hotel Colonial
3 Hotel Pilão
4 Hotel Toffolo
5 Ouro Preto Grande Hotel
6 Pensão D. Conceição
7 Pouso Chico Rei
8 Pensão Vermelha
9 Pousada América
10 Pousada do Mondego
11 Solar N. S. do Rosário

of mining was founded in 1876. After the capital moved to Belo Horizonte, steady decline set in, though the populist government of Getúlio Vargas brought back the bodies of the *Inconfidêntes* (see box p.158 and Museu da Inconfidência on p.157) to a proper shrine, and sensitively restored the crumbling monuments.

Arrival, information and accommodation

Arriving from Mariana, the bus passes through the main square, Praça Tiradentes – where you should get off – before continuing to the *Rodoviária*, some fifteen minutes' walk westwards on Rua Padre Rolim. Buses from Belo Horizonte now stop 1km west of the *Rodoviária*, for the very good reason that the bridge giving access to the town from that direction was washed away in a flood. You're left with a good half-hour walk into the centre, or you can catch the small, regular *Circular* buses from there to the *praça* (the regional buses are too large for the steep, twisting streets taken by the *Circulars*).

Praça Tiradentes itself is dominated by a statue of the martyr to Brazilian independence and lined with beautiful colonial buildings. On the east side at no. 41 is the **municipal tourist office** (Mon–Fri 8am–6pm; ☎031/559-3544 ext. 3269), which sells an excellent city map for $3 (and has a smaller version for free); it can also provide details of some spectacular walks in the surrounding countryside, and has a CD-ROM database which you can access for all sorts of information on Ouro Preto. The town does get crowded at weekends and holiday periods, but there are so many establishments that you can usually find somewhere to stay; the tourist office has details and prices of even the cheapest hotels, and will phone round for you if you have problems, or keep an eye on your luggage while you search. The Banco do Brasil at Rua São José 189 changes money ($100 minimum) from Monday to Friday between 11am and 4pm.

Accommodation

The price codes below are based on weekend (Fri–Sun) and high-season prices; mid-week and in low season, Ouro Preto's hotels offer discounts of around 20–30 percent.

Pousada América, Rua Camilo de Brito 15 (☎031/551-2525). About 100m off Praça Tiradentes along Rua Barão de Camargos (the bus from Mariana passes it), a newish place, family-run and popular with foreign tourists, with good if basic *apartamentos* and *quartos* (same price) though slightly expensive for what it offers. ④.

Hotel Aparecida, Praça Cesário Alvim (☎031/551-1091). Opposite the (freight-only) train station and requiring a steep walk up into the centre. Its *quartos* are the cheapest beds in town. ①–②.

Pouso Chico Rei, Rua Brigador Mosqueira 90 (☎031/551-1274). A small eighteenth-century house converted into a comfortable *pensão*, filled with a collection of relics that would do credit to a museum, with a stunning view from the reading room on the first floor, excellent breakfasts and a tranquil, timeless atmosphere. There are only 6 rooms which means you have to book in advance, but it's certainly the best deal in town. *Quartos* cost $30 per person, but the price for *apartamentos* is the same for singles as for doubles. ⑥.

Hotel Colonial, Travessa Padre Camilo Veloso 26 (☎031/551-3133, fax 551-3361). An excellent place one street back from Praça Tiradentes (it's signposted), with a range of *apartamentos*, all with *frigobar*, TV, air conditioning and telephones. The better rooms are in the wing to the right of the entrance, some of them on two levels. Much better value than the *Pousada América*. ④–⑤.

Pensão D. Conceição, Rua Paraná 90 (☎031/551-1314). Friendly family guesthouse. ③.

Pousada do Mondego, Largo de Coimbra 38 (☎031/551-2528, fax 551-3094). An excellent place in a beautiful restored eighteenth-century building beside the Igreja de São Francisco de Assis, with period furniture in all rooms. ⑦.

Ouro Preto Grande Hotel, Rua Senador Rocha Lagoa 164 (☎ and fax 031/551-1488). If you like airport lounges you'll love this 3-star hotel, built by Niemeyer on one of his bad days – at least staying there you don't have to look at it. All the same, it's central, with good service; a pool is under construction. ⑥.

Hotel Pilão, Praça Tiradentes 51, next to the tourist office (☎031/551-3066, fax 551-3275). Beautiful old rooms overlooking the square (which can be noisy at night), but not the friendliest of places and no single rooms. ③.

Solar Nossa Senhora do Rosário, Rua Getúlio Vargas 270 (☎031/551-5200). The best upmarket place, complete with sauna, scotch bar and a good restaurant. ⑧.

Hotel Toffolo, Rua São José 76 (☎031/551-1322). A beautiful old building in a fine central location – if you can find anyone to let you in. ③.

Pensão Vermelha, Largo de Coimbra, at the corner with Rua Antônio Pereira (☎031/551-1138). Quiet, family-run place, with clean if simple rooms, some overlooking the magnificent façade of the São Francisco church. ②.

The Town

Praça Tiradentes is the best place to start a tour of the town. First stop should be the tourist office (see p.156) to pick up a map and a card that gives the latest opening hours of the churches and museums. The size of the town is deceptive. There's enough to keep you going for days – thirteen colonial churches, seven chapels, six museums and several other sights – and if you want to explore in depth you should buy a copy of the *Guia de Ouro Preto* by Manoel Bandeira, a useful guidebook (Portuguese only) that's sold at the tourist office.

The Escola de Minas

Right on the Praça Tiradentes stands the mining school, the **Escola de Minas**, now housed in the old governor's palace. It's still the best mining school in the country, and its students, with their bars and motorbikes, lend a Bohemian air to the town. The white turrets make the building itself look rather like a fortress: the exterior, with a fine marble entrance, dates from the 1740s, but the inside was gutted during the last century and not improved by it. Attached to the school is the **Museu de Mineralogia** (Mon–Fri noon–5pm, Sat & Sun 9am–1pm; $1), founded in 1877 from the collection of the French geologist Henri Gorceix. Although most of the exhibits are of interest only to geologists, there is one fascinating room where gold and precious stones are beautifully displayed, in contrast to the chaos of the rest of it. One stunning nugget comes from the Gurupi in Maranhão, way to the north – a delicate leaf of gold sprouting out of a lump of quartz.

The Paço Municipal and Museu da Inconfidência

Also in the square are the old city chambers, the **Paço Municipal** (Tues–Sun noon–5pm), a glorious eighteenth-century building that provides a perfect example of the classical grace of Minas colonial architecture. Its beautifully restored interior lives up to expectations: like many colonial town halls it was also a jail, and many of the huge rooms, so well suited to the display of *arte sacra*, were once dungeons.

The building contains the **Museu da Inconfidência** (Tues–Sun noon–5.30pm; $1), interesting enough since the surrounding towns have been stripped of a great deal of their wealth to stock the museum; the only collection that compares with it is in Mariana. There are relics of eighteenth-century daily life, from sedan chairs and kitchen utensils (including the seal the bishop used to stamp his coat of arms on his cakes) to swords and pistols. A ground-floor room is dominated by a vivid life-size effigy of St George, complete with spear, which was propped up on a horse and paraded around during religious processions. And on the table opposite is the museum's highlight: four exquisite, small Aleijadinho statues that are a fitting introduction to the flowing detail of his best work.

Upstairs there's colonial furniture and more art, but the spiritual heart of the place is found at the rear of the ground floor, where the cell in which **Tiradentes**

THE INCONFIDÊNCIA MINEIRA

Ouro Preto is most famous in Brazil as the birthplace of the **Inconfidência Mineira**, the first attempt to free Brazil from the Portuguese. Inspired by the French Revolution, and heartily sick of the heavy taxes levied by a bankrupt Portugal, a group of twelve prominent town citizens led by **Joaquim José da Silva Xavier** began in 1789 to discuss organizing a rebellion. Xavier was a dentist, known to everyone as *Tiradentes*, "teeth-puller". Another of the conspirators was **Tomas Gonzaga**, whose hopeless love poems to the beautiful **Marília Dirceu**, promised by her family to another, made the couple into the Brazilian equivalent of Romeo and Juliet: "When you appear at dawn, all rumpled/like a badly wrapped parcel, no ribbons or flowers/how Nature shines, how much lovelier you seem."

In the event the conspiracy was a fiasco and all were betrayed and arrested before any uprising was organized. The leaders were condemned to hang, but the Portuguese, realizing that they could ill afford to offend the inhabitants of a state whose taxes kept them afloat, arranged a royal reprieve, commuting the sentence to exile in Angola and Mozambique. Unfortunately the messenger arrived two days too late to save Tiradentes, marked as the first to die. He was hanged where the column now stands in the square that bears his name, his head stuck on a post and his limbs despatched to the other mining towns to serve as a warning.

spent the last night of his life is now the **shrine to the Inconfidêntes**. An antechamber holds documents, like the execution order and birth and death register of Tiradentes, reverently framed, and leads into a room containing the remains of the thirteen conspirators and Tiradentes himself – all in the vaguely Fascist style the Vargas era usually chose for its public monuments. Most of the conspirators died in Africa, some in Portugal; all were exiled for the rest of their lives and never returned to Brazil.

The Igreja de Nossa Senhora do Carmo

Next door to the Paço Municipal on Praca Tiradentes is one of the finest churches in Ouro Preto, the **Igreja de Nossa Senhora do Carmo** (Tues–Sun 8–11am). It was designed by Manoel Francisco Lisboa, Aleijadinho's father, and construction began just before his death in 1766. **Aleijadinho** himself then took over the building of the church and finished it six years later. He contributed the carving of the exterior, and worked on the interior, on and off, for four decades. The baptismal font in the sacristy is a masterpiece, as are the carved doors leading to the pulpits. Two of the side chapels in the main church (São João and Nossa Senhora da Piedade) were among the last commissions he was able to complete, in 1809; the accounts book for the time has Aleijadinho complaining he was paid with "false gold". Much the least cluttered of the major churches in Ouro Preto, it's the only one to have *azulejo* tiled panels, to make the Portuguese who patronized it feel at home.

To the side of the church is yet another **museum** of religious art (open same hours as the church), housed in an excellently restored mansion that was once the meeting house for the lay society attached to Nossa Senhora do Carmo. It's a high-quality collection and very well displayed, the best part being the glittering array of gold and silver religious objects downstairs in the Sala de Tesouro.

The Igreja do Pilar

It's a lovely walk from Praça Tiradentes to Ouro Preto's oldest church. **Rua Brigador Mosqueira**, which runs downhill from the square, is one of the quietest and most beautiful streets in Ouro Preto, almost every building worth savouring. Wander down, bear left at the bottom, and you come out onto the incredibly steep Rua do Pilar, from where you can glimpse the towers of the Igreja do Pilar well before the plunging, cobbled path deposits you in front it.

The **Igreja do Pilar** (Tues–Sun 9–10.45am & noon–4.45pm), with an exterior ornate even by Baroque standards, is the finest example anywhere of early Minas Baroque architecture. It was begun in the 1720s and the interior is the opposite of the Carmo's restraint, a wild explosion of glinting Rococo, liberally plastered with gold. The best carving was done by Francisco Xavier de Brito, who worked in Minas from 1741 until his early death ten years later – and about whom nothing is known except that he was Portuguese and influenced Aleijadinho. He was responsible for the astonishing arch over the altar, where the angels supporting the Rococo pillars seem to swarm out of the wall on either side. In the sacristy, there's a small but interesting museum featuring enormous colonial wardrobes and a collection of gold and silver relics, the latter weakened by the theft in 1973 of its most valuable items, which have never been recovered.

The Casa dos Contos

From the Igreja do Pilar, turn right up Rua Rondolfo Bretos and round into **Rua São José** (also, confusingly, called Rua Tiradentes), whose many bars and restaurants make it a good place to take a breather. Crossing the small stone bridge, you come to the perfectly proportioned **Casa dos Contos**, the old treasury building, now a museum (Tues–Sat 12.30–5.30pm, Sun 8.30am–1.30pm; $0.80). Finished in 1787, it was built as a bank-cum-mansion by Ouro Preto's richest family, and in 1803 became the *Fazenda Real*, the place where the Crown extracted its fifth of the gold and assembled armed convoys to escort it down to Rio for shipment to Portugal. The collection is no more than moderately interesting – the usual mixture of *arte sacra* and furniture – but the building is terrific; a magnificent colonial mansion built when Ouro Preto was at its peak. The entrance hall is dominated by an imposing staircase, four storeys high, and built around a beautiful courtyard, large enough for a dozen cavalry troopers. The most interesting places radiate off it: the huge furnace for melting the gold and shaping it into bars, the slave quarters, the stables (horses were definitely better accommodated than slaves) and even an eighteenth-century privy. And don't forget to go right up to the *mirante* on the top floor for one of the best views of Ouro Preto.

The Igreja de São Francisco de Assis

From Praça Tiradentes, Rua Cláudio Manoel winds downhill, lined with stores selling precious stones and jewellery which doesn't come from Ouro Preto (but from eastern Minas) and is rather expensive. Ahead, on the right, is arguably the most beautiful church in Ouro Preto, the **Igreja de São Francisco de Assis** (Tues–Sun 8.30–11.45am & 1.30–4.45pm; $1 entrance ticket also valid for the Matriz de N.S. Conceição and Museu do Aleijadinho). The small square that sets it off – Largo do Coimbra – plays host to a food **market** in the morning and a mediocre arts and crafts market in the afternoon.

The church was begun in 1765, and no other contains more work by Aleijadinho. The magnificent exterior soapstone panels are his, as is virtually all of the virtuoso carving, in both wood and stone, inside; and to top it off, Aleijadinho also designed the church and supervised its construction. You would think the church commissioners would have left it at that, but in 1801 they contracted the best painter of the *barroco mineiro*, **Manoel da Costa Athayde**, to decorate the ceilings. It took him nine years, using natural dyes made from plant juices and powdered iron ore, and his work has stood the test of time far better than other church paintings of the period. The squirming mass of cherubs and saints are framed within a cunning *trompe l'oeil* effect, which extends the real Baroque pillars on the side of the nave into painted ones on the ceiling, making it seem like an open-air canopy through which you can glimpse clouds. There are also painted *azulejos* which look remarkably like the real thing.

The Matriz de Nossa Senhora da Conceição and Museu do Aleijadinho

Returning to Rua Cláudio Manoel, follow the winding Rua Bernardo de Vasconcelos, to the left – this is the back way down to the last of the major churches in Ouro Preto, **Matriz de Nossa Senhora da Conceição** (Tues–Sat 8–11.45am & 1.30–4.45pm, Sun noon–4.45pm; $1 entrance ticket also valid for the Igreja de São Francisco de Assis and Museu do Aleijadinho), and it's a steep descent. Coming this way, you're leaving the main tourist area and everything looks just as it did the day Aleijadinho died: the Matriz is famous as the church he belonged to and where he is buried. The one-time cut-throat Antônio Dias, who founded Ouro Preto and died old and rich in 1727, left his fortune to build this church on the spot of his first camp – so this is where it all began and, with the death of Aleijadinho, also where it can be said to have ended.

Despite Aleijadinho's connection with the church, he never worked on this one. All the same, it is an impressive example of mid-period Minas Baroque, and the painting and carving are very fine, especially the figures of saints in the side altars – look at the expression and movement of St Sebastian, on the left of the nave. Aleijadinho is buried in a simple **tomb** on the right of the nave, marked "Antônio Francisco Lisboa" and covered by nothing more elaborate than a plain wooden plank.

A side door by the main altar of the church leads to the sacristy and the fascinating **Museu do Aleijadinho** (Tues–Sat 8–11.45am & 1.30–4.45pm; $1 entrance ticket also valid for the Igreja de São Francisco de Assis and the Matriz de N.S. Conceição), which is worth lingering over: not so much a museum of Aleijadinho's work as of his life and times. What work there is by him is in the basement, and is quite something – four magnificent lions which once served as supports for the plinth on which coffins were laid. Aleijadinho, never having seen a lion, drew from imagination and produced medieval monsters with the faces of monkeys. The ground floor is taken up by a high-quality collection of religious art, but the highlight is upstairs, in a room dedicated not just to Aleijadinho but to all the legendary figures of Ouro Preto's golden age.

There are reproductions of the birth and death entries in the parish register for Aleijadinho, Marília Dirceu and Manoel Athayde. But even better are the eighteenth-century *ex votos* on the wall, a riveting insight into the tribulations of bygone daily life. One shows a black slave on her sickbed, with the inscription "Ana, slave of Antônio Dias, had me made after finding herself gravely ill, without hope of life, but praying to Our Lord of the Slaves miraculously recovered". Opposite is a gruesome one from 1778 giving thanks for the successful setting of a broken leg, shown in graphic detail. Also on the wall there's a small **portrait**, crude but priceless, of Aleijadinho in middle age. It doesn't flatter so is probably a good likeness: slightly hunched, sharp features, dark and intense.

Igreja de Santa Efigênia

Further out from the centre is the less important but no less fascinating **Igreja de Santa Efigênia**, the church for slaves, located on the east hill some 3km from Praça Tiradentes. To get there, continue along Rua Cláudio Manoel down to the river, cross over and climb up Rua Santa Efigênia. Although poor in comparison to Ouro Preto's other churches, its artwork is well worth the steep climb. The altar was carved by Javier do Briton, the mentor of Aleijadinho; the interior panels are by Manoel Rabelo de Souza; and the exterior image of Nossa Senhora do Rosário is by Aleijadinho himself. Slaves contributed to its construction by smuggling gold in their teeth cavities and under their fingernails. It's currently only open for Sunday Mass, but the municipal tourist office is trying to convince the new *padre* to reinstate the old opening hours (Tues–Sun noon–8pm; enquire at the tourist office).

Mina do Chico Rei

If you don't have time to visit the Mina do Passagem **gold mine** near Mariana, or else balk at its $15 entrance fee, much nearer and cheaper is the **Mina do Chico Rei** (daily 8am–5pm; $2), at Rua Dom Silvério 108 in the eastern *bairro* of Antônio Dias. Founded in 1702, barely seven years after gold was first struck in Sabará, the mine had a working life of nearly two centuries. Though visually not as impressive as the Mina do Passagem, it nonetheless boasts some impressive statistics, which give some idea of just how rich Ouro Preto must once have been: the mine, constructed on five levels, contains an astonishing eighty square kilometres of tunnels, vaults and passages.

Eating and drinking

One of the nice things about Ouro Preto is the number of places where you can eat, drink or just hang out; when the students are out in force on weekend nights, it has none of the quiet atmosphere of a small interior town that you might expect. During termtime, at the weekend, the steep Rua Conde de Bobadela (also called Rua Direita), leading up to Praça Tiradentes, is packed with students spilling out of the **bars** and cafés; more congregate in the square itself, though most of the bars there have been turned into expensive restaurants. The modern wing of the mining school on the square contains a bar and a **live music** venue (see the posters in the lobby). If you prefer a quiet drink away from the crowds, try *Bar Sena*, a local dive on the corner outside the Igreja do Pilar.

There is no shortage of **restaurants**, either; the better-value ones (though still relatively costly) are clustered at the bottom of the hill on Rua São José, of which the best is unquestionably *Restaurante Chafariz* at no. 167 (daily 11am–10pm), which does a superb *mineiro* buffet for about $11 and sometimes has special offers. The decor is pleasantly rustic, the service smooth – altogether highly recommended.

Just off Rua São José at Rua Terceira Amaral 24, there's a good Italian-Mineiro restaurant, *Adega Ouro Preto*, with excellent food for around $10 a head à la carte, or $9 per kilo. More expensive places are clustered at the top of Rua Conde de Bobadela (Rua Direita) and on Praça Tiradentes, where you'll get good regional food in uniformly beautiful surroundings for $15–25 per person, unless you stick to pizza. The only exception on the square itself is *Bar Lampeão*, which has so far resisted the temptation to don evening dress and treble its prices.

Thankfully, for those on a tight budget, there are also several **cheap places to eat**, namely the basic *lanchonetes* on Rua Senador Rocha Lagoa (also called Rua das Flôres) just off the square (the *Vide Gula* here is good, and 20m up, *Lanchonete Ouro Grill* is even cheaper); and one or two bars on Rua Conde de Bobadela, the latter also serving good honey *caipirinhas*.

MOVING ON FROM OURO PRETO

If you're moving on to Mariana, the most convenient place to catch the local Transcotta bus there is from the stop on Rua Conselheiro Quintiliano, by the side of the Escola de Minas (every 20min or so from 5am to midnight). There are also daily services from Ouro Preto to Belo Horizonte (run by Pássaro Verde; ☎031/551-1081; see p.156 for information about where to catch these buses); Rio (Viação Útil; ☎031/551-3166); São João del Rei (Cristo Rei; ☎031/551-1777); São Paulo (Cristo Rei); and Vitória (not Sat; São Geraldo; ☎031/551-1864).

Mariana

MARIANA is one of the major colonial towns, and in the first half of the eighteenth century was grander by far than its younger rival 12km to the west, Ouro Preto. Despite regular riots and the war between Paulistas and the Portuguese, Mariana was the administrative centre of the gold mines of central Minas until the 1750s. The first governors of Minas had their residence here and the first bishops their palace, and the town proudly celebrated its tercentenary in 1996. Yet today Mariana's churches are far less grand than its illustrious neighbour's, and it's really no more than a large village, but it does have a fine museum and a perfectly preserved colonial centre, mercifully free of steep climbs, that is far less crowded and commercialized than Ouro Preto. It's only a twenty-minute bus ride away and if you can't stand the crowds in Ouro Preto you could always stay here instead. There are also at least seven daily buses direct from Belo Horizonte, run by Viação Pássaro Verde, as well as direct services from São Paulo (3 daily; 12hr) run by Cristo Rei.

Mina da Passagem

If you've come on the local bus from Ouro Preto, through steep hills bearing clear traces of centuries of mining, there's a bus stop 4km before Mariana opposite one of the area's more unusual sights – the ancient gold mine of **Mina da Passagem** (or Mina de Ouro).

One of the rare deep-shaft gold mines still operating in Minas, it's also one of the oldest. Gold has been dug here since 1719, although most of the seventeen kilometres of galleries date from the nineteenth century. These days the mine is less successful, and all except one of the eight faces have been closed down. Nevertheless over four hundred people still work here, and it tries hard to halt the decline by running delightfully ramshackle tours every day from 9am until 5pm (☎031/557-1255); the $15 charge is steep, but it's an interesting trip.

Among the series of repair yards is probably the oldest functioning machine in Brazil – a vintage 1825 British steam engine, now adapted to run on compressed air. It powers a drum cable that drives railcars into and out of the mine – safer than it looks, though you do need to be careful of bumping your head once you trundle into the galleries. The young guides are friendly, knowledgeable and speak reasonable English and French; there are bits of nineteenth-century mining equipment knocking around, and the dripping gallery opens out into a small, crystalline floodlit lake, 120m underground. Back up on the surface, the visit is rounded off with a demonstration of gold panning, with real gold – not as easy as it looks.

The history of the mine is a roll-call of economic imperialism. Sold by the Portuguese to the British in 1830, whose owners happily worked it with slaves at the same time as the Royal Navy was intercepting slavers in the Atlantic, it was then offloaded onto the French in 1883. Nationalized by Vargas in 1937, the mine was sold to the South Africans in 1970.

The Town

In Mariana itself, the wealth generated by the mine was transmuted into rows of fine houses. Most now have stores on the ground floor (and not all are colonial), but later builders have taken pains to blend their work in with the colonial core, and everything is carefully maintained. If you're going to tour the sights, then **orientation** is fairly straightforward. The truly colonial area begins at Praça Cláudio Manoel, in front of the large Catedral Basílica; from here, Rua Frei Durão, with several of the noblest eighteenth-century public buildings, leads to the exquisite Praça Gomes Freire, with its bandstand, trees and pond, lined on all sides by colonial *sobrados*, two-storey mansions. Nearby are the two finest churches in Mariana and a lovely *Prefeitura* building in Praça João Pinheiro, complete with *pelourinho*, the old stone whipping post to which slaves and miscreants were tied and beaten.

The Museu Arquidiocesano

Although it has been overshadowed by its neighbour for over two centuries, you can still get a good idea of Mariana's early flourish in one of the best museums in Minas Gerais, the **Museu Arquidiocesano** in the old bishop's palace, on Rua Frei Durão (Tues–Sun 9am–noon & 1– 5pm; $1).

The **building** itself is magnificent, with parts dating from the first decade of the eighteenth century, when it began life, bizarrely, as a prison for erring churchmen. The Franciscans were deeply involved in the Paulista expeditions and were notorious for being the worst cut-throats of all. Between 1720 and 1756 the jail was extended into a palace: the door and window frames are massive, built in beautifully worked local soapstone. Inside, the **collection** is predictable – *arte sacra* and colonial furniture – but is distinguished by its high quality and its age, often predating the earliest material in Ouro Preto by two or three decades. It gives a vivid idea of how Mariana was thriving, with stone buildings and all the trappings of the early eighteenth-century good life, when Ouro Preto was still a collection of hovels.

On the ground floor there's a sobering collection of chains and manacles draped along the walls, and also the "treasure room", containing the ecclesiastical gold and silver. But the bulk of things to see are upstairs. The stairwell is dominated by a taste of things to come, a powerful painting of *Christ's Passion* by Athayde, his best-known work. The stairs lead up to a number of graceful colonial rooms, including the luxurious private quarters of the bishops, which contain an excellent collection of religious art, notably the largest number of Aleijadinho figures anywhere outside a church. They are instantly recognizable: São João Nepomuceno, the bearded São Joaquim in religious ecstacy and a marvellous São Miguel in the corner by the window.

The colonial furniture section, usually the dullest part of Minas museums, is actually worth seeing here: lovely writing desks and chests of drawers, all early eighteenth century and most made of jacaranda wood – there was a glut on the market at the time, as the forests were felled to get at the gold. The most unusual exhibit is a false bookcase, with wooden "books" painted to resemble leather. You can also wander around the bishop's audience room – the throne is also by Aleijadinho, who was nothing if not versatile – and there's a separate gallery of their portraits, incongruously included amongst which are three, rather good, local landscapes by the German artist Nobauer.

Mariana's churches

Mariana's colonial churches are smaller and less extravagant than Ouro Preto's, though most are decorated with paintings by **Athayde**, who came from here and is buried in the Igreja de São Francisco (see below).

The oldest church is the **Catedral de Nossa Senhora da Assunção** on Praça Cláudio Manoel (Tues–Sun 7am–7pm), begun in 1709 and choked with gilded Rococo detail. This is very much an Aleijadinho family venture: his father, Manoel Francisco Lisboa, designed and built it, while Aleijadinho contributed the carvings in the sacristy and a font. The interior is dominated by the massive German organ dating from 1701 and donated by the king of Portugal in 1751. Look closely and you can see Chinese-style decorations carved by slaves, who also worked the bellows. You can hear the organ in action, in recitals given at 11am on Fridays and at noon on Sundays.

The two churches on Praça João Pinheiro, around the corner, show how tastes had changed by the end of the century. Their ornate facades and comparatively restrained

THE GARIMPEIROS OF MARIANA

If you've got time to kill, an interesting place to stroll to is the town *garimpo*, a small **mining camp**. Stand on the last of the bridges over the Carmo creek and you can see figures digging and panning upstream. They are *garimpeiros*, gold-miners, and are using methods almost unchanged since gold was first found here in 1696 – the only difference now is that the pans are metal rather than wood. They dig channels into the stream bed, divert the flow and sift through the gravel with pans. To take a closer look, you can get there easily from Rua Rosário Velho. The *garimpeiros* are friendly, if a little bemused that gringos should find what they are doing interesting. There's another *garimpo* camp 9km out of town on the São Marco road in the *bairro* of Antônio Pereira, where topaz is mined. Again, you're free to wander as you like.

interiors are typical of the third phase of *barroco mineiro*. The **Igreja de São Francisco de Assis** (daily 8am–5pm), finished in 1794, has the finest paintings of any Mariana church, as befits the place where Athayde is buried. The numbers on the church floor are where members of the lay Franciscan brotherhood are buried; Athayde is no. 94. The elaborate interior contains much that is worth seeing: a fine sacristy, and an altar and pews by Aleijadinho, who also put his signature on the church in his usual way, by sculpting the sumptuous soapstone "medal" over the door. The **Igreja de Nossa Senhora do Carmo** (daily 2–5pm), on the other side of the square with a less elaborate exterior, is disappointing in comparison. But the combination of the two churches with the equally graceful **Prefeitura** make the bare grass square a pleasant place to take a break.

From here, it's a short uphill walk via the unspoilt Rua Dom Silvério to the mid-eighteenth-century **Basílica Menor de São Pedro dos Clérigos** (open occasionally Sat & Sun for Mass) which overlooks the town, framed by groves of towering palms; you pass the strange, geometric **Igreja da Arquiconfraria** on the way. The object is not so much to view the Basílica, which was renovated in 1989, but to enjoy the view of the town stretched out before you. If you follow the path along the top the views are even better.

Practicalities

The local **buses from Ouro Preto** leave you right in the centre at Praça Tancredo Neves, opposite an excellent **tourist information post**, the Terminal Turístico (daily 9am–6pm; ☎031/557-1158), which sells a good map for $3 with everything helpfully marked on it, and distributes free brochures and booklets. The Terminal Turístico also has up-do-date bus timetables for planning onward journeys, and supplies accredited guides for tours in the region (around $50 a day). If you're coming from further afield, you'll arrive at the new **Rodoviária** (☎031/557-1122), on the main road a couple of kilometres from the centre; if you can't be bothered to walk into the centre, catch one of the buses from Ouro Preto, which pass through the *Rodoviária* every twenty minutes or so.

All the **places to stay** are within easy walking distance of Praça Tancredo Neves. The best is the *Pousada Solar dos Corrêa*, Rua Josafá Macedo 70 (☎031/557-2080; ⑨), one block up from the Terminal Turístico on the corner with Rua Direita. It's one of Minas' most delightful hotels, with fifteen very different rooms done up with mock-colonial furniture, ranging from small, dark and cosy loft conversions to a gorgeous first-floor room (no. 8) on the street corner flooded with light. It would pay to come mid-week to secure the room of your choice, as at weekends you'd be lucky to get one at all. Cheaper options include the basic *Hotel Central* (☎ and fax 031/557-1630; ③), an outwardly beautiful but inwardly run-down colonial building at Rua Frei Durão 8, overlooking the Praça Gomes Freire; the basic and modern *Hotel Faísca*, Rua Antônio Olinto 48-A (☎031/557-1765; ②–③), which you can see up the street from the tourist office and which offers *apartamentos* or cheaper *quartos* without TVs; *Hotel Müller* (☎031/557-1188, fax 557-2492; ③–④), across the bridge opposite the tourist office at Rua Getúlio Vargas 34, which has a range of rooms to suit all pockets (from $15 per person); and the clean and tidy *Hotel Providência*, Rua Dom Silvério 233 (☎031/577-1444 or 577-1149; ③), along the road that leads up to the Basílica, overlooking the centre and next to a school, which makes it noisy during the day.

Mariana has some excellent **restaurants**, cheaper by far than those in Ouro Preto. The nicest views are to be had from the places that look out onto Praça Gomes Freire (all open daily until midnight): the cosy *Restaurante Pizzeria Senzala* serves good food at lunchtime and is a lively and very friendly bar in the evenings; *Mangiare della Mamma*, three doors up at Rua Dom Viçoso 27, does a topnotch *mineiro comida à kilo* ($6 per kg), presented in heavy iron casseroles sizzling on a hot, wood-fired iron stove; and the *Pousada Solar dos Corrêa*'s restaurant, *Saborearte*, has not only excellent-value, authentic *mineiro* food but surroundings to suit. Just up from the square at Travessa João Pinheiro 26, next to the Igreja São Francisco, is arguably the town's best *mineiro* restaurant, *Tambau* (☎031/557-1406), while at the nearby *Alvorada*, Rua Jorge Marques 101, the food is reasonably good and economical, and the views come free. Similarly good value is the self-service restaurant *Panela de Pedra* attached to the Terminal Turístico, open lunchtimes only.

There are simple **bars** and **sorveterias** on most corners, and at weekends, a couple of **discotheques** open up on Praça Cláudio Manoel, the busiest being *Tatu's Dancing*. Lastly, the *Centro de Cultura SESI-Mariana*, opposite the Museu Arquidiocesano, occasionally hosts local art exhibitions, ballet and dance (☎031/557-1041 for information).

Congonhas

CONGONHAS, a rather ugly, modern town 72km south of Belo Horizonte, sits ill as one of the historic cities. In truth, there's only one reason for coming here: to see the pilgrimage church of Bom Jesus de Matosinhos. It's a long way to come just to see one thing, but this is no ordinary church: if one place represents the flowering of *barroco mineiro*, this is it, the spiritual heart of Minas Gerais.

Getting to Congonhas is relatively easy from both Belo Horizonte (6 buses daily; 1hr) and São João del Rei (5 buses daily, run by the Sandra company; 2hr). There are also two daily buses from Ouro Preto, headed for São Paulo or Barbacena; the ride takes about three hours and is a fascinating journey, much of it on country dirt roads through sleepy villages. It's possible to start out from Belo Horizonte or Ouro Preto, go to Congonhas with enough time to see Bom Jesus, and still get to São João del Rei in the evening (last bus 8.20pm, 10.20pm on Sun), but only if you set out early. To get from the main *Rodoviária*, a couple of kilometres out of town, to Bom Jesus, catch the **local bus** marked "Basílica", which takes you all the way up the hill to the church; it's impossible to miss.

Most people visit Congonhas on a day trip, and there's little reason to **stay**, but the best place is the *Colonial Hotel* (☎031/731-1834; ④), overlooking the church and gardens, with its own pool. The *Max Mazza Hotel* (☎031/731-1970; ⑤) is another good option, at Av. Júlia Kubitschek 410, more modern than the *Colonial*, but without a pool. If you want to eat, head for the *Cova do Daniel*, a good regional **restaurant** next to Bom Jesus.

Bom Jesus de Matosinhos

Built on a hill overlooking the town, with a panoramic view of the hills around it, the **Basílica do Senhor Bom Jesus de Matosinhos** is set in a magnificent sloping **garden** studded with palms and what look like six tiny mosques with oriental domes. These are small **chapels** commemorating episodes of the Passion; each is filled with lifesize statues dramatizing the scene in a tableau, 64 in all. Looking down on them from the parapets of the extraordinary terrace leading up to the church itself are twelve towering soapstone **statues** of Old Testament prophets. Everything, the figures and the statues, was sculpted by **Aleijadinho**, in what he must have known would be his last major commission. His leprosy was already advanced, and he could only work with chisels strapped to his wrists. The results are astonishing, a masterpiece made all the more moving by the fact it was also the farewell piece of a great artist suffering his own Passion.

The whole complex is modelled on the shrine of Bom Jesus in Braga, in northern Portugal. The idea and money came from a Portuguese adventurer, **Feliciano Mendes**, who – towards the end of his life – planned to recreate the pilgrimage church of his native Braga, to house an image of the dead Christ he brought with him from Portugal in 1713. Mendes died in 1756, when work had only just begun, and it was forty years before the local bishop contracted Aleijadinho to produce the figures of the Passion and the prophets. It seems likely that it was a conscious swansong on Aleijadinho's part: there is no other explanation for the way a seriously ill man pushed so hard to finish such a massive undertaking, whose theme was immediately relevant to his own suffering. Somehow, with his apprentices filling in fine detail, he managed to complete everything by 1805 – and the result defies belief that the project was executed by a man who had lost the use of his hands.

The Passion

There are always **guides** hanging around, who do know their stuff and can fill in a lot of interesting detail, but you're not obliged to go around with one.

Start at the bottom of the garden if you want to appreciate the deep religious mysticism that lies behind the design. The **slope** symbolizes the ascent towards the Cross and governs the sequence of tableaux, the scenes leading you up from the Garden of Gethsemane through Christ's imprisonment, trial, whipping, the crown of thorns, and the carrying of the Cross to Calvary. On top, guarded by the prophets, is the church, housing both the wooden image of Christ's body and the real body, in the Communion host: built in the shape of a cross it represents both the Crucifixion and the Kingdom of Heaven.

Two of the chapels are empty as the **figures** are undergoing restoration (you can see them lined up in the museum by the side of the church), but the rest are still in place. Viewing isn't ideal: there are grilles to stop people getting in, and some of the figures are difficult or impossible to see. All are sculpted from cedar and were brightly painted by Athayde, using his preferred natural paints made from ox blood, egg whites, crushed flowers and vegetable dyes. They are marvellously lifelike: you can see Christ's veins and individual muscles, a soldier's cheeks bulge as he blows a trumpet, a dwarf leers as he carries the nail to crucify Christ with. Too savage and realistic to be Baroque art, there is nothing with which to compare it – it's as if Aleijadinho was driven to take his genius for realism to its logical conclusion, and finally shatter the restrictions of the Baroque tradition he had worked in all his life.

Things become even more interesting on the **symbolic** front when you look closely at the figures. Christ is more than once portrayed with a vivid red mark around his neck, which make many think he also represents Tiradentes (see p.158). Support for the theory comes from the Roman soldiers, viciously caricatured, whom Aleijadinho gives two left feet and ankle boots – which only the Portuguese wore. Although nothing is known of Aleijadinho's politics, he was a native Brazilian and lived through the *Inconfidência* in Ouro Preto. He would certainly have known Tiradentes by sight, and it is more than likely that the Congonhas Christ is meant to represent him.

The prophets

If the cedar figures are outside the Baroque tradition, the statues of the **prophets** are its finest expression in all Brazil: carved from blocks of soapstone they dominate both the garden they look down on and the church they lead to. They are remarkably dramatic, larger than lifesize, full of movement and expression; perched on the parapet, you look up at them against the backdrop of either hills or sky. Travellers have left pages of descriptions – the explorer Richard Burton, dreadful Victorian philistine that he was, thought them "grotesque and utterly vile" – but suffice it to say that they are one of the finest works of art anywhere in the world for their period.

The church

The **church** is inevitably something of an anticlimax, but still interesting. The effigy of the dead Christ that Mendes brought over from Portugal is in a glass case in the altar, and through the door to the right of the altar is the cross which carried the image. The lampholders are Chinese dragons, yet more of the Macau influence also to be seen in Sabará and Diamantina.

Next to the church is a fascinating collection of **ex votos**; it keeps irregular hours but the friendly uniformed guards will open it up for you – they're not around at lunchtime. The display will be familiar to anyone who has been to other pilgrimage centres in Brazil, and the photos, pictures and messages from grateful sufferers have a voyeuristic fascination. This collection is remarkable for the number of really old *ex votos*, the earliest from a slave who recovered from fever in 1722. Others record in crude but vivid paintings incidents like being gored by a bull, being seriously burnt or escaping from a bus crash. If you are lucky, you will also find a row of Aleijadinho's Passion figures being restored. The room doubles as a workshop, and you get a better view of them here than in the chapels.

The **bus** to take you back to the *Rodoviária* leaves from the parking bay behind the church.

São João del Rei and around

SÃO JOÃO DEL REI is the only one of the historic cities to have adjusted successfully to life after the gold rush. It has all the usual trappings of the *cidades históricas* – gilded churches, well-stocked museums, colonial mansions – but it's also a thriving market town; easily the largest of the historic cities, with a population of around 80,000. This modern prosperity complements the colonial atmosphere rather than compromising it, and, with its wide central thoroughfare enclosing a small stream, its stone bridges, squares and trees, São João is a very attractive place, well worth lingering in. If possible, stay over on a Friday, Saturday or Sunday when you can take a ride on the "Smoking Mary", a lovingly restored nineteenth-century steam train, to the nearby village of **Tiradentes** – a great day out.

Founded in 1699 on the São João River, the town had the usual turbulent early years, but distinguished itself by successfully turning to ranching and trade when the gold ran out early in the last century. There is still a textile factory, and São João's carpets were once famous. Tiradentes was born here, Aleijadinho worked here, and in more recent times the great *mineiro* politician, **Tancredo Neves**, shepherded Brazil out of military rule when he was elected President in 1985. Tragically, he died before he took office (see "History" in *Contexts*) and is buried in the nearest place the town has to a shrine in the cemetery of São Francisco.

Arrival, orientation and accommodation

The centre of town is fifteen minutes' walk southwest from the **Rodoviária**, or you can take a local bus in: the stop isn't the obvious one immediately outside the *Rodoviária*'s main entrance – instead you need to turn left and take any bus from the stop on the other side of the road. Local buses enter the old part of town along **Avenida Tancredo Neves**, with its small stream and grassy verges to your left, then turn right to leave you at the **Terminal Turístico** (open in high season only), where you can pick up a tourist booklet with a helpful map. **Money changing** is quick, with no commission, at the BEMGE bank, Av. Tancredo Neves 213 (Mon–Fri 11am–4pm).

São João is divided into two main districts, each with a colonial area, separated by a small stream – the **Córrego do Lenheiro** – which runs between the broad Avenida Tancredo Neves on the north side and **Avenida Hermílio Alves**, which turns into **Avenida Eduardo Magalhães**, to the south. Relatively small and easy to find your way around, the districts are linked by a number of small bridges, including two eighteenth-century stone ones and a late nineteenth-century footbridge made of cast iron.

On the south side, the colonial zone is clustered around the beautiful **Igreja de São Francisco de Assis**, at the far western end of town. On the other side is the commercial centre, usually bustling with people, cars and the horse-drawn trailers of rural Minas. This commercial zone sprang up in the nineteenth century and shields the colonial area proper, several blocks of cobbled streets which jumble together Baroque churches, elegant mansions and the pastel fronts of humbler houses. For once you have the luxury of wandering around without losing your breath, as São João is largely flat.

Accommodation

Finding somewhere to stay is not a problem as **accommodation** in São João is plentiful and often excellent value. The best budget option is *Hotel Brasil* (☎032/371-2804; ①) on Av. Tancredo Neves 395, facing the train station, with high-ceilinged rooms and meticulously waxed floorboards (the stairs are positively treacherous). There are also several cheap and basic *dormitórios* nearby, within sight of the Terminal Turístico, the best of which is the friendly *Aparecida Hotel*, Praça Dr. Antônio Viegas 13 (☎032/371-2540; ②), which distinguishes itself in letting you use their kitchen.

Of the medium-range places, best value is the *Pousada Casarão*, Rua Ribeiro Bastos 94 (☎032/371-7447; ⑤), a wonderful converted mansion near São Francisco church, with the added attraction of a swimming pool and a good collection of pottery from the Jequitinhonha valley. At the same price, the *Quinta do Ouro*, towards the western end of Avenida Tancredo Neves on Praça Severiano de Rezende (☎032/371-2565; ⑤), has four lovely rooms, three with salons (reservations essential). Top of the range, with a pool but somewhat soulless, is the smart three-star *Porto Real*, at Av. Eduardo Magalhães 254 (☎ and fax 032/371-7000; ⑥); slightly less expensive, but without a pool, is *Lenheiros Palace*, Av. Tancredo Neves 257 (☎032/371-3914; ⑥).

The Town

São João's colonial sections are complemented by some fine buildings of more recent eras, notably the end of the last century, when the town's prosperity and self-confidence were high. The 1920s and 1930s were also good times – some of the vaguely Art Deco buildings combine surprisingly well with the colonial ones. The main public buildings line the south bank of the stream, best viewed from Avenida Tancredo Neves on the north side, making it very grand for a town centre; there's a sumptuous French-style **theatre** (1893), and the graceful blue **Prefeitura** (town hall) with an imposing Banco do Brasil building facing it. The relaxed atmosphere is reinforced by the number of bars and restaurants, and if you stumble across knots of people staring at walls, take a closer look; in São João a good half dozen traditional "**street newspapers**" still survive. Broadsheets rather than papers, they are posted on the streets for passers-by to catch up on local events, just as they were in the earliest days of the Brazilian press; their content varies from dry commentaries on agricultural issues to peppery tales with headlines like "Cobra-man speaks all!"

The Igreja de São Francisco de Assis and the Memorial Tancredo Neves

The most impressive of the town's colonial churches is the **Igreja de São Francisco de Assis** (Tues–Sun 8am–noon; $1), one block off the western end of Avenida Eduardo Magalhães. Overlooking a square with towering palms – some more than a century old – the church, finished in 1774, is exceptionally large, with an ornately carved exterior by a pupil of Aleijadinho. The master himself contributed the intricate decorations of the side chapels, which can be seen in all their glory now that the original paint and gilding has been stripped off. From the plaques, you'll see that the church has been visited by some illustrious guests, including President Mitterand of France. They came to pay homage at the **grave of Tancredo Neves**, in the cemetery behind the church.

Tancredo was a canny and pragmatic politician in the Minas tradition, but with a touch of greatness; the transition to civilian rule in 1985 would not have happened without his skills. He was born in and spent all his life in São João, where he was loved and is still very much missed. Eerily, to some, he died on the same day of the year as Tiradentes, who was also born in São João – their statues face each other in Praça Severiano de Rezende, on the other side of the Córrego do Lenheiro. Tancredo's black marble grave has a rather fine epitaph from one of his speeches: "You shall have my bones, land that I love, the final blending of my being with these blessed hills."

Just around the corner from the Igreja de São Francisco, on Rua José Maria Xavier at the corner with Avenida Eduardo Magalhães, is the **Memorial Tancredo Neves** (Sat, Sun & holidays 9am–5pm). This small nineteenth-century town house shelters a collection of personal artefacts and documents relating to the president's life. To be honest it's only really of interest to those Brazilians for whom Tancredo was nothing less than a modern saint – *ex votos* used to decorate his grave, thanking him "for graces granted".

The Museu de Arte Sacra

Over on the other side of the stream, one block north from Avenida Tancredo Neves, lies the main street of the other colonial area, **Rua Getúlio Vargas**. The western end is formed by the small Rosário church, which looks onto a cobbled square dominated by two stunning colonial mansions. The one nearest the church is the Solar dos Neves, the family home of the Neves clan for over two centuries, the place where Tancredo was born and lived, and where his widow still lives.

A couple of buildings east along from the Solar dos Neves is an excellent **Museu de Arte Sacra** (Tues–Sun 9am–5pm), contained within another sensitively restored house. The collection is small but very good; highlights are a finely painted St George and a remarkable figure of Christ mourned by Mary Magdalene, with rubies representing drops of blood. As you go around, you're accompanied by Baroque church music, which complements the pieces perfectly. The museum also has a small gallery for exhibitions by São João's large artistic colony.

The Catedral Basílica de Nossa Senhora de Pilar and other churches

Almost next door to the Museu de Arte Sacra on Avenida Getúlio Vargas is a magnificent early Baroque church, the **Catedral Basílica de Nossa Senhora de Pilar** (Tues–Sun 7–11am & 2–4pm), completed in 1721. The interior is gorgeous: only Pilar in Ouro Preto and Santo Antônio in Tiradentes are as liberally plastered with gold. The gilding is seen to best effect over the altar, a riot of Rococo pillars, angels and curlicues. The ceiling painting is all done with vegetable dyes, and there's a beautiful tiled floor.

There are further churches to visit in this part of town, if you're enthusiastic, though none of the same standard as either São Francisco or Pilar. The **Igreja de Nossa Senhora das Mercês**, behind Pilar, dates from 1750 and is notable for the variety and artistry of the graffiti, some of it dating back to the nineteenth century, etched into its stone steps, while the elegant facade of **Nossa Senhora do Carmo** dominates a beautiful triangular *praça* at the eastern end of Avenida Getúlio Vargas.

The Museu do SPHAN

More or less on a level with the cathedral, just off Avenida Tancredo Neves on Praça Severiano de Rezende, is an excellent museum, the **Museu do SPHAN** (Tues–Sun noon–5.30pm), housed in a magnificently restored colonial mansion. Perhaps the most fascinating pieces here are the eighteenth-century *ex votos* on the ground floor, their vivid illustrations detailing the pickles that both masters and slaves got themselves into – José Alves de Carvalho was stabbed in the chest while crossing a bridge on the way home in 1765; a slave called Antônio had his leg broken and was half buried for hours in a mine cave-in. (Happily, the fact they had an *ex votos* made means that they all recovered.) On the first floor are several figures of saints made by ordinary people in the eighteenth century: they have a simplicity and directness that makes them stand out. There's a collection of furniture and relics, too, and one of the oddest items is on the top floor – a machine used until 1928 to select the draft numbers of unfortunate army conscripts.

Eating, drinking and nightlife

On the **north side** of the Lenheiro stream, on Praça Severiano de Rezende, you'll find two of the town's swishest **restaurants**: the *Churrascaria Ramon*, which does a good-value *churrasco*, and the *Quinta do Ouro*, which serves the best *mineiro* food in São João. Both, however, are far beyond the budget pocket. Much cheaper but still good is the self-service *Restaurante Estação* at Av. Tancredo Neves 437 opposite the train station, or else there's an array of basic but filling *lanchonetes* and bars scattered around the sidestreets leading off the *avenida*. Here you'll also find an exceptionally pleasant traditional **coffee-shop**, *Café Tamandaré*, at Av. Getúlio Vargas 234, patronized by the town's older folk.

But the best places, combining good food with lively atmosphere, are on the **south side**, where trippers from Belo Horizonte, as well as young townsfolk and families flock to drink, eat and go to the cinema. Many of the **bars** have live music at weekends and get very crowded later on when people start spilling out onto the pavements. Almost all of the action is concentrated on Avenida Tiradentes, which runs parallel to Avenida Eduardo Magalhães, one block south. The bars are bunched at Tiradentes' western end (near São Francisco), where *Cabana do Zotti* at no. 805 (9pm onwards) is always packed and does good snacks, and halfway along Tiradentes at the junction with Rua Gabriel Passos (the road which runs in from the blue *Prefeitura*). Of the latter bunch, by far the best is *Miaxôu Bar*, at Rua Gabriel Passos 299 (5pm onwards; ☎032/371-8510), with its charming *dona*, excellent food (try the *bolinhos de queijo* or the pizzas) and efficient service. It gets very animated at weekends when whole families get up and shimmy to the live music (around 8pm–3am), often old sambas. For local traditional **sweets**, try *Doces Caseiros*, a family-run business operating from a home almost opposite the Memorial Tancredo Neves at Rua José Maria Xavier 38.

THE TRAIN TO TIRADENTES

If you're in São João between Friday and Sunday, don't miss the half-hour **train ride** to the colonial village of **Tiradentes**, 12km away. There are frequent buses, too (8 daily from São João's *Rodoviária*), but they don't compare to the trip on a nineteenth-century steam train ($15 return fare), with rolling stock from the 1930s, immaculately maintained and run with great enthusiasm. You may think yourself immune to the romance of steam, and be bored by the collection of old steam engines and rail equipment in São João's nineteenth-century station on Avenida Hermílio Alves – the **Estação Ferroviária** (☎032/371-8004; the museum is open Tues–Sun 9–11.30am & 1–5pm) – but by the time you've bought your ticket you'll be hooked: the booking hall is right out of a Thirties movie, the train hisses and spits out cinders, and as you sit down in carriages filled with excited children, it's all you can do not to run up and down the aisle with them.

Built in the 1880s, as the textile industry took off in São João, this was one of the earliest rail lines in Brazil and the trains were immediately christened *Maria-Fumaça*, "Smoking Mary". The service runs only on Friday, Saturday and Sunday, when trains leave São João at 10am and 2.10pm, returning from Tiradentes at 1pm and 5pm. If you want to stay longer, accommodation in Tiradentes is easy to find, or you could get one of the many local buses back to São João. Sit on the left leaving São João for the best views, and sit as far from the engine as you can: steam trains bring tears to your eyes in more ways than one.

The half-hour ride is very scenic, following a winding valley of the **Serra de São José**, which by the time it gets to Tiradentes has reared up into a series of rocky bluffs. You are travelling through one of the oldest areas of gold-mining in Minas Gerais, and from the train you'll see clear traces of the eighteenth-century mine workings in the hills. In the foreground, the rafts on the river have pumps which suck up alluvium from the river bed, from which gold is extracted by modern *garimpeiros*, heirs to over two centuries of mining tradition.

Tiradentes

TIRADENTES was founded as early as 1702, but had already been overshadowed by São João by the 1730s and is now no more than a sleepy village, with a population of only 4000 or so. The core is much as it was in the eighteenth century, straggling down the side of a hill crowned by the twin towers of the **Igreja Matriz de Santo Antônio** (Tues–Sun noon–4pm). Begun in 1710 and completed around 1730, it's one of the earliest and largest of the major Minas Baroque churches, and in 1732 began to acquire the gilding for which it is famous, becoming in the process one of the richest churches in any of the mining towns. It was decorated with the special extravagance of the newly rich, using more gold, the locals say, than any other in Brazil save the Capela Dourada in Recife. Whether this is true or not – and Pilar in Ouro Preto is probably as rich as either – the glinting and winking of the gold around the altar is certainly impressive. You can tell how early it is from the comparative crudeness of the statues and carvings: formal, stiff and with none of the movement of developed Minas Baroque. The exterior already needed restoring by 1810; the beautifully carved soapstone panels on the facade are not by Aleijadinho, as some believe, but by his pupil, Cláudio Pereira Viana, who worked with the master on his last projects.

From the steps of the church you look down an unspoilt colonial street – the old town hall with the veranda has a restored eighteenth-century jail – framed by the crests of the hills. If you had to take one photograph to summarize Minas Gerais, this would be it. Before walking down the hill, check out the **Museu Padre Toledo** (daily except Tues 9am–5pm), to the right of Santo Antônio as you're standing on the steps. Padre Toledo was one of the *Inconfidêntes* and built the mansion that is now the museum. He obviously didn't let being a priest stand in the way of enjoying the pleasures of life: the two-storey *sobrado* must have been very comfortable, and the ceiling paintings may be dressed up as classical allegories but even so are not the sort of thing you would expect a priest to commission. The museum comprises the usual mixture of furniture and religious art, but the interesting part is the yard out back, now converted into toilets but once the old slave quarters.

A more substantial reminder of the slave presence is the **Igreja da Nossa Senhora do Rosário dos Pretos**, down the hill and along the first street to the right. There could be no more eloquent reminder of the harsh divisions between masters and slaves than this small chapel, built by slaves for their own worship. There is gilding even here – some colonial miners were freed blacks working on their own account – and two fine figures of the black St Benedict stand out, but overall the church is moving precisely because it is so simple and dignified.

Tiradentes practicalities

Tiradentes might have a placid and timeless air during the week, but it gets surprisingly lively at weekends as the bars and guesthouses fill up with people attracted by its relaxed atmosphere.

Finding **accommodation** is never a problem, as a good proportion of the town's population have turned their homes into **pousadas** (there are well over forty), most of them exceptionally beautiful and very good value (the majority are priced in the ④ bracket). You'll find a good selection along the road leading into the village from the train station, or around the lovely Praça das Mercês it leads into, and the staff at the **tourist office**, Rua Resende Costa 71 (Tues–Sun 10am–4pm), will help you find available rooms.

Two good **hotels** at the budget end of the range are *Pousada Porão Colonial*, Rua Fogo Simbólico 477 (☎032/355-1231; ②), which has a pool, and the *Wellerson* on the same road (☎032/355-1226; ③). Slightly more expensive, but with a sauna to go with its pool, is the *Villa Real* at Rua Antônio Teixeira de Carvalho 127 (☎032/355-1292; ④). Similar, on the same road at no. 134, is the historic *Pousada Maria Barbosa* (☎032/355-1227; ⑤), whilst the top place to stay in town is the baronial *Solar da Ponte* on Praça das Mercês (☎032/355-1255, fax 355-1201; ⑧): not particularly friendly but in a beautiful old colonial mansion, offering all sorts of comforts and an English-style lawn garden to stroll through.

The best **restaurant** in Tiradentes is *Viradas do Largo*, Rua Jogo de Bola 108 (☎032/355-1157), which sets itself apart from other *mineiro* restaurants with the delicacy of its cooking; a full meal costs around $20–25. Also good is *Canto do Chafariz*, Largo do Chafariz 37 (closed Mon), near the São José fountain, while a number of small cafés and ice-cream parlours line the town's pleasant tree-shaded square, Largo das Forras, just up from Praça das Mercês.

Among Tiradentes' many **bars**, the *Aluarte* has the best atmosphere but is expensive, the *Meninasgerais* at Largo das Forras 66 is a popular dancing place, while *Xiquita Banana*, on Avenida Ministro Gabriel Passos, is the most laid-back. All have live music at weekends.

Diamantina and the Jequitinhonha Valley

DIAMANTINA, home town of Juscelino Kubitschek, the president who built Brasília, is the only historic city to the north of Belo Horizonte and, at six hours by bus, is by some way the furthest from it. Yet the journey itself is one of the reasons for going there, as the road heads into the different landscapes of northern Minas on its way to the *sertão mineiro*. The second half of the 288-kilometre journey is much the most spectacular, so to see it in daylight you need to catch either the 5.30am, 9am or 11.30am Pássaro Verde bus from Belo Horizonte.

MINING IN DIAMANTINA

Uniquely among the *cidades históricas*, large sections of Diamantina still depend on mining for a living, and **diamonds** and **gold** are mined in the whole area using pans and motorized suction pumps called *chupadeiras*. This small-scale mining is known as *garimpagem*, these days best known as a feature of the Amazon gold rush but also a feature of life in Minas since colonial times. Walk around the backstreets in the centre, Rua Rosário for example, and you'll find several **mining stores**, instantly recognizable by the display of zinc pans for gold, and wire mesh pans used to sift the gravel that diamonds are found in. At weekends the *garimpeiros* come in, piling into battered taxis and pick ups for a night on the town, and the centre hums into the small hours – they are on the whole friendly and curious, belying their fearsome media image.

How much longer Diamantina can survive as a mining town is, however, uncertain as the *chupadeiras* are altering the courses and muddying the waterways for miles around. In river-infested Amazonia this wouldn't be a problem, but Diamantina is at the headwaters of the Rio Jequitinhonha, the only river in the *sertão mineiro* which doesn't run dry. For the inhabitants of the *sertão* the issue is simple: if anything happens to the river, they either die or migrate. In 1989, the state government officially closed all the *garimpos* down, and despite a spirited campaign by the *garimpeiros* they are still closed. They may end up having to move out, leaving Diamantina to rely on the little cotton that can grow, and a trickle of tourists.

Diamantina has a very different atmosphere to any of the other colonial towns. Still a functioning diamond-mining town, it is also the gateway to the **Jequitinhonha Valley**, the river valley that is the heart of the Minas *sertão*. The green hills of the southern half of Minas seem very distant in Diamantina, set in a rocky, windswept and often cold highland zone – take a sweater or jacket.

The road to Diamantina

Diamantina itself, scattered down the steep side of a rocky valley, faces escarpments the colour of rust; the setting has a lunar quality you also come across in parts of the Northeastern *sertão*. In fact, at Diamantina you're not quite in the *sertão* – that begins roughly at Araçuaí, some 300km to the north – but in the uplands of the **Serra do Espinhaço**, the highlands that form the spine of the state. Almost as soon as you leave Belo Horizonte, the look of the land changes to the stubby trees and savanna of the Planalto Central, the inland plateau that makes up most of central Brazil. Some 60km from Belo Horizonte you pass the Rei do Mato cave (see p.148), and after another 54km, roughly halfway to Diamantina, the road forks – left to Brasília and the Planalto proper, right to Diamantina and the *sertão*.

You hit the highland foothills soon after the dull modern town of Curvelo, and from then on the route is very scenic. The road winds its way up spectacularly forbidding hills, the granite outcrops enlivened by cactus, wild flowers and the bright yellow and purple *ipê* trees, until it reaches the upland plateau, 1300m above sea level. This heralds yet another change: windswept moorland with few trees and strange rock formations. Look carefully on the left and you'll see traces of an old stone road, with flagstones seemingly going nowhere. This is the old slave road, which for over a century was the only communication line between southern Minas and the *sertão*.

The Town

Even if it were not set in such a striking landscape, Diamantina's **history** would still mark it out from the other *cidades históricas*. The Portuguese Crown had reason to feel bitter about the gold strikes in Minas Gerais: it had been forced to expend blood and treasure in prising the gold from the hands of the Paulistas, and when diamonds were found here in 1720 the same mistakes were not repeated. **Arraial do Tijuco**, as Diamantina was called at first, was put under strict military control. People could only come and go with royal passes and the town was isolated for almost a century. This may have something to do with Diamantina's very distinctive atmosphere. Although it has few buildings or churches to rival the masterpieces of Ouro Preto or Congonhas, the passage of time has had little effect on the large colonial centre of the town, which is the least spoilt of any of the *cidades históricas*. The narrow stone-flagged streets with their overhanging Chinese eaves and perfectly preserved colonial houses are exactly as they have been for generations.

Diamantina takes the *mineiro* penchant for building on slopes to extremes. Although the **Rodoviária** is not far from the centre of town, it's on a steep hill, and the only way back to it once in the centre is by taxi, unless you have the legs and lungs of a mountain goat. The streets are either too narrow or too steep even for Brazil's intrepid local bus drivers. Fortunately the place is small enough for you to get your bearings very quickly. The central square in the old town is **Praça Conselheiro Mota**, which has the Catedral Metropolitana de Santo Antônio built in the middle of it – everyone calls the cathedral and the square "Sé". Most of the sights and places to stay are within a stone's throw of here.

The Museu do Diamante

The **Museu do Diamante** (Tues–Sat noon–5.30pm, Sun 9am–noon) on the cathedral square is the best place to get an idea of what *garimpagem* has meant to Diamantina. It's one of the best museums in Minas, not so much for the glories of its exhibits but the effort it makes to give you an idea of daily life in old Diamantina.

The room behind the entrance desk is devoted to the history of mining in Diamantina: old mining instruments, maps and prints. Dominating everything is an enormous cast-iron English safe, brought by ox-cart all the way from Rio in the eighteenth century – it took eighteen months to get here. It contains a riveting display of genuine gold and diamond jewellery and cut diamonds which are replicas: the originals are stashed in the Banco do Brasil across the road. On the upper shelf is a (genuine) pile of uncut diamonds and emeralds, as they would appear to *garimpeiros* panning – only the occasional dull glint distinguishes them from ordinary gravel. More disturbing is an appalling display of whips, chains and brands used on slaves right up until the late nineteenth century, though the terrifying-looking tongs, underneath the chains, are in fact colonial hair-curlers, and not torture instruments.

The rest of the museum is great to wander through, stuffed with memorabilia from mouldering top-hats to photos of long-dead town bandsmen: Diamantina has strong musical traditions and still supports *serestas*, small bands of accordion, guitar and flute players who stroll through the streets and hold dances around *Carnaval*, or on the evening of September 12, the *Dia da Seresta*.

The Catedral and other churches

Despite the comparative ugliness of the **Catedral Metropolitana de Santo Antônio**, built in 1940 on the site of an old colonial church, the cathedral square is worth savouring. It's lined with *sobrados*, many of them with exquisite ornamental bronze- and iron-work, often imported from Portugal – look closely and you'll see iron pineapples on the balconies. Most impressive of all are the serried windows of the massive *Prefeitura*, and the ornate Banco do Brasil building next to it – possibly unique in Brazil in that it spells the country name the old way, with a "z".

For the **other churches**, you're faced with two problems. Most are closed for restoration, which is taking years, and though the workmen are usually happy to let you in, you're not seeing them at their best. Also, in recent years, a rash of thefts of art-works from churches in and around Diamantina has made people very reluctant to open them up for visitors; the opening hours given on the back of the town map are long obsolete. Disgracefully, some of the thieves were foreigners, and this has made people even more suspicious, so unless you can wheedle in Portuguese you stand little chance of getting in: ask at the nearest house for the *zelador* (guardian), and try your luck. Fortunately, with one exception, the exteriors are actually more interesting than the interiors. Diamantina churches are very distinctive, simple but very striking, with stubby towers and Chinese eaves: street names, like Rua Macau do Meio and Rua Macau de Cima, recall where the Chinese craftsmen imported by the Portuguese lived during the eighteenth century.

The one church worth trying to see the inside of, if at all possible, is the **Igreja de Nossa Senhora do Carmo** on Rua Bonfim, whose exterior is nonetheless also impressive. Built between 1760 and 1765, legend has it that the heir of Diamantina's richest miner made sure the tower was built at the back of the church rather than the front, as was usual, so the bells didn't disturb his wife's beauty sleep. Inside is an atypically florid interior, whose two main features are a rich, intricately carved altar screen and a gold-sheathed organ, which was actually built in Diamantina. Both are currently being restored, so you stand a chance of seeing the painstaking work in progress.

On the cobbled street leading down the hill from here is a local curiosity. The church at the bottom, **Igreja de Nossa Senhora do Rosário**, has a tree growing in front of it: look closely and you can see a large distorted wooden cross embedded in the trunk and lower branches. The story behind this reads like something from Gabriel García Márquez, but did really happen. The year the old Sé church was knocked down, in 1932, the padre of Rosário planted a wooden cross outside his church to commemorate the chapel that old Diamantina had originally been built around. A fig tree sprouted up around it so that at first the cross seemed to flower – there's a photo of it at this stage in the Museu do Diamante – and eventually, rather than knocking it down, the tree grew up around the cross and ended up absorbing it.

The Mercado dos Tropeiros

Diamantina's other important economic role is as the market town for the Jequitinhonha Valley. It's here that the products of the remote *sertão* towns of north-eastern Minas are shipped and stockpiled before making their way to Belo Horizonte. The old **Mercado dos Tropeiros** on Praça Barão do Guaicuí, just a block downhill from the cathedral square, is the focus of Diamantina's trade, and worth seeing for the building alone, an interesting tiled wooden structure built in 1835 as a trading station by the Brazilian army. Its frontage, a rustic but very elegant series of shallow arches, played a significant role in modern Brazilian architecture. Niemeyer, who lived in Diamantina for a few months in the 1950s to build the *Hotel do Tijuco*, was fascinated by it, and later used the shape for the striking exterior of the presidential palace in Brasília, the Palácio da Alvorada.

The market itself has a very Northeastern feel, with its cheeses, blocks of salt and raw sugar, and mules and horses tied up alongside the pick-ups. The food at the stalls here is very cheap, but only for the strong-stomached: the rich *mineiro* sausages (*linguiça*) are worth trying. From the market you have a fine vantage point of a square which is, if anything, even richer than the Praça Conselheiro Mota, a cornucopia of colonial window frames and balconies and exquisite ironwork. Most of the ground floors are still ordinary shops.

There is no *artesanato* section in the market, which is unfortunate since the most distinctive products of the Jequitinhonha Valley are its beautiful clay and pottery figures. The Casa da Cultura, on Praça Antônio Eulálio, has a very good collection which enables you to get a grasp of what the Jequitinhonha potters do, but buying it is difficult. The most reliable place is a friendly and very reasonably priced specialist **shop**, *Relíquias do Vale*, on the same street as the *Hotel do Tijuco*, at Rua Macau de Meio 401. Besides the pottery, they also have a good stock of the rough but very rugged cotton clothes, hammocks, *arraiolos* carpets and wall hangings that are the other specialities of the region. You'll find numerous other carpet shops dotted around town.

Practicalities

Maps are free from the **tourist office** in the Casa da Cultura, tucked away at Praça Antônio Eulálio 53 (Mon–Fri 8am–6pm, Sat 9am–5pm, Sun 9am–noon; ☎038/531-1636). There's also a **tourist post** in the *Rodoviária* (daily 8–11am & 1–6pm), but it's often shut because of staff shortages. The receptions at the *Hotel do Tijuco* and the *Dália Hotel*, and the Museu do Diamante, also hand out maps.

Hotels are plentiful and many are unusually charming and surprisingly cheap. The largest, priciest and most comfortable is the *Pousada do Garimpo*, Av. da Saudade 265 (☎038/531-2523, fax 531-2316; ⑤), on the western continuation of Rua Direita. Much more interesting, however, and cheaper, is the town's Niemeyer creation, the *Hotel do Tijuco*, Rua Macau do Meio 211 (☎ and fax 531-1022; ④). The *Dália Hotel*, Praça J Kubitschek 25 (☎038/531-1477, fax 531-3526; ③), just down from the cathedral, is possibly the best value in town. Housed in a lovely two-storey building, last renovated in 1924, it has bags of character, good rooms and fine views over the square. Another good bet is the *Pousada dos Cristais*, Rua Jogo da Bola 53, west from Rua Direita (☎038/531-2897; ②), a very pleasant family-run place with comfortable, rustic rooms. If you want somewhere cheaper still in the old part of town, *Hotel Carvalho*, Rua Quitanda 20 (☎038/531-1520; ①), is very basic. Other cheap options, with *quartos* upwards of $10, are clustered around the *Rodoviária* in the upper part of town, and are

---

JUSCELINO KUBITSCHEK

Juscelino Kubitschek was born and spent the first seventeen years of his life in Diamantina. His enduring monument is the capital he built on the Planalto Central, Brasília, which fired Brazil's and the world's imagination and which now houses his remains (he was killed in a road accident in 1976). The house he was born and lived in, **Casa de Juscelino**, is preserved as a shrine to his memory (Tues–Sat 9am–5pm, Sun 9am–1pm), on the steep Rua São Francisco, uphill from his statue at the bottom.

Juscelino had a meteoric political career. His energy, imagination and utterly uncompromising liberal instincts make him one of the great postwar presidents. You can understand his lifelong concern with the poor from the small, unpretentious house where he spent the first part of his life in poverty. Restoration has rather flattered it, as the photos of how it was when he lived there make plain – no Brazilian president has yet come from a humbler background. He was of the second generation of poor Czech immigrants: you won't find many family possessions because they didn't have any. The photos and the simplicity of the house are very moving, a refreshing contrast to the pampered corruption of many of his successors.

If you're interested, the **Casa da Cultura** in Praça Antônio Eulálio has a folder of photographs and clippings about Juscelino, relaxing with his *seresta* group – he was an accomplished guitarist – and being feted by the proud inhabitants of the town he clearly never left in spirit. Most of the bars still display his photograph, many dating from before he became president in 1956. And many still don't believe his death was a genuine accident, just as few *mineiros* believe Tancredo really died of natural causes. The massive turnout for Juscelino's funeral in Brasília in 1976 was one of the first times Brazilians dared to show their detestation of the military regime.

ideal if you can't face the prospect of lugging your luggage uphill when it's time to leave: *Hotel JK*, for example, immediately opposite the bus station at Praça Dom João 135 (☎038/531-1142; ②), is perfectly decent.

The streets around the cathedral are the heart of the town, and there's no shortage of simple bars and *mineiro* **restaurants** here. Good ones include the *Capistrana* on Praça Antônio Eulálio, and *Espeto de Prata* on Beco da Pena just off Rua Direita, a sophisticated *churrasco* joint with live music Thursdays to Sundays. Best of all is *Cantina do Marinho* on Rua Direita 113, in front of the cathedral: the food is good and offers the best value for money in town; try a *doce de limão* to round off your meal. There's a good **cake shop** opposite the Casa de Cultura on Praça Antônio Eulálio. The main focus of weekend **nightlife** activity is Rua Direita: the busiest bar is *Oasis Clube* at no. 132 (daily 8am–late), which has live music upstairs on Friday and Sunday evenings and a disco on Saturdays (entrance upstairs costs $3–5). Opposite, the tiny cellar bar *Taberna do Gilmar* (Wed–Sat 8pm onwards) has the town's loudest music system, playing a mixture of Brazilian and rock. The other live music venue is the bar next to the Casa de Juscelino on Rua São Francisco (9pm onwards).

The Jequitinhonha Valley

If you want to get a clearer idea of where the Jequitinhonha *artesanato* comes from, you have to head out into the *sertão* proper, and Diamantina is the obvious place to start your journey. Travelling into the **Jequitinhonha Valley** is not something to be undertaken lightly: it is one of the poorest and remotest parts of Brazil, the roads are bad, there are no hotels except bare flophouse *dormitórios*, and unless you speak good Portuguese you are liable to be looked on with great suspicion. There have been problems in recent years with foreigners buying up mining concessions and kicking out *garimpeiros*, and unless you can explain yourself people will assume you have ulterior motives. The region is so poor and isolated it's difficult for people to understand why outsiders, especially foreigners, would want to go there anyway.

If you need reasons, though, you don't have to look much further than the **scenery**, which is spectacularly beautiful, albeit forbidding. The landscapes are stunning, and bear some resemblance to the deserts of the American Southwest: massive granite hills and escarpments, cactus, rock, occasional wiry trees and people tough as nails speaking with the lilting accent of the interior of the Northeast. Here you're a world away from the developed sophistication of southern and central Minas.

Araçuaí and beyond

It seems wrong to call somewhere as off the beaten track as **ARAÇUAÍ** easy to get to, but it is the most accessible Jequitinhonha destination from Diamantina. You have to be up early – there is one bus a day at 7am (booking the day before is essential) – and the journey is hard: twelve hours of bouncing around on dusty dirt roads, hot as hell during the day and cold at night. The *dormitório* by the bus station is your only option for **accommodation**; take a hammock to avoid having to sleep in one of their beds. Araçuaí is no more than a large village, but it has the best place for buying **artesanato** in the whole region – a producers' co-operative called *Centro de Artesanato*, open Tuesday to Saturday but best to catch on a Saturday morning, when craft workers come in from the surrounding villages to market.

From Araçuaí, if time were no object, you could hop local buses to **Itinga** and then on 30km to the good-quality BR-116 highway into **Bahia** state. Once you get to Vitória da Conquista there are ready connections to all Bahian cities, but it could well take you a couple of days to get that far. It is often quicker to take the bus that leaves every other day to Belo Horizonte and make your connections there; taking the daily bus to Diamantina and connections to Belo Horizonte is also a possibility.

Serro

A much easier trip from Diamantina is the day's outing to the even sleepier colonial village of **SERRO**, 90km away. It takes over two hours to get there, so you'll have to start early. There are only two buses from Diamantina, one at 6am and the other at 4pm, and there are two daily buses back to Diamantina, one at 8.30am and the other at 3.30pm; if you want to return to Diamantina the same day, buy your ticket for the return journey when you arrive. The ride there is always interesting, especially in the early morning when the granite hills loom eerily out of the mist and the clouds seem only a few feet above the ground: warm clothing to keep out the morning cold is essential.

Serro is set in beautiful hill country, dominated by the eighteenth-century pilgrimage church of **Santa Rita** (Sat 3–7pm) on a rise above the centre, reached by steps cut into the slope. Little-visited, this is not so much a place to do and see things in, as somewhere peaceful to unwind and appreciate the leisurely pace of life in rural Minas. There are six colonial churches, but most are closed to visitors and the rest open only for a few hours either on Saturday or Sunday: a spate of thefts has made the keyholders reluctant to let you in, even once you locate them. Founded in 1702, when gold was discovered in the stream nearby, Serro was at one time a rather aristocratic place. Across the valley, easily recognizable from the clump of palms, is the old house of the Barão do Serro which now houses a small **museum** (daily 8am–4pm, though you'll probably have to track down the curator), mostly composed of prints and old newspaper cuttings. The more valuable artefacts are all in storage waiting for the inevitable museum of sacred art; it's currently being constructed in the Igreja do Bom Jesus do Matosinhos, just along the road from the museum on Praça Cristiano Otoni.

From the front of the museum you get a good view of the finest buildings in the village, namely the enormous **Casa do Barão de Diamantina**, clinging to the hillside, beautifully restored and now a school, and the twin Chinese towers of the **Igreja do Matriz** (Sun 8am–7.30pm). The church forms one end of a main street that is completely unspoilt; at the other is the Santa Rita hill.

At the foot of the hill on the eighteenth-century Praça João Pinheiro is the best **place to stay**, *Hotel Itacolomi* at no. 20 (☎038/541-1227; ②), which has a solid *mineiro* **restaurant** open to non-residents. Also good is the *Pousada Vila do Príncipe*, on the main street, Rua Antônio Honório Pires, at no. 38 (☎038/541-1485; ③). There's a cheap *churrascaria* of the same name nearby, and four cheap *pensões*. The *Rodoviária* is almost in the centre: ignore the attentions of the taxi drivers, walk uphill for some 30m, and you're in the heart of the village.

SOUTHERN MINAS: THE SPA TOWNS

The drive from Belo Horizonte **south to Rio** turns into one of the most spectacular in Brazil once you cross the state border and encounter the glorious scenery of the Serra dos Órgãos, but there is little to detain you in Minas along the way. The route passes Juiz de Fora, one of the larger interior cities, but it's an ugly industrial centre, best seen from the window of a bus.

The route **southwest towards São Paulo**, however, is altogether different. The hills, rising into mountains near the state border, make this one of the most attractive parts of Minas. Six or seven hours from Belo Horizonte, to the south of the main route, there's a cluster of **spa towns**, each built around mineral water springs: **Cambuquira**, **São Lourenço**, **Caxambu** and **Lambari**. They are all small, quiet and popular with older people, who flock there to take the waters and baths. Each revolves around a *parque hidromineral*, a park built around the springs, incorporating bath-houses and fountains. Set in spectacular volcanic mountains to the north of the São Paulo road, the city of **Poços de Caldas** is also based around mineral springs, but is much livelier, a traditional place for couples to spend their honeymoon.

From Belo Horizonte to the Circuito das Águas

It's five hours from Belo Horizonte, or three from São João del Rei, before you hit the gateway to the **Circuito das Águas**, the "Circuit of the Waters", as the spa resorts of Cambuquira, São Lourenço, Caxambu and Lambari are collectively known. **TRÊS CORAÇÕES** is a good place for making onward bus connections, and although not a resort town itself, it is more famous, in Brazil at least, than any of the spas. This rather anonymous modern town was the birthplace of Edson Arantes do Nascimento, **Pelé** – the greatest footballer ever – and it's a holy place for any lover of the game. Keep an eye out on the left as the bus winds its way through the centre, and you'll see a bronze statue of him, holding aloft the World Cup, which Brazil (and Pelé) won in 1958, 1962 and 1970. Looking at the steep streets of the poor urban fringes he came from, you can understand why he developed such amazing ball control: one slip and it's a long chase to get the ball back. If you find yourself stuck here overnight while waiting for a bus, the *Cantina Calabresa* **hotel**, Rua Joaquim Bento de Carvalho 65 (☎035/231-2108; ③), has good rooms.

After Três Corações the hill country begins, although it's hardly got going before you run into the first and smallest of the spas, **CAMBUQUIRA**, a pleasant enough place but nothing to compare with the other resorts. If you do want to **stay**, a good cheap option, with its own pool, is *Pousada Passe Fique*, 1km out on the BR-267 Lambari road (☎035/251-1587; ③); more central and upmarket, with a sauna as well as a pool, is *Hotel Santos Dumont*, Av. Virgílio de Melo Franco 400 (☎035/251-1466; ⑤). The baths and massages in the Parque das Águas are open daily between 6am and 7pm.

Caxambu

Just pipping São Lourenço (see below) for the title of nicest of the smaller spas, **CAXAMBU** was a favourite haunt of the Brazilian royal family in the nineteenth century. Dom Pedro II regularly took the waters here, which were meant to restore fertility as well as treating stomach, liver and kidney complaints: they certainly did the trick for his daughter, Princesa Isabel, who produced three children after only two visits and built the small **Igreja de Santa Isabel de Hungria**, overlooking the springs, in gratitude.

The **Parque das Águas** in the centre of town is delightful. Built in the last decades of the nineteenth century and the early years of the twentieth, it's dotted with eleven oriental-style pavilions sheltering the actual springs, and houses an ornate Turkish bath-house which is very reasonably priced – $8 gets you a Turkish bath in turn-of-the-century opulence, and there are also various kinds of sauna and massage available. The bath-house is open Tuesday to Sunday from 8.30am to noon for men, and Tuesday to Saturday 3pm to 5pm for women.

Even if you don't take the waters, wandering around the immaculately kept park, rich with the scent of pine and flowering trees, and overlooked by hills, is a pleasure. Even the bottling plant has an ornate Edwardian facade so that it complements its surroundings. And, next to the bowling track, concealed behind a curtain of pine, is what must be the most elegant urinal in Minas Gerais. As in all the mineral parks, once you've paid the nominal entrance fee you can sample any of the springs and bring bottles to fill up and take away, but drink the waters with caution: a mere mouthful is enough to produce intestinal rumblings and have you bolting to the toilets by the side of the bath-house. Brazilians swear by them for "cleaning out the system".

Next to the park is a good **market**, specializing in honey and home-made syrupy sweets, which leads on to a tree-shaded square, **Praça Dom Pedro**, with yet another oriental pavilion. If you're tired of walking, there's a **chair-lift**, which runs from opposite the bus station up to the *Cristo Redentor* that overlooks the centre – hold tight, as it goes faster than you'd think. At the top there's a tremendous view, not only of the town and the park but also the lovely hill country in which it nestles. There's a restaurant, too, where the views are better than the food. The only drawback is that the chair-lift closes down at 4.30pm, which means you can't appreciate what would be a very spectacular sunset (unless you have excellent night-vision for the two-kilometre descent).

Practicalities

The **Rodoviária** is on the far western edge of town on Praça Castilho Moreira, but Caxambu is so small that it doesn't really matter. A **tourist information post** in the terminal building hands out free town maps, but again, you don't need them to find your way around. Basically, there's one main street, Rua Wenceslau Braz, much of which is taken up by the Parque das Águas, and around which the town is built. Although walking is easy, it's fun to get one of the **horsedrawn cabs**, or *charretes*, that seem especially appropriate to Caxambu's turn-of-the-century surroundings.

For its size, Caxambu has a surprising range of **hotels**. The luxury-class *Grande Hotel*, Rua Dr Viotti 438 (☎ and fax 033/341-3377; ⑤), and the *Hotel Glória*, opposite the park at Av. Camilo Soares 590 (☎ and fax 033/341-3000; ⑦ full board), would make great settings for a costume drama, and both have pools and saunas. The best middle-range place in town – especially out of season when the prices almost halve – is the *Palace Hotel*, Rua Dr Viotti 567 (☎033/341-3344, fax 341-3131; ⑤). Built in 1894, it's crammed with antique furniture, and has a pool and sauna, a children's games room, a drawing room, a massive lounge and a ballroom. Cheaper options include *Hotel Alex*, near Praça Dom Pedro at Rua Oliveira Mafra 223 (☎033/341-1331), and *Hotel Marquês*, in the same building as the *Alex* (☎033/341-1013), both ④. The cheapest places are the *Santa Cecília* on Rua Wenceslau Braz (☎033/341-1073; ③); *Hotel Líder*, Rua Major Penha 225 (☎033/341-1398; ③); and the *Jardim Imperial* (☎033/341-1163; ②), near the bus station on Rua Dr Viotti.

Among **restaurants**, highly recommended is the Danish *La Forelle*, 3km out of town on the BR-354 towards Itamonte (Tues–Sun, open until midnight; ☎033/341-1961); it's expensive, but does an unusual line in Scandinavian *mineiro* cooking, especially good on trout and salmon.

If you decide to **stay in São Lourenço** rather than Caxambu, the last bus is at 7.15pm, or a taxi there costs $20. If you're completely stuck, the midnight Resendense bus to São Paulo goes via São Lourenço, although you will probably have to stand for the forty minutes it takes to get there.

São Lourenço

If Caxambu is the last word in Edwardian elegance, **SÃO LOURENÇO** rivals it with its displays of Art Deco brilliance. Its Parque das Águas is studded with striking 1940s pavilions and has a stunning bath-house, the Balneário, that looks more like a film set for a Hollywood high-society comedy. The most upmarket and modern-looking of the small spas, the town is popular with young and old alike. The **tourist information kiosk** on Praça Duque de Caixas in front of the *parque* (daily 8–11am & 1–6pm; ☎033/332-4455) has free town maps.

The town is built along the shores of a beautiful lake, a large chunk of which has been incorporated into the **Parque** (daily 8am–5pm; the pavilions with the mineral water fountains are closed 11.30am–2pm), and during the day it's here that everything goes on. Much larger than the one in Caxambu, and much more modern, the park is kept to the same immaculate standard: again, a lovely place for a stroll, with its brilliant white pavilions, forested hillside, clouds of butterflies and birds – though steer clear of the black swans on the lake, which have a nasty temper. There are **rowing boats** for rent, and an artificial island in the middle of the lake.

The **Balneário** itself is notable for its *banho carbogasosa*, a fizzy mineral water bath that is a kind of natural jacuzzi. Unfortunately, you can only have a go with a doctor's prescription; it's meant to be good for hypertension. There are ordinary baths (*duchas*), though, and saunas, available for $8–10 (a massage costs $20) and it's worth paying for the surroundings: marbled floors, mirror walls and white-coated attendants. There are separate sections for men and women.

Practicalities

The **Rodoviária** is just off the main street, Avenida Dom Pedro II, which is lined with bars, hotels and restaurants. There is a **youth hostel** at no. 468 with beds for $10, and a good low-price **hotel**, the *Hotel Aliança* (☎ and fax 033/332-4300; ③, full board ④) at no. 505. Of similar standing is the *Hotel Colonial*, Av. Costa 627 (☎033/332-1500; ③, full board ④), by the Praça Duque de Caixas. Much cheaper is the *Santa Rita* at Av. Getúlio Vargas 31 (☎033/332-2522; ②), with basic but clean rooms, all with TVs, but avoid their overpriced full-board package. In the mid-range category, the *Pousada das Alamedas*, Alameda Cecília Meirelles 132, 1km out of town (☎033/331-2608; ⑤), is pleasantly calm, with eight chalets and two apartments, two pools and a sauna, though its singles are the same price as doubles. The *Hotel Brasil*, Alameda João Lage 87 (☎033/332-1313, fax 331-1536; ⑧ full board), which dominates the Praça Duque de Caixas, is luxury class and has the works, including four pools and water-slides.

Buses to Lambari, next town on the circuit, take about ninety minutes, and continue to Varginha. **Buses to Caxambu** leave at 7am, 10am, 2pm, 3.50pm and 6pm, or take a taxi from the post in front of the *parque*. There's no direct bus to Poços de Caldas; you need to get the 11.45am to Pouso Alegre and make a connection there – total journey time is around six hours. Bus timetables do change frequently so it's best to check departure times in advance with the *Rodoviária* (☎033/331-1204).

Lambari

LAMBARI is the nearest you get to a downmarket spa town on the *Circuito das Águas*, though you wouldn't guess it from the prices of its main hotels. It has a beautiful lake and the obligatory spa-park, but lacks the prosperous feel of Caxambu and São Lourenço. The **Rodoviária** is on Avenida Dr José Nicolau Mileo, within easy walking distance of the main square, Praça Conseileiro João Lisboa. Housed in the square, the **Parque das Águas** is small and scruffy, but has six fountains each with different types of water, as well as a fizzy *carbogasosa* pool.

A couple of blocks uphill from the centre are the main – in fact the only – sights in Lambari, the lake and an elegant 1940s building. All colonnades and courtyards, this was originally built as a luxury casino and is now partly used as a town hall and library. It's a shame to see such a magnificent building so under-used – much of it simply lies empty, and nobody stops you wandering around. Next to it is a pleasant park with bars, a waterfall and a surprisingly well-kept public swimming pool; the lake itself is rather polluted.

There are several budget **hotels** near the *Rodoviária*, while mid-range options can be found either on or near the main square. Of these, the *Hotel Ideal*, at Rua Afonso

Vilhena Paiva 245 (☎033/271-1143, fax 271-1650; ④), is probably the best value, basic but comfortable, with a pool and sauna. The *Hotel Itaici* (☎ and fax 033/271-1366; ④) at Rua Dr. José dos Santos 320 is of a similar standard. The *Hotel Glória* (☎033/271-1232, fax 271-1749; ⑤) on the same street at no. 91 offers little more and is overpriced; for the same money you'd be much better off at the town's best hotel, the *Hotel Parque*, Rua Américo Werneck 46 (☎033/271-2000; ⑥), with its own lake, thermal pools, fishing and other sports facilities.

The best place to eat out is the *Restaurante Amigão*, Rua G. Stockler 37, a simple but good *mineiro* **restaurant** whose enormous portions are excellent value. Another good spot worth winkling out is *Ricardo* at Rua Wenceslau Braz 58, while the *Cascata*, overlooking the waterfall in the park, has the best location in town. For digesting all this, a store called *Prince*, one block before the *Amigão*, has shelves marked "Pinga da Roça", on which you'll find a good selection of rums distilled, in the traditional way, on the ranches hereabouts: much smoother and less fiery than the industrially produced varieties.

Poços de Caldas

POÇOS DE CALDAS is the easiest of the Minas spa resorts to get to. Rich Brazilians from the large cities of southern Brazil like to take breaks here, and there are daily bus services to and from Rio and São Paulo as well as from Belo Horizonte. It's some distance from the smaller spa towns, and is an altogether different place; definitely a city rather than a town, it's the most animated spot in Minas after Belo Horizonte.

If possible, you should make the journey in daylight, because the countryside is something special and shouldn't be missed. After the ugly modern town of Pouso Alegre, there is one of the more spectacular climbs into mountains that Brazil has to offer, with superb views of slopes clad in a mixture of pine, eucalyptus and monkey-puzzle, and plains laid out like sheets behind and beneath the road. It is easy to see why the whole region became a resort area.

The city itself, almost on the state line with São Paulo, nestles in the bowl of an extinct volcano – you can trace the rim of what must once have been an enormous crater along the broken horizons. The centre is mostly modern, laid out in a grid pattern with a few skyscrapers, but made very pleasant by huge tree-studded squares, an enormous but elegant bath-house and the closeness of the thickly forested slopes of Alto da Serra, the hill crowned with the obligatory *Cristo Redentor* overlooking the city.

The City

If first impressions counted on arrival, you'd probably take one look at the dirty and decrepit **Rodoviária** and catch the next bus out: its sole redeeming feature is that it is very central, a short distance from the huge central square, **Praça Pedro Sanchez**, easily recognizable by the large Edwardian-style bath-house set in gardens and fountains. Everything goes on around the square and in the blocks to the east of it, and the grid pattern makes it easy to get your bearings.

Unlike Caxambu and São Lourenço, Poços de Caldas doesn't have a single mineral water park that encompasses all the springs; they are scattered all over the city and somehow don't seem as impressive when not set in a garden. The nearest, within easy walking distance of the centre, is **Fonte Frayha**, on the corner of Rua Amazônas and Rua Pernambuco, whose waters are mildly radioactive. You can, however, take the same waters in style in the opulent bath-house, the **Termas Antônio Carlos** (Mon–Sat 8–11.30am & 4–7.30pm, Sun 8–11.30am), whose Edwardian bulk looms over the main square. It specializes in sulphur baths, meant to be good for stomach ulcers, but also offers the usual range of saunas and massages: less personal than the *balneários* in the smaller resorts, but the increase in scale makes a Turkish bath in such splendid surroundings an experience.

On one side of the *praça*, not far from the bath-house on Avenida Francisco Salles, is a **cable car** station (July & Dec–Feb daily 8am–6pm; rest of the year Mon & Wed–Fri 2–6pm, Sat & Sun 8am–6pm; $5 return), from where you're whisked up to the **Alto da Serra** and the Christ statue overlooking the city, at 1678m above sea-level. It's a must: the views at the top are tremendous, there's the usual restaurant with panoramic views, and it's the starting point for an exceptionally scenic walk back down. The cable car's initial stretch carries you just above rooftop level over part of the city, and then rears up over the forest, before trundling into the station at the top of the hill ten minutes later – there's no better way to see Poços de Caldas. A viewing platform is built around the **Cristo Redentor**: take a jacket, because the wind can really blow at this altitude. In front sprawls the city – it's from here that you can best make out the remaining bits of the volcanic crater in which it is built – and behind, a beautiful view frames hills, ranches and a lake.

Practicalities

The **Secretaria de Turismo** is located in the Palace Casino on Parque José Afonso Junqueira (Mon–Sat 8am–noon & 1.30–6pm, Sun 8am–noon; ☎033/722-1551) and they have a good free map of the town. You will find a TELEMIG office just up from the square, on Rua Minas Gerais, where you can make international **telephone** calls.

Accommodation

Accommodation will be the least of your worries. The entire city is geared to catering for visitors and even during holiday periods, when people flock from as far afield as Rio and São Paulo, capacity is never really stretched. Prices are generally very keen, often including full board for what you'd normally pay for bed and breakfast elsewhere.

The best hotels are scattered some way out of town in their own gardens or estates: *Varandas do Sol*, Av. João Pinheiro 8770, 9km out on the Águas da Prata road (☎033/714-2669, fax 714-1615; ⑥), offers splendid views and has the usual pool and sauna, as well as charming chalets and facilities for angling. In town itself, the *Minas Gerais*, Rua Pernambuco 615 (☎033/722-1686, fax 722-1559; ④ full board), constitutes superb value, with two pools, a sauna and a playground for children. Similarly excellent, with two thermal pools and sauna, is *Esplêndido*, Rua Paraná 111 (☎033/722-1177, fax 722-1186; ③, full board ④). The best budget place is the *Excelsior*, Rua Dr Francisco Faria Lobato 153 (☎033/722-1614, fax 721-5835; ③ full board), which also has a pool. For even cheaper places, try the hotels on Rua São Paulo: the *Guarany* at no. 106 is reasonable (☎033/722-2585; ②).

Eating, drinking and nightlife

As you would expect in a place so popular with young couples, the **nightlife** here is very lively, especially at weekends. There are scores of bars and restaurants, many of which put their tables out on the pavement, thronged until late with people seeing and being seen, talking, drinking and listening to music.

Busiest of all is the stretch of **Rua São Paulo** leading down to the square. There is a very good upstairs **bar** here, *Verde Amarelo*, which has high-quality live Brazilian music for free on Friday and Saturday nights; and possibly the best **juice bar** in Minas Gerais, *Casa de Sucos*, on the corner of São Paulo and Assis Figueiredo. It has an amazing variety of freshly made *sucos*, which come in jugs that run to three glassfuls, and an excellent range of sandwiches and desserts – the *doce de arroz* translates literally as "rice pudding", but that doesn't begin to convey how delicious it is, flavoured with vanilla, lemon and cinnamon.

The more expensive **restaurants** are on Rua Assis Figueiredo: a good rule is to avoid the air-conditioned ones, which are vastly overpriced. *Fenícia* is an excellent meat restaurant where the portions are enormous and the beef good enough to satisfy even Argentinians – though vegetarians are equally well catered for with almost seventy types of salads and vegetable dishes, and Sunday lunch features grilled fish; a full meal should cost no more than $15. The *Fenícia* also has a *lanchonete* attached to the restaurant proper which does burgers and sandwiches, and is the only place that rivals the *Casa de Sucos* for a snack lunch. Similarly good and filling is *Fazenda*, 6km out of town on the Caldas road, at Rua Carlos Gomes 333 (☎033/713-1260; closed Mon), which offers thirty types of meat served *rodízio* style – the waiters brandish countless skewers of freshly grilled meat at you, and you're supposed to indicate, with knowing flair, which piece you'd like carved off.

EASTERN MINAS

Eastern Minas Gerais is the least-visited part of the state and, travelling along the BR-262 highway leading to Espírito Santo state and the Atlantic, it seems very clear why. Although the *mineiro* hill country is pretty enough, the towns scattered along it are ugly industrial centres, steel mills belching fumes common even in the gaps between the towns. However, if you persevere right to the border with Espírito Santo, you enter an unrivalled part of Minas, where lush hills are covered with coffee bushes in terraced rows, like contour lines on a map. These hills gradually give way to the craggy, spectacular mountains of the **Parque Nacional do Caparaó** and the highest peak in southern Brazil, the **Pico da Bandeira**. The best time to go is from June to August as at other times of year the mists and rain make it difficult to see the marvellous scenery.

Towards Caparaó

Getting to the park can be complicated, and the fact that Caparaó is the name of both the national park and a village just outside it – which itself is next to another village called Alto do Caparaó – makes things more confusing. You need to head for Alto do Caparaó to get to the park; you can make the journey from either Belo Horizonte or Vitória, the capital of Espírito Santo – Vitória is considerably nearer – but there are no direct buses and you can bank on spending most of the day to get there, and possibly longer, wherever you start from.

Initially, you should head towards the two towns in the vicinity. **Manhuaçu** is served by three daily direct buses from both Belo Horizonte and Vitória, and a midday service from the *Rodoviária* outside Ouro Preto, which calls at Mariana. The town is also a stopping point for the Belo Horizonte–Vitória express buses. From here, local services run the 20km to **Manhumirim**, much closer to the park and a far nicer place to spend the night if necessary. There are two direct buses a day to Manhumirim from Belo Horizonte (at 7am and 10pm), the first going via Ouro Preto (8.45am) and Mariana (9.15am), and two from Vitória (at 9.30am and 3.30pm); all are run by Viação Pássaro Verde. Journey time from either city is about five hours; the afternoon bus from Vitória is the one to Carangola. Wherever you start from you'll need to book your **ticket** the day before if possible, as these routes fill up quickly, especially on Friday and Sunday.

Manhumirim and beyond

Once you get to **MANHUMIRIM**, your next destination will be Alto do Caparaó, 25km further on. It's an exceptionally scenic ride, so it's worth staying the night if you arrive after dark. Manhumirim is, in any case, a pleasant place, a very typical interior town where foreigners rarely appear and the people are curious and friendly. The bars in the centre get surprisingly lively on weekend evenings, and the best (though still basic) **hotel** is the *São Luis* (☎033/341-1178; ②), a short taxi ride from the *Rodoviária*.

The easiest way to reach Alto do Caparaó is by **taxi**, which costs about $15. There are three direct local **buses** a day, too, leaving from the *Rodoviária* at around 9.30am, 2pm and 4.30pm and taking about ninety minutes – check the exact times when you arrive, as they change frequently.

Alto do Caparaó

ALTO DO CAPARAÓ is a small village that lines the sloping asphalted road: wait until the bus makes its final stop opposite the bar at the top of the village before getting off. There are only a few **hotels** in the village itself, but two are unusually good value for money, namely the basic *Pousada Vale Verde* by the bar (no phone; meal and packed lunch provided; ①), and the excellent *Chalé Pico da Bandeira*, Rua das Hortênsias (☎032/747-2626; ③), with ten chalets (all with TV), a bar and a pool. Otherwise, locals rent out **rooms** – ask at the bar for a *casa familiar*, which will cost about $10. Two other hotels lie up the winding signposted road, Rua Vale Verde, that leads from the bus stop. The *Caparaó Parque Hotel* (☎032/747-2559, fax 747-2530; ⑤ B&B or full board) is 1km along, a beautiful place with stunning mountain views out back, and good food and friendly staff. The national park entrance is only a short walk on from the hotel. On the same road, and considerably cheaper, is *Pousada Clube do Bezerra* (☎032/747-2628; ③) which, like the *Caparaó Parque Hotel*, has a pool and a sauna – bliss after a long day's walk. Alternative accommodation for serious hikers is camping in the park, where there are two official campsites that you can use as a base for walking (see below).

Opposite the *Caparaó Parque Hotel* you can **hire horses** for the day ($25) if you feel like exploring the park in a saddle rather than on foot. And there is also a simple, but very friendly, unnamed **bar** in a rustic wooden house with fantastic views back down the valley – a wonderful place from which to watch the sunsets.

Leaving Alto do Caparaó

There are three **buses** a day from Alto do Caparaó to Manhumirim, at 5.30am, 1pm and 6pm, taking about ninety minutes. Otherwise, there are always jeeps outside the entrance of the *Caparaó Parque Hotel* which will take you to Manhumirim for $15 (you can book them in advance from *Transtur Turismo* on ☎032/747-2537). Direct buses from Manhumirim to Belo Horizonte leave at 11am and 10pm – there are four others during the day, but they arrive from other starting points and you may not be able to get a seat.

Parque Nacional do Caparaó

The official **park entrance** (daily 7am–5pm; $2), 4km from the village, is the only way to get into the park. Here you will be handed a useful brochure, also given out free at the reception of the *Caparaó Parque Hotel*, which has a very clear **map** on the back – you'll need it, as the park is huge, 250 square kilometres of some of the most spectacular scenery in Brazil. The Centro de Visitantes marked on the map is still only half built and progressing very slowly, but the main thing you need to know is that the park covers two **ecological zones**. The lower half is extremely beautiful: thickly forested valleys, hills and streams giving way, as the hills lead into mountains proper, to treeless alpine uplands strewn with wild flowers, heather and rock formations. The major **trails** are marked on the map and are just about passable by jeep; there is an (unmapped) maze of smaller trails off these, which you can only explore on foot or horseback (see "Alto do Caparaó" above).

There are two official **campsites** along the trail to the Pico da Bandeira summit, each with piped spring water, a basic shelter and toilets. You need your own equipment and you'll have to **reserve a place** at least a week in advance by ringing the Belo Horizonte branch of *IBAMA*, the national parks authority (☎031/335-6611; only Portuguese spoken), or you can visit their office at Av. Contorno 8121, in the *bairro* of Cidade Jardim, near the centre of Belo Horizonte. You won't be allowed to camp inside the park unless you've reserved a place in advance.

Some twenty minutes into the park, the **main trail** forks: left to the mountains (see below), and right to **Vale Verde**, an enchanting forested valley where a stream forms a series of small waterfalls and shallow pools. A picnic site here is a good base for exploring several trails leading off into the forest. If you carefully pick your way downstream, after about 100m you come to a natural viewing platform looking back down Caparaó valley, framed by forest trees – a wonderfully peaceful spot.

Pico da Bandeira

Despite being 2890m high, the **Pico da Bandeira** is not difficult to climb and the hike takes you through some truly spectacular scenery. That is not to say you shouldn't treat the mountain with the respect it deserves. You will need a thick sweater or jacket to guard against the wind, a packed lunch, a water bottle or a few drinks, and a good pair of walking or training shoes – the climb isn't steep enough for boots to be necessary. Be careful, too, not to be caught out after dark. The path is treacherous in places, and you shouldn't attempt it once the light has gone. Let the rangers at the park entrance know you are going and roughly when you expect to return.

To Tronqueira

The first **campsite** on the route to the summit is called **Tronqueira** and is 8km from the park entrance – uphill all the way, a hike that takes about three hours, or two if you're a seasoned walker. You're rewarded by stunning views, as the road winds its way out of forest into the alpine zone, with panoramic views of the Caparaó valley below. The trail culminates at *Tronqueira* itself, where a viewing platform has been built to allow you to appreciate one of the finest views in the country, as the hills far below recede to the jagged horizon. Just before you get to *Tronqueira*, a fork to the left takes you to **Cachoeira Bonita**, where the José Pedro stream, which forms the state border between Minas Gerais and Espírito Santo, plunges eighty metres down a rockface into a thickly forested gorge; another viewing platform allows full appreciation of the spectacle.

The lazy way to do the Pico, but the only method that allows you to get back to Caparaó the same day if you're not accustomed to long hikes, is to cover the section to *Tronqueira* **by jeep**. There are usually jeeps hanging around the entrance of the *Caparaó Parque Hotel*; if not, the reception will ring for you even if you're not a guest. You need to arrange it the day before, as you have to set out by 8am at the latest to be back the same day. The jeep leaves you at *Tronqueira*, taking about thirty minutes to get there, and returns at 4pm to pick you up – return fare is around $20. If you're staying at the hotel, let them know the day before and they'll prepare a packed lunch.

The hike to the summit

The path up the mountain from *Tronqueira* starts at the opposite end of the campsite from the viewing platform. The return trip to the summit from here is almost 20km, about six hours' walking time for most people, with another couple of hours for rests and lunch along the way. The very first stretch up from *Tronqueira* is extremely steep, but don't be discouraged: it soon flattens out into a pleasant stroll along a mountain valley, with the path hugging a crystalline mountain stream that forms swimmable pools at a couple of points. There is evidence of a forgotten episode in modern Brazilian history along the way, in the shape of bits of a military transport plane that crashed here in 1965. After the 1964 coup a group of left-wing militants took to these hills hoping to foment a Cuban-style popular rebellion, but were either hunted down or driven away – the plane that crashed was supplying the army patrols combing the area.

Halfway to the summit you come to **Terreirão**, the second official **campsite** and a good spot for lunch. A path to the right leads to a point overlooking a valley dominated by two mountains, the rocky crags of **Pico do Calçado** to the left, and **Pico do Cristal** to the right, both only a hundred metres shorter than Pico da Bandeira, and with trails leading up them if you felt so inclined – though only to be attempted if you are camping at *Terreirão*, or you will find yourself still on the mountain at nightfall. Fill your water bottle at *Terreirão*, as there is no drinking water between here and the summit. The path up to Pico da Bandeira continues from the opposite end of the campsite. After the first stretch it hits rocky, treeless moorland where the exact path is sometimes difficult to see, especially when cloud closes in. There are painted arrows to help you get your bearings, but often you only have to follow the trail of rusting cans and plastic rubbish instead; the thoughtlessness of some of the people using the trail is remarkable.

The only really steep part of the climb is right at the end, when you need to scramble up a rocky path to get to the **summit** itself. The arrows disappear, but by now you can get a bearing on the tower that marks the peak. Once there, on a clear day you are rewarded with an absolutely superb 360-degree panorama of the mountains and hills of Espírito Santo and Minas Gerais. On the way back, take special care on the first stretch down from the summit: it's a steep descent and there are many points where undue haste could leave you with a sprained ankle or worse.

ESPÍRITO SANTO

Espírito Santo, a compact combination of mountains and beaches, is one of the smallest states in Brazil (with a population of only 2.6 million), but as Minas Gerais' outlet to the sea it is strategically very important. More iron ore is exported through its capital, **Vitória**, than any other port in the world. Not surprisingly the preponderance of docks, rail yards and smelters limits the city's tourist potential, despite a fine natural location. To a *mineiro*, Espírito Santo means only one thing: **beaches**. The coastline is basically one long beach, some 400km in length and, during weekends and holiday seasons, people flock to take the waters, tending to concentrate on the stretch immediately south of Vitória, especially the large resort town of **Guarapari**. The best beaches, however, lie on the strip of coastline 50km south of Guarapari.

The hinterland of Vitória, far less visited, is exceptionally beautiful, a spectacular mix of lush forest, river valleys, mountains and granite hills. It's here that the state's real pleasures lie. The soils of this central belt are fertile, and since the latter part of the nineteenth century the area has been colonized by successive waves of Italians, Poles, Germans and Russians. Their descendants live in a number of small, very attractive country towns which combine a European feel and look with a thoroughly tropical landscape. All are easy to get to from Vitória, not more than an hour or two over good roads, with very frequent buses. Around the towns, the lack of mineral deposits and the sheer logistical difficulties in penetrating such a hilly area have preserved huge chunks of the **Mata Atlântica**, the lush semi-deciduous forest that once covered all the coastal parts of southern Brazil. Credit should also go to the local Indians, notably the Botocudo, whose dedicated resistance pinned the Portuguese down throughout the colonial period.

Vitória

As a city, **VITÓRIA** is vaguely remniscent of Rio with its combination of sea, steep hills, granite outcrops and irregularly shaped mountains on the horizon. Founded in 1551, it's one of the oldest cities in Brazil, but few traces of its past remain and nowadays most of the centre is urban sprawl. The heart of Vitória is an island connected to the mainland by a series of bridges, but the city has long since broken its natural bounds, spreading onto the mainland north and south: the major beach areas are on these mainland zones, **Camburi** to the north and **Vila Velha** with its beach **Praia da Costa** to the south. Vitória is renowned as the world capital of marlin fishing.

Arrival and information

The enormous, modern *Rodoviária* is only a kilometre from the centre and, outside, all **local buses** from the stop across the road run into town; returning from the centre, most buses from Avenida Jerônimo Monteiro pass the *Rodoviária* and will have it marked as a destination on the route cards displayed on the windscreen or by the door. If you're heading straight for the **beaches** on arrival, any bus that says "Aeroporto", "UFES", "Eurico Sales" or "Via Camburi" will take you to Camburi; to the southern beaches you need "P. da Costa", "Vila Velha" or "Itapoan" – all can be caught at the stops outside the *Rodoviária* or in the centre. As an alternative to the buses, **taxis** are cheap and a good option in this small city, where the distances are relatively short.

Trains from Belo Horizonte pull into the Estação Ferroviária Pedro Nolasco, 1km west of the *Rodoviária*, over in the mainland district of Cariacica; it's connected to the city and *Rodoviária* by yellow buses marked "Terminal Itacibá" and by most of the city's orange buses, including those marked "Jardim America" and "Campo Grande".

The **airport** (Aeroporto Eurico Sales; ☎327-0811) is situated a couple of kilometres from Camburi beach, some 12km from the city centre, and is served by frequent green buses, which can drop you on Avenida Beira Mar, its westward continuation, Avenida Getúlio Vargas, or at the *Rodoviária*.

Information
There's a very helpful CODESPE **tourist information** booth at the *Rodoviária* (Mon–Fri 8am–9pm, Sat 9am–4pm; no phone), which has lists of hotels, brochures and city maps; another booth at the airport keeps the same hours (☎327-2031). The central office of the state tourist company CETUR is at Av. Princesa Isabel 54, 4th floor (Mon–Fri 8am–6pm; ☎322-8888).

Accommodation

The choice for **accommodation** is between dozens of establishments in the beach zones, which tend to be expensive, and hotels in the centre, which generally are not. For really **cheap** places, the row of hotels facing the main entrance of the *Rodoviária* is your best bet. There's a **youth hostel** at Av. Hugo Viola 143, Jardim da Penha, set back a kilometre or so from Camburi (☎223-6010; $12 per person).

Central hotels
Hotel Avenida, Av. Presidente Florentino Avidos 347 (☎ and fax 223-4317). A cheap central place, with a number of reasonable rooms, some with air conditioning, TVs and *frigobar*. Single *quartos* are a particularly good deal at $10. ②.

Cannes Palace Hotel, Av. Jerônimo Monteiro 111 (☎222-1522, fax 222-8061). A mid-range central hotel, with good rooms and parking. ⑤.

Hotel Prata, Rua Nestor Gomes 201 (☎222-4311, fax 223-0943). A good budget option in the centre, with basic rooms with high ceilings and either fans or air conditioning. The better rooms face the pleasant Praça Climaco and the Palácio de Anchieta. Prices drop to ① if you stay over a longer period. ②.

Hotel São José, Av. Princesa Isabel 300 (☎223-7222, fax 322-4556). Bang in the centre on one of Vitória's main streets, but the price is the same as for many of the beach hotels. ⑥.

Hotel Spala, Av. Alexandre Buaiz 495 (☎222-5648). The best of the budget hotels facing the *Rodoviária*, with a range of rooms, some with TVs. The best are at the front, but their $8 *quartos* are windowless and dingy. ①.

> The **telephone code** for Vitória is ☎027.

Beach hotels

Hotel Alvetur Praia, Av. Dante Michelini 877 (☎225-3911, fax 225-3710). A mid- to upper-range hotel on the Praia de Camburi, with pool and sauna. ⑥.

Best Western Porto do Sol, Av. Dante Michelini 3957 (☎337-2244, fax 337-2711). At the furthest end of Praia de Camburi, the beach's most expensive place is up to the usual standards of the chain, but also the nearest hotel to the industrial port. ⑦.

Camburi Praia Hotel, Av. Dante Michelini 1007 (☎325-0455, fax 225-7451). A pleasant medium-size hotel, with sauna and pool, and apartments facing Camburi beach. ⑥.

Pousada da Praia, Av. Saturnino de Brito 1500 (☎ and fax 225-0233). An exception among the beach hotels in that this *pousada* is small (18 rooms) and relatively cheap, and is situated on Ponta Formosa, overlooking the more intimate Praia do Canto. It also has a pool. ⑤.

Senac Ilha do Boi, Rua Bráulio Macedo 417 (☎325-0111, fax 325-0115). A luxury hotel set on the Ilha do Boi facing the beach, with pool, sauna, a very good restaurant and great views. ⑦.

The City

The city is built into a steep hillside overlooking the docks, but the main streets are all at shore level. The name of the street that hugs the shore changes as you go eastwards from the *Rodoviária*, initially called Avenida Elias Miguel, then Avenida Getúlio Vargas, Avenida Mal. de Moraes and finally Avenida Beira Mar, but the whole stretch is generally known to locals as **Avenida Beira Mar**. From the Avenida Beira Mar, you can catch buses to the beach districts; the yellow TRANSCOL bus #500 goes over the massive **Terceira Ponte** (third bridge) to the southern district of town, **Vila Velha**, handy for the **Praia da Costa** and site of the **Convento da Penha**, with its spectacular views over the city. From the bridge itself you can also get a good idea of Vitória's layout.

From **Avenida Jerônimo Monteiro**, the main shopping street, a number of stairways (*escadarias*) lead to the colonial Palácio de Anchieta, now the state governor's palace. Just down from here the pleasant, tree-shaded **Praça Costa Pereira** is the heart of the downtown area with its Teâtro Carlos Gomes, a replica of the Milan Scala built between 1925 and 1927.

At the western end of Avenida Beira Mar is the city's oldest inhabited quarter, a labyrinth of narrow paths and blind alleys that is the **Ilha do Principe**. It occupies a small but very steep hill behind the *Rodoviária*, and although no trace remains of the original dwellings, the atmosphere is of a bygone age, with houses constructed one on top of another, many of them propped up on stilts, complete with the stench of broken sewers and mounds of garbage. Tourists seldom venture here, but it's well worth an hour's ramble for an alternative insight into daily Vitórian life, and harbours a few local bars should you wish to hang out a while longer. But do take care, avoid the area at night, and leave valuables in your hotel.

The centre

The only truly historic building in the centre of Vitória is the fine governor's palace, the **Palácio de Anchieta**, which dates from the 1650s but is closed to visitors. The one part you can see – the **tomb of Padre Anchieta**, in a side entrance – is something of a curiosity. Anchieta was the first of a series of great Jesuit missionaries to Brazil, and is most famous for being one of the two founders of São Paulo, building the rough chapel the town formed around in the sixteenth century and giving his name to one of that city's main avenues, the Via Anchieta. He was a stout defender of the rights of Indians, doing all he could to protect them from the ravages of the Portuguese and pleading their case several times to the Portuguese Crown; he was also the first to produce a grammar and dictionary of the Tupi language. Driven out of São Paulo by enraged Portuguese settlers, he retired to Vitória, died in 1597 and was finally canonized. The tomb is simple, set off by a small exhibition devoted to his life.

There is one museum in the city worth a look, the **Museu do Solar Monjardim** (Tues–Fri 8am–noon & 1–5pm, Sat & Sun 1–5pm), on Avenida Paulino Müller, in the *bairro* of Jucutuquara to the southeast of the centre; take the bus marked "Circular Maruipe" or "Joana d'Arc" from Avenida Beira Mar. It's a restored eighteenth-century mansion filled with a predominantly nineteenth-century collection of furniture and household utensils, and it gives a good idea of the layout and domestic routines of a colonial estate. But if you're used to the fine displays of colonial artwork in the museums of Minas Gerais you'll find it disappointing.

The Convento da Penha

The one reminder of Vitória's colonial past really worth seeing is on the southern mainland in Vila Velha: the chapel and one-time **Convento da Penha**, founded in 1558 (daily 5.30am–5pm; ☎329-0420). Perched on a granite outcrop towering over the city, it's worth visiting not so much for the convent itself, interesting though it is, as for the marvellous panoramic views over the entire city. It is a major pilgrimage centre and, in the week after Easter, thousands come to pay homage to the image of Nossa Senhora da Penha, the most devout making the climb up to the convent on their knees. It also marks the southernmost point the Dutch managed to reach in the sugar wars of the seventeenth century; an expedition arrived here in 1649 and sacked the embryonic city, but were held off until a relief force sent from Rio drove them out – you can see how the 154-metre hill must have been almost impregnable.

You have a choice of **walks** up to the top. The steepest and most direct is the fork off the main road to the left, shortly after the main entrance, where a steep cobbled path (extremely treacherous – take care, especially coming down) leads up to the convent. Less direct, but considerably safer and with better views, is to follow the winding Rua Luísa Grinalda – a very pleasant thirty-minute walk. Once at the top, the city is stretched out below you, the centre to the north framed by the silhouettes of the mountains inland and, to the south, by the golden arcs of Vila Velha's beaches. The builders of the **chapel** thoughtfully included a viewing platform, which you reach through a door to the left of the altar. More interesting than the chapel itself is the **Sala das Milagres**, next door to the café: a collection of photos, *ex votos*, artificial limbs and artefacts from grateful pilgrims.

To **get to the convent** from the centre, take the #500 bus and ask the driver to let you off at the third stop after the Terceira Ponte, which will leave you within easy walking distance of the convent.

Eating, drinking and nightlife

Local cuisine is based around seafood and is pretty good: lobster is plentiful, cheap and tastiest *na brasa* (charcoal-grilled); also worth trying is the *moqueca capixaba*, the local seafood stew where the sauce is less spicy and uses more tomatoes than the better-known Bahian variety. For a taste of local sweets and other delicacies, try the stalls in the Sunday market (8am–noon) on Praça Costa Pereira.

You won't find many classy **restaurants** in the **centre of town**, though there are a number of very good (and cheap) *comida por kilo* places near the Palácio de Anchieta along the Escadaria Maria Ortiz stairway; the best, with a great selection of both *mineiro* and local *capixaba* dishes, as well as vegetarian options, is *D'Barro Restaurante* at no. 29. Otherwise, even the most humble *lanchonete* will tend to have one or two local seafood dishes on offer beside the usual *salgados* and hot dogs.

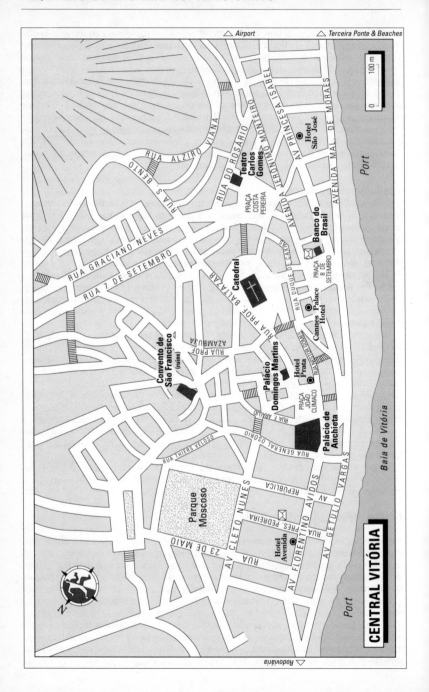

△ Airport   △ Terceira Ponte & Beaches

0 ____ 100 m

Hotel São José

RUA ALZIRO VIANA

RUA DO ROSARIO

RUA S. BENTO

RUA S. BENTO

Teatro Carlos Gomes

PRAÇA COSTA PEREIRA

AV PRINCESA ISABEL

AVENIDA MAL. DE MORAES

AV PRINCESA ISABEL

AVENIDA JERÔNIMO MONTEIRO

Banco do Brasil

RUA GRACIANO NEVES

RUA 7 DE SETEMBRO

Catedral

RUA PROF. BALTAZAR

RUA DUQUE D' CAXIA

PRAÇA 8 DE SETEMBRO

Cannes Palace Hotel

Convento de São Francisco (ruins)

RUA PROF. AZAMBUJA

Palácio Domingos Martins

Hotel Prata

RUA NESTOR GOMES

PRAÇA JOÃO CLIMACO

RUA F. ARAÚJO

Palácio de Anchieta

RUA THIERS VELOSO

RUA GENERAL OSÓRIO

Parque Moscoso

RUA CLETO NUNES

AV REPUBLICA

AV FLORENTINO AVIDOS

RUA PRES. PEDREIRA

AV GETULIO VARGAS

Hotel Avenida

23 DE MAIO

Baía de Vitória

Port

Port

△ Rodoviária

N

CENTRAL VITÓRIA

For better eating, however, the **beaches**, or rather the districts just inland from them, are the places to head for. **Camburi**, especially, has a large concentration of restaurants and nightspots (the green buses to the airport will take you past several). The best eateries include the Portuguese-inspired *Quinzinho*, Rua Aleixo Neto 1370 on the Praia do Canto (☎225-9844), the regional *Papaguth*, Rua Cel. Schwab Filho 127, Bento Ferreira (☎324-0375), and *Pirão*, Rua Joaquim Lyrio 753, also on Praia do Canto (☎227-1165).

As a beach, **Praia da Costa** has the edge over Camburi, but bars and restaurants are thinner on the ground. Still, it does have the advantage of being the place where shrimp boats land their catches; enterprising street-sellers grill them immediately and sell them at several points along the beach – delicious, especially when washed down with the chilled fresh coconut water, also available everywhere. It's worth mentioning one very good Bahian restaurant here, the *Recanto Baiano* at Rua Lucio Bacelar 43 (☎229-3710), which has been going strong for 27 years and is still the best place in town for *vatapá* and other Northeastern delights (see box on p.251).

There are a couple of good **live music** venues on the Praia do Canto: *Boca da Noite*, Rua João da Cruz 80 (☎227-1615), and *Academeia* on the same street at no. 535 (☎225-2428). Currently the hottest **nightclubs** are the dance-obsessed *Rota Brasil*, Rua Constante Sodré 1361, Praia do Canto (Mon–Sat 6pm to late), and the spanking new *Loft Jumping Bar*, with a great big trendy hole in the wall, opposite the university – take the airport bus, and you can't miss it on your right. Popular for cocktails in the same vicinity is the *Bar Picadeiro*, a circus big-top at Rua Francisco Anísio Coelho 240, Jardim da Penha.

Listings

Airlines All airlines have offices at the airport: Nordeste/Rio-Sul (for Belo Horizonte, Rio and São Paulo) ☎227-1588; TAM (for Belo Horizonte and São Paulo) ☎324-1091 or 324-1045; Transbrasil (for Rio and São Paulo) ☎225-9055 or 327-0308; Varig (for Rio, Salvador and São Paulo) ☎222-2322 or 327-0304; VASP (for all main destinations) ☎324-1499 or 327-0296.

Air-taxis *Uniair Táxi Aéreo*, airport (☎327-0244 or 327-0292).

Banks and exchange There's a Banco do Brasil on Av. Princesa Isabel, right in the middle of the banking district, but the best places (avoiding the extortionate bank commissions as well as queues) are the Agencia Esplanada, Av. Princesa Isabel 250, or the Agencia Vila Velha at Av. Champagnat 1077, over the bay in Vila Velha.

Bus companies Vitória has good connections to most of Brazil (see "travel details" at the end of the chapter for frequencies and durations). Companies and destinations are: Itapemirim (Belo Horizonte, Brasília, Fortaleza, Ouro Preto, Rio, Salvador and São Paulo); Rio Doce (São João del Rei); São Geraldo (Belo Horizonte and Ouro Preto in Minas Gerais; Cáceres in the South; Porto Velho in Rondônia); Sudeste (Guarapari and Rio); Viação Alvorada (Guarapari); Viação N.S. das Graças (Santa Leopoldina and Santa Teresa). Enquiries for all services on ☎222-3366.

Car rental Localiza (☎327-0211) at the airport.

Emergencies 24-hour healthcare by Pronto Socorro do Coração, Av. Leitão da Silva 2351, Santa Lúcia (☎227-4833); for police call ☎190.

Taxis Coopertaxi (☎336-5588); Radiotaxi (☎336-7111); Teletaxi (☎325-4343).

Trains The Estação Ferroviária Pedro Nolasco is just over the bridge from the *Rodoviária* in Cariacica (enquiries on ☎226-4169). There are daily services to Belo Horizonte at 6.30am, taking just over 14hr. Tickets are daily sold 5am–7pm and cost $8.50 (2nd class), $11.50 (1st class) and $17.50 (executive).

Beaches

Both the main **city beaches** look good, with palm trees and promenades in the best Brazilian tradition, but you can only swim at **Praia da Costa** to the south. The **Praia**

de Camburi is overlooked by the port of Tubarão in the distance, where iron ore and bauxite from Minas are either smelted or loaded onto supertankers, benefiting the economy but ruining the water: if you swim you'll have oil and chemicals for company. You have to go a little further afield for perfect coast.

The most beautiful beaches lie around and to the south of the burgeoning town of **GUARAPARI**, 54km to the south of Vitória and easily accessible from the *Rodoviária* – Viação Alvorada buses run every half hour from 5am to 9pm. There are dozens of hotels here, mostly white skyscrapers catering for package holidaymakers (prices are generally in the ⑤–⑥ bracket), as well as a very useful eighty-bed **youth hostel**, *Guaracamping*, 800m south of the centre on Avenida F, Quadra 40, Itapebussu (☎ and fax 027/261-0475; $12 per person). If you fancy raucous nightlife and holidaymaking Brazilian style, then Guarapari is the place. On the other hand, if you need some tranquillity to escape to, a mere 10km to the south of Guarapari along the ES-060 are the beaches of **Enseada Azul** and **Dos Padres**. These are amongst the finest in Espírito Santo, relatively unspoilt and with a glorious backdrop of hills covered in tropical vegetation.

To the north of Vitória, by the border with Bahia, is the small village of **CONCEIÇÃO DA BARRA** and the nearby beach of **Itaúnas**, which is composed of huge sand dunes up to 30m high. Beneath these lies a small town that was engulfed in the 1970s after the vegetation surrounding it had been cleared for farmland. It is said that occasionally the dunes shift in the wind to uncover the spire of the old church. There are a number of reasonable **hotels** in town, including the *Pousada do Sol*, Av. Atlântica 226 (☎027/762-1412; ③), which has a pool, and the *Marina Porta da Barra*, Rua Cel. Oliveiro F (☎027/762-1408; ⑤), with the finest views and the added luxury of a sauna.

Inland from Vitória

Inland from the city are several small towns surrounded by superb walking country, great for a day trip or as a base for a relaxing few days. You can easily spot where the first immigrants came from: the houses and churches of **Santa Teresa** look as Italian as those of **Domingos Martins** and **Santa Leopoldina** look German. The smallest of these towns, **Venda Nova**, is home to the remarkable sight of **Pedra Azul**, a grey granite finger almost 2000m high, one of the unsung natural wonders of Brazil. If you're heading for Minas Gerais, Venda Nova lies on the main Vitória–Belo Horizonte highway, Domingos Martins just off it.

Domingos Martins

The closest of the inland towns to Vitória is **DOMINGOS MARTINS**, 42km away on the north side of the Belo Horizonte highway. Confusingly, it has two names: Domingos Martins is the most common, but Campinho is also used. The drive there manages to pack a remarkable amount of scenery into a very short distance – sit on the right-hand side of the bus leaving Vitória for the best views. Almost as soon as the bus leaves the city limits the road starts to climb into the highlands, and very quickly presents wonderful views of hills and forest. Domingos Martins is high enough to be bracingly fresh by day and distinctly cold at night; it looks like a German mountain village, with its triangular wooden houses modelled after alpine chalets.

Get off the bus at the first stop in the town, rather than continuing to the *Rodoviária*. The cheapest **accommodation** is the *Hotel Campinho* near the bus stop (no phone; ②), but if you continue the few metres to the immaculately manicured main square there's a wonderful hotel, the *Imperador*, Rua Duque de Caxias 275 (☎027/268-1115, fax 268-1555; ⑤), built in German style. It's superb value for the quality of accommodation, but at weekends you may well have to phone ahead to reserve a room. If it's luxury you're after, don't miss the *Pousada dos Pinhos*, BR-262 km 90 in Aracê district (☎027/248-1115, fax 248-1283; ⑥) with its stunning views. A good cheap option in town, with a pool, is *Pousada Dom Pedro II*, at Rua Dom Pedro II 10 (☎027/268-1478; ③).

There's not much to Domingos Martins, just a small museum, the **Casa da Cultura**, almost opposite the bus stop at Av. Presidente Vargas 520, which has some old documents and artefacts dating from the colony's early days after it was founded by Pomeranians in 1847. If you're into flora, it's worth the hassle getting to the **Reserva Kautsky** (☎027/268-1209), some way out of town and accessible only by four-wheel-drive, which has a good collection of orchids and camellias – ask at any hotel for details. The main pastime in Domingos Martins in decent weather is **walking** in the surrounding forest and hills; ask at the Casa da Cultura for details and maps of possible itineraries.

In the centre of town, near the Casa da Cultura, is an excellent **restaurant**, *Tia Ria*, which serves homemade food at very low prices. For the authentic German-Brazilian culinary experience, *Hoffmanns Gasthaus* on Ladaria Francisco Santo Silva 50 (closed Mon) is good and reasonably priced. A short bus or taxi ride out of town is the *Restaurante Vista Linda*, where the food is no more than moderate but the view out across a mountain valley is tremendous; the local bus from the *Rodoviária* to the neighbouring town of Marechal Floriano passes by.

When it's time to **move on**, you can get a bus from Marechal Floriano direct to Manhumirim (for the Parque do Caparaó in Minas Gerais – see p.185) without having to trek back into Vitória. Take the local service from Domingos Martins to Marechal Floriano and catch one of the buses run by Aguia Branca to Manhumirim that pass by at 10.30am and 4.30pm. You have to trust to luck there's a seat, but on weekdays you'll probably be lucky. Otherwise you'll have to go into Vitória and get a ticket on the 9.30am or 3.30pm bus to Carangola, which stops at Manhumirim.

Venda Nova and Pedra Azul

VENDA NOVA DO IMIGRANTE, to give it its full name, is an Italian village some 100km further west from Vitória. Even by the standards of the state, the landscape in which it is set is extraordinary, an alpine mix of forests, valleys and escarpments. A few kilometres outside the village is the most remarkable sight in Espírito Santo, a towering bare granite mountain, shaped like a thumb, almost 1000m high – the **Pedra Azul**, or "blue stone". Its peak is actually 2000m above sea level, the other thousand accounted for by the hill country it sprouts out of, an area popular with mountaineers. It's like an enormous version of the Sugar Loaf in Rio, except that no vegetation grows on its bare surface, which rears up from thick forest and looks so smooth that from a distance it appears more like glass than stone. During the day sunlight does strange things to it – it really does look blue in shadow – but the time to see it is either at dawn or sunset, when it turns all kinds of colours in a spectacular natural show.

Venda Nova itself is nothing more than a small village strung along the highway. There are three direct **buses** a day from Vitória, but any bus that goes to Minas Gerais also passes by, as it's on the highway to Belo Horizonte; Aguia Branca buses from Vitória are the best bet. For **accommodation**, an outstanding luxury option, in very carefully maintained regional style – quite possibly Espírito Santo's most charming hotel – lies just outside the village on the rolling hills at the foot of the rock, the *Pousada Pedra Azul* (☎027/248-1101, fax 248-1201; ⑦ full board; closed Mon–Thurs). Its gardens have a Japanese pagoda by a lake, and a sixty-metre waterfall, and the hotel itself has the usual pool, sauna and other accoutrements you'd expect at this price. The *Hotel Alpes* at km 103 of the BR-262 also has its own pool and sauna (☎027/546-1367; ⑤), and there's a cheap place on the main (and only) street in Venda Nova itself, the *Hotel Canal* (no phone; ③). The town has several **restaurants**: *Churrascaria Posso Fundo*, near the Prefeitura, is the best value, but better food is to be had either at the Portuguese *Lusitânia* or the *Peterle*. The countryside around here is excellent for **walking**; even if you don't stay there, the reception desk at the *pousada* gives helpful advice on routes.

Santa Teresa

SANTA TERESA is only 90km northwest from Vitória but the hills between are steep, reducing buses to a crawl for significant stretches and padding the journey out to a good two hours. The initial run up the main highway towards Bahia to the pleasant hill town of Fundão is pretty, but the winding road that takes you the 13km from here to Santa Teresa is something special, with great views on either side of the bus. The soils are rich, and dense forest is interspersed with coffee bushes and intensively cultivated hill farms, framed by dramatic granite cliffs and escarpments.

The closer you get to Santa Teresa, the more insistent the echoes of Europe become. The tiled hill-farms look more Italian and less Brazilian, you see vines, and signs advertising local wines, and when you finally pull into the village you could be arriving somewhere in the hills of northern Italy. The first colonists, mainly Italian but with several families of Polish and Russian Jews, arrived here in 1875; the last shipload of Italian immigrants docked in Vitória in 1925.

The town has grown very little in more recent times, and is still laid out along two streets in the shape of a cross. You go right down the main artery to arrive at the **Rodoviária** at the far end of the village. There is a beautifully tended square, full of flowers, trees and hummingbirds darting around. Along the adjacent street and at the far end, next to the school, is Santa Teresa's main attraction, the Museu de Mello Leitão, a natural history museum and nature reserve covering eighty square kilometres (see below).

From the square, steps cut into the hillside lead to a ridge, and five minutes' walk brings you to an unmistakably Italian **Igreja Matriz**, complete with roundels and cupola; the names of the first colonists are engraved on a plaque on its outside wall. The street leading uphill from here is the oldest in the village, now lined with solid, colonial-looking houses built in the early years of this century. Three hundred metres along it, you come to the surviving two-storey wattle-and-daub houses put up by the first wave of Italians and Poles; oldest of all is the farmhouse opposite the tiny chapel.

The Museu de Mello Leitão

Santa Teresa is full of flowers, and of hummingbirds feeding off them, and early this century they aroused the interest of one of the first generation of Italians to be born here, **Augusto Ruschi**. He turned a childhood fascination into a lifetime of study, and became a pioneering natural scientist and ecologist decades before it was fashionable. Specializing in the study of **hummingbirds**, he became the world's leading expert in the field and, in the later years of his life, was almost single-handedly responsible for galvanizing the state government into action to protect the exceptional beauty of the interior of Espírito Santo; that so much forest remains is due in no small measure to him. He died in 1986, at the age of 71, after being poisoned by the secretions of a tree-frog he collected on one of his many expeditions into the forest.

The **Museu de Mello Leitão**, Av. José Ruschi 4 (Mon–Fri 8am–noon & 1–5pm with guide, Sat & Sun noon–5pm without guide) was named by Ruschi as a tribute to a former professor. It represents Ruschi's life's work, designed and laid out by him since the early 1930s. The museum contains his library and all his collections of animals, birds and insects, as well as a small zoo, a snake farm, a butterfly garden and the richest park in the state, with thousands of species of trees, orchids, flowers and cacti. It is worth timing your journey to catch it open, a beautiful place to wander around and a fine memorial to an extraordinary man.

Practicalities

Regular **buses** run by Viação N.S. das Graças make the trip from Vitória to Santa Teresa (6 daily, 3 on Sun). At present, there are buses on to the nearby German town of Santa Leopoldina at 10am and 2pm (45min), but it's advisable to check the times in Santa Teresa. The best **hotel** is the *Solar dos Colibris*, 4km from the town centre at Av. dos Manacás 400, Jardim da Montanha (☎027/259-1783; ⑤), with pool and sauna. In town itself, *Pierazzo Hotel*, Av. Getúlio Vargas 115 (☎027/259-1233; ④), is quite reasonable. Among **restaurants**, *Mazzolin di Fiori* on Praça Domingos Martins serves local specialities (lunchtimes only), as does *Zitu's* on Avenida Getúlio Vargas, near *Pierazzo Hotel*.

Santa Leopoldina

The drive to **SANTA LEOPOLDINA** (most people shorten it to Leopoldina) from Santa Teresa is fabulous, along a country road winding through thickly forested hills and gorges. There are a few hair-raising drops, which the bus drivers – who know every stone and curve – negotiate with aplomb, grinding gears and holding shouted conversations with the passengers, mostly blonde peasants clutching string bags and chickens. At one point you pass a spectacular waterfall in a gorge choked with forest to the left; even on foot the descent is too steep for you to get close to it. Despite the temporary look of the road and the small settlements you pass through – clearings in the forest uncannily like Amazon highway settlements – these are long-established communities dating from 1919, when the road was finished.

Ironically, the road's completion meant the end of the line for Santa Leopoldina. Founded in 1857 by 160 Swiss colonists, who were followed over the next forty years by over a thousand Saxons, Pomeranians and Austrians, Santa Leopoldina was one of the earliest European colonies in Espírito Santo and also the most successful: coffee grew well on the hills and found a ready market on the coast. Built on the last navigable stretch of the Rio Santa Maria, inland from Vitória, Leopoldina was the main point of entry for the whole region. Once the road was finished, however, Santa Teresa swiftly outgrew it, leaving only a street of solid German houses and trading posts as a reminder of earlier prosperity.

The bus drops you at one end of the main street, **Rua do Comércio**. Back along the street is the interesting **Museu do Colono** (Wed–Sun 9–11am & 1–5pm), housed in the mansion of what used to be the leading German family in town. The museum documents the early decades of German settlement with photographs – including some fascinating ones of the construction of the road to Santa Teresa in 1919 – relics and documents. In a sense the whole village is a museum, with the gables and eaves of the buildings much as they were at the turn of the century, perfectly preserved by the twist of fate that turned the village into an economic backwater many decades ago. Resting quietly in its beautiful river valley, it's a peaceful place to wander around, and there are some fine nineteenth-century buildings on the Rua do Comércio. Several of them are now **bars** or **restaurants**, including one next to the bridge with a great setting overlooking the Rio Santa Maria. Unfortunately, there is nowhere to stay and it's either back to Santa Teresa or to Vitória – buses to the latter leave every couple of hours from the stop on Rua do Comércio, the last one going at 6pm. Buses to Santa Teresa are more infrequent, but you could always **hike** back. The whole area is wonderful walking country, and the 12km to Santa Teresa, with some steep sections, takes about five hours.

travel details

Buses

Belo Horizonte to: Belém (1 daily; 50hr); Brasília (6 daily; 14hr); Campinas (5 daily; 13hr); Campo Grande (4 daily; 23hr); Caxambu (2 daily; 6hr); Congonhas (6 daily; 2hr); Cuiabá (2 daily; 33hr); Curitiba (2 daily; 18hr); Diamantina (6 daily; 6hr); Fortaleza (1 daily; 36hr); Goiânia (6 daily; 16hr); Manhuaçu (3 daily; 4hr 30min); Manhumirim (2 daily; 5hr); Mariana (7 daily; 2hr); Ouro Preto (17 daily; 2hr); Poços de Caldas (4 daily; 8hr); Recife (1 daily; 40hr); Rio (20 daily; 8hr); Sabará (every 15min; 30min); Salvador (2 daily; 28hr); Santa Bárbara (4 daily; 2hr 30min); São João del Rei (6 daily; 4hr); São Lourenço (2 daily; 6hr); São Paulo (15 daily; 12hr); Sete Lagoas (14 daily; 1hr); Vitória (7 daily; 8hr).

Ouro Preto to: Belo Horizonte (17 daily; 2hr); Mariana (every 20min; 30min); Rio (1 daily; 8hr); São João del Rei (2 daily, 4 on Fri; 6hr); São Paulo (3 daily; 12hr); Vitória (1 daily, except Sat; 8hr).

São João del Rei to: Belo Horizonte (6 daily; 4hr); Caxambu (4 weekly; 3hr); São Paulo (2 daily; 8hr); Três Corações (4 daily; 4hr); Vitória (1 daily; 13hr).

Vitória to: Belo Horizonte (7 daily; 8hr); Brasília (1 daily; 22hr); Cáceres (1 daily; 34hr); Domingos Martins (13 daily; 1hr); Fortaleza (5 weekly; 36hr); Guarapari (every 30min; 1hr); Manhuaçu (2 daily; 4hr); Manhumirim (2 daily; 4hr); Ouro Preto (1 daily; 7hr); Rio (9 daily; 7hr); Salvador (1 daily; 17hr); Santa Leopoldina (8 daily; 2hr); Santa Teresa (6 daily, 3 on Sun; 2hr); São João del Rei (1 daily; 13hr); São Paulo (5 daily; 14hr); Venda Nova (hourly; 3hr).

Trains

Calling at all stations, including Governador Valadares and Itabira:

Belo Horizonte to: Vitória (daily at 7am; 14hr).

Vitória to: Belo Horizonte (daily at 6.30am; 14hr).

Planes

Belo Horizonte to: Brasília (9 daily; 1hr); Rio (20 daily; 1hr); São Paulo (25 daily; 1hr); Vitória (6 daily; 1hr).

Vitória to: Belo Horizonte (2 daily; 1hr); Brasília (1 daily; 2hr); Rio (5 daily; 1hr); Salvador (2 daily; 2hr); São Paulo (6 daily; 1hr).

CHAPTER THREE

THE NORTHEAST

T he **Northeast** (*nordeste*) of Brazil covers an immense area and features a variety of climates and scenery, from the dense equatorial forests of western Maranhão, only 200km from the mouth of the Amazon, to the parched interior of Bahia, some 2000km to the south. It takes in all or part of the nine **states** of

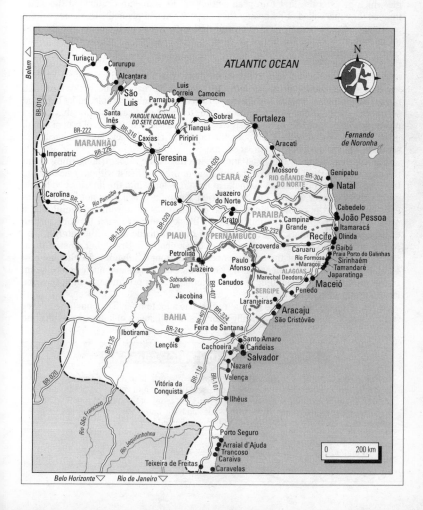

Maranhão, Piauí, Ceará, Rio Grande do Norte, Paraíba, Pernambuco, Alagoas, Sergipe and Bahia, which together form roughly a fifth of Brazil's land area and have a combined population of 36 million. When *nordestinos* living outside the region are included, they make up about a third of Brazil's total population. Within Brazil, the Northeast is notorious for its poverty, and it has been described as the largest concentration of poor people in the Americas. Yet it's also one of the most rewarding areas of Brazil to visit, with a special identity and culture nurtured by fierce regional loyalties, shared by rich and poor alike. You'll come across echoes of Northeastern culture all over Brazil – in the Amazon highway towns or the *favelas* of Rio and São Paulo – engendered by the millions of Northeasterners who migrate out of the region.

It is an identity forged by **geographical** contrasts, as most of the Northeastern states have three distinct areas. First is the flat coastal strip, the **zona da mata**, which literally means "forest zone". Little, apart from the name, is now left of the coastal jungle which greeted the first European settlers in the sixteenth century: at the same time as they marvelled at its beauty they cut it down and planted sugar cane, taking advantage of the heavy tropical rains and rich soils. It was on the coast that the first towns and cities of the Northeast grew up – not for nothing are all the region's state capitals, save one, coastal cities – and to this day the coastal strip is by far the most thickly populated part of the Northeast. Unfortunately, this fertile belt is rather narrow, and nowhere does it extend inland for more than a hundred kilometres. It gives way to an intermediate area, the **agreste**, where hills rear up into rocky mountain ranges and the lush, tropical vegetation of the coast is gradually replaced by highland scrub and cactus. Finally comes the **sertão**, the vast semi-arid interior that covers more than three-quarters of the Northeast but houses a relatively small proportion of its population. The soils here are poor, the rainfall is irregular, and only the hardy can scrabble a living out of the harsh landscape.

The contrast between the coast and the interior is the most striking thing about the region. You could have a fascinating time in the Northeast without ever leaving the *zona da mata*, but unless you make at least one foray into the interior you'll only get a partial view of what is the most varied region in Brazil. It is not just a difference in the way the country looks. Much of it also has to do with the **racial** mix, a product of the region's economic history. Blacks were imported to work on the coastal sugar plantations, and relatively few of them made it into the interior. The Northeast has the largest concentration of black people in Brazil, but most of them still live either on or near the coast, concentrated around **Salvador**, **Recife** and **São Luis**, where African influences are very obvious – in the cuisine, music and religion. In the *sertão*, though, Portuguese and Indian influences predominate in both popular culture and racial ancestry.

As far as specific attractions go, the region has a lot to offer. The **coastline** is over two thousand kilometres of practically unbroken beach, much of it just as you imagine

---

ACCOMMODATION PRICE CODES

In this guide, accommodation has been categorized according to the price codes outlined below, based on US$. These categories represent the minimum you can expect to pay for a **double room in high season** – though note that many of the budget places will also have more expensive rooms. Rates for hostels and basic hotels where guests are charged **per person** are given in US$, instead of being indicated by price code. See p.31 for further information.

| ① under $20 | ③ $30–45 | ⑤ $60–80 | ⑦ $120–175 |
| ② $20–30 | ④ $45–60 | ⑥ $80–120 | ⑧ $175 and over |

tropical beaches to be: white sands, blue sea, palm trees – the stuff advertising campaigns are made of. The **colonial heritage** survives in the Baroque churches and cobbled streets of Salvador, Olinda and São Luis, often side by side with the modern Brazilian mix of skyscrapers and shanty towns. And in Salvador and Recife, with populations of around two million each, the Northeast has two of Brazil's great **cities**. Head **inland**, and the bustling market towns of the *agreste* and the enormous jagged landscapes of the *sertão* more than repay journeys. But above all, in both city and countryside, there's the force of a richly diverse **popular culture** which you will find reflected not only in arts and crafts, but in the texture of everyday life.

We've covered the region starting from Recife, the largest city in the Northeast, then dealt with the *agreste* and *sertão* of **Pernambuco** state, before heading south, via the smaller states of **Alagoas** and **Sergipe**, to the vast state of **Bahia** and its capital Salvador. The account of the northern half of the region, an arc of land which stretches from the eastern tip of Brazil to the fringes of Amazônia, begins with the state of **Paraíba** and heads west, via **Rio Grande do Norte**, **Ceará** and its capital Fortaleza, and **Piauí**, ending in **Maranhão** state. Maranhão marks the geographical and cultural limit of the Northeast. Here the dominant colour changes from brown to green, as the arid *sertão* yields to flat and fertile river plains and palm forests, and the dry heat becomes steamily equatorial. Only a few hundred kilometres west of São Luis, capital of Maranhão, you come to the fringes of the Amazon rainforest proper.

A little history

These very different geographical zones shaped the **history** of the region; the Northeast was the first part of Brazil to be settled by Europeans on any scale. The Portuguese were quick to recognize the potential of the coast, and by the end of the sixteenth century sugar plantations were already importing African slaves. **Salvador** and **Olinda** developed into large towns while Rio de Janeiro was no more than a swampy village. Indeed, Salvador became the first capital of Brazil, and by the end of the sixteenth century the Northeast had become Europe's main supplier of **sugar**. The merchants and plantation owners grew rich and built mansions and churches, but their very success led to their downfall. It drew the attention of the **Dutch**, who were so impressed that they destroyed the Portuguese fleet in Salvador in 1624, burnt down Olinda six years later and occupied much of the coast, paying particular attention to sugar-growing areas. It took more than two decades of vicious guerrilla warfare before the Dutch were expelled, and even then they had the last laugh: they took their new experience of sugar growing to the West Indies, which soon began to edge Brazilian sugar out of the world market.

The Dutch invasion, and the subsequent decline of the sugar trade, proved quite a fillip to the development of the interior. With much of the coast in the hands of the invaders, the **colonization** of the *agreste* and *sertão* was stepped up. The Indians and escaped slaves already there were joined by cattlemen, *vaqueiros*, as trails were opened up into the highlands and huge ranches carved out of the interior. Nevertheless, it took over two centuries, roughly from 1600 to 1800, before these regions were fully absorbed into the rest of Brazil. In the *agreste*, where some fruit and vegetables could be grown and cotton did well, market villages developed into towns. However, the *sertão* became, and still remains, cattle country, with an economy and society very different from the coast.

Life in the **interior** has always been hard. The landscape is dominated by cactus and dense scrub – *caatinga* – the heat is fierce, and for most of the year the countryside is parched brown. But it only takes a few drops of rain to fall for an astonishing transformation to take place. Within the space of a few hours the *sertão* blooms. Its plant life, adapted to semi-arid conditions, rushes to take advantage of the moisture: trees bud, cacti burst into flower, shoots sprout up from the earth, and, literally overnight, the brown is replaced by a carpet of green. Too often, however, the rain never comes, or arrives too late, or too early, or in the wrong place, and the cattle begin to die. The first recorded **drought** was as early as 1710, and since then droughts have struck the *sertão* at ten- or fifteen-year intervals, sometimes lasting for years. The worst was in the early 1870s, when as many as two million people died of starvation; and the early 1990s were also a particularly bad time. The problems caused by drought were, and still are, aggravated by the inequalities in land ownership. The fertile areas around rivers were taken over in early times by powerful cattle barons, whose descendants still dominate much of the interior. The rest of the people of the interior, pushed into less favoured areas, are regularly forced by drought to seek refuge in the coastal cities until the rains return. For centuries, periodic waves of refugees, known as *os flagelados* (the scourged ones), have poured out of the *sertão* fleeing droughts: modern Brazilian governments have been no more successful in dealing with the special problems of the interior than the Portuguese colonizers before them.

Practicalities

You can reach the Northeast from almost any direction. Direct, there are **flights** to Recife and Salvador from Europe and North America, and frequent **buses** to the main Northeastern cities from all parts of Brazil. From **southern and central Brazil**, buses converge upon Salvador, although there are buses to other cities, too. From the **Amazon**, buses from Belém run to São Luis, Teresina, Fortaleza and points east. See *Basics* p.27 and the relevant chapters' "travel details" for more information.

Getting around the Northeast is straightforward thanks to the region's extensive bus network. However, even the main highways can be bumpy at times, and minor roads are often precarious. This is especially true in the **rainy season**: in Maranhão the rains come in February, in Piauí and Ceará in March, and points east in April, lasting for around three months. These are only general rules, though: Maranhão can be wet even in the dry season, and Salvador's skies are liable to give you a soaking at any time of year.

One other thing you should be aware of is that the Northeast splits into two different **time zones** between October and February. Bahia, along with the South and Southeast, moves its clocks forward an hour, while the rest of the Northeast remains three hours behind GMT.

PERNAMBUCO

Recife, capital of the state of **Pernambuco**, shares with São Luis the distinction of not having been founded by the Portuguese: when they arrived in the 1530s, they settled just to the north, building the beautiful, colonial town of **Olinda** and turning most of the surrounding land over to sugar. A century later, the Dutch, under Maurice of Nassau, took Olinda and burned it down, choosing to build a new capital, Recife, on swampy land to the south, where there was the fine natural harbour which Olinda had lacked. The Dutch, playing to their strengths, drained and reclaimed the low-lying land, and the main evidence of the Dutch presence today is not so much their few surviving churches and forts dotted up and down the coast, as the reclaimed land on which the core of Recife is built.

Out of Recife, there are good beaches in both directions. The Portuguese first developed the coastline as far **north** as the island of **Itamaracá**, growing sugar cane on every available inch. This erstwhile fishing village still retains its Dutch fort, built to protect the new colonial power's acquisitions, but these days it's a fairly blighted weekenders' resort. Best is the **coastal route south**, where a succession of small towns and villages interrupts a glorious stretch of palm-fringed beach.

Head **inland** and the scenery changes quickly to the hot, dry and rocky landscape of the *sertão*. **Caruaru** is the obvious target, home of the largest market in the Northeast, and close by is **Alto do Moura**, centre of the highly rated Pernambucan pottery industry. If you plan to go any further inland than this you'll need to prepare well for any kind of extended *sertão* journey, though it's straightforward enough to reach the twin river towns of **Petrolina** and **Juazeiro**.

Recife

Initial impressions are misleading and although **RECIFE** doesn't have the instantly defin-able atmosphere of Rio or Salvador, it's a very distinctive place all the same. The Northeast's largest city, it's lent a colonial grace and elegance by Olinda, 6km to the north and so close that they're considered part of the same conurbation. Recife itself has long since burst its original colonial boundaries and much of the centre is now given over to uninspired mod-ern skyscrapers and office buildings. But there are still a few quiet squares, where an inor-dinate number of impressive churches lie cheek by jowl with the uglier urban sprawl of the past thirty years. North of the centre are some pleasant leafy suburbs, dotted with muse-ums and parks, and to the south there is the modern beachside district of **Boa Viagem**. Other beaches lie within easy reach, both north and south of the city, and there's also all the **nightlife** one would expect from a city of nearly two million Brazilians.

Arrival, information and getting around

The **airport** is fairly close to the city centre, at the far end of Boa Viagem. A taxi to Boa Viagem itself shouldn't be more than $7, to Santo Antônio $12; or take the Aeroporto bus, $3, from right outside, which will drive through Boa Viagem and drop you in the centre. The **Rodoviária**, though, is miles out and arriving here can give you the entirely wrong impression that Recife is in the middle of nowhere. This is not really a problem, since the **metrô**, an overground rail link, whisks you very efficiently into the centre, giving you a good introduction to city life as it glides through various *favelas*. The metrô is very cheap but only serves industrial suburbs, so you're only likely to use it going to and from the *Rodoviária*. It will deposit you at the old train station, called **Estação Central** (or simply "Recife"). To get to your hotel from there, whether in the central hotel district, Boa Viagem or even Olinda, you're best off taking a **taxi** – Recife is a confusing city even when you've been there a few days, and the extra money will be well spent.

Information
Tourist information is not Recife's strong point, and what there is is directed mainly at the upper end of the market. However, some help is available. The state tourist office, EMPETUR, runs a 24-hour information post at the **airport** (☎341-5707), where you may find English-speaking staff and a few maps and calendars of events. They'll also ring hotels for you, but are no good for the cheapest places. EMPETUR has its headquarters inconveniently located at the **Centro de Convenções** (Mon–Fri 8am–6pm; ☎241-2111, ext 2174), an ugly concrete building halfway down the road between Recife and Olinda. A better bet – if it's working – is the **tourist hotline**: just ring ☎1516 (Mon–Fri 8am–6pm) and you should be able to find someone who speaks English. Finally, in **Boa Viagem**, there is a Delegacia do Turista, Rua dos Navegantes 1003 (☎326-9603), which is open 24 hours a day and can help with accommodation at the beach.

The **telephone code** for Recife and Olinda is ☎081.

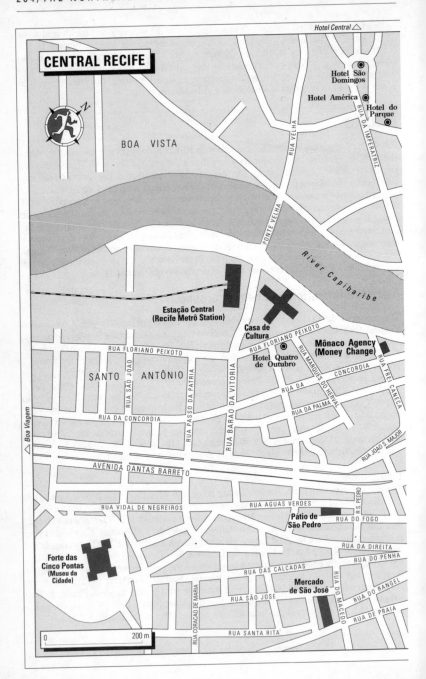

CENTRAL RECIFE

Hotel Central

Hotel São Domingos

Hotel América

Hotel do Parque

BOA VISTA

RUA VELHA

PONTE VELHA

RUA DA IMPERATRIZ

River Capibaribe

Estação Central
(Recife Metrô Station)

Casa de
Cultura

RUA FLORIANO PEIXOTO

Hotel Quatro
de Outubro

Mônaco Agency
(Money Change)

RUA FLORIANO PEIXOTO

RUA MARQUES DO HERVAL

RUA FREI CANECA

CONCORDIA

SANTO ANTÔNIO

RUA SÃO JOAO

RUA PASSO DA PATRIA

RUA BARAO DA VITORIA

RUA DA
PALMA

RUA DA CONCORDIA

RUA JOAO S. MAJOR

△ Boa Viagem

AVENIDA DANTAS BARRETO

RUA VIDAL DE NEGREIROS

RUA AGUAS VERDES

R.S. PEDRO

Pátio de
São Pedro

RUA DO FOGO

RUA DA DIREITA

RUA DO PENHA

Forte das
Cinco Pontas
(Museu da
Cidade)

RUA DAS CALCADAS

RUA DO MACEDO

RUA DO RANGEL

Mercado
de São José

RUA CORAÇAO DE MARIA

RUA SÃO JOSÉ

RUA DE PRAIA

RUA SANTA RITA

0   200 m

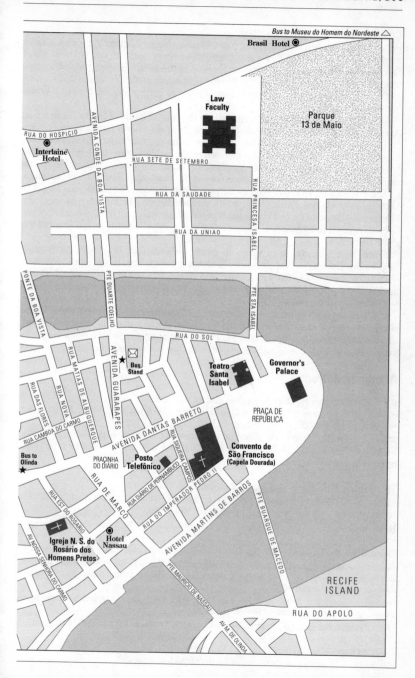

Bus to Museu do Homem do Nordeste △
Brasil Hotel ◉
Law Faculty
Parque 13 de Maio
RUA DO HOSPICIO
Interlainé Hotel
AVENIDA CONDE DA BOA VISTA
RUA SETE DE SETEMBRO
RUA DA SAUDADE
RUA PRINCESA ISABEL
RUA DA UNIAO
PONTE DA BOA VISTA
PTE DUARTE COELHO
PTE STA ISABEL
RUA DO SOL
RUA MATIAS DE ALBUQUERQUE
RUA NOVA
RUA DAS FLORES
AVENIDA GUARARAPES
Bus Stand
Teatro Santa Isabel
Governor's Palace
PRAÇA DE REPÚBLICA
RUA CAMBOA DO CARMO
AVENIDA DANTAS BARRETO
RUA SIQUEIRA CAMPOS
Bus to Olinda
PRAÇINHA DO DIÁRIO
Posto Telefônico
RUA DIARIO DE PERNAMBUCO
Convento de São Francisco (Capela Dourada)
RUA EST DO ROSARIO
RUA DE MARCO
RUA DO IMPERADOR PEDRO II
AV NOSSA SENHORA DO CARMO
Igreja N. S. do Rosário dos Homens Pretos
Hotel Nassau
AVENIDA MARTINS DE BARROS
PTE BUARQUE DE MACEDO
RECIFE ISLAND
PTE MAURÍCIO DE NASSAU
RUA DO APOLO
AV M DE OLINDA

City transport

Recife's **bus network** is an appalling mess. Routes change frequently, the destinations marked on the front of the buses are places you've never heard of, and unlike in Rio or Salvador, there are no helpful signs on the side of the vehicle showing where it stops along the way. To make things worse, the complex layout of the city means that it's hard to get your bearings. What follows is a basic guide to getting around, but you'll probably still have to ask.

Most city buses originate and terminate on the central island of **Santo Antônio**, on Avenida Dantas Barreto, either side of the **Pracinha do Diário** (also known as Praça da Independência). There are other stops nearby on Avenida Guararapes outside the main post office. To get from the city centre **to Boa Viagem**, take buses marked "Aeroporto", "Iguatemi" or "Boa Viagem", or catch the more comfortable *frescão* marked "Aeroporto", just outside the offices of the newspaper, *Diário de Pernambuco*, on the Pracinha do Diário; it goes every twenty minutes and costs about $3. To get **to Olinda** from central Recife, walk south down Avenida Dantas Barreto from the Pracinha do Diário to the last of the series of bus stops, and catch the bus marked "Casa Caiada" – you'll think you're heading in the wrong direction at first, but you will get there eventually.

From Boa Viagem, most buses in either direction can be caught on Avenida Engenheiro Domingos Ferreira, three blocks in from the sea. Buses marked "Dantas Barreto" will get you **to the city centre**, and so should most of those marked "Conde de Boa Vista", though it's probably best to ask. You can get directly from Boa Viagem **to Olinda** on buses marked "Rio Doce".

If you're completely fed up with the buses, there are always **shared taxis**. These small vans race around the city towards the end of the afternoon, offering lifts to various destinations for between $2 and $4. They'll stop almost anywhere and are a pretty good way of getting around as long as you're not too nervous a passenger.

Accommodation

It's cheapest to stay right in the centre, and most expensive in Boa Viagem. The other obvious area to consider staying is Olinda, where prices fall somewhere between the two; hotels there are listed separately under "Olinda" (see p.216).

Recife's **youth hostel**, the *Albergue da Juventude Maracatus do Recife*, is in Boa Viagem at Rua Maria Carolina 185 (☎326-1221), and is superb. Complete with swimming pool and free breakfast, it's excellent value at $15 a night.

The centre: Boa Vista and Santo Antônio

Most central hotels are concentrated around Rua do Hospício, near the bridges linking Santo Antônio with the neighbouring island of Boa Vista.

Hotel America, Praça Maciel Pinheiro 48, Boa Vista (☎221-1300). A 2-star hotel that's not as expensive as it looks. ③.

Brasil Hotel, Rua do Hospício 697, Boa Vista (☎222-3534). A large and rather noisy budget hotel. ①.

Hotel Central, Av. Manoel Borba 209, Boa Vista (☎423-6411 or 423-6604). As its name suggests, this hotel is central and is located on what remains one of Recife's quieter and more elegant streets. Also does a superb breakfast. ③.

Interlaine Hotel, Rua do Hospício 186, Boa Vista (☎433-2941). Decent budget hotel run by an English speaker with a passion for Scotch whisky. ②.

Hotel Nassau, Rua Largo do Rosario 253, Santo Antônio (☎224-3977 or 224-3520 or 224-3517). A comfortable hotel in a good location. ③.

Hotel do Parque, Rua do Hospício 51, Boa Vista (☎222-5427). A little grimy, but redeemed by high ceilings and a broad curving staircase that survives from better days. ①.

Hotel Quatro de Outubro, Rua Floriano Peixoto 141, Santo Antônio (☎424-4477). Close to Recife's main metrô station. ③.

Hotel São Domingos, Praça Maciel Pinheiro 66, Boa Vista (☎231-1388 or 231-1404). Clean and modern 2-star hotel. ③.

Boa Viagem

In **Boa Viagem** finding a hotel is the least of your problems: it sometimes seems as if they outnumber apartment buildings. The difficulty is finding a reasonably cheap one, as the majority cater for international tourists and rich Brazilians. Even so, you should be able to find somewhere for between $30 and $40 a night, certainly if you're prepared to stay a little way back from the seafront.

Hotel 54, Rua Prof. José Brandão 54 (☎465-2396). A pleasant place to stay with all mod cons. ④.

Hotel 200 Milhas, Av. Boa Viagem 864 (☎326-5921). Incredible value given its seafront location. ②.

Pousada Aconchego, Rua Felix de Brito 382 (☎326-2989). This small and comfortable hotel has a swimming pool and good restaurant open 24 hours a day. ④.

Hotel Boa Viagem, Av. Boa Viagem 5000 (☎341-4144). The least expensive of all the 4-star seafront hotels. ⑥.

Casa Grande e Senzala, Av. Cons. Aguiar 5000 (☎462-2974). The exterior is extremely attractive which makes the rooms themselves slightly disappointing for the price. ⑤.

Hotel Pousada da Julieta, Rua Prof. José Brandão 135 (☎326-7860). Inexpensive for its location. ③.

Park Othon Hotel, Rua dos Navegantes 9 (☎465-4666). A large and anonymous high-rise, but just a stone's throw from the beach. ⑥.

Hotel Portal do Sol, Av. Cons. Aguiar 3217 (☎326-9740). Situated just 2 blocks away from the beach and on Recife's principal bus routes. ③.

Recife Monte Hotel, Rua dos Navegantes 363 (☎465-7422). A glorified apartment building with all mod cons and the claim to fame that Chico Buarque and Charles Aznavour once stayed here. ⑦.

Recife Palace Lucsim Hotel, Av. Boa Viagem 4070 (☎465-6688). Superb beach views and all comforts – the cheapest of the 5-star hotels by a long way. ⑦.

Vila Rica Ideale Hotel, Av. Boa Viagem 4308 (☎465-8111). A good deal in this price range with every 4-star luxury. ⑤.

The City

Modern Recife sprawls onto the mainland, but the heart of the city is three small **islands**, Santo Antônio, Boa Vista and Recife proper, connected with each other and the mainland by more than two dozen bridges over the rivers Beberibe and Capibaribe. This profusion of waterways has led to the inevitable description of Recife as the "Venice of Brazil" – a totally ludicrous idea.

Recife island is where the docks are and therefore marks the point where the city began. Until only a few years ago it was a dangerous, run-down area inhabited mainly by drunks and prostitutes, but the investment of millions of dollars by the local authorities and private business have brought about an extraordinary transformation in both the look and feel of the area. The brightly painted colonial buildings make the small, easily negotiable island a pleasant place to wander during the day even though there aren't many specific things to do. And the island now has the best nightlife anywhere in the city centre, its streets jammed with revellers right through the early hours.

Avenida Dantas Barreto splits the island of **Santo Antônio**, home to the central business district and many surviving colonial churches. Just over the river is **Boa Vista**, linked to Santo Antônio by a series of small bridges; the brightly painted criss-cross girders of the **Ponte de Boa Vista** are a convenient central landmark. Santo Antônio and Boa Vista are the dirtiest areas of Recife, and although they bustle with activity during the day they empty at night, when the enormous, largely deserted streets are a little spooky and forbidding. However, they do have the advantage of being cheap: all the most economical hotels are situated here, and you can always cross over onto Recife Island for some nightlife. Residential suburbs stretch to the north, but the bulk of the middle-class population is concentrated to the south, in a long ribbon development along the beach at **Boa Viagem**.

There's no excuse for being bored in Recife. There are literally dozens of **colonial churches** in the city, at least one of which it would be criminal to miss; one excellent and several lesser **museums**; and some lovely public buildings. The churches tend not to have regular opening hours, but if the main door is shut you can often get in by knocking on a side door – if there's anyone inside they'll be only too happy to let you in. Even for the less determined sightseer, there are parks, **beaches** and a number of places where the most interesting thing to do is simply to drift about, absorbing the feel of the city and watching people get on with their lives – something that's particularly true of the city's **markets**.

Avenida Dantas Barreto and São Francisco

The broad **Avenida Dantas Barreto** forms the spine of the central island of Santo Antônio, and is the part of the city where there is most to see and do. In southern Brazil, avenues like this are lined with skyscrapers, but although some have sprouted in Recife's financial district, generally the centre is on a human scale, with crowded, narrow lanes lined with stalls and shops opening out directly onto the streets. Dantas Barreto, the main thoroughfare, ends in the fine **Praça da República**, lined with majestic palms and surrounded by Recife's grandest public buildings – the governor's palace (not open to visitors) and an ornate theatre. One of the charms of the city, though, is the unpredictability of the streets, and even off this main boulevard you'll stumble upon old churches sandwiched between modern buildings, the cool hush inside a refuge from the noise and bustle beyond.

Perhaps the most enticing of the central buildings is the seventeenth-century Franciscan complex known as the **Santo Antônio do Convento de São Francisco**, on Rua do Imperador – a combination of church, convent and museum. Outside, you'll be besieged by crowds of beggars displaying sores and stumps, but negotiate your way through to the entrance of the museum (Mon–Fri 8–11.30am & 2–5pm, Sat 2–5pm), pay the nominal fee, and you'll find yourself in a cool and quiet haven. Built around a beautiful small cloister, the museum contains some delicately painted statues of saints and other artwork rescued from demolished or crumbling local churches. But the real highlight here is the **Capela Dourada** (Golden Chapel), which has a lot in common with the churches in the old gold towns of Minas Gerais. Like them, it's a rather vulgar demonstration of colonial prosperity, from a time when conspicuous consumption often took the form of building grotesque churches. Certainly, this chapel is a classic example of nouveau riche Rococo: finished in 1697, it's the usual wall-to-ceiling-to-wall ornamentation, except that everything is covered with gold-leaf. If you look closely at the carving under the gilt you'll see that the level of workmanship is actually quite crude, but the overall effect of so much gold is undeniably impressive. What really gilded the chapel, of course, was sugar cane: the sugar trade was at its peak when it was built, and the sugar elite were building monuments to their wealth all over the city.

São Pedro and the Mercado de São José

The church of **São Pedro** (Mon–Fri 8–11am & 2–4pm, Sat 8–10am) is situated on the Pátio de São Pedro, just off the Avenida Dantas Barreto. The impressive facade is dominated by a statue of St Peter that looks old but was in fact donated to the church in 1980 by a master sculptor from the ceramics centre of Tracunhaém in the interior. Inside the church there's some exquisite wood carving and a *trompe l'oeil* ceiling, and on another corner of the Pátio is the **Museu de Arte Popular de Recife** (Mon–Fri 9am–7pm) which has some interesting exhibits, including pottery and wooden sculpture. If you've missed the church's opening hours, content yourself with the exterior views, best seen with a cold beer in hand from one of the several bars which set up tables in the square outside. The whole of the Pátio has in fact been beautifully restored, which lends this part of the city a charm of its own.

Recife is probably the best big Brazilian city to find **artesanato** – popular art in all its varieties – and the area around São Pedro is the best place to look for it. If you shop around, even tight budgets can stretch to some wonderful bargains. There are stalls all over the city, but they coagulate into a bustling complex of winding streets, lined with beautiful but dilapidated early nineteenth-century tenements, which begins on the Pátio de São Pedro. The streets are choked with people and goods, all of which converge on the market proper, the **Mercado de São José**, an excellent place for *artesanato*.

If you simply can't face the crowds, there's a very good **craft shop**, Penha, on the corner of the Pátio de São Pedro. It's the main city outlet for some of Recife's excellent woodcut artists. In the same shop you'll also find extremely inexpensive prints on both cloth and paper, known as **cordel**. The usual themes are stock Northeastern stories about cowboys, devils, saints and bandits, although there are also *cordel* based on political events, and educational ballads about disease and hygiene, even poems about how AIDS is transmitted and the need to use condoms. Even if you don't understand a word of Portuguese, the printed covers are often worth having in their own right, and they're extremely cheap, around $1 each. Outside the shop, you can dig out *cordel* around the *mercado* or in Praça de Sebo, next to the *mercado* site, where the secondhand booksellers have stalls. You'll also find books in English here, though hardly any worth buying.

From Largo do Rosário to the Museu da Cidade

Another retreat from the crowds nearby is the **Igreja N.S. do Rosário dos Homens Pretos** (Mon–Fri 8am–noon & 2–7pm, Sat 8am–noon, Sun 8–10am), on Rua Estreita do Rosário. It's an interesting example of a colonial church which catered mainly for slaves, and still has a high proportion of black worshippers. Determined culture vultures could also make the hop from here to Recife's most central museum, the **Museu da Cidade** (Mon–Fri 10am–6pm, Sat & Sun 1–5pm), in the star-shaped fort off the western end of Avenida Dantas Barreto; the best view of it is coming in by bus from Boa Viagem. Built in 1630 by the Dutch, the fort was the last place they surrendered when they were expelled in 1654. The building is actually far more interesting than the museum itself, which is dedicated entirely to the history of the city, with old engravings and photographs.

The Estação Central and Casa da Cultura

Right opposite the **Estação Central**, the forbidding **Casa da Cultura de Pernambuco** (Mon–Sat 9am–7pm, Sun 2–5pm; ☎224-2850) was once the city's prison and is now an essential stop for visitors. It's cunningly designed, with three wings radiating out from a central point, so that a single warder could keep an eye on all nine corridors. The whole complex has been turned into an arts and crafts centre, the cells converted into little boutiques. The quality of the goods on offer here is good, but the prices are a lot higher than elsewhere in the city, so go to look rather than buy. The other reason for visiting is to get information on cultural events: it's the best place to find out what's on, producing a monthly *Agenda Cultural* with listings of plays, films and other entertainments, and things like dancing displays are often laid on, which are free and not at all bad.

Over in the Estação Central itself, the **Museu do Trem** (Tues–Fri 9am–noon & 2–5pm, Sat 9am–noon, Sun 2–5pm) is worth a look, too, tracing the history of the railways that played a vital role in opening up the interior of the Northeast. British visitors can wax nostalgic over the exploits of the Great Western Railway of Brazil Limited, one of whose engines looms over the forecourt of the station, a relic of the days when British companies dominated the Brazilian economy.

The Museu do Homem do Nordeste and Museu do Estado

The **Museu do Homem do Nordeste** (Tues, Wed & Fri 11am–5pm, Thurs 8am–5pm, Sat & Sun 1–5pm) was assembled by anthropologists and is one of Brazil's great museums and the best introduction there is to the history and culture of the Northeast. It's quite a way out of central Recife. Take the "Dois Irmãos" bus from outside the post office or from Parque 13 de Maio, at the bottom of Rua do Hospício; there are two "Dois Irmãos" services, but the one marked "via Barbosa" is the one to get, a pleasant half-hour drive through leafy northern suburbs. The museum is not very easy to spot, on the left-hand side, so ask the driver or conductor where to get off.

The museum is split into several galleries, each devoted to one of the great themes of Northeastern economy and society: sugar, cattle, fishing, popular religion, festivals, ceramics and so on. The historical material is well displayed and interesting, but the museum's strongest point is its unrivalled collection of **popular art** – there are displays not just of handicrafts, but also of cigarette packets, tobacco pouches and, best of all, a superb collection of postwar bottles of *cachaça* (rum). A look at the designs on the labels, very Brazilian adaptations of Western 1950s and 1960s kitsch, leaves you with nothing but admiration for the imagination – and drinking capacity – of the people who put the display together.

The first floor of the museum is largely devoted to the rich regional tradition of clay sculpture and pottery that still flourishes in the *agreste* and *sertão*, especially around Caruaru. The work of **Mestre Vitalino**, a peasant farmer in the village of Alto do Moura, is a highlight. In the 1920s, he began to make small statues depicting scenes of rural life, of an astonishing vitality and power; the feeling and expression in the faces is quite remarkable, for example in the leering devil appearing to a terrified drunk clutching a bottle of rum. As Vitalino grew older, he began to incorporate the changes happening in the countryside around him into his work. There are statues of migrants, and urban themes appear with a series of portraits of professionals: the lawyer, doctors and dentists (very gruesome), the journalist and the secretary. These themes take over in the work of the next generation of artists, the sons of Vitalino and other pioneers, like the almost equally well-known **Zé Caboclo**, whose work fills the next few cases. In the third generation the style changed, and it's interesting that the best contemporary sculptors are women, notably the granddaughters of Zé Caboclo. The statues remain true to the established themes, but they are miniaturized, and the effect comes from the extreme delicacy of detail and painting, which contrasts with the cruder vigour of their male precursors. You'll see reproductions of many of the statues here on market stalls across Brazil, but Pernambuco is the place to get the real thing: certainly, examples of the work of many of the artists displayed in the museum can still be bought fairly cheaply, especially in Alto do Moura itself (see p.227).

The same bus, "Dois Irmãos via Barbosa", is also the one to take for the **Museu do Estado** (Tues–Fri 9am–5pm, Sat & Sun 2–5pm), a fine nineteenth-century mansion at Av. Rui Barbosa 960. It's on the right-hand side about twenty minutes after leaving the city centre, well before the Museu do Homem do Nordeste, but again difficult to spot, so you might need to ask. Here you'll find some fine engravings of Recife as it was in the early part of the last century, all of them English, and upstairs there are good paintings by Teles Júnior, which give you an idea of what tropical Turners might have looked like.

If the bus is crowded, or you can't make the driver understand where you want to get off, don't worry: after the museums it runs on to the **Horto Zoobotânico** (daily except Mon 8am–5pm), a combined zoo and botanical gardens. The gardens are the best part, with outdoor cafés and shady paths to walk along: the zoo, like most Brazilian zoos, is shockingly bad. The animals are confined in concrete boxes far too small for them, where they're constantly taunted by children and adults who ought to know better.

The Olaria de Brennand

If you have time, try and round off your sightseeing with the bizarre **Olaria de Brennand**, an industrial estate in the northern suburbs – there can't be anywhere more impressively offbeat in the whole of Brazil. One of three brothers who inherited a huge tile, ceramic and brickwork factory, Brennand became a very strange kind of tycoon. Although already rich beyond the dreams of avarice, he was driven to become an internationally famous ceramic artist. His factory estate, far from being an industrial wasteland, nestles in the middle of the only part of the old coastal forest still surviving in the metropolitan area. You can see the boundaries of the enormous estate very clearly: the urban sprawl stops dead at the feet of gallery forest, and the asphalt road suddenly becomes a dirt track winding through the jungle, lined with young imperial palms. It's a very beautiful piece of land – and it's sobering to think that without it, nothing at all would remain to show what the coast around Recife looked like before the arrival of the Europeans.

Past the rows of workers' cottages and a brickworks, you come to the *oficina*, an enormous personal gallery (Tues–Fri 9am–noon & 2–4pm; ☎271-2466) containing thousands of Brennand's sculptures, decorated tiles, paintings and drawings. The collection is housed in a shed the size of an aircraft hangar and very obsessive it is, too, although a lot of the work is good, with strong erotic overtones – to say that genitals are a recurring theme is putting it mildly. Most remarkable of all is the space to the right of the gallery, which Brennand has transformed into something which almost defies description: a large area with a fountain, covered in ceramic tiles, dotted with columns and sculpture, and bounded by a huge tiled wall topped with a series of Egyptian-looking statues. It looks like nothing so much as the set for a bizarre film epic, except that everything is real and solid.

The gallery is a long way from the centre, but is definitely worth the effort. A taxi from Santo Antônio will set you back around $12 and if you don't want to walk back you'll have to arrange for it to pick you up again, because no taxis pass anywhere near. Or take the bus marked "CDU–Várzea" from outside the post office to its terminus. Once there you can either take a taxi or walk – it's not far but you'll need to ask the way. Make sure you say "*a oficina de Brennand*" with the stress on the second syllable of *"Brennand"*, or nobody will know what you're talking about. The staff are always pleased to see foreign visitors.

Boa Viagem: the beach

Regular buses make it easy to get down to **Boa Viagem** and the beach, an enormous skyscraper-lined arc of sand that constitutes the longest stretch of urbanized seafront in Brazil. As you'd expect of a city of islands, Recife was once studded with beaches, but they were swallowed up by industrial development, leaving only Boa Viagem within the city's limits – though there are others a short distance away to the north and south. In the seventeenth century, Boa Viagem's name was *Ilha Cheiro Dinheiro*, or "Smell Money Island" – as if whoever named it knew it would become the most expensive piece of real estate in the Northeast.

Much of Boa Viagem is only three or four blocks deep, so it's easy to find your way around. Take your bearings from one of the three main roads: the seafront **Avenida**

Boa Viagem, with the posh hotels and a typically Brazilian promenade of palm trees and mosaic pavements; the broad Avenida Conselheiro Aguiar two blocks up; and then Avenida Engenheiro Domingos Ferreira.

The **beach** itself is longer and (claim the locals) better even than Copacabana, with warm natural rock pools to wallow in just offshore when the tide is out. It gets very crowded at the weekends, but weekdays are relatively relaxed. There's a constant flow of people selling everything the self-indulgent sunbather could possibly want: fresh coconut milk, iced beers, ready-mixed *batidas* (rum cocktails), pineapples, watermelon, shrimp, crabs, oysters, ice creams, straw hats and suntan lotion. The usual cautions apply about not taking valuables to the beach or leaving things unattended while you swim. There have also been a small number of shark attacks in the past few years, but they have almost always involved surfers far from shore.

Eating

Eating out is cheapest in Santo Antônio, more expensive in Recife island and Boa Viagem, with Olinda somewhere in between (for restaurant listings for Olinda see p.218). *Recifense* cuisine revolves around **fish** and **shellfish**. Try *carangueijo mole*, crabs cooked in a spicy sauce until shells and legs are soft and edible, which solves the problem of digging out the meat; small crabs called *guaiamum*; and *agulhas fritas*, fried needle fish. As befits a sugar city, a favourite local drink is *caldo de cana*, the juice pressed from sugar cane by hypnotic Victorian-looking machines.

Cheapest of all, but not to be scorned, are the **foodsellers** and *suco* **stalls** clogging the streets of **Santo Antônio**, with the usual selection of iced fruit juices, kebabs, cakes, sandwiches and *pastel*. There's a row of stalls licensed by the city authorities on the pedestrianized **Rua da Palma**, across the road from the main post office, much patronized by office workers attracted by some very reasonably priced food. The area also has many cheap *lanchonetes* and restaurants, although as their clientele is mainly workers they tend to close down in the early evening. There's also an inexpensive lunchtime-only **vegetarian** restaurant, *O Vegetal*, which has branches on Avenida Guararapes (no. 210, 2nd floor) and Avenida Dantas Barreto (no. 507). Santo Antônio is pretty dead at night, with the exception of the cobbled square around São Pedro church, the **Pátio de São Pedro**, where there are some good regional restaurants, with tables in the square and nice views of the church.

Recife island has plenty of restaurants, and you may want to eat there as a prelude to going on to a bar or a nightclub. But prices are relatively high and the emphasis is on sophistication rather than good old-fashioned hearty Brazilian cooking. *Buon Gustaio*, on Rua do Bom Jesus, does superb Italian food, and *Gambrinus*, at Rua Marquês de Olinda 263, is one of the places where you can get some local dishes. There's also a branch of the vegetarian restaurant, *O Vegetal*, on Rua do Brum (lunchtime only).

Down on **the beach** there are hundreds of places to eat, with one of the biggest concentrations in the **Pina** district, between the city centre and Boa Viagem. Catch a bus in the direction of Boa Viagem and get off on Avenida Herculano Bandeira, which is just where the bus veers round to run parallel to the sea. Almost the whole of the *avenida* is taken up with restaurants, most of them concentrating on seafood; especially recommended are *Marinho's* and *Pra Vocês*.

In **Boa Viagem** itself the best value is to be found at the seafood places on the promenade near the city centre end of the beach, and in the dining rooms of the cheaper hotels, all of which are open to non-residents. *Peixada do Lula*, at Av. Boa Viagem 244, is a reasonably priced seafood restaurant, while *Bargaço*, on the same street at no. 670, does a mixture of seafood and spicier Bahian dishes. If it's meat you're after, try *Edmilson da Carne de Sol*, at Rua José Trajano 82.

Nightlife

As elsewhere in Brazil, **nightlife** in Recife starts late, after 10pm. It's not every country in the world where half the population can dance better than the Temptations, and for sheer fun not many places can beat a good *dancetaria* on a weekend night. The variety of music and dances is enormous, and Recife has its own frenetic carnival music, the **frevo**, as well as **forró**, which you hear all over the Northeast. The dancing to *forró* can be really something, couples swivelling around the dancefloors with ballbearings for ankles. In the past couple of years, Recife island has become the most happening place in the city centre, but there's also plenty of action in Boa Viagem as well as in Olinda. There are other interesting nightspots in suburbs like Graças and Casa Forte, but they're not well served by public transport, so you'll have to take a taxi.

Bars

In **Santo Antônio**, virtually the only place with any zip to it is the **Pátio de São Pedro**, with its bars and restaurants. Occasionally something extra happens here, though: music and dance groups often appear at weekends, and it's one of the centres of Recife's *Carnaval*.

As night falls and the rest of the city centre shuts down, **Recife island** comes to life. There are all kinds of bars here, including quiet places where middle-aged professionals sit and discuss the events of the day. But the scene is mainly young and noisy: **Rua do Apolo** in particular has a string of bars with names like *Armazém da Cerveja* ("Beer Warehouse") and *Arsenal do Chopp* ("Beer Arsenal"), which gives you some idea of the spirit of the place. You should certainly sample the atmosphere here at least once just to get an idea of how seriously young *Recifenses* take enjoying themselves.

In **Boa Viagem**, bars open and close with bewildering speed, which makes it difficult to keep track of them. The liveliest area, though, is around Praça de Boa Viagem (quite a long way down the beach from the city centre, near the junction of Avenida Boa Viagem and Rua Bavão de Souza Leáo); the *Lapinha* bar and restaurant is a popular meeting place, as is *Caktos* bar, Av. Conselheiro Aguiar 2328.

Quieter and classier is the northern suburb of **Casa Forte**. A good place here is *Agua de Beber*, a gem of a bar at Praça de Casa Forte 661: a large house with an expensive restaurant upstairs, but a leafy courtyard in which you can sit and drink magical *caipirinhas*.

Dancing

If you're looking to lay down a few steps, you need to head for a **casa de forró**; the best time to go is around midnight on a Friday or Saturday. In all of them you can drink and eat fairly cheaply, too. They often have rules about only letting in couples, but these are very haphazardly enforced, especially for foreigners. There's a small entry fee, and you may be given a coupon as you go in for the waiters to mark down what you have – don't lose it or you'll have to pay a fine when you leave. Taxis back are rarely a problem, even in the small hours. Two good *casas de forró* are the *Belo Mar* on Avenida Bernardo Vieira de Melo, in Candeias *bairro*, and the *Casa de Festejo* on Praça do Derby in the *bairro* of Torre. Otherwise, look in local papers or ask EMPETUR for details; there are dozens of others. One place that mixes *forró* with samba is the lively *Cavalo Dourado* (Fri & Sat only), at Rua Carlos Gomes 390, in the *bairro* of Prado. More westernized, but still good, is *Over Point Dancing* at Rua das Graças 261 in Graças.

Recife island has a good share of **nightclubs**, though the emphasis is on Western dance music rather than *forró*, at places like *Planeta Maluco* on Rua do Apolo. But the best nights in the docks district are Thursdays between October and March, when a large area along Avenida Marquês de Olinda is given over to hours of live music and open-air dancing, called – appropriately enough – *Dançando na Rua* ("Dancing in the Street").

Carnaval in Recife

Carnaval in Recife is overshadowed by the one in Olinda, but the city affair is still worth sampling even if you decide, as many locals do, to spend most of *Carnaval* in Olinda. The best place for **Carnaval information** is the tourist office, which publishes a free broadsheet with timetables and route details of all the *Carnaval* groups. You can also get a timetable in a free supplement to the local paper, the *Diário de Pernambuco*, on the Saturday of *Carnaval*, but be warned that it's only a very approximate guide.

The *blocos*, or **Carnaval groups**, come in all shapes and sizes: the most famous is called *Galo da Madrugada*; the commonest are the *frevo* groups (trucks called *freviocas*, with an electric *frevo* band aboard, circulate around the centre, whipping up already frantic crowds); but most visually arresting are *caboclinhos*, who wear Brazilian ideas of Indian costume – feathers, animal-tooth necklaces – and carry bows and arrows, which they use to beat out the rhythm as they dance. It's also worth trying to see a *maracatu* group, unique to Pernambuco: they're mainly black, and wear bright costumes, the music an interesting (and danceable) hybrid of African percussion and Latin brass.

In Recife the **main events** are concentrated in Santo Antônio and Boa Vista. There are also things going on in Boa Viagem, in the area around the *Recife Palace Lucsim Hotel* on Avenida Boa Viagem, but it's too middle class for its own good and is far inferior to what's on offer elsewhere. *Carnaval* in Recife officially begins with a trumpet fanfare welcoming *Rei Momo*, the carnival king and queen, on Avenida Guararapes at midnight on Friday, the cue for wild celebrations. At night, activities centre around the grandstands on Avenida Dantas Barreto, where the *blocos* parade under the critical eyes of the judges. The other central area to head for is the Pátio de São Pedro. During the day the *blocos* follow a route of sorts: beginning in the Praça Manuel Pinheiro, and then via Rua do Hospício, Avenida Conde de Boa Vista, Avenida Guararapes, Praça da República and Avenida Dantas Barreto to Pátio de São Pedro. Good places to hang around are near churches, especially Rosário dos Pretos, on Largo do Rosário, a special target for *maracatu* groups. The balconies of the *Hotel do Parque* are a good perch, too, if you can manage to get up there. The day is the best time to see the *blocos* – when the crowds are smaller and there are far more children around. At night it's far more intense and the usual safety warnings apply.

Listings

Airlines Air France, Rua Sete de Setembro 42, Boa Vista (☎231-7735); Air Portugal (TAP), Av. Guararapes 111 (☎224-2700); Transbrasil, Av. Conde de Boa Vista 1546, Boa Vista (☎423-1366); Varig, Av. Guararapes 120 (☎424-2155); VASP, Av. Manoel Barba 488, Boa Vista (☎421-3611).

Banks and exchange Banco do Brasil has branches at the airport (daily 10am–9pm), at Av. Dantas Barreto 541, at Av. Rio Branco 240, 4th floor, and on Rua Sete de Setembro in Boa Vista, all charging $20 commission a time. You're much better off going to a *casa de câmbio* or a travel agency: the Mônaco agency at Praça Joaquim Nabuco 159 in Santo Antônio will change dollars or cheques free of charge. You'll also get reasonable rates in the seafront hotels in Boa Viagem. Exchange rates tend to drop around *Carnaval* time, with the influx of dollars from foreign tourists, so, if you can, delay changing large amounts until afterwards. Don't at any time change money with people who approach you on the street.

Bookstores New books at Livro 7, Rua Sete de Setembro 329, in the city centre, but few in English. Secondhand books (some in English) on corner of Av. Dantas Barreto and Rua Marquês do Recife.

Car rental Hertz at the airport (☎800-8900) and at Av. Conselheiro Aguiar 4214, Boa Viagem (☎325-2907); Avis at the airport (☎800-8787) and next to the airport, at Av. Mascarenhas de Morais 5174 (☎326-5730).

Cinemas Recife's cinema complex is at Shopping Centre Recife, Rua Bruno Veloso, Boa Viagem.

Consulates Denmark, Av. Marquês de Olinda 85, Recife island (☎224-0311); France, Av. Cons. Aguiar 233, 6th floor, Boa Viagem (☎465-3290); Germany, Av. Dantas Barreto 191, 4th floor (☎424-3488); Spain,

Rua Sirinháem 105, 2nd floor (☎326-1006); Sweden, Av. Conde de Boa Vista 1450, Boa Vista (☎231-2581); UK, Av. Eng. Domingos Ferreira 4150, Boa Viagem (Mon–Fri 8–11.30am, Tues & Thurs also 2–4.30pm; ☎325-0247); USA, Rua Gonçalves Maia 163, Boa Vista (Mon–Fri 8am–5pm; ☎421-2441).

Hospital Albert Sabin, Rua Senador José Henrique 141, Ilha do Leite (☎421-5411).

Post office The main post office is the *Correio* building on Avenida Guararapes in Santo Antônio (Mon–Fri 8.30am–5.30pm). There is also a post office on Av. Marquês de Olinda, on Recife island.

Records Disco 7, Rua Sete de Setembro, in a small alley next to the Livro 7 bookstore (see above); small, but the best record shop for Brazilian music in the Northeast (☎222-5932).

Telephones Inter-urban and international telephone offices are located at Rua Diário de Pernambuco 38 and Rua do Hospício 148 (daily 6am–11pm). Also at Rua Bruno Velossa 200, Boa Viagem.

Olinda

OLINDA is, quite simply, one of the largest and most beautiful complexes of **colonial architecture** in Brazil: a maze of cobbled streets, hills crowned with brilliant white churches, pastel-coloured houses, Baroque fountains and graceful squares. Founded in 1535, the old city is spread across several small hills looking back towards Recife, but it belongs to a different world. In many ways Olinda is the Greenwich Village of Recife;

The **telephone code** for Recife and Olinda is ☎081.

it's here that many of the larger city's artists, musicians and liberal professionals live, and it's also the centre of Recife's gay scene. Olinda is most renowned, though, for its **Carnaval**, famous throughout Brazil, which attracts visitors from all over the country, as well as sizeable contingents from Europe.

A city in its own right, Olinda is far larger than it first appears. The old colonial centre is built on the hills, slightly back from the sea, but arching along the seafront and spreading inland behind the old town is a modern Brazilian city of over 300,000 people. Despite its size, Olinda has become effectively a neighbourhood of Recife: a high proportion of the population commutes into the city, which means that **transport links** are good, with buses leaving every few minutes.

Arrival, information and accommodation

From Recife, a number of **buses** run to Olinda, though it's often difficult to know where to catch them; the surest way is to get the "Casa Caiada" bus from the stop on Avenida Dantas Barreto. Buses follow the seafront road; get off in the Praça do Carmo, just by Olinda's main post office, from where it's a two-minute walk up into the old city. **Taxis** from the centre of Recife take around fifteen minutes and cost about $10.

A reasonable **town map** is included in the literature distributed by EMPETUR in Recife; or, in Olinda, pick one up from the **municipal tourist office** at Rua São Bento (Mon–Fri 7.30am–5.30pm; ☎429-1927), or by the central market, the Mercado da Ribeira, at Rua Bernardo Vieira de Melo 160 (mornings only). The office in Rua São Bento can help with information about accommodation during *Carnaval*. There's also an information post on Praça do Carmo, where the buses stop, but it's not particularly useful.

There are a huge number of teenagers offering themselves as **guides** to the city – you'll find yourself besieged as soon as you get off the bus. Some of these youngsters, with yellow T-shirts with the words *Guia Mirim* written on the back, are actually paid by the city council to show you around. They do their job pretty well, though hardly any speak English. If you do choose to engage one of them, bear in mind that they are not drawing huge salaries for their work and will be hoping for a **tip**. All forms of identification other than the yellow T-shirts are out-of-date or false, though you can of course hire anyone as a guide if you don't mind paying. Although hassle is a bit worse in Olinda than in most Brazilian cities, crime is not: doubtless there are a few robberies, especially during *Carnaval*, and all the usual precautions apply, but there's a calm, almost sleepy atmosphere about the place, and wandering around at night feels pretty safe. Finally, note that the beach is awful – polluted and smelly – so you'll need to head out of town if you want to sunbathe or swim.

Accommodation

There are dozens of **hotels** of all price ranges in Olinda. It's probably cheapest to stay in the more modern part of the city, further north down the seafront road from Recife, but you'll be seriously missing out on the old city's atmosphere if you do, and it's worth shopping around for cheaper options in the historic area. Prices vary enormously throughout the year – we've given high-season prices below, but bear in mind that if you go between March and June or between August and November, it will be cheaper. During *Carnaval* it's virtually impossible to get a room unless you've booked months in advance.

If you want to stay for a while and **rent a room**, look out for the signs up outside people's houses saying "*Aluga-se*". There's a **campsite**, *Camping Olinda*, just inside the old city at Rua do Bom Sucesso 262, Amparo (☎429-1365), but do watch your valuables.

Albergue de Olinda, Rua do Sol 233, Carmo (☎429-1592). This excellent you█
night and is just by the seafront.

Costeiro Olinda Hotel, Av. Ministro Marcos Freire 681, Bairro Novo (☎429-487█
hotel in the modern part of the city. ⑥.

Pousada Flor de Manhã, Rua São Francisco 162, Carmo (☎429-2941). One of Olinda's
medium-range options; also runs excursions to places in the surrounding area. ③.

Okakoaras Bungalow Hotel, Av. Claudio J. Gueiros 10927, Praia de Maria Farinha (☎436-1754).
A half-hour bus ride from Olinda, set on a palm-lined beach with a swimming pool and a peaceful
atmosphere. ③.

Pousada d'Olinda, Praça João Alfredo 178 (☎439-1163). This centrally located *pousada* has everything from inexpensive bungalow-style rooms to a penthouse suite. ③–④.

Pousada dos Quatro Cantos, Rua Prudente de Morais 441 (☎429-0220). A beautiful mansion with
idyllic courtyard right in the heart of the old city. ④.

Hotel Pousada São Francisco, Rua do Sol 127, Carmo (☎429-2109). Located on the seafront, with
a swimming pool and all mod cons. ⑤.

Pousada Saúde, Rua Sete de Setembro 8. Definitely a budget option, but probably the best one in
the old city, run by a friendly, noisy family. ②.

The Town

Olinda's hills are steep, and you'll be best rewarded by taking a leisurely stroll around
the town. A good spot to have a drink and plan your attack is the **Alto da Sé**, the highest square in the town, not least because of the stunning view of Recife's skyscrapers
shimmering in the distance, framed in the foreground by the church towers, gardens
and palm trees of Olinda. There's always an arts and crafts **market** going on here during the day, peaking in the late afternoon; a lot of the things on offer are pretty good,
but the large numbers of tourists have driven prices up, and there's nothing here you
can't get cheaper in Recife or the interior.

The **churches** you see are not quite as old as they look. The Dutch burnt them all
down, except one, in 1630, built none of their own, and left the Portuguese to restore
them during the following centuries. There are eighteen churches dating from the seventeenth and eighteenth centuries left today, seemingly tucked around every corner
and up every street. Very few of them have set opening times, but they're usually open
during weekdays, and even when they're closed you can try knocking on the door and
asking for the *vigia*, the watchman.

If you have time to see only one church it should be the **Convento Franciscano**
(Mon–Fri 8–11.30am & 2.30–5pm, Sat 8am–5.30pm), tucked away on Rua São
Francisco. Built in 1585, the complex of convent, chapel and church has been stunningly restored to its former glory; particular highlights are the tiled cloister depicting
the lives of Jesus and St Francis of Asissi, and the beautiful wood-carvings in the sacristy. Among other churches, the **Igreja da Misericórdia**, built right at the top of an
exhaustingly steep hill, has a fine altar, while the **Mosteiro de São Bento** (Mon–Fri
8am–noon & 2–6pm, Sat 8am–noon, Sun 10am–5pm) looks wonderful from the outside
with palm trees swaying in the courtyard, though the interior is less striking.

There's also a good sampling of religious art on display in the **Museu de Arte Sacra
de Pernambuco** (Mon–Fri 8am–1pm), in the seventeenth-century bishop's palace by
the Alto da Sé. The **Museu Regional** (Tues–Fri 9am–5pm, Sat & Sun 2–5pm), at Rua
do Amparo 128, is well laid out, too, although the emphasis is too much on artefacts and
too little on history.

There's more contemporary interest in the colourful **graffiti** in which the old city is
swathed. The local council commissions artists to adorn certain streets and walls,
which has the twin advantage of keeping local talent in work and ensuring Olinda has
the highest-quality graffiti in Brazil. Some are political, urging people to vote for this or

bstract, illustrated poems about Olinda being especial-
, artistic and blend in uncannily well with the colonial
laces to see them is along the municipal cemetery walls
it there are good graffiti all over the old city, especially
il.

is to be found in the **Museu de Arte Contemporânea**, on
market (Tues–Fri 9am–noon & 2–5pm, Sat & Sun 2–5pm):
ry building that was once used as a jail by the Inquisition:
selves are a bit disappointing. Much more interesting is the
(Tues–Fri 9am–5pm, Sat & Sun 2–5pm) at Rua do Amparo 59,
which house_____ nt collection of traditional puppets.

Eating, drinking and nightlife

Olinda's relaxed atmosphere draws many *Recifenses* at night. Tables and chairs are set on squares and pavements, and bars are tucked away in courtyards in spectacular tropical gardens. There is always plenty of music around and, at weekends, a lot of young Brazilians out for a good time – all in all, a good recipe for enjoying yourself.

Eating and drinking

The best place to go for crowds and serious eating and drinking is the **Alto da Sé**. The good, cheap **street food** here, cooked on charcoal fires, can't be recommended too highly; try *acarajé*, which you get from women sitting next to sizzling wok-like pots – beancurd cake, fried in palm oil, cut open and filled with green salad, dried shrimps and *vatapá*, a yellow paste made with shrimps, coconut milk and fresh coriander. It's absolutely delicious and very cheap. If you sit in the Alto da Sé for any length of time, you're bound to be approached by one of Olinda's many **repentistas**, who will try to improvise a song about you (see p.220 under "The Torneio dos Repentistas" for a fuller explanation). The results are sometimes wonderful, sometimes embarrassing, but he will expect a small payment, so if you don't want to shell out, make it clear from the start that you're not interested. However, the only really irritating thing about the Alto da Sé is later in the evening as every stallholder and car-owner tries to prove that he can play his stereo louder than the next. It wouldn't matter so much if they were all tuned to the same radio station, but they aren't, and the resulting din can be quite appalling.

Luckily there are lots of nearby **bars** which you can escape to. The *Cantinho da Sé*, just a few steps down the Ladeira da Sé, is almost always crowded and very lively indeed at night. Further down the same hill, on the corner of Rua do Bonfim, is *Blue's Bar*. It's slightly tucked away and accessible through what looks like a hole in a white wall, but well worth finding as it's a gem of a place. The music is the best in MPB, the service excellent, the atmosphere romantic and the food outstanding: try the stuffed baked potatoes. It's definitely a night-time place though: on most days it doesn't open till 9pm.

Olinda is also extremely well off for **restaurants**. If you want to eat for less than $5, try the *comida a kilo* places along the seafront and in the new part of town. However, for just a little bit more, you can eat far better in the old town. *Ponto 274*, in the garden of an old house at Rua São Bento 274, is moderately priced and does good *carne do sol*, rehydrated dried meat served with roasted manioc. Slightly more expensive – and air-conditioned – is *Mourisco*, at Praça Conselheiro João Alfredo 7, which specializes in seafood. Other good spots at the higher end of the price range are *L'Atelier*, Rua Bernardo Vieira de Melo 91, and *Oficina do Sabor*, Rua do Amparo 335.

Nightlife

Nightlife in Olinda can be very lively, especially at the end of the week. Places to check out, apart from the Alto da Sé, are the seafront restaurants and bars, many of which have *forró* groups on Friday and Saturday nights. If you get bored with *forró* – and the beat does get a bit monotonous after a while – try the *Clube Atlântico* on the Praça do Carmo, easily identifiable by its logo of a couple dancing on a crescent moon. Every Friday and Saturday night (starting at 11pm) it hosts the *Noites Olindenses*, dances to an eclectic variety of music, played very loudly by energetic groups or on record – *frevo*, samba, *forró*, *merengue*, and even non-Brazilian styles like salsa and tango. You pay an entrance fee of about $5, and both the music and the dancing can be quite superb. There are sometimes extras like magicians and *capoeira* displays going on between and even during acts.

Carnaval and other festivals in Olinda

Olinda's Carnaval is generally considered to be one of the three greatest in Brazil, along with Rio and Salvador. It overshadows the celebrations in neighbouring Recife, and attracts thousands of revellers from all over the Northeast. It's easy to see why Olinda developed into such a major *Carnaval*: the setting is matchless, and local traditions of art and music are very strong. Like the other two great Brazilian carnivals, Olinda has a style and feel all of its own: not quite as large and potentially intimidating as in either Rio or Salvador, the fact that much of it takes place in the winding streets and small squares of the old city makes it seem more manageable. The music, with the local beats of *frevo* and *maracatu* predominating, the costumes and the enormous **bonecos**, papier-mâché figures of folk heroes or savage caricatures of local and national personalities, make this *Carnaval* unique.

Carnaval in Olinda actually gets going the Sunday before the official start, when the *Virgens do Bairro Novo*, a traditional *bloco* several hundred strong, parades down the seafront road followed by crowds that regularly top 200,000. By now the old city is covered with decorations: ribbons, streamers and coloured lanterns are hung from every nook and cranny, banners are strung across streets and coloured lighting set up in all the squares. Olinda's *Carnaval* is not only famous for its *bonecos*, which are first paraded around on Friday night and then at intervals during the days, but also for the decorated umbrellas that aficionados use to dance the *frevo*. The tourist office has lists of the hundreds of groups, together with routes and approximate times, but there is something going on all the time in most places in the old city. The most famous *blocos*, with mass followings, are *Pitombeira* and *Elefantes*; also try catching the daytime performances of *travestis*, transvestite groups, which have the most imaginative costumes – ask the tourist office to mark them out on the list for you.

Carnaval practicalities

Inevitably, with so many visitors flocking into the city, **accommodation during Carnaval** can be a problem. It's easier to find a room in Recife, but, unless you dance the night away, transport back in the small hours can be difficult; buses start running at around 5am, and before then you have to rely on taxis. This is not always easy, as many taxi-drivers stop work to enjoy *Carnaval* themselves. Even if you do find one, you either have to pay an exorbitant flat rate or three or four times the metered fare. Also, beware **drunken taxi drivers** and try to avoid travelling by road in the small hours during *Carnaval* as there are far too many legless drivers for comfort, and dozens of people are killed on the road every year.

In Olinda itself you might as well forget about hotels, as they're booked up months in advance. Many locals, though, rent out all or part of their house for *Carnaval* week:

the municipal tourist office has a list of places and prices. Prices start at around $300 for the week, going up to as much as $2000 – get a group together by leaving a note at the tourist office. If all the places on the tourist office lists are full – more than likely if you arrive less than a week before *Carnaval* starts – or if you fancy your chances of getting a cheaper and better deal on your own, wander round the side streets looking for signs saying "*Aluga-se quartos*"; knock on the door and bargain away.

The Torneio dos Repentistas

There are plenty of other festivals of one kind or another besides *Carnaval* in Olinda; its location and cultural traditions make it a popular venue. Definitely worth catching if you happen to be around in late January is the **Torneio dos Repentistas**. A *repentista* is a Northeastern singer-poet who improvises strictly metered verses which are sung in a nasal voice accompanied only by a guitar. And they really do improvise, rather than repeat stock verses. Most *repentistas* make a living singing on street corners and in squares, or at markets, commenting wittily – and often obscenely – on the people going by or stopping to listen, or elaborating on themes shouted out by the audience. Even if you don't understand the lyrics, it's worth catching, especially if you can find a *cantoria*, a sing-off between two or more *repentistas*, who take alternate verses until a draw is agreed or until the audience acclaims a winner. The *Torneio dos Repentistas* in Olinda is one of the most famous events of its kind in the region, bringing in *repentistas* from all over the Northeast, who pair off and embark on singing duels while surrounded by audiences, who break into spontaneous applause at particularly good rhymes or well-turned stanzas. It's centred around the Praça da Preguiça, and lasts for three days.

North from Recife

North from Recife, the **BR-101 highway** runs a little way inland through low hills and sugar cane fields, a scenic enough route but one that offers little reason to stop off anywhere, except perhaps at the small pottery centre of **Goiana**. The **coast** north of Recife is, as you might expect, best explored along the smaller roads that branch off the highway. Nevertheless, it's as well to bear in mind that the Pernambuco coast is thickly populated by Brazilian standards. This isn't to say there aren't relatively peaceful spots, but what seems a deserted retreat during the week can fill up quickly at weekends, with *Recifenses* heading for the beaches, enlivening or destroying the rural atmosphere, depending on your point of view.

Along the BR-101: Goiana and Pitimbu

At **GOIANA**, 80km north of Recife on BR-101, parts of the town are still made up of rows of nineteenth-century terraced houses, built for workers in the local cotton mill, which has been long since bankrupted. Pottery has taken over as the main economic activity, and Goiana is one of the most important centres of the flourishing Pernambucan ceramics industry. The town centre is dotted with workshops, their wares spilling out onto the pavements, and there are some good bargains to be had. You can watch the potters at work in many places, like Zé do Carmo in Rua Padre Batalha. Opposite here, there's a good restaurant, the *Buraco da Giá* at no. 100, where the trained crab which offers you a drink is perhaps the real highlight of any visit to the town. Goiana is served by six buses a day from the Recife *Rodoviária*.

If you want to spend some time in the area it's better to get out of Goiana and head 30km over a country road to the coastal fishing village of **PITIMBU**, just over the border in

Paraíba state. There are four buses a day from Goiana, the last around 2pm; it's a crowded and bumpy ride but Pitimbu is worth it. It has friendly inhabitants and a good beach, 10km in length, although the stretch closest to town can be dirty, and while there's no hotel, camping on the beach is possible, or you can negotiate hammock space with local bar-owners. It's a quiet, sleepy place, ideal for a couple of days of doing nothing at all, with excellent fresh seafood available in several beachside bars. It's also a good place to see *jangadas* in action: the small fishing rafts with huge curving triangular sails, which look impossibly flimsy but are, in fact, well designed to ride waves and surf. They go out at dawn and return in mid-afternoon, quite a sight, as they rear and plunge through the surf.

Along the coast towards Itamaracá

From Olinda, **local buses** continue 11km along the coastal road to the beautiful palm-lined beaches of **Rio Doce**, **Janga** and **Pau Amarelo**. Until recently these were pretty much deserted, and although weekend homes are going up now, development, so far, is less obtrusive than in many places on the coast. Being close to major population centres, however, the water quality at Rio Doce and Janga is not always the best. The area gets busy at weekends, when in Janga especially there's music and dancing in the beachside bars at night. At Pau Amarelo you can still see one of several local star-shaped forts left behind by the Dutch in 1719, and if the original walls were their present height you can see why they lost.

A more popular and even more scenic route north is through the pleasantly run-down colonial villages of **Igarassu** and **Itapissuma** to the island of Itamaracá. Hourly **buses** to Igarassu, with easy connections to Itamaracá, leave from Avenida Martins de Barros, on Santo Antônio island in Recife, opposite the *Grande Hotel*. Another possibility is to go there **by boat**: every travel agency in Recife runs trips, stopping at beaches on the way, for around $35–40.

Igarassu

Turning off the highway past Olinda's ugly industrial suburb of Paulista, the road wends its way through a rich green landscape of rolling hills and dense palm forest. The first town on the route is **IGARASSU**, 25km from Olinda, an old colonial settlement built on a ridge rising out of a sea of palm trees: the name means "great canoe" in the language of the Tupi Indians, the cry that went up when they first saw the Portuguese galleons. The town was founded in 1535, when during a battle with the Indians the hard-pressed Portuguese commander vowed to build a church on the spot if victorious; and the **Igreja de São Cosme e Damião**, one of the oldest churches in Brazil, is still there on the ridge. Down the hill the **Convento de Santo Antônio** is almost as old, built in 1588 and recently restored. Both are simpler and more austere than any of the churches in Recife or Olinda. There's a small museum in an old house near the convent with a dusty collection of nineteenth-century relics from sugar plantations.

Most of the houses in Igarassu are the rows of tied cottages characteristic of the old *engenhos*, or sugar estates. You can get a good idea of what a traditional *engenho* was like at the **Engenho Monjope**, an old plantation that has been tastefully converted into a **campsite** (☎081/543-0528). The *engenho* dates from 1750; there's a decaying mansion, a chapel, water mill, cane presses and a *senzala*, the blockhouse where slaves lived. Minibuses back to Recife from Igarassu drop you at the turn-off (ask for "*o camping*"), and it's an easy ten-minute walk from there. The campsite is separate from the buildings, and you can ask at the entrance to look around even if you don't want to stay. Another accommodation option is the *Pousada Porto Canoas*, Estr. do Ramalho 13km (☎081/436-2220; ④), which has **chalets** to rent and a restaurant.

Itapissuma

Eight kilometres further is **ITAPISSUMA**, where a causeway leads from the mainland to Itamaracá island. Local legend says Itamaracá was once the site of the Garden of Eden, so it's a little ironic that the first building you see is an enormous open prison: all the fields are cultivated by prisoners, easily recognizable in blue and grey uniforms with ID cards pinned to their chests. They own and run a group of cafés and shops on the road just past the prison, selling handmade jewellery and bone carvings. Some old lags still find it difficult to break old habits, overcharging and shortchanging shamelessly. These shops are built near another *engenho*, the **Engenho São João**, much better preserved than Monjope, with most of the original machinery used for pressing cane, boiling the syrup and refining sugar still intact.

Itamaracá

The short drive from Itapissuma across the causeway to Itamaracá town promises much, passing through thousands of palm trees lapped by fields of sugar cane – the rich but sickly smell just before the harvest in March is enough to make you feel distinctly queasy. So it's a shame to have to say that the town of **ITAMARACÁ** is something of a disappointment. It's very crowded and increasingly scarred by the hundreds of weekend homes springing up in ugly rashes along the beaches – alongside the humble wattle huts roofed with palm leaves where the original islanders have managed to hold on. One of the first parts of Brazil to be settled by the Portuguese, Itamaracá was so prosperous as a sugar plantation that it was also the first part of Pernambuco to be occupied by the Dutch, who built a fort here.

Nowadays Itamaracá has a reputation as an idyllic rural retreat, away from the pressures of life in Recife. This might have been true fifteen years ago, but it's stretching things a little now. Nonetheless, there are a couple of places of interest. A turn-off just before the town (you'll probably end up walking as local buses exist but are very infrequent) leads 5km through tacky villas before rewarding you with the **Forte Oranje**, another star-shaped Dutch fort built in 1631 by Maurice of Nassau to protect the newly occupied sugar estates. There's a vicious enfilade at the front gate, where attackers were filtered through a zigzag corridor and exposed to musket fire from slits on all sides, and there are a few old cannons lying around on the ramparts with the makers' crests still visible. The souvenir shop inside is the most overpriced in Pernambuco, but the beachside **bars** opposite are really good value, with excellent food – highlight is the *casquinho de carangueijo*, crabmeat fried with garlic and onions, served in the shell and covered with roasted manioc flour. A couple of iced beers here, looking out across the bay, should be enough to make you feel better disposed towards the island, especially if you catch somebody selling the delicious local oysters out of a bucket. You buy them by the half dozen, for around $1: the seller flicks them open with a knife and supplies a lime to squeeze over them.

Otherwise, it's back to the town itself, which does have a small colonial section, the old port area called **Vila Velha**, where there's an ageing but otherwise unremarkable church, the Igreja do Matriz. There are the usual beachside bars and restaurants, and a couple of **hotels**: *Orange Praia*, Estrada do Forte (☎081/341-4400; ⑥), with a wonderful beachside location, and *Do Maranjo*, Rua Padre Machado 85 (☎081/544-1157; ②). **Camping** on the beach is technically illegal but possible, although not advisable with valuables. The best of the **restaurants** is the *Sargaço*, Rua Santino de Barros 270 (☎081/544-1180), which has fine seafood and a *ciranda* on Friday and Saturday nights, a circular dance to lilting, rhythmic music from flutes, guitars and drums.

The beaches

The **beaches** are very good – wide and lined with palms – and they are a popular night venue for *Carnaval* celebrations, which attract hundreds of visitors. Unfortunately, however, stretches around the town and along as far as the Forte Oranje have been blighted by unregulated building. There are better, deserted beaches round about, but none less than a couple of hours' walk along the shoreline in either direction.

There are *jangadas*, too, but they're a rather poignant symbol of what has happened to the town. A few years ago many families supported themselves by a combination of fishing and farming, and the *jangadas* were very much working fishing boats. A few *jangadeiros* still fish, but most of them now take weekenders and tourists out on trips; a couple of hours is usually around $7. *Jangada* trips are not advisable unless you're a reasonable swimmer, and even then you should be careful if the sea is at all rough; there's nothing to stop you being swept overboard, and no lifejackets are provided.

South from Recife

The coast south of Recife has the best **beaches** in the state and is all too quickly realizing its tourist potential – the sleepy fishing villages are unlikely to remain so for much longer. Almost all **buses** to cities south of Recife take the BR-101 highway, which runs inland through fairly dull scenery, made worse by heavy traffic: as this route eventually leads to the great cities of southern Brazil, lorries sometimes outnumber cars. The trick is to get a bus that goes along the much more scenic **coastal road**, the PE-60, or *via litoral*; they leave from either Avenida Dantas Barreto or the Recife *Rodoviária* for the string of towns down the coast from Cabo, through Ipojuca, Sirinhaém, Rio Formoso, to São José da Coroa Grande. Before São José, where the road starts to run alongside the beach, you may need to get another local bus to get to the beachside villages themselves. In theory, you could hop from village to village down the coast on local buses, but only with time to spare. Services are infrequent – early morning is the usual departure time – and you might have to sleep on a beach or find somewhere to sling a hammock, as not all the villages have places to stay. As you move south, bays and promontories disappear, and walking along the beaches to the next village is often quicker than waiting for a bus.

Gaibu and Santo Agostinho

The first stop out of Recife is the beach at **GAIBU**, some 20km south of Boa Viagem – catch a bus to Cabo from Avenida Dantas Barreto, and then another local one to Gaibu. Gaibu sports the familiar set-up – palm trees, bars and surf – and has a couple of cheap *pensões* and a **youth hostel**: a good base for village-hopping. It gets crowded at weekends, but there's a particularly beautiful stretch of coastline nearby, close enough to explore on foot. Just before Gaibu village, a turning in the dirt road heads off to the right, leading to the cape of **São Agostinho**, a pleasant walk uphill through palms and mango trees, past the odd peasant hut in the forest. Three kilometres up is a ruined Dutch chapel, so overgrown it's almost invisible, and a path to the left leads out onto a promontory where the forest suddenly disappears and leaves you with a stunning view of the idyllic, and usually deserted, beach of **Calhetas**. You can clamber down to the beach, a ring of sand in a bay fringed with palm forest, the distant oil refinery at Suape providing the only jarring note. This is a particularly good beach for surfing.

If you continue on from the ruined chapel, you'll come to the sleepy hamlet of **SANTO AGOSTINHO**, where the present tranquillity masks a violent past. During the Dutch occupation there was vicious guerrilla fighting here, and an infamous massacre took place when Dutch settlers were herded into a church which was then burnt down.

A small chapel still stands on the spot and there are the pulverized remains of a fort. On the cape itself are burnt-out shells of Dutch buildings from the same campaign, and there's also a plaque commemorating the Spanish conquistador, Yanez Piñon, blown south by storms on his way to the Caribbean in 1500. He put in here for shelter a couple of months before Cabral "discovered" Brazil, and sailed off without knowing where he was – thus ensuring Brazil would end up speaking Portuguese rather than Spanish.

Porto de Galinhas to Barra de Santo Antônio

A bus from Avenida Dantas Barreto (run by the Princesa company) will take you direct to another glorious beach, **PORTO DE GALINHAS**, 65km from Recife, and deservedly popular – it's in danger of becoming overdeveloped, but still quiet enough during the week. *Jangadas* will take you out to the small natural coral pools just off the coast and there is some excellent surfing here, too. Good fresh fish is to be had in the beachside cafés; fried needle fish, *agulhas fritas*, is a great snack with a cold beer as you wiggle your toes in the warm sand. There are two **campsites**, if you want to stay. Numerous *pousadas* and *chales* have sprung up as well as an increasing number of upmarket **hotels** on the seafront. Right on the main beach are the luxury *Village Porto de Galinhas* (☎081/552-1038; ⑥) and the smaller *Recanto*, Avenida Beira Mar (☎081/552-1251; ⑤), while the *Pousada dos Coqueiros* (☎081/552-1294; ②) is set on one of the finest beaches in the area, the Praia de Macaripe, 5km away. The *pousada* is basic but it's a good place to stay if you're here to surf.

The sleepiest fishing villages of all are the ones around **ILHA DE SANTO ALEIXO**, reachable by local bus from Sirinhaém, but even here weekend houses for city slickers are going up, and it may well be developed in the not too distant future. For the time being fishing still dominates, with *jangadas* drawn up on the beaches and men repairing nets. In **TAMANDARÉ** (served by direct bus from Recife *Rodoviária* run by the Cruzeiro company), as well as the usual stunning beach, there are the ruins of the fort of Santo Inácio, destroyed in 1646, and a small hotel, *Marinas Tamandaré,* Loteamento Anaisabela, Lote 15A (☎081/675-1388; ⑤). A little way south, in **SÃO JOSÉ DA COROA GRANDE**, where the *litoral* road finally hits the coast (also served by direct bus from Recife *Rodoviária*), there are bars, a huge beach and the overpriced *Hotel Francês*, Rua Antonia Valdemar Acioli Belo 279 (☎081/688-1169; ④).

Into Alagoas

Just 15km over the border into Alagoas state is the even dozier village of **MARAGOGI**, where you'll find the superb *Hotel Salinas*, Rodoviária AL101 km 124 (☎081/296-1122; ⑧), a luxury hotel set on Maragogi beach with every conceivable facility, and *Praia dos Sonhos*, Rodoviária AL101 km 124 (☎081/222-4598; ⑥), on Peroba beach. There are direct buses here from São José da Coroa Grande.

The beautiful, isolated village of **JAPARATINGA** lies 8km to the south, but there are no buses out here; if you're walking, there's a turn-off on the left of the main road, just past Maragogi (no signpost, but anyone can direct you). It's a long but enjoyable hike, passing usually deserted beaches, and if you start early enough and take it easy, going for a couple of swims along the way, you should arrive by lunchtime. Take something to drink, and be careful not to overdo it when the sun is at its height. In Japaratinga, you'll find the cheap *Hotel Solmar* (②) if you want to stay for a couple of days working on the tan.

South of Maragogi, the road loops inland again, passing through low hills dotted with *engenhos* and small market towns, before re-emerging on the coast at the large fishing village of **BARRA DE SANTO ANTÔNIO**. There's a local bus from Maragogi and the village is also a stop for some of the Recife–Maceió interstate buses. Barra is quiet during the week but crowded at the weekend with people making the day trip from Maceió, only 40km down the road. It has a fine beach on a narrow neck of land jutting out from the coast a short canoe-ride away, and good, fresh seafood is served in the cluster of small beachside **hotels**. From here, it's 32km along a series of beaches to Maceió, the capital of Alagoas.

Inland from Recife

In contrast to the gentle scenery of the coastal routes out of Recife, heading **inland** brings you abruptly into a completely different landscape, spectacular and forbidding. The people, too, look and speak differently; the typical *sertanejo* is short and wiry, with the high cheekbones and thin nose of an Indian ancestor. They speak a heavily accented Portuguese, much ridiculed elsewhere, but really one of the loveliest Brazilian accents, irresistibly similar to a strong Welsh lilt.

Buses inland all leave from the Recife *Rodoviária*, and the best place to head for is the market town of **Caruaru**, 130km from Recife and the largest town in the *agreste*. The frequent buses there take two hours and are very comfortable; buy your ticket a day in advance. Seats on the right-hand side of the bus have the best view.

The route to Caruaru: Vitória, Gravatá and Bezerros

The BR-232 highway heads directly away from the sea into gentle hills covered with enormous fields of sugar cane; the size of the estates gives you some idea of the inequality of land distribution in the Northeast, and explains why this part of Pernambuco has been in the forefront of the struggle for agrarian reform in Brazil. It was here in the late 1950s that the Peasant Leagues started, a social movement pressing for land reform through direct action, one of the factors that frightened the military into launching their coup in 1964. Most of the cane is destined for the first town en route, **VITÓRIA DE SANTO ANTÃO**, where, on the left-hand side of the road, is the factory which produces the most widely drunk rum in Brazil, Pitu – you can't miss the thirty-metre-high water tank cunningly camouflaged as an enormous bottle of Pitu.

After Vitória you begin to climb in earnest into the **Serra da Neblina**, threading into the hills of the *agreste* proper. Gradually the air becomes cooler, the heat drier, and highland plants replace the palms and sugar cane of the coastal strip. On a clear day the views are stunning, with rows of hills stretching into the distance on both sides and the coastal plain shimmering in the background. The fertile hills facing the sea get a lot of rain, cotton taking over from sugar as you climb, but deeper inland the hills are brown and parched, and farming becomes more difficult. You begin to see cattle and strange-looking fields filled with neat rows of cactus. This is *palma*, and it's a foretaste of the harshness of *sertão* life: in times of drought, the cactus is chopped down and fed to cattle, thorns and all. It's a feed of last resource, but remarkably, the cactus contains enough water to keep cattle alive for a few more crucial months in the wait for rain.

Gravatá

The next town, 50km down the road, is **GRAVATÁ**, one of several *agreste* towns which has optimistically tagged itself "The Switzerland of Pernambuco" on the strength of its cool hill climate. There are lots of villas and a hotel built in Swiss chalet style, rather incongruous in a landscape that is parched brown as often as not. If you want to break your journey here, the best **hotels** are *Casa Grande*, BR-232 km 87 (☎081/533-0920; ⑥), the chalet-style place; *Portal de Gravatá*, BR-232 km 88 (☎081/533-0288; ⑤), a hotel that looks like a ranch; and *Grande Hotel da Serra*, BR-232 km 83 (081/533-0114; ③), one of the cheapest hotels in the area. After Gravatá, it soon becomes obvious that you are nearing a major market from the activities at the roadside. Boys and men every few hundred yards stand as far into the road as they dare, leaping aside at the last moment, flourishing their wares at passing motorists: chickens, piglets and the delicious fruit of the interior – pomegranates, *jaboticaba* (like a cross between a plum and a sweet grape), *mangaba*, a delicious red berry that stains the mouth black, and *umbu*, which looks like a gooseberry but doesn't taste like one.

Bezerros

BEZERROS, the last town before Caruaru, is the home of a famous artist and printer, **Jota Borges**, some of whose work you may have seen in the Casa da Cultura and Penha (see p.209) in Recife. He has a roadside workshop on the left as you leave town, painted brilliant white with "Ateliê Jota Borges" in large letters across the front. Inside, you can see the carved wooden plates he makes to manufacture the prints on paper and cloth; the smaller ones are for the covers of *cordel*, a large library of which takes up one corner of the workshop. Borges himself is often at the market in Caruaru or delivering in Recife, but a family member is usually on hand to show visitors around. The absurdly inexpensive prints are simple but powerful depictions of peasant life.

Caruaru

Home of the largest market in the Northeast, **CARUARU** is also ideally placed for excursions into the *sertão*. Saturday is the main market day, but Wednesday and Friday are busy, too.

People come from all over the Northeast for the **market**, which takes over the town, with stalls filling the squares and people clogging the streets. It's a slightly less traditional affair than it used to be, with Asian electronic goods playing an increasingly important part, but the atmosphere is still worth savouring. The market is roughly divided into sections: around the bus station are clothes; the centre itself is devoted to food; and on the other side of the river are arts and crafts, songbirds and the famous *troca-troca*, where things are swapped rather than bought. Wandering around the **food market** introduces you to some characteristic sights and smells of the interior: the blocks of hard white *sertão* cheese, delicious with fruit; piles of leaves, roots and barks used in popular medicine; brown blocks of *rapadura*, a sweet made from unrefined sugar with a rich and sickly smell; and rows of mules having their teeth examined by prospective buyers. Across the small bridge is the **songbird market**, illegal but flourishing nonetheless, with dozens of species in small handmade cages. And behind it is the most interesting part of all, the so-called **troca-troca**. Starting early on Saturday morning and finishing by noon, this patch of land is taken over by a crowd of people wandering around with whatever they want to swap: tapes and records, an old radio, used clothes, car parts – things which it would be difficult to sell for cash, which is why you don't see livestock or food being traded. It's fascinating to watch, but keep to the sidelines as locals don't appreciate wandering tourists getting in their way. It's also used by pickpockets unloading hot goods in a hurry, so if you don't want to see your own things being bartered, keep an eye on your bag.

The **mercado de artesanato** is across the road from the songbirds, on a specially constructed site. It is becoming as near to a tourist trap as the interior ever gets, and there is some dross, but there's also a large amount of interesting work at prices far lower than in Recife. Again, it's divided into sections – straw, leather, pottery and so forth – but most popular are the small clay statues for which this area is nationally famous, the *figurinhas de barro*. Caruaru is the main outlet for the renowned potters of Alto do Moura (see opposite), just up the road, and if you've seen the work of Mestre Vitalino in Recife you'll instantly recognize their vivid peasant style. The *figurinhas* are inexpensive, and come expertly wrapped in boxes.

Practicalities

As ever, the **bus station** is out of town, 2km away, but buses from Recife stop in the centre, and you can get off there. It's perfectly possible to see the market, make a trip out to Alto do Moura and get back to Recife in a day – which is what most people do. If you want to stay over, however, or intend to move on the next day further into the interior, there is no shortage of places to sleep. The best **hotels** include: *Hotel do Sol* at the crossroads between the BR-104 and BR-232 (☎081/721-3044; ⑤), a three-star hotel and Caruaru's most luxurious; the central *Hotel Centenário*, Rua Sete de Setembro 84 (☎081/722-4011; ④); and the excellent *Hotel Central*, Rua Vigário Freire 71 (☎081/721-5880; ③). Among **restaurants**, *Le Cottage* at Av. Agamemnon Magalhães 752, slightly north of the centre, serves a good varied cuisine, and *Mestre Vitalino*, Rua Leão Dourado 13 (☎081/721-0499), to the west of town, offers a wide range of local dishes.

Alto do Moura

To explore the tradition of *figurinhas* further, it's worth making the short journey to **ALTO DO MOURA**, 6km up the road from Caruaru: take a taxi or the marked bus (departures every 2hr) from Rua 13 de Maio, one of the roads leading out of the centre towards the *Rodoviária*. It's a dirt road to a small village that seems entirely unremarkable, except that every other house on the only street, **Rua Mestre Vitalino**, is a potter's workshop, with kilns like large beehives in the yards behind. The first house on the left was Mestre Vitalino's, and his widow and grandchildren still live in the simple hut next door. There's a plaque on the adobe wall and, inside, the hut has been kept as Vitalino left it, with his leather hat and jacket hanging on a nail. The only sign that Vitalino was somebody special are the framed photos of him being feted in Rio de Janeiro and introduced to the president. There's a visitors' book, and one of Vitalino's grandchildren is on hand to show you around. It's free, but do leave a donation: disgracefully, Vitalino's widow lives in penury next door without any kind of pension, a sad memorial to a man who brought fame and fortune to the town of his birth.

All the workshops are piled with pottery and *figurinhas* for sale, and are fascinating to browse around; each potter has a unique individual style. One of the most individual, and certainly the most eccentric, is **Gaudino**, on the corner opposite the solitary café. His inspiration comes to him in dreams, and much of his work consists of fantastic clay monsters, each with a poem, describing the dream that gave birth to it, stuffed into its mouth. Apart from his talents as a potter, Gaudino is a very skilled *repentista*: he can immediately improvise a stanza of welcome, rhyming your name to the last word of every line. Of the dozens of other workshops, the best are those of the children and grandchildren of Vitalino and his contemporaries: Manuel Eudócio at no. 151, who specializes in decorative pots; Luiz Antônio at no. 285; and Vitalino's son, Severino Pereira dos Santos, at no. 281. One more essential stopping point is the Casa de Arte Zé Caboclo at no. 63, one of the workshops of the large and extraordinarily talented family of **Zé Caboclo**, along with Vitalino the founder of the *figurinhas* tradition. A crowded cabinet holds a collection of his work that is more extensive even than that held by the Museu do Homem do Nordeste in Recife. His work is larger and cruder than Vitalino's, but has a vivid energy that many of the Alto do Moura potters rate more highly. Here you can also see his granddaughter Marliete's work, most of which is not for sale. She is the best of the younger generation: her delicate miniaturized figurines, superbly painted, show how the special skills of Alto do Moura are revitalized with each generation that passes, a tribute to the strength of popular culture in the interior.

Nova Jerusalém

In Easter week the market crowds are swollen by tourists and pilgrims heading for **NOVA JERUSALÉM**, in the heart of the *agreste*, 50km from Caruaru; the turn-off is on the right just after Caruaru, on the BR-104, marked "Campina Grande". After 24km another turn-off, to the left, the PE-145, leads to the small town of **Fazenda Nova**, just outside which is the site of Nova Jerusalém.

A granite replica of the old city of Jerusalem, it was built in the early 1970s by a local entrepreneur who cashed in on the deep religious feeling of the interior by mounting a Passion play based on that of Oberammergau. Over the years, this *Paixão do Cristo* has become a new tradition of the *agreste*, attracting thousands of spectators to watch five-hundred costumed actors, mostly local amateurs, recreate the Passion and Crucifixion. The "replica" of Jerusalem is in fact a third of the size of the original, and is basically a setting for the twelve stages on which the action takes place, each representing a Station of the Cross. There's an enjoyable sub-Cecil B. De Mille air of tackiness about the whole production, which is very free with the tomato ketchup in the whipping and crucifixion scenes. Next to the site is a sculpture park, where local artists have set up several impressively large granite statues of folk heroes done in the style of the interior, the largest versions you'll see of the *figurinhas de barro*.

Practicalities

The Passion is performed daily from the Tuesday before Easter to Easter Sunday inclusive, taking up most of the day. The most convenient way to see it is to go on one of the day **tours** which many travel agents in Recife – and other Northeastern cities – run there during Holy Week. It's also easy to get there under your own steam, as there are **buses** to Fazenda Nova from Caruaru and a **campsite** when you get there, as well as several simple *dormitórios*. Entry to the spectacle costs about $20.

Into the sertão

The **Pernambucan sertão** begins after Caruaru. There is no sudden transition; the hills simply get browner and rockier, dense thorny scrub takes over from the hill plants, and there are cacti every few yards, from tiny flowering stumps to massive tangled plants as large as trees. And, above all, it is hot, with parched winds that feel as if someone is training a hairdryer on your face. The Pernambucan *sertão* is one of the harshest in the Northeast, a scorched landscape under relentless sun for most of the year. This is cattle country, home of the *vaqueiro*, the Northeastern cowboy, and has been since the very beginning of Portuguese penetration inland in the seventeenth century: one of the oldest frontiers in the Americas.

Travelling in the sertão requires some preparation, as the interior is not geared to tourism. Hotels are fewer and dirtier; buses are less frequent, and you often have to rely on country services which leave very early in the morning and seem to stop every few hundred yards. A **hammock** is essential, as it's the coolest and most comfortable way to sleep, much better than the grimy beds in inland hotels, all of which have hammock hooks set into the walls as a standard fitting. The towns are much smaller than on the coast, and in most places there's little to do in the evening, as the population turns in early to be up for work at dawn. Far more people carry arms than on the coast, but in fact the *sertão* is one of the safest areas of Brazil for travellers – the guns are mainly used on animals, especially small birds, which are massacred on an enormous scale. Avoid tap **water**, by sticking to mineral water or soft drinks: dysentery is common, and although not dangerous these days it's extremely unpleasant.

But don't let these considerations put you off. People in the *sertão* are intrigued by gringos and are invariably very friendly. And while few *sertão* towns may have much to offer in terms of excitement or entertainment, the landscape in which they are set is spectacular. The Pernambucan *sertão* is hilly and the main highway which runs through it like a spinal column winds through scenery unlike any you'll have seen before – an apparently endless expanse of cactus and scrub so thick in places that cowboys have to wear leather armour to protect themselves. If you travel in the rainy season here – March to June, although rain can never be relied upon in the interior – you may be lucky enough to catch it bursting with green, punctuated by the whites, reds and purples of flowering trees and cacti. Massive electrical storms are common at this time of year, and at night the horizon can flicker with sheet lightning for hours at a stretch.

Towards Petrolina

After Caruaru the highway passes through a number of anonymous farming towns. **ARCOVERDE**, 130km to the west, has a market on Saturdays and a reasonable **hotel**, the *Grande Majestic*, Av. Cel. Antônio Japiassu 326 (☎081/821-1175; ②), which doesn't quite live up to its name but is a cheap and handy place to break the journey. You may need to, because the best *sertão* towns to make for are buried deep in the interior, some eight or ten hours by bus from Caruaru. One is the pilgrimage centre of Juazeiro do Norte, just over the border in Ceará state (see p.280). The others are the twin towns of Petrolina and Juazeiro, which have the enormous advantage of being built on the banks of the only river in the Northeast that never runs dry, the **Rio São Francisco**.

The last place that could reasonably be called a town is **SERRA TALHADA**, some 200km west of Arcoverde. Here, the *Pousada da Serra*, Rua Dr Ademar Xavier 1055, Alto da Conceição (☎081/831-1536; ②), is quite reasonable. From here on, the road passes through a succession of flyblown villages, all of which would look vaguely Mediterranean – with their whitewashed churches, café, dusty square and rows of tumbledown cottages – if it weren't for the startling landscape in which they are set. Eighty kilometres beyond Serra Talhada, a turning leads north to Juazeiro do Norte, while one Petrolina bus turns south to follow an alternative route parallel to the São Francisco valley. The others continue for another 110km, across one of the most desolate semi-arid desert landscapes in the Northeast, before reaching **OURICURI**, quite a pleasant place to break your journey with a couple of hotels; from here it's another 213km south along the BR-122 to Petrolina.

Petrolina

After the villages that have gone before, **PETROLINA** seems like a city. Certainly, by the standards of the *sertão*, it's a large, thriving and relatively prosperous town, thanks to the river trade to places downstream. On the **waterfront**, you can occasionally see river boats adorned with *carrancas*, carved wooden figureheads bolted onto the prow, brightly painted and with a grotesque monster's head, meant to frighten evil spirits lurking in wait for unwary mariners. Petrolina also has an interesting **Museu do Sertão** (Mon–Fri 9am–5pm, Sat 2–5pm), on Praça Santos Dumont on the road to the airstrip, about ten minutes' walk from the centre of town. Small but well put together, the museum documents *sertão* life and history through assorted relics and some fascinating photographs, including a couple of the bespectacled social bandit Lampião and his gang, popular heroes who roamed the *sertão* until they were shot in 1938. Lastly, Petrolina has a **market** on Friday and Saturday which brings people in from the *sertão* for miles around.

The **Rodoviária** is quite central and there are a couple of *dormitórios* close by. Better **places to stay** are the *Hotel Central*, on Praça Dom Bosco (②), and the

Petrolina Palace, Av. Cardoso de Sá 845 (☎081/862-1555; ⑤). Excellent regional **food** is served at *O Barranqueiro*, Rua Rio Beberibe 50 (☎081/861-5346), although it's not cheap, while *Chimarrão*, Av. Mons. Angelo Sampaio, Cohab 3, is the place for hungry carnivores. There are three **buses** daily to Petrolina from Recife, which can be picked up at Caruaru.

Juazeiro

Over the bridge, or across the river by boat, and into Bahia state lies Petrolina's poorer sister town, **JUAZEIRO**, not to be confused with Juazeiro do Norte. Many of its inhabitants had their homes flooded when dams created the enormous **Sobradinho lake** just upstream in the 1960s. Since then the area around Juazeiro has become something of a showcase for **irrigation schemes**, and all kinds of fruit – including unlikely products like grapes and asparagus – are grown here.You can ignore the hype about "California in the *sertão*", but a trip to one of the farms might be quite interesting. The town has several **hotels**, a good choice being the *Grande Hotel do Juazeiro*, Rua José Petitinga (☎075/811-7710; ⑤), not as grand as the name would suggest, but situated on the riverfront, and the cheap and clean *Rio* Sol, Rua Cel. João Evangelista 3 (☎075/811-4481; ②). There is an unusual attraction in the form of a nineteenth-century paddle steamer, the *Vaporzinho*, built in 1852 to ply the São Francisco river: it's been restored, turned into a **restaurant** and is now moored on the riverfront.

Juazeiro is the northern terminus for the **river services** of the Companhia de Navegação do São Francisco, which once ran frequent boats downriver as far south as Minas Gerais but is now in decline. It still runs one monthly boat to Pirapora in Minas Gerais, from where there are bus connections to Brasília and Belo Horizonte, but its departure has become increasingly irregular: times and dates are available from tourist information offices in Recife and Salvador. The journey takes three or four days. There are also smaller boats to towns both upstream and downstream leaving from the waterfront in Juazeiro; most of them are river traders and are quite happy to take paying passengers – although always check during negotiations when they return, as it may not be for a couple of days. It's remarkable how appealing the idea of even a short boat trip becomes after the heat and dust of the *sertão*, whose hills crowd right down to the Sobradinho lakeside. Tempting though it is, however, you should **avoid swimming** in still water, as schistosomiasis – also known as bilharzia – is endemic here.

From Juazeiro you can continue south by **bus** along the BR-407 to Feira de Santana (see p.261) and Salvador. Alternatively, if you're interested in the history of the *sertão*, you might want to make the five-hour journey southeast to Canudos (see p.263), from where there are daily buses to Salvador.

Fernando de Noronha

The beautiful archipelago of **FERNANDO DE NORONHA** lies about 350km off the Brazilian coast, and belongs to Pernambuco, even though it's actually nearer to Rio Grande do Norte. European explorers first came here in 1503, and after a struggle between various powers, the islands ended up under the control of the Portuguese. Lisbon considered the archipelago strategically important enough to build the **Forte dos Remédios**, of which only remains are left now.

In recent years the archipelago has become better known as a tourist destination, but most of it is now a **marine national park**, its watchword respect for the environment, in order to maintain the ecological wonders that have been preserved by the islands' isolation from the rest of Brazil. The **wildlife** is magnificent: twitchers will be enthralled by the variety of exotic birds, including several types of pelican, while the crystal-clear sea is full of multicoloured fish, turtles, sharks, whales, sponges and coral. The Aguas Claras company (☎081/619-1225) organizes **scuba-diving** trips, at a price, or will rent out diving equipment.

The main island shelters plenty of stunning **beaches**, notably Praia da Atalaia and Cacimba do Padre, and at Mirante dos Golfinhos you can watch dolphins leaping – tourists used to be able to swim with them, but this has been banned. It's easy enough to hitch-hike your way around the island, but you can also **rent cars and buggies** from several operators, including Eduardo Galvao de Brito (☎081/619-1335) at the *Esmeralda do Atlantico Hotel.*

Practicalities

You can **fly** to Fernando de Noronha from either Recife or Natal with Nordeste airlines; tickets are available from a number of travel agents in both cities. A return flight from Natal will set you back about $300, one from Recife slightly more, though there are more flights from Recife. Bring plenty of local currency with you as you won't be able to change money during your stay, and also bring anything else you think you may need: **prices** in Fernando de Noronha are high, and you should try to avoid doing much shopping while you're there.

Although Fernando de Noronha is an archipelago, only one island – the biggest one – is inhabited and that's where the airport is. The few services that the island has are to be found in the main town, **VILA DOS REMÉDIOS**: the **tourist information** office is called the *Divisão de Turismo* (☎081/619-1352).

As far as **accommodation** is concerned, there are several hotels scattered around the island but most are expensive, and you're probably best off **renting a room** from a local family in Vila dos Remédios. It's not difficult to find such places, and the advantage is that you'll often be able to have your meals included in the price (about $25 per person per night), thus avoiding paying extortionate restaurant bills.

The alternative to all this is to go on an **organized tour**. These can be arranged by travel agencies in Recife or Natal – such as Dolphin Travel, at Av. Eng. Domingos Ferreira 4267 (☎081/326-3815) in Boa Viagem – and usually include a return flight, accommodation, food and tours of the island. Prices start at around $600 for two nights, $660 for three nights and $800 for five nights.

ALAGOAS AND SERGIPE

Alagoas and **Sergipe** are the smallest Brazilian states. Sandwiched between Pernambuco to the north and Bahia to the south, they have traditionally been overshadowed by their neighbours and, to this day, still have a reputation for being something of a backwater. This isn't entirely fair. While it's true that there's nowhere comparable to the cosmopolitan cities of Recife or Salvador, there are the two state capitals of **Maceió** and **Aracaju**, together with some well-preserved colonial towns, and exceptional **beaches** in Alagoas, which many rate as the best in the Northeast. Also, the harshness of the *sertão* here is much alleviated by the São Francisco river valley, which forms the border between the two states.

Alagoas is very poor, as you immediately discover from the potholes in the roads and its rickety local buses. Thousands of *Alagoanos* leave every year, looking for work as far afield as Rio, São Paulo and Amazonia, giving Alagoas the highest emigration rate of any state in Brazil. Sergipe was, for most of its history, in exactly the same position, but since the 1960s a minor offshore oil boom has brought affluence to parts of the coast. Brazil being what it is, this doesn't mean that the poor are proportionately any fewer: it's simply that the rich in Aracaju tend to be richer than the rich elsewhere in the Northeast.

Maceió

Photos of **MACEIÓ**, the state capital of Alagoas, from the 1930s and 1940s show an elegant city of squares and houses nestling under palm trees. Today, while the city is still attractive in places, you can't help wishing the clock could be turned back. Some of the graceful squares and buildings remain, faded yet full of character, but the city as a whole has suffered in recent years from the attentions of planners. Their worst crime was the wrecking of a once famous waterfront parade, facing the harbour around which the city grew. An early nineteenth-century customs house once stood here, framed by offices and the fine houses of traders – all now gone and replaced by grimy concrete boxes.

The city's modern claim to fame – or infamy – is as the place where **Fernando Collor de Melo** cut his political teeth, becoming mayor and then state governor during the 1980s, before being elected Brazil's president in 1990. His term ended in disgrace after he was found to be at the centre of a huge corruption network, and further scandal was to come for Maceió with the violent death of Collor's adviser and chief

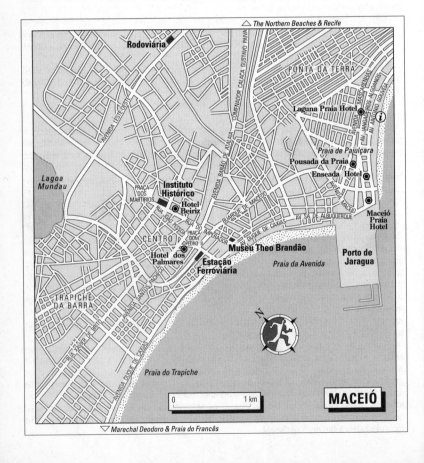

accomplice in crime, **P.C. Farias**. In 1996 he and his girlfriend were found shot dead in a beachside hotel in Maceió – conspiracy theories abounded but it seems to have been a crime of passion.

Arrival, information and accommodation

By Brazilian standards the **Rodoviária** is not far from the centre, though it's still well beyond walking distance; buses marked "Ouro Preto" or "Serraria Mercado" connect it with the centre of town, or take a taxi. The **airport** is 20km from the city, and is served by a bus marked "Estação Ferroviária", which takes you to the train station. A taxi will set you back around $30. Shoals of local buses make **getting around** very simple. All routes pass through the main squares in the centre, notably Praça Deodoro and Praça Dom Pedro II, names you'll often see on route cards propped in the front windows. The *estação ferroviária* is the place to get buses for local routes south of the city, and you may use it to go to nearby Marechal Deodoro or the glorious beach of Praia do Francês.

There's a **tourist information** booth, Av. Duque de Caxias 2014 (Mon–Fri 8am–6pm; ☎082/221-9393), at the small tourist market on the promenade, easily recognizable by the *jangadas* offering trips a mile out to the reef. There are other tourist information offices at the *Rodoviária* (daily 8am–11pm; ☎082/223-4015), the airport (daily 8am–11.30pm; ☎082/322-2288), and at Rua Saldanha da Gama 71, Farol (Mon–Fri 8am–noon & 2–6pm; ☎082/223-4016). The staff are friendly and can provide details of Maceió's lively **out-of-season Carnaval** (mid-December), but are often short of maps and hard information; staff shortages mean they can keep very irregular hours. Information is also often available from booths run by the local telephone company, Telasa. You can **change money** and travellers' cheques at Aero Turismo, Av. Santos Pacheco 65.

Accommodation

Around the **Rodoviária** is a good bet for budget but downmarket hotels. Otherwise, it's a largely one-sided choice between **Centro** and the beach district of **Pajuçara**: the latter is only a short bus ride away, and accommodation is more plentiful and of better quality than in the centre. Buses there are marked "Ponta Verde", "Pajuçara" or "Ponta da Terra" and run one block in from the beach, along **Avenida dos Jangadeiros Alagoanos**. Conveniently, this road is strung with a series of small hotels and *pensões*, with more down the sidestreets. The beach promenade is where the luxury hotels are, and there are good medium-priced hotels on **Avenida Antônio Gouveia**, the first stretch of promenade after the centre.

Hotel Beiriz, Rua João Pessoa 290, Centro (☎082/221-1080). A clean medium-range hotel, but difficult to spot from the road because there's no sign; it's next to a church. ③.

Enseada, Av. Dr Antônio Gouveia 171, Praia da Pajuçara (☎082/231-4726). A comfortable hotel right on the beachfront. ⑤.

Laguna Praia Hotel, Av. dos Jangadeiros Alagoanas 1231, Praia da Pajuçara (☎082/231-6180 or 231-7231). Pleasanter than its ugly modern exterior would suggest, with friendly staff and an outstanding breakfast. ③.

Maceió Praia Hotel, Av. Dr Antônio Gouveia 3, Praia da Pajuçara (☎082/231-6391). A medium-range hotel located just at the beginning of Pajuçara beach. ③.

Matsubara, Av. Brigadeiro Eduardo Gomes 1551, Praia da Cruz das Almas (☎082/235-3000). Every whim is catered for at this beachfront hotel for those who like to throw their (or more likely other people's) money around. ⑦.

Hotel dos Palmares, Praça dos Palmares 253, Centro (☎082/223-7024). A good budget option in the city centre with rooms built around a courtyard, though it can get a bit hot. ②.

Pousada da Praia, Av. dos Jangadeiros Alagoanos 545, Praia da Pajuçara (☎082/231-6843). A good option in the beach area, with chalet-style rooms. You can arrange price reductions if you're staying for longer than a couple of nights. ③.

The City

The small **city centre** is just inland from the modest harbour, and here what remains of Maceió's past is to be found cheek by jowl with the cheap hotels and a central shopping area. The much larger and livelier area of **Pajuçara**, a few minutes away by bus to the east, is built along a spectacular beach, while to the northwest, undistinguished urban sprawl conceals the enormous lagoon of **Mundaú**. It's here that the city ends, an ideal place to watch a sunset and eat cheaply at the simple bars and restaurants that dot its banks.

Maceió is not exactly bursting at the seams with museums and spectacular architecture, and the places worth seeing could all be rushed around in a morning if you were so inclined. There are two museums, but neither are in the same class as the one in nearby Marechal Deodoro (see p.235). The **Museu Theo Brandão**, at Praça Visconte Sinimbu 206, 1st floor (also called the Museu do Folclore; Mon–Thurs 8am–noon & 2–5pm, Fri 8am–noon), has the usual bundles of Indian arrows and moth-eaten feather ornaments. Judged strictly on exhibits, the **Instituto Histórico** at Rua João Pessoa 382 (Mon–Fri 8am–noon & 2–5pm) has the edge, and is worth seeing for the various relics and photographs of the bandit leader Lampião, including the famous "team photo" of his severed head, together with those of his wife, Maria Bonita, and his closest lieutenants. All were preserved in alcohol by the police detachment that shot them in 1938, so that they could be shown in market towns in the interior, the only way to make the people believe he really had been killed. Even now, the Brazilian media occasionally publish pictures of an old man who died in 1996, who bears a striking resemblance to Lampião.

The best place to get some sense of the old Maceió is **Praça dos Martírios**, the finest square in the city, and an object lesson to those who destroyed the waterfront. At one end is the eighteenth-century **Igreja Bom Jesus dos Martírios**, whose exterior, covered with well-preserved blue-and-white *azulejo* tiling, overshadows anything inside. At the other end the colonial **Governor's Palace** faces onto the palm-shaded square, brilliantly white during the day, floodlit at night.

The beaches

Maceió is most famous for its **beaches**, of which *Alagoanos* are justly proud. The main city beach is at **Pajuçara**, whose curving road and wide mosaic promenade are studded with palm trees. The water is not always the cleanest here and many people hire *jangadas* and head 2km out to sea to swim in the natural pools that form at low tide. The bay then curves past the yacht club, into the less crowded beaches of **Ponta Verde** and **Jatiúca**, the beginning of a series of fine sands to the north. The best way to get to them is to take buses marked "Mirante" or "Fátima" from the centre, which take you along the coast as far as **Pratagi** (also called Mirante da Sereia), 13km north, where there are coral pools in the reef at low tide. You can get off the bus anywhere that takes your fancy; the main beaches, in order of appearance, are **Cruz das Almas**, **Jacarecica**, **Guaxuma**, **Garça Torta** and **Riacho Doce**, all of them less crowded than the city beaches during the week, but very popular at weekends.

Most visitors to Maceió flood north to the beaches, which leaves the coast **to the south** in relative calm, though the crowds are now beginning to make their way here too. Hourly buses marked "Deodoro" leave from the bus stop in front of the old train station in Maceió, near the harbour, passing out of the city over the Trapiche bridge into a flat, swampy coastline. Sixteen kilometres south, the road swings left to a beach called **Praia do Francês**, which even by Alagoan standards is something special. An enormous expanse of white sand, surf and thick palm forest, it even boasts a couple of small hotels; the *Hotel Cumarú* (③) is the best value. The last bus back to Maceió leaves at 6pm.

Eating and drinking

The best places to eat and drink in the city are out of the centre, at Mundaú lagoon and Pajuçara beach. From Praça dos Martírios you can take a taxi, or a local bus marked "Mundaú" or "Ponta da Barra", for the short ride to **Lagoa Mundaú**. Have a *caipirinha* at a **waterfront bar** to accompany the routinely spectacular sunset. There are simple but excellent **eating places** here, too, selling fish and shrimp, and the early evening is a good time to watch prawn fishermen at work on punts in the lagoon, their silhouetted figures throwing out nets against the sunset.

At **Pajuçara**, you'll find a series of **bars**, with numbers rather than names, built around thatched emplacements at intervals along the beach. They mix excellent *caipirinhas* and serve cheaper food than you're likely to find in the **seafront restaurants** on the other side of the road, all much of a muchness. Seafood is, naturally, best: the *sopa de ostra* manages to get more oysters into a single dish than most gringos see in a lifetime; they're so common, you can even get an oyster omelette.

Marechal Deodoro

The beautifully preserved colonial town of **MARECHAL DEODORO** lies 22km south of Maceió. Basically it's no more than a small market town, built on rising ground on the banks of a lagoon, with streets that are either dirt or cobbled. But it's immaculately kept, with not a single building that looks as if it were constructed this century. Nor is it simply preserved for tourists to gawp at: the locals spit in the streets, gossip and hang about in bars as they would anywhere else, and there's a real air of small-town tranquillity.

The bus from Maceió drives right to the end of town before reaching its terminus. You should get off a little earlier, in the manicured **Praça Pedro Paulinho**, which is dominated by the imposing facade of the Igreja de Santa Maria Magdalena, with the older **Convento de São Francisco**, finished in 1684, attached. The *convento*'s plain exterior conceals an austere, yet strikingly beautiful interior, which is now turned over to the excellent **Museu de Arte Sagrada** (Mon & Wed–Sat 9am–4pm); entrance to the museum is from the road running down towards the lake from Praça Pedro Paulinho. Restoration has enhanced the character of the complex, preserving a cloistered calm, an appropriate setting for a high-quality collection of religious art. Once inside, you see that the convent is built around a cool courtyard. The main galleries are on the first storey, where the floor is as interesting as many of the exhibits. It's made of rich brown *pau do brasil*, the tropical redwood that gave its name to the country, glistening in a protective coat of varnish. Everything on display is high Catholic religious art, with little concession made to the tropical setting save for the large number of portrayals of São Benedito, the black patron saint of the slaves who manned the *engenhos* all around and built most of Marechal Deodoro itself. The highlight of the collection, extracted from churches all over the state, is the group of seventeenth- to nineteenth-century statues of saints and virgins, in the first gallery to the right. Most are no more than a foot high, made of wood or plaster, and intricately painted. Look, too, for the couple of lifesize (and frighteningly lifelike) carved wooden bodies of Christ, with gruesome wounds. In comparison, the **Igreja de Santa Maria Magdalena** is not as impressive, a typical mid-eighteenth-century building, though less cloyingly Rococo than most. In front of a small side chapel, opposite the entrance from the museum, is a concealed entrance to a secret tunnel, a relic from the original chapel that stood on the site during the Dutch wars.

Down the road curving to the right past the museum is the modest house that was the birthplace of **Marshal Deodoro**, proclaimer and first president of the republic in 1889; it's now preserved as a **museum**, Rua Mal. Deodoro 92 (daily 8am–5pm). Deodoro was the son of an army officer who served with distinction in the Paraguayan war, and rose to become head of the armed forces with the sonorous title "Generalissimo of the Forces of Land and Sea". He was the first Brazilian to mount a military coup, unceremoniously dumping the harmless old emperor Dom Pedro II, but he proved an arrogant and inept president, the earliest in a depressingly long line of incompetent military authoritarians. Dissolving Congress and declaring a state of siege in 1891, he did everyone a favour by resigning when he couldn't make it stick. There's no hint, of course, of his disastrous political career in the museum, which is basically a mildly interesting collection of personal effects and period furniture.

In the streets around you'll find several **lacemakers**, with goods displayed in the windows. Marechal Deodoro is famous for its lace, which you see in any sizeable market in the Northeast. It's high-quality stuff, and costs less than half the price you pay elsewhere when bought at source in the town. The Cooperative Artesanal in Rua Dr Ladislam Netto is a good place to look.

If you want to stay, there's a **pensão**, *Deodoré* (①), on Praça Pedro Paulinho, but there's no sign so you'll have to ask. There's also a **campsite** (☎081/263-1378), clean and with good facilities, half an hour's walk beyond the square; the road is marked by a sign near the small bus company office.

Paulo Afonso and around

Inland from Maceió, 300km to the west, the most popular destination of all in Alagoas is the **Cachoeira de Paulo Afonso**, once the largest waterfall on the Rio São Francisco and the third largest in Brazil, but now largely emasculated by a hydroelectric scheme that diverted most of the flow – a spectacular piece of ecological vandalism surpassed only by the destruction of the even more impressive Sete Quedas waterfall in Paraná by similar means several years ago. These days the only time a considerable amount of water passes over the falls is during the rains of January and February, but the whole surrounding area – a spectacular deep rocky gorge choked with tropical forest and declared a national park – is very scenic all year round.

You can get there by bus from Salvador, but the journey from Maceió is shorter, with two **buses** daily from the *Rodoviária* there. They leave you in the small river town of **PAULO AFONSO**, on the Bahian riverbank, where there are a cluster of reasonable **hotels** near the bus station; the *Belvedere*, Av. Apolônio Sales 457 (☎075/281-1814; ⑤), is more upmarket then the others, but good value.

The **waterfall** is some way out of town and you can only get there by taxi, which will cost you about $5 an hour, but the drivers do know the best spots. Alternatively, you may be able to organize something with the tourist office in the centre of town. Once you get there the best view is from the **cable car**, if it's working.

If you feel like really getting off the beaten track, take the bus from Paulo Afonso to **PIRANHAS**, a picturesque small riverside town 80km south, where there are beaches on the river, a small *pousada*, friendly inhabitants and little to disturb the rural quiet.

Penedo

A couple of hours south of Maceió is the lively colonial town of **PENEDO**. There are several colonial **churches** here which are all marked on a useful map of the town, obtainable at the **tourist office** (Mon–Fri 8–11am & 2–5pm) in the main central square, the Praça Barão de Penedo. Penedo is strategically placed at the mouth of the Rio São Francisco, and while the trading prosperity it might have expected as a result never quite materialized, it's still a busy little place, much of whose life revolves around the river and the waterfront.

The waterfront park, with shaded paths and kiosks selling drinks, is a good place to watch the toing and froing of the boats. You can negotiate with boat-owners to go on **cruises**: the main destinations are **Piassabussu**, a sleepy and little-visited fishing village right on the mouth of the river, and the village of **Neópolis**, opposite Penedo, where there's nothing to do except have a drink and catch the boat back – but it's a nice trip.

If you feel adventurous, have a lot of time and enough Portuguese to make people understand where you want to go, it is possible to go **up the river by boat** as far as Piranhas, and from there get a bus to Paulo Afonso and the falls. Most of the river boats work particular stretches of river, and unless you're very lucky you'll take several days to get as far as Piranhas. Starting from Penedo, the river towns you pass through before Piranhas are Porto Real do Colégio, São Brás, Traipu, Gararu and Pão de Açúcar.

Penedo is served by four **buses** daily from Maceió's *Rodoviária* and for once they leave you in the centre of the town, which is well supplied with good **places to stay**: try *Pousada Colonial*, Praça 12 de Abril (☎082/551-2355; ③), which has excellent views, or *São Francisco*, on Avenida Floriano Peixoto (☎082/551-2273; ④), both in the heart of town; nearer the *Rodoviária*, on Rua Siqueira Campos, are a number of budget hotels with prices starting at around $15. One of the town's better **restaurants** is *Forte da Rocheira* on Rua da Rocheira, specializing in fish dishes.

Aracaju

From Maceió seven buses a day run to **ARACAJU**, capital of the neighbouring state of **Sergipe** with a population of 400,000, a little-visited and rather anonymous place. Built on the flat southern bank of the Rio Sergipe, its American-style grid layout, unusual in Brazil, is the clue to its lack of character. Although the Portuguese founded a colony here in 1592, the capital of the infant state was moved to nearby São Cristóvão. Then, in the mid-nineteenth century, there was a sudden vogue for purpose-built administrative centres (similar to the urge that led to the construction of Brasília a century later), and the core of modern Aracaju was thrown up overnight, becoming the state capital again in 1855. Like the other state capitals planned and built in the last century, Aracaju is – to put it mildly – something of an architectural desert. Oil wealth has stimulated a lot of recent building and given the city council enough money to keep everything clean and tidy, but there is a very un-Brazilian dullness about the place. However, the people are friendly, some of the beaches are good, and the small colonial towns of Laranjeiras and São Cristóvão are only a short bus-ride away.

The spanking new **Rodoviária** is miles out of town, linked to the centre by frequent local buses. The **airport** is also out of town but not far from the beach of Atalaia Velha; buses marked "Aeroporto" will get you into the centre. Sergipe's **tourist office**, EMSETUR, has its headquarters on the corner of Rua Itabaianinha and Rua Geru, on the 13th floor of the Edifício do Estado de Sergipe. But your best bet for information is probably the Centro de Turismo in the shopping centre known as Rua 24 Horas, which is just next to Praça Olímpio Campos and has entrances on Rua Laranjeiras and Avenida Própria. Rua 24 Horas is actually a very pleasant place, set in a restored nineteenth-century building, with cafés, restaurants and a stage where shows are sometimes put on.

The cheaper **hotels** are as usual in the city centre, several of them near the municipal bus station, the *Rodoviária Velha*. For a real budget option you could stay at the *Sergipe Hotel*, Rua Geru 205 (☎079/222-7898; ①), which is perfectly adequate for what you're paying. Two comfortable mid-range hotels in the same area are the *Oásis*, at Rua São Cristóvão 466 (☎079/224-1181; ③), and the *Amado*, at Rua Laranjeiras 532 (☎079/211-9937; ③). Right next to the *Rodoviária Velha* is the plusher and pricier *Grande Hotel*, at Rua Itabaianinha 371 (☎079/211-1364; ⑤). Down at the southern end of the city centre is the *Hotel Jangadeiro*, at Rua Santa Luiza 269 (☎079/211-1350; ④).

The two main **beaches** are Atalaia Velha and Atalaia Nova. **ATALAIA VELHA** lies about 5km south down the road from the city centre and is the more developed of the two. It's easy to get to by bus but, although the beach is OK and doesn't seem to have been polluted by the oil rigs which lie offshore, the whole area is rather soulless and uninspiring. There are, however, a huge number of restaurants and **hotels**, including the *Pousada do Sol*, Rua Atalaia 43 (☎079/255-1074; ④), and the *Hotel Beira Mar* on Avenida Rotary just by the seafront (☎079/243-1921; ⑤). **ATALAIA NOVA** lies on an island in the Rio Sergipe, accessible by boat from the *Hidroviária* in the city centre. The ferry leaves every ten minutes and costs just 40¢; you can then get a bus to Atalaia Nova from the ferry terminal. Although the beach itself isn't great, the island is quite a pleasant place to stay – hotels are expensive, but there are plenty of rooms for rent.

Laranjeiras and São Cristóvão

Sergipe's main attractions are two attractive colonial towns that come as a welcome relief from Aracaju's anonymity, reminders of the time when sugar made the *sergipano* coast one of the most strategically valuable parts of Brazil. Innumerable skirmishes were fought around them during the Dutch wars, but no trace of their turbulent past survives into their tranquil present, as they slide from important market centres into rural backwaters.

The pleasantly decrepit village of **LARANJEIRAS** is forty minutes by bus from Aracaju's *Rodoviária Velha*. Dominated by a hill crowned with the ruins of an old *engenho* chapel, Laranjeiras boasts a couple of small museums as well as the inevitable churches. The **Museu Afro-Brasileiro**, Rua José do Prado Franco 70 (Tues–Sun 8am–noon & 2–5.30pm), concentrates on slave life and popular religion, while the **Centro de Cultura João Ribeiro**, Rua João Ribeiro (Mon–Fri 8am–10pm, Sat 8am–1pm, Sun 2–5pm), is mostly given over to *artesanato* and relics of plantation life. But the main attraction is simply wandering around the winding streets, with quiet squares, pastel-painted houses and small bars where locals sit around and watch the world go by. There are a couple of **pensões**, but no hotels as yet, and with any luck it will stay that way.

The other colonial town worth visiting is the old state capital of **SÃO CRISTÓVÃO**, also reached by local bus from Aracaju's *Rodoviária Velha*. It was founded in 1590 and much of it hasn't changed since, as the shifting of the capital to Aracaju preserved it from the developers. Packed into its small area is the full panoply of a colonial administrative centre, including an old governor's palace, a parliament building and half a dozen period churches, together with the small **Museu de Arte Sacra e Histórico** in the Convento de São Francisco (Tues–Sun 9am–noon & 2–5.30pm).

São Cristóvão is the only place worth stopping on the bus route south to Bahia, which runs inland from Aracaju through parched hill country before emerging some six hours later at Salvador, capital of Bahia state.

BAHIA

The oldest and most historic city in Brazil, **Salvador** was the capital of Brazil for over two centuries, before relinquishing the title to Rio in 1763. The bay on which the city was built afforded a superb natural anchorage, while the surrounding lands of **Bahia state** were ideal country for sugar cane and tobacco plantations. Salvador became the centre of the **Recôncavo**, the richest plantation zone in Brazil before the coming of coffee, and there's a string of colonial towns – like **Santo Amaro** and **Cachoeira** – within striking distance of the city.

The countryside changes to the south, with mangrove swamps and islands surrounding the town of **Valença**, before reverting to a spectacular coastline typical of the Northeast. **Ilhéus** is a thriving beach resort, as is **Porto Seguro** – oldest town in Brazil and site of the first Portuguese landings in 1500. **Inland**, the Bahian **sertão** is massive, a desert-like land which supports some fascinating frontier towns – the mining bases of **Jacobina** and **Lençóis** and the river terminus of **Ibotirama** are just three.

Salvador

SALVADOR is one of that select band of cities which has an electricity you feel from the moment you arrive, and the confident sense of identity you find in a place that knows it's somewhere special. Second only to Rio in the magnificence of its natural setting, on the mouth of the enormous bay of Todos os Santos, there is no better description of Salvador than that by William Scully, who wrote the first guidebook to Brazil in 1866:

> *Here, sheltered from every wind and surrounded by a country exuberantly rich, fleets may ride at anchor in a gulf which seems as if formed by nature to be the emporium of the world and receive its shipping, while the town itself, seen picturesquely crowning the high bluff that circles round the eastern side of the bay, appears a fitting mistress of the lovely scene.*

Salvador's foundation in 1549 marked the beginning of the permanent occupation of the country by **the Portuguese**, though it wasn't an easy occupation. The Caeté Indians killed and ate both the first governor and the first bishop before succumbing, and Salvador was later the scene of a great battle in 1624, when the Dutch destroyed the Portuguese fleet in the bay and took the town by storm, only to be forced out again within a year by a joint Spanish and Portuguese fleet. In a climactic second naval battle in front of the city, legend has it that the Dutch admiral Adrian Patryd, his fleet outgunned and defeated, threw himself into the sea with the words "the ocean is the only tomb worthy of a Batavian admiral".

Much of the plantation wealth of the Recôncavo was used to adorn the city with imposing public buildings, ornate squares and, above all, churches. Today, Salvador is a large, modern city, but significant chunks of it are still recognizably colonial. Taken as a whole it doesn't have the unsullied calm of, say, Olinda but many of its individual churches, monasteries and convents are magnificent, the finest colonial buildings anywhere in Brazil.

The other factor that marks Salvador out among Brazil's great cities is immediately obvious – most of the population is black. Salvador was Brazil's main slave port, and the survivors of the brutal journey from the Portuguese Gold Coast and Angola were immediately packed off to city construction gangs or the plantations of the Recôncavo; their descendants make up the bulk of the modern population. **African influences** are everywhere. Salvador is the cradle of *candomblé* and *umbanda*, Afro-Brazilian religious cults that have millions of devotees across Brazil. The city has a marvellous local **cuisine**, much imitated in other parts of the country, based on African ingredients like palm oil, peanuts and coconut milk. And Salvador has possibly the richest **artistic tradition** of any Brazilian city; only Rio can rival it.

A disproportionate number of Brazil's leading **writers** and **poets** were either born or lived in Salvador, including Jorge Amado, the most widely translated Brazilian novelist, and Vinícius de Morães, Brazil's best-known modern poet. The majority of the great names who made Brazilian **music** famous hail from the city – João Gilberto, the leading exponent with Tom Jobim of *bossa-nova*; Astrud Gilberto, João's daughter,

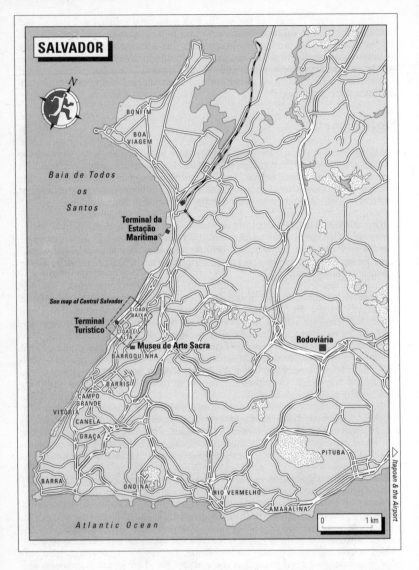

SALVADOR

N

BONFIM

BOA
VIAGEM

Baia de Todos

os

Santos

Terminal da
Estação
Marítima

See map of Central Salvador

Terminal
Turístico

CIDADE
BAIXA

CIDADE
ALTA

Museu de Arte Sacra

Rodoviária

BARROQUINHA

BARRIS

CAMPO
GRANDE

VITÓRIA

CANELA

GRAÇA

PITUBA

BARRA

ONDINA

RIO VERMELHO

AMARALINA

Atlantic Ocean

0   1 km

△ Itapoan & the Airport

whose quavering version of *The Girl from Ipanema* was a global hit; Dorival Caymmi, the patriarch of Brazilian popular music; Caetano Veloso, the founder of *tropicalismo*, Brazil's declaration of musical independence in the 1960s; Maria Bethânia, a fine singer and sister of Caetano; Gal Costa, the loveliest voice in Brazilian music; and Gilberto Gil, who was at one time secretary of culture in the city government. The city's music is still as rich and innovative as ever, and bursts out every year in a **Carnaval** that many think is the best in Brazil.

The **telephone code** for Salvador is ☎071.

Arrival, information and getting around

The **airport** is 20km northeast of the city, and on arrival a shuttle express bus service, $2, from directly in front of the terminal, takes you to Praça da Sé via the beach districts and Campo Grande. The length of the ride varies according to traffic, but if you're going back the other way to catch a plane, make sure you allow an hour and a half. The bus marked "Politeama" also runs to the centre, but gets very crowded and isn't a good idea with luggage. A taxi to the centre will set you back around $30; pay at the kiosk in the arrivals area and hand the voucher to the driver.

Salvador's superb **Rodoviária** – well organized and packed with almost every conceivable facility – is 8km east of the centre. To get to the Cidade Alta and its hotels from here, you could catch an ordinary local bus from just outside the *Rodoviária*: the bus stops are to your left as you come out of the building. The best ones are those marked "Barroquinha" or "Campo Grande", but if you take the latter you'll eventually have to change to another one marked "Campo Grande – Sé". However, if you're loaded down with luggage, it's probably best to give the local buses a miss and either take a taxi (about $10) or catch the comfortable *executivo* bus from the Iguatemi shopping centre across the busy road from the *Rodoviária* – there's a footbridge to stop you getting mown down by traffic. The bus costs $2 and makes a stately progress through the beach districts of Pituba and Rio Vermelho before dropping you in the Praça da Sé.

Information

Salvador's **tourist information** is better than anywhere else in the Northeast. The state tourist agency, **Bahiatursa**, is used to foreigners, most offices have English speakers, and there are a variety of maps and handouts on the city: the best two are the *Mapa Turístico de Salvador da Bahia* (which you have to pay for) and the free *Guia do Pelourinho*. If you're travelling on to other parts of Bahia, you should also ask for whatever material they have on the rest of the state, as elsewhere the service is nothing like as good.

There are **information posts** on arrival at the airport (daily 8.30am–10.45pm) and the *Rodoviária* (daily 8.30am–9.30pm). Bahiatursa's **main office** in Cidade Alta is in the

---

PERSONAL SAFETY: A WARNING

A warning about **personal safety** in Salvador is in order. Although the situation has improved a great deal in recent years, Salvador still has more of a problem with robberies and muggings than anywhere else in the Northeast. The main tourist area around Pelourinho is now heavily policed until quite late at night and is consequently safe. However, the fact that such a large police presence is needed suggests that some **precautions** are still in order. Don't wander down ill-lit sidestreets at night unless you are within sight of a policeman and don't use the Lacerda elevator after the early evening. You should avoid walking up and down the winding roads which connect the Cidade Alta and the Cidade Baixa, and you should be careful about using ordinary city buses on Sundays when there are few people around – the *executivo* bus is always a safe option. Give the Avenida do Contorno a miss too – the seafront road that runs north from the harbour past the *Solar do Unhão* restaurant. It's a shame to put it out of bounds, as it's a very scenic walk, but it's dangerous even in daylight as gangs lie in wait for tourists who don't know any better; if you go to the restaurant, or the Museu de Arte Moderna near it, go and return by taxi.

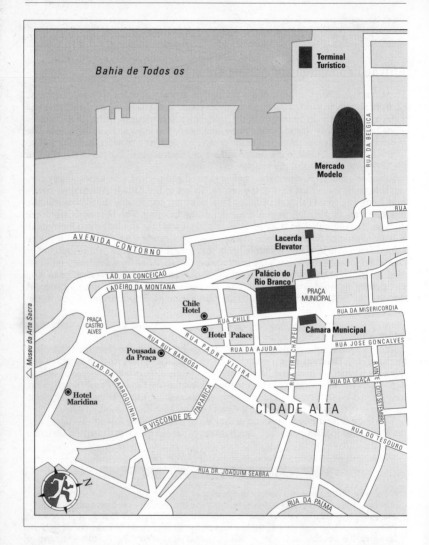

Praça da Sé (daily 8am–6pm; ☎321-1530 or 321-2464), but it's tucked away behind the makeshift Belvedere shopping centre-cum-market, which is just on your left as you come into the square from Rua da Misericórdia: go past the stalls and down the steps at the back. The noticeboard here is a good place to leave messages and information for other travellers, as well as advertising things like air tickets for sale. You can also get information at the nearby Posto Pelourinho, Rua das Laranjeiras 12 (also sometimes called Rua Francisco Muniz Barreto; daily 8am–7pm; ☎321-2463), and Bahiatursa has other offices at the Mercado Modelo (Mon–Sat 8am–6pm; ☎241-0242) and in Barra at Praça Azevedo Fernandes (Mon–Sat 8am–6pm; ☎247-3195). An additional way of get-

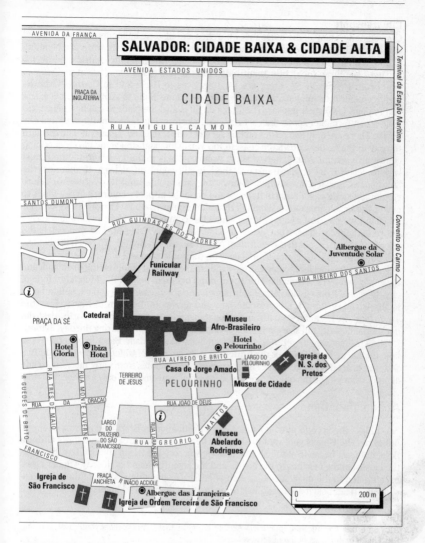

SALVADOR: CIDADE BAIXA & CIDADE ALTA

AVENIDA DA FRANÇA

AVENIDA ESTADOS UNIDOS

PRAÇA DA INGLATERRA

CIDADE BAIXA

RUA MIGUEL CALMON

SANTOS DUMONT

RUA GUINDASTES DOS PADRES

Funicular Railway

Albergue da Juventude Solar

RUA RIBEIRO DOS SANTOS

Catedral

PRAÇA DA SÉ

Museu Afro-Brasileiro

Hotel Gloria

Ibiza Hotel

Hotel Pelourinho

RUA ALFREDO DE BRITO

LARGO DO PELOURINHO

Igreja da N. S. dos Pretos

Casa de Jorge Amado

TERREIRO DE JESUS

PELOURINHO

Museu de Cidade

R GUEDES DE BRITO

RUA TRES DE MAIO

RUA DA ORAÇÃO

RUA MONTE ALVERNE

RUA JOÃO DE DEUS

RUA LARANJEIRAS

RUA DE MATTOS

LARGO DO CRUZEIRO DO SÃO FRANCISCO

RUA GREGÓRIO DE MATTOS

Museu Abelardo Rodrigues

FRANCISCO

Igreja de São Francisco

PRAÇA ANCHIETA

R INÁCIO ACCIOLE

Albergue das Laranjeiras

Igreja de Ordem Terceira de São Francisco

0   200 m

Terminal da Estação Marítima

Convento do Carmo

ting information is via the **tourist hotline**, called "Disque Turismo" – just ring ☎131 from any telephone and you should find an English speaker on the other end. Finally, the city of Salvador has its own tourist authority, **EMTURSA**, which has an office on Largo do Pelourinho (daily 1–7pm; ☎243-6555), but it's nothing like as good.

One thing you should bear in mind when finding your way around the city is that many roads have two **names**: the main seafront road, for example, is sometimes called Avenida Presidente Vargas, but more usually Avenida Oceânica. In general we've gone for the name that actually appears on the street signs, but it's often worth getting used to both alternatives.

City transport

Conveniently, many of the museums, churches and historic buildings are concentrated within **walking** distance of each other in Cidade Alta. Failing that, **taxis** are plentiful, although all the beach areas except Barra are a long ride from the centre.

There are three local **bus terminals**, and the bus system is efficient and easy to use. From **Praça da Sé**, there are local services to Barra and to **Campo Grande**, another central terminus with self-explanatory connections to *Aeroporto*, *Rodoviária* and Itapoan (also spelt Itapoã). The Praça da Sé is also the place to catch the *executivo* ($2), a comfortable express bus service, well worth using instead of the crowded city buses. There are only two routes on this service: buses marked "Iguatemi" run through the city to Barra, head down the coast to Rio Vermelho, and stop at the glossy shopping centre at Iguatemi, from where a short walkway leads to the *Rodoviária* – the fastest way to reach it by public transport, though still count on at least 45 minutes; the "Aeroporto" service, meanwhile, follows the same route until Rio Vermelho, before continuing along past Pituba to Itapoan, and on to the airport – cutting journey times to any of the beach areas to at least half that of a regular city bus. The other city bus terminal is **Estação da Lapa**, in Barris, which has connections to everywhere in the city; it's remarkably well laid out, with destinations clearly labelled, and you catch the "Bonfim" bus here, out to the church of Nosso Senhor do Bonfim. To reach the centre, any bus with "Sé", "C. Grande" or "Lapa" on the route card will do.

Salvador also has **ferry** services to islands in the bay and points on the mainland, and there are two ferry terminals. The **Terminal Turístico**, behind the Mercado Modelo, clearly visible from Cidade Alta, is for launch services – *lanchas* – and excursion boats to the island of Itaparica, across the bay, and ferries to the town of Maragojipe; the **Terminal da Estação Marítima** (or Terminal São Joaquim), to the north, past the docks, handles the full-size car ferries to Itaparica (every 30min during the day; 30min).

The quickest way to get to the ferry terminals – and Cidade Baixa in general – is to take the **Lacerda elevator** or the **funicular railway**, both of which connect Cidade Alta with the heart of Cidade Baixa. They run every few minutes from early morning to late at night (though see the box on "Personal Safety" above), and cost only a few cents a ride.

Accommodation

Salvador is the second most popular tourist destination in Brazil and correspondingly full of **hotels**. Unless you want to stay on a beach, the best area to head for is **Cidade Alta**, not least because of the splendid view across the island-studded bay. **Barra** is the closest of the beaches to the centre and the favoured haunt of the city's upper classes, attracted to the most scenic stretch of coast. Despite this, it's one of the more reasonably priced beach areas and has some good medium-priced hotels.

City centre

Albergue das Laranjeiras, Rua Inácio Acciole 13 (☎321-1366). An excellent youth hostel costing $16 a night in the heart of the historic centre.

Albergue da Juventude Solar, Rua Ribeiro dos Santos 45 (☎241-0055). Another good youth hostel in a slightly quieter part of the Pelourinho district which costs $17 a night with breakfast.

Chile Hotel, Rua Chile 7 (☎321-0245). Very popular with backpackers, a clean and spacious hotel on the road running away from the Praça da Sé towards Praça Castro Alves. ③.

Hotel Glória, Praça da Sé (☎243-1941). A really dingy dive suitable only for the very hard-up. ①.

Hotel Granada, Av. Sete de Setembro 512 (☎243-2301). A good medium-priced option surrounded by the hustle and bustle of Cidade Alta's shopping district. ④.

Ibiza Hotel, Rua do Bispo 6 (☎322-4503). An excellent budget hotel just on the corner of Rua do Bispo and Praça da Sé. ③.

Hotel Maridina, Av. Sete de Setembro 6 (☎242-7176). This hotel just off Praça Castro Alves is mainly frequented by Brazilians and has a friendly, laid-back atmosphere. ③.

Hotel Palace, Rua Chile 20 (☎322-1155). If you want a bit more comfort for a bit more money, this is a good bet. ⑤.

Hotel Pelourinho, Rua Alfredo Brito 20 (☎321-4653). Probably the best-known hotel in Cidade Alta, this has long been an atmospheric and popular place, but it's no longer cheap. ④.

Pousada da Praça Hotel, Rua Ruy Barbosa 5 (☎321-0642). A highly recommended budget hotel offering a magnificent breakfast just off Praça Castro Alves. ②.

The beaches

Amaralina Praia, Av. Otavio Mangabeira 197 (☎248-9998). This comfortable hotel is set in one of the cheapest of all the beach areas, Pituba, and handily close to the airport although a little far from the centre. ④.

Hotel Catharina Paraguaçu, Rua Joao Gomes 128, Rio Vermelho (☎247-1488). Beautifully restored, this is one of Brazil's best hotels – full of character and excellent value. For some reason, taxi drivers have difficulty finding it even though it's on a main road. ⑥.

Fazenda Ilha de Mare, Ilha de Mare, Praia das Neves (☎243-0808). If an island with bananas and mangroves is your thing and you don't mind a half-hour boat journey then this may be the place for you. ④.

Meridien Bahia, Rua Fonte do Boi 216, Rio Vermelho (☎335-8011). A superb luxury hotel standing right on the seafront. ⑦.

Sofitel Quatro Rodas, Rua Passargada, Farol de Itapoa (☎374-9611) Five-star luxury, miles from the city centre. ⑦.

The City

The city is built around the craggy, 50-metre–high bluff which dominates the eastern side of the bay, and splits the central area into upper and lower sections. The heart of the old city, **Cidade Alta** (or simply Centro), is strung along its top, linked to the **Cidade Baixa**, below, by precipitous streets, a funicular railway and the towering Art Deco liftshaft of the Carlos Lacerda elevator, the city's largest landmark. Cidade Alta is the administrative and cultural centre of the city, Cidade Baixa the financial and commercial district.

In the last century the city expanded into the still elegant areas of **Barris** and **Canela**, to the south of Cidade Alta, and up to the exclusive residential suburb of **Barra**, the headland at the mouth of the bay around which the city is built. From Barra, a broken coastline of coves and beaches, large and small, is linked by the twisting **Avenida Oceânica** (also known as the Avenida Presidente Vargas), which runs along the shore through **Ondina**, **Rio Vermelho** and **Pituba**, the main beach areas. Further on is the one-time fishing village of **Itapoan**, after which the city peters out.

Most of Salvador's 25 **museums** and 34 **colonial churches** are concentrated within a short distance of each other in Cidade Alta, which makes sightseeing fairly straightforward. However, the sheer profusion of places worth visiting is a real problem; it's difficult to know where to start in a place so steeped in history. But there's no need to rush. A single meandering walk from the Praça da Sé, taking in all the highlights, but not stopping at any of them, would take no more than an hour; more realistically, you'll need at least two days, and possibly three, if you want to explore the city's history in depth.

From Praça Municipal to Terreiro de Jesus

The best spot to begin a walking tour is at the **Praça Municipal**, the square dominated by the impressive **Palácio do Rio Branco**, the old governor's palace. It was burnt down and rebuilt during the Dutch wars, and the regal plaster eagles were added by nineteenth-century restorers, who turned a plain colonial mansion into an imposing palace. The interior is fine, a blend of Rococo plasterwork, painted walls and ceilings and polished wooden floors. There is also a museum inside, the **Memorial das Governadores** (Mon 2–6pm, Tues–Fri 10am–noon & 2–6pm), but the building itself is the most interesting part. Also facing the square is the **Câmara Municipal**, the seventeenth-century city hall, graced by a series of elegant but solid arches.

To the east, Rua Chile becomes Rua da Misericórdia and leads into **Praça da Sé**, the heart of Cidade Alta, where the *executivo* buses terminate. The **Terreiro de Jesus**, lies to the south in front of the plain **Catedral Basílica**, once the chapel of the largest Jesuit seminary outside Rome. Its interior is one of the most beautiful in the city, particularly the stunning panelled ceiling of carved and gilded wood, which gives the church a light, airy feel that's an effective antidote to the overwrought Rococo altar and side chapels. To the left of the altar is the tomb of **Mem de Sá**, third viceroy of Brazil from 1556 to 1570, and the most energetic and effective of all Brazil's colonial governors. It was he who supervised the first phase of the building of Salvador, and destroyed the Caeté Indians. Look in on the restored sacristy, too, while you're here – portraits of Jesuit luminaries, set into the walls and ceiling, gaze down intimidatingly on intruders. While in the cathedral you may be pestered by self-appointed guides – they have nothing to do with the church and can be extremely irritating.

The Museu Afro-Brasileiro

Next to the cathedral stands one of the best museums in the city, the **Museu Afro-Brasileiro** (Mon–Fri 9am–5pm), contained within a large nineteenth-century building that used to be the university medical faculty; in the shady yard behind is the derelict, circular lecture theatre, now roofless and with trees growing inside, although it is currently being repaired. The main building, however, has been excellently restored, and houses three different collections, one on each of the storeys.

Largest and best is on the **ground floor**, recording and celebrating the considerable black contribution to Brazilian culture. Four rooms are dedicated to different aspects of black culture – popular religion, *capoeira*, weaving, music and *Carnaval* – and everything, for once, is very well laid out. The section on *capoeira*, the balletic martial art the slaves developed, is fascinating, supported by photos and old newspaper clippings. But there are other highlights, too, like the gallery of large photographs of *candomblé* leaders, some dating from the last century, most in full regalia and exuding pride, strength and authority; and the famous carved panels by Carybé, in the exhibition room, past the photo gallery. Carybé, Bahia's most famous artist, was Argentinian by birth but came to Salvador thirty years ago to find inspiration and themes for his work in the city and its culture. The carved panels in the museum represent the gods and goddesses of *candomblé*, figures named for African gods but associated with Catholic saints as well. They are very beautiful, subtly carved and imaginatively decorated with scrap metal.

The **first floor** houses a rather dull museum of the faculty of medicine, dominated by busts and dusty bookcases. A better idea is to look in the **basement**, at the **Museu Arqueológico e Etnológico** (Mon–Fri 9am–5pm). Largely given over to fossils and artefacts from ancient burial sites, it also incorporates the only surviving part of the old Jesuit college, a section of the cellars, in the arched brickwork at the far end. A diagram at the entrance to the museum shows how enormous the college was, extending all the way from what is now the Praça da Sé to Largo do Pelourinho. It was from here that the conversion of the Brazilian Indians was organized, and one of the many Jesuit priests who passed through its gates was Antônio Vieira, whose impassioned sermons defending Indian rights against the demands of the Portuguese slavers are generally regarded as the finest early prose in the Portuguese language. After the Jesuits were expelled in 1759, the vultures moved in. Most of the college was demolished by the rich for building material for their mansions, part of the site was used to found a university, and the rest parcelled out and sold for redevelopment.

The churches of São Francisco

Terreiro de Jesus has more than its fair share of churches; there are two more fine sixteenth-century examples on the square itself. But outshining them both, on nearby **Largo do Cruzeiro de São Francisco** (an extension of Terreiro de Jesus sometimes known as Praça Anchieta), are the superb carved stone façades of two ornate Baroque buildings in a single, large complex dedicated to St Francis: the **Igreja de São Francisco** and the **Igreja da Ordem Terceira de São Francisco**. Of the two the Igreja da Ordem Terceira has the edge: it's covered with a wild profusion of saints, virgins, angels and abstract patterns. Remarkably, the facade was hidden for 150 years, until in 1936 a painter knocked off a chunk of plaster by mistake and revealed the original frontage. It took nine years of careful chipping before the facade was returned to its original glory. The whole church is a strong contender for the most beautiful single building in the city.

The **reliquary**, or *ossuário*, here is extraordinary, the entire room redecorated in the 1940s in Art Deco style, one of the most unusual examples you're ever likely to come across. From here, there's a door into a pleasant garden at the back.

To get into the centre of the complex, you have to go via the Igreja de São Francisco (the entrance is by a door to the right of the main doors). The small cloister here is decorated with possibly the finest single piece of *azulejo* work in Brazil. Running the entire length of the cloister, this **tiled wall** tells the story of the marriage of the son of the king of Portugal to an Austrian princess; beginning with the panel to the right of the church entrance, which shows the princess being ferried ashore to the reception committee, it continues with the procession of the happy couple in carriages through Lisbon, passing under a series of commemorative arches set up by the city guilds, whose names you can still just read – "The Royal Company of Bakers", "The Worshipful Company of Sweetmakers". The vigour and realism of the incidental detail in the street scenes is remarkable: beggars and cripples display their wounds, dogs skulk, children play in the gutter; while the panoramic view of Lisbon it displays is an important historical record of how Lisbon looked before the calamitous earthquake of 1755.

Around Largo do Pelourinho

Heading down the narrow Rua Alfredo de Brito, next to the Museu Afro-Brasileiro, brings you to the beautiful, cobbled **Largo do Pelourinho**, still much as it was during the eighteenth century. Lined with solid colonial mansions, it's topped by the oriental-looking towers of the **Igreja da Nossa Senhora dos Pretos**, built by and for slaves and still with a largely black congregation. Across from here is the **Casa Jorge Amado** (Mon noon–6pm, Tues–Sat 9am–6pm), a museum given over to the life and work of the hugely popular novelist, who doesn't number modesty among his virtues; you can have fun spotting his rich and famous friends in the collection of photographs.

Next door, on the corner of Rua Gregório de Mattos, is the **Museu da Cidade** (Mon–Fri 10am–6pm, Sat & Sun 1–5pm). The lower levels are given over to paintings and sculpture by young city artists, some startlingly good and some pretty dire, while luxuriously dressed dummies show off *Carnaval* costumes from years gone by. There are models of *candomblé* deities and, on the first floor, a room containing the personal belongings of the greatest Bahian poet, Castro Alves, with some fascinating photographs from the turn of the century. Completing the constellation of museums around Pelourinho is the **Museu Abelardo Rodrigues** (Mon–Fri 9am–6pm, Sat 1–5pm, Sun 9am–2pm) at Rua Gregório de Mattos 45, a good collection of Catholic art from the sixteenth century onwards, well displayed in a restored seventeenth-century mansion.

From Largo do Pelourinho, a steep climb up Ladeira do Carmo rewards you with two more exceptional monuments of colonial architecture: on the left as you look at them is the **Convento da Ordem Primeira do Carmo** (Mon–Sat 9am–noon & 2–6pm), and on the right is the **Igreja da Ordem Terceira do Carmo** (Mon–Sat 9am–6pm). Both

ACM AND THE RESTORATION OF PELOURINHO

The Pelourinho district is now an attractive and much-visited area, but it wasn't always thus. As recently as 1991 the area was virtually derelict, with many of the colonial buildings falling to pieces and tourism in decline. The fact that this has changed owes much to Bahia's most famous and most controversial politician, **Antônio Carlos Magalhães**. Widely disliked elsewhere in Brazil as an unreconstructed representative of the country's landed elite, the silver-haired **ACM** (as he's known) is popular in Bahia because of his tireless campaigns on behalf of his home state, and you'll see his picture hanging up in many of the city's bars. The revival of Pelourinho which he undertook as state governor was certainly impressive. Although there's a lot still to be done, much of the stunning colonial architecture has been restored to its original glory, the pastel pinks and blues creating a wonderfully gaudy effect. But the restoration has its critics too. They point to the fact that many local residents have had to be moved out in order for the work to take place, and complain that the area has become too dominated by tourism. There is some truth to this, but you can still see plenty of locals out enjoying themselves alongside the tourists, and the economy of the area is clearly thriving; on the whole, it's hard to argue that Pelourinho was better off as a decaying shadow of its former self.

are built around large and beautiful cloisters, with a fine view across the old city at the back, and have chaotic but interesting museums attached. The convent museum is very eclectic, mostly religious but including collections of coins and furniture, with hundreds of unlabelled exhibits jumbled together in gloomy rooms. The highlight is a superbly expressive statue of Christ at the whipping post by Salvador's greatest colonial artist, the half-Indian slave **Francisco Manuel das Chagas**, whose powerful religious sculpture broke the formalistic bonds of the period – most of Chagas' work was completed in the 1720s. Unfortunately, Chagas died young of tuberculosis, leaving only a small body of work; this statue is appallingly displayed, jumbled together with much inferior work in a glass case in a corner of the rear gallery. In the church museum next door is another Chagas statue, a lifesize body of Christ, this time sensibly displayed alone and, if anything, even more powerful. If you look closely at both statues, you'll find that the drops of blood are small rubies inlaid in the wood.

The rest of Cidade Alta is still largely colonial, and fascinating to wander around – although do it in daylight if you want to get off the main streets, and try to stick to where there are people around. Good streets to try are **Rua Gregório de Mattos** and the road on from the Carmo museums, **Rua Joaquim Távora**, which leads away from the heavier concentrations of tourists to the quiet Largo Cruz Pascoa and eventually ends up at the fort of **Santo Antônio Além do Carmo**, with a spectacular view across the bay. The only difficulty is finding a **bar** perched on the edge of the bluff with a view across the bay, to rest your legs and watch the spectacular sunsets. The best spots are the Praça da Sé itself, the bar of the *Hotel do Pelourinho*, open to non-residents, an unnamed bar on the left just after Largo Cruz Pascoa, and the simple places on Largo Santo Antônio, in front of the fort.

The Museu da Arte Sacra

Despite the concentration of riches in Cidade Alta, you have to leave the old city to find one of the finest museums of Catholic art in Brazil: the **Museu da Arte Sacra** at Rua Sodré 276 (Mon–Fri 12.30–5.30pm). It's slightly difficult to find: if you're coming into Praça Castro Alves from Rua Chile, go straight ahead and up Rua Carlos Gomes. Then take the first turning on your right down the steep Ladeira de Santa Teresa and you'll see the museum in front of you. It's housed in a seventeenth-century convent, a magnificent building with much of its original furniture and fittings still intact, and with galleries on three floors surrounding a cloister. The chapel on the ground floor is lavishly decorated with elaborate, gilded carvings, and it leads into a maze of small galleries stuffed with a remarkably rich collection of colonial art, dating from the sixteenth century. The hundreds of statues, icons, paintings and religious artefacts are enough to occupy you for hours, the only real gap in the collection being the absence of anything by Chagas or by Aleijadinho. There's still some high-quality work, though: small soapstone carvings on the top floor, marvellous tiling in the sacristy behind the chapel and a display of ornately carved religious accessories in solid gold and silver.

Cidade Baixa

Cidade Baixa, the part of the city at the foot of the bluff, takes in the docks, the old harbour dominated by the circular sixteenth-century **Forte do Mar**, the ferry terminals and the main city markets. For the most part it's ugly modern urban sprawl, but for once the developers can't be blamed: the area was always the ugliest part of the city because its low-lying situation deprived it of the sea breezes and cooler air of the higher ground above – William Scully found it "close, swampy, filthy and dilapidated". Since the sixteenth century, the city's inhabitants have only ventured down into the Cidade Baixa to work, choosing to live in the much pleasanter areas above and around.

All the same, it's not completely without interest. You are likely at least to pass through to get to the **ferry terminals**, the municipal one at the far end of the docks for services to towns on the other side of the bay, and the **Terminal Turístico**, in the old harbour, for excursions to Itaparica (see p.256). And there is one essential stop: the old covered market called **Mercado Modelo**. This is the large building set on its own by the old harbour, across the road from the foot of the Lacerda elevator. It houses a huge and very enjoyable arts and crafts market, always crowded with Bahians as well as tourists, with the best selection of *artesanato* in the city. Not everything is cheap, so it helps to have the confidence to haggle. Some of the nicest souvenirs are the painted statues of *candomblé* deities – look for signs saying *artigos religiosos* – and if nothing here takes your fancy, there is also a store on Praça de Sé. Even if you don't buy anything the building is a joy, a spacious nineteenth-century cathedral to commerce. There is always something going on in and around the market; displays of *capoeira* are common, and there is an **information post** to the left of the front entrance. Upstairs you will find a couple of good **restaurants**, *Maria de São Pedro* and *Camafeu de Oxóssi*, looking out across the harbour.

The Igreja do Bonfim

If the Museu da Arte Sacra is the finest expression of high Catholic devotion, then the Igreja do Bonfim, as everyone calls the **Igreja do Nosso Senhor do Bonfim** (Tues–Sun 6am–noon & 2–6pm), in the western suburbs, is the centre of popular worship, focal point of colourful religious festivals which attract thousands of devotees from all over Brazil. To get there, take the buses marked "Bonfim" or "Ribeira" from the Estação da Lapa, or the bottom of the Lacerda elevator.

The church is not, by any means, the oldest or most beautiful in the city – completed in 1745 with a plain white exterior and simple interior – but it's easily the most interesting. The force of popular devotion is obvious from the moment you leave the bus. The large square in front of the church is lined with stalls catering for the hundreds of pilgrims who arrive every day, and you'll be besieged by small children selling *fitas*, ribbons in white and blue, the church colours, to tie around your wrist for luck and to hang in the church when you make your requests; it's ungracious to enter the church without a few. It's always at least half-full of people worshipping, often with almost hypnotic fervour: middle-class matrons and uniformed military officers rub shoulders with peasants from the *sertão* and women from the *favelas*.

For a clearer idea of what this place means to the people of Bahia, go to the right of the nave where a wide corridor leads to the **Museu dos Ex-Votos do Senhor do Bonfim** (Tues–Sat 8.30–11.30am & 2.30–7pm, Sun 8.30–11.30am). The *ex votos* here are offered by people to remind Jesus of who they are and what they want Him to do for them, or as a gesture of thanks and a commemoration of His power, something called *pagando a promessa*, paying the promise. An incredibly crowded antechamber gives you an idea of what to expect: lined to the roof with thousands of small photographs of supplicants, with notes pinned to the wall requesting intervention or giving thanks for benefits received. Every spare inch is covered with a forest of ribbons, one for each request, some almost rotted away with age, and many of the written pleas are heart-rending: for the life of a dying child, for news from a husband who emigrated south, for the safe return of sailors and fishermen, for success in an exam, for money to pay for a college education, for a favourite football team to win a championship – in short, a snapshot of popular worries and hopes. Hanging from the roof are dozens of body parts – limbs, heads, even organs like hearts and lungs – made of wood or plastic for anxious patients asking for protection before an operation, silver for relieved patients giving thanks after successful surgery. Some people blessed by a particularly spectacular escape pay tribute by leaving a pictorial record of the miracle: photos of smashed cars which the driver walked away from, or crude but vivid paintings of fires, sinkings and electrocutions.

Upstairs in the museum proper is the oldest material and recent offerings judged worthy of special display. It's not only the poor who come asking for help: there are several university classbooks deposited here, and military insignia commemorating promotion up to the rank of general. The more valuable *ex votos* are displayed here in ranks of cases, classified according to part of the body: silver heads and limbs you might expect, even silver hearts, lungs, ears, eyes and noses, but the serried ranks of silver kidneys, spleens, livers and intestines are novel. There are football shirts – the city's two big teams always make a visit at the start of the season – models of the church, and dozens of paintings, especially of fires and shipwrecks. Other paintings are vivid to the point of gruesomeness: people falling from horses, lying sweating with cholera or displaying bullet wounds.

Eating, drinking and nightlife

Eating out is one of the major pleasures Salvador has to offer, and the local cuisine (*comida baiana*) is deservedly famous. There's a huge range of restaurants, and although Cidade Alta has an increasing number of stylish, expensive places, it's still quite possible to eat well for less than $10. You should certainly treat yourself to at least one slap-up feed before leaving the city.

Restaurants
The cheapest places for a sit-down meal are around **Praça Castro Alves** and in **Cidade Baixa**. Restaurants in the **Pelourinho** area and the **beach districts** are classier and tend to be more expensive, though this isn't a hard-and-fast rule.

The best place for **beginners** is undoubtedly the *Restaurante do SENAC* (closed Sun), a municipal restaurant school in a finely restored colonial mansion on Largo do Pelourinho, opposite the Casa Jorge Amado. It looks very expensive from the outside, but it's good value for what you get. You pay a set charge – about $17 – and take as much as you want from a quality buffet of around fifty dishes, all helpfully labelled so that you know what you're eating. Off-season it can be a strange place to eat, as the large numbers of waiters stand lining the walls of the enormous dining rooms, outnumbering customers five or ten to one. If you go for dinner (served Thurs–Sat), try to finish before 10pm, when there's a rather touristy folklore show.

Once you've identified and sampled the dishes at *SENAC*, you can tackle the menus at other restaurants with more confidence. Two excellent, unnamed restaurants are

COMIDA BAIANA: DISHES AND INGREDIENTS

The secret of Bahian cooking is twofold: a rich seafood base, and the abundance of traditional West African **ingredients** like palm oil, nuts, coconut and ferociously strong peppers. Many ingredients and **dishes** have African names: most famous of all is *vatapá*, a bright yellow porridge of palm oil, coconut, shrimp and garlic, which looks vaguely unappetizing but is delicious. Other dishes to look out for are *moqueca*, seafood cooked in the inevitable palm-oil based sauce; *caruru*, with many of the same ingredients as *vatapá* but with the vital addition of loads of okra; and *acarajé*, deep-fried bean cake stuffed with *vatapá*, salad and (optional) hot pepper, available on many street corners from the *baianas*, women in traditional white dress. Bahian cuisine also has good **desserts**, less stickily sweet than elsewhere: *quindim* is a delicious small cake of coconut flavoured with vanilla, which often comes with a prune in the middle.

Some of the best food is also the cheapest, and even gourmets could do a lot worse than start with the street-corner *baianas*, thick on the ground near bus stops and office buildings. Be careful of the *pimenta*, the very hot pepper sauce, which newcomers should treat with respect, taking only a few drops. The *baianas* also serve *quindim*, *vatapá*, slabs of maize pudding wrapped in banana leaves, fried bananas dusted with icing sugar, and fried sticks of sweet batter covered with sugar and cinnamon; all absolutely wonderful.

side by side on **Rua Ruy Barbosa**, off Praça Castro Alves and just next to the *Pousada da Praça Hotel*. Both serve marvellous Bahian food at extremely moderate prices. Back in the **Pelourinho** area there are any number of very good places where the atmosphere is almost as much worth savouring as the food. The *Aquárius Restaurant*, at Rua Ribeiro Santos 37, is inexpensive, does good *carne do sol* and has a lovely view over the old city, while there's excellent African food at *Casa do Benin*, Padre Agustinho Gomes 17, at the bottom of Largo do Pelourinho. A very popular restaurant which specializes in Northeastern food from both the coast and the interior is *Uauá*, at Rua Gregório de Mattos 36. More expensive but highly recommended are *Restaurante Encontro dos Artistas*, Rua das Laranjeiras 15, and *Maria Mata Mouro*, Rua Inácio Acciole 8. Finally, if you want maximum indulgence for both your eyes and your tastebuds, try *Restaurante Contos dos Réis*, at Rua do Carmo 66, beyond Pelourinho and on the way to the fort of Santo Antônio Além do Carmo. It's by no means cheap but the setting – with the whole of the Bahia de Todos os Santos spread out beneath you – is breathtaking.

There are two more good Bahian restaurants next to each other, on the first floor of the Mercado Modelo in **Cidade Baixa**, the *Maria de São Pedro* (Mon–Sat 11am–6pm, Sun 11am–3pm) and the *Camafeu de Oxóssi* (daily 11am–8pm), with little to choose between them and both with great views across the bay if you can get a table on the terrace. Further along the coast, on the seafront Avenida do Contorno that heads left from the harbour, is the *Solar do Unhão*, which has a marvellous setting in the old slave quarters of a seventeenth-century mansion but doles out overpriced and mediocre food; go and return by taxi, as the area is dangerous even by day.

The other main area for eating out is at **the beaches** to the south. Especially at Barra and Rio Vermelho, the seafront promenade is lined with bars, cafés and restaurants, and the best option is to take a bus and hop off wherever you fancy. The non-Brazilian cuisines tend to be concentrated in **Barra**, where Salvador's upper middle class lives: there's a good Chinese restaurant, *Yan Ping*, at Rua Marquês de Leâo 253; an excellent Japanese restaurant, *Sukiyaki*, Av. Oceânica 3562, near to the Ondina seafront; and an Arabic place, the *Matbah*, at Rua Barão de Sergy 14 – getting a taxi from the Barra seafront is the easiest way to get there, as the road is a little obscure. In **Pituba**, there are restaurants that specialize in Bahian cuisine, including the highly recommended *Yemanjá*, at Av. Otávio Mangabeira 9292 (☎231-5770); it's a far better bet than the large, overpriced restaurants at the far end of Pituba.

Nightlife

Salvador's most distinctive **nightlife** is to be found in **Pelourinho**. The whole area is always very lively, and there are any number of bars where you can sit and while the evening away. However, undoubtedly the biggest attraction of the area is the chance to hear **live music**. The best way to do this is to attend the rehearsals of the *Carnaval blocos*, which take place throughout the year, and with special frequency in the couple of months leading up to *Carnaval*. The most famous are Oludum: they rehearse on Sunday nights from 6.30pm onwards in the Largo do Pelourinho itself and on Tuesdays from 7.30pm in the *Teatro Miguel Santana* on Rua Gregório Mattos. On Friday night, it's the turn of Ara Ketu, who start their show at 7pm in Rua Chile, and Ilê Aiyê rehearse on Saturdays from 8pm near the fort of Santo Antônio Além do Carmo. These rehearsals get very crowded so be careful with your belongings.

However, you may eventually find it a bit claustrophobic in Cidade Alta, in which case the thing to do is head for the **beaches**, where there are far more nightclubs. For **dancing** into the small hours, Amaralina and Pituba are probably the liveliest areas to head for, and Friday and Saturday nights are best. Bars, too, often have **live music**, with listings given in the local papers at weekends; try the Sunday edition of *A Tarde*. As far as specific places go, *Travessia* at Av. Otávio Mangabeira 168 in Pituba (open 24hr Fri–Sun only) gets crowded and lively; and there's often good music, too, at *Canteiros*, Rua Minas Gerais in Pituba, starting after 9pm on Friday and Saturday.

CAPOEIRA AND CANDOMBLÉ

Music and food are areas where the African influence in Salvador is very clear, but less well known to visitors are **capoeira**, which began in Angola as a ritual fight to gain the nuptial rights of women when they reached puberty, and has evolved into a graceful semi-balletic art form somewhere between fighting and dancing; and **candomblé**, the Afro-Brazilian religious cult that permeates the city.

CAPOEIRA

Capoeira is not difficult to find in Salvador. It's usually accompanied by the characteristic rhythmic twang of the *berimbau*, and takes the form of a pair of dancers/fighters leaping and whirling in stylized "combat" – which, with younger *capoeiristas*, occasionally slips into a genuine fight when blows land by accident and the participants lose their temper. There are regular displays, largely for the benefit of tourists but interesting nevertheless, on Terreiro de Jesus and near the entrances to the Mercado Modelo in Cidade Baixa, where contributions from onlookers are expected. But the best *capoeira* is in the **academias de capoeira**, organized schools which have classes that anyone can watch free of charge. All ages take part, many of the children astonishingly nimble: although most *capoeiristas* are male, some girls and women take it up as well. The first and most famous *academia* is still the best, the Associação de Capoeira Mestre Bimba, named after the man who popularized *capoeira* in the city from the 1920s; it's on the first floor of Rua das Laranjeiras 1, Terreiro de Jesus, and may have classes open to tourists. Other schools are at the other end of Cidade Alta, at the Forte de Santo Antônio Além do Carmo: the Grupo de Capoeira Pelourinho, with classes on Tuesday, Thursday and Saturday from 7pm to 10pm; and the Centro Esportivo de Capoeira Angola, open all day to 10.30pm on weekdays, though you have to turn up to find out when the next class is – late afternoon is a good time, as afternoon and evening sessions are generally better attended.

CANDOMBLÉ

Candomblé is a little more difficult to track down. Many travel agencies offer tours of the city that include a visit to a *terreiro*, or cult house, but no self-respecting *terreiro*

There is also a lively **gay scene**; *Holmes 24th*, on Rua Gamboa de Cima, opposite the Rua Banco dos Ingleses, near Campo Grande (safer by taxi), is particularly frequented by transvestites.

Salvador's festivals

The two main **popular festivals** of the year, besides *Carnaval*, take place either in or near the Igreja do Bonfim. On New Year's Day is the **Procissão no Mar**, the "Sea Procession", when the statues of the seafarers' protectors, *Nosso Senhor dos Navegantes* and *Nossa Senhora da Conceição*, are carried in a decorated nineteenth-century boat across the bay from the old harbour to the church of Boa Viagem, on the shore down from Bonfim. The boat leaves at around 9am from Praça Cairú, next to the Mercado Modelo in Cidade Baixa, and hundreds of schooners and fishing boats wait to join the procession as the statues boat passes: you can buy a place on the phalanx of boats that leaves with the statues, but the crowds are thick and if you want to go by sea you should get there early. On the shores of Boa Viagem, thousands wait to greet the holy images, there's a packed Mass in the church, and then *Nossa Senhora da Conçeicão* is taken back by land in another procession to her church near the foot of the Lacerda elevator. The celebrations around both churches go on long into the night, with thousands drinking and dancing the night away.

would allow itself to be used in this way – those which do are to be avoided. The best alternative is to go to the main Bahiatursa office, behind the Belvedere market on Praça da Sé, which has a list of less commercialized *terreiros*, all fairly far out in the suburbs and best got to by taxi. Make sure that the *terreiro* is open first: they only have ceremonies on certain days sacred to one of the pantheon of gods and goddesses, and you just have to hope you strike lucky – though fortunately there's no shortage of deities.

Each *terreiro* is headed by a *mãe do santo* (woman) or *pai do santo* (man), who directs the operations of dozens of novices and initiates. The usual object is to persuade the spirits to descend into the bodies of worshippers, which is done by sacrifices (animals are killed outside public view and usually during the day), offerings of food and drink, and above all by drumming, dancing and the invocations of the *mãe* or *pai do santo*. There's a central dance area, which may be decorated, where devotees dance for hours to induce the trance that allows the spirits to enter them. A possession can be quite frightening: sometimes people whoop and shudder, their eyes roll up, and they whirl around the floor, bouncing off the walls while other cult members try to make sure they come to no harm. The *mãe* or *pai do santo* then calms them, blows tobacco smoke over them, identifies the spirit, gives them the insignia of the deity – a pipe or a candle, for example – and lets them dance on. Each deity has its own songs, animals, colours, qualities, powers and holy day; and there are different types of *candomblé*, as well as other related Afro-Brazilian religions like *umbanda*.

If you go to a *terreiro*, there are certain **rules** you must observe. A *terreiro* should be respected and treated for the church it is. Clothes should be smart and modest: long trousers and a clean shirt for men, non-revealing blouse and trousers or long skirt for women. The dancing area is sacred space and no matter how infectious you find the rhythms you should do no more than stand or sit around its edges. And don't take photographs without asking permission from the *mãe* or *pai do santo* first, or you will give offence. You may find people coming round offering drinks from jars, or items of food: it's impolite to refuse, but watch what everyone else does first – sometimes food is not for eating but for throwing over dancers, and the story of the gringos who ate their popcorn is guaranteed to bring a smile to any Brazilian face.

The spectacle, with the bay as an enormous backdrop, is impressive enough: participating in it is exhilarating.

Soon afterwards, on the second Thursday of January, comes the **Lavagem do Bonfim**, second only to *Carnaval* in scale; it means "the washing of Bonfim". Hundreds of *baianas*, women in the traditional all-white costume of turban, lace blouse and billowing long skirts, gather in front of the Igreja de Nossa Senhora da Conceição, and a procession follows them the 12km along the seafront to the Igreja do Bonfim, with tens of thousands more lining the route: the pace is slow, and there is no shortage of beer and music while you wait. At the church, everyone sets to scrubbing the square spotless, cleaning the church and decorating the exterior with flowers and strings of coloured lights, and that evening, and every evening until Sunday, raucous celebrations go on into the small hours, the square crowded with people. If you have the stamina, the focus switches on Monday to Ribeira, the headland beyond Bonfim, for a completely secular preview of *Carnaval*. Here you can freshen up after dancing in the hot sun by swimming at the excellent beaches.

Music and Carnaval

Musically, Salvador marches to a different beat from the rest of Brazil. Instead of being connected to a single style, as Rio is to samba and Recife is to *frevo*, Salvador has spawned several, and in recent years it has overtaken Rio to become the most creative centre of Brazilian music. A good example of this was the way the city absorbed and transformed reggae during the 1980s, so that by the end of the decade a new Bahian sound, exemplified by groups like *Reflexus*, dominated *Carnaval* processions throughout Brazil.

Some of the best music in the city comes from organized **cultural groups**, who work in the communities that spawned them, have clubhouses and a *bloco* or two for *Carnaval*. They are overwhelmingly black and a lot of their music is political. Two of the best are the Grupo Cultural Olodum, who have a house on Largo do Pelourinho, and Ara Ketu. In the weeks leading up to *Carnaval*, their *blocos* have public rehearsals around the clubhouses, and the music is superb (see also "Nightlife" above). For the rest of the year, the clubhouses are used as bars and meeting places, often with music at weekends.

Having steadfastly resisted commercialization, **Carnaval** in Salvador has remained a street event of mass participation. The throbbing heart is Cidade Alta, especially the area around Praça Castro Alves, which turns into a seething mass of people that once joined is almost impossible to get out of – not for the claustrophobic, but hugely enjoyable. You're more or less stuck with whatever you get swept up behind, which might be a sound system, a *trio elétrico* on a specially built lorry with banks of speakers on all sides, or an *afoxé*, Salvador's Africanized version of a *bloco*, hundreds strong.

From December onwards *Carnaval* groups hold public rehearsals and dances all over the city. Good spots are the Igreja da Nossa Senhora da Conceição near the foot of the Lacerda elevator, Terreiro de Jesus, Largo do Pelourinho and the area around the fort of Santo Antônio Além do Carmo. One of the oldest and best loved of the *afoxés* is Filhos de Gandhi ("Sons of Gandhi"), founded in the 1940s, who have a clubhouse in Rua Gregório de Matos, near Largo do Pelourinho, easily recognized by the large papier-mâché white elephant in the hall. Their rehearsals attract the whole Pelourinho area to join in. The other focal point of *Carnaval* is the northern beaches, especially around the hotels in Rio Vermelho and Ondina, but here it's more touristy and lacks the energy of the centre.

Information about Carnaval is published in special supplements in the local papers on Thursday and Saturday. Bahiatursa and EMTURSA offices also have schedules, route maps, and sometimes sell tickets for the Campo Grande grandstands. One point worth bearing in mind is that all-black *blocos* may be black culture groups who won't appreciate being joined by non-black Brazilians, let alone gringos, so look to see who's dancing before leaping in amongst them.

Listings

Airlines Air France, Rua Portugal 17, Ed. Regente Feijó, Cidade Baixa (☎242-4955); Lufthansa, Rua Miguel Calmon 555, Ed. Citibank, Cidade Baixa (☎241-5100); TAP Air Portugal, Av. Estados Unidos 137, Ed. Cidade de Ilhéus, Cidade Baixa (☎243-6122); Transbrasil, Rua Portugal 3, Cidade Baixa (☎326-1044); Varig Cruzeiro, Rua Carlos Gomes 6, Cidade Alta (☎322-1611), or Rua Miguel Calmon 19, Cidade Baixa (☎243-9311); VASP, Rua Chile 27, Edifício Chile, Cidade Alta (☎243-7277), Rua Miguel Calmon 27, Cidade Baixa, or Rua Marquês de Leão 455, Barra.

Banks and exchange There are now several places where you can change money in the Pelourinho area, including Olímpio Turismo on Largo do Cruzeiro de São Francisco and Vert-Tour on Rua das Laranjeiras. You'll get lower, but still reasonable, rates for dollars cash and travellers' cheques at the smarter beach hotels in Ondina and Pituba. On no account change on the street, especially around the Lacerda elevator: your wad will be snatched as soon as you get it out. Banco do Brasil has branches at Av. Sete de Setembro 254 in Cidade Alta and at Av. Estados Unidos 561 in Cidade Baixa.

Car rental Avis Rentacar is at Av. Sete de Setembro 1796 (☎237-0154), and Nobre Rent a Car is at Av. Oceânica 409 (☎245-8022).

Consulates UK, Av. Estados Unidos 4, Room 1109, Cidade Baixa (Mon–Thurs 9–11am & 2–4pm, Fri 9–11am; ☎243-9222); USA, Avenida Antônio Carlos Magalhães, Ed. Cidadella Center, Room 410 (Mon–Fri 9–11am & 2.30–4.30pm; ☎358-9166).

Football Salvador has a couple of good teams. The most popular, Bahia, have a tradition of playing open, attacking football in the best Brazilian tradition. The biggest matches take place on Sunday afternoons in the Estádio Octávio Mangabeira, close to the centre; take the bus marked "Nazaré" from Campo Grande, or it's a short taxi ride.

Laundry Lavanderia Lavalimpo, Rua do Pilar 31, Cidade Baixa; Lav–Lev, Av. Manoel Dias da Silva 2364, Pituba.

Post office At the airport; Marquês de Caravelas 101, Barra; Av. Amaralina 908, Amaralina; Rua J. Seabra 234; the *Rodoviária*; Rua Ruy Barbosa 19, Cidade Alta; and at the Praça da Inglaterra, Cidade Baixa. Opening hours are Mon–Fri 8am–6pm.

Shopping The main place for *artesanato* is the Mercado Modelo in Cidade Baixa (see p.249). Good, cheap leatherwork from the street stalls of Barroquinha, the steep street leading downhill just before Praça Castro Alves; and clothes and shoes in the commercial area further down, too.

Taxis Chame Táxi (☎241-2266); Teletáxi (☎321-9988).

Telephones You can make international collect calls from a booth on Terreiro de Jesus; other *postos telefônicos* are in the airport, the *Rodoviária*, in Campo da Pólvora in Cidade Alta, and in the Iguatemi shopping centre.

Theatres Big names in Brazilian music play the Teatro Castro Alves on Campo Grande. The SENAC building on Largo do Pelourinho has an outdoor arena and basement theatre, used for plays, concerts and displays. Also scan posters and local papers (under *Lazer*), or ask at the tourist office.

Around Salvador

Salvador looks onto a bay, the **Bahia de Todos os Santos**, ringed with beaches and dotted with tropical **islands**. To the **northeast** of the city a string of fishing villages lies along a beautiful coastline – in short, no lack of places to explore.

Northeast to Arembepe

Buses from Salvador's *Rodoviária* run along the coastal road to **AREMBEPE**, 50km away, a former hippy hangout now gone up in the world, though still peaceful and very pretty. The journey there takes you through some fine beaches and small, friendly villages, and you can get off wherever takes your fancy. **Accommodation** is easy everywhere along this route, from chic *pousadas* to simple *pensões*, as you're heading along a well-beaten tourist track. Don't be put off, though – it's a beautiful coastline and the beaches are long enough to swallow the crowds.

The bay: Ilha de Itaparica

Itaparica is always visible from Salvador, looking as if it forms the other side of the bay, but in reality it's a narrow island, 35km long, that acts as a natural breakwater. After the local Indians were driven out, it was taken over by the Jesuits in 1560, making it one of the earliest places to be settled by the Portuguese. Its main town, also called **ITAPARICA**, was briefly the capital of Bahia before the Portuguese were expelled from Salvador, though little evidence remains here of these times, apart from a couple of small seventeenth-century chapels. The lovely island is now very much seen as an appendage of the city, whose inhabitants flock to its beaches at weekends, building villas by the score as they go. It's quiet enough during the week, though, and big enough to find calmer spots even at the busiest times. Apart from the beaches, Itaparica is famous for its fruit trees, especially its mangoes, which are prized throughout Bahia.

Most **ferries** (see p.244) leave you at the **Bom Despacho** terminal in Itaparica town, although some smaller boats also go to the anchorage at **Mar Grande**, a couple of kilometres away. For **getting around** once you're there, use the Kombis and buses which ply the coastline, or rent **bicycles** (the places easily spotted by the bikes piled up on the pavement). If you want to stay on the island, there are some reasonable **hotels**, but most are on the expensive side thanks to Itaparica's popularity as a resort for Salvador's middle classes. Cheaper ones are often full from December to *Carnaval*; if you're on a budget, try the **campsite** and **youth hostel** in Itaparica town. Good hotels on the island include *Club Mediterranée*, Estr. Praia da Conceição (☎071/880-7141; ⑦), a luxurious hotel set directly on the beachfront; *Pousada Jardim Tropical*, Estr. da Rodagem, Praia Ponta de Areia 3.5km (☎071/831-1409; ④), with a pool and a reasonable restaurant; and *Recanto do Guiga*, Praia da Barra do Pote (☎071/880-7268; ③), a small *pousada* on the seafront near a fishing village.

To see anything of the **other islands** scattered across the bay – 31 of them, most either uninhabited or home to a few simple fishing villages – travel agents in Salvador offer daylong cruises in private schooners; the kiosks in the city's Terminal Turístico are the easiest places to buy tickets. It's less busy during the week, but crowded schooners have their advantages. If you manage to get on one full of Brazilian trippers you're likely to have a very lively time indeed, and drinks are often included in the price.

The Recôncavo and Valença

The **Recôncavo** proper, the early Portuguese plantation zone named after the concave shape of the bay, arcs out from Salvador along 150km of coastline, before petering out in the mangrove swamps around the town of **Valença**. It's one of the most lush tropical coastlines in Brazil, with palm-covered hills breaking up the green and fertile coastal plains. And it's still one of the most important agricultural areas in Bahia, supplying the state with much of its fruit and spices. Only the sugar plantations around Recife could match the wealth of the Recôncavo, but, unlike Pernambuco, the Recôncavo survived the decline of the sugar trade by diversifying into tobacco and spices – especially peppers and cloves. It was the agricultural wealth of the Recôncavo which paid for most of the fine buildings of Salvador and, until the cocoa boom in southern Bahia in the 1920s, **Cachoeira** was by some way the second city of the state. The beauty of the area and the richness of its colonial heritage make it one of the more rewarding parts of the Northeast to explore.

Access is good as there's a main highway, the BR-324, which approximately follows the curve of the bay, with good local roads branching off to the towns in the heart of the Recôncavo. Thirty kilometres out of Salvador, a turn-off leads to Candéias, continuing on to Santo Amaro and the twin towns of Cachoeira and São Félix. Regular **buses** go to all these places from the *Rodoviária* in Salvador.

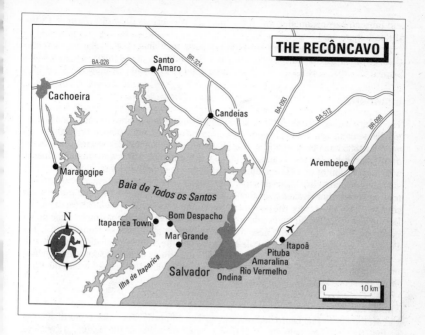

Candéias and Santo Amaro

CANDÉIAS is nowhere special, a modern market town 30km from Salvador, but 7km outside there's a good introduction to the history of the area in the **Museu do Recôncavo** (Tues, Thurs & Sun 9am–5pm), situated in a restored plantation called the Engenho da Freguesia. It's much like the plantation museums in Pernambuco and elsewhere, with pictures and artefacts from three centuries illustrating the economic and social dimensions of plantation life. But here, the owners' mansion and the slave quarters have been impressively restored, juxtaposing the horrors of slave life – there's a fearsome array of manacles, whips and iron collars – with the elegant period furniture and fittings of the mansion. The only problem is that no bus service passes the museum: if you don't go by car you have to take a taxi from Candéias, around $17.

SANTO AMARO, 73km from Salvador, is a lovely colonial town straddling the banks of a small river. It was the birthplace and is still the home of **Caetano Veloso**, one of Bahia's most famous singers and poets, who sings Santo Amaro's praises on many of his records. There's no tourist office, and the best thing to do is simply to wander around the quiet streets and squares, absorbing the atmosphere.

If you're arriving on the bus from Salvador, wait till it stops at the *Rodoviária* before getting off, then turn left as you come out of the *Rodoviária* in order to get into the centre. A few minutes' walk will bring you into the main square, the Praça da Purificação, where you'll find one of the town's most attractive sights, the **Igreja da Purificação**: beautifully restored, the church shelters a wonderfully elaborate eighteenth-century painted ceiling. The other building you should definitely see is the tranquil **Convento dos Humildes**, nearby on Praça Frei Bento, which has a museum attached, and plenty of friendly if slightly under-employed guides waiting to show you around. Elsewhere there are various ruined mansions that once belonged to the sugar and tobacco barons, among which the most atmospheric is the **Solar Araújo Pinto**, at Rua Imperador 1.

If you feel like staying, there are a few **pensões**, including the very basic *Pousada do Coronel* on Praça da Purificação (①), and the much better *Amarós*, on Rua Cons. Saraiva 27 (☎075/241-1202; ①), which has a good **restaurant** at the back.

Cachoeira

The twin towns of Cachoeira and São Félix are only a few kilometres apart across the Rio Paraguaçu, which is spanned by an iron box-girder bridge built by British engineers in 1885 and opened by Emperor Dom Pedro himself. **CACHOEIRA** is easily the more impressive of the two, one of the most beautiful colonial towns of the Northeast, with a profusion of fine old buildings as evidence that, in the eighteenth century, this was an important city. The rich sugar plantations of the Paraguaçu valley supported a trading centre that rivalled Salvador in size and wealth until the beginning of the last century. The town was the site of a short but vicious war in 1822 to expel the Portuguese from Bahia, when a docked Portuguese warship was stormed by the inhabitants, the city becoming the first in Brazil to declare allegiance to Dom Pedro I. The Portuguese general, Madeira de Melo, bombarded the town in retaliation, but this only provoked the countryside into general revolt, and troops from Cachoeira led a victorious assault on Salvador. After that began the long decline that turned it into the beautifully preserved small town it is today.

The Town

Get off the bus in Rua Lauro de Freitas at the bus company office; don't wait till it crosses the river into São Félix or you'll have to walk back across the bridge. A couple of blocks back along Rua Lauro de Freitas past the market you'll come to the fine Praça Doutor Milton, with its Baroque public fountain and the early eighteenth-century bulk of the **Santa Casa da Misericórdia**, which has a beautiful small garden. Leaving Praça Doutor Milton in the direction of the river, go up the narrow, cobbled Rua da Ajuda, and after a short climb you'll come to a peaceful little square which contains the **Capela da Nossa Senhora da Ajuda**, the city's oldest church. Begun in 1595 and completed eleven years later, it just about qualifies as sixteenth century, which makes it a rarity. Sadly, the simple but well-proportioned interior is often closed to visitors for fear of thieves, but if you knock on the door there might be someone around to let you in.

If you go straight on down the hill as you come out of the Capela da Nossa Senhora da Ajuda, you'll find yourself in Rua 13 de Mayo. On your right is the **Museu da Irmandade da Boa Morte**, which is connected with the August festival known as Nossa Senhora da Boa Morte (see "Candomblé in Cachoeira" below). Just a few steps in the other direction is a renovated building which houses the small **Museu Hansen Bahia**, dedicated to the work of a German engraver who settled in the town. The first turning on your left out of Rua 13 de Mayo takes you up to Rua Ana Néri and the impressive **Igreja Matriz de Nossa Senhora do Rosário**. Again, the church has been robbed all too frequently and is sometimes shut, but if you can get in, you'll see two huge (five-metre-high) *azulejo* panels dating from the 1750s.

But the biggest treat is yet to come. At the end of Rua Ana Néri, in the opposite direction from Praça Doutor Milton, is the finest and most spacious square in the town, **Praça da Aclamação**. On one side it's lined with civil buildings from the golden age of Cachoeira in the eighteenth century, including the Prefeitura Municipal, the town hall, and the old city chambers. The other side of the square is dominated by the huge bulk of the **Conjunto do Carmo**, built in the eighteenth century and now beautifully restored, in four parts: a church, a museum, a *pousada* and a conference centre. The museum contains rare seventeenth-century furniture and some fine sacred art, including carvings and statues from Macau which bring an unexpectedly Chinese flavour to the collection. The cloister leads to the church, decorated with seventeenth-century tiles and an extravagant Rococo gold-leaf interior.

There's a lively tradition of **woodcarving** in town and several sculptors have studios open to the public. One of the best is **Louco Junior**, who displays his wonderful elongated carvings in his studio on Rua 13 de Mayo.

On the stretch of waterfront nearest the old centre is Praça Teixeira de Freitas, from where you can take a launch out to the Ilha do Farol in the river, and over to **SÃO FÉLIX**. The main reason for going is the great view back across the river, with the colonial facades reflected in the water.

Candomblé in Cachoeira

The other thing Cachoeira is known for is **candomblé**, with some *terreiros* still conducting rituals in African dialects that nobody now speaks, recognizable as variants of West African and Angolan languages. One of the best known *candomblé* events is Cachoeira's fiesta of **Nossa Senhora da Boa Morte**, but its date varies (it always begins on the first Friday before August 15) so ask Bahiatursa in Salvador if in doubt. It's staged by a sisterhood, the Irmandade da Boa Morte, founded by freed women slaves in the mid-nineteenth century, partly as a religious group and partly to work for the emancipation of slaves, by acting as an early co-operative bank to buy people their liberty. All the local *candomblé* groups turn out with drummers and singers, and although the name of the fiesta is Catholic, it's a celebration of *candomblé*, with centre stage held by the dignified matriarchs of the sisterhood. The other great day in the *candomblé* year is the **Festa de Santa Barbara**, on December 4 in São Félix, dedicated not to the saint but to the goddess Iansã. There are several other fiestas worth catching, like the **São João** celebrations, from June 22 to 24, while five saints' days are crammed into the last three months of the year; check with Bahiatursa for exact dates.

Practicalities

Cachoeira has no **Rodoviária**, just an office by the bus stop in Rua Lauro de Freitas. There's a **Bahiatursa** office in Praça da Aclamação, where you can get a map and some basic information. The nicest **place to stay** is the *Pousada do Convento de Cachoeira* (☎075/725-1716; ④) which is part of the Conjunto do Carmo on Praça da Aclamação. Other options include the basic *Hotel Colombo*, at Rua Sete de Setembro 19 (①), the *Hotel Santo Antônio* on Praça Maciel (①), the *Pousada do Guerreiro*, at Rua Treze de Maio 14 (②), and the excellent *Pousada do Pai Thomaz*, at Rua 25 de Junho 12 (③).

Valença and around

After Cachoeira, the coast becomes swampy and by the time you get to **VALENÇA**, five hours by bus from Salvador, you're in mangrove country. Alternatively, you can take the ferry to Nazaré and from there take a bus to Valença, reducing the journey by 150km. Fortunately, though, instead of alligators, the swamps are dominated by shellfish of all kinds, most of them edible. Valença lies on the banks of the Rio Una, about 10km from the sea, at the point where the river widens into a delta made up of dozens of small islands, most of which support at least a couple of fishing villages. At one time it was an industrial centre – the first cotton factory in Brazil was built here – but it has long since reverted to fishing and boatbuilding. It's increasingly popular for trippers from Salvador, but is not yet over-commercialized.

The Town

Valença's **Rodoviária** is right in the centre of town: cross the bridge opposite and you're in the heart of things. There are a couple of colonial churches – the most interesting is the Igreja de Nossa Senhora do Amparo near the market – but Valença is a place for walks, boat trips and lazing on beaches rather than sightseeing. By far the most interesting thing the town has to offer is the **boatyards**, the *estaleiros*, along the waterfront to the left of the bridge as you cross it from the bus station. They build a whole series of wooden boats here, largely by hand, ranging from small fishing smacks to large schooners, and local boatbuilders are renowned throughout the Northeast for their skill. You can easily appreciate their work: boats in various stages of completion, some just a ribbed keel, others ready to be painted, lie under palm or tile shelters with no sides. Provided you don't get in the way – try going around midday, when work stops for a couple of hours – and ask permission, people are pleased to let you take a closer look and often take pride in showing off their work. The plain wooden schooner hulls, with hand-fitted overlapping planks, have beautiful curves that even landlubbers can admire.

Practicalities

Accommodation is easy to find. There are several hotels and *pensões*: the *Hotel Tourist*, Rua Marechal Floriano 167 (②), and the *Guaibim* on Praça da Independência (☎075/741-1110; ③), are friendly and good value, while the *Portal Rio Una* on Rua Maestro Barrinha (☎075/741-2321; ⑤) is a more luxurious option. If you're on a tighter budget, the rented hammock space on Tinharé island costs next to nothing. A good way of getting around is by **bicycle**. They can be rented cheaply all over the place: look out for signs saying *Aluga-se bicicleta*.

The **restaurants** in the town are simple and reasonably priced, and the food is excellent; the combination of fresh seafood and palm oil – Valença is famous for its *dendê* – is definitely special. Try the seafood *rodízio* (where you pay a flat fee and have all you can eat from a succession of dishes) at the *Akuarius*, on Praça da Independência, or the mouthwatering *moqueca* at the *Makulelê*, on Rua Governador Gonçalves, which has the added attraction of live music.

From Valença there are five daily **buses** back to Salvador, or you can continue south to Ilhéus and Porto Seguro.

Around Valença

The town is a good base from which to explore the countryside around, a project best undertaken by **boat**. The obvious place to head for is the island of **Tinharé** and its famous beaches at **MORRO DE SÃO PAULO**. These provided an anchorage for the British admiral Lord Cochrane in 1822: as head of the Brazilian navy, he was instrumental in driving the Portuguese out of Brazil, as he had driven the Spanish a few years before from Peru and Chile, working together with Simón Bolívar. The **beaches** are superb, and the views from the hill, crowned with a simple nineteenth-century church, are breathtaking. At the weekends, especially between December and March, Morro de São Paulo gets unbearably crowded, but it's quite pleasant the rest of the time.

There are several **boats** a day from Valença to Tinharé which cost about $3 and take one-and-a-half hours to get there, or there is a quicker and more expensive launch. In high season there is also a direct boat from Salvador which you can catch from the Terminal Turístico (it's also worth enquiring in low season, as it may operate on certain days then, too). It costs about $30 for a one-way trip and takes about three hours, but the sea can be rough so avoid it if you have problems with sea-sickness. There are a huge number of **places to stay** on the island: good bets include the excellent *Pousada Porto da Cima* (③) in the town of Morro de São Paulo itself, and the *Pousada Farol do Morro* (☎075/783-1036; ③) down on the beach.

On the opposite side of the small island, in a hamlet called **PRAINHA**, is the **Casa da Sogra**, which looks like a bar but is the home of a local poet and sculptor, who has papered the walls with his poems and with decorative painted maps of the region and the road to Rio. There are no hotels here, but if you want **to stay** for a few days of idyllic tranquillity, the locals – mainly fishing families – rent out hammock space: there is little except grilled fish and shellfish to eat, but it's a lifestyle you could easily get used to. At least one boat calls every day when you want to get back to Valença.

The best beaches elsewhere are at **GUAIBIM**, 15km north of Valença, and it seems that half the population of the town piles onto buses heading this way at weekends; the last one back is at 5pm.

Otherwise, the best **walks**, apart from on Tinharé, are just before Valença, where there's a dirt road leading off to the left as you arrive. Three kilometres down you'll find a series of gentle rapids on the Rio Una, the **Cachoeira de Candengo**, where you can cool off by plunging into the natural pools and lying on the rocks with the water flowing around you. There are paths along the riverbank, too, which allow you to explore further.

Inland: the Bahian sertão

The **Bahian sertão** is immense: an area considerably larger than any European country and comprising about a third of the total land area of the Northeast. Much of it is semi-desert, endless expanses of rock and cactus broiling in the sun. But it can be spectacular, with ranges of hills to the north and broken highlands to the west, rearing up into the tableland of the great **Planalto Central**, the plateau that extends over most of the state of Goiás and parts of Minas Gerais. No part of the Bahian *sertão* is thickly populated, and most of it is positively hostile to human habitation: in places, no rain falls for years at a stretch. Its inhabitants suffer more from drought than anywhere else in the Northeast, and in parts of the *sertão* there's still desperate poverty.

Despite its reputation, not all the *sertão* is desert. Winding through it, like an enormous snake, is the **Rio São Francisco**, sprawling out into the huge hydroelectric lake of **Sobradinho**. River and lake support a string of towns, notably Paulo Afonso (see p.236) and Juazeiro (see p.230). Other possible destinations to the north are **Jacobina**, in the midst of spectacular hill country, where gold and emeralds have been mined for nearly three centuries, and **Canudos**, site of a mini-civil war a hundred years ago, and a good place to get a feel for *sertão* life. The other main route into the *sertão* is westwards, along the BR-242, which eventually hits the Belém–Brasília highway in Goiás: possible stop-off points on this route are the old mining town of **Lençois** – one of the most popular spots in the interior for hiking – and the river town of **Ibotirama**.

Feira de Santana

Whether you choose the route north or west, you're likely to pass through **FEIRA DE SANTANA**, 112km from Salvador, which if it weren't for the different landscape would bear a striking resemblance to Caruaru in Pernambuco. Like Caruaru, it styles itself "The Gateway to the *Sertão*" – with some justification – and it, too, supports an enormous market, the **Feira do Couro**, literally "leather market". Leatherwork is the main form of *artesanato* in the *sertão*, as you'd expect from cattle country. The market happens every Monday, taking over the centre of town with thousands of stalls and tens of thousands of customers, and you can find virtually anything. It's the best place to buy leatherwork in the Northeast, with cheap and very high-quality wallets, handbags, satchels, cases and bags of every shape and size, many of them beautifully tooled. You should get there early, as the market starts to wind down after lunchtime, although it does go on all day. **Buses** leave every fifteen minutes from Salvador on market day, every half-hour the rest of the week; the journey takes about two hours.

If you can't make it there on a Monday the permanent **Mercado de Artesanato** in the centre has a wide range of leather goods every day of the week. Apart from the market, though, there's little reason to come, or to stay. The town itself is rather ugly and the countryside around is nothing special; it's best to make a day trip from Salvador.

North: Jacobina

After Feira de Santana, the BR-324 strikes into the interior proper. The scenery is dull for the first couple of hours, but then the road climbs into the highlands of the **Chapada Diamantina**, with rock massifs rising out of the scrub, vaguely reminiscent of the American Southwest. At the small town of Capim Grosso the BR-407 branches off on a 300-kilometre journey north to Juazeiro, but sticking with the BR-324 for another hour brings you to the old mining town of **JACOBINA**. It nestles on the slopes of several hills with panoramic views over the **Serra da Jacobina**, one of the first parts of the *sertão* to be settled in strength by the Portuguese. The clue to what attracted them is the name of one of the two fast-flowing rivers that bisect the town, the Rio de Ouro, "Gold River". **Gold** was first found here in the early seventeenth century, and several *bandeirante* expeditions made the trip north from São Paulo to settle here. Although cattle and farming are now more important, mining still continues: there are emerald mines at nearby Pindobaçu, two large gold mines, and the diamonds which gave the Chapada Diamantina its name. The last big rush was in 1948, but miners still come down from the hills every now and then to sell gold and precious stones to traders in the town – you'll notice that many of them have precision scales on their counters.

The **town** itself is notably friendly – they don't see many tourists and people are curious – while the altitude takes the edge off the temperature most days, which makes it a good place to walk. It's a typical example of an interior town, quiet at night save for the squares and the riverbanks, where the young congregate, especially around the *Zululândia* bar in the centre, while their parents pull chairs into the streets and gossip until the TV soaps start. In all directions, **paths** lead out of the town into the surrounding hills, with spectacular views, but it still gets hot during the day and some of the slopes are steep, so it's best to take some liquid along. The *Hotel Serra do Ouro* runs trips out to the **emerald mines** of Pindobaçu, around 60km to the north, and to the **gold mines** of Canavieiras and Itapicuru, though these are a bit disappointing in some respects: to the untrained eye uncut emeralds look like bits of gravel.

Practicalities

It's about a six-hour ride to Jacobina on the two daily **buses** from Salvador. There's no tourist office, although you might be able to get hold of a pamphlet with a street map from Bahiatursa in Salvador. Still, it's small enough to get by without one. The bus leaves you near the centre, where there are several cheap **hotels** and *pensões*. The best, the *Hotel Serra do Ouro* (☎075/621-3325; ④), is on the outskirts, built on a hillside with a magnificent view of the town. A cheaper, though less attractive option is the *Jacobina Palace Hotel*, Rua Manoel Navares 210 (☎075/621-2600; ②).

Jacobina is a good place for getting acquainted with the **food** of the interior: *carne do sol com pirão de leite* is rehydrated dried meat with a delicious milk-based sauce; *bode assado* is roast goat, surprisingly tender when done well; and *buchada*, a spicy kind of haggis made from intestines, is much nicer than it sounds but not for delicate stomachs. Good **restaurants** are *Carlito's*, on the banks of the Rio

Ouro, and the *Cheguei Primeiro*, which only serves *caça* (game): the best dish is *tatu*, armadillo, which has a tender white flesh that tastes vaguely like pork. You should also try *doce de buriti*, a tangy, acidic-tasting paste made from the fruit of the buriti palm; it's sold in neat boxes made from the wood of the palm, which keep it fresh almost indefinitely.

There is even a **nightspot** called *Status* on the slopes of the Serra da Caixa above the town, only accessible by taxi – it calls itself a nightclub, but is more of a *dancetaria*, worth checking out on Friday and Saturday nights.

North: Canudos

A different route north from Feira de Santana along the bumpy BR-116 takes you to **CANUDOS**, site of Antônio Conselheiro's rebellion in the 1890s (see box). The main reason for coming here is to get a taste of these remarkable events, but it's also a chance to sample the atmosphere of a typical small town in the *sertão*, with life still dominated by the all-important question of rain or the lack of it. Despite the obvious poverty, it's a rewarding place to visit: everything centres on the main square, with weather-beaten *sertanejos* trudging around during the day, and the local youngsters taking over at night. If you've come from a big city, you'll certainly notice the sense of isolation provided by the *caatinga* all around.

You have to leave the town if you want to visit the **site of the war of Canudos**. The valley where it all happened was flooded by a dam in the 1960s and the new Canudos is the result of a shift a few miles down the road. There is a bus which will drop you at the battlefield (ask for "Velho Canudos") but you'll have to wait a long time to be picked up again so it may be better to arrange your own transport if you can find someone to take you. Alternatively, you could walk it in a couple of hours, but it's very hot and you should take plenty of sun protection. When you get to the edge of the valley you'll see a few houses, a statue of Antônio Conselheiro and a small museum, but it's usually closed. More interesting is the valley itself, where the water has sunk to such a low level that you can now see the tops of trees and houses which may have formed part of

---

ANTÔNIO CONSELHEIRO'S REBELLION

The Bahian *sertão* provided the backdrop to one of the most remarkable events in Brazilian history, the **rebellion** of the messianic religious leader, **Antônio Conselheiro**, who gathered thousands of followers, built a city called Canudos, and declared war on the young republic in 1895 for imposing new taxes on an already starving population. The rebels held out for two years. The forces sent confidently north from Salvador were terribly mauled by the *sertanistas*, who proved to be great guerrilla fighters, with an intimate knowledge of the harsh country, which the city troops found as intimidating as their human enemies. Twice military columns were beaten, and then a third force of over a thousand troops commanded by a national hero, a general in the Paraguayan war, was sent against the rebels. In the worst shock the young republic had suffered up to that point, it was completely annihilated: the next expedition discovered the bleached skulls of the general and his staff laid out in a neat row in front of a thorn tree. Not until 1897, when a fourth expedition was sent, did Canudos fall, and almost all of its defenders were killed; Antônio Conselheiro himself had died of fever a few weeks before the end. One member of the force, **Euclides da Cunha**, immortalized the war in his book, *Os Sertões*, generally recognized as the greatest Portuguese prose ever written by a Brazilian – it was translated into English as "Rebellion in the Backlands". It's a good introduction to the Bahian *sertão*, but a more entertaining read is *The War of the End of the World* by the Peruvian novelist Mario Vargas Llosa, which gives a haunting fictionalized account of the incredible events in Canudos.

the original Canudos. It's incredible to think that this valley was once a place that was thought to threaten the future of the Brazilian Republic.

Back in the new Canudos, there are – surprisingly – two or three **places to stay**: it may be that the increased interest in the history of the place is bringing in a few extra visitors; *Grapiuna* on Praça Monsenhor Berenguer (☎075/275-1157; ③) is a good bet. **Transport** there and away is also not a problem: there's a daily bus to Salvador and another daily service to Juazeiro, on the border with Pernambuco. The **food** isn't great: the local speciality is *bode assado*, roast goat, which is not particularly popular with outsiders, and there's a distinct lack of fresh fruit and vegetables. But there are plenty of biscuits in the shops, so you won't starve.

West: Lençóis and Ibotirama

The route **west** into the *sertão* is along the BR-242, which skirts Feira de Santana and swings south, where a turn-off signposted to Brasília heads inland, into the heart of the *sertão*. The scenery is remarkably similar to that along the Jacobina road 200km to the north: you're still in the tablelands of the Chapada Diamantina, with its rock spurs and mesas forming an enormous chain of foothills to the Planalto Central.

Lençóis

Five hours' ride down the BR-242, **LENÇÓIS** is another mining town and the main tourist centre in the Chapada Diamantina. It's a funny name for a town – it means "sheets" – and it derives from the camp that grew up around a diamond strike in 1844. The miners, too poor to afford tents, made do with sheets draped over branches. Lençóis is a pretty little town, in the midst of walking country that, if anything, is even more spectacular than the Serra da Jacobina. Most of its fine old buildings date back to the second half of the last century, when the town was a prosperous mining community, attracting diamond buyers from as far afield as Europe. The **Mercado Municipal**, next to the bridge over the Rio Lençóis that runs through the centre, is where most of the diamonds were sold – it has Italian- and French-style trimmings tacked on to make the buyers feel at home. The centre of the town, between two lovely squares, Praça Otaviano Alves and Praça Horácio de Matos, is made up of cobbled streets, lined with well-proportioned two-storey nineteenth-century houses with high, arched windows. On Praça Horácio, the **Subconsulado Francês**, once the French consulate, was built with the money of the European diamond buyers, who wanted an office to take care of export certificates. **Tourist information** is available from an office on Avenida Senhor dos Passos, on the other side of the river. You'll also find several people offering themselves as guides to the town: at a dollar or two for an extensive tour they're not expensive, and as life is not easy around here, it might help someone out.

There are two **buses** a day from Salvador to Lençóis, one at 7.30am, the other at 10pm, for a seven-hour journey. The best, and most expensive, **place to stay** in town is the *Pousada de Lençóis*, Rua Altina Alves (☎075/334-1102; ⑤). Cheaper, but still good, are the *Colonial*, Praça Otaviano Alves 750 (☎075/334-1114; ③), and the *Tradiçao*, Rua José Florêncio (☎075/334-1120; ③). There's a **campsite** in the centre, *Lumiar Camping*, on Praça do Rosário (☎075/240-2798).

Local **artesanato** is very good, particularly the bottles filled with coloured sand and arranged into intricate patterns; get a guide to take you to the **Salão das Areias** on the outskirts of town, where you can see the sand being gathered and put into bottles by local artisans – even children do it. You can buy the finished product at Gilmar Nunes, Rua Almirante Barroso, or at Manoel Reis, Rua São Félix.

Walks around Lençóis

The countryside around Lençóis is promising walking territory. Some places you could just about manage unaided, like the **Gruta do Lapão**, a remarkable grotto over a kilometre long, with a cathedral-like entrance of layered rock and stalactites. It's a short drive or a long walk from the centre, but it's probably better to have someone take you there. The only other place within easy reach is the **Cascatas do Serrano**, where the river flows over a rock plate forming a series of small waterfalls and pools that are good for swimming – very popular with the town's children.

Anywhere more distant and you'll need a proper **guide**, as the countryside can be difficult to negotiate: at an *artesanato* shop, Funkart, in the centre there's a resident American guide, Roy Funch; he may not be able to guide you himself, but can certainly recommend someone and suggest places to head for. Standard rates for a guide are between $20 and $30 a day and you may need to go the first part of the journey by car or taxi, as some places are up to 30km away. You can usually negotiate this with the guide, who will know somebody – and you'll have to arrange a place and time for them to pick you up if you don't feel like walking all the way back. Sunglasses, a hat and protective cream are all essential, as well as taking along liquids: it can get very hot and several of the walks are strenuous.

Places you're likely to have suggested to you as possible destinations are **Morro do Pai Inácio**, a 300-metre-high mesa formation 27km from Lençóis (don't be deceived about how near it looks). It is, though, much more easily climbed than seems possible from a distance, and you're rewarded with quite stunning views across the tablelands and the town once you get to the top, which is covered in highland cacti, trees and shrubs. Thirty kilometres away, but with much easier road access, is **Rio Mucugezinho**, another series of small waterfalls and pools that are fun to swim in; a closer river beach is the **Praia do Rio São José**, also called **Zaidā**. Finally, and most spectacular of all, is the highest waterfall in Brazil, the **Cachoeira Glass**, a small stream that tumbles 400m down over a mesa, becoming little more than a fine mist by the time it reaches the bottom. It's closer to town than most of the other places, and if you only feel up to one day's walking it's the best choice.

Ibotirama and the Rio São Francisco

Another couple of hundred kilometres down the road is the small river town of **IBOTI-RAMA**, where the São Francisco is almost a kilometre wide and all highway traffic crosses a high bridge at the northern end of town. The **waterfront**, where there's a market and a crowd of riverboats with flat tops and open sides, is by far the most interesting part of the town. Fishing is important here, and the enormous river fish can be seen piled up all over the riverbank, ready for salting.

There are several **hotels** and *dormitórios*; the best is the *Velho Chico* on the riverfront at Rua Teixeira Lott, Alto do Fundao (☎073/698-1113; ④). A cheaper option is the *Dourado*, Rua João Borges Figueiredo 665 (☎073/698-1015; ②), and there's also the friendly family-run *Pousada and Lanchonete California*, on the main road where the buses stop (☎073/698-1431; ①). Salvador–Brasília **buses** and local services connect Lençois with Ibotirama. Heading east, unless there are empty spaces on a bus passing through from Brasília you'll have to get up sharp to catch the Salvador bus, which leaves in the early hours of the morning.

Apart from the waterfront, the town's not much, but it is an important river trading centre and a good starting point for **boat** trips. Small launches make runs to **river towns** in both directions, while canoes from Ibotirama will ferry you to two islands, **Gado Bravo** and **Ilha Grande**, half an hour's paddling away. Both have fine sandy beaches during the dry season, approximately March to October.

South from Salvador

The BR-101 highway is the main route to the **southern Bahian coast**, a region immortalized in the much-translated and filmed novels of Jorge Amado. From the bus window you'll see the familiar fields of sugar replaced by huge plantations of *cacau*, cocoa, the raw material of chocolate and cocoa. Southern Bahia produces two-thirds of Brazil's cocoa, almost all of which goes for export, making this part of Bahia the richest agricultural area of the state. The *zona de cacau* seems quiet and respectable enough today, with its pleasant towns and prosperous countryside, but in the last decades of the nineteenth century and the first decades of this, it was one of the most turbulent parts of Brazil. Entrepreneurs and adventurers from all over the country carved out estates here, often violently – a process chronicled by Amado in his novel *The Violent Lands*.

Ilhéus and around

In literary terms **ILHÉUS**, Amado's birthplace, is the best-known town in Brazil, scene of his most famous novel, *Gabriela, Cravo e Canela*, translated into English as "Gabriela, Clove and Cinnamon" – by far the most renowned Brazilian novel internationally. If you haven't heard of it before visiting Ilhéus, you soon will; it seems that every other bar, hotel and restaurant is either named after the novel or one of its characters.

The town is on the coast 400km south of Salvador, where the local coastline is broken up by five rivers and a series of lagoons, bays and waterways. Much of it is modern but it's still an attractive place, with the heart of Ilhéus perched on a small hill that overlooks one of the largest and best beaches in Bahia. Before you head for the beaches however, take time to look around the town. The modern cathedral, built in the 1930s with extravagant Gothic towers and pinnacles, is a useful landmark. Nearby, the oldest church in the city, the **Igreja Matriz de São Jorge**, on Praça Rui Barbosa, finished in 1556, has a religious art museum, while the domed roof and towers of the **Igreja de Nossa Senhora de Lourdes** dominate the shoreline nearest to the centre. Domes are rare in church architecture in Brazil, and this combination of dome and towers is unique.

The main leisure options in Ilhéus have changed little from Amado's time: hanging around in the **bars** and squares, and heading for the beaches. The *Vezúvio* on Praça Dom Eduardo, the cathedral square, is the most famous bar in Brazil; in Amado's book it's owned by the hero Nacib, and is a watering hole of the cocoa planters. You pay a little extra for drinks, but it's a good bar, with renowned Arab food. Apart from the centre, the main concentration of bars is along the fine beach promenade of the Avenida Atlântica, the beach itself called simply **Avenida**, though much of it is now polluted and not recommended for bathing. There are other **beaches to the north**, past the port; the first is **Isidro Ramos** (bus from the centre or Avenida), followed by **Praia do Marciano** and **Praia do Norte**.

Most locals prefer the coastline to the **south**, including the village of **OLIVENÇA**, served by local buses from the centre. Half an hour out of town is the beautiful beach at **Cururupe**, where Governor Mem de Sá trapped the Tupiniquim Indians in 1567 between his troops and the sea. It was called the "Battle of the Swimmers", after the Indians' desperate attempts to escape by water, but it was more of a massacre than a battle, and the tribe was almost wiped out. Today there are a series of bars and some holiday homes, peaceful groves of palm trees and no hint of the place's dark past. In Olivença itself the main attraction is the **Balneário**, public swimming baths built around supposedly healthy mineral water from the Rio Tororomba, which flows through the place. The healing powers of the water are exaggerated, but the baths complex is very pleasant, with an artificial waterfall, and bar and restaurant attached. The coast between Ilhéus and Olivença is very beautiful: you can **camp** virtually anywhere along the way.

Practicalities

The **Rodoviária** is on Praça Cairu, a little way from the centre of Ilhéus, but buses outside marked "Centro" or "Olivença" take you into town. There's a **tourist information** post at the *Rodoviária*, with good town maps, and also one in the centre on Praça Castro Alves.

Your best bet for **accommodation** in Ilhéus is probably on one of the beaches, although there's no shortage of places elsewhere if you prefer. *Pousada Vitória* (①) is a budget option on Praça Cairu, next to the *Rodoviária*. In the centre, *Ilhéus*, Rua Estáquio Bastos 144 (☎073/634-4242; ⑤), is good value, and the *Britânia*, Rua 28 de Junho 16 (☎073/231-1722; ③), is one of the cheapest central *pousadas* you'll find. Probably the best place to stay in town, though, is *Morada da Praia do Cristo* on Avenida Dois de Julho (⑤). As well as boasting a superb breakfast, it has four levels with plenty of open spaces to relax and read a book. There are also several places along the Ilhéus–Olivença road worth trying: frequent buses run into town.

Buses to Ilhéus from Salvador take around six hours and are run by Expresso São Jorge: the only one you can catch if you want to see the pleasant countryside en route is in the morning, for which you have to book at least a day in advance; otherwise take one of the three night departures. There are direct buses from Ilhéus, once a week, to Rio and São Paulo, but book at least two days ahead for these.

Porto Seguro

The most popular destination in southern Bahia is the resort area around the town of **PORTO SEGURO**, where Cabral "discovered" Brazil in 1500, a couple of thousand years after the first Indians populated the country. Founded in 1526, it has some claim to being the oldest town in Brazil, and buildings still survive from that period.

The story goes that in 1500 **Pedro Alvares Cabral** and his men, alerted to the presence of land by the changing colour of the sea and the appearance of land birds, finally saw a mountain on the horizon, which must have been Monte Páscoal, to the south of today's Porto Seguro. First landfall was made on Good Friday, on a beach to the north of Porto Seguro, and the anchorage Cabral used was probably the cove where the village of Santa Cruz de Cabrália now stands. The Indians were friendly at first – they might have been better advised to massacre everyone, since Cabral claimed the land for the king of Portugal, and thus began over three centuries of Portuguese rule.

These days Porto Seguro is about as far as you can get from pre-colonial tranquillity. It's become one of the biggest holiday resorts in Brazil, and heaves with Brazilian tourists throughout the year, reaching saturation point at New Year and *Carnaval*. You may actually enjoy yourself here if your main interest is nightlife; but you've got to like crowds, and don't expect much peace and quiet. All the same, Porto Seguro has somehow managed to retain its reputation as a fairly classy destination.

The Town

The colonial area, **Cidade Alta**, is built on a bluff overlooking the town, with fine views out to sea and across the Rio Buranhém. The **Igreja da Misericórdia** here, begun in 1526, is one of the two oldest churches in Brazil. The **Igreja de Nossa Senhora da Pena**, nearby, dates from 1535 and has the oldest religious icon in Brazil, a St Francis of Assisi, brought over in the first serious expedition to Brazil in 1503. There are the ruins of a Jesuit church and chapel (dating from the 1540s) and a small, early fort; the squat and thick-walled style of the churches shows their early function as fortified strongpoints, in the days when Indian attacks were common. Near the ruins of the Jesuit college is the **Marca do Descobrimento**, the two-metre-high column sunk to mark Portuguese sovereignty in 1503; on one side is a crude face of Christ, almost unrecognizable now, and on the other the arms of the Portuguese Crown.

Cidade Baixa, below, is where the modern action is. The riverside Avenida 22 de Abril and its continuation, Avenida Portugal, are a mass of bars, restaurants and hotels – so much so in fact that Avenida Portugal changes its name at night to become the Passarela do Álcool, or "Alcohol Street". There's one stretch of road which particularly merits this name: here competing stallholders urge you to try their fiendishly strong cocktails. These sweet, lethal concoctions are supposed to improve your sex life, or at least to make you wish you had one, but will probably merely hasten your descent into slumber.

Practicalities

The **Rodoviária** is a little way out of town, but taxis are cheap and plentiful. Águia Branca runs three **buses** a day on the eleven-hour journey from Salvador, but one of these is an extremely expensive *leito* service, and you should book well ahead. There are now direct **flights** from Rio and Salvador, and there's talk of flights from Europe as well. **Tourist information** offices are at the *Rodoviária* and the airport, and in the centre of town, Pataxó Turismo, Av. dos Navegantes 333 (☎073/288-1256), and Taípe Viagens e Turismo, Av. 22 de Abril 1077 (☎073/288-3127), are helpful.

Finding **accommodation** should be the least of your worries as Porto Seguro is jammed with hotels. However, prices vary astonishingly between high and low season: a budget hotel in, say, November, could triple in price by Christmas. You need to bear this in mind when considering the high-season prices we've quoted.

If you want to be right in the thick of the nightlife, you could try the *Pousada da Orla*, at Av. Portugal 404 (☎073/288-2434; ③). A couple of roads back from the riverfront, in a heavy wooden building pretending to be from the colonial era is the *Hotel Terra Á Vista*, Av. Getúlio Vargas 124 (☎073/288-2035; ④), which is actually a relatively peaceful place to stay. A hotel with some genuine colonial character is the *Pousada Oásis do Pacatá*, at Rua Marechal Deodoro 286 (☎073/288-2221; ④). It's run by a Frenchwoman, and has a swimming pool and a friendly atmosphere. Chalet-style accommodation is provided at the *Pousada São Luiz*, Av. 22 de Abril 329 (☎073/288-2238; ④), and greater luxury can be found at the *Park Palace Hotel*, Av. 22 de Abril 400 (☎073/288-3777; ⑤).

The best-equipped **campsite** is *Camping da Gringa* (☎073/288-2076), at the edge of town; there's another on Mundaí beach (☎073/288-2287), which starts in front of Cidade Alta.

There are a huge number of **places to eat** in Porto Seguro, though the more sophisticated ones tend to be quite expensive. You can dine more cheaply at *Tché*, on Travessa Augusto Borges, just off the Passarela do Álcool, where a half-portion of *carne do sol* will satisfy even the most ravenous carnivore.

South of Porto Seguro

South of Porto Seguro are three less developed, more relaxed beach resorts generally preferred by backpacking foreigners, though there are plenty of Brazilian tourists as well. You'll definitely enjoy yourself here if you're looking for beaches and nightlife, and the resorts get quieter the further south you go.

Arraial d'Ajuda

ARRAIAL D'AJUDA is the closest of the three to Porto Seguro and the easiest to get to: catch the ferry from the centre of Porto Seguro for the ten-minute journey across the Rio Buranhém. From the other side there are buses which climb the hill and drop you in the centre of town: don't stay on the bus after this or you'll find yourself making a very boring round trip. In the centre itself and on the roads running down the steep hill to the beach are an incredible number of **places to stay**. The nicest of these is the *Hotel*

Pousada Marambaia, at Alameda dos Flamboyants 116 (☎073/875-1275; ④), which has clean, chalet-style rooms around a peaceful courtyard, complete with swimming pool and gently jangling cowbells. The *Hotel Pousada Buganville*, at Alameda dos Flamboyants 170 (☎073/875-1007; ④), also has a friendly atmosphere, while the *Pousada Vento Sul*, on the Caminho da Praia, the hill which runs down to the beach (☎073/875-1294; ③), is for those with a taste in loud rave music, thumping out from the bar below.

The **beach** is lively and can get very crowded in places, though the further you get from the bars and the restaurants, the easier it is to find somewhere peaceful to sit in the sun. The main problem with Arraial d'Ajuda is that it's become too popular too quickly – whatever rubbish collection there is simply can't cope with the huge amounts of litter left by tourists.

Trancoso and Caraíva

Further south down the coast – more peaceful, but next in the developers' sights – is **TRANCOSO**. You can get there either **by bus** (about five a day from Arraial d'Ajuda for a fifty-minute journey) or **on foot**. It's a beautiful walk – 12km down the beach from Arraial – but you have to ford a couple of rivers so be prepared to get wet. Once again, there's no shortage of **accommodation**: *Gulab Mahal* (③), on the main square, the Quadrado, is highly recommended.

If you really want to get away from civilization in this part of Bahia, you have to go even further south, to **CARAÍVA**. It has no electricity apart from that provided by generators, and no cars, but the real reason for its simplicity is that it's time-consuming to get to. There are **boats** from Porto Seguro (consult a travel agent) and Trancoso which take four and two hours respectively, and two **buses** a day from Trancoso – a bumpy ride, ending with a boat journey across a river. Once there, you'll find superb beaches, a few rustic places to stay, some good food and plenty of peace and quiet.

Caravelas

On the banks of the Rio Caravelas, in the extreme south of Bahia, lies **CARAVELAS**, an attractive, unpretentious colonial town which makes an ideal farewell or introduction to the Northeast. Founded in 1503, it became an important trading centre in the seventeenth and eighteenth centuries. Today both the town and its nearby beach are – despite the growth of tourism – extremely relaxing places to hang out. Caravelas is also the jumping-off point for the **Parque Nacional Marinho dos Abrolhos**, one of the best places in Brazil to see exotic marine life, including – at certain times of year – whales.

Apart from organizing your trip to Abrolhos, there aren't a huge number of specific things to do in Caravelas, but it's an extremely agreeable place to wander round. Most of the interest lies in the streets between the river and the *Rodoviária*, which is located on Praça Teófilo Otoni in the centre of town. One block to your left as you come out of the *Rodoviária* is Praça Quinze, the liveliest square in this sleepy town. Another block further on and running parallel to the river is Rua Marcílio Diaz, which becomes Rua Sete de Setembro and eventually leads to the beautiful **Praça de Santo Antônio**. This is definitely the architectural highlight of Caravelas and contains the eponymous **Igreja de Santo Antônio**, which you may – if you're lucky – find open.

Practicalities

In order to get to Caravelas, you have to go first to **Teixeira de Freitas**, further inland. Águia Branca run five **buses** a day on the four-hour journey between Porto Seguro and Teixeira de Freitas. From the south, you can get there from Minas Gerais or Espírito Santo or, if you want to miss out those two states altogether, São Geraldo run a daily service from Rio which leaves in mid-afternoon and takes fifteen hours. It's an *executivo* and will set you back about $50.

Once at the *Rodoviária* in Teixeira de Freitas, you can get yourself a ticket for the onward journey to Caravelas. Expresso Brasileiro run five buses a day along this route, an agreeable two-hour meander through lush tropical fields.

There's an excellent **place to stay** near the *Rodoviária* on Praça Teófilo Otoni, the *Pousada Caravelense* (☎073/297-1182; ②), which offers friendly service and has a pool table. There are several other hotels, most of them to your left as you come out of the *Rodoviária*. The *Pousada da Ponte*, on Rua Anibal Benevolo (②), is a simple, charming place built right on the riverbank. The *Pousada Caravelas* (②), on Rua Sete de Setembro, just next to the Banco do Brasil, is friendly, modern and clean, while for a real budget option, you could try the *Hotel Shangri-La* (①) further down the same road. There's also accommodation **on the beach**, called Praia do Grauçá or Barra de Caravelas – a half-hour journey from the *Rodoviária* in Caravelas and well worth a visit even if you don't stay there. The *Pousada das Sereias* (☎073/874-1033; ③) is the obvious choice if you don't want to spend too much money, while the *Hotel Marina Porto Abrolhos* (☎073/874-1082 or 874-1060; ⑥) is for beachside luxury.

There are number of good **restaurants** in town. *Carenagem*, just by the petrol station on Praça Quinze, offers very good value, as does the extraordinarily named *Muroroa Reggae Night*, which is on the riverbank at the other end of town, near the Praça de Santo Antônio. It seems to get very little business in low season but deserves much more as the *carne do sol* is awesomely good. There's another good place to eat down on the beach at Barra de Caravelas, the *Museu da Baleia*, which owes its name to the enormous whale skeleton partially assembled outside – but rest assured that whale meat is not on the menu.

Parque Nacional Marinho dos Abrolhos

For all Caravelas' attractions, there's no doubt that the main reason people come here is to see the extraordinary profusion of marine and bird life in the **Parque Nacional Marinho dos Abrolhos**. The park consists of an archipelago of five islands lying 52km offshore. Among the clear waters and coral reefs you can see all kinds of rare fish, sea turtles and birds, and between July and early November the waters are home to **whales** taking refuge from the Antarctic winter.

There are two main **tour companies** in Caravelas which offer trips to Abrolhos: the well-established Abrolhos Turismo, on Praça Dr Imbassay (☎073/297-1149), and the slightly cheaper Abrolhos Embarcações, at Av. das Palmeiras 2, more or less on Praça Quinze (☎073/297-1172). Abrolhos Turismo offers a basic day trip to the national park in a launch, leaving at 7am and returning at 5pm, for about $120. The same sort of trip costs about $100 at Abrolhos Embarcações, though the day is shorter, starting at 8am and returning at 4pm. In either case, you can pay extra to hire snorkels, masks and more sophisticated diving equipment. Both companies also offer longer yacht-trips to Abrolhos of up to three nights, for which you pay just over $100 a day at Abrolhos Turismo and about $75 at Abrolhos Embarcações. Again, hiring diving equipment costs extra.

PARAÍBA

Most people who are travelling north from Recife head directly for Ceará and Rio Grande do Norte's beaches, missing out **Paraíba state** and its capital of **João Pessoa** altogether. This is a big mistake, as it is the most attractive of the smaller Northeastern cities, with everything you could reasonably ask for: fine beaches, a beautiful setting on the mouth of the Rio Sanhauá, and colonial remains, including one of Brazil's most striking churches. In addition, not enough foreign travellers make it to the city for the *Pessoenses* to have become blasé about them, and you're likely to be approached by smiling kids who are anxious to practise their hard-learned English.

Out of the city, there are fine beaches to the north and south, while the highway inland leads to **Campina Grande**, a market town strategically placed at the entrance to the *sertão*. The main target of the interior, though, is actually in neighbouring Ceará state, but dealt with here since it's most easily accessible from Paraíba – the fascinating pilgrim town of **Juazeiro do Norte**.

João Pessoa

JOÃO PESSOA is one of the oldest and one of the poorest cities in Brazil, and has the air of dilapidated elegance you find in Brazilian cities that have been left behind by modern development. Walking around, it feels as if you have slipped back to the Thirties, as of all the Northeastern cities this is the one least scarred by modern developers. As a result, **Cabo Branco** and **Tambaú** are two of the region's finest urban beaches, though it's not the beaches themselves that are unique, but the ageing style of the seafront: three storeys is the maximum height here and the absence of skyscrapers on the shoreline comes as a pleasant surprise.

Arrival, orientation and information

The **Rodoviária** in João Pessoa is conveniently near the city centre. Any bus from the **local bus station**, opposite the *Rodoviária*'s entrance, takes you to the city's one unmistakable, central landmark: the circular lake, the Parque Solon de Lucena, which everybody simply calls **Lagoa**, spectacularly bordered by tall palms imported from Portugal. All **bus routes** converge on the circular Anel Viário skirting the lake, and it's from here that you can catch buses for the beach districts, as well as buses further afield – to the northern beaches, the neighbouring town of Cabedelo and the village of Penha to the south of the city.

Orientation

João Pessoa's **centre** is just to the west of the Lagoa. To the east **Avenida Getúlio Vargas**, leads out of town towards the beachside *bairros* of Cabo Branco and Tambaú. At the city's core is **Praça João Pessoa**, which contains the state governor's palace and the local parliament; most of the central hotels are clustered around here. The oldest part of the city is just to the north of Praça João Pessoa, where **Rua Duque de Caxias** ends in the Baroque splendour of the **Igreja de São Francisco**. The steep **Ladeira de São Francisco**, leading down from here to the lower city and the bus and train stations, offers a marvellous view of the rest of the city spread out on the banks of the **Rio Sanhauá**, framed by trees.

The two sweeping bays of **Cabo Branco** and **Tambaú** are separated by the futuristic, circular, luxury *Hotel Tambaú*, where the highest concentration of nightspots is found. The southern boundary of the city is the lighthouse on Ponta de Seixas, the cape at the far end of Cabo Branco. Locals claim it as the most easterly point of Brazil, a title disputed with the city of Natal to the north – though the *Pessoenses* have geography on their side.

Information

Official **tourist information** is available at the *Rodoviária*, run by the state tourist board, PB-Tur. Theoretically it opens during office hours but in practice sometimes closes because of staff shortages. Far more helpful is the tourist office in the Centro de Turismo in Tambaú, opposite the *Tambaú Hotel* at Av. Almirante Tamandaré 100 (daily 8am–7pm; ☎083/226-7078). You can also find a post office and a *posto telefônico* here.

The **main post office** is on Praça Pedro Américo, two blocks downhill from Praça João Pessoa in the direction of the bus stations. Domestic and international **telephone calls** are cheapest from the TELPA building, off Rua Visconde de Pelotas in the centre, open until 10pm daily. You can **change money** and travellers' cheques at Câmbio Turismo, which has branches at Rua Visconde de Pelotas 54 in the city centre (Mon–Fri), and in the shopping centre on Tambaú beach (Mon–Sat).

Accommodation

The very cheapest places to stay are the *dormitórios* opposite the *Rodoviária*. You can find good budget and medium-range hotels both in the centre and on the beaches, but five-star luxury is only available by the sea. For some reason, hotels in João Pessoa rarely seem to charge the full price displayed at the reception desk, and you can get some pretty hefty discounts.

City centre hotels

Hotel Franklin, Rua Rodrigues de Aquino 293 (☎083/222-3001). Fairly downmarket hotel, gloomy and basic. ①.

J.R. Hotel, Rua Rodrigues Chaves 87 (☎083/241-2104). A good modern option. ②.

The martial art of dancing – *capoeira* in Olinda

Patio de São Pedro and Cathedral, Recife

The cloister adjoining the Capela Dourada, Recife

Igreja de Santo Antônio, Recife

Rooftops in Olinda

Ladeira do Carmo, Salvador

Jericoacoara

Salvador

Popcorn cart in Olinda

Bananas

Sliding down the dunes, Jericoacoara

Largo de Pelourinho, Salvador

Lagoa Park Hotel, Parque Solon de Lucena 19 (☎083/241-1414). Not as expensive as it looks, with great views over the Lagoa. ③.

Paraíba Palace, Praça Vidal de Negreiros (☎083/221-3107). Very centrally located and good value. ③.

Pousada Raio de Luz, Praça Venancio Neiva 44 (☎083/221-2169). A surprisingly inexpensive hotel offering by far the best value in the city centre. ①.

Beach hotels

Hotel Gameleira, Av. João Maurício 157 (☎083/226-1576). Not the cleanest of hotels, but its location is good, right on the seafront at Tambaú. ②.

Pousada Malibu, Av. Cabo Branco 3056 (☎083/226-1152). Budget accommodation near Cabo Branco beach. ②.

Mar Azul Hotel Pousada, Av. João Maurício 315 (☎083/226-2660). Despite not providing breakfast, this seafront budget hotel at Tambaú offers excellent value. ②.

Ouro Branco Praia, Av. Nossa Senhora dos Navegantes 431 (☎083/247-1010). An attractive 4-star hotel a couple of blocks from Tambaú beach. ⑥.

Hotel Tambaú, Av. Almirante Tamandare 229 (☎083/226-3660). Luxury beachside hotel and one of the landmark modernist buildings of the city, reminiscent of a camouflaged flying saucer. Anyone catching a taxi from here stands a good chance of being classed as a rich sucker and charged accordingly. ⑦.

Pousada Verdes Mares, Av. Nossa Senhora dos Navegantes 400 (☎083/226-3082). A useful road to be in for both beach and bus connections at a reasonable price. ④.

Camping

The beautiful **campsite**, on a promontory past the Ponta de Seixas, can be reached by taking the Cabo Branco bus to its terminal and then walking (for about 45min) past the lighthouse and along the road down the other side until the signposted fork to the left. Easier on the legs is taking the Penha bus from the Anel Viário or the local bus station: it passes near the campsite but only runs every couple of hours. Clean and well run, on a fine beach with a spectacular view of the city, the campsite is often full, especially from January to March, so it's advisable to book beforehand in the centre at Sala 18, Rua Almeida Barreto 159 (☎083/221-4863).

The City

The centre of João Pessoa is dotted with **colonial churches, monasteries and convents**, some of which are extremely beautiful. Until a few years ago they were all being allowed to fall into ruin but, not a moment too soon, the state government and the Ministry of Culture mounted a crash restoration programme, for once using historians and archeologists to return the buildings to their original glory, rather than gutting them.

São Francisco

João Pessoa's most spectacular church is the **Igreja de São Francisco** (Tues–Sun 8–11am & 2–5pm), which sits in splendid isolation atop the hill that bears its name, at the end of Rua Duque de Caxias, and now forms part of the **Centro Cultural de São Francisco**.

The exterior alone is impressive enough. A huge courtyard is flanked by high walls beautifully decorated with *azulejo* tiling, with pastoral scenes in a series of alcoves. These funnel you towards a large early eighteenth-century church that would do credit to Lisbon or Coimbra: its most remarkable feature is the tower topped with an oriental dome, a form that the Portuguese encountered in Goa and appropriated for their own purposes. Older than the church by a few decades is the stone cross opposite the courtyard, at the foot of which is a group of finely carved pelicans, symbolizing Christ: pelicans were once believed to tear flesh from their own chests to feed their young, and were often used to represent selfless love. You reach the church through an entrance which has marvellously carved wooden panels and doors. Beyond the church are the chapels and cloister of the **Convento de Santo Antônio**, and upstairs there's an excellent **museum** of popular and sacred art.

Around São Francisco

The other places worth seeing in the centre are within a short walk of São Francisco. Down the steep Ladeira de São Francisco is the oldest building in town, the **Casa da Pólvora**, a relic of the times when the Dutch and Portuguese fought for control over this sugar-rich coastline. It's a squat, functional building that was once the city arsenal and is now the local museum (Mon–Fri 8am–noon & 1–5pm), mostly given over to a collection of enlarged photographs of the city in the early decades of this century. Much of it is still recognizable, and were it not for the absence of charabancs and men wearing hats you could step outside and imagine yourself walking around the photographs.

If you go back up the Ladeira de São Francisco, turn right and right again, you'll end up on Rua General Ossório. Here you'll find the cathedral, **Igreja de Nossa Senhora das Neves**, which boasts a well-proportioned interior that, for once, forgoes the Rococo excesses of many colonial cathedrals. Further down Rua General Ossório, the seventeenth-century **Mosteiro de São Bento** (Tues–Sat 2–5pm) has a simple, beautifully restored interior with a lovely curved wooden ceiling. Other colonial churches are cheek by jowl on Rua Visconde de Pelotas, two blocks to the east: the **Igreja de Nossa Senhora do Carmo** here is well worth a look.

The beaches

The beach areas of Tambaú and Cabo Branco are linked to the centre by frequent buses from the Anel Viário and the local bus station. The **Cabo Branco** seafront is especially stylish, with a mosaic pavement and thousands of well-tended palm trees to complement the sweep of the bay. This is best viewed from the **Ponta de Seixas lighthouse**, where there is a plaque and a monument to mark Brazil's easternmost point. From here, it's only 2200km to Senegal in Africa, less than half the distance to Rio Grande do Sul in the south of Brazil or the state of Roraima in the north. To get to the lighthouse, take the "Cabo Branco" bus to its terminal on the promontory at the end of the bay, and walk up the hill. There is a park at the top and a couple of tacky souvenir shops, but the main thing is the **view**, which is glorious – Cabo Branco beach stretches out before you in an enormous arc, 6km long, which the absence of tall buildings makes all the more impressive. Cabo Branco itself is the city's exclusive upper-class suburb, where the rich stay hidden in their large detached houses, whose high walls shut out both the people and the view. This leaves the fine beach indecently bereft of the usual string of bars and hotels, and only the rustle of wind in the palm trees disturbs the calm elegance of the mansions, a universe away from the poverty of the rest of Paraíba.

Far livelier is **Tambaú**, dominated by its eponymous hotel, which forms one end of a small square. Nearby, on the corner of Avenida Nossa Senhora dos Navegantes and Avenida Rui Carneiro, is a modern building housing the **Mercado de Artesanato Paraíbano**. Although not up to the standards of Pernambuco, Paraíba has distinctive *artesanato* that's worth checking out: painted plates and bowls, and striking figurines made out of sacking and wood.

From the market onwards you do begin to encounter the familiar clusters of beachside bars and restaurants, and at weekends they and the beach get crowded. The **beach** itself (confusingly called Praia de Manaíra as well as Tambaú) is dirtier than

Cabo Branco but more fun: there are the usual simple cafés and vendors selling fruit and fish, and *jangadas* aplenty. Anywhere here is a good place for a *caipirinha* and a view of an invariably spectacular sunset.

Eating, drinking and nightlife

As usual in a coastal capital, the centre tends to get deserted after dark, as people looking for a night out head for the beaches, particularly Tambaú. However, there are several **restaurants and bars** in the centre worth looking at.

João Pessoa has a surprisingly rich but fluctuating **music scene** for a city of its size, concentrated at the beaches: the only nights it is difficult to catch something are Sunday and Monday. Venues open and close with bewildering frequency, so it's best to ask the tourist office for a current list of venues and suggestions. They will direct you to the more expensive upmarket clubs unless you are persistent; alternatively, look in the entertainments guide of the local paper.

City centre

The *Casino da Lagoa* is a bar-restaurant in a small park looking out across the Anel Viário, on the right coming down from the centre: the food is no more than average but the view is excellent, especially at night. Some of the best **sertão food** in the city is served at *Recanto do Picuí* (☎083/244-1400), a restaurant on the Avenida Beira-Rio, which runs parallel to the river behind the *Rodoviária*. The *carne do sol* here is excellent, best accompanied by green beans and *batata doce assado*, roast sweet potatoes.

Finally, stop by the *Bar do Pólvora*, behind the Casa de Pólvora, down the hill from the Igreja de São Francisco. No more than a bar with tables set out on the patio behind the old arsenal, serving only beer, *caipirinhas* and soft drinks, it has two major advantages: one is the setting, beneath the ancient walls of the arsenal, with a stunning view out across the river; the other is the clientele – young, student-dominated and very Bohemian. Best time to go is Thursday evening, when a small fee is charged for a table and there's a show, whose basic format is a few groups/poets/singers doing spots, plus whoever else in the audience feels like doing a turn. As you might expect, some of the acts are appalling, notably the local poets reading interminable extracts from their work, but the music is sometimes excellent.

Vegetarians can try the *Natural*, Rua Rodrigues de Aquino 177, down from Praça João Pessoa – unfortunately only open for lunch.

The beaches

The more expensive **restaurants** in the beach areas ($20–35 range) are in **Cabo Branco**: *Olho de Lula*, for example, on the seafront at Av. Cabo Branco 2300, is a good seafood place. Further down, at no. 5100, is *Marina's*, one of the few seafront bars in Cabo Branco, which also does seafood. A local speciality is *polvo ao leite de coco*, octopus in coconut milk.

If you're looking for meat and *sertão* food, head for *Tábua de Carne*, at Av. Rui Carneiro 648, one of the roads running away from the beach at **Tambaú**. *Mangai*, Av. Edson Ramalho 696, boasts a wide range of dishes with much of the produce coming fresh from their own ranch; this is regional cooking at its best, though it's not cheap.

The square in front of the *Hotel Tambaú* is a relaxed place for a drink and to catch **live music**. It's surrounded by restaurants and bars, and on Friday and Saturday nights tables and chairs are put out in the square, drink starts flowing and after about 9pm things start getting very lively. Every other bar has a *forró* trio, and guitarists and accordion players stroll through the crowds. There's no shortage of good, cheap food sizzling on the charcoal grills of the street vendors if your budget doesn't stretch to a restaurant. In the streets behind there are any number of small **bars and clubs**, which close down and reopen too quickly to keep track of them, so just wander around and stop by anywhere you see lights and music. These smaller bars tend not to get going until 11pm at the earliest, as they rely on people moving on from the seafront places.

Finally, note that there are a couple of **gay bars** in the streets behind Avenida Nossa Senhora dos Navegantes in Tambaú, but it's not an exclusively gay area.

Along the coast

Like so much of Brazil, Paraíba is blessed with many wonderful **beaches** along its 140-kilometre coastline. Unlike some other parts of the Northeast, however, many of its beaches are, for the time being, largely undeveloped and many require somewhat difficult journeys by bus and then on foot or by taxi to reach them.

Penha

Just to the **south** of João Pessoa is the fishing village of **PENHA**, served by local buses from outside the *Rodoviária* or from the Anel Viário. Strung out along a fine beach set in the midst of dense palm forest, Penha is distinguished from other fishing villages roundabout by a nineteenth-century church, the **Igreja de Nossa Senhora da Penha**, which is a pilgrimage centre and focus of much popular devotion. The beach near the church is also used by followers of *candomblé*, who identify the Virgin with Iemanjá, the goddess of the sea. The legend is that over a century ago an image of the Virgin was dredged up by fishermen in their nets, and worked so many miracles that the community adopted her as their patron saint and built the simple chapel to house her icon. Along the beach there are several rustic **bars** where you can eat and also string a hammock for a nominal fee. Discreet camping on the beach is also possible.

Tambaba

TAMBABA is set on a volcanic outcrop and lies some 30km to the south of João Pessoa. It's the first officially recognized nudist beach in the Northeast and is well off the beaten track. Getting here involves a bus ride from the *Rodoviária* to the small seaside town of **Jacumã** followed by a walk of 8km along a rough road. If you don't want to walk, it's probably better to take a taxi than risk bringing a rented car along here as the dirt-track road is more difficult than it looks. The beach is superb and there's a small if somewhat overpriced bar here. Alternatively, and a little nearer to Jacumã, is the **Praia Coqueirinho**, which is a popular spot for the local children in the surrounding villages. Again, you'll need to take a taxi here. **Camping** is possible at the beach of Tabatinga, just to the north, or there are places to stay in Jacumã.

North towards Cabedelo

Penha apart, most of the readily accessible **beaches** are to the **north**, off the road that leads to Cabedelo, 18km or 45 minutes by frequent local buses from the Anel Viário in João Pessoa – they get very crowded at weekends. The road runs a little inland and there are turn-offs leading to the beaches on the way: it seems to depend more on the drivers' whim than a timetable as to whether the bus takes you right to the beach, but hop on the Cabedelo bus anyway, and get off at the relevant turn-off if need be; it'll only be a short walk to the sea.

BESSA is the generic name for the stretch of coastline immediately north of Tambaú. Six kilometres out of town is a turn-off that leads to the yacht club and a cluster of bars, which have a rather more upmarket clientele than the next village along, **POÇO**, where there is a chapel, some weekend homes, a fine palm-fringed beach with the obligatory bars and several good fish restaurants: *Badionaldo* serves delicious crab stew (*ensopado de carangueijo*), a local speciality, while at the *Bar e Restaurante do Marcão*, Rua Carolino Cardoso, four crabs for $5 will satisfy even the greediest of appetites. From there, you could walk the 10km along the beach to Cabedelo; otherwise hourly buses to Cabedelo, or back to João Pessoa, leave during the day from the bus stop near the church.

Cabedelo and around

CABEDELO itself is older than it looks. It was much fought over in the Dutch wars, and the star-shaped fort of **Santa Caterina** (Tues–Sat 8am–5pm), dating from 1585, is the major sight in the village. Unfortunately, Petrobrás have built a series of oil storage tanks right up to its ramparts, and it's difficult to get a sense of its strategic position, commanding the only deep-water anchorage on this stretch of coast.

Nowadays, Cabedelo's main claim to fame is as the starting point for the famous **Transamazon highway** – the *Transamazônica* – and there's a sign proving it over the João Pessoa road. It has a certain logic. The Transamazon was always as much a grand symbolic gesture as a physical thing in the minds of its creators, so it had to stretch from the extreme west of Brazil to the extreme east. On top of that, it was also seen as the conduit along which would flow the "people without land" to the "land without people", as poor Northeasterners were funnelled towards Amazonia: a political signal to the large landowners of the Northeast that the government had no intention of tackling the region's problems by implementing agrarian reform. So the only thing the poor of Paraíba got was a convenient escape route.

There's no reason to hang around in Cabedelo and plenty of reason to continue 20km to two superb and largely unspoilt beaches. For the more adventurous camper there is the **Praia do Oiteiro**, a wild and beautiful beach with hills covered with tropical vegetation but little in the way of modern comforts. **Campina**, just north of Oiteiro, is similarly idyllic but with the addition of a small fishing settlement. You can get to both beaches on the same bus which takes you through Cabedelo from João Pessoa or you could try renting a boat in Cabedelo as it's only half the distance along the coast.

Inland to Campina Grande

The BR-230 highway, a good-quality asphalt road, bisects Paraíba and leads directly into the *sertão*. The green coastal strip is quickly left behind as the road climbs into the hills; two hours' driving and you arrive in the second city of Paraíba, **CAMPINA GRANDE**, linked to João Pessoa by hourly bus. It's a large town, similar in many ways to Caruaru in Pernambuco: even the slogan you see at the city limits – "Welcome to the Gateway of the *Sertão*" – is identical. Like Caruaru, Campina Grande owes its existence to a strategic position between the *agreste* and the *sertão* proper. It's a market town and centre of light industry, where the products of the *sertão* are stockpiled and sent down to the coast, and where the people of the *sertão* come to buy what they can't make. There's a large Wednesday and Saturday **market** where you can see this process unfolding before your eyes.

You may also see evidence of the fierce competition between Campina Grande and João Pessoa. *Campinenses* proudly contrast their industries and commercial ability with the decadence and stagnation of João Pessoa, and there is concerted pressure from the people of Campina Grande to make this the new capital of Paraíba. To the traveller,

CAMPINA GRANDE'S FESTIVALS

In June there is a month-long **festival** that uses the São João holiday – the **festas juninas** – as an excuse for a general knees-up, and is the best time to visit. The wonderfully named **forrodrómo** in the centre of town, an enormous cross between a concert hall and a *dancetaria*, is where it all happens.

Campina Grande is also famous for its out-of-season carnival, the **Micarande**, an event in late April which attracts some 300,000 people over a period of four days and which is the largest of its kind in Brazil. The music is best described as frenetic electric and reaches fever pitch as the *trio eletricos,* with live *frevo* bands playing on top, work their way through the crowds with their followers in train. The music goes on until dawn. Accommodation during this period is particularly scarce and expensive even for the humblest of abodes, so it is best to get in touch with one of the leading organizers, the state tourist authority, before setting out. A word of warning, however: although the event itself is very well policed, it is best to take care when making your way to it.

though, João Pessoa's elegance is something of a contrast with Campina Grande, which even locals admit is rather ugly. Still, it's a good place to sample the distinctive culture of the *sertão*, without having to suffer its discomforts, and also to experience some unforgettable **festivals**.

The **climate** in Campina Grande is always pleasant, as its height takes the edge off the coastal heat without making it cold, though you may need a sweater at night during the rainy season.

The City

Although the city sprawls out into anonymous industrial suburbs, the **central layout** is compact and easy to get the hang of. The city's heart, and most useful landmark, is the obelisk of the **Parque do Açude Novo**, straddling the **Avenida Floriano Peixoto**, which bisects Campina Grande from west to east. The stretch of the avenue from the obelisk to the cathedral is the centre proper, where most of the things to do and see are concentrated.

The highlight of Campina Grande is its **market**, held every Wednesday and Saturday. The market takes over the area around the cathedral and the municipal market behind it, and although not quite on the scale of Caruaru or Feira da Santana in Bahia, it is the largest in the northern half of the Northeast. Saturday is busiest, but to catch it at its peak you either need to arrive on the Friday or make an early start from João Pessoa, as it starts to wind down from around noon. A highlight are the cries, improvised verses, chants and patters of the scores of streetsellers: you may be lucky enough to come across hawkers going head to head, when two vendors set up shop next to each other and try to outdo the other in extravagant claims and original turns of phrase. Sometimes sellers of *cordel* (see p.209) recite chunks of the ballads to whet the public's appetite, and clusters of people gather around to shout comments and enjoy the story. If you miss the market, but still fancy trying to get hold of **artesanato and cordel**, good places are the co-operative *Casa do Artesão*, Rua Venâncio Neiva 85, near the Rique Palace, and *Kaboclinha*, nearby at Rua Vidal de Negreiros 36.

There are two **museums** in Campina Grande. By some way the best is the **Museu de Arte Assis Chateaubriand**, part of the complex of buildings in the Parque do Açude Novo (Mon–Fri 9am–noon & 2–10pm; Sat & Sun 2–10pm). It's a source of justifiable civic pride, boasting a good gallery of modern art, devoted entirely to Brazilian artists, with a special emphasis on work from the Northeast. Some of Brazil's greatest modern painters are represented, notably Cândido Portinari, whose large canvases fuse social realism with modernist technique in their depiction of workers and work-places. The most intriguing part of the museum is the *atelier livre*, a kind of gallery of work in progress by local artists, where there are temporary exhibitions: local painters, carvers and sculptors bring things to exhibit or sell. They are not very cheap, but for the quality and originality the price is often more than reasonable.

A total contrast, the **Museu do Algodão** (Mon–Fri 8am–noon & 2–6pm) is in the tourist centre in the old train station. It concentrates on the history of the cotton plantations of the area, including some fearsome chains, stocks, iron collars and whips used on the slaves.

Lagoa Seca

The village of **LAGOA SECA** is just a short bus or taxi ride away from Campina Grande: buses leave from Avenida Floriano Peixoto. Like Alto do Moura outside Caruaru it's a village of craft workers that has turned out *artesanato* for two genera-tions. The people are friendly, and you can see many of the artists at work carving reli-gious figures in their yards and in front of their houses. It was in Lagoa Seca that the sacking and wood figurines that you find throughout Paraíba originated.

Practicalities

The **Rodoviária** is on the outskirts of town; local buses marked "Centro" take you downtown. The **tourist office** is situated at Praça Clementino Procópio (Mon–Fri 8am–5pm; ☎083/321-7717) and you can get a useful city map here.

There's a good choice of **accommodation** in Campina Grande. The cheaper *dor-mitórios* are clustered around the old train station and there are plenty of mid-range places close to each other around the city centre. The centrally located *Belfran*, Av. Floriano Peixoto 258 (☎083/341-1312; ②), is one of the best budget choices in town and the *Mahatma Gandhi*, Av. Floriano Peixoto 338 (☎083/321-5275; ②), is worth a visit just for the name. Apparently plans are afoot to build a luxury version called the *Indira Gandhi*. Also in the heart of the city are the comfortable *Majestic*, Rua Marciel Pinheiro 216 (☎083/341-1881; ④), and the *Ouro Branco*, Rua Cel. Joao Lourenço Porto 20 (☎083/341-2929; ⑤), one of Campina Grande's luxury hotels. Some way out from the centre but in a beautiful location near a lake, the *Lago Dourado*, Acude Boqueiro, Municipio de Boqueirao (☎083/226-1686; ③), is excellent value.

Two of the best **restaurants** in town are *Manoel da Carne-de-Sol*, Rua Felix de Aranjo 263, and the *Dona Nina*, Rua Augusto dos Anjos 183, both specializing in regional cui-sine. A cheaper option is *Tábua de Carne*, Av. Manoel Tavares 1040.

Into the sertão

The BR-232 continues threading its way though the *sertão* to the town of **PATOS**: hot, fly-blown, and looking like a spaghetti western set with pick-ups instead of horses. If you need to stop, use the *Hotel JK*, Praça Getúlio Vargas (☎083/421-2811; ②). Then it's on to **SOUSA**, an otherwise unremarkable *sertão* town five hours west of Campina Grande, with two hotels and one of the Northeast's more unusual sights, the **Vale dos Dinosauras**, "Dinosaur Valley", formed by the sedimentary basin of the Rio Peixe. At one time, difficult though it is to imagine in this searing semi-arid landscape, all was swamp and jungle. Various prehistoric reptiles left their footprints, preserved in stone, at several sites in the area around the town. The only way to get to them is by battered taxi over the dusty road. The nearest site is called *A Ilha*, about 5km out of town, which will cost you around $15 in a taxi. Here the prehistoric tracks are striking. The beast clearly lumbered along the riverbed for a while and then turned off, and you can see a regular series of footprints the size of dinner plates, some with two claws visible at the front.

Juazeiro do Norte

The main centre of the deep *sertão* is 160km west – actually in the south of Ceará state – where a series of hill ranges, higher ground blessed with regular rainfall, provides a welcome respite. Food crops can be grown here, and every available inch of land is used to grow fruit and vegetables, or graze cattle. Here there are two towns within a few kilometres of each other, Crato and **JUAZEIRO DO NORTE**, and it was in this area that one of the most famous episodes in the history of the Northeast took place (see box). It is still the site of a massive annual pilgrimage.

Making the pilgrimage

If you want to do what the pilgrims do, the first stop is Padre Cícero's **tomb** in the church of **Nossa Senhora do Perpétuo Socorro**, to the left of the square. There is a small monument outside, always decorated with *ex votos*, tokens brought by those praying for help – you will offend if you pick up or handle them. Inside the plain church there is a constant stream of *romeiros* praying intensely and queueing to kiss the marble slab by the altar, which you might think is the grave but isn't: that is outside to the left, an unpretentious tomb covered in flowers and ribbons. The church is surrounded by souvenir shops, which specialize in the figurines of Padre Cícero with hat and walking stick that you can find all over the Northeast.

The next destination is the **statue** of Padre Cícero on the peak of the **Serra do Horto**, the hill that looks down on the town. The soft option is to take a taxi or bus for 3km along a road that winds up the hill – a route which can be walked if you want to see the fine

---

MIRACLE AT JUAZEIRO

In 1889 Juazeiro was no more than a tiny hamlet. There was nothing unusual about its young priest, **Padre Cícero Romão Batista**, until women in Juazeiro claimed the wine he gave them at Communion had turned to blood in their mouths. At first it was only people from Crato who came, and they were convinced by the women's sanctity and the evidence of their own eyes that Padre Cícero had indeed worked a miracle. As his fame grew, the deeply religious inhabitants of the *sertão* came to hear his sermons and have him bless them. Despite himself, Padre Cícero came to be seen as a living saint: miraculous cures were attributed to him, things he had touched and worn were treated as relics. The Catholic Church began a formal investigation of the alleged "miracle", sent him to Rome to testify to commissions of enquiry, rejected it, sent him back to Brazil and suspended him from the priesthood – but nothing could shake the conviction of the local people that he was a saint. Juazeiro mushroomed into a large town by *sertão* standards, as people flocked to make the pilgrimage, including legendary figures like the bandit chief Lampião.

By the end of his long life, Padre Cícero had become one of the most powerful figures in the Northeast. In 1913 his heavily armed followers caught the train to the state capital, Fortaleza, and forcibly deposed the governor, replacing him with somebody more to Padre Cícero's liking. But Padre Cícero was a deeply conservative man, who restrained his followers more often than not, deferred to the Church, and remained seemingly more preoccupied with the next world than with this. When his more revolutionary followers tried to set up a religious community nearby at Caldeirão, he didn't deter the authorities from using the air force against them, in one of the first recorded uses of aerial bombs on civilians. When he finally died, in 1934, his body had to be displayed strapped to a door from the first floor of his house, before the thousands thronging the streets would believe he was dead. Ever since, pilgrims have come to Juazeiro to pay homage, especially for the anniversary of his death on July 20; an enormous white statue of the priest looks out from a hillside over the town he created.

views of the **valley of Cariri** unfold, with the town of Crato visible to the west. The other way is to follow the **pilgrim route**, a track from the town directly up the hill: it isn't sign-posted but people will willingly direct you to it if you ask for *a picada dos romeiros* or *a Via Sacra*. It's a brisk hour to the top, and at several points the pilgrims have cut steps to help you up. Thousands walk the trail on July 20, "paying the promise", performing penances for help received: a few hardy souls make the journey on their knees.

Once on top, the main attractions are not so much the statue – 27m high but hardly a masterpiece – as the panoramic views and the **chapel** and **museum of ex votos** next to it. Room after room is piled high with stacks of offerings from the grateful thousands for whom Padre Cícero interceded over the decades: countless artificial limbs, wooden models of bits of body, photos of disasters escaped and crashes survived, even football jerseys from victorious players, including one from Brazil's winning 1970 World Cup team. As a demonstration of the hold popular religion has on the daily lives of millions of *nordestinos*, only the *ex votos* at the church of Bonfim in Salvador rival it.

You finish up with Padre Cícero's **house**, signposted from the church where he is buried, and now a cross between a museum and shrine. It's a simple dwelling, with large rooms, a garden and glass cases displaying everything anybody could find that was even remotely connected to the great man: his glasses, underwear, hats, type-writer, bed linen, even the bed he died in. Just for good measure, there are bundles of Indian arrows, fossils and a coin collection thrown in.

The last act of pilgrimage is to be **photographed** to prove to the folks back home that you've made the trip. This ensures a steady flow of work for the many photogra-phers clustered around the last church on the way to the hill, the **Igreja Matriz de Nossa Senhora das Dores**. They all have a series of props to help you pose: lifesize statues of Padre Cícero, dozens of hats, toy elephants and so forth, and although the snap takes two or three hours to develop it comes ready mounted in a mini-viewer, far more durable than a photo proper – the ideal souvenir.

Practicalities

When booking a ticket to Juazeiro make sure you specify Juazeiro *do Norte*, or you run the risk of ending up in Juazeiro in Bahia, several hundred kilometres south. The **Rodoviária** is a couple of kilometres out of the town, which is smaller than its fame suggests. There is one central square where you'll find the best and most expensive **hotel**, the *Panorama* (☎088/512-3100; ④), but finding somewhere to stay is the least of your worries in a town geared to putting up pilgrims: there are small hotels and *dormitórios* everywhere. Among these, the *Hotel Municipal* on Praça Padre Cicero (②) is a good budget option.

Leaving town, seats fill up fast on the daily buses to João Pessoa, Recife and Fortaleza, so if you're staying overnight book a ticket when you arrive. Alternatively, it is usually possible to get a seat on one of the **pilgrim buses** parked around town; their drivers sell seats for the same price as on the regular bus – you don't choose the desti-nation, but as coachloads come from all the major cities that shouldn't be a problem.

RIO GRANDE DO NORTE

Until the late 1980s, the small state of **Rio Grande do Norte** and its capital, **Natal**, were sleepy, conservative backwaters rarely visited by tourists. It's still true to say that there's little of historical interest among Natal's modern hotels and office buildings, and the interior is poor and thinly populated, the only place of any size being the town of **Mossoró**. But two things have transformed Rio Grande do Norte into one of the Northeast's biggest tourist centres: **beaches** and **buggies**. The beaches were always there, but the sometimes hair-raising buggy rides for which the state is famous have taken off only in the past ten years.

One big difference between Rio Grande do Norte and the states to the south is in its **landscape**, for this is where the Northeastern sugar belt finally peters out, drastically changing both history and landscape. **North of Natal**, the *sertão* drives down practically to the coast, and the idyllic palm-fringed beaches give way to something wilder as the coastline changes character, massive sand dunes replacing the flat beaches and palm trees. There is practically no *agreste* to provide insurance against hard times in the form of rich soil and market towns. Instead, the coast is dotted, more and more sparsely, with small fishing villages, rather than the prosperous old sugar towns further south; the *sertão* is flatter and less flinty, and given over almost completely to cattle, mostly scrawny, scratching a living along with the people. The black Brazilian population shrinks with the sugar zone, and in Rio Grande do Norte dwindles to almost nothing.

Natal

NATAL is a small city of about 600,000 people, built on the banks of the Rio Potengi, and founded sixty years later than planned, after the Potiguar Indians stifled the first Portuguese landing on the coast in 1538. They continued to hold the invaders off until 1598, when the Portuguese built the star-shaped fort at the mouth of the river – the city's most enduring landmark. Natal is at the heart of one of the most spectacular strings of beaches in the Northeast: in fact, given that you could rent a beach buggy in Genipabu, just north of Natal, and drive along 250km of dunes uninterrupted until Areia Branca, practically on the border with Ceará, Natal is at one end of what amounts to a single enormous beach.

Stranded at the eastern tip of the Northeast, away from the main international tourist routes, and with little industry to provide employment, Natal has lately been developing tourist facilities with the desperation of a place with few other economic options. It's become a popular destination for Brazilian holidaymakers, lured by the sun and sand rather than the city itself, which is mostly modern and has a sloppily developed seafront: you will look in vain for the colonial elegance of João Pessoa or Olinda. But the glorious beaches do compensate, and amid the development and hotels there are some good nightspots and *dancetarias*.

Arrival, city transport and information

Natal's **airport**, Augusto Severo, is about 15km south of the centre on the BR-101 highway; a taxi to the centre will cost you about $24, or you can catch the bus marked "Parnamirim–Natal". The **Rodoviária** is also a long way out from the centre, at Av. Capitão Mor-Gouveia 1237 in the suburb of Cidade de Esperança (☎231-1170), but you can get a local bus into town at the bus stop on the other side of the road, opposite the *Rodoviária* entrance; the stops immediately outside are a setting-down point for buses to the outer suburbs only, and will take you in the wrong direction. Most buses from across the road pass through the centre: those marked "Av. Rio Branco", "Cidade Alta" and "Ribeira" are the most common. Taxis from the *Rodoviária* into the centre are also plentiful and should cost around $8.

Natal's main thoroughfare is the **Avenida Rio Branco**, which runs past the oldest part of the city, **Cidade Alta** (where precious little that's old remains), and terminates just to the right of a scruffy square, Praça Augusto Severo, site of the useful local bus station. From Cidade Alta, steep descents lead to the **city beaches** and the coastal road

The **telephone code** for Natal is ☎084.

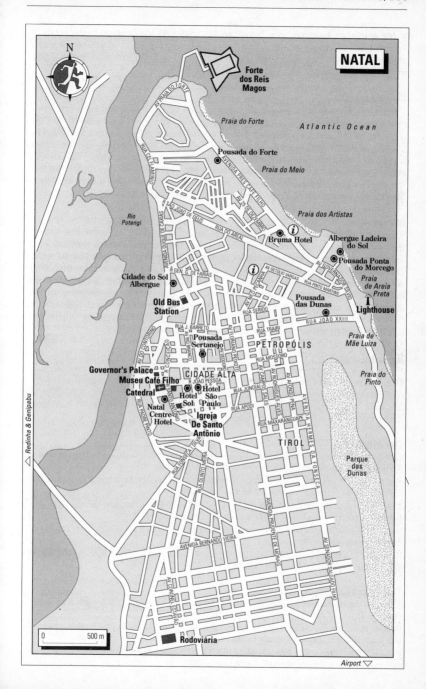

NATAL

N

Forte
dos Reis
Magos

Praia do Forte

Atlantic Ocean

AV PRAIA DO FORTE

RUA CEL LAMIND

Pousada do Forte

AVENIDA PRES CAFÉ FILHO

Praia do Meio

AV 15 DE ABRIL

R SÃO JOÃO DE DEUS

RUA DO AREAL

Rio
Potengi

Praia dos Artistas

Bruma Hotel

Albergue Ladeira
do Sol

AVENIDA DE CAXIAS

R GEN. G. DE FARIAS

AV GOVERNADOR SILVIO

Pousada Ponta
do Morcego

Cidade do Sol
Albergue

AV GETÚLIO VARGAS

RUA PINTO MARTINS

Praia
de Areia
Preta

Old Bus
Station

RUA SERIDÓ

Pousada
das Dunas

Lighthouse

RUA JOÃO XXIII

AV CONTORNO

RUA J. BARRETO

RUA TRAIRI

Praia de
Mãe Luiza

R CONCEIÇÃO

R FLORIANO

AV LOPES DE MACEDO

PETRÓPOLIS

Pousada
Sertanejo

RUA MOSSORÓ

CIDADE ALTA

R JOÃO PESSOA

AV RODRIGUES ALVES

AV CAMPOS SALES

Praia do
Pinto

Governor's Palace
Museu Café Filho
Catedral

Hotel
Sol

Hotel
São
Paulo

RUA JUNDIAÍ

RUA APODI

AVENIDA HERMES DA FONSECA

Natal
Centre
Hotel

RUA PADRE PINTO

Igreja
De Santo
Antônio

RUA MAXARANGUAPE

TIROL

R AFONSO PENA

Parque
das
Dunas

RUA DR QUINTO MEIRA

AVENIDA PRUDENTE DE MORAIS

AVENIDA BERNARDO VIEIRA

AV SENADOR SALGADO FILHO

◁ Redinha & Genipabu

0   500 m

Rodoviária

Airport ▽

to the **southern beaches**, now being rapidly developed; the beaches to the north are less crowded and more beautiful. Just out of the centre are the quiet and pleasant grid-pattern suburbs of **Petrópolis** and the incongruously named **Tirol**, after the birthplace of the Austrian planner who laid them out in the 1930s.

City transport
Natal's **bus system** is easy to master, and in a hot city with hills and scattered beaches it's worth spending a little time getting used to it. At the old **bus station** on Praça Augusto Severo, and from **Avenida Rio Branco**, you can get local buses to most of the places you might want to go to: all the buses to the southern beaches, like Areia Preta and Ponta Negra, can be caught from here or the seafront; buses marked "Via Costeira" head along the southern coastal road out to Ponta Negra. Several bus routes run from the centre to the *Rodoviária*, taking at least half an hour and often longer because of their circuitous routes; "Cidade da Esperança" is the most direct.

Information
There is a **tourist information post** at the *Rodoviária*, which has good free maps of the city and can organize accommodation for you. The main headquarters of the state's tourism secretariat is inconveniently located at the **Centro de Convenções**, on the Via Costeira on the way to Ponta Negra. You're better off trying the **tourist centre** (daily 9am–5pm) in the old prison, perched on top of a hill at Rua Aderbal de Figueiredo 980 in Petrópolis, where there are beautiful views of the beaches and city and various over-priced stalls selling *artesanato*. There's also an information booth on Avenida Presidente Café Filho, at Praia dos Artistas. Alternatively, you can ring the **tourist hotline** (☎219-4226) where you may find someone who speaks English.

Accommodation

Hotels are plentiful in both the city centre and the beach areas. A good alternative option is to stay at one of the beaches outside the city, like Ponta Negra – site of Natal's campsite –and Pirangi to the south or Redinha and Genipabu to the north (accommodation details are given in the text under the relevant places).

The city centre
Cidade do Sol Hotel e Albergue, Av. Duque de Caxias 190 (☎211-3233). A youth hostel near the old bus station, which has decent rooms and a nice garden at the back. $10 a night per person.

Natal Center Hotel, Rua Santo Antônio 665 (☎221-2355). This is the most upmarket option in the city centre, with restaurant, swimming pool and sauna. ⑥.

Hotel São Paulo, Av. Rio Branco 697 (☎211-4485). This budget hotel has been recently refurbished and does a good breakfast. The entrance is on Rua General Osório. ②.

Hotel Pousada Sertanejo, Rua Princesa Isabel 481 (☎221-5396). A good reasonably priced place right in the city centre. ③.

Hotel Sol, Rua Heitor Carilho 107 (☎221-1157). A good-value medium-range hotel in the older part of the upper city, with its own restaurant. ③.

The beaches
Albergue de Juventude Ladeira do Sol, Rua Valentim de Almeida 8 (☎202-1699). A good youth hostel on Praia dos Artistas which costs $10 a night per person.

Bruma Hotel, Av. Pres. Café Filho 1176, Praia dos Artistas (☎211-4947). This hotel overlooks the beach and is worth staying in mainly for the beautiful, relaxing design of the building. ④.

Pousada das Dunas, Rua João XXIII 601 (☎202-1820). A friendly, family-run *pousada* just a bus-ride from the Praia dos Artistas in the Mãe Luiza district. ②.

Pousada do Forte, Av. Pres. Café Filho 786, Praia do Meio (☎211-6080). Large, clean rooms with all mod cons on the beachside opposite the statue of Iemanjá.

Pousada Ponta do Morcego, Rua Valentim de Almeida 10 (☎202-2367). An extremely inexpensive place to stay right next to the youth hostel. ①.

Hotel Vila do Mar, Via Costeira 4233 (☎211-6000). A luxury hotel close to the sea with all facilities including pool and tennis courts. ⑦.

The City

For a city that was founded nearly four centuries ago there is surprisingly little of historical interest in Natal itself, apart from the distinctive, whitewashed star of the **Forte dos Reis Magos** (daily 8am–4.45pm), dominating the river entrance. Like most of Brazil's colonial forts it looks very vulnerable, directly overlooked by the hill behind it and with thick, surprisingly low walls. Although there is not much to see apart from a token museum of local culture, it's interesting to wander around.

The oldest part of the city is formed by the closely packed streets and small squares of **Cidade Alta**, but the street plan itself is one of the only things that remains from colonial times. Instead, the architecture that has survived the modern thrust for development is clustered around the administrative heart of the city, **Praça Sete de Setembro**, which is dominated by the **governor's palace**, built in tropical Victorian style in 1873, and the town hall. In the neighbouring Praça Albuquerque is the **Catedral**, built in 1768 but unexceptional for all that. Smaller, and rather more interesting, is the nearby **Igreja de Santo Antônio**, also known as the Igreja do Galo, after the eighteenth-century bronze cock crowing on top of its Moorish tower. Just off Praça Sete de Setembro is the most interesting museum in a city largely bereft of them, the **Museu Café Filho** (Mon–Fri 8am–5pm, Sat 8–10am), dedicated to the only *Rio Grandense* to become president of Brazil – a corrupt and incompetent paternalist, despite the attempts by the museum to present him as a statesman. But he had the good taste to live in a fine two-storey mansion, at Rua da Conceição 630, which is worth seeing – more than can be said for the yellowing papers and heavy furniture of the long-dead president.

The beaches

What Natal lacks in attractions for the culturally minded, it makes up for in facilities for the beach bum. There are fine **beaches** right inside the city, beginning at the fort where arcs of sand sweep along the bay to the headland and **Mãe Luiza lighthouse**, a useful point to take bearings from. Buses marked "Mãe Luiza" take you from the seafront to the foot of the hill crowned by the lighthouse, which you can walk up but you will be besieged by children offering guided tours. From the top there is a magnificent view of the **Praia do Meio**, the beach that stretches from the fort to the headland of the Ladeira do Sol, and the **Praia da Areia Preta**, curving between the headland and the lighthouse. Technically the Praia do Meio is composed of three beaches: the small **Praia do Forte** next to the fort, the Praia do Meio and the **Praia dos Artistas**. All the beaches are lined with stalls serving the usual array of cold drinks and food, and numerous **hotels** and **bars** are strung along the inland side of the seafront, which gets lively on weekend evenings.

On the other side of the lighthouse is another enormous beach, **Praia de Mãe Luiza**, accessible along the tourist development highway known as the Via Costeira, which takes you to the out-of-town beaches of Ponta Negra, 10km away. The beaches near the centre of town ought to be treated with respect: the combination of a shelving beach and rollers roaring in from the Atlantic often makes the surf dangerous, and a few tourists are drowned every year.

BEACH BUGGIES

Going to Natal without riding a **beach buggy** is a bit like going to Ireland and not drinking Guinness – you may or may not enjoy it, but you might as well try it seeing as you're there. Buggies have become a way of life in Natal, providing employment for the young drivers or *bugeiros* who race around the city and its beaches in their noisy, low-slung vehicles. After a period of explosive, unregulated growth during which unqualified cowboy *bugeiros* risked their and their passengers' necks, the buggy industry has settled down a little bit, though you should still check that your driver has **accreditation** and **insurance** – most of them have.

There are two basic kinds of buggy rides. One possibility is to go on a **day** or **half-day trip**, which involves riding either north or south down the coast, mainly along the beaches. Many firms offer a full day's outing with the *litoral norte* in the morning and the *litoral sul* in the afternoon, or vice versa. The *bugeiro* will perform a few stunts along the way, surfing the sand dunes, but it's mainly an opportunity to explore the beautiful coastline around Natal. A day trip costs about $100 for four people.

However, the real thrills and spills are to be found on specific beaches, especially at **Genipabu** to the north of Natal. Here you pay by the ride or by the hour for fairground-type stuff, with the *bugeiros* making full use of the spectacular sand dunes to push your heart through your mouth. These rides are not cheap, and you may find yourself paying over $40 for an hour's entertainment.

Conditions inside the buggies are cramped. Most *bugeiros* will try and fit three or four people in on each trip, with two people sitting outside at the back hanging on to a metal bar. You'll need plenty of **sun protection** and an extremely tight-fitting **hat**. However, there's no doubt that it's an exhilarating business, with the wind whipping through your hair as you bounce around the sand dunes.

Most hotels have deals with buggy companies, and you'll find yourself besieged by offers of rides wherever you are in Natal. If you want to deal with the **companies** directly, try Hot Buggy, at Av. Eng. Roberto Freire, Ponta Negra (☎219-2540), or Top Buggy, at Estrada de Pirangi 1, Ponta Negra (☎219-2820).

Eating, drinking and nightlife

Restaurants are one of Natal's strongest points, and the regional cuisine has, if anything, been strengthened by the influx of Brazilian tourists, as many see Northeastern food as part of their holiday (consider also the *Canto do Mangue*, described under "Nightlife" below).

Bar do Cação, on the seafront near the fort. Good oyster and shellfish dishes.

Carne de Sol Benigna Lira, Rua Dr José Augusto Bezerra de Menezes 9, Praia dos Artistas (☎202-3914). The speciality of this moderately priced restaurant is sun-dried meat, as good as you'll find anywhere in Brazil.

Casa da Mãe, Rua Pedro Afonso 230, Petrópolis. The speciality here is *galinha cabidela*, chicken stewed in a sauce enriched by its own blood and giblets. The giblets are sieved out before serving, and it's delicious and inexpensive.

Chaplin, Av. Presidente Café Filho 27 (☎211-7457). Somewhat overpriced international restaurant set on the Praia dos Artistas.

Macrobiótica, Rua Princesa Isabel 529. As the name suggests, a macrobiotic restaurant, in the centre of Natal (Mon–Sat 11am–2pm).

O Crustáceo, Rua Apodi 414 (☎222-1122). Excellent, inexpensive seafood in unpretentious surroundings right in the city centre (daily 11am–midnight).

Saborosa, Av. Campos Sales 609, Petrópolis (☎222-7338). Formerly known as *Raizes*, this inexpensive restaurant now serves an excellent range of regional food by the kilo.

Nightlife

Most of Natal's nocturnal action takes place on or around the beaches rather than in the centre. One good spot to head for is **Praia dos Artistas**, the stretch of beach about halfway between the fort and the headland, which hosts plenty of live music at night, especially on weekends. *Coconut* specializes in MPB, while *Bar do Caranquejo* has *forró* on Fridays and Saturdays.

If all you want to do is sip a *caipirinha* and watch the sun set, a good place is the *Canto do Mangue* on the banks of the Rio Potengi: it's a taxi-ride away near the municipal fish market in the *bairro* of **Ribeira**, where Rua Coronel Flaminio runs into Rua São João. It's also one of the best places to eat fish in the city: a speciality is fresh fish fried and served in tapioca with coconut sauce (*peixe ao molho de tapioca*). Be warned, however, that Ribeira can be a fairly rough neighbourhood, especially at night, so take care.

South of Natal

Talking of things to do and places to go around Natal boils down to talking about **beaches**. The easiest southern beach to get to from Natal, and also the liveliest in either direction, is **PONTA NEGRA**, 10km out of town along the Via Costeira, with regular buses from the local bus station that you can also catch from the seafront. The beach, running along a sweeping bay, is magnificent. It's a popular destination for people from the city, especially at weekends; there are bars with live music on Friday and Saturday nights and Sunday afternoons, and several **hotels** and *pousadas* if you feel like staying, as well as a **campsite**, *Vale das Cascatas* (☎236-3229). Some of the better hotels include *Ponta do Mar*, Rua Skal 2056 (☎084/236-2509; ③), with its own pool, and *Bella Napoli Praia*, Av. Beira Mar 3188 (☎084/219-2667; ④), right on the beach and with a good restaurant.

After Ponta Negra, the sands get less crowded. The only problem is getting to them without a car, as there are usually only one or two buses a day to most of the villages from Natal's bus station. Check the times with the tourist office, but they usually leave early in the morning and you may not be able to get back to Natal the same day. This is not a problem, though, since the coastline is being rapidly developed. The villages normally have a *pousada* or two, and it is easy to come to an arrangement about stringing up hammocks in bars and houses. An alternative way of reaching the beaches is to take a **bus** along the main BR-101 highway to Recife from the *Rodoviária*, and get off at Nízia Floresta, from where there are pick-ups, lorries and a local bus service along the dirt road to the coastal fishing villages and beaches of **BÚZIOS** and **BARRA DE TABATINGA**, 20km and 25km from Natal.

More direct is to take the bus from the Natal *Rodoviária* to **PIRANGI DO NORTE**, 30km out of town. Apart from the beach, the village's other famous attraction is the biggest **caju tree** in the world. Although Brazilians know *caju* as a fruit, its seeds, once roasted, become the familiar cashew nut. It's difficult to believe this enormous (over 7000 square metres) expanse of green leaves and boughs could be a single tree; it looks more like a forest. But it is, centuries old and with branches that have spread and put down new roots. It still bears over a ton of fruit annually, so it's not surprising that Pirangi is known for its *caju*-flavoured rum.

To get away from people, you have to travel further south to **Praia da Pipa**, 80km south, and **Praia Sagi**, which virtually lies on the border with Paraíba state some 120km from Natal. The latter is particularly inaccessible and can only be approached by four-wheel drive or on foot, but the result is that it is virtually untouched. The Praia da Pipa ("Kite Beach"), on the other hand, is set in idyllic surroundings with dolphins regularly swimming near the beach and sports a decent selection of facilities: an increasing number of *pousadas* are springing up all over the place and there are also well-established bars like *Yahoo!* where all the nightlife takes place. Once again access is only realistically possible by car or on foot although there are some irregular local bus services.

North of Natal

Most of the recent hotel-building and development has been funnelled south of Natal by the building of the Via Costeira, which makes the **northern beaches** an attractive option. The two main places to head for are Redinha and Genipabu.

REDINHA, 16km from Natal, is a small fishing village facing the city on the northern mouth of the Rio Potengi, and marks the southern end of the enormous beach that effectively makes up the state's northern coastline. The beaches are notable for their huge shifting **sand dunes**, many metres high, which cluster especially thickly to tower over Genipabu. Redinha itself (hourly buses from the local bus station in Natal) is surprisingly underdeveloped for somewhere so close to the city, retaining the air of a simple fishing village, with a small chapel and beachside stalls that fry the freshly caught fish and chill the beer.

There are regular buses to **GENIPABU** leaving from Natal's local bus station, every two hours from Monday to Saturday and hourly on Sunday. Genipabu is still a fishing village, but these days depends more on tourism for its income. There's no need to look down your nose at it, though, as the beach is large enough for you to get away from the crowds. The massive dunes are spectacular and great fun to run down: the sand is so fine it often looks like it came from an egg-timer. A favourite local pastime is to roar up and down them in **beach buggies**, exhilarating but not for those who get travel sick easily (see box p.286). Good excursions along the dunes are to the mineral water spring at Pitangui, and the lovely beach of Jacumã. There are plenty of *pousadas* in Genipabu, so accommodation is no problem. However, the beach stalls operate a cartel and are very expensive for what they offer; the restaurant, *O Pedro*, just to the side, compares very favourably for similar prices and serves a wide range of seafood.

West towards Ceará

The highway **west** to Fortaleza, capital of Ceará state, would be one of the most dramatic in the region if it followed the coast; sadly, though, the BR-304, a good-quality asphalt road, takes a more direct inland route and is pretty dull as a result. The **interior** of Rio Grande do Norte is flatter than the *sertão* of the states to the south, plains of scrubby *caatinga* and cacti only rarely broken up by hills or rocky escarpments. Even on a moving bus you can feel the heat, and you get some idea of why this is one of the poorest and most unforgiving areas in the Northeast. From Natal three daily **buses** make the 500-kilometre run to Fortaleza, taking around nine hours. It's a good stretch of road to do overnight: about the right length to get some sleep, and no spectacular scenery for you to regret missing.

Mossoró

The one place you might think of stopping off at before crossing into Ceará state is **MOSSORÓ**, in many ways an archetype of the *sertão* town in which so many of the inhabitants of the Northeastern interior live. Mossoró has a population of about 190,000 and is growing fast, although you wouldn't guess it from the centre, very much that of a small market town: market, square and a couple of ornate 1930s public buildings, with white plasterwork set off against walls of bright pink, looking for all the world like wedding cakes.

The Town

It's easy to get your bearings in Mossoró, despite the lack of town maps and tourist information. The main street is **Avenida Augusto Severo**, which runs down past the municipal market and local bus station to the two linked squares which are the hub of the city, **Praça Vigário Antônio Joaquim**, where the cathedral is, and **Praça da Independência**. To the left is the road leading to the old jail and town museum; straight on takes you to the Rio Apodi, where – over the bridge – is a small *artesanato* market.

The quickest way to get a flavour of Mossoró is by wandering around the **municipal market**. It gives you an instant handle on the social and economic fabric of the *sertão*, both from the goods on sale – dried meat, medicinal herbs and barks, slabs of salt – and the wiry, straw-hatted peasants and townspeople milling around. The brightly painted lorries and buses, most of which you wouldn't see outside a museum in the developed world, are the more remote villages' only link with Mossoró and, through it, to the outside world. On the fringes of the market simple stalls sell food and rum and iced *caldo de cana* (sugar cane juice) to the shoppers, and small vendors spread their wares out on the pavement. Look for the *funilaria*, kerosene lamps and other simple household items made with great ingenuity from old tins.

However, the main places of interest in the city have to do with Mossoró's enduring claim to fame, a glorious moment in 1924 when the townspeople fought off a full-scale attack by the legendary bandit leader **Lampião** and his band. It's an event that's still celebrated every June 13 with Masses and re-enactments. To follow the Lampião trail, first stop is the **Igreja de Santo Antônio**, near the centre. In accordance with Northeastern form there was no question of a surprise assault when Lampião mounted his attack. He had announced his intention to hold the town to ransom well in advance and had taken landowners in the surrounding countryside hostage to show he meant business: an audacious thing to do, since even then Mossoró was the second city of Rio Grande do Norte. He sent two notes to the mayor demanding money, but the townspeople decided to resist him, digging trenches in the main streets and fortifying public buildings. On June 13, 1924, Lampião attacked with a band of about fifty outlaws, or *cangaçeiros*, and there was fierce fighting, concentrating on the church, where the mayor, his family and retainers had barricaded themselves in. By late afternoon the bandits were driven off with several wounded, one dead, and one famous black outlaw, Jararaca, wounded and captured. Despite being a humiliating defeat for him, the battle of Mossoró became one of the most famous events in Lampião's much celebrated life. On the church there's a plaque commemorating the event, and you can still see the walls and tower pockmarked with bullet holes, carefully preserved.

The next step is to make your way to the **Museu Histórico Municipal**, Praça Antônio Gomes 514 (Tues–Fri 8am–8pm, Sun 8–11am), housed in the oldest building in town, a solid late nineteenth-century building that was once a jail and is now a combined museum and council chamber: it's signposted to the left from Praça Vigário Antônio Joaquim. It contains a remarkable collection of photographs and newspaper articles of the attack and its aftermath, together with things like guns used, clothing taken from the bandits and maps of how the action developed. The most fascinating pieces are the powerful and eloquent photographs of the wounded **Jararaca**, kept in a cell in the very building which houses the museum. Jararaca was in jail for a day, treated by the town doctor, interviewed by the local paper, visited by town luminaries, constantly photographed by the town photographer, and then was taken out at dawn to the municipal cemetery, stabbed, thrown into an already open grave, and shot.

Reading what he said that day, it's clear he knew his fate, but he expressed no fear or regret, only his determination to die like a man, which by all accounts he did. The final stop on the tour is a visit to his grave, in the **cemitério municipal** near the church. The grave isn't signposted, but anyone, except a priest, will point you in its direction, left of the single path as you enter: just say *Jararaca* and look quizzical. The final twist is that the outlaw got his own back in death, becoming a mythical figure and saint for the poor of the region, despite attempts by the Church and the municipal authorities to put a stop to it – hence the lack of a signpost and the fact there is no path to his grave. His grave is covered with flowers, candle stumps, *ex votos* and prayers written on scraps of paper, and regularly visited by supplicants. The best time to see this popular devotion in action is on December 13, when thousands flock to Mossoró from all over the interior of Rio Grande do Norte to celebrate the holy day of Santa Luzia, the city's patron saint.

Practicalities

Mossoró is 276km from Natal, about four hours' drive, and served by several buses a day. The *Rodoviária* is on the edge of town and there are regular **local buses** into the centre; or it's about ten minutes by taxi. **Leaving**, you can get a bus to the *Rodoviária* from the local bus station on the fringes of the municipal market.

The best **hotel**, the *Hotel Thermas*, Av. Lauro Monte 200 (☎084/321-1200; ⑦), is a couple of kilometres out of town, built around some thermal pools. The others are simple and all in the centre of town: try the *Del Prata*, Avenida Augusto Severo, Rua Tiradentes 50 (☎084/321-3846; ②). There's a pleasant **bar**, *O Sujeito*, built on the riverbank just by the *artesanato* market.

CEARÁ

Ceará, covering a vast area, but with only eight million inhabitants, has long borne the brunt of the vagaries of the Northeastern climate. Droughts were recorded here as early as the seventeenth century. In the 1870s, as many as two million people may have died in a famine provoked by drought, and as recently as the early 1980s people were reduced to eating rats, while the populaton of Fortaleza grew by about a third as people fled drought in the interior.

Yet for all its problems Ceará has kept a strong sense of identity, making it a distinctive and rewarding state to visit. Its capital, **Fortaleza**, is the largest and most cosmopolitan city in the Northeast after Recife and Salvador. The **sertão** is unforgiving to those who have to live in it, but in Ceará it rewards the traveller with some spectacular landscapes: as you travel west the flat and rather dull plains of Rio Grande do Norte gradually give way to ranges of hills, culminating in the extreme west of the state in the highlands and lush cloud forest of the **Serra da Ibiapaba**, the only place in Brazil where you can stand in jungle and look down on desert. To the south there are the hills and fertile valleys of **Cariri**, with the pilgrim city of Juazeiro do Norte (see p.280). And the coastline boasts some of the wildest, most remote and beautiful **beaches** in Brazil.

Save for a few sheltered valleys with relatively reliable rainfall, sugar cane does not grow in Ceará and it never developed into the plantation economy of other Northeastern states. Ceará was and remains **cattle** country, with the main roads and centres of population in the state following the route of the old cattle trails. As settlement by the Portuguese and serious economic development began over a century later than in the sugar zone states, and only really got going in the last century, there are very few buildings that date back to colonial times – and, indeed, nothing colonial remains in Fortaleza.

In recent years, Ceará has developed a reputation as one of the best-governed states in Brazil. Successive governors from the **PSDB**, the Social Democratic party of President Fernando Henrique Cardoso, have done much to reduce poverty and disease through imaginative health and education schemes. For the visitor, all this gives Ceará the feeling of an up-and-coming place where things are changing fast.

Fortaleza

FORTALEZA is a sprawling city of around 1.8 million inhabitants, and for well over a century it has been the major commercial centre of the northern half of the Northeast. More recently it has poured resources into expanding its tourist trade, lining the fine city beaches with gleaming luxury hotels. Taken together, this means that no trace remains of the city's eventful **early history**, the clue to which is in its name: Fortaleza means "fortress". The first Portuguese settlers arrived in 1603 and were defeated initially by the Indians, who killed and ate the first bishop (a distinction the city shares with Belém), and then by the Dutch, who drove the Portuguese out of the area in 1637 and built a fort of their own. In fact the Portuguese were restricted to precarious coastal settlements until well into the eighteenth century, when the Indians were finally overwhelmed by the determined blazing of cattle trails into the interior.

It was from Fortaleza that the independence movement from Portugal in northern Brazil was organized, and it was one of the few places where the Portuguese actually made a fight of it, massacring the local patriots in 1824 before being massacred themselves a few months later. The city did well in the **nineteenth century**, as the port city of a hinterland where ranching was expanding rapidly. For decades, though, one of the city's most important exports was the people of the state: shipping lines transported *flagelados* wholesale from Fortaleza during drought years to the rubber zones of the Amazon and the cities of southern Brazil. These days, Fortaleza has something of the same atmosphere as Rio, especially when it comes to the good things in life. It's not a beautiful city but it has a safe, relaxed atmosphere, and the nightlife is superb.

Arrival, city transport and information

The **Rodoviária** and **airport** are some way from the centre in the southern suburb of Fátima, but getting into town has been made easy thanks to the introduction of a comfortable *frescão* service by the Top Bus company ($3). The buses will stop to let you off – or can be flagged down – wherever you want along their circular route, which takes in both the airport and the *Rodoviária* before winding its way through the crowded city centre on its way to the beach areas; it's supposed to run throughout the night, but the service is less frequent then, and you should check with the tourist office if you're relying on it to catch an early-morning bus or plane.

Fortaleza also has plenty of **local buses**. Useful routes that take you out to the main beach areas and back to the city centre are those marked "Grande Circular", "Caça e Pesca", "Mucuripe" and "P. Futuro". Two buses, the "Circular 1" and "Circular 2", run services that cover the outskirts and central part of Fortaleza respectively. There are loads of **taxis**, too, which are essential for getting around late at night. You may also choose to **walk** around Fortaleza quite a lot: the city is heavily policed and feels much safer than many other Brazilian cities, though the usual basic precautions are still in order.

The **telephone code** for Fortaleza is ☎085.

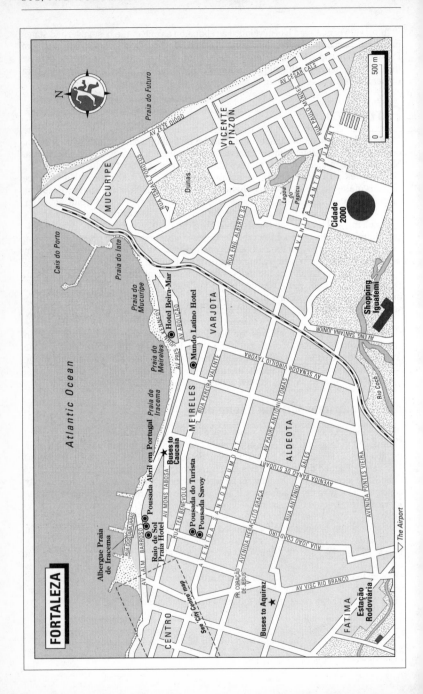

Information

Fortaleza is geared towards catering for visitors and the **tourist information posts** of the *Secretaria de Turismo*, **SETUR**, are friendly and efficient. They give out free city maps, and if you're planning to travel in the state outside Fortaleza you should stock up on the relevant information here. There are information posts at the airport (24hr) and at the *Rodoviária* (daily 6am–6pm). The **main information office** (Mon–Fri 7am–6pm, Sat 8am–2pm, Sun 8am–noon) is in the *Centro de Turismo* in the centre, on Rua Dr João Moreira, and should be your first port of call; the staff know their stuff, and are especially good on the complicated bus journeys that are often necessary to get to the out-of-town beaches. The best maps of the city are to be obtained from the municipal tourist organization, **FORTUR**, who have an information post on Praça do Ferreira in the centre.

You can **change money** at numerous places down on the beach and, in the city centre, at Tropical Viagens, Rua Barão do Rio Branco 1233 (Mon–Fri normal business hours, Sat 8am–noon).

Accommodation

The budget hotels, as ever, tend to be in the centre, which hums with activity during the day but empties at night, and the more expensive ones are generally out by the beaches, notably Iracema and Meireles. But this is not a hard and fast rule; there are literally hundreds of hotels of all shapes and sizes in the city, including luxury hotels in the centre and cheap ones in the beach areas, although very few bargains are to be had on the seafront itself. You should remember that Fortaleza can get very hot, and either air conditioning or a fan is essential.

The city centre

Hotel Caxambu, Rua General Bezerril 22 (☎231-0339). A clean and comfortable place to stay with air conditioning, bar and restaurant. ④.

Lidia Hotel, Rua Rufino de Alencar 300 (☎221-1365). This is a friendly, modern hotel which meets all the basic requirements for comfort. ③.

Nordeste Palace Hotel, Rua Assunção 99 (☎221-1999). Right in the centre of town, on the next street down from Rua Floriano Peixoto – good value for its location and quality. ④.

Hotel Passeio, Rua Dr João Moreira 221 (☎252-2104). A good, though rather musty place to stay at the lower end of the city centre price range. ③.

Hotel Sol, Rua Barão do Rio Branco 829 (☎211-9166). A classy option with airy rooms and a swimming pool. ⑤.

The beaches

Albergue Praia de Iracema, Av. Almirante Barroso 998, Praia de Iracema (☎252-3267). Fortaleza's youth hostel is in an excellent location near the best nightlife and costs $15 a night per person.

Pousada Abril em Portugal, Av. Almirante Barroso 1006, Praia de Iracema (☎231-9508). A good-value budget hotel near the youth hostel. ②.

Hotel Beira-Mar, Av. Beira-Mar (Av. Presidente Kennedy) 3130, Praia de Meireles (☎244-9444). A luxury hotel right next to the Praia de Meireles. ⑦.

Mar Aberto, Av. Zezé Diogo 2322, Praia do Futuro (☎234-3279). Twelve kilometres from the centre of town on Futuro beach, this is a comfortable place with its own pool. ⑤.

Mundo Latino Hotel, Rua Ana Bilhar 507, Praia de Meireles (☎261-8778). This lovely hotel set back from the beach at Meireles offers a high level of comfort for a relatively low price. ③.

Raio de Sol Praia Hotel, Av. Almirante Barroso 772, Praia de Iracema (☎251-1057). A fairly luxurious place to stay near Iracema beach. ⑤.

Pousada Savoy, Rua Dom Joaquim 321 (☎226-8426). Next door to the *Pousada do Turista*, your chance to stay at the *Savoy* at a fraction of the usual price – and comfort. ②.

Pousada do Turista, Rua Dom Joaquim 351 (☎231-6607). A budget hotel run by French-speakers, in a peaceful area a 10min walk from both the city centre and the beach. ②.

The City

The only visible legacy of its crowded history in modern Fortaleza is the city's name, and a **gridded street pattern** laid out in the nineteenth century by a French architect, Adolphe Herbster. He was contracted by the ambitious city fathers to turn Fortaleza into "the Paris of the North" – you can only hope they got their money back.

The **layout of the city** is easy to grasp, despite its size. The **centre**, laid out in blocks, forms the commercial, administrative and religious heart, with markets, shops, public buildings, squares and a forbiddingly ugly concrete cathedral. To the west of the centre, undistinguished urban sprawl finally gives way to the beaches of **Barra do Ceará**, but most of the action is to the **east**, where the main city beaches and the chic middle-class *bairros* of **Praia de Iracema** and **Meireles** are to be found, linked by the

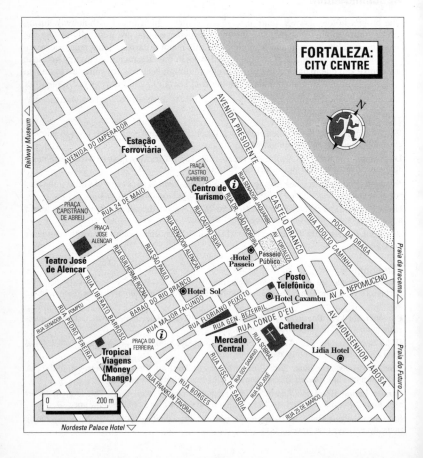

FORTALEZA:
CITY CENTRE

main seafront road, **Avenida Presidente Kennedy**, usually known as **Avenida Beira-Mar**. These give way to the *favelas* and docks of the port area, **Mucuripe**, the gateway to the eastern beaches, notably **Praia do Futuro**, beyond which the city peters out.

While not the most visually attractive Brazilian city centres, there is enough going on in the heart of Fortaleza to merit more attention than it usually gets from visitors. It certainly can't be faulted for being boring: the streets are very crowded, with shops and hawkers colonizing large areas of pavement and squares, so that much of the centre often seems like a single large market. Fortaleza is an excellent place for **shopping**, and you should stock up here if you're heading west, as you won't get comparable choice until you hit Belém, 1500km away. Clothes are plentiful and cheap, and Fortaleza is the largest centre for the manufacture and sale of hammocks in Brazil. As ever, there is also good *artesanato* to be had, notably lace and leather. Tourists tend to do their shopping in a couple of obvious places, like around the tourist centre in the old prison and in front of the seafront hotels in Praia de Iracema – you'll be able to bargain but the prices are, by Brazilian standards, relatively high.

The Mercado Central

Much better and more interesting, if you can take the dirt, the potholes, the smells and the crowds, is the **Mercado Central**, a huge commercial complex where hundreds of small stores and shops are jammed into a series of narrow streets and alleys. It's next to the cathedral, and if you can't see it you will probably be able to smell it, as it includes a large fish and meat market. (There are plans afoot to move the entire market to a new indoor complex down the road, so by the time you read this it may have moved.) This is the best place to **buy a hammock** in the city: if you're going to use one on your travels, purchase it with care. Cloth ones are the most comfortable, but are heavier, bulkier and take longer to dry out if they get wet. Less comfy in the heat, but more convenient, much lighter and more durable are nylon hammocks. Aesthetically, however, nylon hammocks are no match for cloth ones, which come in all colours and patterns. You ought to be able to get a perfectly adequate cloth hammock, which will stand up to a few weeks' travelling, for around $10 for a single and $19 for a double; for a nylon hammock, add $5 to the price. If you want a more elaborate one – and some handwoven hammocks are very fine – you will pay more. Easing the path to slinging hammocks once you get home are metal *armadores*, which many hammock and most hardware shops sell: these are hooks mounted on hinges and a plate with bolts for sinking into walls. When buying a hammock you are going to use, make sure it takes your body lying horizontally across it: sleeping along the curve is uncomfortably bad for your back.

The Centro de Turismo and the Museu de Arte e Cultura Popular

When you've finished shopping, drop in on the **Centro de Turismo** in the old prison overlooking the sea at the bottom of Rua Senador Pompeu. This is not just to visit the tourist information post here, but to sit having a beer in a bar in the one-time exercise yard, shaded by mango trees, and to see the best museum in the city, the **Museu de Arte e Cultura Popular** (Mon–Fri 8am–6pm, Sat 8am–1pm). Well laid out in a single huge gallery on the first floor, this is a comprehensive collection of *Cearense artesanato* of all kinds, together with a sample of the painting and sculpture produced by the best of the state's modern artists. The imaginative juxtaposition of more traditional popular art with modernism is what distinguishes it, and the two collections dovetail neatly. Both are of very high quality: the modern art is often startlingly original, as in the sculptures of bolts, nuts and scrap metal of Zé Pinto, but in style and subject matter you can see how profoundly it is rooted in the tradition of popular art all around it. There is work here in all Ceará's considerable range of materials and styles: leather, ceramics, wood-carvings, lace, cloth, prints, *ex votos*, saints, *cordel* and much more – all beautiful-ly displayed. Wandering around is made easier by the design of the building, whose thick walls keep the heat out, leaving the interior pleasantly cool.

The Passeio Público

Two blocks from the Centro de Turismo is another survivor of nineteenth-century Fortaleza: the old municipal boulevard, the **Passeio Público**, now a pleasant shady square popular with children and families – as well as prostitutes. It looks out over the waterfront, and stallholders set up chairs and tables under the trees, from where they sell cold drinks and simple food. It's a good place to go in the late afternoon or early evening, when the workers stroll around after they get out of their offices watching the variety of street entertainers and hawkers. The municipality often lays something on: small fairs, dances – the ubiquitous *forró* pumped out by tannoy or thumped out by trios – or concerts. Even without entertainment, it has a relaxing feel, and is certainly the best place, away from the beaches, to watch the sunset.

Praça José de Alencar

The nerve centre of this part of the city, however, is its largest square, **Praça José de Alencar**, four blocks inland from the train station at the heart of the commercial dis-trict. In the late afternoon and early evening, the crowds here attract *capoeira* groups, streetsellers of all kinds and especially *repentistas*. Fortaleza seems to specialize in these street poets, who with great skill and wit gather an audience by improvising a verse or two about those standing around watching, passing around a hat for you to show your appreciation. If you refuse, or give what they consider too little, the stream of innuendo and insults, in a variety of complicated metres, is unmistakable, even if you don't understand a word.

On the square you'll also find the one truly impressive building in the city, the beautiful **Teatro José de Alencar**, named after the great nineteenth-century novel-ist and poet, a native of the city. Built in the first decade of this century, the fine trop-ical Edwardian exterior is in fact only an elegant facade, which leads into an open courtyard and the main body of the theatre. It was built in ornate and beautifully worked cast-iron sections, bolted together, which were brought over complete from Scotland and reassembled in 1910. Surprisingly, for a building made out of iron, it is extremely cool and pleasant to be in, even when the sun is at its height: the ironwork is open and lets in the air without trapping heat, a masterly example of Scottish design in the least Scottish setting imaginable. In 1991 it was superbly restored and is now a key venue for theatrical performances and concerts. The best time to see it is at night, when it opens for business, a favourite venue for *Cearense* music of all vari-eties and exhibitions in the courtyard. Friday and Saturday are the likeliest nights to find something on: the staff can let you know what's happening, or try looking under the heading *Lazer* in the local papers.

Transport museums

Museums are not Fortaleza's strong point. However, if you get bored with the beach-es and you are into transport then there are a couple of museums worth visiting: the **Centro da Preservaçao da Historia Ferroviária do Ceara** at Av. São Francisco Sa 4829 (Tues–Sat 9am–noon & 2–5pm, Sun 9am–1pm), which deals with the develop-ment of the rail network throughout Ceará; and the **Museu do Automovel**, at Av. Des. Manoel Sales de Andrade 70 in the Água Fria district on the southern edge of the city (Tues–Sat 9am–noon & 2–5pm, Sun 9am–1pm), which charts the history of the motor car in Brazil.

The city beaches

The main city beach is the **Praia de Iracema**, whose scores of apartment buildings and hotels laid out on a grid pattern are a resort by day and the main focus for Fortaleza's nightlife. The water is not as clean as it could be, due to the proximity of docks both east and west: the further away from the centre, the better for swimming. That said, Iracema is the best bet for sunset watching: the seafront boulevard is well laid out, punctuated by clumps of palm trees, and there is no shortage of watering holes.

If you're a beach devotee, cleaner water, higher rollers and better seafood are to be had further out past Mucuripe at **Praia do Futuro**: take buses marked "Caça e Pesca" or "P. Futuro" from Rua Castro e Silva in the centre, or "Mucuripe" to its terminal and make a connection. The beach *barracas* here are very good: the fried fish is fresh and comes in enormous portions. The only disadvantage is the irregularity of buses back to town after 10pm, which makes watching the sunset here difficult unless you are prepared to pay $8 for a taxi. The ultimate surfing beaches, however, are 6km beyond the Praia do Futuro, at **Porto das Dunas** and **Prainha**, 11km in combined length. Porto das Dunas also has an aquatic theme park called **Beach Park** (daily 9am–5pm; ☎360-1150), the largest of its kind in Latin America.

Eating, drinking and nightlife

You'll be all right in the centre during the day if you want something to eat as there are countless places to grab a snack. However, most of what Fortaleza has to offer your palate is to be found on the beaches, especially around **Rua dos Tabajaras** on Praia de Iracema. There's a pier here known as *Ponte dos Ingleses*, which is a lovely place to have a beer and watch the sunset. Rua dos Tabajaras itself is a joy to wander around, with its brightly coloured bars and **restaurants**, and glamorous young people out enjoying themselves. The *Restaurante Estoril* makes the best of its setting at Rua dos Tabajaras 397, but it's quite pricey. Slightly cheaper is the *Colher de Pau* at no. 412, while *La Bohéme* at no. 380 combines a French menu at moderate prices with an art gallery. An excellent seafood restaurant is the *Restaurante Tia Nair*, just down the seafront road, on the corner of Avenida Beira-Mar and Idelfonso Albano.

Two **bars** on Avenida Beira-Mar, just along from Rua dos Tabajaras, offer a wonderful combination of eating, drinking and live music: the *Pontal de Iracema* at no. 680 and the *Cais Bar* at no. 696 are extremely trendy nightspots where you have to arrive pretty early to get a seat.

Forró: dancing and clubs

Fortaleza is justly famous for its **forró**. Nowhere is it so popular, and there is no better way to see what *Cearenses* do when they want to enjoy themselves than to spend a night in a *dancetaria* in Fortaleza. And spending the night is literally what you need to do: although most *dancetarias* open at 10pm, people don't really start arriving until around midnight, and peak time is in the early hours of the morning. There always seems to be *forró* on somewhere but the venue changes every night.

On Mondays the place is *Pirata*, one of the most easily accessible nightclubs in Fortaleza, at Rua dos Tabajaras 3235. It's a great night out but not cheap: entrance costs about $15. *Subindo ao Céu*, at Av. Zezé Diogo out on Praia do Futuro, is the main venue on Tuesday nights. On Wednesdays the scene shifts to the *Clube do Vaqueiro* (☎276-2014), a taxi-ride away out on the periphery of the city along the BR-116 highway leading east to Natal. As its name implies, the club has everything for the cowboy: the huge complex is sometimes used for rodeos during the day, and on Wednesday nights the cavernous interior throbs with *forró* rhythms and hundreds of dancing couples. On Thursdays you can eat crab and enjoy live music at *Chico do Caranguejo*, at Av. Zezé Diogo 4930 on Praia do Futuro. Finally, on Fridays the venue for *forró* is the *Parque do Vaqueiro* (☎296-1159), west of Fortaleza on the BR-020.

Around Fortaleza: the beaches

The **beaches** of Ceará are what attract most visitors, and both east and west of Fortaleza they stretch unbroken for hundreds of kilometres. They are invariably superb, a mixture of mountainous sand dunes, palm trees and Atlantic breakers, wilder than the sheltered reef beaches of the southern states of the Northeast. Even some of the most remote beaches have been "discovered" by tourists, but there is no need to scorn them on that account: the coastline is more than big enough to swallow large numbers of property developers and visitors without getting crowded. It's easy to bewail the passing of the simple life in the fishing villages, but talk to their inhabitants and you'll find they are still functioning communities, making money from tourists on the side. What travellers see as an idyllic, rustic existence seems more like poverty to those who live it.

Any description of the beaches becomes repetitive: they are all stunning. Travelling along the coast, while often leisurely, is not difficult. To reach the beaches, as a rule, you will need to get off at a town and catch a connection to the nearby coast, and the local bus network covers most places: at the better-known beaches, shoals of pick-ups and beach buggies meet the buses from Fortaleza.

East to Aracati and Canoa Quebrada

East of Fortaleza there are two basic routes. The first heads along a coastal road that branches off the BR-116 just south of the city to Beberibe. The first coastal village along this route is **AQUIRAZ**, where there are the beaches of **Iguape** and **Prainha**. Buses to Aquiraz are run by the São Benedito company and leave from a stop on the corner of Avenida Domingos Olímpio and Avenida Aquanambi. For anywhere east of Aquiraz, buses can be caught at the *Rodoviária*. Thirty kilometres beyond Aquiraz is Cascavel, 12km inland but a starting point for two more beaches: **Caponga** and, less crowded, **Aguas Belas**. Twenty kilometres further on is **BEBERIBE** itself, the drive there a lovely one on a country road through palm forests and dunes. The irregularly shaped dunes of Beberibe's beach, **Morro Branco**, are fifteen minutes away. Five kilometres from here is the small fishing village and mineral-water spring of **PRAIA DAS FONTES**, which also boasts a luxury hotel of the same name, reasonably priced and serving excellent food (☎085/338-1179; ⑤).

A more direct route east takes you to **ARACATI**, two hours from Fortaleza, a once-prosperous small textile town with half-a-dozen derelict, and a couple of functioning, eighteenth-century churches. It is also the jumping-off point for one of Ceará's better-known and most fashionable beaches, **Canoa Quebrada**, half an hour along a dirt road from Aracati: pick-ups meet every bus from the city, so access is no problem. Canoa Quebrada is popular with foreigners and young Brazilians alike, the atmosphere is relaxed, and it's fairly lively at night. Certainly, if you want company and *movimento* it's the beach to head for. The dusty approach road to Canoa Quebrada is flanked by dozens of boards advertising *pousadas* and restaurants and there's no shortage of either. Curiously, the beach served directly by asphalted road from Aracati, **Majorlândia**, is less crowded and a lot quieter. It's certainly as good as Canoa Quebrada, there are *jangadas* on the beach and surf here as well, and it's just as easy to find places to stay.

West to Jericoacoara

The choice of strands **west of Fortaleza** is equally rich. Only 8km from Fortaleza is the town of **Caucaia**, which is served by buses from Avenida Ruy Barbosa (outside the Ideal Clube) on Praia de Meireles. From Caucaia, local buses head out to the beaches of **Icaraí** (not to be confused with another Icaraí more than 150km to the west), **Pacheo** and **Tabuba** where, even by *Cearense* standards, the coastline is really something, with dunes, lagoons, palm forests and enormous expanses of sand; the road ends up in the fishing village of Cumbuco.

Frequent buses from the Fortaleza *Rodoviária* (tickets from Brasileiro Transporte) go to **SÃO GONÇALO DO AMARANTE**, only an hour and 57km away. From here, you can head on to the beaches of **Pecém**, 15km away, and the glorious beach of **Taíba**, 6km on. Not all buses to São Gonçalo continue to the beaches, but if they don't there are pickups and local buses. The beach town of **PARACURU**, 80km from Fortaleza (frequent buses from the *Rodoviária*, also with Brasileiro Transporte), is being rapidly developed and gets crowded during weekends, but is less frenetic during the week.

After Paracuru, you head out of Fortaleza's influence and the further west you go, the less crowded the beaches become. A good place to head for, reasonably remote but not impossible to get to, is **TRAIRI**, 118km from Fortaleza, served by direct buses from the *Rodoviária*, which take around three hours. From here it's a few kilometres to the beautiful and usually deserted beaches of **Mundaú** and **Fleixeiras**. When the tide is out, you can walk for an hour along the beach to the fishing hamlet of **GUAJIRU**. There is no electricity or running water, but the people are friendly and the scenery marvellous.

Ceará's most famous beach, **JERICOACOARA**, lies 291km west of Fortaleza, a remote hangout with huge dunes. Two buses a day from Fortaleza cover the seven-hour journey to the village of Gijoca, where pickup trucks and buggies will meet you for the hour-long ride over the sands to Jericoacoara. It's still a primitive place, unconnected to the main electricity grid, but there are plenty of places to stay, or you can rent a house.

On to Piauí: the Serra da Ibiapaba

Apart from the beaches, there is little to detain you as you head west from Fortaleza, though it's a fine drive, with rocky hills and escarpments rising out of the *sertão* and the road snaking through occasional ranges of hills. You pass through the town of **SOBRAL**, an ugly industrial centre nestling in the middle of a spectacular landscape very typical of the interior of the Northeast: fiercely hot, cobalt blue skies, flinty hills and *caatinga*. It would be very easy to sit back, enjoy the scenery and head directly west for Piauí and Maranhão in one go, but if you did you'd miss one of the finest sights Ceará state has to offer: the beautiful cloudforest and hills of the highlands that run down the border between Ceará and Piauí – the **Serra da Ibiapaba** – and the caves of **Ubajara**.

Serra da Ibiapaba

You reach the Serra on buses arriving from either east or west, along the BR-222 highway that links Fortaleza with Teresina, capital of the neighbouring state of Piauí. You can get off at **TIANGUÁ**, a pleasant, sleepy town on the *Cearense* side of the border: from here there are frequent local connections to Ubajara (see p.300), also served by direct buses from Fortaleza (Ipu Brasília line). In Tianguá, there is a good **hotel**, the *Serra Grande* (☎085/671-1818; ⑤), but it's best to press on to Ubajara, 15km away.

Whether you approach from Teresina or Fortaleza the effect is the same. The buses drive across a bakingly hot plain, which begins to break up the nearer you get to the state border, rearing up into scattered hills and mesas covered with scrub and enormous cacti. Then on the horizon, in view hours before you actually start to climb it, all the hills seem suddenly to merge into a solid wall that rears up 900m from the parched plain below, its slopes carpeted with thick forest: the **Serra da Ibiapaba**.

Ironically, the abundance of the highland forest is part of the explanation for the parched landscape below. The sheer slopes of the serras are well watered because they relieve any clouds of their surplus water before they drift over the plains below. As the bus begins to climb, winding its way through gorges choked with forest, the broiling heat of the plain is left behind and the air gets fresher and more comfortable. When you reach the tableland on top, it seems another world. Everything is green and fertile: the temperature, warm but fresh with cool breezes, is an immense relief, and the contrast with the conditions only half an hour's drive away below couldn't be more marked.

Ubajara

En route to Ubajara you'll see how *Nordestinos* treasure those few parts of the interior blessed with fertile soil and regular rainfall: the highlands are intensively farmed by smallholders and supply fruit, vegetables, sugar and manioc for the whole region. **UBAJARA** itself is a small, friendly town nestling in beautiful hills. There are a couple of simple but perfectly adequate **hotels** near the single church and quiet square, together with one or two **bars** and **restaurants**. It's a pleasant place to stay, but probably the best option is to head a couple of kilometres out of town, along the road leading away from Tianguá, to the comfortable *Pousada da Neblina*, Estrada do Teleférico (☎085/634-1270; ②). Standing in splendid isolation at the foot of a hill covered with palm forest, it has a restaurant and swimming pool, and is remarkable value; you can also camp here. Another option is *Sitio Santana*, known as "*Sitio do Alemão*" by the locals, which provides small chalets on a coffee plantation (②). The view from the chalets is spectacular and it's only a short taxi-ride away, or the owner will pick you up from town; just ask anyone in town to put you in touch with him.

Parque Nacional de Ubajara

A twenty-minute walk along the road from the *pousada* will bring you to the gatehouse of the **Parque Nacional de Ubajara**, which ensures that the magnificent forest remains untouched. Continue past the gatehouse and you come to the *mirante*, a viewing platform with a small café built onto the rim of an escarpment. North and south the serra breaks into ridges covered with forest and tumbles down into the plain, which stretches as far as the eye can see. The view is broken up by jagged hills, towns and villages connected by vein-like roads, and the whole panorama is laid out as if seen from the cockpit of an aeroplane.

From here a **cable car** swoops down 400m to the cave complex of the **Grota de Ubajara**. It's an unforgettable ride, plunging down and skimming the top of the forest before arriving at the caves. If you feel more adventurous, there is a **path** down which can be negotiated with a guide. On no account try it on your own; though it's not dangerous, you need somebody to make sure you don't stray off the path. The forest wardens, one of whom is always on duty at the gatehouse, will take you down if you make arrangements the day before. You'll be met at the gatehouse early in the morning, so you do the bulk of the walk before the heat gets up: take liquids, and wear trainers or decent walking shoes. Going down takes a couple of hours, returning twice that, but there are streams and a small waterfall to cool off in along the way. There are also **caves** to explore: huge caverns with grotesque formations of stalactites and stalagmites. Technically, the wardens are meant to guide you as part of their job, but as they're extremely badly paid they appreciate some recompense for spending several hours of their time making sure you come to no harm.

PIAUÍ

Piauí is, as its inhabitants say, shaped like a ham, with a narrow neck of coastline 59km long that broadens out inland. It's a very distinctive state, but unfortunately most of the reasons for this are depressing. Despite its size it has less than two million inhabitants and by far the lowest population density in the Northeast. With virtually no natural resources except the *carnaúba* palm, and subject to drought, it is Brazil's poorest state.

Few travellers spend much time in Piauí. The capital, **Teresina**, is strategically placed for breaking the long bus journey between Fortaleza and São Luis, but it's a modern, rather ugly city where the heat can be oppressive. The southern half of the state merges into the remoter regions of Bahia and forms the harshest part of the Northeast. Much of it is uninhabited, largely trackless, arid badlands, in the midst of which lies, ironically, the oldest inhabited prehistoric site yet found in Brazil. Cave paintings show that this desert was once jungle. Other than the capital, there are two places worth making for: the pleasant coastal town of **Parnaíba**, which has excellent beaches, and the **Parque Nacional de Sete Cidades**, good walking country with weird and striking rock formations. For some reason, this poorest of states has an excellent **highway** system and the main roads between Teresina and Parnaíba and towards Ceará are very good: as the country is largely flat, the buses really fly.

Piauí was sparsely settled by cattle drovers moving westwards from Ceará in the second half of the eighteenth century and has a violent history. The few Indians were never really conquered and were assimilated with the newcomers rather than being defeated by them, leaving their imprint in the high cheekbones and copper skin of a strikingly handsome people. Apart from cattle, the only significant industry revolves around the **carnaúba palm**, a graceful tree with fan-shaped leaves that grows in river valleys across the northern half of the state. The palm yields a wax that was an important ingredient of shellac, from which the first phonogram records were made, and for which there is still a small export market. It's also a source of cooking oil, wood, soap, charcoal and nuts, and many livelihoods depend on it.

Parque Nacional de Sete Cidades

The **Parque Nacional de Sete Cidades** comprises thirty square kilometres of nature reserve which could hardly be more different from the forest reserve of Ubajara a couple of hundred kilometres east. Here it's the spiky, semi-arid vegetation of the high *sertão* that is preserved – gothic cacti and stubby trees. The really special feature of the reserve is its eroded **rock formations**, many streaked with prehistoric rock carvings. From the air they look like the ruins of seven towns, hence the name of the area, and their striking shapes have given rise to all sorts of ridiculous theories about the area having been a Phoenician outpost in the New World. In fact the rock sculpting is the entirely natural result of erosion by wind and rain.

There are two ways of **getting to the park**, depending on whether you approach from Ceará state or elsewhere in Piauí. Coming **from Fortaleza or Ubajara**, get off the bus at the town of **Piripiri**, from where a free bus or transit van leaves at 6am (Tues–Fri) and takes you to the national park hostel run by the IBDF, the Brazilian forestry service. If you arrive too late, or on a day when the bus isn't running, you could take a local bus from Piripiri to the turn-off to the park 15km north, and walk (3hr) from there. Coming **from Teresina or Parnaíba**, get a bus to Piracuruca and take a taxi to the park – the taxi-ride costs about $20. There are perfectly adequate, cheap and clean **hotels** near the bus stations in both Piripiri and Piracuruca, as well as the accommodation in the park itself (see p.302).

Despite its good facilities and its position near the main Teresina–Fortaleza highway, not as many people visit the park as you might expect. Consequently, it's the ideal place to get off the beaten track without actually venturing far from civilization.

Into the park

There are two **places to stay** in the park, both of them more than acceptable. At the entrance is the *Fazenda Sete Cidades* (☎086/276-2222; ⑤), with a restaurant, pool and regular pick-up shuttle into the park itself, which you can use whether you stay there or not. More convenient for walking, and just as comfortable, is the cheaper *Abrigo do Ibama* (②) in the centre of the park, again with a restaurant and bathing nearby in a natural spring.

Walking in Sete Cidades is not difficult. There are a series of **trails** and several **campsites**, and the staff at both the *fazenda* and the *Abrigo do Ibama* are good at suggesting routes; there are very cursory sketch maps on sale, but don't rely on their accuracy. The walks are not especially strenuous, but take care all the same. It gets extremely hot and a stout pair of shoes, plenty of liquids and a broad-brimmed hat are essential. Start out as near sunrise as you can manage, when the park is at its most beautiful. And when you approach the rocks make some noise: rattlesnakes sometimes sun themselves on them, but they are very shy and slither away if they can hear you coming. The **rock formations** themselves make very good landmarks and their different shapes have lent them their names: the "Map of Brazil", the "Tortoise", the "Roman Soldier", the "Three Kings", the "Elephant" and so on.

Carnaúba country

Heading **west** from Ceará or from Sete Cidades towards Amazonia, there are two routes you can follow. The fastest and most direct is simply to take the highway through Teresina and on to São Luis or, a day from Teresina, to Belém and Amazonia proper. But if you have the time, there is a much more interesting and scenic route **north** up the BR-343 highway, a fine drive through a plain studded with *carnaúba* palm plantations to **Parnaíba** and the coast. From Parnaíba there is a direct bus service, over country dirt roads that get seriously difficult to travel in the rainy season, to São Luis, capital of neighbouring Maranhão state, where the Amazon region begins.

Parnaíba

PARNAÍBA, with its attractive natural anchorage on the Rio Igaraçu, was founded over fifty years before Teresina. For the Portuguese, it was the obvious harbour from which to ship out the dried meat and *carnaúba* of the interior and, in the nineteenth century, it was a thriving little town; you can still see the chimneys of the cotton factories put up by British entrepreneurs a century ago. Then the river silted up, the port moved to Luiz Correia at the mouth of the river, and the town slipped into decline. Today, Parnaíba has a lazy feel, but is still the second largest city in the state with around 128,000 inhabitants. Located anywhere else it would be a thriving resort town; the **beaches** nearby are excellent.

There is not too much to do in Parnaíba except waste time pleasantly. The commercial area in the centre is busy, and **Praça da Graça**, with its palms and cafés, is an enjoyable place to hang about. The liveliest place in town, though, is the riverfront **Avenida Nações Unidas**, a grandiose name for a small promenade lined with cafés and restaurants. There are also boat trips to the islands at the mouth of the Rio Parnaíba, organized by the state tourist authority PIEMTUR based in the Complexo Turístico at the end of Avenida Getúlio Vargas (☎086/322-3692).

The modern **Rodoviária** is on the edge of town, and buses for the short ride to the centre leave from outside. The centre is small and contains all Parnaíba's **hotels**, the best of which is the *Cívico*, Av. Chagas Rodrigues 474 (☎086/322-2470; ④). There's also cheap, clean accommodation at the *Pousada Rio Igaraçu*, Rua Almirante Gervásio Sampaio 390 (☎086/322-3342; ②), and the *Casa Nova Hotel*, at Praça Lima Rebelo 1094 (☎086/322-3344; ②). Or you could stay out at the coastal village of Luiz Correia (see below) and its beaches Atalaia and Coqueiro.

The beaches

You might as well follow the locals and head off to the **beaches** if you want to relax. Not served by bus, but only a short taxi ride away, is the **Lagoa do Portinho**, a freshwater lake with palms and chalets to stay in, and a good restaurant.

There are simple hotels and *dormitórios* if you want to stay in **LUIZ CORREIA**, basically a fishing village 8km north of Paranaíba, with a small modern port attached. From here you can either walk or get the bus to the huge and popular **Praia de Atalaia**. At weekends practically the entire population of Parnaíba decamps here and the crowded bars reverberate to *forró* trios. A less crowded beach, **Coqueiro**, is 12km from here, but there are only a couple of buses a day.

Hourly **local buses** to Luiz Correia and Praia de Atalaia leave from the terminus next to Praça Santo Antônio in Parnaíba, three blocks along the pedestrianized shopping street that leads down from Praça da Graça; they take about twenty minutes to arrive in Luiz Correia, and another five to hit the beach – stay on till the end of the line to be dropped at the liveliest stretch.

Teresina

People from **TERESINA** tell a joke about their city: "Why do vultures fly in circles over Teresina? Because they glide with one wing and have to fan themselves with the other!" Brazil's hottest state capital, Teresina sits far inland on the east bank of the Rio Parnaíba, where it bakes year round in an *average* temperature of 40°C (which means it regularly gets hotter than that). The rains, meant to arrive in February and last for three or four months, are not to be relied upon – though ironically, twice in the last ten years, they have actually flooded Teresina. Unless you're used to such heat, you'll find it tiring to move around; rooms with at least a fan, and preferably air conditioning, are a necessity.

There's not a great deal to do or see in Teresina, but there's enough to occupy yourself for a day if you feel like breaking the long bus journey from Ceará. Besides having some comfortable hotels, it's the only place between Fortaleza and São Luis where you can do things like have money cabled out to you and cash travellers' cheques.

The City

Thankfully, in such a hot place, most of the things worth seeing and doing are reasonably close to each other. The best place to start is the **market** that occupies most of the main square of the city, technically called Praça da Bandeira, but universally known by its old name, **Marechal Deodoro**. It's a smaller, more urbanized version of the typical Northeastern market, with packed stalls forming narrow streets, determined shoppers, energetic sellers, noise, loud music and plenty of *caldo de cana* kiosks, where you can slurp freshly crushed sugar cane and watch the city at work. There is *artesanato* scattered around, and the hammocks from the interior are high quality; both are cheaper here than in the craft shops run by PIEMTUR.

Overlooking the market, in one of the very few fine old buildings in the city, the **Museu do Piauí** at Marechal Deodoro 900 (Tues–Fri 8am–5pm, Sat & Sun 8am–noon) is definitely worth seeing. A governor's palace, built in 1859, it has been beautifully restored, with the exhibits well displayed in simple, elegant rooms, many with high arched windows and balconies perched just above the crowded market stalls. The collection is the usual eclectic mix, and pride of place must go to a collection of early radios, televisions and stereograms, a must for lovers of 1950s and 1960s kitsch. There are also fine examples of the two things that distinguish *artesanato* in Piauí: sculpture in straw and beautifully tooled leather. The art is vivid, simple and varies widely in quality.

You might also want to investigate the crafts and culture complex run by PIEMTUR, the **Centro de Comercialização Artesanal**, also known as the Mercado Central, in the old military barracks at Rua Paissandu 1276, overlooking Praça Dom Pedro Segundo. It's small, but a pleasant place to wander around. The *artesanato* is laid out in booths and is good quality, although a little expensive; the leatherwork is especially fine. Upstairs is a nice café with restaurant attached, where the *carne do sol* is excellent.

Practicalities

The **Rodoviária** is on the outskirts of the city and has a **tourist information post** (Mon–Fri 8am–noon & 2–6pm, Sat 8am–noon) run by the state tourist organization PIEMTUR, where you can pick up free booklets with a centrefold city map. Frequent buses run into the centre from outside, and there are cheap taxis, too. You will also find an information post on the corner of Magalhaes Filho and Alvaro Mendes in the centre of town five blocks from the Praça da Liberdade. It's very easy to find your way around as the streets are organized in a grid pattern.

There are a number of good **hotels** opposite the *Rodoviária*. Both the *Elite* (①) and the *São Francisco* (②) are good value. In the city centre overlooking the river is the luxury *Luxor Hotel do Piauí*, Praça Mal. Deodoro 310 (☎086/221-4911; ⑦), while cheaper places nearby are around Praça Saraiva. Mid-range hotels include the *Sambaiba*, Rua Gabriel Ferreira 230 (☎086/222-4911; ③), and the *Teresina Palace*, Rua Paissandu 1219 (☎086/221-2770; ④), both in the city centre.

There are good **restaurants** in the city, although the prices are medium to expensive, rather than cheap. Good regional food is served at *Celsos*, Rua Agelica 1059 (☎086/232-2920), a short taxi-ride away from the centre in the *bairro* of Fátima. You'll find excellent seafood at *Camarão de Elías*, Av. Pedro Almeida 457, in the *bairro* of São Cristóvão (☎086/232-5025; closed Sun). *Piauienses* excel at meat: a good place to try the *cabrito*, young goat, deliciously tender and served either roasted over charcoal or *ao leite de coco*, stewed in coconut milk, is *Asa Branca*, Av. Frei Serafim 2037, in the centre, with live music (Thurs–Sat). If you're after a meat feast, the *rodízio* at *Rio Poty*, Av. Mal. Castelo Branco 616, is the place to go.

The city's **nightlife** lacks the focus of the coastal capitals, but there is life after dark. The bank of the Rio Parnaíba is the best place from which to enjoy the sunset. A kilometre or so south of the centre, along the riverfront road, is **Prainha**, a series of bars and restaurants built along the riverbank, shaded by planted trees: buses run there, but are very infrequent by late afternoon – use the taxis in Teresina, which are cheap.

MARANHÃO

Maranhão is where the separate but interlinked worlds of the Northeast and Amazonia collide. Although classed as a Northeastern state by Brazilians, its climate, landscape, history and capital of **São Luis** are all *amazônico* rather than *nordestino*. Maranhão is the only state in the Northeast which more people migrate to than emigrate from. Drought is not a problem here; the **climate** is equatorial – humid, hot and very wet indeed. The rainy season peaks from January to April, but most months it rains at least a little, and usually a lot – although only in concentrated, refreshing bouts for most of the year. Maranhão has more fertile, well-watered land than the rest of the Northeast put together. Much of it is flat, the east and north covered with palm forest, and the centre and west riddled, in typical Amazonian fashion, with large rivers and fertile riverine plains – one of the main rice-producing areas of Brazil.

Further west begins the tropical forest and savanna of Amazônia proper, as you hit the eastern boundary of the largest river basin in the world. The **coast** also changes character: the enormous beaches give way, from São Luis westwards, to a bewildering jumble of creeks, river estuaries, mangrove swamps and small islands, interspersed with some of the most remote beaches in Brazil – three hundred miles of largely roadless coastline with towns and villages accessible only from the sea.

Like most zones of geographical transition, Maranhão also marks a historical and cultural divide. The **people** are a striking contrast to the ethnic uniformity of the states immediately to the east: here blacks, Indians and Europeans form one of the richest cultural stews to be found in Brazil. Catch the great popular festival of **Bumba-meu-boi** in June and you'll get some idea of how different from the rest of the Northeast Maranhão really is.

The main centres of population in the state are on and around the island of São Luis, and deep in the interior along the banks of the **Rio Tocantins**, a tributary of the Amazon but a mighty river in its own right. The contrast between the two regions could hardly be more stark. Only thirty years ago the Rio Tocantins was the boundary between Brazil and largely unknown Indian country. Today, as people flood into eastern Amazonia, **Imperatriz**, with 276,000 inhabitants, is the second city of the state, and even dozy, historic São Luis, founded in 1612, is being transformed by docks and factories linked to the huge development projects of eastern Amazonia – the subject of much international controversy.

Routes into Maranhão

There are two **routes** into Maranhão from the east: scooting along the good asphalted highway that links Teresina to São Luis, a six-hour bus ride; or lurching along country roads from Parnaíba, which is more interesting but not to be attempted in the rainy season, when the non-asphalted roads in Maranhão become quagmires. Either way, there's little to detain you before you get to São Luis, as you watch the land transforming itself into the tropics along the way. The *carnaúba* palm of Piauí gives way to the taller trunk and straight fronds of the most common tree in Maranhão, the **babaçu palm**, on which even more livelihoods depend than on *carnaúba*: it provides nuts, cooking oil, soap, charcoal, rope fibre, timber and thatch.

São Luis

SÃO LUIS is a poor city, the most emphatically Third World of all the state capitals of the Northeast. There are power cuts, things don't work, some of the historic city centre is literally falling to pieces, and the infant mortality rate is 136 per thousand live births, putting São Luis up there with poor African countries. Sometimes it even looks like an African city as it has a huge black population, a legacy of plantation development during the eighteenth and nineteenth centuries. It is also far larger than it seems from the compact city centre; about 700,000 people live here, most of them in sprawling *favelas*, with the middle classes concentrated in the beach areas of Ponta da Areia, São Francisco and Olho d'Agua, linked to the rest of the city by a ring road and the bridge built out from the centre across the Rio Anil.

The **telephone code** for São Luis is ☎098.

△ The Beaches

SÃO LUIS

Palácio dos Leões
PRAÇA PEDRO II
Prefeitura
Terminal de Integração
Vila Rica Hotel
Cathedral
Hotel Estrela
ZONA
Pousada Ilha Bella
Lord Hotel
PR JOÃO LISBOA
Pousada do Francês
Fonte do Ribeirão
Cafuá das Mercês
Museu de Arte Sacra
Santo Antônio
Convento das Mercês
São João
Igreja do Desterro
PRAÇA ODÓRICO MENDES
Athenas Palace Hotel
Banco do Brasil
PRAÇA DEODORO
0   500 m

Rodoviária & Airport ▽

But, for all its problems, São Luis is still a fascinating place, undeservedly neglected by travellers. Built across the junction of two rivers and the sea, on an island within the larger delta formed by the **Pindaré** and **Itapicuru** rivers, it has the umbilical connection with rivers that marks an Amazon city, but is also a seaport with ocean beaches. Since 1989, two hundred buildings in its historic centre (many of which are tiled mansions typical of the colonial period) have benefited from a large-scale restoration programme, the **Projeto Reviver**, reputed to have cost anything between $25 million and $100 million. If there is any truth in the latter figure then someone must have made a lot of money in the process. Meanwhile, other parts of the colonial heritage continue to crumble but have their own unique atmosphere: there are people packed cheek by jowl, workshops, stalls, brothels, *dormitórios* – in short, a living and breathing heart of a city, not something lifelessly preserved for consumption by outsiders.

The **beaches**, too, are magnificent, and for the most part have been spared intrusive urban development. Above all, try to visit in June, when you can enjoy the festival for which the city is famous, **Bumba-meu-boi** (see box p.308); here, it counts for more than *Carnaval*.

Arrival, information and accommodation

Both the airport and the *Rodoviária* are some way from the city centre. A taxi from the **airport** to the centre will cost you about $20: pay at the kiosk on the left as you come out of the luggage collection area and hand the coupon to the driver. Alternatively you can catch the bus outside marked "São Cristóvão". From the **Rodoviária** a taxi to the centre costs about $10. Buses connect the *Rodoviária* with the local bus station, the

Terminal de Integração at Praia Grande, by the waterfront in the city centre. Once there you shouldn't need to use public transport very much: the area of interest is small and most things are within walking distance.

The availability and quality of **tourist information** in São Luis seems to fluctuate considerably. The latest scheme of the state governor, Roseana Sarney, is to have all public employees working a shorter day, starting at about noon and going on till about 6pm. It's not clear exactly what she aims to achieve by this, but you may find some of the information posts shut during the morning. The main office of the state tourist organization, MARATUR, is in a small road just off Praça Dom Pedro Segundo (Praça Pedro II) in the city centre. Other offices which you may find open are at the Casa da Cidade in Praça João Lisboa, and at Rua Djalma Dutra 61a, in the heart of the Zona. You can **change money** at the Banco da Amazônia on Praça Dom Pedro Segundo or at Casa 711, Av. Beira Mar 544, right next to the bridge which connects the old city with São Francisco and the other beach areas.

One other thing you should bear in mind is that as in Salvador, many streets have two **names**: Rua Trapiche, for example, is also known as Rua Portugal.

Accommodation

Places to stay are divided between the beaches, where there are a few medium-range hotels but no cheap ones, and the centre. To get a flavour of the atmosphere of the city there's no substitute for staying in the historic centre, but you should be aware that there are sometimes extremely loud reggae nights which may keep you awake.

Athenas Palace Hotel, Rua Antônio Rayol 431 (☎221-4163 or 221-4225). Quite good value as a place to stay, but not ideally located for trips into the Zona. ②.

Hotel Estrela, Rua da Estrela 370 (☎232-7172). A budget option right in the heart of the old city. ②.

Pousada do Francês, Rua 7 de Setembro 121 (☎232-0879). An outstanding luxury-class *pousada* on the edge of the Zona in a restored eighteenth-century mansion. Probably the best value in São Luis. ④.

Pousada Ilha Bella, Rua da Palma 92 (☎231-3563). One of the cleanest and least expensive of the budget hotels in the Zona. ①.

Lord Hotel, Rua Joaquim Távora 258 (☎222-5544). Set in a colonial building, this is a slightly faded 2-star hotel which may be the ideal option if you want to stay just on the edge of the historic centre without spending too much money. ②.

Sofitel Quatro Rodas, Av. Aviscência (☎235-4545). Set above Calhau beach, this hotel appears to lend support to the proposition that when it comes to Brazilian hotels, luxury is almost invariably in inverse proportion to architectural good taste. However, it's endowed with all possible comforts and boasts a wide range of sports facilities including tennis, basketball, swimming and football. ⑦.

Hotel Vila Rica, Praça Dom Pedro Segundo 299 (☎232-3535). This 5-star hotel is superbly located on the edge of the Zona and offers an astonishing breakfast. It's as expensive as you'd expect but you may be able to negotiate hefty discounts if you pay in cash. ⑧.

The City

The city's central **layout** is easily grasped. Built on a headland that slopes down to rivers on two sides, the largest square is **Praça Deodoro**, from where the narrow but crowded Rua da Paz and Rua do Sol, each only with room for one lane of traffic and perilously tight pavements, lead down to **Praça João Lisboa**, which marks the edge of the **Zona** – the nickname for the colonial core of the city. From here steep streets lead down to the river waterfront. It's on the buildings fronting Praça João Lisboa that you will first see the lovely, glazed tile frontages, the **azulejos**, that are the city's signature. Salvador has finer individual examples of *azulejo*, but taken as a whole the *azulejos* of

BUMBA-MEU-BOI

Bumba-meu-boi, which dominates every June in São Luis, is worth making some effort to catch: there's no more atmospheric popular festival in Brazil. A dance with distinctive music, performed by a costumed troupe of characters backed by drummers and brass instruments, it blends the Portuguese, African and Indian influences of both the state and Brazil. It originated on the plantations, and the troupes the *Maranhenses* rate highest still come from the old plantation towns of the interior – Axixá, Pinheiro and Pindaré. To mark the day of São João on **June 24**, the interior towns send their bands to São Luis, where at night they sing and dance outside churches and in squares in the centre. Seeing the spectacular dances and costumes, and hearing the spellbindingly powerful music echoing down the colonial streets, is a magical experience.

Although the climax comes over the weekend nearest to June 24, *bumba* takes over the city centre at night for the whole month. Dozens of stalls spring up in the areas where the troupes rehearse before setting off to the two churches in the centre around which everything revolves: the **Igreja de São João Batista**, on Rua da Paz, and the **Igreja de Santo Antônio**, four blocks north. Along the waterfront, stalls go up selling simple food and drinks, including lethal *batidas* with firewater rum – try the *genipapo*. Many choose to follow the **bois**, as the troupes are called, through the streets: if you feel less energetic, the best place to see everything is Praça de Santo Antônio, the square in front of the church where all the *bois* converge, where you can sit and drink between troupes.

Bumba-meu-boi has a stock of characters and re-enacts the story of a plantation owner leaving a bull in the care of a slave, which dies and then magically revives. The bull, black velvet decorated with sequins and a cascade of ribbons, with someone inside whirling it around, is at the centre of a circle of musicians. The songs are belted out, with lyrics declaimed first by a lead caller, backed up only by a mandolin, and then joyously roared out by everyone when the drums and brass come in. You couldn't wish for a clearer symbol of the cultural influences that make Brazil what it is: the brass sounds Mediterranean, the dancers dress as Indians, and the drumming is like nothing you'll have ever heard. *Bumba* drums are unique: hollow, and played by strumming a metal spring inside, they give out a deep, haunting, hypnotically powerful backbeat.

The troupe is surrounded by people singing along and doing the athletic dance that goes with the rhythm. There are certain old favourites which are the climax of every performance, especially *São Luis*, the unofficial city anthem: *São Luis, cidade de azulejos, juro que nunca te deixo longe do meu coracão* – "São Luis, city of *azulejos*, I swear I'll never keep you far from my heart", it begins, and when it comes up there is a roar of recognition and hundreds of voices join in. The sound of the people of the city shouting out their song radiates from Praça de Santo Antônio across the centre, turning the narrow streets and alleys into an echo chamber.

Bumba-meu-boi starts late, the troupes not hitting the centre until 11pm at the earliest, but people start congregating, either at the waterfront or in the square, soon after dark. *Bois* don't appear every night, except during the last few days before the 24th: ask at the place you're staying, as everyone knows when a good *boi* is on. *Bumba-meu-boi* troupes are organized like samba schools; towns and city *bairros* have their own, but thankfully the festival hasn't been ruined by making them compete formally against each other. Informal rivalries are intense, all the same, and *Maranhenses* love comparing their merits: most would agree that Boi de Madre de Deus is the best in the city, but they are eclipsed by the troupes from the interior, Boi de Axixá and Boi de Pinheiro.

The best day of all is **June 29** (St Peter's Day) when all the *bois* congregate at the Igreja de São Pedro from 10pm until dawn.

colonial São Luis are unmatched for the scale of their use and their abstract, almost Arabic beauty. Most are early nineteenth century; some, with characteristic mustard-coloured shapes in the glazing, date back to the 1750s. Remarkably, many of the oldest tiles arrived in São Luis by accident, as ballast in cargo ships.

The Zona

The **Zona** – also called the **Reviver** after the project to restore it – covers a small headland overlooking the confluence of the Rio Anil and the Atlantic Ocean, and though it may not look like much, a defensible harbour on this flat coastline was of some strategic importance. Now the waterfront is no more than a landing place for fishing boats and ferries, but slave ships once rode at anchor here, bringing in workers for the cotton and sugar plantations upriver. Then, the harbour was crowded with cargo boats, mostly from Liverpool, shipping out the exports of what – from about 1780 to 1840 – was a prosperous trading centre, for the first and last time in its history.

But the Zona predates even that colonial boom. São Luís shares with Rio the distinction of having been founded by the French, and is the only city in Brazil to have been ruled by three European countries. The French, decimated by a lethal combination of malaria and Indians, were soon dislodged by the Portuguese in 1615; then the Dutch sacked the city and held the area for three years from 1641, building the small fort that now lies in ruins on a headland between Calhau and Ponta da Areia. Over the next hundred years, the original shacks were replaced by some of the finest colonial buildings in northern Brazil.

The only way to **explore the Zona** is on foot. A good place to begin is **Praça Dom Pedro Segundo**. The cathedral here is ugly, but the official buildings that line the square are splendidly proportioned survivors of the pre-Baroque colonial era. The oldest is the municipal hall (on the corner next to the *Base da Lenoca* restaurant), which dates from 1688: it still houses the *prefeitura* and is called the **Palácio La Ravardiere**, after the French buccaneer who founded São Luís and is commemorated by a piratical bust on the pavement outside. In November 1985 the building was torched by an angry crowd, with the newly elected mayor inside, after an election acrimonious even by *Maranhense* standards. While it was encouraging to see the people participating so directly in the political process, it's a pity this historic building was the one to be damaged. Next door, barring another outburst of popular discontent, is the tropical Georgian elegance of the state governor's residence, the **Palácio dos Leões**, built between 1761 and 1776 and currently closed for restoration.

On the other side of the square from the Palácio dos Leões, steps lead down to the steep colonial street, **Beco Catarina Mina**, that takes you to the heart of the Zona, block after block of buildings, many restored whilst others are in an advanced state of decay. With its cobbled streets, *azulejos* and the vultures on the tile roofs, the Zona remains physically much as it was 150 years ago, although the colonial merchants and plantation owners who built it would have turned up their noses at its modern inhabitants. As economic decline bit deep, they sold up and moved on.

Beco Catarina Mina runs into the finest array of *azulejos* in the city, the tiled facades of the **Rua do Trapiche**, with the **Mercado da Praia Grande**'s gorgeous arches perfectly set off by the piercing blue tiles and symmetrical windows and balconies. This area is the best-restored part of the Zona, given a magical feel by the brightly coloured *azulejos*, and has plenty of bars and restaurants.

The **churches** have exteriors that date for the most part from the seventeenth century. The most beautiful is the **Igreja do Desterro**, with its Byzantine domes, at the southern end of the Zona, but none of the church interiors has survived successive restorations. It was in these churches that the Jesuit **Padre Antônio Vieira** preached his sermons three hundred years ago, berating the plantation owners for enslaving Indians before the Jesuits had a chance to do so – sermons which are often taken to be the finest early Portuguese prose ever written.

Museums

There are two **museums** worth visiting on Rua do Trapiche (Rua Portugal). The **Salão de Bens Culturais** (daily 9am–9pm), at no. 303, houses an interesting collection of sacred and contemporary art, but the highlight is the display of brightly coloured cloth *bois*, or bulls, used in the festival of *Bumba-meu-boi* (see box p.308). There's also a video of the festival permanently playing in the museum. (Part of this collection used to be in the Centro de Cultura Popular Domingos Vieira Filho, Rua 28 de Julho 221, an excellent museum that's been closed for restoration for some time now, though it's due to reopen soon.) Still on Rua do Trapiche, at no. 273, is the **Museu de Artes Visuais** (daily 9am–9pm), a gallery which displays work by local artists.

Down at the other end of the Zona is the **Cafuá das Mercés**, the old slave market, which now houses the **Museu do Negro**. Slaves who survived the journey across from West Africa were marched up here from the harbour and kept in the holding cells until they could be auctioned off in the small square outside. This used to be an excellent museum but for some reason the collection of objects illustrating the slave trade has been severely depleted. Nearby on Rua da Palma is the **Convento das Mercés**, an attractive spacious wooden building which houses a selection of presidential memorabilia belonging to one of Maranhão's most famous sons, the walrus-lookalike José Sarney. Despite having been a mediocre president, Sarney obviously benefits from having a sense of humour: many of the photographs and pictures on display mock him in one way or another.

One of São Luis's best museums lies outside the Zona. The **Museu de Arte Sacra**, Rua 13 de Mayo (Rua São João) 500, houses some superb religious art from the seventeenth, eighteenth and nineteenth centuries (Tues–Sat 9am–6pm). One of the outstanding pieces is a small wooden statue of St Paul embedded with incredibly lifelike glass eyes. There's also a statue of St John the Baptist with an incision in the neck: the space was used to hide jewels that were being smuggled out of the country.

The beaches

São Luis is blessed with a chain of excellent **beaches**, though development is proceeding apace as a new road is driven along the coast past the nearest, **Ponta da Areia**, to Calhau. All these beaches can be reached by bus from the *Terminal de Integração*. One word of **warning**: although they don't shelve steeply, these are ocean beaches and the surf can be dangerous. People drown every month, so take care. It's also worth noting that swimming after sunset is not a good idea, as there are occasional attacks by sharks which are attracted to these waters by the kitchen waste dumped by ships off shore.

Calhau is larger and more scenic than Ponta da Areia: when the tide is out there is a lovely walk along the sands to Ponta da Areia, two hours' leisurely stroll west. After Calhau comes **Olho d'Agua**, equally fine, and finally **Araçagi**, 19km out of town, the loveliest beach of all. It's served by hourly buses, but unless you rent a car you won't make it back the same day; there is a small hotel, though, the *Araçagi Praia* (☎226-3299; ③).

Eating, drinking and nightlife

At weekends virtually the entire city moves out to the beaches, which are large enough to swallow up the masses without getting too crowded. You will quickly discover one of the delights of this coast: the **seafood**. The seas and rivers around here teem with life, most of it edible. The beach stalls do fried fish, the prawns are the size of large fingers, and whatever they don't cook you can buy fresh from a stream of vendors – juicily tender crabs, battered open with bits of wood, or freshly gathered oysters, dirt cheap, sold by the bagful, helpfully opened for you and sprinkled with lime juice. One thing you won't find outside Maranhão is *cuxá* – a delicious dish made of crushed dried shrimp, garlic and the stewed leaves of two native plants.

Except during *Bumba-meu-boi* and *Carnaval*, São Luis is quieter than most Brazilian cities of its size. The largest concentration of nightspots is just over the bridge, in **São**

Francisco, a little on the tacky side for the most part, although there is a good Japanese restaurant, the *Samurai*, at Av. Castelo Branco 21. However, there are now plenty of bars and restaurants in the Zona, and Wednesday nights are when the historic centre really lets its hair down, with loud reggae music blasting out till dawn.

Eating out in town is rewarding, thanks to the abundant seafood. The best in São Luis is the *caldeirada de camarão* (shrimp stew) at the *Base do Edilson* restaurant (☎222-7210), served with *pirão*, a savoury manioc porridge that's the perfect accompaniment. The restaurant is buried deep in the *bairro* of Vila Bessa, at Rua Alencar Campos 31, but the short taxi journey from the centre is well worth the effort. Good *caldeirada* is also to be had at the *Base do Germano*, also a short taxi-ride from the centre on Avenida Wenceslau Brás (☎222-3276), in the *bairro* of Camboa. The *Restaurante São Luis*, Praça Benedito Leite 20 (☎222-4131), offers a wide selection of local dishes by the kilo and is excellent value. Salvador's *SENAC* restaurant school (see p.250) has a branch at Rua de Nazaré 242 (☎221-4931), in the Zona.

Along the coast

Travel in Maranhão outside São Luis is made difficult by a road system that is limited and – given the rains – often precarious. If you want to travel **along the coast** the most practical way is by boat, an option, however, that is not to be taken lightly as it's hard going: no schedules or creature comforts, and no one who speaks English. Don't do it unless you're healthy, a good sailor, not fussy about what you eat, have at least basic Portuguese and aren't too worried about time. But if you want to get completely off the beaten track, there's nothing to rival a sea journey.

The place to start is the **Estação Marítima** in São Luis, on the waterfront at the end of Praça Dom Pedro Segundo. This is the local station for boats, which supply the nearby coastal villages and towns, take on passengers and cargo and wait for the tides. Brightly painted, many with masts, rigging and sails that make seadogs growl with approval, these boats are built by artisans along the coast who still know how to put an ocean-going vessel together from timber.

There are sailings to the main coastal towns to the **west** about once a week. Pick a destination and ask at the booth in the *Marítima* station for the day and time: you either buy your passage there and then, or negotiate with the captain. The main coastal towns, as you head west, are Guimarães (half a day away), Turiaçu (two days) and Luis Domingues and Carutapera (three days). Take plenty of food and drink; *Maranhenses* scratch limes and smell them to guard against seasickness, and it does seem to help.

São José do Ribamar

Fortunately, not all the interesting places are difficult to get to. Easiest of all are the fishing towns on the island of São Luis: Raposa, a simple village on a beach, an hour away by bus from Deodoro or Rua da Paz; and **SÃO JOSÉ DO RIBAMAR**, which you can reach on the bus marked "Ribamar" from the same stops, or from outside the *Athenas Palace Hotel*.

It's 32km to São José, about an hour's drive, a lovely route through thick palm forest and small hills. The bus deposits you in the small town centre, where straggling houses on a headland have sweeping views of a fine bay; it's easy to stay over, as there are several **pensões** in the centre. São José is an important fishing town, as well as being a centre of skilled boatbuilding by traditional methods – you can see the yards, with the half-finished ribs of surprisingly large boats, behind the houses running inland from the small landing quay and large beach. There's a very relaxing feel to the town. The people are friendly, the scenery splendid, and it's not difficult to while away a few days doing nothing in particular. There are some good **restaurants**, too: the *Ribamar* has a terrace looking out to the bay, and the rustic *barracas* on the waterfront are ideal spots to chat and watch the sunset from.

A lot of the **boats** that ply the coast both east and west drop in at São José, and it's a convenient place to begin a boat trip. Easiest places to head for, and with a fair degree of certainty that there'll be a boat back within a day or two, are Icatu, the mainland village on the other side of the bay, and Primeira Cruz on the east coast. From the latter, it's a short hop to the interior town of Humberto De Campos, where you can catch a bus back to São Luis.

Parque Nacional dos Lençóis

From Primeira Cruz, you can also continue to what is arguably one of the most beautiful sights in Brazil, the **Parque Nacional dos Lençóis**, a desert some 370km to the east of São Luis covering more than 200 square kilometres. What makes it so special is that it is composed of hundreds of massive sand dunes that reach towering heights but which are subject to prolonged rainfall. The result is that the dunes are sprinkled with literally hundreds of crystal-clear freshwater lagoons. To get there either continue from the small town of Primeira Cruz, or, direct from São Luis, catch the bus to Barreirinhas which leaves the *Rodoviária* at 7am (hours variable so check beforehand with MARATUR) and takes about eight hours to get there. There are some very modest *pousadas* if you wish to stay overnight. Then it's a three-hour journey down the Rio Preguiças to the dunes themselves. If you don't fancy organizing the trip for yourself then there are a couple of agencies in São Luis that will: *Giltur*, Rua do Giz 46, in the Zona (☎232-6041), and *Taguatur*, Rua do Sol 141, inside the shopping centre (☎231-4197 or 232-0906), which both organize trips by bus and boat or by plane. The overland trip takes three days and will set you back about $100; the plane trip takes a day and costs about $180.

Across the bay: Alcântara

Set in a wonderful tropical landscape on the other side of the **bay of São Marcos** from São Luis, **ALCÂNTARA** is now no more than a poor village built around the ruins of what was once the richest town in northern Brazil. São Luis had already eclipsed it by the end of the eighteenth century, and for the last two hundred years it has been left to moulder quietly away. The measure of its decline is that there are now no roads worthy of the name to get there; the only way is by sea from the Estação Marítima at the end of Praça Dom Pedro Segundo in São Luis.

Alcântara is a ninety-minute chug across the bay, which can still sometimes get choppy enough to make you thankful you've arrived. The alternative is a large motorboat – the Batevento – which takes half the time but at twice the price ($6). The ordinary boat leaves at 7am, the motorboat around 9.30am. There's a fine view of ruins and the houses of the town as you arrive, strung out along a headland, the skyline dominated by imperial palms; you face a short walk uphill after you disembark. Most of the **ruins** you see are from the seventeenth century: Alcântara, founded in 1648, was the first capital of Maranhão and the main centre of the first stretch of coastline that the Portuguese converted to sugar plantations.

The main square, **Praça da Matriz**, gives you an idea of how grand it must have been in its heyday, surrounded on three sides by colonial mansions. In the centre of the square is a curious corroded stone post, erected in 1647, on which you can still see the carved arms of the Portuguese Crown: this is the *pelourinho*, a whipping post, set up to mark the king of Portugal's claim to the coast.

If you thought some of the buildings in the colonial zone of São Luis were in bad repair, Alcântara proves how much worse things can get notwithstanding its more recent efforts at restoration. Very few of the oldest buildings survive; for the most part only the facade and walls are standing, many with coats of arms still discernible. The roofs went generations ago and most have large trees growing out of them. On the main square is a small **museum**, in a restored mansion with a fine *azulejo* frontage, which has a good collection of artefacts and prints to give you an idea of what the place was once like. It doesn't keep regular opening hours, but they will open it up for you if you ask nicely; they'll know where the key is at the *Hotel Pelourinho* (see below).

The ruins, the views, the beaches and the friendliness of the people combine to make Alcântara a very atmospheric place. Short **walks** or **canoe rides** in either direction take you to deserted **beaches** where there are rustic cafés and bars with chilled beer, and, provided you don't mind eating fish, you won't starve. Better still are boat trips through the mangroves where you will see guarás, birds resembling flamingos except they are bright red instead of pink; against the green background they look extraordinary.

Practicalities

The last boat back to São Luís leaves daily at 4pm, so if you want to stay for more than eight hours you'll have to spend the night. It's worth doing, as the moonlight shows the ruins to best effect, and the two **hotels** on Praça Matriz are both good: *Pousada do Imperador* (no phone; ③) and the clean and comfortable *Hotel Pelourinho* (no phone; ②). There's also the more expensive *Pousada do Modomo Régio*, Rua Grande 134 (☎098/337-1197; ④). The cheapest option is to string your **hammock** in a house: groups of children meet incoming boats looking for tourists for exactly that purpose, so finding somewhere is easy. The deal will include an evening meal and breakfast, simple but wholesome; just don't drink the water. The best **restaurant** in town is at *Hotel Pelourinho*, with home-brewed fruit liqueurs a speciality; try the guava (*goiaba*). Just off the main square there's a TELMA post, from where you can make **telephone calls**.

The interior

Travel in the **interior** of Maranhão is limited by the road system: there is only one highway out of São Luís, which forks east to Teresina and west to Belém. Although asphalted now, chunks of it often get washed away during the rainy season. You'll usually get through eventually – even if you have to push with the rest of the passengers – but things like timetables cease to have any meaning. The worst part of the road is the bit from São Luís to Santa Inês, but you can avoid this by going on the train bound for Carajás (see below).

The **road to Belém** is now a lot better than it was, although the link southwest to Imperatriz can still be a bit dodgy. There's little to keep you in central Maranhão, although the journey is interesting: travel by day if you can. The area you pass through was first populated on a large scale thirty years ago and the towns, the largest en route being Bacabal and Santa Inês, are young but growing rapidly. By the time you get to Santa Inês you're in Amazonia, but don't expect to see any forest en route to Belém; most was cut down for cattle ranching twenty years ago.

Although there's nowhere worth getting off the bus, this final western stretch of Maranhão is fascinating. Inland, a **gold rush** has been going on since 1982. Watch the people who get on and off at the roadside villages past Santa Inês, especially at the town of Maracassumé – many are *garimpeiros*, gold-miners. Just over the border with Pará you even get to see a gold camp, Cachoeira, where a village has developed around a gold strike; you can just about see the diggings from the road, but it's not advisable to get off for a closer look.

South to Imperatriz and Carolina

At Santa Inês a fork heads southwest to **IMPERATRIZ**, a mushrooming city on the Belém–Brasília highway: 276,000 people where as recently as twenty years ago there was only a small town of about 10,000. You can also get there by **train** from São Luis, along the rail line to the **Carajás** iron and bauxite deposits built by the Brazilian CVRD mining company. Tickets cost just over $20 if you want to go first class, and they're available either from the Estação Ferroviária de São Luis on Avenida dos Portugueses, or from the optician Ótica Baluz, Rua do Sol, Edifício Colonial, loja 14. To get to the train station, catch a "Villa Nova" bus from the *Terminal de Integração*; it's a twenty-minute ride.

There's little reason to go to Imperatriz for its own sake. The town is teeming with people on the move, and even basic facilities have been swamped. The atmosphere here is made worse by the violent **land conflicts** in the region, and Imperatriz is where the gunmen hang out between contracts. However, it does lie en route to Brasília and, more immediately, **CAROLINA**, the only town in southern Maranhão of any conceivable interest to tourists. Situated on the banks of the Rio Tocantins, Carolina's attraction is that it lies in a region of spectacular waterfalls, the most famous being those at **Pedra Caída**, more than 30km out of town. If you're coming from São Luis, you should get the train as far as Imperatriz before changing to the bus for a four-hour ride to Carolina. There are a few **places to stay**, including the *Recanto Pedra Caída* (☎098/731-1318; ④), right by the falls.

travel details

Buses

João Pessoa to: Cabedelo (every 30min; 45min); Campina Grande (hourly; 2hr); Fortaleza (3 daily; 9hr); Juazeiro do Norte (2 daily; 10hr); Mossoró (several daily; 4hr); Penha (every 2hr; 45min).

Maceió to: Aracaju (7 daily; 5hr); Paulo Afonso (2 daily; 4hr); Penedo (4 daily; 2hr).

Recife to: Amarelo (every 30 min; 1hr); Aracaju (2 daily; 8hr); Belém (1 daily; 35hr); Belo Horizonte (3 daily; 35hr); Brasília (3 daily; 48hr); Caruaru (at least hourly; 2hr); Fortaleza (4 daily; 12hr); Goiânia (6 daily; 2hr); João Pessoa (10 daily; 2hr); Maceió (20 daily; 4hr); Natal (20 daily; 4hr 30min); Petrolina (4 daily; 12hr); Porto de Galinhas (every 30min; 1hr); Rio (3 daily; 42hr); Salvador (7 daily; 13hr); São José da Coroa Grande (hourly; 1hr 30min); São Paulo (4 daily; 48hr).

Salvador to: Belém (1 daily; 35hr); Brasília (6 daily; 26hr); Cachoeira (hourly; 2hr 30min); Feira de Santana (hourly; 2hr); Ilhéus (6 daily; 6hr 30min); Jacobina (2 daily; 6hr); Lençois (2 daily; 7hr); Porto Seguro (3 daily; 11hr); Recife (3 daily; 13hr); Rio (2 daily; 30hr); Santo Amaro (every 30min; 2hr); São Paulo (2 daily; 35hr); Valença (6 daily; 5hr).

Teresina to: Belém (1–2 daily; 24hr); Fortaleza (at least 1–2 daily; 15hr); São Luis (several daily; 10hr).

Ferries

Salvador to: Itaparicá (every 30min; 30min); Maragojipe (1 daily at 3pm; 1–2hr).

CHAPTER FOUR

THE AMAZON

The Amazon is a vast forest and a giant river system. It covers over half of Brazil and a large portion of South America. The forest extends into Brazil's neighbouring countries – Venezuela, Colombia, Peru and Bolivia, where the river itself begins life among thousands of different headwaters. In Brazil only the stretch between Manaus and Belém is actually known as the **Rio Amazonas**: above Manaus the river is called the **Rio Solimões** up to the border with Peru, where it once again becomes the Amazônas. The daily flow of the river is said to be enough to supply a city the size of New York with water for nearly ten years, and its power is such that the muddy Amazon waters stain the Atlantic a silty brown for over 200km out to sea. This was how its existence was first identified by the Spaniard, Vicente Yanez Pinon, sailing the Atlantic in search of El Dorado. He was drawn to the mouth of the Amazon by the sweet freshness of the ocean or, as he called it, the *Mar Dulce*.

To many Indian tribes, the Amazon is a gigantic mythical anaconda, a source of life and death. In its upper reaches, the Rio Solimões from Peru to Manaus, it is a muddy yellow, but at Manaus it meets the darker flow of the Rio Negro and the two mingle together at the famous "meeting of the waters" to form the Rio Amazonas. There are something like 80,000 square kilometres of **navigable river** in the Amazon system, and the Amazon itself can take ocean-going vessels virtually clean across South America, from the Atlantic coast to Iquitos in Peru. Even at the Óbidos narrows, the only topographical obstruction between the Andes and the Atlantic, the river is almost 2km wide and for most of its length it is far broader – by the time it reaches the ocean the river's gaping mouth stretches further apart than London and Paris.

Ecology and development

The Amazon is far more than just a river. Its catchment basin contains, at any one moment, over one-fifth of all the world's fresh water, and the **rainforest** it sustains covers an area of over six million square kilometres, stretching almost right across the continent and forming the largest tract of forest on Earth. The Amazon forest is a vitally important cog in the planet's biosphere controls. There are over a thousand tributaries (several larger than the Mississippi), whose combined energy potential is estimated at over 100,000 megawatts daily (an endlessly renewable supply equivalent to five million

---

ACCOMMODATION PRICE CODES

In this guide, accommodation has been categorized according to the price codes outlined below, based on US$. These categories represent the minimum you can expect to pay for a **double room in high season** – though note that many of the budget places will also have more expensive rooms. Rates for hostels and basic hotels where guests are charged **per person** are given in US$, instead of being indicated by price code. See p.31 for further information.

① under $20	③ $30–45	⑤ $60–80	⑦ $120–175
② $20–30	④ $45–60	⑥ $80–120	⑧ $175 and over

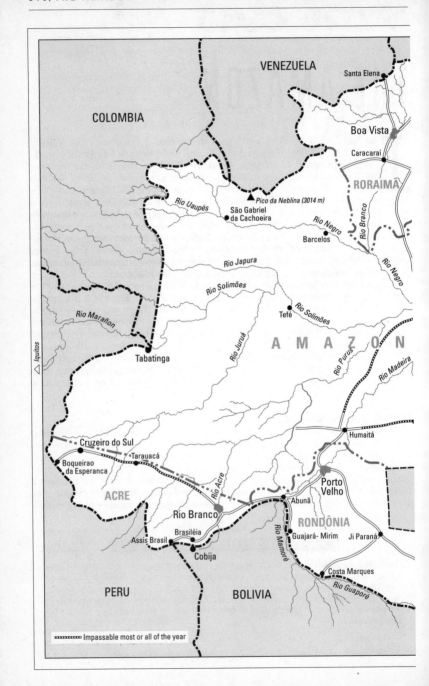

Impassable most or all of the year

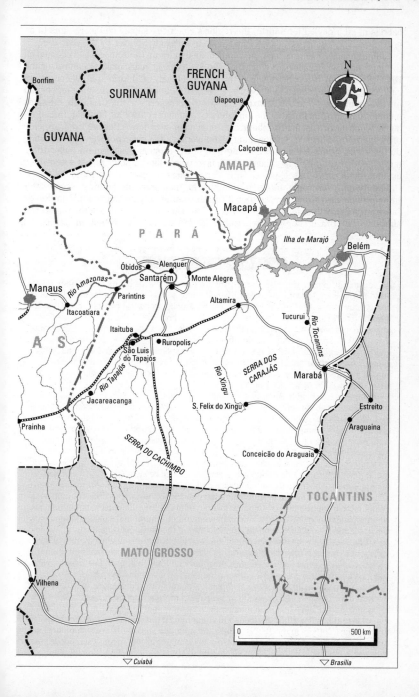

barrels of oil a day). Eletronorte, the region's electricity supply company, aims to be providing 22,000 megawatts from Amazonian hydroelectric power by the year 2000.

Although in 1639 Pedro Teixeira travelled 2000 miles up the Amazon and claimed all the land east of Ecuador for Portugal, the Portuguese really gained control of the Brazilian Amazon, in a political sense, through the Treaty of Madrid in 1750. Four years later, Governor Mendonça Furtado was appointed Boundary Commissioner and began his tour of inspection in the Amazon. He saw the prosperity of the Carmelite missions on the Rio Negro and initiated the Directorate System of controlling "official" Indian villages which were essentially labour camps. Having seen how effective the Carmelite missionaries had been in manipulating native workers, the governor was determined to do the same. Some Indians, remaining free in the regions upstream on major tributaries, tended to gather in villages at portage points like difficult rapids where they acted as guides and muscle-power for traders. Others retreated deeper into the forest.

The region was only integrated fully into the Brazilian political scene after Independence in 1822. And even then it remained safer and quicker to sail from Rio de Janeiro to Lisbon than to Manaus. Within a few years of Independence the region was almost lost to Brazil altogether when the bloody **Cabanagem Rebellion** (see p.323)

AMAZON CUISINE

As you might expect from the richest freshwater ecosystem in the world, **fish** takes pride of place in Amazonian cooking. You'll come across dozens of species, the best being *peixe nobre* (the noble fish), which Amazonians prize above all others for its flavour. There are many kinds of huge, almost boneless fish, including *pirarucu*, *tambaqui* and *filhote* which come in dense slabs sometimes more like meat, and are delicious grilled over charcoal. Smaller, bonier fish, such as *surubim*, *curimatã*, *jaraqui*, *acari* and *tucunaré* can be just as succulent, the latter similar to a large tasty mullet. Fish in the Amazon is commonly just barbecued or fried; its freshness and flavour need little help. It's also served *no escabeche* (in a tomato sauce), *a leite de coco* (cooked in coconut milk) or stewed in *tucupi* (see below).

The other staple food in Amazonia is **manioc**. *Farinha*, a manioc flour and a staple food throughout Brazil, is supplied at the table in granulated form – in texture akin to gravel – for mixing with the meat or fish juices with most meals, and is even added to coffee. Less bland and more filling, manioc is also eaten throughout Amazonia on its own or as a side dish, either boiled or fried (known as *macaxeira* in Manaus and Western Amazonia or *mandioca* elsewhere). A more exciting form of manioc, **tucupi**, is produced from its fermented juices. This delicious sauce can be used to stew fish in or to make *pato no tucupi* (duck stewed in *tucupi*). Manioc juice is also used to make *beiju* (pancakes) and *doce de tapioca*, a tasty cinnamon-flavoured tapioca pudding. A gloopy, translucent manioc sauce also forms the basis of one of Amazonia's most distinctive dishes, *tacacá*, a shrimp soup gulped from a gourd bowl and sold everywhere from chichi restaurants to street corners. Other typical regional dishes include *maniçoba*, pieces of meat and sausage stewed with chicory leaves, and *vatapá*, a north Brazil version of the Bahian shrimp dish.

Finally, no stay in the Amazon would be complete without sampling the remarkable variety of **tropical fruits** the region has to offer, and which form the basis for a mouthwatering array of *sucos* and ice creams. Most have no English or even Portuguese translations. Palm fruits are among the most common; you are bound to come across *açai*, a deep purple pulp mixed with water and drunk straight, with added sugar, with tapioca or thickened with *farinha* and eaten. Other palm fruits include *taperebá*, which makes a delicious *suco*, *bacuri* and *buriti*. Also good, especially as *sucos* or ice cream, are *açerola* (originally Japanese, although Amazonians will swear blind it is regional; it came over with the first Japanese settlers in the 1920s), *peroba*, *graviola*, *ata* (also called *fruta de conde*) and, most exotic of all, *capuaçu*, which looks like an elongated brown coconut and floods your palate with the tropical taste to end all tropical tastes.

overthrew white rule and attempted to establish an independent state. When things had quietened down a little, in the mid-nineteenth century, US Navy engineers were sent to the Amazon to check out its potential resources. They reported that it was wealthy in forest gums, fruits, nuts and excellent timber, and provided with a ready-made transport network in the form of rivers which gave direct contact with the Atlantic. Within a few years one of those forest gums – **rubber** – was to transform the future of the Amazon.

Until Charles Goodyear invented the rubber tyre, the Amazonian economy had ticked over at a bare subsistence level, sustained by the slave trade and lumber. But the new demand for rubber coincided handily with the introduction of steamship navigation on the Amazon in 1858, beginning an economic boom as spectacular as any the world has seen. By 1900 both Manaus and Belém were extraordinarily rich cities, and out in the forest were some of the wealthiest and most powerful men in the world at that time, beyond the reach of the newspapers, conscience and worries of nineteenth-century Europe: men like Nicolas Suárez, who earned a reputation as an autocratic ruler of a rubber-tapping region larger than most European countries. Controlling the whole of the region around the upper Rio Madeira and into modern-day Peru, he was a legendarily harsh employer even by the standards of the day.

When the rubber boom ended, almost as suddenly as it had begun, following the success of rubber plantations established in the Far East (with smuggled Brazilian seeds), development of the region once again came to an almost complete halt, relying on the export of the traditional products of the forest to keep the economy going at all. There was a brief resurgence during World War II, when the rubber plantations in the Far East were controlled by the Japanese, but it is only in the last thirty years or so that large-scale **exploitation – and destruction – of the forest** has really taken off, along with a massive influx of people from other parts of Brazil, the Northeast in particular, in search of land.

The destruction and survival of the forest

There are three main **types of Amazon forest**: the *várzea* or floodplain zones, regularly flooded by the rivers; the *igapós*, which are occasionally flooded; and the *terra firma*, generally unflooded land which forms the majority of the surface area. Each forest type differs in the nature of its vegetation and the potential of its land use. Much of the *terra firma* is high forest where life exists as much in the upper canopies as it does on the ground. In the extreme northern and southern limits of the Amazon Basin, and to some extent taking over where mankind has caused most devastation, there are extensive coverings of wooded and scrubby savannas. When the forest is destroyed the land generally remains productive for only a few years before turning to scrub. There's also the contribution to the greenhouse effect from burning the cleared forest and, from a global perspective, the forest can be seen as the kidneys and lungs of the planet – cleaning toxic substances from the atmosphere and putting vital oxygen back through photosynthesis.

The destruction of the Amazon forest obviously takes a severe toll on the area's unique **flora and fauna**. There are believed to be as many as 15,000 animal species in the Amazon – thousands of which have still to be identified – and untold numbers of so far unclassified plants. Since they remain unknown, it is impossible to say quite what damage the destruction of the rainforest is doing; but there can be no doubt that many animal and plant species will be lost before anyone has had a chance to study them. The loss of this gene pool – with its potential use for medicines, foods and others unknown – is really serious; perhaps only the indigenous people of the forests will really know what has been lost – if they survive.

The Brazilian riposte, of course, is that the Western nations have no right to occupy any moral high ground, or to stand in the way of what they see as the essential economic development of their country. And they generally further add that the area being lost is insignificant compared to what survives. For all the damage to the ecology and the peoples of the Amazon, it is hard to argue that Brazil should be denied the right to exploit the mineral and natural resources by people who have already raped so much of the rest of the world.

One hopeful sign is that people are increasingly discovering that cultivation – particularly cattle ranching – is not an efficient way to use the jungle, and that the productivity of the land decreases rapidly after the first few years. Scientists are just beginning to demonstrate (and developers to accept) that the virgin forests – with their fruits, roots, nuts, medicinal plants, dyes, game etc – are an endless resource that can actually be more profitable than cleared land. For more on the Amazon environment see p.615. Another good sign is the growth of interest, among tourists and Brazilians alike, in **eco-tourism**. This pursuit, properly managed, brings money into the region and provides employment for its inhabitants, through an industry which conserves rather than exploits the natural environment.

Getting around the Amazon

Most people who visit Brazil will, at some time or other, have dreamt about taking **a boat up the Amazon** (see box below). This is not hard to do, though it's not as comfortable or easy-going as daydreams might have made it seem. Given the food on some

---

RIVER JOURNEYS

Any journey up the Rio Amazonas is a serious affair. The river is big and powerful and the boats, in general, are relatively small, top-heavy-looking wooden vessels on two or three levels. As far as **spotting wildlife** goes, there's very little chance of seeing much more than a small range of tropical forest birds – mostly buzzards around the refuse tips of the ports en route – although your chances increase the smaller the craft you're travelling on, as going upriver, the smaller boats tend to hug the riverbanks, bringing the spectacle much closer. Going downstream, however, large and small boats alike tend to cruise with the mid-stream currents, taking advantage of the added power they provide. Whichever boat you travel with, the river is nevertheless a beautiful sight and many of the settlements you pass and tie up in are fascinating to the traveller's eye.

It's important to **prepare** properly for an Amazon river trip if you want to ensure your comfort and health. The most essential item is a **hammock**, which can be bought cheaply (from about $10) in the stores and markets of Manaus, Santarém or Belém, plus two stout pieces of rope to hang it from – hooks are not always the right interval apart for your size of hammock. Loose **clothing** is OK during daylight hours but at night you'll need some warmer garments and long sleeves against the chill and the insects. A **blanket** and some **insect repellent** are also recommended. Enough **drink** (large containers of mineral water are the best option, available in the bigger towns) and extra **food** – cookies, fruit and the odd tin – to keep you happy for the duration of the voyage may also be a good idea. A lot of the boats now provide their own mineral water, and the food, included in the price, has improved on some vessels, but a lot of people get literally sick of the rice, meat and beans served on board most boats, which is, of course, cooked on river water. If all else fails, you can always buy extra provisions in the small ports the boats visit. There are toilets on all boats, though even on the best they can get filthy within a few hours of leaving port. Again, there are exceptions, but it's advisable to take your own roll of **toilet paper** just in case. **Yellow fever inoculation** checks are common on boats leaving Belém to travel upriver, and for travellers unfortunate enough not to have a **valid certificate of vaccination**, you risk having a compulsory injection. Chances are that shared needles are now a thing of the past, but it's obviously safer to have had a yellow fever inoculation beforehand.

There are a few things to bear in mind when you're choosing **which boat** to travel with, the most important being the size and degree of comfort. The size affects the length of the journey, small wooden boats taking anything over 7 days to cover Belém to Manaus, with the larger vessels generally making the journey in 5–6 days (4–5 days downriver). The three ENASA three-deck **catamarans** are the largest boats connecting Belém with

boats, the trip can be tough on the stomach, and you'll need meditative patience to appreciate the subtle changes in the forest scene on the often-distant riverbanks. But with a bar on the top decks of most boats, most passengers, whether Zen adepts or not, make a great time of it.

The classic journey is the five or six days from **Belém**, a friendly coastal city worth visiting in its own right, to **Manaus** in the heart of the jungle; and perhaps on from there on a wooden riverboat to Iquitos in Peru via Tabatinga on the Brazilian frontier. But sticking only to the main channel of the Amazon is not the way to see the jungle or its wildlife: for that you'll want to take trips on smaller boats up smaller streams, an option which is particularly rewarding in the west where the rivers aren't quite so wide.

Thirty years ago river travel was virtually the only means of getting around the region, but in the 1960s the **Transamazônica** – Highway BR-230 – was constructed, cutting right across the south of Amazonia and linking the Atlantic coast (via the Belém–Brasília highway) with the Peruvian border at Brazil's western extremity. It remains an extraordinary piece of engineering, but is now increasingly bedraggled. Lack of money to pay for the stupendous amount of maintenance the network needed has now made much of it impassable. West of Altamira it has practically ceased to exist,

Manaus, each with at least 25 cabins ($225 upriver, $155 downriver; or $430/370 for a private bath and decent air conditioning) and room for around 300 hammocks on the middle deck (around $90 upriver, $65 downriver). Like all riverboats, the catamarans call at Breves, Santarém, Óbidos, Oriximiná and Parintins along the way; however, their departure times are erratic and at times there may be no service for weeks. Note also that ENASA has a poor reputation for its cuisine, and the boats tend to stick to the middle of the river, so you don't really see all that much. Their addresses are given under the "Listings" for Belém, Santarém and Manaus.

Better value, and usually more interesting in the degree of contact it affords among tourists, the crew and locals, is the option of choosing a **wooden riverboat**, carrying both cargo and passengers. There are plenty of these along the waterfront in all the main ports, and it's simply a matter of going down there and establishing which ones are getting ready to go to wherever you are heading, or else enquiring at the ticket offices; like the ENASA boats, these vessels stop at most towns along the way. You'll share a deck with scores of other travellers, mostly locals or Brazilians, which will almost certainly ensure that the journey never becomes too monotonous. The most organized of the wooden riverboats are the larger **three-deck vessels**, on which the Belém–Manaus trip costs $86 for hammock space ($70 downriver); this is bargainable if you're really stuck for cash, and will often come with a small discount if you buy your tickets two or more days before departure. The smaller **two-deck boats** are cosier, but often only cover shorter legs of the river. This is fine if you don't mind spending a day or two waiting for your next connection to load up. All of these wooden vessels tend to let passengers stay aboard a night or two before departure and after arrival, which saves on hotel costs.

There's room for debate about whether hammock space is a better bet than a **cabin** (*camarote*; currently around $140 upriver), of which there are usually only a few. Though the cabins can be unbearably hot and stuffy during the day (whilst other passengers swing coolly in their hammocks), they do offer **security** for your baggage, as well as some privacy (though the cabins are shared, with either 2 or 4 bunks in each). The hammock areas get extremely crowded, so arrive early and establish your position: the best spots are near the front or the sides if you like the wind (it doesn't really matter which side, as the boat will alternate quite freely from one bank of the river to the other). If it really gets unbearably crowded, you can always take your chances slinging your hammock on the lower deck with the crew, though you'll also have to share your space with cargo and throbbing engine noise.

apart from the Porto Velho–Rio Branco run and odd stretches where local communities find the road useful and maintain it. The same fate has met other highways like the Santarém–Cuiabá and the Porto Velho–Manaus, on which great hopes were once pinned. With the exception of the Belém–Brasília and Cuiabá–Rio Branco highway corridors, transport in the Amazon has sensibly reverted to rivers. Access to what remains of the Transamazônica from Belém or Brasília is via Estreito, the settlement at the junction where the BR-230 turns west off the old north–south highway, the BR-153/BR-010.

One thing to bear in mind while travelling is that there are three **time zones** in the Amazon region. Belém and eastern Pará are on the same time as the rest of the coast, except from October to February when Bahia and the states of the southeast and the South switch to summertime, leaving Belém an hour behind. At the Rio Xingú, about halfway west across Pará, the clocks go back an hour to Manaus time. Tabatinga, Rio Branco and Acre, in the extreme west of the Amazon, are another hour behind again.

EASTERN AMAZONIA

Politically divided between the states of Pará and Amapá, the eastern Amazon is essentially a vast area of forest and savanna plains centred around the final seven hundred miles or so of the giant river's course. **Belém**, an Atlantic port near the mouth of the estuary, is the elegant capital of Pará and a worthwhile place to spend some time. It overlooks the river and the vast **Ilha de Marajó**, a marshy island in the estuary given over mainly to cattle farming, but with a couple of good beaches.

Pará has always been a relatively productive region. In the late eighteenth century it was an important source of rice (allowing Portugal to be "self-sufficient" in the commodity), and it also exported cacao and, later, rubber. Very little of the wealth, however, ever reached beyond a small elite, and falling prices of local commodities on the world markets have periodically produced severe hardship. In the 1830s resentment exploded in the Cabanagem Rebellion, ruthlessly fought and equally harshly suppressed.

Today, the state is booming once again, largely thanks to vast mineral extraction projects in the south. The landscape of southern Pará, below **Marabá** and the Tocantins-Araguaia rivers, is essentially a scrubby savanna known locally as *caatinga*: traditionally the home of the *Gê*-speaking Indians, it forms the major part of the central Brazilian plateau or shield. Over the last twenty years some of the most controversial developments in the Amazon have been taking place here: particularly the vast **Grande Carajás** industrial scheme, based around a huge deposit of iron and other ores, and the associated hydroelectric operation at **Tucurui**, whose dam has flooded an enormous area of forest and Indian land. Not far away are the once infamous **Serra Pelada** gold mines.

Amapá, in the northeastern corner of the Brazilian Amazon, is a fascinating place in its own right. A poor and little-visited area, it nevertheless offers the possibility of an adventurous overland route to French Guyana and on into Surinam, Guyana and Venezuela. It's possible to do much of this journey by ocean-going boat.

Connections in the region are pretty straightforward, in that you have very few choices. The main throughway is still the Amazon, with stops at **Santarém** – a sleepy town entirely dominated by the river – and **Óbidos**, far less enticing. As far as **roads** go there are good highways south from Belém towards Brasília (the BR-010) and east into the state of Maranhão (the BR-316). In the north there's just one road from **Macapá**, the capital of Amapá, up towards the border with French Guyana. The BR-010 crosses the powerful Rio Tocantins near Estreito (in Maranhão) close to the start of the **Transamazônica**. If you're coming from the south, connections with westbound buses and other traffic are best made at Araguaina (in Tocantins) where there's a small *Rodoviária* and several hotels. The first stop on the Transamazônica within Pará is **Marabá**, some 460km (12hr) by bus from Belém. Continuing from here, the Transamazônica reaches **Altamira** on the navigable Rio Xingu, a small new city over 300km west of Marabá where there's another massive hydroelectric dam scheme. With a population that's grown from 15,000 in 1970 to over 100,000 today, it's at the centre of an area of rapidly vanishing jungle. Beyond Altamira, the Transamazônica becomes impassable.

Belém

Strategically placed on the Amazon river estuary close to the mouth of the mighty Rio Tocantins, **BELÉM** was founded by the Portuguese in 1616 as the City of Our Lady of Bethlehem (Belém). Its original role was to protect the river mouth and establish the Portuguese claim to the region, but it rapidly became established as an Indian slaving port and a source of cacao and spices from the Amazon. Such was the devastation of the local population, however, that by the mid-eighteenth century a royal decree was issued in Portugal to encourage its growth: every white man who married an Indian woman would receive "one axe, two scissors, some cloth, clothes, two cows and two bushels of seed".

Despite the decree, a shrinking labour force and, in the 1780s, the threat of attack by a large contingent of Munduruku Indians meant that Belém was deep in decline before

THE CABANAGEM REBELLION

The **Cabanagem Rebellion** ravaged the region around Belém for sixteen months between January 1835 and May 1836, in the uncertain years following independence and the abdication of Pedro I. Starting with political division among Brazil's new rulers, it rapidly became a revolt of the poor against racial injustice: the *cabanos* were mostly black and Indian or mixed-blood settlers who lived in relative poverty in cabana huts on the floodplains and riverbanks around Belém and the lower Amazon riverbanks. Following years of unrest the pent-up hatred of generations burst into Belém in August 1835. After days of bloody fighting, the survivors of the Belém authorities fled, leaving the *cabanos* in control. In the area around the city many sugar mills and *fazendas* were destroyed, their white owners being put to death. Bands of rebels roamed throughout the region, and in most settlements their arrival was greeted by the non-white population's spontaneously joining their ranks, looting and killing. The authorities described the rebellion as "a ghastly revolution in which barbarism seemed about to devour all existing civilization in one single gulp".

The rebellion was doomed almost from the start, however. Although the leaders declared independence from Brazil and attempted to form some kind of revolutionary government, they never had any real programme, and nor did they succeed in controlling their own followers. A British ship became embroiled in the rebellion in October 1835, when it arrived unwittingly with a cargo of arms which had been ordered by the authorities before their hasty departure a couple of months previously. The crew were killed and their cargo confiscated. Five months later, the following March, a British naval force arrived demanding compensation from the rebels for the killings and the lost cargo. The leader of the *cabanos*, Eduardo Angelim, met the British captain and refused any sort of compromise; British trade was threatened, too, and the fleet commenced a blockade of the fledgling revolutionary state. Meanwhile, troops from the south prepared to fight back, and in May 1836 the rebels were driven from Belém by a force of 2500 soldiers under the command of Francisco d'Andrea. Mopping-up operations continued for years, and by the time the Cabanagem Rebellion was completely over and all isolated pockets of armed resistance had been eradicated, some 30,000 people are estimated to have died – almost a third of the region's population at that time.

> The **telephone code** for Belém is ☎091.

the end of the century. In the nineteenth century, it sank still further, as the centre of the nation's bloodiest rebellion (see box p.323), before the town experienced an extraordinary revival as the most prosperous beneficiary of the Amazon rubber boom. By the end of the nineteenth century, Belém was a very rich town, accounting for close to half of all Brazil's rubber exports. At this time rubber was being collected from every corner of the Amazon. As a result of the boom, thousands of poor people moved into Belém from the Northeast, bringing with them new cultural inputs such as music and dance, plus, of course, the *candomblé* and *macumba* Afro-Brazilian religions. After the crash of 1914, the city suffered another disastrous decline – but it kept afloat, just about, on the back of Brazil nuts and the lumber industry.

The wealth generated by the rubber boom is still evident in the shape of the modern city, whose elegant central avenues lead from the luxuriant Praça da República down to the port, past a historical sector which is replete with Portuguese colonial architecture. It's a friendly city with a Parisian feel and a surprisingly modern skyline. Always warm and often hot (and often wet, too), the **climate** is generally very pleasant, with an average temperature of 25°C. Belém remains the economic centre of the north, and the chief port for the Amazon.

Arrival, orientation and information

Belém's **Rodoviária** is situated some 2km from the centre on Avenida Governador José Malcher, near the Almirante Barroso ring road: any bus from the stops opposite the entrance to the *Rodoviária* will take you downtown. If you want Praça da República, take one with "P. Vargas" on its route card. There are excellent facilities and services at the *Rodoviária*, including a Parátur information office (not always open, even when it's meant to be). If you're coming by scheduled airline, you'll arrive at Belém **airport**, 15km out of town (☎211-6039), which also has a Parátur office with unreliable opening hours. There's the usual system of co-op taxis opposite the arrivals hall, for which you buy a ticket at the kiosk, but this is a ludicrously expensive way of getting into town ($20 for a 15-minute ride). Instead, you can walk to the opposite end of the terminal where you'll find the taxi stand for ordinary city cabs, which are drastically cheaper. Or you can take the "Marex Arsenal" bus from the airport to the *Rodoviária* and continue into town from there. **Boats** dock on the river near the town centre, from where you can walk or take a local bus up Avenida Presidente Vargas (not recommended if you have luggage or late at night), or catch a taxi. For information on boat services see p.330.

Presidente Vargas is the modern town's main axis, running from the Praça da República and the landmark Teatro da Paz right down to the riverfront. Buses coming into Belém centre from the airport and *Rodoviária* travel down Avenida Assis de Vasconcelos, which is more or less parallel. Most of the hotels, restaurants, shops and businesses are along Presidente Vargas, or just off it. On block 7, you'll find the FUNAI office and shop and the Varig offices, and on block 6, the VASP office and the telephone company. The central post office, one of the most impressive in South America, is on block 4 and the ENASA riverboat company building at the end of the *avenida* on the riverfront.

As well as the somewhat erratic offices at the airport and *Rodoviária*, **tourist information** is available at Parátur offices downtown at the Feira de Artesanato do Estado on Praça Kennedy (☎224-9633). **Maps** and town guides can be bought cheaply from the newspaper stands on Avenida Presidente Vargas.

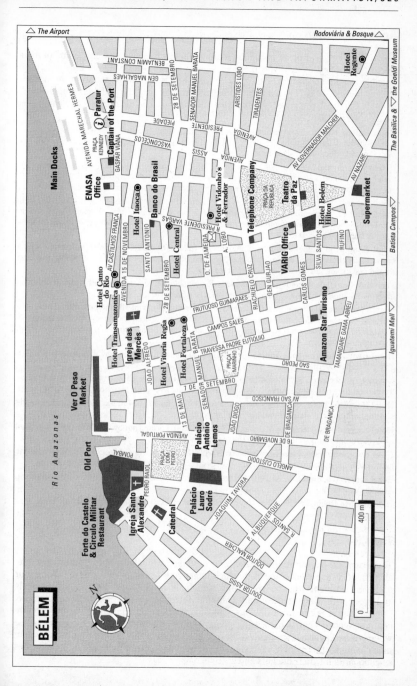

BÉLEM

The Airport

Rodoviária & Bosque

Rio Amazonas

Main Docks

Ver O Peso Market

Old Port

Forte do Castelo & Círculo Militar Restaurant

Igreja Santo Alexandre

Catedral

Palácio Lauro Sodré

Palácio Antônio Lemos

Praça Dom Pedro

POMBAL

AVENIDA PORTUGAL

PEDRO RAIOL

13 DE MAIO

7 DE SETEMBRO

SENADOR MANUEL BARATA

JOÃO ALFREDO

Hotel Vitória Regia

Hotel Fortaleza

Igreja das Mercés

Hotel Transamazônica

Hotel Canto do Rio

AV CASTILHOS FRANCA

AVENIDA 15 DE NOVEMBRO

28 DE SETEMBRO

SANTO ANTONIO

FRUTUOSO GUIMARAES

CAMPOS SALES

TRAVESSA PADRE EUTIQUIO

Praça MARINHO

ENASA Office

AVENIDA MARECHAL HERMES

PRAÇA KENNEDY

GASPAR VIANA

Paratur

Captain of the Port

BENJAMIN CONSTANT

GEN MAGALHÃES

PIEDADE

28 DE SETEMBRO

SENADOR MANUEL BARATA

PRESIDENTE VASCONCELOS

ASSIS

AVENIDA PRESIDENTE VARGAS

Banco do Brasil

Hotel Itaoca

Hotel Central

Hotel Vidonho's & Ferrador

O. DE ALMEIDA

A. LOBO

RIACHUELO CRUZ

GEN GURJAO

CARLOS GOMES

Amazon Star Turismo

SÃO PEDRO

AV SÃO FRANCISCO

DE BRAGANÇA

16 DE NOVEMBRO

JOÃO DIOGO

ANGELO CUSTODIO

DOUTOR MALCHER

DOUTOR ASSIS

JOAQUIM TÁVORA

P. ALBUQUERQUE

R. SANTOS

TAMANDARE GAMA ABREU

ARISTIDES LOBO

TIRADENTES

AV GOVERNADOR MALCHER

AV NAZARE

Telephone Company

Praça DA REPÚBLICA

Teatro da Paz

VARIG Office

Hotel Belém Hilton

Supermarket

Hotel Regente

Iguatemi Mall

Batista Campos

The Basílica & the Goeldi Museum

SILVA SANTOS

RUFINO

400 m

0

N

Accommodation

There are plenty of **hotels** in Belém, many of them expensive and only some of them worth the money asked. The more expensive and mid-price hotels are located on Avenida Presidente Vargas. Other, more basic hotels tend to be found in the narrow streets behind, between Avenida Presidente Vargas and the old heart of town by Avenida Portugal, the government palace and the fort. The nearest place to camp is at Benfica, some 15km east of town.

Hotel Belém Hilton, Av. Presidente Vargas 882 (☎223-6500). Belém's best and most expensive hotel dominates the Praça da República. Although usually exorbitant, the *Hilton* occasionally has radical price reductions at slack times of year. ⑦.

Hotel Canto do Rio, Av. Castilhos Franca (☎224-7473). Situated very close to the port, this hotel has friendly staff but offers very basic accommodation in a dubious neighbourhood more or less opposite one end of the Ver O Peso market. The *Canto do Rio* also acts as an agent for boats going upstream. ①.

Hotel Central, Av. Presidente Vargas 290 (☎222-3011). Probably the best value in town, this well-situated hotel is a splendid old building with a wide range of comfortable, elegant rooms and an excellent rooftop breakfast. Some of the rooms have windows opening onto corridors, so put valuables in the hotel safe. ①–③.

Hotel Equatorial Palace, Av. Bras de Aguiar 621 (☎241-2000). Slightly less expensive and with a more cosy ambience than the international-flavoured *Hilton*, this hotel has a small rooftop pool and a good restaurant, just over 500m east of Praça da República. ⑥.

Ferrador, Rua O. de Almeida 476 (☎242-1444). Reasonable and very central, with a mainly Brazilian business clientele. Shares the building with *Vidonho's Hotel*. ③.

Hotel Fortaleza, Rua Frutuoso Guimaraes 275 (no phone). Undoubtedly the best value of the very cheapest places – a safe, family-run establishment with large shared rooms in a modest and pleasant colonial house. Just a few streets behind Avenida Vargas, the *Fortaleza* is pretty central and can also organize boat trips. ①.

Hotel Itaoca, Av. Presidente Vargas 132 (☎241-3434). Situated near the port, this hotel is comfortable but rather overpriced. ④.

Novotel, Av. Bernardo Sayão 4804 (☎249-7111). A bus- (Guamá or UFA) or taxi-ride from the centre in the *bairro* of Guamá. Part of the international chain, with great views out across the river. ⑤.

Hotel Regente, Av. Governador Malcher 485 (☎224-0755, fax 224-0343). Excellent value in a handy location, with good restaurant and a swimming pool. ③.

Hotel Sagres, Av. Governador Malcher 2927 (☎228-3999). Located out by the *Rodoviária*, this hotel with restaurant and pool is well worth the money. ③.

Hotel Transamazônica, Travesia da Industria 17 (☎222-5232). This is one of the cheapest dives in Belém, located near the dockers' and miners' bars. Less clean or friendly than the nearby *Canto do Rio*. ①.

Hotel Vidonho's, Rua O. de Almeida 476 (☎242-1444). Good value, central and modern, just off the Avenida Vargas. ③.

Hotel Vitoria Regia, Rua Frutuoso Guimaraes 260 (☎224-2833). A modern-fronted little hotel; very reasonable and clean. ②.

The City

The **Praça da República**, an attractive central park with plenty of trees affording valuable shade, is a perfect place from which to get your bearings and start a walking tour of Belém's downtown and riverfront attractions. The *praça* itself is sumptuously endowed with fine statues and columns focusing on its fountain centrepiece. Overlooking it is the most obvious sign of Belém's rubber fortunes: the nineteenth-century Rococo **Teatro da Paz**, dripping with Neoclassical fixtures, the opera house where Anna Pavlova once danced. Beside it, modern reality is reflected in the young men cleaning other people's big cars on the pavement, using the roots of the old trees as cupboards for their buckets and sponges.

Cidade Velha

Heading down Presidente Vargas towards the river, the old part of town – the **Cidade Velha** – lies off to the left, full of crumbling Portuguese colonial mansions and churches. The oldest church of all is the **Igreja das Mercês**, Rua Frutuoso Guimarães 31. Architecturally it's nothing special, but as a living, working relic it's totally fascinating, full of quaint little touches. The holy water, for example, is dispensed from an upside-down rum bottle with the label half torn off.

This is a pleasant area to wander, and it's not much further to the river docks and the hectic and anarchic market in Amazonian produce, overlooked closely by the old fort. **Ver O Peso market** is not quite the colourful spectacle it once was, but it remains the liveliest spot in town early in the morning (apart from one or two of the more energetic nightclubs). Ver O Peso ("see the weight") was originally a slave market, but these days its main commodities are fish, fruit and vegetables, manioc flour, nuts and other jungle produce. There's not much that is aimed at tourists, but Ver O Peso is one of the most interesting traditional markets in all South America and is a good reason in itself to visit Belém. There are sections devoted to medicinal plants and herbs, and an expanding sector selling locally produced craft goods. It can be a dangerous place, so leave your valuables somewhere safe, and it's not a good idea to go to the market area at any time other than the morning.

The nearby square offers views across to the old Portuguese fort, which has been taken over by a bar on the battlements and the *Círculo Militar* restaurant. Opposite the fort are two more important churches: the **Catedral de Nossa Senhora da Graça**, in Praça Frei Caetano Brandão, which was built in 1748 and is hung with some fine paintings, and the **Igreja Santo Alexandre**. The latter, also an eighteenth-century construction, now houses a small religious art museum.

The architectural highlights of Cidade Velha, however, dominate the square behind the old port and Ver O Peso. Together with the Opera House in Manaus, the magnificent **palaces** of Lauro Sodré and Antônio Lemos are the finest buildings left by the rubber boom. Until recently the seat of the mayor and state governor respectively, and more than a little run-down, they have been sensitively restored, with the addition of museums, and thrown open to the public (Tues–Fri 10am–5pm). No visit to Belém would be complete without seeing them.

The **Palácio Lauro Sodré**, completed in the 1890s at the height of the rubber boom, has an elegant blue and white Neoclassical colonnaded exterior and a series of airy arched courtyards which are occasionally used as galleries for travelling exhibitions. Upstairs is the Salão Nobre, a huge suite of reception rooms running the entire length of the frontage with crystal chandeliers, beautiful inlaid wooden floors and Art Nouveau furniture marred only by a few grim paintings.

Next door, painted a dazzling white, is the **Palácio Antônio Lemos**, built in the 1770s by Antônio Landí, a talented emigré Italian, who was also an artist and sketched the first scientifically accurate drawings of Amazonian fauna. It was from here that the joint Portuguese–Spanish border commissions set out to agree the frontiers of Brazil in colonial times. Pará's independence from Portugal in 1822 and adhesion to the Republic in 1888 were declared from here, and it was on the staircase here that President Lobo de Souza was shot down on January 7, 1835, in the early hours of the Cabanagem Rebellion (see p.323). The *palácio* later became the centre of days of street fighting at the rebellion's height, which left hundreds dead. Today it houses the museum of the state of Pará, which itself is nothing special, but the building is glorious. Apart from the magnificent central staircase, carved from marble during the rubber boom, the ground floor and half of the first floor are still much as they were in the eighteenth century, uncluttered and elegant. The reception rooms overlooking the square were rebuilt at the turn of the century with no expense spared and, perhaps even more than the Manaus Opera House, give an idea of what an extrordinary period the rubber boom was.

Avenida Nazaré: the Basílica and Museu Goeldi

Two of the most important and worthwhile sights in Belém lie about fifteen minutes' walk inland from the Praça da República along Avenida Nazaré. The first is the **Basílica de Nossa Senhora de Nazaré** on Praça Justo Chermont. Created in 1908, and supposedly modelled on St Peter's in Rome, it rates – internally at least – with the most beautiful temples in South America. It somehow manages to be both ornate and simple at the same time, a cruciform structure with a fine wooden ceiling and attractive Moorish designs decorating the sixteen main arches. Most importantly, however, this is home to one of the most revered images in Brazil, **Nossa Senhora de Nazaré**. The story of the image is littered with miracles: it is said to have been originally sculpted in Nazareth in the early years of Christianity, from where it found its way to Spain by the eighth century. Here it had to be hidden from the Moors, and somehow survived to end up in Portugal, where the first important miracle occurred in the twelfth century, when the mayor of Porto de Mós, Fuas Roupinho, was saved from certain death (plunging off the edge of a cliff on horseback) by the intervention of the Virgin. He built a chapel in celebration, and from there the Jesuits brought the image to Brazil in the seventeenth century. On the first attempt to bring it to Belém, the image was lost in the jungle, and rediscovered in 1700 by a rancher. He built a rough shrine to house the Virgin, and word of its miraculous properties rapidly spread; today that shrine has grown to an impressive church, and the cult of Nossa Senhora de Nazaré is stronger than ever.

The most obvious sign of the thriving cult is the annual **Cirio de Nazaré** (Festival of Candles), for which something approaching a million people flock to Belém on the second Sunday in October. A copy of the image is carried in a vast parade from the cathedral to the basilica, and two weeks later it returns: in between are all the usual secular festivities of a Brazilian celebration. If you hope to stay at this time of year, you'll need to book a room well in advance.

Two long blocks up Avenida Magalhães Barata (the continuation of Nazaré) from the basilica, you'll find the excellent **Museu Paraense Emílio Goeldi** at no. 376 (Tues–Thurs 9am–noon & 2–5pm, Fri 9am–noon, Sat & Sun 9am–5pm; museum $2, zoological gardens $3). The gardens alone are worth a visit, and quite apart from the collections of plants, birds, animals and Indian artefacts, any money you spend here goes not only to the upkeep of the museum and its grounds but also to a wide programme of research in everything from anthropology to zoology. Founded in 1866, this is one of only two Brazilian research institutes in the Amazon, and plays a vital role in developing local expertise.

Set in the compact but beautifully laid-out botanical gardens here is a small **zoo**. Tapirs, manatees, big cats, huge alligators, terrapins, electric eels and an incredible selection of birds make this place an important site for anyone interested in the forest. By Brazilian standards the animals are reasonably kept, too – although the jaguars barely have room to turn round, and the larger birds seem horribly cramped. The **museum**, particularly the geology, ecology, archeology and anthropology sections, is equally fascinating and well organized. There's an excellent description of the region from its pre-ceramic hunter-gatherer stage (10,000–1000 BC) through the period of early ceramics and incipient agriculture (3000–200 BC) until the emergence of forest agriculture as encountered by the Portuguese in the sixteenth and seventeenth centuries. Some of the early Marajó island ceramics are particularly impressive: marvellous pots and bowls which are virtually the only reminder of a culture that had already vanished when the Portuguese arrived. Finally, the museum's **souvenir shop** has probably the best selection of T-shirts and other souvenirs in Belém – it's not the cheapest place in town, but quality is high and the money goes to a good cause.

The Bosque Rodrigo Alves

About half an hour by yellow bus marked "Avenida Almirante Barroso" from Ver O Peso market, the **Bosque Rodrigo Alves** botanical gardens (Tues–Sun 9am–noon &

3–4.30pm) are actually a small reserve of relatively virgin plantlife – or as virgin as is possible within the confines of a large modern city. There's also a well-stocked lake and mini-zoo, and archeological exhibits from the region are on display. Recently restored to its original, turn-of-the-century grandeur, it's a worthwhile outing for a breath of fresh air (or you could head for the beaches – see p.331), and limited refreshments are available.

Eating, drinking and nightlife

Belém is a great place to eat out, and an opportunity to get acquainted with the distinctive cuisine of the Amazon region (see box p.318). For quick Brazilian **snacks** and plenty of local atmosphere try the *Café Milano* on Avenida Presidente Vargas and the *Bar do Parque* (see below) at Praça da República. The best places for **ice creams** are the *Casa dos Sucos* on Presidente Vargas, offering a wide variety of local fruit flavours, and *Tribon*, Rua Municipalidade 1643. There are dozens of good **restaurants** in town including:

Restaurant Akilu's, 28 de Setembro 38. Perhaps the best value in town and offering a great choice, this is a self-service *comida por kilo* restaurant where you pay for the food you have chosen by weight.

Avenida, Av. Nazaré 1086 (☎223-4015). One of Belém's best restaurants with a great setting overlooking the basilica, excellent food and air conditioning – though it's fairly expensive and a bit short on atmosphere.

Restaurant Casa Portuguesa, Senador Manuel Barata 897. Located directly behind *Restaurant Inter* with typical, moderately priced local food, *cabaña*-style decor and a quiet atmosphere.

Cheiro Verde, Av. Bras de Aguiar, near the *Equatorial Palace Hotel* and Praça de Nazaré. Excellent and cheap self-service restaurant, where you pay by the weight of your plate; vegetarian options as well as meat and fish, and very good salad bar. Always packed and lively; live music after 9pm on Fri and Sat nights.

Circulo Militar, Praça Frei Caetano Brandão (☎223-4374). Situated within the grounds of the city's historic fort, this expensive restaurant serves delicious food – try the lobster or *filhote na brasa* (an Amazon fish, charcoal-grilled), and *pudim de cupuaçu* for dessert – and offers panoramic views over a busy part of the Amazon.

Restaurant Gostosão, Rua Aristides Lobo 388. Just off block 4 of Avenida Presidente Vargas, this inexpensive restaurant serves good evening meals – and very good fish salads.

Restaurant Inter, 28 de Setembro 304. Superb value, large delicious helpings and local specialities, frequented mostly by Belém's office workers at lunchtime.

Lá em Casa, Av. José Malcher 247 (☎222-9164). Good, moderately priced food, eaten underneath an enormous mango tree, with a retractable roof in case of rain. Regional dishes are recommended: the menu has a helpful English translation.

Miako, Trav. 1 de Março 766 (☎223-4485). The city's large Japanese population supports this pricey restaurant, located behind the *Hilton*, which serves great Japanese food and a wide selection of *sucos* made from Amazonian fruit.

Sabor da Terra, Av. Souza Franco (also called Docas) 600. The food is nothing special but the highlight is the floor show afterwards, which is touristy but very good as these things go: regional dances and music, well staged, with especially good dancers. Reasonably priced: around $20 a head, excluding drinks.

Nightlife

Belém can be a very lively place, especially at weekends, but one of the best **bars** is also the quietest, the *Bar do Forte* on the battlements of the old Portuguese fort overlooking Ver O Peso market; the entrance is just past the *Circulo Militar* restaurant. Here you sit outside, among eighteenth-century cannon pointing out to sea, and the view is marvellous especially at sunset. The other outdoor bar in the centre is a famous meeting spot right in the heart of the Praça da República, in front of the theatre, the *Bar do*

Parque. It's open all day and there's always something going on, including, very often, a *batucada* playing live music on weekend nights.

Belém's real **nightlife** rarely begins much before 10 or 11pm, when the focus switches to the western *bairro* of **Condor**, on the banks of the Rio Guamá (the area is named after the German Kondor flying-boat that established the first regular air service in the Amazon, between Belém and Manaus, in the 1920s). There are numerous clubs to choose from, particularly lively on Thursday, Friday and Saturday, and you'll need to take a taxi there and back. *Lapinha*, Trav. Padre Eutiquio 3901 (☎229-3188; no entry charge), is the best known and most enjoyable, though it rarely gets going much before midnight. It's not too glitzy, there's usually good food and a live band at weekends (again, after midnight), and it may be the only club in the world which has three toilets – "Men", "Women" and "Gay". Other places to try are the *Palácio dos Bares* in Condor and, much more upmarket but a place which often has good samba bands, the *Bar Teatro Maracaibo*, Alcindocacela 1299 (☎222-4797).

Another good area after dark is the **Avenida Souza Franco**, which everyone calls Docas, a short taxi-ride or walk from the centre: head up Avenida José Malcher from Praça da República, turn left down Quintino Bocaiuva, take the second right and keep going for another five minutes – it's the broad street with a canal in the middle to your left. It has two nightclubs, *Spectrum* and *Back Street Bar*, which usually have DJs playing a mixture of international and Brazilian dance music to a young crowd; they occasionally host live shows by local bands. It's hard to call it more sedate, but at least you can sit down at the nearby *Miralha*, which has good live Brazilian music on weekend nights, and good food every night.

The other live music spot, and current hottest place in town, is the *African Bar* on the dock road just past the start of Avenida Presidente Vargas; it has great pseudo-African decor, complete with thatched roof, and is surprisingly cheap. Both Brazilian and international music – mostly electronic dance – is played, and it's always lively and crowded with the fashionable young.

Belém is a good place for a night at the **cinema**. A couple of fine old theatres with cavernous interiors and refreshingly enormous screens make even bad films enjoyable to watch: check out the *Olímpia*, on Presidente Vargas almost next door to the *Hilton*, and the *Nazaré*, on the *praça* by the cathedral, which show mainstream releases. There's a good triple-screen arthouse, *Cinema 1-2-3*, behind the Iguatemi mall in Batista Campos: take any bus with an "Iguatemi" card in front, get out at the mall, and walk through it. Plenty of bars and restaurants in the same street cater for the after-show crowd, if you want to make a night of it.

Listings

Airlines Transbrasil, Av. Presidente Vargas 780 (☎212-6977); Varig, Av. Presidente Vargas 768 (☎224-3344); VASP, Av. Presidente Vargas 620 (☎211-6083).

Banks and exchange The Banco do Brasil (2nd floor, Av. Presidente Vargas 248) and many of the larger shops, travel agents and hotels will change both travellers' cheques and dollars cash. The *Hotel Central* generally offers reasonable rates, and there are several *casas de câmbio* on Av. Presidente Vargas.

Boats See also box pp.320–321. Boats leave Belém regularly for upstream Amazon river destinations, even as far as Porto Velho (at least one a day to Macapá, Santarém and Manaus) and for coastal cities such as Salvador and Rio; there are also boats every day to the port of Souré on the Ilha de Marajó (4hr). However, boats don't have set times of departure, as this depends on tides and river conditions, and there are a huge number of different companies, with no central place where you can get information. Any travel agent will book a ticket for you (just say when and where you want to go), or speak to the captains on the docks. ENASA (Av. Presidente Vargas 41; ☎223-3878) has large boats heading upstream four or more times a month.

Consulates UK, Rua Gaspar Viana 490 (☎224-4822); USA, Rua Oswaldo Cruz 165 (☎223-0800).

Hospital Hospital Guadalupe, Rua Arcipreste Manoel Teodoro 734 (☎241-8940).

Post office The central post office (Mon–Sat 9.30am–6pm) is an impressive building on Av. Presidente Vargas. However, as this is frequently crowded, it's often quicker to walk to the small post office at Av. Nazaré 319, 3 blocks beyond the Praça da República.

Shopping Belém is one of the best places in the world to buy hammocks (essential tackle if you are about to go upriver) – look in the street markets between Avenida Presidente Vargas and Ver O Peso, starting in Rua Santo Antônio, for these and anything from digital watches to unusual rubber-crafted knives and keyrings.

Travel agents Ciatur, Av. Presidente Vargas 645 (☎241-2347), operates tours on large boats, often taking up to 100 people at a time. More personal service with a greater choice of tours around Belém and to the Ilha do Marajó, is offered by Amazon Star Turismo, Rua Carlos Gomes 14 (☎212-6244), a French-run agency specializing in ecological tourism.

Around Belém

Although Belém is over a hundred kilometres from the ocean, there are some good **river beaches** nearby, all of them popular with city crowds at weekends and holidays. At the village of **ICOARAÇI**, only 18km or about half an hour by bus from the bus stop next to the *Hotel Central* on Avenida Presidente Vargas, there's a reasonable beach and this is also the best place to visit local **ceramic workshops** and the cheapest place to buy the very fine pottery. Still very much based on the ancient designs of the local Indians, the skill involved in shaping, engraving, painting and firing these pots is remarkable. Some of the ceramics are very large and, except to the expert eye, barely distinguishable from the relics in the Goeldi museum.

Apart from Icoaraçi, the closest and most popular of the beaches are Outeiro and Mosqueiro, both easy day trips. **OUTEIRO**, a picturesque and often busy little town, can be reached in under an hour by bus and ferry. **MOSQUEIRO**, some 70km north of Belém, is actually an island, though it's well connected by road and bridge. The beaches are beautiful and relatively unspoilt, but they can get very crowded at holiday times; there are all the usual beach facilities – stalls selling chilled coconut milk, bars, good restaurants and a few hotels. **Praia Murubira**, with safe swimming and sailing, is probably the best of those close to Mosqueiro town. Of the other beaches here, Praia Farol is popular and preferable to Praia Areão, which is closer to the main *praça* and bus terminal. Buses run frequently from Belém's *Rodoviária*, a journey of around two hours. At *Carnaval* and during the July Festival de Verão, Mosqueiro is particularly lively, with *blocos* on the beach.

Just 18km east from Belém is the island haven of **Cotijuba**, replete with beautiful beaches, rainforest and access to *igarapé* creeks. It's the perfect place for birdwatching and nature walks. Trips are arranged by Amazon Star Turismo (see above), with accommodation in native-style bungalows.

Ilha do Marajó

The **Ilha do Marajó** is a vast island of some 50,000 square kilometres in the estuary opposite Belém. Created by the accretion of silt and sand over millions of years, it's a wet and marshy area, the western half covered in thick jungle, the east flat savanna, swampy in the wet season (Jan–June), brown and firm in the dry season (June–Dec). On this savanna are *fazendas* where huge water buffalo are ranched – some 60,000 of them roam the island – and supplying meat and hides to the markets in Belém is still Marajó's main trade. The island is also famous for its giant *pirarucu* fish which, at over

180kg, is the biggest freshwater breed in the world. Other animal life abounds, including numerous snakes, alligators and venomous insects, so be careful where you walk. There are also some beautiful sandy beaches, and the island has become a popular resort for sunseekers and eco-tourists alike.

Although it was settled by Jesuits at an early stage, the island has something of a reputation for lawlessness stemming from its violent treatment of foreign visitors during the nineteenth-century Cabanagem Rebellion. Its earliest inhabitants have left behind burial mounds, 1000 years old and more, in which many examples of the distinctive Marajó pottery were found. Large pieces, decorated with geometric engravings and painted designs, these are virtually the only reminder of a vanished people – the best examples are in the Museu Goeldi in Belém. When the Jesuits arrived and established the first cattle ranches, the island was inhabited by Nhemgaiba Indians; later its vast expanses offered haven to runaway slaves and to free Indians who wanted to trade with Belém without too much direct interference from the white man's culture. Water buffalo, ideally suited to the marshy local conditions, were imported from India around the turn of the century – or, if you believe local legend, were part of a French cargo bound for Guyana and escaped when the ship sank. River navigation around Marajó is still a tricky business, the course of the channels constantly altered by the ebb and flow of the ocean tides.

Practicalities

The main port of **SOURÉ** is a growing resort offering pleasant beaches where you can relax under the shade of ancient mango trees (watch out in March and April though, when the ripe mangoes begin to fall). The *Hotel Souré*, just a few blocks from the docks in the town centre (①), is very basic, while the *Hotel Marajó*, Praça Inhangaiba (☎091/224-5966; ④), offers more comfort and a pool. Other magnificent empty **beaches** can be found all around the island – the **Praia do Pesqueiro**, about 13km from Souré, is one of the more accessible and well served with places to eat, such as the *Restaurant Maloca*. If you want to see the interior of the island – or much of the wildlife – you have to be prepared to camp or pay for a room at one of the *fazendas*: book with travel agents in Belém or take your chance on arrival. One of the best rural lodgings, the *Pousada dos Guará* (☎091/241-0891; ⑤), is situated close to Praia Grande.

Organized trips can be booked at most travel agencies in the city (see p.331). It is also easy enough to get to Marajó yourself. By river – a four-hour trip each way – **boats** leave in the mornings on weekdays (be at the port before 8am to be sure of finding an early one if you don't want to stay overnight). There are also larger boats, usually leaving Wednesday and Friday at 8pm and Saturday around 2pm.

Southern Pará

The southern half of Pará, south and west of Belém, is real frontier territory containing the notorious Serra Pelada gold mines and harbouring the Grande Carajás project (see box on pp.334–335). The region does have its fascination, but it doesn't constitute a tourist attraction, nor do locals on the whole welcome overcurious outsiders: wherever you go, take care.

Marabá

MARABÁ, on the banks of the Rio Tocantins, almost 600km south of Belém and 400km north of Araguaina on the Belém–Brasília road, is often described as the worst of all Amazon towns. It's the market centre for the region, and also the place where the ranchers, construction workers, truckers and goldminers come for entertainment: it has a bad reputation for theft and violent crime, and it's not a place you should (or would want to) hang around any longer than you have to.

Marabá is a city of three parts, all of them easily reached by bus from Araguaina or from Belém. The earliest part of town was founded on the south side of the river on ground which was liable to flooding; later settlers created the Cidade Nova on the north side, hoping to escape the waters. Then in the 1970s the completion of the Transamazônica led to the foundation of Nova Marabá, back on the south side. All three parts are linked by bridges across the river, and, although each has its own church, the rapid growth of the town is eroding the physical distinctions between them. All around the town, development is reflected in rising land values and the influx of new settlers – and with them further conflict between *fazendeiros* and landless arrivals (see box on pp.334–335).

Buses will drop you at the *Rodoviária* at Km 4 on the Transamazônica in Nova Marabá; small local buses or taxis run from here to just about every part of town. The **airport** (☎091/324-1243 or 324-1383) is just 3km out of town near the Cidade Nova. The choice of **accommodation** is relatively small: in Nova Marabá there's the *Hotel Itacaiúnas*, Folha 30, Quadra 14, Lote 1 (☎ and fax 091/322-1715; ④); and the *Hotel Vale do Tocantins*, Folha 29, Quadra Especial, Lote 1 (☎091/322-2321, fax 322-1841; ④), both with pool, bar and restaurant; in the Cidade Nova the choice is essentially between the *Hotel Vitória*, Av. Espírito Santo 130 (☎091/528-1175; ②), and the *Hotel Keyla*, Transamazônica 2427 (☎091/324-1175; ③). Nearer the *Rodoviária* there's also the basic and somewhat noisy *Pensão Nossa Senhora do Nazaré* (①). The town's best fish **restaurant** is *Bambu*, Travessa Pedro Carneiro 111, Cidade Nova (☎091/324-1290), and there's an excellent Japanese restaurant, *Kotobuki*, Av. Tocantins 746, Novo Horizonte (closed Mon).

Money can usually be changed (dollars cash only) in the larger hotels and shops, but generally at poor rates – you'd do better to change it before you arrive. **Cars** can be rented from Interlocadora (☎091/321-1266) or Localiza (☎091/322-1414).

THE SERRA PELADA GOLD MINES

About 100km to the southwest of Marabá, in the **Serra Pelada**, a number of huge gold nuggets were discovered in 1980. The discovery sparked off the biggest gold rush of the century, and within a couple of years there were as many as 100,000 *garimpeiros* hacking away at the landscape. The scene here – the mountainside stripped of all vegetation, the landscape pock-marked with vast craters scraped out by the most basic of methods – is familiar from dozens of colour magazine spreads: a vision of hell unseen outside the imaginings of Hieronymus Bosch, as thousands of prospectors scraped away at the mud, barely distinguishable from it. One or two made their fortunes – above all the famous José Maria who struck a patch with over 1000 kilos of gold and became one of the richest men in Brazil overnight. But far more barely made a living, and many lost their lives. Now the mines are in terminal decline, the gold all but played out.

Serra Pelada and the surrounding Carajás region are not a tourist attraction, though they were visited by a lot of journalists in the 1980s. There have been frequent violent disturbances at the workings: in 1988, for instance, ten gold prospectors were shot dead by military police while protesting for improved safety precautions. Around 5000 miners blockaded the road and rail bridges over the Rio Tocantins until fired on indiscriminately by charging policemen. The mines are now closed to all visitors. The prospectors, too, have been forced out to make way for monstrous mechanical extractors, although the official line is that the area has been closed to encourage environmental recuperation.

THE MINERAL PROVINCE OF CARAJÁS

The **Serra dos Carajás** is a range of steep hills about 160km west of Marabá. Even today, much of it is heavily forested and astonishingly beautiful, fed with moisture by the clouds and mists that are a feature of the local climate. It is also the heart of the most extensive, ambitious and destructive "development" project in the Amazon and one of the largest mining operations in the world today. Its story starts in the 1960s, when the military authorities were making determined efforts to discover whether the Amazon's rumoured mineral deposits really existed. In 1968 a geological survey helicopter, off course, developed engine trouble and landed on one of the hills in the Carajás range. While it was being repaired the geologists on board discovered, to their astonishment, that they were standing on a hill composed almost entirely of high-grade iron ore. Further exploration established rich deposits of many other minerals, too.

Today **Carajás** has good roads, a modern airport and neatly planned towns where miners and technicians live, and is entirely unlike the rest of Amazonia. There are no villages strung out along the roads, no roadside vendors, no bars or cheap hotels and no bus stations. The explanation is that no one without a permit may enter: along the roads are police checkpoints, and outside them huddle the familiar shanty towns filled with people hoping for work within the officially declared **Mineral Province of Carajás**. Carajás itself is effectively a no-go zone: supplied by air, sealed off by road, with a permanent cheap labour pool to be admitted as needed and then expelled. Within the region, the massive CVRD (*Companhia do Vale do Rio Doce*), the recently privatized mining company, is in complete control. In the past, as a state-owned civil body, it could and did call upon military and police support whenever it needed it. Now a privately owned concern, there are even fewer controls on its more blatantly damaging activities, and with talk of the company being resold to foreign multinationals at a cut-down price, the environment and the Indians are last things on anyone's mind.

The scale of it all is hard to comprehend: apart from the sophisticated open-cast mining operation itself, extracting iron, manganese, bauxite, copper and gold, a completely new network of power generation, transport and processing plants has been created, with a rail line to the coast connecting with new port facilities and aluminium factories, and an enormous hydroelectric scheme at nearby Tucurui. The original plan was for a total investment of 62 billion dollars – a substantial proportion of Brazil's current foreign debt. Under military rule construction targets were met, but at an enormous environmental and political cost.

Tucurui

TUCURUI town, some 225km to the north of Marabá, was until 1977 no more than a pin on a surveyor's map. Today over 60,000 people live here amid air-conditioned office buildings, supermarkets, a modern hospital and even green tennis courts; it has a dusty red main street and a tendency to noise, with construction by day and rowdy construction workers by night. The entire city was built by Eletronorte to house the workers building Brazil's largest dam – over 12km long and with a flooded reservoir covering 4000 square kilometres of rainforest, the fourth largest artificial lake in the world. Now on stream, the **Barragem da Hidrelétrica de Tucurui** is projected to supply eight million kilowatts a year throughout the 1990s, making it the largest hydroelectric dam project in the world.

The cost of building the dam is unknown, but it's estimated that at one stage three million dollars were being spent every day. Corruption was almost inevitable, and the "Capemi case" was one of the most public scandals of the years of military rule. Rather than simply drowning the vast tracts of forest in the area of the reservoir,

Communities living in the path of the development were simply moved (usually without compensation) or ignored. The rail line, for example, cuts through the Gaviões Indian reserve, a problem which was solved by simply getting dispensation from FUNAI to build there. The construction of the **Alcoa aluminium plant at São Luís** is a good example of the way environmental issues and the needs of local people were simply ignored. Some 22,000 people were moved from their homes, without compensation, to allow the plant to be built, and environmental guarantees, though given, appear to have been ignored. Resentment in São Luís is fuelled by the plant's thirst for water and electricity. Power to the plant comes from new lines direct from Tucurui: they stop at the factory, keeping it brightly lit even when the city is suffering one of its frequent power cuts. Many locals believe that the plant has priority when it comes to water, too.

More recently, attention has switched to the **sem terras**, the landless rural workers who face eviction from a number of *fazendas* in the province to make way for large-scale mining and agricultural projects. Their plight hit the headlines in April 1996, when 1200 protestors blockaded the PA-150 highway near **Eldorado do Carajás**, some 100km south of Marabá, in protest against legal moves to expel them from a local *fazenda*. After two days of protest, military police responded to the stones and chants of the *sem terras* with a two-hour volley from automatic weapons, killing or summarily executing 19 protestors (including 2 babies), and wounding 69 others. The massacre brought a wave of international outcry, and bolstered the cause of the **Movimento de Trabalhadores Rurais Sem-Terra (MST)**, yet the trial of those responsible for the massacre will probably end only in the year 2010. A small memorial museum, a red roadsign and 19 wooden crosses mark the site of the massacre, 9km north of Eldorado.

Meanwhile, in the *serra* itself the lands of several thousand **Indians**, and a huge chunk of **rainforest**, are being transformed into a giant industrial park. Hundreds of Indians have already died, others are now suffering as a result of disease, pollution, deforestation and land invasions on the fringe of the project. Twelve fully loaded trains, each over 2km long, run daily through the territory of the Guajajara and Gaviões Indians, while landless settlers moving up from Marabá are also laying claim to their lands and destroying brazil-nut groves vital to the local economy. In the Xikrin Indian reserve, which lies close to the central mines, *garimpeiros* who have managed to penetrate the cordon have polluted local rivers with mercury, used to separate out gold after panning.

Electronorte invited tenders for the timber to be cleared and sold by 1983. There were plenty of companies with all too much experience of clearing rainforest, but the contract was won, in 1979, by a company called Capemi – a company which dealt mainly with investing military pensions and had no experience of the lumber industry. The decision caused outrage, millions of dollars went missing, and clearance started two years late, succeeding in removing less than a quarter of the high-quality hardwood available. It was a textbook example of the widespread corruption that marked the final years of military rule, and has never been properly investigated: part of the deal by which the military relinquished power was that there should be no investigation of human rights or financial abuses involving military personnel. In human terms the cost was high, too. The lake flooded a section of the Parakanan Indian Reserve and necessitated the re-routing of the Transamazônica through another part of it. It also destroyed the homeland of the Trocara, a group of Indians who had been "discovered" by FUNAI only in 1970.

The new city of Tucurui is served by an older settlement about 9km distant. Today this old town is the site of brothels and other entertainment for the region's workers.

Many of the people working and living in the old town are refugees from the flooded area, and their number grows steadily as year after year floods strike the region, causing roads to be cut and washing away homes. There's not a great deal in Tucurui, and although it's only 350km from Belém, it's not really on the way to anywhere. Nevertheless, the dam is spectacular and worth the trip. For **permission to visit the dam**, phone ☎091/787-2010 at least three days in advance for a guided tour (at 8.30am Tues, Thurs & Fri).

Practicalities

If you want **to stay** in the city there are a number of possibilities. The *Hotel HTA*, Praça França (☎091/787-1232; ④), and the *Hotel Rio Doce*, Rua Lauro Sodré 663 (☎091/787-1146; ③), are reasonable value. Next door to the latter, the *Hotel Marajoara*, Rua Lauro Sodré 685 (☎091/787-1489; ②), is another central option. The *Restaurante Kurika's*, on Rua M #18 (Jardim Paraíso), is a good **place to eat**, as is *Restaurant Hilda* on Praça Jarbas Passarinho at no. 84. The **Rodoviária** is close by on Rua Lauro Sodré and the **airport** (☎091/787-2571) is a six-kilometre taxi-ride away.

Amapá

The **state of Amapá**, north of the Amazon, is one of Brazil's poorest regions. Traditionally it was dependent primarily on rubber exports, but manganese was discovered in the 1950s and this, together with timber and other minerals, is now the main source of income. A standard-gauge rail line links the mining camps to the northwest with the Amazon port of **Porto do Santana**, near the capital Macapá, crossing the dry, semi-forested plains of the region en route. Amapá doesn't have much going for it, other than as a transit route **to French Guyana**, and it suffers the most marked dry season in the Amazon, running from June through December, when it can get extremely hot. Macapá fights it out with Palmas in Tocantins for the title of dullest state capital in Brazil, but at least it's cheap – like Manaus, it's a freeport, exempt from customs duties.

Macapá

MACAPÁ, on the north bank of the Amazon and right on the equator, is the gateway to the state of Amapá and home to three-quarters of its population. Surrounded by uninhabited forests and hills, it dominates the northern section of the Amazon estuary. If you're coming by ferry from Belém you'll actually arrive to the southwest at **Porto do Santana**, just twenty minutes by bus or an hour by boat from Macapá, though it lies on the other side of the equator. The **airport** is 4km from town on Rua Hildemar Maia (☎096/222-2881). The **Rodoviária** faces the Polícia Técnica, 5km outside town on the BR-156; from there, local buses run to Praça Veiga Cabral in the centre.

The countryside around Macapá is, like the Ilha do Marajó in the estuary, roamed by large herds of water buffalo. In town there is not a great deal to do. The highlight is the **Fortaleza de São José** (daily 8am–6pm), one of the largest colonial forts in Brazil, built in 1764 out of material brought over as ballast in Portuguese ships, in response to worries that the French had designs on the north bank of the Amazon. It is often closed, but nobody will mind if you slip through the enormous main gates for a stroll along the battlements. There's an interesting daily artisan market nearby on Canal da Fortaleza, and you could fill some more time checking out the eighteenth-century **Igreja São José de Macapá** on the Praça Veiga Cabral and the **Museu Histórico** at Av. Mário Cruz 17 (Tues–Sun 8am–noon & 2–6pm). There's also a small private museum, the **Instituto de Estudos e Pesquisas de Plantas Medicinais (IEPA)** at Av. Feliciano Coelho 1509, holding the Valdemiro Gomes collection of minerals, Amazon woods and medicinal plants (Mon–Fri 9am–noon).

For **accommodation** the *Hotel Tropical*, Av. Antônio Coelho de Carvalho 1399 (☎096/231-3759; ②), is excellent value. The *Hotel São Antônio* (①) is better placed on the main *praça*, and even cheaper, but not quite as good; or there's the clean and friendly *Hotel Mara* in Rua São Jose (☎096/222-0859; ③). Out near the airport, the *Hotel San Marino*, Av. Marcílio Dias 1395 (☎096/223-1522, fax 223-5223; ⑥), offers more comfort and a pool, whilst top of the range for creature comforts is the *Novotel* on Av. Azarias Neto 17 (☎096/223-1144, fax 223-1115; ⑦). But by far the best option, if you can afford it, is the *Pousada Ekinox*, a short walk from the centre at Rua Jovino Dinoa 1693 (☎096/222-4378; ④). This small but lovely *pousada*, which doubles as the **French consulate**, is owned by a Frenchman and his Brazilian wife, and the food is as good as that combination suggests. It's a popular place to stay, so you'll need to ring ahead and make a reservation.

As for **food**, Macapá's position as a river and sea port means that there's plenty of excellent fish. The *Lennon Restaurant* downtown is a popular eating place, but greater variety can usually be found at the *Restaurant Boscão*, Rua Hamilton Silva 997. Excellent but expensive fish is served at *Martinho's Peixaria*, Av. Beira-Rio 140. The coast road in either direction from the fort has the pleasantest **bars** in town, always well ventilated by the sea breeze. For unrestrained night-time entertainment, try the *Marco Zero* **nightclub**, 5km out on the Fazendinha road near the equator mark.

Listings

Airlines Penta, Canal de Fortaleza 45, almost opposite the Banco do Brasil building (☎096/223-5226), covers the eastern Amazon and Manaus, including reasonably priced flights to Santarém ($120); VARIG to Belém, Brasília, Rio and São Paulo (Rua Cândido Mendes 1039; ☎096/223-1755).

Air taxis Pena (☎096/223-5226); Rio Norte (☎096/222-0033).

Boats For information about boats to the north or to Belém, the Captain of the Port, Av. FAB 427 (☎096/222-0415), can be contacted at his offices most weekdays between 8am and 5pm. The main companies, all based at Porto do Santana, are: ENAVI (☎096/242-2167), with irregular sailings via Belém as far as Santarém; Senava (☎096/223-9090) for sailings to Belém (Tues & Fri); and Silnave (☎096/223-4011) for car-carrying boats to Belém (Tues & Fri).

Car rental Localiza (☎096/223-2799 or 224-2336).

Trains As there are no fixed schedules to the interior, and officially no passenger service, it's a matter of enquiring at the station in Porto do Santana.

Into French Guyana

The main reason to come to Amapá is to get to **French Guyana**: the key road in the state connects Macapá with the town of **OIAPOQUE**, on the river of the same name which delineates the frontier. The road is only asphalted for the first 100km out of Macapá, but the dirt road that takes over is good quality: if you want to make it in one run, the regular buses to Oiapoque take 15 hours, though they can take nearer 24 in the worst periods of the rainy season. It's unfortunately a rather boring drive, largely through savanna rather than forest, with mile after mile of scrubby pine plantations blocking any view. You could break the journey in **CALÇOENE**, eight hours by bus from Macapá, a pleasant, sleepy town built around rapids on the river of the same name, with several cheap hotels and regular bus connections out to Oiapoque. While there you may feel tempted to visit the nearby goldmining town of Lourenço – don't, it's dangerous and very malarial.

A more leisurely option is to go by **boat** from Macapá to Oiapoque, a journey of two days (one night); boats depart once a week or so, but there's no regular schedule. If you're interested in this possibility, you simply have to go to the docks and ask around: if a boat is leaving, seek out its captain and negotiate for hammock space, which should cost no more than $20 in either direction. The best hammock spaces are those with open sides, preferably on the middle deck.

If you are not a citizen of a European Union country, the USA or Canada, you will need a **visa** to enter French Guyana. There is a French consulate in Macapá at Rua Jovina Dinoa 1693 (☎096/222-4378), though it's better to try to arrange this before you leave home. If you're going to travel overland, buy **French francs** in Belém or Macapá. You can get them in Oiapoque but the rates are worse, and you can't depend on changing either Brazilian currency or US dollars for francs in Saint-Georges.

Dug-out taxis are the usual means of transport between Oiapoque and Saint-Georges, about ten minutes downriver. Brazilian **exit stamps** can be obtained from the *Polícia Federal* at the southern road entrance into Oiapoque; on the other side you have to check in with the *Gendarmes* in Saint-Georges. The border along the Rio Oiapoque is still a sensitive one, although the last time there were actual hostilities was in 1808–17, when a Brazilian force crossed the border and occupied Cayenne. It was during this period that Brazil obtained the lucrative cayenne pepper seeds for its own export market.

Most travellers, in fact, cross the border the easy way – by **flying** from Macapá to the capital at Cayenne (around $170). Once you're across the border you'll probably want to fly from the border settlement of Saint-Georges to Cayenne in any case – or else catch a boat – since overland transport is atrocious.

Santarém

Around 700km west of Belém – but closer to 800 as the river flows – **SANTARÉM** is the first significant stop on the journey up the Amazon, a small city of around 120,000 people, which still makes it the fourth largest in the Brazilian Amazon. It is a pleasant, rather sleepy place which feels more like a large town than a city – a world away from the bustle of Belém and Manaus. But don't be deceived by its languid atmosphere, there are plenty of things to do here, and Santarém, positioned right in the centre of the area often referred to as the middle Amazon, a region still largely (and inexplicably) unvisited by tourists, is the perfect base for exploring some of the most beautiful river scenery the Amazon basin has to offer.

It is likely that this area once supported one of the highest populations in the Americas before Europeans arrived, with towns and villages stretching for miles along the riverbanks, living off the rich stocks of fish in the river, and farming corn on even richer alluvial soils, replenished annually when the Amazon flooded. On all the distinctive flat-topped hills around Santarém, there is evidence of **prehistoric Indian occupation**, easily identified by the *terra preta do Indio* (Indian black soil), a black compost deliberately built up over the generations by Indian farmers. If you do any walking up and down these hills, especially around Belterra, keep your eyes open for ceramic shards. Over the last few years, thanks to the work of an American archeologist, Anna Roosevelt, it has become clear that Santarém and its surrounding area is one of the most important archeological sites in the Americas.

Thirty kilometres east of Santarém, more easily accessible by river than by road, is a nineteenth-century sugar plantation called **Taperinha**. In an excavation there in 1991, Roosevelt unearthed **decorated pottery** almost 10,000 years old – twice as old as the

The **telephone code** for Santarém is ☎091.

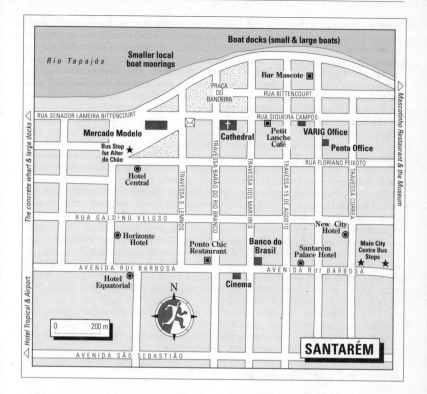

oldest ceramics found anywhere in the Americas. This suggests that the Amazon basin was settled before the Andes, and that the Americas had been settled much earlier than previously thought. Later excavations in **Monte Alegre** confirmed that the middle Amazon played an important role in the prehistory of the Americas with cave and rock paintings dotting the surrounding hills also being dated at around 10,000 years old. About two thousand years ago, Indian culture in the region entered a particularly dynamic phase, producing some superbly decorated ceramics comparable in their sophistication with Andean crafts; there are beautiful pieces of Santarém-phase pottery in the small museum in Santarém, and even more in the Museu Goeldi in Belém.

The very first European accounts of the middle Amazon, dating from the early six-teenth century, which talk of swarms of canoes coming out to do battle and of Indian long-houses lining the riverbanks, are probably true. The river asssumed its current lightly populated look in the centuries after first contact, as disease and slaving wiped out the Indians or drove them way upriver; as late as 1960 some two hundred Indians were massacred by settlers on a sandbank just south of Itaituba.

Development and the rubber boom

Santarém in its modern form began life as a Jesuit mission in the seventeenth century. It grew only slowly during subsequent centuries, but its convenient location made it popular as a base for the several European naturalists who wrote the first travel books about the Amazon in the 1840s and 1850s. It was then a town of five thousand people locking themselves up after dark as jaguars prowled the streets. It was the **rubber boom** that proved the making of Santarém and the town became an important trading centre. The region also became a refuge for two diametrically opposed groups: escaped slaves, who founded communities along the Trombetas and Maicuru rivers on the Amazon's north bank, which were never conquered, and for refugee Confederates, who made the big mistake of moving to Santarém under the misapprehension that they could grow cotton there. By the time they realized they had been misinformed, most of them had died of malaria and yellow fever; the survivors moved into sugar and prospered, although in time their descendants intermarried with locals and adopted their language and now the only trace of them is the occasional surname of Higgins or Macdonald.

Meanwhile, in 1874 an Englishman named **Henry Wickham** settled at Santarém with his wife. He was to be almost single-handedly responsible for the collapse of the Amazon rubber boom, smuggling quantities of valuable rubber seed from the heart of the Amazon (at a price of £10 for every 1000 seeds). The seeds he collected were transported to Kew Gardens, in London, for germination, before being sent on to British-owned plantations in Asia which were already prepared and waiting. It took over twenty years for the first crop to mature to anywhere near peak production, but when it did the bottom fell out of the Brazilian rubber market. British plantations produced 4 tons of rubber in 1900, but 71,000 tons by 1914. This was not only more than Brazil was producing, but also a great deal cheaper, since the plantations were far more efficient than the labour-intensive wild rubber-tree tapping practised in the Amazon. Rubber was to feature again in local history through the development of **Fordlândia** (see p.345). More recently, Santarém underwent explosive growth after the Santarém–Cuiabá highway was completed in the early 1970s, but as the highway deteriorated and finally become impassable in the mid-1980s and gold-mining continued to decline in the interior, the town slumped. Tourists are therefore very welcome here and you will find prices in Santarém and the surrounding area very low.

Arrival and accommodation

Santarém is a busy port, serving river communities for over 300km around as well as operating long-distance services to Manaus and Belém. **Boats** to and from Manaus and Belém arrive and leave most days: the journey time is two to three days in either direction and the cost varies enormously, so it's worth shopping around. The appalling state of the roads in the region means that the **Rodoviária** on the outskirts of town is largely symbolic; there are no inter-city buses in or out of the region. Buses to places within an hour or two of Santarém – notably Alter do Chao, Belterra and Fordlândia – leave from the Mercado Modelo or along Avenida Rui Barbosa, not from the *Rodoviária*.

Santarém does have a useful little **airport** 13km from the centre with a bus connection to Avenida Rui Barbosa. (Travelling from the town centre take the "Aeroporto" bus, not to be confused with "Aeroporto Velho" which goes nowhere near the airport.) There is also a Kombi connecting the *Hotel Tropical* and the airport most mornings. The airport may not look it, but it's a regional hub, thanks to being the headquarters of Penta, a good local airline. They run daily flights to Belém and Manaus at half Varig or Riosul rates, and have routes to Macapá and São Luís which save you at least a day by not passing through Belém.

Local buses in Santarém are sometimes useful, despite the small size of the city, to save you roasting yourself in the heat. Any bus heading left down the riverfront as you stand facing the river will take you to the Mercado Modelo, a hideous large concrete structure which houses a very useful market for stocking up on fruit and other essentials for a river journey.

Accommodation

Santarém is well supplied with hotels to suit every pocket. It's one of the best places to take a break from a long-distance boat-trip, and you could well find yourself staying a few days.

Arco-Iris Hotel, corner of 15 de Novembro and Avenida Tapajos (no phone). A wonderful location towards the western end of the riverfront, but music from the nearby bars might keep you awake at weekends. Some rooms with air conditioning, some just with fan. ②–③.

Hotel Central, Praça Rodrigues dos Santos 887 (☎522-2981). Opposite the Mercado Modelo and one of the best of the budget places. ②.

Hotel Equatorial, corner of Avenida Rui Barbosa and Silvino Pinto (☎522-1135). Centrally located, a clean and airy place on the first floor, which offers excellent value. Some rooms have air conditioning. ①–②.

New City Hotel, Trav. Francisco Correa 200 (☎522-4719 or 523-2351). Clean, modern and very friendly. River tours are also organized by this hotel. ③.

Santarém Palace, Av. Rui Barbosa 726 (☎523-2820). A good medium-range hotel in the centre of town. Also runs reasonably priced river tours. ④.

Hotel Tropical, Av. Mendonça Furtado 4120 (☎523-2800). The flashiest hotel in town, built in hyper-modern style by Varig to celebrate the opening of the Santarém–Cuiabá highway, and now, with the highway effectively gone, something of a relic. Never more than a fraction full, it is comfortable, has nice views out across the river and a good restaurant, but there's also a strange atmosphere as your footsteps echo down empty corridors.You don't have to stay here to use the excellent pool. ⑤.

The city and its beaches

By far the most interesting place in Santarém, at any hour of the day or night, is the **waterfront**. There are always dozens of boats tied up, with the accompanying bustle of people and cargoes being loaded and unloaded, and constant activity in the shops and outfitters lining the riverfront. You will probably have to wander along the front anyway to find boats to points around, but a sunset walk is reason enough to venture down here. Many of the city's restaurants and nightspots line the riverfront, but it is especially lively during the rainy season, when the beaches are under water. On Sundays, hundreds of young people clog the riverfront along the centre of town, where they get their kicks riding their bikes off raised planks into the river.

The waterfront also boasts a surprisingly good **museum**, a fine turn-of-the-century building constructed during the rubber boom and standing in splendid isolation just past the *Mascotinho* restaurant. The highlight of the collection is some stunning Indian pottery, small but elaborately decorated and around 2000 years old. The building itself is also very pleasant and the shady internal courtyard is a good spot to hide from the sun on a hot day.

Beaches

Unlike the eastern and western reaches of the Amazon, the region around Santarém has a very distinct **dry season**, stretching from June to December. In the dry season, Santarém and its surroundings get extremely hot, even by Brazilian standards, with a particularly enervating dry heat. Fortunately this is also the time of year, especially between July and February, when the Amazon drops and the region's magnificent **river beaches** are exposed for you to cool off. If you are unlucky enough to be in Santarém in hot weather while the beaches are still flooded, gringos can use the swimming pools at the *Hotel Tropical* or the *Yacht Clube*, a short taxi-ride from the centre.

PIRANHAS AND STINGRAYS

One thing definitely worth bearing in mind if you are swimming anywhere in the middle Amazon is that **piranhas** and **stingrays** (*raia*) are common. Piranhas are actually much less of a problem. Forget any films you have seen; they don't attack in shoals, and prefer still water to currents. Nevertheless, they can give you a nasty bite and are indeed attracted to blood. They frequent particular spots, which locals all know about and avoid, so ask for advice.

Stingrays are more of a problem. They love warm, shallow water and are so well camouflaged that they are practically invisible. If you tread on one, it will whip its sting into your ankle causing a deep gash and agonizing pain for at least 24 hours and possibly twice that. However, stingrays really hate noise and crowds and so are rarely found on regularly used beaches, such as Alter do Chao, near Santarém. But off the beaten track, they are an ever-present danger. You can minimize the danger by wearing canvas boots or trainers and by splashing and throwing sand and stones into shallow water if you intend to swim there.

In the city itself, the beach which forms at the waterfront in the dry season is definitely not recommended despite the number of locals you'll see swimming there: you can count the raw sewage outlets draining directly into the water as you walk along the promenade. A much better option is to get the local bus to **Maracana** on the far side of town, which is clean. There are lots of small bars and restaurants here serving delicious freshly caught fish. The very best beach near Santarém however is 15km away at **Alter do Chao** (see p.344).

Eating, drinking and nightlife

You'll find many of Santarém's **restaurants** along the waterfront, but the city's sidestreets are also a good hunting ground, as is the beach at Maracana. As you'd expect, **fish** is the main cuisine, but there's also Italian, Japanese and plenty of traditional Brazilian food to be had. For delicious home-made **ice cream** using regional fruits go to *Nido* on Mendonça Furtado between Assis Vasconcelos and 2 de Junho; try the *castanha*, the best brazil-nut ice cream you'll ever have.

Bar Mascote, Praça do Pescador 10. One of the city's popular waterfront places, with regular live music at weekends. Serves a wide range of moderately priced fish and meat dishes.

Bom Paladar, Av. Cuiabá. Regional fish any way you want it – the *caldeirada* (fish stew) is particularly recommended. Live music on Friday and Saturday nights.

Canta-Galo, Trav. Professor Antônio Carvalho. Serving very reasonably priced *carne do sol* – sundried meat grilled as you watch – this restaurant is a short taxi-ride from the centre; all the taxi drivers know it.

Churrascaria Tapajós, Av. Tapajós. Along the waterfront, by the gas station and just past the Mercado Modelo, this is the best option for carnivores tired of eating fish. Good range of salads as well.

Lumi, Av. Cuiabá 1683. A good and moderately priced Japanese restaurant and the best option for vegetarians – the tempura is delicious.

Mascotinho, on the waterfront. This is the place to come for pizza and to enjoy a wonderful location – the restaurant is built out onto the river right in the heart of town.

Petit Lanche, Rua Siqueira Campos. Just down from the church, this place is cheap and simple; good for snacks and breakfast.

Ponto Chic Restaurant, Av. Rui Barbosa. Always lively at lunchtime and very good value.

Uirapiru, on the waterfront opposite *Mascotinho*. Unpronounceable name, but pretty good atmosphere and great views out across the river.

Vapt Vupt, Av. Rui Barbosa, near Banco do Brasil. A *comida por kilo* buffet only open at lunchtime. Excellent quality and value, and a good option for vegetarians. You pay by the weight of your food and if you guess the weight correctly, they halve the price. An incorrectly guessed but hefty lunch will set you back around $4.

Vinhoca, Rua Turiano Meira 387. Just past the corner with Mendonça Furtado, this Brazilian restaurant is easily walkable from the centre. It serves extremely cheap and wonderful regional food including *tacacá, manicoba* and duck in *tucupi* sauce, but you have to get there by about 7pm or there won't be anything left.

Yacht Clube. The restaurant here serves excellent fish and is walkable from the *Hotel Tropical*; otherwise take a taxi and arrange for it to pick you up again as no buses pass this way. Despite its name, it's not at all exclusive, nor are you likely to come across any sailing types. Good-value food, around $12 for a meal for two, and lovely views across the Tapajós.

Nightlife

There's no shortage of options when it comes to **nightlife**. On Friday and Saturday nights, the *Mascote, Mascotinho* and other waterfront dives have live music; people start here and then head out to the serious music places. The *Yacht Clube* usually has something going on starting at around midnight, and *Sygnus*, a *boite* (nightclub) on Avenida Borges Leal gets going around the same time – most local buses from the centre pass by. If you want to make an all-nighter of it, *Denis Bar* on Mendonça Furtado is the place to go and, unlike the other clubs, it has no cover charge. Not far away on Mendonça is the *Babilônia*, a cavernous hangar with a stage, live music and wild crowds every weekend night. The *Bom Paladar* restaurant on Avenida Cuiabá becomes a *boite* on Friday and Saturday nights and there's good dancing here, but it's the sort of place you might expect to see Popeye and Bluto trading blows in the corner – get under the table if you hear any shots.

Listings

Airlines Penta, Rua Floriano Peixoto 220 (☎522-2857); Varig, Rua Silveira Campos 277 (☎522-2084).

Banks and exchange Changing money can be a problem in Santarém. None of the banks changes foreign currency (though cash advances on Visa cards only are available upstairs at the Banco do Brasil; bring your passport), and you have to do the rounds of the travel agents in the centre (see below). One possibility is to try at Fundação Esperanca (see below under "Health"), where, if they don't change the money themselves they will be able to tell you who will; dollars cash only.

Boats Head for the docks nearer the large concrete wharves for riverboats to Manaus and Belém, where you can ask the various captains when they're leaving and how much they'll charge. The *Rio Nilo* line and the *Cisne Branco* to Manaus and Belém have a good reputation, though like most boats they get crowded at times. ENASA is at Trav. Correa 34 (☎522-1934). Wandering along the waterfront is also the best way to find boats heading to the towns between Belém and Manaus; although the larger boats stop at them as well, it's better to get one of the medium-sized boats which only ply that route, since everyone on it will be local and it will probably be less crowded. These boats usually have placards hanging from their side, or set out on the concrete promenade, advertising their destinations and departure times. They are very cheap, and most serve beers and soft drink en route, but take your own food.

Health Any health or dental problems, contact Fundação Esperanca, Rua Coaracy Nunes 3344, a clinic and health centre which runs a volunteer programme for foreign health professionals, so you will be seen by an English-speaking physician or dentist, and get the best treatment in the region at minimal cost. Santaremzinho, Starenzinho, Aeroporto Velho and Amparo/Conquista buses take you right to the door.

Tour operator Amazon Turismo, Trav. Turiano Meira 1084 (☎522-2620), run by Steve Alexander, an expatriate American, operates trips to Belterra and Fordlândia, and reasonably priced forest and boat tours including bird-watching and dolphin-spotting.

Around Santarém

The area around Santarém is richly rewarding, with a variety of day trips possible out to **Alter do Chao**, **Belterra** or **Fordlândia** or boat journeys further afield. Due north, on the opposite bank of the Amazon, some six hours away by boat, is the town of **Alenquer**, the jumping-off point for the stunning waterfall of Veu da Noiva, on the Rio Maicuru. Similar journey times west along the Amazon will land you in **Óbidos**, east takes you to the beautiful town of **Monte Alegre**, and a slightly longer trip south up the Rio Tapajós, through gorgeous river scenery, will bring you to **Itaituba**, a classic gold-rush town, 250km from Santarém.

Alter do Chao

The municipality of Santarém, which is slightly bigger than Belgium, has just 32km of asphalted road. A good two-thirds of this is accounted for by the road that leads from Santarém to its beach resort of **ALTER DO CHAO**, and you can't fault their transport priorities. Alter do Chao is a beautiful bay in the Rio Tapajós overlooked by two easily climbable hills, one the shape of a church altar, giving the place its name. Most of the year the bay is fringed by **white sand beaches**, which combine with the deep blue of the Tapajós to give it a Mediterranean look. In the dry season a sand-bank in the middle of the bay is accessible either by wading or by canoe, and simple stalls provide the fried fish and chilled beer essential to the full enjoyment of the scene. During the week you'll almost have the place to yourself, unless you're unlucky enough to coincide with one of the periodic invasions by hundreds of elder-ly tourists from a cruise ship docked at Santarém. Weekends see the tranquillity shat-tered, as *Santarenhos* head out en masse for the beach – be careful if you're heading back to Santarém on a weekend afternoon as many drivers on the road will be drunk. If the beach is too crowded, get a canoe to drop you on the other side of the bay at the entrance to the path leading up to the higher conical hill. It's a half-hour walk through the forest and finally up above it to the top and a breathtaking view of the meeting of the Tapajós and Amazon rivers.

One essential sight is the **Centre for the Preservation of Indian Art** (daily 9am–noon & 1–5pm; $3.50), a spectacular collection of Indian artefacts from all over the Amazon basin put together by an American and his Indian wife who settled in Alter do Chao. The centre is not difficult to find: it's by some way the largest building in the vil-lage, and might look more at home in New Mexico, with its painted adobe walls, were it not for the Indian masks nodding in the breeze outside. The collection is good and there is the bonus of a **gift shop** stuffed with far better Indian goods than those in any FUNAI shop, as well as a good range of books. Although prices are in dollars, and can therefore seem expensive, the reason is an honourable one: this shop is unusual in that a fair price is paid to the makers of the goods on sale.

Practicalities

The problem with Alter do Chao is transport. There are only three **buses** a day from in front of the Mercado Modelo in Santarém, with two daily returning to town. If you don't feel like getting the last bus back, you might as well make a night of it and stay at one of the three **pousadas** in town, all of them cheap and clean: *Pousada Alter do Chao* (①) on the waterfront, which has a good restaurant open to non-residents as well; *Pousada Tia Marilda* on the street leading up from the square (①); and *Pousada Tupaiulandia* (②), a block further up, which is the best of the bunch. Away from the beach, the town square is surrounded by **restaurants** all dependably cheap if you stick to the fish.

Fordlândia and Belterra

Fordlândia and Belterra are the fruits of an attempt by Henry Ford to revive the Amazon rubber trade in the first half of this century. Ford's intention was to establish a Brazilian plantation to challenge the growing power of the British- and Dutch-controlled rubber cartels, based in the Far East. He was sold a vast concession on the banks of the lower Rio Tapajós by a local man named Villares. What no one seemed to notice at the time was that Villares also organized the Amazon survey, which ended up visiting only his piece of land. Though it was vast – almost 25,000 square kilometres in all – the tract of land he sold had marginal potential for a plantation of any kind. It depended on seasonal rather than regular rains, it was hilly and therefore awkward to mechanize, the soil was sandy and overleached and it was beyond the reach of ocean-going vessels for several months every year.

Nevertheless, Henry Ford went ahead with a massive investment, and the construction of **FORDLÂNDIA**, 100km south of Santarém, began in 1928. Cinemas, hospitals and shops were built to complement the processing plants, docks and neat rows of American staff homes; there was even an independent power supply, designed in Detroit. Nothing like it existed within a thousand kilometres in any direction. Unfortunately the rubber planting proceeded at a much slower rate. Difficulties were encountered in trying to clear the valuable timbers which covered the land, and even when it was cleared there was a shortage of rubber-tree seeds. After five years only about ten square kilometres a year were being cleared and planted, at which rate the process would still have been only half completed in the year 3000.

In the 1930s a new site for the plantation was established at **BELTERRA**, and high-yield rubber seeds were imported back from Asia. Belterra is a plain, around 150m above sea level, about 20km from Santarém on the east bank of the Tapajós, at a point where the river is navigable all year round. Even here, though, Ford never looked likely to recover his money, and poor labour relations combined with poor growth to ensure that he didn't. Although the plantations are still operative, they have always suffered from loss of topsoil and from South American Leaf Blight (the fungus *microcycous uli*), and have never made a significant contribution to the world's rubber supply. By the late 1930s Ford himself had lost interest and in 1945 he sold out to the Brazilian government for $250,000, having already invested well in excess of $20 million.

If you do visit, these are pretty bizarre places. They mimic small-town America exactly, with whitewashed wooden houses, immaculate gardens, fire hydrants, churches and spacious tree-lined streets. The only jarring note is the potholed roads. Belterra is built on a bluff overlooking the Tapajós, with spectacular views down to the river. Fordlândia, with its water towers and the ruined hulk of the rubber-processing factory, is actually on the river and more easily accessible by boat. All boats to Itaituba stop at Fordlândia, the journey taking six to twelve hours depending on the time of year. There's no accommodation but you can probably string your hammock up in the school; bring your own food as there isn't a restaurant. A daily bus runs to Belterra from the Mercado Modelo, but the road is difficult during the rains. There is one bus a day back, but in the morning – and there's no accommodation – so it's not a practical proposition unless you have a car, or can get on an excursion organized by a travel agent in Santarém.

Alenquer

Some five or six hours away from Santarém by boat, through a maze of islands and lakes on the north bank of the Amazon, is **ALENQUER**, a typical small Amazon river town rarely visited by tourists. The town is interesting enough, but wouldn't on its own detain you for more than a day. The streets are pleasant, the waterfront occasionally bustles and has a good view of the river, and there are a couple of atmospheric public buildings from the days of the rubber boom. However, the surrounding countryside is strikingly beautiful with **lakes**, an abundance of wildlife and the gorgeous **waterfall of Veu da Noiva**, all accessible either by road or boat.

Renting a boat for the day costs about the same as hiring a taxi for a day – around $30 – and although the birdlife in the lakes surrounding Alenquer is not as rich as around Monte Alegre (see below), the creeks and islands you can explore are if anything more scenic. The lakes are actually quite heavily populated, by Amazonian standards, and your boatman is almost certain to take the chance to stop off and visit a relative somewhere on the way, giving you the chance to glimpse some rural life. *Botos* (river dolphins) are common and, with luck, you might even see a group of them leaping out of the water together. Unfortunately, piranhas are also common, so be careful about swimming. You will need to take food and water for you and the boatman.

Practicalities

There is a good **hotel** in town, the *Hotel Cirio* (☎091/526-12138; ①), on the waterfront street to the right as you arrive at the quayside. Quite apart from its being by far the best option for accommodation, the owner Donna Maria José can arrange boats for exploring the lakes and taxis for visiting the waterfall. As tourists in Alenquer are still relatively rare, things are cheap and both of these trips will set you back about $30 if you arrange them through the hotel; they're well worth it. As Donna Maria only speaks Portuguese, you will have to try out yours; the waterfall is *a cachoeira* and to rent a boat is *alugar um barco*.

There are **boats** most days between Santarém and Alenquer, but you need to check on boats back before leaving Santarém if you are on a tight schedule – the crew of the boat leaving will always be able to tell you when the next boat back is. There are also boat connections from Alenquer to Belém, Manaus and Monte Alegre, and in the dry season there are **buses** to Óbidos, Oriximina and Monte Alegre, but the schedule is irregular and depends on the condition of the road, usually bad but passable.

Véu da Noiva

The **Véu da Noiva waterfall** is on the Rio Maicuru, a couple of hours' drive from Alenquer on a dirt road which eventually leads to Monte Alegre. A taxi will take you as far as it can and you have to walk the last 3km or so, a beautiful stroll down a forested valley with occasional glimpses of river, before the path drops down right in front of the magnificent waterfall, over 6m high and about 45m wide. The waterfall cascades into a glade in the forest with deep pools of deliciously cool water to swim in. You can also clamber to spots where you can lie down and let the waterfall pour over you – the most exhilarating hydromassage you're ever likely to have. Below the falls you can wade with care through shallow rapids, but watch your step; it's easy enough to lose your balance and whilst the rapids are not deep, there are sharp-edged rocks. It's an idyllic spot and well worth the effort involved getting here. You will need to take everything for the day with you, including lunch for yourself and your taxi driver (who will wait for you at the end of the road), some water (don't drink the river water no matter how clear it looks) and, most importantly, a note from the owner of the private land on which the waterfall is located – who happens to be a relative of Donna Maria at the hotel, hence the advantage of arranging the trip through her. Without a note, the watchman on the estate won't let you in.

Monte Alegre

If you only have time to visit one river town in the middle Amazon, it should be **MONTE ALEGRE**. Most of the town is built along the brow of a steep hill with spectacular views out across marshes and freshwater lakes, with the Amazon to the south and jagged hills to the north and west, the only pieces of high ground between Belém and Manaus. With its obvious strategic advantages, this was one of the first places on the Amazon to be colonized by Europeans; a small group of English and Irish adventurers settled here in the 1570s, almost fifty years before Belém was founded. They were soon expelled by the Portuguese, and Monte Alegre was a ranching and farming settlement, then a centre of the rubber trade, before becoming the prosperous river town it is today. However, there is a much longer history of human settlement in the region. At various points the hills behind the town are covered in spectacular **Indian rock paintings**, one of the main reasons for visiting Monte Alegre. The paintings have been dated at just over 10,000 years old, making Monte Alegre one of the most important archeological sites in South America.

The paintings are only accessible by **four-wheel drive transport** and you will need a **guide**; expect to pay around $60 for the two. Depending on how many people you can get together this can be very reasonable as it is an all-day expedition. Nelsi Sadeck, Rua do Jaquara 320 (☎091/533-1430 or 533-1215), can arrange trips. Everyone knows him and will point you in the direction of his house. Although he only speaks Portuguese, he is used to taking parties of tourists around the hills, and if he knows people are coming he can usually rustle up a few local people interested in coming along, which will bring the price of the truck rental down. The paintings range from abstract geometric patterns through stylized representations of animals and human stick figures to the most compelling images of all – palm prints of the ancient painters themselves. Some of the paintings are on rockfaces large enough to be seen from the road, but others are hidden away, requiring a steep climb to see them, so wear good shoes. The itinerary also includes a visit to a cave with another set of paintings, and several gnarled rock formations on hilltops with stunning views across the floodplains and rivers. Whatever time of year you go, it is likely to get very hot during the day. Take plenty of water, a hat and sunscreen.

Nelsi can also arrange **boat rental** for around $25 a day. The water world around Monte Alegre is one of the richest **bird** sites in Amazonia. All along the banks of the Amazon, huge freshwater lakes are separated from the river by narrow strips of land. Depending on the time of year, the lakes either flood over the surrounding land, become marshland or even, in places, sandy cattle pasture. The whole area is a fluctuating region – neither water nor land but a constantly shifting mixture of the two. It is thick with birdlife: huge herons, waders of all kinds and a sprinkling of hawks and fish-eagles. At sunset, thousands of birds fly in to roost in the trees at the foot of the town. The stunning waterscapes set against the dramatic backdrop of hills make a boat trip really worth doing, even if you can't tell an egret from your elbow. Take everything with you for the day, including lunch for you and the boat owner.

Practicalities

Monte Alegre hasn't even begun to realize its tourist potential; it's only rarely visited by foreigners and still very cheap. There is just one **hotel** in town, which has a number of chalets overlooking the river on a road off the main square; it's basic but clean, friendly and perfectly adequate (①). The square itself has a fabulous view out across the Amazon and the lakes, and there's a bar here conveniently situated for you to watch the sunset. Monte Alegre's one **restaurant** is conveniently attached to the hotel, and serves a wonderful range of fish dishes. They also do good packed lunches for your day in the hills; you need to order these a day in advance. To get to the hotel and restaurant from the main square, take the road leading down from the square to the left, turn second left, first right and keep going following the street as it curves left. Anyone in town can direct you if you get lost.

Transport connections are good. Monte Alegre is one of the main stops on the Belém–Santarém–Manaus **boat** route, and there are also dedicated services from both Santarém and Belém which are usually less crowded. Boats from Prainha and Macapá also stop here. Leaving, you won't wait more than two days wherever you're headed.

Itaituba

Heading south down the Rio Tapajós, between twelve and fourteen hours from Santarém depending on the time of year (the current is much stronger in the rainy season), is another face of the Amazon, the gold-rush town of **ITAITUBA**. The **boat journey** here is one of the main reasons for going – the broad mouth of the Tapajós, over 30km wide where it joins the Amazon just west of Santarém, soon narrows enough so you can appreciate the forest on either side. There is usually plenty of wildlife to be seen, including anteaters swimming across the river, dolphins and parrots galore.

Gold prospecting and **mining** began in the headwaters of the Tapajós in the 1950s with a few skilled prospectors from former British Guyana. Itaituba remained no more than a tiny village, living more from trade in rubber and animal pelts than gold until the early 1970s when the Transamazon highway arrived and changed everything. The highway itself was only open for a few years; it was too expensive to maintain and was soon reclaimed by forest. Nevertheless, it was long enough to channel a new wave of migrants into the area, and when the price of gold started to rise after 1974, there was capital and labour available to start exploiting the mines in a big way. The city mushroomed, and its current population of 50,000 makes it by far the biggest town on the Tapajós, even in its current depressed state (the gold has been giving out and the price has fallen since the boom years in the mid-1980s). Many mine owners are forming partnerships with big Brazilian mining companies now that the easily available gold has been mined, and Itaituba will continue to be a mining town for the foreseeable future, albeit with fewer miners and nothing like as wild a nightlife as it used to have.

The Town

Itaituba seems unprepossessing at first, all of its buildings modern and most of them ugly, but there is a certain energy and frontier feel about the place. You'll soon start to see the **gold-buying shops** in the commercial area, dominating everything with their signs "Compra-se Oura" (we buy gold). Go inside and you can watch miners bringing in gold dust and fragments which are then burned (don't get too close, the smoke is mercury vapour), weighed and purchased with bundles of notes. Miners, despite their fearsome reputation, are quite friendly if you're polite, and are usually proud to show off their gold. Things are quieter now than they used to be but Itaituba is still the trading centre of the largest goldfield in the Brazilian Amazon, supplying scores of mines (*garimpos*) scattered in the forest to the south of town and usually only accessible by air.

There is a waterfront, with several **bars** and **restaurants**, a market and no shortage of **hotels**; the best is the *Juliana Park* (☎091/518-0548; ②) with excellent breakfasts and air conditioning – essential because it's hot here all the time. The nicest bar is the *Bar do Chico* at the far end of the waterfront, on the first corner past the church; it serves excellent *frango a caipira* (chicken in spicy gravy). It is possible to rent boats to go further upriver but you can only go about an hour or so before major rapids just past the village of São Luis do Tapajós make the river impassable. Boats back to Santarém leave every day, usually in the early evening; ask at the waterfront. The Banco do Brasil on Travessa 13 de Maio does cash advances on Visa cards only.

Óbidos

Around forty million years ago, when the Andes began to form themselves by pushing up from the earth, a vast inland sea burst through from what we now know as the main Amazon basin. The natural bursting point was more or less the site of modern-day **ÓBIDOS**. The huge sea squeezed itself through where the Guyanan shield to the north meets the Brazilian shield from the south, and cut an enormous channel through alluvial soils in its virgin route to the Atlantic. The river is some seven kilometres wide at Santarém, while at Óbidos, about 100km upstream, it has narrowed to less than two kilometres. Physically then, Óbidos is the gateway to the Amazon; there's an old fort to protect the passage, and most boats going upstream or down will stop here for an hour or two at least.

In the Cabanagem Rebellion (see box p.323), most of the town's leading white figures were assassinated by rebels and Óbidos was looted and left ungoverned for years. Describing this period, the English botanist Richard Spruce remarked that anti-white feeling ran so strong in Óbidos that the mob considered that to have a beard was a crime punishable by death.

The town and around

Óbidos is now a pretty river town with a very attractive **waterfront**, little changed since the 1920s. It makes a good stopover if you feel like breaking the journey between Manaus and Santarém or Belém. The sights won't keep you more than a morning, but it is a pleasant town to stroll around. The main thing to see is the seventeenth-century **Forte Pauxis** on the Praça Coracy Nunes, which played a crucial role in Amazon history. It was the jumping-off point for the settlement of the upper Amazon, and the cannon still in position on the ramparts command the whole width of the river. Its strategic importance meant that Óbidos was the largest town on the middle Amazon during colonial times, but the fort is the only colonial relic. Elsewhere the town has some fine buildings dating from the rubber boom and identified by metal plaques giving their history (in Portuguese only of course). Most of them are in the commercial area just off the waterfront, constructed by trading families as emporiums on the ground floor with living quarters above. Most are still shops selling simple hammocks and pots and pans.

There is an interesting little **museum** in town which, like most small museums, depends on the enthusiasm of a single person, Donna Maria, who lives next door, on the road leading down from the main square. Everyone knows her so just ask for her by name. If the museum isn't open, knock on her door and she will be only too pleased to let you in. The collection is eclectic, ranging from Indian pottery to imported British household luxuries from rubber-boom days. There are also some intriguing old photographs: you can see that the town has hardly changed since the early years of the century. Entrance is free, but leave some money for its upkeep and sign the visitors' book; Donna Maria will insist and likes exotic signatures.

The town's other attractions are river-based, as you might expect. Just 25km from Óbidos along the PA-254, you can go bathing in the beautiful **Igarapé de Curuçambá**, which is served by local buses. There are also organized trips to the narrowest of Amazon river straits with impressive forested river cliffs and close-up views of riverbank homesteads and jungle vegetation. Ask at the port or the *Braz Bello* hotel.

If you end up **staying** try the *Braz Bello*, Rua Marios Rodrigues de Souza 86 (☎091/547-1411; ②), which is a reasonable mid-range hotel, while along the waterfront you'll find several decent bars and restaurants. **Boats** travel in and out of Óbidos every day. If you're heading to Santarém, take the smaller boats that only ply that route rather than hopping onto one of the larger Manaus–Belém boats.

WESTERN AMAZONIA

An arbitrary border, a line on paper through the forest, divides the state of Pará from the western Amazon. Encompassing the states of **Amazonas**, **Rondônia**, **Acre** and **Roraima**, the western Amazon is dominated even more than the east by the Amazon and Solimões rivers and their tributaries. In the north, the forest revolves around the Negro and Branco rivers, before phasing into the wooded savannas of Roraima. To the

BOI BUMBA IN PARINTINS

Parintins, an otherwise unremarkable small river town roughly halfway between Santarém and Manaus, has in recent years become the unlikely centre of one of the largest mass events in Brazil, the **Boi Bumba** celebrations every June (the date varies, but it's always the weekend before June 24). Thanks to astute marketing, what began as a local custom has now become a megabucks spectacle, which attracts tens of thousands of spectators to a stadium unforgettably called the Bumbódromo, constructed in the shape of a stylized bull. It hosts a wild, energetic parade by something resembling an Amazonian version of Rio samba schools – and the resemblance to Rio is not coincidental, the organizers having consciously modelled themselves on Rio's *Carnaval*.

Boi Bumba in Parintins revolves around two schools, Caprichoso and Garantido. Each year they vie for a championship by parading through the Bumbódromo, where custom has it that supporters of one have to watch the opposing parade in complete silence. You thus have the strange spectacle of 20,000 people going wild while the other half of the stadium is as quiet as a funeral, with roles reversed a few hours later. Much like the *Bumba meu boi* of São Luis (see p.308), Parintins' *Boi Bumba* has its high point with the acting out of the death of a bull, part of the legend of the slave Ma Catirina who, during her pregnancy, developed a craving for ox tongue. To satisfy her craving, her husband, Pa Francisco, slaughtered his master's bull, but the master found out and decided to arrest Pa Francisco with the help of some Indians. But, as the legend would have it, the priest and the witch doctor managed to resuscitate the animal, thus saving Pa Francisco; with the bull alive once more, the party begins again at fever pitch, to a frenetic rhythm that pounds away well into the hot and smoke-filled night.

The parade is undeniably spectacular, and the music infectious, if rather monotonous after a while. But don't be deceived by all the references to tradition and Indian culture: the parades have only existed on this scale since the 1990s, and have about as much to do with Indian culture as the Rio samba schools that served as a model. All the same, it is enjoyable, and is an enormous benefit to the people of town, which has precious little else going for it economically. Thousands of people get through the rest of the year on the proceeds of catering for the huge influx of visitors during the festivities.

The number of people who descend on Parintins is considerably larger than the town's population. Forget about **accommodation** in any of the town's few hotels: they are booked up months in advance. The best option is simply to stay on the boat: in all the towns and cities of the region – notably Manaus and Santarém – you will find boats and travel agencies offering all-in packages for the event, with accommodation in hammocks on the boats, and this is by far the easiest way to do it. Seeing the town harbour crammed with hundreds of boats is a sight in itself. Most of the riverboat companies offer 3- or 4-day packages, costing between $100 and $350. The trips are often booked well in advance, and are advertised from March onwards on banners tied to the boats. As you might expect, there is a lot of petty thieving and pickpocketing, so take extra care of anything you take with you.

south, the Madeira, Purús and Juruá rivers meander through the forests from the prime rubber region of Acre and the recently colonized state of Rondônia.

The hub of this area is **Manaus**, more or less at the junction of three great rivers – the Solimões/Amazonas, the Negro and the Madeira – which between them support the world's greatest surviving forest. There are few other settlements of any real size. In the north, **Boa Vista**, capital of Roraima, lies on an overland route to Venezuela by bus. South of the Rio Amazonas there's **Porto Velho**, capital of Rondônia, and, further west, **Rio Branco**, the main town in the relatively unexplored rubber-growing state of Acre – where the now famous Chico Mendes lived and died, fighting for a sustainable future for the forest.

Travel is never easy or particularly comfortable in the western Amazon. **From Manaus** it's possible to go by **bus** to Boa Vista and Venezuela: currently around eighteen hours to Boa Vista on the partially paved BR-174 through the stunning tropical forest zone of the Waimiris tribe, with over fifty rickety wooden bridges en route. You can also head east to the Amazon river settlement of Itacoatiara, but the road south to join the Transamazônica at **Humaitá** for the connection to Porto Velho is no longer open, having been repossessed by the rains and vegetation for most of its length. **From Porto Velho** the Transamazônica continues, newly paved, into Acre and **Rio Branco**, from where the route on to Peru is possible, although only in the dry season; alternatively the paved BR-364 offers quick access south to Cuiabá, Mato Grosso, Brasília and the rest of Brazil.

The rivers are an equally important if not dominant means of communication. Entering from the east, the first places beyond Óbidos are the small ports of **Parintins** and **Itacoatiara** – which has bus connections with Manaus if you're really fed up with the boat, though the roads, too, are often very hard going in the rainy season, between December and April. From here it's a matter of hours till Manaus appears near the confluence of the rivers Negro and Solimões. It takes another five to eight days by boat to reach the Peruvian frontier – and even here the river is several kilometres wide, and still big enough for ocean-going ships.

It rains a lot in the western Amazon – up to 375cm a year in the extreme west and about 175cm around Manaus. The humidity rarely falls much below eighty percent, and the temperature in the month of December can reach well above 40°C. This takes a few days to get used to: until you do it's like being stuck in a sauna with only air conditioning or cool drinks to help you escape. The heaviest rains fall in January and February most years, with a relatively dry season from June to October.

Manaus and around

MANAUS is the capital of Amazonas, a tropical forest state covering around one and a half million square kilometres. It is also the commercial and physical hub of the entire Amazon region. Most visitors are surprised to learn that Manaus isn't actually on the Amazon at all. Rather it lies on the Rio Negro, six kilometres from the point where that river meets the Solimões to form (as far as Brazilians are concerned) the Rio Amazonas. Just a few hundred metres away from the tranquil life on the rivers, the centre of Manaus perpetually buzzes with energy: always noisy, crowded and confused. Everywhere you turn, shops and stalls are selling everything from imported Persian rugs to Taiwanese toys and plastic sunglasses. Escaping from the frenzy is not easy, but there is the occasional quiet corner, and the sights of the port, markets, Opera House and some of the museums make up for the hectic pace in the downtown area. In the port and market areas, where the infamous *Porto do Manaus* smell is inescapable, pigs and chickens line the streets and there's an atmosphere which seems unchanged in centuries.

For the Amazon hinterland, Manaus has long symbolized "civilization". Traditionally, this meant simply that it was the **trading centre**, where the hardships of life in the forest could be escaped temporarily and where manufactured commodities to make that life easier could be purchased – metal pots, steel knives, machetes and the like. Virgin jungle seems further from the city these days – just how far really depends on what you want "virgin forest" to mean – but there are still waterways and channels within a short river journey of Manaus where you can find dolphins, alligators, kingfishers and the impression, at least, that man has barely penetrated. Indeed, most visitors to Manaus rightly regard a **river trip** as an essential part of their stay; various **jungle tour and lodge** options are set out on pp.364–365 (see also box pp.320–321 for longer river

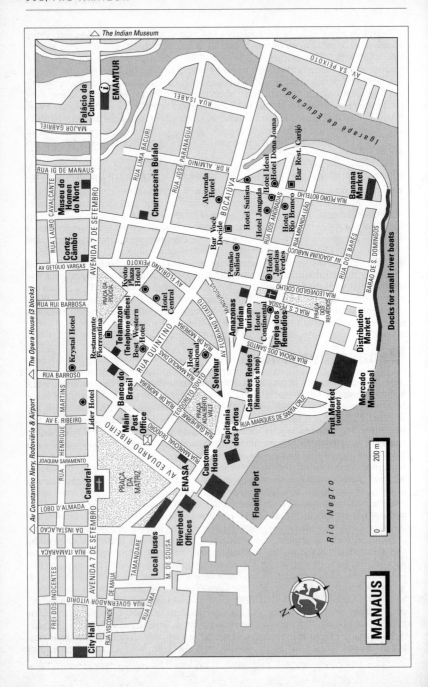

△ The Indian Museum

EMAMTUR

Palácio da Cultura

MAJOR GABRIEL

AV SÁ PEIXOTO

RUA ISABEL

RUA IG DE MANAUS

Museu do Homem do Norte

RUA JOSÉ PARANAGUÁ

R DR ALMINO

Igarapé de Educandos

RUA LIMA BACURI

Churrascaria Búfalo

CAVALCANTE

RUA LAURO

Cortez Câmbio

AV GETÚLIO VARGAS

AVENIDA 7 DE SETEMBRO

BOCAIUVA

Alvorada Hotel

Hotel Ideal

Hotel Dona Joana

Bar Rest. Carijó

Banana Market

RUA PEDRO BOTELHO

Hotel Sulista

Hotel Jangada

RUA DOS ANDRADAS

Hotel Rio Branco

RUA MIRANDA LEÃO

Bar Você Decide

AV JOAQUIM NABUCO

RUA RUI BARBOSA

(The Opera House (3 blocks)

Krystal Hotel

AV FLORIANO PEIXOTO

Kyoto Plaza Hotel

Pensão Sulista

Hotel Janelas Verdes

RUA DOS BARÉS

BARÃO DE S. DOMINGOS

Restaurante Fiorrentina

Hotel Central

RUA LEOVEGILDO COELHO

Telamazon (Telephone offices)

Best Western Hotel

RUA QUINTINO

Amazonas Indian Turismo

RUA S. PESSOA

RUA MARCILIO DIAS

RUA DR MOREIRA

Hotel Nacional

AV FLORIANO PEIXOTO

Hotel Continental

Igreja dos Remédios

PRAÇA DOS REMÉDIOS

Distribution Market

Docks for small river boats

RUA BARROSO

Lider Hotel

MARTINS

HENRIQUE

Banco do Brasil

RUA QUINTINO

TEODORETO SOUTO

Selvatur

RUA ROCHA DOS SANTOS

Casa des Redes (Hammock shop)

Mercado Municipal

AV E. RIBEIRO

JOAQUIM SARAMENTO

Main Post Office

RUA GUILHERME MOREIRA

PRAÇA ADALBERTO VALLE

RUA MARQUÉS DE SANTA CRUZ

Fruit Market (outdoor)

AV EDUARDO RIBEIRO

Capitania dos Portos

Catedral

PRAÇA DA MATRIZ

RUA MARECHAL DEODORO

Customs House

LOBO D'ALMADA

DA INSTALAÇÃO

ENASA

Floating Port

Rio Negro

Riverboat Offices

AVENIDA 7 DE SETEMBRO

TAMANDARE

DE MAUÁ

Local Buses

M. DE SOUSA

RUA ITAMARACA

FREI DOS INOCENTES

RUA GOVERNADOR VITÓRIO

RUA LIMA

RUA VISCONDE

City Hall

0   200 m

N

MANAUS

> The **telephone code** for Manaus is ☎092.

journeys, and boat details under "Listings" on p.360). Even if you can't afford the time to disappear up the Amazon for days at a stretch, however, there are a number of sites around Manaus that make worthwhile day excursions, most notably the **meeting of the waters** of the yellow Rio Solimões and the black Rio Negro, and the lily-strewn **Parque Ecólogico Janauary**.

The **weather** in Manaus is often dramatic. During the rainy season (Jan–June), it pours down for at least one hour every day and the temperatures generally range from 22°C to 30°C, though it feels much more in the humidity. Between July and December, it rains much less, is generally less cloudy and the temperatures fluctuate between 27°C and 40°C.

Some history

The name Manaus came originally from the Manau tribe which was encountered in this region by São Luis do Maranhão, exploring the area in 1616. He called the spot São Luis del Rio. But it was Francisco do Motta Falco who really founded Manaus by building up the settlement and encouraging others to remain there with him.

The city you see today is primarily a product of the **rubber boom** and in particular the child of visionary state governor **Eduardo Ribeiro**, who from 1892 transformed Manaus into a major city. Under Ribeiro the Opera House was completed, and whole streets were wiped out in the process of laying down broad Parisian-style avenues, interspersed with Italian piazzas centred on splendid fountains; an English company built the city's drainage system. In 1899 Manaus was the first Brazilian city to have trolley buses and only the second to have electric lights in the streets.

Around the turn of the century Manaus was an opulent metropolis run by elegant people, who dressed and housed themselves as fashionably as their counterparts in any large European city. The rich constructed palaces and grandiose mansions; time was passed at elaborate entertainments, dances and concerts. But this heyday lasted barely thirty years, and by 1914 the rubber market was collapsing fast; Ribeiro himself had committed suicide in 1900. There was a second brief boost for Brazilian rubber during World War II, but today's prosperity is largely due to the creation of a **Free Trade Zone**, the *Zona Franca*, in 1966. Over the next ten years the population doubled, from 250,000 to half a million, and many new industries moved in, especially electronics companies. An impressive new international airport was opened in 1976 and the floating port, supported on huge metal cylinders to cope with variations of as much as 14m in the level of the river, was modernized to cope with the new business.

Today, with over three million inhabitants, Manaus is an aggressive commercial and industrial centre for an enormous region – the Hong Kong of the Amazon. Over half of Brazil's televisions are made here and electronic goods are around a third cheaper here than in the south. All of this helps encourage domestic tourism – Manaus airport is crowded with Brazilians going home with their arms laden with TVs, hi-fis, computers and fax machines.

Arrival, information and accommodation

Try to avoid arriving on a Sunday, when the city is very quiet, with few places open. If you arrive in Manaus by river, your **boat** will dock right in the heart of the city, either by the Mercado Municipal or a short way along in the floating port. If you're arriving from Peru or Colombia, don't forget to have your passport stamped at the Customs House, if you haven't already done so in Tabatinga. The **Rodoviária** is some 10km north of the centre: #306 buses run every twenty minutes down Avenida Constantino Nery, two streets from the bus station, to Praça da Matriz in the heart of town. The **airport** (Aeroporto de Eduardo Gomes, Avenida Santos Dumont; ☎621-1210 or 654-2044 for information) is 17km from town in the same direction: also bus #306 (last run around 11pm), or there are taxis for $24.

The main EMAMTUR **tourist office** is next to the Palácio da Cultura at Av. Sete de Setembro 1546 (Mon–Fri 7am–7pm, Sat 7am–1pm; ☎633-2983 or 633-2850); their *promoção turística* office has a huge range of brochures, maps and information packs about Manaus and Amazonas. There is also an EMAMTUR agent at the airport.

Accommodation

Plenty of travellers end up in Manaus, so there's a wide range of places to stay, with a number of perfectly reasonable **cheap hotels**, especially in the area around Avenida Joaquim Nabuco and Rua dos Andradas. The downtown centre is just a few blocks from here, with the docks for boats up and down the Amazon and Rio Negro. Even cheaper are those along Rua José Paranaguá, though that road is said to be unsafe at night. If you want to **camp**, the only secure option is beyond the *Tropical Hotel* at the sites around Praia Ponta Negra.

Alvorada Hotel, Rua Quintino Bocaiúva 583 (☎233-5740). By far the best of the many cheap hotels on this road, most of them rented by the hour to local prostitutes and their clients. This one is clean and friendly, and the rooms are remarkably well appointed, with TV, *frigobar* and air conditioning. ②.

Best Western Hotel, Rua Marcilio Dias 217 (☎622-2844, fax 622-2576). Very plush, the best hotel in central Manaus and reasonable value, but no pool. ⑦.

Central Hotel, Rua Dr Moreira 202 (☎622-2600, fax 622-2609). Wide choice of rooms all with TV, *frigobar* and air conditioning; it has a good restaurant, too. Excellent value at the price. ④–⑤.

Hotel Continental, Rua Coronel Sergio Pessoa 189 (☎233-3342). Large, clean rooms, with good showers and TVs, some rooms overlooking the Rio Negro and others facing on to the Praça and Igreja dos Remédios. Lower end of the price range. ③.

Hotel Dona Joana, Rua dos Andradas 553 (☎233-7553). Their rooms, though large, are usually dirty, but to compensate many have superb views over the river, which the other budget hotels lack. ②.

Hotel Ideal, Rua dos Andradas 491 (☎233-9423). Opposite the *Rio Branco* and much the same, although the rooms tend to be darker. Choice between fan and air conditioning. ①–②.

Hotel Janelas Verdes, Rua L. Coelho 216 (☎233-1222). Tucked away, this is one of Manaus's best hotels, a small, traditional family-run place with 15 neat and comfortable rooms, much nicer than its multistorey rivals on Av. Getúlio Vargas. Great breakfasts. ⑤.

Hotel Jangada, Rua dos Andradas 473 (☎232-2248). Although slightly run-down, this place has reasonably friendly staff, a decent little restaurant, and always seems busy. Guests can use their kitchen and laundry. ①.

Krystal Hotel, Rua Barroso 54 (☎233-7305, fax 233-7882). Near the cathedral and very good value for its modern, well-kept rooms, all with TV, phone and *frigobar*. ⑤.

Kyoto Plaza Hotel, Rua Dr Moreira 232 (☎232-6552 or 232-6773). Very central, a lower mid-range hotel with a friendly atmosphere. ③.

Líder Hotel, Av. Sete de Setembro 827 (☎633-3648 or 633-1326, fax 633-3393). In the commercial centre, a calm, upmarket place, but it lacks a pool. ⑥.

Hotel Nacional, Rua Dr Moreira 59 (☎233-7533). Quite basic rooms with the usual accessories (fridge and TV). ③.

Plaza Hotel, Av. Getúlio Vargas 215 (☎232-7766, fax 622-1761). Next door to the similar but twice-as-expensive *Hotel Imperial*, the towering *Plaza* has well-appointed rooms and a pool – good value, though at this price the service could be better. ⑤.

Hotel Rio Branco, Rua dos Andradas 484 (☎ and fax 233-4019). During the early 1990s this place became the main haunt of backpacking gringos, and is currently favoured by overland trucks. It's a safe, family-run hotel with spartan, clean rooms (shared bathrooms for some), offering a basic breakfast. Ground-floor rooms can be damp, and some others don't have windows. The hotel is a base for *Jungle Experience* tours (see p.364), although they can be a bit pushy. ①.

Pensão Sulista, Avenida Joaquim Nabuco 347 (☎234-5814). A pleasant old colonial-style building with clean, but small, rooms. Along with the *Rio Branco*, the only cheap hotel which doesn't admit whores. Their annexe at Rua Pedro Botelho 162, the *Hotel Sulista* (☎233-4538), has better rooms and is marginally more expensive. ①.

Tropical Hotel, Estrada da Ponta Negra (☎658-5000, fax 658-5026). This popular 5-star hotel, 15km northwest of town and 8km from the airport, is right by the chic city beach, Praia Ponta Negra. Facilities include pool, tennis courts, good nightlife, fine river beaches and even water-skiing on the Rio Negro, and the service is excellent. The *Tropical* has its own buses from the airport; from downtown, take the #120 bus from Praça da Matriz. ⑧.

The City

It's not hard to get used to the **layout** of the city, and most things of interest huddle close to the water. From the floating port where the big ships dock, riverboat wharves extend round past the market, from one end of Rua dos Andradas to the other. The busiest commercial streets are immediately behind, extending up to the Avenida Sete de Setembro, with the cathedral marking one end of the downtown district, the Praça da Polícia the other. Beyond Avenida Sete de Setembro, towards the Opera House, it's a bit calmer, with more offices and fewer shops. The busy Praça da Matriz by the cathedral is the main hub of city communications, with **buses** to local points around the city and suburbs; another good connection point for city buses and taxis is the east side of Avenida Getúlio Vargas just north of Avenida Sete de Setembro.

Manaus is above all a **river port**, and it's this reality that you'll come back to time and time again as you wander the streets. Only in the main shopping districts in the middle of the day, or in clubs at night, can you forget the location, but in one way or another virtually everything in Manaus seems related to either the river or the forest – from the fish on your plate and the rotting fruit in the gutters to the powerful tropical rainstorms that catch every visitor to Manaus by surprise at some time or another.

Around the docks

Since it's the docks that have created Manaus, it seems logical to start your exploration here – and it's certainly the most atmospheric part of town. The **port** itself is an unforgettable spectacle. A constant throng of activity stretches along the riverfront while the ships tied up at the docks bob serenely up and down. Boats are getting ready to leave, or having just arrived are busy unloading. People cook fish at stalls to sell to the hungry sailors and their passengers, or to the workers once they've finished their shift of carrying cargo from the boats to the distribution market. There's produce of every kind: manufactured goods, sacks of rice and beans and cement, and bunches of bananas by the thousand. Hectic and impossibly complex and anarchic as it appears to the unaccustomed eye, the port of Manaus is in fact very well organized, if organically so. During the day there's no problem wandering around, and it's easy enough to find out which boats are going where just by asking around. At night, however, this can be a dangerous area and is best avoided: many of the rivermen carry guns.

From the Praça Adalberto Valle, the impressive **Customs House** stands between you and the floating docks. Erected in 1906, the building was shipped over from Britain in prefabricated blocks. The floating docks, too, were built by a British company, at the beginning of the century. To cope with the river rising over a 14m range, the concrete pier is supported on pontoons which rise and fall to allow even the largest ships to dock here all year round (the highest recorded level of the river so far was in 1953, when it rose some 30m above sea level). A covered yard in the Customs House, just on the left as you enter, is the best place to check which boats are going where and when. Around the yard, different boats staff a number of small kiosks displaying pictures of their vessels, departure times and prices. This is a good place to buy advance tickets, for which you can often get a reasonable discount.

Following Rua Marques de Santa Cruz down towards the new docks will bring you to the covered **Mercado Municipal**, whose elegant Art Nouveau roof was designed by Eiffel and is a copy of the former Les Halles market in Paris. Here tropical fruit and vegetables, jungle herbs, scores of different fresh fishes and Indian craft goods are jumbled together on sale. Just to the east of this market is the wholesale **port distribution market**, whose traders buy goods from incoming boats and sell them on wholesale to shops, market stall-holders and restaurants. There's also a substantial number of retail traders here where you too can buy the goods at prices only a little over wholesale. It's at its busiest first thing in the morning; by the afternoon most of the merchants have closed shop, and the place looks abandoned. In the early 1990s, this market was modernized – turning rat-infested wood and mayhem into concrete-based organized chaos. Much of the original charm has given way to the clinicality of the twentieth century, but the port and markets are still fascinating places to wander.

The commercial centre and the Opera House

Things are almost as busy in Manaus's downtown **commercial centre**, but although it starts only a few metres inland, the atmosphere is totally different. Essentially an electronics market which has evolved out of the Free Trade Zone era, this is the hub of the modern city. Everything from shoes to hi-fis can be bought – very cheap by Brazilian standards, but expensive for foreigners given the current exchange rate.

The city's most famous symbol, the **Teatro Amazonas** or **Opera House** (Mon–Sat 9am–4pm; $4 including guided tour; ☎234-0508), seems even more extraordinary coming in the midst of this rampant commercialism. Until you actually see it, it's hard to believe that the Ballet Russe danced here and Jenny Lind once sang. The whole incongruous, magnificent thing, designed in a pastiche of Italian Renaissance style by a Lisbon architectural firm, cost in the region of $3 million. The wrought-iron skeleton of the building was brought from Scotland and the stone from Italy. After twelve years of building, with virtually all the materials – apart from the regional wood – brought from Europe, the Opera House was finally completed in 1896. Its main feature, the fantastic cupola, was created from 36,000 tiles imported from Alsace in France. The theatre's main curtain, painted in Paris by Brazilian artist, Crispim do Amaral, represents the theme of the meeting of the waters and the local Indian water goddess Iara. The four painted pillars on the ceiling depict the Eiffel tower in Paris, giving visitors the impression, as they look upwards, that they are actually underneath the tower itself. The chandeliers are of Italian crystal and French bronze, and the theatre's seven hundred seats and its main columns and the balconies are made of English cast iron. Greek masks representing different European artists – Shakespeare, Moliere, Mozart and Verdi – adorn the pillars around the auditorium. If you include the dome, into which the original curtain is pulled up in its entirety, the stage is a vertical 75m high.

Major restorations have taken place in 1929, 1960, 1974 and, most recently, in 1990, when the outside was returned from blue to its original pink. Looking over the upstairs balcony down onto the road in front of the Opera House, you can see the black driveway made from a special blend of rubber, clay and sand, originally to dampen the noise of horses and carriages as they arrived. Yet the building is not just a relic, and it hosts regular concerts, including in April the **Festa da Manaus**, initiated in 1997 to celebrate thirty years of the *Zona Franca*.

In front of the Teatro, the wavy black-and-white mosaic designs of the **Praça São Sebastião** are home to the "Monument to the Opening of the Ports", a marble and granite creation with four ships that represent four continents – America, Europe, Africa and Asia/Australasia – and children who symbolize the people of those continents. Across the *praça* is the beautiful little **Igreja de São Sebastião**, built in 1888, which, like many other churches in Brazil, has only one tower due to the nineteenth-century tax payable by churches with two towers. Nearby is the **Palácio da Justiça**, which was supposedly modelled on Versailles.

Some three blocks further away from the river, up Rua Tapajós, you'll find the old **Central Post Office**, another imposing reminder of the glorious years of the rubber boom. On the pavement around the back there's an ornate, much-photographed antique post box, dated 1889.

Along Avenida Sete de Setembro

Heading back towards the river, the **Catedral** on Avenida Sete de Setembro is a relatively plain building, surprisingly untouched by the orgy of adornment that struck the rest of the city. But judging by the number of people who use it, the cathedral plays a more active role in the life of the city than many more showy buildings. Around it is the Praça da Matriz, a shady park popular with local courting couples and sleeping drunks. There are a number of outdoor bars here, open in the daytime only.

About 500m west of the cathedral along Avenida Sete de Setembro is the **Instituto Geográfico e Histórico do Amazonas** (Mon–Fri 2.30–5pm), Rua Bernardo Ramos 117. The institute's small museum includes a collection of ceramics from various tribes, a range of insect displays and indigenous tools like stone axes and hunting equipment.

The **Museu do Homen do Norte** (Museum of Northern Man; Mon–Thurs 9am–noon & 1–5pm, Fri 1–5pm), in the opposite direction at Av. Sete de Setembro 1385, near Avenida Joaquim Nabuco, offers a quick overview of human life and ecology in the Amazon region. Also worth at least a quick visit is the recently renovated **Palácio da Cultura**, the former Palácio Rio Negro, a gorgeous colonial-period mansion which from 1998 will house the archives (manuscripts, drawings and plans) of the nineteenth-century Portuguese naturalist and scientist, Alexandre Rodrigues Ferreira. Regular video screenings, Indian ceremonial dances and rituals, and related activities are also planned; it certainly justifies the short walk to find out what's on, and the building itself is a treat anyway.

The excellent **Museu do Índio**, Rua Duque de Caxias 356 (Mon–Sat 8–11am & 2–5pm), lies about 500m further east along Avenida Sete de Setembro. The museum is run by the Salesian Sisters, who have long-established missions along the Rio Negro, especially with the Tukano tribe. There are excellent, carefully presented displays, with exhibits ranging from sacred ritual masks and inter-village communication drums to fine ceramics, superb palm-frond weavings and even replicas of Indian dwellings. Neatly complementing this collection is the **Museu Amazonico da Universidade do Amazonas**, to the north of the centre at Rua Ramos Ferreira 1036, which houses a small collection of sixteenth-century documents and engravings relating to the first explorations of the interior.

The meeting of the waters and the Parque Ecólogico Janauary

The most popular and most widely touted day trip around Manaus is to the **meeting of the waters**, some 10km downstream, where the Rio Negro and the Rio Solimões meet to form the Rio Amazonas. For several kilometres beyond the point where they join, the waters of the two rivers continue to flow separately: the muddy yellow of the Solimões contrasting sharply with the black of the Rio Negro. It's a strange sight, and one well worth seeing. If you're going under your own steam, take the "Vila Burity" **bus** (#713)

from Praça da Matriz to the end of the line, where there is a free half-hourly government ferry over the river, passing the meeting of the waters.

Most **tours** to the meeting of the waters leave the docks at Manaus and pass by the
shanty town of Educandos and the Rio Negro riverside industries before heading out
into the main river course. Almost all will also stop in at the **Parque Ecológico
Janauary**, an ecological park some 7km from Manaus on one of the main local tributaries of the Rio Negro. Usually you'll be transferred to smaller motorized canoes to
explore its creeks (*igarapés*), flooded forest lands (*igapós*) and abundant vegetation.

One of the highlights of the area is the abundance of *Vitória Regia*, the extraordinary giant floating lily for which Manaus is famous. Found mostly in shallow
lakes, it flourishes above all in the rainy months. The plant, named after Queen
Victoria by an English naturalist in the nineteenth century, has huge leaves – some
over a metre across – with a covering of thorns on their underside, as protection
from the teeth of plant-eating fish. The flowers are white on the first day of their life,
rose-coloured on the second, and on the third they begin to wilt: at night the
blooms close, imprisoning any insects that have wandered in, and releasing them
again as they open with the morning sun. In the rainy season you'll explore the
creeks and floodlands by boat; during the dry season – between September and
January – it's possible to walk around.

Praia Ponta Negra and the Cachoeira do Tarumã

The river beach at **Praia Ponta Negra**, about 15km northwest of Manaus near the
Hotel Tropical, is another very popular local excursion, and at weekends is packed with
locals. It's an enjoyable place to go for a swim, with plenty of bars and restaurants serving freshly cooked river fish. The beach is at its best between September and March,
when the river is low and exposes a wide expanse of sand, but even when the rains
bring higher waters and the beach almost entirely disappears, plenty of people come to
eat and drink. Soltur's Ponta Negra bus (#120) leaves every half hour: catch it by the
cathedral on Praça da Matriz.

The nearby military-run **CIGS Zoo** (Tues–Sat 8.30am–5pm), Estrada Ponta Negra
750, is also an army jungle training centre, and many of the animals in it were captured,
so they say, on military exercises out in the forest. There's a wide variety of wildlife
including what is claimed to be the largest number of jaguars bred in captivity anywhere,
though all the cages are pretty small and squalid. To get there take the #120, or the
"Compensa" or "São Jorge" bus from the military college on Avenida Epaminondas.

The waterfalls of **Cachoeira do Tarumã**, about 20km northwest of the city, are the
last of the local beauty spots within easy reach of Manaus. They don't offer unspoiled
beauty any more, thanks to commercialization and weekend crowds, but the place is
fun, there's good swimming, and on busy weekends you'll often find live music in the
bars. The cascades themselves, supplied by the Rio Negro, are relatively small white-
water affairs which more or less disappear in the rainy season (April to August). Soltur
buses (#11) run approximately every twenty minutes from the Praça da Matriz, taking
about half an hour.

Eating and drinking

There are very few places in Manaus where you can sit down and enjoy any peace: in
the parks you're certain to be interrupted by someone hassling you or wanting to practise their English, while on the streets every square centimetre seems to be used by
someone – usually as a sales pitch. Even the cafés and bars are too full to give you much

elbow room. One advantage of the crowds is that there's **street food** everywhere: especially around the docks, the Mercado Municipal and in busy downtown locations like the Praça da Matriz, where a plate of rice and beans with a skewer of freshly grilled meat or fish costs about $2. One traditional dish you should definitely try here is **tacacá** – a soup that consists essentially of yellow manioc root juice in a hot spicy dried-shrimp sauce. It's often mixed and served in traditional gourd bowls, *cuias*, and is usually sold in the late afternoons by *tacacazeiras*.

For your own food, there's a **supermarket** at the corner of Avenida Joaquim Nabuco and Avenida Sete de Setembro, and another towards the market on Rua Rocha dos Santos. The following **restaurants** are closed Sundays unless otherwise stated, and be warned that prices in Manaus are roughly double what you might find in the rest of the country.

Restaurante Anavilhaus, Av. Joaquim Nabuco 498. One of the cheapest places in town for good cooked meals. It's a no-frills night-dive stacked with beer crates, playing loud music all the time, but it serves excellent fish dishes – try the *tucunaré*. Daily.

Churrascaria Búfalo, Av. Joaquim Nabuco 628A. Excellent *rodízio* but expensive at $12 a head.

Restaurante Canto da Peixada, Rua Emilio Moreira 1677. Considered by many to be Manaus's best regional and river-fish restaurant, and therefore not cheap, but good value nonetheless.

Restaurante Fiorentina, Praça da Polícia. Upmarket Italian restaurant – good food but it's expensive and the service can be overbearing, verging on unfriendly.

Restaurante Floresteiro, Rua Dr Moreira, two doors down from *Central Hotel*. This new basement place, strong on fish, has good regional *comida por kilo* ($8 per kg) lunchtimes, and moderately priced à la carte evenings. Closed Sat evening as well as Sun.

Bar Restaurante Galo Carijó, Rua dos Andradas 536. Opposite the *Hotel Dona Joana*, this is a simple, inexpensive but excellent local fish restaurant and bar. Mon–Fri 7am–9pm and Sat lunchtime.

Kaktus Churrascaria, Av. Getúlio Vargas, 4 blocks up from Av. Sete de Setembro. Cheap and open Sun.

Lanche Alternativa, Rua Marques de Santa Cruz, by the Mercado Municipal. Grilled meat and beer accompanied by the biggest and loudest PA rig in Manaus. Daily.

Mandarim, Av. Eduardo Ribeiro 650, at the corner of Rua 24 de Maio. Excellent and reasonably priced Chinese restaurant, with a *comida por kilo* system for lunch and à la carte evenings (6–10.30pm). Their *chopa* (sizzling platter) dishes are recommended.

Restaurante Mister Kilo, Av. Sete de Setembro next to *Krystal Hotel*, first floor. Popular and friendly lunchtime *comida por kilo* joint.

O Naturalista, Rua Sete de Setembro 752, 2nd floor. A large, clean and enjoyable vegetarian restaurant one block east from the cathedral. Mon–Fri lunchtime.

Suzurau, Av. Boulevard Alvaro Maia 1683, Praça 14, 3km east of the city along Av. Sete de Setembro. This very good Japanese restaurant is the best of the three in Manaus. Closed Tues.

Nightlife

Like most large port towns, Manaus is busiest in the early mornings, and again at night, with plenty of bars, clubs and other venues that are worth exploring if you're in town for a few days; Friday editions of *Amazonas Em Tempo* carry fairly comprehensive listings.

The best – and rowdiest – **bars** are bunched around and in the Mercado Municipal, and along the entire length of Avenida Joaquim Nabuco south of Avenida Sete de Setembro. The usual starting place, for beer, snacks and a lively atmosphere, is the bar *Você Decide*, hemmed in by a wrought-iron fence on the corner of Avenida Joaquim Nabuco and Rua Quintino Bocaiuva, opposite the *Pensão Sulista*. Open daily to around 1 or 2am, it's usually very busy and has pool tables and loud music; for the unwary, it's probably worth mentioning that it's frequented by ladies (and gentlemen) of the night. Around the Mercado Municipal, the popular *Lanche Alternativa* (see above) sometimes has live music. Further around the port, to the west of Praça da Matriz on Rua M. Sousa, a couple of even louder places – *Holanda Bar* and *Recanto da Natureza* – stay open all night, and are wilder than anything you're likely to see on a jungle tour.

As to **clubs**, the most exciting are undoubtedly those around Praia Ponta Negra. Their names change frequently, though the music is invariably a danceable blend of old and modern sambas – it's worth coming just to see the formation dancing of the crowds. Given Manaus's prohibitive taxi fares, most of the Praia Ponta Negra clubs remain open all night, so you might as well bring a towel for a sobering early morning dip in the river. Similarly distant is the relatively new *Zazoueira Disco*, located out near the airport on Estrada Torquato Tapajós at Km12 – Flores. This is one of the best straight clubs in town and is good for *boi* dancing (or whatever else is fashionable when you get there), but drinks and entrance are expensive. Not as chic, but far more central, are the touristy *Jet Set*, Rua 10 de Julho 439, near the Opera House, where most foreigners seem to end up and a lot of hookers hang out; and, nearby, the more pop-orientated *Mykonos Disco*, facing the Opera House at the corner of Rua J. Clemente and Avenida Eduardo Ribeiro. The *Cheik Clube*, Av. Getúlio Vargas 773, has a solid reputation for modern dance music (house and techno as well as salsa). **Brazilian music** venues include the *Sabor Brasil Clube*, Rua Leonardo 1840, for samba (☎234-4520 for details), and the *Havai Club*, Estrada da Ponta Negra (☎651-2797), which is great for any sort of dancing. For a more studenty feel and some live bands, try *Coração Blue*, Estrada da Ponta Negra 3701, Km6 (starts 10pm; ☎984-1391).

Listings

Airlines You'll find travel agents selling flight tickets on every street, but the main airlines are: Penta, Rua Barroso 352 (☎234-1046; airport ☎621-1161), covering the eastern Amazon; Tavaj, airport (☎621-1483 or 621-1214); Transbrasil, Rua Guilherme Moreira 150 (☎622-3462 or 622-3738); Varig, Rua Marcilio Dias 284 (☎622-3090 or 622-1552); and VASP, Av. Sete de Septembro 993 (☎621-1258 or 622-3470).

Air taxis Girassol (☎651-1959); Cruzeiro (☎651-3571); Rico (☎621-1164).

American Express agent at Selvatur, Praça Adalberto Valle.

Banks and exchange Câmbio e Turismo Cortez (Mon–Fri 9am–5pm, Sat 9am–12.30pm), at the corner of Av. Getúlio Vargas and Av. Sete de Setembro, has good rates and a fast service for both cash and travellers cheques, unlike the Banco do Brasil, Rua Guilherme Moreira 315, which keeps its usual low standards and high commission ($20).

Boats There are regular passenger boat services to: Belém, Santarém and all ports along the Rio Amazonas; along the Rio Solimões to Tabatinga; and up the Rio Madeira to Porto Velho. Less frequent services go up the Rio Negro to São Gabriel da Cachoeira and up the Rio Branco to Caracaraí. Tickets for the regular services can be bought from the riverboat offices – booths inside the port building off Praça da Matriz – and most boats are tied up at the port there. Smaller boats with no regular schedules are found to the east of the Mercado Municipal. They usually display signs with their destinations marked up. The main ENASA ticket office is at Rua Marechal Deodoro 61 (☎633-3280, fax 633-3093). See also the "River Journeys" box pp.320–321.

Buses The *Rodoviária* is at Rua Recife 2800 (☎236-8305), 10km north of the centre. Three daily departures to Boa Vista with União Cascavel (book in advance as they're often full); and other local services to Manacapuru and Itacoatiara. From the city centre, take local bus #306 to the *Rodoviária* from Praça da Matriz; taxis cost around $12.

Car rental Avis (☎234-4440); Interlocadora (☎232-1558); Unidas (☎651-2558).

Cinemas *Cine Chaplin*, Av. Joaquim Nabuco 1094 (☎232-7531); *Cinema Novo*, Av. Joaquim Nabuco 1447 (☎233-0476). There are 6 more cinemas at *Amazonas Shopping Center* (see "Shopping" below). Ticket prices vary between $4 and $6.

Consulates Bolivia, Rua Fortaleza 80, Adrianópolis (☎232-0077); Colombia, Rua D. Libânia 62 (☎234-6777); France, Av. Joaquim Nabuco 1846 (☎233-6585); Italy, Rua Belo Horizonte 240, Adrianópolis (☎611-4877); Japan, Rua Ferreira Pena 92 (☎232-2000); Peru, Rua A – C/19 – Conj. Aristocratico, Chapada (☎656-3267 or 656-1015); Portugal, Rua Terezina 193 (☎633-1577); USA, Rua Recife 1010 – CCI – Adrianópolis (☎234-4546); Venezuela, Rua Ferreira Pena 179 (☎233-6004).

Environmental information Up-to-date eco-info from the German-backed INPA (Instituto Nacional de Pesquisas de Amazónia), Av. A. Araújo 1756 (☎643-3377; daily 9am–noon & 2–5pm), who have free two-hour video screenings at weekends (at 10am and 2pm) and a very large tame anteater, too. Try also the Museu de Ciências Naturais da Amazônia, Colônia Cachoeira Grande, Estrada Belém (☎644-2799; Mon–Sat 9am–5pm; $2), where there are fish, insects and a 37,000-gallon aquarium. FUNAI's offices, from whom you need authorization (rarely given) to visit any Indian reserves, are on Av. Joaquim Nabuco 294 (☎633-3132 or 233-7103).

Hospital The main state hospital is Hospital dos Acidentados, Av. Joaquim Nabuco 1775 (☎633-2200). For an ambulance call ☎192.

Laundry Amazonas, Rua Costa Azevedo 63; Super Rápida, Rua Paraíba 1.

Maps *Mundo dos Mapas*, Rua Saldanha Marinho 773 (☎233-4909), two blocks north from Av. Sete de Setembro.

Police ☎190.

Post office The main one, with a reliable *poste restante* service (first floor; they keep mail for 2 months), is just off the Praça da Matriz on Rua Marechal Deodoro at the corner with Rua Teodoreto Souto (Mon–Fri 8am–6pm, Sat 8am–noon).

Shopping *Artesanato* is available from the Museu do Índio (see p.357). *Artesanato da Amazônia*, near the Opera House on Rua José Clemente 500, has a wide range of well-priced stock, as does *Casa do Beija-Flor* (House of the Hummingbird), Rua J. Clemente 632. *Artíndia*, in the pink pavilion on Praça Adalberto Valle, is more central but expensive. Indian crafts are also sold at the Mercado Municipal. Interesting *macumba* and *umbanda* magico-religious items such as incense, candles, figurines and bongos, can be found at *Cabana São Jorge* at Rua da Instalação 36. Duty-free electronic and all kinds of other luxury items can be bought everywhere in the centre. The most modern shopping centre is *Amazonas Shopping*, on the airport road, 15km by taxi or bus #306, with hundreds of shops and cafés, plus 6 cinemas. A good hammock shop is *Casa des Redes* on Rua dos Andradas.

Taxis Rádio Táxi ☎622-1122 or 622-4040.

Jungle trips from Manaus

Manaus is the obvious place in the Brazilian Amazon to find a **jungle river trip** to suit most people's requirements. It's not necessarily the best place if you are serious about spotting a wide range of wildlife, but it does offer mostly well-organized tours bringing visitors into close contact with some of the world's finest tropical rainforest. Unfortunately, though, since Manaus has been a big city for a long time, the forest in the immediate vicinity is far from virgin. Over the last millennia it has been explored by Indians, missionaries, rubber gatherers, colonizing extractors, settlers, urban folk from Manaus and, more recently, quite a steady flow of eco-interested tourists.

The amount and nature of the **wildlife** you get to see on a standard jungle tour depends mainly on how far away from Manaus you go and how long you can devote to the trip. Birds like macaws, jabarus and toucans can generally be spotted; and you might see alligators, snakes and a few species of monkey on a three-day trip (though you can see many of these anyway at the Parque Janauary – see p.357). For even a remote chance of glimpsing wild deer, tapirs, armadillos or wild cats then a week-long trip is the minimum, preferably more. On any trip, make sure that you'll get some time in the smaller channels in a canoe, as the sound of a motor is a sure way of scaring every living thing out of sight.

There are a few Brazilian **jungle terms** every visitor should be familiar with: a *regatão* is a travelling boat-cum-general-store, which can provide a fascinating introduction to the interior if you can strike up an agreeable arrangement with one of their captains; an *igarapé* is a narrow river or creek flowing from the forest into one of the larger rivers (though by narrow around Manaus they mean less than 1km wide); an *igapó* is a patch of forest which is seasonally flooded; a *furo* is a channel joining two rivers and therefore a short cut for canoes; a *paraná*, on the other hand, is a branch of the river which leaves the main channel and returns further downstream, creating a river island.

There are scores of different **jungle tour companies** in Manaus offering very similar services and the competition is intense. On the down side this means you'll get hassled by touts all over town, and the sales patter is unrelenting. On the positive side this means that you'll be able to bargain the price down a bit; large groups can always get a better deal than people travelling alone. Unfortunately, even the most established companies, including those listed in the box below, will try to get the best price out of naive-looking tourists, who are sometimes charged almost double the normal rate. Your best bet is to shop around, talk to other tourists who have already been on trips and be wary of parting with wads of cash before you know exactly what you'll be getting in return (see below). Ideally, you should arrange a pay-half-now, half-later deal, though even with the smoothest of silver tongues you might find that nigh impossible. If you have time to spare, the best ploy is simply to name your price to the tour companies, give your hotel address and wait for them to find other tourists to make up a group.

It's always a good idea to pin your tour operator down to giving you specific details of the trip and you should always ask about the accommodation arrangements, what the food and drink will consist of, exactly where you are going; ask to see photos. A circular trip may sound attractive, but the scenery won't change very much, whatever the name of the *rio*. You should also check that the guide speaks English, whether the operator has an environmental policy and what insurance cover they offer (usually nil in the case of the cheaper operators). What is not included in the price? Can you get your money back, or part of it, if the trip turns out to be disappointing? On a more upmarket tour, you should ensure that binoculars and reference books are provided on the boat, and, on any tour, you of course have the right to expect that any promises made – regarding maximum group size, activities and so on – are kept. If not, then a promise to complain to EMAMTUR (see p.354) may give you some leverage in obtaining redress.

The most dependable and comfortable way to visit the jungle is to take a package tour that involves a number of nights in a **jungle lodge** – though for the more adventurous traveller the experience can be a little tame. The lodges invariably offer hotel-standard accommodation, full board and a range of activities including alligator spotting, piranha fishing, trips by canoe, as well as transport to and from Manaus. You can

---

YANOMAMI TOURS: A WARNING

Some tourists are offered trips to the Yanomami or other Indian reserves. However, this is only possible with valid permission from IBAMA and FUNAI (see p.361) which you have to obtain yourself; if a company says they already have permission, they're lying, as each visit needs a new permit. In any case, permission is generally impossible to get, so that the trips offered are actually illegal and could land you in serious trouble. Of course, the ethics of such visits are in any case clear: isolated groups of Indians have no immunity to imported diseases, and even the common cold can kill them with devastating ease (see p.371).

either book a jungle lodge tour through a tour operator, or approach the lodges direct at their offices in Manaus (see box).

If you want to forgo organized tours entirely and travel independently, **milk boats** are a very inexpensive way of getting about on the rivers around Manaus. These smaller vessels, rarely more than 20m long, spend their weeks serving the local riverine communities by delivering and transporting their produce. You can spend a whole day on one of these boats for as little as $10, depending on what arrangement you make with the captain. The best place to look for milk boats is down on Flutuante Tres Estrelas, one of the wooden wharves behind the distribution market. Approach the ones that are obviously loading early in the morning of the day you want to go, or late in the afternoon of the day before. Other commercial boats bound for the interior – some of them preparing for trips up to a month long – can be found at the docks off the Mercado Municipal.

Tour itineraries

The **basic options** for jungle tours run from one-day through to three-, five-, or even fifteen-day expeditions into the forest – almost all of them dominated by river travel. They usually include the services of local guides and forest experts. Some offer accommodation on boats, some in hammocks in forest clearings, others offer both in the same three-day trip. The more expensive ones offer the added luxury of jungle lodges.

The **one-day river trip**, usually costing around $60 per person, generally includes inspecting the famous meeting of the waters, some 10km downriver from Manaus (see p.357). Here you can see clearly how the darker flow of the Rio Negro meanders downstream separately from the much lighter Rio Solimões for some 6km before the two rivers visibly merge (at which point the Rio Solimões becomes called the Rio Amazonas again). More often than not, this trip will also visit one or two fairly typical riverine settlements and take a side trip up a narrow river channel to give at least some contact with birdlife and a tantalizing taste of the forest itself. One-day river trips usually leave port around 8 or 9am, returning before 6pm, though some last barely six hours.

The other most popular jungle river trips tend to be the **three-to-five-day expeditions**. If you want to sleep in the forest, either in a lodge or, for the more adventurous (and perhaps those with a low budget), swinging in a hammock outside in a small jungle clearing, it really is worth taking as many days as you can to get as far away from Manaus as possible. The usual price for guided tours, including accommodation and food, should be between $35 and $60 a day per person (no matter the sales pitch), more again if you opt for an upmarket jungle lodge.

The most commonly operated tours are three-day trips combining both the **Rio Negro** and **Rio Solimões**, although some trips only cover the former, as it is more accessible from Manaus and, due to the acidity of the vegetation and waters, has less of a mosquito problem. Unfortunately, for the same reasons, there is also less wildlife on the Rio Negro. Four-day trips should ideally also include the **Anavilhanas archipelago** on the Rio Negro, one of the world's largest river island complexes with around four hundred isles, as well as a good day's walk through the jungle.

On the Solimões, some of the three-to-five-day options include trips to Lago Mamori or Manacapuru. Although well visited and only half a day's travel by road and boat from Manaus, **Lago Mamori** offers reasonably "virgin" forest conditions where you'll see plenty of birds and alligators and have the chance to do some piranha fishing. **Manacapuru**, also accessible by road and boat, offers more in the way of plant familiarization walks, including access to Brazil-nut tree trails. It's also an area where visitors can make interesting excursions up smaller tributaries in search of birdlife, alligators and spectacular flora, such as the gigantic **samaumeira tree** with its buttress base (one of the tallest trees in the Amazon).

JUNGLE TOUR OPERATORS AND LODGES IN MANAUS

Tour Operators

Amazonas Indian Turismo, Rua dos Andradas 311 (no ☎). A rough-edged operator, but the least pushy of the budget crowd, specializing in tours up the Rio Urubu, a tributary of the Amazonas some 180km east of Manaus. Jungle trekking, wildlife (mainly birds – including toucans – dolphins and alligators), exploring *igarapés* in small canoes, piranha fishing and visits to local communities. Guides vary in quality (some speak only Portuguese, and not very fluently at that), as do the prices quoted: $60–80 a day is too much and needs sharp bargaining skills to bring it down; $40–50 is more reasonable. However, the groups tend to be smaller than most, and more personalized itineraries are also possible: you might consider doing a deal for a week or more, using a guide for only a few days, and spending the rest of the time exploring alone by canoe or on foot, based at their native-style hammock-camp miles away from anywhere else. They also offer longer tours, but their expertise in this is lacking.

Amazon Clipper Cruises, Rua Sucupira 271, Kíssia (☎656-1246, fax 656-3584). Operators of luxury cruises aboard their own boats, with regular departures (most other cruise companies expect you to hire the entire boat, one week minimum, for $1300–2000 a day!).

Amazon Cristovão Tour, Rua Marechal Deodoro 75, room 201 (☎233-3231). One of the biggest names, operating trips from 1 to 10 days on all the rivers in the region, but at over twice the price of the cheapies ($100–150 per day) for largely similar tours. Their claim that quality and experience naturally cost more would be more credible if more attention were given to details.

Amazon Explorers, Praça Adalberto Valle (☎232-3052, fax 234-6767). In a glass kiosk at the southern edge of the square (the main office is at Rua Nhamundá 21), a reputable and very helpful company offering a reservations service for upmarket jungle lodges, luxury boat hire and fishing trips, as well as operating their own jungle tours with accommodation on boats (from around $100 per person a day, mimimum two people for two days) and a 6-hour trip to the meeting of the waters and Parque Janauary for $60.

Amazon Nut Safaris, Av. Beira Mar 43, São Raimundo (☎671-3525, fax 671-1415). Upmarket ecological expeditions to the Anavilhanas archipelago. They also operate a small 9-room lodge, *Apurissawa*, on the Rio Cuieiras, 4hr by boat from Manaus.

Amazon Wild Tours, Rua dos Andradas 371 (☎ and fax 234-5238). An established company which seems to have grown complacent of late, with a litany of complaints to their name. Their 3-day trips are still cheap, but there's no guarantee of quality, and we mention them only because their touts will find you before others do.

David Rios, Av. Joaquim Nabuco 201, Apt. 102. An independent guide specializing in tours to the Jau National Park, encompassing 27,000 square kilometres of primary forest – the largest protected zone in the state of Amazonas and just one day's river travel up the Rio Negro.

Jungle Experience, currently at hotels *Ideal* and *Rio Branco* on Rua dos Andradas (contact Christopher Gomes; ☎645-4108, fax 233-9423). A new company with old faces, notably one of the best guides in the region, Gerry Hardy, an English-speaking Guyanese. Three-to-five-day jungle trips in and around the seldom-visited Paraná do Mamori and Lago de Juma, south of Manaus. $60–80 a day.

Selvatur, Praça Adalberto Valle (☎622-1173, fax 622-2177). Rather on the expensive side (around $140 per day) and their boats are very big, too large really to see any significant wildlife; at the time of writing they'd cut down on most of their operations, concentrating on day trips to the meeting of the waters and Parque Janauary ($60).

Swallows and Amazons, Rua Quintino Bocaiúva 189, 1° sala 13 (☎622-1246). A small company with a high reputation, operating guided tours along the tributaries of the Rio Negro.

LODGES AND CAMPS

Apart from Amazon Explorers (who also operate their own jungle tours – see opposite), the only **agency** which handles bookings for a variety of jungle lodges is Tarumã Turismo, Av. Eduardo Ribeiro 620, Loja/F, Edifício Cidade de Manaus (☎633-3363, fax 633-3310).

The following **lodges and camps**, listed with their contact addresses in Manaus, are a recommended selection. Contact Amazon Explorers, Tarumã Turismo or EMAMTUR (see p.354) for details of other jungle lodges.

Adventure Jungle Lodge, Rua Silva Ramos 20 (☎234-7308, fax 233-5615). Situated on Lago Janauaca, this new but very basic floating lodge with 25 rooms specializes in fishing holidays, although it does have a cheaper *ecológico* package which includes forest walks, alligator spotting and other activities. From $189 per person for 3 days and 2 nights.

Amazon Ecopark, Praça Auxiliadora 4, grupo 103 (☎658-3506). A nature reserve on the west bank of the Rio Tarumã, just over 20km from Manaus and an easy day visit. A wide variety of monkeys, birds, ungulates, rodents and reptiles are presented in their natural environments at the adjacent "Amazon Monkey Jungle". $60 per person for a day trip, or $260 for an overnight stay; if you can get there under your own steam (phone for transport options and opening times before setting off) it's possible to stay overnight in a forest camp for $15.

Amazon Lodge, Nature Safaris, Rua Santa Quitéria 15, Presidente Vargas (☎622-4144, fax 622-1420). Powerful motor boats take you 80km upriver to Lago Juma and their floating lodge with 14 double rooms and a restaurant. Expensive.

Amazon Swiss Lodge, Av. Eduardo Ribeiro 620, sala 215 (☎633-2322). Situated on the Rio Urubu and reached by road (182km to Lindóia), then 30min by boat. It's relatively small, with 16 wooden cabin-style rooms, collective toilets and a restaurant. Overnights in the jungle possible. $70 per person per night, or $16 to camp.

Amazon Village, Grand Amazon Turismo, Rua Ramos Ferreira 1189, sala 403 (☎633-1444, fax 633-3217). On Lago Puraquequara, 30km from Manaus; much larger than the *Amazon Lodge* (32 rooms), with more and better facilities but not quite as wild.

Ariau Amazon Towers, Rio Amazonas Turismo, *Hotel Monaco*, Rua Silva Ramos 41 (☎234-7308, fax 233-5615). Just 65km up the Rio Negro from Manaus (3hr by boat) by Ariau lake, this is one of the largest and most developed of the jungle lodges with a helicopter pad, swimming pool, almost 100 rooms, mostly in wooden chalets, and a 35m viewing tower from which you get an exceptionally close and breathtaking view of the forest canopy. It's a must if your budget isn't restricted ($340 per person for three days and two nights).

Hotel Ecológico Terra Verde (Green Land Lodge), Av. Getúlio Vargas 657 (☎234-0148, fax 238-1742). Located in the Forest of Life 10,000-hectare ecological reserve, 50km from Manaus beyond Manacapuru on the Tiririca river, this lodge has 14 relatively luxurious apartments, a floating swimming pool and horse-riding facilities. A comfortable and interesting place, but probably a bit tame for the adventurous traveller. $250 per person for 3 days and 2 nights.

Ecomazon Jungle Lodge, Rua Henrique Martins 561B (☎232-8186, fax 663-5464). A floating hotel located near the Parque Janauary and so not far from Manaus, but somewhat basic for the price. An overnight stay is $250 a double; alternatively, a 10-hour day trip to the lodge and the *parque* costs $70 a head.

Malocas Jungle Lodge, Iaratur, Rua Guilherme Moreira 297, sala 1 (☎633-2330). Native-style (hammocks) lodge near the Rio Preta da Eva, well-organized, upmarket and reasonably priced.

The Rio Solimões and the journey to Peru

The stretch of river upstream from Manaus, as far as the pivotal frontier with **Peru** and **Colombia** at Tabatinga, is known to Brazilians as the **Rio Solimões**. Once into Peru it again becomes the Rio Amazonas. Although many Brazilian maps show it as the Rio Marañon on the Peru side, Peruvians don't call it this until the river forks into the Marañon and Ucayali headwaters, quite some distance beyond Iquitos.

From Manaus to Iquitos in Peru, the river remains navigable by large ocean-going boats, though few travel this way any more. Since the collapse of the rubber market and the emergence of air travel, the river is left to smaller, more locally orientated **riverboats**. Many travellers do come this way, however; and, although some complain about the food and many get upset stomachs (especially on the Peruvian leg), it can be a really pleasant way of moving around – lying in your hammock, reading and relaxing, or drinking at the bar. Against this, there are all the inherent dangers of travelling by boat on a large river, especially at night. Boats have been known to sink (though this is rare) but they do frequently break down, causing long delays, and many captains seem to take great pleasure in overloading boats with both cargo and passengers. In spite of the discomforts, however, the river journey remains popular; and it's unarguably an experience that will stick in the memory.

The river journey is also, of course, by far the cheapest way of travelling between Brazil and Peru. There are reasonable facilities for visitors in the border town of **Tabatinga**, where you'll almost certainly have to stop: most boats will terminate at the border whichever direction they've come from.

The boat trip from Manaus to Tabatinga – five to eight days upstream – costs around $70 inclusive of food (though bring some treats, as the fare on board, though good, does get a bit monotonous). The downstream journey takes three to four days and costs around $50. If you want to break the journey, you can do so at **Tefé**, around halfway; but there's no reason to stop here unless you really can't face the boat any longer (there are several weekly flights from Tefé to Manaus and Tabatinga if you're really fed up). Five large boats currently ply the river on a regular basis, all pretty similar and with good facilities (toilets with paper, showers, mineral water and enough food). Smaller boats also occasionally do the trip, but more often terminate at Tefé, from where other small boats continue. On the other side of the border, the boat trip to **Iquitos** from Tabatinga costs around $25–35 and takes three or four days; sometimes more, rarely less. Coming downstream from Iquitos to Tabatinga ($20) gives you one and a half days on the river. Again, it's advisable to take your own food and water – all normal supplies can be bought in Tabatinga. Following the cessation of flights in the early 1990s, there are now super-fast 16-seater powerboats connecting Tabatinga and **Leticia** (the town on the Colombian side of the border) with Iquitos. They cost upwards of $50 and take roughly ten to twelve hours.

The three-way frontier

The point where Brazil meets Peru and Colombia is known as the **three-way frontier**, and it's somewhere you may end up staying for a few days sorting out red tape or waiting for a boat. Some Brazilian boats will leave you at Benjamin Constant, across the river from Tabatinga, but, if you do have to hang around, then Tabatinga, or the neighbouring Colombian town of Leticia, are the only places with any real facilities. A fleet of motorboat taxis connect these places, and Islandia and Santa Rosa in Peru: Benjamin Constant to Tabatinga takes half an hour and costs around $2.50; Tabatinga to Islandia or Santa Rosa takes fifteen minutes and costs $1.50. When you're making plans, bear in

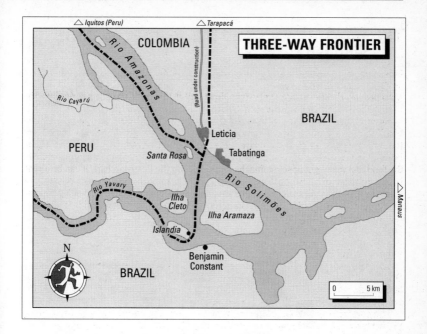

mind that the three countries have differing time zones: make sure you know which you are operating on (Tabatinga is an hour behind Manaus).

Tabatinga

TABATINGA is the place to complete Brazilian exit (or entry) formalities with the Polícia Federal, on Avenida da Amizade (daily 8am–noon & 2–6pm), and it also has an airport with regular flights to Manaus. Many of the boats into Peru leave from here, and if you're coming the other way most downstream boats start their journeys here too (south down Rua Tamandaré, then right after the Marine base), before really filling up at Benjamin Constant.

Accommodation is generally awful in Tabatinga, a good reason to stay on the boat if you can. If you really need a night of luxury, the neighbouring Colombian town of Leticia (see below) has a couple of charming hotels. In Tabatinga, your choice is limited to the *Hotel Pajé*, Rua Pedro Teixeira 367 (☎092/412-2774; ①), friendly but very basic; the fairly pleasant *Hotel Rasgo da Lua* at the start of Rua Marechal Mallet (☎092/412-2571; ③), the best in town; and along the same road at no. 440, *Hotel Alto Solimões* (☎092/412-2827; ③–④), the most expensive but a dump, not redeemed by having TVs in all rooms. There is apparently a "tourist" hotel being planned for the future on Avenida da Amizade, opposite *Drinks Bar*, though the building is currently derelict and shows no sign of life.

On Avenida da Amizade, you'll find a number of good **restaurants**, including *Canto do Peixada* and *Te Contei?* which both do excellent river fish. Further along the *avenida*, towards Leticia, a number of lively **bars and discos** cater for the sleepless. In the other direction, *Scandalo's* (Fri–Sun) and *Amazonas Clube* (Sun only, 8pm–5am) are the places

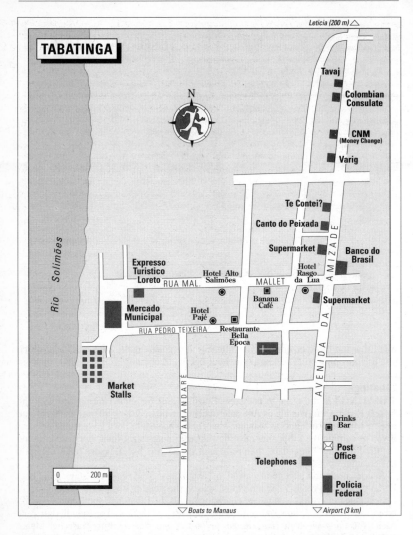

Leticia (200 m) △

TABATINGA

N

Tavaj

Colombian Consulate

CNM (Money Change)

Varig

Te Contei?

Canto do Peixada

Supermarket

Banco do Brasil

Expresso Turistico Loreto

Hotel Alto Salimões

RUA MAL.

MALLET

Hotel Rasgo da Lua

Banana Café

Supermarket

Rio Solimões

Mercado Municipal

Hotel Pajé

RUA PEDRO TEIXEIRA

Restaurante Bella Epoca

AVENIDA DA AMIZADE

Market Stalls

RUA TAMANDARE

Drinks Bar

⊠ Post Office

Telephones

Polícia Federal

0   200 m

▽ Boats to Manaus   ▽ Airport (3 km)

for serious dance freaks – and prostitutes – as is *Banana Café* (Sat & Sun) on Rua Marechal Mallet. For **live music** (Fri & Sat), try *Restaurante Bella Epoca* on Rua Pedro Teixeira, or *Bar Porto Segurro*, a couple of kilometres west beyond the port for Manaus boats. For **money changing**, forget the *Banco do Brasil* (expensive and slow); you'll get a better deal for travellers' cheques at *Câmbio CNM* (Mon–Fri 8am–5pm, Sat 8am–noon), on Avenida da Amizade, whereas for cash you're best off crossing the border into Leticia.

Leticia

If you are staying around for a few days then **LETICIA**, an old, more established river port – little over twenty minutes' walk away and with a steady trickle of connecting

Volkswagen vans ($1) if it's really too hot – is a more interesting place. With an economy based on tourism and contraband (mostly cocaine), it has more than a touch of the Wild West about it – there are no entry formalities at all, though you should carry your passport with you.

There are endless kiosks **changing dollars** into Brazilian, Colombian and Peruvian currency, mostly on the riverfront, but also on the boundary between Tabatinga and Leticia. Leticia is also a good place to buy hammocks, and if you're looking for a little pampering, there are a couple of very good **hotels** in town: *Hotel Colonial*, on the main street, Carrera 10, is a delightful colonial-period wood-framed house, similar to its sister hotel, the *Hotel Parador Ticuna*, one block closer to the waterfront on Carrera 11 (both ☎0057-819/27273 or 27243 from Brazil; ⑥). For **food**, there are a number of excellent places, including *Buccaneer* and *La Taguara*, both on Carrera 10. Amazons Explorer's, 1st floor Edificio Matiz, no. 785 Carrera 10, can arrange **trips** out to Monkey Island or visits to local Indian communities. The *Hotel Parador Ticuna* also runs tours: day trips for around $30 including lunch, and three- to five-day trips up the Rio Cayaru in Peru to Bellavista for around $70 a day.

Onward practicalities

If you want to go further **into Colombia** you'll need to pick up a tourist card from the Colombian consulate in Tabatinga (Av. da Amizade, near the border; Mon–Fri 8am–2pm). From Leticia, Avianca operates flights to the main Colombian cities. Alternatively, an extremely adventurous option would be to cut across overland along the planned road to Tarapacá, due north of Leticia, to connect with the Rio Putumayo, where canoes to Puerto Asis connect with the Colombian road and bus system.

Heading **into Peru** many of the boats actually leave from Tabatinga, although Peruvian authorities and passport control are in **Santa Rosa**, a military post over the river, where all Peru-bound boats have to stop for passport and customs control. The Peruvian consulate is on the main street in Leticia (Mon–Fri 9am–3pm). Powerboats (*lanchas*) to Iquitos are run by Expresso Turistico Loreto, on Rua Marechal Mallet in Tabatinga in one of the last shacks on the left as you walk down towards the river. Other, slower boats can be found at the port in both Leticia and Tabatinga.

Up the Rio Negro

The **Rio Negro** flows into Manaus from northwestern Amazonas, one of the least explored regions of South America. There's virtually nothing in the way of tourist facilities in this direction, but it's possible to make your way up the Rio Negro boat by boat (see below) from Manaus to Barcelos, from Barcelos to São Gabriel, and from there on to the virtually uncharted borders with Colombia and Venezuela. Alternatively, there are now reasonably fast boats from Manaus every Friday, run by Asabranc, which call in at Barcelos (2 days; $35–50) on their way to São Gabriel (about 5 days up, 3 downriver; $60–80). There are also daily Tavaj **flights** to São Gabriel from Manaus (3hr; around $170), stopping off en route on alternate days at either Barcelos or Tefé on the Rio Solimões. To leave Brazil via these routes requires expedition-level planning, but it's an exciting trip. One piece of good news is that the black colour of the Rio Negro is caused by vegetable acidity leached from the surrounding forested basins and the Colombian foothills where the river's source lies: this acidity helps keep down the number of insects (particularly mosquitoes) along the river, making it much more comfortable to sleep on the river beaches than on those of most major Amazonian tributaries.

The first part of the journey, from Manaus to **BARCELOS**, is relatively easy. As well as the Asabranc boat, there are ordinary boats at least twice a week ($15), taking fifty to sixty hours; the *Irmaos Feraes* is particularly recommended, with good, fresh river food aboard. Other boats leave fairly frequently but with no predictable regularity from the docks behind the Mercado Municipal: look for the destination signs. Alternatively, you can hire a river taxi from the floating port to help you find a boat bound for Barcelos since they also moor to the west of the main port. Fix a price with the taxi first; it should cost no more than $6. In Barcelos the Nara family offer accommodation and good food to visitors who are going on their **jungle tours**. Run by Tatunca Nara, a local native, they take you deep into the forest where there's a better chance of spotting wildlife than there is closer to Manaus. Contact Tatunca's wife, who speaks English, in advance: Dr Anita Nara, c/o Unidade Mista, Barcelos, Amazonas 69700 (☎092/721-1165).

At least two days further upriver, the town of **SÃO GABRIEL DA CACHOEIRA** is the next settlement of any size. Besides the Asabranc service, boats from Barcelos leave at irregular intervals, but generally several times a week; expect to pay between $25 and $35. It's a beautiful place where the jungle is punctuated by volcanic cones, one with a Christ figure standing high on its flank. Superb views can be had across the valley from the slopes around the town, and there's a good **pensão** and several **restaurants**.

A little further upriver you reach the **Rio Negro Forest Reserve**, where local guides will take you camping from around $20 a day. At present this park zone – a massive triangle between the headwaters of the Rio Negro and its important tributary the Rio Uaupés, both of which rise in Colombia – is crawling with military personnel. It's a sensitive zone, partly because of fears of narcotics smuggling, but also in terms of the national frontier: Venezuela, Brazil and Colombia meet here, and the Rio Negro itself forms the border between Venezuela and Colombia for some way. There are also plans to put a highway through the park – the projected BR-210 or Perimetral Norte – which is destined to run from Macapá on the Atlantic coast to São Gabriel, passing south of Boa Vista on the way. From São Gabriel it should eventually make its way, if the plans go ahead, across the Amazon via Tabatinga to Cruzeiro do Sul, where it would link up with the westerly point of the Transamazônica, making it feasible to do an enormous circle by road around the Brazilian Amazon. Exactly when this will happen is anybody's guess, and some of the regions they are talking about putting this road through are incredibly remote.

You may also be able to get a guide to take you into the **Parque Nacional do Pico da Neblina**. The Pico da Neblina itself, Brazil's highest peak at 3014m, is on the far side of the park, hard against the Venezuelan border.

To proceed **beyond São Gabriel** by river is more difficult, particularly in the dry season from May till October. The river divides a few hours beyond São Gabriel. To the right, heading more or less north, the Rio Negro continues (another day by boat) to the community of Cucui on the Venezuelan border – there's also a very rough road from São Gabriel. It is just about possible to travel on from here **into Venezuela** and the Orinoco river system, through the territory of Yanomami Indians. But this involves a major expedition requiring boats, guides and considerable expense: cost aside, it is also potentially dangerous, and you should get a thorough update on the local situation before attempting this route. One of the main problems at present is the fact that the region has become the focus for the *garimpeiros* or gold-miners who were effectively pushed out of the Yanomami territory in Roraima during the early 1990s. They have moved further west into this region, which is clearly one of the last Amazonian frontiers. The left fork is the **Rio Uaupés** where the **Araripirá waterfalls** lie a day or two upstream, just before the border settlement of Iaurete. The Uaupés continues, another day's journey, along the border to the Colombian town of Mitu. Again, this is a potentially hazardous area, home to Maku Indians and, more worryingly, to coca-growing areas and members of the Colombian underworld.

Roraima

The **state of Roraima**, in the far north of Brazil butting against Guyana and Venezuela, only came into existence in 1991. It's an active frontier zone, pushing forward the bound-aries of "development", indigenous "acculturation" and, in some regions, perhaps even international borders. When the grasslands here were discovered in the mid-eighteenth century they were thought to be ideal cattle country, and it was the Portuguese who first moved in on them. But the current national borders weren't finally settled until the early part of this century. During the late 1980s, there was a massive gold rush here, with an influx of as many as 50,000 *garimpeiros* (compared to a total population of around 200,000 previously). This was centred above all in the northwest, up against the Venezuelan bor-der in the Serra Pacaraima, formerly the territory of the Yanomami Indians.

In 1989 the plight of the **Yanomami**, a relatively recently "discovered" people living on both sides of the border, whose lands were being invaded by prospectors, brought about an international outcry which forced the Brazilian government to announce that they would evacuate all settlers from Yanomami lands. But the project was abandoned almost as soon as it began: protection of the region's valuable mineral reserves was deemed to necessitate the strengthening of the country's borders and the settlement of the area, and the military have a strong vested interest in its development. As a result of all this, tourists are often treated with some suspicion, especially in Boa Vista where talk of the Yanomami invariably attracts long sideways glances. But you'd be extreme-ly unlucky to encounter any real trouble.

Up the Rio Branco

It's now relatively easy to get from **Manaus to Boa Vista**, the capital of Roraima, by road, usually taking eighteen hours by **bus** ($55). The road is tarmacked in places,

---

THE YANOMAMI

The major problems facing the **Yanomami** as a result of the land invasions by prospec-tors are primarily to do with political control of their own **territory** and, more immediately serious, considerable **health problems**. In fact, thousands of Yanomami have died of imported diseases, mainly malaria, since the *garimpeiros* first moved into the area in large numbers in the mid- to late 1980s. Other new sicknesses, including hepatitis, TB, sexual-ly transmitted diseases and skin infections, are all taking their toll at the present moment.

Following the successful **demarcation** of Yanomami lands in 1992, and, with the help of international pressure from organizations such as Survival International, the territo-ry's official recognition by the Federal State, things have improved slightly. There are now fewer *garimpeiros* prospecting in Yanomami forests. Some have moved west towards the Colombian border, others are now panning for gold along the Guyanan bor-der, or in Guyana. Many have also crossed over illegally into Venezuela, where they con-tinue to prospect on non-Brazilian, but still Yanomami, land.

In the long run there appear to be some serious political problems regarding the rights of the Yanomami to control their own territory. The **Calhe Norte project**, by which the northern part of Roraima comes under military control, was reactivated in the early 1990s, and the army has apparently begun building new roads within the Yanomami's demarcated areas. There are also high-level moves, within the state and in Brasília, to take some of the land back from the Yanomami. Many vested interests were thwarted when the Yanomami's land was officially demarcated in their favour during the early 1990s. For the moment, however, the constitutional reform, which included moves to reduce the size of Yanomami reserves, has fortunately been paralysed, but the battle for the Yanomami's land rights continues.

though there are plenty of nail-biting sections across plank bridges and through run-off zones after rain to keep you on the edge of your seat. In the rainy season you may find yourself getting bogged down several times along the way, and if a bridge has collapsed, you might find yourself arriving a day or two later than planned. It is also possible to take a **boat** all the way from Manaus up the Rio Negro and Rio Branco as far as the waterfalls of **Caracaraí**, from where you can join the bus to Boa Vista (some boats also go from Caracaraí to Boa Vista, but they're few and far between). It isn't an easy trip and it has been known to take over two weeks, with lots of stopping and starting and depending on local riverside people for hospitality and food. If you can get a boat which is going direct, all the better. Expect to pay at least $100 for the trip, more if you're boat hopping. It's sometimes easier to travel first to Barcelos from where there are occasional boats bound up the Rio Branco, but it's all very much hit and miss once you're on the rivers.

Those who do make it up the Rio Branco are generally rewarded for their steadfastness by the sight of river dolphins, alligators, plenty of birdlife and even the odd snake. At Caracaraí there are very few tourist facilities, but the police station has been known to offer free hammock space to travellers, and there are two very basic **hotels**, the *Hotel Márcia*, Rua Dr Zanny (☎095/232-1208; ①), and, marginally better, *Hotel Maroca*, Av. Pres. Kennedy 1140 (☎095/232-1292; ②).

Boa Vista

BOA VISTA must be one of the largest small towns on earth. Unrelentingly hot, modern and concrete, its planners laid it out on a grand but charmless scale, with broad tree-lined boulevards divided by traffic islands and a vast Praça do Centro Cívico, swirling with traffic, from which streets radiate just unevenly enough to confuse the otherwise perpendicular grid. Clearly this is meant to be a fitting capital for the development of Roraima – and there are large stores full of ranching and mining equipment which reflect that growth. Busy as it is, though, Boa Vista has far to go to fill its ambitious designs. The huge streets seem half empty, reflecting the waning of the gold boom after the initial rush in the late 1980s and early 1990s, and many of the old hotels and gold-trading posts have closed down, or have turned into travel agencies, small-time banks and restaurants. The new layout obliterated many of the town's older buildings, which means that there's little to see of interest in the city itself.

Arrival

On the edge of the city, surrounded by timber yards and agricultural supply stores, stands the large, modern **Rodoviária**, with several stores, a *lanchonete*, a local **tourist office** (Mon–Sat 10am–5pm) and a private tour agent's office, AMATUR (☎095/224-0004). **Taxis**, which are relatively expensive here, line up outside; on the main road beyond them (from the same side as the terminal) you can catch a **local bus** towards the centre. This takes something of a detour, round past an army base and some outlying areas, before heading back to near the *Rodoviária* where it turns down past the prison and heads down the broad Avenida Benjamin Constant towards the central *praça*. Buses for the *Rodoviária* from town, which bear the "Joquie Clube" sign on the route card, can be caught either at the urban bus terminal (the *Rodoviária Urbana*) on Rua Dr Silvio Botelho, or along the Avenida Ville Roy.

Coming from the **airport**, some 3km outside town, you'll have to take a taxi ($14). Arrival in Boa Vista can be awkward because, thanks to the gold rush, international interest in the plight of the Yanomami Indians and the fact that the area is increasingly used by cocaine smugglers, there are lots of military personnel about who are very suspicious of foreigners: you're likely to have your luggage taken apart and to be questioned about your motives. The best bet is probably to play the dumb tourist, and say you're heading for Venezuela or Manaus.

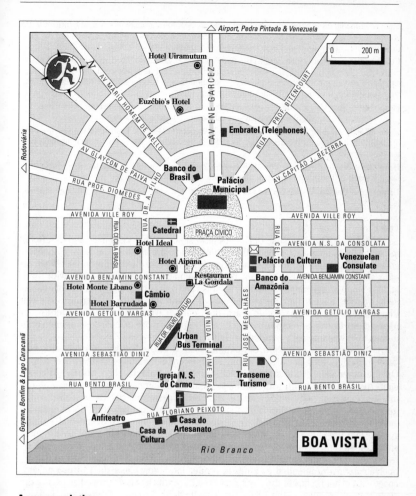

Accommodation

Budget **accommodation** in Boa Vista, mainly along Avenida Benjamin Constant, is pretty dire, as most hotels were originally designed to meet the needs of the now-ailing *garimpeiro* market, and few of them are accustomed to tourists. There are a couple of good places close to the *Rodoviária* though, while in the centre of town you'll find a handful of upmarket places, aimed at businessmen, with their own swimming pools and restaurants.

Hotel Aipana Plaza, Praça do Centro Cívico 53 (☎095/224-4800, fax 224-4116). The best hotel in Boa Vista with a pool, bar and a good restaurant, but it's overpriced, at double the rates of its nearest competitor. ⑥.

Hotel Barrudada, Rua Araújo Filho 228 (☎095/224-9335). Once a charming private house of a hotel, its popularity was such that it was knocked down in 1996 and replaced by a modern 6-storey edifice, but the staff remain helpful and the rooms are good value. ③.

Pousada Beija Flor, Av. Nossa Senhora da Consolata (☎095/224-8241, fax 224-6536). A gem of a place recently opened by a Brazilian–Belgian couple who are tuned in to backpackers' requirements.

The accommodation is basic but clean, and Néa and Jean offer a range of reasonably priced tours around Roraima, and are a wealth of information. From the *Rodoviária*, walk 6 blocks down Av. Ville Roy, turn right at the lights and then left onto Av. Consolata, and it's 2 blocks further down. ①.

Euzébio's Hotel, Rua Cecilia Brasil 1107 (☎095/224-0300, fax 224-8690). The most popular of the town's upmarket hotels, and often full, but not particularly central. It has a swimming pool and an expensive restaurant, yet much of its accommodation is in small, surprisingly dingy units. Make sure you get a room worth the money you're paying. ③–④.

Hotel Ideal, Rua Araújo Filho 467 (☎095/224-6342). Spectacularly fails to live up to its name: the rooms are smelly, but slightly more spacious than other budget options. ①.

Hotel Monte Libano, Av. Benjamin Constant 319 (☎095/224-7232). Probably has the edge over other budget hotels in the centre, in that the staff are friendlier and the rooms are in marginally better condition. ①.

Hotel Três Nações, Av. Ville Roy 1885 (☎095/224-3439). Virtually opposite the *Rodoviária*, this place is spick and span with pleasant rooms around an open courtyard. ②.

Uiramutum Palace, Av. Ene Garcez 427 (☎095/224-9912). Good value with a pool, though the food is poor. ⑤.

The City

As capital city of Roraima, one of Brazil's newest states, Boa Vista makes great efforts to establish its identity. Opposite the biggest landmark in town, the huge cylindrical concrete tube pointing towards the skies from the roof of the Embratel telephone offices on the Avenida Ene Garcez, there's a semi-circular **amphitheatre** with three statues – one of a *garimpeiro* holding a shovel and a gold-panning bowl; one of a *fazendeiro* wielding a lasso; and, the central one, an Indian with a bow and arrow. Just down the road, in the centre of the Praça do Centro Cívico, there's the better-known **Monument to the Garimpeiro**, which clearly speaks more to local businessmen than it does to environmentally minded foreign visitors.

On the south side of the *praça*, the modest-sized **Cathedral** has an interesting curvaceous design, very airy, with a ceiling reminiscent of the hull of a huge wooden boat. On the other side of the square is the brand new **Palácio da Cultura** (Mon–Fri 8am–7pm, Sat 8am–1pm), with its well-stocked public library and very smart auditorium which occasionally holds theatre and music performances (☎095/623-2280 for information on events). The *palácio* is the most visible symbol of the local council's laudable **Projeto Raízes** which is designed to inject some badly needed cultural venues into the city. The old waterfront district, connected to the *praça* by the main shopping street, Avenida Jaime Brasil, has been particularly targeted. Works include the renovation of the small Portuguese-style **Igreja Nossa Senhora do Carmo**, an open-air *anfiteatro* intended as a music venue, and a new **Casa da Cultura** gallery-space – an exact replica of the city's first Prefeitura which was destroyed as part of the zealous modernization of the 1960s. But lest you think the council's gone soft, facing it is an imposing concrete **Monument to the Pioneers of Roraima**. The huge bust of a Yanomami chief dominates the sculpture, his shoulder somewhat ambiguously being trampled over by a pioneer on horseback.

The **Casa do Artesanato**, on the riverbank, is also worth a visit: its selection of handicrafts is not wide but there's some interesting stuff and it's all very cheap (Mon–Sat 8am–6pm). There are great views from the *Restaurante Panorama* and the river bank near the Casa do Artesanato out across the Rio Branco towards the large-span, modern concrete bridge and the forest stretching beyond.

Eating and drinking

Lanchonetes are everywhere in Boa Vista, though more substantial **restaurants** are surprisingly scarce as well as expensive. In the centre, the *Restaurante La Gondola*, on the corner of Avenida Benjamin Constant and the Praça do Centro Cívico, is fine for *comida por kilo* (daily 10.30am–3pm & 6–10.30pm) and very popular. At night, the *Hotel Euzébio*'s restaurant serves good meals and, virtually next door, the lively *Pigalle* (daily 4pm–2am) has good pizzas and fish, but neither place is exactly on the cheap side; both also function as bars. More reasonable, and with excellent views, are a growing number of restaurants along the riverfront: the *Restaurante Panorama*, close to the Casa do Artesanato at Rua Floriano Peixoto 114 (☎095/224-8227), is highly recommended, as is the fish restaurant *Ver O Rio* (☎095/224-6964; closed Mon lunchtime), two buildings down on the same road. For more evening atmosphere, but without the river outlook, try the *Black and White Restaurant*, one road back on Rua Barreto Leite 11 (☎095/224-5372; closed Mon).

As to **bars and clubs**, *Clube ABB* near the airport is the most popular nightspot (Fri & Sat only); also well worth trying is the *Zanzibar*, corner of Avenida Sebastião Diniz and Rua Coronel Pinto, which hosts local bands (Fri & Sat only, 9pm onwards; ☎095/224-0093). Straightforward drinking bars are surprisingly few, the best being *Meu Cantinho* opposite the *Panorama*, with equally good views (daily until midnight).

Listings

Banks and exchange The best place to change money in Boa Vista is the private backroom office of Casa Pedro José, Rua Araújo Filho 287 (☎095/224-4277), which gives excellent rates and a fast, efficient service. Otherwise, the Banco do Brasil, on the *praça* near the Palácio Municipal changes money between 8am and 12.30pm (arrive early), charging a flat $20 commission.

Car rental Localiza (☎095/224-0010) or Unidas (☎095/224-0062).

Consulate Venezuela, Av. Benjamin Constant 525 (☎095/224-2182). If you hope to get a visa in a single day then arrive early: hours are officially 8–11.45am but they may open in the afternoon to give your completed visa back. You'll need to show your passport and have a photo and an onward ticket – though you may be able to get round the latter by having plenty of money and a good excuse. From the consulate they'll send you to a doctor for a cursory medical examination ($10 for this privilege) and from there you go to a clinic for a blood test (free) which they claim is for malaria. Having passed these you can usually go back in the afternoon, clutching the certificates, to pick up your passport and visa.

Flights To and from Manaus, planes can be solidly booked for days if not weeks ahead, especially at holiday times, though you might get lucky with the waiting list: Varig have an office at Av. Getúlio Vargas 242 (☎095/224-4143 or 224-2226), and there are several air-taxi companies based at the airport, including Macuxi (☎095/224-3772).

Post office Praça do Centro Cívico (Mon–Fri 9am–5pm).

Taxis ☎095/225-2223 or 224-4823.

Around Boa Vista

Situated as it is on the northern edge of the Amazon forest, where it meets with the savanna of Roraima, the region around Boa Vista boasts three different forms of eco-system: tropical rainforest, grassland savanna plains and the "Lost World"-style *tepius* mountain, flat plateau-like rock rising out of the savanna. Still fairly underdeveloped in terms of its tourism infrastructure, the area is exceptionally beautiful, with a wealth of river beaches, and has a very pleasant climate (hot with cooling breezes). As the options for eco-tourism are developed, more opportunities will no doubt emerge for visitors to explore Roraima in some depth.

Your first port of call in Boa Vista should be the Roraima Tourism Office at Rua Coronel Pinto 241 (Mon–Fri 7.30am–1.30pm & 3.30–5.30pm; ☎095/623-1230), who have details on new destinations, circuits and accommodation options in the state. At present, **independent travel** in the region can be problematic, with only sketchy bus services, so you might find it easier simply to hire a car (see "Listings" above). **Organized tours**, usually dependent on enough tourists filling spaces, are operated by

Anaconda Tours, Av. Silvio Botelho 12 (☎095/224-4132), and ECOTUR, Rua Barreto Leite 46 (☎095/224-6010), whilst the agency inside *Euzébio's Hotel* deals in six-day packages for around $450–500. Much cheaper, and virtually the only outfit in town able to arrange tours for small groups, is *Pousada Beija Flor* (see p.373), who combine enthusiasm with a wealth of knowledge about the state.

Places to head for include the famous painted rock, **Pedra Pintada**, en route to Santa Elena and Venezuela; the ruined eighteenth-century **Forte Sao Joaquim**, two hours from Boa Vista by boat; the ecological island reserve of **Ilha do Maracá**, located on the fairly remote Rio Uraricoera; and the very pleasant **Lake Caracaranã** with its fine beaches fringed by shady cashew trees, 180km from Boa Vista in Normandia. This is currently almost the only place in the state outside Boa Vista which has adequate facilities for tourists, with fifteen chalets and ten apartments for hire, the four-bed chalets a bargain at $40; ☎095/262-1254, or contact Transeme Turismo in Boa Vista, Av. Sebastião Diniz 234 (☎095/224-9409 or 224-6271).

Into Venezuela and Guyana

It's now relatively straightforward to go from Boa Vista to Santa Elena in **Venezuela**, and beyond to Ciudades Guyana and Bolívar – even right on to Puerto La Cruz on the north coast if you're that anxious to escape the interior – with a daily União Cascavel bus leaving at 7am. Santa Elena is also served by six other daily Eucatur buses (3hr, plus 2hr for border formalities). The road is now fully tarmacked, which means that the União Cascavel bus arrives at the border for lunch instead of supper, though it stops at a very expensive restaurant; bring your own lunch if you're running short. The journey from Boa Vista, across a vast flat savanna that is dusty in the dry season, boggy in the wet, offers very little in the way of scenery, but there is a great deal of wildlife, especially birds: white egrets, storks and all sorts of waders in the rainy season, flycatchers and hawks; and also the chance of some fairly large animals, including giant anteaters. As the border approaches the land begins to rise slightly: to the northeast lies **Monte Roraima**, the fourth highest peak in Brazil at 2875m, at the point where Brazil, Guyana and Venezuela meet.

Allow a couple of hours to cross the border itself (the bus waits while everyone has passports stamped and luggage checked); **SANTA ELENA DE UAIRÉN** is barely twenty minutes further. It is no longer necessary to spend the night here, as the União Cascavel bus now continues further up into Venezuela, but if you fancy a break, Santa Elena is a tiny place with the real feel of a border town in its low, corrugated-roofed houses and dusty streets. You can see the whole place in an hour's walk, but the *Hotel Frontera* also runs tours to local waterfalls and native communities. If you're staying overnight, good **hotels** include the *Frontera* (③), the simple *Hotel Marcia* (②), and the *Hotel Lucas* (⑤) which has a casino. There's good **food** at the *Restaurante Itália* (the spaghetti is the cheapest thing to eat in a relatively expensive town). **Money** is hard to change here: various traders will accept cash dollars or Brazilian currency – try the *Hotel Frontera* – but there's nowhere at all to change travellers' cheques. **Leaving**, there's a 5am bus to Ciudad Bolívar (12hr), as well as the União Cascavel bus late at night, and a daily flight (2hr). If you're heading for Brazil, there are at least seven buses a day. Don't forget to get your Venezuelan exit stamp from the office next to the police station on the hill behind the bus terminal, and get there early as they don't open until 8am.

Guyana is less straightforward. It's easy enough to get to **Bonfim** on the border, just over 100km away (two daily buses with Eucatur), though the road is pretty grim, but it's much less easy to continue beyond there. Get your Brazilian exit stamp in Bonfim and then walk – about 5km – to the border marked by the Rio Tucutu, where you can rent a boat to row you across to the Guyanan settlement of **LETHEM** for Guyanan border formalities. This is a friendly enough town, but there's only one expensive hotel (though the Government Rest House may put you up free) and no public road transport to anywhere: to continue on to Georgetown you can either try to hitch on the cargo lorries, or you have to fly (1 daily Mon–Sat on Guyana Airways). One further problem is that Guyanan entry regulations are very strict, and they're worried about people moving in from Brazil – you may simply be refused entry. All in all, if you want to go to Guyana, it's easier to fly; there are flights from Manaus to Georgetown, but no longer any services from Boa Vista.

Rondônia and Porto Velho

A large, partially deforested region in the southwest corner of the Brazilian Amazon, the **state of Rondônia** has undergone the first phase of its environmental destruction. Roads and tracks, radiating like fine bones from the spinal highway BR-364, have already dissected almost the entire state as scores of thousands of settlers and many large companies move in on the land. Poor landless groups, the surviving representatives of once proud Indian tribes, are a common sight huddled together under plastic sheets at the side of the road.

The state was only created in 1981, having evolved from an unknown and almost entirely unsettled zone (then the Territory of Guaporé) over the previous thirty years. The new, fast-changing Rondônia was named after the famous explorer, Indian "pacifier" and telegraph network pioneer Marechal Cândido Rondon. It's not exactly one of Brazil's major tourist attractions, but it is an interesting area in its own right, and it also offers a few stopping-off places between more obvious destinations. **Porto Velho**, the main city of the region, is an important pit-stop between Cuiabá and the frontier state of Acre. Rondônia also offers border crossings to Bolivia and access to overland routes into Peru.

Given that it is such a recently settled region, the system of road **transport** is surprisingly good, and combines well with the major rivers – Madeira, Mamoré and Guaporé. The main focus of human movement these days is the fast BR-364, which caused another surge of development after its completion in the 1980s. Manaus to Porto Velho remains possible by boat, with usually three leaving weekly in either direction.

Porto Velho

The capital of Rondônia state, **PORTO VELHO** overlooks the Amazon's longest tributary, the mighty Rio Madeira. With over 350,000 inhabitants these days, Porto Velho has evolved from a relatively small town in just twenty years. In the 1980s, settlers arrived in enormous numbers in search of land, jobs and, more specifically, the mineral wealth of the region: gold and casserite (a form of tin) are found all over Rondônia. As in most regions, the gold boom has bottomed out and the empty gold-buying stores are signs of the rapid decline. Seen from a distance across the river, Porto Velho looks rather more impressive than it does at close quarters. The two bell towers and Moorish dome of the cathedral stand strikingly above the roof tops, while alongside the river three phallic, black water towers sit like waiting rockets beside a complex of military buildings. A little further downstream the modern port and the shiny cylindrical tanks of a petrochemical complex dominate the riverbank.

In the town itself, the main street – Avenida Sete de Setembro – has an almost festival atmosphere about it. Noise is used as much as visual display to attract shoppers and *garimpeiros* in town to sell their gold. Music stores blare out their sounds; the "Compro Ouro" stores shout out their gold-buying prices; and market stall-holders chatter on about their predominantly cheap plastic wares. Every other lamp post seems to have a loudspeaker attached to it.

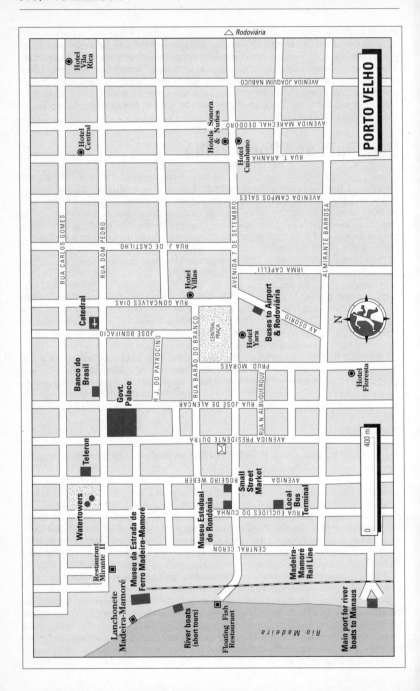

△ Rodoviária

PORTO VELHO

AVENIDA JOAQUIM NABUCO

AVENIDA MARECHAL DEODORO

Hotel
Vila
Rica

Hotels Sonora
& Nuñes

Hotel
Cuiabano

RUA T. ARANHA

Hotel
Central

AVENIDA CAMPOS SALES

RUA CARLOS GOMES

RUA DOM PEDRO

RUA J. DE CASTILHO

AVENIDA 7 DE SETEMBRO

ALMIRANTE BARROSA

IRMA CAPELLI

Hotel
Villas

RUA GONÇALVES DIAS

Catedral

JOSÉ BONIFACIO

Buses to Airport
& Rodoviária

CENTRAL
PRAÇA

AV OSORIO

N

Banco do
Brasil

R J. DO PATROCINO

RUA BARÃO DO BRANCO

Hotel
Yara

PRUD. MORAES

Hotel
Floresta

Govt.
Palace

RUA JOSÉ DE ALENCAR

RUA N. ALBUQUERQUE

Teleron

AVENIDA PRESIDENTE DUTRA

400 m

Watertowers

ROGEIRO WEBER

Small
Street
Market

AVENIDA

0

Restaurant
Mirante II

Museu Estadual
de Rondônia

RUA EUCLIDES DO CUNHA

Local
Bus
Terminal

Museu da Estrada de
Ferro Madeira-Mamoré

CENTRAL CERON

Madeira-
Mamoré
Rail Line

Lanchonete
Madeira-Mamoré

River boats
(short tours)

Floating Fish
Restaurant

Rio Madeira

Main port for river
boats to Manaus

Arrival and accommodation

Porto Velho's **airport**, Belmont, is 7km out of town, served by local buses and taxis. The **Rodoviária**, with daily connections to Guajará-Mirim and the Bolivian border, Cuiabá and Rio Branco, is also some way out on Avenida Kennedy; catch a local bus into town from here to Sete de Setembro. Regular **boats** link Manaus and Porto Velho, and the docks are located just 1km west of the main waterfront area.

There is plenty of **accommodation** to choose from in Porto Velho as it's a settlement serving a large hinterland of farmers, prospectors and businessmen as well as a growing number of tourists.

Hotel Central, Rua Tenreiro Aranha 2472 (☎069/224-2099). A good mid-range place, clean but characterless. ④.

Hotel Cuiabano, Av. Sete de Setembro. A good budget place with rooms set around a courtyard, but it's noisy during the day, as it's located on the main commercial drag. ①.

Hotel Floresta, Rua Almirante Barroso 502 (☎069/221-5669). A popular place, with a pool and a relatively quiet location, though within easy walking distance of the town centre. ③.

Hotel Nunes, Av. Sete de Setembro. Opposite the *Cuiabano*, this good-value place is clean, cool and very conveniently located. ①.

Hotel Rondon Palace, Av. do Aeroporto (069-223-3422). Close to the airport some way from the centre, this is a modern, soulless hotel with pool and good restaurant. ⑥.

Hotel Sonora, Av. Sete de Setembro. Next door to the *Nunes*, and a very dingy neighbour; only worth checking out if there's no room elswhere. ①.

Hotel Vila Rica, Rua Carlos Gomes 1616 (☎069/221-2333). This hotel is unmissable as it is by some way the tallest building in the centre; luxury class, it is nevertheless good value. ⑥.

Hotel Villas, Gonçalves Dias. Friendly but rather basic, located just off Sete de Setembro. ①.

Hotel Yara, Av. Osório. Clean and modern. ①.

The Town

Although it's a lively town and an enjoyable place to spend some time, Porto Velho doesn't have much in the way of a developed tourist scene. The main attraction, the wonderful **Madeira-Mamoré Railway** museum, closed in 1994, but, for railway buffs, there's still plenty to see around the old railway terminal on the riverbank. The Madeira-Mamoré (or Mad Maria) Railway was closed in 1960. It was built to provide a route for Bolivian rubber to the Atlantic and the markets of Europe and the eastern USA, but was completed, in 1912, just in time to see the price of rubber plummet and the market dry up. Some estimates say that as many as fifty thousand men died – mostly of malaria – building the rail line, though in truth the figure was probably a tenth of that. The project was first attempted by British engineers in 1872; by 1874, two British companies had already been forced to admit defeat with most of their labour force – mainly Irish workers – having died on the job. In 1878 a North American company, P.T. Collins, took nearly a year to lay six kilometres of track before again being stopped by epidemics. In 1883 Brazilian engineers started a sixteen-month scheme which also ended in tragedy. By 1903, with the price of rubber still rising, Brazil agreed to attempt the rail link with Bolivia once again, in part as compensation for having annexed the Bolivian territory of Acre. But it wasn't until Jekyll and Randolf – the US company who had helped build the Panama Canal – appeared on the scene in 1907 that the rail line really began to make headway. By this time advances in engineering technology and medical practice gave them a better chance, but it was still five more years before the first train ran. The line was nationalized in 1931, and in 1972 many of the tracks were ripped up to help build a road along the same difficult route.

The other museum in town, the **Museu Estadual de Rondônia** on Sete de Setembro, has an interesting collection of ethnographic artefacts gathered from indigenous tribes of the region. There's little else to see: the **Government Palace** is not a very inspiring building, and the **Cathedral** is better appreciated from the far side of the river.

One of the best things to do while you're here is to take a short trip on a **floating bar** – Fluvetur or Baretur are competing outfits which both offer much the same deal. They set out at intervals during the day – there's almost always a 5pm sundowner tour, and more frequent sailings at weekends – and for a few *reais* and the price of a beer or two you can spend a pleasant couple of hours travelling up and down the Madeira, sharing the two-storey floating bar with predominantly local groups. The atmosphere is invariably lively, and there's often impromptu music. You can find the bars down at the port, directly behind the old rail station.

Eating, drinking and nightlife

There are some excellent places to **eat and drink** in Porto Velho, though beer here is three times as expensive as it is on the coast. Food, on the other hand, tends to be a little cheaper.

It may not look like it, but Porto Velho does have one of the best **restaurants** in Brazil. Tucked away down an obscure side street on the riverfront, it's impossible to find without a taxi but every taxi driver knows where it is. *A Caravela do Madeira*, Rua Jose Camacho 104, Arigolandia (☎069/221-6641; closed Sun evening), is an amazing place, an enormous wooden construction looming out over a hillside overlooking the Rio Madeira. It would be magical even if the food was dreadful, which it most certainly isn't. It specializes in river fish; try *costeleta de surubim*, which is like a huge meat chop, except that it's fish, or the equally delicious *pirarucu na brasa*. A meal with taxi to and from the centre will set you back around $20 and there's sometimes live music on Saturdays.

Otherwise, the best place for restaurants is the stretch of Avenida Joaquim Nabuco behind the *Hotel Vila Rica*, where there is a cluster of restaurants including, extraordinarily, a genuine Chinese restaurant, *Oriente*, Av. Amazônas 1280 (closed Mon), catering for the Taiwanese gold buyers attracted to the region by the gold rush of the late 1980s. There's also an excellent Arabian restaurant, *Habibe*, Av. Lauro Sodre 1190 (closed Mon). A very pleasant spot, the *Lanchonete Madeira*, overlooking the port side of the railway sheds, serves drinks, snacks and fish meals in a friendly if primitive environment and is popular in the early evenings. Nearby, the floating restaurant *Flutuante Rio Madeira* is a flashy eating barge on the railyard docks. Close to the military complex on the hill above the town, the *Restaurante Mirante II* has a good view over the river and often has live music on Friday evenings. As the night progresses, the *Wau Wau* bar, in the Hotel Vila Rica, generally offers good entertainment.

Listings

Airlines Tavaj, with an office at the airport (☎069/225-2999), covers most of the Western Amazon.

Banks and exchange Banco do Brasil at the corner of José Alencar and Dom Pedro II (*câmbio* upstairs). Cash can also be changed at the *Hotel Floresta* and the *Vila Rica*.

Boat departures The main commercial port is easily located about 1km upstream from the rail yards; you'll have to go there to check out all the possibilities. For Manaus there are frequent boats offering first- and second-class passages for the four-day trip. Even in first class you'll need a hammock for sleeping and some extra food and drink to make the trip more enjoyable and easier on the stomach. The boats at the port generally display their destinations; otherwise it's a matter of asking the crew of each vessel and making a deal with the captain whose itinerary suits you best.

Environmental information For information or permission to enter ecological reserves, contact IBAMA, Av. Jorge Teixeira 3477 (☎069/223-33607).

Post office The main post office is in Avenida Presidente Dutra, just off Sete de Setembro (Mon–Fri 9am–5pm).

Telephones The Teleron office, for international calls, is at the corner of Avenida Rogeiro Weber and Dom Pedro II, uphill slightly from the centre, just behind the main government building (Mon–Fri 9am–6pm).

Around Porto Velho

There are several places where you can get deeper into the forest around Porto Velho. The *Pousada Rancho Grande*, c/o Haarald Schmitz, Fazenda Rancho Grande, Lote 23, Linha C20, Cacaulandia (☎069/535-4301; ④), is a unique lodge run by a German family in the middle of rainforest and plantations. You need to make a reservation in advance, and the *fazenda* is located about 260km south of Porto Velho, about 28km off BR-364. They offer bird-watching, horseriding, jungle walks and a visit to the biggest tin mine in the world at Bom Futuro. Much nearer to Porto Velho, but around the same daily rate, the *Tapiri Selva Hotel* offers jungle lodge accommodation near Lago de Cujubim (☎069/221-4785; phone for transport arrangements).

West from Porto Velho

The backbone of modern Rondônia, the **BR-364** highway links the state more or less from north to south, connecting Porto Velho with Cuiabá, Brasília and the wealthy south coast markets. The state's main towns are strung out along the BR-364, almost all of them – including Porto Velho itself, Ji Paraná and Vilhena at the border with Mato Grosso – marking the points where the road crosses major waterways. It's a fast road, and in the final analysis there's little to stop for anywhere in this direction: you're better off heading straight through to Cuiabá.

Heading **west from Porto Velho** is a very different matter, and soon begins to feel like real pioneering. The further you go, the smaller and wilder the roads, rivers and towns become. The main attractions for the traveller are Rio Branco (see p.382) and the border crossings into Peru, in the state of Acre; and **Guajará-Mirim**, where you can cross into Bolivia or undertake an adventurous visit to the Forte Príncipe da Beira. The BR-364 in this direction has recently been asphalted, although heavy rains still have a habit of washing great sections of it away.

Most of the land beside the road between Porto Velho and Abunã has already been bought up by big companies, and much of the forest has suffered initial clearing and burning. Only rarely does it come closer than two or three kilometres from the road, and in parts it's already been cleared as far as the eye can see. Meanwhile many of the smaller *fazendas* have started actively producing beef cattle and other tropical cash crops. Waterbirds like the *garça real* (an amazing white royal heron) can frequently be spotted from the bus, fishing in the roadside streams and ditches, but the general picture is one of an alarming rate of destruction with columns of wood-smoke rising wherever you look and endless tracts of charred trunks sticking up into the sky like gnarled hands (for further details of the Amazonian environmental crisis, see p.432).

At **ABUNÃ** – some five hours out of Porto Velho – there are often long lines at the ferry which takes vehicles over the wide Rio Madeira into Acre. It's not a particularly pleasant town, caught at the end of a gold rush in which it expanded too fast for its own good, and the river itself is awash with wrecked gold-mining machinery half-sunk on large steel cylinders. Following the road towards Rio Branco, Bolivia lies across the Rio Abunã to your left, but if you want to cross the border, the closest place to do so is Guajará-Mirim to the south. The road there turns off to the east of the ferry crossing at Abunã, following the Rio Mamoré via the small settlement of Taquaras.

Guajará-Mirim and beyond: Bolivia and the Rio Guaporé

GUAJARÁ-MIRIM is easy enough to reach by bus from Porto Velho (6 daily), and once you get there it's a surprisingly sophisticated place with several **hotels**, the best of which are the *Hotel Mini-Estrela*, Av. 15 de Novembro 460 (☎069/541-2399; ③), and *Hotel Lima Palace*, Av. 15 de Novembro 1613 (☎069/541-3421; ③). There are, however, only two reasons you might come here – to get to Bolivia or to head up the Mamoré and Guaporé rivers on a trip probably destined for the Forte Príncipe da Beira.

The valley of the **Rio Guaporé**, around 800km in length, is an obvious destination for an adventurous break from routine town-to-town travelling. Endowed with relatively accessible rainforest, a slow-flowing river and crystal-clear creeks, it is a favourite fishing region with townspeople from Porto Velho. Likely catches include the huge *dourado*, the *tambaqui*, the *pirapitanga* and *tucunaré*. Heading towards the Guaporé, there are amazing rapids on the Rio Mamoré just south of Guajará-Mirim, close to the place where the Rio Pacaás Novas flows in.

If you want a purpose to your river trip, the star-shaped **Forte Príncipe da Beira** is the place to head for. Built in 1773 by pioneering Portuguese colonists, this was an advanced border post designed to mark out Portuguese territory from the Spanish lands across the river in the Bolivian jungle. Underground tunnels and passages lead directly down to the river by the small settlement of Costa Marques. By river, it will take at least three days to reach the fort from Porto Velho: the first day by bus to Guajará-Mirim, then two or three more by boat 150km to the fort itself or 20km further to the town of Costa Marques where there is a hotel, restaurants and even a small airstrip. If you go by bus from Porto Velho you can get there quicker: along the BR-364, just south of Ji Paraná, to Presidente Médici where you have to change buses and roads for the BR-429 to Costa Marques. Another major attraction in the area is the **Reserva Biologica do Guaporé**, a swampy forest home to many birds. Contact IBAMA in Porto Velho before going to this reserve (see p.380).

As for **Bolivia**, if all you want to do is see it, join a sightseeing tour by motor barge from Guajará-Mirim; ask at *Hotel Jamaica*, Av. Leopoldo de Matos 755 (☎069/541-3721). These leave frequently, visiting the main sights, and often stopping at the islands between Guajará-Mirim and Guayaramerin, on the Bolivian side. If you actually want to cross the border it's equally easy to get a boat over the Rio Mamoré to **GUAYARAMERIN**. This is something of a contrast to the Brazilian town – far more of a border outpost, with no roads, though there is a good air-taxi service to La Paz, Cochabamba and Santa Cruz with TAM and Lloyd Aéreo Boliviano. If you intend travelling into Bolivia, get your passport stamped by the Bolivian consul in Guajará-Mirim, Av. Costa Marques 495, and an exit stamp from the Polícia Federal, Av. Presidente Dutra 70 (☎069/541-2437), before crossing the river. If you want to stay in Guayaramerin, try the *Hotel Plaza*, four blocks from the port.

Rio Branco

Crossing from Rondônia into the state of **Acre**, territory annexed from Bolivia during the rubber-boom days in the first years of this century, there's nowhere to stop before you reach the capital at **RIO BRANCO**. The state is a vast frontier forest zone, where it comes as a real surprise to find that Rio Branco is one of Brazil's funkiest cities. It's a small place with little of specific interest to point at, but it's exceptionally lively, with a strong student influence that means plenty of music and events to fill a stay of a few days. Arriving at night (as you usually do) after an eight-hour journey through the desolation of what's left of the jungle between here and Porto Velho, the brightly coloured lights and animated streets can make you wonder if you've really arrived at all, or simply drifted off to sleep. By the light of day Rio Branco doesn't have quite so much obvious charm, but it remains an interesting place full of interesting people.

Much of the reason for all this life is that Rio Branco is a federal **university town**, second only to Belém (and before Manaus) on the student research pecking order for social and biological studies associated with the rainforest and development. Consequently the place has more than its fair share of young people, and of Brazilian

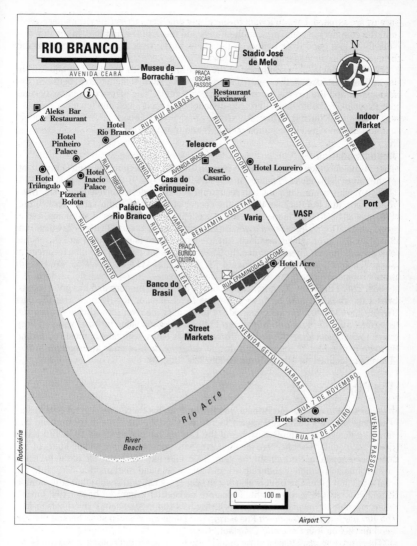

intellectuals. On top of this, the region's burgeoning development means that Rio Branco is also a thriving and very busy market town, pivotally sited on the new road and with an active, if tiny, river port.

Arrival, information and accommodation

Rio Branco is divided in two by the **Rio Acre**, whose old Indian name was Macarinarra, or "River of Arrows", because on it were found the flowering bamboos from which arrows were cut. You'll probably arrive in the south, where both the *Rodoviária* and the airport are situated, but you'll want to spend any time here across the river where you'll find the commercial zone, most of the hotels and much of the nightlife. In the dry season, there is a good river **beach** on the curve in the river – just upstream from the bridges and on the *Rodoviária* side of town.

The **Rodoviária**, 3km southwest of the river in the Cidade Nova, is just about within walking distance of the centre, or take a taxi; note that the area between the *Rodoviária* and the river is considered unsafe at night. The **airport** is not far beyond the *Rodoviária*, though from here you definitely will want a taxi into town.

The regional **tourist office**, Av. Getúlio Vargas 659 (☎068/224-3997), can supply maps of the town and information on hotels and travel in the region.

Accommodation

There is no shortage of **hotels** in Rio Branco, though the better ones aren't cheap. Top of the range is the *Hotel Pinheiro Palace*, Rua Rui Barbosa 91 (☎068/224-7191, fax 224-5726; ⑥), with swimming pool, bar, restaurant and all modern conveniences. The *Hotel Rio Branco*, Rua Rui Barbosa 193, on the corner of Avenida Getúlio Vargas (☎068/224-1785, fax 224-2681; ③), is modern, with excellent service and TVs in all rooms, and is great value. The *Hotel Inácio Palace*, on the same street at no. 82 (☎068/224-6397, fax 224-5726; ⑤), is of similar standard, but the atmosphere is impersonal and the rooms overpriced, though guests can use the *Pinheiro*'s pool. Cheaper but still overpriced is *Hotel Triângulo*, Rua Marechal Peixoto 727 (☎068/224-4117, fax 224-9265; ④), though some rooms overlook the river. The *Hotel Loureiro*, Rua Marechal Deodoro 196 (☎068/224-3110 or 224-9627, fax 224-6806; ③), is central, modern and has good rooms, whilst the cheapest (and dirtiest) in town is *Hotel Acre*, on Rua Jacomé near the port (☎068/224-6341; ①). On the other side of town, over the river towards the *Rodoviária*, the *Hotel Sucessor*, Rua 7 de Novembro 1149 (②), is good value for what you get. Very close to the *Rodoviária*, the *Hotel Uirapuru* (①) is clean, with fans in most rooms and its own pool table. There is also a decent *Albergue de Juventude* at Fronteira Verde, Travessa Natanael de Albuquerque (☎068/225-7128; ②).

The City

If you set out to explore Rio Branco, you'll soon find that there's not a great deal to see. The main square – the large **Praça Plácido de Castro** – has little to recommend it in terms of design, its main feature being the Lion's Club plaque dated 1984. But it is a lively and popular social centre for the town, with concerts, mime and all kinds of live activities happening throughout the year. It's events like these, the life of the bars and restaurants and simply wandering around the streets and markets that constitute the real attraction here. The **port** is also worth seeing – small and shabby, but still an interesting spectacle in its own right. There are no regular organized **boat trips**, but it's often possible to travel on the rivers with traders and in *fazendeiros*' riverboats: ask in the *Bar dos Linguarudos*, down Rua Sergipe and onto the wooden steps behind the covered market on Rua Benjamin Constant.

There are two main tourist attractions in the town. More interesting of the two is the **Museu da Borrachá**, Av. Ceará 1177 (Mon–Fri 7am–5pm; free), essentially an ethno-historical collection focusing on archeological finds, ethnographic items such as feather crafts and basketry, and a range of exhibits dealing with the rubber boom. More relevant to recent history, perhaps, though closed at the time of writing for renovations, is the **Casa do Seringueiro**, Av. Brasil 216 (Tues–Fri 7am–1pm & 2–5pm, Sun 4–7pm), near the corner with Avenida Getúlio Vargas, which houses displays about Chico Mendes and the life and times of rubber tappers in general.

Acre, and in particular Rio Branco, is a strong centre for some of Brazil's fastest-growing **religious cults**. A number of similar cult groups are based in the region, con-

---

ACRE AND THE RUBBER CONFLICT

The relaxed air of Rio Branco masks many tensions, above all to do with population movement – people are still arriving here from the east – and the development of the jungle by small ranchers and multinational companies. When the leader of the rubber tappers' union, **Chico Mendes**, was shot dead by hired gunmen working for the cattle ranchers in 1988, the plight of the forest peoples of Acre came to the attention of the world. The political situation in Acre remains uneasy, with the second- and third-generation tappers and gatherers joining forces with the native population in resisting the enormous economic and armed might of the advancing cattle-based companies. The basic conflict in Acre is fairly simple to understand – on the one side there are people who have lived here for a long time and who know how to manage the forests in a sustainable way; on the other, newcomers who aim to turn the trees into pasture for beef cattle and short-term profit, destroying not only the forest but also many local livelihoods.

---

nected essentially by the fact that they use forest "power plants" – like the hallucinogenic vine *banisteriopsis* – to induce visionary states. Having evolved directly out of native Indian religious practice and belief, these cults are deeply involved in a kind of green nature worship which relates easily to the concept of sustainable forest management. If you want to visit a "Santo Daime" village, contact Acretur (see below) for details. The groups operate in a vaguely underground way, keeping their sanctuaries secret to non-participants. Interestingly, these cults have now spread to the fashionable coastal areas of Brazil where, behind closed doors in São Paulo and Rio de Janeiro, intellectuals participate in visionary ceremonies.

Eating, drinking and nightlife

For **eating out** it is hard to beat the *Restaurant Casarão*, at Av. Brazil 110 (☎068/224-6479; closed Sun lunchtime) by the bottom end of the Praça Plácido de Castro, near the Teleacre office. The food here, though not what it once was (it's now all *comida por kilo*) is still good; and, at weekends, there's live music and the atmosphere is excellent. On just about any evening it's also a good place to meet people – a hangout of students, musicians and poets. The *Hotel Triângulo* has a good *churrasco* restaurant, and *Oscar's*, Rua Franco Ribeiro 73, is also a popular meat-house, but for a broader range of regional dishes, try the *Kaxinawá*, Rua Rui Barbosa on the corner with Avenida Ceará (closed Wed and Sun) – it's also a lively night spot. The *Pizzeria Bolota*, Rua Rui Barbosa 62, is a relatively quiet spot, next to the *Hotel Inácio Palace*. For **street food** you'll find some good, extremely cheap stalls by the outdoor market, near the old bridge at the bottom of Avenida Getúlio Vargas.

There are a couple of typical wooden verandah **bars** overlooking the river and port area, down the alley leading into the main commercial market zone, by the Praça da Bandeira. A great place to meet people in the evening is in the small triangular Praça Oscar Passos which is stuffed with chairs and tables served by a number of small bars. You might also try *Alek's Bar* on Rua Rio Grande do Sul near Rua Marechal Peixoto, which to all appearances is in someone's back garden. As to **clubs**, currently packing them in is *14 Bis* right next to the airport (take a taxi) which has live salsa bands (Thurs to Sat, 7pm to very late).

Listings

Airlines Tavaj, at the airport (☎068/223-2701), covers most of the Western Amazon including Cruzeiro do Sul, São Gabriel do Cachoeira and Tabatinga; Varig, Rua Marechal Deodoro 115 (☎068/224-2226), and at the airport (☎068/224-2719), has daily flights to Brasília, Campo Grande,

Cuiabá, Manaus, Porto Velho, Rio and São Paulo; VASP, Rua Quintino Bocaíuva 105 (☎068/224-6535). A company called Andino (☎068/223-3666) organizes charter flights to Peru for between $120 and $300 (return), and there are half a dozen air-taxi companies based at the airport such as Táxi-Aéreo Rio Branco (☎068/224-1384).

Airport Aeroporto Internacional Presidente Médici (☎068/224-6692).

Banks and exchange The Banco do Brasil, Rua Arlindo P. Leal 85, set back from the Praça Eurico Dutra (Mon–Fri, *câmbio* between 8am and 12.30pm), will change US dollars and travellers' cheques for a $20 commission – arrive early as it takes around two hours; you can also change dollars at the bigger hotels.

Buses Viação Rondônia operates five buses daily to Porto Velho; Empresa Transportes Acreana has several daily services south to Xapuri and the frontier at Brasiléia. Tickets for both companies can be bought at the offices in the *Rodoviária* (☎068/224-1182 or 224-6179) between 9am and 5pm Mon–Sat.

Post office Rua Epaminodas Jácome (Mon–Fri 9am–5pm).

Shopping The street market along Avenida Getúlio Vargas is the best place to shop for almost anything you might need. As well as the usual fruit and vegetables, there's an indoor section for everything from machetes, fishing nets and medicinal herbs to umbrellas and Michael Jackson tapes.

Telephones The Teleacre office is at Av. Brasil 378, near the bottom of Praça Plácido de Castro (daily 6am–10pm).

Travel agents Ocitur, corner of Av. Getúlio Vargas and Rua Rui Barbosa; Acretur, Rua Rui Barbosa 193 (☎068/224-2404), next to the *Hotel Rio Branco*, which offers organized trips to Brazil-nut forest ranges and *seringais* (rubber-tapping zones), starting at about $25 a day.

On to Peru: Brasiléia and Cruzeiro do Sul

There are really only two onward routes from Rio Branco, and both of them end up in Peru. You can either head south to Brasiléia (which is actually on the border with Bolivia) and from there continue to Assis Brasil for the border crossing, or head west to Cruzeiro do Sul and Brazil's westernmost extremity. The Peruvian jungle region of Madre de Dios, where you arrive after crossing the border between Assis Brasil and Inapari is wild territory. Cocaine smuggling on this frontier is on the increase and you should not undertake this route lightly.

Brasiléia and Assis Brasil

The small town of **BRASILÉIA** is six hours by bus from Rio Branco and if you're crossing the border this is where you have to visit the Polícia Federal for your exit (or entry) stamp. The office (daily 8am–5pm) is just to the right of the church as you head from the international border with Bolivia, the bus terminal just to the left. If you have to stay the night, the *Hotel Major*, Rua Salinas 326 (①), is cheap and cheerful. Much better rooms, with air conditioning, are at *Pousada Las Palmeras*, on Avenida G. Assis (☎068/546-3284; ③). You can change money at the Casa Castro, over the river on the road towards Assis Brasil.

It's possible to cross to Bolivia here but there seems little point. The small town of **Cobija** on the other side, once an important rubber-collecting station, has a few expensive hotels and, at present, no onward land transport, though you can fly out, or attempt an adventurous river trip onwards to Riberalta. However, a road link between Cobija and Riberalta and the rest of Bolivia is planned.

ASSIS BRASIL is a further 90km beyond Brasiléia, and the rough road can be slow going by bus. If you can't get across the border the same day – which should be just about possible if you set off early enough from Rio Branco, and the buses connect – you can camp near the river and it's safe to leave your bags at the police station. It's then just a two-kilometre walk across the border to **Inapari** in Peru. The *Hotel Aquino* here is basic (①); or you can camp by the football pitches over the road from the hotel. Trucks leave Inapari most days for Puerto Maldonado, a journey that can take several days even in the dry season (May to September) and can be horrific in the rainy season (November to March). From Puerto Maldonado there are decent road and regular air links with Cuzco and the rest of Peru.

Cruzeiro do Sul

Totally isolated on the western edge of the Brazilian Amazon, **CRUZEIRO DO SUL** is a town of some fifty thousand inhabitants, many of whom, as in Rio Branco, are social science or biology students; many others are involved in cocaine smuggling. The only dependable links with the outside world are by air either to Rio Branco (daily; 2hr) and from there the rest of Brazil, or to Pucallpa, a jungle city in the Peruvian Amazon. The road to Rio Branco is generally only passable between June and October and even then there is no bus service.

There is little obvious attraction to Cruzeiro, though it's possible to make **river trips** to extraordinarily isolated *seringais*: they can be booked through most **hotels** from around $30 a day. The *Hotel Novo Acre* (①) is very good value, and the *Hotel Flor de Maio* (①), overlooking the Rio Ituí, is cheaper still. Of a better standard, *Sandra's Hotel*, Av. Celestino M. Lima 248 (☎068/322-2481; ②), is probably the cleanest in town, and is similar to *Savone Hotel*, Trav. M. Lobão 53 (☎068/322-2349; ②).

But the only reason people come here is to cross from Brazil to Peru or vice versa – and even then this is one of the more obscure border crossings. The quickest way to Peru once you're here is to **fly** direct to Pucallpa – about one hour in a small plane which generally leaves on Tuesdays (check with SASA, Boulevard Taumaturgo 25; or with TASA, Peoreira 84, ☎068/322-3086). There is no bus link between the airport and Cruzeiro town centre some 7km away; taxis cost $6–10. The aggressively adventurous option, only possible in the rainy season between November and March, is to go **by boat**, which takes anything between one and two weeks and involves at least two or three days' walking between the Ucayali and Juruá watersheds. This involves travelling through a remote and relatively dangerous part of the Peruvian jungle, where terrorism and smuggling make tourism rather risky, and is not recommended.

If you've arrived from Peru, you can get up-to-date information about the road to Rio Branco from the land transport group Organização Geral Transportes, Av. Celestino M. Lima 79 (☎068/322-2093). Airlines that operate **flights within Brazil** from Cruzeiro include: VASP, Av. Celestino M. Lima 220 (☎068/322-2106); Taxi Aéreo Vale Jurua, Rua Barbosa 132 (☎068/322-2587); Tavaj, at the airport (☎068/322-2587); and Varig, Av. Celestino M. Lima 90 (☎068/322-2359).

travel details

Buses

Belém to: Brasília (1 daily; 36hr); Marabá (1 daily; 14hr); Salvador (1 daily; 32hr).

Boa Vista to: Bonfim (2 daily; 4hr); Manaus (3 daily; 18hr); Santa Elena (6 daily; 3hr 30min).

Manaus to: Boa Vista (3 daily; 18hr).

Marabá to: Araguaina (several weekly; 13hr); Belém (1 daily; 14hr); Tucurui (several weekly; 6hr).

Porto Velho to: Cuiabá (1 daily; 22hr); Guajará-Mirim (5 daily; 4hr); Rio Branco (5 daily; 8hr); São Paulo (2 daily; 34hr).

Rio Branco to: Brasiléia (3 daily; 6hr); Porto Velho (5 daily; 8hr).

Boats

Belém to: Macapá (several weekly; 1–2 days); Manaus (several weekly; 4–6 days); Santarém (several weekly; 2–3 days).

Macapá to: Belém (several weekly; 1–2 days); Puerto La Cruz, Venezuela (1 daily; 18hr); Oiapoque (1 weekly; 2 days).

Manaus to: Belém (several weekly; 4 days); Caracaraí (irregular; 4–8 days); Humaitá (4 weekly; 3–4 days); Porto Velho (3 weekly; 5 days); Santarém (daily; 2 days); São Gabriel da Cachoeira (weekly; 5–7 days); Tabatinga (several weekly; 5 days plus upstream, 3–4 downstream).

Porto Velho to: Manaus (1 weekly; 3–4 days).

Santarém to: Belém (several weekly; 2–3 days); Macapá (several weekly; 2–3 days); Manaus (1 daily; 2–3 days).

Tabatinga to: Iquitos (several weekly; 3 days); Manaus (several weekly; 4–5 days).

Planes

Belém to: Boa Vista (1 daily; 4hr); Brasília (1 daily; 2hr); Manaus (2 daily; 2hr); Porto Velho (1 daily; 5hr); and daily to all other main Brazilian cities.

Manaus to: Alta Floresta (1 daily; 1hr 30min); Barcelos (3 weekly; 1hr); Belém (2 daily; 2hr); Boa Vista (2 daily; 2hr 30min); Brasília (4 daily; 3hr); Cuiabá (1 daily; 3hr); Porto Velho (1 daily; 2hr); Rio Branco (several weekly; 2hr 30min); Rio de Janeiro (several daily; 3hr 30min); São Gabriel da Cachoeira (1 daily; 3hr); São Paulo (several daily; 3hr 30min); Tabatinga (1 daily; 2hr 30min); Tefé (3 weekly; 1hr).

From **Porto Velho**, **Rio Branco** and **Marabá**, there are daily services to major Brazilian cities. Tavaj Linhas Aéreas covers most towns in the Western Amazon mentioned in this chapter, including a helpful link from Rio Branco to Tabatinga (2 weekly; 2hr).

CHAPTER FIVE

BRASÍLIA, GOIÁS AND TOCANTINS

lmost 1000km from Rio and located in the barren *sertão* of the Goiás highlands – very much in rural, peasant Brazil – **Brasília** is the largest and most interesting of the world's "planned cities". Declared the national capital in 1960, the futuristic city is located in a federal zone of its own – Brasília D.F. (Distrito Federal) – right in the centre of Goiás state. But until the city's construction this was one of Brazil's most isolated regions, and the opening up of communications, coupled with a concerted drive to exploit the hinterland, has led to a process of rapid transformation.

Much of the finance for Brasília, and for the Transamazonian road network which has appeared over the last three or four decades, was borrowed by the Brazilian authorities on a more or less conditional basis – the condition being that they agreed to a massive "development" campaign for the region. Funds and tax incentives were made available to persuade some of the largest national and international companies to take part, and by the late 1960s it suddenly became feasible (because of the new roads) and economically viable (because of the favourable bureaucratic assistance from Brasília) to drop bulldozers by helicopter into the interior. The bulldozers felled trees around the edge of a clearing until the perimeter met the path of another incoming bulldozer. In this way, **forest clearance** on a gigantic scale led, in a matter of years, to the creation of enormous pasturelands for beef cattle, mostly for the European and American fast-food markets. One of the worst aspects of this kind of development was that – technically – the tax relief was only available to companies who were utilizing at least half of the land they had claimed. This sounds reasonable until you realize that all that the companies were expected to do was to clear half the land by felling the trees and burning off the stubble. For many of the largest companies, forest involvement was little more than a financial game, the cost of which was the extermination of huge tracts of the world's remaining virgin forest. Although **cattle ranching** is still one of the leading industries in the region, there are signs that this particular type of "development" is slowing down: the tax advantages are now much less, and, on top of that, most of the best and easily accessible land has already been claimed and at least partly cleared.

Brasília's only real attraction – but reason enough to stop – is its unique **city architecture**. The futuristic forms of the National Theatre, cathedral and Congress buildings are a sight you'll never forget: cold, concrete and utterly compelling. There are parks and the large man-made **Lago Paranoá** close to the city and, within day-trip distance, there's the small rural town of **Cristalina** where crystals and semi-precious stones are more common than bread. When it's time to move on, Brasília is surrounded by rivers, hills and well-farmed countryside. It's also well connected by long, but good-quality, **roads** to the rest of the country – to the Mato Grosso to the west, to Belém and the Northeast, to Rio, São Paulo and the South and, more recently, to Rondônia and Acre in the Western Amazon.

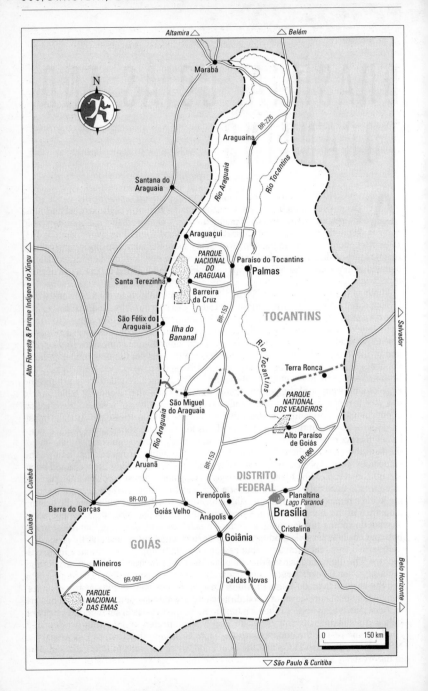

At the heart of Brazil **the states of Goiás and Tocantins** give birth to the mighty Araguaia and Tocantins rivers which divide the Amazon basin and much of the Mato Grosso from the more populated areas around Rio, Minas Gerais and the Northeast. It's a huge, wild area, largely off the beaten tourist track. The state of Goiás itself remained largely unexplored until this century. Much of the northern half was composed of relatively virgin forest, a haven for previously unknown Indian tribes. Today, long bus-rides take you into the scenic **Chapada dos Veadeiros** national park and, in Tocantins, to the world's largest river island, the **Ilha do Bananal**. Goiás is just beginning to open up to eco-tourism with a tenuous but fresh infrastructure based on the extensive *sertão* wilderness areas and the historic towns of **Pirenópolis** and **Goiás Velho**. In the south, **Goiânia**, another planned city, is the state – as opposed to the national – capital.

BRASÍLIA

The idea of a **Brazilian inland capital** was first mooted in 1789, and a century later (in 1891) the concept was written into Article 3 of the Republic's Constitution, which stated "from now on an area of 14,400 square kilometres will belong to the government for the creation of a new capital." Many sites were considered; indeed, in 1913 US President Theodore Roosevelt visited the western edge of the *planalto* and remarked that "any sound northern race could live here; and in such a land, with such a climate, there would be much joy of living." But the idea had to wait for fulfilment until 1956 when **Juscelino Kubitschek** became president, on the promise that he would build the city if he won the election. He had to get it finished by the end of his term of office, so work soon began in earnest.

The site was quickly selected by aerial surveys of over 50,000 square kilometres of land. In less than four years a capital city had to be planned, financed and built in the face of apparently insurmountable odds: the building site was 125km from the nearest rail line, 190km from the nearest airport, over 600km from the nearest paved road; the closest timber supply was 1200km distant, the nearest source of good steel even further. Still, in **Oscar Niemeyer**, the city's architect, Brasília had South America's most able student of Le Corbusier, founder of the modern planned city and a brilliant designer of buildings. Alongside Niemeyer, who was contracted to design the buildings, **Lúcio Costa** was hired for the awesome task of Brasília's urban planning.

Design and construction

Costa produced a **city plan** described variously as being in the shape of a bow and arrow, a bird in flight or an aeroplane. Certainly, on maps or from the air, Brasília appears to be soaring, wings outstretched, towards the eastern Atlantic coast. The main public buildings, government ministries, palace of justice and presidential palace, line the "fuselage", a five-mile-long dusty and windswept grass mall known as the **Eixo Monumental** (Monumental Axis). The main residential districts wing out to the north and south, in the arc of the bow, while the commercial areas are clustered where the wings join the fuselage (or the bow and arrow meet).

Money for the **construction** came from all over the world in the form of grants and loans, and from the printing of more paper money, a move which didn't do the Brazilian inflation rate much good. The whole operation was incredibly expensive, not least because everything – workers, food, cement etc – had to be flown in, as work started long before the first access roads appeared. At the time of construction, and even after inauguration, many considered the whole scheme to be a complete waste of time and money: Rio's *Correio da Manhã* newspaper coined the phrase "The Limit of Insanity".

Nevertheless, exactly three years, one month and five days after the master plan was unveiled, 150,000 people arrived in Brasília for the official **inauguration**, in April

1960. It must have been a hectic time. There were only 150 first-class hotel rooms completed (for 5000 visiting dignitaries), but the celebrations went ahead, topped by a spectacular 38-tonne firework display.

When the smoke cleared in the morning it was apparent to everyone that, despite the finished government complexes, 94 apartment buildings, around 500 one- and two-storey houses plus their local schools and shops, there were still years of work left to do. Road junctions were not the super-slick lane mergers that had been promised, pedestrians and apartments still had to be separated from traffic, and the accommodation units had none of their intended leafy surroundings – the flats supposedly close enough to the ground for a mother to call her child. Indeed, thirty years on, user-friendly touches such as these are only obvious in the more established suburbs.

The costs: financial and environmental

On the face of it at least, Kubitschek had lived up to his electoral campaign promise of fifty years' progress in five. What he hadn't made clear before, though, was just how much it would cost Brazil. When Kubitschek stood down in 1960, his successor, **Janio Quadros**, broadcast an important message to the nation, saying "All this money, spent with so much publicity, we must now raise – bitterly, patiently, dollar by dollar, *cruzeiro* by *cruzeiro*." With outstanding foreign loans of two billion dollars, to many the city seemed an antisocial waste of resources, while for most economists, it was responsible for Brazil's hyper-inflationary spiral.

The costs were obviously very high, but they did also include the construction of two new **major highways** – one connecting Brasília with Belém, on the mouth of the Amazon, the other connecting the city (and therefore the Atlantic coast) with the first ever **transcontinental** road. This might not have been particularly well constructed at its western edges, but – in good weather – it now became more or less possible to drive from Brasília across the southern Amazon and on to the Pacific Ocean, via Peru and the Andes. Ever since the 1960s, these roads have been quietly revolutionizing the interior, though their success – like Brasília's – has been patently double-edged: with the burgeoning of the new "Green" consciousness, the roads' contribution to the disappearance of huge chunks of tropical rainforest can no longer be seen as development. These days even Andreazza (Minister of Transport in the early 1970s) admits that the large cattle ranches in the forest were a "serious mistake".

The City

Imagine what it would be like touching down on another planet, and you'll have some idea of what confronts you when you first arrive in **BRASÍLIA**: there is a clinical, science-fiction logic at work in the city. Other visitors have had less kind things to say about the city. Simone de Beauvoir, visiting in 1963 with Jean-Paul Sartre in tow, described the place as "elegant monotony", while the Royal Institute of British Architects poked fun by renaming Brasília "The Moon's Backside".

The city was intended for a population of half a million by the year 2000. However, there are already almost two million people living in and around Brasília and within twenty years this could easily double again. There are also substantial and rapidly growing shanty towns – which are euphemistically named "pioneer settlements" – ringing the ultramodern city. Most of the people who live here do so for economic reasons. A large service sector followed the bureaucrats and businessmen into the new city and, behind that, a whole trail of retailers and smaller merchants arrived to compete for the new markets.

Brasília's good points are all fairly obvious **architectural** ones, but there are other attractions, too. Magnificent sunsets send a golden glow over the twin concrete towers of the National Congress building; pleasant parks, popular for weekend picnics, encircle the entire city; and in the downtown zone, by the central bus station, the lively atmosphere revolves around a busy mess of people and trade. Brasília's design also has a **mystic** side to it. On Brazilian Republic Day – April 21 – the sun rises through the concrete "H" shape of the parallel twin towers which poke out of the National Congress building, provoking images of a futuristic Stonehenge. Other curious theories associate modern Brasília with the stars, with the lost city of Atlantis and with ancient Egypt's pyramids and temples. The aerial view of the city, the winged bird shape, is vaguely reminiscent of the mystical Egyptian ibis bird, and the cemetery is laid out in the shape of a spiral – life's symbol and essential pattern.

Brasília can be as alienating as any city and, unlike most other Brazilian cities, people here seldom stop or smile to acknowledge a fellow human being. Moreover, on some very basic points, Brasília has certainly failed as a planned city. Thirty years on, few people have got anything good to say about it as a real live city – no one would dream of comparing it to Paris, London or Rio for nightlife and entertainment. Many officials arrive for work on Monday and leave for home on Thursday because they find the city either too oppressive or just plain boring at the weekend. At the most basic level, there's a devastating lack of street-corner bars and ad hoc market places, things which provide a major social hub elsewhere in Brazil. Despite this, there is a substantial middle class living and working happily in Brasília, mostly based around the university and the civil service.

> The **telephone code** for Brasília is ☎061.

Growth and development

Part of the problem is that the **city plans** were too simplistic and out of date. Based on Le Corbusier's original theories, which equated urban progress with geometrical order, rectilinear planning and a mechanized, bureaucratic organization, Costa failed to make long-term provision for future growth of the entire Federal District. The most fundamental short-sightedness of the city plan is Brasília's total domination by the **road traffic** system, and to the traveller walking the footways, this is the obvious gripe against the city. To be fair though, at the very centre of the city, Costa had imagined an area resembling the streets and squares of Venice – smaller in scale but giving colour to the centre of the Eixo Monumental. The political reality for Kubitschek, however, was to deal with the large, costly parts of the plan first – so the area soon became dissected and taken over by large roads, in direct contradiction to the master plan.

In a similar way, the area to the south of Lake Paranoá has developed in a haphazard manner. The north side, originally planned as a series of parks and public places, is occupied by private clubs belonging to the elite, which effectively cuts the rest of the city off from the lake. Temples of a fast-developing nation, the two ultra-modern banks – Banco Central and Banco do Brasil – dominate the downtown landscape with their huge dark glass presence. Meanwhile, in spite of incipient crime, growing slums, water shortages, transportation problems and lack of entertainment, the city continues to grow faster than anyone ever imagined.

Orientation, arrival and information

Although initially quite confusing, Brasília is laid out with geometric precision. Unlike most cities, it has no true heart or centre. Instead, it is neatly divided into sectors: there are residential sectors – each with their own shopping and other facilities – hotel sectors, embassy sectors and banking and commercial sectors. Roads are numbered, rather than named, with digits representing their position and distance north or south of the **Eixo Monumental**, and east or west of the other main axis, the **Eixo Rodoviário**. The different sectors are given acronyms, most fairly easy to work out – see the box on "Addresses".

The central *Rodoviária*, the urban bus station, is the main hub of movement within Brasília, with the Eixo Monumental passing around it and the Eixo Rodoviário crossing over the top of it. Up above the *Rodoviária*, on a level with the Eixo Rodoviário and the main commercial blocks, you can see at a glance the main areas of interest to the visitor. Looking east, towards the main government buildings which resemble great green dominoes, is the unmistakable Aztec form of the **Teatro Nacional**, recently renovated, and the conical crown of the **Cathedral** a little further away to the right: both are within easy walking distance. Slightly further away, but still within a half-hour's stroll, are the strange bowls and towers of the **Congresso Nacional** buildings. Immediately on either side of the *Rodoviária* there are two separate shopping centres, the **Conjuntos de Diversões**, one to the north, another to the south. Twenty years ago these vast concrete boxes were overshadowed only by the TV Tower, but nowadays the modern towers of the nearby **Setors Hoteleiros** dominate the scene, together with the bank buildings on either side of the Eixo Monumental to the east.

Arrival

The **airport** is 12km south of the centre, and bus #102 runs every hour from there into Brasília, dropping you at the downtown *Rodoviária*. *Lotação* minibuses run more frequently. Inter-city and long-distance buses use the **Rodoferroviária**, the bus and

ADDRESSES IN BRASÍLIA

Most people in Brasília live in *superquadras* – massive apartment complexes, some of which you can see coming in along the Eixo Rodoviário Sul from the airport. Finding out where someone lives or works can seem impossible from the **address**, but there is an almost perfect internal logic to the system. For example, the address

SQN 208
Bloco H – 304
70000 Brasília DF

means *superquadra* north no. 208, building H, apartment 304. The three-digit *superquadra* number here (208) gives the location: the first digit represents the position east or west of the Eixo Rodoviário, with odd numbers to the west, evens to the east, increasing the further away from the centre you get. The last two digits represent the distance north or south of the Eixo Monumental in streets, so that, for example, SQN 208 is five streets north from SQN 203, SQS 208 five south from SQS 203. Unfortunately, addresses are rarely written out in full: you'll have to watch out for "Q" (*quadra*, and often used for *superquadra*, too), "L", "lj" or "lt" (*loja* or *lote*, meaning "lot" or "shop", used for commercial addresses), "B" or "bl" (*bloco*) and "cj" (*conjunto* meaning "compound"). The other terms you are most likely to come across are:

Asa Norte/Asa Sul General terms for the two "wings" (*asas*) of the city, comprising the avenues Eixo Rodoviário Norte and Eixo Rodoviário Sul, and the roads running off and parallel to them (the latter lettered "W" to the west, and "L" to the east, eg Avenida W-2 Norte, Avenida L-3 Sul).

SBN/SBS Setor Bancário Norte/Sul. The two banking sectors either side of the Eixo Monumental.

SDN/SDS Setor de Diversões Norte/Sul. The two shopping centres (*conjuntos*) either side of Eixo Monumental.

SEN/SES Setor de Embaixadas Norte/Sul. The embassy sectors, east of the bank sectors.

SHN/SHS Setor Hoteleiro Norte/Sul. The hotel sectors either side of the Eixo Monumental, west of the *Rodoviária*.

SCN/SCS Setor Comercial Norte/Sul. The two commercial office block areas, set back from the Conjuntos de Diversões shopping centres. Often confused with CLN/CLS (see below).

SQN/SQS or SHCN/SHCS Superquadras Norte/Sul. The individual *superquadras* in the main residential wings, Asa Norte and Asa Sul.

CLN/CLS or SCLN/SCLS (Setor) Comércio Local Norte/Sul. These terms describe the shopping blocks which are interspersed throughout the residential *superquadras* which comprise Asa Norte and Asa Sul. Their numbering follows that of the *superquadras*, so that CLN 208 is near SQN 208.

SHIN/SHIS Setor de Habitações Individuais Norte/Sul. The two peninsulas that jut into Lago Paranoá, the northern one accessible from the end of Eixo Rodoviário Norte, the southern one, also called Lago Sul, connected by bridges from Avenida das Nações.

former train station at the far western end of the Eixo Monumental (☎233-7200). From here, the #131 bus covers the 5km of the Eixo Monumental to the downtown *Rodoviária*, passing the famous statue of Juscelino Kubitschek. Once at the downtown *Rodoviária*, go up the escalators to the second level for the shopping centres and upper roads, from where you can see most of central Brasília.

Information

Tourist information is hard to access in Brasília. Apart from city tours, it's either a matter of getting leaflets from the main hotels such as the *Nacional* or buying a map or booklet (when they have them) from the *Pause* bookshop, Galeria Hotel Nacional 59, just a few doors from the hotel. The state tourist office, SETUR, at the unusual and futuristic Centro de Convenções Dr Ulisses Guimarães, Eixo Monumental (☎321-3318), may just about be able to help you if you have a special request, but they're short on brochures and more mundane information. The numerous travel agents and airline offices in the gallery around the base of the *Hotel Nacional* may also have some information, but are more geared to selling long-haul air tickets, and have more details on Rome, New York and London than they do on Brasília.

Getting around

By dividing the city into a few geographically distinct zones – essentially the head, heart and tail of the design – it is not difficult to see most of Brasília's sights **on foot** in one or two days, though it can't be stressed too highly that it gets extremely tiring wandering around the open city in the heat of the day. There are two or three **city bus routes**, instead, which can save you a lot of shoe-leather. Details of these are given in the text, and there are two **circular bus routes** which are very handy for a cheap overview of the city: buses #105 and #106 leave from and return to the downtown *Rodoviária* (☎223-0557) after a long outer city tour; just try to avoid these routes between 4pm and 6pm on weekdays when the buses are particularly crowded. It's also a good idea to keep a watchful eye out for pickpockets when standing in line for the buses, though, once on the bus, you should be all right.

The city has a good **taxi** service, which costs a minimum of $2 even for the shortest ride. Flag a taxi down when you want one, or pick one up at the many ranks throughout the city. Most people, if they can, drive their own cars, and if you want to join them, see p.404 for addresses of **car rental** firms; it'll cost you from $70 a day, much less if you rent over a longer period.

City tours

For some people, one day is enough in Brasília, and if you want someone else to take care of things then the expensive but reliable **city tours** might be the thing for you. Most hotels in Brasília are keen to offer city tours to their guests. These are centrally organized, with the hotels usually taking a percentage of the fee for themselves. It's worth shopping around – the *Hotel El Pilar* can be up to 25 percent cheaper than the *Hotel Nacional* – or you can book direct with the tour organizers, Power Turismo, Galeria Hotel Nacional 48 (☎332-6699). Tours range from a variety of three-hour programmes (around $60) covering commercial, banking and residential sectors as well as prominent buildings, to the night-time tour ($70–90) which ends with an evening meal. While not necessarily the best time to see most of the sights, the evening tour does give you the chance to experience the city by neon. In many ways Brasília seems easier to comprehend in the light-studded darkness when the wide open spaces melt away.

Accommodation

Brasília is not one of the most hospitable of Brazilian cities. The urban and alienating atmosphere is made worse by the fact that inexpensive accommodation is very difficult to find. The **central sectors** are geared to cater for expense accounts, offering only top- or middle-range beds from $40 (rare) to $200 per person per night. For cheaper accommodation and more of a small-town, less alienating environment, the only viable option is to stay in the satellite settlement of **Núcleo Bandeirante**, a few kilometres south

ACCOMMODATION PRICE CODES

In this guide, accommodation has been categorized according to the price codes outlined below, based on US$. These categories represent the minimum you can expect to pay for a **double room in high season** – though note that many of the budget places will also have more expensive rooms. Rates for hostels and basic hotels where guests are charged **per person** are given in US$, instead of being indicated by price code. See p.31 for further information.

① under $20	③ $30–45	⑤ $60–80	⑦ $120–175
② $20–30	④ $45–60	⑥ $80–120	⑧ $175 and over

near the zoo and the airport (which means frequent low-flying planes – bring earplugs if you're a light sleeper). Once the base for construction workers building Brasília, and so actually the city's oldest district, Núcleo Bandeirante was originally known as *Cidade Livre* (Free City) because, unlike Brasília itself, it wasn't split up into sectors and it was possible to build more or less where you liked. This zone is well connected by buses (#160 to and from the downtown *Rodoviária*, #159 to and from the *Rodoferroviária*) and by *lotaçao* minibuses (#82 to and from the *Rodoferroviária*), which take around 15 to 25 minutes to enter the heart of Brasília (traffic permitting).

The central sectors

All Brasília's central hotels, even the poshest, offer discounts at weekends and at other times when they're not too busy (25–30 percent is normal), though you do sometimes have to ask for them.

Hotel das Américas, SHS 04, Bloco D (☎321-3355). Comfortable and modern, with an excellent restaurant, but overpriced if you don't get a discount. ⑦.

Bristol Hotel, SHS 04, Bloco F (☎321-6162). Luxurious and with a rooftop swimming pool, this is a good-value hotel without being top of the range. ⑦.

Byblos Hotel, SHN 03, Bloco E (☎223-1570, fax 322-4208). Unlike most of the hotels in SHS and SHN, this one is low-rise. Clean and spartan, but its rooms aren't as nice as the *Casablanca*'s and are more expensive to boot. ⑥.

Hotel Casablanca, SHN 03, Bloco A (☎321-8586, fax 224-8273). Close to the Eixo Monumental and within sight of the TV Tower, a small and friendly hotel in the style and colour that its name suggests, with excellent rooms and a nice restaurant. Good value at the lower end of this price bracket. ⑥.

Hotel El Pilar, SHN 03, Bloco F (☎224-5915). The cheapest hotel in downtown Brasília, in a low-rise building, but slightly run-down and with indifferent service. The cheaper rooms are without views, TVs or fridge-bars, which makes you wonder what they do with your money. ⑤.

Kubitschek Plaza, SHN 02, Bloco E (☎316-3333, fax 321-9365). Currently the best 5-star hotel, in a strange blend of Space Age and ancient Egyptian styles. Everything you'd expect at this price – plus free medical insurance throughout your stay. ⑧.

Manhattan Flat, SHN 02, Bloco A (☎319-3060, fax 321-5683). Less extravagant than its stable-mate the *Kubitschek Plaza*, but still extremely smart, attracting a slightly younger clientele. ⑦.

Metropolitan Flat, SHN 02, Bloco H (☎323-3030, fax 323-6141). A quarry died for the marble floors and walls in here, but the effect, though plush, is soulless and bare. Bizarre modern art hangs in the bedrooms, presumably designed to distract you from the cost. Comes complete with shopping centre, steam bath and whirlpool. ⑧.

Hotel Nacional, SHS 01, Bloco A (☎321-7575, fax 223-9213). The oldest of the big hotels, and still brimming over with well-to-do business people. Well run and marginally more central than most other places. Bargaining possible. ⑧.

Núcleo Bandeirante

Hotel Europa, Av. Central 410 (☎552-4831). Basic but adequate, and cheaper than most in Núcleo Bandeirante, with lighter rooms, too. Forget the *Hotel Líder* next door, which is squalid. ②.

Hotel Portugal, Av. Central 380 (☎552-0033). The best rooms in Núcleo Bandeirante, but also the most expensive. Try to get a room with a window to the street. No breakfast. ③.

St Moritz Hotel, Av. Central 460 (☎552-1039). Large and largely empty rooms, but friendlier than the others on this street. ②.

Hotel Valadares, Av. Central 336 (☎552-0338). Best value for a double room in Núcleo Bandeirante, but singles cost the same, and it's not the cheeriest of places. ②.

Camping

Camping de Brasília, Setor Áreas Isoladas Norte, behind the Palácio Buriti and Kubitschek Monument. The most central of the campsites and the cheapest place in the city, at under $2 a day, but keep your valuables in a locker; take the #109 bus from the downtown *Rodoviária*.

Bela Vista, 46km out of town on Estrada da Ponte Alta/Estrada da Marila (☎226-2663). A good site which more or less lives up to its name.

Downtown

Brasília's overriding attraction is the bizarre environment produced by its stunning **architecture**. The blue sky which normally hangs over the city contrasts well with the modern buildings and the deep red, dusty earth of the *planalto*. There are no exceptional museums or historical sites; it's the city itself that's on show, which – in many ways – is less than satisfying since, unlike other Brazilian cities, there is little human contact to be made.

It's a very strange place to tour around. To some, it appeals as a futuristic metropolis, to others it seems like an open-air prison, but perhaps the most apt comparison is with a gigantic *Rodoviária*, a great concrete complex dominated by road systems. Class and race barriers do exist here, though the most obvious dividing line in Brasília is the question of **car** ownership, which confers status and power. If you haven't got a car, you're part of the underclass. The open spaces are vast and daunting, and traditionally no one walks if they can help it, but on foot you can get a closer, more intimate look at the city.

Below, the main sights in downtown Brasília are divided into three basic sections, following the head, body and tail concept of the bird or aeroplane that the city resembles; the outlying areas of the city are dealt with afterwards.

The Power Complex

Separated from the commercial centres and the downtown *Rodoviária* by the esplanade of ministry buildings, the area known as the **Power Complex** comprises the Congresso Nacional, Palácio da Justiça, Palácio Itamarati, Palácio Planalto, Museu Histórico and the Supremo Tribunal. All of these places are within a few minutes' walk of each other, entrance is free and they can be seen in half a day, though you can easily spend more time than this exploring if you get sidetracked.

At the centre of the complex is the **Praça dos Três Poderes** (Square of Three Powers), representing the forces emanating from the Congress, the judiciary and the Foreign Office. The **Congresso Nacional** (Mon–Fri 9am–6.30pm, sometimes only to 10.30am; ☎311-4141 for information on entry times to the Senate, ☎318-5151 for information on entry times to the House of Representatives) is the heart of legislative power and one of the most obvious landmarks in Brasília – in a way, everything else flows from here. If you accept the analogy of the city built as a bird, then the National Congress is the beak of the beast, something it clearly resembles with its twin 28-storey towers. The two hemispheres, one on either side of the towers, house the Senate Chamber (the smaller, inverted one) and the House of Deputies. They were designed

so that the public could climb and play on them, but no more: the only people allowed to play there now are the patrolling soldiers of the Polícia Militar. Still, the egalitarian principle survives elsewhere: the Congresso Nacional permits visitors to attend debates when in session, something you might want to enquire about.

The **Palácio da Justiça** (Mon–Fri noon–6pm) is beside the Congress building, on the northern side of the Esplanada dos Ministerios. Created in 1960 with a concrete facade by the socialist architect Niemeyer (who eventually won the Lenin Peace Prize for his overall work), the building was covered with fancy – and, to many, elitist – marble tiles by the military government during the dictatorship. Now that democracy rules once again, the tiles have been removed, laying bare the concrete, artificial waterfalls flowing between the pillars. On the southern side of the Congress building stands the **Palácio Itamarati** (Mon–Fri; ☎211-6161 for permission to visit), the vast Foreign Office structure. Combining modern and classical styles, it's built around elegant courtyards, sculptures and gardens. Outside, the marble *Meteor* sculpture by Bruno Giorgi is a stunning piece of work, its five parts representing the five continents, the water underneath symbolic of the divinity. There are also some fascinating water gardens here and, inside, a good art collection of Brazilian and other works.

Behind the Congresso Nacional, on the northern side, the **Palácio do Planalto** (Sun 8am–2pm; ☎211-1221) houses the president's office. This has been closed to visitors recently, but there's usually a changing of the guard out front at 8.30am and 5.30pm daily. Nearby in Praça dos Três Poderes, the **Museu Histórico de Brasília** (Mon–Sat 9am–1pm & 2–5pm) is of limited interest to most, telling the tale of the transfer of the capital from the coast to the central *planalto*. The **Supremo Tribunal**

Federal (Mon–Fri 1–7pm) – the Supreme Court – is open to the public, although entrance is with formal dress only (ie no shorts and T-shirts); outside there's a concrete monument to Justice.

From here, you can take a **bus** to the downtown *Rodoviária*, or it's a twenty-minute walk west through the esplanade of ministry buildings to the cathedral and downtown commercial centre.

The cathedral and the commercial sectors

Between the Power Complex and the downtown *Rodoviária*, and within walking distance of either, lies the **Catedral Metropolitana Nossa Senhora Aparecida**, one of Brasília's most striking edifices (daily 7am–6.30pm; visitors requested not to wear shorts). It marks the spot where the city of Brasília was inaugurated in 1960 and is built in the form of an inverted chalice and crown of thorns; its sunken nave means that most of the interior floor is below ground level. Outside, a moat surrounds the incredible stained-glass domed roof. Some of the glass roof panels in the interior reflect rippling water from outside, adding to the sense of airiness in the cathedral, while the statues of St Peter and the angels suspended from the ceiling (the inspired gravity-defying creation of Ceschiatti) help to highlight the feeling of elevation. Nevertheless, although some 40m in height and with a capacity of 2000, the cathedral is surprisingly small inside.

Around ten minutes' walk away, closer to the shopping centres and *Rodoviária* on the northern side of the Eixo Monumental, is the **Teatro Nacional**. Built in the form of an Aztec temple, it's a marvellous, largely glass-covered pyramid set at an angle to let light into the lobby, where there are often good art exhibitions with futuristic and environmental themes. Inside are three completed halls: the Martins Pena, the Villa-Lobos (the largest, seating 1200) and the much smaller Alberto Nepomuceno. Unfortunately, the theatre can only be of limited interest to foreigners, since most productions are in Portuguese.

The two shopping centres, the **Conjuntos de Diversões**, one on either side of the downtown *Rodoviária*, provide proof that human life does exist in Brasília, and together are the closest the city gets to having a heart. Both stand three storeys high, crammed with all kinds of shops and eating places. Contained in a huge concrete block that's covered with massive product advertisements, the **northern conjunto** is much more upmarket than its neighbour across the way, essentially a modern indoor shopping centre, always very busy and generally entertaining. The flashy jewellery and furniture shops combine with restaurants and fast food outlets, and unlike the modern shopping centres in other Latin American cities, the *conjuntos* are not just a playground for the rich; everyone seems to frequent the place. The **southern conjunto**, reached by following the pavement over the top of the *Rodoviária*, is rather down at heel in appearance, but has dozens of specialist bookshops, a theatre and drama school, and boasts an excellent vegetarian restaurant and New Age shop – *Cheiro Verde* – with great views from its terrace, overlooking the cathedral. Stuck underground between the two giant shopping blocks, the downtown *Rodoviária* is also on three levels, and here you'll find more shops, toilets, snack bars and a bus information office.

The TV Tower, Kubitschek Memorial and Parque Rogério Pithon Farias

The tail end of Brasília's layout provides less gripping an attraction, though there are several places you'll want to visit on any extended stay in the city. The **TV Tower**, at Eixo Monumental, Setor Oeste, is an obvious city landmark and easily reached on foot or by bus (the #131 from the *Rodoviária*). The 218-metre-high tower's viewing platform (Mon 2–9pm, Tues–Sun 9am–9pm; free) is a great place from which to get Brasília into perspective. Lower down, above its weird concrete supports, is the **Museu Nacional**

da Gemas (Tues–Fri 3–8.30pm, Sat & Sun 10.30am–6.30pm; $1), which is actually little more than a glorified and quite expensive gem shop. At the weekend, the tower is also popular for its **craft market**, held around the base.

If you're so inclined, the **Planetarium**, on Eixo Monumental at the side of the Centro de Convenções, is a relatively short walk from the TV Tower, but it's only open on Saturdays and Sundays, at 4.20pm for children ($1) and 5.20pm for adults ($2); weekdays are reserved for school groups. Also close to the convention centre, but on the western side, is the famous **Juscelino Kubitschek (JK) Memorial** (daily 9am–6pm; small entrance fee), the statue standing inside an enormous question mark. More interesting than the monument itself is the **museum** below, covering both the history of Brasília and Kubitschek's life, with some fascinating photographs and documentary records. A little stroll to the north of Eixo Monumental from the JK Monument brings you to the **Palácio do Buriti**, administrative seat of the Federal District, set in its own little square with pretty illuminated fountains.

Finally, if you're tired of contending with so much concrete and traffic, you might appreciate the city park, **Parque Rogério Pithon Farias**, south of the TV Tower. There's a heated public swimming pool, a boating lake, snack bar and woods. You can get there on bus #152 from the *Rodoviária*, or from the JK Memorial by walking back towards the *Rodoviária* – it's signposted on the right 300–400m to the east. From the entrance it's a good two-kilometre walk through a relatively barren section of the park to the main recreation zone.

The rest of the city

Beyond the central sights, there's little to Brasília that warrants a longer stay, though there are some low-key city destinations that can fill in the time. Most are dotted along Asa Sul and Lago Sul pensinsula, with the exception of a couple of decent museums. The **Museu de Arte de Brasília** (Tues–Sun 2–6pm), which lies east of the Power Complex near the lake, between the Concha Acústica and the presidential residence, Palácio da Alvorada (bus #104 or taxi, $5 return, from the *Rodoviária*), has a collection of modern Brazilian art from 1970 to the present day. In Asa Norte (take an L-2 Norte bus), the **Museu Etnográfico**, Av. L-2 Norte 609, Bloco D (Mon–Fri 8am–noon & 2–6pm), contains some excellent archeological, prehistoric and ethnographic exhibits.

On the south side of the city, the nearest sight to the Eixo Monumental is the mock-Gothic **Santuário Dom Bosco**, Av. W-3 Sul 702 (Mon–Fri 8am–noon & 2–5pm, Sat 8am–noon), named after an Italian priest who, in 1833, had a dream that "between the 15th and 20th parallels, where a lake had formed, a great civilization will be born". It would be churlish not to accept that Brasília fulfils the prophecy and the Sanctuary, glass-based and blue-tinted, is a suitably modern affair. The crucifix standing above the main altar is over 7m tall and carved from one piece of wood. Fifteen minutes walk south from here is the very first building inaugurated in Brasília; built by Oscar Niemeyer and looking like a cross between a nun's wimple and a marquee, the **Igreja Nossa Senhora de Fátima** (or *Igrejinha)* lies between *superquadras* 307 and 308, in front of commercial sectors 107 and 108. Buses marked "W3-Sul" will take you to within walking distance.

Much further south is the city's most visited building, the **Templo da Boa Vontade**, SGAS 915, Lotes 75/76 (open 24hr daily), an unusual seven-sided pyramid-shaped building, looking rather like a giant concrete tepee. Inaugurated in 1989 by the Legion of Goodwill, this "temple of goodwill" is meant to be a monument to universal solidarity with its architectural features linked to the number of perfection, 7. Covering over 2000 square metres, it rises to a height of 21m with the world's largest crystal, from Cristalina, at its pinnacle. Inside there's an unusual spiral pavement and a Silence Room on the lower floor, designed as a meditative space.

Over on the Lago Sul peninsula in the sprawling new residential district, SHIS (take the "Lago Sul" bus from the *Rodoviária*), you'll find the lively **Centro Comercial Gilberto Salomão**. Particularly active in the evenings, this offers a range of nightclubs, beer gardens and restaurants – and the world's oldest three-in-one (270-degree panorama) screen cinema. Created in 1985, the **Jardim Botânico**, Setor de Mansões Dom Bosco, Cj. 12, Lago Sul (Tues–Sun 8.30am–5pm), isn't really the world leader that it claims to be, but it is a calm and well-organized retreat nonetheless and gives you the chance to experience the flora and fauna of the *sertão* at first hand. There's an information centre, a large display of medicinal plants of the region, ecological trails and over forty square kilometres of nature reserve right on the edge of the city. It's a long way out of town, too far to walk, but only about fifteen minutes on bus #147 from the downtown *Rodoviária*. The entrance is by Quadra 1, 23, to the side of the Escola Fazendeira.

Eating, drinking and nightlife

The wide variety of **bars and restaurants** is one of the best things about Brasília, though prices are comparatively steep for Brazil. Cheaper eats can be found in the street markets and stalls scattered around the *Rodoviária*; in a number of self-service canteens inside the two *Conjuntos de Diversões*; and all over Núcleo Bandeirante, which has the widest choice. The problem, of course, is getting to places. Buses from the *Rodoviária* cover most corners, but you'll need time to find the right one and the patience to queue. Taxis can be found everywhere (or see the "Listings" section below for phone numbers); you shouldn't have to pay more than $10 for any but the longest rides. If you're walking, you should have no problems at night security-wise in Asa Norte and Asa Sul, whilst Núcleo Bandeirante simply goes to sleep.

Restaurants

Atalaia Restaurante, CLN 102, Bloco C, Loja 49 (☎224-1278). Typical Brazilian food with meat dishes from most regions. Moderately priced.

Bar Beirute, CLS 109, Bloco A, Loja 2 (☎244-1717). Middle Eastern food has always been popular in Brasília (a legacy of the thousands of Lebanese and Syrians who were instrumental in the country's turn-of-the-century rubber boom), and this is the most traditional of the Arab dives and very popular at night.

Barriga Verde, CLN 203, Bloco B, Loja 47 (☎224-7729). Excellent but expensive Brazilian restaurant particularly well known for its seafood.

Beda, CLN 714/715. Cheap – and therefore popular – regional restaurant, with a range of good food both à la carte and self-serve.

Cheiro Verde, SDS, Edifico Eldorado (☎224-8365 or 226-3160). This superb vegetarian restaurant, facing east from the first floor of the southern shopping block, is a great lunchtime spot (Mon–Sat 11.30am–3pm). There's a *comida por kilo* self-service system and splendid views from the patio over towards the cathedral, Teatro Nacional and Congress areas.

China Restaurante, CLS 103, Bloco D, Loja 2 (☎224-3339). Popular Chinese place with a moderately priced home delivery service.

Comida Brasileira, CLS 302, Bloco A, Loja 13/15 (☎226-0560). Moderately priced Brazilian restaurant serving a whole range of meat, fish, vegetables and salads. Open lunchtimes only.

Hikaru, SHN 2, Bloco J "Garvey Park" (☎224-5151). Located under the *Hotel Garvey*, this very expensive Japanese restaurant serves an astonishing range of sushi and sashimi, among other dishes, largely to business types, as well as operating a home delivery service. Mon–Fri 7pm–midnight, Sat noon–midnight.

Lagash, CLN 308/309, Bloco B, Loja 11/13 (☎273-0098; closed Mon). Among the top five restaurants in Brasília, with a mouth-watering range of Lebanese and North African delicacies. About $40–50 a head, excluding wine or *arak*.

Mãe Natureza, CLS 505 (Av. W-2 Sul), Bloco A, Loja 54 (☎244-8025). Along with the *Cheiro Verde*, one of Brasília's main vegetarian restaurants.

Picanhas do Sul, CLN 706/707, Bloco E, Loja 06. A good-value meat and beer restaurant, which sometimes has live music on Wed, Thurs and Fri nights.

Pizza In, CLN 310, Bloco E, Loja 58/66 (☎349-5511). Like the dozens of other pizzerias scattered throughout Brasília, quite good but quite expensive. Delivery service.

Requinte Self-Service, CLS 404, Bloco A, Loja 13. Good value with a wide choice of fine food (around $8–9 a kilo).

San Marino Restaurante, CLS 209. One of the few good, inexpensive pasta and pizza parlours.

Bars and discos

In a city like Brasília, where there's a large middle class plus plenty of students, politicians, press and civil servants, it's not surprising that there are a lot of bars. Even discounting the hotel bars – and there are plenty of those – there's a good selection of **places to drink**, though the scene as a whole is nothing like as lively as in Rio.

One of the most popular bars is *Gate's Pub*, CLS 403, Bloco B, Loja 34 (☎225-4576), which has live bands (11pm onwards) Friday and Saturday, and a disco Thursday and Sunday. The *Gang Executive Bar* in the *Hotel Torre Palace*, SHN 4, Bloco A, and *Piantella*, CLS 202, Bloco A, Loja 34, are also worth a fling. The popular *Manhattan Café*, CLN 207, Bloco A, Loja 06, often has cultural exhibitions and art on display, while the very trendy *Martinica*, CLN 303, attracts much the same sort of *"yuppy alternativo"* crowd to its music jams. For a more alternative and intimate feel, *Bar Beirute* (see "Restaurants" above) is the place for yuppy hippies and skinheads alike, while more artistic and theatrical folk like to be seen in the *Café da Rua 8*, CLN 408 (Mon–Sat till 3am or so), which also does great salads.

For **dancing**, your best choice is in the Conjunto Venâncio shopping centre – notably the gay club, *Aquarius*. You should also check out *Galeria*, CLN 304, for live mixes of modern club dance, and *Fabrica*, a nightclub complex complete with sushi and tequila bars, SIA Trecho 3, southwest of the *Rodoferroviária* in the industrial sector (take a taxi). Failing all this, there are a number of good clubs in the Centro Comercial Gilberto Salomão.

Listings

Airlines Mostly found around the *Hotel Nacional* in various agents' shops. The main Brazilian companies are Nordeste, airport (☎365-1802); TAM, SHS 1, Galeria Hotel Nacional 61 (☎223-5168), and at the airport (☎365-1000); Transbrasil, CLS 305, Bloco C, Lojas 31–33 (☎243-6133); Varig, SCN 4, Bloco B (☎329-1111), and at the airport (☎365-1169); and VASP, SHS 1, Galeria Hotel Nacional 53/54 (☎321-3636). Among overseas airlines are Air France, SHS 1, Galeria Hotel Nacional 39/40 (☎223-4152); Iberia, Conjunto Venâncio 2000, Bloco B, Loja 40-A Terreo (☎226-1908 or 226-0456); KLM, SHS 1, Galeria Hotel Nacional 51 (☎321-3636 or 225-5915); Lufthansa, SHS 1, Galeria Hotel Nacional 1 (☎223-5002).

Airport enquiries ☎365-1941, 365-1224 or 365-1947.

American Express The Amex representative is at Buriti/Brasília, CLS 402, Bloco A, Lojas 27/33.

Art galleries and exhibitions Good international photography and art exhibitions are often held in the lobby of the Teatro Nacional (Mon–Fri 1–6pm; ☎321-6002; see p.400), as well as in the Espaço Cultural, CLS 508 (☎224-0411) on the east side of Av. W-3 Sul, which recently hosted an exhibition of Sebastião Salgado's photographs; take buses #161, 162 or 163 (marked W-3 Sul) to block 708, and it's opposite. The Aliança Francesa building, Av. W-4 Sul, CLS 708/907 (☎242-7500), is usually worth a browse. Also of some repute are Performance, CLS 116, Bloco A, Loja 7 (☎245-5131); Cavalier Galeria de Arte, CLN 307, Bloco E, Loja 34 (☎274-0797); and Itaugaleria, SCS 3, Bloco A, Loja 30, which occasionally links up with the university's Department of Visual Arts for interesting exhibitions.

Banks and exchange Given that Brasília is the banking centre of Brazil, it's annoying to find that the exchange rates offered in the city are uniformly bad. You can change cash and travellers' cheques at Banco do Brasil, SBS, Edifício Sede 1, Terreo (Mon–Fri 10am–5pm), but they charge their usual $20 commission. Reasonable rates with no commission apply at the *câmbio* in the *Hotel Nacional* (Mon–Fri 9am–6pm, exceptionally Sat), which is the best bet for travellers' cheques (avoid the other *câmbio*-travel agencies around the hotel, whose rates are terrible, as are those touted by most other big hotels).

Bookstores English-language novels can be found on the ground level of the Conjunto de Diversões Norte; enter from opposite the Teatro Nacional.

Car rental Hertz, at the *Eron Brasília Hotel*, SHN 5, Bloco A (☎234-4656); Unidas, SHS 1, Galeria Hotel Nacional 60 (☎225-5191), and the airport, stand 24 (☎248-6227).

Doctors and clinics Dr. C. Menecucci, Centro Medico, Av. W-3 Sul 716, Bloco D, sala 16, speaks good English. For quick blood tests, the Clínica SOS Check-Up de Brasília, SHIS 9, Bloco E, Loja 312 (☎248-4093), at the Centro Clínico do Lago, is efficient.

Embassies For the Setor de Embaixadas Sul (SES), take a bus to Avenida das Nações, or just walk. Argentina, SHIS 1, cj. 5, casa 28 (☎365-3000); Australia, SHIS 9, cj. 16, casa 1 (☎248-5569); Austria, SES 811, Lote 40 (☎243-3111); Bolivia, SHIS 1, cj. 15, casa 52 (☎248-7744); Canada, SES 803, Lote 16, sala 130 (☎321-2171); Colombia, SES 803, Lote 10 (☎225-3254); Ecuador, SHIS 1, cj. 1, casa 24 (☎248-5560); French Guyana, SBN 2, Bloco J, 13° (☎224-9229); Germany, SES 807, Lote 25 (☎244-7273); Paraguay, SES 811, Lote 42 (☎242-3732); Peru, SES 811, Lote 43 (☎242-9831); Portugal, SES 801, Lote 2 (☎321-3434); South Africa, SES 801, Lote 6 (☎223-4873); Switzerland, SES 811, Lote 41 (☎244-5500); UK, SES 801, Lote 8 (☎225-2710); USA, SES 801, Lote 3 (☎321-7272); Venezuela, SES 803, Lote 13 (☎223-9325).

Emergencies Medical ☎192; police ☎197; fire brigade ☎193.

Festivals Festa da Cidade on April 21 (inauguration anniversary); Feira dos Estados in last week of June; Dom Bosco's Day, a procession on Lake Paranoá on Aug 31; Grande Prêmio Automobilistico (motor racing over 1000km) on Sept 7; Festival of Brazilian Cinema in Oct.

FUNAI SEPS 702/902, Bloco A (☎226-4887 or 226-8211). This is the main headquarters for FUNAI, the federal agency for Indian affairs, which is the only organization authorized to grant permits for visitors to Indian Reserves. Though their permits are usually impossible to obtain, they should be able to fill you in on recent politicking, on what might be possible and on what certainly isn't.

Hospitals Da Base do Distrito Federal, SMHS 101 (☎325-5050); Santa Lúcia, SHLS 716, Bloco C (☎245-3344).

Lost property ☎217-2323.

Newspapers and magazines English, American and European newspapers are often available from the *Pause* bookstore at the Galeria Hotel Nacional 59, just a few doors away from the hotel.

Post office Brasília's main post office (Mon–Sat 9am–6pm) is the small, white building in the open grassy space behind the *Hotel Nacional*. Collect your poste restante from here, too.

Shopping You can buy almost anything in the Conjuntos de Diversões (see p.400). For *artesanato* and other craft goods, there's a good market underneath the TV Tower on Sat, Sun and most public holidays. A smaller market next to the cathedral sells an incredible range of dried and dyed flowers. For regional craft specialities try the *Galeria dos Estados*, in the subway connecting the Setor Bancário Sul with Setor Comercial Sul. Great value gems and jewels are available from *Pedras Nativas*, Conjunto Venâncio 2000, Terreo. For incense, tiger balm, tie-dye wraps, rizlas and the like, try the *Mercado Alternativo* in the Centro Cultural Le Corbusier, at Centro Comercial Gilberto Salomão.

Taxis ☎322-2090, ☎325-3030, ☎223-1000 or ☎224-1000.

Theatres *Teatro Nacional* (☎325-6240; see p.400); *Scenaria*, Centro Comercial Gilberto Salomão, Bloco A (☎248-5153), which plays new Brazilian and other modern works; *Teatro Galpão*, Av. W-2 Sul 508 (☎244-0411); *Teatro Dulcina de Moraes*, Conjunto de Diversões Sul (☎226-0188), which has comedy and music too. Next door, the Faculdade Brasileira de Teatro is a good place to enquire about other venues and events; if the porter can't help, wait around till a seminar ends and ask the students, or try the *Café Belas Artes* around the corner.

Travel agents For local tours and air tickets try Buriti, SCS 402, Bloco A, Loja 27 (☎225-2686); Presmic, SHS 1, Galeria Hotel Nacional 33/34 (☎225-5598); and Power Turismo, SHS 1, Galeria Hotel Nacional 48 (☎332-6699).

Around Brasília

The main attraction beyond the city limits is **Catetinho** (Tues–Sun 9am–5pm), the very first building in Brasília, and once the residence of Kubitschek. Built on stilts, it was constructed in 1956 for the financiers, planners and designers to work from. Luciano Pereira, the present curator, actually helped to build the place. A quaint, mostly timber, construction, it still retains some of the president's furniture and other objects. To reach it, take the bus to Belo Horizonte from the *Rodoferroviária* and get off after 27km at Catetinho.

Eight kilometres from the city, but in the opposite direction (along the road towards Formosa and Salvador), the **Parque Nacional de Brasília** is a popular place for picnics amongst the woodlands, with natural springs, swimming pools and baths – take the Estrada to Sobradinho, along the BR-020. Residents of the city flock here in their thousands at weekends, but designated areas have been set aside for the protection of local flora and fauna, and there's an orchid house containing rare species.

Lago Paranoá

Covering forty square kilometres, **Lago Paranoá** is a man-made recreation area, created by the diversion of three rivers to humidify the dry climate. It's already suffering from an algae problem, but it's the scene of water sports, clubhouses and the **Ermida Dom Bosco**. This small conical hermitage, sitting alone on the edge of the lake, around 30km from the downtown *Rodoviária*, offers fine views over the lake towards the Alvorada Palace, while below the nearby Paranoá dam there are amazing waterfalls during the heavy summer rains. **Buses** from the *Rodoviária* go right around the lake in a couple of hours: #123 and #125 cover the southern half, finishing up in a shanty settlement after crossing the main dam; for the northern end of the lake, take the buses #136-1 or #136-2 "Clube do Congresso".

Planaltina and Cristalina

The historic but sleepy town of **PLANALTINA** is a possible, though not compelling day trip from Brasília. It's around 40km east of the city, and three-quarters of the way there the road crosses the divide between the Amazon and Plate watersheds. Like many communities on the Planalto Central, Planaltino was founded by *bandeirantes* and evolved into a small market town. Nowadays, there are a few unremarkable colonial buildings left in the centre, making it into one of the few historic towns in the region. There's also a museum and some good restaurants, but there's a distinct air of small-town tedium here. As soon as it gets dark, the streets empty as the locals settle down to watch the TV soaps behind their shutters.

A longer but more interesting trip can be made to the settlement of **CRISTALINA**, around 100km south of Brasília in the Goiás plateau highlands. Indeed, the journey itself is one of the main reasons to come, through the distinctive, savanna scenery of the Planalto along the BR-040 towards Belo Horizonte. Prospectors came here looking for gold in the early eighteenth century when they came across a large quantity of rock crystal. This crystal mountain did not have much value until over a century later when the European market opened up. Today Cristalina is an attractive, rustic town, based around the mining, cutting, polishing and marketing of semi-precious stones, and quartz crystals and Brazilian amethyst can be bought here at very reasonable prices. If you want to **stay**, *Hotel Attie*, Praça José Damian 34 (☎061/612-1252; ④), and *Hotel Goyá*, Rua da Saudade 41 (☎061/612-1301; ④), are both good. For **food**, *Restaurante do Petrônio*, Av. Kaled Cozac 47, is an excellent *churrasco* joint.

406/BRASÍLIA, GOIÁS AND TOCANTINS

THE STATES OF GOIÁS AND TOCANTINS

Beyond the city and Federal District of Brasília, the hill-studded, surprisingly green plains of **Goiás state** extend towards another planned city, **Goiânia**, and the historic old towns of **Pirenópolis** and **Goiás Velho**. Although gold mining started here in a small way during the seventeenth century, the first genuine settlement was not until 1725. These days agriculture is the main activity: cattle in their millions, pigs, rice, maize, soya, sugar cane and fruits.

In the north of Goiás rises the mystical mountain range and national park of the **Chapada dos Veadeiros** with its deep, impressive cave system of **Terra Ronca**. In the south, the well-serviced thermal springs of **Caldas Novas** and **Rio Quente** bubble up into giant hotel complexes, while, over on the western border with Mato Grosso, the **Emas National Park** is packed with wildlife, in particular the large American rhea.

The mighty Rio Araguaia (which means Macaw River in Tupi Indian language), with its many beautiful, sandy beaches forms the 1200-kilometre-long western frontier of both Goiás and Tocantins states. The **state of Tocantins**, created for political rather than geographic or economic reasons in 1989, contains the huge river island, **Ilha do Bananal**, and its **National Park of Araguaia**. The main and central section (BR-153) of the 2000-kilometre-long highway from Goiânia and Brasília to Belém also runs through Tocantins. The only town of any significance is **Araguaína**, a flyblown settlement in the middle of a largely deforested savanna.

Both Goiás and Tocantins are fairly well served by **bus** but, in many ways, this is new territory for travellers to explore, most foreign visitors travelling straight through the region en route to better-known destinations such as the Amazon and Mato Grosso. If you have the time, however, Goiás in particular offers a variety of interesting stops. The area is popular with Brazilian holidaymakers, and the tourist industry is beginning to get organized. There is already a wide range of good hotels throughout the region and, as usual in South America, some excellent eating places if you know where to look.

Goiânia

The other modern, planned city in central Brazil, **GOIÂNIA** was founded in 1933, becoming the state capital four years later. Over a million strong, cheaper than Brasília, with some good hotels and only 209km from the federal capital, Goiânia might well be a stopping-off point, since it is very well connected by road to most other Brazilian cities.

Goiânia hit the international headlines in 1987 when a salvaged X-ray machine was broken open by a scrap merchant's family and the radioactive crystals inside were unwittingly spread around the town. The purple, glowing crystals caused serious illness, and sections of the city were sealed off for weeks. However, don't let this put you off: life has returned to normal, and Goiânia is back to earning its living as a market centre for the surrounding agricultural region which specializes in rice and soya. In the Bosque dos Buritis in downtown Goiânia there's a powerful modern monument to Peace created by Siron Franco, actualized in the wake of the radioactivity incident.

Arrival, information and accommodation

Both the **Rodoviária** and **airport** lie in the northern sectors of town. The *Rodoviária* is around twenty minutes by foot from Setor Central along Avenida Goiás, or a short ride by local bus, and the airport is also linked to the centre, 6km away, by bus (#190

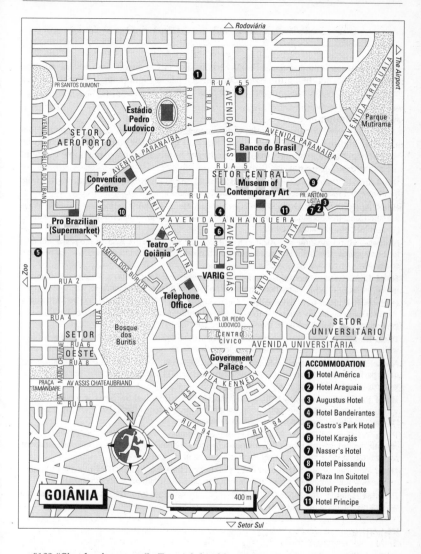

△ Rodoviária

PR SANTOS DUMONT

Estádio
Pedro
Ludovico

SETOR
AEROPORTO

Banco do Brasil

Convention
Centre

SETOR CENTRAL
Museum of
Contemporary Art

Pro Brazilian
(Supermarket)

Teatro
Goiânia

VARIG

Telephone
Office

Bosque
dos
Buritis

SETOR
OESTE

PRAÇA
TAMANDARÉ

SETOR
UNIVERSITÁRIO

AV ASSIS CHATEAUBRIAND

AVENIDA UNIVERSITÁRIA

Government
Palace

N

GOIÂNIA

0   400 m

▽ Setor Sul

△ Zoo

ACCOMMODATION

❶ Hotel América
❷ Hotel Araguaia
❸ Augustus Hotel
❹ Hotel Bandeirantes
❺ Castro's Park Hotel
❻ Hotel Karajás
❼ Nasser's Hotel
❽ Hotel Paissandu
❾ Plaza Inn Suitotel
❿ Hotel Presidente
⓫ Hotel Principe

or #162 "Circular Aeroporto"). To catch local buses in town, there are main stops on Avenida Araguaia just south of Rua 4, and along Avenida Goiás opposite Hotel Paissandu. There's a **tourist information** booth at the airport which has free maps, though better maps ($1.50) can be bought from the newsagent opposite.

The wide central streets are almost handsome in their blend of pre-war continental-style grandeur with modernist concrete and glass, skyscraping offices and homes for the rapidly growing middle-class population of the city. The main node of the concentric city plan is the Centro Cívico and Praça Dr Pedro Ludovico, at the head of the massive Avenida Goiás, whose broad and leafy pavement extends all the way down its

> The **telephone code** for Goiânia is ☎062.

middle between both directions of busy traffic. The city is divided into several sectors, the most important being the Setor Central, Setor Oeste and Setor Universitário, and many of the streets have numbers rather than names.

Accommodation

Goiânia has a wide range of **hotels**, wider, in fact, than in Brasília. As well as giving you a greater choice of places to bed down, this also means that you're more likely to be able to negotiate discounts – many of the larger hotels as a matter of course discount their prices out of season by 20–40 percent.

Hotel América, Rua 74, #262, Centro (☎223-2864). Clean and family-run, this is a little way out from the centre, but its *quartos* are probably the cheapest rooms in town. ①.

Hotel Araguaia, Av. Araguaia 664, Centro (☎ and fax 224-1830). Overlooking the little Praça Antônio Lisita, this hotel has an impressive lobby, which the rooms conspicuously fail to live up to. Good value only with a discount. ⑤.

Augustus Hotel, Av. Araguaia 702, Centro (☎224-1022, fax 224-1410). Also on the *praça* and next to the *Araguaia*, this hotel is much flashier, with good rooms – though a little dark – a pool and sauna. ⑥.

Hotel Bandeirantes, Av. Anhangüera 3278, Centro (☎ and fax 224-0066). Flashy and air-conditioned but with no pool; it's particularly worth bargaining over room prices here. ⑦.

Castro's Park Hotel, Av. República do Líbano 1520, Setor Oeste (☎223-7766, fax 225-7070). A 5-star hotel with immaculate service, three pools and numerous restaurants; outside holiday times, a good place to try for discounted rooms. ⑦.

Hotel Karajás, Rua 3, #860, Centro (☎224-9666, fax 229-1153). Very comfortable 20-storey block with good-sized rooms. Same price for singles, however. ⑤.

Nasser's Hotel, Av. Araguaia 640 (☎212-2317, fax 212-7262). A run-down place in the busier and older part of town with fist-sized depressions in the doors. The rooms themselves are OK, though, with *frigobar* and air conditioning. ④.

Hotel Paissandu, Av. Goiás 1290, Centro (no ☎). Situated beyond the heart of the city, though within walking distance, this hotel is pretty good value, if a touch basic, but there are TVs in all rooms, and singles are considerably cheaper than doubles. ③.

Plaza Inn Suitotel, Rua 20, #930, corner of Praça Antônio Lisita (☎212-8500, fax 212-7911). With smooth service, superb rooms (all with en-suite lounges), and a pleasant ground-floor restaurant, by far the best value in town; 30 percent discount out of season. ⑥.

Hotel Presidente, Av. Anhangüera 5646, Centro (☎224-0500, fax 224-0551). Once a great budget option, now mid-range veering on luxury – modern and clean with great breakfasts. ⑤.

Príncipe Hotel, Av. Anhangüera 2936, Centro (☎224-0085 or 224-0962, fax 224-2831). Modern place with rather small rooms. Cheaper *quartos* with shared bathrooms. ②–③.

The City

One of the first things visitors note when they arrive in Goiânia is the size of the place, its modern skyline dominating the horizon for some time before you reach the city's limits. It is one of Brazil's ten biggest cities, created to function as a regional agricultural and livestock market centre as gold became less important in Goiás. Like several cities throughout South America it has an eternally springlike climate, of which it takes good advantage through its extensive network of established green spaces – mainly large *praças*, public parks and sports grounds. Pleasant enough in its own right, Goiânia lacks any sights of outstanding interest or stunning architectural gems.

The Bosque dos Buritis and the museums

Just two blocks due west of the Centro Cívico lies the **Bosque dos Buritis** (daily 9am–6pm). The woods, spread over 140,000 square metres and containing a huge water-jet fountain, have been managed since Goiânia was a mere twinkle in the eye of its then 60-year-old founder, Pedro Ludovico Teixeira. In the Buritis woods, you're quite likely to find the **Museu de Arte**, Rua 1, #605, West Sector (Tues–Sun 8am–6pm), by accident if not on purpose. It's a free and reasonably interesting museum in a relaxed atmosphere with paintings of the city and stone sculptures on display. For a better selection of paintings with a faster changing range of exhibits, try the **Museu de Arte Contemporanea**, lost in the concrete depths of the city's business heart in the Parthenon Centre, Rua 4, #515 (Tues–Sat 9am–6pm, Sun 9am–2pm; ☎233-6773).

Only if you're really kicking your heels is it worth visiting Goiânia's other museums, which include, in the east of the downtown area, the anthropological museum, Praça Universitária 1166 (Tues–Fri 9am–5pm) and, nearby, the even less interesting archeological museum, Praça Universitária 1440 (Mon–Fri 8am–6pm). If you're en route for some eco-tourism and birdwatching in Goiás or the Mato Grosso, the **Museu Ornitológia**, Av. Para 395, Setor Campinas (daily 8am–10pm), which displays around six thousand stuffed birds, may hold greater charm.

Jardim Zoológico and Parque Mutirama

One of the town's main outdoor features, the **Jardim Zoológico** (Tues–Sun 8am–5pm; $2), located some nine long blocks west along Avenida Anhangüera from the Teátro Goiânio, is a pleasant and well-managed public park. It's focused at its northern end around the muddy Lago das Rosas, home to a number of semi-tame monkeys, while the southern corner houses a large and well-stocked zoo, which is a must for anyone going on to the Goiás *sertão*, the Mato Grosso or the Amazon in search of wildlife. You'll see *emas* (rheas), *tuiuius* (red-throated storks) and *jacarés* (alligators) closer here than you will in the wild.

The other main public park in Goiânia, **Parque Mutirama**, in the northeast of the city at the junction of *avenidas* Araguaia and Contorno (Tues–Sun 9am–6pm), is very popular with local kids, who enjoy the delights of its ingenious amusement centre, skating rink, and its planetarium (Sun 3.30pm & 4.30pm; ☎224-5787). Opposite the park, the woods of the **Parque Botafogo** (closed Mon), with their reforested native trees, help the centre of the city to breathe; on the last Sunday of every month, there's good live music here.

The Feira Hippie and Feira da Lua

The **Feira Hippie** (hippy fair), is a fascinating and useful street market open every Sunday from early in the morning until mid-afternoon. It dominates the centre of Avenida Goiás from the Centro Cívico right down to Praça Bandeirante, whose elegant bronze monument impassively watches the intense and frantic weekly ritual. Originally a market for local craftspeople, it has evolved to incorporate a wide range of more general alternative handicrafts, plus the global variety of socks, underwear, watches, electrical goods and all kinds of imported plastics. And if you're around on a Saturday, head for the **Feira da Lua** (moon fair), which sells mainly *artesanato* in the tree-studded and lively Praça Tamandaré, a few blocks west of the Centro Cívico, where there are plenty of bars and restaurants.

Eating, drinking and nightlife

Legend has it that, being a remote frontier in the eighteenth and early nineteenth centuries, the state of Goiás developed an exquisite **cuisine** in order to prolong the stay of passing travellers. Even today, in Goiânia as in Goiás Velho, the people are justly proud of their cooking. Local delicacies range from rice with *pequi* fruit through pasties (*empadões*) to roast sow with fried banana (*leitão assada com banana frita*). You may find, however, that the increasing popularity of the self-service *comida por kilo* system means that it's nigh impossible to track down seriously good food at lunchtime unless you're happy dining at the most expensive restaurants. There are however a number of cheap and good *lanchonetes* around Praça Tamandaré and around the cheaper hotels in Setor Centro. The basic rule is the further south you go, the more expensive the restaurant.

Anhangüera, Av. Anhangüera near the corner with Av. Paranaíba, Setor Central. Next to the Pro Brazilian supermarket, one of the cheapest and busiest lunchtime *comida por kilo* places.

Tacho do Cobre, Rua 72, #550, Jardim Goiás (☎242-1241). Located in an outer suburb to the southeast of the centre (take a taxi), this expensive restaurant serves the very best local dishes.

Dragão, Rua Maria Cruvinel 1111 (☎215-1442). Just off Av. República do Líbano on the south side of Praça Tamandaré, good Chinese food, better in the evenings and weekends when the *comida por kilo* system makes way for old-fashioned à la carte. Home delivery service for the truly lazy.

A Peixisqueira, Praça Walter Santos 164, Setor Coimbra (☎233-9333). Hard to beat for moderately priced fish-based cuisine, but you will need to take a taxi to get here (it's west beyond the Jardim Zoológico).

Restaurante Piquiras, Av. República do Líbano 1758, Setor Oeste (☎224-9239). One of the city's better fish restaurants, always good quality and good value.

Tropeiro Chopera e Restaurante, Rua 10. Located just off the western edge of Praça Tamandaré and open evenings only, this popular, moderately priced restaurant has a great atmosphere whether you're just drinking or having a meal. This is a good place to try *mandioca frita* (fried manioc).

Restaurante Vegetariano, Rua 7, #475, Centro (☎225-7290). Simple, well-presented vegetarian dishes.

Restaurante Sabor Tradição, Rua 74, #194, Setor Central. Close to the corner with Rua 55, one of a number of good lunchtime *comida por kilo* places in the centre (closed Sun).

Nightlife

Goiânia has quite a lively nightlife, but most of the best **clubs** change names and venues every few months as they go in and out of fashion. Prices tend to be high, with some places charging $10 entrance as well as imposing a minimum spending limit once inside (usually also $10). Praça Tamandaré is always a good place to start your evening, with a number of bars and cafés and, later on, nightclubs. The best of these is currently the terminally designer *Draft Casual Bar & Diner*, south down Avenida República da Líbano on the corner of Rua 22 and Rua 23, Setor Oeste (Tues–Sun). A little further west, *Chocolate Chic*, Av. Portugal 719, is full of the tackiness that passes as style among Goiânia's monied youth, but it's still a fun night out. Also fairly reliable for a good night out are the *Bavária*, Rua T–51, #1054, Setor Bueno (☎251-6083), and *Boate People*, Rua 7, #1000, Setor Oeste (☎215-1623). As to straight drinking **bars**, there aren't that many. Very busy is *O Ceará*, on the corner of Rua 2 and Rua 8. Try also the new *Cervejaria Brasil* on Praça Antônio Lisita (closed Sun), which has a good range of bottled beers and cocktails.

Listings

Airlines Lufthansa, Rua 4, #1042, Setor Central (☎223-0036); Pantanal Linhas Aéreas, Rua Dona Gercina Borges 34, Setor Sul (☎224-4286); TAM, Av. 85, #944, Setor Sul (☎207-1700); Transbrasil, Rua 6, #370, sala 26, Setor Oeste (☎225-1966); Varig, Av. Goiás 285, Centro (☎224-5049, airport ☎207-1743); VASP, Rua 1, #157, Centro (☎224-6389, airport ☎207-1350).

Airport enquiries ☎207-1288.

Air taxis Goiás (☎207-1616); Anhangüera (☎207-2727).

Banks and exchange Good money-changing service on the first floor at the Banco do Brasil, Av. Goiás 980 (Mon–Fri 10am–6pm). The Lufthansa office (see "Airlines" above) changes cash at good rates.

Bus enquiries ☎224-8466.

Car rental First, Av. Araguaia 185 (☎212-3736); Hertz, Av. República do Líbano 1880 (☎223-6000); Localiza, Av. Anhangüera 3520 (☎261-7111).

Hospital Hospital do Inamps, Av. Anhangüera 4379, Setor Oeste (☎223-5601).

Shopping Goiânia's large modern shopping complex, Bougainville, is at Rua 9, #1855, Setor Oeste (Mon–Sat 10am–10pm). Crafts are available from the hippy fair along Avenida Goiás on Sun mornings and the Feira da Lua on Sat (see p.409), or from the Handicraft Centre, Praça do Trabalhador, a producers' shop located in the old train station (daily 8am–6pm).

Taxis ABC (☎285-1366); Coopertaxi (☎229-0800); Rádio-Táxi Link (☎295-1513).

Tour guides SINGTUR (Sindicato dos Guias de Turismo), Alameda Progresso 511 (☎271-6970) is the regional tour-guide syndicate, and provides accredited guides for the Parque Nacional das Emas and the Parque Nacional Chapada dos Veadeiros.

Travel agents Grupo Nativa, Rua 10, #849, Setor Oeste (☎224-6299 or 241-7585), eco-tourism specialists; Nature Tur, Av. República do Líbano 2417, Setor Oeste (☎215-2000), especially for visits to Caldas Novas; Toriua Turismo, Av. Tocantins 319, Centro (☎223-2333), for flights, tickets and hotel bookings.

Pirenópolis

The picturesque town of **PIRENÓPOLIS** straddles the Rio das Almas, 112km north of Goiânia in the scrubby mountains of the Serra dos Pireneus. Founded in 1727 as a gold-mining settlement, it's now one of the prettiest and friendliest towns in Brazil, and a popular weekend retreat for residents of Brasília.

The main street, **Avenida Sizenando Jayme**, is a broad, peaceful, tree-lined avenue where the old men, with their ponies and carts, and visiting *fazendeiros* hang out chatting in the shade; on Sunday morning there's a market here. Just a couple of blocks down the hill is the oldest church in Goiás, the **Igreja Nossa Senhora do Rosário de Meia Ponte** (1728–32), an attractive colonial edifice built mainly of mud, clay and sand, with an impressive ceiling painted by the Brazilian artist, Inacio Periera Leal. It's currently undergoing much-needed structural repairs, and renovation work on the more ornate paintings and baroque naves is set to continue for some time, though the workmen will be happy to let you in. Opposite the church, the ruined turn-of-the-century **theatre** is also being rebuilt, and should, when finished, be once more the venue for plays and other distractions.

East of the church, along Rua Bonfim do Serra dos Pireneus, **Igreja Nosso Senhor do Bonfim**, built between 1750 and 1754, is famous for its image of Nosso Senhor do Bonfim originally brought here by two hundred slaves. Also in the upper part of town, at Rua Direita 39 between the Igreja N.S. do Rosário and the *Rodoviária*, you'll find the small **Museu das Cavalhadas** ($0.50), located in a family's front room (knock if it appears closed). The museum contains displays of incredible carnival costumes from the *Festo do Divino Espírito Santo*, a lively and largely horse-mounted religious festival which takes place in the town exactly six weeks after Easter Sunday. The festival combines dances with mock battles from the Crusades, and the costumes include ornate metal armour, demonic masks and animal heads. Another tiny museum, the **Museu da Família Pompeu**, in the family's home on the same road at no. 28, may in future become the *museu municipal*, with its odd collection of colonial and later bric-a-brac, including an old printing press, municipal newsletters and silver jewellery.

Below the Igreja N.S. do Rosário, the town has a different atmosphere. Swimming and sunbathing spots line the river by the old stone and wood bridge, which links the main settlement with the Carmo section of town on the north bank, and there's a vibrant **alternative scene** reflected in a handful of interesting bars, organic cafés and New Age stores. *Homeostratum* at Rua do Rosário 12 sells homeopathic products, natural foods, alternative magazines and *artesanato*. *Nataraja* has a wide range of hippy clothes, crystals and alternative medicines. However, Pirenópolis is most famous in Brazil for its **silverwork**, mostly inset with semi-precious stones. The craft was introduced barely twenty years ago by the hippies who came and stayed, and nowadays, with over two hundred artisans working in around a hundred workshops, you'll find jewellery for sale in dozens of shops, much of it inspired by Asian designs.

On the north side of the river, housed in the eighteenth-century Igreja Nossa Senhora do Carmo, the **Museu Sacro** displays an image of the town's patroness, which was originally brought from Portugal. A couple of hours' easy walk from town heading out north past the church (about 6km and well signposted) is the **Santuário Vagafogo** (Tues–Sun 8am–5pm; $5), a very good wildlife sanctuary, which also serves special brunches at weekends and on holidays.

Practicalities

Pirenópolis is well connected by road to the other major towns of the region. There's one direct **bus** a day from Goiânia, and four from the important junction town of Anápolis (which in turn has frequent connections with Goiânia). Brasília is just 172km east along the BR-070 (8 buses daily). The *Rodoviária* is on the eastern edge of town, five minutes' walk from the centre.

Accommodation

As Pirenópolis is a popular local resort, here are dozens of **hotels** to choose from, many of them merely private homes with a few rooms for rent. The quality is generally well above average, and discounts are available mid-week or out-of-season. The best-located hotel is the *Pousada das Cavalhadas*, Praça da Matriz (☎ and fax 062/331-1261; ④), opposite the Igreja N.S. do Rosário, although its singles are overpriced. On the small square to the right of the church, the *Hotel Rex*, Praça Emmanoel Lopes 15 (☎062/331-1121; ②), has several quaint rooms, some self-contained, along the edge of a traditional courtyard. Further up, *Lanchonete Pousada Central* (☎062/331-1625) rents out five beds in two rooms at $10 a person. One road away, at Rua Nova 25, is one of the town's nicest hotels, the *Pouso do Sô Vigário* (☎062/331-1206; ⑤), housed in the old priest's residence, but now embellished with a pool and sauna. On the main street, at Av. Sizenando Jayme 21, is the new *Pousada Imperial* (☎062/331-1382; ④), a friendly and well-appointed place, with nice views of the Serra dos Pireneus over the river and half-price singles. On the other side of the river, the *Pousada dos Pireneus* (☎062/331-1028, fax 331-1345; half-board ⑦) is the main upmarket place, with its own rambling gardens, a small waterpark with chutes that kids will love, and horseriding facilities – including amusing half-hour jaunts by carriage through town for a mere $4.40 for four people. The *pousada* also rents bicycles at $4.40 the hour, but insists you stay in town, which is most unhelpful for visiting any of the surrounding attractions.

Eating and drinking

There are several good **restaurants** along Avenida Sizenando Jayme, including *As Flor* at no. 16, unprepossessing in appearance but good at lunchtimes for regional cooking, though evening fare can dip in quality. *Pamonharia*, around the corner going down to the church, is also cheap. Other good, but much more expensive, restaurants can be found in the lower part of town around the river; try *Restaurante Dona Cida* (Fri–Sun only) on Rua do Carmo 22A for *galinha caipiri*, small succulent chicken oven-baked with saffron, or else baked in its own blood, *galinha cabidela molho pardo*. For good basic food, the *Churrascaria Pireneus*, on the corner of Praça Matriz opposite the church, is open daily. There are small **supermarkets** at Av. Sizenando Jayme 30 and by the river opposite the police station. The best **bars** are down by the river, notably the communally run *Aravinda Bar* on Rua do Rosário 25, a place where beer hogs meet patchouli oil and incense in a very relaxing and friendly way (open Thurs–Sun only; live New Age music Sat night); it also serves food, including excellent *peixa na telha* (fish baked in an earthenware dish). Throughout the week, the *Pousada Central*'s bar is a popular meeting place.

Tours

A number of guides and agencies offer ecological **tours** of the surrounding region, taking in sites such as the Abade, Inferno and Corumbá waterfalls. Based at Rua Emílio de Carvalho 18 (☎062/331-1392), Dinis, who during the week drives a school bus, runs guided eco-tours ($50 for 3–4hr), as do Cerrado Ecoturismo, Rua do Bonfim 46 (☎062/331-1240), who are agents for a number of private wildlife sanctuaries in the region. More alternative guided tours (bicycles a speciality) are offered by Calango Expedições, Bairro do Carmo (☎062/331-1564); they may just rent you a bike if you're nice enough. Another guide worth contacting, though you'll need your own transport, is silversmith Alcides dos Santos Filho, at Rua Anduzeiro 20 (☎062/331-1416). For further information, the council publishes an excellent annual *Guia do Turista* (free), available in most of the hotels and establishments mentioned above.

Goiás Velho

Some 144km northwest of Goiânia, the attractive historic town of **GOIÁS VELHO** – originally known as Vila Boa, and now often just called Goiás – is no longer the vital centre it once was. Goiânia has taken over as the state's commercial and political fulcrum and, in many ways, Pirenópolis has more old-world charm. Nevertheless, Goiás Velho is still on the tourist circuit for Brazilians and foreign visitors alike, and has useful bus connections north towards the Ilha do Bananal (p.417).

Founded in 1726 as a gold-mining settlement by the *bandeirantes*, it remained the state capital until 1937. There is still a strong sense of the colonial past here, impregnating the cobbled streets and the many well-preserved eighteenth- and nineteenth-century buildings, and a preservation order was placed on the town in 1950. Stone houses and the occasional metallic clopping of mule hooves combine to produce an almost timeless atmosphere that's enhanced annually during the colourful torchlit Easter *Fogareu* procession. Famous for its *doces caseiros* (homemade fruit compotes) and local crafts, mainly ceramics and soapstone carvings, Goiás Velho also possesses a few particularly outstanding churches and houses. The **Palácio Conde dos Arcos**, built in 1743, on the Praça Castelo Branco, has some fine period furniture (Tues–Sat 8am–5pm, Sun 8am–noon). The **Museu das Bandeiras** situated on the Praça Brasil Ramos Caiado covers the story of the gold rush (Tues–Sat 8am–noon & 1–5pm, Sun noon–5pm), and there is a **Museu de Arte Sacra** in the Igreja da Boa Norte on Praça Castelo Branco (Tues–Fri 8am–5pm, Sat & Sun 8am–noon).

If you need to cool off in the afternoon after a day walking the old city streets, there's a natural swimming pool out by the **Cachoira Grande waterfalls** on the beautiful Rio Vermelho, just 7km east of town (access at km138 on the BR-070).

Practicalities

The *Rodoviária*, with connections to Goiânia and Anápolis, is on Praça Vinicius Fleury (☎062/371-1510). The *Villa Boa Hotel*, Av. Dr Deusdete Ferreira de Moura s/n (☎062/371-1000; ⑥), with a decent pool and sauna, is the best **hotel** in town. The *Hotel*

Serrano, in the same street, is cheaper and more central (☎062/371-1825; ③), while the *Araguaia* at no. 8 (☎062/371-1462; ③) is especially popular with Brazilian tourists. Cheapest of all, but still very pleasant, is *Pousada do Sol* at Rua Americano Brasil 17 (☎371-1717; ②). **Camping** is possible at *Chafariz da Carioca* near the town centre, as well as on the banks of the Rio Bacalhau, 3km towards Goiânia. One of the best places for **food** is the *Restaurante Caseiro*, Rua D. Cândido 31, which serves regional dishes for lunch and between 7pm and 10pm at night.

West of Goiânia

The shiny and mighty **Rio Araguaia** is the glory of Goiás. Even though most of the river now falls within the state of Tocantins (see p.417), the Goiás section has hundreds of fine **sandy beaches** suitable for camping, and some quite well-established resorts, very popular with the residents of Goiânia and other towns in Goiás. Rich in fish, the Araguaia is particularly popular during the dry season from May to September when the river is not so high, and serious enthusiasts come from São Paulo and Goiânia to compete. The gateway to the river is **ARUANÃ**, a small town served by only a few hotels, just over 380km northwest of Goiânia. The *Recanto Sonhado Hotel*, Avenida Altamiro Caio Pacheco (☎062/376-1230 or, in Goiânia, ☎062/212-3955 for reservations; ⑤), is very good and has a pool with water-tobogganing, a sauna and facilities for jet-skiing. At the same price but with less on offer (you should get a discount) is *Hotel Araguaia*, Praça Couto Magalhães 53 (☎062/376-1251; ⑤), also with a pool. Cheaper still, there's the *Hotel Do Sesi* (☎062/376-1221; ②). You can arrange boat trips to go fishing or rent your own boat in Aruanã, and it's one of the main ports of access for the Ilha do Bananal (see p.417). July is the busiest month when it can prove difficult even to get a room.

Parque Nacional das Emas

Right down in the southwestern corner of Goiás state, the **Parque Nacional das Emas** is beginning to open up to regular tourist visits now that it is possible to fly here from Goiânia or Brasília. Until the growth in eco-tours, this national park was only frequented by zoologists and botanists. Located in the central Brazilian highlands near the Mato Grosso do Sul border, it consists of about 1320 square kilometres of fairly pristine *cerrado*, a unique form of Brazilian savanna. As you might expect, the national park supports an enormous population of **emas** (South American rheas) and also large herds of **veado-campeiro deer**. Both are more easily spotted here than anywhere else in Brazil. The Emas park is also famous for its wide range of variously coloured and extremely large **anthills**. They are used by *coruja-do-campo* owls as lookout posts dotted across the flat plain, and are a good source of food for *bandeira* anteaters. Some of the anthills glow phosphorescently green and blue due to the activity of larvae living inside them – an amazing sight on a dark night.

There is no **accommodation** in the park and almost all visitors come by small plane from Brasília or Goiânia. The nearest hotels are just over 100km away in the small town of **Mineiros**, the best of which is *Pilões Palace*, Praça Dep. José Alves Assis (☎062/661-1547; ⑤). Although you no longer need official permission to travel individually to the park, you're still advised to contact Ibama, the national parks authority: in Goiânia at Rua 229, #95, Setor Universitária (☎062/224-2488); in Brasília, at Av. W-3 Norte 513, Edifício Imperador, Loja 301-320. Tours and flights can be organized through most travel agents in either city.

Caldas Novas and Rio Quente

More easily accessible than many of Goiás's attractions, the adjacent **thermal resorts** of Caldas Novas and Rio Quente, around 185km south of Goiânia, are incredibly popular with Brazilians from beyond the state. Taken together they lay claim to being the world's largest hot-spring aquifers, a massive and very hot natural subterranean reservoir. The healing reputation and the sheer joy of relaxing in the natural spa resorts lure plenty of people from the urban sprawl of the São Paulo region.

CALDAS NOVAS sometimes gets crowded in the dry season, from May to September, but there are thousands of hotel beds and over seventy hotels (which is over half the hotels in the entire state) within the relatively small town of only around forty thousand people. The therapeutic properties of the waters are said to include reduction of blood pressure, dissolving of kidney stones, reduction of blood viscosity, improved digestion, analgesic effect on rheumatic symptoms and even, it is claimed, the stimulation of endocrine glands and sexual vitality. While some people do come for long expensive courses of treatment, most visitors are simply on holiday, relaxing, sunbathing and taking the waters for a few days or a week.

Reservations are best made in advance, usually from Goiânia. Among the better **hotels**, *Thermas di Roma*, Rua São Cristóvão, Solar de Caldas, on the exit for Morrinhos (☎062/453-1718, fax 453-1945; half-board ⑦), has a beautiful location out of town with panoramic views, nine thermal pools, and a sauna. On the whole, it's excellent value, as is *Taiyo Thermas*, in town itself at Rua Presidente Castelo Branco 115 (☎ and fax 062/453-1334; ⑥), with three pools and a sauna. Much less expensive, although singles are the same price as doubles, is the slightly smaller *Hotel Roma*, Praça Mestre Orlando 368 (☎062/453-1335, fax 453-1340; ⑤), with six thermal pools. Cheaper still is *Hotel Triângulo*, Av. Orozimbo Correia Neto 157 (☎ and fax 062/453-1709; ④), with only one pool, but the waters are no doubt just as efficacious. Poolless, but with reasonable rooms, is *Hotel Santa Clara*, Rua América 226 (☎ and fax 062/453-1764; ②). For **camping**, *CCB-GO-2*, 4km along the road for Ipameri (☎062/223-6561), is in a beautiful location. The better hotels have their own **restaurants** or you could try the *Restaurante Papas* at Praça Mestre Orlando 12, which serves a wide variety of Brazilian dishes. The Banco do Brasil is at Rua Santos Dumont 55.

Nearby **RIO QUENTE** consists of a huge hotel complex attached to a small service town of only 2000 inhabitants. Here, hot springs emerge from the riverbed at an average temperature of around 40°C. The main feature, the dominant *Pousada do Rio Quente* complex (☎062/452-1122; reservations in São Paulo ☎011/883-1688, in Goiânia, through Nature Tur ☎062/215-2000), offers superb-quality accommodation in two hotels: the four-star *Hotel Pousada* and the five-star *Hotel Turismo* (both well into the ⑧ category). The whole complex is arranged around a natural hydrothermal spa, and in high season the minimum stay is two nights, with cheaper (but still ⑧) four-day packages offered Sunday to Wednesday.

Parque Nacional Chapada dos Veadeiros

Within Brazil, the state of Goiás is gaining a reputation as a major eco-tourism destination and the **Parque Nacional Chapada dos Veadeiros**, in the north of the state, has long been recognized as a significant site of natural beauty. Meaning "Deer Mountains" (named after the commonly spotted *Veado-campeiro* wild deer), the thousand-metre-high Chapada dos Veadeiros is the source of both the Tocantins and Parana rivers. Magnificent **waterfalls** can be seen at the Cachoeiras de Rio Preto, and armadillos, anteaters, wild pigs, capibaras and guara wolves still abound, while to the north of the park are the spectacular **cave systems** of Terra Ronca and São Domingos.

The stunning scenery, wild and sparse vegetation, cave systems and river rapids of this area have brought peace and enlightenment seekers from all over Brazil and even further afield in more recent years. A number of alternative communities have been set up in this region where there are regular UFO sightings. Although **permission** to visit the park is no longer officially needed, you do still need a guide, which can be arranged at the park gate at Sede (☎062/646-1109). And you might just as well contact Ibama anyway in either Goiânia or Brasília (see p.414), for up-to-date information and advice on the sensitive **ecological issues** at play in the region.

Practicalities

Facilities for visitors are scarce and quite basic and, though things are changing fast, an **organized tour** is still the simplest way to explore the region. Grupo Nativa, for example, based in Goiânia (☎062/224-6999), charge roughly $70 a day per person for their tours. From São Paulo, Novo Tempo (☎011/543-2677) run occasional alternative package tours (around $780 for 6 days), combining the main sights with the insights of a number of weird local sects such as the Order of the Holy Grail, the Solar Brotherhood and the Holistic Association of the Valley of the Sun. If you're determined to **go it alone**, note that there is no accommodation within the park itself, so your options are either to **camp**, for which you will need to take your own equipment and food as well as a guide, or to be based outside the park and to take day trips in.

The main settlement for access is **ALTO PARAÍSO DE GOIÁS**, some 240km north of Brasília and connected by regular **buses**; local buses run from here every day to the National Park base settlement of São Jorge. In Alto Paraíso, there's a **tourist office** on Praça do Centro Administrativa, 1km south of the centre on the GO-118 (☎062/646-1159), which can sometimes help organize trips. Two recommended official **guides** are Paulo Emilio Lemos (☎061/646-1102) and his friend Jorge Virgilio Ruppenthal. There are two main **hotels** here, but neither is outstanding or cheap. The better of the two is the clean and friendly *Hotel Grande Paraíso*, Av. Ari Valadão Fernando 18 (☎062/646-1177; ⑤), whilst the *Pousada Alfa & Ômega*, Rua Joaquim de Almeida 15 (☎061/646-1225 or 272-6156; ⑤), is only marginally less expensive. For more reasonable options, you'll have to ask around if anyone has **rooms** to rent (around $15–20 a night). A good choice for somewhere to **eat** is the *Creperie Alfa e Ômega*, Avenida Ari Valadão near the *Grande Paraíso* (evenings only, closed Mon).

But no one really travels to the Chapada to stay in an urban setting, and by far the most attractive and useful place to stay is the *Pousada Casa das Flores* in the district of São Jorge (reservations ☎061/234-7493; ③–④). Located 32km out of town along the GO-239, the *pousada* offers six rooms in stone chalets and good breakfasts. There are also a couple of basic hotels in São Jorge. From São Jorge village you can walk the 4km to the park entrance at Sede where you'll be charged a nominal fee (around $2), but beyond this you will also require the services of a **guide** ($50 a day). From the park gate, it's a further 6km to the much-photographed canyon, an astonishing natural linear trough gouged into the rock by the bluest water imaginable. Nearby is the Cachoeira das Cariocas and some of the most beautiful countryside you are likely to see in Brazil.

North of the park: Terra Ronca and São Domingos

Over 100km to the north of the Chapada are the **cave systems** of Terra Ronca and São Domingos. **Terra Ronca** has a mouth opening over 90m high and 120m wide and can be penetrated for almost 6km, at times with virtual hills inside vast caverns. The **São Domingos** complex includes more than twenty limestone caves. In 1972, yet another magnificent cave, the Caverna Angelica Bezerra, was discovered in the region.

Buses from Alto Paraíso will take you to the small towns of Monte Alegre or Campos Belos where you can rent a pickup with driver and guide out to the caves (this is likely to cost anything from $40 a day upwards). Be warned that the last 38km to Terra Ronca is a very bumpy dirt track. It's very early days tourism-wise and, all in all, it's probably best to see the caves as part of a tour; try Grupo Nativa in Goiânia (see opposite).

Tocantins

Created in 1989, the new **state of Tocantins** is not an obvious geographical or cultural unit, merely a political and bureaucratic invention. Most visitors tend to pass through the region rather than spending time around the state's hot and flyblown towns. Apart from the main north–south artery, the BR-153 highway, **transport** is difficult, and getting to the state's main attraction – the **Ilha do Bananal** – can be an expensive headache unless you're taking a guided tour (usually from Goiânia or Barra do Garças on the Mato Grosso border). As Brazilians switch on to the attractions of eco-tourism, however, things are bound to change, and probably quite rapidly. The few options that do exist for the independent traveller are detailed below.

The Ilha do Bananal

Most travellers spending time in Tocantins come to explore the **Ilha do Bananal** and the **Parque Nacional do Araguaia** in the island's northern reaches, an emerging eco-tourist destination. Bananal is the world's largest river island, over 300km long from head to tail, and home to the intrepid, canoe-faring Karajá tribe, still renowned for their fine feather craftsmanship and clay dolls. Like most parks in the region, you need **permission** to enter from Ibama in Brasília or Goiânia – addresses on p.414.

Although designated a national park, the Ilha do Bananal has lost over fifty percent of its area to settlers and development. In 1958, the British explorer, Robin Hanbury-Tenison, visited the island and its communities of several thousand Indians and witnessed two shamans performing ritual dances. Yet just thirteen years later, there were only eight hundred Indians left on the island, and today the few hundred survivors are far outnumbered by the many thousands of non-Indian Brazilian settlers. These days Indian dances are only performed on the command of government officials. This apart, it's an easy place to immerse yourself in the wonders of the forest. **Wildlife** is varied and plentiful, and it's even possible to spot a maned wolf or otters if you've the time to spend searching during the rainy season. However, as there are no roads on the island, travel is only possible by boat, which means either renting one, with a boatman as guide, in one of a small number of settlements on the island fringes or in Aruanã (see p.414); or taking an organized tour from Barra do Garças on the Mato Grosso border (see p.434) or from one of the big cities. Travel agents in Goiânia (see p.411) and Brasília (see p.404) can put together tours; in São Paulo, Iate Clube, Rua Maurício Jaquei 62 (Rudge Ramos), São Bernardo do Campo (☎011/457-3277), offers fishing trips on the Rio Cristalino, a tributary of the Araguaia, including stays in their four-bed cabins in the national park.

Access to the southern part of the island is usually from **SÃO MIGUEL DO ARAGUAIA**, some 480km northwest of Goiânia, where the Rio Araguaia starts to split to form the boundaries of the island. The nearby fishing port of Porto Luís Alves functions picturesquely as the starting point on the river, and has a couple of good but expensive **accommodation** options: try the *Hotel Mirante do Araguaia* (☎ and fax 062/271-5815; information ☎062/702-1155; ⑤) which has boats for hire, or the *Hotel Jabaru* (☎062/271-5355, fax 271-5815; ⑤) which has a pool, and offers guided walks and information on boat trips, especially for fishing. You should also try the boat crews themselves at the docks for possible river journeys. São Miguel itself is much cheaper for accommodation. Outstanding value, with good, clean rooms, all with TVs and fridges, is *Pousada Luz do Araguaia*, Rua 12, no. 371, Setor Oeste (☎062/772-1122; ③); singles are especially cheap here. Another good option is the *Hotel Paraíso*, Av. Jose Pereira Nascimento 317 (☎062/774-1061; ②). There are daily overnight **buses** to São Miguel and Porto Luís Alves from Goiânia.

Further north, about halfway along the western edge of the Ilha do Bananal, is the port of **SÃO FÉLIX DO ARAGUAIA**. The only settlement of any size around the island, São Félix is one of the few places where you can buy much in the way of stores. There's a nice beach, the **Praia do Morro**, 2km north of town. The *Pousada Kuryala*, 20km away, is a good if expensive base (⑦); you can make reservations at their Goiânia office on Avenida República do Líbano (☎063/215-1313). The *Hotel Xavante*, Av. Severiano Neves 391 (☎063/522-1305; ②), is more central and much better value. For boat trips, ask at the port along Avenida Araguaia. Irregular **buses** link the town with Barra do Garças along the BR-158. São Félix is also served by air taxis from Brasília and Goiânia; you can arrange flights at the airstrip itself.

Some 150km further north is **SANTA TEREZINHA**, the nearest point of access to the Parque Nacional do Araguaia. Situated on the western bank of the Rio Araguaia, it also backs onto the small **Tapirapé Karajá Indian Reserve**, for which you should seek permission from FUNAI in Brasília to enter. There are no facilities for tourists as yet, and access to the town is along a very bad dirt road or else by air. As there are no bus services, you could try hitching a lift from Santana do Araguaia (300km north), which is connected by bus to Araguaína.

Much easier to access is the small settlement of **PARAÍSO DO TOCANTINS**, another base for visiting the northern section of Ilha do Bananal and the Parque Nacional do Araguaia. It's due west of Palmas on the BR-153, and has one excellent-value hotel, *Serrano's Park*, Av. Bernardo Sayão 250 (☎063/602-1410, fax 602-1463; ④), with a pool and sauna. From Paraíso, a long dirt road runs to the settlement of Araguaçui, 200km northwest on the Rio Araguaia, from where it should be possible to hitch a lift on a boat south along one of the two rivers flanking the Ilha do Bananal. Alternatively, another dirt road swings off west from the BR-153 some 40km south of Paraíso to connect with the even smaller settlement of Barreira da Cruz on the eastern side of the Ilha; here there are no facilities at all for visitors and the success of your trip will depend entirely on your skills in negotiating boat rental and guides with local *fazendeiros*.

Palmas

The capital of the state, **PALMAS** lies just under 1000km north of Brasília and just over 1200km south of Belém. The town itself, though, is inconveniently set back on the banks of the Rio Tocantins, some 150km by minor roads from the main Brasília–Belém highway BR-153, and to be honest there's little reason in coming here. If you do get stuck in Palmas, the best **hotel** is the *Rio do Sono*, ACSUSO 10, conj. 1, lote 10 (☎ and fax 063/215-1733; ⑤) with nice bright rooms and a pool. Slightly cheaper, but also with a pool, is *Casa Grande*, Av. Joaquim Teotônio Sugurado, ACSUSO 20, conj. 1, lote 1 (☎ and fax 063/215-1813; ④).

Araguaína

Lying 400km north of Palmas, **ARAGUAÍNA** is many times larger, but no more attractive a place to stay. It dominates the road network in northern Tocantins, located as it is almost exactly halfway between the Araguaia and Tocantins rivers. If you do end up staying here, perhaps while changing from one bus to another, there are a few possible

places to stay. The best, with all-important cool pools, are *Tarcisio's Palace*, Av. Perimetral 1, Qd. 3, Setor Manoel Gomes, off the BR-153 (☎063/813-1110, fax 813-1177; ④), and *Olyntho Estância*, BR-153 Sul, Km 125, Gurupi exit (☎ and fax 063/813-1377; ⑤). For **restaurants**, *Gaúcha*, at Rua das Mangueiras 1246, does good *rodízio*, and more or less opposite, at no. 1213, *Don Fabrício* has a solid reputation for traditional regional cooking.

travel details

Buses

Brasília to: Araguaína (1 daily; 18hr); Belém (daily; 36hr); Belo Horizonte (6 daily; 14hr); Campo Grande (daily; 24hr); Alto Paraíso de Goiás (several weekly; 3hr); Cuiabá (daily; 20hr); Goiânia (hourly; 2hr 30min); Ibotirama (several daily; 14hr); Pirenópolis (8 daily; 3hr); Rio (daily; 20hr); São Miguel do Araguaia (daily; 9hr); São Paulo (daily; 16hr).

Goiânia to: Anápolis (20 daily; 1hr); Araguaína (1 daily; 19hr); Brasília (hourly; 2hr 30min); Caldas Novas (3 daily; 3hr); Campo Grande (daily; 18hr); Cuiabá (1 daily; 17hr); Goiás Velho (daily; 3–4hr); Pirenópolis (1 daily; 45min); Rio (daily; 18hr); São Miguel do Araguaia (daily; 9hr 30min); São Paulo (daily; 14hr).

Planes

From Brasília and Goiânia to Belém, Belo Horizonte, Manaus, Rio and São Paulo, there are several flights every day. Other daily flights to Campo Grande, Cuiabá, Fortaleza, Foz de Iguaçú, Macapá, Recife, Salvador and Santarém; less frequent flights to São Felix de Araguaia and Teresina.

CHAPTER SIX

THE MATO GROSSO

Very Brazilian, in both its vastness and its frontier culture, the **Mato Grosso** region is essentially an enormous plain rippled by a handful of small mountain ranges. Equally Brazilian, there's a firm political boundary, a line on a map, across the heart of the Pantanal swamp marking the competing ambitions of two mammoth states: **Mato Grosso** and **Mato Grosso do Sul**. The northern half of the region – the state of Mato Grosso – is sparsely populated with the only settlements of any size – Cuiabá, Rondonópolis and Cáceres – having a combined population of little over a million. Most of the state of Mato Grosso do Sul, which is marginally more populous, is either seasonal flood plain or open scrubland. Bolivian swamps and forest border it to the west; the mighty rivers **Araguaia** and **Paraná** (one flowing north, the other south) form a natural rim to the east, while the **Rio Paraguai** and the country named after it complete the picture to the south. The name Mato Grosso, which means "thick wood", is more appropriate to the northernmost state, where thorny scrubland passes into tropical rainforest and the land begins its incline towards the Amazon.

The simple road network and the limited sprinkling of settlements make **getting about** within the Mato Grosso fairly hard work. Distances are enormous, and although most of the buses and trunk roads are good, any journey is inevitably a long one. But the variety of landscape alone makes the trip a unique one and, for the adventurous traveller, there's any one of a wide range of fascinating locations – from swamps and forests to endless cattle ranches, riverine villages or jungle Indian reservations. The Mato Grosso, however, was too much for one adventurer: Colonel Fawcett, a British explorer, disappeared into its interior in 1925, never to be seen again.

The cities of the Mato Grosso are particularly deceptive. Although surprisingly modern and developed, they've only recently received the full trappings of civilization. Portuguese colonists began to settle in the region fairly late, at the time of the great **Cuiabá** gold rush of the early eighteenth century, though Cuiabá town itself remained almost completely isolated from the rest of Brazil until its first telegraph link was installed in the 1890s. Masterminded and built by a local boy made good – a down-to-earth army officer called Rondon – the telegraph lines were the Mato Grosso's first real attempt to join the outside world. These days, with the completion of Highway BR-364, Cuiabá has again become a staging post for pioneers; this time for thousands of Brazilian peasants in

---

ACCOMMODATION PRICE CODES

In this guide, accommodation has been categorized according to the price codes outlined below, based on US$. These categories represent the minimum you can expect to pay for a **double room in high season** – though note that many of the budget places will also have more expensive rooms. Rates for hostels and basic hotels where guests are charged **per person** are given in US$, instead of being indicated by price code. See p.31 for further information.

① under $20	③ $30–45	⑤ $60–80	⑦ $120–175
② $20–30	④ $45–60	⑥ $80–120	⑧ $175 and over

search of land or work in the freshly opened western Amazon states of Rondônia and Acre. Cuiabá can't exactly claim to be a resort town, but it is a natural stepping stone for exploring either the Pantanal, or the mountainous scenery of Chapada dos Guimarães.

Until 1979 Cuiabá was capital of the entire Mato Grosso. **Campo Grande** in the south, however, was also growing rapidly and playing an increasingly important financial and administrative role within Brazil. The old state was sliced very roughly in half – Campo Grande becoming capital of the brand-new state of **Mato Grosso do Sul**. This tightening of political control over the various Mato Grosso regions reflects their rapid development and relative wealth – a complete contrast to the poorer, even more expansive and much more remote wilderness of the Amazon basin.

Topographically, and in terms of its tourist potential, the Mato Grosso will always be dominated by the **Pantanal**, one of the world's largest swamps, which extends into both the states of Mato Grosso and Mato Grosso do Sul. Despite over a hundred years of cattle ranching, the swamp is renowned as one of the best places for spotting wildlife in the whole of South America, and so far seems to have absorbed Brazil's typically bovine attack on the environment. Between two million and five million cayman alligators are "culled" annually from the Pantanal, though it's better known for its array of birdlife and its endless supply of piranha fish – the latter used in an excellent regional soup dish. So far it's proved impossible to put a road right through the Pantanal, so travelling anywhere around here is slow.

After Cuiabá and Campo Grande, **Corumbá**, on the western edge of the swamp, is probably the next most popular urban destination. A very small city, it's only half an hour from Bolivia, but seven or eight from Campo Grande, the nearest Brazilian outpost. It is possible to travel through the Pantanal by river from Corumbá, directly to the port of Cáceres near Cuiabá, though unless you can afford a luxury tour this adventurous fluvial route takes at least a week, and often longer.

Getting around

There are three main **routes** through the Mato Grosso. Two fan out around the main Pantanal swamplands in tweezer-like form and run east to west: the most heavily used road, the BR-364 through Cuiabá, and the BR-262, which runs through Campo Grande to Corumbá. The third road, the BR-163, runs from south to north, connecting Campo Grande with Cuiabá, and extending north to Santarém on the Amazon river (currently impassable) and south to Paraguay and Asunción. Given the distances involved, anyone in possession of a Brazilian **air pass**, or simply limited by time, might well consider the occasional plane hop; however, you should bear in mind that Varig stopped flying to Corumbá in the mid-1990s.

The Mato Grosso is officially one hour behind the standard **time** of Brasília and the coast. In Campo Grande, however, not everybody operates on Mato Grosso time so it's always a good idea to synchronize with the right authority when arranging bus or plane reservations.

THE STATE OF MATO GROSSO

The state of Mato Grosso is dominated completely by **Cuiabá** in spite of the fact that this city is located in the very south of the state. Roads radiating from this commercial and administrative centre appear on a map like the tentacles of a gigantic octopus extending hungrily over the plains in every direction. The city is over 1000km from Brasília, almost 1500km from Porto Velho and more than 1700km from São Paulo: an opportune place to break a long overland haul. Beyond its strategic importance, though, Cuiabá's friendly personality, interesting city centre and superb ice-cream parlours can easily trap you into staying longer than planned.

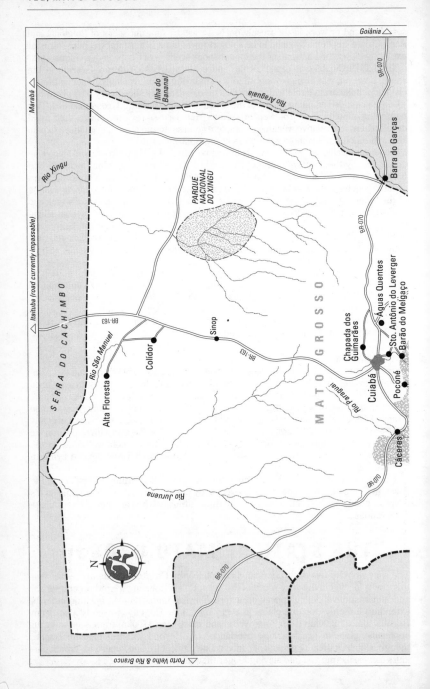

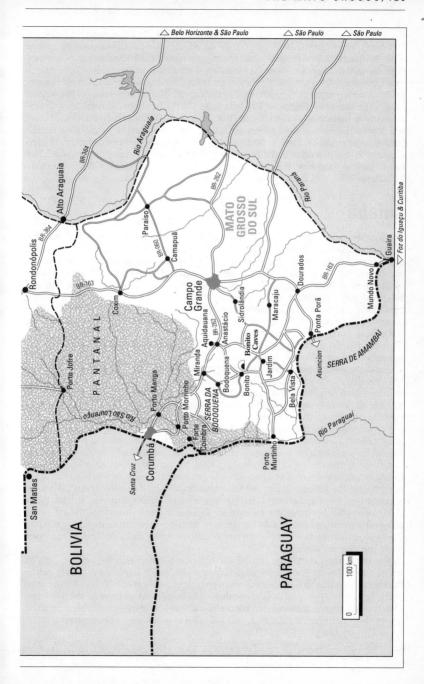

Cuiabá is a good springboard for a trip into or through the **Pantanal** (see p.454 and following) but as far as other long expeditions go, the state has disappointingly little to offer. No longer a true frontier zone, it's an established cattle-ranching region where cows are much bigger business than tourism. With almost no tourist development outside Cuiabá and the Pantanal, the reality for most travellers will be an intrepid journey by bus (and perhaps river) to some other distant city. The most arduous of the options used to be the awful **Highway BR-163** from Cuiabá to Santarém, which, in theory, connects at Itaituba with the BR-230 *Transamazônica* Highway for Altamira, Marabá and Belém. However, around 400km of road has been reclaimed by jungle along the Rio Janamxim in southern Pará, making it impassable for the foreseeable future: the furthest north you can drive is the Serra do Cachimbo on the fringes of Pará state. The fastest road is **Highway BR-364** through Cuiabá, which ultimately links São Paulo with Porto Velho and Rio Branco.

Cuiabá

The southern gateway into the Amazon, **CUIABÁ** has always been firmly on the edge of Brazil's wilderness. Following the discovery of a gold field here in 1719 (one version of the town's name means the "river of stars"), the town mushroomed as an administrative and service centre in the middle of Indian territory, thousands of very slow, overland miles from any other Portuguese settlement. To the south lay the Pantanal and the dreaded Paiaguá people who frequently ambushed convoys of boats transporting Cuiabá gold by river to São Paulo. The fierce Bororo tribe, who dominated the Mato Grosso east of Cuiabá, also regularly attacked many of the mining settlements. Northwest along a high hilly ridge – the Chapada dos Parecis, which now carries Highway BR-364 to Porto Velho – lived the peaceful Parecis people, farmers in the watershed between the Amazon and the Pantanal. By the 1780s, however, most Indians within these groups had either been eliminated or transformed into allies: the Parecis were needed as slave labour for the mines; the Bororo either retreated into the forest or joined the Portuguese as mercenaries and Indian hunters; while the Paiaguá fared worst of all, almost completely wiped out by cannon and musket during a succession of punitive expeditions from Cuiabá.

The most important development came during the 1890s, when a young Brazilian army officer, Lieutenant **Cândido Rondon**, built a telegraph system from Goiás to Cuiabá through treacherous Bororo territory – assisted no doubt by the fact that he had some Bororo blood in his veins. By 1903 he had extended the telegraph from Cuiabá south to Corumbá, and in 1907 he began work to reach the Rio Madeira, to the northwest in the Amazon basin. The latter expedition earned Rondon a reputation as an important explorer and brought him into contact with the Nambikwara Indians. Since then, Cuiabá has been pushing forward the frontier of development and the city is still a stepping stone and crossroads for pioneers, with a population approaching 800,000. Every year, thousands of hopeful settlers stream through Cuiabá on their way to a new life in the western Amazon.

The established farmlands around the city now produce excellent crops – maize, fruits, rice and soya. But the city itself thrives on the much larger surrounding **cattle-ranching region**, which contains almost a quarter of a million inhabitants. Future prosperity is assured, too: a large lead ore deposit is being worked close to the town, and some oil has been discovered at Várzea Grande; but it is more sustainable industries, like rubber and palmnut gathering, that will provide exports in years to come.

The **telephone code** for Cuiabá is ☎065.

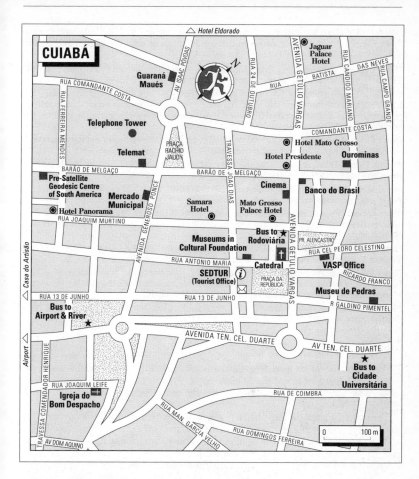

Arrival, information and accommodation

The **Rodoviária** on Avenida Marechal Rondon is an ultra-modern complex, 3km north of the city centre: it's a fifteen-minute ride into Cuiabá on buses #202, 304 or 309, or by taxi ($8–10). The **airport** , 8km south in Várzea Grande, is connected to the centre by buses marked "Tuiuiú" and taxis.

You'll be able to get **tourist information** on arrival at the airport (☎381-2211) and *Rodoviária* (☎321-0102); the offices at both open daily between 8am and 6pm. The local tourist board, SEDTUR, also has an office in the city centre, on Praça da República 131 (Mon–Fri 8am–6pm; ☎624-9060).

Accommodation

With the *Rodoviária* relatively close, most people prefer to stay in or near the busy city centre. The main area for budget hotels and *dormitórios* (all ①) has traditionally been around the old bus station, four or five blocks south of the centre along Rua

Baltazar Navarro, but many of them are now closing down or are just simply run-down. There are numerous two- and three-star hotels around the airport and on the way into town.

Hotel Central (☎321-8309) and **Hotel São Marcos** (☎624-2300), both on Rua Galdino Pimentel. Two budget options in the heart of the old town. Very basic. ①.

Colorado Palace Hotel, Av. Jules Rimet 32 (☎621-3763). One of a dozen 3-star hotels along the main road from the *Rodoviária* into town, this one's right opposite the bus station. The rooms are predictably noisy and not particularly good value, but convenient if you're leaving by bus early the next day. ④.

Hotel Eldorado, Av. Isaac Póvoas 1000 (☎624-4000, fax 624-1480). Five stars and top of the range with 182 rooms, a pool and arctic air conditioning. ⑦.

Jaguar Palace Hotel, Av. Getúlio Vargas 600 (☎322-9044, fax 322-6698). Very good value, with a restaurant and pool which non-residents may be able to use for a fee. ⑥.

Hotel Mato Grosso, Rua Comandante Costa 166 (☎321-9121, fax 321-2386). Within 3 blocks of the *praça*, with excellent-value rooms. ③.

Mato Grosso Palace, Rua Joaquim Murtinho 170 (☎624-7747, fax 321-2386). Part of the Best Western Group. Situated in a grand building behind the Fundação Cultural, with excellent service. No pool. ⑦.

Hotel Panorama, Praça Moreira Cabral 286 (☎322-0866, fax 322-0072). On the corner with Rua Ferreira Mendes, basic but good value with views over the city from its upper floors. ②.

Hotel Presidente, Av. Getúlio Vargas 345 (☎321-6162). Just two blocks from Praça da República, in a crumbling building on the corner of Rua Barão de Melgaço, this place has seen better days but is reasonable at the price (air conditioning extra). Can be loud. ②.

Hotel Samara, Rua Joaquim Murtinho 270 (☎322-6001). Clean and friendly, cheaper than *Hotel Presidente* and just as centrally located. ①.

The City

Perhaps because of its busy feel, Cuiabá is an exciting place to spend a few days. There's certainly a lot to see and do in the city's relatively self-contained centre, where modern skyscrapers jostle for attention with the ornate façades of crumbling, pastel-shaded colonial villas.

The central **Praça da República** is a hive of activity from daybreak onwards. It's the city's main meeting spot, and the cathedral, post office, the cultural foundation and university all face onto the square, while under the shade of its large trees, hippies from the Brazilian coast sell crafted jewellery and leather work. The most interesting old mansion in town, the **Palaçio da Instrução**, is on the square at no. 151. Now the **Fundação Cultural de Mato Grosso**, it houses three excellent **museums** of history, natural history and anthropology, with exhibits ranging from prehistoric through to colonial times (Mon–Fri noon–6pm, natural history section also open Sat morning; $0.50). There are some fascinating old photos of Cuiabá, along with rooms full of stuffed creatures from the once-forested region; and, best of all, a superb array of Indian artefacts. The **Catedral do Bom Jesus**, next to the cultural foundation, was built in the 1960s to replace the old cathedral, a beautiful Baroque affair which was then thought old-fashioned. Constructed of pinkish concrete with a very square Moorish facade, the new cathedral has a predictably vast, rectangular interior; its main altar is overshadowed by a mural reaching from floor to ceiling which depicts a sparkling Christ, floating in the air above the city of Cuiabá and the cathedral.

The only other church of any real interest in Cuiabá is the **Igreja de Nossa Senhora do Bom Despacho** (Mon–Fri 7am–6pm, Sat & Sun 2–6pm), which is worth seeing as much for its religious art collection as for its architecture. Sitting on the hill to the south, across the Avenida Tenente Coronel Duarte from the cathedral side of town, Bom Despacho used to dominate the cityscape before office buildings and towering hotels sprang up to dwarf it in the latter half of this century.

Just to the northeast of Praça da República, a few narrow central lanes – Pedro Celestino, Galdino Pimentel and Ricardo Franco – form a crowded pedestrian shopping area. It's here that you'll find the unusual **Museu de Pedras**, Rua Galdino Pimentel 195 (Mon–Fri 8–11am & 12.30–5pm; $2). Packed tightly into just two rooms, the museum contains the marvellously eccentric collection of Ramis Bucair, comprising gemstones, crystals, fossils, Stone Age artefacts, stuffed animals, birds and snakes. The exhibits are a hotchpotch of genuinely fascinating pieces – rocks containing liquid and loose diamonds, and a dried catfish tongue, once used as a rasp for grating *guaraná* – mixed with some outrageous fakes, such as the inch-high carved stone purported to be a shrunken human skull from some remote Indian tribe, and a display case containing a large fossilized bone, discovered locally and boldly claimed to be that of a *Tyrannosaurus rex*. An equally dubious claim is made in **Praça Moreira Cabral**, along Rua Barão de Melgaço by the state assembly buildings: a small post enclosed by a tall thin pyramid marks what was considered to be, until the advent of satellite topography, the geographical centre of the South American continent. The actual place, for what it's worth, is actually 67km away in Chapada dos Guimarães.

Having exhausted the central possibilities, there are a couple of other museums in Cuiabá, which are worth an hour or so of your time if you have any interest at all in the indigenous culture. The **ethnographic collection** belonging to the offices of FUNAI, the Foundation for Indian Affairs, is difficult to track down, as they keep moving location; it's currently on Avenida C.P.A. (☎644-1850), but it's worth checking with the tourist office. Easier to find is the smaller university-run **Museu do Índio Marechal Rondon**, on Avenida Fernando Corrêa da Costa (Mon–Fri 8–11am & 1.30–5.30pm), which also focuses on local Indian culture: it's beside the university pool, 5km east of town off Highway BR-364, in the sector known as Cidade Universitária; buses #133, #505, #513, #514 and others from Avenida Tenente Coronel Duarte will take you there. Also in the Cidade Universitária is a small army-run **zoological garden** (daily 8am–5pm), ideal if you have no time for a Pantanal tour.

Finally, focusing mainly on work by early Republican and modern Brazilian artists, there are two **art galleries** in Cuiabá – one in the Casa da Cultura, Rua Barão de Melgaço, the other, Laila Zharan, at Av. Marechal Deodoro 504.

Eating, drinking and nightlife

Cuiabá has a surprising range of cuisine and some excellent **restaurants**. Here, as in most of Brazil, eating out is very much part of the way of life and is often combined with live musical entertainment, although you'll find almost everything closed on Sundays. Avenida Getúlio Vargas hosts an array of very swish and expensive modern Italian restaurants, such as *Adriano* at no. 985 and *Tavola Piena* at no. 676; *Getúlio's* here offers decently priced drinks and cocktails, if you want to watch the cream of Cuiabá cruise by in their dream wagons in the evenings. For **cheaper eating** and *lanches* there are plenty of places in the area around Praça Alencastro, at the north end of Travessa João Dias near Rua Comandante Costa, and in the shopping zone between Rua Pedro Celestino and Rua Galdino Pimentel. **Ice-cream parlours** are an essential ingredient of any city with temperatures often over 40°C. The best in Cuiabá are *Alaska*, Rua Pedro Celestino 215, *Patotinha*, Av. Generoso Ponce 761, and *Flocky's* on Avenida Isaac Póvoas. For your own supplies, the *Mercado Municipal* is on Avenida Generoso Ponce (Mon–Sat 7.30am–6pm, Sun 7.30am–noon).

Restaurants

Barranco Bar, Rua Pedro Celestino. Inexpensive food and drinks and live Brazilian music, in a modest but friendly place – as good as any to meet the local people. One of the few cheapies open Sun.

Casa Branca, Rua Comandante Costa 565. Cheap and cheerful restaurant, 500m east of *Hotel Mato Grosso*. Closed Sun.

Choppão, Praça 8 de Abril (☎322-9101). Sleek Brazilian restaurant, 2km up Av. Getúlio Vargas, with excellent service at similar prices to its stable-mate Papagaio.

Chopp Dourado, Av. Ten. Cel. Duarte. Large and very busy place on the *avenida* with good and reasonably priced meals (about $10 a head). It tends to get packed at night with crowds dancing to its frequent live music.

Le Bam, Rua Comandante Costa. Around the corner from *Hotel Presidente*, a gem of a *lanchonete*: cheap and delicious food with exceptionally friendly owners. Mon–Sat 8am–9pm.

O Regionalíssimo, Rua 13 de Junho (☎322-3908). Excellent, moderately priced regional dishes. On Wed they serve a speciality of beef with green bananas, and there's sometimes live music at the weekends. Closed Mon.

Papagaio Grill, Av. Mato Grosso 764. Five blocks down from Av. Getúlio Vargas, presently Cuiabá's trendiest restaurant-bar and the evening focus for brash, young *Cuiabanos*, with excellent but expensive food (which works out cheapest in a group of 4 or more) and infamous cocktails. Daily 4pm–3am.

Peixaria Flutuante, Ponte Nova, 6km out of town. The best-known restaurant in Cuiabá, this is a floating eating-house specializing in fresh river fish. To get there, take the airport bus towards Várzea Grande; the restaurant is by the bridge. Daily 11am–11.30pm. Similar, on the opposite bank, is *La Barca*.

The Best, Rua Pedro Celestino 8. Refreshingly cool coffee bar with friendly service. Mon–Fri 7am–6pm, Sat 7am–4pm.

Tio Ari Natural Restaurante, Rua Comandante Costa 770. Excellent, largely vegetarian food near the Caixa Econômica bank, at very low prices.

Bars and nightlife

Although beer is twice as expensive here as it is on the coast, you'll find that **nightlife** in Cuiabá revolves mainly around the bars and restaurants in the town centre, especially along Rua Isaac Póvoas. Some places with a good atmosphere have already been mentioned under "Restaurants", like *Barranco Bar* and *Papagaio Grill*. Beyond the downtown area, along the large Avenida C.P.A. (the easterly continuation of Avenida Tenente Duarte), there are several more bars and clubs, continuously opening and closing at the fickle whim of Cuiabá's monied youth. Currently recommended – provided you have plenty of cash – are *Deck Avenida*, *Tucano* (with great sunsets) and *Terraço* with live music. The *Veneza Palace Hotel*, Av. Cel. Escolástico 738 in Bandeirantes (☎661-1480 or 321-4847), has occasional big-name bands from Rio playing live. The main gay venue, though not exactly a scream, is the bar under Hotel Presidente. Lastly, if you're desperate for a fix of Hollywood, the main **cinema** is Cine Bandeirantes, Rua Pedro Celestino 199 (☎624-3550), which screens reasonably new releases.

Listings

Airlines TAM, Rua Isaac Póvoas (☎624-0055; airport ☎682-3650); Varig, Av. 15 de Novembro 230 (☎624-6498); VASP, Rua Pedro Celestino 32 (☎624-2770; airport ☎682-3737).

Airport enquiries ☎682-2252.

Air taxis Cheap if you're travelling in a big group, an air-taxi service is a useful way of getting to some of the more remote places, and the only way during the rains to reach most of the Pantanal

TOUR OPERATORS AND GUIDES IN CUIABÁ

All of Cuiabá's travel agents offer trips into the Pantanal (see also the list of upmarket operators on p.495) or to the closer sites, like Chapada dos Guimarães, although their real work is selling flights within Brazil to businessmen and local well-to-do families. For more personal service, however, you'd do better to contact one of the **tour operators**: Anaconda Pantanal Operator, Rua Comandante Costa 649 (☎624-4142 or 624-5128, fax 624-6242), is the biggest; Tuiu Tur, Rua Barão de Melgaço 3508, sala 601 (☎624-7740), runs occasional charter flights to Bolivia, as well as being specialists in arranging Pantanal hotel bookings. If you're short of time, Ametur, Av. Joaquim Murtinho 242 (☎624-1000), runs day trips by boat to Barão de Melgaço (see p.460).

Tours within the region tend to cost upwards of $70 a day per person (though it's often worth bargaining). Note that in low season, you may have to wait a few days for enough tourists to make up your group, unless you're happy paying more. Individual **guides** to the Pantanal tend to approach arriving passengers at the airport, as well as leaving their brochures at the SEDTUR office on Praça da República.Well worth contacting for their more personal tours are Joel Souza, an excellent guide who operates from an office next door to *Hotel Presidente*, at Av. Getúlio Vargas 155-A (☎624-1386, fax 321-4323), and the ever-enthusiastic Munir of Natureco, Rua Barão de Melgaço 2015 (☎ and fax 624-5116).

pousadas. About ten companies are based at the airport, among them Guara (☎682-2288), JM (☎381-5462) and Universal (☎381-2352).

Banks and exchange Cuiabá is the only place in the region where you're likely to be able to change travellers' cheques – both cheques and notes can be exchanged in the Banco do Brasil (first floor) on Praça Alencastro (Mon–Fri 10am–4pm; $20 commission). Dollars cash can be exchanged at good rates at a number of *casas do câmbio* along Rua Ricardo Franco, at Ourominas at Rua Cândido Mariano 401 (Mon–Fri 8am–5.30pm), or in some of the larger hotels.

Buses For information phone ☎321-4803. Note that the road to Manaus is now impassable, and that buses heading for Porto Velho are frequently overloaded with personal luggage, agricultural tools and household effects. For local bus information, detailed routings of all services are listed in the *Lista Telefônica* phone book, along with a host of other useful facts.

Car rental Vitória Rent a Car, Av. Comandante Costa 1350 (☎322-7122, fax 322-7363); Trescinco Locadora, Av. Fernando Corrêa da Costa 1751 (☎627-3500, fax 627-2944) which also has a branch at the airport.

Festivals There are no truly spectacular festivals in or around Cuiabá, but June and July is the most eventful period. At São Antônio do Leverger, the dry and relatively cool month of July is designated a beach festival (see p.431); and at the same time of year there's a summer festival in Chapada dos Guimarães (see p.430).

Health Amecor Hospital (Clinica do Coração), Av. Rubens de Mendonça 898 (☎623-0770). There is an alternative health centre at Rua Balneário São João 322 (☎361-2215).

Photo equipment There are two decent photographic shops on Rua Joaquim Murtinho: Cuiabá Color at no. 789 (☎321-5031) and the friendly Artcolor next door.

Post office Praça da República (Mon–Fri 9am–6pm, Sat 9am–noon).

Shopping Try Casa do Artesão, corner of Rua 13 de Junho and Rua Senador Metello (Mon–Sat 8am–5pm), or FUNAI's Artíndia shop, Rua São Joaquim 1047 (☎323-1673; Mon–Fri 8am–noon & 1.30–4pm), for local handicrafts. More curious is the magic shop on Avenida Tenente Duarte, near the corner with Avenida Generoso Ponce – its shelves are stacked with coloured candles, ceremonial swords, North American Indian ceramic figurines, incense, diabolic pots, strings of jungle beads and seed pods. Also worth a visit is the shop Guaraná Maués, Av. Isaac Póvoas 611 (Mon–Fri 7am–7pm, Sat 7am–1pm), which specializes in the caffeine-packed natural stimulant *guaraná*, grown locally in Mato Grosso state.

Telephones National and international telephone facilities at Telemat, Rua Barão de Melgaço (Mon–Sat 7.30am–5.30pm), and phone booths outside.

Around Cuiabá

Although it's a major staging post for the Pantanal, there isn't a lot in terms of organized tourism in the immediate region **around Cuiabá**, and what there is is mostly aimed at local people. Nevertheless, the scenery around **Chapada dos Guimarães** makes a fascinating side-trip from the city – much more of a draw than either the hot springs of **Águas Quentes** or the beach at **São Antônio do Leverger**.

Chapada dos Guimarães

A paved road winds its way up to the scenic mountain village of **CHAPADA DOS GUIMARÃES**, 64km from Cuiabá, with nine daily **buses** from the *Rodoviária* covering the one-hour journey.

It is here that the true geodesic centre of South America was pinpointed by satellite, much to the chagrin of the Cuiabanos who stick resolutely to their old 1909 mark; the actual spot is marked down the southern continuation of Rua Clariano Curvo from Praça Wunibaldo. Parochial disputes aside, Chapada is an interesting settlement in its own right, containing Mato Grosso's oldest church: the **Igreja de Nossa Senhora de Santana**, a fairly plain colonial temple built in 1779. But these days, with a population nearing 14,000, the town has something of a reputation as a centre for the Brazilian "New Age" movement, and health food stores and hippy communities have sprung up here in the last fifteen years. If this doesn't grab you, Chapada dos Guimarães' other attraction is its public **swimming pool**, supplied by a natural spring, that provides welcome relief from the heat all year round. However, the pool has got somewhat smelly recently, so most locals now prefer swimming in the river a few kilometres west of town – though even that isn't totally unpolluted.

If you're here in July, you're in for a treat, with the staging of the **Festival de Inverno**. This includes drama and exhibitions, but mainly music, ranging from performances of traditional, sacred and Indian musics, to funk and rap.

Most of the year, however, it's not the town itself which brings most people out to Chapada. With over 300 square kilometres protected as a *parque nacional*, the stunning countryside consists of a grassy plateau – at 800m, the highest land in Mato Grosso – scattered with low trees, a marvellous backdrop for photographing the local flora and birdlife. Within walking distance, there are waterfalls, weird rock formations and precipitous canyons, as well as some interesting, partially excavated archeological sites. The most spectacular of all the sights around the village is the **Véu de Noiva waterfall**, which drops over a sheer rock face for over 60m, pounding into the forested basin below. You get there by walking or, if you're lucky, hitching from the village of Buruti, on the road from Cuiabá, about 12km before Chapada dos Guimarães. Alternatively, the falls lie within a couple of kilometres of the road if you jump off the bus some 6km beyond Salgadeira (ask the driver to show you the track).

If you're thinking of **staying**, both food and accommodation are available in Chapada dos Guimarães. The *Quincó* on Praça Dom Wunibaldo is the cheapest hotel, and perfectly reasonable (☎065/791-1284; ②), or try *Hotel Turismo*, Rua Fernando Corrêa 1065 (☎065/791-1176; ④), one of several mid-range options. There's a good **tour agent** in town, ECO Turismo on Praça Wunibaldo (☎065/791-1393), which organizes tours of the region and has an English-speaking guide. Joel Souza, who operates from Cuiabá (see p.429), is also worth contacting as a guide.

Águas Quentes and São Antônio

The hot baths of **ÁGUAS QUENTES**, 86km east of Cuiabá in the Serra de São Vicente, just off Highway BR-364 towards Rondonópolis, function as a weekend and honeymoon resort for locals. Apart from the baths, though, there is little of interest. The water, said to be mildly radioactive, comes in four different pools, the hottest at around 42°C, and is regarded as a cure for rheumatism, liver complaints and even conjunctivitis. There are daily **buses** from the *Rodoviária* in Cuiabá, but be warned that the resort has only one **hotel**, the expensive hydrotherapy centre of *Hotel Águas Quentes* (⑥); you can book in advance at the *Hotel Mato Grosso Palace* in Cuiabá.

The closest **beach** to Cuiabá is at **SÃO ANTÔNIO DO LEVERGER**, 35km south of the city on the Rio Cuiabá. It's as much fun as most of the beaches on the coast, even if it seems a little incongruous given the jungle backdrop, but the waters are now far from clean, carrying with them much of Cuiabá's effluent. Again, there are **buses** every day from the *Rodoviária* in Cuiabá.

On from Cuiabá

Cuiabá is a central point for all sorts of long-distance trips within Brazil, and a launching pad for onward travel into neighbouring countries. The two main regional highways, the BR-163 and the BR-364, are accessible from the city: the BR-364 is particularly important as a link between the Amazon and almost all other regions, although parts of its westernmost sections are impassable for much of the year. Whether you're coming from São Paulo, Rio, Brasília or the Northeast, this is the route to take if you want to travel overland into the western Amazon. What follows is a brief rundown of the onward possibilities from Cuiabá, taking in some of the more important stopovers. Some of the places mentioned are covered elsewhere in the text; page references will tell you where to find the relevant accounts.

To the Pantanal

It's little more than 200km by road from Cuiabá to the two main northern ports of the **Pantanal**, Porto Jofre and Cáceres. And if you decide to go to Corumbá, it's downriver from Cáceres, so it takes only four to six days, rather than the six to ten required to complete the same journey upstream. There are a number of tourist agencies in Cuiabá running organized tours; see p.429. All round – in terms of communications, buses and planes – it's well worth considering Cuiabá as a first stop for travel into the Pantanal. A full description of the Pantanal, including more detailed information about routes from Cuiabá, can be found in the section on "The Pantanal" beginning on p.454.

West to Rondônia and Porto Velho

Heading **west from Cuiabá**, Porto Velho and Rio Branco are both possible destinations in their own right, or would serve as relaxing stops on the way to Manaus, Peru or Bolivia. Following Rondon's telegraph link to Manaus in the early twentieth century, **Highway BR-364** to northern Mato Grosso and southwestern Amazon was the next development to open up the region. Paving the BR-364 cost around $600 million – partly financed by the World Bank – but construction was held up for a while when anthropologists realized that it was planned to cut straight through **Nambikwara** tribal lands. The road was eventually completed by making a large detour around these Indians, who still live in small, widely scattered groups which have very little contact with each other.

Leaving the industrial fringes of Cuiabá, the road soon enters the well-established pastoral farmlands to the west. At **Cáceres** (see p.464), three hours out of Cuiabá, the highway starts to leave the Pantanal watershed and climbs gradually towards the inhospitable but beautiful ridges of the **Chapada dos Parecis** and the state frontier with Rondônia. Here everyone has to pass through the **yellow fever checkpoint**: busloads of people spend half an hour either getting inoculated or showing their vaccination certificates. The Nambikwara and Sararé Indians live to the south of the Chapada escarpment, while to the north there are settlements of Parecis and various other groups. The process of occupation in this region is so recent and intense that the Indians have suffered greatly. Most of their demarcated lands have been invaded already and the situation is worsening all the time; local newspapers are full of reports concerning police operations aimed at removing the illegal *garimpeiros* from the reserves. The Indians don't generally come out to the highway, though sometimes you'll see a family or two selling crafted goods – bows and arrows, beads or carvings – beside the road at small pit-stops.

The second half of the 23-hour trip to Porto Velho passes through the remains of tropical rainforest. There's the occasional tall tree left standing, but more usually it's acres of burnt-out fields and small frontier settlements, crowded with people busy in mechanics' workshops or passing the time playing pool. This is **Rondônia** (see p.377), a relatively recently established jungle state, which has already, even by official reckoning, lost over fifteen percent of its original forest. Seen from the air, Rondônia looks like a fish skeleton, with parallel feeder roads running at right angles in both directions for a hundred kilometres or more into the forest, on either side of the highway. These bureaucratically designed roads, little more than 30km apart, carved up the region for rapid "development" and, by amassing the plots of disillusioned or intimidated peasants, some people were able to establish vast, though officially illegal, claims. Without government support and ill-adapted to the forest environment, convoys of landless peasants can be seen camping beside the road on their way to find a new life in the west. However, these thousands of colonists, mostly from Brazil's poor Northeast, are now being pushed on out of Rondônia, as the official programme has already been overrun by a spontaneous influx of settlers far larger than anyone dreamed of. The official attitude is that the opening up of western Amazonas is a great opportunity for a generation of the landless poor, but even if you ignore the plight of the indigenous Indians, the reality is very different. And it will become disastrous if the warnings now emanating from ecologists and other scientists are proved true: if the region turns to desert by the twenty-first century, as some currently predict, then the same generation who initially benefited will lose everything, and future generations will face real suffering.

JI PARANÁ is the only town of any real size along the BR-364, with a population that's grown from 9000 in 1970 to over 120,000. Now Rondônia's second-largest city, its main drag is dominated by a massive Ford showroom, while thousands of gigantic tree trunks sit in enormous piles. Even from the bus you can hear the electronic grating noise of circular saws, slicing the forest into manageable and marketable chunks. And on the outskirts of town, hundreds of small, new wooden huts are springing up every month. It's another five hours, through decimated jungle scenery, before you reach the jungle frontier town of Porto Velho (see p.377), capital of Rondônia state.

North towards the Serra do Cachimbo

Crossing the hills to the **north of Cuiabá**, the BR-163 heads up towards the Serra do Cachimbo (the 2000-kilometre continuation to the Amazon and Santarém, a bold but untenable attempt to cross what is still essentially a vast wilderness, is currently impassable). As the road climbs towards the rim of the Amazon basin, the forest becomes thicker and the climate muggier, and the road surface soon deteriorates. This transitional zone is one of the best areas south of Boa Vista for large-scale ranching, and there are plenty of open grasslands, it being dry enough in the dry season to burn off the old pastures to make way for fresh shoots with the first rains. Interspersed among the grasses and tangled bamboo and creeper thickets there are large expanses of cane, grown as fodder for the cows after the pasture has been burnt. Yet it's still very much a frontier land, with small settlements of loggers and brick-firers springing up along the roads as the forest is cleared away for ever.

Colonel P.H. Fawcett, the famous British explorer, vanished somewhere in this region in 1925, on what turned out to be his last attempt to locate a lost jungle city and civilization. He'd been searching for it, on and off, for twenty years, the story entertainingly told in his edited diaries and letters, *Exploration Fawcett*. This last expedition was made in the company of his eldest son, Jack, and a schoolfriend of Jack's, and following their disappearance various theories were put forward as to their fate: existing as prisoners of a remote tribe or, more fancifully, adopted chiefs. Possibly, they were murdered out in the wilds, as were dozens of other explorers over the years, although Fawcett had travelled for years among the Indians without coming to any harm. More likely, they merely succumbed to one of the dozens of tropical diseases which were by far the biggest killer at the time. The fate of the colonel remains shrouded in mystery: in 1985, the same team who had identified the body of the Nazi Josef Mengele announced that they had identified bones found in a shallow grave to be that of the colonel; but in 1996 another expedition, Expedição Autan, dissatisfied with the Mengele team's proofs, set off to try to make a DNA match, but found no trace of either the colonel or his companions.

Alta Floresta

Turning west off the BR-163 some 150km before the Serra do Cachimbo, a dirt road leads to **ALTA FLORESTA**, a rapidly growing frontier town of around 70,000 people. Located almost 800km north of Cuiabá, it's a remote but thriving agricultural settlement with regular bus and plane connections to Cuiabá and elsewhere. There's little of immediate interest unless end-of-road towns are your thing, but the town has recently opened its doors to **ecotourism** in the form of a four-star **hotel**, the *Floresta Amazônica*, Av. Perimetral Oeste 2001 (☎065/521-3601; ⑥), a tastefully developed place with expansive jungle grounds which serves as a base for the associated *Cristalino Jungle Lodge* (⑦). Deeper in the forest on a tributary of the Rio Teles Pires, which ultimately flows into the Amazon, the lodge offers a wide choice of trips and activities (around $100–150 per person per day), including visits to an *escola rural productiva* where you can buy paintings and other artefacts from local Kayaby Indians. The forest around here is particularly rich in **birdlife**, and there are several set birding trails, where you can also see alligators and capuchin, spider and howler monkeys. A similar but even more remote development, accessible only by air taxi, lies 140km northwest of Alta Floresta on the Rio São Benedito on the Pará state border: *Pousada Thaimaçu* (☎065/521-3587; ⑦) offers fishing, boat trips and pleasant chalet accommodation.

Back in town, the *Grande Hotel Coroados*, Rua F – 1, 118 (☎065/521-3111; ②), offers exceptional value and has an excellent pool, as well as a sauna, as though the climate weren't enough. Difficult to find as there are few street signs in Alta Floresta, it's one street back from Avenida Ludovico da Riva Nato in "Bloco F" at the end of a cul-de-sac. *Lisboa Palace Hotel*, at the start of Avenida do Aeroporto (☎065/521-2876 or 521-2969, fax 531-3500; ③), has larger rooms but no pool. A surprisingly good budget option is the *Hotel e Restaurante Luz Divina*, opposite the *Rodoviária* on Avenida Ludovico da Riva Nato (☎065/521-2742 or 521-4080; ①), with a wide choice of clean, modern rooms.

As buses no longer connect Cuiabá with Santarém, **flying** is the only way **northwards from Alta Floresta**. The **airport**, 2km northwest of Alta Floresta (☎065/521-2696; $10 by taxi), has daily flights (valid on Varig air passes) north to Itaituba, Santarém and Belém, and south to Cuiabá and São Paulo.

Southeast to Rondonópolis and São Paulo

For those who have arrived in Cuiabá from the Amazon, the city acts as a gateway to the rest of Brazil. From the earliest times, São Paulo was the main source of settlers arriving in the Mato Grosso, though until this century the route followed the river systems. These days, the **BR-364** runs all the way (over 1700km) from Cuiabá to São Paulo, with several daily buses taking around 24 hours minimum.

On the headwaters of the Pantanal's Rio São Lourenço, two to three hours from Cuiabá, the industrial town of **RONDONÓPOLIS** acts as a base for visiting the local **Bororo Indians**. In the present political climate, visits to Indian reservations are not always permitted – and you might consider the ethics of such visits before you decide to go. In any case, permission must be obtained first from FUNAI (see below), and they'll decide if, when and where you can go. Meanwhile, if you decide to stay here, there's a range of **hotels** in Rondonópolis, including the cheap but clean *Turis Hotel* on Rua Alagoas 61 (☎065/421-7487; ②). Good mid-range hotels include the *Hotel Nacional*, right by the *Rodoviária* at Av. Fernando Corrêa 978 (☎065/421-3245; ④), and the *Monte Libano*, Rua Rui Barbosa 1872 (☎065/421-4618; ③).

JATAÍ is almost halfway to São Paulo, about ten hours from Cuiabá in the state of Goiás. This is where many passengers will be getting off and on the bus, changing to one of the other routes which emanate from here – to Brasília, Goiânia, Belo Horizonte, Rio de Janeiro, the Northeast and Belém.

East towards Goiânia and Brasília: Barra do Garças

An alternative route from Cuiabá to Goiás Velho, Goiânia and Brasília runs east via the **BR-070**. Over 500km from Cuiabá, on the frontier between Mato Grosso and Goiás states, **BARRA DO GARÇAS** is a useful and interesting point at which to break a long bus journey. This small, isolated town of some 50,000 people sits astride the Rio das Garças, one of the main headwaters of the Araguaia, underneath low-lying wooded hills. It's a surprisingly good base for a variety of nature-based hikes or relaxing in hot-water springs, and the nearest beach is barely 1km away, the **Praia de Aragarças**. In the mountainous terrain which stretches from Barra do Garças up to the Serra do Cachimbo, the most impressive feature is the highly eroded red-rock cliff of the 700-metre Serra do Roncador, 150km due north of the town. Waterfalls and caves abound in the region; 100km to the west, there are fourteen waterfalls in the Serra Azul alone, a range which rises to over 800m.

Much nearer, just 6km northeast of town, there are more fine river beaches and the popular natural hot baths of the **Parque Balnéario das Águas Quentes** (daily 6am–9.30pm). Besides curing all the usual complaints (ulcers, kidney problems, liver disease etc), the waters are proudly proclaimed by the town's tourist office to have the capacity to augment one's *vitalidade sexual* – you have been warned! Nearby, too, there are the reserves of the Xavante and Bororo Indians. For information and to find out about written authorization to enter one of the reserves, contact FUNAI at Rua Muniz Mariano 3, Setor Dermat (☎065/861-2020), though you may find that only the Brasília offices of FUNAI can grant permission (see p.404 for address).

Practicalities

The swishest **place to stay** is the *Toriuá Parque*, with a beautiful pool some 4km beyond Barra do Garças on Avenida Min. João Alberto (BR-158), Chácara Rio Araguaia (☎ and fax 065/638-1811; ⑤). In the centre, the *Hotel Presidente*, Av. Joao Alberto 55 (☎065/861-2108; ③), and the *Novo Mundo*, opposite at no. 48 (☎065/861-1762; ②), are both reasonable. There are also two **camp sites**, one at the Porto Bae on the banks of the Rio Araguaia (access from Avenida Marechal Rondon) and the other at the Parque das Águas Quentes, 6km from town.

There's not a huge choice of **restaurants** in Barra do Garças, but the food is reasonably good and not particularly expensive. The floating *Restaurante El Barco*, at the Porto dos Pioneiros, is great for fish and open from 10am to midnight every day. Another interesting place, the *Rock Café*, Av. Rio das Garças 4 (opposite the *Aquarius Pizzeria*), is a trendy place to be seen eating and drinking in the evenings.

You can **change money** at the Banco do Brasil on Praça Tiradentes and you'll find the central **post office** at Rua I de Maio 19. There is a municipal **tourist office**, FUNDATUR, on Praça Tiradentes (☎065/861-2227 or 861-2344).

Bus connections along the BR-070 between Cuiabá and Brasília are good and there is also an **airport**, Julio Campos, 15km out of town (☎065/861-2218). Interestingly, there are three **environmental organizations** in town: CELVA, Centro Etno-Ecologico do Vale do Araguaia (☎065/861-2018); União Eco-Cultura do Vale do Araguaia, Av. João Alberto 100; and the Fundação Cultura Ambiental do Centro Oeste (Caixa Postal 246). These may be able to help with information on the region and eco-tours, as well as possibilities for **rock-climbing**, **pot-holing** and **canyoning** (abseiling down waterfalls). Lastly, Barra do Garças also serves as a possible starting point for visits to the world's largest river island, the Ilha do Bananal, in Tocantins state (see p.417).

MATO GROSSO DO SUL

A fairly new state, **Mato Grosso do Sul** is nevertheless considered to be one of Brazil's better-established economic regions. It has a distinct Wild West flavour: close to the border with Paraguay and just a bit further from Argentinian *gaúcho* territory, it's not uncommon to end up dancing Spanish polkas through the night in some of the region's bars. Until the eighteenth century the whole region was Indian territory and was considered an inhospitable corner of the New World. A hundred and fifty years and numerous bloody battles later, the Mato Grosso do Sul might now be developed and "civilized" but – thankfully – it's still a place where you can forget about industrial ravages and wonder at nature's riches.

The region's wealth comes predominantly from cattle ranching, something you don't even escape in the state capital, **Campo Grande**, which sports cowboy supply shops along its modern city streets. It's a useful base from which to delve deeper into the Mato Grosso. The road connection to Corumbá is well served by buses, so reaching the Pantanal is fairly easy. But the swamp is vast, stretching into the state from north to southwest, so you can also get a good look at the wildlife from a variety of road-linked places closer to Campo Grande – like **Coxim**, north of the city, or **Aquidauana**, to the west.

The south of the state is favoured by the beautiful hills of the **Serra da Bodoquena** and **Serra da Maracaju** and, deep in the Bodoquena hills, you can visit the spectacular **Bonito caves**. Further south, 319km from Campo Grande, **Ponta Porã** sits square on the Paraguayan border, from where there's a two-day overland route to Asunción. There are also several daily bus services from Campo Grande via **Dourados** and **Mundo Novo** to Guaira and the amazing falls of Foz do Iguaçú in the neighbouring state of Paraná.

Campo Grande

Nicknamed the "brunette city" because of its chestnut-coloured earth, **CAMPO GRANDE** has in less than forty years been transformed from an insignificant settlement into a buzzing metropolis, with a population rapidly approaching a million. Founded in 1889, the city was only made the capital of the new state of Mato Grosso do Sul in the late 1970s, since when it has almost doubled in size, though it retains a distinctly rural flavour: its downtown area manages to combine skyscraping banks and apartment buildings with ranchers' general stores and poky little shops selling strange forest herbs and Catholic *ex votos*. Unnervingly reminiscent of Dallas in parts, it's a relatively salubrious market centre for an enormous cattle-ranching region; it's also an

> The **telephone code** for Campo Grande is ☎067.

important centre of South American trade routes from Paraguay, Bolivia, Argentina and the south of Brazil.

An obvious place to break a long journey between Cuiabá or Corumbá and the coast, Campo Grande tries hard to shake off the feeling that it's a city stuck in the middle of nowhere. Apart from the *gaúcho* influence on some of the shops, the town centre is much like that of any other medium-sized city; the people are friendly and there's little manifest poverty. The generally warm evenings inspire the locals to turn out on the streets in force. Chatting over a meal or sipping ice-cold beers at one of the restaurants or bars between Avenida Afonso Pena and Rua Maracaju, the guitars, maracas and congas are often brought out for an impromptu music session.

Arrival and accommodation

The **Rodoviária** is a ten-minute walk west of the central Praça Ari Coelho at Rua Joaquim Nabuco 200 (☎383-1678). A surprisingly large bus terminal, it also houses six hairdressers, a cinema, bookstores and several bars. A **word of warning**, however: the *Rodoviária* is known for its unsavoury types, and though you should have no problems during the day, the area is best avoided at night unless you're confident of yourself and haven't much to lose. (Similarly, the district south of Avenida Afonso Pena is also acquiring a dodgy reputation.) If in doubt, take a **cab**: there's a taxi rank in the bus station, or phone Rádio Táxi on ☎787-1414.

The other point of arrival is the **airport**, Aeroporto Internacional Antônio João (☎763-2444), 7km out of town on the road towards Aquidauana. Buses from there to the *Rodoviária* cost around $1, taxis $6. **Tourist information** and hotel bookings can be had at the very helpful, privately run tourist office, the Morada dos Bais (☎724-5830; Tues–Fri 9am–8pm, Sat 9am–noon), at Av. Noroeste 5140 on the corner with Avenida Afonso Pena.

Accommodation

With the demise of passenger trains, the majority of **hotels** around the *Rodoviária* have smartened up their act, now offering quite acceptable alternatives to both the downtown and rather defunct train station options. The better budget ones are around the junction of Rua Barão do Rio Branco and Rua Allan Kardek, one street west of the *Rodoviária*.

Hotel Caçula, Av. Calógeras 2704 (☎721-4658). One of Campo Grande's most basic hotels, rather squalid but exceptionally friendly. ①.

THE CAMPO GRANDE RAILROAD

Look at any map of the region, and you'll see a thin black line tracing the path of a long railroad which connects São Paulo on the Atlantic with Campo Grande, where it forks to Corumbá on the Bolivian border, and to Ponta Porã on the Paraguayan frontier. Unfortunately, the privatization of the Brazilian railways has led to the closure of all passenger lines west of Bauru, perhaps forever. This is a real shame, not least because the Corumbá line formed part of an even longer rail system, connecting with the Bolivian Tren de los Mortes to Santa Cruz; from there it's still possible to continue by train into Chile or via La Paz into Peru, over Lake Titicaca (by boat or around it on a bus) and on to Cuzco. There seems little chance in the immediate future of the lines being reopened (though freight trains are still running), but hopefully, with ever-increasing tourist interest in the Pantanal and Mato Grosso do Sul, services may in the course of time resume.

Hotel Campo Grande, Rua 13 de Maio 2825 (☎721-6061, fax 724-8349). Campo Grande's top hotel, with 4 stars and all the modern conveniences and luxuries one expects. ⑦.

Exceler Plaza Hotel, Av. Afonso Pena 444 (☎721-0102, fax 721-5666). Another plush parlour where you'll be coddled and swaddled in all the usual 4-star treats. ⑧.

Grande Hotel Gaspar, Av. Mato Grosso 2, near the train station (☎ and fax 383-5121). Plenty of laid-back charm, though crumbling a bit around the edges. ④.

Hotel Iguaçú, Rua Dom Aquino 761, next to the *Rodoviária* (☎384-4621, fax 721-3215). Not particularly clean, but reasonable value nonetheless. The *Cosmos* next door is similar. ③.

Indaiá Park Hotel, Av. Afonso Pena 354 (☎384-3037, fax 721-0359). 3-star hotel with pool, restaurant and piano bar, but rather impersonal. Better value than the *Hotel Vale Verde*, on the same road at no. 106. ⑥.

Hotel Internacional, Rua Allan Kardek 223 (☎384-4677, fax 721-2729). The largest and flashiest of the hotels around the *Rodoviária*, and surprisingly well appointed, with TVs and phones in all rooms and even a pool for the weary to sink into. Well worth the extra few *reais*. ③.

Hotel Jandaia, Rua Barão do Rio Branco 1271 (☎721-7000, fax 721-1401). Excellent new 4-star hotel on the corner with Rua 13 de Maio. ⑦.

Hotel Nacional, Rua Dom Aquino 610 (☎ and fax 383-2561). Probably the best value of the budget places around the *Rodoviária*, with plenty of character. Choice of fans or air conditioning. ③–④.

Palace Hotel, Rua Dom Aquino 1501 (☎384-4741, fax 382-3604). A central, rather faceless, mid-range hotel. ③.

Turis Hotel, Rua Allan Kardek 200 (☎382-7688). One block from the *Rodoviária*, safe and good value for its clean rooms. ②.

Hotel União, Av. Calógeras 2828 (☎382-4213). Close to the train station, simple and run-down but clean and excellent value. ①.

Hotel Zys, Rua Barão do Rio Branco 342 (☎383-3778). Basic but one of the cheapest downtown. ①.

The City

The surprisingly modern heart of Campo Grande is based around the Praça Ari Coelho, five blocks east of the *Rodoviária*. Tourism is fairly low key in the city, but there's enough to keep you interested for a couple of days. One of the best-known attractions is the **Museu Dom Bosco** (Mon–Fri 8am–6pm, Sat 8am–5pm, Sun 8–11.30am & 1–5pm), in the university building facing the Praça da República, at Rua Barão do Rio Branco 1811–43. A fascinating place, it's crammed full of exhibits, ranging from superb forest Indian artefacts to over 10,000 terrifying dead insects – and some astonishingly beautiful butterflies. Most impressive of all is the vast collection of stuffed birds and animals, including giant rheas (the South American version of an ostrich), anacondas and examples of the Brazilian marsupials – the gamba and the quica. Closer to the city centre, the **Casa do Artesão** (Mon–Fri 8am–6pm, Sat 8am–noon), on the corner of Avenida Calógeras and Avenida Afonso Pena, is slightly disappointing considering the huge region it is supposed to represent (not least the Terena, Kadiwéu and Guato peoples). Housed in a refurbished two-storey hall (once Campo Grande's only bank), it sells mostly local craft works, the best pieces without a doubt being the wood-carvings, often depicting mythical symbols like fish-women and totemic figures. In general, though, the feel is of a modern arts and crafts gallery rather than anything truly ethnic.

If you're desperate for culture, there is another museum, the small **Museu José A. Pereira** (Mon–Fri 8–11am & 1–4.30pm), which deals with local history, out at Cidade Universitária, several kilometres from the city centre: to get there, take a taxi which will cost $5–6, or it's a forty-minute walk following the street signs south along Avenida Calógeras. Closer to the centre are two **galleries** specializing in local, contemporary art: Museu de Arto Contemporânea de Mato Grosso do Sul (MARCO), Av. Calógeras 2499 (Tues–Fri 9am–6pm, Sat & Sun 9am–4pm), and the Centro Cultural de Mato Grosso, Rua 26 de Agosto 463. The Banco do Brasil, Rua 13 de Maio 2691 at the corner

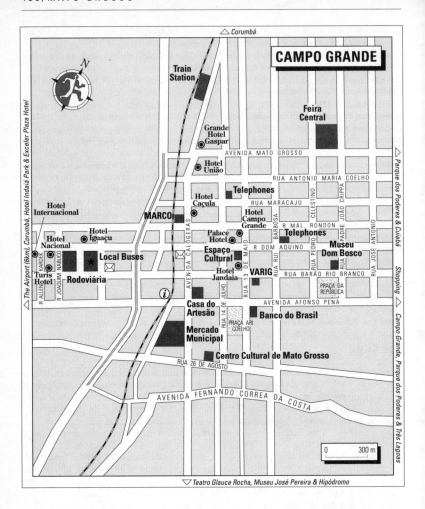

△ Corumbá

CAMPO GRANDE

Train Station

Feira Central

Grande Hotel Gaspar

AVENIDA MATO GROSSO

Hotel União

RUA ANTONIO MARIA COELHO

Hotel Internacional

Telephones

Hotel Caçula

RUA MARACAJU

MARCO

Hotel Campo Grande

Hotel Iguaçu

Palace Hotel

Telephones

Hotel Nacional

Espaço Cultural

R DOM AQUINO

Museu Dom Bosco

Local Buses

Turis Hotel

Rodoviária

Hotel Jandaia

VARIG

RUA BARÃO RIO BRANCO

PRAÇA DA REPÚBLICA

AVENIDA AFONSO PENA

Casa do Artesão

Banco do Brasil

PRAÇA ARI COELHO

Mercado Municipal

Centro Cultural de Mato Grosso

RUA 26 DE AGOSTO

AVENIDA FERNANDO CORREA DA COSTA

0   300 m

▽ Teatro Glauce Rocha, Museu José Pereira & Hipódromo

with Rua Dom Aquino, also has an *espaço cultural* with regular exhibitions of art and photos (daily 10am–5pm).

If all this feels too static, much more immediate encounters with the *indígenos* are to be had at two local markets: the **Feira Indígena** by the Mercado Municipal (daily, closed Mon morning) and the more compelling **Feira Central**, Rua Abrão Julio Rahe, off Avenida Mato Grosso. The latter takes place twice a week, overnight from 3pm to 6am, starting Wednesdays and Saturdays, and attracts a large number of forest Indians selling weird potions and bundles of bark, beads and leatherwork, as well as a few Paraguayans selling toys. The eclectic blend of peoples is further compounded by the variety of foods on offer, ranging from *churrasquinho* to Japanese *yaki soba*.

For the flip side to contemporary Mato Grosso culture, the **cowboy shops** along Rua 14 de Julho are just as strange, selling gunbelts, holsters, saddles and boots. You can see some of this gear in action at the **horseracing**, out at the Hipódromo, run by the

Jóquei Clube de Campo Grande; the Hipódromo is 5km along Highway BR-167, beyond the exit for Dourados.

If all this is too much for you, head for the **Parque dos Poderes**, beyond the town centre at the end of Avenida Mato Grosso (Mon–Fri noon–6pm), a calm ecological reserve that's home to a variety of native plants and a small selection of the region's wild animals.

Eating, drinking and nightlife

Eating out is an important part of the local lifestyle and this is reflected in the diversity of restaurants. There are scores of **lanchonetes**, especially around the *Rodoviária* and east along Rua Dom Aquino, and, during the hot afternoons, the city's many **juice bars** are popular: you'll find them on most street corners. As a cattle-ranching market centre, a lot of cows get roasted daily in Campo Grande, so if you're mad for **beef** you're in for a treat; however, there are vegetarian options and several good Chinese restaurants. As restaurants in Campo Grande have a habit of disappearing or moving location with annoying rapidity, telephone numbers are given in the listings below.

Cantina Romana, Rua da Paz 237 (☎383-4204). Wonderful Italian food, fair prices.

Casa do Peixe, Rua João Rosa Pires 1030 (☎382-7121). A very popular venue for good regional food, often with live music. It's exceptional value and the service is excellent.

Kallil Karnes, Av. Furnas 142, near the Shopping Campo Grande shopping centre towards the eastern end of Av. Afonso Pena (☎726-3715). New meat house with a good reputation, but somewhat out of the way unless you're thinking of clubbing afterwards (see below).

Multiplus Vegetallis, Rua 13 de Junho 756 (☎725-8109). Good vegetarian restaurant despite its steroid-sounding name.

Rádio Clube, Rua Padre João Crippa 1280 (☎721-0131). Brisk and cheap, popular with students.

Rei da Picanha, Av. Afonso Pena 1907 (☎384-5701). The most popular meat house in town, with the added bonus of live music every evening.

Restaurante Casa Grande e Senzala, Rua 14 de Julho 757 (☎721-2605). Traditional and rural Brazilian cooking, but expensive.

Restaurante China, Rua Pedro Celestino 750 (☎382-4476). One of the best Chinese restaurants in town, with very reasonable prices; the fried duck (*pato frito*) is particularly recommended.

Restaurante Hong Kong, Rua João Rosa Pires 761 (☎724-3237). Another excellent Chinese restaurant, specializing in local tofu and regional curries; moderately priced.

San Marino Pizzas, Av. Afonso Pena 2716 (☎721-5084). One of several reasonable pizzerias on Afonso Pena, with delivery service.

Seriema Restaurante, Av. Afonso Pena 1919 (☎721-2475). Next door to *Rei da Picanha*, this is also a lively steak house, with cheap lunchtime *rodízio*.

Viva a Vida, Rua Dom Aquino 1354, 1st floor (☎384-6524), and Av. Fernando Corrêa da Costa 2177 (☎721-3208). Campo Grande's favourite vegetarian restaurants (meat also available), self-service, open lunchtimes only. Closed Sat.

Nightlife

Most of Campo Grande's action happens at weekends, when the *churrascarias* and other large restaurants generally serve their food to the energetic sounds of Paraguayan polkas (*Rei da Picanha* has them weekdays also). **Nightclubs** tend to change quickly, but those currently popular are *Limit* (200m off Av. Afonso Pena by Shopping Campo Grande), *Nix Club* on Avenida Afonso Pena near Rua 25 de Dezembro, and *Mr. Dam* at 197 Pajuçara off Avenida Ceará (turn right from Av. Afonso Pena, and it's on the left). All three are well to the east of the city centre, and play a mix of Brazilian, European, Stateside and underground sounds.

The *Glauce Rocha* **theatre** is out of town, in Cidade Universitária, but often hosts interesting Brazilian works (☎387-3311 for details, or see the local press). *Peña Eme-Ene*, on the corner of Avenida Afonso Pena and Rua Barbosa, is a popular meeting place for artists and musicians, which has live **regional music** every Thursday night from 8pm – no entrance fee but you're expected to take dinner (☎383-2373; Mon–Wed & Fri 7.30am–6pm, Thurs 7.30am–midnight, Sat noon–6pm).

Listings

Airlines Pantanal Linhas Aéreas, Rua Maracaju 1525 (☎383-3238 or 763-3859); TAM, Av. Afonso Pena 1974 (☎383-2933); Varig, Rua Barão do Rio Branco 1356 (☎383-4070); VASP, Av. Calógeras 2129 (☎382-4491). All are open Mon–Fri 8am–4pm, Sat 8am–noon.

Air taxis Mato Grosso do Sul, Av. Duque Caxias (☎763-1131, fax 763-2766).

Banks and exchange You can change money in the Banco do Brasil, just off the main square at Av. Afonso Pena 133 (Mon–Fri 10am–5pm); at the *Câmbio*, Rua 13 de Maio 2484; at the airport bank; or, if you're persuasive, in one of the larger hotels.

Bingo Only recently introduced to Brazil, bingo has proved very popular with young and old alike. The *Salas do Bingo* are at Av. Mato Grosso 3566 and Rua 14 de Julho 1453.

Bus departures There are numerous daily services from the *Rodoviária* to Aquidauana, Belém, Belo Horizonte, Bonito, Brasília, Corumbá, Cuiabá, Dourados, Ponta Porã on the Paraguayan frontier and São Paulo, with less frequent connections to other places described in this chapter. There are also services along a relatively well-worn trail to Asunción. See "travel details" on p.464 for further details of frequencies and durations. Tickets out of the city should be bought in advance from one of the kiosks on the first floor of the *Rodoviária*.

Car rental Brascar, Rua Fernando Corrêa da Costa 975 (☎383-1570); Unidas, Av. Afonso Pena 829 (☎384-5626).

Consulates If you're heading into either Paraguay or Bolivia from Campo Grande, you should check on border procedures and visa requirements. The Paraguayan consul is at Rua Padre João Crippa 1065 (☎721-4430), and the Bolivian consul at Rua Dom Aquino 1354 (☎382-2190); both are open Mon–Fri 9am–5pm.

Hospital Santa Casa, Rua Eduardo Santos Pereira 88 (☎382-5151).

Police ☎190.

Post offices The branch at Av. Calógeras 2309 on the corner with Rua Dom Aquino is open Mon–Sat 9am–5pm; the one on Rua Barão do Rio Branco by the *Rodoviária* stays open till 6pm.

Shopping The busiest shopping streets are mostly congregated in the square formed by Av. Calógeras, Av. Afonso Pena, Rua Cândido Mariano Rondon and Rua Pedro Celestino. For music cassettes, a street market selling plastic goods and electronics sets up daily along Rua Barão do Rio Branco between the *Rodoviária* and Av. Calógeras.

Travel agencies and tour guides Dallas, Rua Barão de Rio Branco 1484 (☎384-2030), and NPQ Turismo, Av. Afonso Pena 2081, on Praça da Ari Coelho (☎725-6789), are best for flights. For help in sorting out an organized tour to one of the local sites, like the Pantanal or Bonito, try Pantanal Express, Av. Afonso Pena 2081, facing the *praça* but hidden away at the back of the shopping arcade (☎382-5333); expect to pay $100–150 a day. Impacto Turismo, Rua Padre João Crippa 1065, sala 106 (☎382-5197), also runs good Pantanal tours; Ney Gonzalves is an excellent guide. Also in Campo Grande, Lilian Borges Rodrigues is a very good English-speaking guide; contact her at Rua Octavio de Souza 464, Monte Libano (☎067/742-2204). See also the box "Upmarket Pantanal Agents and Operators" on p.459.

North to Coxim

The area of scrub forest to the east of Coxim and north of Campo Grande used to be the territory of the **Caiapó** Indian nation, who ambushed miners along the routes to Goiás and Cuiabá from São Paulo, posing a serious threat to Portuguese expansion and development in the mid-eighteenth century. In reaction to the successful use of Bororo

Indian mercenaries against their main villages in the Camapua area, the Caiapó took their revenge on the growing numbers of Portuguese settlers and their farm slaves in the area. In 1751 – the same year that the governor of Brazil declared an official military campaign against them – the Caiapó went as far as attacking the town of Goiás, beyond the northern limits of their usual territory.

Today, **COXIM** is a quiet place, easily reached by bus from Campo Grande in around three to four hours (six or seven hours from Cuiabá). Situated on the eastern edges of the Pantanal, it's a fantastic **fishing** centre: the fisherman Pirambero runs excellent trips into the swamp, down the Rio Taquari, to catch piranhas (ask for him at the port). If you're really serious about angling, contact the local fishing club, the Iate Clube Rio Verde, at Rua Ferreira, Bairro Piracema (☎067/291-1246). Besides fishing, **swimming** in the Rio Taquari, around Campo Falls, is a popular pastime, too, in spite of the razor-teethed fish, and, nearby on the Rio Coxim, the **Palmeiras Falls** are a good place for a picnic or to camp a while. From November through to January, the two falls are the best places to see the incredible *piracema* spectacle – thousands of fish, leaping clear of the river, on their way upstream to the river's source to lay their eggs.

Coxim offers plenty of **accommodation** possibilities, including the *Hotel Neves* one block from the *Rodoviária* in an old brick farmhouse (☎067/291-1273; ③); the very basic *Aconchega* right opposite the bus station (no ☎; ①); and the more upmarket *Hotel Santa Ana*, Rua Miranda Reis (☎067/291-1602; ③), with a pool and bar. There are many more hotels, mostly aimed at fishing holidaymakers, 5km away in Silviolândia. When it's time to move on, it might be worth enquiring about **river boats to Corumbá**. The Rio Taquari has silted up considerably in recent years – the effect of land clearance for cattle grazing and agriculture, leading to huge amounts of topsoil being shifted into the river systems – and as a result, boats along the river, once common, are now rare – though there are still a few.

South to the Paraguayan border

There's no great draw – in fact, no draw at all – in the towns south of Campo Grande en route to the Paraguayan border. The only settlement of any size is **DOURADOS**, 224km from the state capital, a violent, rapidly expanding place which recently overtook Corumbá as Mato Grosso do Sul's second largest city. Its name is a reminder of the fact that the spot was first settled by travellers en route to the Cuiabá gold mines. These days, it's the region's most important agricultural centre, but there's little of interest to the tourist except bus connections to points further south and west (the daily bus to Bonito currently leaves at 3pm). Should you get stranded overnight, three reasonable **accommodation** options are *Hotel Bahamas*, Rua João Cândido da Câmara 750 (☎067/421-4714; ③), *Figueira Palace Hotel*, Rua Toshinobu Takayama 553 (☎067/421-5661; ③), and, best value of all, *Turis Hotel*, Av. Marcelino Pires 5932 (☎067/422-1909, fax 421-8827; ②).

MUNDO NOVO, about eleven hours by bus from Campo Grande, is another transport terminus, if anything even less attractive. From here, buses run to the crossing point for ferries to Guaira, and to Porto Frajelli and Foz do Iguaçu. If you get stuck overnight, the *Hotel Marajoara*, Av. Castelo Branco 93 (☎067/474-1692; ②), has decent **rooms**.

Ponta Porã

Despite the distinctly unthrilling towns that have gone before, **PONTA PORÃ** itself is an attractive little settlement, right on the Paraguayan border up in the Maracaju hills. The **Avenida Internacional** divides the settlement in two – on one side of the street you're in Brazil, on the other in the Paraguayan town of **Pedro Juan Caballero**. On the Paraguayan side you can polka the night away, gamble your money till dawn or, like most people there, just buy a load of imported goods at the duty-free shops. There's a strange blend of language and character, and even a unique *mestizo* cuisine, making it an interesting place to spend a day or two. Ponta Porã also has a tradition as an distribution centre for *maté* herb – made into a tea-like drink containing caffeine.

There are plenty of **hotels** to choose from, though most budget travellers tend to go for the *Alvorada* (②) or *Dos Viajantes* (①), over the road from the train station, both of which are cheap and friendly. The *Internacional*, Av. Internacional 2604 (☎067/431-1243; ③), is a mid-range hotel with regular hot water, while for a plusher stay, it's hard to beat the *Pousada do Bosque*, just outside of Ponta Porã at Av. Presidente Vargas 1151 (☎067/431-1181, fax 431-1741; ⑤), with its welcoming swimming pool. Other reasonable options include *Porta do Sol Palace Hotel*, Rua Paraguai 2688 (☎067/431-2664; ④), *Barcelona Hotel*, Rua Guia Lopes 45 (☎067/431-3061; ④), and *Frontier Palace Hotel*, Av. Brasil 1119 (☎067/431-2825; ③).

Crossing the border is a simple procedure for most non-Brazilians. An exit stamp must be obtained from the Polícia Federal at Rua Mal. Floriano 1483 (☎067/431-1428) on the Brazilian side, then it's a matter of walking four or five blocks down Rua Guia Lopes to the Paraguayan customs and control. If you need a visa for Paraguay you can get this from the consulate on Avenida Internacional on the Brazilian side. If you're pushed for time, catch a cab from the bus station to complete exit and entry formalities; the fare is about $10, including waiting time. Once in Paraguay, there's a reasonably good road direct to Concepción, a major source of imports and contraband for Brazilians; daily buses make the five- or six-hour trip in good weather. It's another five hours from there to Asunción; there's also a direct service (8–10hr) from the bus station in Pedro Juan Caballero. There's no problem **changing money** at decent rates on Avenida Internacional. However, it's impossible to change travellers' cheques on Sundays and holidays.

Bela Vista and Porto Murtinho

The two other interesting destinations on the Paraguayan border are Bela Vista and Porto Murtinho. Both are to the west of Ponta Porã and though they're harder to reach, they do have hotels and restaurants once you're there. Although it's not technically legal to cross the frontier into Paraguay at these places, they are worth visiting for their natural splendour alone. Both towns are served by **bus** from Dourados (a good day's journey), and from Jardim (8hr), which in turn is connected daily with Anastácio (4hr).

Bela Vista
In **BELA VISTA** you can explore the natural delights of the Piripacu and Caracol rivers, behind which are the unspoilt peaks of the Três Cerros and Cerro Margarida. There's also the extraordinary **Nhandejara bridge**, with a natural underground passage over 30m long. Most Brazilians, however, come here for the opportunity to buy imported goods: over the border is the Paraguayan town of Bela Vista, which has a road connection (a day's travel) to Concepción. If you need to stay, try the *Pousada da Fronteira*, Av. Teodoro Sativa (☎067/439-1487; ③).

Porto Murtinho
Remote and tranquil, **PORTO MURTINHO** owes its foundation to the thriving trade in the tea-type herb, *erva maté*. The town, of 13,000 inhabitants, sits on the banks of the Rio Paraguai, over 470km southwest of Campo Grande, near where the river finally leaves Brazilian territory. Well blessed with abundant wildlife and luxuriant vegetation,

it marks the very southern limits of the Pantanal swamplands. Porto Murtinho is quite a cheap place from which to make excursions in riverboats, though you might be expected to haggle over the price a little, since there are often several boatmen to choose from at the riverfront.

For **accommodation**, *Hotel Americano*, Rua Dr Corrêa 430 (☎067/287-1344, fax 287-1309; ⑤ full board), has 38 large, air-conditioned rooms and boats for residents' use (rowing boats $15, motorboats $45); 1km out of town, in the Fazenda Saladero, is the similar *Saladero Cue* (☎067/287-1113, fax 287-1352; ④), which has a beautiful riverside location and also has boats for hire; slightly cheaper but not as nice is the *Pousada do Pantanal*, Rua Alfedo Pinto 141 (☎067/287-1325; ③). Lastly, the *Americano* owns and runs *Hotel Nabileque* (⑥), 120km upriver on the Rio Nabileque, and primarily a base for anglers. The hotel is actually built on the river, supported on stilts, and has boats for hire ($20–45). Daily boats (3hr) from the *Americano* will get you out there.

West towards Corumbá

Several **buses** daily connect Campo Grande with Aquidauana/Anastácio (2hr) and Corumbá (7hr), the scenery becoming increasingly swamp-like the further west you travel. It may still be worth enquiring about the axed passenger train to Corumbá (see p.436) in case someone has had the good sense to restart it.

West of Campo Grande, the savanna becomes forested as the road approaches the first real range of hills since leaving the Atlantic coast. Sticking up like a gigantic iceberg in the vast southern Mato Grosso, the **Serra de Maracaju** provided sanctuary for local Terena Indians during a period of Paraguayan military occupation in the 1860s. Under their somewhat crazy and highly ambitious dictator, Lopez, the Paraguayans invaded the southern Mato Grosso in 1864, a colonial adventure that resulted in the death of over half the invasion force, mostly composed of native (Paraguayan) Guarani Indians. It was one period in Brazilian history when Whites and Indians fought for the same cause, and it was in the magnificent Serra de Maracaju hills that most of the guerrilla-style resistance took place. Beyond, interesting geological formations dominate the horizon: vast towering tors, known as *torrelones*, rise magnificently out of the scrubby savanna.

Further along, around the small station of **Camisão**, is a relatively lush valley supporting tropical fruits, sugar cane and, of course, beef cattle. Further west, the green hills of the Serra do Bodoquena appear to the south: although rarely peaking over 500m, this range stretches from the attractive country resort of Bonito in the east as far as Corumbá in the west.

Aquidauana and Anastácio

The next town, **AQUIDAUANA**, 130km from Campo Grande, is a lazy-looking place and very hot, sitting under the beating sun of the Piraputanga uplands. Since the demise of the passenger trains to Corumbá, it sweats somewhat uncomfortably some distance from the main BR-262 highway, and though it still serves as one of several gateways into the Pantanal (see p.458), it's better known for fishing and walking, with some superb views across the swamp. It's worth enquiring about two nearby but seldom visited sites: the ruins of the **Cidade de Xaraés**, founded by the Spanish in 1580 on the banks of the Rio Aquidauana; and the **Morro do Desenho**, a series of prehistoric inscriptions on the riverbank and in the nearby hills.

The river running through the town boasts some pleasant sandy **beaches**, quite clean and safe for swimming especially between May and October; **fishing** championships are an integral part of the annual São João festival here. There's a reasonable choice of **hotels**, including the quiet *Hotel Pantanal* (☎067/241-1929; ②) at Rua Estevão Alves

Correa 2611 opposite the *Rodoviária*, and the *Hotel Tropical*, Rua Manoel Aureliano Costa 630 (☎067/241-4113; ③), which is one of the best in town. One of several decent **restaurants** in town is the *Restaurante Palladar*, Rua Mal. Mallet 1047(☎067/241-3727), which is expensive but serves good Brazilian dishes (closed Sun evening).

The neighbouring town of **ANASTÁCIO** – half an hour's walk on the other side of the river – has some nice beaches of its own, but is best known for the large *jaú* fish (often weighing over 75 kg) that live in its river. Anastácio is the transport hub of the region, with daily bus services to Bela Vista, Bonito, Miranda and Ponta Porã, as well as Campo Grande and Corumbá. If you're lucky enough to have your own wheels, there's an infrequently taken road which skirts the southeastern rim of the Pantanal right up to **Rio Verde do Mato Grosso**, 200km north of Campo Grande on the way to Cuiabá, which has ample opportunities for bathing in the transparent waters and cascades which feed the Rio Verde.

Fifty kilometres south of Aquidauana on the road towards Bonito, the *Cabana do Pescador* **luxury fishing lodge** on the Rio Miranda (reservations ☎067/241-3697), is another relaxing destination and a possible base from which to take a tour to the Bonito caves; there are frequent buses from the *Cabana* to both Aquidauana and Bonito.

Bonito and around

Nestling in the Bodoquena Hills, three hours by bus from Aquidauana, five from Campo Grande and Dourados, **BONITO** is a small, somewhat sleepy sprawl of a town. But the dirt tracks that make up the region's roads conceal the fact that things have developed very significantly in Bonito over the last few years, especially since it starred as an "undiscovered" ecological paradise on TV Globo in 1993. In short, Bonito has discovered **eco-tourism**, and, needless to say, tourists have been swarming to the town ever since (especially over Christmas and Easter, and in July and August). Nowadays, an estimated seventy percent of the town's 10,000 inhabitants work one way or another for the industry, and at the time of writing there were over thirty hotels and twenty tour companies (see "Listings" p.447) with trained and authorized guides.

Yet the mood, out of season, is surprisingly relaxed and not at all pushy. The tour companies offer identical trips at identical – and very reasonable – prices which are set by the *prefeitura*. The municipality also limits the numbers of visitors to Bonito's natural wonders and systematically enforces a whole array of annoying –for the individual traveller – but ultimately wise regulations intended to protect this ecologically "pure" region. Many of the sites charge for entry, and for some, such as the famous Lago Azul cave, you require both authorization and a guide to visit. Such permits and guides are usually arranged by the tour companies or hotels, but if you're arranging your own visits, the *prefeitura* gives formal permission (see "Listings" p.447). The main catch for DIY tours, though, is that almost all the sites require transport (roughly $20 via the tour companies), which means you save almost nothing by going it alone. Some hotels, like *Pousada Muito Bonito*, can arrange **car hire** for around $30, and someone may be happy to rent you their **bicycle** for the day – ask around.

Bus schedules to and from Bonito usually mean that you'll have to stay two nights if you want to include a trip to the caves or rivers (organized tours leave around 7.30am). There are daily services to and from Anastácio and Campo Grande, Dourados, Ponta Porã and Corumbá via Miranda.

Accommodation

There are plenty of **places to stay** in Bonito, so finding a room should be easy even in high season. Most accommodation is budget-range – there are over a dozen cheapies on **Rua Pilad Rebuá**, two blocks up from the *Rodoviária* – but there are also a fair number of classier options.

Outside of town, by far the nicest place is *Pousada Bacuri*, 7km away beside the Aquario Natural (☎067/255-1632; reservations in Bonito at Rua 15 de Novembro 632; ④). It's a perfect little paradise run by a charming family, with a number of basic but clean dormitories, and a gorgeous stretch of the Rio Formosinho for swimming, complete with four waterfalls and virgin forest inhabited by monkeys and macaws; **camping** is also allowed ($10 per person, including electricity).

A brand-new fifty-bed **youth hostel** opened in town in July 1997: *Albergue de Juventude Yacanga*, Rua Lício Borralho 716 (☎067/255-1462; ②), ten blocks north of the *Rodoviária*.

Hotel Gemila Palace, Rua Luiz da Costa Leite 2085 (☎067/255-1421, fax 255-1754). The best mid-range choice, a friendly, family-run place with air-conditioned rooms and a great buffet breakfast. ⑤.

Pousada Olho d'Água, Estrada Baia das Garças, 3km from the centre (☎067/255-1430, fax 255-1470). No less luxurious than the *Zagaia Resort*, but more personal and affordable, this offers delightful bungalow accommodation in intimate wooded surroundings and excellent food. ⑥.

Pousada Muito Bonito, Rua Pilad Rebuá 1448 (☎067/255-1645). The best value in town, friendly with spotless but rather dark rooms. Check the showers work before dropping anchor. ①.

Paraiso Tour, Rua Pilad Rebuá 1800 (☎067/255-1477). The cheapest beds in town but rather mangy. $5 a head in *dormitórios*.

Hotel Pousada da Praça, Rua Pilad Rebuá 2097 (☎067/255-1312). Basic but clean. Similar are the *Hotel Florestal* at no. 2084 (☎067/255-1409), and *Pousada Aconchego* at no. 1777-A. All three let you choose between ventilators (②) and air conditioning (③).

Zagaia Resort Hotel, 2km from the centre by the airfield (☎067/255-1777). Top of the range, an ultra-modern complex with 3 swimming pools, various playing fields, horseriding, numerous restaurants and even a cabaret – the holidaymakers from Rio love it. ⑧.

The Gruta do Lago Azul

The **Gruta do Lago Azul** (daily 8am–2pm, 7am–4pm on holidays; no children under 5) is a cave some 20km from Bonito, out beyond the tiny municipal airstrip. It's set in forested hills which are evidently rich in limestone, granite and marble, and full of minerals – as well as a growing number of mercury, uranium and phosphorus mines. Even before the mines, though, these hills, which reach up to about 800m above sea level, were full of massive caves, most of them inaccessible and on private *fazenda* land. Nine kilometres from town, there's a sign to the left for the Lago Azul cave. This takes you through a *fazenda*, where you should see *emas* (South American rheas) and other wildlife, until you come to the cave guardian's hut. This is where you show your authorization, pay the small entrance fee ($5) and receive the key to open the metal gates which protect the enormous cave entrance.

Rediscovered in 1924 by local Terena Indians, the entrance to the cave is quite spectacular. Surrounded by around 250,000 square metres of ecological reserve woodland, it looms like a monstrous mouth inviting you into the heart of the earth. At first you climb down a narrow path through vegetation, then down deeper into dripping stalactite territory some 100m below to the mists hovering above the cave's lake. The pre-Cambrian rocks of the cave walls are striated like the skin of an old elephant and there are weird rock formations such as the easily recognized natural Buddha. Light streams in from the semi-circular cave opening, but only penetrates right to the lake level in the bottom of the cave for 45 minutes on 30 days each year. No smoking or drinking is allowed in the cave and you are not permitted to remove rocks or plants.

Until twenty years ago the cave was used much like a local rubbish tip, but tourism revived the local council's interest in the cave and since 1989 a number of expeditions have attempted to fathom the depths of the lake, but with no success (70m is the deepest exploration to date). One of these, a joint French–Brazilian expedition, discovered the bones of prehistoric animals (including a sabre-toothed tiger) and even human remains. The blue waters of the lake extend into the mountain for at least another 300m and are exceptionally clear, with only shrimps and crustacea able to survive in the calcified water.

There is another spectacular cave in the area, **Nossa Senhora Aparecida**, 30km from Bonito, which can only be visited with a guide and special permission from the *prefeitura*.

The Aquario Natural and Ilha do Padre

The **Aquario Natural** (daily 9am–6pm; all-in price, including transport, $30, children under 11 $20), for which you need a guide and authorization (also included in the price), is justifiably Bonito's next most popular attraction. Located at the source of the stunning Rio Formoso, 7km from town, this is a small sanctuary with water so clear and full of fish that it's like looking into an aquarium. In fact, visitors are encouraged to put on a floating jacket, mask and snorkel, and to get into the water with the mainly *piripitanga* and *dourado* fishes – a tickling experience with no danger from *piranhas* who never swim this far upriver. If you're particularly skint, the nearby *Pousada Bacuri* (see p.445), 500m from the Aquario Natural, has a stretch of river all of its own ($3 admission), with *dourado* fishes, four small waterfalls and a small forest in which you're free to wander about.

Further down the Rio Formoso, about 12km from Bonito, there's an interesting island, **Ilha do Padre**, which, bought by a priest in 1971, has been turned into a public nature reserve and **campsite**. It costs $5 to enter (no guide or authorization is required) and $8 per person to camp, or you can pay a little more ($12) to use the primitive wooden chalets. The island is surrounded by 22 waterfalls of varying sizes and covers almost 50,000 square metres. The Formoso is an active white-water rafting river, but there are also delightful natural swimming spots, lots of exotic birdlife and luxuriant vegetation. Its not quite as beautiful as the Aquario Natural at the river's source, but still very pleasant, although come prepared for the biting flies and mosquitoes. The island is annoyingly busy at peak holiday times (such as Easter).

Also in the region there are a number of river-bathing resorts and waterfalls well worth visiting. The ones nearest town tend not to require guides, but the grander sites, such as the eight-metre-high **Mimosa River Falls** ($10, or $18 with lunch), 18km from town, and the **Aquidaban River Trail** ($10), which leads to falls 120m high some 54km from Bonito in the Kadiwéu Reserve, do require a guide.

Fazenda da Barra Projeto Vivo

The **Fazenda da Barra Projeto Vivo** is a recently opened ecological visitor centre, 31km from Bonito at the point where the *rios* Formoso and Miranda meet, which provides a vivid example of how the apparently conflicting interests of ecology and business can be combined for profit, pleasure and education. The centre is one of the first of its kind in Brazil and deserves to succeed; judging by the numbers of visitors it already attracts, there is little doubt it will. Full- and half-day trips from Bonito are organized by the local travel agencies: a full day costs $55, a half-day $35 (children half-price), including transport to and from Bonito, a guided forest walk, river-rafting, horseriding and meals. There's a small eco-library for those who read Portuguese and, needless to say, it's an excellent place for children, with plenty of additional hands-on activities (painting, paper-recycling etc) to keep them happy. If you really take a shine to the place, you can **stay** in one of their two chalets sited 200m from the Rio Formoso: *Chalé das Artes* (③) with eight beds, or *Chalé Eden* (⑦) with only two (for details ☎ or fax 067/255-1500).

Eating and drinking

Although Bonito is a small town, there are a large number of **restaurants** catering for the summer tourist trade; out of season, their quality is somewhat variable. Consistently the best are the *Pousada Olho d'Água* (see p.445) and the *Restaurante*

Tapera, Rua Pilad Rebuá 1961, both serving excellent but pricey fish dishes in the evening. There are plenty of ice-cream parlours on Rua Pilad Rebuá, while for a quick lunch, *Pousada Muito Bonito* has good home cooking in pleasant surroundings, or try *Bôca Pizzeria* at Rua 29 de Maio 967.

Listings

Bank There's only a Banco do Brasil, which takes ages and charges the standard $20 commission for the privilege.

Permits The *prefeitura* is opposite the post office at Rua Pilad Rebuá 1759 (☎067/255-1351).

Tour companies Bonito-based tour companies are unusually well tuned in to the requirements of overseas visitors, and all offer the same packages at the same prices (trips to all the places described above, plus a range of snorkelling and excellent white-water rafting activities). Hapankany Tours, Rua Pilad Rebuá 1837 (☎067/255-1315), and, a couple of doors down at no. 1853, Ygarapé Tours (☎ and fax 067/255-1733) distinguish themselves by also offering scuba-diving (from $90 for half an hour for beginners).

Miranda

As an alternative base for visiting Bonito (128km) or the Pantanal swamp, **MIRANDA** is certainly worth considering. A small town straddling the BR-262, it sits at the foot of the Serra de Bodoquena by Rio Miranda. Once the scene of historic battles, Miranda has been somewhat ignored by visitors since the demise of the passenger rail service, but it's a pleasant town which has a reputation for excellent fishing and for Terena and Kadiwéu artefacts.

If you plan on staying, there are several reasonable **hotels**, including *Pantanal Hotel*, Av. Barão do Rio Branco 609 (☎067/242-1068; ④), which has a pool, and a good cheap option, the *Hotel Roma*, Praça Agenor Carrillo 356 (☎067/242-1321; ③). *Hotel Chalé*, just up from the *Rodoviária* on Rua Barão do Rio Branco (☎067/242-1216; ③), is similarly good value, with clean, modern rooms, all with air conditioning. The best hotel, though, is the *Águas do Pantanal*, Av. Afonso Pena 367 (☎067/242-1314, fax 242-1242; ⑦), with a pool and excellent service. They also run the *Fazenda San Francisco*, 36km

---

THE TERENA INDIANS

West beyond Aquidauana lies the traditional territory of the **Terena people**, for whom there was little peace even after the Paraguayan occupation of the 1860s. The late nineteenth century saw an influx of Brazilian colonists into the Aquidauana and Miranda valleys as the authorities attempted to "populate" the regions between Campo Grande and Paraguay – the war with Paraguay had only made them aware of how fertile these valleys were. Pushed off the best of the land and forced, in the main, to work for new, white landowners, the Terena tribe remained vulnerable until the appearance of **Lieutenant Rondon** (after whom the Amazonian state of Rondônia was named). Essentially an engineer, he came across the Terena in 1903 after constructing a telegraph connection – poles, lines and all – through virtually impassable swamps and jungle between Cuiabá and Corumbá. With his help, the Terena managed to establish a legal claim to some of their traditional land rights. Considered by FUNAI (the federal agency for Indian affairs) to be one of the most successfully "integrated" Indian groups in modern Brazil, the Terena have earned the reputation of possessing the necessary drive and ability to compete successfully in the market system – a double-edged compliment, which could be used by the authorities to undermine their rights to land as a tribal group. They live mostly between Aquidauana and Miranda, the actual focus of their territory being the town and train station of **Taunay** – an interesting little settlement with mule-drawn taxi wagons and a peaceful atmosphere. You'll find Terena handicrafts on sale in Campo Grande.

down the road to Bonito (☎067/242-1497; ⑦), which offers lots of activities, but at extra cost. For **camping**, ask the staff at *Perqueiro Camping Lopes* around the corner from the *Rodoviária* (☎067/242-1116) about their site 12km away.

Corumbá and around

Far removed from mainstream Brazil, hard by the Bolivian border and 400km west of Campo Grande, the city of **Corumbá** provides a welcome stop after the long ride from either Santa Cruz (in Bolivia) or Campo Grande. As an entrance to the Pantanal, Corumbá has the edge over Cuiabá in that it is already there, stuck in the middle of a gigantic swamp, only 119m above sea level. Its name, in Tupi, means the "place of stones" and, not surprisingly, Corumbá and the Pantanal didn't start out as a great source of attraction to travellers. As early as 1543, the swamp proved an inhospitable place to an expedition of 120 large canoes on a punitive campaign against the Guaicuru tribe. Sent by the Spanish governor of Paraguay, it encountered vampire bats, stingrays, biting ants and plagues of mosquitoes. And while it doesn't seem quite so bad today, it's easy to understand why air conditioning is such a big business here. It was Corumbá's unique location on the old rail link between the Andes and the Atlantic which originally brought most travellers to the town, but ironically, the same swamp which deterred European invaders for so long has rapidly become an attraction, at the same time as the Brazilian part of the rail link has been closed down.

The **telephone code** for Corumbá is ☎067.

Arrival and accommodation

As there are now only freight trains to and from Corumbá, you're likely to arrive either by bus or plane. The **Rodoviária** is close to the train station on Rua Porto Carrero (☎231-3783) and is served by daily buses from Campo Grande, São Paulo and even further afield. From the *Rodoviária*, it's a fifteen-minute walk into town, or there are buses and taxis ($5) plying the route. The **airport** (☎231-3322) is a half-hour walk or a $10–15 taxi ride west of the city centre.

What little **tourist information** there is can be obtained from the Pan Tur travel agency, Rua Frei Mariano 1013 (☎231-2000), Emcotur opposite (☎231-6996) or in the Casa do Artesão, Rua Dom Aquino Correa 405 (☎231-2715).

Accommodation
Hotels in Corumbá vary considerably but their sheer quantity (the following are just a selection) means you should have no trouble finding a room, even from August to October. Out of season, especially January–Easter, there are heavy discounts all round, and prices can be bargained even lower.

The most centrally located for shops and the port, and so noisiest at night, are the clutch of cheapies around **Rua Delamare** west of Praça da República; they tend to be very popular with backpackers and are good places to meet companions for trips into the Pantanal. For those travelling in a group, *Urcabar*, by the river at Rua Manoel Cavassa 181 (☎231-3039), have a house to rent (9 beds in 2 rooms) for $50 a day.

Hotel Angola, Rua Antônio Maria Coelho 124 (☎231-7233). Safe, perfectly reasonable, and cheapest of the bunch around Rua Delamare in low season (singles from $5). Colibri Pantanal tours are based here. ③.

Hotel Beatriz, Rua Porto Carrero 896 (☎231-7441). Facing the *Rodoviária* and very cheap, so useful if you arrive late at night by bus and can't face the 2km hike into town. ①.

Hotel Beira Rio, Rua Manoel Cavassa 109 (☎231-2554, fax 231-3313). One of the more characterful hotels right by the shore, with cheerful management. Its best rooms overlook the river and the Pantanal, and there are boats for guests' use. ③.

Hotel Brasil, Rua Delamare 903 (☎231-4753). Clean rooms, but the mood is a little impersonal and the management pushily expect you to take their Pantanal tours. ②.

Hotel Caçula, Rua Cuiabá 795 (☎231-5745, fax 231-1976). Next door and similar to *Laura Vicuña*, with good clean rooms, each with TV. ③.

Hotel Laura Vicuña, Rua Cuiabá 775 (☎231-5874, fax 231-2663). A peaceful place, very neat and tidy in traditional fashion. All rooms have phone and TV. ③.

Nacional Palace Hotel, Rua América 936 (☎231-6868, fax 231-6202). Top of the range in Corumbá: it's convenient and has a pool, but is a bit flashy and overpriced. ⑥.

Hotel Nelly, Rua Delamare 902 (☎231-6001, fax 231-7396). Long a favourite haunt for budget travellers and kids from Rio and São Paulo, and excellent value, if a little dank. Rooms with TV cost more. ①–②.

Pousada Pantaneira, Rua Ladário 271 (no ☎). A delightful family-run place 2 blocks east of Praça da República, very cheap with spacious rooms, but unfortunately closed out of season. ①.

Hotel Salette, Rua Delamare 893 (☎231-3768, fax 231-4948). Similar to neighbouring *Nelly* and *Brazil* but more expensive. Cheaper rooms share bathrooms; all rooms have TV. ①–③.

Santa Mônica Palace Hotel, Rua Antônio Maria Coelho 345 (☎231-3001, fax 231-7880). Corumbá's largest hotel and best mid-range option, offering excellent value: bedrooms with all mod cons including air conditioning and fridges, and the added luxury of a pool, sauna and river boats for hire. ⑤.

Hotel Santa Rita, Rua Dom Aquino Correa 860 (☎231-5453, fax 231-4834). Clean and airy rooms, the more expensive ones with air conditioning and TV. Value for money, although the mattresses might just as well be given to the piranhas. ②–③.

La Siesta Hotel (Carandá Hotel), Rua Dom Aquino Correa 47 (☎231-2023, fax 231-4558). In similar vein to the *Nacional Palace Hotel*, with a swimming pool, but cheaper. ⑤.

Hotel Timoneiro, Rua Cabral 879 (☎231-5530). A budget place near the *Rodoviária*, quieter than the clutch around Rua Delamare. The ground-floor rooms are grotty, but cheaper than those on the first floor, which have fans and more light. ②–③.

The City

Commanding a fine view over the Rio Paraguai and across the swamp, the city is small (about 100,000 inhabitants) and is really only busy in the mornings – indeed it's one of Brazil's most laid-back towns south of the Amazon, basking in intense heat and overwhelming humidity. Even at the port nothing seems to disturb the slow-moving pool games taking place in the bars. Because of the heat, there's a very open-plan feel to the city and the people of Corumbá seem to be equally at home sitting at tables by bars and restaurants, or eating their dinners outside in front of their houses. In every street, there's at least one television blaring away on the pavement, and it's not unusual to be invited into someone's house for food, drinks or – at weekends – for a party.

Corumbá's life revolves around its **port**, while its transport connections are at the other end of town around the *Rodoviária* and airport; if you're intending to stay more than one night, the port end is your best bet. Within a few blocks of the riverfront you'll find the **Praça da Independência**. A large, shaded park, the *praça* has ponds, a children's playground and a few unusual installations dotted around: a streamroller, imported from England around 1921, whose first job was flattening Avenida General Rondon, and an antique waterwheel, also English, which served in a sugar factory until 1932. Early in the day, the *praça* is alive with tropical birds, and by evening it's crowded with couples, family groups and gangs of children relaxing as the temperature begins to

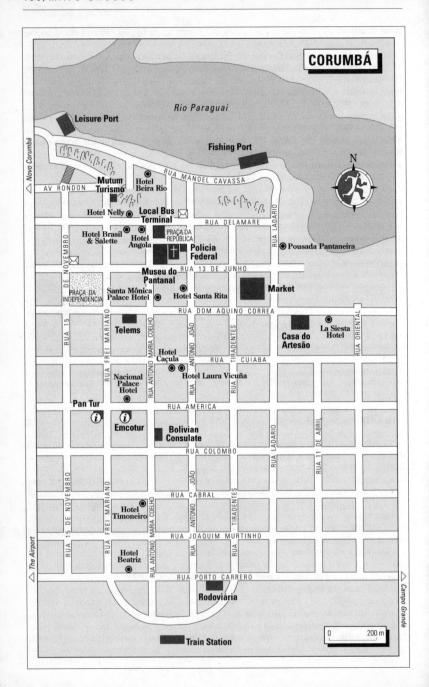

CORUMBÁ

Rio Paraguai

Leisure Port

Fishing Port

Novo Corumbá

RUA MANOEL CAVASSA

AV RONDON

Mutum Turismo
Hotel Beira Rio

Hotel Nelly
Local Bus Terminal

RUA DELAMARE

RUA LADARIO

Pousada Pantaneira

Hotel Brasil & Salette
Hotel Angola
PRAÇA DA REPÚBLICA
Polícia Federal

DE NOVEMBRO

RUA 13 DE JUNHO

Museu do Pantanal

PRAÇA DA INDEPENDENCIA
Santa Mônica Palace Hotel
Hotel Santa Rita
Market

RUA DOM AQUINO CORREA

RUA 15

RUA FREI MARIANO

Telems

RUA ANTONIO MARIA COELHO

RUA ANTONIO JOAO

RUA TIRADENTES

Casa do Artesão
La Siesta Hotel

RUA ORIENTAL

Hotel Caçula

RUA CUIABA

Nacional Palace Hotel

RUA

RUA

Hotel Laura Vicuña

Pan Tur

RUA AMERICA

i
i
Emcotur

Bolivian Consulate

RUA COLOMBO

RUA LADARIO

RUA 11 DE ABRIL

DE NOVEMBRO

RUA FREI MARIANO

RUA JOAO

RUA TIRADENTES

RUA CABRAL

Hotel Timoneiro

RUA ANTONIO MARIA COELHO

RUA ANTONIO

RUA JOAQUIM MURTINHO

RUA 15

RUA FREI MARIANO

Hotel Beatriz

RUA

RUA

RUA PORTO CARRERO

The Airport

Campo Grande

Rodoviária

N

0   200 m

Train Station

drop. The large but otherwise unimpressive church on this square is useful as a prominent landmark to help you get your bearings in this very flat, grid-patterned city.

A stone's throw away on the smaller **Praça da República** stands the decrepit Igreja Matriz Nossa Senhora da Candelária. Next door at Rua Delamare 939, facing the local bus terminal, is the fascinating **Museu do Pantanal** (Mon–Fri noon–5pm), but at the time of writing it was closed for structural repairs due to last "a few years". When rebuilt, the museum should once more be home to some fine natural history exhibits – if you need advice or information about the local flora or fauna, contact the museum office. The only other thing to see is the **Casa do Artesão** at Rua Dom Aquino Correa 405 (Mon–Fri 8–11.30am & 2–5.30pm, Sat 8am–noon). It's housed in Corumbá's most historic edifice – the old prison, dating from 1900 – and is a great place to track down some local craft work (especially wood and leather), as well as local liquors and *Farinha da Bocaiúva*, a flour made from palm-tree nuts and reputed to be an aphrodisiac.

Eating, drinking and nightlife

For **self-catering**, there's a branch of Supermercado Ohara on the corner of Rua Dom Aquino Correa and Rua Antônio João, and three butchers opposite. The covered market, one block north, should complete your provisions.

There is no shortage of **restaurants** in Corumbá. The best are to be found on Rua Frei Mariano and Rua 15 de Novembro, though there are plenty of cheap snack bars throughout town, especially on Rua Delamare west of the Praça da República, serving good set meals for less than $5. For upmarket local cuisine try *Peixaria do Lulu*, Rua Antônio João 410 (☎231-4936), for superb fish, or the smart *Cantina Casa Mia*, opposite the telephone office on Rua Dom Aquino Correa (closed Mon). There's a huge choice of meat and fish in vast portions from *Galpão*, Rua 13 de Junho 797 at the corner of Rua Antônio Maria Coelho; more modest is the calm *Restaurante Trivial* at Rua 15 de Novembro 146. For **pizza** freaks, *Fiorella Pizza* is on the eastern corner of Praça da República and Rua Delamare, while for the truly lethargic, *Palador Pizza* operates a dial-a-pizza service (☎231-4581).

As to **bars**, you'll find these all over town, though with few exceptions they're spit-and-sawdust joints, rough-looking and a little intimidating at first. Among the more relaxed are those down on the riverfront, where you can usually get a game of pool with your drink, and the friendly *Bar da China* on Rua Ladário off Rua Dom Aquino Correa. For **coffee**, try *Café Nectar*, Rua Antônio Maria Coelho 34, and for **ice cream**, *Scorpius Sorvetes* at the corner of Rua Cuiabá and Rua Frei Mariano, and *Sorvetaria Cristal* on the corner of Rua Delamare and Rua 7 de Setembro.

Nightlife, beyond the stagger of bars, is thin on the ground: the only club is the distinctly sleazy *Xodó*, right at the end of Rua Frei Mariano where it meets Rua Porto Carrero. Otherwise, *Restaurante Estalagem (Canecão)*, cornering Rua Frei Mariano and Rua Dom Aquino Correa, brightens up its undistinguished menu with occasional live music.

Lastly, for those who like to cruise with their food, the **restaurant-boat** *La Barca Tur* (☎231-5222) does five-hour lunch trips in high season, including the inevitable piranha soup, for $25.

Listings

Airlines Note that the Varig air pass is not valid for Corumbá. Aerosul flies twice daily to Santa Cruz in Bolivia (☎231-6939; office at the *Rodoviária* open 8am–noon, office at the airport from 2pm), and Lloyd Boliviano fly there daily, both companies charging $58. TAM (☎231-7299) and Pantanal Linhas Aéreas (☎231-1818 or 231-7095) fly regularly from Corumbá to Campo Grande, and thereon elsewhere. Should VASP resume a regular service, you can get information from their office at Rua 15 de Novembro 392 (Mon–Fri 8am–noon & 2–6pm, Sat 8am–noon; ☎231-4441, fax 231-3471).

Tickets for all companies can be brought from Mutum Turismo (see "Travel and tour agencies" below), or at the airport after 9.30am.

Air taxis Visa Aérotáxi (☎231-1745) are the best; Ocorema (☎231-3823) are also reliable; check at their airport desks.

Banks and exchange You can change cash and travellers' cheques at the casa de câmbio at Rua 15 de Novembro 212 (Mon–Fri 8.30am–5pm). Otherwise, there's a host of banks to try your luck at on Rua Delamare west of Praça da República (all Mon–Fri 10am–3pm), as well as the Banco do Brasil, Rua 13 de Junho 914 (10am–5pm). Out-of-hours exchange might be possible at the desk in the *Nacional Palace Hotel*, Rua América 936.

Boats There are plenty of boats waiting on the riverfront off Rua Manoel Cavassa which will take you into the Pantanal swamp or Bolivia. See box on p.459 for details of Pantanal operators, or ask around at the numerous offices on the waterfront. Small motorboats can be hired (2–4 passengers) from *Beiro Rio Hotel* and Urcabar, also on Rua Manoel Cavassa, for about $60–70 a day (gas is extra, and costs around $1 a litre – you'll need up to 50 litres in a day). The demise of the luxury liner *Sabrina* means there are no direct passenger connections to the Atlantic. Those vessels which still cover part of the route invariably now begin in Paraguay, although a ship called *Presidente Strousner* is rumoured to appear occasionally in August. Another option, equally hit or miss, is the opportunity of joining a cargo boat bound for Asunción. If you do find a Paraguayan trading boat, you should check with the Polícia Federal (Praça da República) and the Paraguayan consulate (see below) before leaving town, as well as with the Capitania dos Portos (☎231-6444) at Rua Delamare 806, next to the post office.

Bus departures When leaving Corumbá, it's a good idea to buy bus tickets at least an hour in advance, or the day before in high season (Easter, Aug–Oct & Christmas), from the *Rodoviária* or a travel agent (see below). It's about 7 hours by bus to Campo Grande, from where onward connections cover most of Brazil. The Andorinha bus company (office at the *Rodoviária*, ☎231-3783) has monopolized the route, and has 11 buses daily via Miranda and Aquidauana. Buses to Puerto Suárez (for the Bolivian frontier) leave on the hour from the local bus station in the Praça da República (see box "Crossing the Bolivian border").

Cameras and film There are numerous photographic shops throughout town; Fotocor, Rua Delamare 871, has a good reputation.

Car rental UNIDAS, Rua América 810 (Mon–Sat 8am–6pm; ☎231-1239, fax 231-6992), has reliable Volkswagens which can be taken out of Brazil, but must be returned to Corumbá. Localiza is at Rua Frei Mariano 51 (☎231-6000). Both charge $115 a day upwards.

CROSSING THE BOLIVIAN BORDER

Crossing into or out of Bolivia from Corumbá is a slightly disjointed procedure. **Leaving Brazil**, you should get an exit stamp from the Polícia Federal at the Praça da República in Corumbá (easiest before 11am or between 7pm and 9pm), before picking up a Bolivian visa (if you need one) from the consulate at Rua Antônio Maria Coelho 852 (☎067/231-5606). After that, it's a matter of taking the bus (every hour from Praça da República) the 10km to the border, checking through Bolivian immigration and receiving your passport entry stamp. **Money** can be changed at decent rates at the border.

Train tickets for Santa Cruz should be bought at La Brasilena train station in **Quijarro**, a few minutes by *colectivo* ($1) or bus from the Bolivian immigration office. First class to Santa Cruz costs $24, second class $16. The first-class carriages are comfortable, with videos, but everything sways and the toilets are dirty. Limited food is available on board, and also from the track-side villages during the train's frequent stops. Insect repellent and clothes which cover your flesh are essential, as the lights of the carriages attract all manner of biting insects at night. Drinking water and a torch are also useful. As timetables vary considerably, check at the station in Corumbá or Quijarro at least a couple of days in advance. It's worth going to Quijarro the day before departure to actually make your booking.

Entering Brazil from Bolivia is essentially the same procedure in reverse, although US citizens should remember to pick up visas in the Brazilian consulate in Santa Cruz before leaving.

Cinema About 2km (12 blocks) west down Rua Delamare; rarely the latest films.

Consulates Bolivia, Rua Antônio Maria Coelho 852 (☎231-5606); Paraguay, Rua Cuiabá (☎231-4803).

Guides Mutum Turismo (see "Travel and tour agencies" below) has a list of approved Pantanal guides. Other tour agencies should also be able to fit you up with reputable dragomen, or else you'll find free-lance guides down by the waterfront off Rua Manoel Cavassa or in any of the cheap hotels around Rua Delamare – if they don't find you first. Giltour, Crocodile Tourism and Colibri Pantanal (run by Claudine, a Swiss girl) are currently the best bets, though things can change quickly – ask around.

Hospital Rua 15 de Novembro, between Rua América and Rua Colombo.

Laundry There's an expensive same-day laundry service at Apae, Rua 13 de Junho 1377.

Post office The main one is at Rua Delamare 708, opposite the church on Praça da República (Mon–Fri 9am–5pm, Sat 8am–noon). A smaller office is situated near Praça da Independência on Rua 15 de Novembro (same hours).

Shopping For the Casa do Artesão and for food shopping, see p.451. Two of the shops on Praça da Independência are devoted entirely to hunting, fishing and cowboy paraphernalia, like saddles and guns, and there's a shop on Rua Antônio Maria Coelho, three blocks from the river, stuffed with garish Catholic *ex votos* and plastic icons.

Swimming pools Non-residents can use the pools at hotels *Nacional Palace* ($10) and *Santa Mônica Palace* ($5).

Taxis ☎231-7057. The taxi rank is at the southeast corner of Praça da Independência.

Trains Unlikely as it is, the collective wailings of frustrated tourists might one day convince the authorities to reopen the rail connection with Campo Grande, so it might be worth enquiring at the station nonetheless (☎231-2876). Some people talk of hitching rides atop the freight cars which are still running, an option which might be possible but is not recommended: officials might cause problems down the line, and the insects will have a feast on the 11-hour journey.

Travel and tour agencies Corumbátur, Rua Antônio Maria Coelho 852 (☎ & fax 231-1532), is an upmarket operator dealing with *fazendas* and luxury angling cruises, which also does half-day cruises to Puerto Suárez in Bolivia ($15; no passport required), a good place for silverwork and tax-free goods; a similar service is offered by Pan Tur, Rua Frei Mariano 1013 (☎231-2000, fax 231-6006); Mutum Turismo, Rua Frei Mariano 17 (☎231-1818 or 231-1768, fax 231-3027), deals with flights and ticketing; Tucantur, Rua 13 de Junho 744 (☎231-5323), speaks good English. Office opening times are invariably Mon–Fri 7am–4pm, and Sat 7am–noon. See also "Guides" above, and the list of upmarket Pantanal operators on p.459. Budget Pantanal tours are run by all the cheap hotels around Rua Delamare, whose touts will probably find you as soon as you get off the bus.

Around Corumbá

Apart from the Pantanal itself (see p.454), there isn't a great deal to visit around Corumbá. Probably the most interesting place is the **Forte de Coimbra**, 80km to the south. Theoretically, the fort can only be visited with previous permission from the Brigada Mista in Corumbá, Av. General Rondon 1735 (☎067/231-2861), although visitors unaware of this fact are sometimes allowed in. On the other hand, the Brigada Mista is as good a place as any to find out about transport to the fort.

The fort is accessible only by water, and is most easily reached via Porto Esperança, an hour by bus from Corumbá (buses leave from outside *Hotel Beatriz* several times a day). The journey there is an interesting one along the edge of the swamp, and once in Porto Esperança you should have little difficulty renting a boat, or finding a guide, to take you a couple more hours downriver to the fort. It's also possible to approach the fort in traditional fashion, by following the Rio Paraguai all the way from Corumbá in a boat, but this takes around seven hours and involves going through a tour agency in town.

The Forte de Coimbra (daily 8.30–11.30am & 1.30–4pm) was built in 1775, three years before Corumbá's foundation, to defend this western corner of Brazilian territory and, more specifically, to protect the border against invasion from Paraguay. In 1864 it was attacked by the invading Paraguayan army, which had slipped upriver into the southern

Mato Grosso. Coimbra provided the first resistance to the invaders, but it didn't last for long as the Brazilian soldiers escaped from the fort under cover of darkness, leaving the fort to the aggressors. Nearly 3000 Paraguayans continued upstream in a huge convoy of ships and, forging its way north beyond Corumbá, the armada crossed the swamps almost as far as the city of Cuiabá, which was saved only by the shallowness of its river. Nowadays the fort is a pretty dull ruin (except perhaps for military enthusiasts), but it's a fine trip there, especially for two little-visited natural caves, **Gruta do Inferno** and **Buraco Soturno**, sculpted with huge finger-like stalactites and stalagmites. The caves are in a military area, which means you need a guide: trips (3–4hr by boat from Coimbra) can be arranged through local travel agencies in Corumbá.

You may also be able to visit one of the planet's largest **manganese** deposits, currently being mined in the Urucum hills, just south of Corumbá off the BR-262. The hills rise more than 950m above the level of the swamp, and although much of the area is technically out of bounds, organized visits to the Minas do Morro do Urucum at **Mineradora**, 24km from Corumbá, with their subterranean galleries (Grutas dos Belgas), can still be arranged through most tour agencies in Corumbá – or contact the company office at Av. General Rondon 1351 (☎067/231-1661). If you chance a visit unaccompanied, buses to Urucum depart from a lot next to *Hotel Beatriz* on Rua Porto Carrero.

Finally, if you're not going to have the time to get any further into the Pantanal, you can get a taste of the swamp life without spending a lot of money at two settlements on the Rio Paraguai. **PORTO MORRINHO** is the easier to get to, 67km or an hour by bus from Corumbá, just west of Porto Esperança on the main road to Campo Grande, with ample birdlife and creeks to explore. It has a few cheap **hotels**, as well as the mid-range *Hotel Tuiuiú*, 200m by *balsa* from Porto Morrinho on the banks of the river (⑤). The hotel rents out motorboats at $40 a day, rowing boats at $15. About the same distance from Corumbá on the old Campo Grande road (the unsurfaced MS-184/MS-228) is **PORTO MANGA**, which is renowned as a centre for wildlife and fishing on the Rio Paraguai, particularly in September. There are a couple of **hotels**, including the *Hotel Pesqueiro* (☎067/231-1987; ③), some riverboats and boatmen for hire and various potential **camping** locations in and around the settlement. From Porto Manga onward it's only 70km via Passo do Lontra to rejoin the main highway.

THE PANTANAL

An open swampland larger than France, extending deep into the states of Mato Grosso and Mato Grosso do Sul, **THE PANTANAL** is a slightly daunting region to visit, one of the rare places in Brazil where you're more likely to find wildlife than nightlife. In fact, you see so many birds and animals that you start to think you're in a well-stocked wildlife park – the wildlife *is* wild, but not at all shy. *Jacarés* (alligators), jaguars, anacondas and *tuiuiú* (giant red-necked storks) are all quite common sights in the Pantanal, and it's probably the best place for wild mammals and exotic birds in the whole of the Americas. Having said that, it's only fair to mention that you'll still see more cattle than any other creature.

Taking off into the Pantanal is what most independent travellers have in mind when they arrive in Mato Grosso, but as no road or rail track crosses the swamp, it's a tricky place to travel. The easiest and one of the best ways to experience the Pantanal is by taking an **organized tour**, perhaps spending a night or two at a **fazenda-lodge** (called **pousadas** in the northern Pantanal). The *fazenda*-lodges, mostly converted ranch-houses with decent facilities, are generally reached by jeep; those which require access by boat or plane are usually deeper into the swamp, which increases your chances of spotting the more elusive wildlife. At least one night in the swamp is essential if you want to see or do anything other than sit in a bus or jeep the whole time; three- or four-day excursions will

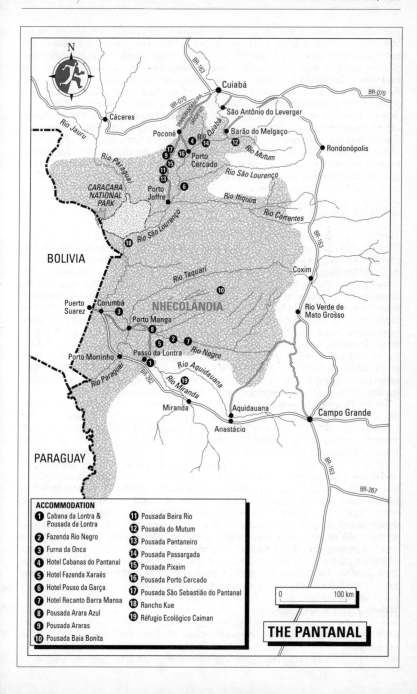

N

BR-163

Cuiabá

BR-070

Cáceres

São Antônio do Leverger

Rio Jauru

BR-070

Poconé

Barão do Melgaço

Rondonópolis

Rio Paraguai

Porto Cercado

Rio Mutum

Rio São Lourenço

CARACARA NATIONAL PARK

Porto Joffre

Rio Itiquira

Rio Correntes

BR-163

Rio São Lourenço

BOLIVIA

Coxim

Rio Taquari

NHECOLÂNDIA

Puerto Suarez

Corumbá

Rio Verde de Mato Grosso

Porto Manga

Porto Morrinho

Passo da Lontra

Rio Negro

Rio Aquidauana

PARAGUAY

Rio Paraguai

BR-262

Rio Miranda

Miranda

Aquidauana

Campo Grande

Anastácio

BR-163

BR-267

ACCOMMODATION

1 Cabana da Lontra & Pousada da Lontra
2 Fazenda Rio Negro
3 Furna da Onca
4 Hotel Cabanas do Pantanal
5 Hotel Fazenda Xaraés
6 Hotel Pouso da Garça
7 Hotel Recanto Barra Mansa
8 Pousada Arara Azul
9 Pousada Araras
10 Pousada Baia Bonita
11 Pousada Beira Rio
12 Pousada do Mutum
13 Pousada Pantaneiro
14 Pousada Passargada
15 Pousada Pixaim
16 Pousada Porto Cercado
17 Pousada São Sebastião do Pantanal
18 Rancho Kue
19 Réfugio Ecológico Caiman

0   100 km

THE PANTANAL

give you a couple of full days in the swamp. Without an organized trip, unless you've got bags of money or are travelling in a large group in which case you can hire boats to get you almost anywhere, you're dependent on local **cargo boats**, which inevitably take much longer than expected. Organized tours are also more likely to go out of their way to show you the wildlife than will a captain whose boat is brimming over with livestock. **Renting a car** is also a slim possibility, though without 4WD you're limited only to a few tracks on the fringes of the swamp where the wildlife makes itself scarce.

Most organized tours enter the Pantanal by road and spend a couple of days exploring in canoes, small motorboats or on horseback from a land base. The most obvious initial target is **Corumbá** in Mato Grosso do Sul. There's lots of accommodation here and no end of agencies and operators running trips into the swamp. Other routes into the swamp are from **Campo Grande** in the east or **Cuiabá**, to the north, through settlements like **Porto Jofre** and **Cáceres**.

Some background

There are very few places on earth where it is so easy to see so much wildlife as in the Pantanal, which occupies an arguably unique ecological niche as an unparalleled biogenetic reservoir. It's almost unnerving spending the afternoon on the edge of a remote lagoon in the swamp surrounded by seemingly endless streams of flying and wading birds – toucans, parrots, red and even the endangered hyacinth macaws, blue herons, and the symbol of the Pantanal, the magnificent *jabiru*, or giant red-throated storks, known locally as *tuiuiú*. Unlike most other areas of wilderness, the birdsong in the Pantanal lives up to the soundtrack of Hollywood jungle movies, and in the middle of the swamp it's actually possible to forget that there are other people in the world – though it's very difficult to forget the **mosquitoes**. (Malaria is supposedly absent in the Pantanal, so you'll only have the insufferable itching to worry about.) The mosquitoes should be no surprise really, given that it's the biggest inland swamp in the world, covering some 200,000 square kilometres of the upper Rio Paraguai basin. It acts as an immense sponge, seasonally absorbing the swollen waters of three large rivers – the Paraguai, Taquari and Cuiabá.

During the **rainy season** (Jan–April), it's a vast flooded plain with islands of scrubby forest amidst oceans of floating vegetation. Transport is necessarily dominated by the rivers, natural water channels and hundreds of well-hidden lagoons. The small islands of vegetated land created during the rains crawl with wild animals – jaguars, tapirs, capybaras (the world's largest rodents) and wild boar living side by side with domesticated cattle.

At other times of the year, much of the Pantanal is still very boggy though interspersed with open grassy savannas studded with small wooded islands of taller vegetation, mainly palm trees. The **dry season**, from August to January, with its peak normally around September, transforms the swamp into South America's most exciting natural wildlife reserve. Its infamous piranha and alligator populations crowd into relatively small pools and streams, while the astonishing array of aquatic birds follows suit, forming very dense colonies known here as *viveiros*. Treeless bush savanna alternates with wet swamp, while along the banks of the major rivers grow belts of rainforest populated with colonies of monkeys (including spider monkeys and noisy black gibbons). Note, however, that the previously metronomic **regularity of the seasons** has become most unpredictable of late, with the onset of global warming.

History and development

Very little is known about the Pantanal's **history**. At the time of early Portuguese explorations, and the first unsuccessful attempts at populating the region by the Spanish in the sixteenth century, the region was dominated by three main tribes. In the south lived the horseriding **Guaicuru**, who adopted stray or stolen horses and cattle from the advancing white settlers, making the tribe an elite group amongst Indians. Wearing only jaguar skins as they rode into battle, they were feared by the neighbouring **Terena** (Guana) tribe, who lived much of their lives as servants to Guaicuru families. In many ways, the nature and degree of their economic and social interaction suggests that the two might once have been different castes within the same tribe. Another powerful people lived to the north – the **Paiaguá**, masters of the main rivers, lagoons and canals of the central Pantanal. Much to the chagrin of both Spanish and Portuguese expeditions into the swamps, the Paiaguá were superbly skilled with both their canoes and the bow and arrow.

It wasn't until the **discovery of gold** in the northern Pantanal and around Cuiabá during the early eighteenth century that any genuine settlement schemes were undertaken. A rapid influx of colonists, miners and soldiers led to several bloody battles. In June 1730 hundreds of Paiaguá warriors in 83 canoes ambushed the annual flotilla carrying some 900kg of gold south through the Pantanal from Cuiabá. They spared only some of the women and a few of the stronger black rowers from the flotilla: all of the gold and most of the white men were lost. Much of the gold eventually found its way out of Brazil and into Spanish Paraguay where Cautiguacu, the Paiaguá chief, lived a life of luxury in Asunción until his death 55 years later.

The decline of the gold mines during the nineteenth century brought development in the Pantanal to a standstill and the population began to fall. This century has seen the establishment of unrestricted **cattle-grazing** ranches – *fazendas* – with, at the time of writing, over 23 million head of cattle roaming the swamp. To the east, the BR-163 between Campo Grande and Cuiabá skirts around the Pantanal, and Ministry of Transport plans for a *Transpantaneira* road from Cuiabá to Corumbá have been shelved for the sake of the region's ecological balance. For all that, tourism has developed greatly in the region over the last few years, which has coincided with a slump in the price for cattle. The papers are full of auction notices for *fazendas*, livestock and equipment, though some *fazendeiros* have been quick to realize the potential of converting their farms and land into ecological reserves.

The Pantanal, however, is still **under threat** from the illegal exploitation of skins, fish and rare birds, and even gold panning. The chemical fertilizers and pesticides used on the enormous *fazendas* to produce cash crops such as soya beans are also beginning to take their toll. **Eco-tourism** has been heralded as a potential saviour for the swamp, but this will only work if sufficient money is ploughed back into conservation. The Pantanal has its own Polícia Florestal who try to enforce the environment-friendly regulations now being strictly applied to visitors and locals alike: no disposal of non-biodegradable rubbish, no noise pollution, no fishing without a licence (it costs $100) or between November and January during the breeding season, no fishing with nets or explosives and no removal of rocks, wildlife or plantlife.

Practicalities

If you talk to locals about visiting the Pantanal they will almost certainly recommend going in by road. This is usually cheaper and quicker than renting a boat or going on one of the cruises. The main problem, though, is knowing where and how to go, and which company or lodge to choose. This section gives a rough overview of the various options, together with a box listing a selection of recommended **tour operators**. The following sections describe some possible **routes**, from Corumbá and from Cuiabá, together with details of **accommodation** in *fazenda*-lodges and *pousadas*. The box on p.462 describes the options for **boat trips** from Cáceres and Corumbá.

If you want to go **independently** remember that the Pantanal is a difficult and dangerous place to travel in. There are very few roads, and although hundreds of tracks sneak their way into the swamp, they are only used by *fazenda* workers who know them inside out. An inexperienced driver or hiker could easily get lost – or worse. That said, there's no better way to see the wildlife than to camp or stay on a boat deep in the swamp, away from roads, tracks or *fazenda*-lodges, but to do this you will need a **local guide**; these are generally available only at lodges or in end-of-the-track settlements like Porto Jofre. Also, it's important to take all the **equipment** you need with you if you're going it alone like this in the Pantanal – food, camping gear, a first-aid kit and lots of mosquito repellent. It's possible to take **buses** and **boats** from Cuiabá and Corumbá to places such as Cáceres, Coxim, Porto Jofre or Aquidauana, and it's then a matter of finding a boat going your way deeper into the swamp or paying a local guide or *fazendeiro* to take you on a trip. This will cost around $20–50 per person per day, including canoe or vehicle transport and a guide/boatman/driver. Local guides and *fazendeiros* usually prefer to use the road networks to reach *fazenda*-lodges within the swamp, and explore in canoes or on horseback from there. Cheaper still, and certainly the most unusual alternative, is to buy a passage (around $10–20 a day; hammock essential) on one of the few **trading boats** still crossing the Pantanal between Corumbá and Cáceres, and occasionally Porto Jofre (both connected by road to Cuiabá).

Most people, however, go on **organized tours**, entering the swamp in jeeps or trucks and following one of the few rough roads that now connect Corumbá, Aquidauana, Coxim and Cuiabá (via Poconé or Cáceres) with some of the larger *fazenda* settlements of the interior. The short **jeep trips**, often run by freelance operators, are relatively cheap (especially from Corumbá, where a hammock and truck tour can cost as little as $20–25 a day per person; from Cuiabá, it's more like $50–60), but they offer little more than a flavour of the swamp. Details of these freelance operators are given on p.429 (Cuiabá), p.440 (Campo Grande) and p.453 (Corumbá). Instead, it's better to seek out **small boat trips** (around $40–80 a day, from Corumbá, Porto Jofre or Cáceres; there are no agencies for this, so just ask around), or a **combination of jeep and boat**, over four or five days, which would certainly give the trip a taste of adventure, and could work out cheaper if you and your companions (there's usually a minimum number of passengers needed for boats) are happy braving the mosquitos in hammocks. Note that if you're in Campo Grande, the trips you might be offered will invariably be luxury cruises.

Swamping it **upmarket** is much easier, at one of an increasing number of **fazenda-lodges** in the Pantanal, well away from towns and main roads. However, with few exceptions these cost upwards of $100 a night per person, and $200 is not uncommon. In their favour, though, is that the prices invariably include various activities, including trips by boat or jeep, horseriding, guided walks or fishing expeditions, as well as meals. Prices are generally more reasonable in the northern Pantanal (accessible from Cuiabá) than in the south (Corumbá, Miranda and Aquidauana). Also including nights in *fazenda*-lodges are **all-inclusive package tours**, though their prices vary wildly, sometimes undercutting the official lodge price, at other times almost doubling it – it's worth shopping around and bargaining (the tour operators listed in the box opposite all have a selection). As a general rule, however, you'll pay less if you deal direct with a *fazenda*-lodge owner in Porto Jofre, Cáceres, Aquidauana and even Corumbá, rather than through their agents. Most of the *fazenda*-lodges are located east and northeast of Corumbá, and also on either side of the Rio Cuiabá in the north, accessible for the most part via the aborted *Transpantaneira* road between Poconé and Porto Jofre. If you really have money to burn, signing up for a **luxury** cruise, or even **hiring a boat** for a week or so is the ideal option – see the box on p.462. If you want to arrange tours from home before you leave for Brazil, see "Basics" for operators.

UPMARKET PANTANAL AGENTS AND OPERATORS

The following is a selection of the more upmarket Pantanal operators who deal both with complete packages and bookings for boats and lodges; for other agents and guides, see the "Listings" for Cuiabá, Campo Grande and Corumbá.

Águas do Pantanal, Av. Afonso Pena 367, Miranda (☎067/242-1314, fax 242-1242). This company owns and runs several *pousadas* around Miranda, Passo do Lontra and Porto Morrinho on the Rio Paraguai.

Confiança Turismo, Rua Cândido Mariano 434, Cuiabá (☎065/623-4141, fax 322-1580). A well-established company with a strong track record operating a variety of Pantanal tours.

Corumbátur, Rua Antônio Maria Coelho 852, Corumbá (☎ & fax 067/231-1532). Corumbá's leading upmarket agency, dealing with all the main *fazendas* and luxury boat cruises, as well as organizing its own fishing and photography tours (anything from $120 per person per day). Prices for the fishing cruises (departing Sun on a variety of boats) range from $675 to $1300 per person per week.

Fish World, Rua Lucélia 85, Vila Castelo, Campo Grande (☎067/383-3709, fax 382-8152). Efficient agents for a large number of luxury boat trips, specializing in angling trips, as well as *fazenda*-lodges.

Impacto Turismo, Rua Padre João Crippa 1065, sala 106, Campo Grande (☎067/382-5197). This company runs very good eco-tours to the Pantanal.

Pantanal Explorers/Expediturs, Av. Gov. J.P. Arruda, Várzea Grande, Cuiabá

(☎682-2800 or 682-1260). Agents and operators for tours and boats based around Cuiabá and Cáceres.

Pantanal Express, Av. Afonso Pena 2081, Campo Grande (☎067/382-5333). Agents for some of the more upmarket tour operators and *fazenda* experiences.

Pan Tur, Rua Frei Mariano 1013, Corumbá (☎067/231-2000, fax 231-6006). Agents for almost everything, who also run their own Pantanal tours, from around $70 a day.

Pérola do Pantanal, Rua Manoel Cavassa 255, Corumbá (☎067/231-1460/70, fax 231-6585). Agents for upmarket cruises from Corumbá.

SuperPesca Pantanal, Rua Marechal Cândido Rondon 2300, Campo Grande (☎067/721-5713). Specialists in angling tours, and especially knowledgeable on which boats go down which rivers, which could be useful in hitching a ride.

Transtur/La Barca Tur, Rua Manoel Cavassa, Corumbá (☎231-3016, 231-2871 or 231-5222). This company has a fleet of barges, imaginatively converted into floating bars and hotels, down at the waterfront in Corumbá. The large floating hotels cost over $600 a day out of season for eight people (ie $75 per person including food but not drink) – add another $60 a day for any additional passengers.

Into the swamp: routes from Corumbá

Of the three main Pantanal towns, **Corumbá** is best placed for getting right into the Pantanal by bus or jeep, and has a welter of guides and agencies to choose from, as well as boats for hire. Currently the most popular **fazenda-lodges** are those in **Nhecolândia**, roughly speaking the area between the *rios* Negro and Taquari east of Corumbá. These benefit from a well-established dirt access road, the MS-184/MS-228 (the old Campo Grande road), which loops off from the main BR-262 highway 300km from Campo Grande near **Passo do Lontra** (it's well signposted), and crosses through a large section of the swamp before rejoining the same road some 10km before Corumbá. The track also passes through **Porto Manga** (see p.454).

Fazenda-lodges in the southern Pantanal

The following *fazenda*-lodges are accessible from either Corumbá, Miranda or Aquidauana, offer full-board accommodation and swamp trips, and can be booked through the addresses given below or through the upmarket Pantanal operators listed in the box on p.459.

Baia Bonita, Nhecolândia (☎ and fax 067/231-4009). On reasonably dry land approximately 160km northeast of Passo do Lontra (turn right before you reach Porto Manga), a 2-storey block beside a ranch house. Homely atmosphere with safari-style tours. Minimum 2 people for 2 nights. ⑦.

Cabana da Lontra, Passo do Lontra (☎067/383-4532). Situated near where the MS-184 crosses the Rio Miranda, some 100km southeast of Corumbá and 7km off the main BR-262. With over 20 rooms and its own motorboats, this is located in a good spot for most wildlife; excellent for fishing. ⑤.

Fazenda Rio Negro, Rio Negro (owned by Orlando Rondon, Rua Antônio Correa 1161, Bairro Monte Libano, Campo Grande; ☎067/725-7853). One of the Pantanal's oldest ranches, founded in 1895 by Cicíaco and Thomázia Rondon. Located up the Rio Negro with access from Aquidauana, this is a small, upmarket place with boats, horses and good guides. Air transfer from Campo Grande or Aquidauana is $99 return. ⑧.

Furna da Onca, Ladário (☎067/231-5463). This is a great little place situated on the Rio Paraguai 25km east from Corumbá, with swimming pool and good access to the rivers. ⑥.

Hotel Fazenda Xaraés, Rio Abobral (bookings Rua América 969, Corumbá; ☎067/231-6777, fax 231-6006). 130km from Corumbá on the Rio Abobral (Nhecolândia), accessible from Miranda. Well-appointed but not particularly luxurious lodge. Horseriding, but in a rather tame corner of the swamp. Astonishingly overpriced ($280 for the cheapest single). ⑧.

Hotel Recanto Barra Mansa, Rio Negro (owned by Guilherme Rondon, ☎067/383-5088). Further east from Fazenda Rio Negro on the north shore of the river, 130km from Aquidauana, a new place with room for 12 guests. Daily buses from Corumbá. ⑧.

Pousada Arara Azul, Rio Negrinho (information ☎067/383-3709 or 383-1924). Close to the Rio Negro in Nhecolândia 38km up the MS-184 past Passo do Lontra, this *pousada* offers all the comforts you could want, plus amazing guaranteed access to virtually all the bird and mammalian wildlife apart from the rarer jaguars and wolves. Excellent for piranha fishing, night-time *jacaré* observation and horseriding. Camping allowed, too ($10 a night), though they may require a minimum stay of 2 or days in the lodge. ⑦.

Pousada da Lontra, Passo do Lontra (owned by J.A. Venturini, ☎067/241-2406/7). Not far from the *Cabana da Lontra*, and one of the rare cheap options (with substantial reductions in low season), although a mimimum of 6 guests may be required. They allow camping. ⑥.

Réfugio Ecológico Caiman, Rio Aquidauana (owned by Roberto Klabin, ☎067/883-6622), with agents in Campo Grande (☎067/725-5267), Corumbá (☎067/242-1102) and São Paulo (☎011/246-5016, fax 521-9082). *The* luxurious 5-star Pantanal experience, the *réfugio* is located some 240km west of Campo Grande, 36km north of Miranda, and covers over 530 square kilometres. There are five *pousadas* which you can choose from and combine, staying in a different one every night if you wish, all with good facilities and a distinctive style to match the surroundings. The only niggle is that the reserve is too much on the margins of the swamp to be really exciting or wild. Still, it's the only place which offers horseback cattle ranching to its residents, as 70 percent of the reserve's income still derives from cattle. The *réfugio* has its own airstrip, and the minimum stay is 3 nights. Very expensive (from around $400 a double for one night). ⑧.

Into the swamp: routes from Cuiabá

One of the simplest ways into the swamp is to take a **bus** (3hr) from Cuiabá south to **BARÃO DO MELGAÇO**, a small, quiet village on the banks of the Rio Cuiabá. Although not quite in the true swamp, and therefore with less in the way of wildlife, Barão is perfect if you're short on time and just want a taste of the Pantanal. There's a reasonable **hotel** by the river in town, the *Barão Tour Pantanal Hotel* (bookings at Rua

Joaquim Murtinho 1213, Cuiabá; ☎065/713-1166, fax 624-8743; ③), which also has boats for hire, while the exclusive *Pousada do Mutum* lodge is just an hour away by boat, in a stunning location on the Baía de Siá Mariana bay near the Rio Mutum (☎065/713-1223; or book through Eldorado Exec. Centre, Av. Rubens de Mendonça 917, sala 301, Cuiabá, ☎ and fax 065/321-7995; ⑥). Although Barão is no longer served by regular boats from Corumbá, it might still be worth asking around should a shallow-draught vessel be covering the journey – an unforgettable experience right through the centre of the swamp.

Poconé and Porto Jofre

The most exploited option from Cuiabá is to follow the route south to Poconé and Porto Jofre. There are daily **buses** from Cuiabá's *Rodoviária* as far as **POCONÉ** along a paved and fairly smooth hundred-kilometre stretch of road. Like Barão do Melgaço, Poconé is not real Pantanal country, but it's a start and there are plenty of **hotels in town** if you need to stay over. On the main square, Praça Rondon, the *Hotel Skala* at no. 64 (☎065/721-1407; ③) and a couple of restaurants take most of the trade. At the southern end of town at the start of the road to Porto Jofre, the cheaper *Hotel Santa Cruz* (☎065/721-1439; ③) is recommended. Cheaper still is *Dormitório Poconé* (①), near the *Rodoviária*.

The swamp proper begins as you leave the town going south, along the aborted *Transpantaneira* road. In fact it's just a bumpy track, often impassable during the rains, but you'll see plenty of wildlife from it, as well as signs marking the entrances to a number of *fazenda*-lodges and *pousadas* set back from the road around various tributaries of the Rio Cuiabá, notably the Pixaim. Although pricey, they're cheaper than their counterparts in the southern Pantanal, and all have restaurants and facilities for taking wildlife day trips into the swamp by boat, on horseback or on foot. Another track from Poconé, in an even worse state, trails off southeast to **Porto Cercado** on the banks of the Rio Cuiabá itself, and also has a few *pousadas*.

After 145km, having crossed around a hundred wooden bridges in varying stages of dilapidation, the track eventually arrives at **PORTO JOFRE**. After Cuiabá, Porto Jofre appears as little more than a small fishing hamlet, literally the end of the road. This is as far as the *Transpantaneira* route has got, or ever looks like getting, thanks to technical problems and the sound advice of ecological pressure groups. As far as **accommodation in town** goes, the *Hotel Porto Jofre* (☎065/322-6322; closed Nov–Feb; ⑦) has the monopoly and therefore charges through the nose. In the future, the *Hotel Santa Rosa* may reopen after its indefinite rebuilding, but will more likely than not charge much the same; in its favour though is its exceptional location on the banks of the Rio Cuiabá. If you have a hammock or a tent, it's usually all right to sleep outside somewhere, but check with someone in authority first (ask at the port) and don't leave your valuables unattended. There are no other options unless you can get someone to invite you to their house.

From Porto Jofre, there are irregular cargo **boats** to Corumbá (about twice a month), normally carrying soya or cattle from Cáceres, and the journey takes between two and five days, depending on whether the boats sail through the night. It's also possible to arrange a day or two's excursion up the Piquiri and Cuiabá rivers from Porto Jofre.

Pousadas around Poconé and Porto Jofre

All of the following can be booked through the addresses given below or through upmarket travel agents in Cuiabá (see p.429); some lodges insist on advance reservation and won't let you in unannounced, but others might relent if you just drop by. All the lodges below offer full-board accommodation, with swamp trips included in the price; they're listed in loose geographical order, from northeast to southwest.

Pousada Passargada (bookings through Cuiabá's travel agents, or in Rio ☎021/235-2840 or São Paulo ☎011/284-5434). Linked in the dry season by the Porto Cercado track, most of the year it's 1hr 30min by boat from Barão do Melgaço. A good place directly on the Rio Pixaim. ⑤.

Hotel Cabanas do Pantanal (Confiança Turismo, Rua Cândido Mariano 434, Cuiabá; ☎065/623-4142, fax 322-1580). Situated 50km from Poconé on the Rio Piraim, left off the Porto Cercado track. Confiança prefer you take one of their various 3- to 5-day packages, including trips to Águas Quentes and Chapada dos Guimarães. ⑧ full board.

Pousada Porto Cercado (☎065/721-1726; reservations ☎065/682-1300). Near the end of the Porto Cercado track, 79km from Poconé with direct access to the Rio Cuiabá. It has 30 double rooms, and a restaurant specializing, not surprisingly, in fish. Pool and boats for messing about in. ⑤.

Pousada São Sebastião do Pantanal (☎065/322-0178, fax 321-0710). 34km from Poconé at Km27 of the aborted *Transpantaneira* road, and usually reachable even in bad weather. A first-class estab-

PANTANAL BOAT JOURNEYS

At present, two basic types of **cargo boat** cross the swamp between Cáceres and Corumbá on a fairly regular basis – **soya** and **cattle barges**. Neither have fixed schedules or itineraries, so it's a matter of checking on departure dates when you arrive at either town. The trip usually takes about six to ten days upstream from Corumbá, three to six downstream, with plenty of time for relaxing and looking out for wildlife. The barges, though, do tend to keep to the main channel of the Rio Paraguai, which obviously doesn't give you a very good chance of spotting anything particularly shy or rare. However, if you can find space on one of these boats, then it's a very inexpensive as well as unusual way of seeing some of the Pantanal. As well as your hammock, take some extra food (tins, biscuits, bottled drinks etc), insect repellent and a few good books. And a bottle of whisky or good *cachaça* wouldn't go amiss with the captain.

The only other problem is that travelling on the barges hasn't been strictly legal since 1985, when the son of a naval minister accidentally died while on board one of the cement barges which used to ply the same route. Passengers have consequently been "smuggled" aboard in dinghies, under cover of darkness. However, you might find it's still possible to buy a ride simply by asking the *commandante* of Portobras, one of the barge companies – offices on the waterfront in both Corumbá and Cáceres (☎065/222-1728). The cattle barge between Corumbá and Cáceres run by Serviço de Navegação da Bacia da Prata also often picks up passengers from the ports at either end, but leaves at irregular intervals. Other cattle boats leaving Corumbá are willing to take passengers on return journeys within the swamp, delivering and picking up cattle from various *fazendas*.

Luxury fishing boats are the other option, prohibitively expensive for most, but an ideal way to meet the swamp's wildlife on the end of a line and ultimately on your plate. Essentially floating hotels designed with the Brazilian passion for angling in mind, one of these for a week costs anything from $800 to $3000 a head, though the price is full-board and usually includes ample drink, food and unlimited use of their small motorboat tenders for exploring further afield. Note that for **families with small children**, any river trip is inadvisable as none of the boats currently in use has guard-rails safe enough to keep a toddler from falling in.

Most of the boats are based in Corumbá, with some others in Cáceres, Barão do Melgaço and Cuiabá, and all can be booked through the upmarket agents on p.459. In high season, they tend to run pre-scheduled trips, departing and returning Sundays; routes are mentioned where they remain fixed from year to year. Out of season, they're up for rent, with a minimum number of passengers and days invariably demanded, though bargaining is possible. You can find them tied up at their home ports.

Luxury boats from Cáceres
Barco Hotel São Lucas, bookings through upmarket agent SuperPesca in Campo Grande. Similar to the *Botel Pantanal Explorer II*, covering the Rio Paraguai, Rio Jauru and Ilha Taiamã. $150 per person per day.

lishment located close to the river in pleasant wooded surroundings, offering horse and boat safaris. Pool. Good for families. ⑥.

Pousada Araras (office at Cuiabá airport, or Av. Ponce de Arruda 670, Varzéa Grande; ☎065/682-2800, fax 682-1260). At Km32 of the *Transpantaneira*, this long-established *pousada* is an old brick ranch building, more atmospheric than most of the more modern *pousadas*, with a pool, as well as boats and horses, but its 14 rooms are likely to be full in high season. ⑤.

Pousada Pixaim (☎065/721-1899; reservations ☎065/721-1172). At Km64 on the Rio Pixaim, and not always reachable by road (this and the more southerly *pousadas* are often cut off in the rains, but all have airstrips). Ten wooden 3-bed rooms on stilts, with motorboats for hire and a number of swamp tracks to follow on foot. ⑤.

Pousada Beira Rio (☎065/321-9445). Km65. On the opposite bank of the Rio Pixaim and more upmarket, with 35 apartments, boats and horseriding for guests; mainly used by package tours. ⑥.

Botel Pantanal Explorer II (☎065/381-4959). Mainly covering the Rio Paraguai, this boat is very small with only 3 quadruple cabins. $130 per person per day.

Rei do Rio and **Velho do Rio**, contact Moretti Serviços Fluviais, Cuiabá (☎065/361-2082, fax 322-6563). A couple of Louisiana-style houseboats intended primarily as bases for fishing expeditions.

Luxury boats from Corumbá

Albatroz (☎067/231-4851). An 18-room boat (72 passengers) which specializes in photo safaris on the Rio Paraguai. $200 per person per day, 5 days minimum.

Arara Pantaneira II, Rua Manoel Cavassa 47, Corumbá (☎067/231-5888 or 231-4851). A slightly smaller boat doing much the same thing as the *Albatroz*. $250 per person per day, 5 days minimum.

Barco Hotel Falcão, Rodrigues Turismo, Rua Manoel Cavassa 331, Corumbá (☎067/231-5186, fax 231-6746). For 6 to 8 passengers, conceived as a floating base for sports anglers. There's a five-day minimum rent, $180 per person per day. The Falcão is also available for return trips along the Rio Paraguai to Cáceres, at $2000 per person (the trip takes around 8 days upriver, 5 days down).

Botel Joia Pantaneira (☎065/231-3372). With room to take only 8 people, this is a more intimate way to explore the flora and fauna of the Rio Paraguai. $244 per person per day.

Cabexi I & II, Pantanal Tours, Rua Manoel Cavassa 61, Corumbá (☎067/231-4683 or 231-1559, fax 231-2523). Two 2-tiered riverboats for rent, similar in style to the *Kalypso* but, with a maximum of 8 passengers each, rather more exclusive. Motorboats and fishing accessories provided. Five day minimum period, $200 per person per day. Reservations and $3000 deposit required.

Cidade Barão do Melgaço, bookings through upmarket agent Fish World. This converted tour boat with 8 double cabins used to do monthly 7-day trips from Corumbá to Barão de Melgaço. Alas, it's now only for rent from Corumbá: 5 days and 8 people minimum, from $180 per person per day.

Kalypso, bookings through agents Corumbátur or Pan Tur. Brazil's answer to Nile cruisers, the *Kalypso* is a spacious three-tier affair with berths for 120 passengers, and looks for all the world like a pile of portacabins on a barge (which is what it once was). The interior is wood-panelled, the restaurant is self-service, and there's a pool on top in which to escape the mosquitoes and the heat. Originally designed as a base for fishing trips, it has a number of small motorboats and a giant fridge in which you can keep your catch. Prices start at $125 per person per day, with a minimum stay of 6 nights.

Pousada Pantaneiro (bookings through Cuiabá's travel agents). Approximately 100km south of Poconé, a small place (5 rooms) and one of the more reasonably priced *pousadas* which, although not on a river itself, offers swamp trips on horseback. It should be OK to camp here, too, and they also have tents for hire. ④.

Hotel Pouso da Garça (☎065/322-8823 or 322-4916; bookings at Rua Miranda Reis 38, Cuiabá). On the Rio São Lourenço near its confluence with the Rio Cuiabá (access by light aircraft), with a pool, motorboats and horses at the service of visitors. ⑥.

Rancho Kue (☎067/241-1875). This is one of the best-located *fazendas*, right in the centre of the swamp and close to the confluence of the big *rios* Paraguai and São Lourenço. Access by plane. ⑧.

Cáceres

Although less frequented than the Porto Jofre route, **CÁCERES** is another good target from Cuiabá, 233km west of the city. It's a very pleasant, laid-back place, and given the prices of accommodation along the *Transpantaneira*, definitely deserves consideration as a base for visiting the Pantanal. It's a three- to four-hour journey by **bus**, several daily leaving from the *Rodoviária* in Cuiabá. On the upper reaches of the Rio Paraguai, which is still quite broad even this far upstream, Cáceres is a relatively new town, apparently made up of wooden shacks, bars and pool rooms. There are lots of cheap **hotels**, the best of which is the *Santa Terezinha*, Rua Tiradentes 485 (☎065/223-4621; ②), which is clean and hospitable. *Hotel Fênix*, Rua do Operários 600 (☎065/223-1027; ③), is more expensive and has little extra to offer. The *Hotel Comodoro*, Praça Duque de Caxias 561 (☎065/223-2078; ④), has boats for hire.

About 60km away on the confluence of the *rios* Paraguai and Jauru is the touristy, Japanese-owned *Hotel Fazenda Barranquinho* (☎065/223-1081; ⑦), which can be reached by track or boat in around three hours from Cáceres. It's a beautiful spot, but is still not far enough into the swamp for the best chance of spotting **wildlife**. Best bet for this is to take one of the cargo **boats** to Corumbá from Cáceres – see the box on p.462, which also gives details of luxury fishing boats. For an even more adventurous option, you might be able to hire a small boat with an outboard motor for a week or two, which would certainly give you greater freedom, though a guide would be advisable. The Cáceres Iate Clube, Rua Maravilha (☎065/223-2148) may be of help. Other potentially useful contacts are on Rua Boa Vista: the Oficina Náutica São Luiz at no. 115 (☎065/223-1427), and Nautica Turismo at no. 119 (☎065/223-1565).

The only road to go further into the Pantanal is the track that leads on to the **Bolivian border** settlement of San Matias; from here you can fly to Santa Cruz.

travel details

Buses

Except the Campo Grande–Corumbá route, which is monopolized by Andorinha, there are scores of different bus companies competing for the same routes as well as opening up new ones. Each company advertises destinations and departure times at its ticket office windows, making it relatively easy to choose a route and buy a ticket. Note that going north from Cuiabá, buses only go as far as Alta Floresta, or to Rio Branco via Porto Velho. Manaus, Itaituba, Santarém and Belém are all advertised by the bus companies, but are reach-able only by enormous detours taking several days via Goiânia. Cruzeiro do Sul has no reliable road access.

Anastácio to: Bonito (1 daily; 4hr); Campo Grande (10 daily; 2hr); Corumbá (10 daily; 5hr); Ponta Porã (2 daily; 4–6hr).

Bonito to: Anastácio (1 daily; 4hr); Campo Grande (1 daily; 5hr); Corumbá (Mon–Sat 1 daily; 9hr); Douradas (1 daily; 5hr); Miranda (Mon–Sat 1 daily; 4hr); Ponta Porã (1 daily; 7hr).

Campo Grande to almost everywhere in Brazil, including: Alta Floresta (3 daily; 22hr);

Anastácio/Aquidauana (10 daily; 2hr); Belo Horizonte (1 daily; 23hr); Bonito (1 daily; 5hr); Brasília (1 daily; 24hr); Corumbá (11 daily; 7hr); Coxim (4 daily; 3–4hr); Cuiabá (6 daily; 11hr); Dourados (6 daily; 4hr); Foz do Iguaçu (10 daily; 15hr); Miranda (11 daily; 3hr); Ponta Porã (4 daily; 5–6hr); Rio de Janeiro (4 daily; 22hr); São Paulo (8 daily; 14hr). There is also a weekly service to Asuncíon in Paraguay, leaving Sunday mornings (Amambay company).

Corumbá to: Campo Grande, via Anastácio/Aquidauana and Miranda (11 daily; 7hr; change in Campo Grande for most onward destinations); Rio de Janeiro (4 daily; 32hr); São Paulo (4 daily; 26hr).

Cuiabá to: Alta Floresta (4 daily; 12hr); Brasília (6 daily; 20hr); Campo Grande (6 daily; 11hr); Coxim (6 daily; 6–7hr); Goiânia (6 daily; 14hr); Porto Velho (4 daily; 23hr); Rio Branco (4 daily; 32hr); Rio de Janeiro (1 daily; 31hr); Rondonópolis (10 daily; 3hr); São Paulo (1 daily; 24hr-plus).

Planes

Campo Grande Several daily flights (VASP, Varig, TAM, Pantanal Linhas Aéreas) to Brazil's main cities; also to Vilhena (halfway between Cuiabá and Porto Velho).

Cuiabá VASP, Varig and TAM cover the main cities. Rio-Sul flies daily to Alta Floresta, Itaituba, Santarém and Belém, and Lloyd Aéreo Boliviana flies Mon and Fri to Santa Cruz.

Corumbá Daily flights (TAM and Pantanal Linhas Aéreas) to Campo Grande, Rio de Janeiro and São Paulo; and to Santa Cruz in Bolivia (Aerosul, Lloyd Aéreo Boliviano or air-taxi service). Note that Corumbá flights are not valid on the Varig air pass.

CHAPTER SEVEN

SÃO PAULO

The citizens of the **state of São Paulo**, *Paulistas*, never tire of saying that their state is Brazil's economic powerhouse, and they produce a mountain of statistics to sustain the boast. The state's forty million inhabitants represent about a quarter of Brazil's total population, yet the state contributes forty percent of the federal tax revenues, and consumes sixty percent of the country's industrial energy to produce two-thirds of its industrial output. A highly capitalized agricultural sector produces eighty percent of Brazil's oranges, half of its sugar, forty percent of its chickens and eggs, and 22 percent of its coffee. Yet while *Paulistas* crow that without their muscle, Brazil's economy would collapse, other Brazilians feel that São Paulo has developed at their expense. The state, it's argued, attracts capital away from the other regions, which are basically seen as sources of cheap labour and as guaranteed markets for São Paulo's products.

This economic pre-eminence is a relatively recent phenomenon. In 1507, São Vicente was founded on the coast near present-day **Santos**, the second oldest Portuguese settlement in Brazil, but for over three hundred years the area comprising today's state of São Paulo remained a backwater. The inhabitants were a hardy people, of mixed Portuguese and Indian origin, from whom – in the seventeenth and eighteenth centuries – emerged the **bandeirantes**: frontiersmen who roamed far into the South American interior to secure the borders of the Portuguese Empire against Spanish encroachment, capturing Indian slaves and seeking out precious metals and gems as they went.

Not until the mid-nineteenth century did São Paulo become rich. Cotton production received a boost with the arrival of Confederate refugees in the late 1860s, who settled between **Americana** and **Santa Bárbara d'Oeste**, about 140km from the then small town of **São Paulo** itself. But after disappointing results with cotton, most plantation owners switched their attentions to coffee and, by the end of the century, the state had become the world's foremost producer of the crop. During the same period, Brazil abolished slavery and the plantation owners recruited European and Japanese immigrants to expand production. Riding the wave of the coffee boom, British and other foreign companies took the opportunity to invest in port facilities, rail lines, power and water supplies, while textile and other new industries emerged, too. Within a few decades, the town of São Paulo became one of South America's greatest commercial and cultural centres, sliding from a small town into a vast metropolitan sprawl.

Even if the thought of staying in the city of São Paulo doesn't particularly appeal to you, the state does have other attractions. The beaches north of Santos, especially on **Ilhabela**, and around **Ubatuba**, rival Rio's best, while those to the south – near **Iguape** and **Cananéia** – remain relatively unspoiled. **Inland**, the state is dominated by agribusiness, with seemingly endless fields of sugar cane, oranges and soya interspersed with anonymous towns where the agricultural produce is processed. But for the novelty in tropical Brazil of a winter chill, or to escape scorching summer temperatures, make for **Campos do Jordão**, São Paulo's enticing mountain resort.

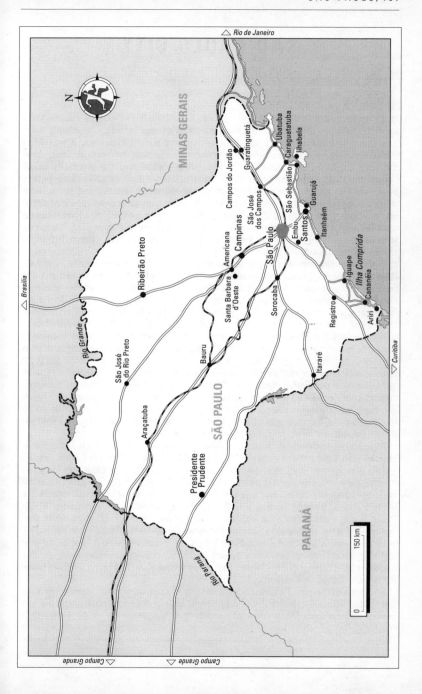

SÃO PAULO CITY

Rio is a beauty. But São Paulo – São Paulo is a city.

Marlene Dietrich

In 1554, the Jesuit priests José de Anchieta and Manuel da Nóbrega established a mission station on the banks of the Rio Tietê in an attempt to bring Christianity to the Tupi-Guarani Indians. Called São Paulo dos Campos de Piratininga, it was 70km inland and 730m up, in the sheer, forest-covered inclines of the Serra do Mar, above the port of São Vicente. The gently undulating plateau and the proximity to the Paraná and Plata rivers facilitated traffic into the interior and, with São Paulo as their base, roaming gangs of *bandeirantes* set out in search of loot. Around the mission school, a few adobe huts were erected and the settlement soon developed into a trading post and a base from which to secure mineral wealth. In 1681, São Paulo – as the town became known – became a seat of regional government and, in 1711, it was constituted as a municipality by the king of Portugal, the cool, healthy climate helping to attract settlers from the coast.

With the expansion of **coffee** plantations westwards from Rio de Janeiro, along the Paraibá Valley, in the mid-nineteenth century, São Paulo's fortunes looked up. The region's rich soil – *terra roxa* – was ideally suited to the growth of coffee, and from about 1870, plantation owners took up residence in the city, which was undergoing a rapid transformation into a bustling regional centre. British, French and German merchants and hoteliers opened local operations, British-owned rail lines radiated in all directions from São Paulo, and foreign water, gas, telephone and electricity companies moved in to service the city. In the 1890s, enterprising "coffee barons" began to place some of their profits into local industry, hedging their bets against a possible fall in the price of coffee, with textile factories being a favourite area for investment.

As the local population could not meet the ever-increasing demands of plantation owners, factories looked to **immigrants** to meet their labour requirements. As a result, São Paulo's **population** soared, almost tripling to 69,000 by 1890 – and, by the end of the next decade, increasing to 239,000. By 1950 it had reached 2.2m and São Paulo had clearly established its dominant role in Brazil's urbanization.

As industry, trade and population developed at such a terrific pace, buildings were erected with little time to consider their aesthetics; in any case, they often became cramped as soon as they were built, or had to be demolished to make way for a new avenue. However, some grand **public buildings** were built in the late nineteenth and early twentieth centuries, and a few still remain. None, though, are as splendid as those found in Buenos Aires, a city that developed at much the same time. In São Paulo, beauty counted for little and when, occasionally, graceful buildings raised their heads, they were almost always immediately overshadowed by some new monstrous edifice, or simply knocked down. Even now, conservation is seen as not being profitable, and São Paulo's concerns are more to do with rising population, rising production and rising consumption – factors that today are paralleled by rising levels of homelessness, pollution and violence.

Residents of the city, *Paulistanos*, talk smugly of their work ethic, supposedly superior to that which dominates the rest of Brazil, and speak contemptuously of the idleness of *cariocas* (in reply, *cariocas* joke sourly that *Paulistanos* are simply incapable of

The **telephone code** for São Paulo is ☎011.

enjoying anything, sex in particular). But work and profit aside, São Paulo does have its attractions: the city lays claim to have long surpassed Rio as Brazil's **cultural** centre, and São Paulo is home to a lively music and arts world. The city's **food**, too, is excellent, thanks to immigrants from so many parts of the world.

Orientation

The prospect of arriving in a city of sixteen million inhabitants, spread over an area of 30,000 square kilometres, is likely to seem a little daunting. However, while it's true that urban development has been carried out with an almost complete lack of planning, **SÃO PAULO** is far more manageable than you might imagine. Greater São Paulo is enormous, but the main shopping, entertainment and hotel districts are easy to move between, and the areas of historic interest are extremely limited. Even so, São Paulo's streets form something of a maze and even for the briefest of visits it's well worth buying a **map**. The *Guia Quatro Rodas*, a street guide available at any newspaper kiosk, is particularly good.

São Paulo's traditional centre is seen as the areas around **Praça da Sé** and **Praça da República**, the two sections of the city bisected by a broad avenue, the **Vale do Anhangabaú**, which in turn is bridged by a pedestrian crossing, the **Viaduto do Chá**. The area around Praça da Sé is where you'll find the Pátio do Colégio, which dates back to the early years of the Jesuit mission settlement, and the commercial district of banks, offices and shops, known as the **Triângulo** – originally comprising Rua Direita, Quinze de Novembro, São Bento, and Praça Antônio Prado. The area around Praça da República now forms an extension of the main commercial district, but there are many hotels and apartment buildings here, too.

The *bairros* to the **east** of the centre contained some of the city's first industrial suburbs and were home for many immigrants, but with the exception of the Museu da Hospedaria do Imigrante there's hardly anything of interest here. **North** of the centre is the neighbourhood of **Bom Retiro**, in the past the home of the Jewish community in São Paulo, and due north of here, across the Rio Tietê, is the **Rodoviária Tietê**.

Just **south** of the commercial district is **Bela Vista**, usually referred to as "Bixiga", São Paulo's "Little Italy", centred on **Rua 13 de Maio**. And immediately to the south of Praça da Sé is **Liberdade**, the Japanese neighbourhood, with its centre around Praça da Liberdade and Rua Galvão Bueno.

To the southwest of the centre is **Avenida Paulista**, an avenue of high-rise office buildings which effectively divides the traditional centre from the **Jardins**, the middle- and upper-class garden suburbs. Rua Augusta, which begins in the centre at Praça

---

AVOIDING TROUBLE IN SÃO PAULO

Use a little common sense and you're unlikely to encounter any real problems in the city. With such a mixture of people in São Paulo, you're far less likely to be assumed to be a foreigner than in most parts of Brazil, and therefore won't make such an obvious target for pickpockets and other **petty thieves**.

At night, though, pay particular attention around the central district of **Luz**, location of the city's main train stations and red-light districts, and – though not as bad – around **Praça da República**, and take special care late at night in **Bixiga** (Bela Vista) and **Praça Roosevelt**. Always carry at least some money in an immediately accessible place so that, if you are accosted by a **mugger**, you can quickly hand something over before he starts getting angry or panicky. If in any doubt at all about visiting an area you don't know, don't hesitate to take a taxi.

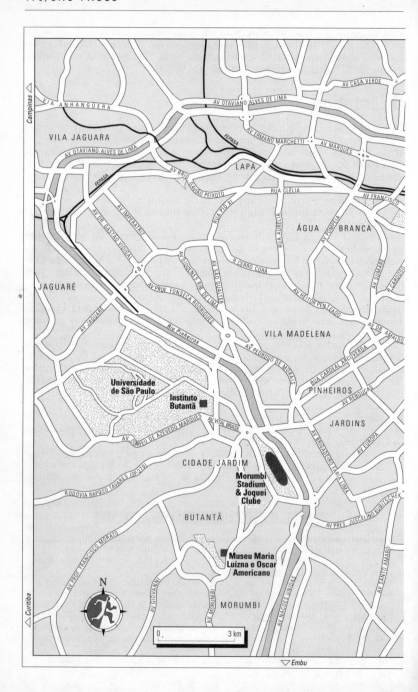

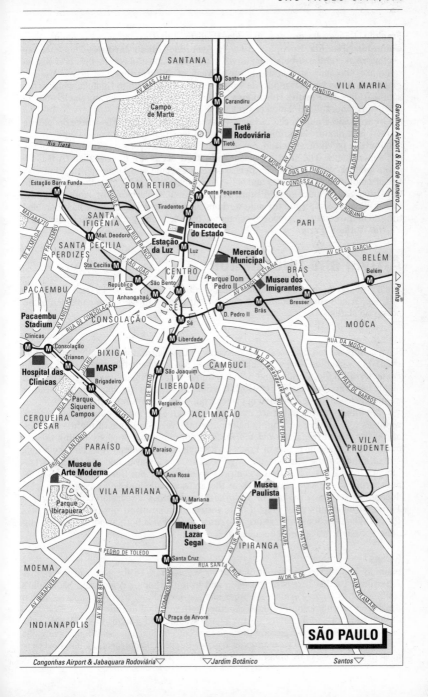

SANTANA

AV BRÁS LEME

Campo
de Marte

Rio Tietê

SANTANA
Carandiru

Tietê
Rodoviária
Tietê

AV MARIA CANDIDA

VILA MARIA

AV MORIAH DIAS DE FIGUEIREDO

Garulhos Airport & Rio de Janeiro ▷

Estação Barra Funda

MATARAZZO

DE ALMEIDA
DE PACAEMBU

BOM RETIRO

AV RUDGE

AV RIO BRANCO

Tiradentes

PARI

Ponte Pequena

AV CONDESSA ELIZABETH DE
ROBIANO

SANTA
IFIGÊNIA

SANTA CECÍLIA
PERDIZES

PACAEMBU

Mal. Deodoro

Pinacoteca
do Estado

Estação
da Luz
Luz

AV SÃO JOÃO

Sta Cecília

República

São Bento

CENTRO

Mercado
Municipal

Parque Dom
Pedro II

AV CELSO GARCIA

BELÉM

Belém

BRÁS

Museu dos
Imigrantes

◁ Penha

RUA DE CONSOLAÇÃO

Anhangabaú

SÉ

Sé

Pacaembu
Stadium

AV ANGÉLICA

Clínicas

Hospital das
Clínicas

Consolação

Trianon

MASP

Brigadeiro

Parque
Siqueira
Campos

CONSOLAÇÃO

BIXIGA

RUA R DE

AV PAULISTA

22 DE MAIO

São Bento

Liberdade

São Joaquim

Vergueiro

D. Pedro II

Bresser

Brás

Bresser

MOÓCA

RUA DA MOÓCA

CAMBUCI

AVENIDA DO ESTADO

Rio Tamanduatei

AV PAES DE BARROS

CERQUEIRA
CÉSAR

AV BRIG LUIS ANTÔNIO

PARAÍSO

Museu de
Arte Moderna

Parque
Ibirapuera

LIBERDADE

ACLIMAÇÃO

Paraíso

Ana Rosa

VILA MARIANA

V. Mariana

Museu
Lazar
Segal

Museu
Paulista

AV RICARDO JAFET

IPIRANGA

RUA BOM PASTOR

RUA DOM PEDRO

AV NAZARÉ

VILA
PRUDENTE

RUA DO MANIFESTO

MOEMA

AV IBIRAPUERA

INDIANÁPOLIS

AV RUBEM BERTA

R PEDRO DE TOLEDO

Santa Cruz

RUA SANTA CRUZ

AV DR. G. DE

AV DOMINGOS DE MORAIS

Praça de Árvore

SÃO PAULO

Franklin Roosevelt, crosses Avenida Paulista into the Jardins, becoming **Rua Colômbia**, **Avenida Europa** and finally **Avenida Cidade Jardim** – this interconnecting road and the streets running off it are where most of São Paulo's best restaurants and shopping streets are located. **West of the Jardins** just across the Rio Pinheiros, is the **Universidade de São Paulo** and the Instituto Butantã, while to the southeast lies the **Parque Ibirapuera**, one of the city's great parks and the location of more museums and exhibition centres.

Greater São Paulo includes huge, sprawling, industrial suburbs where people are housed in a mixture of grim-looking high-rise tenements, small houses and, on just about every patch of wasteland, *favelas* – the slum homes for some two million of the city's inhabitants. The most important **industrial areas** are the so-called "A B C D" *municípios* of Santo André, São Bernardo, São Caetano and Diadema, the centre of Brazil's motor vehicle industry and of the city's militantly left-wing political tradition. In the 1940s, Santo André elected Brazil's first Communist Party mayor, while out of the Metal Workers' Union and the auto workers' strikes of the late 1970s, which heralded the end of the country's supposed economic "miracle", emerged Lula, the leader of the PT, the Workers' Party.

Arrival and information

You'll probably **arrive** in São Paulo by plane or bus, though there is a train connection with Rio. Watch your belongings at all times, as thieves thrive in the confusion of airports and stations.

By air

São Paulo is served by two airports. Nearer to the centre, to the south, **Congonhas** (☎531-7444) handles services within the state of São Paulo and the shuttle services (the *Ponte Aérea*) to Rio, Curitiba and Belo Horizonte. Other domestic, and all international flights use **Garulhos** airport (☎945-2111), 30km from the city. Note that bad weather frequently leads to the diversion of planes from Garulhos to Congonhas.

Congonhas and Garulhos are connected to each other by air-conditioned *executivo* buses ($8) leaving at roughly half-hourly intervals (or 45min at night), stopping off on the way at the Tietê *Rodoviária*. At similar intervals, buses ($8) link the airports with the western side of Praça da República, from where you can take a taxi, bus or metrô to elsewhere in the city. Taxis are readily available at both airports – the fare from Congonhas to the centre is around $30, from Garulhos about $40. At both airports there are taxi desks in the arrivals halls and you pay a fixed price depending on the distance of your destination. SET (Secretaria de Esportese Turismo) maintains very helpful state **tourist information** desks at the airports (daily 7.30am–10.30pm); there are also *casas de câmbio* at both airports for changing dollars, cash or travellers' cheques.

By bus

Inter-city bus services arrive at one of two *Rodoviárias*. To the south of the centre, **Jabaquara** (☎235-0322) is for buses to and from the Santos region and São Paulo's south coast as far as Peruíbe. All other bus services to and from destinations within Brazil and neighbouring countries use the **Tietê** terminal to the north (☎235-0322). Both Jabaquara and Tietê are on the metrô system, and a night bus (#510M) runs between the *Rodoviárias*, passing through the centre at Praça da Sé. When leaving São Paulo you can probably save an extra trip out to either *Rodoviária*, as bus tickets to most destinations can be bought at travel agents in the city.

By train

There are very few train services now to São Paulo's **Estação da Luz** at Praça da Luz, at the edge of the city centre to the north. The train still runs to Bauru in the interior of the state of São Paulo, but the connection on to Campo Grande for Corumbá has been suspended. The only other services are to Campinas and to Rio de Janeiro. To or from the city centre itself, take the metrô (from the Luz station) or a taxi, which will cost $20.

Information

There are several **tourist offices** and booths scattered about the city (and at the airports) that provide information on the city and state of São Paulo.

The city's **information booths** are especially helpful for general directions, or for local bus and metrô details, and give away free a very good map of the downtown area. There are booths along Avenida Ipiranga, on Praça da República (daily 9am–6pm); at Praça da Liberdade (daily 9am–6pm); Teatro Municipal (Mon–Fri 9am–6pm, Sat 9am–1pm); along Avenida Paulista opposite MASP (Mon–Fri 9am–6pm); and at the Morumbi (Mon–Fri 9am–6pm) and Ibirapuera (Mon–Fri 9am–6pm, Sat noon–4pm) shopping centres (see p.494).

A good map, but otherwise very limited information on the state of São Paulo, is available from the **tourist office** at Praça Antônio Prado 347 (Mon–Fri 10am–5pm). There are also **information points** with a video-text tourist service in English; you can call ☎267-2122 to find out where the nearest one is.

Getting around

São Paulo's **public transport** network is excellent and, despite the traffic congestion and an almost perpetual rush hour, you can move around the city by metrô, bus or taxi with remarkable ease. The one time *not* to attempt to travel is when it rains: São Paulo's drainage system is hopelessly inadequate to cope with the tropical storms and, as roads are transformed into rivers, the city grinds to a halt – just take cover in a bar or *lanchonete* and sit it out. As a **safety precaution**, always make sure you have some small notes at hand, so as not to attract attention to yourself when fumbling through your wallet or bag for change.

The metrô

Clean, quiet, comfortable and fast, São Paulo's **metrô** would be by far the easiest way to move around the city were it not limited to just three lines. The **north–south** line has terminals at Santana and Jabaquara (the *Rodoviária* from where buses to Santos depart) and also serves the Tietê *Rodoviária* and Luz train station. One of the **east–west** lines has terminals at Corinthians–Itaquera and Barra Funda, and intersects with the north–south line at Praça da Sé. The shorter east–west line crosses underneath Avenida Paulista from Ana Rosa to Clinicas stopping at the Museu de Arte (Trianon-Masp station).

The metrô operates every day from 5am until midnight, although the stations along Avenida Paulista close at 8.30pm. **Tickets** cost 60 cents for a one-way journey and come either as singles (*ida*), doubles (*dople*), or valid for ten journeys (*bilhete com dez unidades*). You can also buy integrated bus/metrô tickets, as many buses stop at the metrô stations, with the names of their destinations well marked.

Buses

Traffic congestion rarely allows São Paulo's **buses** to be driven at the same terrifying speeds as in Rio. The network is efficient and includes trolley buses as well as ordinary buses; there is a flat fare of 50 cents.

SOME USEFUL BUS ROUTES

The *Guia Quatro Rodas* for São Paulo, available at any newspaper kiosk, gives the numbers and routes taken by all the city's buses. Below are listed a few buses to some likely destinations.

From Praça da República along Avenida Paulista (via Liberdade): #595P.

From Praça da República to Avenida Brigadeiro Faria Lima (via Rua Augusta): #702P.

From Praça da República to Butantã (via Rua Augusta and Avenida Brigadeiro Faria Lima): #7181 and 107P.

From Avenida Ipiranga to Butantã and Universidade de São Paulo: #702U.

From metrô Ana Rosa along Avenida Paulista: #875P.

From *Rodoviária* Tietê to *Rodoviária* Jabaquara via Largo de São Bento and Avenida Liberdade: #501M (midnight–5am only).

On the down side, **bus routes** often snake confusingly through the city, and working out which bus to take can be difficult. The number of the bus is clearly marked at the front, and there are cards at the front and the entrance (towards the back) which indicate the route. At **bus stops** (usually wooden posts) you'll have to flag down the buses you want: be attentive or they'll speed by. Buses run between 4am and midnight, but avoid travelling during the evening rush hour (5–7pm) when they are overflowing with passengers.

Taxis

Taxis in São Paulo are abundant and cheap. With irregular – or no – bus services at night, taxis are really the only means of transport after midnight. There are two main types: the yellow *comuns* and the *radiotáxis*.

The **comuns**, generally small cars that carry three passengers, are the cheapest and are found at taxi ranks or hailed from the street. **Radiotáxis** are larger and more expensive, and are ordered by phone: try Coopertax (☎941-2555) or Ligue Táxi (☎272-9960). Both types of taxi have meters, with two fare rates, and a flag, or *bandeira*, is displayed on the meter to indicate which fare is in operation: fare "1" is charged from 6am to 10pm Monday to Saturday, but after 10pm and on Sunday and public holidays, fare "2" is charged, costing twenty percent more. Just in case the driver is tempted to take a longer than necessary route to your destination, it's a good idea to keep an eye on your map as you go.

Accommodation

Hotels in São Paulo tend to be busiest during the week when people visit the city for work. Nevertheless, finding somewhere to stay is rarely a problem and, as there are several areas where hotels are concentrated, you should get settled in quite quickly. The **prices** of hotels remain pretty much the same throughout the year, but in the quieter summer months (December and January) they may be lower. Weekend **discounts** of up to fifty percent are often given, especially at the better hotels that otherwise cater largely to business executives.

Hotels tend to be geared to business travellers on expense accounts and, as such, it's difficult to find a comfortable room in a pleasant location for under around $70. Those budget and medium-priced places that do exist are often in rather seedy parts of the city where walking alone at night may feel uncomfortable. However, the dangers are often more imaginary than real and, by simply being alert and taking taxis late at night, you should have no problems.

Praça da República and around

In the traditional centre of São Paulo, there are lots of medium-priced hotels in the streets around Praça da República. Cheaper rooms can be found in hotels towards Estação da Luz in the Santa Ifigénia district, but many of these are aimed at either long-stay guests or couples checking in for an hour or two, and the area has a distinctly dangerous edge to it. At night, the Praça da República area has a more comfortable feel than around Luz, but there are still a lot of seedy-looking individuals milling around.

Alfa, Av. Ipiranga 1152 (☎228-4188). Good value and entirely respectable. There are several other hotels of a similar category along this street, too. ③.

Cineasta Hotel, Av. São João 613 (☎223-8024). This once elegant hotel has seen better days, but it remains comfortable, safe and well located. ④.

Copacabana, Rua Aurora 26 (☎222-0511). A basic crashpad, offering less expensive rooms without bath. There are plenty of similar, cheap hotels on this street. ②.

Gávea Palace, Rua Conselheiro Nébias 445 (☎222-4655). Situated just behind Praça da República towards Avenida São João, this is a clean and comfortable hotel. ③.

Grande Hotel Broadway, Av. São João 536 (☎222-2811). A good-value hotel, serving excellent breakfasts and situated not far from the square. ④.

Joamar, Rua Dom José de Barros 187 (☎221-3611). This hotel is just a block from República metrô station and is clean and friendly; others on this street are similar. ③.

Luanda, Rua Santa Ifigénia 348, on the corner of Rua Aurora (☎222-2441). A good cheap hotel with shared bathrooms. ①.

Ofir, Rua das Andradas 258 (☎223-8822). Good, clean rooms all with bathrooms, on the next street along from Rua Santa Ifigénia. ②.

Paulicéia, Rua do Timbiras, on the corner of Rua Santa Ifigénia (☎220-9733). Rooms here are with or without shower, safe and well kept. ①–②.

Plaza Apolo, Rua Santa Ifigénia 163 (☎229-8198). A large, good-value hotel. ②.

São Paulo Center, Rua Santa Ifigénia 40 (☎228-6033). Part of the Best Western chain, but otherwise little to recommend it. ⑥.

São Sebastião, Rua Sete de Abril 364 (☎257-4988). Clean and quiet rooms, some with shower, just moments from the entrance to the Praça da República metrô station. A popular choice with European backpackers, with safe night-time access. ②–③.

Vale Verde, Praça da Bandeira 39 (☎607-2833). A highly recommended place to stay, clean, secure and extremely friendly. Well located near the Anhangabaú metrô station.

Rua Augusta and around

Rua Augusta is best known for the *Cá d'Oro* and *Caesar Park*, two of São Paulo's finest and most expensive hotels. However, along and just off this same road are some far more affordable options worth seeking out. The hotels here are ideally located, midway between the city centre and Avenida Paulista; it's the northern boundary of the more fashionable Jardins, and the area is very safe at night.

Augusta Palace Hotel, Rua Augusta 467 (☎256-1277). This hotel is nearer to Rua da Consolação than Avenida Paulista which makes it handy for the Praça da República area. Very much a business hotel and worth calling in advance for weekend discounts. ⑥.

Augusta Park Residence, Rua Augusta 922 (☎255-5722). A comfortable little hotel with friendly service. ④.

Augusta Plaza Hotel, Rua Augusta 1255 (☎284-0866). Dark, but otherwise very comfortable rooms with bathrooms. ⑥.

Cá d'Oro, Rua Augusta 129 (☎256-8011). Well located and like a European grand hotel in style, with facilities to match. ⑧.

Caesar Park, Rua Augusta 1508 (☎285-6622). Almost on the corner with Avenida Paulista, this is one of the most comfortable hotels in the city. ⑧.

Pousada Dona Ziláh, Alameda Franca 1621 (☎852-1444). A large house converted into a simple, very friendly hotel. Its location makes it an especially attractive place to stay – on the north side of Avenida Paulista near the bars, restaurants and shops of Jardins. Discounts offered for stays of one week or more. ④.

Estela, Rua Augusta 1047. Basic rooms. ②.

Savoy Palace Hotel, Rua Augusta 1272 (☎288-6459). A good-value and very pleasant small hotel in a convenient location. ⑤.

Liberdade

As well as great food, Liberdade, São Paulo's Japanese *bairro*, also has a few medium-priced hotels, mainly for Brazilian-Japanese and visiting Japanese businessmen, who are seeking Japanese-style food, baths and cleanliness.

Banri, Rua Galvão Bueno 209 (☎270-8877). A very popular and comfortable hotel with Japanese bath tubs. ③.

Isei, Rua da Gloria 290 (☎278-6646). Provides comfortable, but not recognizably Japanese rooms, verging on the kitsch. ②.

Nikkey Palace Hotel, Rua Galvão Bueno 425 (☎270-8511). Even if you can't afford to stay at this luxury hotel, try their Japanese buffet breakfast ($12). ⑦.

The City

For visitors and locals alike, the fact that São Paulo's history extends back for over four centuries, well beyond the late nineteenth-century coffee boom, usually goes completely unnoticed. Catapulted virtually overnight from being a sleepy, provincial market town into one of the western hemisphere's great cities, there are few places in the world that have as comprehensively turned their backs on the past as São Paulo has done. In the nineteenth century, most of colonial São Paulo was levelled and replaced by a disorganized patchwork of wide avenues and large buildings, the process constantly repeating itself ever since; today, not only has the city's colonial architectual heritage all but vanished, but there's little physical evidence of the coffee boom decades either.

Nevertheless, a few relics have, somehow, escaped demolition and offer hints of São Paulo's bygone eras. What remains is hidden away discreetly in corners, scattered throughout the city, often difficult to find but all the more thrilling when you do. There is no shortage of **museums**, but with a few significant exceptions they are disappointing for a city of São Paulo's importance. Collections have frequently been allowed to deteriorate and exhibits are generally poorly displayed. Fortunately, museum **charges** are negligible, around $1, and are only given in the text below where they are unusually high.

There are several sights associated with the vast influx of immigrants to the city (see p.480), and it's worth visiting some of the individual *bairros*, detailed in the text, where the immigrants and their descendants have established communities: the food, as you'd expect, is just one reason to do this.

Around Praça da Sé

Praça da Sé is the most convenient starting point for the very brief hunt for **colonial São Paulo**. The square itself is a large expanse of concrete and fountains, dominated by the **Catedral Metropolitana**, a huge neo-Gothic structure with a capacity of 8000 but otherwise unremarkable. Completed in 1954, it replaced São Paulo's eighteenth-century cathedral, which was demolished in 1920. During the day the square outside bustles with activity, always crowded with hawkers and people heading towards the commercial district on its western fringes. At night it's transformed into a campsite for homeless children, who survive as best they can by shining shoes, selling chewing gum or begging.

Along Rua Boa Vista, on the opposite side of the square from the cathedral, is where the city of São Paulo originated. The whitewashed Portuguese Baroque **Pátio do Colégio** is a replica of the college and chapel that formed the centre of the Jesuit mission founded here in 1554. Although built in 1896 (the other buildings forming the Pátio were constructed this century), the chapel (Mon–Fri 7.30am–4pm) is an accurate reproduction, but it's in the **Casa de Anchieta** (Tues–Sun 1–4.30pm), part of the Pátio, where the most interesting sixteenth- and early seventeenth-century relics – mostly old documents – are held.

Virtually around the corner from the Pátio do Colégio at Rua Roberto Simonsen 136 is the **Museu da Cidade** (Tues–Sun 9am–5pm). More interesting than the museum's small collection chronicling the development of São Paulo is the building that it's housed in, the **Solar da Marquesa de Santos**, an eighteenth-century manor house that represents the sole remaining residential building in the city from this period. A couple of hundred metres from here, at Av. Rangel Pestana 230, is the well-preserved **Igreja do Carmo** (Mon–Fri 7–11am & 1–4pm, Sat & Sun 7.30–9.30am), which was built in 1632 and still retains many of its seventeenth-century features, including a fine Baroque high altar.

In these streets, particularly around Rua 25 de Março, São Paulo's Lebanese and Syrian community is concentrated. At Rua Comandante Abdo Schahin 40, the Empório Syrio sells Middle Eastern delicacies, and on the same road there are some excellent Arab **restaurants**, always full with local merchants. The community is fairly evenly divided between Muslims and Christians, and hidden away at Rua Cavalheiro Basilio Jafet 15 there's a beautiful **Orthodox church**.

Over the other side of the Praça da Sé, a two-minute walk down Rua Senado Feijó to the Largo de São Francisco is the **Igreja de São Francisco** (Mon–Fri 7.30am–7pm, Sun 7.30–11am & 4–6pm), a typical late seventeenth-century Portuguese colonial church which features intricately carved ornaments and an elaborate Baroque altar. While here, step inside the courtyard of the Faculdade de Direito de São Paulo – founded in 1824, one of Brazil's first higher education institutions – which adjoins the church and take a look at the huge 1930s stained-glass window depicting the Largo de São Francisco in the early ninetenth century. Before leaving this area, at Praça do Patriarca, by the Viaduto do Chá (the pedestrian bridge linking the two parts of the commercial centre), the **Igreja de Santo Antônio** is worth a visit. Built in 1717, its yellow and white facade has been beautifully restored; the interior has been stripped of most of its eighteenth-century accoutrements, though its simple painted wooden ceiling deserves a glance.

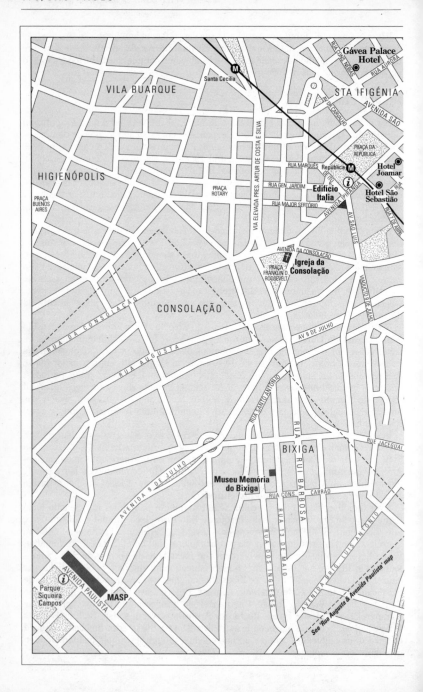

Gávea Palace
Hotel

STA IFIGÉNIA

VILA BUARQUE

Santa Cecilia

AVENIDA SÃO

PRAÇA DA
REPÚBLICA

HIGIENÓPOLIS

RUA MARQUÊS   República   Hotel
Joamar

RUA GEN. JARDIM   Edifício
Itália

PRAÇA
ROTARY

RUA MAJOR SERTÓRIO   Hotel São
Sebastião

PRAÇA
BUENOS
AIRES

VIA ELEVADA PRES. ARTUR DE COSTA E SILVA

AVENIDA IPIRANGA

AV SÃO LUIS

AVENIDA DA CONSOLAÇÃO

Igreja da
Consolação

PRAÇA
FRANKLIN D
ROOSEVELT

CONSOLAÇÃO

VIADUCTO DE JULHO

AV 9 DE JULHO

RUA DA CONSOLAÇÃO

RUA AUGUSTA

RUA SANTO ANTONIO

RUA AUGUSTA

RUE JACEGUAI

BIXIGA

RUI BARBOSA

AVENIDA 9 DE JULHO

Museu Memória
do Bixiga

RUA CONS. CARRÃO

RUA 13 DE MAIO

RUA DOS INGLESES

AVENIDA PAULISTA

Parque
Siqueira
Campos

MASP

AVENIDA BRIG. LUIS ANTONIO

See 'Rua Augusta & Avenida Paulista' map

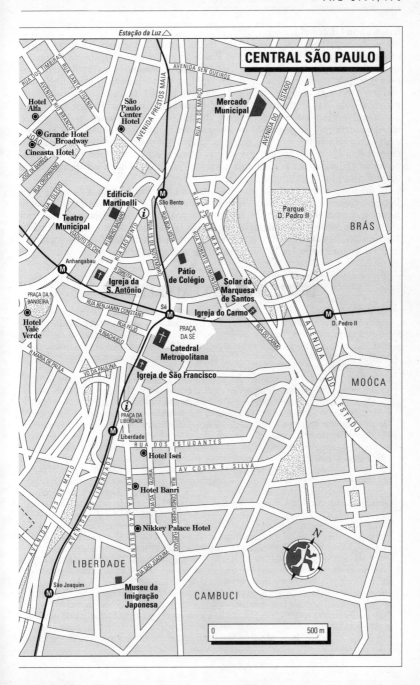

Estação da Luz △

CENTRAL SÃO PAULO

RUA DOS TIMBIRAS
RUA SANTA IFIGÉNIA
AVENIDA RIO BRANCO

AVENIDA SEN QUEIRÓS

AVENIDA PRESTES MAIA

RUA 25 DE MARÇO

AVENIDA DO ESTADO

Hotel Alfa

São Paulo Center Hotel

Mercado Municipal

JOÃO

Grande Hotel Broadway

Cineasta Hotel

JOSÉ DE BARROS

RUA CRISPIANO

RUA TOLEDO

Edifício Martinelli

RUA BARÃO BUENO

M São Bento

RUA BOA VISTA

RUA 15 DE NOVEMBRO

RUA ROBERTO SIMONSEN

Parque D. Pedro II

BRÁS

Teatro Municipal

VIADUTO DO CHÁ

RIBEIRO BADARÓ

R DIREITA

Anhangabaú M

Igreja da S. Antônio

Pátio de Colégio

Solar da Marquesa de Santos

PRAÇA DA BANDEIRA

RUA BENJAMIN CONSTANT

Sé M

Igreja do Carmo

M D. Pedro II

AVENIDA DO ESTADO

Hotel Vale Verde

RUA FEIJÓ

PRAÇA DA SÉ

RUA DO CARMO

RUA RIACHUELO

Catedral Metropolitana

MOÓCA

R MARIA DE PAULA

VD DA PAULINA

Igreja de São Francisco

PRAÇA DA LIBERDADE

M Liberdade

RUA DOS ESTUDANTES

Hotel Isei

AV COSTA E. SILVA

AVENIDA 23 DE MAIO

AVENIDA DA LIBERDADE

RUA DA GLÓRIA

RUA VIA VIA

RUA CONSELHEIRO

Hotel Banri

Nikkey Palace Hotel

FURTADO

N

RUA SÃO JOAQUIM

LIBERDADE

São Joaquim M

Museu da Imigração Japonesa

CAMBUCI

0 ____ 500 m

Bixiga and Liberdade

Since the early twentieth century, the Italian immigrant population of the *bairro* of **Bixiga**, lying to the southwest of Praça da Sé, has given it the name "Little Italy" (it's also known as Bela Vista). Calabrian stonemasons built their own homes with leftover materials from the building sites where they were employed, and the narrow streets are still lined with such houses. In an otherwise ordinary house at Rua dos Ingleses 118, the **Museu Memória do Bixiga** (Wed–Sun 2–5.30pm) enthusiastically documents the history of the *bairro*, and there's a small collection of photographs and household items. You'll find Italian **restaurants** throughout the city, but the area of greatest concentration is Bixiga. The central Rua 13 de Março, and the streets running off it, are lined with *cantinas*, pizzerias and bars, and at night this normally quiet neighbourhood springs to life (see "Eating" for restaurant listings).

To the south of the Praça da Sé is the bairro of **Liberdade**, home of the city's large Japanese community. Rua Galvão Bueno and intersecting streets are largely devoted to Japanese restaurants and shops selling semi-precious stones, Japanese food and clothes. The **Museu da Imigração Japonesa** (Wed–Sun 1.30–5.30pm), at Rua São Joaquim 381, has excellent displays on the contribution of the Japanese community to Brazil since their arrival in 1908 to work on the coffee plantations.

IMMIGRATION AND SÃO PAULO

São Paulo is a city built on **immigrants**: largely due to immigration, São Paulo's population grew a hundred-fold in 75 years to make it the country's second largest city by 1950. Besides sheer numbers, the mass influx of people had a tremendous impact on the character of the city, breaking up the existing social stratification and removing economic and political power from the traditional elite groups at a much earlier stage than in other Brazilian cities.

Although there had been attempts at introducing Prussian share-croppers in the 1840s, mass immigration didn't begin until the late 1870s. Initially, conditions were appalling for the immigrants, many of whom succumbed to malaria or yellow fever while waiting in Santos to be transferred inland to the plantations. In response to criticisms, the government opened the **Hospedaria dos Imigrantes** (Rua Visconde de Paraíba 1316, near Brás metrô station) in 1887, a hostel in the eastern suburb of Brás. Now partly used as an immigration research centre and excellent museum (Tues–Sun 10am–5pm; research facilities available only 1–5pm), featuring period furniture, documents and photographs, the building is an imposing structure – one which had its own rail siding and platform for unloading immigrants and their baggage. Near the entrance, a separate building contained the rooms where new arrivals met their prospective employers, the government providing interpreters to help the immigrants make sense of work contracts. Designed to hold 4000 people, the hostel housed as many as 10,000 at times, the immigrants treated little better than cattle. In its early years, it was a virtual prison: the exit ticket was securing a contract of employment. Control was considered necessary since few immigrants actually wanted to work in the plantations, and there was a large labour leakage to the city of São Paulo itself. The Hospedaria is little visited – perhaps due to its grim location, an unpleasant walk from Brás metrô station – but it is definitely one of the best museums in São Paulo.

Immigration to São Paulo is most closely associated with the **Italians**, who constituted 46 percent of all arrivals between 1887 and 1930. In general, soon after arrival in Brazil they would be transported to a plantation, but most slipped away within a year to seek employment in the city or to move on south to Argentina. The rapidly expanding factories in the districts of Brás, Mooca and Belém, east of the city centre, were desperately

North of Praça da Sé

The coffee boom that led to the dismantling of São Paulo's colonial buildings provided little in terms of lasting replacements. In the city's first industrial suburbs, towering brick chimneys are still to be seen, but generally the areas are now dominated by small workshops and low-income housing, and even in the city centre there are very few buildings of note, most of the area given over to unremarkable shops and offices.

To the north of Praça da Sé, at Rua da Cantareira 306, you'll find the **Mercado Municipal**, an imposing, vaguely German neo-Gothic hall, completed in 1933. Apart from the phenomenal display of Brazilian and imported fruit, vegetables, cheese and other produce, the market (Mon–Sat 5am–4pm) is most noted for its enormous stained-glass windows depicting scenes of cattle raising, market gardening and coffee and banana plantations. Just across the Viaduto do Chá, in the direction of Praça da República, is the **Teatro Municipal**, São Paulo's most distinguished public building, an eclectic mixture of Art Nouveau and Italian Renaissance styles. Work began on the building in 1903, when the coffee boom was at its peak and São Paulo at its most confident. The theatre is still the city's main venue for classical music, and the auditorium, lavishly decorated and furnished with Italian marble, velvet, gold leaf and mirrors, can be viewed only if you're attending a performance.

short of labour, and well into the twentieth century the population of these *bairros* was largely Italian. But it is **Bixiga** (or, officially, Bela Vista) where the Italian influence has been most enduring, as catalogued in the **Museu Memória do Bixiga** (see above). Originally home to freed slaves, by the early twentieth century Bixiga had established itself as São Paulo's "Little Italy". As immigration from Italy began to slow in the late 1890s, arrivals from other countries increased. From 1901 to 1930 **Spaniards** (especially Galicians) made up 22 percent, and **Portuguese** 23 percent, of immigrants, but their language allowed them to assimilate extremely quickly. Only Tatuapé developed into a largely Portuguese *bairro*.

The first 830 **Japanese** immigrants arrived in 1908 in Santos, from where they were sent on to the coffee plantations. By the mid-1950s a quarter of a million Japanese had emigrated to Brazil, most of them settling in the state of São Paulo, and unlike most other nationalities, the rate of return migration among them has always been small: many chose to remain in agriculture, often as market gardeners, at the end of their contract. The city's large Japanese community is centred on **Liberdade**, a *bairro* just south of the Praça da Sé and home to the excellent **Museu Histórica da Imigração Japonesa** (see above).

São Paulo's **Arab** community is quite substantial. Commonly associated with petty commerce, Arabs started arriving in the early twentieth century from Syria and the Lebanon and, as they were then travelling on Turkish passports, they're still usually referred to as *turcos*. Family ties remain strong and, with the 1980s civil war in the Lebanon, the community has been considerably enlarged. Many of the boutiques in the city's wealthy *bairros* are Arab-owned, but it's in the streets **around Rua 25 de Março**, north of Praça da Sé, where the community is concentrated (see p.477).

The **Jewish** community has also prospered in São Paulo. Mainly of East European origin, many of the city's Jews started out as itinerant pedlars before concentrating in **Bom Retiro**, a *bairro* near Luz train station. As they became richer, they moved to the suburbs to the south of the city, but some of the shops in the streets around Rua Correia de Melo are still Jewish-owned and there is a synagogue here. And as the Jews move out, **Koreans** – São Paulo's latest immigrant arrivals – are moving in.

Luz

Further north, the once affluent and still leafy *bairro* of Luz is home to São Paulo's two main train stations. Built between 1926 and 1937, the **Estação Júlio Prestes** at the intersection of Rua Duque de Caxias and Rua Mauá is worth a visit for railway buffs, not least to admire the large stained-glass windows depicting the role of the train in the expansion of the Brazilian economy in the early twentieth century. Nearby, by the corner of Rua Mauá and Avenida Tiradentes, is the older **Estação da Luz**, an imposing part of the British-owned rail network that did much to stimulate São Paulo's explosive growth in the late nineteenth century. Built in 1901, on the site that had been occupied since 1864 by a much smaller terminal, everything was imported from Britain for its construction, from the design of the project to the smallest of screws. Although the refined decoration of its chambers was destroyed by fire in 1946, interior details – iron balconies, passageways and grilles – bear witness to the majestic structure's original elegance.

Nearby, on Avenida Tiradentes, the **Parque da Luz** was São Paulo's first public garden, whose intricate wrought-iron fencing and rich foliage provides evidence of the garden's former glory. Sadly, it's long since been overcome by the general squalor around Luz station, and it's one of the seediest red-light areas of the city. Also on Avenida Tiradentes, at no. 141, is the **Pinacoteca do Estado** (Tues–Fri 11am–6pm, Sat & Sun 1–6pm), the state of São Paulo gallery, containing an extensive and important collection of beautifully displayed nineteenth- and twentieth-century Brazilian art, including works by Larsar Segall, Di Cavalcanti, Cândido Portinari, Tarsilla do Amaral and Almeida Junior.

By the Tiradentes metrô station, at Av. Tiradentes 676, is one of the city's few surviving colonial churches, the **Igreja e Convento da Luz** (daily 8–11am & 2–4.30pm), a rambling structure of uncharacteristic grandeur. Built on the site of a sixteenth-century chapel, the former Franciscan monastery and church date back to 1774, though they've been much altered over the years and today house the **Museu de Arte Sacra** (Tues–Sun 1–6pm). The museum's collection includes examples of Brazilian seventeenth- and eighteenth-century wooden and terracotta religious art and liturgical pieces.

Formerly a predominantly Jewish neighbourhood, the adjoining *bairro* of **Bom Retiro** is now the home of the city's Korean population, with numerous shops selling cheap clothes and fabric.

Around Praça da República

Praça da República is now largely an area of offices, hotels and shops but was once the site of the lavish **mansions** of the coffee-plantation owners who began to take up residence in the city from about 1870. However, no sooner than they were built, the mansions, constructed from British iron, Italian marble, Latvian pine, Portuguese tiles and Belgian stained glass, were abandoned as the city centre took on a brash and commercial character, and the coffee barons moved to new homes in the Higienópolis district, a short distance west of Praça da República. The central mansions were all knocked down, though a few remain in Higienópolis: the Art Nouveau-influenced **Vila Penteado**, on Rua Maranhão, is a fine example and one of the last to be built in the area.

The Edifício Martinelli and Edifício Itália

Southeast of the Praça da República, lies the **Triângulo**, the traditional banking district and a zone of concentrated vertical growth. At the northern edge of the Triângulo, on Avenida São João, stands the thirty-storey **Edifício Martinelli**, the city's first skyscraper. Modelled on the Empire State Building, Martinelli was inaugurated in 1929 and remains an important landmark, only dwarfed by Latin America's tallest office building, the 42-storey **Edifício Itália**, built in 1965 on Avenida São Luís, the street leading south from the *praça*. On cloud- and smog-free days, the Itália's 41st-floor restaurant, the *Terraço Itália*, is a good vantage point from which to view the city; the food's expensive and not very good, so you're best off just having afternoon tea or an early evening drink at the bar. In the 1940s and 1950s **Avenida São Luís** itself was São Paulo's version of Fifth Avenue, lined with high-class apartment buildings and offices, and, though no longer fashionable, it still retains a certain degree of elegance. Admirers of the Brazilian architect Oscar Niemeyer will immediately pick out the serpentine Edifício Copan, the largest of the apartment and office buildings on the avenue.

Along Avenida Paulista

By 1900, the coffee barons had moved on again, flaunting their wealth from their new mansions, set in spacious gardens stretching along the three-kilometre-long **Avenida Paulista** – then a tree-lined avenue set along a ridge 3km southwest of the city centre. In the late 1960s, and throughout the 1970s, Avenida Paulista resembled a giant building site, with banks and other companies competing to build ever taller buildings. There was little time for creativity, and along the entire length of the avenue it would be difficult to single out one example of decent modern architecture. There are, however, about a dozen Art Nouveau or Art Deco mansions along Avenida Paulista, afforded official protection from the developers' bulldozers. Some lie empty, the subjects of legal wrangles over inheritance rights, while others have been turned into branches of McDonalds or prestigious headquarters for banks. One mansion that is well worth visiting is the French-style **Casa das Rosas**, Av. Paulista 35 (Tues–Sun noon–8pm), near Brigadeiro mêtro station at the easterly end of the *avenida*. Set in a rose garden with a beautiful Art Nouveau stained-glass window, it stunningly contrasts with the mirrored-glass and steel office building behind it. The Casa das Rosas is now a cultural centre owned by the state of São Paulo, where interesting art exhibitions are often held.

Museu de Arte de São Paulo (MASP)
The **Museu de Arte de São Paulo**, Av. Paulista 1578 (Tues–Sun 11am–6pm, Thurs until 8pm; $5, free on Thurs), is considered to be the most important museum of Western art in Latin America and is the great pride of São Paulo's art lovers. It houses a fine collection of work of great European artists from the last five hundred years, though very little space is devoted to Brazilian and other Latin American artists. For most North American and European visitors, notable though some of the individual works of Hieronymus Bosch, Rembrandt and Degas may be, the highlights of the permanent collection are likely to be the seventeenth- to nineteenth-century landscapes of Brazil by European artists, none more important than those of Frans Post. MASP is one of Brazil's few museums that regularly receives important visiting exhibitions; and the museum's excellent and very reasonably priced restaurant is open for lunch and afternoon tea, an excellent escape from the crowds, exhaust fumes and heat of Avenida Paulista outside.

Parque Siqueira Campos
Almost directly across Avenida Paulista from MASP is one of São Paulo's smallest but most delightful parks, the **Parque Siqueira Campos**, created in 1912 when building in the area began. It was planned by the French landscape artist, Paul Villan, based around local vegetation with some introduced trees and bushes, and in 1968, underwent thorough renovation, directed by the great designer, Roberto Burle-Marx. The park consists of 45,000 square metres of almost pure Atlantic forest with a wealth of different trees, and there's a network of trails, as well as benches to sit and relax on away from the intense summer heat. The park is well patrolled by wardens but a degree of alertness is still called for – don't doze off.

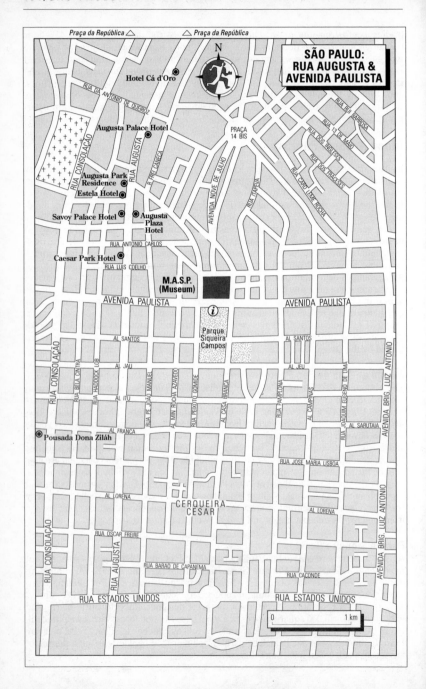

Praça da República △   △ Praça da República

N

**SÃO PAULO:
RUA AUGUSTA &
AVENIDA PAULISTA**

Hotel Cá d'Oro

RUA DA ANTONIO DE QUEIROZ

Augusta Palace Hotel

PRAÇA
14 BIS

RUA CONSOLAÇÃO

RUA AUGUSTA

R. FREI CANECA

AVENIDA NOVE DE JULHO

RUA ITAPEVA

RUA RUI BARBOSA

RUA 13 DE MAIO

RUA DOS INGLESES

RUA DOS FRACESES

RUA CARD LEME ROCHA

Augusta Park
Residence

Estela Hotel

Savoy Palace Hotel

Augusta
Plaza
Hotel

RUA ANTONIO CARLOS

Caesar Park Hotel

RUA LUIS COELHO

**M.A.S.P.
(Museum)**

AVENIDA PAULISTA   AVENIDA PAULISTA

ⓘ

Parque
Siqueira
Campos

AL SANTOS   AL SANTOS

RUA CONSOLAÇÃO

RUA BELA CINTRA

RUA HADDOCK LOB

AL JAU   AL JEU

AL ITU

RUA PE JOÃO MANUEL

RUA MIN ROCHA AZAVEDO

RUA PEIXOTO GOMIDE

AL CASA FRANCA

RUA PAMPLONA

AL CAMPINAS

RUA JOAQUIM EUGENIO DE LIMA

AVENIDA BRIG. LUIZ ANTONIO

AL SARUTAIA

AL FRANCA

Pousada Dona Ziláh

RUA JOSE MARIA LISBOA

AL LORENA

**CERQUEIRA
CESAR**

AL LORENA

RUA OSCAR FREIRE

RUA CONSOLAÇÃO

RUA AUGUSTA

RUA BARAO DE CAPANEMA

RUA CACONDE

AVENIDA BRIG. LUIZ ANTONIO

RUA ESTADOS UNIDOS   RUA ESTADOS UNIDOS

0   1 km

The Jardins and the Parque do Ibirapuera

Avenida Paulista marks the northeastern boundary of **Cerqueira César**, and beyond that are the **Jardins**, laid out in 1915 and styled after the British idea of the garden suburb. From the city centre, Rua Augusta crosses Avenida Paulista, and passes through the middle of Cerqueira César, joining with Rua Colômbia and – dividing Jardim América and Jardim Paulista – Avenida Europa and Avenida Cidade Jardim. Cerqueira César largely consists of apartment buildings for the city's upper middle class, while the Jardins themselves are dominated by luxury houses – protected from Third World realities by high walls, complex alarm systems, guards and fierce dogs. These exclusive residential neighbourhoods have long since taken over from the city centre as the location of most of the city's best restaurants and shopping streets, and many residents never stray from their luxurious ghettos.

Parque do Ibirapuera

The **Parque do Ibirapuera** (daily 6am–9pm), southeast of the Jardins, is the most famous of São Paulo's parks and is the main sports centre for the city. It's a ten-minute bus ride from the bus stops on Avenida Brigadeiro Luís Antônio. The park, officially opened in 1954, was created to mark the 400th anniversary of the founding of the city of São Paulo. Most of the buildings were designed by Oscar Niemeyer and impressive designs for landscaping were produced by Burle-Marx. Unfortunately, these plans remained on paper only.

The park contains the peaceful and unusual *Bosque de Leitura* (reading woods) where you can borrow books and sit amongst the trees reading them, and is home to several of the city's museums. The **Museu de Arte de Contemporânia** (Tues–Sun noon–6pm), located in the Pavilhão da Bienal in the park – and also on a second site at Rua da Reitoria 160 (Mon–Fri noon–8pm, Sat 9am–1pm) in the university complex – regularly alters its displays, drawing upon its huge stored collection. Although the collection includes work by important European artists, such as Picasso, Modigliani, Léger and Chagall, and Brazilians including Tarsila do Amaral, Di Cavalcanti and Portinari, the pieces that are selected for exhibition can be disappointing.

Next door to the Pavilhão da Bienal in the Marquise do Parque do Ibirapuera, the **Museu de Arte Moderna** (Tues–Fri 1–6pm, Sat & Sun 11am–7pm) is a much smaller museum holding a good collection of contemporary Brazilian art, with works by Di Cavalcanti and Portinari alongside more recent Brazilian artists. Also in the park is the **Museu de Folclore** (Tues–Sun 2–5pm), an extremely cramped collection of musical

---

THE SÃO PAULO BIENAL

The **São Paulo Bienal** has been held in the Parque do Ibirapuera every two years since 1951. It's widely considered to be the most important exhibition of contemporary visual art in Latin America and is only rivalled in the world by the similar event held in Venice. Each country sponsors work by its most influential living artists, and a select few artists (living or dead) are chosen by the Bienal's curators. At best, the Bienal can be an exhilarating venue to see important retrospectives and to experience a wealth of innovative art, but at worst it can be not much more than an embarrassing – or amusing – exposure of fourth-rate global art. The Bienal was traditionally held in October and November in odd-numbered years, but the 1993 event was postponed until 1994 and it is now scheduled for even-numbered years, with especially grand shows planned for 2000. For advance information contact the cultural attaché of any Brazilian embassy, or write directly to São Paulo Bienal, Parque do Ibirapuera, Portal 3, 04090-900 São Paulo – SP (fax 549-0230).

instruments, household appliances, handicrafts, costumes and exhibits relating to traditional medicine; courses on Brazilian folklore are also held here.

If you're on the art-museum trail, the *bairro* due east of the park, Vila Mariana, contains the **Museu Lasar Segall** at Rua Afonso Celso 388 (Tues–Sun 2–6.30pm; $4). As most of Lasar Segall's work is contained in this museum, the Latvian-born naturalized-Brazilian painter is relatively little known outside Brazil. Originally a part of the German Expressionist movement at the beginning of the twentieth century, his later work was influenced by the exuberant colours of his adopted homeland.

Butantã and Morumbi

In the southwest of the city, the two *bairros* of Butantã and Morumbi are worth the long trek. No houses from the colonial era remain standing in the city centre, but out here in the suburbs a few simple, whitewashed adobe **homesteads** from the time of the *bandeirantes* have been preserved. The easiest to visit is the **Casa do Bandeirante**, by the university at Praça Monteiro Lobato, Butantã (Tues–Fri 10.30am–5pm, Sat & Sun 9am–5pm): it's no more than a small, typical *paulista* dwelling containing eighteenth-century farm implements.

One of the city's more popular attractions is also situated in the *bairro* of Butantã. Founded in 1901, the **Instituto Butantã**, Av. Vital Brasil 1500 (Tues–Sun 9am–5pm), was one of the world's foremost research centres for the study of venomous snakes and insects and the development of anti-venom serums. Sadly, financial cuts have had a devastating effect on the institute, and what was once one of the highlights of a tour of São Paulo is now, despite its enduring reputation, a large disappointment. There's a dark and dusty museum that documents the history of the institute's work, huge, mostly empty, snake pits, and rooms where spiders and scorpions are bred; the work of the institute, however, now goes on almost entirely behind closed doors.

Fundação Maria Luiza e Oscar Americano

Situated in the elegant suburb of Morumbi, the **Fundação Maria Luiza e Oscar Americano**, Av. Morumbi 3700 (Tues–Fri 11am–5pm, Sat & Sun 10am–5pm; $5; ☎842-0077), is a sprawling modernist house full of eighteenth-century furniture, religious sculptures and collections of silver, china, coins and tapestry. Amongst the most valuable works are Brazilian landscapes by the seventeenth-century Dutch artist Frans Post, and drawings and important paintings by Cândido Portinari and Emiliano di Cavalcanti. There's a superb tearoom, serving high teas (expensive at $18 per person) until 6pm daily, on Sundays there are concerts and, during the week, courses on music, art and architecture are held here. The house is set on a hill top, and the beautiful tree-filled park-like gardens make this an excellent place to escape the city.

Eating

Eating out is an important pastime for middle- and upper-class *Paulistanos*. The vast number of restaurants in the city is a source of great pride; people like to claim that São Paulo's range of restaurants is second only to New York's. Certainly, the variety of eating options is one of the great joys of São Paulo, though the quality can be somewhat disappointing, especially at the more expensive end of the scale.

Fast food, coffee, tea and ice cream

Paulistanos are reputed to be always in a hurry and on just about every block there's somewhere serving **fast food**. *Lanchonetes* do snacks and cheap, light meals and – in direct competition – *McDonalds*, *KFC* and *Pizza Hut* are opening at a frightening rate. Claiming to have invented the traditional *Bauru* sandwich (made with roast beef, salad and melted cheese) is the *Ponto Chic* at Largo do Paissandu 27, Centro, while **sandwich bars** popular with a younger crowd include the *Frevo*, Rua Oscar Freire 603, Cerqueira César, the *Companhia Paulista de Sanduíches* at Rua Prof. Arthur Ramos 395, Jardim Europa, and *The Bagel Factory*, Rua Padre João Manoel 881, Jardim Europa. There are plenty of **pizzerias**, with the *Margherita*, at Alameda Tietê 255, Cerqueira César, the *Marco Polo*, Rua Franz Schubert 35, Jardim Europa, *Castelões*, Rua Jairo Góis 126, Brás (one of the most traditional pizza houses in the city), and the long-established *Camelo*, Rua Pamplona 1873, Jardins, all highly recommended.

Oddly, for a city built on immigrants and coffee, São Paulo has no **café** tradition. **Coffee**, though, is drunk endlessly in the form of *cafézinhos* (small cups of strong, black coffee). It's not usually lingered over, but if you want to take your time, look out for one of the ever-increasing numbers of places with an *espresso* machine. Among several branches of *Fran's Café* in downtown São Paulo, the most popular is on the ground floor of the Edifício Italia just round the corner from Praça da República. Open 24 hours a day, it serves delicious *canelinha*, espresso with milk and cinnamon. *Café Floresta* in the Edifício Copan shopping mall also serves excellent coffee.

There are a few good **tearooms**, among which *Jasmin* at Rua Haddock Lobo 932 and *La Baguette* at Rua Haddock Lobo 1604 (both in Cerqueira César) are especially inviting. At *As Noviças*, Av. Cotovia 205, Moema, waitresses dressed as nuns serve teas against a background of religious music. For a major splurge and to escape the city crowds and fumes, head out to the *Fundaçâo Maria Luiza e Oscar Americano* (see p.486) where superb English-style high teas are served.

La Basque at Alameda Lorena 1444, Cerqueira César, sells good-quality **ice cream**, but for Italian-style ice cream and fruit sorbets at their absolute best try *Gelateria d'Atre* at Alameda Lorena 1784, Cerqueira César.

Restaurants

São Paulo's restaurants are concentrated where the money is, in the city centre and in the middle- and upper-class suburbs of the city's southwest. You can get away with paying $5 or so for a standard dish of rice, beans and meat at a small, side-street restaurant, but at the most elegant of restaurants in the wealthiest neighbourhoods, you'll be very hard-pressed to pay less than $75 per person. Fortunately, though, there's a huge choice of good restaurants between these price extremes, so you're unlikely to have much trouble finding places to suit your tastes and budget. The listings below are arranged alphabetically and, though it's impossible to be comprehensive, they do give an idea as to the range of available options.

Arab

In Brazil, "Arab" restaurants serve Lebanese or Syrian food, typically a large variety of small dishes of stuffed vegetables, salads, pastries, pulses, minced meat, spicy sausages and chicken, with a strong emphasis on meat in individual dishes. In general, Arab restaurants in São Paulo are extremely reliable and excellent value.

Al Kaukab, Rua Com. Abdo Schahin 130, Centro. A meeting point for the local Arab community, the food's excellent and cheap, the atmosphere always lively.

Arabe, Rua Com. Abdo Schahin 102, Centro. Crowded at lunchtime with Lebanese diners, for the rest of the day the inexpensive restaurant is a focus for dawdling, elderly Arabs.

Arábia, Rua Haddock Lobo 1397, Cerqueira César. Excellent Lebanese food served in pleasant suroundings. The fixed-price lunch menus are very good value and include some unusual choices.

Au Liban, Rua Jerónimo da Veiga 30, Itaim Bibi. Near Jardim Paulista, this is quite an expensive choice, but the menu is more sophisticated and varied than is typical.

El Tarbuch, Rua Com. Abdo Schahin 144, Centro. Another restaurant and café serving the Lebanese community; good food, huge portions and lots of atmosphere.

Esfiha Chic, Rua da Consolação, junction with Av. Paulista, Cerqueira César. Delicious food and very low prices with excellent service.

Folha de Uva, Rua Bela Cintra 1435, Cerqueira César. A combination of fast food and a buffet of Middle Eastern snacks.

Brazilian

Apart from *lanchonetes* and *churrascarias* (see below), Brazilian food is surprisingly hard to come by in São Paulo. This may be because of the immigrant origins of so many of the city's inhabitants, or simply because Brazilian food is for the home, not for occasions when you go out to eat. Still, the selection below should prove good enough for most tastes.

Andrade, Rua Artur de Azevedo 874, Pinheiros. This moderately priced restaurant specializes in Northeastern food, in particular *carne do sol* (sun-dried meat served with manioc flour).

Bargaço, Rua Oscar Freire 1189, Cerqueira César. A reasonably priced Bahian restaurant specializing in spicy seafood.

Bolinha, Av. Cidade Jardim 53, Jardim Europa. Brazilian food at moderate prices; the restaurant is especially noted for its *feijoadas*.

Dona Lucinha, Av. Chibarás 399, Moema. Medium-priced dishes from Minas Gerais with an excellent fixed-price buffet.

O Profeta, Alameda dos Aicás 40, Indianópolis. Authentic, and fairly inexpensive, food from Minas Gerais, with a buffet containing over thirty different dishes.

Tia Carly, Alameda Ribeirão Preto 492, Bela Vista. Excellent, cheap "home cooking" with *feijoadas* served on Wed and Sat. Closed Sun dinner.

Tucupy, Rua Bela Cintra 1551, Cerqueira César. If you don't make it to the Amazon, this is your opprtunity to try the food of the state of Pará. Closed Mon.

Ver-o-Peso, Alameda Nhambiquaras 1360, Moema. Interesting and inexpensive Amazonian and Northeastern food and drinks. Closed Mon.

CHURRASCOS

Beef in a bewildering variety of cuts is the centre of any **churrasco** (barbecue), but lamb, chicken and pork are also usually served.

Baby-Beef Rubaiyat, Av. Viera de Carvalho 116, Centro. A popular *churrascaria* with business diners, where the meat – especially the baby beef – is very good and reasonably priced. There's also a branch at Av. Brigadeiro Faira Lima 533, Jardim Paulistano.

Bar das Putas, Rua da Consolação (near the intersection with Rua Maceió), Consolaçâo, Cerqueira César. Fantastic steaks at unbelievably low prices. More of a snack place than a proper restaurant.

Bassi, Rua 13 de Maio 334, Bixiga. Expensive without being extortionate, you're unlikely to find better meat in São Paulo.

Costela de Ripa, Rua João Cachoeira 298, Itaim Bibi. Beef ribs are the speciality of this unpretentious and reasonably priced *churrascaria*. Closed Sun dinner.

Dinho's Place, Alameda Santos 45, Paraíso. One of the city's oldest *churrascarias*, distinctive because of its Wed and Sat *feijoada* buffets, where the ingredients are cooked and served separately; fairly expensive but consistently high quality.

Esplanada Grill, Rua Haddock Lobo 1682, Jardins. A very fashionable and expensive place, one of the best in the city.

Galeto's, Alameda Santos 1112, Cerqueira César. Barbecued chicken only here.

Rodeio, Rua Haddock Lobo 1498, Cerqueira César. The *couvert* is an excellent small meal in itself, so be sure to hold back until the expensive but high-quality meat is served.

The Place, Rua Haddock Lobo 1550, Cerqueira César. Come here to mingle with the trendy, rich and famous at the bar rather than for the food.

French

There are several excellent, but expensive French restaurants in São Paulo. Expect to pay at least $50 a head, and possibly even double that amount.

L'Arnaque, Rua Oscar Freire 518, Cerqueira César. Interesting, but not always successful, French-Brazilian *nouvelle cuisine*. Pleasant surroundings attract a trendy clientele; the fixed-priced menu is good value, but still not for the budget-conscious.

La Casserole, Largo do Arouche 346, Centro. An old favourite for a romantic evening out, with ever-reliable – though fairly expensive – food. Closed Sat lunch and Mon.

Le Coq Hardy, Av. Adolfo Pinheiro 2518, Alto da Boa Vista. Arguably São Paulo's best traditional French restaurant, and almost certainly its most expensive. Closed Mon.

Roanne, Rua Henrique Martins 631, Jardim Paulista. *Nouvelle cuisine* of a high standard. The daily changing *menu confiance* helps to limit – but only slightly – the damage to your wallet in this relaxed, yet sophisticated restaurant. Closed Sat lunch and Sun.

German

German restaurants in São Paulo – in fact throughout Brazil – are unimaginative in their range of dishes, with menus usually based on pork, potatoes and sauerkraut. But you'll eat heartily for $10–15 a meal.

Alt Nürnberg, Av. João Carlos da Silva Borges 543, Santo Amaro. São Paulo's swankiest German restaurant; the menu's still pork-based, but there's a wide range of accompanying dishes. Closed Sat lunch and Sun.

Bierquelle, Av. Professor Papini 169, Interlagos. A cosy place serving German and Swiss dishes – try their fried, grated potato with apple jam.

Juca Alemão, Rua Min. José Galotti 134, Brooklin Paulista. Plain German food of the kind Brazilians go for. Cheap, with a following of mainly young people.

Kakuk, Alameda Glete 1023, Santa Cecília. Medium-priced restaurant with plenty of choice and high standards.

Miguel, Av. Moema 684, Moema. Inexpensive but run-of-the-mill food, served with excellent *chopp*.

International

Restaurants that claim to have "international" menus are often best avoided, since the dishes tend to be characterless and expensive. However, in São Paulo this is not completely true: there are some attempts at creativity, though most places are still pricey and rather formal.

Manhattan, Rua Bela Cintra 2238, Cerqueira César. A friendly atmosphere, superb Brazilian cocktails, fresh oysters, steak tartare and crepes attract the trendy set, who can afford the price tag of $30-plus a head.

Massimo, Alameda Santos 1826, Jardins. An expensive menu that changes daily, covering everything from simple spaghetti to elaborate roasted meats.

Paddock Jardins, Av. Brigadeiro Faria Lima 1541, Jardim Paulistano. An expensive and elegant place that combines Brazilian and foreign recipes to good effect. Closed Sun.

Italian

With so many immigrants from Italy, it's hardly surprising that the city has a huge number of Italian restaurants, ranging from family-run *cantinas* and pizzerias to elegant, expensive establishments. For the most part, São Paulo's Italian restaurateurs are the children or grandchildren of immigrants, and have adapted their mainly northern recipes to suit Brazilian tastes and the availability of ingredients. For a fun night out, head for Bixiga, São Paulo's "Little Italy", where there are countless inexpensive restaurants.

Bricola, Alameda Gabriel Monteiro da Silva 1040, Cerqueira César. Pretty courtyard restaurant serving a simple, low-priced menu.

Capuano, Rua Conselheiro Carrão 414, Bixiga. One of the oldest trattorias in Bixiga, where simple Italian cooking is produced in a lively environment. Closed Sun night and Mon.

Famiglia Mancini, Rua Avanhandava 81, Centro. The food's not that great but the atmosphere is, especially late at night when it's crowded with young people.

Fasano, Rua Haddock Lobo 1644, Cerqueira César. Renowned for its fine ingredients and unusual vinegar marinades, but expensive.

Gero, Rua Haddock Lobo 1629, Cerqueira César. Very good, moderately priced food served in a relaxed, somewhat trendy, setting.

Gigetto, Rua Avanhandava 63, Centro. Just off Rua Augusta on a road where there are several other Italian restaurants, this one is always crowded with lively Brazilian families. The food's excellent and very inexpensive.

Jardim de Napoli, Rua Dr Martinico Prado 463, Higienópolis. A simple *cantina* where some of São Paulo's best Italian food is served at astonishingly low prices. Closed Mon.

La Locandeira, Rua Dr Mário Ferraz 465, Itaim Bibi. Fine pasta dishes in this modestly priced, lunchtime-only restaurant, sited in one of the city's most exclusive shopping districts.

Roma Jardins, Av. Cidade Jardim 411, Haim. A mid-range restaurant specializing in *antipasti* and fine wines. The roast lamb here is excellent.

Roperto, Rua 13 de Maio 634, Bixiga. A *cantina* serving northern Italian dishes.

Japanese

With the largest Japanese community outside Japan, São Paulo has many excellent Japanese restaurants that serve food as good as that in Japan itself. Where Brazilian-Japanese food does differ is in the emphasis placed on meat and fish; you get much more of both all round in Brazil. Make for Liberdade, São Paulo's "Japanese quarter", where restaurants and sushi bars (serving raw fish) are everywhere. The three restaurants listed below are recommended wholeheartedly.

Sushi-Yassu, Rua Tomás Gonzaga 110 A, Liberdade. Excellent sushi and other fish dishes, but not cheap (about $25 a person). Closed Mon.

Tanji, Rua dos Estudantes 166, Liberdade. Specializing in sushi, the quality of the food depends on the owner's general mood. Evenings only; closed Wed.

Yamaga, Rua Thomaz Gonzaga 66, Liberdade. Small and mainly attracting Japanese diners, an excellent meal here will cost around $30 a head.

Jewish

Few members of São Paulo's sizeable Jewish community have opened restaurants, and fewer still have opened Jewish restaurants. The ones that do exist, though, are very cheap and – with only one exception – are located in Bom Retiro. Expect heavy Eastern European dishes that are rather unsuited to the tropics.

Cecília, Rua Amazonas 63, Bom Retiro. A small, neighbourhood restaurant. Lunch only; closed Mon.

Europa, Rua Correia de Mello 56, Bom Retiro. A simple restaurant with an extensive menu and extremely good food.

Sara, Rua da Graça 32, Bom Retiro. Busy café/snack bar. Mon–Fri 11am–7pm, Sat & Sun 11am–3pm.

Z-Deli, Alameda Lorena 1214, Cerqueira César. Trendy people who live or work in the neighbourhood come to this small restaurant, modelled on a New York gourmet deli. There are two other branches, operating with the same hours: Alameda Lorena 1449, Cerqueira César; Alameda Gabriel Monteiro da Silva 1350, Jardim Paulistano. Mon–Fri 9am–6.30pm, Sat 9am–4pm.

Miscellaneous: seafood, Eastern, Far Eastern and European

There's a mixed bunch of other restaurants in São Paulo, the best of which are detailed below, including a couple that are something of a novelty for Brazil. Seafood is usually good, too, as – little more than an hour from the coast – São Paulo can always count on extremely fresh fish. Most of the city's seafood restaurants are expensive, but worth trying if you're not on a tight budget.

Acrópoles, Rua da Graça 364, Bom Retiro. A popular and inexpensive restaurant serving traditional Greek food. Daily noon–4pm.

Chamonix, Rua Pamplona 4146, Jardim Paulista. São Paulo's best fondue restaurant – don't expect genuine Swiss quality, but be prepared for genuine Swiss prices. Evenings only; closed Mon and last Sun of month.

China Massas Caseiras, Rua Mourato Coelho 140, Pinheiros. Huge quantities of extremely cheap Chinese-style food, served in a lively atmosphere.

Ganesh, Av. Rogue Petroni, Júnior 1089 (Shopping Morumbi), Brooklin. Dishes from all over India and you choose how hot you want it.

Govinda, Rua Princesa Isabel 379, Brooklin Paulista. The oldest Indian restaurant in the city, with dishes tempered to suit unfamiliar Brazilian tastebuds. Very expensive, the restaurant isn't worth going to for the food but for the lavish decoration. Closed Sun evening.

Key West, Rua da Consolação 3452, Jardins. A moderate–expensive place serving traditional Brazilian dishes combined with Cajun and Caribbean cuisine (meat and seafood).

Korea House, Rua Galvão Bueno 43, Liberdade. One of the very few Korean restaurants in the city, despite the large Korean community. Many dishes are prepared at the table, and the often spicy meals are very different to Chinese or Japanese cooking. Around $4 per person.

La Trainera, Av. Brigadeiro Faria Lima 511, Jardim Paulistano. The best and probably the most expensive seafood in the city.

Mr Fish Grill, Alameda Lorena 1430, Cerqueiro César. Simply prepared but extremely fresh fish served with a choice of sauces and accompaniments. Pleasant environment and, at less than $25 per person, reasonable prices.

Valência, Av. Lavandisca 365, Moema. Excellent fish dishes and decent paellas characterize this moderate–expensive Spanish restaurant. Closed Mon.

Vivenda do Camarão, Rua Groenlândia 513, Itaim Bibi. Wonderful prawn dishes at moderate prices.

Portuguese

There are very few Portuguese restaurants in São Paulo, and you pay for what you get: if it's cheap, it tends not to be very good.

Antiquarius, Alameda Lorena 1884, Cerqueiro César. Excellent – but extremely expensive – food and wine, though uncomfortably formal. Closed Mon lunchtime & Sun evening.

O Rei do Bacalhau, Av. Brigadeiro Faria Lima 2174, Pinheiros. Specializing in cod dishes; expect to pay upwards of $15 per person. Closed Mon.

Presidente, Rua Visconde de Parnaíba 2424, Brás. Very good food, reasonably priced, in an area which once had a large Portuguese community. Closes daily at 9.30pm and all day Sun; Sat lunch only.

Vegetarian

There's nowhere easier in Brazil to be vegetarian than in São Paulo: barring *churrascarias*, most restaurants offer non-meat dishes. The following, specifically vegetarian restaurants are very inexpensive, and have unusually varied menus extending well beyond brown rice and beans.

Cheiro Verde, Rua Peixoto Gomide 1413, Cerqueira César. An especially pleasant vegetarian restaurant, whose simple menu changes with the season but is always inexpensive.

Da Fiorella, Rua Bernardino de Campos 294, Brooklin Paulista. Vegetarian Italian food. Their staple dish is a cold tomato, herb and mozzarella sauce served over hot pasta. Closed Sun evening and Mon.

Mel, Rua Araújo 75, Centro (Mon–Fri lunch only), and Av. Brigadeiro Faria Lima 1138, Jardim Europa (Mon–Fri lunch only). One of the best places for a light lunch downtown. The menu is only half vegetarian – fish and chicken are also served.

Sativa, Rua da Consolação 3140, Jardins. Very comfortable place with reasonably priced food. One of the few vegetarian restaurants that serve beer.

Bars, nightlife and entertainment

Whether you're after "high culture", live music, a disco or just a bar to hang out in, you won't have much of a problem in São Paulo. Some ideas are detailed below, but for the full picture of what's on and where, consult the supplement in the São Paulo edition of the weekly magazine *Veja*, or the daily newspaper *Folha de São Paulo*, which lists cultural and sporting events. São Paulo has a large gay population but clubs and bars tend to be mixed rather than specifically gay, with the scene mainly in the Jardins area.

Bars

The bars that you'll find scattered throughout the city depend largely upon the neighbourhoods that they're in for their character. Some of the liveliest, a few with live music, are found around Rua 13 de Maio in Bixiga (Bela Vista), and in the fashionable Jardins neighbourhoods.

Balcao, corner of Alameda Tiête and Rua Melo Alves, Cerqueira César. A pleasant neighbourhood bar attracting well-heeled trendies.

Bar Brahma, corner of Avenida São João and Avenida Ipiranga, Centro. Cheap beer in one of the city's oldest bars.

Cachaçaria Paulista, Rua Mourato Coelho 593, Pinheiros. A great place for sampling *cachaça*: there are over 200 kinds here and it's open from 6pm until the last customer leaves.

Café do Bixiga, Rua 13 de Maio 76, Bela Vista. Excellent *chopp* and a carefully nurtured Bohemian atmosphere.

Elephante, Rua Pinheiros 534, Pinheiros. Usually packed with São Paulo's younger crowd.

Ferros Bar, Avenida Radial Leste–Oeste, near Praça Franklin Roosevelt, Centro. Especially popular with gay women.

Fidalga, Rua Fidalga 32, Jardins. Live jazz and Brazilian music during the week, and its own small bookstore.

Finnegan's, Rua Cristiano Viana 358, Pinheiros. Very friendly and busy late into the evening with live blues and jazz.

Ritz, Alameda Franca 1088, Cerqueira César. During the day a quiet restaurant serving hamburgers and sandwiches, at night a lively bar for young people, popular with the gay crowd.

Supremo, Rua Oscar Freire 996, Jardins. Established downtown tourist haunt with good food, too.

Live music and dancing

São Paulo has quite an imaginative **jazz** tradition. The *Bourbon Street Music Club*, Rua dos Chanés 127, Moema, has a consistently good programme including visiting international artists and frequent festivals. In Bixiga, the *Café Piu-Piu* (closed Mon), at Rua 13 de Maio 134, is a lively venue for some very good jazz and *choro*, as well as the most appalling rock and country-and-western music.

If it's more obviously **Brazilian music** that you're seeking, check the newspaper entertainment listings for touring artists or, if feeling slightly adventurous, you could go to a **gafieira**, a dance hall that's the meeting place of working-class and Bohemian chic. A *gafieira* that's always packed to the rafters with migrants from the Northeast dancing to *forró* is *Pedro Sertanejo*, Rua Catumbi 183, Brás (Sat 9pm–4am, Sun 8pm–midnight). Be warned that *gafieiras* tend to be out of the centre and can seem rather alien and disconcerting places if you've only just arrived in Brazil. The *Som de Cristal* at Rua Rego Freitas 470, Centro, is a good place to discover how the *lambada* should really be danced. Regular performances of Brazilian folk, popular and New Wave music are given at the Centro Cultural de São Paulo, at Rua Vergueiro 1000 (by the Vergueiro metrô station), and are either free or charge only a modest admission fee. If you're around, one of the most enjoyable outings is to the *Clube do Choro*, held on Saturday and Sunday nights in Jardim América (at Rua João Moura, between Rua Artur Azevedo and Rua Teodoro Sampaio); the street is closed off, a stage erected and tables and chairs put out so that you can sit and listen to some excellent music. There's a small cover charge and food and drink are available, too.

Discos and clubs

Aeroanta, Rua Miguel Isasa 404, Pinheiros. A good old-fashioned rock 'n' roll joint.

Balafon, Rua Sergipe 160, Higienópolis. Very busy at weekends, mainly a reggae venue.

Banana Banana, Av. 9 de Julho 5872, Jardins. A traditional disco playing all the hits from the FM stations.

Cais, Praça Franklin Roosevelt 134. A broad mix of dancers participating in a well-cultivated acid house image.

Cha Cha Cha, Rua Tabapuã 1236, Itaim. Plenty of space here and a good mix of hip-hop, acid jazz and house.

Clube Massivo, Alameda Itú 1548, Jardins. Open from midnight onwards, this is a shrine to the sounds of the 1970s.

Columbia, Rua Estados Unidos 1570, Jardins. One of the best clubs in São Paulo, with all-night parties on Saturdays.

Nostromondo, Rua da Consolação 2554, Jardins. A mainly gay venue; best night Sunday from 6pm until midnight.

Paparazzi, Rua da Consolação 3046, Jardins. Plenty of TV sets around the bar and big screens showing dance music videos. The beer's cheap and it's a popular meeting place at the beginning of the evening.

Roof, Av. Cidade Jardim 400, Jardim Europa. Rather vulgar and full of well-heeled yuppies, but compensated for by its magnificent views across the city.

Ursa Major, Rua Augusta 2203, loja 19, Jardins. Definitely an "in" place, located underneath a traditional shopping mall. A big gay venue playing jazz rap, garage, techno and house.

Cinema, theatre and classical music

In general, **films** arrive in São Paulo simultaneously with release in North America and Europe, and are subtitled rather than dubbed. Charging around $6, most cinemas are on Avenida Paulista, but there are also several downtown on Avenida São Luís. All the shopping centres (see p.494) have cinema complexes and show the latest blockbusters. Keep a special eye out for what's on at CineSesc, Rua Augusta 2075, Cerqueira César, Bixiga, Rua 13 de Maio (Bixiga), and the Centro Cultural de São Paulo, Rua Vergueiro 1000, by the Vergueiro metrô station, which are devoted to Brazilian and foreign art films. Art-house films are also shown at the Belas-Artes at Rua da Consolação 2423, on the corner of Avenida Paulista.

São Paulo is Brazil's theatrical centre and boasts a busy season of classical and avant-garde productions; a visit to the **theatre** is worthwhile even without a knowledge of Portuguese. Seats are extremely cheap, available from **ticket offices** that have details of all current productions: Casa do Espectador, Rua Sete de Abril 127, Centro (Mon–Fri 10am–6pm), and Vá ao Teatro, Shopping Ibirapuera, Moema (Mon–Fri 9am–9pm, Sat 9am–3pm). The Brasileiro de Comédia, Rua Major Diorgo 311, and the Teatro Sérgio Cardoso, Rua Rui Barbosa, both in Bixiga, have particularly good reputations.

The focal point for São Paulo's vibrant **opera** and **classical music** season is the Teatro Municipal, in Praça Ramos de Azevado, in the city centre, where, in the 1920s, Vila Lobos himself performed. As an operatic and classical music centre, traditionally São Paulo was less important than Rio, but now Brazilian and foreign performers divide their time between the two cities. Many of São Paulo's churches have free **recitals**, most notably the beautiful Gregorian chant at the Basílica de São Bento, Largo de São Bento, Centro, every Sunday at 10am and 5pm.

Shopping

São Paulo's **shopping** possibilities are as varied as the city's restaurants and, for *Paulistanos* with the means, as important an activity. In the wealthy southwestern suburbs of Cerqueira César and the Jardins, shops are far more impressive than those in just about any other Brazilian city, and the quality way above par. Even if you're not intent on a spree, the shopping centres and stores are worth a tour to experience the opulent surroundings. And there's a fine selection of **markets**, too, where you can pick up a decently priced souvenir or two and some good food. For books, maps, newspapers and recorded music, see "Listings".

Shopping centres
The rich victors of the Brazilian economic "miracle" wander São Paulo's shopping centres – air-conditioned temples to hedonism – able to feel utterly insulated from their less fortunate fellow citizens. Each centre tries to outdo the other, with mirrored walls and ostentatious fountains – you won't feel closer to North America than this during your stay in Brazil. All the shopping centres are open 9am–10pm Monday–Friday and 9am–6pm on Saturdays; their cinemas are also open on Sundays.

Center Norte, Trav. Casal Buono 120, Vila Guilherme (bus from Av. Brigadeiro Luíz Antônio, corner of Av. Paulista).

Eldorado, Av. Rebouças 3970, Pinheiros (bus from Praça da República).

Ibirapuera, Av. Ibirapuera 3103, Moema (bus from metrô Ana Rosa, or Praça da República).

Iguatemi, Av. Brigadeiro Faria Lima 1191, Jardim Europa (bus from Av. Ipiranga).

Jardim Sul, Av. Presidente Giovanni Gronchi 5899, Vila Andrade (bus from Praça da República).

Morumbi, Av. Roque Petroni Jr. 1089, Morumbi (bus from metrô Ana Rosa).

Plaza Sul, Avenida Dr Ricardo Jafet, Ipiranga (bus from Praça da República).

Downtown shopping
The main shopping streets in the centre of the city are near **Praça da República**, especially the roads running off Avenida Ipiranga: Rua Barão de Itapetinga, Rua 24 de Maio, Rua do Arouche and, between them, Rua Dom José de Barros. Most of the stores around here sell clothes, but you'll rarely find the latest fashions.

Cerqueira César and the Jardins
This is where the money is, and where all the best stores are. There are lots of trendy boutiques selling clothes but, compared to Europe or North America, prices are high. Rua Augusta, Avenida Europa and Avenida Cidade Jardim, and the streets running parallel and off them, are where you'll find most of the stores. There are no obvious "**sou-**

venirs" of São Paulo, but the following places are worth checking out for unusual Brazilian items:

Ana (Arte Nativa Aplicada), Rua Melo Alves 184. Beautiful, high-quality cotton and wool fabrics, and scarfs printed with Indian motifs. Also features a small but interesting selection of ceremics.

Arte-India (FUNAI), Rua Augusta 1371. Basketwork and feather handicrafts made by Indians. Fair prices and authenticity guaranteed.

Kabuletê, Rua Dr Melo Alves, Cerqueira César. An unusual choice of unique – but expensive – Brazilian crafts.

O Bode, Rua Bela Cintra 2009, Cerqueira César. Carefully selected handicrafts from throughout Brazil, including items from the state of São Paulo.

Markets

There's lots of choice here, from handicrafts to flowers, and one – the Mercado Municipal – that ranks as one of the best **markets** in Brazil. The different *bairros* also have their own markets.

Comunitária de Trocas do Bixiga, Praça Dom Orioni, Bixiga (Sun 10am–4pm). A flea market with little worth purchasing, but lots of atmosphere.

Feira de Antiguidades, Museu de Arte de São Paulo (MASP), Av. Paulista 1578 (Sun 10am–5.30pm). A fun place to browse, but don't expect much worth buying.

Feira de Arte e Artesanato, Praça da República, Centro (Sun 8am–1pm). Handicrafts from throughout Brazil, semi-precious gems and spicy food from the Northeast.

Feira Oriental, Praça da Liberdade, Liberdade (Sun 2–6pm). Japanese-Brazilian handicrafts and Japanese food.

Mercado de Flores, Largo de Arouche, Centro. A dazzling daily display of flowers.

Mercado Municipal, Rua da Cantareira 306, Centro (Mon–Sat 5am–4pm; see also p.481). About the most fantastic array of fruit, vegetables and fish that you're likely to find anywhere in Brazil.

Listings

Airlines Aerolíneas Argentinas, Praça D. José Gaspar 16, Centro (☎214-4233); Aeroperu, Rua da Consolação 329, Centro (☎257-4866); Air France (☎289-2133); Alitalia, Av. São Luis 123, Centro (☎257-1722); American Airlines (☎214-4233); Avianca, Av. São Luis 50, Centro (5th floor; ☎259-8455); British Airways, Av. Ipiranga 331, Centro (☎259-6144); Canadian, Av. São Luis 50, Centro (cj. 71; ☎259-9066); Iberia, Av. Ipiranga 318, bl. B, Centro (12th floor; ☎257-6711); KLM, Garulhos Airport (☎945-3111); Lan Chile, Av. São Luis 165, Centro (2nd floor; ☎259-2900); Líneas Aéreas Paraguayas, Av. São Luis 50, Centro (12th floor; ☎259-2477); Lloyd Aéreo Boliviano, Av. São Luis 72, Centro (☎258-8111); Lufthansa, Av. São Luis 59, Centro (☎236-7700); Pluna, Av. São Luis 174, Centro (☎231-2822); SAS, Av. São Luis 50, Centro (28th floor; ☎259-1522); Swissair (☎251-4000); TAP, Av. São Luis 187, Centro (☎259-5155); Transbrasil, Av. São Luis 250, Centro (☎231-1529); Varig-Cruzeiro, Rua da Consolação 368, Centro (☎231-9400); VASP, Rua Libero Badaró 106, Centro (☎220-3622).

Airports Flight information: Congonhas (☎532-1068); Garulhos (☎945-2945).

Banks and exchange Banco do Brasil is not your best bet in São Paulo as currently they will not change amounts less than $500. Instead try Citibank, Av. Paulista 1111, or Banco Real, Av. Paulista 1374. Faster than the banks are the many travel agents around Praça da República and the adjoining Av. São Luís, or Turist Câmbio at Av. Paulista 529 (at the intersection with Alameda Eugênio de Lima). If you need to change money at weekends, try the souvenir shops and jewellers in Liberdade, the Japanese *bairro*.

Books and maps The following stores stock English-language **books**: Bestseller, Av. Tietê 184, Cerqueira César; Cultura, in the Conjunto Nacional building, Av. Paulista 2073, Cerqueira César with a good general stock of Brazilian and English-language books, including excellent travel and coffee-table book sections; MFV – Livraria de Turismo, Rua Oscar Freire 1141, Cerqueira César, a small and welcoming travel bookshop with lots of titles in English; Livraria Corrêa do Lago, Rua João Cachoeira 267, Itaim, which has what is probably Brazil's most extensive collection of rare and out-of-print books for sale; Kosmos, Av. São Luis 162, Centro. More English-language books, plus a wide selection of Portuguese works on Brazilian history and politics, from branches of Brasiliense, scattered around the city; Seridó, Edifício Copan shopping mall, Av. São Luis near Praça da República; and Seibo, Rua da Consolaçâo, Centro. There's an excellent **map** shop, Mapolândia, on Rua Sete de Abril just off Praça da República, which has maps of the city, the state and many other regions of Brazil.

Car rental The main difficulty in driving in São Paulo is finding a parking space. Otherwise, roads are well signposted and it's surprisingly easy to get out of the city. Car rental firms are: Avis, Rua da Consolação 335, Centro (☎258-8833); Hertz, Rua da Consolação 439, Centro (☎256-9722); Interlocadora, Largo Sta. Cecília 140, Centro (☎222-2037); Localiza, Rua da Consolação 419, Centro (☎231-3055); Nobre, Rua Martins Fontes 205, Centro (☎255-8922); Unidas, Rua da Consolaçâo 347, Centro (☎256-2233).

Consulates Argentina, Av. Paulista 1106 (9th floor; ☎284-1355); Austria, Rua Augusta 2516, Cerqueira César (10th floor; ☎282-6223); Belgium, Av. Paulista 2073, Cerqueira César (13th floor; ☎287-7892); Bolivia, Rua Quirino de Andrade 219, Centro (3rd floor; ☎255-3555); Canada, Av. Paulista 1106, Bela Vista (5th floor; ☎287-2122); Colombia, Rua Peixoto Gomide 996, Cerqueira César (10th floor; ☎255-6863); Denmark, Rua João Tibiriçá 900, Lapa (☎831-9799); Germany, Av. Brig. Faria Lima 1383, Jardim Paulistano (12th floor; ☎814-6644); Ireland, Av. Paulista 2006, Cerqueira César (5th floor; ☎287-6362); Netherlands, Av. Brig. Faria Lima 1698, Jardim Paulistano (3rd floor; ☎813-0522); Norway, Rua Oscar Freire 379, Cerqueira César (3rd floor; ☎883-3322); Paraguay, Av. São Luis 112, Centro (10th floor; ☎255-7818); Peru, Rua Suécia 114, Jardim Europa (☎531-0943); Sweden, Rua Oscar Freire 379, Cerqueira César (3rd floor; ☎883-3322); Switzerland, Av. Paulista 1754, Cerqueira César (4th floor; ☎289-1033); UK, Av. Paulista 1937, Cerqueira César (17th floor; ☎287-7722); Uruguay, Av. Campinas 433, Cerqueira César (7th floor; ☎284-5998); USA, Rua Pe. João Manoel 933, Cerqueira César (☎881-7917); Venezuela, Rua Veneza 878, Jardim Paulista (☎887-2318).

Cultural institutes Alliance Française, Rua Gen. Jardim 182, Vila Buarque (☎259-8211); Cultura Inglesa, Av. Ipiranga 877, Centro (☎222-3866); Goethe Institut, Rua Lisboa 974, Pinheiros (☎280-4288); Instituto Italiano de Cultura, Rua Frei Caneca 1071, Bela Vista (☎285-6933); União Cultural Brasil-Estados Unidos, Rua Cel. Oscar Porto 208, Paraiso (☎885-1022).

Dentists Expensive, but with good reputations, are Dental Office Augusta, Rua Augusta 878, Cerqueira César (☎256-3104), and Dr José Miotto Adura Neto, Av. Pavão 224, Moema (☎531-2236).

Football There are three First Division teams based in São Paulo: Corinthians, who play at Parque São Jorge (Rua São Jorge 777; metrô Bresser and bus #278A); São Paulo, at Morumbi Stadium (metrô Ana Rosa and bus #775P; or simply bus #775P from Av. Paulista); and Palmeiras, at Palestra Itália (Parque Antártica; bus #208A or #208C from Av. São João). Matches are generally on Wed and Sat.

Hospital The private Albert Einstein Clinic (Av. Albert Einstein 627, Morumbi; ☎845-1233) is considered to be the best hospital in Brazil, and one where strict precautions are taken against the spread of AIDS.

Laundry There are very few self-service laundries in São Paulo and it is extremely expensive to have your hotel wash your clothes. One conveniently located self-service place is at Alameda Tiête 96, near the intersection with Rua Augusta, Cerqueira César.

Newspapers and magazines Most newspaper kiosks downtown and in Jardins sell English-language newspapers. Farah's, Rua Haddock Lobo 1503, Cerqueira César (open until midnight), has a very good selection of European magazines and newspapers (including the *International Herald Tribune*, the *Sunday Times* and *Guardian Weekly*), as does Jardim Europa, corner of Av. Europa and Rua Groenlândia (open 24hr). Some of the kiosks on Avenida Ipiranga near Praça da República and Edifício Itália sell *The Times*, *Melody Maker* and *The Face*.

Pharmacies 24-hour service at São Paulo, Rua Teodoro Sampaio 2014, Pinheiros (☎815-8829); Tabajara, Rua Brig. Luís Antônio 1628, Bela Vista (☎288-3483); Drogadec, Av. 9 de Julho 3606, Jardim Paulista (☎853-5413).

Police Emergencies ☎190. To extend your visa, visit the Polícia Federal, Av. Prestes Maia 700, Centro (Mon–Fri 10am–4pm; ☎223-7177 ext. 231).

Post office The main post office is downtown at Pràça Correio, at the corner of Av. São João, and is open 8am–10pm. There are postal kiosks scattered throughout the city, including several along Av. Paulista.

Public holidays Most things in São Paulo close on the following days: January 1; January 25 (Founding of the City); *Carnaval*; Ash Wednesday; Good Friday; April 21 (Remembrance of Tiradentes); May 1 (Labour Day); June 2 (Corpus Christi); September 7 (Independence Day); October 12 (Nossa Senhora Aparecida); November 2 (Finados); November 15 (Proclamation of the Republic); December 25.

Record stores The widest selection of Brazilian music in the city is from Música da República, Praça da República, Centro; secondhand Brazilian records (good for rarities) from Sebo do Disco, Rua Lisboa 45, Jardim América.

Telephones For long-distance calls, TELESP (the state telephone company) have a 24hr office on Rua Sete de Abril (just off Praça da República).

Women's groups Centro Informação Mulher, Rua Leôncio Gurgel, casa 11, Luz (☎229-4818); Coletivo de Mulheres Negras, Rua Estado Unidos 346, Jardim América (☎852-1750; evenings only); Grupo Ação Lésbico-Feminista, Caixa Postal 62618, São Paulo 01214; União de Mulheres de São Paulo, Rua Sto. Antônio 1395, Bela Vista. There are several Delegacias da Mulher (women's police stations), with the main one at Praça Dom Pedro II, Brás (☎228-6101 or 254-3361).

Around São Paulo

What only a few years ago were clearly identifiable small towns or villages have become swallowed up by Greater São Paulo. But, despite the traffic, escaping from the city is surprisingly easy, and there are even points on the coast that can make good day trips (see p.502).

Embu

Founded in 1554, **EMBU** remained a mere village until São Paulo's explosive growth in the twentieth century. But, just 27km west of the city, Embu couldn't have expected to remain unaffected by its growth; what is surprising is that it has somehow managed to retain its colonial feel. Despite having a population of over 100,000, simple colonial-style buildings predominate in the town's compact centre.

In the 1970s, Embu was a favourite retreat for writers and artists from São Paulo, and many set up home in what was then still little more than a village. Today, the Sunday **handicraft market** (7am–6pm) in the main square, Largo 21 de Abril, makes the town a favourite with *Paulistano* day-trippers, although during the week Embu is far quieter. The shops around the main square stock a more or less similar selection of ceramics, leather items, jewellery and homemade jams to what's on offer in the market but they are open daily. Nearby, on Largo dos Jesuitas, the basic structure of the eighteenth-century **Igreja Matriz Nossa Senhora do Rosário** is typical colonial Baroque, but its interior retains almost no original features. Otherwise, you might as well sit down and eat: there are several **restaurants** on Largo 21 de Abril and along the adjoining streets, and the town is a very good place to sample traditional *Paulista* cooking.

It takes less than an hour to get to Embu from São Paulo; catch the "Embu Cultural" **bus** from outside the Tietê *Rodoviária*.

Paranapiacaba

For most of its history, communications from São Paulo to the outside world were slow and difficult. In 1856 the British-owned São Paulo Railway Company was awarded the concession to operate a rail line between Santos and Jundaí, north of São Paulo, and the 139-kilometre line was completed in 1867. Overcoming the near vertical incline of the Serra do Mar, the line was an engineering miracle and is slowly being restored today.

Every Sunday at 8.30am, **trains** leave São Paulo's Estação da Luz (☎991-3212) for the two-hour ride to **PARANAPIACABA**, southeast of the city and the last station before the line plunges down the coastal escarpment. As there's nowhere to stay in

Paranapiacaba, and only snacks in the way of food, it's necessary to return to São Paulo on the same day, the trains departing at 4pm.

Paranapiacaba was the administrative centre for the rail line and at one time was home to four thousand of its workers. Neatly laid out in the 1890s, the village has remained largely unchanged over the years, and the workers' cottages, train station and other rail buildings are in excellent order; some are open to the public. At the **Centro Preservação da História de Paranapiacaba** (Sat & Sun 9am–5pm), there's a display of old photographs of the rail line's early years, and the attendants are a mine of information. (Serious rail buffs who want to find out more about the preservation work on this line, and plans for others in Brazil, should visit the Associação Brasileira de Preservação Ferroviária in São Paulo, at Rua Economizadora 10, Luz; it's best to go on Thursday when there are meetings open to the public, held from 8.30pm.) At weekends there are short steam-engine excursions from Paranapiacaba along the most amazing stretch of the line, a cog-wheel section heading towards the coast, from where there are stunning views.

THE STATE OF SÃO PAULO

Away from the city, it's the state's coastline that has most to offer. **Santos**, Brazil's leading port, retains many links with the past, and lots of the **beaches** stretching north and south from the city are stunning, particularly around **Ubatuba**. The towns and cities of the state's **interior** are not so great an attraction – the rolling countryside is largely devoted to vast orange groves and fields of soya and sugar. Good-quality roads run through this region, including major routes to the Mato Grosso and Brasília.

The interior

Although there's not much to detain you inland from São Paulo, **Americana** and **Santa Bárbara d'Oeste** do have traces of Confederate history, and you can take one of the few remaining train services out of São Paulo as far as **Bauru**. To escape the summer heat, the resort of **Campos do Jordão**, northeast of the city, offers some attractive hill scenery and plenty of walking possibilities.

Campinas

One hundred kilometres northwest of São Paulo is **CAMPINAS**, in decline since the nineteenth century when it was by far the more important of the two cities. It started life as a sugar plantation centre, produced coffee from 1870 and, most recently, has made its money as an agricultural processing and hi-tech centre. An attractive city, with a reasonably small centre, there aren't too many reasons for visiting, though it's interesting enough to take a tour around Largo do Rosário, with its **Catedral**, inaugurated in 1883. A few blocks southwest of here – around the train station – is the **Vila Industrial**, rows of small houses built for the city's new working class in the late nineteenth century. Better known as **Unicamp**, the Universidade Estadual de São Paulo, 13km from the city centre. The university was founded in 1969 on land belonging to Colonel Zeferino Vaz and, during the worst years of military terror, became – thanks to the protection afforded by Vaz – a refuge for left-wing teachers who would otherwise have been imprisoned or forced into exile. Unicamp rapidly acquired an international reputation and today is considered one of Brazil's best universities.

With a student population of 100,000, Campinas has a reasonably lively cultural life, centred on the **Centro de Convivência Cultural**, at Praça Imprensa Fluminense in the centre. It has a theatre and art galleries and is home to the fine Orquestra Sinfonia. To the south of the *praça*, the folklore, history, Indian and natural history **museums** (Tues–Sat 9–10.50am & 1–5pm, Sun 9am–noon & 1–5pm) in the **Bosque dos Jequitbás** contain little of any interest, though the park itself is a pleasant place to while away an hour or two.

Practicalities

Campinas is a major transport hub, and there are **buses** from the city to most places in the state and many beyond. The highway to São Paulo itself is one of Brazil's best, and the hourly buses take an hour and a quarter. The **Rodoviária** in Campinas is at Rua Barão de Itapura, a twenty-minute walk from the city centre down Rua Saldanha Marinho. There are also several daily **trains** between Campinas and São Paulo's Estação da Luz, though they take around twenty minutes longer to make the same journey.

With São Paulo so close you won't need to stay in Campinas, but you might want to grab something **to eat**. The three branches of *Giovanetti* in Praça Carlos Gomes and Largo do Rosário are popular student meeting points, selling drinks and excellent sandwiches. *Cenat*, at Rua Barão de Jaguara 1260, serves excellent vegetarian food; *Tevere* (owned by a *Unicamp* philosophy professor), Av. Coronel Silva Teles 439, has good Italian dishes; the tiny *Cantina Alemã* at Rua Luzitana 981 offers reasonable German food; the *Santa Gertrudis* at Rua Olavo Bilac 54 is the city's best *churrascaria*; *The Old Dutch*, Rua Padre Almeida 214, serves Dutch specialities and is a bit more upmarket; and the *Éden*, Rua Barão de Jaguara 1224, is just a large hall serving huge portions of cheap, plain food.

Americana and Santa Bárbara d'Oeste

Although there are perhaps as many as 100,000 Brazilians of Confederate descent, there are few obvious signs of this in the two towns most associated with them. **AMERICANA**, an hour beyond beyond Campinas, is a bustling city of about 150,000 people, but there are only 25 English-speaking families. If curiosity does bring you here, the **Rodoviária** is just a short walk from the centre of town; walk across the bridge in front of the building and keep straight on for about ten minutes. On the main square, Praça Comendador Muller, you'll find the simple, but perfectly adequate **hotel** *Cacique* (no

---

CONFEDERATES IN SÃO PAULO

In the face of humiliation, military defeat and economic devastation, thousands of former American **Confederates** resolved to "reconstruct" themselves in often distant parts of the world, forcing a wave of emigration without precedent in the history of the United States. Brazil rapidly established itself as one of the main destinations, offering cheap land, a climate suited to familiar crops, political and economic stability, religious freedom and – more sinisterly – the possibility of continued slave ownership. Just how many Confederates came is unclear: suggested numbers vary between 2000 and 20,000, and they settled all over Brazil, though it was in São Paulo where they had the greatest impact. Although Iguape, on the state's southern stretch of coast, had a large Confederate population, the most concentrated area of settlement was the Santa Bárbara colony, in the area around present-day **Americana** and **Santa Bárbara d'Oeste**.

The region's climate and soil were ideally suited to the growing of **cotton** and the Confederates' expertise soon made Santa Bárbara one of Brazil's biggest producers of the crop. As demand for Brazilian cotton gradually declined, many of the immigrants switched to **sugar cane**, which remains the area's staple crop, though others, unable to adapt, moved into São Paulo city or returned to the United States.

phone; ②), and for a bit more comfort, there's the *Nacional* at Rua Washington Luís 399 (☎019/461-8210; ④) and the *Florença Palace*, Av. Cillos 820 (☎019/461-6393; ③). For **food** there are plenty of *lanchonetes*, as well as a very good *churrascaria*, the *Cristal*, at Av. Fortunato Faraoni 613. But apart from the odd Confederate emblem, don't expect much to do with the South.

Santa Bárbara d'Oeste

Thirteen kilometres west of Americana, **SANTA BÁRBARA D'OESTE** has more Confederate ties. Much the smaller of the two, there are about thirty families of Confederate origin here, most of whom still speak English with more than a touch of Dixie in their voice. Near the main square, a short walk from the *Rodoviária*, the excellent **Museu da Imigração** (closed Sun) has displays relating to the history of the Confederates in the area, and to that of other nationalities, chiefly Italian. About 10km from town, the **Cemitério do Campo** is a cool and shaded cemetery on a hill overlooking endless fields of sugar cane. It dates back to 1910 and all the tombstones, as well as the monument commemorating the Confederate immigrants, bear English inscriptions. There's a small chapel here, too, and a picnic area where, four times a year (the second Sunday of January, April, July and October) around 250 members of the *Fraternidade Descendência Americana* arrive from throughout Brazil to renew old ties. The cemetery is very isolated and can only be reached by car: a taxi will charge around $25 to take you there, and will wait for you while you look around. However, as not all taxi drivers know exactly where the cemetery is, ask the museum attendant to order a taxi for you and give your driver precise directions.

As for **accommodation** in Santa Bárbara, there's only one hotel, the very simple *Municipal* (no phone; ①), right by the *Rodoviária*; and there's only one **restaurant**, too, the *Bela Mesa*, at Rua General Osório 676.

Campos do Jordão

When temperatures plunge to 15°C, São Paulo's citizens generally shiver and reach for their mothballed woollens. But to experience something approaching genuine cold weather they have to head into the highlands. East of the city, in the direction of Rio, is the **Serra da Mantiqueira**, which boasts the lively winter resort of **CAMPOS DO JORDÃO**, 1628m above sea level. The town lies on the floor of a valley, littered with countless Swiss chalet-style hotels and private houses, and divided into three sections: **Abernéssia**, the older commercial centre and location of the *Rodoviária*; and, a fifteen-minute bus ride away, **Juaguaribe** and **Capivari,** where most of the boutiques, restaurants and hotels are concentrated.

The novelty of donning sweaters and legwarmers draws the crowds, who spend their days filling in the time before nightfall when they can light their fires. In all directions from Capivari there are good walks, and **trails** are well signposted. Much of the land has been stripped of forest cover to make way for cattle pasture, but in the higher reaches you'll still come across remains of the graceful araucaria (Paraná pine) trees that once dominated the natural vegetation hereabouts. For a good **view** over Campos do Jordão and the surrounding Paraíba valley, take the **ski lift** from near the small boating lake in the centre of Capivari: it whisks you up to the **Morro do Elefante**, where you can hire horses.

Practicalities

With about sixty **hotels** to choose from, finding a room is easy. But finding an affordable one – at any rate during the winter months of June and July – can be difficult. You're best off walking along the tree-lined Avenida Macedo Soares (Capivari), where many of the cheaper hotels are located, including the *Itália* at no. 306 (☎012/262-2846;

②), the *Casa São José* at no. 827 (☎012/262-8206; ②) and the *Nevada* at no. 27 (☎012/262-3735; ③). Before accepting a room, check that it has an electric fire as even on warm summer days it can get quite chilly at night. Also in Capivari there's a small **youth hostel**, *Elis Regina II* (☎012/263-2732; $12 a night), at Rua Benigno Ribeiro 320, but at the weekend it's often fully booked. One of Campos de Jordão's more interesting hotels, the *Duas Quedos Park*, Rua Manoel Ribeiro de Toledo 255, Vila Britânia (☎012/262-2492; ⑤), is situtated in a beautiful park with waterfalls nearby; the hotel also has chalets to rent which sleep 6–8 people for $60–100 per chalet. Another scenic place is the *Veredas* (☎012/263-2626; ③) at Rua 5, Vila Floresta, in the hills 6km from town, offering panoramic views and dinner included in the room price.

Most people eat in their hotels, so the choice of **restaurants** is comparatively limited. But you won't go hungry since there are several pseudo-Swiss restaurants in which you can take pot-luck: try *Só Queijo*, Av. Macedo Soares 642, or the *Matterhorn*, Rua Djalma Forjaz 10. **Nightlife** is very much hotel-oriented, but people also congregate around the splendidly kitsch "medieval" shopping arcade in Capivari, drinking hot mulled wine at the top of the arcade's tower or – for a really big evening out – watching the electronic thermometer.

The coast

Until fairly recently – despite its proximity to the city – most of the four hundred kilometres of the *Paulista* **coast** were overlooked by sun and beach fiends in favour of more glamorous Rio. Now, though, the beaches northeast of the port of Santos are easily accessible on the new BR-101 coastal highway, and the area is becoming increasingly commercialized. This part of the coast offers great contrasts, ranging from long, wide stretches of sand at the edge of a coastal plain, to idyllic-looking coves beneath a mountainous backdrop. Having the use of a car is an advantage as the beaches near places accessible by bus are generally quite developed (see p.496 for car rental addresses in São Paulo). Southwest of Santos, however, tourism has still to take hold, in part because the roads aren't as good, but also because the beaches simply aren't as beautiful.

The route to Santos: Cubatão

About 75km south of São Paulo, Santos is Brazil's most important port, but until the construction of the rail line, travel between the two cities was a major trek. Today, buses take less than an hour to make the journey, along a multi-lane highway that offers no sense of how formidable a barrier the escarpment behind Santos used to be. Roughly midway between the two cities, the SP-150 highway passes **CUBATÃO**, said to be one of the most polluted towns on the planet. Although control of the level of factory emissions is minimal, it's not this which makes Cubatão stand out from other Brazilian industrial centres. The main problem with Cubatão is that the town lies in a valley where the toxic clouds are unable to disperse. The results are disastrous: the rich tropical vegetation is dying and long-term health damage is a serious problem for the workers and residents of the area. Efforts, of doubtful effectiveness, are under way to improve the conditions.

Santos

SANTOS was founded in 1535, a few kilometres east of São Vicente, one of Portugal's first New World settlements. The city stands on an island, its port facilities and old town facing landwards with ships approaching by a narrow, but deep, channel. In a dilapidated kind of a way, the compact centre retains a certain charm that has not yet been extinguished by the development of an enormous port complex.

Arriving in Santos and getting orientated couldn't be easier. The **Rodoviária**, at Praça dos Andradas, is within easy walking distance of everywhere in Centro, on the north side of the island: from it, walk across the square to Rua XV de Novembro, one of the main commercial streets. One block on, turn left at **Rua do Comércio**, along which are the remains of some of Santos' most distinguished buildings. Sadly, only the facades remain of most of the mid- and late nineteenth-century former **merchants' houses** that line the street, but the elaborate tiling and wrought-iron balconies offer a hint of their lost grandeur. At the end of Rua do Comércio is the **train station**, built between 1860 and 1867, and while the city's claim that the station is an exact replica of London's Victoria is a bit difficult to swallow, it is true that the building wouldn't look too out of place in a British town. Next to the station is the **Igreja de Santo Antônio do Valongo** (in Largo Marquês de Monte Alegre), built in 1641 in colonial Baroque style but with its interior totally "restored" over the following centuries. Back on Rua XV de Novembro, at no. 95, is the **Bolsa de Café**, where coffee prices are fixed and the quality assessed. And at the end of the street is another Baroque building, the **Convento do Carmo**, again sixteenth century in facade only.

Across town from Centro on the south side of the island, twenty minutes by bus from Praça Maua by Rua do Comércio, are Santos' **beaches**. They're huge, stretching around the Atlantic-facing Baía de Santos, and are attractive in a Copacabana kind of way. The problem, though, is that while the beaches themselves are kept tidy, the water is of doubtful cleanliness; stick to the sands.

Practicalities

Coming from São Paulo, be sure to remember that buses to Santos leave from the Jabaquara *Rodoviária* and not from Tietê. In Santos, there are **tourist offices** at the *Rodoviária* in Centro, and at the corner of Avenida Ana Costa and the seafront Avenida Presidente Wilson in Gonzaga, but their opening hours are very haphazard. **Changing money** in Santos is easy, with banks and *câmbios* on Praça da República in Centro and on Rua XV de Novembro.

Hotels in Santos are concentrated in **Gonzaga**, a *bairro* of apartment buildings, restaurants and bars alongside the beach, facing the Baía de Santos. Good places include the comfortable *Gonzaga*, at Av. Presidente Wilson 36 (☎013/244-1411/; ②), and the *Ritz*, set back at Av. Marechal Deodoro 24 (☎013/284-1171; ③). There are some reasonable seafood **restaurants** in Centro (try *Café Paulista* at Praça Rui Barbosa 8, or *Rocky* at Praça dos Andradas 5), but otherwise they are almost all in Gonzaga. For souvenir hunters, the most distinctive local items are embroideries, the product of the descendants of immigrants who came to Santos in the late nineteenth century from the island of Madeira. The best source is the Unidade Regional de Produção do Morro de São Bento, Largo do São Bento 120, near the Igreja do Valongo in Centro (☎013/232-8984).

Guarujá, Boiçucanga and Maresias

GUARUJÁ is São Paulo's most important beach resort, and getting there is easy. There are half-hourly buses from the city's Jabaquara *Rodoviária* that take little more than an hour to travel the 85km to the resort. From Santos, take a bus from Gonzaga east along the beach avenue to Ponta da Praia, from where a ferry makes the ten-minute crossing of the Santos channel, and then it's a fifteen-minute bus ride on to Guarujá itself. The resort features a set of large apartment buildings alongside lengthy, rather monotonous beaches. In the summer, finding space on the main beach, **Pitangueiras**, can be difficult, and the beaches within walking distance, or a short bus ride, to the northeast are little better. In fact, without a car and considerable local knowledge, Guarujá is best avoided; in any case, finding a reasonably priced **hotel** in the summer can be almost impossible. Your best bet around Praia das Pitangueiras is the small and friendly *Hotel*

Rio Guarujá at Rua Rio de Janeiro 131 (☎013/286-6081; ③), just a block from the sea, or at the adjoining Praia Guarujá, the *Guarujá Praia*, Praça Brigadeiro Franco Faria Lima 137 (☎013/286-190; ③). For a local map, detailed instructions on outlying beaches and hotel information, there's a helpful **tourist office** at Rua Quintano Bocaiúva 248 (Mon–Fri 9am–6pm, Sat & Sun 9am–noon).

From Guarujá's *Rodoviária* there are buses east as far as Ubatuba (see p.505), stopping off at points along the way. For much of the first 90km the road passes inland, but approaching **BOIÇUCANGA**, it again skirts the coastline, and the landscape grows increasingly mountainous as the forested Serra do Mar sweeps down towards the sea. Boiçucanga is a quiet resort, much more attractive than Guarujá, consisting of a few simple **hotels**, a campsite and a couple of **restaurants**. The rooms at the *Pousada da Barra* (☎012/465-1391; ④) are highly recommended, but cheaper alternatives are available including the *Dani* (☎012/465-1299; ②). *Le Bistrot* produces some surprisingly good French dishes. There's a **tourist office** at Rua Hilário de Mattos (daily 8am–7pm). The beaches, especially those in the direction of Maresias, are small and extremely pretty, all within walking distance or within a short drive or bus ride of the resort. There are a few places to stay over in neighbouring **MARESIAS**; try the comfortable *Pousada Refúgio de Maresias* (☎012/465-1280; ④), or the youth hostel (☎012/465-1561; $12 per person).

São Sebastião

Twenty-seven kilometres further northeast is **SÃO SEBASTIÃO**, a bustling little town on the mainland directly opposite the island of Ilhabela (see below). After its foundation in the first years of the seventeenth century, sugar cane and coffee farms were responsible for São Sebastião's growth until the eighteenth century, when the town entered a period of decline. Emerging from this stagnation only in the last few decades, the town has retained many of its colonial buildings. Unlike in other similar towns, they've not been taken over by wealthy city-dwellers, since São Sebastião's beaches, in both directions from the centre, are poor and completely cut off from the open sea by the much more beautiful Ilhabela, directly opposite.

Praça Major João Fernandes is the heart of São Sebastião and the location of the **Igreja Matriz**, built in 1636, almost as old as the town (though its interior is twentieth-century plaster). Along the waterfront near the square are innumerable **bars** and seafood **restaurants**, where excellent meals cost about $10. Because of the proximity to Ilhabela, there's a large selection of **hotels**, the best of which – well worth the splurge – is the *Pôrto Grande* (☎012/452-1101; ⑤), a whitewashed colonial-style building, with a pool in park-like gardens stretching down to its own beach. The hotel is a ten-minute walk from the centre, at Av. Guarda Mór Lobo Viana 1440. Cheaper hotel options include the friendly and comfortable *Roma*, Praça Major João Fernandes (☎012/452-1016; ②), which offers an attractive garden and good, inclusive breakfasts; and the good-value *Beira Mar*, Rua Expedecionários Brasileiros 258 (②), with attractive sea views. There are plenty of other choices (①–②) on Rua Três Bandeirantes, one street from the main square by the sea. The **tourist office** on the waterfront at Av. Dr Altino Arantes 174 (daily 8am–7pm) covers the town and the mainland villages to the southwest.

Ilhabela

Without a shadow of a doubt, **Ilhabela** is one of the most beautiful spots on the coast between Santos and Rio. Of volcanic origin, the island's startling mountainous scenery rises to 1370m and is covered in dense, tropical foliage. Its dozens of waterfalls, beautiful beaches and azure seas have contributed to its popularity; old or new, most of the buildings are in simple Portuguese colonial styles, as far removed from brash Guarujá as you can get. The island is a haunt of São Paulo's rich who maintain large and discreetly located homes on the coast, many with mooring facilities for luxury yachts or with helicopter landing pads. The hotels are expensive and are often fully booked, so many people choose to stay in São Sebastião instead – not a bad idea, since transport connections are good. **Ferries** (daily 4.30–1.30am, 24hr in summer; pedestrians free, cars $5) depart from São Sebastião's waterfront every half an hour and the crossing takes about twenty minutes. The ferry is met by a bus, which goes to **Vila Ilhabela** at the northwestern end of the island.

Vila Ilhabela

Almost all of the island's 6000 inhabitants live along the sheltered western shore, with the small village of **VILA ILHABELA** the only population centre. A few kilometres before you enter the village, look out on the right-hand side of the road for the grand eighteenth-century main house of the **Fazenda Engenho d'Agua**. This was one of the largest plantations on the island, famous for its high-quality *cachaça*. Today there's virtually no agricultural production on the island, its economy completely geared to tourism. On the outskirts of the village at Rua Bartolomeu de Gusmão 140, there's a **tourist office** (daily 9am–6pm) which produces a very detailed map.

The village has a few pretty colonial buildings, and is dominated by the **Igreja Matriz**, a little church completed in 1806. There is a branch of Banespa, the only bank on the island and the only place to change travellers' cheques, a few grocery stores, some excellent snack bars and boutiques selling overpriced T-shirts and yachting gear. In the evenings, people congregate on the pier catching swordfish with remarkable ease.

The rest of the island

Getting around the island can be a problem as the only bus route is along the island's western shore north as far as the lighthouse at Punta das Canas and south to Porto do Frade – the limits in both directions of good-quality roads. The beaches along this mainland-facing shore are small, but pleasant enough, and are popular with windsurfers; the water's calm but of questionable cleanliness. Far more attractive are the small beaches in the coves along the northern coast, such as the **Praia do Jabaquara**, but access is generally difficult, involving clambering down steep trails hidden from view from the road. It's along this stretch of coast that some of the island's most exclusive villas are located, and their owners have an interest in making sure the road remains in a poor condition and that the beaches are difficult to reach. The road is also poor along the southern shore, but this is where some of the best beaches are located, especially around **Praia do Bonete**, where there's a small fishing settlement.

The east coast beaches of the **Baia de Castelhanos**, 22km across the island via a steep mountain road often washed out by heavy rain, have the most surf and are considered by many to be the island's most beautiful. They are linked to one another by cliff-top trails. Seven kilometres along the road, stop at the *Jardim Tropical* (daily 9am–6pm; $3, including insect repellent) for a drink and a refreshing shower under a waterfall or a dip in a natural pool.

Buses are few and far between and the routes limited. You can try hitching lifts, or rent a **jeep** at *Locatudo*, Av. Princesa Isabel 1634, Praia do Perequê, near the ferry landing (☎012/472-2468; $100 per day).

Practicalities

In the summer it's difficult to find a **place to stay** on the island, and throughout the year the place is extremely expensive. Reservations are essential over summer weekends and, to avoid disappointment, it's sensible to make them for summer weekdays, too.

In Vila Ilhabela the cheapest place to stay is the *Hotel Costa Azul* (☎012/472-1365; ④), just to the north of the main commercial area and next to the yacht club at Rua Francisca Gomes da Silva Prado 71. For the price, the hotel provides very basic accommodation, though it's extremely friendly. A little more expensive, more comfortable and with a large, pleasant garden leading down to the beach is the *Hotel da Praia* (☎012/472-1218; ⑤), located at Av. Pedro Paulo de Moraes 578 on the southern outskirts of the village. Nearby on the same street, at no. 151, is the *Hotel Ilhabela* (☎012/272-1083; ⑤), completely devoid of character but with large rooms and a good-sized pool. Much prettier, at no. 720, is the *Pousada dos Hibiscos* (☎012/472-1375; ④), also with a pool. Further south at Saco do Capela, the *Porto Pousada* (☎012/472-2255; ④) has beautiful rooms with verandahs, lush tropical gardens and a pool, while the *Pousada d'Ajuda* (☎012/472-042; ④) offers basic accommodation. Near the ferry landing at Praia do Perequê there are a number of hotels, the cheapest of which is the *Hotel Rafimar* (☎012/472-1539; ④), small but with a pool, while the *Hotel Perequê* (☎012/472-1813; ④) is simple but attractive.

Ilhabela has several **campsites** including the *Camping Clube de Ilhabela* (☎012/472-9147) at Praia do Perequê and, south of the ferry landing, *Camping Porto Seguro* (☎012/472-9147) at Praia Grande. In general, camping on beaches is strictly forbidden, but no one cares if you camp on the virtually uninhabited eastern side of the island.

Eating, like everything else on Ilhabela, is expensive. Restaurants come and go rapidly, but most are concentrated in and just south of Vila Ilhabela and at Praia do Perequê. When it's time to **move on**, you can either take the twice-daily bus to São Paulo from near the pier in the main village of Ilhabela, or from São Sebastião there are buses in both directions along the mainland coast.

Ubatuba and beyond

From São Sebastião, the highway continues along the coast passing frustratingly close to deserted beaches of dazzling beauty. Buses stop in Caraguatatuba, an ugly little town with a long, gently curving beach alongside the main road, but you're better off carrying on towards **UBATUBA**. The town is only slightly more attractive than Caraguatatuba, but that's of little importance when you consider the local beaches, 72 in all, on islands and curling around inlets.

Ubatuba is centred on Praça 13 de Maio, a couple of blocks from the *Rodoviária* on Rua Conceição. On the square there's a very helpful **tourist office** (daily 8am–6pm) which supplies maps of the coast and will make hotel reservations for you. As far as **accommodation** goes, Ubatuba makes a good base if you plan to explore the outlying beaches, but the hotels are expensive, especially during the summer; they are concentrated in the area around Rua Conceição, towards the beach. On Rua Conceição itself, comfortable and reasonably cheap are the *Parque Atlântico* at no. 185 (☎012/432-1336; ④) and the *São Nicolau* at no. 213 (☎012/432-1267; ④), while the *Xaréu*, around the corner at Rua Jordão Homem da Costa 413, is slightly more expensive (☎012/432-1525; ④). For travellers on tight budgets, the only alternative is to head for a **campsite** – the nearest to town is the *Sítio Usina Velha* (☎012/432-3629), some 3km north on the road to Parati, where you can pitch a tent for $10 per night or rent a small cabin (②). Most **restaurants** are on Avenida Iperoig, which curves alongside the town's beach, the Praia de Iperoig, and you'll find a good variety of seafood, Italian and other types to choose from.

The beaches

Although there's nothing wrong with the town's **Praia de Iperoig**, Ubatuba is best used as a base from which to visit some of the 71 other beaches accessible by bus or private boat. The least developed are to the **northeast** of town, with the furthest,

Camburi, 46km away on the border with the Rio state. To get to these beaches, take the **local bus** marked "Promirim" from the *Rodoviária* and ask the driver to stop at whichever stretch takes your fancy.

To the south of town are the more popular beaches, again easily reached by bus from the town centre. **ENSEADA**, 9km away, is lined with beach-front hotels, none of which have rooms for less than $60. In a bay protected from the lively surf, the beach is popular with families, and in the summer it's always uncomfortably crowded.

Across the bay from Enseada are a series of beautiful isolated beaches that draw fewer people. Walk out of town on the main road for about 2km until you reach **RIBEIRA**, a yachting centre and colourful fishing port. From here, there are trips on sailing **boats** to the **Ilha Anchieta**, a nearby island where only a few fisherfolk live, or further afield along the coast: these will cost between $20 and $35, depending on the itinerary. Beyond Ribeira are sandy coves that you can reach by clambering down from the trail on the cliff above the sea.

Southwest of Santos

The coastal escarpment **southwest of Santos** begins its incline 20–30km inland from the sea. Lacking the immediate mountain backdrop, and with large stretches of the coast dominated by mangrove swamp, this region was for years left more or less untouched by tourism. However, holiday development companies have been moving in recently, aiming at *Paulistanos* who can't afford places further north.

Heading south from Santos, the road follows the coast as far as Peruíbe, then moves inland onto higher, firmer terrain before heading back to the coast down the Serra do Mar. The road is slow, but passing through small fishing villages, banana and sugar plantations and cattle-grazing land, you're reminded that there's more to Brazil than just beaches. Incidentally, from São Paulo, rather than travelling via Santos it's much faster to take a direct bus to Iguape and Cananéia.

Itanhaém

The coastline between Santos and **ITANHAÉM**, 61km south, is, in effect, one long beach which – were it not for the new holiday complexes that line the entire stretch – would be simply unremarkable rather than unattractive. Founded in the sixteenth century, there are a few remaining facades from Itanhaém's early years, most notably the **Covento de Nossa Senhora da Conceição**, a semi-ruined chapel and monastery.

If you do decide to stay over, you're likely to have problems finding a **hotel** room in the summer. Most of the people coming on holiday here are lower-middle-class *Paulistanos* staying in holiday complexes owned by workers' associations, but there are a few, small hotels. Your best bet is the *Hotel Atlântico* (☎013/292-3154; ③) at Rua Cunha Moreira 68 or, failing that, the bigger and more expensive *Pollastrini* (☎013/422-3222; ④) at Praça 22 de Abril.

Iguape

IGUAPE, roughly two and a half hours further south by bus, was founded in 1538 by the Portuguese to guard against the possibility of Spanish encroachment on the southern fringes of the empire. On the southern tip of the estuarine island of Papagaio, Iguape was well placed as a base for exploring the southern *Paulista* interior, up the Rio Ribeira do Iguape. Far from possible markets, however, it was slow to develop and attempts to settle immigrants – most notably Confederate refugees – were met with abject failure. But because Iguape remained a backwater for so long, many of its colonial buildings survive today, albeit in extremely dilapidated states.

During the summer, Iguape is popular with *Paulista* holidaymakers, seeking a beach vacation away from the sophistication, crowds and expense of resorts further north. Facing the town is an island, the **Ilha Comprida**, 86km long and 3km wide, whose interior is of light forest, while on the Atlantic-facing side an uninterrupted beach stretches the entire length of the island. In the summer it gets very crowded near the access road across the island, but if you want to be alone just walk south for a few kilometres. Continual **ferries** make the five-minute crossing to the northern part of the island and, until 7pm, **buses** take passengers across the island to the beach.

A couple of kilometres south of the access road crossing the island, there are several **campsites**, bars and *lanchonetes*. The island also has several **hotels**: budget choices include the *Alpha* (☎013/842-1270; ②) and the *Vila das Palmeiras* (☎013/842-1349; ②). There's also the *Pousada Aconchego*, on Avenida Beira Mar, Balneario São Martinho (②), a simple building facing the sea with rooms for up to four people. You'll get good inexpensive steak, fish, chicken, rice and beans at the *Nordestão* on Avenida Beira Mar, and there are numerous restaurants serving up cheap fresh fish.

A much better choice of hotels, though, is to be found in Iguape: the *Zé Juca* at Av. Ademar de Barros 598 (☎013/841-1920), the *De Martis* at Rua Rebello 258 (☎013/841-1325) and the *Rio Verde* at Rua Antônio José de Moraes 86 (☎013/841-1745) are amongst the cheapest (③). For food, *Aconchego do Amigo Fritz*, Rua São Paulo 26, Barra do Ribeira, is a small, reasonably priced place serving German food, fish and seafood. The *Barra Bar* at Rua São Pedro 120, Barra do Ribeira, serves traditional sandwiches and huge portions of prawns and is the only place open late at night. For Italian food, there's the *Maratea*, Av. Papa João XXIII 420, also in Barra do Ribeira, specializing in fish and homemade pasta ($8–15 per person).

Cananéia

Like Iguape, **CANANÉIA**, 50km further south, is on an island, lying between the mainland, to which it's linked by a short bridge, and the Ilha Comprida. There's a constant **ferry** service between the town and the Ilha Comprida, from where you can either take a bus (every hour) or walk the 3km to the beach. Where the road hits the beach, there are a couple of simple hotels and bars. In the summer it gets quite crowded here but, as in the north of the island (see above), you don't have to wander far for a quiet piece of sand.

In the centre of Cananéia, in particular along *ruas* Tristão Lobo, Bandeirantes and Dom João II, there are many simple ochre-coloured and whitewashed colonial and nineteenth-century buildings. Except for a few, such as the seventeenth-century church, they're in very poor condition and for many only the facade remains. The area to the south of Cananéia is a protected **nature reserve** with isolated beaches and fishing villages which can be reached by chartering a small motor-launch. Karl Beitler (☎ & fax 013/851-1683) a German long resident in Cananéia, knows the area well and leads tours into the Mâta Atlantica and the islands.

Cars are permitted to drive along the beach between Iguape and Cananéia. Otherwise, **buses** have to take a circuitous route inland and the trip is over 80km. There are several buses a day between the towns, or you can travel by **boat**; departures are from Iguape on Monday and Thursday, and continue south to Ariri (see p.530), returning the following day.

Cananéia's grandest **hotel** is the *Glória* (☎013/851-1377; ③–④), across from the *Rodoviária*, but its rooms are damp, the staff unfriendly and general atmosphere institutional – one to avoid. Most other hotels are along or near the waterfront in the same vicinity: good bets are the *Beira-Mar* at Av. Beira Mar 219 (☎013/851-1115; ③), the *Recanto do Sol* at Rua Pedro Lobo 271 (☎013/851-1162; ③), or, with swimming pools, the *Cabana do Bugre* (☎013/851-1101; ④) and the *Coqueiro* (☎013/851-1255; ③), both on Avenida Independência. You can eat extremely well in Cananéia, with the menus of the mainly Japanese-owned **restaurants** including clams, mussels, conch, octopus and, Cananéia's speciality, oysters; especially recommended are the *Silencio Naguissa*, Av. Luiz Wilson Barbosa 401, *Reconto do Sol*, Rua Pero Lobo 271, *Beira-Mar*, Av. Beira Mar 219, and the *Caldeirada*, which serves a superb seafood soup for $15.

On from Iguape and Cananéia

If travelling south to Paraná, you'll have to change buses in **REGISTRO**, an hour from both Iguape and Cananéia. Registro is in the heart of a Japanese tea-growing region, and if you're unlucky with connections and need to **stay**, try the *Lito Palace* (☎013/821-1055; ②), Av. Jonas Banks Leite 615, or the cheaper *Regis* (☎013/821-1988; ②), at Rua São Francisco Xavier 83. The *Ebissuya*, Rua Getúlio Vargas 401, is one of the town's better **restaurants**, while the *Estoril* at Rodoviária BR-116, km 442, on the way to São Paulo, has a good varied menu specializing in Brazilian dishes.

travel details

Buses

Campinas to: Curitiba (5 daily; 6hr); São Paulo (hourly; 1hr 15min).

São Paulo to: Bauru (7 daily; 4hr 30min); Belo Horizonte (hourly; 12hr); Campinas (hourly; 1hr 15min); Campo Grande (8 daily; 16hr); Cananéia (4 daily; 4hr 30min); Corumbá (4 daily; 26hr); Curitiba (hourly; 6hr); Florianópolis (8 daily; 12hr); Guarujá (every 30min; 1hr); Iguape (4 daily; 3hr 30min); Recife (4 daily; 40hr); Rio (every 30min; 6hr); Salvador (4 daily; 30hr); Santa Bárbara d'Oeste (8 daily; 2hr); Santos (every 15min; 1hr); Ubatuba (6 daily; 3hr 30min).

Santos to: Cananéia (2 daily; 4hr 30min); São Paulo (every 15min; 1hr).

Ubatuba to: Parati (3 daily; 1hr 30min); Rio (2 daily; 5hr); São Paulo (6 daily; 3hr 30min).

Trains

São Paulo to: Bauru (4 daily; 5hr 30min); Campinas (8 daily; 1hr 50min).

CHAPTER EIGHT

THE SOUTH

T he states forming the **South** of Brazil – **Paraná, Santa Catarina** and **Rio Grande do Sul** – are generally considered to be the most developed part of the country. The smallest of Brazil's regions, the south maintains an economic influence completely out of proportion to its size. This is largely the result of two factors: the first is an agrarian structure that, to a great extent, is based on highly efficient small and medium-sized units; and the second is the economically over-active population which produces a per capita output considerably higher than the national average. With little of the widespread poverty found elsewhere in the country, Brazilians tend to dismiss the South as being a region that has more in common with Europe or the United States than with South America.

Superficially, at least, this view has much going for it. The inhabitants are largely of European origin anyway and live in well-ordered cities where there's little of the obvious squalor prevalent elsewhere. However, beneath the tranquil setting there are tensions: due to land shortages people are constantly forced to move vast distances – as far away as Acre in the western Amazon – to avoid being turned into mere day-labourers, and *favelas* are an increasingly common sight in Curitiba, Porto Alegre and the other large cities of the South. From time to time these tensions explode as landless peasants invade the huge, under-used *latifúndios* found in the west and south of the region, but little has been done to appease demands for genuine land reform.

For the tourist, though, the region offers much that's attractive. The **coast** has a subtropical climate that in the summer months (November to March) attracts Brazilians who want to avoid the oppressive heat of northern resorts, and a vegetation and atmosphere that feel more Mediterranean than South American. Much of the *Paranaense* coast is still unspoilt by the ravages of mass tourism, and building development is virtually forbidden on the beautiful islands of the **Bay of Paranaguá**. By way of contrast, tourists have encroached along Santa Catarina's coast, but only **Balneário Camburiú** has been allowed to develop into a concrete jungle. Otherwise, resorts such as most of those on the **Ilha de Santa Catarina** around **Florianópolis** remain small and do not seriously detract from the region's natural beauty.

ACCOMMODATION PRICE CODES

In this guide, accommodation has been categorized according to the price codes outlined below, based on US$. These categories represent the minimum you can expect to pay for a **double room in high season** – though note that many of the budget places will also have more expensive rooms. Rates for hostels and basic hotels where guests are charged **per person** are given in US$, instead of being indicated by price code. See p.31 for further information.

① under $20	③ $30–45	⑤ $60–80	⑦ $120–175
② $20–30	④ $45–60	⑥ $80–120	⑨ $175 and over

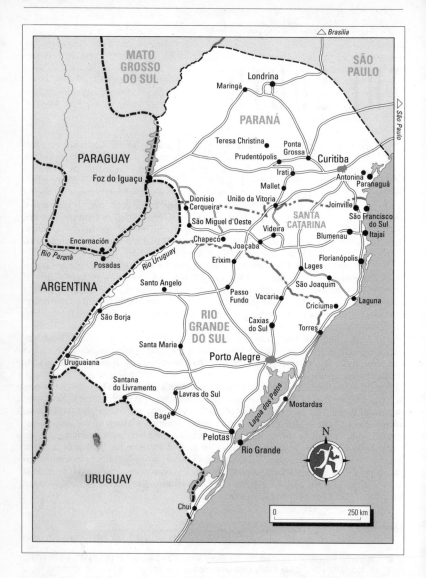

The **interior** is even less frequently visited. Much of it is mountainous, the home of people whose way of life seems to have altered little since the arrival of the European pioneers last century. Cities in the interior that were founded by Germans (such as **Blumenau** in Santa Catarina), Italians (**Caxias do Sul** in Rio Grande do Sul) and Ukrainians (**Prudentópolis** in Paraná) have lost most of their former ethnic character, but only short distances from them are villages and hamlets where time appears to have stood still. The highland areas between **Lages** and **Vacaria**, and the grass-lands of southern and western Rio Grande do Sul, are largely given over to vast cattle ranches, where the modern *gaúchos* (see box p.586) keep alive many of the skills of their forebears.

Travelling around the South is generally easy, and there's a fine **road** network. Most north–south **buses** stick to the road running near the coast, but it's easy to devise routes passing through the interior, perhaps taking in the Jesuit ruins of **São Miguel** or the spectacular **Iguaçu** waterfalls.

PARANÁ

Paraná is the northernmost of Brazil's southern states and one of the wealthiest in all Brazil. Its agricultural sector is based on small and medium-sized land holdings, modern industries which, unlike those of neighbouring São Paulo, have been subject to at least limited planning controls, and a population comprised largely of the descendants of immigrants. All of which combine to give Paraná something of the vague feel of an American Midwestern state transplanted to the subtropics.

For several decades after breaking away from São Paulo in 1853, Paraná's economy remained based on pig-raising, timber extraction and *erva maté* (a South American bush, the leaves of which are used to make a tea-like beverage), and in its early years the province was linked to the rest of Brazil only by a network of trails along which cattle and mules passed between Rio Grande do Sul's grasslands and the mines and plantations of the northern provinces. Paraná was sparsely populated by Indians, Portuguese and mixed-race *caboclos*, who worked on the *latifúndios*, scratched a living as semi-nomadic subsistence farmers or, on the coast, fished.

Then, because of a labour shortage in Brazil brought about by the end of the slave trade, the provincial government turned to **immigration** as a means to expand Paraná's economy and open up land for settlement. The first immigrant colonies of British, Volga-Germans, French, Swiss and Icelanders were utter failures, but, from the 1880s onwards, others met with some success. As mixed farmers, coffee or soya producers, Germans moved northwards from Rio Grande do Sul and Santa Catarina; Poles and Italians settled near the capital, Curitiba; Ukrainians centred themselves in the south, especially on Prudentópolis (see box p.531); Japanese spread south from São Paulo, settling around Londrina and Maringa; and a host of smaller groups, including Dutch, Mennonites, Koreans, Russian "Old Believers" and Danube-Swabians established colonies elsewhere with varying success rates. Thanks to their isolation, the immigrants' descendants have retained many of the cultural traditions of their forebears, traditions that are only now gradually being eroded by the influences of television and radio, the education system and economic pressures that force migration to the cities or to new land in distant parts of Brazil. Nevertheless, this multi-ethnic blend still lends Paraná its distinct character and a special fascination.

Unless you're heading straight for the **Iguaçu** waterfalls, **Curitiba** makes a good base. Transport services fan out in all directions from the state capital and there's plenty to keep you occupied in the city while you're waiting for connections. The **Bay of Paranaguá** can be visited as a short excursion from Curitiba, but the bay's islands and colonial towns could also easily take up a week or more of your time. Inland, the strange geological formations of **Vila Velha** are usually visited as a day trip from Curitiba, but – by changing buses in Ponta Grossa – you can head west to the Ukrainian-dominated region around the towns of **Prudentópolis** and **Irati**; and from there, head yet further west to Foz do Iguaçu.

Curitiba

Founded in 1693 as a goldmining camp, **CURITIBA** was of little importance until 1853 when it was made capital of Paraná. Since then, the city's population has steadily risen from a few thousand, reaching 140,000 in 1940 and some 1.5 million today. It's said that Curitiba is barely a Brazilian city at all, a view that has some basis. The inhabitants are descendants of Polish, German, Italian and other immigrants who settled in Curitiba and in surrounding villages that have since been engulfed by the expanding metropolis. On average, *Curitibanos* enjoy Brazil's highest standard of living: the city boasts health, education and public transport facilities that are the envy of other parts of the country. There are *favelas*, but they're well hidden and, because of the cool, damp winters, sturdier than those in cities to the north. The wooden houses of Curitiba's lower and middle classes often resemble those of frontier homesteads and frequently betray their inhabitants' central or eastern European origins, with half-hip roofs, carved window frames and elaborate trelliswork. As elsewhere in Brazil, the rich live in mansions and luxury condominiums, but even these are a little less ostentatious, and need fewer security precautions, than usual.

Many nineteenth- and early twentieth-century buildings have been saved from the developers who, since the 1960s, have ravaged most Brazilian cities, and there's a clearly defined **historic quarter** where colonial buildings have been preserved. Much of the centre is closed to traffic and, in a country where the car has become a symbol of development, planners from all over Brazil and beyond descend on Curitiba to discover how a city can function effectively when pedestrians and buses are given priority. Thanks in part to the relative lack of traffic, it's a pleasure just strolling around and, what's more, you can wander the city, day or night, in safety.

One result of its being so untypical of Brazil is that few visitors bother to remain in Curitiba longer than it takes to change buses or planes. At most, they stay for a night, prior to taking the early morning train to the coast. But it deserves more than this: although there's some truth in the image of northern European dullness, Curitiba's attractive buildings, interesting museums and variety of restaurants make a stay here pleasant – if not overly exciting.

Arrival, information and city transport

Curitiba is easy to reach from all parts of Brazil and, once here, you'll find yourself in a Brazilian city at its most efficient. Flights to most major Brazilian cities depart from ultramodern Afonso Pena **airport**, about thirty minutes from the city centre. The airport features a good range of shops (including several excellent souvenir and local handicraft shops), a post office and *casas de câmbios*, but there is no tourist information office. Taxis from the airport charge about $25, or take a bus marked "Aeroporto" (in the centre, they leave about every hour from outside the *Hotel Presidente* on Rua Westphalen by Praça Rui Barbosa).

The main bus and train stations (the **Rodoferroviária**) are located adjacent to one another, about ten blocks from the city centre. The only remaining passenger trains to Curitiba run along the line from Morretes and Paranaguá (see p.522), which has become a major tourist attraction. From the *Rodoferroviária*, it takes about twenty minutes to walk to the centre, or there's a minibus from almost in front of the station: catch it at the intersection of Avenida Afonso Camargo and Avenida Sete de Setembro, to the left of the entrance to the station's drive.

The **telephone code** for Curitiba is ☎041.

In the backwaters near Manaus

Amazon lilies

Drum tree in the Amazon

The German Festa Pomerana, Pomerode, Santa Catarina

Houses on stilts by the old port of Manaus

Amazon piranha

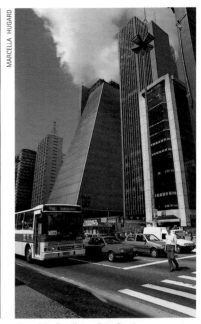
Avenida Paulista, São Paulo

Graffiti taunting the gridlock in
São Paulo

Daniela beach, Santa Catarina island

PETER WILSON

Viewing platform, Iguaçu Falls

DILWYN JENKINS

The Cathedral in Brasília

PETER WILSON

Iguaçu Falls from the Brazilian side

Information

The *Secretaria Especial do Esporte e Turismo* (*SETUR*), the state **tourist information** organization, has its headquarters near the Palácio Iguaçu at Rua Deputado Mário de Barros 1290, on the third floor of Edifício Caetano Munhoz da Rocha (Mon–Fri 9am–6pm). They keep up-to-date information on changes to rail and boat schedules and provide useful maps of trails in state parks; many of the employees speak English. Closer to the city centre, and an easy walk from the *Rodoferroviária*, there's also a branch at the Centro de Convenções, Rua Barão do Rio Branco 370 (same hours). For information specifically on Curitiba, go to the very helpful and well-organized tourist office on Rua Ébano Pereira 477 (Mon–Fri 8am–noon and 2–6pm), which has a branch supplying basic information in the Galleria Schaffer at Rua XV de Novembro 416 (same hours).

City transport

Curitiba is small enough to be able to **walk** to most places within the city centre. For exploring outlying areas, there's an extremely efficient municipal **bus** network that's considered the envy of all other Brazilian cities. In the city centre, the two main bus terminals are at Praça Tiradentes and Praça Rui Barbosa, from where buses head out into the suburbs as well as to neighbouring *municípios*. **Taxis** are easy to come by and, as distances are generally small, they're not too expensive.

If you have limited time in Curitiba, an excellent way to view the city's main attractions is to take a **bus tour**. There are two routes, both starting from Praça Tiradentes and stopping at fifteen attractions: the *Jardineira* line (Tues–Sun 9am–5.30pm, every half hour) makes stops at the city's much-heralded parks and environmental attractions; the *Volta ao Mundo* line (Tues–Sun 9.10am–5.20pm, every 45min) stops at monuments and parks associated with the city's many ethnic communities. Both the itineraries take two hours, but tickets ($5) allow passengers to get off at three of the stops and rejoin the tour on a later bus.

Accommodation

If your sole reason for being in Curitiba is to catch the dawn train to the coast, there are numerous cheap and medium-priced **hotels** within a few minutes' walk of the *Rodoferroviária*. Otherwise, places to stay in the city centre are widely scattered but within walking distance of most attractions. Many of the better hotels offer discounts at weekends as they are primarily used by business executives. Curitiba's **youth hostel** is at Rua Padre Agostinho 645 (☎233-2746). It's friendly and has no curfew but is located twenty minutes' walk from the city centre in the pleasant residential suburb of Mercês, and on the opposite side of town from the *Rodoferroviária*.

Hotel Boa Viagem, Av. Presidente Afonso Camargo. Next door to the *Império*, this is one of the cheapest places to stay in town, but don't expect too much in the way of comfort. ①.

Hotel Bourbon, Rua Cândido Lopes 102 (☎322-4001). The best hotel in the city, the *Bourbon* has recently undergone thorough renovation to create an atmosphere of traditional elegance combined with every modern facility, including a pool and very good restaurants. ⑧.

Curitiba Palace Hotel, Rua Ermelino de Leão 45 (☎322-8081). Centrally located and modern, all the rooms have balconies. ⑤.

Hotel Eduardo VII, Rua Cândido Leão 15 (☎322-6767). Perfectly located near the historic centre, close to Praça Tiradentes and surprisingly quiet. Friendly service, good-sized rooms but somewhat overpriced. ⑤.

Elo Hotel Universidade, Rua Amintas de Barros 383 (☎262-7131). A large, modern, characterless hotel with a pool, situated next to the university's main administrative building. The rooms are comfortable and excellent value. ④.

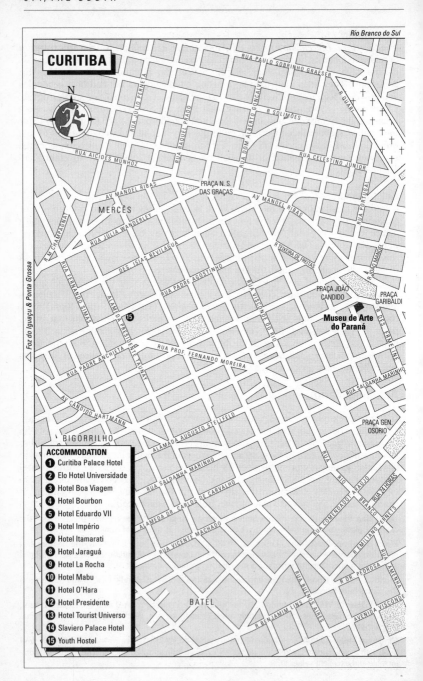

Rio Branco do Sul

CURITIBA

N

◁ Foz do Iguaçu & Ponta Grossa

RUA JÚLIO PERNETA

RUA PAULO SOBRINHO GRAESER

RUA RAQUEL PRADO

R SOLIMÕES

RUA DOM ALBERTO GONÇALVES

RUA AICIDES MUNHOZ

RUA CELESTINO JUNIOR

R M CHAMPAGNAT

AV MANOEL RIBAS

PRAÇA N. S.
DAS GRAÇAS

AV MANOEL RIBAS

RUA PORTUGAL

MERCÊS

RUA JULIA WANDERLEY

RUA FERNANDO SIMAS

DES ISIAS BEVILAGUA

R TEIXEIRA DE FREITAS

R JOAQUIM MANOEL

RUA PADRE AGOSTINHO

PRAÇA JOÃO
CANDIDO

PRAÇA
GARIBALDI

ALAMEDA PRESIDENTE TAUNAY

⑮

RUA VISCONDE DO RIO

**Museu de Arte
do Paraná**

R DES ERMELINO

RUA PADRE ANCHIETA

RUA PROF. FERNANDO MOREIRA

RUA SALDANHA MARINHO

AV CÂNDIDO HARTMANN

PRAÇA GEN
OSORIO

BIGORRILHO

ALAMEDA AUGUSTO STELLFELD

ACCOMMODATION

❶ Curitiba Palace Hotel
❷ Elo Hotel Universidade
❸ Hotel Boa Viagem
❹ Hotel Bourbon
❺ Hotel Eduardo VII
❻ Hotel Império
❼ Hotel Itamarati
❽ Hotel Jaraguá
❾ Hotel La Rocha
❿ Hotel Mabu
⓫ Hotel O'Hara
⓬ Hotel Presidente
⓭ Hotel Tourist Universo
⓮ Slaviero Palace Hotel
⓯ Youth Hostel

RUA SALDANHA MARINHO

ALAMEDA DR. CARLOS DE CARVALHO

RUA VICENTE MACHADO

RUA COMENDADOR ARAÚJO

RUA 24 HORAS

RUA BRANCO

R EMILIANO PERNETS

RUA AMÉLIA

R DR PEDROSA

AVENIDA VISCONDE

BATÉL

R BENJAMIN LINS

RUA BUENOS AIRES

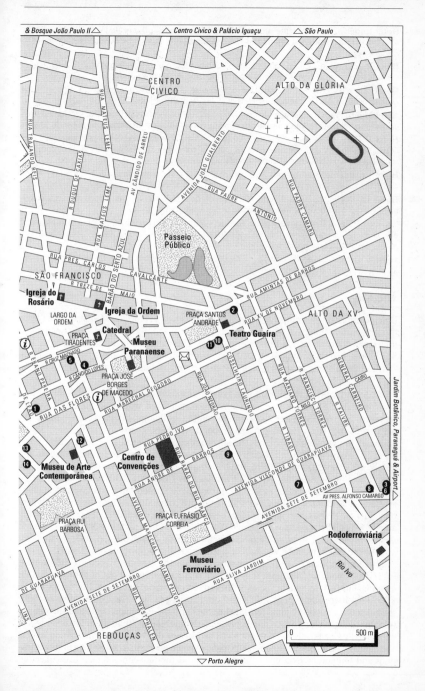

△ & Bosque João Paulo II   △ Centro Cívico & Palácio Iguaçu   △ São Paulo

CENTRO
CÍVICO

ALTO DA GLÓRIA

RUA TRAIANO REIS
RUA MATEUS LEME
R DUQUE DE CAXIAS
AV CÂNDIDO DE ABREU
AVENIDA JOÃO GUALBERTO
RUA PADRE
ANTÔNIO
RUA PADRE CAMARGO

Passeio
Público

RUA PRES. CARLOS CAVALCANTE
BARÃO DO SERTO AZUL

SÃO FRANCISCO

RUA AMINTAS DE BARROS

**Igreja do
Rosário**

R TREZE DE
MAIO

Igreja da Ordem

PRAÇA SANTOS
ANDRADE ❷

RUA XV DE NOVEMBRO

ALTO DA XV

LARGO DA
ORDEM

Catedral

PRAÇA
TIRADENTES

**Museu
Paranaense**

❶❶ ❿

Teatro Guaíra

ⓘ

R EBANO PEREIRA
R CRUZ MACHADO
❺ ❹
R CÂNDIDO LOPES

PRAÇA JOSÉ
BORGES
ⓘ DE MACEDO

RUA MARECHAL DEODORO

RUA DAS FLORES

❶

RUA JOÃO NEGRÃO
RUA COSELHEIRO TAURÃFIO
RUA MARIANO TORRES
NILO TORRES
RUA FRANCISCO TORRES
RUA TIBAGI
GENERAL CARNEIRO
CAIRO
R FAIVEL

❿

RUA PEDRO IVO
RUA ANDRÉ DE BARROS
RUA BARÃO DO RIO BRANCO

**Centro de
Convenções**

❾

AVENIDA VISCONDE DE GUARAPUAVA

❼

AVENIDA SETE DE SETEMBRO

❽ ❸
❻

**Museu de Arte
Contemporânea**

❶❸
❶❹
❶❷

AV PRES. ALFONSO CAMARGO

Jardim Botânico, Paranaguá & Airport △

PRAÇA RUI
BARBOSA

AVENIDA MARECHAL FLORIANO PEIXOTO

PRAÇA EUFRÁSIO
CORREIA

AVENIDA SETE DE SETEMBRO

Rodoferroviária

Rio Ivo

**Museu
Ferroviário**

RUA SLIVA JARDIM

DE GUARAPUAVA

RUA WESTHALEN
RUA SETE DE SETEMBRO
LINS

REBOUÇAS

0   500 m

▽ Porto Alegre

Hotel Império, Av. Presidente Afonso Camargo 367 (☎264-3373). Located virtually opposite the *Rodoferroviária*, with good rooms and a nice atmosphere, this is the best budget option here-abouts. ②.

Hotel Itamarati, Rua Tibagi 950 (☎222-9063). Only a few minutes' walk from the *Rodoferroviária* towards the centre of town, this hotel is fairly quiet and excellent value. ②.

Hotel Jaraguá, Av. Presidente Afonso Camargo 279 (☎362-2022). Directly opposite the *Rodoferroviária*, this has the best facilities of all hotels in the vicinity. ⑤.

Hotel Mabu, Praça Santos Andrade 830 (☎322-1122). Good location and attentive service but over-priced – presumably for the convenience of being part of the Best Western Hotel network. ⑥.

Hotel O'Hara, Praça Santos Andrade 770 (☎232-6044). A well-located city centre hotel on a con-tinuation of Rua XV de Novembro, just ten minutes' walk from the *Rodoferroviária*. The rooms are small but comfortable – one of the best mid-range options in the city. ③.

Hotel Presidente, Rua Westphalen 33 (☎322-5141). It's worth spending a little more here to get one of the larger, lighter rooms. The restaurant serves reasonable and moderately priced meals. ⑤.

Hotel La Rocha, Rua João Negrão 532 (☎233-6479). Basic rooms with private showers, conve-niently located for both the *Rodoferroviária* and the city centre. ②.

Slaviero Palace Hotel, Rua Senador Alencar Guimarães 830 (☎322-7271). Situated a couple of blocks from Rua das Flores, this well-established hotel is popular with business travellers. The rooms are pleasant, large and fully equipped. ⑦.

Tourist Universo, Praça Osório 63 (☎322-0099). Attractively situated with the nicest rooms over-looking the tree-lined square. Friendly atmosphere and well-equipped rooms. ⑤.

The City

Being comparatively compact, much of Curitiba is best explored on foot and, apart from the museums – many of which are located in the central commercial district – most interest is concentrated in the historic centre. The main commercial district, with Rua das Flores (part of Avenida XV de Novembro) at its heart, is only a couple of blocks south of the historic quarter, which is concentrated around the Largo da Ordem.

The commercial district: Rua das Flores and around

The **Rua das Flores** – a pedestrianized precinct lined with graceful, and carefully restored, pastel-coloured early twentieth-century buildings – is the centre's main late afternoon and early evening meeting point, its bars, tearooms and coffee shops crammed with customers. Few of the surrounding streets are especially attractive, but the former city hall, at Praça Generoso Marques, across from the flower market is def-initely worth a visit. Built in 1916, the building is a magnificent Art Nouveau construc-tion that now houses the **Museu Paranaense** (Mon–Fri 9.30am–5.30pm). One of Curitiba's more interesting museums, it displays a limited but attractive collection of artefacts charting the history of Paraná from pre-colonial times into the twentieth cen-tury. Just off Praça General Osório, at the far end of Rua das Flores, there's a shopping arcade especially popular with people returning from late parties and dinners, as well as with insomniacs, the *Rua 24 Horas*. As its name suggests, businesses here are open around the clock, useful if you have a 4am urge to buy a postcard or a T-shirt.

There are a number of other museums within the commercial centre (the tourist office has a complete list), but only two are really worth going out of your way for. Of obvious interest to rail buffs, the **Museu Ferroviário**, in Praça Eufrásio Correia (Tues–Fri 10am–5pm), contains relics from Paraná's railway era. The building housing the museum was the original terminus of the Curitiba–Paranaguá line, and the display relating to the history of the line is particularly interesting (though, unfortunately, the explanatory text is only in Portuguese). The **Museu de Arte Contemporânea**, at Rua Westphalen 16 (Mon–Fri 10am–7pm), concentrates on *Paranaense* artists in its perma-nent and temporary exhibits. A brief look round the museum's diminutive collection will be enough to recognize that Paraná is unlikely to establish itself as a trendsetter in the Brazilian contemporary art scene.

A couple of blocks north from Rua das Flores is Praça Tiradentes where the **Catedral Metropolitana** is located. Inaugurated in 1893, and supposedly inspired by Barcelona's cathedral, it's a totally unremarkable neo-Gothic construction. If you feel the need for a break from the city crowds, head east for a few blocks to the **Passeio Público**, Curitiba's oldest park. Opened in 1886, it has two large boating ponds at its centre and a network of paths to wander along, shaded by tall trees. Of particular interest here are the aviaries housing local species of brightly feathered birds.

The historic quarter

Near the cathedral, a pedestrian tunnel leads to Curitiba's **historic quarter**, an area of impeccably preserved eighteenth- and nineteenth-century buildings. With few exceptions, the whitewashed buildings of the old town are of a style that would not be out of place in a small village in Portugal. Today the buildings all have state preservation orders on them and do duty as bars, restaurants, art and craft galleries and cultural centres.

Two of Curitiba's oldest churches physically dominate the historic quarter. Dating from 1737, with the bell tower added in the late nineteenth century, the **Igreja da Ordem Terceira de São Francisco das Chagas**, on Rua São Francisco, is the city's oldest surviving building and one of the best examples of Portuguese ecclesiastical architecture in southern Brazil. Plain outside, the church is also simple within, its only decoration being typically Portuguese blue and white tiling and late Baroque altars. The church contains the **Museu de Arte Sacra** (Tues–Fri 9am–noon & 1.30–6.30pm, Sat & Sun 9am–1pm), with relics gathered from Curitiba's churches. Opposite the church is the mid-eighteenth-century **Casa Romário Martins**, Curitiba's oldest surviving house, now the site of a cultural foundation and exhibition centre for *Paranaense* artists. A short distance uphill from here, on the same road, the church of **Nossa Senhora do Rosário** dates back to 1737, built by and for Curitiba's slave population. However, after falling into total disrepair, the church was completely reconstructed in the 1930s and remains colonial in style only.

Carrying on up the hill, the **Museu de Arte do Paraná**, on Praça João Cândido (Tues–Fri 10am–noon & 1–6pm), contains work by mainly *Paranaense* artists of the nineteenth and early twentieth centuries, who were important if only for documenting the local landscape of their time.

The outskirts

North of the old town, about 3km from the centre of Curitiba, the **Bosque João Paulo II** (daily 6am–8pm) was created to commemorate the papal visit to Curitiba in 1980. In the heart of the park, the **Museu da Imigração Polonêsa** (Tues–Sun 9am–6pm) celebrates Polish immigration to Paraná. It's made up of several log cabins, built by Polish immigrants in the 1880s and relocated here from the Colônia Thomaz Coelho. The cabins contain displays of typical objects used by pioneer families, and one building has been turned into a shrine to the "Black Madonna of Czestochowa". There's a **shop** attached to the museum selling Polish handicrafts and wonderful postcards marking the papal visit. The museum's staff are extremely helpful and are pleased to offer information about the museum and Paraná's Polish community. On the side road as you enter the park, there's a tea room, *Kawiarnia Krakowiak* (daily 10am–9pm) where you can get delicious homemade Polish–Brazilian cakes, light meals and superb locally produced vodkas.

To get to the park, take the yellow #182 or #183 bus going to Abranches (a suburb with a high concentration of Poles) from Praça Tiradentes and get off at the **Portal**

Polaco, a huge concrete structure extending over the road leading north out of town. Alternatively, take any bus that goes to the Palácio Iguaçu, a massive complex of state government buildings bordering the park. You can enter via a back gate and then follow the footpaths through the wood to the museum.

A short distance north of the park is the **Universidade Livre do Meio Ambiente**, hardly a university in the traditional sense but more a park and exhibition centre promoting environmental awareness. Established in 1991 as one of the centrepieces of Curitiba's self-proclaimed status as the "environmental capital of Brazil", the grounds – a former quarry – are certainly an attractive place for a stroll. The "university's" building (daily 8am–8pm) is visually striking – it forms an arch and aims at evoking the four elements of fire, earth, wind and water – and hosts stimulating exhibits on themes such as the regeneration of the Atlantic forest, recycling and alternative forms of energy. The easiest way to get there is to catch a bus marked "Bosque Zaninelli" from Praça Tiradentes.

On the other side of town is the **Jardim Botânico** (daily 8am–8pm), another high-profile project promoting the city's green image. Also created in 1991, in the formal style of a French garden, the Jardim Botânico is still in its infancy, its limited attraction being its flowerbeds and the small Museu Botânico. To get to the gardens, take any bus from Praça Tiradentes marked "Jardim Botânico".

Eating, drinking and nightlife

Given Curitiba's prosperity and its inhabitants' diverse ethnic origins, it's not surprising that there's a huge range of **restaurants**. What is strange, however, is that although *Curitibanos* take eating out very seriously, there are few genuinely excellent restaurants. Snacking on cakes in the excellent **cafés** is a good alternative. There's a fair amount of evening **entertainment**, too, based around the usual bars, cinemas and theatres.

Restaurants

Acrótona, Rua Cruz Machado 408. A cheap Brazilian restaurant where the speciality is unusual soups. Evenings only.

Alpendre, Av. Visconde do Rio Branco 1046. The best of the city's Portuguese restaurants, right in the centre of town. Expensive.

Bologna, Rua Carlos de Carvalho 1367. Most of Curitiba's Italian restaurants are concentrated in Santa Felicidade (see p.520); this is one of the few close to the downtown area. The moderate-to-expensive food is quite good – if somewhat pretentious – and served in pleasant surroundings. Closed Sun evening and all Tues.

Le Boulevard, Rua Voluntarios da Pátria 539. By far the best French restaurant in the city, with prices to match, in a somewhat vulgar atmosphere. Closed Sat lunch and all Sun.

A Camponesa do Minho, Rua Padre Anchieta 978, Mercês. A good Portuguese restaurant, but fairly expensive as many of the dishes are based on imported dried cod (*bacalhau*). Closed Sun lunch and all Mon.

Estrela da Terra, Rua Lycio de Castro Velloso 180, Mercês. An excellent and moderately priced restaurant, providing *Paranaense* cooking at its most refined, although everything is served with the ubiquitous semi-dry beans and pork rind. On Sunday an excellent buffet lunch is served. Tues–Fri lunch only; closed Sun evening and all day Mon.

Galleria Schaffer, Rua XV de Novembro 416. There are two restaurants here in an attractive turn-of-the-century building, also housing an arts cinema. Good value, though somewhat dull Brazilian and "international" meals, snacks and desserts. Being right in the city's commercial centre, this is a useful and pleasantly quiet spot to relax over lunch.

Green Life, Rua Carlos Carvalho 271. An unimaginative but inexpensive vegetarian restaurant located downtown; closed Sun.

A Landerna, Rua Padre Agostinho 690. Just across the road from the youth hostel in Mercês, this is a very good, though fairly expensive pizzeria. Mon–Sat evenings and Sun lunch.

Mali, Rua Francisco Torres 427. Large portions of Japanese food at very reasonable prices and located within walking distance of the centre; closed Mon.

Mineira Gostosa, Rua Mateus Leme 491. An inexpensive self-service restaurant with a range of typical Minas Gerais dishes.

Oriente Arabe, Rua Ébano Pereira 26. Central and cheap, offering large helpings of simple, but fairly good, Lebanese food.

Tung Lok, Rua Prudente de Morais 175. Acceptable and moderately priced Chinese food. Closed Mon.

Verão Natural, Rua João Negrão 150. Curitiba's other vegetarian restaurant, on a par with the *Green Life*. Lunch only, closed Sat.

Warsóvia, Av. Batel 2059. Inexpensive traditional Polish dishes, out of the centre in Batel, a southern suburb reached by bus from Praça Tiradentes. Closed Sun evening & all day Mon.

Cafés and tearooms

Modern Paraná was founded on coffee and European immigrants, and one result in Curitiba has been a profusion of old world-style cafés and tearooms, most concentrated on the Rua das Flores. Virtually unchanged in style and clientele since opening in the 1920s (elderly ladies and gentlemen in ill-fitting grey suits predominate) are the *Confeitaria Schaffer* (at no. 424), the *Confeitaria das Famílias* (no. 372) and the *Confeitaria Cometa* (no. 410), at all of which the coffee's good, the tea's bad and the cakes are sticky. For superb cakes, it's well worth making the trek out to the Bosque João Paulo II where there's an excellent Polish tearoom, the *Kawiarnia Krakowiak* by the entrance (see p.517). For a pre-dawn coffee or snack, you can always join the crowds at *Rua 24 Horas* (see p.516).

Bars

During the late afternoon and early evening locals congregate in the pavement cafés at the Praça Osório end of Rua das Flores, but as the evening progresses the historic centre comes to life, its **bars** and restaurants attracting a mainly young and well-heeled crowd. On Praça Garibaldi, and the streets extending off it, there are numerous bars, many with **live music** – typically Brazilian rock music, jazz and what seem to be parodies of country-and-western.

Cinema and theatre

Films reach Curitiba fast, and details of the latest releases are found in *Bom Programa*, a weekly events leaflet distributed by the tourist office and most hotels. There are two good arts cinemas showing non-Hollywood productions, the Cine Groff in the Galleria Schaffer, Rua das Flores 424, and the Cine Ritz in the same street.

During the winter, the Teatro Guaira at Praça Santos Andrade, across from the Federal University, has a varied schedule of **theatre**, **ballet** and **classical music**. With three excellent auditoriums, the Guaira is justified in its claim of being one of the finest theatres in Latin America and is often host to companies from the rest of Brazil, and even international tours.

Listings

Airlines Transbrasil, Rua Mal. Deodoro 410 (☎382-1234); Varig, Rua XV de Novembro 614 (☎322-5535); VASP, Rua XV de Novembro 537 (☎221-7422).

Car rental Interlocadora (☎322-4322); Localiza (☎253-0330); Unidas (☎322-4000).

Consulates Austria, Rua Mal. Floriano Peixoto 228 (☎224-6795); France, Av. Paraná 968 (☎253-4249); Germany, Av. Joâo Gualberto 1237 (☎252-4244); Italy, Rua Atilio Borio 680 (☎262-4042); Netherlands, Rua Mal. Floriano Peixoto 96, Sala 172 (☎222-0097); Switzerland, Av. Sete de Setembro 6780 (☎244-4363); UK, Rua Pres. Faria 51 (☎322-1202).

Exchange Main offices of banks are concentrated at the Praça Osório end of Rua das Flores. The travel agents on Rua XV de Novembro are convenient for changing travellers' cheques (try Jade Turismo at no. 477).

Hospitals In emergencies use the Pronto-Socorro Municipal at Av. São José 738 (☎262-1121). Otherwise, go to Nossa Senhora das Graça at Rua Alcides Munhoz 433 (☎222-6422).

Laundry There's a self-service laundry on the corner of Trajano Reis and Treze de Maio, near Praça João Cândido in the historic quarter.

Market Every Sunday (9am–3pm), at Praça Garibaldi in the historic centre, there's a handicraft market but you're unlikely to find anything terribly distinctive amongst the hippyish jewellery and leather items.

Post office The main office is at Rua XV de Novembro 700, by Praça Santos Andrade.

Shopping Several stores in the historic centre sell *Paranaense* crafts, especially African-influenced wood-carvings from the coast. The Centro do Artesanato Paranaense, Alameda Dr Muricy 950, has a good general selection. However, Polish and Ukrainian items are as "typical" a souvenir of Paraná as you're likely to find. For Ukrainian crafts, Vecelko, Rua Brigadeiro Franco 898, midway between the youth hostel and city centre, sells simple embroideries and intricately painted eggs. Artesanato Tipico Polonês, in the Bosque Joâo Paulo II, also sells Polish items, including painted eggs. There's a surprisingly good selection of handicrafts, T-shirts and other souvenirs available at the airport.

Telephones Next to the main post office on Praça Santos Andrade and in small kiosks along Rua das Flores.

Women's organization Contact the Conselho Municipal da Condição Feminina, Rua Claudino dos Santos 104, in the historic centre. There is an excellent feminist bookstore on the second floor of the Galleria Schaffer, Rua XV de Novembro 416.

Around Curitiba

Apart from heading down to the coast (see "Bay of Paranaguá", p.522) there are several places easily reachable by bus that are well worth seeing on day trips from Curitiba. On the city's outskirts, **Santa Felicidade** is near enough to visit for an evening, to eat at one of the many Italian restaurants there, while **Lapa**, a small colonial country town 80km southwest of the city is a pleasant place to go for a typical *Paranaense* Sunday lunch. **Araucária** offers interesting insights into Polish pioneer life, while just under 100km west of Curitiba is **Vila Velha**, home of a strange rock formation that's the basis of a state park.

Santa Felicidade

Now almost an outer suburb of Curitiba, about 8km northwest of the city, **SANTA FELICIDADE** was founded as a farming colony in 1878 by Italians transferred from failed coastal settlements and by newly arrived immigrants from northern Italy. Only the oldest inhabitants still speak the language of their immigrant forebears and Santa Felicidade now has little Italian feel to it; the European legacy is essentially that of grape and wine production, culinary traditions and periodic music and folk-dancing festivals. Across the road from the church there's an interesting **cemetery**, dating from 1886, but the only real reason to visit Santa Felicidade is for the **restaurants** which line the main road, Avenida Manoel Ribas, alongside shops selling plants, wicker items, wine and other produce of the local smallholders.

The restaurants compete fiercely for the custom of Curitiba's *nouveaux riches*, each vying to surpass the next in vulgarity – it's easy to think you're entering the kind of lavish motel Brazilians surreptitiously check into. As far as the food goes, in theory most varieties of Italian regional cooking can be found, but it's best to avoid those claiming to specialize in Sicilian or Neapolitan dishes and instead try those with no particular regional claim. These places generally offer the northern Italian food in which the local cooking is rooted. Don't expect the same style of food (not to say wine, made from locally grown American grapes) that you may have tasted in Italy. Dishes have been adapted according to the availability of ingredients and the results are, at best, an interesting blend of local Brazilian and Italian influences – rustic dishes as eaten by the *colonos* themselves. At worst, they're simply poor imitations of Italian cooking. Whether in a restaurant decked out to look like a pseudo-Italian *palazzo*, a medieval castle or somewhere less pretentious, charges remain much the same: about $7 per person for the *rodízio di pasta*, a continuous round of pasta, salad and meat dishes.

Yellow **buses** to Santa Felicidade can be caught on Travessa Nestor de Castro, at the intersection of Rua do Rosário, just below Curitiba's historic quarter; the journey out along Avenida Manoel Ribas takes about 45 minutes.

Lapa

Also worth visiting for culinary reasons, if for little else, is **LAPA**, a sleepy provincial town founded in 1731 on the trail linking Rio Grande do Sul to the once important cattle market in Sorocaba. It's only because Lapa is one of the very few towns in Paraná's interior that has made any efforts to preserve its late eighteenth- and early nineteenth-century buildings – though they're of no great architectural interest – that the town has become a favourite place for Sunday excursions from Curitiba.

Four blocks behind the *Rodoviária*, Lapa's main church, the **Igreja Matriz de Santo Antônio**, dominates the principal square, Praça General Carneiro. Built in the late eighteenth century, but reformed over subsequent years, the church's interior displays – all too typically – no original features. However, there are several small museums of mild interest, most notably the **Museu de Epoca** (Tues–Sun 1.30–5pm), an early nineteenth-century house furnished in period style, on Rua XV de Novembro 67, opposite the Panteon dos Herois. The **Museu de Armas** (Sat & Sun 9–11.30am & 1–5pm), on the corner of Rua Barão do Rio Branco and Rua Henrique Dias, in a house of the same period, contains a poor collection of nineteenth-century weaponry.

It's to sample **Paranaense cooking**, rare in Curitiba itself, that makes Lapa really worth a visit. A few metres uphill from the *Rodoviária* at Av. Manoel Pedro 1855 is the excellent *Lipski Restaurante*, and behind the bus terminal is the cheaper, but similarly good, *Restaurante Santa Rita*, at Rua Barão do Rio Branco 1240. There are ten **buses** a day between Curitiba and Lapa covering the 80km in less than an hour; if you want to **stay** over, your best bet is the *Pousada da Lapa*, Av. Manoel Pedro 2069 (☎041/822-1422; ②).

Araucária

The ethnic group most often asociated with Paraná are the Poles who settled in tightly knit farming communities around Curitiba in the late nineteenth and early twentieth centuries. Poles came to Brazil in three main waves: the smallest number between 1869 and 1889, the largest during the period of so-called "Brazil fever" that swept Poland and Ukraine between about 1890 and 1896, and the next largest contribution in the years just before World War I. Most of the Poles settling in the vicinity of Curitiba arrived in the 1880s with subsequent immigrants settling further afield in south-central Paraná.

Well into the twentieth century, the Polish community was culturally isolated, but as Curitiba expanded, absorbing many of the Polish settlements, assimilation accelerated and today the lives of most *Paranaenses* of Polish origin is indistinguishable from their non-Polish neighbours. In recent years, however, there has been a tremendous revival in interest in people's Polish heritage, and wherever there are large concentrations of Poles, children are encouraged to join Polish language classes, and folk dance and music groups are being established to preserve folk traditions.

One small town within easy reach of Curitiba that is making a strong effort to promote and preserve elements of the Polish immigrant heritage is **ARAUCÁRIA**, situtated some 30km south of the state capital. In most respects, a thoroughly unremarkable agricultural processing town, Araucária has made particular efforts to record its history. Within walking distance of the town centre is the **Parque Cachoeira**, a large recreational area with a small lake, dotted with distinctive *Araucária* (Paraná pine) trees that once characterized the region's landscape. The park is the location of the **Museu da Mata e Imigração Polonêsa** (closed Mon), an outdoor musuem that serves as a tribute to the area's first Polish settlers who arrived in 1886. The museum, resembling a small village, is similar to the one in Curitiba's Bosque João Paulo II, but larger. Abandoned buildings from outlying parts of this largely rural *município* have been transported to the park and renovated and, so far, the village consists of early pioneer log cabins, a granary, chapel and school, as well as a pig pen, bee hive and various agricultural implements. There's an excellent book and gift store, and traditional Polish food is available.

Buses leave Curitiba's Praça Rui Barbosa for the 45-minute journey to Araucária hourly. **Tourist information** and details of special cultural events in and around Araucária are available from the very active Secretaria Municipal de Cultura e Turismo at Praça Dr Vicente Machado 25 (Mon–Fri 9am–noon & 2–6pm; ☎041/843-1300).

Parque Estadual de Vila Velha

At **Vila Velha** stand 23 rock pillars, carved by time and nature from glacial sandstone deposits, and looking from a distance like monumental, abstract sculptures. The sandstone formation is a result of sand deposited between 300 and 400 million years ago during the Carboniferous period, when the region was covered by a massive ice sheet. As the glaciers moved, the soil was affected by erosion and the ice brought with it tons of rock fragments. When the ice thawed, this material remained, and as natural erosion took its course and rivers rose, these deposits were gradually worked into their current formations.

The **Parque Estadual de Vila Velha** (daily 8am–6pm) is 97km, an hour and a half by **bus**, from Curitiba. From the city's *Rodoviária*, take a *semi-direito* bus (roughly every two hours) to Ponta Grossa and ask to be let off at the park's entrance, a half-hour walk from the rock formations. If you're lucky, the driver may enter the park itself, leaving you only a few metres from the beginning of the area where you can wander between and above the fantastically shaped stones and in the partially wooded section behind. Views over the surrounding countryside from here are tremendous. There's a small entrance charge to the park, but it gets you a detailed map, an elevator-ride into a crater-lake (located 4km away from the pillars) and use of the **swimming pool** – a welcome relief from the midday heat since, at an altitude of 1000m, the sun is deceptively strong.

In the park there are a couple of simple **restaurants**, but apart from a **campsite**, there's no overnight accommodation available. However, there are good late afternoon bus services back to Curitiba, so there's no chance of being left stranded. If you're travelling on to Iguaçu, there's no need to return to Curitiba: instead, take a bus the 20km to Ponta Grossa from where you can catch an overnight bus to Foz do Iguaçu.

The Bay of Paranaguá

Sweeping down from the plateau upon which Curitiba lies, the **Serra do Mar** has long been a formidable barrier separating the coast of Paraná from the interior. Until 1885 only a narrow cobblestone road connected Curitiba to the coast and the **Bay of Paranaguá**, and it took two days for carriages to cover the 75km from what was, at the time, the main port, **Antonina**. In 1880, work began on the construction of a **rail line** between Curitiba and **Paranaguá**. Completed in 1885, this remains a marvel of late

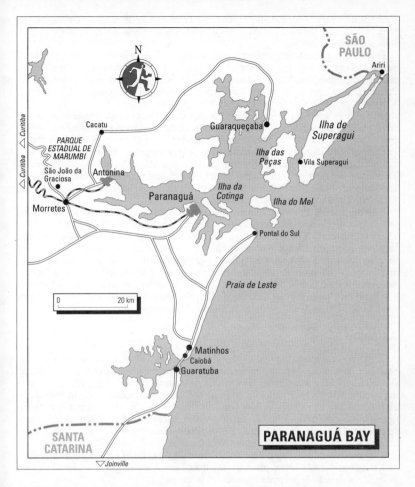

nineteenth-century engineering and the source of much local pride, as it is one of the country's few significant rail lines developed with Brazilian finance and technology. Sufferers from vertigo be warned: the line grips narrow mountain ridges, traverses 41 bridges and viaducts and passes through 14 tunnels as the trains gradually wind their way down to sea level (see below for details of schedules). Passing through the **Parque Estadual de Marumbi**, on a clear day the views are absolutely spectacular, and the towering Paraná pines at the higher altitudes at the beginning of the journey and the subtropical foliage at lower levels are unforgettable.

If the fight to save the Amazon rainforest is now on, that for the **Mata Atlântica**, the Brazilian Atlantic forest, today covering barely three percent of its original area, has been all but lost. But the forbidding terrain of Paraná's Serra do Mar has provided limited natural protection from exploitation by farming and lumbering interests and, since 1986, legal protection for a wider area has been granted by the state government. In theory, the region's future development must serve the needs of local communities, but the regulations are being blatantly flouted, most persistently by ranchers and plantation owners in remote regions. It remains to be seen to what extent the *Paranaense* coastal zone will remain unspoilt.

There are regular passenger **trains** from Curitiba's *Rodoferroviária* to the coast daily during December, January and February and on Wednesday, Saturday and Sunday during the rest of the year. The train leaves at 7am, arriving at Morretes at 10.15am and at Paranaguá at 11.20am; the return train departs Paranaguá at 4.30pm and Morretes at 5.38pm, arriving in Curitiba at 8.20pm. It's advisable to buy tickets in advance ($9 return). There's also an air-conditioned tourist train, the *Litorina*, stopping at scenic points daily in January and February, and on Saturday, Sunday and holidays during the rest of the year. It departs Curitiba at 9am and arrives in Morretes at 11.25am and in Paranaguá at 12.15pm; it leaves Paranaguá at 3.30pm and Morretes at 4.15pm to arrive in Curitiba at 6.35pm. At the weekend, there's also a *Litorina* service to Antonina. Tickets for the *Litorina* ($16 return) must be purchased several days before and only hand luggage can be carried. For the best views, sit on the left-hand side going down to the coast and on the right when returning.

If timing doesn't allow you to travel by train to the coast, take a **bus** from Curitiba which follows the Graciosa road (2 daily), a route almost as beautiful as the rail line's. There are also hourly buses between Curitiba and Antonina and Paranaguá by the new highway (journey time approximately 1hr 30min); many people return by bus rather than on the train. Buses between Guaraqueçaba and Curitiba take six hours (2 daily), and between Guaraqueçaba and Paranaguá four hours (2 daily), both services going via Antonina. If travelling to or from Santa Catarina, Curitiba can be avoided by taking a bus between Paranaguá and Guaratuba (15 daily, most via Pontal do Sul for access to the Ilha do Mel), and another between Guaratuba and Joinville.

Antonina

An important port until the mid-1940s, **ANTONINA** has all the atmosphere of a town that has long since become an irrelevance. As ships grew larger and access to Antonina's harbour was restricted by silt, the town abandoned its role as Paraná's main port and entered a long period of stagnation. Due to its decline, many of Antonina's eighteenth- and nineteenth-century buildings have largely been saved from the developers, leaving the town with a certain dilapidated, backwater charm. With neither masterpieces of colonial architecture, nor beaches immediately accessible, the town attracts few other than Sunday visitors from Curitiba. Nonetheless, along with its much smaller neighbour, Morretes, Antonina is the most pleasant of Paraná's coastal towns, and is a considerably better place to stay than Paranaguá, only a 45-minute bus ride away. It also has an important *Carnaval*.

The **Rodoviária** is located right in the town centre. Turn right onto Rua XV de Novembro, the main commercial thoroughfare, and walk two blocks, past once-elegant nineteenth-century merchants' houses, then one block along Rua Vale Porto to reach Antonina's main square and evening meeting point, **Praça Coronel Macedo**. From the **train station** turn right and right again onto Rua Cons. Alves de Araujo, which leads to the square. The **tourist office** is at Rua XV de Novembro 150.

On Praça Coronel Macedo is the town's principal church, **Nossa Senhora do Pilar**. Imposing rather than interesting, the church dates back to 1715 and is built in typical Portuguese colonial style. Its interior has sadly been completely remodelled and preserves no original features – removed and sold abroad, say locals, by priests from the United States who are attached to the church and run the town's radio station. Across from the church, at Praça Cel. Macedo 214, is Antonina's oldest house, which is of late seventeenth-century origin.

If you want to **stay**, the *Hotel Regency Capela* (☎041/432-1357; ④), built amid the ruins of an eighteenth-century Jesuit mission right on the main square, is worth a splurge, especially if you want a pool. If you're not tempted, directly opposite on the same square is the comfortable and much cheaper *Hotel Monte Castelo* (②).

As for **meals**, avoid the *Regency Capela*'s extremely mediocre "international" restaurant and go instead to one serving seafood or the regional speciality, **barreado**, a dish only available on the *Paranaense* coast and most easily found in Antonina. Barreado used only to be eaten by the poor during *Carnaval* as it can provide food for several days and requires little attention while cooking. Traditionally, it's made of beef, bacon, onion, cumin and other spices, placed in successive layers in a large clay urn, covered and then "*barreada*" (sealed) with a paste of ash and *farinha* (manioc flour); and then slowly cooked in a wood-fired oven for twelve to fifteen hours. Today pressure cookers are often used (though not by the better restaurants), and gas or electric ovens almost always substitute for wood-fired ones. *Barreado* is served with *farinha* which you spread on a plate; place some meat and gravy on top and eat with banana and orange slices. In Antonina excellent *barreado* (as well as good seafood) is found at the *Restaurante Maré Alta*, Rua XV de Novembro 122. For lunch try the excellent food stalls in the municipal market by the *Rodoviária*, serving fresh seafood at very low prices.

Morretes

MORRETES, a small colonial town founded in 1721, lies 16km inland of Antonina at the headwater where the Rio Nhundiaquara meets the tidal waters of Paranaguá Bay. Buses constantly pass Morretes on their way between Curitiba and Antonina, and Antonina and Paranaguá, but it's an unremarkable place noted only for its production of excellent *cachaças*, and for *fandango*, a local dance introduced into the area during Spanish colonial times. However, Morretes is a good base for visiting the Parque Estadual de Marumbi. You can get park information from the **tourist office** in the Casa Rocha Pombo, Largo José Pereira 43 .

There are two **hotels** in Morretes, the nicer of which is the *Nhundiaquara Hotel*, Rua Carneiro 13 (☎041/464-1228; ②), picturesquely positioned on the river in the town centre. With less character, but more expensive and with air conditioning, is the *Porto Real*, Rua Visconde do Rio Branco 85 (☎041/462-1228; ③). As well as sampling the excellent local *cachaças*, you can eat extremely well in the town's **restaurants**, mostly specializing in seafood and *barreado*. For the best *barreado*, try the *Nhundiaquara Hotel* or the *Casa do Barreado* on Largo José Pereira. For similar regional dishes in slightly more elegant surroundings, there's *Armazém Romano*, Rua Visconde do Rio Branco 144.

Parque Estadual de Marumbi

The original **Graciosa trail** (*Caminho Colonial da Graciosa*), constructed between 1646 and 1653 to link Curitiba with the coast, passes through the **Parque Estadual de Marumbi** alongside the newer road, and is slowly being reclaimed from the forest. A network of other trails provides stunning views on clear days, and there's a wealth of flora and fauna in this, one of the largest and least spoilt stretches of Mata Atlântica (Atlantic forest). If you're travelling by car, the Graciosa road takes you through the park, with rest areas, picnic tables and fire grills.

From Morretes, there's a **bus** to the village of São João de Graciosa, a two-kilometre walk from the park's entrance; if you're coming directly from Curitiba, get off the train at the Marumbi stop. At the park entrance you can pick up a trail map and information about the very basic **camping sites**; the only site hereabouts that's equipped with any kind of facilities is in São João. In any case, it's not the best spot to camp because of the heavy rainfall and mosquitoes which are characteristic of the entire region. If you don't camp, you're best off staying either in Morretes or in São João's only **pousada** (②), situated on the main road through the village. In the park itself there are no places to eat, but São João sports numerous small **restaurants** and bars.

Paranaguá

Propelled into the position of Brazil's second most important port for exports within a couple of decades, **PARANAGUÁ** has now lost most of its former character, becoming just another victim of the Brazilian "miracle". It was founded in 1585, and is one of Brazil's oldest cities, but only recently have measures been undertaken to preserve its colonial buildings. While both Antonina and Morretes boast less of interest than Paranaguá, they have at least remained largely intact and retain instantly accessible charm. Paranaguá doesn't, though what is worth seeing is conveniently concentrated in quite a small area, allowing you the possibility of spending a few interesting hours between boats, trains or buses.

The **train station** is three blocks from the waterfront on Avenida Arthur de Abreu. Inside the building is a very helpful **tourist office** which has useful maps of the city, hotel lists and boat, bus and train information. The **Rodoviária** is located on the waterfront, a few hundred metres beyond the Jesuit college. Both bus and train stations are only a few blocks from Paranaguá's historic centre, and in walking from one to the other you'll pass most of what's worth seeing of the city. Left out of the train station, it's three blocks or so to Rua XV de Novembro. Here, on the corner, is the **Teatro da Ordem**, housed in the very pretty former **Igreja São Francisco das Chagras**, a small and simple church built in 1741 and still containing its eighteenth-century Baroque altars. Along Rua XV de Novembro is the **Mercado Municipal do Café**, a turn-of-the-century building that used to serve as the city's coffee market. Today the Art Nouveau structure contains handicraft stalls and simple restaurants serving excellent and very cheap seafood.

Just beyond the market, Paranaguá's most imposing building, the fortress-like **Colégio dos Jesuítas**, the old Jesuit college, overlooks the waterfront. The *colégio* has had an unfortunate history. In 1682 the Jesuits were invited by Paranaguá's citizens to establish a school for their sons, and sixteen years later construction of the college began. Because it lacked a royal permit, the authorities promptly halted work on the college until 1738, when one was at last granted and building recommenced. In 1755 the college finally opened, only to close four years later with the Jesuits' expulsion from Brazil. The building was then used as the headquarters of the local militia, then as a customs house, and today is home to the **Museu de Arqueologia e Etnología** (Tues–Sun noon–5pm). The stone-built college has three floors and is divided into 28 rooms and a yard where the chapel stood, until it was destroyed by a fire in 1896. None of the museum's exhibits relates to the Jesuits, concentrating instead on prehistoric archeology, Indian culture and popular art. The displays of local artefacts are of greatest interest, and there are some fine examples of early agricultural implements and of the basketry, lace-making and fishing skills of the Tupi-Guarani Indians, early settlers and *caboclos*.

Away from the waterfront, in the area above the Jesuit college, remaining colonial buildings are concentrated on Largo Monsenhor Celso and the roads running off it. The square is dominated by a cathedral that dates from 1575 but which has since suffered innumerable reforms. On nearby Rua Conselheiro Sinimbu is the charming, little **Igreja São Benedito**, a church built in 1784 for the use of the town's slaves, and one that is unusual for not having been renovated. Beyond the church is the **Fonte Velha** or **Fontinha**, a mid-seventeenth-century fountain, and Paranaguá's oldest monument.

Practicalities

In the end, though, Paranaguá remains basically a place to pass through – it's worth getting details about leaving immediately you get here, and only later setting out to explore the city. If you find you have no alternative but to spend a night, there are several inexpensive and centrally located **hotels**. The *Hotel Litoral* at Rua Correiade Frietas 65 (☎041/422-0491; ①) is excellent value and just a few blocks back from the waterfront. More comfortable (and more expensive) hotels nearby include the *Monte Líbano* at Rua Júlia da Costa 152 (☎041/422-2933; ③) and the *Karibe* on Rua Fernando Simas (☎041/423-4377; ②). **Restaurants** specialize in seafood and the best two are the *Restaurante Bobby* at Rua Faria Sobrinho 750 (closed Mon evening) and, with a waterfront view, *Restaurante Danúbio Azul* at Rua XV de Novembro 95. Alternatively, for lunch only, try the excellent and inexpensive seafood restaurants in the Mercado Municipal do Café.

For information about **boat departures** ask at the fish market below the Jesuit college. Every morning, fishermen from all around the bay land their catches in Paranaguá and it's usually possible to find boats returning to most points (see "Guaraqueçaba", p.529). Keep a careful eye on the weather as storms blow up quickly, making crossings uncomfortable and potentially dangerous, as few boats carry lifejackets. Apart from short tourist excursions from the new municipal market near the bus station, the only **scheduled boat service** from Paranaguá – and one which does pay heed to safety – is for Guaraqueçaba, stopping off at the Ilha das Peças and at the Ilha de Superagüi; departures are in the early afternoon on Wednesday and Friday.

The Ilha do Mel and the southeast coast

To the east of Paranaguá are Paraná's main beach resorts, principally attracting visitors from Curitiba seeking open sea and all the familiar comforts of home. The surrounding countryside is relentlessly flat and the beaches can't really compare with those of Santa Catarina or, for that matter, most other parts of Brazil. There is, however, one notable exception, the Ilha do Mel, which, despite being Paraná's most beautiful island, has been protected from tourism's worst effects by being classified as an ecological protection zone – building is strictly regulated and the sale of land to outsiders is carefully controlled.

The Ilha do Mel

The **Ilha do Mel** is reached by hourly buses from Paranaguá or Guaratuba to **PONTAL DO SUL** (where you'll find the *Hotel Jhonny*, at the bus stop, if you're stuck); the last bus stop is the beach, where small boats depart. If travelling by car, there are private parking areas where you can safely park for a charge of $8 per day. As there are no shops on the island, it is worth coming well supplied with a flashlight or candles (electric current is available for only a few hours a day), mosquito coils, fruit and fruit juices. The **boat crossing** to Encantada (also refered to as Prainha) or Nova Brasília, the only villages on the island, takes between twenty and forty minutes, with the last boats in both directions at about 6pm ($2). If you miss the last boat, it's easy to find a small launch to take you to the island at a charge of $20–25 for the ten-minute crossing. These boats can take up to four passengers and there are always people around to share the costs with.

ENCANTADA is the smaller of the two settlements but the one that attracts most of the day-trippers. Apart from fishermen's clapboard houses, all there is to Encantada is some **bars**, three or four **pousadas** offering basic but good-value accommodation (②–③), a few simple but excellent restaurants, a campsite and a police post. In a sheltered position facing the mainland, it can feel rather claustrophobic due to the mountains all around, but only minutes' walk behind the village on the east side of the island is the **Praia de Fora** where powerful waves roll in from Africa.

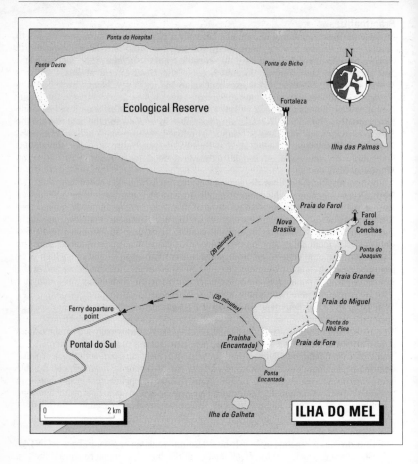

Livelier than Encantada, but lacking the intimate fishing-village atmosphere, is
NOVA BRASÍLIA, where the bulk of the island's 1200 inhabitants are concentrated.
Stretched between two gently curving, sheltered bays on a narrow strip of land linking
the flat western section of the island to the rugged, smaller, eastern portion, this is the
area of the island where most tourist facilities (such as they are) are located. Close to
the jetty where the passenger boats land, there's a **campsite**, the ecological station, a
police, medical and telephone post, and beyond this an immense beach along which are
several *pousadas*, **restaurants** and **bars** which are crowded with young people in the
evenings. These are not always immediately visible, as many are hidden along paths
leading from the beach, up to a 45-minute walk from Nova Brasília's "centre". For a
pleasant and undemanding stroll, wander along the beach towards the ruins of
Fortaleza, the Portuguese fort (built in 1769 to guard the entrance of the Bay of
Paranaguá), in the opposite direction from the clearly visible lighthouse.

If you plan to visit in the height of summer, it's best to arrive during the week and as
early as possible in the morning as **accommodation** is scarce. There's only one genuine **hotel**, the *Park Hotel Ilha do Mel* (☎041/223-2585; ⑤) out towards Fortaleza – they

will send a boat to Nova Brasília to take you directly to the hotel. Following the trail leading from the jetty, one of the first **pousadas** is the justly popular *Pousadinha* (☎041/978-3662; ③). The young, multilingual employees are friendly, and rooms are simple but comfortable. A little further along the trail another excellent possibility, the *Pousada das Meninas* (☎041/978-2872; ③), is more intimate but otherwise similar. The owner, Suzy, speaks some English and, if you gather together a small group, her husband will take you to outlying islands with his motorboat.

The most beautiful part of the island is the series of **beaches** along its mountainous southeast side, between Encantada's Praia de Fora and the lighthouse at Nova Brasília – an area of quiet coves, rocky promontories and small waterfalls. It takes about three hours to walk between the two settlements but, because of the need to clamber over rocks separating the beaches, the journey is best undertaken at low tide. As the tide comes in, be extremely careful on the rocks: it's easy to slip or get pulled into the ocean by a wave. Let someone where you're staying know where you're going to, and carry a bottle of water (there's a clean mountain stream about halfway for a refill) and enough money to be able to return by boat if need be. If you're carrying too much luggage to walk between Encantada and Nova Brasília, it's usually easier and cheaper to return to the mainland and pick up another boat from there rather than wait for a boat going directly between the two settlements.

The southern Paranaense coast

In contrast to the Ilha do Mel, it's hard to find anything positive to say about the rest of the **southern Paranaense coast**, except that it's easy to get to it from Curitiba, thus making it a popular location for second homes for the city's inhabitants. Twenty kilometres south of Pontal do Sul is the first such resort, **PRAIA DE LESTE**, attracting families and campers. **MATINHOS**, 20km further down the coast, is Paraná's surfing capital and, during the summer months, **hotels** here are expensive – though, in any case, they tend to be fully booked. If you're stuck, however, the *Casarão* (②) and the *Beira-Mar* (②), both on Rua Reinoldo Schaffer, and the *Praia e Sol* on Rua União (②), are the cheapest hotels in town and worth a try.

Ten kilometres further south down the coastal road, and a ten-minute ferry ride from Caiobá, across the entrance of Guaratuba Bay, is **GUARATUBA** itself, Paraná's most upmarket resort. The best beaches are only accessible by car or private boat, so unless you enjoy being surrounded by luxury hotels and multistorey apartment buildings, Guaratuba offers little but the buses going to and from Santa Catarina.

Guaraqueçaba and its islands

North of Paranaguá, directly across the bay, lies Guaraqueçaba, Paraná's poorest and fifth-largest *município*. With 55 isolated settlements, a few poor roads and a widely scattered population of only 10,000 (including a few surviving Tupi-Guarani Indians, sometimes seen by roadsides selling basketware), Guaraqueçaba's mountainous interior, coastal plain and low-lying islands give the authorities huge administrative headaches. The only town, also called **GUARAQUEÇABA**, is really only visited by the most dedicated of fishing enthusiasts and people interested in the conservation zone which, in theory at least, encompasses ninety percent of the *município*. Guaraqueçaba is marked by a tremendous feeling of isolation, connected as it is to the outside world only by sea and an unpaved and severely potholed road, which winds about the interior for the convenience of the *latifúndios*. The owners – usually São Paulo-based corporations – are illegally cutting down the forest, most of which falls within the Guaraqueçaba conservation zone, for development as buffalo pasture or banana and *palmito* plantations. Isolation apart, the town's lack of beaches, its one **hotel**, the air-conditioned but cockroach-infested *Hotel Guarakessaba* on the waterfront (☎041/482-1217; ②), two very plain **restaurants** (the *Barbosa* is slightly preferable to the *Guarakessaba*), and rain that seems to pause only long enough to enable mosquitoes to breed, do little to encourage visitors.

None of the town's buildings bears witness to the fact that, in the seventeenth century, Guaraqueçaba was a more important port than Paranaguá. Nor, apart from the former banana producers' co-operative building (now headquarters for APA, the regional environmental protection body, Rua Dr Ramos Figueira 3), do more than a few buildings remain from its heyday between 1880 and 1930 when ships sailed from here to Europe and the River Plate laden with bananas and timber. Today, a shadow of its former self, the port is used only by local fishermen and by boats belonging to the ecological station and municipal authorities, which are used to visit otherwise inaccessible parts of the *município*. In the APA building, there's a fascinating small **museum** depicting the history of the *município*; reproductions of the paintings of William Michaud, a settler from Switzerland, provide vivid images of the area in the nineteenth century.

Boats and islands

The only scheduled **boat services** are run by the *município*; precise times are available at the *prefeitura* (☎041/482-1222) and you would be wise to confirm the schedule before going to Guaraqueçaba. If there are no municipal boats for your destination, ask at the waterfront whether a fishing boat's heading there. Alternatively, it's easy, but very expensive, to charter a boat. Though rare, good weather is highly desirable for exploring this, one of the more inaccessible and least spoilt parts of Brazil's coastline, but what is absolutely essential is plenty of time, patience, mosquito repellent and anti-mosquito coils for overnight stays. You may get stuck somewhere for days if there are storms.

Twice a week (Wed & Fri at 5am) a boat makes the crossing to Paranaguá, stopping off at the **Ilha das Peças**, which forms part of the Parque Nacional de Superagüi and is noted for its marine and Atlantic forest birds. You can be let off on the island and collected again later in the day on the boat's return journey (though confirm that the boat will in fact collect you).

The other regular service is a fortnightly boat to **ARIRI** (first and third Thursday of the month, returning the next day), a small fishing village just within Paraná on the border with São Paulo. On this extremely rewarding trip, the boat stops off at **VILA FATIMA**, a tiny settlement on the northwest coast of the island of Superagüi (see below), before passing through the **Canal da Varadouro**, a long, narrow mangrove-fringed channel. Ariri is only a very short boat-trip from **ARARAPIRA**, a village just inside the state of São Paulo, from where another boat leaves the following day (though schedules are extremely fluid) for Cananéia and Iguape.

An occasional boat service also links Guaraqueçaba with the island of **Superagüi** and its village, **VILA SUPERAGÜI**, but as departures depend on the islanders' medical needs, the village is more easily reached by fishing boat from Paranaguá. In the mid-nineteenth century, Superagüi was the site of a Swiss farming colony led by William Michaud which, not surprisingly given the subtropical climate and soil utterly unsuitable for cultivation, soon collapsed. Today, the island's inhabitants depend, rather more sensibly, on fishing for their livelihoods. By asking around, it's easy to find **accommodation** either with a family or in the one basic *pousada*, but in a village where tourism is still hardly known, don't expect much comfort.

On the east side of the island, just a short walk from the village, is **Praia Deserta**, a beach stretching 34km which, despite its name, boasts a total population of three. It's probably safe to camp on the beach, but isolation does have its risks, so unless you are in a group, ask villagers where you should pitch your tent.

South-central Paraná

The hilly – and in places almost mountainous – region of **south-central Paraná** makes a good stopover between Curitiba and Iguaçu Falls for anyone interested in European, especially **Ukrainian**, immigration. As none of the towns in the region are especially distinctive, it's better to use them more as bases from which to visit nearby villages and hamlets where the pioneering spirit of the inhabitants' immigrant fore-bears remains. The houses, made of wood and sometimes featuring intricately carved details, are typically painted in bright colours and are usually surrounded by flower-filled gardens. Because of the ethnic mix, even small villages contain **churches** of sev-eral denominations; most hamlets have at least a chapel with someone on hand to open it up to the rare visitor.

Prudentópolis and around

The administrative centre of a *município* where 75 percent of the inhabitants are of Ukrainian origin, **PRUDENTÓPOLIS** is heralded as the capital city of Ukrainian Brazil. However, in common with the other regional urban centres, there's little in the city of Prudentópolis to indicate the ethnic background of most of its citizens.

UKRAINIANS IN PARANÁ

In the late nineteenth and early twentieth centuries, European and North American com-panies were contracted to construct a rail line linking the state of São Paulo to Rio Grande do Sul. As part payment, large tracts of land were given to the companies and, as in the United States and the Canadian West, they subdivided their new properties for sale to land-hungry immigrants who, it was hoped, would generate traffic for the rail line. Some of the largest land grants were in southern central Paraná, which the companies quickly cleared of the valuable Paraná pine trees that dominated the territory. Settlers came from many parts of Europe, but the companies were especially successful in recruiting **Ukrainians**, and between 1895 and 1898, and 1908 and 1914, over 35,000 immigrants arrived in the Ukraine's "other America". Today, there are some 300,000 Brazilians of Ukrainian extraction, of whom eighty percent live in Paraná, largely con-centrated in the southern centre of the state.

As most of the immigrants came from the western Ukraine, it's the Ukrainian Catholic rather than the Orthodox Church that dominates – and dominate it certainly does. Throughout the areas where Ukrainians and their descendants are gathered, domed churches and chapels abound. While the Roman Catholic hierarchy, in general, is grad-ually becoming sensitive to the need to concentrate resources on social projects rather than in the building of more churches, new Ukrainian Catholic churches are proliferat-ing in ever more lavish proportions. In Brazil, the **Ukrainian Catholic Church** is extremely wealthy, and its massive landholdings contrast greatly with the tiny properties from which the vast majority of the poverty-stricken local population eke out a living. Priests are often accused of attempting to block measures which will improve conditions: they are said to fear that educational attainment, modernization and increased prosperi-ty will lessen the populace's dependence on the Church for material and spiritual com-fort, so reducing their own influence.

The Ukrainians' neighbours (*caboclos*, Poles, Germans and a few Italians and Dutch) fre-quently accuse them and their priests of maintaining an exclusiveness that is downright racist in character. While inter-communal tensions are easy to detect, the few non-Brazilian visitors to this part of Paraná are treated with the utmost civility, and if your Portuguese (or Ukrainian) is up to it you should have no problem finding people in the region's towns and hamlets who will be happy to talk about their traditions and way of life.

Blonde heads and pink noses do predominate, but if you're expecting plump, Tolstoyesque peasants wearing elaborately embroidered smocks and chatting to one another in Ukrainian against a skyline dominated by gold- or silver-domed eastern-style churches, or have a craving for cabbage rolls, *borscht* and *pirogies*, you'll be extremely disappointed.

At a glance, Prudentópolis is much like a thousand other nondescript small towns in the interior of southern Brazil. At the heart of the city is a large Roman (not Ukrainian) Catholic church set in a park-like square totally disproportionate in size to the town. The surrounding buildings are the usual mix of anonymous breeze-block and concrete-slab municipal buildings, houses, *lanchonetes* and small stores. Still, committed Ukrainophiles should not despair. A closer look around town will reveal some traces of the Ukraine: many of the older houses bear a resemblance to peasant cottages of Eastern Europe, in particular in the style of the window frames and roofs. As throughout the region, the Ukrainian Catholic Church displays a strong presence, most visibly in the form of the **seminary**, a large mustard-coloured building located next to the Ukrainian Catholic **Catedral** that overlooks the city centre. Across the road from the seminary is the church's printing press where Ukrainian-language propaganda is churned out on machinery that has remained unchanged since soon after the first Ukrainians arrived in Brazil. A few doors away is a stationery shop, whose Ukrainian owner sells simple, locally produced embroidery of classic Ukrainian design.

A couple of blocks from the main square is Prudentópolis' only **hotel**, *Hotel Lopes*, Av. São João 2595 (☎042/446-1476; ②), close to the town's sole **restaurant**, the *Churrascaria do Penteado*, at Rua Domingos Luiz de Oliveira 1378, run by a cheerful Hawaiian-clad Ukrainian Brazilian. If you need to change money, there's a branch of the Banestado in town, but you'll get better rates in Curitiba or Foz do Iguaçu.

It's a fairly simple matter to reach Prudentópolis, well served by **bus** from Curitiba (4 daily), Foz do Iguaçu (3 daily) and most nearby centres. However, as one of Paraná's largest and most sparsely populated *municípios*, travelling far beyond the city without a car is difficult. To see some of the rural environs, though, you could always take a **local bus** (2 daily) about 10km northwest of town to the village of **ESPERANÇA**, where there's a large domed church, and a school staffed by Ukrainian nuns; and then turn off the road and head north for 6km to **BARRA BONITA**, another extremely poor and overwhelmingly Ukrainian settlement.

Bairro dos Binos

While descendants of Ukrainian immigrants form the great majority of Prudentópolis' population, immigrants have arrived from elsewhere as well. Germans from Rio Grande do Sul bought up land vacated by Ukrainians moving into urban centres or north towards the Amazon. However, perhaps the strangest (as well as earliest) arrivals are the **French** of **BAIRRO DOS BINOS**. In 1858, 87 French families arrived in Brazil to form a farming community in what was then – and still is – an extremely isolated part of Paraná. After a few years the colony all but disintegrated, with only a few families remaining. Disappointingly, but not surprisingly, there remains barely the faintest trace of Bairro dos Binos' French origins – the odd family carrying French surnames, and some uncharacteristic stone houses of the early settlers.

Getting to Bairro dos Binos is very time-consuming; it's reached by a **bus** from Prudentópolis to **Teresa Cristina** (140km north), and then a ten-kilometre walk west. Still, the journey to Teresa Cristina is fascinating, with the road passing through isolated communities and mountainous terrain, while Bairro dos Binos itself is quite pretty. Aim to return to Prudentópolis on the same day, but if you don't, ask the priest at Teresa Cristina's church if he can help find a bed for the night.

Irati, Mallet and around

Smaller, and with a greater ethnic diversity than Prudentópolis to the north, **IRATI** and **MALLET** are not especially interesting in themselves, but both are useful jumping-off points for visiting the Ukrainian villages and hamlets nearby. The two towns are very similar in character, both straddling the rail line to which they owed their existence and growth during the first decades of the twentieth century. Mallet – smaller and generally less developed – is marginally the more attractive of the two, and its small Ukrainian Catholic Church is worth a visit, as is the train station which dates back to 1903.

Regular **buses** link Irati and Mallet with each other, as well as with União da Vitoria, useful if you're travelling to or from Santa Catarina; and there are three buses a day to and from Prudentópolis, and two to and from Curitiba. On weekdays, finding **accommodation** in Irati can be a problem, but if the *Hotel Colonial Palace*, across from the bus station (☎042/423-1144; ②) is full, try the *Hotel Luz*, Rua 15 de Julio 522: walk downhill to the end of the road, turn left and take the second right (☎042/422-1015; ①). In Mallet, there's always room at the *Hotel Brasil* (①), next to the bus station. As in Prudentópolis, **food** means meat, with *churrascarias* located near the bus stations of both towns.

Gonçalves Júnior

About 12km west of Irati, the small village of **GONÇALVES JÚNIOR** is well worth a visit if you want to get an idea of local rural traditions. Of the village's four **churches** (Lutheran, Roman Catholic, Ukrainian Catholic and Ukrainian Orthodox) the only one that deserves much attention is the Orthodox, which serves 24 local families. The small church, built in 1934, has an extremely beautiful interior featuring Orthodox icons, and a ceiling and walls bearing intricately painted traditional frescoes. From Gonçalves Júnior, take the Linha "B" road, along which there's a pretty chapel cared for by Ukrainian Catholic nuns. If you're walking to the chapel (allow at least an hour), you will no doubt come across plenty of *colonos*, Ukrainian-, Polish-, German-, Italian- and Dutch-speaking peasant farmers who live in the colourful wooden houses that front the dirt road, who will be happy to chat to you about their lives and those of their parents and grandparents.

Serra do Tigre

Without any doubt, the most interesting and most beautiful Ukrainian church hereabouts is in **SERRA DO TIGRE**, a small settlement south of Mallet. Built in 1904, the church, spectacularly positioned high upon a mountain-top near the heart of the village, is the oldest Ukrainian Catholic church in Paraná. In traditional fashion, the church was constructed totally of wood – including, even, the roof tiles – and both the exterior and the elaborately painted interior frescoes are carefully maintained as a state monument.

Almost all Serra do Tigre's inhabitants are of Ukrainian origin but, rather curiously, amongst them lives Dorothea Roepnack, a charming elderly American woman. Donna Dorothea, as everyone calls her, is making an admirable effort to preserve the forest around her home as a nature reserve, and it's one of the very few places in the area where **howler monkeys** still survive. If you do drop in on Donna Dorothea, watch out for her vicious guard dogs and the almost equally aggressive pet orphaned howler monkeys – and, if at all possible, leave her any books that you have finished with.

Getting to Serra do Tigre is not terribly easy. Immediately on arrival in Mallet, go to the *prefeitura* and ask for a lift to Serra do Tigre on the school bus, which departs very early in the morning and then again at about noon. Alternatively, take a bus the 10km from Mallet to **DORIZON** from where it takes about an hour to walk up the very steep hill to Serra do Tigre. The *Hotel Dorizon* is a spa resort with good food and a natural swimming pool (☎042/542-1272; ⑤).

The Iguaçu Falls and around

The **Iguaçu Falls** are, unquestionably, one of the world's great natural phenomena. To describe their beauty and power is a tall order, but for starters cast out any ideas that Iguaçu is some kind of Niagara Falls transplanted south of the equator – compared to Iguaçu, with its total of 275 falls that cascade over a precipice 3km wide, Niagara is a ripple. But it's not the falls alone that makes Iguaçu so special: the vast surrounding subtropical **nature reserve** – in Brazil the Parque Nacional do Iguaçu, in Argentina the Parque Nacional Iguazú – is a timeless haunt that even the hordes of tourists fail to destroy.

The Iguaçu Falls are a short distance from the towns of **Foz do Iguaçu** in Brazil, **Puerto Iguazú** in Argentina and **Ciudad del Este** in Paraguay – which makes the practical details of getting in and out that bit trickier. Foz do Iguaçu and Puerto Iguazú are both about 20km northwest of the entrance to the national park, while Ciudad del Este is 7km northwest of Foz do Iguaçu. Most tourists choose to stay in Foz do Iguaçu, much the largest of the three towns. It has the greatest choice of hotels, including the least expensive options, and is also well positioned midway between the falls and the casinos and tax-free shops in Ciudad del Este.

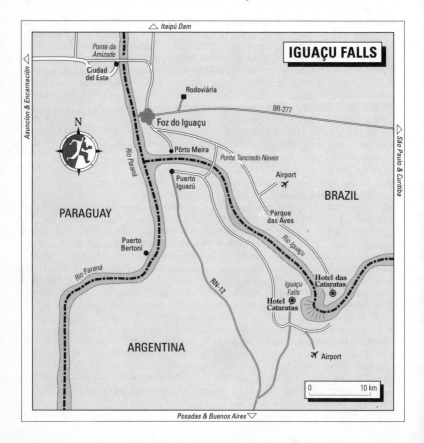

Foz do Iguaçu

The **airport** at **FOZ DO IGUAÇU** is served by flights from throughout Brazil and from Ascunción (Paraguay) and Buenos Aires (Argentina). Regular buses (5am–midnight) head to the **local bus terminal** in the centre of town on Avenida Juscelino Kubitschek. If you want to take a taxi, there's a desk in the arrivals hall where you purchase a fixed-price voucher ($18). Arriving by bus, Foz do Iguaçu's **Rodoviária** is located on the northern outskirts of town by the road to Curitiba and is served by buses from throughout southern Brazil, Ascunción in Paraguay and from as far north as Rio and Mato Grosso do Sul. Buses #01, #02 and #03 link the *Rodoviária* with the local bus terminal in town; taxis cost around $10.

Accommodation

Finding **somewhere to stay** in Foz do Iguaçu is easy, but it's likely to cost more than in other places in Brazil. Many of the **hotels**, including some of the best, are located some distance from town on the road leading to the falls, and most of the cheaper ones cater exclusively to shoppers bound for Paraguay. During the summer months, the town is generally very hot, but most mid-range hotels have air conditioning and pools. Outside the peak tourist months of January, February and July, most hotels offer substantial discounts, usually around thirty percent.

There's an excellent **campsite** run by the *Camping Club do Brazil* (☎045/574-1310) situated near the entrance to the *parque nacional*; at $10 per person, it's a little expensive but facilities are good (including a laundry area, clean swimming pool, and praiseworthy, inexpensive meals), and the experience of sleeping surrounded by jungle is unforgettable.

Hotel das Cataratas, Parque Nacional do Iguaçu (☎045/523-2266). The only hotel within the national park, discreetly located just out of sight from the falls. The rooms are comfortable and furnished with character. Even if you can't afford to stay here, you can wander around the hotel's grounds or, for $25, sample their wonderful buffet lunch featuring a vast range of Brazilian dishes. Reservations, through a Varig agent, are essential if you want to stay here. ⑦.

Dany Palace Hotel, Av. Brasil 509 (☎045/523-1530). No frills but prides itself on cleanliness. Centrally located. ③.

Hotel Diplomata, Av. Brasil 678 (☎045/523-1615). A large good-value hotel with pool. Rooms are spacious and all have minibar and colour TV. ④.

Hotel Internacional Foz, Rua Almirante Barroso 2006 (☎045/523-1414). The best hotel in town with all luxury facilities including a large pool, gift shop and nightclub. ⑥.

Pousada da Laura, Rua Naipi 629 (☎045/574-3628). Laura is incredibly friendly and her simple bed and breakfast-style accommodation has become a firm favourite for backpackers. $10 per person.

Hotel Master, Rua Mem de Sá 435 (☎045/523-1823). Right next to the local bus terminal, rooms are comfortable and well equipped for the price. ③.

Hotel Rafain Centro, Rua Marechal Deodoro 984 (☎045/523-1213). The rooms are large here, with balconies, and the service friendly. Ask for a room overlooking the pool at the rear of the building. ⑤.

Hotel Três Fronteiras, Av. Jorge Schimmelpfeng 605 (☎045/523-2202). Modern, clean and comfortable. The buses to Argentina and the Brazilian falls stop on this avenue. ④.

Pousada Verde Vale, Rua Rebouças 335 (☎045/574-2925). Well located for the local bus station, shops and restaurants, and open 24 hours. However, it's renowned for being hot and airless. Tolerable for a night or two. $10 per person.

Eating and drinking

Foz do Iguaçu is certainly no gastronomic paradise, but it's possible to **eat** reasonably well without paying too much. On Rua Marechal Deodoro there are numerous buffet-style restaurants offering good, standard Brazilian food where you pay by the weight of what you've put on your plate. Nearby, on Avenida Schimmelpfeng, at the intersection

with Rua Marechal Deodoro, the *Bier Kastell* is a lively beer garden where you can enjoy ice cold *chopp* and German-style sausage and other snacks. If you're really on a tight budget, follow the Ciudad del Este-bound shoppers to dinner.

There are also a number of decent, more upmarket restaurants. For reasonably priced and remarkably good Portuguese food try the *Restaurante Antônio Maria* at Rua Edmundo de Barros 391 (Mon–Sat dinner only, Sun lunch only), while for overpriced but otherwise acceptable Lebanese food, there's the *Carneiro de Ouro* at Rua Almirante Barroso 1741. On the same road, at no. 1717, is the *Cantina Santino Pezzi* in an attractive 1940s house, surely one of the oldest buildings in town. Avoid the soggy pizzas and other Italian dishes and go for the *surubi*, the excellent local freshwater fish; portions are easily enough for two people. A superb three-course meal for two, including drinks, will cost around $30. Most hotels have restaurants, but the only one worth trying is that of the *Hotel das Cataratas* in the national park, with an excellent buffet of Brazilian dishes for $25.

Listings

Airlines Transbrasil, Av. Brasil 1225 (☎045/574-3836); Varig/Rio-Sul, Av. Brasil 821 (☎045/523-2111); VASP, Av. Brasil 845 (☎045/523-2212).

Consulates Argentina, Rua Dom Pedro II 28 (☎045/574-2969); Paraguay, Rua Bartolomeu de Gusmão 777 (☎045/523-2898).

Exchange Dollars (cash or travellers' cheques) can be easily changed in travel agents along Av. Brasil in Foz do Iguaçu.

FISHING ON THE RIO PARANÁ

The upper reaches of the Rio Paraná are the home of one of the world's greatest fresh-water game fish, the **dourado**, a beautiful silver and gold fish with deep orange marking on its fins and tail. Known as the "golden salmon", these immensely powerful fish have long been popular with South American and European anglers alike. Similar in character to the better-known East African tiger fish, the migrating *dourado* is found as far north in Brazil as the Pantanal, but it's in the fast-flowing stretch of the Rio Paraná between Argentina and Paraguay around Iguaçu that the largest fish can be caught. *Dourado* are caught from boats positioned side on and allowed to drift with the current, and they weigh between 13 and 18 kg. The *dourado* season is from October to March, with the best time to fish being November, December and January.

A British-run company, Dourado Sports Fishing (☎045/523-2076), which operates out of Foz do Iguaçu's Cataratas Yacht Club, organizes well-equipped fishing trips in large, safe aluminium launches. For half a day (4 hours) on the river, including collection from your hotel and all fishing equipment and bait, the rate is $100 per person for a minimum of two people. A full day costs $150 and includes lunch. For fishing enthusiasts, basic accommodation is also available for an additional $40 per person in a small old fishing lodge on the Paraguayan side of the river, an hour from the club. The lodge has a large open terrace and a barbecue area and is surrounded by dense vegetation. It's a wonderful and easy way of experiencing the jungle close up. Advance reservations are essential for staying at the lodge and can be made in the UK with their London office (☎0181/563-1988) or in the US through Pan Angling (☎1-800/533-4353). Shorter fishing trips can be booked on the spot through hotels and travel agents in Foz do Iguaçu.

Post office Praça Getúlio Vargas near Rua Barão do Rio Branco.

Tourist offices At the airport (daily 9am–11pm), at the *Rodoviária* (daily 6am–6pm), on the Brazilian side of the Ponte Tancredo Neves (daily 8am–6pm); in town, at the local bus terminal (daily 9am–6pm), on Rua Barão do Rio Branco (daily 7am–10pm), and at Rua Almirante Barroso 1300 (Mon–Fri 9am–5pm).

Puerto Iguazú

If you want to avoid the crowds, **PUERTO IGUAZÚ** is a better place to stay than Foz do Iguaçu, especially if you're on a tight budget, as simple **hotels** are more pleasant on the Argentine side of the border. Near the bus terminal there are several basic, family-run hotels, including the recommended *Residencia Paquita*, at Av. Córdoba 731 (☎0757/20434; ②), and the *Residencial Arco Iris*, Curupi 152 (☎0757/20636; ②), which is particularly good value. Only a little more expensive, *Residencial King*, Av. Victoria Aguirre 916 (☎0757/20360; ③), has an attractive garden setting and a small pool. The best mid-range place, however, is the *Hotel Saint George* at Av. Córdoba 148 (☎0757/20633; ③), which has a pool. At the luxury end, the rather hideous *Hotel Internacional Iguazú* (☎0757/20748; ⑦) offers views of the forest or the falls. If you want to **camp**, use the good site at Puerto Canoas in the national park on the Argentine side (see p.540).

Puerto Iguazú is a sleepy town and what action there is takes place in the "down-town" **bars** on Avenida Victoria Aguirre. This being Argentina, **food** means meat, with a couple of excellent *parrillas* (grills), *Charo* and *La Rueda*, near the bus terminal on Avenida Córdoba.

There's a **tourist office** at Av. Victoria Aguirre 396 (daily 8am–8pm). Puerto Iguazú has daily **flights** to and from Buenos Aires, Cordoba and elsewhere in Argentina. Aerolíneas Argentinas, with an office on Avenida Victoria Aguirre y Eppens (☎0757/20237), also runs direct flights (3 weekly) to Rio at much cheaper rates than airlines operating out of Foz do Iguaçu. Puerto Iguazú's combined local and long-distance **bus terminal** is in the town centre with several daily departures to Buenos Aires and Posadas, near the Jesuit ruins of San Ignacio Miní.

Ciudad del Este and around

At first sight, **CIUDAD DEL ESTE** must rank as one of South America's more unpleasant cities. When it rains, the city is awash with mud and it can be dangerous to cross a road for fear of vanishing into one of the many potholes. In dry weather, the place is coated with a thick layer of red dust. Whatever the weather, Ciudad del Este's tax-free status is a magnet for Brazilian shoppers who travel from afar to purchase cheap electronic equipment and cigarettes. Most of the small, scruffy, bazaar-like shopping centres are on the main Avenida Monseñor Rodriguez, but the only item that you're likely to find worth buying is film. However, by late afternoon the Brazilians return to Foz do Iguaçu, and Ciudad del Este becomes tranquil.

The **bus terminal** is located just south of the centre, to which it is linked by local buses. If you arrive from Asunción or Encarnación after dark it makes sense to cross into Brazil the next morning. Buses between Foz do Iguaçu and Ciudad del Este (daily 7am–8.50pm) stop on Avenida Monseñor Rodriguez and the parallel Avenida Adrián Jara. Depending on traffic, it can take between twenty minutes and two hours to go from city centre to centre – heading out of Ciudad del Este, it's often faster to walk across the international bridge and pick up a bus heading into Foz do Iguaçu. Day and night there are taxis available for around $6. If you're just crossing for a day you need only wave your passport at the immigration officials, but otherwise remember to be stamped in or out of the respective countries. The Brazilian **consulate** is at Tenente Coronel Pampliega 337 (☎061/31-2309).

Ciudad del Este's **tourist office** is at the Paraguayan immigration post. Dollars, *pesos* and *reis* are all accepted in town, but if you're travelling further into Paraguay, you'll need Paraguayan **guaranies**, available at similar rates in *casas de câmbio* in Foz do Iguaçu, Puerto Iguazú and, in Ciudad del Este, on the main Avenida Monseñor Rodríguez. The **post office** is opposite the bus station at Alejo García and Oscar Rivas Ortellado (the Paraguayan postal service is much cheaper than the Brazilian or the Argentine).

If you need **accommodation**, there are two good hotels located opposite one another on Avenida Adrián Jara, near the intersection with Alejo Garcia. The *Mi Abuelo* (☎061/62373; ②) is friendly, quiet and has an attractive courtyard, and the *Convair* (☎061/62349; ④) is more impersonal but with air conditioning, TV and minibars. German-speakers may be attracted to the *Hotel Munich* (☎061/62371; ②) or the *Hotel Vienna* (☎061/68614; ②), both in Calle Emiliano Fernández, between Calle Miranda and Calle Morgelos; the two hotels are predictably clean and remarkably friendly. It's worth crossing into Ciudad del Este just for dinner: you can **eat** very well and inexpensively here, and Paraguayan beer is excellent. Like the shops, most restaurants are owned by Arab and east Asian immigrants and cater mainly for the shop owners. On Avenida Adrián Jara, the *Oriental* serves excellent Japanese food – the mixed tempura is particularly good value. Also check out the side roads, such as Calle Abay, where many of the smaller Chinese, Japanese and Korean restaurants are located. For more traditional Paraguayan offerings, try *Mi Ranchito*, an outdoor *parrilla* at the corner of Calle Curupayty and Avenida Adrián Jara.

Colonia Iguazú and Puerto Bertoni

If you're interested in agricultural settlement schemes, **Colonia Iguazú**, 41km west of the city in an area carpeted with soya fields and cattle pasture, deserves a visit. The prosperous Japanese community was established in 1960; to reach it take any Asunción-bound bus and get out at the Esso Servicentro where there's also an excellent restaurant serving Japanese food.

Definitely worth the effort is a visit to **Puerto Bertoni**, home of the late-nineteenth-century Swiss naturalist and ethnologist, Moises Bertoni. Bertoni's house and outbuildings are gradually rotting away in the jungle, as are the few mementos of his work held in the small museum. To get to Puerto Bertoni, you can take a launch, by prior arrangement, from Porto Meira, the old Brazilian ferry landing. At the Puerto Bertoni landing, there's a steep fifteen-minute walk up the river embankment along a jungle trail to get to the house. The trip lasts about three and a half hours and costs $45. Tickets are available from travel agents in Foz do Iguaçu or directly from the British organizer, Paraná River Safaris, based in Foz do Iguaçu's Cataratas Yacht Club (☎045/523-2076).

The falls

The **Iguaçu Falls** are formed by the Rio Iguaçu, which has its source near Curitiba. Starting at an altitude of 1300m, the river snakes westward, picking up tributaries and increasing in size and power during its 1200-kilometre journey. About 15km before joining the Rio Paraná, the Iguaçu broadens out, then plunges precipitously over an eighty-metre-high cliff, the central of the 275 interlinking cataracts that extend nearly 3km across the river. There is no "best time" to visit since the falls are impressive and spectacularly beautiful whatever the season. That said, the rainy season is during the winter months of April to July, and at this time the volume of water is at its greatest – but then the sky is usually overcast and the air, especially near the falls themselves, is quite chilly. By the end of the summer dry season, around March, the volume of water crashing over the cliffs is reduced by a third (only once, in 1977, did the falls dry up altogether), but even then there's no reduction in impact, with the added attraction of the rainbow effects from the splashing of falling water and the deep-blue sky.

Although many people arrive at Iguaçu in the morning and depart the same evening, the falls should really be viewed from both the Brazilian and the Argentine sides of the river: at least two days are needed to do them justice. Crossing the **frontier** to see both sides is easy, and if you're of a nationality that normally requires a visa to visit either Argentina or Brazil, you won't need one just for a day trip. If, however, you're not returning to Foz do Iguaçu or Puerto Iguazú the same day, you'll have to go through normal **immigration** formalities on either side of the **Ponte Presidente Tancredo Neves**, the bridge that crosses the Rio Iguaçu between the two towns.

The Brazilian side

The finest overall view of the falls is obtained from the Brazilian side, best seen in the morning when the light is much better for photography. You'll only need about half a day here, since although the view is magnificent and it's from here that you get the clearest idea as to the size of the falls, the area from which to view them is fairly limited.

From the local bus terminal in central Foz do Iguaçu, there are hourly **buses** (daily 8am–7pm except at 5pm) to the "Cataratas do Iguaçu", which cost around $2 and take about 45 minutes. Once there, entrance to the park costs around $6. Buses stop on the road beneath the renowned *Hotel das Cataratas* (see p.535), where you're only a couple of minutes' walk from the first views of the falls.

From the bus stop, there's a stairway which leads down to a 1.5-kilometre cliff-side **path** near the rim of the falls. From spots all along the path there are excellent views, at first across the lower river at a point where it has narrowed to channel width. At the bottom of the path, where the river widens again, there's a catwalk leading out towards the falls themselves. Depending on the force of the river, the spray can be quite heavy, so if you have a camera, be sure to carry a plastic bag. From here, you can either walk back up the path or take the elevator to the top of the cliff and the road leading to the hotel.

Every fifteen minutes or so you'll hear the extremely irritating buzzing from a **helicopter** flying overhead. It takes off from near the hotel, and offers seven-minute flights over the falls for about $50 or a 35-minute flight over the falls and Itaipu for $100. In recent years the helicopter has been the cause of a minor rift between Brazil and Argentina: the Argentines refuse to allow it to fly over their side of the falls as they rightly claim that it disturbs the wildlife.

The Argentine side

For more detailed views, and greater opportunities to experience the local flora and fauna at close range, Argentina offers by far the best vantage points. The falls on the Argentine side are much more numerous and the viewing area more extensive and this, combined with the fact that many people only visit the Brazilian side, means that you'll rarely be overpowered by fellow tourists. With a good eye, toucans and other exotic birds can be spotted, and brilliantly coloured butterflies are seen all about. In warm weather, be sure to bring your bathing gear as there are some idyllic spots to cool off in, beneath cataracts, in pools and the river itself.

Getting to the Argentine side of the falls from Foz do Iguaçu is straightforward enough, but if your time is very limited it makes sense to join an **excursion**, which most travel agencies and the better hotels organize. Otherwise, from Foz do Iguaçu's local bus terminal take a **bus to Puerto Iguazú** ($2; departures at least every half-hour 7am–9pm; 30min). From Puerto Iguazú's bus terminal, there are buses every hour ($5) which take thirty minutes to reach the park. At the park's entrance there's a fee of $5, and you'll be given a very useful map; the bus then continues on to the national park's visitors' centre. Bear in mind that the Argentine time is one hour behind the Brazilian, and that you'll need US currency or Argentine *pesos* (pegged on a one-to-one basis to the dollar) for the bus fare between Puerto Iguazú and the falls, snacks and drinks, and the Argentine park entrance charges.

The **visitors' centre** itself makes a good first stop and there's a small but useful **museum** focusing on the region's natural history. It's here that you'll have the best chance of seeing the extremely shy, and mainly nocturnal, forest animals – though they're all stuffed. From the centre, follow the **Circuito Inferior**, a walk that, with a few interruptions to admire the scenery, is likely to take a couple of hours. Despite not being as dramatic as the falls upriver, few parts of the park are more beautiful and the path passes by gentler waterfalls and dense vegetation. At the river shore, **boats** ($5 return) cross to the **Isla San Martín**, whose beaches are unfortunately marred by the streams of sand flies and mosquitoes present. One of the many enchanting spots on the island is **La Ventana**, a rock formation that's framed, as its name suggests, like a window. From here you can continue around the marked circuit, but, if you are at all agile, haul yourself instead across the rocks in front and behind La Ventana where, hidden from view, is a deep natural **pool** fed by a small waterfall, allowing some relaxing swimming.

The Argentine falls embrace a huge area, and the most spectacular spot is probably the **Garganta del Diablo** (Devil's Throat) at **PUERTO CANOAS**. The Garganta del Diablo marks a point where fourteen separate falls combine to form the world's most powerful single waterfall in terms of the volume of water flow per second. Catwalks lead into the middle of the river, but they are currently closed for renovation with no indication when they might reopen. However, for $5 you can take a 200-metre boat-ride to the old central viewing platform from where it's easy to feel that you will be swallowed by the tumbling waters. From Puerto Canoas there's no need to return to the visitors' centre, as there are frequent buses that link directly with Puerto Iguazú.

The forest

One of the remarkable aspects of the park is that visitors can gain access to a **tropical rainforest** without much difficulty and without posing a threat to people or nature. Even by keeping to the main paths around the falls, it's easy to get a taste of the jungle. The forest is home to over two thousand plant varieties, four hundred bird species, dozens of types of mammals and innumerable insects and reptiles. It's essentially made up of four levels of vegetation: a nearly closed canopy reaching over 35m; a layer of trees between 3 and 10m in height; a lower layer of shrubs; and a herbaceous ground level. In reality the levels are not so pronounced, as epiphytes and other plants inter-twine, at times creating a mass of matted vegetation.

Within the forest lives a rich diversity of **wildlife** species, but they are spread out over a wide area, are often nocturnal and are usually extremely timid. However, if you get up early, walk quietly away from other people and look up into the trees as well as towards the ground, you have a good chance of seeing something. Jaguars and mountain lions have been seen in Iguaçu, but they keep so well hidden and so few remain that realistically your chances of observing them are minimal. Around the water's edge, you may occasionally see **tapirs**, large animals shaped rather like a pig with a long snout. Smaller, but also with a pig-like appearance is, the **peccary**, dangerous when cornered, but shy of humans.

Far more common is the **coatimundi**, the size of a domestic cat but related to the racoon. Even on the main paths on the crowded Brazilian side of the falls, you often come face to face with coatimundi, begging food from tourists. The *caí*, or **capuchin monkey**, is also often seen and is recognizable by its long legs and tail, small size and black skullcap mark which gives it its name. These monkeys travel the forest canopy in large groups and emit strange bird-like cries. Far bigger and with a deep voice is the howler monkey. You may not see any, but you're likely to hear their powerful voices emanating from the jungle.

The forest is also home to a rich variety of **birdlife**, and with a good eye you should be able to see toucans, parakeets and hummingbirds even without straying from the main paths. Again, their most active hours are soon after dawn when it's cooler. For a more reli-able view of local birdlife, a visit to the **Parque das Aves** (daily 8.30am–6.30pm; $8) is highly recommended. Located just 100m from the entrance to the national park on the Brazilian side of the falls, the bird park maintains both small breeding aviaries and enor-mous walk-through aviaries, still surrounded by dense forest. Photo opportunities are tremendous, and, if you stand quietly on the paths leading between aviaries you may be able to spot the yellow and red beak of a toucan. There's also a large walk-through but-terfly cage – butterflies are bred throughout the year and released when mature. All the butterflies and eighty percent of the birds are Brazilian, most of them endemic to the Atlantic forests, the main exception being those in the Pantanal Aviary.

Expeditions into the forest are organized in both the Brazilian and Argentine parks, and hotels and travels agents sell tickets for the most basic of these. A typical trip lasts about two hours ($30) and involves driving by jeep along a rough dirt road, a walk down a narrow trail to the river and a wild boat-ride down some rapids or very close to a set of waterfalls. Don't expect to see any wildlife, apart from butterflies, but guides will point out some of the flora. On the Argentine side you can rent **mountain bikes** and will be given a map with which you can explore some of the trails. Also on the Argentine side, at Puerto Canoas you can rent an inflatable boat and float smoothly downriver 4km to the Puerto Tres Marinas. Expert guides are also available who can lead serious birdwatchers, botanists and photographers into the forest. The two most reliable expe-dition organizers are, on the Argentine side, *Iguazú Jungle Explorer* (☎0757/20295), based in the park next to the visitors' centre, and, on the Brazilian side, *Macuco Safari de Barco* (☎045/574-4244), also based in the park, 3km from the falls.

Itaipu

While there's complete agreement that Iguaçu is one of the great natural wonders of Brazil, there's bitter debate as to what **Itaipu** – the world's largest hydroelectricity scheme – represents. Work on the dam, 10km north of Foz do Iguaçu, began in the early 1970s at a cost of US$25 billion, and its eighteen 700,000 kilowatt generators became fully operational in 1991. Proponents of the project argue that the rapidly growing industries of southeastern Brazil needed nothing less than Itaipu's huge electrical capacity, and that without it Brazilian development would be greatly impeded. However, critics claim that Brazil neither needs nor can afford such a massive hydroelectric scheme and that the country would have been much better served by smaller and less prestigious schemes nearer to the centres of consumption. In addition, they point to the social and environmental upheavals that have been caused by the damming of the Rio Paraná and the creation of a 1350-square-kilometre reservoir: forty thousand families have been forced off their land; a microclimate with as yet unknown consequences has developed; and – critics say – the much-publicized animal rescue operations and financial assistance for displaced farmers barely address the complex problems.

Visiting Itaipu is easy, with hourly **buses** from Foz do Iguaçu's local bus terminal. You're dropped at the **Visitors' Centre** where a film about the project, in English and other languages, is shown, and from where **free guided tours** depart (Mon–Sat 6 daily; 1hr). The film is extremely slick and, until you stand on the dam and look across the massive reservoir stretching into the horizon, it's easy to be convinced by Itaipu's PR machine that the project was, at worst, no more than a slight local inconvenience.

SANTA CATARINA

Santa Catarina shares a similar pattern of settlement with other parts of southern Brazil, the indigenous Indians rapidly being displaced by outsiders. In the eighteenth century the state received immigrants from the Azores who settled along the coast; cattle herders from Rio Grande do Sul spread into the higher reaches of the mountainous interior around **Lages** and **São Joaquim**; and European immigrants and their descendants made new homes for themselves in the fertile river valleys. Even today, small communities on the **island of Santa Catarina**, and elsewhere on the coast, continue a way of life that has not changed markedly over the generations. Incidentally, to prevent confusion with the name of the state (though barely succeeding at times), most people call the island of Santa Catarina **Florianópolis**, which is actually the name of the state capital – also situated on the island. Elsewhere, cities such as **Blumenau** and **Joinville**, established by German immigrants, have become totally Brazilianized, but in the surrounding villages and farms many people still speak the language of their forebears in preference to Portuguese.

On the coast, tourism has become very important and facilities are excellent; in only a surprisingly few spots has the natural beauty been totally destroyed. Inland, though, visitors rarely venture, despite the good roads and widely available hotels. Here, with the minimum of discomfort, it's possible to get a sense of the pioneering spirit that brought immigrants into the interior in the first place – and keeps their descendants there.

The island of Santa Catarina

The **island of Santa Catarina** is noted throughout Brazil for its Mediterranean-like scenery, attractive fishing villages and the city of Florianópolis, the state's small and prosperous capital. The island has a subtropical climate, rarely cold in winter and with a summer heat tempered by refreshing South Atlantic breezes; the vegetation is much softer than that further north. Joined to the mainland by two suspension bridges (the longest, British-designed, has been closed for several decades to all but cyclists and pedestrians), the island is served by frequent **bus** services connecting it with the rest of the state, other parts of Brazil, Buenos Aires, Asunción and Santiago. During January and February the island is extremely popular with middle- and upper-

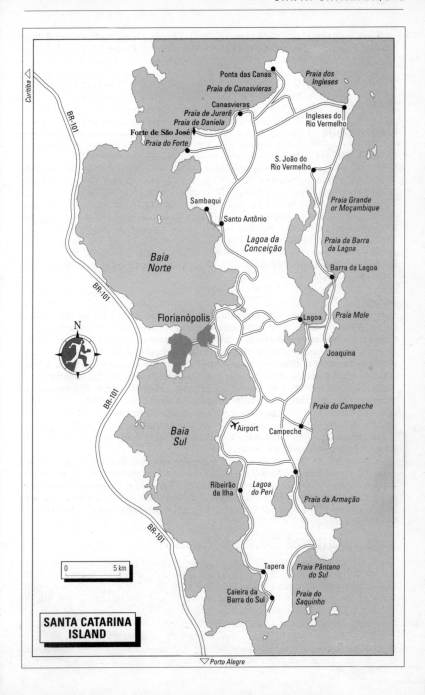

SANTA CATARINA ISLAND

> The **telephone code** for Florianópolis and the island of Santa Catarina is ☎048.

middle-class Argentine, Uruguayan and Paraguayan tourists who, during periods of favourable exchange rates, can enjoy a summer holiday here for much less than the cost of one at home.

Florianópolis

FLORIANÓPOLIS – or "Desterro" as it was originally called – was founded in 1700 and settled by immigrants from the Portuguese mid-Atlantic islands of the Azores. Since then, it's gradually developed from being a sleepy provincial backwater into a sleepy state capital. With the construction of the bridges linking the island with the mainland, Florianópolis as a port has all but died, and today the city thrives as an administrative, commercial and tourist centre. Land reclamation for a multi-laned highway and new bus terminals has totally eliminated the character of the old seafront and, with it, vanished much of the city's former charm. Despite all the changes, though, the late nineteenth-century pastel-coloured, stuccoed buildings still recall faint "old world" images, while the relaxed, small-town atmosphere provides a total contrast to the excitement of São Paulo or Rio.

Arrival

Buses arrive at the modern **Rodoviária** situated between the two bridges that link the island to the mainland. Outside the main entrance, beyond the car park and dual carriageway, is the former waterfront area where one of the **municipal bus terminals** is situated. From here, frequent buses set out for most parts of the city as well as to all points in the south of the island. Otherwise, buses to the northern and eastern beach resorts depart from the corner of Rua José da Costa Moelmann and Avenida Mauro Ramos, a fifteen-minute walk around the hillside. These buses run to a surprisingly accurate timetable (check times at the information booths) and are cheap, though generally crowded. Alternatively, from the terminal nearest to the *Rodoviária*, there are faster, more comfortable and more expensive minibuses to most of the beaches.

The **airport** is 12km south of the city and is served by taxis ($18) and "Aeroporto" buses, which take about forty minutes.

In Praça XV de Novembro, there's a **tourist information kiosk** (Dec–March Mon–Sat 7am–10pm, Sun 7am–7pm; rest of the year Mon–Sat 8am–6pm), where very good, free maps of the island and city are available. For **changing money**, travel agents in the Ceisa Center, a modern shopping mall on Rua Vidal Ramos, offer good rates for dollars and travellers' cheques. Banks are located on Rua Felipe Schmidt and by Praça XV de Novembro.

Accommodation

Try to arrive in Florianópolis early in the day as cheap **accommodation** is snapped up quickly during the peak holiday periods, and it's especially difficult to get a bed at the well-cared-for **youth hostel** at Rua Duarte Schutel 59 (☎222-3781; open year round). Many of the cheapest **hotels**, charging around $15, are located on, or just off, Rua Felipe Schmidt, only a few minutes from both Praça XV and the bus terminals. If you get really desperate, and don't have too strong an aversion to cockroaches, the *Dormitório da Ilha* (next to the *Colonial*) offers very basic accommodation.

Hotel Baia Norte, Av. Beira Mar Norte (☎223-3144). Pleasant rooms with balconies over the ocean, situated a short walk from good bars and restaurants. ⑤.

Hotel Cacique, Rua Felipe Schmidt 423 (☎222-5359). Always popular but difficult to get a room. Good for the price and location. ②.

Hotel Colonial, Rua Conselheiro Mafra 399 (☎222-2302). Simple, good-sized rooms, often none too clean, but the staff are friendly. ②.

Faial Palace, Rua Felipe Schmidt 603 (☎224-2766). Friendly old-style comfort near Praça XV de Novembro. ⑥.

Felipe, Rua João Pinto 26, at the intersection with Rua Antônio Luz (☎222-4122). The rooms here are clean and small, with ten percent discounts offered to youth hostel association card-holders. ②.

Florianópolis Palace, Rua Artista Bittencourt 2 (☎222-9633). The one five-star hotel in the city centre, with excellent facilities. The hotel has a minibus service to its private beach at Canasvieras. ⑦.

Hotel Ivoram, Av. Hercílio Luz 652 (☎224-5388). Good-value, though rather small rooms with mini-bars and TV. It's often full with Argentine package tourists. ⑤.

Hotel Majestic, Rua Trajano 4. Situated near the former markets, basic accommodation that's noisy and often full. ②.

Oscar Palace, Av. Hercílio Luz 760 (☎222-0099). Another favourite with Argentine tourists. Comfortable rooms and friendly service. ⑤.

The City

With the notable exception of *Carnaval* – rated as the country's fourth most elaborate, and certainly the liveliest south of Rio – few tourists visit the island for the limited charm and attractions of Florianópolis itself. However, being so centrally located, and with hotels much cheaper here than in the beach resorts, the city does make a good

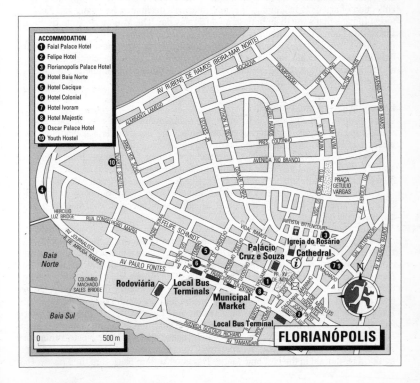

base for exploring the rest of the island, as most points are easily reached within an hour by bus. Take time, though, at least for a stroll around Florianópolis before heading out to the beaches.

On the former waterfront, you'll find the two ochre-coloured **municipal market and customs house** (*Alfândega*) buildings, now converted to contain good craft stalls, the official Ministry of Labour handicraft shop, an art gallery, the **Museu de História e Arte** and snack bars. From here, there's a steep walk up to the Praia de Fora, the "new town", centred on the main, tree-filled square, **Praça XV de Novembro**. On one side of the square is Florianópolis's main post office, and across from it is the **Palácio Cruz e Souza**, an imposing pink building built between 1770 and 1780 as the seat of provincial government. It's now open to the public as the **Museu Histórico de Santa Catarina** (Tues–Fri 10am–7pm, Sat 1–7pm, Sun 3–7pm) and, as there's no admission charge, it's worth taking a brisk walk around the building to admire the nineteenth-century interior decoration, rather than to examine the unexciting collection of guns, swords and official scrolls. Overlooking the square from the highest point is the utterly unremarkable **Catedral Metropolitana**; it was originally constructed between 1753 and 1773, but was enlarged and totally remodelled in 1922, so you'd be hard pressed to identify any original features. The only church in the city centre dating back to the colonial era, and retaining some of its original Portuguese Baroque architectural character, is the **Igreja de Nossa Senhora do Rosário**, higher up from the cathedral and best approached by a flight of steep steps from Rua Marechal Guilherme.

On the campus of the Federal University (UFSC), twenty minutes by bus from the city centre, the **Museu de Antropologia** (Mon–Fri 9am–noon & 1–5pm) has a small collection of artefacts belonging to Santa Catarina's decimated Kaingang and Xokleng forest Indians that's worth an hour or so on a rainy day. The **Museu de Arte de Santa Catarina** (Tues–Fri 9am–noon & 1–9pm, Sat & Sun 5–10pm), in the Centro Integrado de Cultura (reached by buses marked "Agronomica"), hosts permanent and temporary exhibitions by local and national artists of often dubious talent. The centre itself boasts an arts cinema showing less commercial films; a detailed programme is published in the *Jornal de Santa Catarina*.

Eating, drinking and nightlife

In the centre, on the roads which run off the main square in all directions, are numerous cheap, but largely uninspiring **restaurants**. The *Lanterna* is a fair attempt at a pizzeria, at Rua Esteves Júnior 63; and directly across the road the *Restaurante Nostra Damus* has a reasonable, so-called "international" menu. Good **vegetarian** meals are available at *Vida*, Rua Visconde de Ouro Preto 62 (closes Mon–Fri at 8.30pm, Sat at 3pm and all day Sun), and both *Sol da Terra*, Rua Nereu Ramos 13, and *Natural Familia Doll*, Rua Vidal Ramos 43a, also serve decent vegetarian meals, but close at 6pm. *Box 32* in the Mercado Público is a popular meeting point, serving cold beer and tasty snacks, especially fish (closed Sun).

Come evening, there's very little life in the commercial centre around Praça XV. Instead, people concentrate in the **bars and restaurants** that spread out along the **Beira Mar Norte** (or Avenida Rubens de Arruda Ramos as it is officially called), a dual carriageway that skirts the north of the city along reclaimed land starting at the Hercilio Luz bridge. Places move in and out of fashion rapidly and in summer you'll find that the bars – the first two of which are situated virtually under the bridge itself – are either packed solid with wealthy young people or, for no apparent reason, totally empty. Unfortunately there are no outstanding restaurants here either, but there is at least a fair choice, which is more than can be said for the commercial centre. Towards the far end of Beira Mar Norte (take any bus which reads "via Beira Mar Norte") there are several worth noting: on the avenue itself, the *Moçambique* is probably the best **seafood** restaurant in the city, and nearby two good **Italian** places are the *Pizzeria Don*

Pepe, Rua Bocaiúva 20 (closed Mon), and the *Macarronada Italiana*, Rua Bocaiúva 170. At no. 210 on the same road, the *Restaurante Kaffa* offers huge portions of good and very reasonably priced **Lebanese** food. Cold beer and hearty **German** dishes are available at the *Bierplatz* on Beira Mar Norte until late into the night. In the *Beira Mar Norte Shopping Center* (Mon–Sat 10am–10pm) there are a dozen fast food outlets including the usual hamburgers and some decent seafood; at *Batatas e Poemas*, you'll be treated to a poem written by the owner, for the price of a baked potato.

The rest of the island

Most people arriving in Florianópolis head straight for the beaches, undoubtedly the best of which are found on the **north** and **west** coasts. With 42 beaches around the island to choose from, even the most crowded are rarely unbearably so, and they're all suited to a few days' winding down. Despite the existence of a good **bus network**, this is one place where **renting a car** (ask at any travel agency) should be considered, especially if you have limited time and want to see as much of the island as possible: the roads are excellent and drivers fairly civilized.

The north coast

The island's increasingly built-up **north coast** offers safe swimming in calm, warm seas and, as such, is particularly popular with families. The long, gently curving bay of **CANASVIERAS** is the most fashionable of the northern resorts, largely geared towards wealthy *Paulista*, Argentine and Uruguayan families who camp or rent houses near to the beach. Most of the bars along the beach cater to the tourists, playing Argentine and North American pop music, and serving Paraguayan or Uruguayan beer far superior to Brazilian varieties – accompanied by Argentine snacks. By walking away from the concentration of bars at the centre of the beach, towards the east and Ponta das Canas, it's not too difficult to find a relatively quiet spot. Unless you're renting a house for a week or more (agencies abound), finding **accommodation** is difficult. However, by asking in the souvenir shops and restaurants you'll eventually be directed to someone with a spare **room to rent**. Otherwise, there are plenty of well-organized **campsites**, many of which – as throughout the island – rent out **cabins** suitable for two or more people. The local **restaurants** mostly offer the same menu of prawn dishes, pizza and hamburgers, with only the *Restaurante Tropical* and its Bahian dishes standing out as different.

Heading westwards, almost an extension of Canasvieras, from which it is separated by a rocky promontory, is **JURERÊ**, another long beach that also almost exclusively attracts families. Still further west, a series of coves fringed by luxuriant vegetation – reached by clambering down from the road skirting the coast; or by climbing over the rocks that separate one cove from another – link Jurerê to **DANIELA**, a smaller and less developed beach. Though it amounts to nothing special, the turquoise waters of the nearby coves are well worth the small effort needed to reach them; and **rooms** are available next to the *Lancheria Palheiro*. Roughly midway between Jurerê and Daniela, stunning views of the coast and across to the mainland can be appreciated from the ruins of the **Forte de São José** (usually referred to as Forte Jurerê), built in 1742 to guard the northern approaches to Desterro. Next to the fort there's a small eighteenth-century chapel.

The east coast

If you find the north coast too crowded and developed and the ocean too calm, head for the **east coast**, where Atlantic rollers scare away most of the families. Take extreme care yourself, though, as the undercurrents here make for dangerous swimming.

There are a couple of places to avoid. **PRAIA BRAVA** (the most northerly of the east coast beaches) is dominated by huge Argentine-owned condominium complexes that have resulted in this beautiful stretch of coast becoming the island's ugliest corner. Similarly, **INGLESES**, a little further south, is rapidly undergoing uncontrolled development and, as the sea is not too ferocious at this point, is fast becoming a downmarket alternative to Canasvieras. Instead, you're better off returning to Florianópolis and crossing the island to **LAGOA**, once a fishing hamlet but long since taken over by seafood restaurants, many of which are excellent. Lagoa is approached by a winding road from which there are truly breathtaking views across the **Lagoa da Conceição**, a large saltwater lagoon by which the village is situated. There's an excellent place to stop for lunch here, *Andrinus*, serving superb freshly caught fish. In contrast to Lagoa, **BARRA DA LAGOA**, at the entrance to the lagoon, has succeeded fairly well in allowing tourism to develop without destroying the inhabitants' traditional main activity – fishing. Azorean fishermen prepare their nets and launch their boats from the lagoon's narrow channel and Barra da Lagoa's beach, seemingly oblivious to the sunbathers and swimmers all around them. Barra da Lagoa has several **restaurants** (though not as good as Lagoa's), a good **campsite**, and there are also a couple of cheap **hotels** near the beach, a **youth hostel** (☎232-0169; open all year), and plenty of **rooms** to rent. If there's no space in the campsite or all the rooms are occupied, walk back along the road fronting the lagoon towards Lagoa and you're sure to come across empty rooms or campsite cabins. Stretching north for kilometres, Barra da Lagoa's beach at some point merges with Praia Grande (also known as Praia da Moçambique) and you don't have to walk too far to get away from the crowds.

South of Barra da Lagoa, the road climbs steeply, passing mountain-sized sand dunes to **PRAIA MOLE**, whose beautiful beach is slightly hidden beyond sand dunes and beneath low-lying cliffs. Mole has become extremely popular with young people but, rather surprisingly, commercial activity has so far remained low key. Approached by a road passing between gigantic dunes, the next beach is at **JOAQUINA**, always crowded with surfers, particularly so during the Brazilian national surf championships, held annually in the last week of January. Despite the crowds near the bars and restaurants, the beach stretches to the south, where it merges with **PRAIA DO CAMPECHE**, so by walking for fifteen minutes or so you can be almost alone. Accommodation here is limited, and the hotels by the beach itself are expensive and often full. On the whole the beach **restaurants** are good, though for a really superb (and expensive) meal go to the *Martim-Pescador* (closed Sun evening & Mon), on the approach road to Joaquina, which is noted for being one of the best seafood restaurants in southern Brazil.

Campeche, which merges into Morro das Pedras and Armação, is considered by many to be the most beautiful stretch of the island's coast. Due, however, to the strong current and often ferocious surf, fewer people are attracted here than to the beaches to the north. Consequently, there's been comparatively little building work, and only slowly are bars and beach houses appearing. For sleeping, there's the *Estalgem das Açores*, a very pleasant medium-sized hotel with a Portuguese feel to it, and a youth hostel (☎222-6746; open Dec 20–Feb 25), or you'll need a **tent**. If you're sleeping under the stars, be prepared for late night thunderstorms; you're unlikely to have any hassles camping wild, at least if there's a group of you.

South again, you reach **PANTANO DO SUL**, a small fishing village at the end of a well-protected bay with a mountainous backdrop. There are several restaurants, while for **accommodation** there's the very pleasant *Pousada Sol de Costa* (☎222-5071; ③) or it's down to asking around for a room. The village itself is not at all attractive, but the water is calmer than elsewhere on the east coast, the views of the small, offshore, uninhabited islands are pleasant and there are some fine bars in which to while away the hours. The *Restaurante do Arantinho*, next to the beach, offers a modestly priced daily special with a choice of fish or prawns, accommpanied by all the usual trimmings, but also *piráo de caldo de peixe*, a fish soup served with *farinha*.

The west coast

The principal places of interest on the **west coast** are **SAMBAQUI** and **SANTO ANTÔNIO** to the north of Florianópolis, and **RIBEIRÃO DA ILHA** to the south. As the island's oldest, most attractive and least spoilt settlements, the houses in these places are almost all painted white and have dark blue sash windows – in typical Azorean style – and each village has a simple colonial church. As was the case with most of the island's settlements, these villages were founded by immigrants from the Azores, and their present-day inhabitants – who still refer to themselves as being Azorean – retain many traditions of the islands from which their forefathers came. Fishing, rather than catering to the needs of tourists, remains the principal activity, and it is quite a spectacle watching their boats being prepared for sailing or returning with their catch. Azorean immigrants brought their lace-making skills to Santa Catarina, too, and intricately fashioned lace tablecloths, mats and other items are displayed for sale outside many of the houses – or you can buy them at the *Casa Açoriana*, Rua Cônego Serpa, in Santo Antônio. Because the beaches are small and face the mainland, tourism has remained minimal, the few visitors that are about on day trips from resorts elsewhere on the island. They stay just long enough for a meal: the *Restaurante Rosemar*, outside Sambaqui towards Santo Antônio, and the *Pizzeria Lisboa*, in Santo Antônio itself, both serve excellent seafood.

South of Ribeirão da Ilha, hugging the steep hillside as it passes tiny, deserted coves, the dreadfully pot-holed road leading to Barra do Sul runs through some of the most stunning scenery on the island. The rainfall here is extremely heavy, nurturing a profusion of rich foliage, most noticeably flamboyants and bougainvillaea.

If you choose to stay in the west coast villages, **finding a room** can be quite a problem and involves, as ever, some asking around. But you'll be rewarded by complete tranquillity of a kind lost to most of the rest of the island over the course of the last couple of decades.

Around Florianópolis: the mainland

On the mainland, 30km inland and southwest of Florianópolis, lies the small resort of **SANTO AMARO DA IMPERATRIZ** served by four buses daily from Praça da Bandeira. In the late nineteenth century, Imperatriz (the name commemorating the visit in 1845 of Brazil's emperor, Dom Pedro II and his wife, the Empress Teresa Cristina) was quite a fashionable spa town. The *Hotel Plaza Caldas da Imperatriz* (☎048/245-1333; ⑤ full board) was opened to celebrate the imperial visit, and for years afterwards succeeded in mimicking the European idea of the Grand Hotel, attracting wealthy Brazilians from as far away as Rio. Today most of the hotel's visitors are elderly *Catarinenses* and *gaúchos*, especially chronic sufferers of rheumatism and those with digestive or nervous disorders, though the baths are also open to non-guests on payment of a small fee.

A few kilometres up the narrow, tree-filled valley is another spa, the more recently developed **ÁGUAS MORNAS** and its luxury *Palace Hotel* (☎048/245-1315; ⑤ full board), favoured by the seriously rich. The spa itself is not particularly attractive, but the approach road and general setting are delightful.

Parque Estadual da Serra do Tabuleiro

For anyone with even a vague interest in the fauna of Santa Catarina, a visit to the nature reserve of the **Serra do Tabuleiro** is a must. Animals and birds from throughout the state live in as near to natural conditions as is possible, and endangered species are bred in the hope that they will eventually be returned to the wild. You'll see alligators, tortoises, twenty species of birds (including rheas, emus and flamingos – and even the odd lost penguin from Patagonia), anteaters and deer and, best of all, get no feeling that you're in, essentially, a zoo.

To get to the reserve from Florianópolis, take a **bus** (Empresa Paulo Lopez line, or any bus heading south along the main coastal highway, the BR-101) and ask to be let off at the entrance to the "Parque da Serra". From the park's entrance, it takes about half an hour to walk to the reserve. As the journey time there is about two hours, you'd do best to take the 7am or, at the latest, the 10.30am bus from Florianópolis; count on returning on the 2pm or 4.30pm bus. It's a tiring excursion, but well worth it.

The north coast to São Francisco do Sul

If you're going to travel on Santa Catarina's coastal highway (the BR-101) **north of Florianópolis** in the Brazilian summer you're best off keeping your eyes firmly closed. The bumper-to-bumper traffic moves at terrifying speeds, with cars, trucks and buses constantly leapfrogging one another for no apparent advantage; the wrecked cars that litter the highway are enough to make you get out of the bus and walk to your destination – something that, at times, might be faster anyway. But worse, if you don't have a car of your own, is that much of the BR-101 passes alongside absolutely stunning beaches, most of which are totally devoid of buildings and people. If you're on the bus, there's no hope of stopping for a refreshing dip, and you'll just have to make do with the idyllic images out of the window.

Porto Belo

Although the stretch immediately north of Florianópolis is probably the most beautiful part of the *Catarinense* coast, there's only one spot that is both easy to reach by bus and still not overrun by Argentine and *Paulista* tourists: the peninsula and city of **PORTO BELO**. With luck, it's less than two hours from Florianópolis, and although the local authority's claim that there are 32 beaches around Porto Belo is highly suspect, the beaches there certainly are numerous and large enough to cope with the visitors.

The "city" of Porto Belo is, in reality, just a small village containing a tourist office, post office and a couple of reasonable seafood restaurants, but from here frequent local buses fan out to **beaches** around the peninsula, stopping along the road to pick up passengers. The most attractive beaches are **Bombas** and **Bombinhas**, 5km and 8km east of Porto Belo respectively and separated from one another by a rocky promontory. The bay in which they're found is very pretty, with rich vegetation behind, and the waves here are suitable for inexperienced surfers. South of Bombinhas, for open sea and more powerful waves, the east-facing **Praia do Mariscal** is better, but should be braved by only the most expert of surfers. In complete contrast, the nearby **Praia do Canto** is ideal for anyone merely seeking a gentle swim.

All the beaches around Porto Belo are geared to **campers**, with sites mainly concentrated at Bombas and Bombinhas. Some of the campsites also rent out **cabins**, and at Bombas there are a couple of small, overpriced **hotels**, the cheapest of which is the *Bomar* (☎047/369-4136; ③). Expensive, but worth every *real*, is the *Pousada do Arvoredo* (☎047/369-2355; ⑥), on Praia de Bombinhas, which has accommodation in individual cabins, and a pool. Back in Porto Belo itself, try the *Hotel Baleia Branca* (☎047/369-4011; ⑤) or the more basic *Pousada das Flores* (☎047/369-4590; ③). However, at $10 a bed, the best bargain around is the **youth hostel** (☎047/369-4327), about ten minutes' walk away, on Av. Governador Celso Ramos 1442, the approach road to town. It has a very relaxed atmosphere, cooking facilities and no curfew.

Balneário Camboriú

Just 20km north of Porto Belo, but a world away from it in style, lies **BALNEÁRIO CAMBORIÚ**, Brazil's answer to Benidorm. It's got the lot, though you probably won't want any of it: high-rise hotels, a towel-sized patch of beach per person, and nightclubs which celebrate *"Carnaval"* all summer, with dance troupes imported from the tropical, more "exotic" Brazil to the north.

Stretching for 5km along the Avenida Atlântico, Camboriú is only a few streets deep. With the mountains behind the resort plunging almost straight into the sea, it's just about possible to imagine how beautiful it once was before the developers moved in, back in the 1930s. Today, there's precious little natural beauty still in evidence, but if you do want to stick around, there's rarely a problem finding a **room**. How much you'll have to pay is totally unpredictable and depends largely on the state of the economy in Argentina, where the overwhelming majority of the tourists come from. When the Argentine currency is strong, hotels can demand gold as payment; in other years rooms are almost given away in the hope that guests will at least run up a bill in the hotel's bar and restaurant. In theory, however, the cheapest hotels are near the *Rodoviária* (from where buses leave for just about every city in South America south of Rio), and on the streets set back from the beach. The **tourist office** (Dec–March daily 8am–8pm, April–Nov Mon–Fri 8am–noon & 2–6pm) with branches at Praça Papa João Paulo I 320 and Praça Tamandaré, provides helpful information on hotel availability, a list of the phenomenal number of **restaurants**, most of which only open between December and March, and the latest information on the constantly changing nightclub and disco scene.

Itajaí

Santa Catarina's most important port, **ITAJAÍ** is located at the mouth of the Rio Itajaí-Açu, 10km north of Balneário Camboriú. Although founded in the early eighteenth century, Itajaí only really started to develop in the mid-nineteenth century when surrounding parts of the state started to receive European immigrants who generated business for the port. Towards the close of that century, the town itself received a considerable influx of Italian and, to a lesser extent, German and Polish immigrants, whose – completely assimilated – descendants now make up the bulk of the population.

Despite its relative age, Itajaí looks fairly new, with few buildings dating back to before 1950 – and with nothing of any tourist interest. However, it's an important transport centre, and it may not be possible to avoid the city altogether. Fortunately, most buses pass straight by it, with only a minority actually stopping to pick up and put down passengers in the city. And as there's a constant flow of buses to Blumenau, Joinville and Florianópolis, as well as further afield in all directions, there are few reasons actually to stay in Itajaí. One reason might be to catch an early morning plane from nearby Navegantes **airport**, from where you can fly to Porto Alegre and São Paulo. To get to the airport, take the ferry from Avenida Argentina, across the river, and then a taxi; or, a little more expensive, taxis will take you direct from Itajaí, via the ferry, to the airport.

Should you need a **hotel**, there are a couple clearly visible from the *Rodoviária*: the *Itajaí Tur* (☎047/348-4600; ③–④) is convenient and has rooms of varying degrees of comfort. A few blocks away from the *Rodoviária* on the way to the centre, is the *Hotel San Remo* (☎047/348-0968; ③), offering basic accommodation. Downtown at Rua Felipe Schmidt 44, the *Grande Hotel* (☎047/348-3747; ④) is a comfortable, executive-style place.

If for some reason you really can't get out of Itajaí, and have some time to spare, the city's **beaches** aren't bad. From the local bus terminal in the city centre, near the intersection of Rua Joinville and Avenida Victor Konder, buses take about twenty minutes to reach the nearest beaches, **Atalaia** and **Geremias**, or a little longer to get to the cleaner **Praia Cabecudas**.

The Ilha de São Francisco

North of Itajaí, the highway gradually turns inland towards Joinville (see p.554), but 45km east of here is the **Ilha de São Francisco**, a low-lying island separated from the mainland by a narrow strait which is spanned by a causeway. As Joinville's port and the site of a major Petrobras oil refinery, it might be reasonable to assume that São Francisco should be avoided. However, this isn't the case. Both the port and refinery keep a discreet distance from the main town, São Francisco do Sul, and the beaches, and the surprisingly few sailors that are around blend perfectly with the slightly dilapidated colonial setting.

São Francisco do Sul

The island was first visited by European sailors as early as 1504, though not until the middle of the following century was the town of **SÃO FRANCISCO DO SUL** established. It's one of the oldest settlements in the state and also one of the very few places in Santa Catarina where colonial and nineteenth-century buildings survive concentrated together. During most of its first two hundred years, São Francisco do Sul was little more than a naval outpost, its simple local economy based on fishing and sugar cane production. In the nineteenth century, with the opening of nearby areas to immigrants from Germany, the town grew in importance as a transhipment point for people and produce. Merchants established themselves in the town, building grand houses and dockside warehouses, many of which remain today – protected from demolition and gradually undergoing restoration. Dominating the city's skyline is the **Igreja Matriz**, the main church, originally built in 1665 by Indian slaves, but completely reconstructed in 1884, losing all of its original features. You might want to visit the **Museu Histórico** (daily 9am–6pm) on Rua Coronel Carvalho, housed in São Francisco's nineteenth-century prison building (which, incidentally, stayed in use until 1968). The former cells have been converted into small exhibition halls; the most interesting exhibits are nineteenth-century photographs of the town. São Francisco do Sul is still one of the most important ports in southern Brazil and has been chosen as the location of the **Museu Nacional do Mar** (daily 9am–6pm). Located at Rua Manoel Lourenço de Andrade, the museum aims at being a research centre and is developing a collection relating to the technology of ocean travel and the people who make their living from the sea.

Most of the island's visitors bypass the town altogether and head straight for the beaches to the east, so, even in midsummer, there's rarely any difficulty in finding a **hotel** with room. Quite comfortable, and with sea views, is the *Hotel Kontiki* (☎047/444-0232; ③) at Rua Camacho 33, near the market. Eating out holds no great excitement, with the relatively luxurious *Hotel Zibamba* (☎047/444-0077; ⑤) at Rua Fernandes Dias 27 having the best **restaurant** of a generally poor bunch. Alternatively, on Praça Badeira, the *Restaurante Panaroma* sports – as you might expect – very nice views across the bay, which take your mind off the totally uninspiring meals of rice, beans and fried fish.

From the market in the town centre, there are **buses** to the *Rodoviária*, beyond the town's limits, from where there are hourly connections to Joinville as well as daily services to São Paulo and Curitiba. Travelling to Joinville, a more scenic, cheaper, less crowded and generally more civilized way is by **train**. The station, near the centre of town, no longer has regular services, but in the summer, special trains are laid on for tourists – you'll need to make enquiries on the spot.

The island's beaches

The prettiest beaches, **Paulos** and **Ingleses**, are also the nearest to town, just a couple of kilometres to the east. Both are small, and have trees to provide shade, and surprisingly few people take advantage of the protected sea, ideal for weak swimmers. On the east coast, **Praia de Ubatuba** and the adjoining **Praia de Enseada**, about 15km from town, are the island's most popular beaches, with enough surf to have fun but not enough to be dangerous. At Enseada there are a couple of **campsites** and an over-priced hotel, while Ubatuba caters mainly for families who rent or own houses that front the beach. By way of contrast, a ten-minute walk across the peninsula from the eastern end of Enseada leads to **Praia da Saude** (or just Prainha), where the waves are suit-able for only the most macho *surfista*.

Buses to Enseada and Ubatuba leave from the market in the town centre, with the last buses in both directions departing at about 9.30pm.

Northeast Santa Catarina

Although the northeast of Santa Catarina is populated by people of many ethnic origins, it's an area most associated with **Germans**, who so obviously dominate both cultural-ly and economically. **Joinville** and **Blumenau** vie with each other not only to be the economic powerhouse of the region, but also the cultural capital. However, both cities lose out in terms of tourist interest to the small towns and villages of the interior where old dialects continue to be spoken and survive. One such community is **Dona**

GERMAN SANTA CATARINA

In the nineteenth century, as it became more difficult to enter the United States, land-hungry European immigrants sought new destinations, many choosing Brazil as their alternative America. Thousands made their way into the forested wilderness of Santa Catarina, attempting to become independent farmers, and of all of them, it was the **Germans** who most successfully fended off assimilationist pressures. Concentrated in areas where few non-Germans lived, there was little reason for them to learn Portuguese, and as merchants, teachers, Catholic priests and Protestant pastors arrived with the immigrants, complete communities evolved, with flourishing German cultural organizations and a varied German-language press. After Brazil's entry into World War II, restrictions on the use of German were introduced and many German organizations were proscribed, accused of being Nazi fronts. Certainly, "National Socialism" found some of its most enthusiastic followers among overseas Germans, and though the extent of **Nazi activity** in Santa Catarina is a matter of debate, for years after the collapse of the Third Reich, ex-Nazis attracted sympathy in even the most isolated forest homesteads.

Later, due to the compulsory use of Portuguese in schools, the influence of radio and television and an influx of migrants from other parts of the state to work in the region's rapidly expanding industries, the German language appeared to be dying in Santa Catarina. As a result, in **Joinville** and **Blumenau** – the region's largest cities – German is now rarely heard. However, in outlying hamlets and villages such as **Pomerode**, near Blumenau, and **Dona Francisca**, near Joinville, German remains very much alive, spo-ken everywhere but in classrooms and government offices. Recently, too, the German language and Teuto-Brazilian culture have undergone a renaissance and the German government has provided financial support. Property developers are encouraged to heed supposedly traditional **German architectual styles**, resulting in a plethora of buildings that may be appropriate for alpine conditions, but look plain silly in the Brazilian sub-tropics. A more positive development has been the move to protect and restore the hous-es of the early settlers, especially those built in the most characteristic local building style, that of **enxaimel** ("Fachwerk" in German) – exposed bricks within an exposed tim-ber frame. These houses are seen throughout the region, concentrated most heavily in the area around Pomerode and Dona Francisca. Keen to reap benefits from the new eth-nic awareness, local authorities have also initiated pseudo-German **festivals**, such as Blumenau's Munich-inspired "Oktoberfest" and Pomerode's more authentic "Festa Pomerana", both of which have rapidly become major tourist draws.

Francisca, which is set amidst flat and fertile terrian dotted with attractive nineteenth-century farmhouses. Further into the hilly interior, **Pomerode** is set in a particularly attractive area and does much to promote its German heritage.

Joinville

An hour from São Francisco, the land on which **JOINVILLE** was settled was originally given as a dowry by Emperor Dom Pedro to his sister, who had married the Prince of Joinville, the son of Louis-Philippe of France. A deal with Hamburg timber merchants meant that, in 1851, 191 Germans, Swiss and Norwegians arrived in Santa Catarina, to exploit the 25 miles of virgin forest, stake out homesteads and establish the "Colonia Dona Francisca" – later known as Joinville. As more Germans were dispatched from Hamburg, Joinville grew and prospered, developing from an agricultural backwater into the state's foremost industrial city. This economic success has diluted much of Joinville's once solidly German character, but evidence of its ethnic origins remains: the largely Germanic architecture and the impeccably clean streets produce the atmosphere of a rather dull small town in Germany.

The Town

Shops and services are concentrated along Rua Princesa Isabel, while Rua XV de Novembro and Rua IX de Março run parallel to each other, terminating at the river. However, the points of interest associated with Joinville's German heritage are more widely scattered. The first place to head for is the **Museu Nacional de Imigração e Colonização** at Rua Rio Branco 229, near Praça da Bandeira (Tues–Sun 9am–5.30pm), an excellent introduction to the history of German immigrants in Santa Catarina in general and Joinville in particular. In the main building, formerly the Prince of Joinville's palace, built in 1870, there are some late nineteenth- and early twentieth-century photographs, though the museum's most interesting features are an old barn containing farm equipment used by early *colonos*, and a typical nineteenth-century *enxaimel* farmhouse with period furnishings. If you've more than a passing interest in Joinville's history, also visit the superbly organized (and German-funded) **Arquivo Histórico** (Mon–Fri 8am–noon & 2–9pm, Sat 8am–noon), on Rua Rio de Janeiro, where temporary, mainly photographic, exhibitions are held.

As throughout the region, Joinville's municipal authorities are making efforts to preserve the surviving **enxaimel houses**. Although scattered throughout the city, they can be seen in some concentration along the former main approach road, the cobbled **Rua XV de Novembro**. On the same road, about twenty minutes' walk from the centre, is the **Cemitário do Imigrante**, the final resting place of many of Joinville's pioneer settlers. Covering a hillside from where there are fine views of the city, the cemetery has been preserved as a national monument, the tombs and headstones serving as testimony to Joinville's ethnic origins. If you have some time on the way to the cemetery, take a brief look around the **Museu de Arte**, Rua XV de Novembro 1400 (daily 9am–9pm). The museum, housed in a small German-style mansion built in 1864, has a small collection of works by mainly local artists, hosts visiting exhibitions and has a **cinema** featuring non-commercial, often German, films.

It's also worth popping into the **Mercado Municipal**, near the local bus terminal, which sells food and some handicrafts produced by local German *colonos*. On the second Saturday of each month a **handicraft market** is held in the nearby Praça Nereu Ramos.

Practicalities

The **Rodoviária** is 2km from the city centre, reached in five minutes by bus or in half an hour on foot by walking down Rua Ministro Calógeras and then left along Avenida

Kubitschek. Bus services to neighbouring cities are excellent. The terminal for **city buses** and those to Dona Francisca is in the centre, at the end of Rua IX de Março.

Opened in 1910, Joinville's **train station** – an imposing construction with a German half-hipped roof – is the oldest one still functioning in Santa Catarina. Today, the only passenger trains go east to São Francisco do Sul, laid on for tourists in the summer months; the trip takes around an hour and a half one way, so if you want you could use the train for an afternoon's excursion. There's a **tourist information** post at Praça Nereu Ramos 372 (daily 7am–9pm).

Finding a comfortable, spotlessly clean and reasonably priced **hotel** is easy. Opposite the train station is the *Colonial* (②), a simple, hospitable hotel with a definite German feel to it. In the city centre, on Rua Jeronimo Coelho near the local bus terminal, is the *Ideal* (☎047/422-3660; ②) at no. 98, and the much nicer *Principe* (☎047/422-8555; ②) at no. 27. Nearby is the slightly more expensive *Trocador*, Rua Visconde de Taunay 185 (☎047/422-1469; ③), along the road from Joinville's priciest hotel, the *Tannenhof* (☎047/433-8011; ⑤) at no. 340. However, the best place to stay is the *Anthurium Parque Hotel*, Rua São Jose 226 (☎047/422-6299; ④), a curious building claiming to be in a "Norwegian–German" style of architecture, located in pretty grounds near the cathedral. Another attractive city centre option with a pleasant European atmosphere is the *Hotel Germânia* (☎047/433-9886; ⑤) at Rua Ministro Calógeras 612.

Further out of town and back down the price scale is the pleasant but noisy *Hotel Mattes* (☎047/422-3582; ②), at Rua XV de Novembro 811, which charges $10 per person and is conveniently located across the road from the Cemitário do Imigrante.

Not surprisingly, **German restaurants** abound, but all are of the sausage, pig's knuckle, potato and sauerkraut level of sophistication. The *Bierkeller*, Rua XV de Novembro 497 (closed Mon), is friendly; the *Tante Friede*, Av. Visconde de Taunay 1174 (closed Sun evening), has an excellent-value buffet; and the *Juca Alemão*, Rua Jerônimo Coelho 188 (closed Sun), is reasonably priced, though with a limited menu. **Vegetarians** and other non-pork eaters should try the *Cozinha Natural*, at Rua Marinho Lobo 38 (Mon–Sat 11am–2.30pm), or try a pizza at *O Fornão* at Av. Visconde de Taunay 299. You'll get good **cakes** at the *Cafeteria Brunkow*, Rua IX de Março 607, and the upscale hotels all serve a good *café colonial* (high tea).

There's a cultural institute in Joinville, the Instituto Cultural Brasil-Alemanha on Rua Princesa Isabel, near Rua Sergipe, and students congregate in the nearby **bars** in the evenings after classes. Since 1937, the **Festa das Flores** has been held for ten days during the second half of November, the height of the orchid season – flower shows, German folk dancing, music and food are the main attractions.

Dona Francisca

Close to Joinville, 20km west and 45 minutes away by bus (hourly from the local bus terminal), is **VILA DONA FRANCISCA**, adminstrative centre of the *município* of the same name. Of little interest itself, the *município* on the other hand contains some of the oldest and best-cared-for *enxaimel* houses in Santa Catarina which, though difficult to find, are well worth seeking out.

Supported by the German government, the **Projeto Memória de Joinville** is slowly renovating fifty of the oldest and architecturally most significant houses. The project has an office in Dona Francisca's *prefeitura* (open Mon–Fri) and the workers are very welcoming to visitors. Thanks largely to the efforts of the project, the level of local awareness of the historic importance of the region's old buildings is high, and many people delight in showing their homes to visitors.

As the most interesting houses are scattered over a wide area and are often rather hidden in the forest, you're best off accompanied by someone who knows the area well. If you show up at the *prefeitura* early, you may be able to arrange to join someone from

Memória de Joinville who's due to visit the restoration sites. Alternatively, ask for the name of a taxi driver who's familiar with the area and negotiate a price (say, about $15) for a couple of hours of back-road driving.

On foot, head for the Estrada Dona Francisca (SC-280) by crossing the main road (BR-101) just out of town. In an old barn and *enxaimel* farmhouse, at the intersection of the BR-101 and SC-280, there's a museum of *colonos* life, the **Museu Rural** (daily 9am–5pm), and a shop selling local produce. From the museum, follow the SC-280 and, by keeping to the following directions, you'll see a fair amount; though be aware that the distances mentioned are only approximate and that the summer sun is very powerful. One kilometre along the SC-280 is Dona Francisca's only **hotel**, the modest, yet extremely comfortable *Angler Hof* (☎047/424-1359; ③); 2km further down the road, turn left on the Estrada Mildrau, along which you'll find the first restored *enxaimel* farmhouse. After another 3km on the SC-280, turn right on the Estrada do Pico: soon after crossing a stream, the road divides; take the right fork and continue along the road (much of the time right alongside the river) and you'll come to a perfectly restored nineteenth-century wooden covered bridge. Along the same road for another couple of hundred metres and you'll hit the SC-280 again. From here, about 7km further along the SC-280, you'll come to the Estrada Quiriri, a dirt road passing through one of Dona Francisca's prettiest and most fertile valleys. Two kilometres away, on the left, is a stunning house, the bricks and timber frame of which form a particularly intricate pattern.

Allow an entire day to see something of Dona Francisca – and be prepared for blistered feet at the end of the day. If you have time for a **meal** or need a **drink** at the end of the day, the *Restaurante Serra Verde* in the village makes a pleasant place to pause and sample *colono* dishes. On the BR-101, soon after crossing the Rio Cubatão, in the direction of Curitiba, turn left on the Estrada Bonita marked by a wooden gateway extending over the road: the pretty farmhouses along this road have signs advertising their produce, including pies, *cachaça* and liqueurs, jams and cheese, while at the end of the road, about 8km along, is the excellent *Recanto Tia Marta* (☎047/435-1722), a restaurant set in the grounds of a typical local farmhouse.

Blumenau

Despite Joinville's challenge, **BLUMENAU** has succeeded in promoting itself as the "capital" of German Santa Catarina. Picturesquely located on the right bank of the Rio Itajaí, Blumenau was founded in 1850 by Dr Hermann Blumenau, who served as director of the colony until his return to Germany in 1880. Blumenau always had a large Italian minority, but it was mainly settled by Germans and, as late as the 1920s, two-thirds of the population spoke German as their mother tongue. In the surrounding rural communities an even larger proportion of the population were German-speakers, many of them finding it completely unnecessary to learn Portuguese. Well into this century Blumenau was isolated, with only poor river transport connections with the Brazil beyond the Itajaí valley – something that enabled its German character to be retained for longer than was the case in Joinville.

Today, Blumenau's municipal authority never fails to miss an opportunity to remind the world of the city's German origins, the European links helping tourism and attracting outside investors. And, superficially, at least, Blumenau certainly looks, if not feels, German. The streets are sparkling clean, parking tickets are issued by wardens dressed in a uniform that Heidi would have been comfortable in, most buildings are in German architectural styles and geranium-filled window boxes are the norm. But since German is almost never heard, and the buildings (such as the half-timbered Saxon-inspired department store and the Swiss chalet-like *prefeitura*) are absurd caricatures of those found in German cities, the result is a sort of "Disneyland" interpretation of Germany.

It's easy to sneer, but tourists from São Paulo are impressed by Blumenau's old-world atmosphere and visit in large numbers, especially during the annual **Oktoberfest**. Held, since 1984, during the second and third weeks of October, the festival is basically an advertising gimmick thought up by Hering, the Blumenau-based textile and agroindustrial giant. Besides vast quantities of beer and German food, the main festival attractions are the local and visiting German bands and German folk-dance troupes. Performances take place at PROEB, Blumenau's exhibition centre, located on the city's outskirts (frequent buses during the festival period), as well as in the downtown streets and the central Biergarten. So successful has the Oktoberfest been in drawing visitors to Blumenau – some 800,000 attended the festivities during its peak year in 1993 – that the city's authorities are now trying to cut back on attendance, believing that the local flavour of the event has been totally swamped by outsiders.

The rest of the year, local German bands perform every evening from 5pm in the **Biergarten**, the city's main meeting point, in the tree-filled Praça Hercílio Luz. In the oldest part of Blumenau, across a small bridge on the continuation of the main street, Rua XV de Novembro, the Biergarten is only a short walk from the **Museu Histórico da Família Colonial**, one of the city's few museums, at Alameda Duque de Caxias 78 (daily 8.30–11.30am & 1.30–5.30pm). The museum's buildings, constructed in 1858 and 1864 for the families of Dr Blumenau's nephew and secretary-librarian, are two of the oldest surviving *enxaimel* houses in Blumenau. Exhibits include nineteenth-century furniture and household equipment, documents relating to the foundation of the city, photographs of life in the settlement during its early years, and artefacts of the Kaingangs and Xoklengs – the indigenous population displaced by the German settlers. But it's in the beautiful forest-like garden that you'll find the most curious feature: a cemetery, the final resting place for the much-loved cats of a former occupant of one of the houses.

A good half-hour walk from Praça Hercílio Luz, on the river at Rua Itajaí 2195, is the **Museu de Ecologia Fritz Müller** (Mon–Fri 8–11.30am & 2–5.30pm), built in 1867 and the former home of the eponymous German-born naturalist. Born in 1822, Müller lived in Santa Catarina between 1852 and 1897, and was a close collaborator of British naturalist Charles Darwin; the small museum is dedicated to the work of the lesser-known of the two scientists.

Practicalities

The **Rodoviária** is 7km from the city centre in the suburb of Itoupava Norte (the "Cidade Jardim" bus runs into the centre). There are hourly services to Florianópolis, Joinville and Itajaí, and frequent services to western Santa Catarina, Curitiba and São Paulo. Buses to Pomerode leave roughly hourly from Rua Paulo Zimmermann, located near the *prefeitura* and Praça Victor Konder; if in doubt, ask for the bus stop of the Volkmann company.

Tourist information offices are found at Rua XV de Novembro 420, at the corner of Rua Nereu Ramos (daily 9am–9pm), at the *Rodoviária*, and in the *prefeitura* (Mon–Fri 9am–5pm) at Praça Victor Konder. If you need official help, there's a **German consulate** at Rua Caetano Deeke 20 (11th floor); and an **Italian** one at Rua Guilherme Siebert 333 (☎047/322-2552).

Centrally located **hotels** are plentiful, so accommodation shouldn't pose a problem, except during the Oktoberfest. At the lower end of the price range, look no further than the wonderful *Hotel Hermann* (☎047/322-4370; ②), an early twentieth-century *enxaimel* building in the heart of the city at Rua Floriano Peixoto 213, by the intersection with Rua Sete de Setembro. Another small German-style hotel, on Rua Ângelo Dias, is the *Christina Blumenau* (☎047/322-1198; ③), owned by a granddaughter of the town's founder. Blumenau's most expensive hotel is the *Plaza Hering*, Rua Sete de Setembro 818 (☎047/326-1277; ⑥), but there are several other medium-priced hotels on the same road, including the *Glória* at no. 954 (☎047/322-1988; ⑤). There's a very good **youth**

hostel at Rua Paraíba 66 (☎047/322-1900) in the centre near the *prefeitura*. If you want to stay with a German-speaking family, contact the tourist information office.

The cheaper hotels don't serve **breakfast**, but a superb one – a $7 buffet affair – can be found at the *Café Haus* in the *Hotel Glória*, around the corner from the *Hotel Hermann*. The same place also serves the best cakes in Blumenau and is an excellent spot for afternoon tea. In general, though, food in Blumenau is poor and largely takes the form of **snacks** to accompany beer.

There are several **German restaurants**, by far the most pleasant of which is the *Frohsinn* (closed Sun). The food here is not at all special, but the location – on a beautiful, cool, pine-clad hill with excellent views over the city – makes the slight effort to get there worthwhile. From Praça Hercílio Luz, walk for about fifteen minutes along Rua Itajaí and turn right on Rua Gertrud Sierich – the restaurant is at the top of this very steep road. Nearer to the centre, huge portions of passable German food are served at the *Cavalinho Branco*, Alameda Rio Branco 165, but it's accompanied by loud Teutonic music. If you're sick of pork, cross the bridge to the *Restaurante Moinho do Vale* at Rua Paraguai 66, which serves more typically Brazilian and international food. It's rather expensive but worth it for the beautiful setting overlooking the river. If you're craving something really different, there are several cheap **Chinese restaurants** – one of the best is the *Chinês* at Rua XV de Novembro 346.

You could also take a **dinner cruise** down the river. Cruises depart at noon, 4pm and 8pm (dinner served only on this one) from Avenida Castelo Branco, near the intersection with Rua Nereu Ramos – a two-hour paddle-steamer excursion that costs from $10, food extra.

Pomerode

Thirty kilometres to the north of Blumenau, **POMERODE** probably has the best claim to be the most German city in Brazil. Not only are ninety percent of its 15,000 inhabitants descended from German immigrants, but eighty percent of the *município*'s population continue to speak the language. Unlike Blumenau, in Pomerode German continues to thrive and is spoken just about everywhere, except in schools. There are several reasons for this: almost all the immigrants – who arrived in the 1860s – came from Pomerania, and therefore did not face the problem of mixing with other immigrants speaking often mutually unintelligible dialects; as ninety percent of the population are Lutheran, German was retained for the act of worship; and, until recently, Pomerode was isolated by poor roads and communication links. This isolation has all but ended, though. The road to Blumenau is now excellent, buses are frequent, car ownership is common and televisions are universal. However, despite the changes, German looks more entrenched than ever. The language has been reintroduced into the local school curriculum, cultural groups thrive and, where the government has exerted pressure, it has been to encourage the language's survival.

Pomerode is renowned for its **festivals**, the chief of which is the **Festa Pomerana**, a celebration of local industry and culture held annually for ten days, usually from around January 7. Most of the events take place on the outskirts of town, on Rua XV de Novembro, about 1km from the tourist office, and during the day thousands of people from neighbouring cities descend on Pomerode to sample the local food, attend the song and dance performances and visit the commercial fair. By late afternoon, though, the day-trippers leave and the Festa Pomerana comes alive as the *colonos* from the surrounding areas transform the festivities into a truly popular event. Local and visiting bands play German and Brazilian music, and dancing continues long into the night. In July, Pomerode organizes the smaller, though similar, **Festa da Tradição Alema**.

There are more regular festivities too, as every Saturday the local hunting clubs take turns to host **dances**. Visitors are always made to feel welcome, and details of the week's venue are displayed on posters around town, or ask at the tourist office. As many of the clubs are located in the *município*'s outlying reaches, a bus is laid on, leaving from outside the post office, on Rua XV de Novembro.

The main activity for visitors, other than attending the town's famous festivals and dances, is **walking**. Pomerode has Santa Catarina's greatest concentration of *enxaimel* buildings, the largest number found in the Wunderwald region: to reach them, cross the bridge near the Lutheran Church, turn left and walk for about twenty minutes, then turn right just before a bridge across a small stream.

Practicalities

Buses to and from Blumenau stop outside the *Hotel Schroeder* and the Lutheran Church on Rua XV de Novembro, the main street, which sprawls alongside the banks of the Rio do Testo. At no. 555 the very helpful **tourist office** (Mon–Fri 8am–5pm, Sat & Sun 10am–5pm) provides a good map and details of forthcoming events, and has a small selection of local wooden and ceramic handicrafts for sale.

Accommodation is always easy to find, even during the Festa Pomerana. The best hotel in town is the *Hotel Bergblick* (☎047/387-0952; ⑤), on the outskirts of town at Rua George Zepelin 120, while the *Hotel Schroeder*, on the main street (☎047/387-0933; ③), is comfortable if rather soulless. If the latter is full or too expensive, the tourist office just across the road can find you a **room** with a local family.

You can **eat** well in Pomerode, too. There's no attempt to reproduce "old world" cooking, but instead simple local dishes are prepared. Pork is, of course, ever present, but it's duck that's considered the local speciality. The *Pommerhaus* at Rua Presidente Costa e Silva 708 (closed Mon), just before the turn-off for the Testo Alto road, is, without doubt, Pomerode's best restaurant, serving typical regional food. The *Hotel Bergblick* also has a very good restaurant. Nearer the town centre, there are several others, the best of which is the more orthodox German *Stettiner Klause*, just across the river from the post office and opposite the unremarkable zoo. For a good *café colonial* (high tea) try the *Torten Paradies* at Rua XV de Novembro 211. There are almost hourly **buses** to and from Blumenau, but as the last goes to Blumenau at 6pm and returns at 10.30pm, going into the city for an evening out is only just about possible.

The south coast to Laguna and Criciúma

Unlike the northern stretch of coast, heading south from Florianópolis doesn't offer as many temptations to leap off the bus and into the sea. Most of this part of the BR-101 highway is too far inland to catch even a glimpse of the sea but, in any case, south of Laguna, the beaches are less attractive and more exposed. Many of the coastal settlements were founded by Azorean immigrants in the late seventeenth century and early eighteenth century, and they've retained the fishing and lace-making traditions of their ancestors. Inland, settlement is much more recent and the inhabitants are a blend of Germans, Italians and Poles, whose forebears were attracted in the late nineteenth century by promises of fertile land and offers of work in the region's coal mines. However, apart from a handful of farms and villages where Portuguese-influenced Italian dialects are spoken, only surnames and scattered wooden and stone houses of the early settlers remain of the immigrant heritage.

Garopaba and Imbituba

The first accessible spot worth stopping at is **GAROPABA**, a fishing village inhabited by people of Azorean origin, which, despite attracting more and more people every summer, has not yet been totally overwhelmed by tourism. In the 1970s, Garopaba was "discovered" by hippies from Porto Alegre, attracted to the area by the peaceful atmosphere and beautiful beaches. During the 1980s, surfers from throughout Brazil and beyond descended on the village, which fast developed a reputation for having some of the best surfing in the country. In recent years, the region has been increasingly threatened by major tourist development.

The **beaches** are excellent, but are located a short distance from the village. The main village beach is fine, and large enough to take the summer crowds, but try to make it to the outlying beaches. Ten kilometres to the north is Praia Siriú, backed by huge dunes, while 6km further on, Praia da Gambora is a good beach for swimming, with a beautiful mountain backdrop. The best beaches for surfing are to the south, the most challenging being Praia do Silveira (3km) and Praia do Rosa (18km).

Facilities in Garopaba are mainly geared to campers and there are very few **restaurants**, mainly simple places serving fried fish. Of Garopaba's half-dozen **hotels**, the cheapest is the *Pousada Casa Grande e Senzala* at Rua Dr Elmo Kiseki 444 (☎048/254-3177; ③), but being small, it's often full in summer. However, by asking around, there's rarely a problem in finding a room in a private house. There's a small, and in the summer usually full, **youth hostel** at Estrada Geral do Capão, Praia da Ferrugem, opposite the Paulotur bus terminal. There's a greater concentration of places to stay at Praia do Rosa, 18km to the south; *pousadas* there, however, are expensive, and even at around $80 per night they're snapped up quickly.

Despite Garopaba's size, **bus** services are good, with buses to Florianópolis leaving from Rua Marques Guimarães, and those destined for points south as far as Porto Alegre leaving from Praça Silveira.

Thirty kilometres south of Garopaba, **IMBITUBA**, once one of the most attractive points along the coast, should be avoided at all costs. Imbituba's main function is that of a port serving the nearby coalfields; from here coal is sent north to the steel mills of Volta Redonda for coking. The town's beaches are polluted and, should you want putting off further, so too is the air, thanks to the carbo-chemical plant.

Laguna

LAGUNA, on the other hand, 125km from Florianópolis is an excellent place to break your journey: the closest Santa Catarina gets to having a near-complete colonial town. Located at the end of a narrow peninsula, at the entrance to the Lagoa Santo Antônio, Laguna feels like two distinct towns. Facing west onto the sheltered lagoon is the old port (long surpassed by Imbituba) and Lagoa's historic centre, protected as a national monument. Two kilometres away, on the far side of a granite outcrop of mountainous proportions that separates the city's two parts, is the new town, facing east onto the Atlantic Ocean.

The Town

As a beach resort, Laguna's attraction is limited. The city's importance lies in its **old town** which, even during the height of the summer tourist season, attracts few people – just as well, as it's quite small and could easily be overwhelmed. The one time of year that Laguna gets unbearably crowded is during *Carnaval* as the town is rated as having one of the best celebrations south of Rio.

Laguna was significant as early as 1494, being the southern point of the line dividing the Americas between Spain and Portugal (the northern point was at Belém), 370 leagues west of the Cape Verde Islands. A **monument**, near the *Rodoviária*, a few minutes' walk from the centre, marks the exact spot. However, a permanent settlement wasn't established until 1676, but it rapidly became the pre-eminent port of the southern fringes of the Portuguese Empire, and a base for the exploration and colonization of what is now Rio Grande do Sul.

Although by no means all of Laguna's old town dates from the eighteenth century, its general aspect is that of a Portuguese colonial town. The oldest streets are those extending off **Praça Vidal Ramos**, the square which holds the **Igreja Santo Antônio dos Anjos**. Built in 1694, the church retains its late eighteenth-century Baroque altars and, though simple enough, is considered the most important surviving colonial church in Santa Catarina.

On the same square as the church is the **Casa de Anita** (daily 8am–noon & 2–6pm), a small museum housed in a simple early eighteenth-century house and dedicated to Anita Garibaldi, the Brazilian wife of Giuseppe Garibaldi, maverick military leader of the Italian unification movement. Garibaldi was employed as a mercenary in the Guerra dos Farrapos, between republicans and monarchists, and it was in Laguna that a short-lived republic was declared in 1839. There are some fine photographs of nineteenth-century Laguna on display, but – oddly perhaps – there's little on Anita's life and republican activities; scissors and hairbrushes that once belonged to her are typical of the exhibits. In Praça República Juliana in the former town hall and jail, built in 1747, is the **Museu Anita Garibaldi** (daily 8am–noon & 2–6pm) with a rather dreary collection of local Indian artefacts and items relating to the Guerra dos Farrapos. Close by, on Praça Lauro Muller, the **Fonte da Carioca** is the oldest surviving fountain in Laguna, dating back to 1863, covered in blue and white Portuguese tiles and located next to the former slave market.

Practicalities
The **Rodoviária** is at Rua Arcângelo Bianchini, a couple of minutes' walk from the waterfront and the old town. Located above the old market on the waterfront is the **tourist office**, which provides excellent maps of Laguna and the surrounding area.

Most of Laguna's hotels and restaurants are located in the new town, alongside and parallel to the **Praia do Mar Grosso**, the city's main beach. **Hotels** here tend to be large and expensive, but two moderately priced exceptions are the *Mar Grosso*, Av. Senador Galotti 644 (☎048/644-0298; ③), and the *Monte Libano*, Av. João Pinho 198 (☎048/644-0671; ④). The seafood **restaurants**, concentrated in the middle of Avenida Senador Galotti, are good, if much of a muchness.

Apart from during *Carnaval*, **rooms** in the **old town** are easy to find. The *Hotel Farol Palace* (☎048/644-0596; ②), on the waterfront opposite the market, is comfortable and friendly. There are also a couple of extremely cheap *dormitórios* behind the hotel. **Restaurants** in this part of town are poor, the best being two pizzerias on Praça Juliana, but there's a very pleasant little *confeitaria*, the *Docelândia*, at Rua Voluntário Carper 78.

Around Laguna
About 15km out of town to the south is the **Farol Santa Marta**, a lighthouse (the third tallest in the Americas) which was transported piece by piece from Scotland in 1891. It's surrounded by bleak but beautiful scenery offering wild seas (suicidal for even the strongest of swimmers) and protected beaches. Between June and September the lighthouse is a popular spot from which to watch the migrating humpback whales: a good eye and powerful binoculars are required. There are no buses, but if you do find a way of getting here, you'll discover a luxurious **hotel**, *Farol de Santa Marta* (☎048/644-0370; ④), complete with a heated pool, as well as another very simple hotel, houses renting rooms, and a couple of **restaurants**.

South to Criciúma

The **coastline** between Laguna and the Rio Grande do Sul border is effectively one long beach – though it's of no great beauty and can be passed without much pain. The coastal plain, which stretches inland some 30km, provides little in the way of natural attraction, and the region's two largest towns, Tubarão and Criciúma, were founded as coal-mining centres; the area remains one of Brazil's very few producers of the mineral. Should you need to stay, **CRICIÚMA** is marginally the more pleasant and less polluted of the two.

The **Rodoviária** is centrally located on Avenida Centenário, the main artery which bisects the town, and as there are frequent buses to all points in Santa Catarina, it's unlikely that you'll have to stay the night. However, if you arrive late, there are two very good **hotels**, virtually alongside the *Rodoviária* – the luxury *Crisul* (☎048/437-4000; ⑤) and the medium-priced *Turis Center* (☎048/633-8722; ③) – and two basic *dormitórios*. Cheap and comfortable, the *Cavaller Palace* (②) is on Rua Anita Garibaldi, near the town's central square, Praça Nereu Ramos. The square is also where you'll find the **tourist office**, a five-minute walk from the back of the *Rodoviária*.

Killing time in Criciúma is fairly easy if you're interested in immigration history. The **Centro Cultural Teuto-Brasileiro** (reached by the "Forquilhinha" bus) contains a small museum related to the German settlers, while exhibits in the **Museu da Colonização**, Rua Cecília Daros Casagrande (Mon–Fri 8am–noon & 1–6pm; take the "Bairro Comerciario" bus), largely relate to the Italian community. If you've only got a couple of hours to spare, a visit to the **coal mine** (daily 8–11.30am & 2–6pm), Criciúma's prime tourist attraction, is really the best idea. It's 3km from the city centre: take the "Minha Model" bus from the local bus terminal, which is next to the *Rodoviária*. Coal seams were discovered around Criciúma in 1913, and this mine entered production in 1930. Visitors are taken through the coal mine by retired miners who spiel out, in exhausting detail, information about the local geological structure and mining techniques. The squeamish should note that the mine is home to huge numbers of – quite harmless – fruit bats.

Central and western Santa Catarina

Until the road-building programme of the 1970s, mountainous **central and western** Santa Catarina was pretty much isolated from the rest of the state. Largely settled by migrants from neighbouring states, the inhabitants of this territory are of diverse origins including Germans and Italians in the extreme west, Austrians, Italians and Ukrainians in the central Rio do Peixe Valley, and *gaúchos* – and even Japanese – in the highlands of the Serra Geral. In the more isolated areas, dominated by a single ethnic group, traditions and languages have been preserved but, as elsewhere in southern Brazil, they are under threat.

Any route taken to reach the **Serra Geral** is spectacular, but if you enter the region directly from the coast the contrasts of landscape, vegetation and climate unfold most dramatically. From the subtropical lowlands, roads have been cut into the steep escarpment and, as the roads slowly wind their way up into the Serra, dense foliage unfolds – protected from human destruction by its ability to cling to the most precipitous of slopes. Waterfalls can be seen in every direction until suddenly you reach the *planalto*, a virtual plateau. Here, the graceful Paraná pine trees are fewer in number but much larger, their branches fanning upwards in a determined attempt to re-form the canopy that existed before the arrival of cattle and lumber interests.

For tourists, towns in the Serra are generally places to travel towards rather than destinations in their own right. Even if it means going a considerable distance out of the way, most **bus** services to Lages, from the coast, travel via the BR-470 – Santa Catarina's main east–west highway – before turning onto the BR-116, that cuts north–south through the state. To and from Florianópolis, for example, it's usually much faster and more comfortable for buses to travel via Blumenau, but the twice-daily services from Florianópolis direct to Lages via Alfredo Wagner are far more picturesque. From the southern coast of Santa Catarina, the Serra can be approached by bus from Criciúma on the even more spectacular road leading up via São Joaquim to Lages.

Urussanga and Orleans

The route into the Serra Geral from Criciúma at first passes through a gently undulating landscape inhabited largely by the descendants of northern Italian immigrants who settled in the region in the 1880s, before climbing the steep escarpment into the highlands. If possible choose a clear day to make the trip as the views east towards the coast are absolutely spectacular.

Some 20km from Criciúma the road passes through **URUSSANGA**, a small agricultural processing town. Urussanga and the surrounding country is noted for its stone farm buildings dating from the arrival of the first Italian settlers and, with federal government support, the authorities have been making tremendous efforts to restore them. A handful are located in the town itself, but to see those in outlying areas you'll need to get detailed directions from the local Secretaria de Cultura at the *prefeitura*.

A further 20km along the road is **ORLEANS** lying on a fairly busy crossroads from where it's easy to pick up buses to São Joaquim, Criciúma or Laguna. If you decide to stop over, there are a couple of modest **hotels**, the *São Francisco* (☎048/666-0282; ③), at Rua Aristiliano Ramos 120, and the *Brasil* (②), at Rua Getúlio Vargas 9. An unremarkable little town in most ways, Orleans boasts the excellent outdoor **Museu ao Ar Livre** (Tues–Sun 10am–5pm). The museum records early immigrant life and industry and features a water-powered saw mill and other buildings moved here from the surrounding area.

São Joaquim

Formerly a small ranching centre, **SÃO JOAQUIM**, ninety steep kilometres beyond Orleans, has only really been on the Brazilian map since the mid-1970s when apple orchards were introduced here. Within twenty years, Brazil changed from importing nearly all the apples consumed in the country to becoming a major exporter of fruit. At an altitude of 1360m (the highest town in Brazil), apple trees are in their element in São Joaquim, benefiting from the very pronounced seasonal temperature variations. Temperatures in the winter regularly dip to -15°C and, as one of the few parts of Brazil that sees regular snowfalls, there is a surprising amount of tourism in the winter with camping being especially popular amongst Brazilians as a way of truly experiencing the cold. Anyone with a specific interest in apples can visit the **Estação Experimental de São Joaquim**, on the outskirts of town, where research into fruit takes place. Or if you're just plain hungry visit the **shop**, owned by an English-speaking Israeli farmer, just below the main square, which sells a vast variety of apples. On Sundays there's a handicrafts market on the square itself, with stalls selling local food produce too, including more apples.

The **Rodoviária** (good services to Lages and Criciúma) is a couple of minutes' walk from the city centre. Opposite one another on Rua Manoel Joaquim Pinto are the town's only **hotels**, the *Nevada* (☎0492/33-0259; ②) and *Maristela* (☎0492/33-0007; ②), both of which are perfectly comfortable. Despite the presence of some fifty Japanese apple-growing families, the only **restaurant** is a pizzeria, the *Agua na Boca* on Rua Marcos Batista 907, although you can get a good *café colonial* (high tea) at *Quitutes da Rogéria*, Rua Manoel Joaquim Pinto 62 (Sept–Feb 8am–8pm).

Lages

Although founded in 1766, nothing remains in **LAGES** from the days when it was an important resting place on the route northwards to the market in Sorocaba, to which cattle and mules were herded. Nowadays, Lages, 76km northwest of São Joaquim, is a collection of anonymous post-1950s buildings, and only the presence in town of visiting ranchers and cowhands, dressed in the characteristic baggy pantaloons, waist sash and poncho, reminds you that the town is at the northern edge of *gaúcho* country. Because of the presence of so many knife-carrying men, who come into town at the weekend for supplies and a good time, Lages is reputed to be the most violent town in the state. However, the general atmosphere is dull rather than menacing, and tourists are unlikely to get caught up in any trouble.

The reason for visiting Lages is for a taste of life in *gaúcho* country. The tourist office promotes the *Turismo Rural* project, which provides opportunities for people to visit typical cattle *fazendas* and catch a glimpse of life in outlying parts of the Serra – otherwise extremely difficult for tourists to see. For day trips, only groups are catered for, so ask at the tourist office whether you can join one that has already been formed. However, several *fazendas* accept guests, who are encouraged to participate in the everyday activities of the rugged Serra cattle stations. Otherwise, the best way to get a feel of the region is to attend one of the periodic **rodeios**; again, the tourist office can provide information. Lages' great event is the *Rodeio Criola*, held over a two-week period in January. As at neighbouring Vacaria's *rodeio* (see p.581), thousands of *gaúchos* from throughout southern Brazil come to watch and compete.

Practicalities

The **Rodoviária** is a half-hour walk southeast of the centre, or take a bus marked "Dom Pedro". The **tourist office** (Mon–Fri 8am–noon & 2–6pm) is in the centre of town, in the Casa do Artesão on Praça João Costa (near the *prefeitura*), and distributes a good map of Lages and sells rustic leather and wooden *gaúcho*-related items.

Reasonable, modestly priced **hotels** are easy to come by, even during the *Rodeio Criola* (when most people camp). The *Hotel Presidente*, Av. Presidente Vargas 106 (☎0492/24-0014; ③), and the *Hotel Map*, Rua Hercílio Luz 520 (☎0492/22-1058; ③), are both quite good and only minutes' walk from the cathedral and main square, Praça Waldo da Costa Avila. If you want a bit more luxury, try the *Grande Hotel Lages*, Rua João de Castro 23 (☎0492/22-3522; ④). However, to really experience *serra* life you should arrange to stay on a cattle **fazenda**. Recommended are *Pedras Brancas* (☎0492/23-2073), *Rancho do Boqueirão* (☎0492/26-0354) and *do Barreiro* (☎0492/22-3031); all $50 per person including full board. Reservations are essential because accommodation is limited and it's important to make arrangements to be met in Lages, or, if driving, to get clear instructions. And while the landscape of the *serra* is extremely rugged and the life of the highland *gaúcho* is often harsh, the *fazendas* provide very comfortable accommodation, excellent food and facilities such as swimming pools.

Restaurants are, of course, largely meat-orientated, the best being the *Laghões*, at Rua João de Castro 27. There are also a number of vaguely Italian restaurants: *Cantina d'Italia*, at Rua Francisco Furtado Ramos 122, is worth a try.

Rio do Peixe valley

Immigrants were introduced to the **Peixe valley** in around 1910 by the American-owned Brazil Railway Company. For completing the São Paulo–Rio Grande rail line, the company received land from which they could extract valuable timber and which they could divide for sale to homesteaders. Due to the region's isolation, war in Europe, anti-immigration legislation and the discovery that the soil was not as fertile as had been believed, fewer people than hoped moved into the area. Of those who did come, most were from neighbouring states, mainly Slavs from Paraná, and Germans and Italians from Rio Grande do Sul.

Joaçaba and around

The region's most important town is **JOAÇABA**, 462km west of Florianópolis, on the Peixe's west bank, directly across the river from the smaller town of Herval d'Oeste.

Perhaps due to the narrowness of the valley, whose slopes rise precipitously along one entire side of town, Joaçaba has an oppressive, almost menacing, atmosphere. Although the population is dominated by people of Italian extraction, no obvious Italian influences remain, and as Joaçaba developed into an important centre of light industry and agribusiness, it lost its former frontier charm. However, if you're visiting the Rio do Peixe area, Joaçaba is difficult to avoid altogether. Buses serve all surrounding districts and towns to the west, and there are regular departures to Blumenau, Florianópolis, São Paulo and Foz do Iguaçu.

With the **Rodoviária** located just minutes' walk from the town centre, arriving in Joaçaba couldn't be easier. On leaving the *Rodoviária*, turn right onto Avenida XV de Novembro, the road that follows alongside the river through town; turn right again on Rua Sete de Setembro and you'll find an inexpensive **hotel**, the *Hotel Comércio* (☎0495/22-2211; ②). A few doors away is the modern luxury *Hotel Jaraguá* (☎0495/22-4255; ⑤), which has a pool and a reasonable restaurant. Also on Avenida XV de Novembro are a couple of *churrascarias* and pizzerias, the best of which is the *Plaza Center* at no. 818.

Really though, it makes little sense to stay in Joaçaba except, possibly, to use it as a base from which to visit the surrounding area. In every direction from Joaçaba the countryside ranges from hilly to mountainous, and by selecting at random a neighbouring small town, you'll be sure to be rewarded with a bus ride through some beautiful scenery. The road to **PIRATUBA**, 50km to the south, is especially attractive and at the journey's end you can relax in the natural thermal pools there. Most of the *colonos* along this road are of Italian origin, with those around **LACERDÓPOLIS** still retaining elements of the dialects and traditions of past generations.

Treze Tilias

Of the region's ethnic groups, it is one of the smallest – the Austrians – who have been most stubborn in resisting cultural assimilation. The claim of the *município* of **TREZE TILIAS** to be the "Brazilian Tyrol" is by no means a baseless one. In 1933, 82 Tyroleans led by Andreas Thaler, a former Austrian minister of agriculture, arrived in what is now Treze Tilias. As the dense forest around the settlement was gradually cleared more settlers joined the colony, but after Germany's annexation of Austria in 1938, immigration came to an end – as did funds to help support the pioneers during the difficult first years. With the onset of war, communications with Austria ceased altogether and, with no country to return to, abandoning the colony was not an option. During the immediate postwar years, contacts with Europe were minimal, but as Austria grew more prosperous, Treze Tilias began to receive assistance. The area came to specialize in dairy farming and today its milk products are sold in supermarkets throughout Santa Catarina.

Treze Tilias is only an hour north of Joaçaba and west of Videira and it's perfectly practical to use it as a base for getting to know the wider region. All buses stop outside the *Hotel Áustria* (☎0495/37-0132; ② with a huge breakfast included), the oldest and cheapest of the town's **hotels**. Excellent inexpensive meals, incorporating Austrian and Brazilian influences, are served at the *Áustria*, and the hotel is a mine of local knowledge. If you're staying there, you can ask the manager, Andreas Moser, to take you to the smallholding where all the food consumed in the hotel is produced. The *Hotel Tirol* (☎0495/37-0239; ③), a Tyrolean-style chalet, right in the centre, complete with geraniums hanging from every balcony, has comfortable rooms and a swimming pool. You'll get similar floral comforts at the more intimate *Campestre Recanto da Áustria* (☎0495/37-0287; ③). Both these hotels have good restaurants serving simple Austrian dishes at lunch, and *café colonial* in the late afternoon and evening. One place to avoid is the restaurant in the cultural centre, next to the Banco do Brasil: a limited menu and Brazilian food at its most uninspired. If you want to stay with a local family, enquire at the tourist office in the centre of the village.

But for the absence of snow-capped mountain peaks, the general appearance of Treze Tílias is not dissimilar to that of a small alpine village. Walking in any direction, you'll pass through peaceful pastoral landscapes. The seven-kilometre walk to the chapel at **Babenberg** is particularly rewarding, while if you set out to visit the local **waterfalls**, get very detailed directions beforehand.

In the village itself, try and visit some of the **wood carvers**, the best of whom learned their craft in Europe, and whose work is in demand throughout Brazil. Farmers and craftsmen alike respond very openly to interest in their work from outsiders. The small **Museu do Imigrante** (Mon–Fri 2–5pm, Sat & Sun 9–11am) features a small collection of photographs of the area in the 1930s and 1940s, as well as items brought with the immigrants from Austria. The **Festa da Imigração Austríaco** during the first two weeks of October is a lively display of Austrian folk traditions including singing and dancing.

Videira

On the eastern fringes of Treze Tílias, along the Linha Pinhal road leading to **VIDEIRA**, the population is mainly of Italian origin, descended from migrants who came from Rio Grande do Sul in the 1940s. Vines dominate the landscape, and if you visit a *colônia*, you'll probably be invited to taste their home-produced salami, *cachaça* or the wine – it's only polite to buy a bottle before leaving. If you want to take the matter further, in Videira itself the small, but well-organized **Museu do Vinho** (Mon–Fri 8.30–11am, Sat & Sun 2–5pm) next to the main church, is worth half an hour or so. The displays relate to the local wine-making skills in the early years of settlement.

Videira itself doesn't justify more than the briefest of pauses between buses which are, unfortunately, far less frequent than those from Joaçaba. If you need a **hotel**, and there's no time to go to Treze Tílias, walk down the hill on Avenida Dom Pedro II from the *Rodoviária* and turn right at the Shell station onto Rua Brasil (the main commercial street); the inexpensive *Savannah Hotel* (②) and **restaurant** is the first building on the left. Alternatively, crossing the river over the bridge at the bottom of Rua Brasil, next to the local bus terminal, you'll come to Videira's luxury *Hotel Verde Vale Palace* (☎0495/66-1622; ⑤), whose reasonably priced restaurant serves the best food in town – not that there's much competition.

The extreme west

Until the 1950s, most of the population of the extreme west of Santa Catarina were Kaingang Indians and semi-nomadic *caboclo erva maté* harvesters. With land availability in Rio Grande do Sul increasingly difficult, peasant farmers moved north into Santa Catarina and the area has since become the state's foremost producer of pigs and chickens.

Chapecó and around

Without an interest in agriculture, **CHAPECÓ** – or indeed any other town in the region – is unlikely to hold your attention for longer than it takes to change buses. Fortunately, Chapecó is well served with **buses** to points throughout Santa Catarina and Rio Grande do Sul, to Dionísio Cerqueira (for Argentina), Curitiba and Cascavel (for connections to Foz do Iguaçu) in Paraná. If you have to stick around for a while, frequent buses connect the *Rodoviária*, on the city's outskirts, with the local bus terminal, which is located virtually on the main square. There are a couple of **places to stay** near the bus terminal – *Hotel Eston* is comfortable (☎049/723-1044; ③) – and two more on the main street, Avenida Getúlio Vargas.

Chapecó's self-proclaimed status as regional capital simply means that its slaughterhouses are larger than those in the surrounding towns. If you happen to be in town during the month of August, you'll coincide with the **Festa Nacional do Frango e do Peru**, an absurdly contrived affair celebrating chicken and turkey production – almost as ridiculous as its **Würstfest**, an annual jamboree in November in celebration of the sausage. Otherwise there's not much to delay you, though if you're stuck, browse around Bolicho do Gauderio, on the main square, a general outfitters aiming at fashion-conscious young *gaúchos*; it's a good place to pick up souvenirs. On a rather sadder note, souvenirs can also be purchased from forlorn-looking Kaingang Indians, who wander around town attempting to sell their brightly coloured basketwork and bows and arrows.

If you do have a day to spare, head into the outlying **countryside** where the *colonos* cultivate maize, beans and manioc on even the most precipitous of mountain slopes. A typical village within an hour of Chapecó (buses from the central bus terminal) is **SAUDADES**, from where you can take another bus to **SÃO CARLOS**, 25km south along the winding valley of the Rio Chapecó. From São Carlos, there are frequent buses to Chapecó (1hr) or, 3km to the east, stop off at **ÁGUAS DE CHAPECÓ**, a small thermal springs and beach resort beautifully located overlooking the mighty Rio Uruguai. There are **camping** facilities here and two simple **hotels**.

Abelardo Luz

Ninety kilometres north of Chapecó is **ABELARDO LUZ**, a small town near the *Paranaense* border. With a total population of just 15,000, in the mid-1980s Abelardo Luz briefly hit the headlines in Brazil, when thousands of landless peasants from neighbouring areas moved onto the huge estates of absentee landowners in this, one of the poorest and most sparsely populated parts of Santa Catarina.

The unrest has long since subsided and the reporters from throughout Brazil who descended on this little town are now just an exciting memory for the otherwise sleepy place. However, small numbers of tourists do stop off in Abelardo Luz, on their way between eastern Santa Catarina and Rio Grande do Sul and Foz do Iguaçu. The attraction is the beautiful waterfalls, **Quedas do Rio Chapecó**, a 45-minute walk from town. To reach the falls, walk up Abelardo Luz's main street and, at the top, turn left and walk until you reach an asphalted highway where you turn right. Walk along the road past the horseshoe-shaped entrance to the park, cross a bridge and continue past a hotel (very basic) until you come to signs for the *quedas*, indicating a road to the left. You'll be charged a small entrance fee, but facilities are good; there's a **campsite**, a **restaurant** and snack bar. The falls themselves extend across the river and take the form of eight steps varying in breadth and width. Walkways cross parts of the waterfalls and there are numerous small natural pools by the side of the tourist complex. But to swim properly, you need to go 3km upriver to **Prainha**, a beach where there's also a campsite.

Unless you're camping, apart from the hotel on the way to the falls the only **place to stay** is a very grim, but cheap, hotel on the main street in town, across from two poor **restaurants**. **Buses** leave from virtually outside the hotel and there's an hourly service to Xanxerê, from where there are frequent connections to points within Santa Catarina and Rio Grande do Sul. If you're travelling to or from Foz do Iguaçu, take a bus to Cascavel (Paraná) or Dionísio Cerqueira and change there.

Dionísio Cerqueira

Situated in the extreme northwest corner of Santa Catarina, **DIONÍSIO CERQUEIRA** virtually merges with the smaller *Paranaense* town of **Barracão** and, just across the Argentine border, **Bernardo de Irigoyen**. Dionísio Cerqueira has become quite a busy shopping centre, attracting Argentines eager to purchase cheap food, household goods and clothes in Brazil, but it's an unremarkable border town and you're unlikely to want to stay over longer than is needed to catch a bus out. Fortunately each of the border towns is well served by **bus** companies. Dionísio Cerqueira's *Rodoviária*, a few blocks back from the border, has frequent departures to all main towns in Santa Catarina, Rio Grande do Sul and Posadas in Argentina. The nearby Barracão *Rodoviária* serves Paraná, including Curitiba and Foz do Iguaçu. From Bernardo de Irigoyen's bus station, there are services throughout the Argentine province of Misiones including Posadas (for the nearby Jesuit ruins or travel further south or west into Argentina) and Puerto Iguazú. The **road to Iguaçu** through Argentina is more varied and slightly faster than the one through Brazil. The first part of the journey is through an intensely logged area, the original subtropical vegetation having been replaced by fast-growing pine trees and small farms. The bus makes occasional detours to stop at the small settlements that have developed by the road since the 1970s when German-Brazilian pioneers moved into the area. For the last 40km or so, the road passes through the Parque Nacional del Iguazú, the only remaining large expanse of the rainforest that once covered the entire region.

If you do need to stay over, it's easy to find a **hotel**. The best place is the *Motel ACA* (☎0751/92218; ④) near the bus station in Bernardo de Irigoyen. In Barracão, the *Hotel Província* (☎049/844-1261; ③) is comfortable and has a restaurant, while in Dionísio Cerqueira there's the very basic *Hotel Iguaçú* (☎049/844-1029; ②), at Rua Mário Cláudio Turra 260. Dionísio Cerqueira has only one real **restaurant**, the *Medieval* at Av. Santa Catarina 190.

The **border crossing** is very relaxed and is open between 7am and 7pm. Argentine passport control is located right on the border, whereas the Brazilian Polícia Federal is two blocks back from the border on Dionísio Cerqueira's main road, at Rua República Argentina 259.

RIO GRANDE DO SUL

For many people the state of **Rio Grande do Sul**, bordering Argentina and Uruguay, is their first or last experience of Brazil. More than most parts of the country, it has an extremely strong regional identity – to the extent that it's the only state where the possibility of independence is discussed. Today, the Santa Cruz do Sul-based **Movimento Pro-Pampa** campaigns for the separation of Brazil's three southernmost states to create the República Federal da Pampa Gaúcha. Central government's authority over Brazil's southernmost state has often been weak: in the colonial era, the territory was virtually a no-man's land separating the Spanish and Portuguese empires. Out of this emerged a strongly independent people, mostly pioneer farmers and the descendants of European immigrants, isolated fishing communities and, best known, the *gaúchos* (see p.586), the cowboys of southern South America whose name is now used for all inhabitants of the state, whatever their origins.

The **road and bus network** is excellent and it's easy to zip through the state without stopping if need be. However, Rio Grande do Sul is as Brazilian as Bahia or Rio and it would be foolish to ignore the place. The capital, **Porto Alegre**, is southern Brazil's most important cultural and commercial centre but, like all the other cities in Rio Grande do Sul, has little to detain tourists. However, it's also the state's transportation axis and at some point you're likely to pass through the city. For a truer flavour of Rio Grande do Sul, visit the principal region of Italian and German settlement, around the towns of **Caxias do Sul**, **Bento Gonçalves** and **Nova Petrópolis**, a couple of hours north of Porto Alegre. And for the classic image, head for the cattle country of the *serra* and *campanha* where old *gaúcho* traditions still linger.

Porto Alegre

The capital of Rio Grande do Sul, **PORTO ALEGRE** lies on the eastern bank of the Rio Guaiba, at the point where five rivers converge to form the **Lagoa dos Patos**, a giant freshwater lagoon navigable by even the largest of ships. Founded in 1755 as a Portuguese garrison, to guard against Spanish encroachment into this part of the empire, it wasn't until Porto Alegre became the port for the export of beef that it developed into Brazil's leading commercial centre south of São Paulo.

With a rather uninteresting feel to it, like a cross between a southern European and a North American city, most people will be tempted to move straight on from Porto Alegre. However, as it's a major transport centre, a stop here might be unavoidable. Fortunately the city has considerable life, if not much visible history, and you'll find many ways to occupy yourself.

> The **telephone code** for Porto Alegre is ☎051.

Arrival, information and accommodation

There's hardly an airport in southern Brazil which doesn't serve Porto Alegre, and there are international services to Buenos Aires, Montevideo and Santiago, too. The **airport** is linked by metrô to the Mercado Público, in the city centre, or take the L.05 bus, which links the airport with Praça Parobe (next to the Mercado Público). Taxis into the city will cost about $10.

Buses from throughout Brazil and neighbouring countries stop at Porto Alegre's **Rodoviária**, which is within walking distance of the centre; however, because the *Rodoviária* is virtually ringed by a mesh of highways and overpasses, it's far less confusing, and safer, to use the metrô from here. Porto Alegre used to be a major **rail** hub but, apart from suburban routes, the only remaining services are to Santa Maria, from where the line branches out to Santana do Livramento and Uruguaiana. Trains depart from the new *Ferroviária*, also accessible by metrô.

The **metrô** (Mon–Fri 6am–11pm, Sat & Sun 5am–10pm; 60¢) has its city centre terminal at the Mercado Público, but as the system is very limited in extent, it's only really of use when you arrive and leave Porto Alegre.

EPATUR, the city's **tourist office** (Mon–Fri 8.30am–noon & 1.30–6pm), has very helpful branches at the airport, in Praça XV de Novembro and at Travessa do Carmo 84 (Largo dos Açorianos). CRTur, the state tourist office, has a very helpful kiosk at the *Rodoviária* (daily 7am–7pm). Both agencies hand out excellent free maps of Porto Alegre.

Accommodation

Hotels are scattered all around the city centre, but distances are small and it's possible to walk to most places, although great care should be taken at night. The **Tchê Youth Hostel** is at Rua Fernando Machado 681 (☎225-3581), conveniently located in the heart of the city. It's a small hostel accepting members and non-members alike, and there are kitchen and laundry facilities; rates are $12 per person.

Hotel Metrópole, Rua Andrade Neves 59 (☎226-1800). Basic but clean rooms, popular with business travellers from outlying parts of the state. One of several places to stay on this busy road in the heart of the commercial district; less expensive, but similar hotels on the same road include *Hotel Marechal* (☎228-3076) and *Hotel Glória* (☎224-6433). ③.

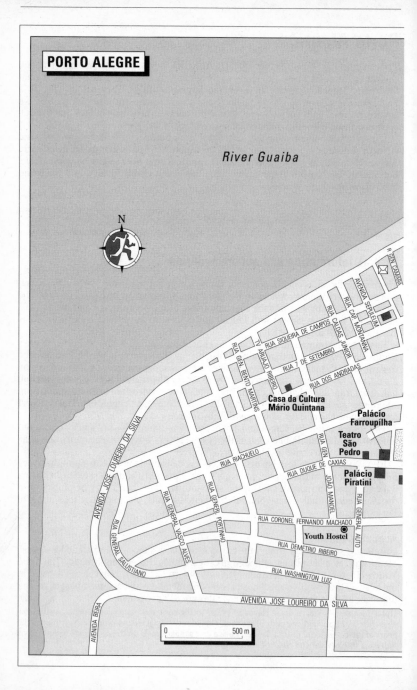

PORTO ALEGRE

River Guaiba

N

RUA SIQUEIRA DE CAMPOS

RUA GEN. BENTO MARTINS

TV ARUJÃO RIBEIRO

RUA 7 DE SETEMBRO

RUA CALDAS JUNIOR

RUA CAP. MONTANNA

AVENIDA SEPÚLEÚM

R. GENT. CAMARÁ

RUA DOS ANDRADAS

Casa da Cultura Mário Quintana

Palácio Farroupílha

Teatro São Pedro

RUA GEN.

Palácio Piratini

RUA RIACHUELO

RUA DUQUE DE CAXIAS

AVENIDA JOSÉ LOUREIRO DA SILVA

RUA GENERAL VASCO ALVES

RUA GENERAL PORTINHO

RUA JOÃO MANOEL

RUA GENERAL AUTO

RUA CORONEL FERNANDO MACHADO

Youth Hostel

RUA DEMETRIO RIBEIRO

RUA GENERAL SALUSTIANO

RUA WASHINGTON LUIZ

AVENIDA JOSÉ LOUREIRO DA SILVA

AVENIDA BEIRA

0   500 m

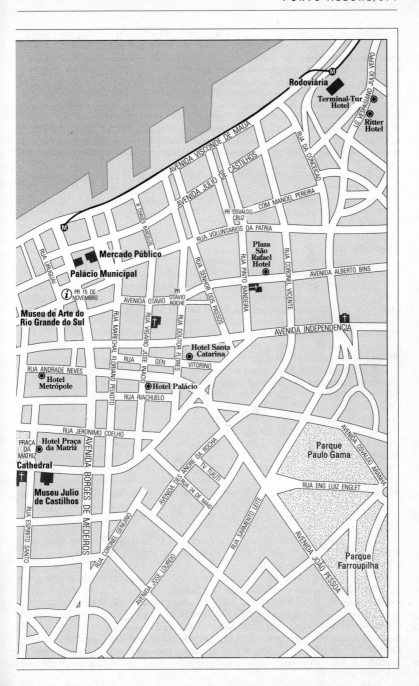

Hotel Palácio, Rua Vigario José Inácio 644 (☎225-3467). Friendly, secure and popular with travellers, this hotel is situated in the commercial district and is somewhat noisy. ②.

Plaza São Rafael Hotel, Av. Alberto Bins 514 (☎221-6100). All the features you'd expect in the city's best hotel. Ask for a room overlooking the river. ⑦.

Hotel Praça da Matriz, Largo João Amorim do Albuquerque (☎225-5772). Located in an early nineteenth-century house on a large tree-lined square near the cathedral and a few blocks back from the main commercial district, the hotel has clearly seen better days. However, the ornate building retains its original grace, the rooms are large and there's an attractive courtyard. ③.

Ritter Hotel, Largo Vespasiano Júlio Veppo 55 (☎228-4044). Across the road from the *Rodoviária*, this hotel is totally devoid of character but is clean, efficient and serves an inexpensive buffet supper. You can use the swimming pool, sauna and other facilities of the adjoining upmarket *Porto Alegre Ritter Hotel*. ⑤.

Santa Catarina, Rua General Vitorino 240 (☎224-9044). A well-equipped medium-category hotel in the heart of downtown. ④.

Terminal-Tur, Largo Vespasiano Júlio Veppo 125 (☎227-1656). Small rooms but with air conditioning, very important for a Porto Alegre summer. This is the cheapest secure hotel near the *Rodoviária*. ③.

The City

Porto Alegre sprawls out over a series of hills with the centre spread between two levels, the older residential area on the higher level and the commercial area below. In the 1960s and 1970s the city centre underwent dramatic redevelopment with new urban highways, ever larger office buildings and landfill schemes to improve the docks. Despite the destruction accompanying the construction boom, many of Porto Alegre's nineteenth- and early twentieth-century buildings escaped demolition, and the city has succeeded in retaining some of its former dignity. In the city centre itself, everything is within an easy walk, and a half-day or so is enough to visit most places of interest.

The ochre-coloured **Mercado Público** is at the heart of the lower town, located alongside Praça Rui Barbosa and Praça XV de Novembro. Dating back to 1869 and said to be a replica of Lisbon's Mercado da Figueira, this imposing building, with its intricate, typically Portuguese, stuccoed detail, has recently undergone restoration. It contains an absorbing mix of stalls selling household goods, food, a vast variety of herbs, *erva maté* of all grades of quality and regional handicrafts. As part of the municipal authority's project to "humanize" Porto Alegre, much of the maze of streets around the market has been pedestrianized; the bar and restaurant on Praça XV de Novembro, formerly the meeting place of the city's artists and intellectuals, is an especially good spot from which to watch everyone pass by. To the left of the market is the **Palácio Municipal**, the old *prefeitura*, built in Neoclassical style between 1898 and 1901, its impressive proportions an indication of civic pride and self-confidence during the period when Porto Alegre was developing from being a mere southern outpost into an important city. Between about 1880 and 1930, Porto Alegre attracted large numbers of southern and Eastern European immigrants and in front of the palace is a **fountain**, a gift to the city from its once considerable Spanish community.

The streets along the steep slope rising from the low-lying parts of the centre (Rua dos Andradas, Rua General Vitorino and Rua Andrade Neves, which becomes Avenida Senador Salgado Filho) mark Porto Alegre's main **commercial district** of clothing stores, travel agents and banks. Further up the hill are Praça da Matriz (officially called Praça Marechal Deodoro) and Largo João Amorim do Albuquerque, where the former legislative assembly and some of Porto Alegre's oldest buildings are concentrated. Despite the buildings in this part of the city having late eighteenth- to mid-nineteenth-century origins, they have undergone so many renovations and additions over the past couple of centuries that only vaguely, if at all, do they bear any resemblance to their colonial predecessors. Though the foundations of the **Catedral Metropolitana** are built over those of a church that dates back to 1772, the present Italianate structure was only begun in 1921, and wasn't completed until 1986. Work on the former legislative assembly also started in 1772 but, likewise, it has undergone innumerable renovations over the years. The **Palácio Piratini** (the state governor's residence) dates from only 1909, while across from it, the **Teatro São Pedro** was inaugurated in 1858. Surprisingly, its Portuguese Baroque appearance has remained largely unmolested, and the theatre is an important venue for local and visiting companies. The **Consulado Italiano** (Italian consulate) is an impressive mansion and its prominent position, on the east side of the Praça da Matriz (no. 134), is a symbol of the important role Italians maintained in Porto Alegre and elsewhere in Rio Grande do Sul.

Porto Alegre's **museums** are a poor bunch, which is somewhat surprising for a city that has long been prosperous and is the most important cultural centre south of São Paulo. One that does stand out is the **Casa de Cultura Mário Quintana**, Rua dos Andradas 736 (Tues–Fri 9am–8pm, Sat & Sun 9am–6pm), one of Latin America's largest cultural centres. Designed in Neoclassical style by the German architect Theo Wiederspahn in 1923, the extremely elegant rose-coloured building was a hotel until 1980 and as such was once a popular meeting point for local artists, intellectuals and politicians, including presidents Vargas and Goulart. The poet Mário Quintana was a long-time resident, hence the name. Apart from numerous exhibition galleries, the Casa de Cultura houses a library, a cinema, a decent restaurant and a café. The **Museu de Arte do Rio Grande do Sul**, Praça da Alfândega (Tues–Sun 10am–5pm), has been devastated by thefts but still has a reasonable collection of work by *gaúcho* artists, among which the nineteenth-century landscapes deserve particular attention; it also hosts occasional special exhibitions. The **Museu Julio de Castilhos**, Rua Duque de Caxias 1231 (Tues–Fri 9am–5pm, Sat & Sun 1–5pm), presents a patchy and poor history of the state. A curiosity – rather than intrinsically interesting – is the **Museu da Força Expedicionária Brasileira** at Av. João Pessoa 567 (Mon–Wed & Fri 2–5pm, Thurs 8–11.30am), where exhibits relate to the Brazilian battalions who served in the Italian campaign of World War II.

Eating, drinking and nightlife

As you'd expect, meat dominates menus here and *churrascarias* abound. However, the city centre has only a limited selection of **restaurants** of any sort, with the best located in the suburbs – which, fortunately, are not more than a $6 taxi-fare away.

Although during the daytime you can walk around most places in the city with reasonable safety, take care after dark, as Porto Alegre is developing a reputation for street crime to rival the worst of Brazilian cities. Nevertheless, it's a lively place with plenty going on until late into the evening.

Restaurants

Al Dente, Rua Mata Bacelar 210. There are several very good Italian restaurants in the suburb of Auxiliadora, 3km northeast of the centre, and this is one of the best. Moderate to expensive; evenings only, closed Sun.

Associação Macrobiotica, Rua Mal. Floriano 72. Vegetarians will have a hard time in Rio Grande do Sul, and even its comparatively cosmopolitan capital is no exception. This is one of the few oases for non-meat eaters in Porto Alegre. Inexpensive. Mon–Fri 9am–6pm, Sat 9am–2pm.

Casa de Portugal, Av. João Pessoa 579. Portuguese and one of the few good restaurants in the centre of town. Moderate to expensive; closed Mon.

Chef's Grill, Rua Miguel Tostes 424. East of the centre in the suburb of Rio Branco, this is one of the city's best *churrascarias*. Moderate to expensive.

El Chiriinguito, Rua Coronel Bordini 882. The city's best Spanish restaurant. Moderate to expensive; Mon–Sat evenings, Sun lunch.

Il Gattopardo, Rua 24 de Outubro 1585. Another superb Italian restaurant out in Auxiliadora. Moderate to expensive; evenings only.

Ilha Natural, Rua Andrade Neves 42, 1st floor. One of Porto Alegre's rare vegetarian restaurants, but the inexpensive food is fairly unimaginative. Mon–Fri lunch only.

O Galo, Av. Aureliano Figueiredo Pinto 904. Located in Cidade Baixa, this is the best Portuguese restaurant in the city centre. Moderate to expensive; Tues–Sat evenings, Sun lunch, closed Mon.

Polska, Rua João Guimarães 377. Unsophisticated, fairly inexpensive Polish cooking that tastes excellent on a cold Porte Alegre winter's day. Tues–Sat evenings, Sun lunch, closed Mon.

Pulperia, Trav. do Carmo 76. Good, moderately priced regional food, a short walk from Largo João Amorim de Albuquerque. Dinner only.

Recanto do Seu Flor, Av. Getúlio Vargas 1700. If you've only time for one meal in Porto Alegre, it's definitely worth the trip out to this place in the suburb of Menino Deus (just beneath Morro Santa Teresa), where regional food at its best is served. The moderately priced menu is inspired by *gaúcho* traditions and concentrates on unusual stews. You may have to endure a floor show featuring dancing *gaúchos* and rowdy customers breaking into song in accompaniment.

Stübel, Rua Quintino Bocaiúva 940. Hearty, moderately priced German food in the suburb of Moinhos de Vento. Evenings only, closed Sun.

Nightlife and entertainment

Bars, some with live music and most with a predominantly young and trendy clientele, are spread out along, and just off, Avenida Osvaldo Aranha, alongside the Parque Farroupilha and near the Federal University. Favourites change constantly, but the *Doce Vicio*, Rua Vieira de Castro (off Avenida José Bonifácio at the park's southern edge), and, for dancing, the *Ocidente*, on Avenida Osvaldo Aranha itself, are usually lively. Be warned, though, things don't get going until around 11pm.

Throughout the year, Porto Alegre's numerous Centros de Tradição Gaúcha organize traditional meals, music and dance performances. Tourist offices have only limited information on the events, but full details are available from the Movimento Tradicionalista Gaúcho, Rua Guilherme Schell 60 (☎223-5194).

Porto Alegre boasts a good popular **music scene** and a considerable **theatrical** tradition. Foreign performers of all kinds usually include Porto Alegre on any Brazilian or wider South American tour. The Sala Jazz Tom Jobim at Rua Santo Antônio 421 (☎225-1229) features the city's best **jazz** or there are live afternoon jazz sessions at the *Café Concerto* within the Casa de Cultura (see p.573), which also has a good art-house **cinema**. The Instituto Goethe (see "Listings") regularly shows German films, though it doesn't take long for American films to be released in Porto Alegre. To find out **what's on** at any of these venues, consult the monthly *Programa*, produced by the tourist office, or the events listings in the newspaper *Zero Hora*.

Listings

Airlines Aerolíneas Argentinas, Av. Salgado Filho 267 (☎221-3300); Air France, Rua Sete de Setembro 1069 (☎224-6085); Iberia, Rua dos Andradas 1273 (☎233-6288); KLM, Rua dos Andradas 1535 (☎225-8666); Lufthansa, Praça da Alfândega 12 (☎226-9455); Swissair, Rua Gen. Andrade Neves 100 (☎225-7045); TAP, Rua dos Andradas 1237 (☎226-1211); Transbrasil, Av. Borges de Medeiros 410 (☎225-8300); Varig/Cruzeiro, Rua dos Andradas 1107 (☎221-6333); VASP, Rua Uruguai 396 and Av. Farrapos 2059 (☎342-4233).

Banks and exchange There are numerous banks and *casas de câmbio* (Mon–Fri 10am–4.30pm) along Rua dos Andradas and Avenida Senador Salgado near Praça da Alfândega. The *casa de câmbio* at the *Rodoviária* accepts travellers' cheques. The Banco do Brasil (Mon–Fri 10am–2.30pm) at the corner of Rua Uruguai and Rua dos Andradas changes travellers' cheques but at a minimum of $100 per transaction, and the airport branch levies the typical $20 fee.

Boat excursions Two-hour excursions on the Rio Guaiba leave from the tour-boat berth (*Doca Turistica*) on Avenida Maua, near the train station. Schedules vary seasonally, so check with the tourist office.

Consulates Argentina, Rua Prof. Annes Dias 112, 1st floor (☎224-6810); Austria, Av. Carlos Gomes 111 (☎345-1566); Belgium, Rua Uruguai 240, cj. 406 (☎226-0509); Denmark, Av. Ipiranga 321 (☎233-4600); Finland, Rua Com. Azevedo 224 (☎222-7140); Germany, Rua Prof. Annes Dias 112, 11th floor (☎424-9592); Italy, Praça Mal. Deodoro 134 (☎228-2055); Netherlands, Rua José Salgado Martins 145 (☎330-3132); Norway, Av. Ipiranga 321 (☎233-4600); Sweden, Av. Sen. Salgado Filho 327, cj. 1301 (☎227-1289); Switzerland, Av. Viena 327, cj. 1301 (☎222-2025); Uruguay, Av. Cristovão Colombo 3133 (☎224-3499); USA, Rua Cel. Genuino 421 (☎/226-4177); UK, Rua Itapeva 110 (☎341-0720).

Cultural institutes Instituto Cultural Brasileiro-Norte Americano, Rua Riachuelo 1257 (☎224-4358); Instituto Gaúcho de Tradição e Folclore, Av. Siqueira Campos 1184, 5th fl (☎221-5411); Instituto Goethe, Av. 24 de Octobro 112 (☎222-7832).

Festivals Main folklore events are the Festa de Nossa Senhora dos Navegantes (Feb 2), the high point of which is a procession of fishing boats; and Semana Farroupilha (Sept 13–20), featuring traditional local folk dancing and singing.

Medical emergencies Pronto-Socorro Municipal, Av. Oswaldo Aranha at the intersection with Venâcio Aires (☎231-5900); or get advice from your consulate.

Post offices At Rua Siqueira Campos 1100, Rua Sete de Setembro 1020 and Rua General Camara, near the waterfront Avenida Maua.

Shopping Handicrafts from throughout the state are available at Artesanato Rio Grande do Sul, Av. Senador Salgado Filho 366, and the Feira do Artesanato on Praça da Alfândega (between *ruas* da Praia and Sete de Setembro) is worth a look, too. The Museu de Arte do Rio Grande do Sul (see p.573) has a small gallery where reasonably priced original prints and paintings by local artists are offered for sale.

The Serra Gaúcha

North of Porto Alegre is the **Serra Gaúcha**, a range of hills and mountains populated mainly by the descendants of German and Italian immigrants. The Germans, who settled in Rio Grande do Sul between 1824 and 1859, spread out on fairly low-lying land, establishing small farming communities, of which **Nova Petrópolis** is just one that still retains strong elements of its ethnic origins. The Italians, who arrived between 1875 and 1915, settled on more hilly land further north and, being mainly from the hills and mountains of Veneto and Trento, they adapted well and very quickly specialized in **wine production**. Caxias do Sul has developed into the region's most important administrative and industrial centre, but it is in and around smaller towns, such as **Bento Gonçalves** and **Garibaldi**, where the region's – and, in fact, Brazil's – wine production is centred.

To the **east**, and at much higher altitudes, are the resort towns of **Gramado** and **Canela**, where unspoilt landscapes, mountain trails, refreshing temperatures, *cafés coloniais* (high teas: a vast selection of cakes, jams, cheeses, meats, wine and other drinks produced by the region's *colonos*) and luxurious hotels attract visitors from cities throughout Brazil.

Nova Petrópolis and around

The main road north from Porto Alegre passes **São Leopoldo** and **Nova Hamburgo** (Rio Grande do Sul's first two German settlements but now mere industrial satellites of the city) before entering more hilly terrain inhabited by peasant farmers. In most of the family farms, German-based dialects are still spoken, but in the majority of towns and villages, Portuguese is the dominant language. However, in architecture and culture, the ethnic origins of the townsfolk are quite obvious, and considerable pride is taken in the German heritage.

In most respects thoroughly unremarkable, **NOVA PETRÓPOLIS**, 100km north of Porto Alegre, makes the greatest effort in promoting its German character, and the German language is almost universally spoken here. The municipal authorities encourage new building to be in "traditional" German architectural styles (which is why there's a plethora of alpine chalet-like structures around), and **festivals** take on a distinct German flavour. Principal amongst these are the Festa de Verão (weekends during Jan & Feb), the Festa do Folklore (weekends in July) and the Oktoberfest (October weekends), all held in the **Parque do Imigrante**. But while clearly German-inspired, the events have little in common with the popular culture of the region's *colonos*. Indeed, of rather more interest is the Parque do Imigrante itself, where a village much like many in the region during the late nineteenth century, has been created (daily 8am–6pm). The black-and-white half-timbered buildings, dating between 1870 and 1910, were brought to the park from outlying parts of the *município* and include a Protestant chapel and cemetery, a general store with a dancing salon, a credit agency (*Bauernkasse*), a school house and a smithy.

Disappointingly, Nova Petrópolis is not a place for walks. Instead, take a bus to the nearby hamlet of **Linha Imperial** and walk from there. The scenery is hilly and pastoral and it's a good area to view rural life close up. There's a hotel here, the *Veraneio Schoeler* (☎054/281-1778; full board ④) which is remarkably comfortable for such a backwater.

Practicalities

The **Rodoviária** is centrally located just off Avenida XV de Novembro with good connections to Porto Alegre, Gramado and Caxias do Sul. You'll find the helpful **tourist office** (daily 8am–6pm) at the entrance to the Parque do Imigrante.

As you might expect of somewhere so German-influenced, **hotels** here are always clean and usually relatively expensive. The most pleasant is the *Hotel Recanto Suíço*, Av. XV de Novembro 2195 (☎054/281-1229; ③–④), on the principal road running through town. The main building of the hotel feels like a diminutive Swiss inn, and in the extensive tree-filled gardens there's a small pool and chalets. The friendly owner speaks excellent English and, of course, German. There are several other hotels on the same road or just off it, all providing similar facilities at around the same price. Typical of the rather characterless alternatives is the *Hotel Petrópolis*, near the *Rodoviária* at Rua Coronel Steglich 81 (☎054/281-1091; ④), in a modern chalet-style building with an attractive garden and a beautiful mountain view.

You can **eat** well in town, too, and the *Hotel Recanto Suíço* has an excellent and inexpensive restaurant featuring simple German dishes. If you want to have supper there, advance notice is required. *Opa's Kaffeehaus* at Rua João Leão 96 (closed Mon) offers a wonderful *café colonial* in a spot with spectacular views. If you need a break from German influence, a good alternative is the *Galeto Picollo Pollo* at Av. XV de Novembro 2680, a five- to ten-minute walk from the centre towards Gramado. The restaurant serves vaguely Italian-style local dishes centred on chicken, polenta and excellent locally produced country wine.

Gramado

Thirty-six kilometres due east of Nova Petrópolis, along a beautiful winding road, is **GRAMADO**, Brazil's most exclusive mountain resort. At 825m you're unlikely to suffer from altitude sickness, but Gramado is high enough to be refreshingly cool in summer and positively chilly in winter. Architectually, Gramado and the neighbouring resort of Canela try hard to appear Swiss, with alpine chalets and flower-filled window boxes the norm. It's a mere affectation, though, since hardly any of the inhabitants are of Swiss origin – and only a small minority are of German extraction. The most pleasant time to visit the area is during the spring (Oct & Nov) when the parks and gardens are full of flowers, but the hydrangeas remain in bloom well into January. Gramado's attractions lie mainly within the town itself: excellent and varied restaurants and the large and very pretty **Parque Knorr** (daily 9am–6pm) and the secluded **Lago Negro**. The whole region is magnificent but it's difficult to explore properly without a car.

Practicalities

Gramado can easily be reached by **bus** from Porto Alegre and Caxias do Sul, and in the summer from Torres. The **Rodoviária** is on the main street, right in the centre of town. The **tourist office**, at Av. Borges de Medeiros 1674 (daily 9am–9pm), is extremely well organized and provides several excellent maps and comprehensive lists of local hotels and restaurants.

Many **hotels** offer discounts outside the peak summer and winter months, especially during the week. The lowest-priced are the *Planalto* across from the *Rodoviária*, at Av. Borges de Medeiros 554 (☎054/286-1210; ③), and, also in the centre, the *Dinda*, Rua Augusto Zatti 160 (☎054/286-2810; ③). There's no lack of more expensive places to stay: worth considering is the small *Hospedaria Andrade* at Av. Borges de Medeiros 3585 (☎054/286-3356; ④), or the *Hotel Cavalo Branco* (☎054/286-1254; ④), with a pool set in beautiful grounds. Overlooking the town centre in a private park is the *Hotel Serrano* (☎054/286-1332; ⑦) at Av. das Hortênsias 1160, a good choice if you're after luxury hotel facilities with rustic pretensions.

As far as **restaurants** are concerned, many claim to be "Swiss" or "Italian" and, in general, the Italian ones are cheaper while the Swiss tend to be better. One of the best in town is the *Belle du Valais*, Av. das Hortênsias 1432. You'll get a superb *café colonial* in Gramado featuring all the local goodies – try *Tia Nilda*, Av. das Hortênsias 765.

Canela

CANELA, 8km further east, down a road bordered on both sides by hydrangeas, is slightly lower, smaller and less commercialized; but otherwise, it's much like its neighbour. Canela offers little of particular beauty within its small urban area, but it is better situated for the **Parque Estadual do Caracol**, 8km to the north. You can reach the park by bus – marked "Caracol Circular" (4 daily) – which leaves from next to the old steam engine in the centre of Canela; get off at the restaurant-tourist complex in the park. From here, a path leads down to the foot of a waterfall, the park's main attraction, and other paths lead to different small falls at higher levels, from where there are panoramic views into the deep canyon of the Rio Caí. There's also a good **campsite** in the park.

Canela's **Rodoviária** is on the central main street, and there are regular buses here from Porto Alegre and Caxias do Sul. The **tourist office**, in Praça João Correia (Mon–Sat 8am–6pm, Sun 8am–1pm), tries to be helpful but is less useful than the one in Gramado.

There's a good **youth hostel** across the road from the *Rodoviária* at Rua Ernesta Urbani 132 (☎054/282-2017), but over winter weekends and in the summer it can be difficult to find a bed. The cheapest **hotel** is the *Turis Serra* (☎054/282-2136; ②) at Av. Osvaldo Aranha 160, while there are a number of small *pousadas* providing accommodation in cabins. The nicest of these is the *Pousada Alpes Verdes* (☎054/282-1162; ④), set in park-like gardens. The *Grande Hotel Canela*, Rua Getúlio Vargas 3000 (☎054/282-1285; ⑤), has a carefully cultivated "old world" atmosphere with a beautiful garden and lake. Canela is home to the finest hotel in the state, the *Laje de Pedra* (☎054/282-4300; ⑦), and even if you're not staying, you can visit for the spectacular views of the Rio Caí which snakes around in the valley below. There's a minibus from town which plies the three-kilometre route out to the hotel, where there's an expensive restaurant and a *chimarrão* salon where you can sip *maté*.

Parque Nacional dos Aparados da Serra

The dominant physical feature of south central Brazil is a **highland plateau**, the result of layer upon layer of ocean sediment piling up and the consequent rock formations being lifted to form the Brazilian Shield. Around 150 million years ago, lava slowly poured onto the surface of the shield, developing into a thick layer of basalt rock. At the edge of the plateau, cracks puncture the basalt and it is around the largest of these that the **Parque Nacional dos Aparados da Serra** was created.

The park lies 100km east of Canela. Approaching it from any direction, you pass through rugged cattle pasture, occasionally interrupted by the distinctive umbrella-like Paraná pine trees and solitary farm buildings. As the dirt road enters the park itself, forest patches appear, suddenly and dramatically interrupted by a canyon of breathtaking proportion, **Itaimbezinho**. Some 5800m in length, between 600 and 2000m wide and 720m deep, Itaimbezinho is a dizzying sight. The canyon and the area immediately surrounding it have two distinct climates and support very different types of vegetation. On the higher levels, with relatively little rainfall, but with fog banks moving in from the nearby Atlantic Ocean, vegetation is typical of a cloud forest, while on the canyon's floor, a mass of subtropical plants flourishes. The park has abundant birdlife and is home to over 150 different species.

In the park, there's a **visitors' centre**, a **campsite**, a **restaurant** and simple **accommodation** at the *Paradouro do Itaimbezinho* (☎054/251-178; ②). From here, you can hire a guide to lead you down the steep trail (including a five-metre vertical incline which you have to negotiate by rope) to the canyon floor. You'll need to be physically fit, have good hiking boots and be prepared for flash floods.

Visiting the park

Aparados da Serra can be visited throughout the year, but spring (Oct & Nov) is the best time for flowers. In the winter, especially in July, it can get very cold and occasionally snows. Summers are warm and mainly sunny, but heavy rainfall sometimes makes the roads and trails impassable. Without your own transport, or if you're not travelling as part of an organized tour, the park can be difficult to reach. Although part of the park is located in Santa Catarina, access is much easier from Rio Grande do Sul.

To get to the park, take a bus from Porto Alegre, Gramado or Canela to **São Francisco de Paula**, 69km from the park's entrance. From São Francisco, you need to take another bus northeast to **Cambará do Sul** and ask to be let off at the entrance to the park. From here it's a further 15km to Itaimbezinho. Buses occasionally run between São Francisco or Cambará and Praia Grande (which has a couple of basic hotels, one on the main square and the other at the *Rodoviária*), on the Santa Catarina side of the state line. These will drop you just 3km from Itaimbezinho. In São Francisco, you may be able to join a tour group headed for the park. Coming from Cambará, the park entrance is only 3km away and you should be able to get a taxi to take you.

São Francisco de Paula and Cambará do Sul

São Francisco and Cambará are both good places to use as a base for visiting the park. In **SÃO FRANCISCO DE PAULA**, you'll pass the **tourist office** on the way into town (daily 8am–7pm) where you may be able to gather advice on how to get to the park. There's a wide choice of places **to stay** in São Francisco, much the larger though the less attractive of the two towns. Two good places to try are the *Estrela Parque* (☎051/644-

1338; ③) at Rua Tiradentes 732 which has a small pool or, also with a pool and set in pleasant gardens, the *Hotel Cavalinho Branco* (☎051/644-1263; ④) at Praça Tiradentes 50. The best place **to eat** is in the *Hotel Veraneio Hampel* (☎051/644-1363; reservations essential), 4km out of town on the road to Canela, which serves superb home-style meals.

In **CAMBARÁ DO SUL**, the **tourist office** is situated in the *prefeitura* on Rua Dona Úrsula (Mon–Fri 8.30–11.30am & 2–5pm). The only **place to stay** is the simple but pleasant *Pousada Fortaleza* (☎054/251-1224; ②), and the best place **to eat** is the *Restaurante São Cristóvão* (11.30am–1pm) at Rua Oswaldo Kroeff 209 which serves excellent local dishes. In the evening there's a rustic but good *churrascaria, Pampa,* at Rua João Francisco Ritter 504.

Caxias do Sul

Around 70km west of Gramado and 37km north of Nova Petrópolis is **CAXIAS DO SUL**, Rio Grande do Sul's third largest city. Italian immigrants arrived in Caxias (as the city is known) in 1875, but the only obvious indication of the city's ethnic origins are its *adegas,* now huge companies or co-operatives that produce some of the state's poorest wine. Caxias' most important wine producer is the Chateau Lacave but, 9km from town, it's not worth the effort involved in getting there. A better bet are the *cantina* **tours** offered by several wine producers in the city centre, followed by free tastings: Riograndense, Rua 18 do Forte 2346, are especially used to receiving visitors. If you're interested in the history of the region, the **Museu Casa de Pedra** (Tues–Sun 9am–noon & 1–5pm) is worth a look. Housed in a late nineteenth-century stone farmhouse, it contains artefacts relating to the first Italian immigrants. The most important festival in Caxias is the **Festa Nacional da Uva** (odd-numbered years), a celebration of Italian traditions and local industry – most importantly wine production.

Inexpensive **hotels** are located just off the main square, Praça Rui Barbosa, and you'll find the tourist office here, too. **Food** in this "Italian" city is not at all sophisticated but there are a few simple restaurants serving fairly authentic dishes: try the *Alvorado*, Rua Os 18 do Forte 200 (closed Sun evening), for chicken and polenta, or *Belaria*, Rua Marques do Herval 1124, for homemade pasta.

Caxias is a major transport centre and **buses** run to towns throughout Rio Grande do Sul, and to states to the north, from the **Rodoviária**, seven blocks from Praça Rui Barbosa.

Flores da Cunha and around

Virtually all the towns and villages in the area to the north and west of Caixas do Sul were founded by northern Italian immigrants and, set amidst the almost mountainous landscape, **FLORES DA CUNHA** is considered to be the most Italian of Brazilian towns, retaining thriving Italian folk traditions. The town itself is quite unremarkable in appearance, but the **Museu Histórico** (Mon–Fri 8–11.30am & 1–5.30pm, Sat 2–5pm), in the old town hall on Rua 25 de Julho, provides a good overview of the region's history. The **tourist office** is located in the same building. There's just one **hotel**, the very plain but clean *Fiório* (☎054/292-2535; ③) on the way into town, and one excellent **restaurant**, *Lola's* at Rua Ernesto Alves 2107 (evenings only, closed Mon), where a delicious buffet meal with wine costs just $7. The town is a good base from which to explore the surrounding countryside and stop off at some of the *colônias* selling their homemade cheeses, salamis, liqueurs and wine. Both in town and in the region around, there are innumerable *cantinas* that welcome visitors for wine tasting.

A particularly attractive hamlet to head for is **OTÁVIO ROCHA**, 13km southwest of town (two buses daily). The people here are almost entirely of Veneto origin and still maintain their pioneer forebears' dialect and customs. The best time to visit is in the last two weeks of July when the **Festo do Colono** takes place, but throughout the year the hamlet is delightful. Vines are planted on just about every patch of land, extending down to the main street itself, and the smell of fermenting grapes is remarkable. If you want to stay over in Otávio Rocha, there's a good **hotel** which serves wonderful *colono* food, the *Hotel Dona Adélia* (☎054/292-1519; ②). A further 7km west, the village of **NOVA PÁDUA** makes a good place to stop, as the *Albergue Belvedere Sonda* (☎054/292-1899; ③) is a pleasant hotel with beautiful views of the Rio das Antas and serves superb local dishes, even better than those in Otávio Rocha.

Thirty-four kilometres north of Flores da Cunha, **ANTÔNIO PRADO** was founded in 1886 by another group of northern Italian immigrants. The **Museu Municipal** in Praça Garibaldi (Mon–Fri 8.30–11.30am, Sat & Sun 2–4pm) tells the usual story of the first pioneers, but it's Antônio Prado's wealth of **stone houses** and farm buildings that makes it particularly interesting. Until about 1940 the area prospered, but over the following decades, the local economy stagnated and *colonos* moved as far away as the western Amazon. The town was left with dozens of disused late nineteenth- and early twentieth-century buildings, and 47 of them now have preservation orders served on them. For a local map, and information on the farm buildings scattered along the *município*'s backroads, ask at the helpful **tourist office** in the *prefeitura* at Praça Garibaldi 57 (Mon–Fri 9am–5pm) or at the museum. The *Hotel Piemonte* (☎054/293-1280; ②), across from Praça Garibaldi, is the only place **to stay** in Antônio Prado. There are numerous simple **restaurants** around serving country-style food.

Bento Gonçalves and around

Approach **BENTO GONÇALVES**, 40km west of Caxias, from any direction and there's no doubting that this is the heartland of Brazil's wine-producing region. On virtually every patch of land, no matter the gradient, vines are planted. Wine production entered a new era in the late 1970s as huge co-operatives developed, local *cantinas* expanded and foreign (mainly French) companies set up local operations. But the results have been somewhat mixed. In the past, the locals relied almost exclusively on North American grape varieties and produced their own distinctive wines. Gradually, though, they were encouraged to join a co-operative or agree to sell their grapes exclusively for one company. New European and, more recently, Californian vines enabled companies to produce "finer" wines of a type until then imported. All this means that the *colonos* now rarely produce more than their own family's requirements, and hi-tech stainless steel vats and rigidly monitored quality control have rapidly replaced the old oaken barrel tradition; the resulting wines are, at best, mediocre.

Bento Gonçalves itself is an undistinguished-looking town whose economy, of course, totally revolves around grape and wine production. There are numerous **cantinas** in the centre of town offering free tours and tastings and a **Museu do Imigrante**, at Rua Erny Dreher 127 (Tues–Fri 8–11am & 1.30–5.30pm), documenting the history of Italian immigration and life in the area. There's a **youth hostel**, the *Pousada Casa Mia* at Traversa Niterói 71 (☎054/451-1215; $12 per person), while **hotels**, of which there are none too shortage, are mainly found in the streets around the very helpful **tourist office**, Rua Mal. Deodoro 70 (Mon–Fri 8–11.45am & 1–7pm, Sat 9am–5pm). **Restaurants** are generally poor, serving overcooked pasta and undercooked pizza. One exception, however, is the *Casa Colonial Felicità*, a half-hour walk from the centre in the Parque da Fenavinho, serving excellent local food with strong Italian influences.

The surrounding area

It's worth visiting the surrounding countryside and villages, where, on the surface at least, the way of life has changed little over the years. The calendar revolves around the grape, with weeding, planting, pruning – and the maintenance of the characteristic stone walls – the main activities during the year, leading up to the harvest in February and March. An excellent way to admire the beautiful countryside is to take the Saturday tourist **steam train** (at 2pm from Bento; tickets $10 from Giordani Turismo, Rua Erny Hugo Dreher 197; ☎054/451-2788) into the vine-dominated countryside. Along its 48-kilometre route (formerly part of a line extending south to Porto Alegre), the train stops at some of the more scenic spots, of which the most spectacular is the view over the **Vale do Rio das Antas** where the river's path takes the form of a horseshoe.

Many of the villages around Bento could, from a distance at least, be mistaken for Italian ones. One of the nicest is **MONTE BELO**, from where there are fine views in all directions. With a simple, but very cheap **hotel** whose **restaurant** serves authentic *colono* food – a complete meal costs just $5 – Monte Belo is a fine base from which to wander along pathways and tracks between the vineyards. There are several buses a day to Monte Belo, but try to take one that goes along the **Linha Leopoldina**, a beautiful road along which there are old stone farmhouses and other farm buildings, and a chapel, the Capela das Neves. If you are travelling by car, take the RS-470 out of Bento and turn off the road at Km68.5. You can get a map and detailed directions from the tourist office in Bento. Quite unusual in an area where wine production has become so thoroughly industrialized is the Casa Valduga, a small winery owned and run by a local family. It produces, in limited quantities, some of Brazil's finest wines – wines that are otherwise only available at some of São Paulo's best restaurants. The best time to go is January–March when the grapes are harvested, but passing visitors are welcomed throughout the year for tastings.

Vacaria

On the northeastern plateau, 955m above sea level, **VACARIA** is a quiet administrative and commercial centre for the surrounding cattle country. The road to Vacaria from Caxias do Sul, 100km to the south, is extremely beautiful, rising sharply from vine-clad hill slopes before reaching the near treeless *planalto* cattle country. Normally there would be absolutely nothing to detain you in town, but once a year Vacaria comes to life when people from throughout southern Brazil and beyond come to participate in the **Rodeio Crioulo Internacional**, one of the country's most important *rodeios* (see the box on p.586), held in the last week of January.

All the **events** that you'd expect are included, like lasso-throwing, horse-breaking and steer-riding competitions, in addition to the real purpose behind a *rodeio*, the accompanying cattle and horse shows, and song and dance events. While nattily dressed urban *gaúchos* show up in impeccably tailored *bombachas* and distinguished-looking capes, Vacaria's *rodeio* is first and foremost a popular event, attended by ordinary people of the *campanha* and cattle-ranching *serra*.

Huge **tents** are erected at the *rodeio* grounds on the outskirts of town (reached by constant buses from Vacaria's main square), in which most of the spectators and competitors stay, despite the often bitterly cold midsummer temperatures. Several simple **hotels** are on, and just off, the main square: there's usually space, even during *rodeio* week. The two best are the *Pampa*, Rua Júlio de Castilhos 1560 (☎054/231-1333; ④), and the *Granetto*, Rua Dr Flores 437 (☎054/231-1046; ③), while cheaper are the *Real*, Rua Ramiro Barcelos (②), and the *Querencia*, Rua Mal. Floriano (②). At the *rodeio*, **food** means meat – and only meat – and at the *rodeio* ground's restaurants you're expected to come equipped with your own sharp knife. However, in the town centre, just off the main square, there's a pizzeria where you can retreat, having sworn never to touch another steak.

Finally, throughout the period of the *rodeio*, the state **tourist office** maintains an office just outside the gates of the exhibition grounds; it also has a detailed programme of events.

The coast: the Litoral Gaúcho

The **coast** of Rio Grande do Sul is a virtually unbroken 500-kilometre-long beach, along which are dotted resorts popular with Argentines, Uruguayans and visitors from Porto Alegre and elsewhere in the state. In winter the beaches are deserted and most of the hotels closed, but between mid-November and March it's easy to believe that the state's entire population has migrated to the resorts. The attraction of this, the **Litoral Gaúcho**, is essentially one of convenience: from Porto Alegre many of the resorts can be reached within two or three hours, making even day trips possible. But for anyone travelling to or from points north, the beaches here can easily be ignored. Those resorts that are accessible are crowded, while – due to the influence of the powerful Rio Plate – the water is usually murky; and, even in summer, Antarctic currents often make for chilly bathing.

Torres

The northernmost point on the Litoral Gaúcho, 197km from Porto Alegre, **TORRES** is the one spot along the coast that is actually worth going out of your way for. It's considered the state's most sophisticated coastal resort, and the beaches behind which the town huddles, **Praia Grande** and **Prainha**, are packed solid on summer weekends. However, by walking across the Morro do Farol (identifiable by its lighthouse) and along the almost equally crowded Praia da Cal, you come to the **Parque Estadual da Guarita**, one of the most beautiful stretches of the southern Brazilian coast. The development of the park was supervised by the landscaper Roberto Burle Marx together with Brazil's foremost environmentalist, José Lutzenberger.

The state park is centred on a huge basalt outcrop, with 35-metre-high cliffs rising straight up from the sea, from where there are superb views up and down the coast. At several points, steps lead down from the clifftop to basalt pillars and cavern-like formations, beaten out of the cliff face over the years. Although there are areas where it's both possible, and safe, to dive from the rocks, generally the sea is inaccessible and ferocious. Continue along the clifftop, and you'll eventually reach the **Praia da Guarita**, a fairly small beach that is never as crowded as those nearer town. Just beyond a further, much smaller outcrop, there's another beach, this time stretching with hardly an interruption all the way to the border with Uruguay.

Practicalities

From the **Rodoviária**, served by buses from Porto Alegre, Florianópolis, São Paulo, Curitiba, Buenos Aires and Santa Fe, walk down Avenida José Bonifacio to Avenida Barão do Rio Branco. Here, turn right for the centre and the beach (six blocks) or left for the **tourist office** (one block). Torres has countless **hotels**, with many of the cheaper ones located on Barão do Rio Branco and the two streets running parallel to it. Even on a midsummer weekend, accommodation is surprisingly easy to track down, but try to arrive early in the day. You won't find a cheaper hotel than the excellent *Medusa* at Av. Barão do Rio Branco 828 (☎051/664-2378; ①) but, more typically, expect to pay at least $40 for a double room. Others worth trying are the *Mar Del Plata*, Av. Barão do Rio Branco 148 (☎051/664-1665; ③), or the *Bauer*, Rua Ballino de Freitas 260 (☎051/664-1290; ③). Basic **youth hostel** accommodation is available in summer at Rua Júlio de Castilhos 875 (☎051/664-1865; closed March to mid-Dec), opposite the *Rodoviária*.

All the best **restaurants** are by the river, twenty to thirty minutes' walk from the centre. Either walk along Praia Grande in the opposite direction from the lighthouse or, quicker, along Rua Sete de Setembro, a couple of streets back from the beach.

Especially recommended are *Gaviota* and the *Cantinho do Pescador*, which serve a wide variety of seafood. In the centre, there are plenty of beachside **bars**, some serving light meals, while at Rua José Luís de Freitas 800, the *Galeto Régis* serves excellent chicken dishes (closed April–Nov).

With Argentine tourists in mind, scattered about the centre are a number of **câmbios** giving a good rate for the dollar.

Capão da Canoa and Tramandi

Typical of resorts popular with day-trippers and weekend visitors are **CAPÃO DA CANOA** and **TRAMANDI**, respectively 140km and 120km northeast of Porto Alegre. Unless you're spending time in Porto Alegre and want to get away briefly from the often intense summer heat, neither resort has much to recommend it. Tramandi is the larger of the two, with more hotels, more restaurants and even more people. Both share an identical lack of character, based on wide open beaches with little in the way of vegetation, and plenty in the way of beachside bars.

There are no really cheap **hotels** in Tramandi, the most reasonable ones being the *Paulinho* at Av. Rio Grande 1060 (☎051/661-1209; ③), the *Centenário* at Trav. Pellegrini 42 (☎051/661-1778; ④) and the *São Jorge*, Rua Fernando Amaral 19 (☎051/661-1154; ④). In the centre of Capão da Canoa try the *Maquine* at Rua Andira 320 (☎051/665-2323; ③) or the *Acapulco* at Rua Venâncio Aires 363 (☎051/665-3121; ③).

Parque Nacional da Lagoa do Peixe

If you are travelling south along the coast from Torres down to the Uruguayan border at Chuí, it's normally necessary to go inland via Porto Alegre. But if time's no problem, it is possible to take buses from village to village along the RS-101 road and the narrow peninsula that protects the Lagoa dos Patos from the sea. The road is unpaved and often in the most appalling state, while the landscape is barren and windswept, but the remote fishing communities along the way have consequently been protected from the ravages of tourism. The inhabitants, largely of Azorean stock but also descendants of shipwreck survivors and renegades fleeing other parts of Rio Grande do Sul, make a living by fishing, growing onions and raising chickens and sheep.

At the midpoint of the peninsula is the **Parque Nacional da Lagoa do Peixe**, centred on an area surrounding a long and narrow lagoon – so shallow that trucks can drive across it. The park is one of the most important **bird sanctuaries** in South America. Migrating birds stop here, as well as a fair number of lost penguins, albatrosses and other sea birds, attracted by the clean, brackish water rich in algae, plankton, crustacea and fish. The best time to visit is in the winter months, particularly July. There is no infrastructure for receiving visitors, so you'll need to track down someone with considerable local knowledge if you want to see anything of the park. It's best to head for the village of **MOSTARDAS** where basic **accommodation** (②) is available at the *Hotel Mostardense* (☎051/673-1368) or the *Hotel e Churrascaria Scheffer* (☎051/673-1277). For help in finding a guide, ask at the *prefeitura* (Mon–Fri; ☎051/673-1166). You'll need plenty of time to enjoy the area, not only because of difficulties in gaining access to the park but because of the appalling state of the RS-101, often washed out by flash floods, and because of poor bus services between the peninsula's small settlements. If you're driving, you may find it much easier to head down the peninsula on the Atlantic beach, as the sand is hard enough to take the weight of a car, although you will have to negotiate the few streams which cut across the beach and watch out for sudden tidal surges or weather changes.

Pelotas

Rio Grande do Sul's second largest city, **PELOTAS**, 270km to the south of Porto Alegre, is situated on the left bank of the Canal de São Gonçalo which connects the Lagoa dos Patos with the Lagoa Mirim. The town was founded in 1812 as a port for the *charque* (dried meat) producers of the surrounding region, and with the introduction of refrigeration in the late nineteenth century, demand for beef increased, and with it Pelotas' importance as a port and commercial centre. However, by the turn of the century, Rio Grande's port, able to take larger ships, had superseded it.

While a slowdown in investment might have been bad for the city's economy, it saved Pelotas' nineteenth-century Neoclassical centre from the developers. **Praça Coronel Pedro Osório**, the main square, is the city's heart, and most of the very elegant, stuccoed buildings with wrought-iron balconies overlooking the square date from the last century. Nearby, on Praça José Bonifácio, the **Catedral de São Francisco de Paula** is slightly unusual for these parts: while its interior has undergone reforms over the years, the exterior has not been fundamentally altered since it was built in 1832.

As a railhead, port and an important commercial centre, late nineteenth-century Pelotas was home to a considerable British community. Bearing witness to this is an Anglican church, the **Igreja Episcopal da Redentor**, a couple of blocks from the main square on Rua XV de Novembro. Built in 1883, the ivy-covered church would go unnoticed in any English town, but in Brazil it looks completely alien. In fact, though, in Rio Grande do Sul such churches have become a normal part of the urban landscape, with 52 others dotted around the state.

Practicalities

The **Rodoviária** is way out of town, with buses running into the centre every fifteen minutes. Long-distance services arrive in Pelotas from Rio Grande (1hr) and Porto Alegre (3hr) almost hourly, and less frequently from Santo Angelo, Santa Maria, Uruguaiana and Montevideo. There's an unhelpful **tourist office** (Mon–Fri 9am–6pm) at Praça Coronel Pedro Osório 6. On Praça Coronel Osório you'll find several cheap **hotels**, of which the best are the *Rex* (②) and the *Grande* (②). In general, **restaurants** are pretty poor but, on the main commercial street, decent (if dull) German meals are available at the *Bavária*, Rua Sete de Setembro 306, directly opposite a Chinese restaurant, the *Shangai*. More interesting are *El Paisano*, Rua Deodoro 1093 (closed Mon; March–Sept lunchtimes and evenings, Oct–Feb evenings only), an excellent Uruguayan *churrascaria*, and a good Portuguese restaurant, the *Vila do Conde*, Rua Andrade Neves 1321 (closed Mon), both inexpensive. Pelotas is famous for its **sweets and cakes**, and a good place to try them is *Otto Especialidades*, Rua Sete de Setembro 304. On a different note, as a supposed **gay** centre Pelotas has a reputation for being Brazil's San Francisco. If this is true, the gay community is extremely discreet – even for Rio Grande do Sul, one of Brazil's most homophobic states – since there are no obvious gay bars or clubs.

Rio Grande and around

On the entrance to the Lagoa dos Patos, **RIO GRANDE** was founded in 1737 at the very southern fringe of the Portuguese empire. With the growth of the *charque* and chilled beef economy, Rio Grande's port took on an increasing importance from the mid-nineteenth century. Rather more spread out than Pelotas, it does not share that city's instant charm. However, colonial and late nineteenth-century buildings are to be found in the area around Rua Floriano Peixoto and **Praça Tamandaré** (the main square), which is almost next to Largo Dr Pio and the much renovated eighteenth-century **Cathedral**. On Rua General Osório, by the corner of Rua General Neto, is the **Biblioteca Rio-grandense** (Mon–Fri 8am–noon & 2–6pm, Sat 8am–noon), dating from 1846, the oldest and still the most important library in the state. The library is especially significant for its nineteenth-century collection featuring many rare volumes. A number of museums are also worth a look. The **Museu Oceanográfico** at Rua Reito Perdigão 10 (Mon–Fri 9–11am & 2–5pm) is perhaps the most important of its type in Latin America, featuring a huge collection of fossils and preserved sea creatures. Containing a photographic archive and objects relating to the city of Rio Grande, the **Museu Histórico da Cidade** (Tues–Fri 9.30–11.30am & 2.30–5pm) is located in the old customs house (*alfândega*), a Neoclassical building built in 1879 on Rua Riachuelo.

At the **waterfront**, just moments' walk from the cathedral, there's always a lively mixture of ocean-going ships, fishing vessels and smaller boats. From here boats cross the mouth of the Lago dos Patos to the small village of **São José do Norte**, one of the oldest settlements in the state, with a simple church, **Nossa Senhora dos Navegantes**, built in 1795.

As far as **beaches** are concerned, though, you'll need to go to **Cassino**, a resort facing the Atlantic that's very popular with Uruguayans, 25km south of Rio Grande and served by buses from Praça Tamandaré. Like most of the rest of the Litoral Gaúcho, the beaches here are long, low and straight and only merit a visit if you have time between buses.

Practicalities

A few blocks from Praça Tamandaré is Rio Grande's **Rodoviária**, served by buses from most cities in Rio Grande do Sul, and from cities as far north as Rio de Janeiro. Though rarely open, the **tourist office** is at Rua Riachuelo 355, in front of the Câmara de Comércio, by the waterfront.

Built in 1826, the *Paris Hotel,* on the waterfront at Rua Marechal Floriano 112 (☎0532/32-8944; ②), was once *the* place **to stay** in Rio Grande and – with some imagination – a little of its former "Grand Hotel" feel remains. More expensive, more comfortable but with no character is the *Taufik,* near the cathedral at Rua General Neto 20 (☎0532/32-7455; ③). For **eating**, try the *Pescal*, Rua Aarechl Andrea 269 (closed Sun), which specializes in fish, or the *Angola*, Rua Benjamin Constant 163 (closed Mon), with Portuguese specialities. Unusual, very sweet **cakes** are sold at *Especialidades Milano*, Praça Tamandaré 282, or for Arab cakes or snacks, try the friendly Egyptian-owned *Lancheria Oriental* at Rua General Bacelar 421, opposite the Transbrasil office.

The Uruguayan border: Chuí

Unless you're shopping for cheap Scotch whisky or visiting the casino, there's absolutely nothing in **CHUÍ** (or "Chuy" on the Uruguayan side of the frontier) to stick around for. **Buses** entering and leaving Brazil stop at an immigration office a short distance from town for passports to be stamped. The Brazilian **Rodoviária** (frequent services from Pelotas, Rio Grande and Porto Alegre), on Rua Venezuela, is just a couple of blocks from Avenida Brasil, which divides the Brazilian and Uruguayan sides of town; you can cross back and forth quite freely. Onda, one of Uruguay's main bus companies, stops on the Uruguayan side of Avenida Brasil and has frequent departures for Punta del Este and Montevideo. If you are travelling to or from western Uruguay and Treinta Y Tres, you will have to walk 3km down Calle General Artigas (follow the signs to Montevideo) to the Uruguayan immigration post for an entry or exit stamp in your passport. If you need a **visa** to enter Brazil, there's a Brazilian consulate on the Uruguayan side of town at Calle Fernández 147, while in Brazil the Uruguayan consulate is at Rua Venezuela 311.

Change money at a Uruguayan *casa de câmbio* or bank before travelling on into Brazil as you will receive the equivalent of the best rates available in Brazilian cities. If you can, try to avoid **staying** in Chuí as hotels are overpriced and unpleasant; as a rule, those on the Brazilian side of the common avenue are cheaper, those on the Uruguayan side cleaner and more comfortable. **Restaurants** – even the most simple – are better on the Uruguayan side of the avenue. Finally, if you plan to send parcels abroad, Uruguayan postage rates are a fraction of Brazil's.

Gaúcho country: Lavras and Santa Maria

If you want to witness the everyday working life of the pampas close up, **LAVRAS DO SUL** is the place to head for. Located some 300km southwest of Porto Alegre and 100km north of Bagé, there's nothing to mark out the town from countless others in the region, dedicated to raising cattle, horses and sheep. What does make Lavras different is the local **fazenda** owners who have started taking guests, turning part of either the main house or their outhouses into *pousadas*. On arrival at a *fazenda*, you first have to show whether you can handle a horse. If you can't, you're quickly coached to develop some basic equestrian skills. Guests then join the *fazenda's* workers in their day-to-day

---

GAÚCHOS

During the colonial era and well into the nineteenth century, Rio Grande do Sul's southern and western frontiers were ill-defined, with Portugal and Spain, and then independent Brazil, Argentina and Uruguay, maintaining garrisons to assert their claims to the region. Frontier clashes were frequent, with central government presence weak or non-existent. If anyone could maintain some measure of control over these border territories it was the **gaúchos**, the fabled horsemen of southern South America. The product of miscegenation between Spanish, Portuguese, Indians and escaped slaves, the *gaúchos* wandered the region on horseback, either individually or in small bands, making a living by hunting wild cattle for their hides. Alliances were formed in support of local *caudilhos* (chiefs), who fought for control of the territory on behalf of the flag of one or other competing power. With a reputation of being tough and fearless, the *gaúcho* was also said to be supremely callous – displaying the same indifference in slitting a human or a bullock's throat.

As the nineteenth century ended, so too did the *gaúcho's* traditional way of life. International boundaries became accepted, and landowners were better able to exert control over their properties. Finally, as fencing was introduced and rail lines arrived, cattle turned into an industry with the animals raised rather than hunted. Gradually *gaúchos* were made redundant, reduced to the status of mere *peões* or cattlehands.

Still, more in Rio Grande do Sul than in Argentina, some *gaúcho* traditions persist, though for a visitor to get much of a picture of the present-day way of life is difficult. In general, the cities and towns of the state's interior are fairly characterless, though travelling between towns still brings forth echoes of former times, especially if you get off the beaten track. Here, in the small villages, horses are not only a tool used to herd cattle, but remain an essential means of transport. While women are no differently dressed than in the rest of Brazil, men appear in much the same way as their *gaúcho* predecessors: in *bombachas* (baggy trousers), linen shirt, kerchief, poncho and felt-rimmed hat, shod in pleated boots and fancy spurs. Also associated with the interior of Rio Grande do Sul is *chimarrão* (sugarless *maté* tea), which is sipped through a *bomba* (a silver straw) from a *cuia* (a gourd). In the towns themselves, cattlemen are always to be seen, purchasing supplies or just around for a good time. But undoubtedly your best chance of getting a feel of the interior is to attend a **rodeio**, held regularly in towns and villages throughout *gaúcho* country, and most notably at Vacaria (see p.581). Branches of the state tourist office, CRTur, will have information about when and where *rodeios* are due to take place.

duties minding the livestock around the property. There are natural pools and streams for cooling off in on hot summer days, while the extremely comfortable *fazenda* buildings all have open fires for the often bitterly cold winter evenings.

Four *fazendas* in Lavras do Sul accept guests: *Fazenda do Sobrado* (☎055/736-1008), *Fazenda Quero-Quero* (☎055/736-1223), *Fazenda São Crispin* (☎055/736-1207) and *Fazenda Quantrilho* (☎055/736-1291) The rate of $70 for a double room includes three very full meals a day. **Reservations** are essential as the *fazendas* only have room for between six and eight guests each and need some notice in order to collect you from town. You can book by phoning the association formed by the four *fazendas*, Hotéis Fazenda de Lavras do Sul (☎055/736-1239), which can also provide information on local events such as *rodeios*.

Santa Maria and around

In the centre of Rio Grande do Sul, just at the point where the *campanha* hits the escarpment leading up into the *serra*, is **SANTA MARIA**, a city of some 300,000 inhabitants. A farming, cattle, administrative and educational centre and rail junction, Santa Maria is probably the most important city west of Porto Alegre. And, with a very pleasant and relaxed atmosphere, it makes a good stopping-off point on the way into or out of Brazil.

Founded in 1797, it wasn't until the late nineteenth century, with the rise of the cattle economy and the arrival of the rail line, that Santa Maria became of significance. However, while there are a number of interesting buildings dating back to about 1900, nothing much remains from earlier times. On the main square in the heart of the city is the **Catedral**, Baroque in style, but built at the beginning of the twentieth century. On the same square there's another church, Anglican and – like the others in the state – built for the employees of the once-important British rail line and meat exporting interests. On Rua Daudt, a few blocks from Praça Saldanha Marinho, is another typically English building, from the same period but of otherwise uncertain origin – a curious ivy-clad house set in a beautiful garden. Many of the rail engineers at the beginning of the twentieth century were from Belgium, and they were housed in the **Vila Belga**, a row of very pretty, but dilapidated cottages built in 1903 on Rua Ernesto Beck, Rua Dr Valtier, Rua Manoel Ribas and Rua André Marques near the train station.

Practicalities

The commercial, largely pedestrianized streets run off, and parallel to, the main square on the side of town where the train station, the **Ferroviária**, is located (3 trains a week from Santana do Livramento, 3 from Uruguaiana and 6 from Porto Alegre). To get to the cathedral square from here, head straight along Avenida Rio Branco. Buses from all points in Rio Grande do Sul arrive at the **Rodoviária**, those from Curitiba and São Paulo use the Pluma depot, next door, while those from Montevideo run out of Planalto Turismo, beside the luxury *Itaimbé Palace Hotel*. The *Rodoviária* is about fifteen minutes' walk from the city centre; cross the road and walk across the Parque Itaimbé and at the *Itaimbé Palace Hotel* turn left and walk straight on for about three blocks. There's a helpful **tourist office** on Praça Saldanha Marinho, near the main square.

Several cheap **hotels** are gathered near the *Ferroviária*, but better (though a little more expensive) is the *Gloria*, Av. Rio Branco 639 (☎055/222-5656; ②), and the *Hotel Dom Rafael*, Av. Rio Branco 192 (☎055/221-2423; ③). The best place to stay is the *Itaimbé Palace Hotel* (☎055/222-1144; ⑤), which is large, modern, very comfortable and has a swimming pool and a good restaurant. Other **places to eat** include the vaguely German *Fritz Krüg* at Rua Tuiuti 2373, the *churrascaria, Bovina*, at Rua Venâncio Aires 1596 or, for chicken, the *Vera Cruz* at Av. Medianeira 1869.

Around Santa Maria

The immediate area around Santa Maria is now mainly given over to cattle and soya. Italians from northeastern Rio Grande do Sul have had some considerable success farming the very picturesque **Vale Veneto** (take a bus to Nova Palma), about 45 minutes from Santa Maria, but Bessarabian Jews were not so fortunate. In 1904, eighty Jewish families arrived in Santa Maria with the intention of establishing a farming colony. They were given land 15km north of the city, but it slowly became apparent that the soil would only be of use for cattle. Over a forty-year period, settlers drifted from the **Colônia Philippson** – as it was known – into Santa Maria, where there survives a small and very elderly Jewish community who still maintain a synagogue (at Rua Otavio Binato 49, Santa Maria). Virtually in the middle of nowhere, on a hill surrounded by cattle pasture, is the colony's small cemetery, located within what is now the Fazenda Philippson: to get there, take any bus heading north on the BR-158 and, on the left, a few kilometres past the Oasis swimming centre (45min from Santa Maria), is the *fazenda*'s clearly marked entrance. From there, ask for directions to the cemetery.

With even just a faint interest in geology you should find a visit to **MATA** worthwhile, an hour by bus from Santa Maria. Scattered everywhere in the small town are massive petrified tree trunks. The **Museu Guido Borgomanero** (Mon–Fri 8–11.30am & 1.30–4.30pm, Sat & Sun 9–11.30am & 2–5pm) has a well-catalogued collection of fossils of all kinds, and the steps leading to the local Catholic church – itself unremarkable – are made entirely of fossilized wood. If you need a **hotel** in Mata, there's the very simple *Paleon* (☎055/259-1165; ②) by the Catholic church, and a basic **restaurant**, too.

The Jesuit missions and Iraí

For much of the seventeenth and eighteenth centuries, the **Guarani Indians** of what is now northeastern Argentina, southeastern Paraguay and northwestern Rio Grande do Sul were only nominally within the domain of the Spanish and Portuguese empires, and instead were ruled – or protected – by the Society of Jesus, the **Jesuits** (see p.604). The first **redução** – a self-governing Indian settlement based around a Jesuit mission – was established in 1610 and, within a hundred years, thirty such places were in existence. With a total population of 150,000, these mini-cities became centres of some importance, with *erva maté* and cattle the mainstay of economic activity, though spinning, weaving and metallurgical cottage industries were also pursued. As the seventeenth century progressed, Spain and Portugal grew increasingly concerned over the Jesuits' power, and Rome feared that the religious order was becoming too independent of papal authority. Finally, in 1756, Spanish and Portuguese forces attacked the missions, the Jesuits were expelled and many Indians killed. The missions themselves were dissolved, either razed to the ground or abandoned to nature, surviving only as ruins.

Brazil, Argentina and Paraguay each have one fine ruin of a Jesuit mission and, without too much diffculty, it's possible to combine a visit to all three. There are direct bus services every day between Santo Ângelo, which serves the **São Miguel** site in Brazil, and Posadas in Argentina, crossing the border at São Borja (see p.597). Posadas is a short distance from Argentina's **San Ignacio Miní** ruins and Paraguay's **Trinidad**. Alternatively, these latter two missions are an easy side-trip from the Iguaçu falls.

São Miguel and around

Of the thirty former mission towns, sixteen were in present-day Argentina, seven in Paraguay and only seven were situated in what is now Brazil, and almost all were completely levelled. The one exception in Brazil is **SÃO MIGUEL** (daily 8am–8pm; $5), not to be compared in significance to San Ignacio Miní in neighbouring Argentina, but still

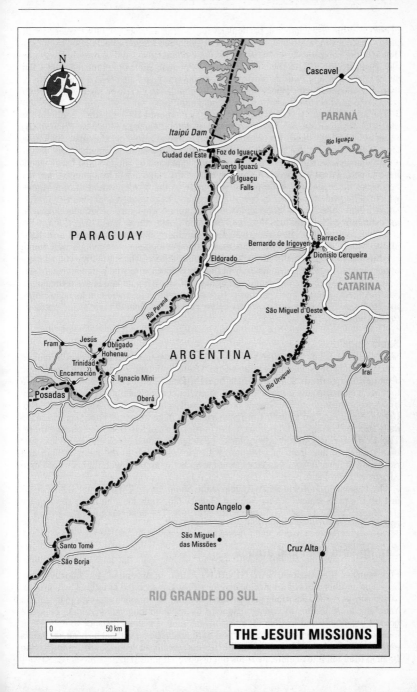

THE JESUIT MISSIONS

of considerable visual interest, particularly for its dramatic location on a treeless fertile plain. Despite vandalism and centuries of neglect, São Miguel's ruins offer ample evidence of the sophistication of Guarani Baroque architecture, and of *redução* life generally. Founded in 1632, to the west of the Rio Uruguai, São Miguel moved only a few years later to escape *Paulista* slavers, and then a few years after that it was destroyed by a violent windstorm. After being rebuilt, its population increased rapidly and in 1687 it was relocated across the river to its present site.

The initial priority was to provide housing, so not until 1700 did work begin on the **church**, designed by the Milanese Jesuit architect, Giovanni Baptista Primoli, the ruins of which still stand. The facade is a handsome example of colonial architecture. One of the church's two towers is missing, but otherwise its stone structure is reasonably complete, the lack of a vault or dome explained by the fact that these would have been finished with wood. Other aspects of the ruins are of less interest, but the outline of the *redução*'s **walls** provides a guide to the former extent of São Miguel which, at its peak, was home to over 4000 people. The **museum** (daily 9am–6pm) has an excellent collection of stone and wood sculptures, which are beautifully displayed in Jesuit-influenced buildings designed by Lúcio Costa, the architect of Brasília.

Every evening (6pm in winter, 8.30pm in summer; $5) there's a **sound and light show**, which, even if you don't understand the Portuguese narrative, is well worth staying for. You can actually stay in the quiet village here, which will give you an ideal opportunity to wander the ruins early in the day before the tourist buses arrive. In any case, if you're attending the sound and light show, there are no late buses returning to Santo Ângelo. There's one very basic, though perfectly clean and comfortable **hotel**, the *Brilhante* ($10 per person) with a better **restaurant** than the one at the entrance to the ruins.

Santo Ângelo

São Miguel is 55km from **SANTO ÂNGELO**, a town in a farming region inhabited predominantly by people of German origin. There's not much to see in the town itself, although the **cathedral**, on the main square, Praça Pinheiro Machado, is worth a look as it's supposedly a replica of São Miguel's church. Santo Ângelo is served by buses from throughout Rio Grande do Sul as well as from Curitiba, São Paulo and Rio. If you're planning on visiting the Jesuit ruins in Argentina and Paraguay, there's a daily **bus** to Posadas, or take a bus to the border town of São Borja and change there. The **Rodoviária** is within a few blocks of Praça Pinheiro Machado; there are four buses a day to and from São Miguel, with the last going to the ruins at 5pm and returning at 7pm. A few kilometres out of town is the **airport** with flights from Porto Alegre and São Paulo.

The best cheap **hotel** in Santo Ângelo is the *Santo Ângelo Turis* (☎055/312-4055; ②) just off the main square at Rua Antônio Manoel 726, while for a bit more comfort try the *Maerkil* at Av. Brasil 1000 (☎055/312-2127; ④). The best **restaurant** in town is a *churrascaria*, the *Chico*, at Rua Antônio Manoel 1421.

San Ignacio Miní and around

Like many of the missions, **SAN IGNACIO MINÍ**, in Argentina, was initially established on another site and later relocated for safety. Consecrated in 1609 as San Ignacio-guazú across the Rio Paraná in present-day Paraguay, the mission was moved to the Rio Yabebiry in 1632 due to constant attacks by slave-hunting *bandeirantes*. This site proved unsuitable and in 1695 the mission was moved a short distance to its present location, developing into one of the largest of the *reducciónes* with, at its peak, an Indian population of over 4000. Following the Jesuits' expulsion from South America, San Ignacio Miní fell into decline, its ruins not discovered until 1897.

Of all the mission ruins, those of San Ignacio Miní (daily 7am–7pm; $2.50) are the best preserved, one of the largest in area and feature some of the most interesting museum displays. Throughout the site the buildings, trees and bushes are labelled in Spanish, so it's helpful to carry a dictionary. As you enter the site, be sure not to miss the **Centro de Interpretación**, its elaborate stage-prop style displays depicting an idyllic pre-Hispanic past, the voyages of "discovery", the clash of cultures and the enslavement of the Guaraní, and finally the rise and fall of the Jesuit *reducciónes*. Among the thoroughly entertaining and thought-provoking displays is a detailed scale model of the mission prior to its abandonment.

The mission is centred around the **Plaza de Armas**, dominated by the church. Visitors can wander into the ruins of the red sandstone buildings flanking the plaza: these served as workshops, schools, cloisters and living quarters for the Indians and missionaries. Completed in 1724, and designed by the Italian Jesuit architect, Giovanni Brasonelli, the huge Guarani Baroque church was, and still is, the focal point of mission, although only part of the facade and a few other parts of the structure remain standing. The church, like many of the other buildings, is decorated with delicate, mainly floral design, bas-relief sculptures by Guaraní artisans. Near the exit from the ruins is a small **museum** where sculptures excavated over the years are displayed. For an excellent view across the entire mission area, climb to the top of grandstand at the edge of the *plaza*. The stand itself is used for the **sound and light shows** (daily 7.30pm; $2): you'll obviously get more out of the show if you understand Spanish, but the music, sound effects and lighting are enough to be able to enjoy the event.

San Ignacio

San Ignacio Miní is located 60km north of Posadas, just off the main highway to Puerto Iguazú. The ruins are a few hundred metres from the centre of the sleepy little village of **SAN IGNACIO**, a pleasant place to spend a night. Especially over weekends, San Ignacio can be crowded during the day, but it empties at night. Apart from the ruins, San Ignacio is best known as the home of Uruguayan-born writer **Horacio Quiroga**, who lived here from 1910 until 1917, when his wife committed suicide, and this is where he set many of his short stories. Quiroga's home, on Calle San Martin, has been converted into a **museum** (daily 8.30am–7.30pm). Attached to San Ignacio's **church** is a shop with interesting **basketwork and wood-carvings** – most of the proceeds return to the Guaraní producers. In contrast, the handicrafts sold in the shops and stalls near the ruins' entrance are mainly produced in Brazil and Paraguay. Next to the church, the Jesuit and Guaraní artefacts collected by a Romanian archeologist and ethnologist in the **Museo Miguel Nadasdy** (daily 7.30am–noon & 3.30–7pm) are worth a brief look.

San Ignacio is well served by **buses**, which arrive outside the church on the main *plaza* every hour or so from Puerto Iguazú (4hr) and Posadas (1hr). By staying in San Ignacio you can get to the ruins early and wander around virtually alone. There are two good **accommodation** options. On the village's central *plaza* is the comfortable, air-conditioned *Residencial San Ignacio* (☎0752-70047; ③), while near the ruins' entrance, around the corner from the *Restaurante El Jardin*, is the friendly, German-run *Hospedaje Los Salpeter* with clean rooms at $10 per person. Nearby are numerous **restaurants,** catering primarily to tour groups. There's little to choose between them, except that *La Carpa Azul* has a swimming pool, wonderful on a hot summer afternoon.

Posadas

Travelling to San Ignacio Miní you're likely to pass through **POSADAS**, the capital of the Argentine province of Misiones. Apart from the pervasive red dust and a multi-ethnic population that includes descendants of German, Ukrainian, Scandinavian and other immigrants who settled in Misiones during the course of the twentieth century, the city has little of the province's frontier atmosphere. There's not much of touristic interest in Posadas but it's a useful place to stay, convenient for both the Argentine and Paraguayan ruins. Summers are intensely hot and humid, but the streets and *plazas* are well shaded by trees, and the ice cream is good, a legacy of the country's strong Italian presence.

An important commercial centre, Posadas is still small enough for you to walk to most places. Few buildings date from the city's foundation in 1870, but there are some attractive houses near the harbour in the oldest area, **La Bajada Vieja**. The city is centred on Plaza 9 de Julio, with banks and shops concentrated on Bolívar between Azara and Junín. The Argentine *peso* is maintained at exact parity with the US dollar, and Posadas is a good place to change travellers' cheques into dollar bills and to arrange cash advances on credit cards.

The **airport**, with flights from Buenos Aires and Córdoba, is located 12km west of Posadas; buses into town cost $4. The **bus terminal**, on the corner of *avenidas* Mitre and Uruguay, is twelve blocks south of the city centre: most provincial centres are served, and there are regular services to and from other Argentine cities, Asunción and Rio Grande do Sul. Buses for Encarnación, across the river in Paraguay, leave from across the road from the bus terminal every fifteen minutes, picking up passengers in the city centre. Midway between the bus terminal and the centre at Rioja and Colón is the well-organized **tourist office** (Mon–Fri 7am–12.30pm & 2–8pm, Sat & Sun 8am–noon & 4–8pm) which provides good maps of Posadas and local and provincial information.

Posadas is a relatively expensive city, with food and drink costing fifty per cent more than in Brazil. **Restaurants** are concentrated on the streets extending off Plaza 9 de Julio and along Calle San Lorenzo and, as throughout Argentina, beef features prominantly on menus; however, look out for *surubi*, the delicious local fish. Reasonably priced **hotels** are easy to find. Next to the bus terminal are several basic places to stay, charging around $25 for a double room, but it's worth walking a couple of blocks in the direction of the centre to the comfortable and quiet *Residencial Córdoba*, at Santiago del Estero 2162, between Junín and Ayacucho (☎0752-35451; ③). In the centre, the least expensive place to stay is the *City Hotel* (☎0752-33901; ③), but being on Plaza 9 de Julio it's rather noisy. On the same *plaza* is the more luxurious *Hotel Continental* (☎0752-38966; ⑤) with large but impersonal-feeling rooms – ask for one with a river view. A block away at Bolívar 272, but quieter and friendlier, is the *Hotel Posadas* (☎0752-30801; ⑤). Pleasant and with excellent river views from the upper-floor balconies is the *Hotel Turismo* (☎0752-37401; ③), nearby at the corner of Bolívar and Junín.

Brazil maintains a **consulate** at Av. Mitre 1242 with a same-day visa service, and Paraguay's consulate is at San Lorenzo between Santa Fé and Sarmiento. For **telephone calls** the Entel office is at Colón and Santa Fé, while the **post office** is at Bolívar and Ayacucho; both are within three blocks of Plaza 9 de Julio. At Colón 1574, El Pale has a very good and varied selection of regional **handicrafts**.

Trinidad and Jesús

Of the three best-preserved Jesuit mission ruins, those of **TRINIDAD** (Mon–Sat 7.30–11.30am & 1.30–5.30pm, Sun 1.30–5.30pm; $1) in Paraguay are the least visited. Founded in 1706, Trinidad was one of the last *reducciónes*, but it grew quickly and by 1728 it had a Guarani population of over 4000. The mission was designed by the Milanese Jesuit architect, Giovanni Baptista Prímoli, and the work wasn't completed until 1760, just a few years before the Jesuits' expulsion from South America. Trinidad prospered, developing *maté* plantations, cattle *estancias* and a sugar plantation and mill, and its Guarani artisans became famous for the manufacture of organs, harps and other musical instruments, bells and statues, exported throughout the Rio Plate region and beyond. One of the most grandiose of missions, Trinidad is thought to have been the regional centre for Jesuit activity in Paraguay. Following the departure of the Jesuits, the community fell into rapid and terminal decline, the final blow coming in 1816 when Paraguay's dictator, Francia, ordered the destruction of all Indian villages as part of his infamous scorched earth policy.

Nonetheless, Trinidad is Paraguay's best-restored Jesuit ruin and there is intense local pride in its status as a a UNESCO World Heritage Monument. Occupying a hilltop position surrounded by vast areas of soya fields and cattle pasture, the site is not as extensive and the church not as large nor as complete as at San Ignacio Miní and São Miguel. Even so, much of the **church** remains in remarkable condition, including the elaborate pulpit and some of the most beautiful and intricate of **Guarani Baroque frescoes**. Especially charming is the procession of little angels carved in sandstone that have somehow survived the centuries. Behind the ruins of the church is a small chapel: ask the guard to let you in as it contains yet more stunning wood and stone statues of angels. For an excellent view of the entire mission site and across the surrounding countryside climb the church's bell tower.

Trinidad is located 28km northeast of Paraguay's second largest city, Encarnación. There aren't many facilities in Trinidad, which is visited by far fewer people than either San Ignacio Miní or São Miguel. By the entrance there's a restaurant that's rarely open, but at the main road at the turn-off to the ruins there are bars selling snacks and drinks. While there are no hotels, **camping** is sometimes allowed near the ruins' entrance. Most visitors stay in Posadas and cross the border for the day, or stay in Encarnación.

Ten kilometres to the north lies the Jesuit mission of **JESÚS**. Not strictly speaking ruins, Jesús (same hours and fees as Trinidad), founded in 1685 but only settled in 1763, is really an unfinished construction site, the large **church** half built when the Jesuits were ordered out of South America. The church has been restored, its beautiful arched portals resembling shamrocks, and it has an enormous half-erected guardian tower. Lacking the wealth of other missions, Jesús was not such a target of treasure seekers and remained relatively intact.

Encarnación and around

It's much cheaper to stay in **ENCARNACIÓN** than Posadas and just as convenient if visiting the missions on both sides of the river, but bear in mind that Paraguayan time is one hour behind that of Argentina. Although just one-third the size of Posadas, Encarnación is Paraguay's second largest city. It's far from being a typical Paraguayan town, being in the centre of a region largely populated by European and Japanese immigrants and their descendants. Ukrainians and other Slavs have settled to the southwest around Fram, Germans to the northeast in the so-called *Colonias Unidas* (including Hohenau and Obligado) and Japanese to the west around La Paz and Pirapo. Unlike most other parts of the country, Spanish is heard far more than Guaraní, the national language, which is abandoned even by the migrant workers drawn from central Paraguay. For a glimpse of a more traditional Paraguay head 150 km northwest to **Yuty**, a delightful village on the way to Villarica where ox-drawn carts are still more common than Toyota pickup trucks.

There are still two parts to Encarnación (the old and the new) with the rail track being the rough dividing line. Avenida Estigarriba, the main commercial artery, extends through both parts of the city. However, the **old city**, on the slopes leading down to the river, is due to be flooded when the huge Yacyretá dam is completed. For now, the area is one of decaying houses, public buildings and small stores selling inexpensive electronics, cameras (stock up with very cheap Fuji film) and other imports to Argentine tourists. The **post office** is near the river at Capellán Molas 377, at the intersection with Avenida Estigarribia; postage is around one-fifth of Brazilian rates. The **new city** on the higher ground, centred around the Plaza Artigas, is where most of the better hotels and restaurants are found and where government offices, banks and businesses are gradually being relocated.

Practicalities

US, Argentine and Brazilian **currency** are all accepted by hotels and restaurants, but Paraguayan *guaranies* are needed for bus tickets and stamps. **Changing money** is straightforward and rates are good. Banks (Mon–Fri 8.45am–12.15pm) are concentrated along Avenida Estigarribia around Plaza Artigas and give cash advances on credit cards. There are also numerous *casas de câmbio* (Mon–Fri 8.30am–5pm) along Avenida Estigarribia towards the river, and at other times money changers offer reasonable rates at the bus terminal.

The chaotic **bus terminal** is located five blocks south of the new city centre. **From Posadas**, there are buses every fifteen minutes which pass by the Encarnación bus terminal before continuing to the city centre and port. The trip takes 45 minutes and **immigration procedures** on the bridge spanning the Rio Paraná are completed rapidly. If you're just crossing the border for the day you'll be waved through, but otherwise you'll have to leave the bus to have your passport stamped and then take the next bus at no extra cost. US, Australian and other citizens requiring an Argentine visa should be sure that they have valid ones.

Two types of bus services operate in Paraguay, *servicio removido* which stop to pick up or put down passengers as requested, and more expensive but much faster *servicio directo* which stop at fixed locations in towns en route and may take the form of *ejecutivo* buses which are faster, more comfortable and have toilets. There are hourly departures for Asunción and constant departures to centres in eastern Paraguay. If you're heading on **to Iguaçu Falls**, travelling via Ciudad del Este rather than Posadas is almost as fast and less expensive. The paved road passes through gently rolling terrain, until recently densely forested but now cleared by German and German-Brazilian settlers, who produce soya and farm cattle. There are buses every two hours **to Trinidad**, or take any bus going to Jesús or to the *Colonias Unidas* and ask to be let off at the side of the main road near the ruins' entrance. There's an Argentine **consulate** in Encarnación at Dr Juan L. Mallorquín 788 on the corner with Cabañas, while the Brazilian consulate is at Memmel 452; both are less than a block from the bus terminal.

There's also a **train station**, six blocks west of Plaza Artigas, with snail-pace services for Asunción; even if you're not a train buff look out for the amazing nineteenth-century steam engines billowing out smoke as they pass through town.

Inexpensive and comfortable **hotels** are easy to find. The cheapest are near the train station (the only decent one being the *Repka* at Tomás Romero Pereira 44; ①) and directly across from the bus terminal (the best choice being the *Itapua*; ☎071/3346; ①), but most of these are best avoided unless desperate. An excellent budget choice is the *Hotel Viena* (☎071/3486; ①), a couple of blocks behind the bus terminal at Calle P.J. Caballero 568, near Carlos Antonio López, set in a neighbourhood of vulgar mansions (the results, it is widely believed, of rake-offs from the Yacyretá dam project). The rooms are basic but clean, the courtyard attractive and while the German family that runs the hotel may at first appear dour, they are informative and even quite friendly. Near Plaza Artigas is the modern *Hotel Paraná*, at Av. Estigarribia 1414 (☎071/4480; ④), while the *Cristal* at no. 1157 (☎071/2371; ④) is the best hotel in town, offering excellent value and with a good restaurant.

There are numerous *heladerías* throughout the city, but the ice cream is not nearly as good as in Argentina. Instead try the refreshing national drink *terere* – *maté* served ice cold – or Paraguayan beer which is excellent and cheap. There are some good **parrillas** (grills): on Avenida Mariscal Estigarribia near Plaza Artigas is the excellent

Rancho Grande, while the *Cuarajhyon*, actually on Plaza Artigas, is also reasonable. Meat, of course, dominates menus, but vegetarians can enjoy huge salads and should try *sopa paraguaya*, a national staple which is not, as its name suggests, soup but corn bread made with onion and cheese. Alternatively, the *Restaurante Chino Rubi* at Av. Mariscal Estigarribia 519, towards the river, serves large portions of acceptable, though hardly exciting, Chinese food.

Iraí

On the Rio Mel, a tributary of the Rio Uruguai, near the border with Santa Catarina's extreme western region, is the small spa town of **IRAÍ**, whose waters are claimed to offer relief from rheumatism and digestive disorders. If you don't suffer from these complaints, avoid it – it's one of the most depressing places of its kind imaginable. Most of the visitors are elderly and they spend their days in the thermal pools of the **Balneário Cruz** (8.30–10.45am & 2–5.30pm), while nights are predictably quiet, with the main action found in Iraí's late-night chemist. The town's unfortunate youth hang out at a snack bar called *K-Chorrão*, located across from the cinema (expect a 1950s *Zorro* film). Having a far worse time, however, are the 150 Kaingang Indians who camp in the most miserable conditions on the banks of the Rio Mel, beneath the gardens of the *balneário*, trying to make a living by selling "typical" Indian basketwork and bows and arrows.

If you reckon that Iraí will do you more good than harm, **accommodation** won't be a problem. All the hotels are right in the centre of town; the cheapest two, both with their own cold-water pools, are the *São Luiz* (☎055/345-1324; ③) and the *Internacional* (☎055/345-1216; ③). The only good **place to eat** is the *Restaurante Panorâmico*, just over a kilometre out of town on the road to the north, overlooking the Rio Uruguai, and serving excellent freshwater fish. Next to the *Internacional* is the **Rodoviária**, and there are mercifully frequent buses to Santa Catarina and points throughout Rio Grande do Sul.

The border towns

Apart from Chuí (see p.585), the most commonly used **border crossing** into Uruguay is at **Santana do Livramento**. While most buses cross into Argentina via **Uruguaiana**, you may find **São Borja** quicker if you're travelling between Jesuit mission sites or making your way north to Iguaçu Falls. Rarely do people remain in the border towns longer than it takes to go through immigration formalities, but if you're trying to get a taste of *gaúcho* life, check to see if there's a *rodeio* about to be held somewhere around. Alternatively, use a smaller border crossing point, like **Aceguá**, near Bagé, where at least your first impressions of Uruguay or Brazil will be of cattle and ranch-hands rather than duty-free shops and casinos.

Bagé and Aceguá

Of all the towns on or very near Rio Grande do Sul's border with Argentina and Uruguay, **BAGÉ** is the only one with any charm, remaining first and foremost a cattle and commercial centre, rather than a tourist transit point. Like all towns in the *campanha*, Bagé has its own lively events, which attract people from the surrounding cattle ranches. The most important **festival**, held in January in odd-numbered years, is the **Semana Crioula Internacional**, but the Semana de Bagé (a folklore festival held annually from July 10 to 17), or even the Exposição (first half of Oct), will give you a taste of the *campanha*. For details of these and other events ask at the **tourist office** at Praça Silveira Martins (Mon–Fri 9–11.30am & 2–6pm, Sat 9am–noon). For an understanding of the region's history, a visit to the **Museu Dom Diogo de Souza**, Av.

Guilayn 5759 (Tues–Fri 8.30–11.30am & 1.30–5.30pm, Sat & Sun 1.30–5.30pm), is a must. Also worth visiting is the **Museu da Gravura Brasileira** at Rua Coronel Azambuja 18 (Mon–Fri 1.30–7.30pm & Sat 1.30–6pm; closed Jan), which has a small but important collection of engravings: Rio Grande do Sul has a long tradition of this art form and some of the most important artists worked in Bagé.

Arriving from the Uruguayan border (Melo is the nearest Uruguayan town) ask to be let off at the **Polícia Federal**, a few blocks from the main square, Praça General Osório, at Rua Barão do Trunfo 1572. It's here, not at Aceguá (see below), where you'll need to have your passport stamped. Arriving in Bagé from elsewhere, take a "Santa Tecla" bus into the centre from the main road next to the **Rodoviária** (3 daily buses from Santa Maria and Porto Alegre, 1 each from Santo Ângelo and, via Curitiba, São Paulo). If you're leaving Brazil, have your passport stamped; failing to report to the Polícia Federal here will mean that you're likely to have difficulties entering or leaving Brazil later on.

Hotels in Bagé are plentiful, with the clean and friendly *Mini*, Avenida Sete de Setembro, near Praça General Osório (②), the centre's cheapest; there are also two inexpensive hotels near the *Rodoviária*. If you want something more refined, the best hotel in town is the *Charrua*, at Av. Sete de Setembro 901 (☎0532/42-2211; ⑤).

ACEGUÁ, 60km south and the actual frontier crossing point, is very much a back door into Brazil and Uruguay, with only a Uruguayan immigration post (remember to be stamped in or out of the country) and a few houses and stores – certainly not a place to spend a night. However, as the four buses a day in each direction between Bagé and Aceguá connect with others to and from Melo, this shouldn't be a problem – but check bus times carefully before setting out.

Changing money is best done at a *casa de câmbio* in Melo, but in Aceguá there are always plenty of men milling about offering reasonable rates for dollar bills. In Bagé, if you can't wait for the border, you can change dollars at Bradesco and many of the other banks in town are equipped with an ATM.

Santana do Livramento and around

Apart from Brazilians attracted to the casino and the duty-free shopping in Rivera, the Uruguayan border town into which **SANTANA DO LIVRAMENTO** (or, simply, Livramento) merges, few people stay here long. Unless you're in pursuit of *gaúchos* and intent upon taking local buses to outlying villages, the only time when Livramento is actually worth visiting in its own right is when there's a livestock exhibition, *rodeio* or cultural event on. The most important such **events** are the Charqueada da Poesia Crioula (last two weeks in April), the Exposição Internacional do Corriedale (March 5–12) and the Exposição Agropecuária (last two weeks in Sept), but check with the **tourist office** at Rua Tamandaré (Mon–Sat 7am–1pm & 3–6pm, Sun 3–8pm) to see if there are any other smaller events due, in or around the town. Livramento is also a very good place to purchase *gaúcho* **clothing and accessories**, with Correaria Gaúcha, Rua Rivadávia Correia 184, and Correari Nova Esperança, Rua Duque de Caxias and Rua 24 de Maio, having good selections.

Otherwise, the only possible reason not to move straight on would be a visit to **Vila Palomas**, a village 15km from Livramento, the centre of the new and increasingly important wine industry. Of all Brazil's commercial **wineries**, Almadén is about the best, and their *cantina* can be visited if you give them 24 hours' notice (☎055/242-5151).

Practicalities

Livramento's **Rodoviária**, at Rua Sen. Salgado Filho 335, serves most points in Rio Grande do Sul, while the **Ferroviária**, in Praça Castello Branco, receives three trains a week from Santa Maria and Porto Alegre. **From Rivera**, there are several departures a day for Montevideo from the bus terminal.

If you need to stay, **hotels** are cheapest in Livramento. The *Laçador* (②) near the park, at Rua Uruguai 1227, is good, or try the *Livramento*, opposite the *Rodoviária* (☎055/242-5444; ③). There's a **youth hostel** at Rua Manduca Rodrigues 615 (☎055/242-3340; $12 per person), about five blocks from the *Rodoviária*, while across in Rivera there's another hostel at Uruguay 735. **Restaurants** are better in Rivera: the best is the *Dan Servanda*, Calle Carambula 1132, around the corner from the immigration office.

Before **leaving** Livramento and Rivera, you'll need a Brazilian exit (or entry) passport stamp from the Polícia Federal, Rua Uruguai 1177, near the central park, and a stamp from Uruguay's Dirección Nacional de Migracíon, Calle Suarez 516 (three blocks from Plaza General José Artigas, Rivera's main square). If you have problems, Brazil's **consulate** in Rivera is at Calle Caballos 1159 (☎0622/244-3278), and Uruguay's is in Livramento at Av. Tamandaré 2110 (☎055/242-1452). **Change money** at a *casa de câmbio* or bank in Rivera, where exchange rates are as good as you'll find in Brazil and the process much faster.

Uruguaiana

The busiest crossing point on Rio Grande do Sul's border with Argentina, **URUGUAIANA** is also one of the state's most important cattle centres. However, unless you're around while there's a livestock show or folklore festival, there's little incentive to remain here: ask about festival dates at the **tourist office** (Mon–Sat 8.30am–6pm), in the *prefeitura*, Praça Barão do Rio Branco. The most important annual events are the Campeira Internacional (a festival of regional folklore) held in the first half of March, Semana Farroupilha (another folklore festival) held September 13–20, and a huge livestock show, the Expo-feira Agropecuária, held in the first half of November. Otherwise, the **Museu Crioulo, Histórico e Artístico** (Mon–Fri 8.30am–noon & 2–5.30pm), in the cultural centre on the corner of *ruas* Santana and Duque de Caxias (by the main square), is worth a look for its interesting collection of *gaúcho*-related items.

Uruguaiana is connected to Argentina and the town of Paso de los Libres by a 1400-metre-long bridge spanning the Rio Uruguai. Frequent **local buses** connect the train and bus stations, and the centres of each city, and **immigration** formalities take place on either side of the bridge. If you have problems entering Argentina, the **consulate** in Uruguaiana is at Rua Santana 2496 (☎055/412-1925). The Brazilian consulate in Paso de las Libres is at Calle Mitre 918. You're best off **changing money** in Paso de los Libres, but travel agents in Uruguaiana give reasonable rates. If you need **accommodation**, hotels in Uruguaiana are cheaper: best bargains are at the *Wamosy* (☎055/412-1326; ②) and *Mazza Tur* (☎055/412-3404; ③), at Rua Sete de Setembro, nos 1973 and 1088 respectively. **Restaurants** (for carnivores only) are better over the border in Argentina but, in Uruguaiana, the *Casa d'Itália* at Rua Dr Maia 3112 has a varied menu to choose from.

Bus services from Uruguaiana are excellent, and you can get to or from most of the important centres, from Rio southwards. From Paso de los Libres, there are equally good services to points within Argentina, including Buenos Aires, Posadas and Puerto Iguazú. Finally, there are three **trains** a week to and from Santa Maria and Porto Alegre. There are daily **air services** from Uruguaiana to Porto Alegre and from Paso de los Libres to Buenos Aires.

São Borja

Today a fairly major border crossing point and regional trading centre, **SÃO BORJA** is best known in the rest of Brazil as the birthplace of two of the country's most controversial presidents: **Getúlio Vargas** and **João Goulart**. In São Borja, if nowhere else in Brazil, the populist Vargas remains a venerated figure, and his former home, at Av.

Presidente Vargas 1772, is now open to the public as the **Museu Getúlio Vargas** (Mon–Fri 8–11am & 2–5pm), containing his library and personal objects and furniture. Goulart, whose incompetent presidency led to the military's seizure of power in 1964 followed by 25 years of often ruthless rule, is someone that São Borja tries to forget.

As a **border crossing**, São Borja is most useful when travelling between the Brazilian Jesuit mission of São Miguel and those in Argentina and Paraguay. São Borja has good **bus** connections with Santo Ângelo (for São Miguel), most other important towns in Rio Grande do Sul and Curitiba, São Paulo and Rio. The **ferry** (Mon–Fri 8am–5.30pm, Sat 8am–4pm, Sun 8am–3pm) across the Rio Uruguai leaves every hour from the suburb of Passo, 5km from the centre of town and connected by local buses. There's a **tourist office** next to the ferry landing (Mon–Fri 8am–6pm). On the Argentine side of the river, the ferry docks at Puerto Hormiguero, 10km south of Santo Tomé, to which it's connected by bus. From Santo Tomé there are several bus services a day to Posadas, Puerto Iguazú, Buenos Aires and other towns in Argentina.

If you need to stay over in São Borja, the cheapest **hotel** is the *Itaipu* at Rua Aparício Mariense 1167 (☎055/431-1577; ②), while the *Executivo* at Av. Presidente Vargas 2515 (☎055/431-3741; ③) offers greater comfort. In Santo Tomé, the *Residencial Paris*, at Calle Mitre 890 on the corner of Calle Beltrán (②), is a favourite with budget travellers, while the best place in town is the *Hotel Santo Tomé* (☎0756/20161; ③).

travel details

Buses

Blumenau to: Florianópolis (6 daily; 3hr); Itajaí (hourly; 2hr); Joinville (hourly; 2hr); Pomerode (hourly; 1hr).

Curitiba to: Blumenau (10 daily; 4hr); Buenos Aires (2 daily; 37hr); Florianópolis (14 daily; 5hr); Foz do Iguaçu (12 daily; 10hr); Guaraqueçaba (2 daily; 6hr); Paranaguá (hourly; 2hr); Porto Alegre (10 daily; 11hr); Prudentópolis (4 daily; 6hr); Rio (9 daily; 11hr); São Paulo (hourly; 6hr).

Florianópolis to: Blumenau (6 daily; 3hr); Buenos Aires (2 daily; 30hr); Curitiba (14 daily; 5hr); Foz do Iguaçu (2 daily; 16hr); Joinville (hourly; 3hr); Porto Alegre (10 daily; 7hr); Rio (8 daily; 19hr); Santo Amaro da Imperatriz (4 daily; 1hr); São Paulo (10 daily; 12hr).

Foz do Iguaçu to: Itaipu (hourly; 1hr); Prudentópolis (3 daily; 7hr); Rio (6 daily; 22hr).

Joinville to: Blumenau (hourly; 2hr); Curitiba (hourly; 2hr 30min); Florianópolis (hourly; 3hr); Porto Alegre (2 daily; 10hr); Rio (1 daily; 15hr); São Francisco do Sul (hourly; 1hr); São Paulo (7 daily; 9hr); Vila Dona Francesca (hourly; 45min).

Porto Alegre to: Buenos Aires (2 daily; 22hr); Curitiba (10 daily; 11hr); Florianópolis (10 daily; 7hr); Livramento (4 daily; 7hr); Montevideo (3 daily; 12hr); Pelotas (hourly; 3hr); Rio (6 daily; 26hr); Rio Grande (hourly; 1hr); São Paulo (8 daily; 18hr).

Trains

Curitiba to: Paranaguá (1 daily; 4hr 20min).

Porto Alegre to: Livramento (3 weekly; 14hr); Santa Maria (daily except Sat; 7hr).

Ferries

Guaraqueçaba to: Ariri (2 weekly; 10hr); Paranaguá (2 weekly; 2hr).

THE

CONTEXTS

THE HISTORICAL FRAMEWORK

Brazil's recorded history begins with the arrival of the Portuguese in 1500, although it had been discovered and settled by Indians many centuries before. The importation of millions of African slaves over the next four centuries completed the rich blend of European, Indian and African influences that formed modern Brazil and its people. Achieving independence from Portugal in 1822, Brazil's enormous wealth in land and natural resources underpinned a boom-and-bust cycle of economic development that continues to the present day. The eternal "Land of the Future" is still a prisoner of its past, as industrialization turned Brazil into the economic giant of South America, but sharpened social divisions. After a twenty-year interlude of military rule, the civilian "New Republic" has struggled, with some success, against deep-rooted economic crisis and has managed to consolidate democracy. Although social divisions remain, the current economic and political outlook is the best it has been for a generation.

EARLY HISTORY

Very little is known about the thousands of years that Brazil was inhabited exclusively by **Indians**. The first chroniclers who arrived with the Portuguese – Pedro Vaz da Caminha in 1500 and Gaspar Carvajal in 1540 – saw large villages, but nothing resembling the huge Aztec and Inca cities that the Spanish encountered. The fragile material traces left by Brazil's earliest inhabitants have for the most part not survived. The few exceptions – like the exquisitely worked glazed ceramic jars unearthed on Marajó island in the Amazon – come from cultures that have vanished so completely that not even a name records their passing.

The Indians fascinated the Portuguese, and many of the first Europeans to visit Brazil sent lengthy reports back home. The most vivid account was penned by a German mercenary, **Hans Staden**, who spent three nervous years among the cannibal **Tupi** after being captured in 1552. He tells how they tied his legs together, ". . . and I was forced to hop through the huts, at which they made merry, saying 'Here comes our food hopping towards us.'" Understandably, his memoirs were one of the first bestsellers in European history, and contained much accurate description of an Indian culture still largely untouched by the colonists. The work of Staden and the first explorers and missionaries is a brief snapshot of Indian Brazil in the sixteenth century, a blurred photograph of a way of life soon to be horribly transformed.

It was unfortunate that the Portuguese first landed in the only part of Brazil where ritualized cannibalism was practised on a large scale; away from the Tupi areas it was rare. Nowhere was stone used for building. There was no use of metal or the wheel, and no centralized, state-like civilizations on the scale of Spanish America. There are arguments about how large the Indian population was: Carvajal described taking several days to pass through the large towns of the Omagua tribe on the Amazon in 1542 but, away from the abundant food sources on the coast and the banks of large rivers, **population** densities were much lower. The total number of Indians was probably around five million. Today there are two hundred thousand in Brazil.

CONQUEST

The Portuguese discovery of Brazil, when **Pedro Alvares Cabral** landed in southern Bahia on April 23, 1500, was an accident, an episode in Portugal's thrust to found a seaborne empire in the East Indies during the sixteenth century. Cabral was blown off course as he steered far to the west to avoid the African doldrums on his way to Calcutta: after a cursory week exploring the coast he continued to India, where he drowned in a shipwreck a few months later. King Manuel I sent **Amerigo Vespucci** to explore further in 1501. Reserving the name of the continent for himself, he spent several months sailing along the coast, calendar in hand, baptizing places after the names of saints' days: entering Guanabara Bay on New Year's Day 1502, he called it Rio de Janeiro. The land was called *Terra do Brasil*, after a tropical redwood that was its first export; the scarlet dye it yielded was called *brasa*, "a glowing coal".

Portugal, preoccupied with Africa and the lucrative Far East spice trade, neglected this new addition to its empire for the first few decades. Apart from a few lumber camps and scattered stockades, the Portuguese made no attempt at settlement. Consequently, other European countries were not slow to move in, with French and English privateers using the coast as a base to raid the spice ships. Finally, in 1532, João III was provoked into action. He divided up the coastline into **sesmarias**, captaincies fifty leagues wide and extending indefinitely inland, distributing them to aristocrats and courtiers in return for undertakings to found settlements. It was hardly a roaring success: Pernambuco, where sugar took hold, and São Vicente, gateway to the Jesuit mission station of São Paulo, were the only securely held areas.

Irritated by the lack of progress, King João repossessed the captaincies in 1548 and brought Brazil under direct royal control, sending out the first governor-general, **Tomé da Sousa**, to the newly designated **capital** at Salvador in 1549. The first few governors successfully rooted out the European privateers, and – where sugar could grow – wiped out Indian resistance. By the closing decades of the century increasing numbers of Portuguese settlers were flowing in. Slaves began to be imported from the Portuguese outposts on the African coast, as **sugar plantations** sprang up around Salvador and Olinda. Brazil, no longer seen merely as a possible staging point on the way to the Far East, became an increasingly important piece of the far-flung Portuguese Empire. When Europe's taste for sugar took off in the early seventeenth century, the Northeast of Brazil quickly became very valuable real estate – and a tempting target for the expanding maritime powers of northern Europe, jealous of the Iberian monopoly in the New World.

WAR WITH THE DUTCH

The **Dutch**, with naval bases in the Caribbean and a powerful fleet, were the best placed to move against Brazil. A mixture of greed and pressing political motives lay behind the Dutch decision. From 1580 to 1640 Portugal was united with Spain, against whom the Dutch had fought a bitter war of independence, and they were still menaced by the Spanish presence in Flanders. Anything that distracted Spain from further designs on the fledgling United Provinces seemed like a good idea at the time. As it turned out, neither the Spanish nor the Portuguese crowns played much of a role in the war: it was fought out between the Dutch, in the mercantile shape of the Dutch West India Company, and the Portuguese settlers already in Brazil, with Indian and *mameluco* (mixed race) backing. Although the Dutch occupied much of the Northeast for thirty years, they were finally overcome by one of South America's first guerrilla campaigns, in a war made vicious by the Catholic–Protestant divide that underlay it: few prisoners were taken and both sides massacred civilians.

In 1624 a Dutch fleet appeared off Salvador, taking the governor completely by surprise, and the city by storm. After burning down the Jesuit college and killing as many priests as they could find (like the good Calvinists they were), they were pinned down by enraged settlers for nine months and finally expelled in 1625 by a hastily assembled combined Spanish and Portuguese fleet – the only direct intervention made by either country in the conflict. When a Dutch force was once more repulsed from Salvador in 1627, they shifted their attention further north and found the going much easier: Olinda was taken in 1630, the rich sugar zones of Pernambuco were occupied, and Dutch control extended up to the mouth of the Amazon by 1641. With settlers moving in, a strong military presence and a fleet more powerful than Portugal's, Dutch control of the Northeast looked like becoming permanent.

Maurice of Nassau was sent out as governor of the new Dutch possessions in Brazil in 1630, as the Dutch founded a new capital in Pernambuco: Mauritzstaadt, now Recife. His enlightened policies of allowing the Portuguese freedom to practise their religion, and including them in the colonial government, would probably have resulted in a Dutch Brazil were it not for the stupidity of the Dutch West India Company. They insisted on Calvinism and heavy taxes, and when Maurice resigned in disgust and returned to Holland in 1644, the settlers rose. After five years of ambushes, plantation burnings and massacres, the Brazilians pushed the Dutch back into an enclave around Recife. The Dutch poured in reinforcements by sea, but their fate was decided by two climactic battles in 1648 and 1649 at **Guararapes**, just outside Recife, where the Dutch were routed and their military power broken. Although they held onto Recife until 1654, the dream of a Dutch Empire in the Americas was over, and Portuguese control was not to be threatened again until the nineteenth century.

THE BANDEIRANTES: GOLD AND GOD

The expulsion of the Dutch demonstrated the toughness of the early Brazilians, which was also well to the fore in the penetration and settling of **the interior** during the seventeenth and eighteenth centuries. Every few months, expeditions set out to explore the interior, following rumours of gold and looking for Indians to enslave. They carried an identifying banner, a *bandeira*, which gave the name **bandeirantes** to the adventurers; they became the Brazilian version of the Spanish *conquistadores*. São Paulo, thanks to its position on the Rio Tietê, one of the few natural highways that flowed east–west into the deep interior, became the main *bandeirante* centre.

The average *bandeira* would be made up of a mixed crew of people, reflecting the many – and often conflicting – motives underlying the expedition. None travelled without a priest or two (*bandeirantes* may have been cut-throats, but they were devout Catholic cut-throats), and many *bandeiras* were backed by the Jesuits and Franciscans in their drive to found missions and baptize the heathen. The majority combined exploration with plundering and could last for years, with occasion-

al stops to plant and harvest crops, before returning to São Paulo – if they ever did: many towns on the Planalto Central or Mato Grosso have their origins in the remnants of a *bandeira*. The *bandeirantes* had to fight Indians, occasionally the Spanish, and also themselves: they were riven with tension between native-born Brazilians and Portuguese, which regularly erupted into fighting.

The journeys *bandeiras* made were often epic in scale, covering immense distances and overcoming natural obstacles as formidable as the many hostile Indian tribes they encountered, who were defeated more by diseases to which they had no resistance, than by force of arms. It was the *bandeirantes* who pushed the borders of Brazil way inland, practically to the foothills of the Andes, and also supplied the geographical knowledge that now began to fill in the blanks on the maps. They explored the Amazon, Paraná and Uruguai river systems, but the most important way they shaped the future of Brazil was in locating the Holy Grail of the New World: gold.

Gold was first found by *bandeirantes* in 1695, at the spot that is now Sabará, in Minas Gerais. As towns sprang up around further gold strikes in Minas, gold was also discovered around Cuiabá, in Mato Grosso, in 1719, adding fresh impetus to the opening-up of the interior. The 3500-kilometre journey to Cuiabá, down five separate river systems, took six months at the best of times; from São Paulo it was easier to travel to Europe. Along the way the *bandeirantes* had to fight off the Paiaguá Indians, who attacked in canoes and swam like fish, and then the Guaicuru, who had taken to the horse with the same enthusiasm of the Plains Indians of North America were later to show. They annihilated entire *bandeiras*; others following left descriptions of "rotting belongings and dead bodies on the riverbanks, and hammocks slung with their owners in them, dead. Not a single person reached Cuiabá that year."

But the *Paulista* hunger for riches was equal even to these appalling difficulties. By the mid-eighteenth century, the flow of gold from Brazil was keeping the Portuguese Crown afloat, temporarily halting its long slide down the league table of European powers. In Brazil, the rush of migrants to the gold areas changed the regional balance, as the new interior communities drew population away from the Northeast. The gateways to the interior, Rio de Janeiro and São Paulo, grew rapidly. The shift was recognized in 1763, when the capital was transferred from Salvador to Rio, and that filthy, disease-ridden port began its transformation into one of the great cities of the world.

THE JESUITS

Apart from the *bandeirantes*, the most important agents of the colonization of the interior were the **Jesuits**. The first Jesuit missionaries arrived in Brazil in 1549 and, thanks to the influence they held over successive Portuguese kings, they acquired power in Brazil second only to that of the Crown itself. In Salvador they built the largest Jesuit college outside Rome, and set in motion a crusade to convert the Indian population. The usual method was to congregate the Indians in **missions**, where they worked under the supervision of Jesuit fathers. From 1600 onwards, dozens of missions were founded in the interior, especially in the Amazon and in the grasslands of the southeast.

The role the Jesuits played in the conversion of the Indians was ambiguous. Mission Indians were often released by Jesuits to work for settlers, where they died like flies; and the missionaries' intrepid penetration of remote areas resulted in the spread of diseases that wiped out entire tribes. On the other hand, many Jesuits distinguished themselves in protecting Indians against the settlers, a theological as well as a secular struggle, for many Portuguese argued that the native population had no souls and could therefore be treated like animals.

The most remarkable defender of the Indians was **Antônio Vieira**, who abandoned his position as chief adviser to the king in Lisbon to become a missionary in Brazil in 1653. Basing himself in São Luís, he struggled to implement the more enlightened Indian laws that his influence over King João IV had secured, to the disgust of settlers clamouring for slaves. Vieira denied them for years, preaching a series of sermons along the way that became famous throughout Europe, as well as Brazil: "An Indian will be your slave for the few days he lives, but your soul will be enslaved for as long as God is God. All of you are in mortal sin, all of you live in a state of condemnation, and all of you are going directly to Hell!" he thundered from the pulpit in 1654, to the fury of settlers in the congregation. So high did feelings run that, in 1661, settlers forced Vieira onto a ship bound for Portugal, standing in the surf and shouting "Out! Out!"

But Vieira returned, with renewed support from the Crown, and Jesuit power in Brazil grew. It reached a peak in the remarkable theocracy of the **Guarani missions**, where Spanish and Portuguese Jesuits founded over a dozen missions on the pampas along the Uruguayan border. Left alone for the first fifty years, they effectively became a Jesuit state, until the Treaty of Madrid in 1752 divided up the land between Spain and Portugal; the treaty ordered the missions abandoned, so that settlers could move in. The Guarani revolted immediately, and while the Jesuit hierarchy made half-hearted efforts to get them to move, most of the priests stayed with their Guarani flocks. Resistance was heroic but hopeless: the superior firepower of a joint Spanish-Portuguese military expedition decimated both Guarani and Jesuits in 1756.

Jesuit involvement in the Guarani war lent added force to the long-standing settler demands to expel them from the colony. This time, they were helped by the rise to power of the **Marquis de Pombal**, who became the power behind the Portuguese throne for much of the eighteenth century. Seeing the Jesuits as a threat to Crown control, he seized upon the Guarani wars as an excuse to expel the Order from Brazil in 1760. The Jesuits may have been imperfect protectors, but from this time on the Indians were denied even that.

INDEPENDENCE

Brazil, uniquely among South American countries, achieved a peaceful transition to independence. The odds seemed against it at one point. Brazilian resentment at their exclusion from government, and at the Portuguese monopoly of foreign trade, grew steadily during the eighteenth century. It culminated, in 1789, in the **Inconfidência Mineira**, a plot hatched by twelve prominent citizens of Ouro Preto to proclaim Brazilian independence. The rebels, however, were betrayed almost before they started – their leader, **Tiradentes**, was executed and the rest exiled. Then, just as the tension seemed to be becoming dangerous, events in Europe once again took a hand in shaping Brazil's future.

In 1807, **Napoleon** invaded Portugal. With the French army poised to take Lisbon, the British navy hurriedly evacuated **King João VI** to Rio, which was declared the temporary capital of the Portuguese Empire and seat of the government-in-exile. While **Wellington** set about driving the French from Portugal, the British were able to force the opening-up of Brazil's ports to non-Portuguese shipping, and the economic growth that followed reinforced Brazil's increasing self-confidence. João was entranced by his tropical kingdom, unable to pull himself away even after Napoleon's defeat. Finally, in 1821, he was faced by a liberal revolt in Portugal that threatened to topple the monarchy, and he was unable to delay his return any longer. In April 1822 he appointed his son, **Dom Pedro**, as prince regent and governor of Brazil; when he sailed home, his last words to his son were "Get your hands on this kingdom, before some adventurer does."

Pedro, young and arrogant, grew increasingly irritated by the strident demands of the *Côrtes*, the Portuguese assembly, that he return home to his father and allow Brazil to be ruled from Portugal once again. On September 7, 1822, Pedro was out riding on the plain of Ypiranga, near São Paulo. Buttoning himself up after an attack of diarrhoea, he was surprised by a messenger with a bundle of letters from Lisbon. Reading the usual demands for him to return his patience snapped, and he declared Brazil **independent** with the cry "Independence or death!" With overwhelming popular support for the idea, he had himself crowned **Dom Pedro I**, Emperor of Brazil, on December 1, 1822. The Portuguese, preoccupied by political crises at home and demoralized by Pedro's defection, put up little resistance. Apart from an ugly massacre of Brazilian patriots in Fortaleza, and some fighting in Bahia, the Portuguese withdrawal was peaceful and by the end of 1823 no Portuguese forces remained.

EARLY EMPIRE: REVOLT IN THE REGIONS

Although independence had been easily achieved, the early decades of empire proved much more difficult. The first problem was Dom Pedro himself: headstrong and autocratic, he became increasingly estranged from his subjects, devoting more attention to scandalous romances than affairs of state. In April 1831 he abdicated, in a fit of petulance, in favour of the heir apparent, **Dom Pedro II**, and returned to Portugal. Pedro II would later prove an enlightened ruler, but as he was only five at the time there were limits to his capacity to influence events. With a power vacuum at the centre of the political system, long-standing tensions in the outlying provinces erupted into revolt.

There were common threads in all the **rebellions** in the provinces: slaves rebelling against masters, Indian and mixed-race resentment of white domination, Brazilians settling scores with Portuguese and the poor rising against the rich. The first, and most serious, conflagration was the **Cabanagem Rebellion** in Pará, where a mass revolt of the dispossessed began in 1835. The rebels took Belém, where, in a great moment of retribution, the Indian Domingues Onça killed the governor of Pará. The uprising spread through the Amazon like wildfire and took a decade to put down. A parallel revolt, the **Balaiada**, began in Maranhão in 1838. Here the rebels took Caxias, the second city of the state, and held out for three years against the army. Similar risings in Pernambuco, Bahia and Rio Grande do Sul punctuated the 1830s and 1840s; the disruption was immense, with large areas ravaged by fighting which threatened to tear the country apart.

The crisis led to Dom Pedro II being declared emperor four years early, in 1840, when he was only fourteen. Precociously talented, he was a sensible, scholarly man, completely unlike his father. His instincts were conservative, but he regularly appointed liberal governments and was respected even by republicans. With government authority restored, the provincial rebellions had by 1850 either blown themselves out or been put down. And with **coffee** beginning to be planted on a large scale in Rio, São Paulo and Minas, and the flow of European immigrants rising from a trickle to a flood, the economy of southern Brazil began to take off in earnest.

THE WAR OF THE TRIPLE ALLIANCE

With the rebellions in the provinces, the **army** became increasingly important in Brazilian political life. Pedro insisted they stay out of domestic politics, but his policy of diverting the generals by allowing them to control foreign policy ultimately led to the disaster of the war with Paraguay (1864–70). Although Brazil emerged victorious, it was at a dreadful cost. The **War of the Triple Alliance** is one of history's forgotten conflicts, but it was the bloodiest war in South American history, with a casualty list almost as long as that of the American Civil War: Brazil alone suffered over 100,000 casualties.

It pitted, in unequal struggle, the landlocked republic of Paraguay, under the dictator **Francisco Lopez**, against the combined forces of Brazil, Argentina and Uruguay. Although the Paraguayans started the war, by invading Uruguay and parts of Mato Grosso in 1864, they had been sorely provoked by Brazilian meddling in Uruguay. The generals in Rio, with no more rebels to fight within Brazil, wanted to incorporate Uruguay into the empire; Paraguay saw Brazil blocking its access to the sea and invaded to pre-empt a Brazilian takeover, dragging Argentina reluctantly into the conflict through a mutual defence pact with Brazil.

The Brazilian army and navy were confident of victory as the Paraguayans were heavily outnumbered and outgunned. Yet the Paraguayans, for the first time, demonstrated the military prowess that would mark their history: united under the able leadership of Lopez, the Paraguayan army proved disciplined and fanatically brave, always defeated by numbers but terribly mauling the opposition. It turned into a war of extermination and six terrible years were only ended by the killing of Lopez in 1870, by which time the male adult population of Paraguay is said to have been reduced (by disease and starvation as well as war) to under twenty thousand, from over a million in 1864.

THE END OF SLAVERY

From the seventeenth to the nineteenth century around ten million Africans were transported to Brazil as **slaves** – ten times as many as were shipped to the United States – yet the death rate in Brazil was so great that in 1860 Brazil's black population was half the size of that in the USA. Slavery was always contested: slaves fled from the cities and plantations to form refugee communities called *quilombos*; the largest, **Palmares**, in the interior of the northeastern

state of Alagoas, was several thousand strong and stayed independent for almost a century.

But it was not until the nineteenth century that slavery was seriously challenged. The initial impetus came from Britain, where the abolitionist movement became influential just when Portugal was most dependent on British capital and British naval protection. Abolition was regarded with horror by the large landowners in Brazil, and a combination of racism and fear of economic dislocation led to a determined rearguard action to preserve slavery. A complicated diplomatic waltz began between Britain and Brazil, as slavery laws were tinkered with *para inglês ver* – "for the English to see" – a phrase that survives in the language to this day, meaning doing one thing and intending another. The object was to make the British believe slavery would be abolished, while ensuring that the letter of the law kept it legal.

British abolitionists were not deceived, and from 1832 to 1854 the Royal Navy maintained a squadron off Brazil, intercepting and confiscating slave ships, and occasionally entering Brazilian ports to seize slavers and burn their ships – one of history's more positive examples of gunboat diplomacy. The slave trade was finally **abolished** in 1854, but to the disgust of the abolitionists, slavery itself remained legal. British power had its limits and ultimately it was a passionate campaign within Brazil itself, led by the fiery lawyer **Joaquim Nabuco**, that finished slavery off. The growing liberal movement, increasingly republican and anti-monarchist, squared off against the landowners, with Dom Pedro hovering indecisively somewhere in between. Slavery became the dominant issue in Brazilian politics for twenty years. By the time full **emancipation** came, in the "Golden Law" of May 13, 1888, Brazil had achieved the shameful distinction of being the last country in the Americas to abolish slavery.

FROM EMPIRE TO REPUBLIC

The end of slavery was also the death-knell of the monarchy. Since the 1870s the intelligentsia, deeply influenced by French liberalism, had turned against the emperor and agitated for a republic. By the 1880s they had been joined by the officer corps, who blamed Dom Pedro for lack of backing during the Paraguayan war. When the large landowners withdrew their support, furious that the emperor had not prevented emancipation, the **monarchy collapsed** very suddenly in 1889.

Once again, Brazil managed a bloodless transition. The push came from the army, detachments led by **Marechal Deodoro da Fonseca** meeting no resistance when they occupied Rio on November 15, 1889. They invited the royal family to remain, but Dom Pedro insisted on exile, boarding a ship to France, where he died in penury two years later in a shabby Parisian hotel. Deodoro, meanwhile, began a Brazilian tradition of hamfisted military autocracy. Ignoring the clamour for a liberal republic, he declared himself dictator in 1891, but was forced to resign three weeks later when even the army refused to support him. His deputy, **Marechal Floriano de Peixoto**, took over, but proved even more incompetent; Rio was actually shelled in 1893 by rebellious warships, demanding Peixoto's resignation. Finally, in 1894 popular pressure led to Peixoto stepping down in favour of the first elected civilian President, **Prudente de Morais**.

COFFEE WITH MILK – AND SUGAR

The years from 1890 to 1930 were politically undistinguished, but saw Brazil rapidly transformed economically and socially by large-scale **immigration** from Europe and Japan; they were decades of swift growth and swelling cities, which saw a very Brazilian combination of a boom–bust–boom economy and corrupt pork-barrel politics.

The boom was led by **coffee** and **rubber**, which – at opposite ends of the country – had entirely different labour forces. Millions of *nordestinos* moved into the Amazon to tap rubber, but the coffee workers swarming into São Paulo in their hundreds of thousands came chiefly from Italy. Between 1890 and 1930 over four million migrants arrived from Europe and another two hundred thousand from Japan. Most went to work on the coffee estates of southern Brazil, but enough remained to turn São Paulo into the fastest growing city in the Americas. Urban industrialization appeared in Brazil for the first time, taking root in São Paulo to supply the voracious markets of the young cities springing up in the *Paulista* interior. By 1930, São Paulo had displaced Rio as the leading industrial centre.

More improbable was the transformation of **Manaus** into the largest city of the Amazon. Rubber turned Manaus from a muddy village into a rich trading city within a couple of decades. The peak of the **rubber boom**, from the 1870s to the outbreak of World War I, financed its metamorphosis into a tropical *belle époque* outpost, complete with opera house. Rubber exports were second only to coffee, but proved much more vulnerable to competition. Seeds smuggled out of Amazonia by Victorian adventurer Henry Wickham in 1876 ended up in Ceylon and Malaya, where – by 1914 – plantation rubber pushed wild Amazon rubber out of the world markets. The region returned to an isolation it maintained until the late 1950s.

Economic growth was not accompanied by political development. Although not all the early presidents were incompetent – **Rodrigues Alves** (1902–06), for example, rebuilt Rio complete with a public health system, finally eradicating the epidemics that had stunted its growth – the majority were corrupt political bosses, relying on a network of patron–client relationships, whose main ambition seemed to be to bleed the public coffers dry. Power was concentrated in the two most populous states of São Paulo and Minas Gerais, which struck a convenient deal to alternate the presidency between them.

This way of ensuring that both sets of snouts could slurp away in the trough uninterrupted was called **"café com leite"** by its opponents: coffee from São Paulo and milk from the *mineiro* dairy herds. In fact, it was coffee with milk and sugar: the developing national habit of the sweet *cafezinho* in the burgeoning cities of the south provided a new domestic market for sugar, which ensured support from the plantation oligarchs of the Northeast. In a pattern that would repeat itself in more modern times, the economy forged ahead while politics went backwards. The saying "Brazil grows in the dark, while politicians sleep" made its first appearance.

THE REVOLUTION OF 1930

The revolution of 1930 that brought the populist **Getúlio Vargas** to power was a critical event. Vargas dominated Brazilian politics for the next quarter-century, and the Vargas years were a time of radical change, marking a decisive break with the past. Vargas had much in common with his Argentinian contemporary, Juan Perón: both were charming, but cunning and ruthless with it, and rooted their power base in the new urban working class.

It was the **working class**, combined with disillusion in the junior ranks of the military, that swept Vargas to power. Younger officers, accustomed to seeing the armed forces as the guardian of the national conscience, were disgusted by the corruption of the military hierarchy. When the **Great Depression** hit, the government spent millions protecting coffee growers by buying crops at a guaranteed price; the coffee was then burnt, as the export market had collapsed. Workers in the cities and countryside were appalled, seeing themselves frozen out while vast sums were spent on landowners, and as the economic outlook worsened the pressure started building up from other states to end the São Paulo and Minas grip on power. This time, the transition was violent.

In 1926, **Washington Luis** was made president without an election, as the elite contrived an unopposed nomination. When Luis appeared set to do the same thing in 1930, an unstoppable **mass revolution** developed, first in Vargas's home state of Rio Grande do Sul, then in Rio, then in the Northeast. There was some resistance in São Paulo, but the worst fighting was in the Northeast, where street battles left scores dead. The shock troops of the Revolution were the young army officers who led their units against the *ancien régime* in Minas and Rio, and the *gaúcho* cavalry who accompanied Vargas on his triumphant procession to Rio. Although São Paulo rose briefly against Vargas in 1932, the revolt was swiftly crushed, and Getúlio, as Brazilians affectionately knew him, embarked on the longest and most spectacular political career in modern Brazilian history.

VARGAS AND THE ESTADO NOVO

It was not just Vargas who took power in 1930, but a whole new generation of young, energetic administrators, who set about transforming the economy and the political system. Vargas played the nationalist card with great success, nationalizing the oil, electricity and steel industries, and setting up a health and social welfare system that earned him unwavering working-class support which continued even after his death.

Reforms this fundamental could not be carried out under the old constitutional framework. Vargas simplified things by declaring himself **dictator** in 1937 and imprisoning political opponents – most of whom were in the trade union movement, the Communist Party or the *Integralistas*, the Brazilian Fascists. He called his regime the "New State", the **Estado Novo**, and certainly its reforming energy was something new. Although he cracked down hard on dissent, Vargas was never a totalitarian dictator. He was massively popular and his great political talents enabled him to outflank most opponents.

The result was both political and economic success. The ruinous coffee subsidy was abolished, industry encouraged and agriculture diversified: by 1945 São Paulo had become the largest industrial centre in South America. With the federal government increasing its powers at the expense of state rights, regional government power was wrestled out of the hands of the oligarchs for the first time.

It took **World War II** to bring Vargas down. At first Brazil stayed neutral, reaping the benefits of increased exports, but when the United States offered massive aid in return for bases and Brazilian entry into the war, Vargas joined the Allies. Outraged by German submarine attacks on Brazilian shipping, Brazil was the only country in South America to play an active part in the war. A **Brazilian Expeditionary Force**, 5000-strong, fought in Italy from 1944 until the end of the war; when they returned, the military High Command was able to exploit the renewed prestige of the army, forcing Vargas to stand down. They argued that the armed forces could hardly fight for democracy abroad and return home to a dictatorship, and, in any case, after fifteen years a leadership change was overdue. In the election that followed in 1945, Vargas grudgingly endorsed the army general **Eurico Dutra**, who duly won – but Getúlio, brooding on his ranch, was not yet finished with the presidency.

THE DEATH OF VARGAS

Dutra proved a colourless figure, and when Vargas ran for the presidency in 1950 he won a crushing victory, the old dictator "returning on the arm of the people", as he wrote later. But he had powerful enemies, in the armed forces and on the right, and his second stint in power was turbulent. Dutra had allowed inflation to climb, and Vargas proposed to raise the minimum wage and slightly increase taxation of the middle classes. In the charged climate of the Cold War this was denounced by the right as veering towards communism, and vitriolic attacks on Vargas and his government were made in the press, notably by a slippery, ambitious journalist named **Carlos Lacerda**.

Vargas's supporters reacted angrily and argument turned into crisis in 1954, when shots were fired at Lacerda, missing their target but killing an air force officer guarding him. The attempt was traced to one of Vargas's bodyguards, but Vargas himself was not implicated. Even so, the press campaign rose to a crescendo, and finally, on August 25, 1954, the military High Command demanded his resignation. Vargas received the news calmly, went into his bedroom in the Palácio de Catete in Rio and shot himself through the heart.

He left an emotional suicide note to the Brazilian people: "I choose this means to be with you always . . . I gave you my life; now I offer my death. Nothing remains. Serenely I take the first step on the road to eternity, as I leave life and enter history." The initial popular reaction of stunned shock gave way to fury, as Vargas's supporters turned on the forces that had hounded him to death, stoning the newspaper offices and forcing Lacerda to flee the country. Eighteen months of tension followed, as an interim government marked time until the next election.

JK AND BRASÍLIA

Juscelino Kubitschek, "JK" to Brazilians, president from 1956 to 1961, proved just the man to fix Brazil's attention on the future rather than the past. He combined energy and imagination with integrity and great political skill, acquired in the hard school of the politics of Minas Gerais, one of the main nurseries of political talent in Brazil. Although the tensions in the political system were still there – constitutionalists in the armed forces had to stage a pre-emptive coup to allow him to take office – Kubitschek was able to serve out his full term, still the only elected civilian president to do so in modern times. And he left a permanent reminder of the most successful postwar presidency in the form of the country's new capital, Brasília, deep in the Planalto Central.

"Fifty years in five!" was his election slogan, and his economic programme lived up to its ambitious billing. His term saw a spurt in growth rates that was the platform for the "economic miracle" of the next decade; the economic boom led to wider prosperity and renewed national confidence. Kubitschek drew on both in the flight of inspired imagination that led to **the building of Brasília**.

It could so easily have been an expensive disaster, a purpose-built capital miles from anywhere, the personal brainchild of a president anxious to make his mark. But Kubitschek implanted the idea in the national imagination by portraying it as a renewed statement of faith in the interior, a symbol of national integration and a better future for all Brazilians, not just those in the south. He brought it off with great panache, bringing in the extravagantly talented **Oscar Niemeyer**, whose brief was to come up with a revolutionary city layout and the architecture to go with it. Kubitschek spent almost every weekend on the huge building site that became the city, consulted on the smallest details and had the satisfaction of handing over to his successor, **Jânio Quadros**, in the newly inaugurated capital.

1964: THE ROAD TO MILITARY RULE

At the time, the **military coup of 1964** was considered a temporary hiccup in Brazil's postwar democracy, but it lasted 21 years and left a very bitter taste. The first period of military rule saw the famous economic miracle (see below), when the economy grew at an astonishing *average* annual rate of ten percent for a decade, only to come to a juddering halt after 1974, when oil price rises and the increasing burden of debt repayment pushed it off the rails. But most depressing was the effective end of democracy for over a decade, and a time – from 1969 to 1974 – when terror was used against opponents by military hardliners. Brazil, where the *desaparecidos* numbered a few hundred rather than the tens of thousands butchered in Argentina and Chile, was not the worst military regime on the continent. But it is difficult to overestimate the shock even limited repression caused. It was the first time Brazilians experienced systematic brutality by a government, and even in the years of economic success the military governments were loathed right across the political spectrum.

The coup of 1964 was years in the brewing. It had two root causes: a constitutional crisis and the deepening divides in Brazilian society. In the developed south, relations between trade unions and employers went from bad to worse, as workers struggled to protect their wages against rising inflation. But it was in the Northeast that tension was greatest, as a result of the **Peasant Leagues** movement. Despite industrial modernization, the rural Northeast was still stuck in a timewarped land tenure system, moulded in the colonial period and in many ways unchanged since then. Peasants, under the charismatic leadership of **Francisco Julião** and the governor of Pernambuco, **Miguel Arrães**, began forming co-operatives and occupying estates to press their claim for agrarian reform; the estate owners cried communism and openly agitated for a military coup.

The crisis might still have been avoided by a more skilful president, but Kubitschek's immediate successors were not of his calibre. Quadros resigned after only six months, in August 1961, on the anniversary of Vargas's suicide. He apparently wanted popular reaction to sweep him back into office, but shrunk from suicide and ended up shooting himself in the foot rather than the heart. The masses stayed home, and the vice-president, **João Goulart**, took over.

Goulart's accession was viewed with horror by the right. He had a reputation as a leftist firebrand, having been a minister of labour under Vargas, and his position was weakened by the fact that he had not succeeded by direct popular vote. As political infighting began to get out of control, with the country polarizing between left and right, Goulart decided to throw himself behind the trade unions and the Peasant Leagues; his nationalist rhetoric rang alarm bells in Washington, and the army began to plot his downfall, with tacit American backing.

The coup, in the tradition of Brazilian coups, was swift and bloodless. On March 31, 1964, troops from Minas Gerais moved on Rio; when the military commanders there refused to oppose them, the game was up for Goulart. After futile efforts to rally resistance in Rio Grande do Sul, he fled into exile in Uruguay, and the first in a long line of generals, **Humberto Castelo Branco**, became president.

MILITARY RULE

The military moved swiftly to dismantle democracy. Congress was dissolved, those representatives not to military taste being removed. It then reconvened with only two parties, an official government and an official opposition ("The difference," ran a joke at the time, "is that one says Yes, and the other, Yes Sir!"). All other parties were banned. The Peasant Leagues and trade unions were repressed, with many of their leaders tortured and imprisoned, and even prominent national politicians like Arrães were thrown into jail. The ferocity of the military took aback even those on the right who had agitated for a coup. Ironically, many of them were hoist with their own petard when they voiced criticism, and found themselves gagged by the same measures they had urged against the left.

The political climate worsened steadily during the 1960s. An **urban guerrilla campaign** took off in the cities – its most spectacular success was the kidnapping of the American ambassador in 1969, released unharmed in return for over a hundred political detainees – but it only served as an excuse for the hardliners to crack down even further. General **Emílio Garrastazu Médici**, leader of the hardliners, took over the presidency in 1969 and the worst period of military rule began. Torture became routine, censorship was strict and thousands were driven into exile: this dark chapter in Brazilian history lasted for five agonizing years, until he gave way to **Ernesto Gel** in 1974. The scars Médici left behind him, literally and metaphorically, have still not completely healed.

THE ECONOMIC MIRACLE

Despite the cold winds blowing on the political front, the Brazilian economy forged ahead from the mid-1960s to 1974, the years of the **economic miracle** – and the combination of high growth and low inflation indeed seemed miraculous to later governments. The military welcomed foreign investment, and the large pool of cheap but skilled labour was irresistible. Investment poured in, both from Brazil and abroad, and the boom was the longest and largest in Brazilian history. Cities swelled, industry grew, and by the mid-1970s Brazil was the economic giant of South America, São Paulo state alone having a GNP higher than any South American country.

The problem, though, was uneven development. Even miraculous growth rates could not provide enough jobs for the hordes migrating to the cities, and the squalid **favelas** expanded even faster than the economy. The problem was worst in the Northeast and the Amazon, where industry was less developed, and drought combined with land conflict to push the people of the interior into the cities. It was also the miracle years that saw the origins of the **debt crisis**, a millstone around the neck of the Brazilian economy in the 1980s and 1990s.

After 1974, a lot of petrodollars were sloshing around the world banking system, thanks to oil price rises. Anxious to set this new capital to work, international banks and South American military regimes fell over themselves in their eagerness to organize deals. Brazil had a good credit rating: its wealth of natural resources and jailed labour leaders saw to that. The military needed money for a series of huge development projects that were central to its trickle-down economic policy, like the **Itaipu dam**, the **Carajás** mining projects in eastern Amazonia, and a **nuclear power programme**. By the end of the 1970s the debt was at $50 billion; by 1990 it had risen to $120 billion, and the interest payments were crippling the economy.

OPENING UP THE AMAZON

The first step towards opening up the vast interior of the **Amazon** was taken by Kubitschek, who built a dirt highway linking Brasília to Belém. But things really got going in 1970, when Médici realized that the Amazon could be used as a huge safety valve, releasing the pressure for agrarian reform in the Northeast. "Land without people for people without land!" became the slogan, and an ambitious programme of highway construction began that was to transform Amazonia. The main links were the **Transamazônica**, running west to the Peruvian border, the **Cuiabá–Santarém** highway into central Amazonia, and the **Cuiabá–Porto Velho/Rio Branco** highway, opening access to western Amazonia.

For the military, the Amazon was empty space, overdue for filling, and a national resource to be developed. They set up an elaborate network of tax breaks and incentives to encourage Brazilian and multinational firms to invest in the region, who also saw it as empty space and proceeded either to speculate with land or cut down forest to graze cattle. The one group that didn't perceive the Amazon as empty space was, naturally enough, the millions of people who already lived there. The immediate result was a spiralling land conflict, as ranchers, rubber tappers, Brazil-nut harvesters, gold-miners, smallholders, Indians, multinationals and Brazilian companies all tried to press their claims. The result was – and is – chaos.

By the late 1980s the situation in the Amazon was becoming an international controversy, with heated claims about the uncontrolled destruction of forest in huge annual burnings, and the invasion of Indian lands. Less internationally known was the **land crisis**, although a hundred people or more were dying in land conflicts in Amazonia every year. It took the assassination in 1988 of **Chico Mendes**, leader of the rubber tappers' union and eloquent defender of the forest, to bring it home. Media attention, as usual, has shed as much heat as light, but there are grounds for hope. Deforestation follows highways and there's unlikely to be a comparable highway building programme in the future, so the worst may well be about to come to an end. And for all the destruction, Amazonia is very large – there is still time for more sensible development to protect what remains. (See also "Amazon Ecology and Indian Rights", p.615.)

THE ABERTURA

Growing popular resentment of the military could not be contained indefinitely, especially when the economy turned sour. By the late 1970s debt, rising inflation and unemployment were turning the economy from a success story into a joke, and the military were further embarrassed by an unsavoury chain of corruption scandals. Gel was the first military president to plan for a return to civilian rule, in a slow relaxing of the military grip called *abertura*, the "opening-up". Yet again, Brazil managed a bloodless – albeit fiendishly complicated – transition. Slow though the process was, the return to democracy would have been delayed even longer were it not for two events along the way: the **metalworkers' strikes** in São Paulo in

1977 and the mass **campaign for direct elections** in 1983–84.

The São Paulo strikes began in the car industry and soon spread throughout the industrial belt of São Paulo, in a movement bearing many parallels with Solidarity in Poland. Led by unions that were still illegal, and the charismatic young factory worker **Lula (Luis Inácio da Silva)**, there was a tense stand-off between army and strikers, until the military realized that having São Paulo on strike would be worse for the economy than conceding the right to free trade unions. This dramatic re-emergence of organized labour was a sign that the military could not control the situation for much longer.

Reforms in the early 1980s lifted censorship, brought the exiles home and allowed normal political life to resume. But the military came up with an ingenious attempt to control the succession: their control of Congress allowed them to pass a resolution that the president due to take office in 1985 would be elected not by direct vote, but by an electoral college, made up of congressmen and senators, where the military party had the advantage.

The democratic opposition responded with a counter-amendment proposing a direct election. It needed a two-thirds majority in Congress to be passed, and a campaign began for **diretas-já**, "elections now". Even the opposition was surprised by the response, as the Brazilian people, thoroughly sick of the generals, took to the streets in their millions. The campaign culminated in huge rallies of over a million people in Rio and São Paulo, and opinion polls showed over ninety percent in favour; but when the vote came in March 1984 the amendment just failed. The military still nominated a third of Senate seats, and this proved decisive.

It looked like defeat; in fact it turned into victory. The moment found the man in **Tancredo Neves**, ex-minister of justice under Vargas, ex-prime minister, and a wise old *mineiro* fox respected across the political spectrum, who put himself forward as opposition candidate in the electoral college. By now it was clear what the public wanted, and Tancredo's unrivalled political skills enabled him to stitch together an alliance that included dissidents from the military's own party. In January 1985 he romped home in the electoral college, to great national rejoicing, and military rule came to an end.

Tancredo proclaimed the civilian **Nova República** – the "New Republic".

THE NEW REPUBLIC: CRISIS AND CORRUPTION

Tragically, the New Republic was orphaned at birth. The night before his inauguration, Tancredo was rushed to hospital for an emergency operation on a bleeding stomach tumour: it proved benign, but in hospital he picked up an infection and six weeks later died of septicaemia. His funeral was the largest mass event in Brazilian history; a crowd of two million carried his coffin from the hospital where he had died in São Paulo to Garulhos airport. The vice-president, **José Sarney**, a second-league politician from Maranhão, who had been fobbed off with a ceremonial post, suddenly found himself serving a full presidential term.

His administration was disastrous, though not all of it was his own fault: he was saddled with a ministerial team he had not chosen, and a newly powerful Congress which would have given any president a rough ride. But Sarney made matters worse by a lack of decisiveness, and wasn't helped by the sleaze that hung like a fog around his government, with **corruption** institutionalized on a massive scale. No progress was made on the economic front either. By 1990 inflation accelerated into **hyperinflation** proper, and, despite spending almost \$40 billion repaying interest on the foreign debt, the principal had swollen to \$120 billion at the end of the decade. Popular disgust was so great that on every occasion Sarney found himself near a crowd of real people, he was greeted with a shower of bricks and curses. The high hopes of 1985 had evaporated: Sarney had brought the whole notion of civilian politics into disrepute, and achieved the near-impossible of making the military look good.

BRAZIL IN THE 1990S

Despite everything, Brazil still managed to begin the new decade on a hopeful note, with the inauguration in 1990 of **Fernando Collor de Melo**, the first properly elected president for thirty years, after a heated but peaceful campaign had managed to consolidate democracy at a difficult economic moment. In the last months of his administration, Sarney had presided over the take-off into hyperinflation, and it was clear the new president would have to come up with fast economic answers if he was to survive.

The campaign had passed the torch to a new generation of Brazilians, as the young Collor, playboy scion of one of Brazil's oldest and richest families, had squared off against **Lula**, who had come a long way since the São Paulo strikes. Now a respected – and feared – national politician, head of the Workers' Party that the strike movement had evolved into, Lula took most of the cities, but Collor's conservative rural support was enough to secure a narrow victory.

Collor's presidency began promisingly enough, as he pushed for a long-overdue opening-up of the economy and implemented the most draconian currency stabilization plan yet, the infamous **Plano Collor**, hated by the middle classes because it temporarily froze their bank accounts. The economy resisted all attempts at surgery, and inflation began to climb again. Collor seemed to become more unstable than the economy; he was increasingly erratic in public, and rumours grew about dark goings-on behind the scenes. Thanks to fine journalism and a denunciation by Collor's own brother, apparently angry that Fernando had made a pass at his wife, it became clear that a web of **corrupt dealings** masterminded by Collor's treasurer, **P. C. Farias**, had set up what was effectively a parallel government. Billions of dollars had been skimmed from the government's coffers, in a scam breathtaking even by Brazilian standards.

Impeachment proceedings were begun in Congress, but few politicians expected them to get anywhere. Demonstrations began to take place in the big cities, led initially by students, but soon spreading to the rest of the population and numbering hundreds of thousands of angry but peaceful citizens. It rapidly became clear that if Congress did not vote impeachment through, there would be hell to pay. In September 1992, Collor was duly impeached and replaced by his vice-president, **Itamar Franco**. Farias was jailed, later to die in mysterious circumstances: he was allegedly murdered by a girlfriend who then committed suicide, but it is likely the full story of his death will never be known. His master, Collor, who may know more than most about the murder, lives in gilded exile in Miami, to the fury of most Brazilians.

Specimen corruption charges failed, and his continued liberty is testimony to the weakness of the Brazilian legal system.

Franco, like Sarney before him, proved an incompetent buffoon left minding the shop. The real power in his government was the finance minister, **Fernando Henrique Cardoso**, who staked his claim to the succession by implementing the **Plano Real** in 1994. This finally tamed inflation and stabilized the economy, for the first time in twenty years. A grateful public duly gave him an overwhelming first-round victory in the presidential election later that year, when he trounced Lula in every state bar Brasília and the Distrito Federal.

CARDOSO: STABILITY AND REFORM

Uniquely among modern Brazilian presidents, Cardoso, a donnish ex-academic from São Paulo, proved able and effective. Ironically, before he became a politician he was one of the world's most respected left-wing theorists of economic development. However, his political career has moved along a different track, as his government has opened up the Brazilian economy and pushed through vital political reforms. The stabilization of the economy that he achieved through the Plano Real has not been forgotten by the Brazilian poor, who were the most affected by hyperinflation, and now that a constitutional amendment permitting re-election has been passed, Cardoso is certain to be overwhelmingly re-elected in 1998.

Cardoso entered office with a clear vision of Brazil's economic and political problems, and how to cure them. On the economic front, he has built on the Plano Real by pushing through a privatization programme in the teeth of fierce nationalist opposition, cutting tariff barriers, opening up the economy to competition and making Brazil the dominant member of **Mercosul**, a regional trade organization which also includes Argentina, Uruguay and Paraguay, with Bolivia and Chile in the queue to join. The result has been healthy growth, falling unemployment and low inflation, an achievement without precedents in modern Brazilian history.

Politically, he has steered a skilful middle course between dinosaurs of right and left, corrupt *caudilhos* and their patron–client politics on the one hand, and time-warped nationalists still clinging to protectionism and suspicious of the outside world on the other. In a steady, if unspectacular process, a series of constitutional amendments has been passed reducing the role of the state and reforming the political system. Corruption still plagues political life, and further reforms are necessary, but his achievements to date are impressive.

Brazil approaches the twenty-first century in better shape than seemed possible a few years ago. The bad press it often – and usually deservedly – gets abroad can obscure the positive side of the coin: an increasingly deep-rooted democracy, where people and the media were able to bring down a corrupt president, and now, finally, a stable, growing economy. There are still difficulties, of course. The judicial system is a joke, which is much more of a problem than it seems: it underlies the frightening level of violence in Brazilian society, since those using it know they will almost certainly not be brought to book, and it also encourages corruption, for the same reason. Economic growth needs to be linked to stronger social action, if it is not to widen inequalities that are already yawning. Agrarian reform, an explosive issue, has still to be properly dealt with. And although the environment has slipped down the agenda in recent years with the decline in Amazonian deforestation, a growing economy will force many hard environmental choices in the years to come.

All the same, the achievements of the New Republic have been impressive. For all its faults, Brazil is a vibrant, functioning democracy. Its economy has an increasingly modern look to it, and the recent improvements have, crucially, reached down to lower-income families as well. Cardoso is clever enough to realize that his place in history depends on reducing inequality, as well as encouraging growth. If – a big if – Brazil's politicians build on Cardoso's achievements rather than concentrate on lining their wallets, Brazilians, justly famous for their optimism, can extend it to fields other than a football pitch.

AMAZON ECOLOGY AND INDIAN RIGHTS

The Amazon rainforest is not just an icon for the environmental movement, it is the largest and most biodiverse forest left on Earth. More, too, than a future world breadbasket, the Amazon is home to over a million indigenous Indians. The two issues that predominate in the environmental debate, the destruction of the rainforest and the plight of the indigenous Indian population, are in many cases inextricably linked. Brazilians tend to react with outrage at being lectured on the preservation of their environment and the protection of native peoples by North Americans and Europeans, who less than fifteen years ago were still accusing Brazil of failing to exploit the very resources they now seek to save. Justifiable as Brazilian accusations of hypocrisy may be, however, they cannot hide the fact that there is a real environmental crisis in Brazil, a reality that is finally gaining acceptance among domestic politicians.

THE AMAZON

The Amazon is larger than life. It contains one fifth of the world's fresh water, sustaining the world's largest rainforest – over six million square kilometres – which in turn supports thousands upon thousands of animal and plant species, many of them still unknown. It possesses one in five of all the birds on earth. But perhaps the most startling statistic is the extraordinary rate at which the forest has been **destroyed** over the past thirty years. In the state of Maranhão, over fifty percent of the forest had disappeared by 1989. Most of the remainder had gone by 1994, cleared largely by well-armed and well-organized loggers, hired guns, squatters and speculators.

It is impossible to understand the Amazon without grasping that the rivers and the forest are essentially different aspects of the same organic whole. The Amazon rainforest has taken over fifty million years to evolve. If small clearings are made in virgin forest they may more or less regenerate within 100–150 years. But the enormous regions being decimated these days are unlikely ever to grow back as they were.

In 1983, official Brazilian statistics showed that some two to four percent of the trees had already disappeared from the Amazon region – according to Friends of the Earth it was closer to thirty percent. Even if you bear in mind their respective bias, plus the fact that secondary regenerative growth is often mistaken for true forest in satellite photos, then the real figure was probably between ten and fifteen percent; by 1997 this was more like 25 percent.

The rainforest is still seen by many in Brazil as a resource to be exploited until it no longer exists, much as we see fossil fuels and mineral deposits. The indigenous Indians and many of the modern forest-dwellers – including rubber tappers, nut collectors and, increasingly, even peasant settlers – view the forest differently. For them it is one of nature's gifts which, like an ocean, can be harvested regularly if it is not overtaxed. One of the most **hopeful signs** in the Amazon is that this view is increasingly gaining scientific and economic credibility, as people come to realize that sensible exploitation of the forest can in the long term be more profitable than clearance. Another piece of good news is that clearance has so far followed **road** building: much of the land easily accessible from existing roads has already been devastated, and major new roads seem unlikely when jungle is growing back over some Amazon roads because they are used so little.

Until the Amazon was opened up by roads, many areas were inhabited and exploited only by **Indian tribal peoples**, who had long since retreated from the main rivers. They had done so in order to escape the white man's deadly influence and to continue their traditional forms of life. When the Spanish and Portuguese first explored the Amazon they noted that a well-established, highly organized, apparently agriculturally based Indian society thrived along the banks of the main rivers. Within a hundred years this relatively sophisticated Indian culture had vanished. Although many had died from the initial effects of new diseases (flu, smallpox, measles, etc), a large proportion had escaped into more remote areas of the forest.

When a road reaches into new territories it brings with it the financial backing and interests of big agricultural and industrial companies, plus an onslaught of land-seeking settlers. These days the **areas most endangered** by roads are Rondônia (already largely devastated by the early 1990s), large areas in southern Pará (notably the giant Carajás industrial scheme, where a new rail line provides the transport), the whole Transamazonian belt to the south of the Amazon river, a large region around Manaus, and what's left of the corridor formed by the Brasília–Belém highway.

Chico Mendes, the Brazilian rubber tappers' union leader who was shot dead in 1988, was the best-known voice on the side of the established Amazon-dwellers: "the forest is our mother, our source of life," he argued. He became a victim of the oppression of forest-dwellers by large land-owning interests when he was killed by hired gunmen outside his house in the state of Acre in the southwest Amazon. His "crime" had been to stand up and be vocal in the face of financial and physical attack, mainly from large cattle-ranching companies. In February 1989, a few months after Mendes was shot, over 4000 Amazonian forest people gathered in Altamira along with environmental groups, scientists and government officials to thrash out the environmental and socio-cultural issues involved in rainforest destruction and the taking of indigenous land for national developments (see below).

The forest is a very fragile but potentially sustainable source of harvested fruits, nuts and oils, but some agronomists are of the probably dangerous opinion that with the same investment in chemical, mechanical and genetic manipulation the Amazon could be a highly productive zone. Even on a relatively small farm level, if properly logged, the forest can provide low levels of capital while at the same time safeguarding the biodiversity and forest resources for the future. The Brazilian government-funded agroforestry research institute, **EMBRAPA**, based in Manaus, has experimented successfully with incorporating and weaving in trees and replanted mixed tree species with agricultural production. There are apparently many advantages to the well-being of plants and soil encouraging or maintaining tree species diversity. Sustainable and appropriate matching of cash crops, tree and timber-related products to available resources could make for a viable agroforestry industry in many areas of

the Amazon. The Amazon can, many argue, best be preserved by managing it, not destroying it. The line is a fine one, but it is not impossible to clarify.

DESTRUCTION OF THE FOREST: THE REGIONAL CONSEQUENCES

In regional terms, the most serious effects of the destruction of the Amazon rainforest are threefold:

• Climatic experts have predicted that **deserts and droughts** will be created by the disappearance of large tracts of the Amazon rainforest. This has already happened in the Northeastern coastal regions where barely any of the original forest cover survives. Drought- and poverty-stricken peasants from the Northeast form the majority of the landless settlers moving into the recently cleared areas of the Amazon today.

• The **devastation of indigenous tribal groups** is a second major problem associated with the destruction of the Amazon. The chief culprit is disease, introduced to people who have no natural resistance, but physical violence has also taken its toll. Gold-miners have polluted rivers (and the water and fish therein) with mercury, and people have been forced to move from their traditional homes to areas less able to support them.

• The **loss of the forest itself** is also serious. This may sound a circuitous argument, but the fact is that as the forest goes, so does an endless potential supply of rubber and other valuable gums, medicines, nuts, fruits, fish, game, skins and the like. A wide variety of ways to harvest the natural products of the forest are emerging, and, as time goes on, it seems more and more apparent that there is a greater long-term value in this approach if the forest can be saved.

THE GLOBAL CONSEQUENCES

In world terms too, the loss of the Amazon rainforest has serious consequences:

• The destruction of the forest has two effects on the earth's atmosphere. The smoke from the vast forest clearances makes a significant direct contribution to the **greenhouse effect**. Less immediately, the fewer trees there are to absorb carbon dioxide, the faster the greenhouse effect is likely to build.

• The **loss of resources** is a world problem almost as much as it is a regional one. Only a small proportion of the plants that exist in the Amazon have been studied, and there is a real danger of losing a genetic pool of vital importance. Already, as many as one in four of the chemicals or medicines found in a high-street chemist originate from rainforest products, and there can be little doubt that there are many more medical breakthroughs waiting to be discovered. In 1982 a US National Academy of Sciences report estimated that an average 10 square kilometres of rainforest contains 750 tree species; 125 mammal types; 400 varieties of birds; 100 different kinds of reptiles; 60 amphibians; and that a typical individual tree might support over 400 insect species.

• The potential loss of **the world's last major forest** is perhaps enough in itself to make the Amazon worth saving.

WHY IS THE FOREST GOING?

A number of reasons are put forward for the continuing destruction of the rainforest. A complete answer should include the following four major factors, though none of them is particularly convincing on its own:

• **Population and land pressures**. Perhaps the most popular theory of all, certainly in Brazil, is that an unstoppable tide of humanity is swamping the forest. Although certainly an important factor, the invasion of the Amazon by small-scale settlers contributes far less to the destruction of the rainforest than large-scale, big-business agriculture. Farming and clearance on a small scale do relatively little damage, and in any case many of the small settlers are either moving from regions like the Northeast which have already been environmentally decimated (by large-scale agriculture) or have been squeezed off their old patches by large companies wanting to ranch or mine the place.

• **Debt**. Brazil's billion-dollar external debt is another popular scapegoat, but again not a particularly convincing one in isolation. In agricultural terms, few of Brazil's export crops come from the Amazon, and the beef cattle raised here are largely for domestic consumption. Many of the area's mineral resources do go for export, but on the other hand it was the development of extraction schemes like the Grande Carajás project that largely created the debt in the first place.

• **Greed**. Underlying the continuing destruction of the rainforest is greed. In Brazil this is manifested mostly by the powerful alliance between big business and the armed forces which began back in the early 1960s. The opening-up of the Amazon had always been a "national dream" and, with the building of Brasília, the 1960s seemed an appropriate time to forge ahead with the vision. There were millions of dollars to be made in foreign investment, and throughout the "economic miracle" of the 1960s and 1970s plenty of cash was available to be shared around between the construction industry, mining companies, land speculators and the authorities. Internationally, the greed of the industrial-consumer nations, like Britain and the United States, has also played its part: both at the level of individual consumer behaviour – using tropical hardwoods rather than sustainable plantations, for example – and at the level of governments and financial institutions which have been only too happy to invest in environmentally damaging schemes like Grande Carajás.

• **Ignorance**. Only the "greening" of Brazil at the level of national and individual consciousness will ultimately determine how quickly, if at all, the devastation of the Amazon can be halted. It is easy to forget just how recently environmental concerns have been widespread: as little as fifteen years ago Brazil was being actively encouraged to exploit the Amazon "hinterland" by European and world banks. It is only the sudden global awareness of potentially very serious environmental problems that has caused a change of heart.

tHE FUTURE

Until the Earth Summit in Rio in 1992 (see p.618), the Brazilian **response** to foreign environmental advice had been negative. After all, why should they listen to US scientists when the USA continues to push more pollutants into the atmosphere than any other nation? In 1989, President Sarney introduced new legislation to create sanctions against unauthorized forest clearance, to create more national reserves, to do away with incentives for large-scale cattle-ranching and to guarantee the Yanomami Indians the right to at least some of their traditional lands. As usual, the political decisions were made too late and the political will was too small for these decisions on paper to have any lasting or noticeable effect on the real world, but they were a start.

More significantly, Sarney's successor, Collor, committed himself in the media to the "greening" of Brazil. He outlined a plan for an alternative to military service – **Green Soldiers**, to work in areas of ecological importance like national parks and reserves. He talked of debt-for-nature swaps and of enforcing severe punishments for "ecological crimes".

Meanwhile the infamous dry-season **queimadas** – the annual torchings of the felled forest – continue as a serious threat to the planet's climate. To try and control the *queimadas* in 1989 and 1990, Brazil's environmental protection agency, IBAMA, organized helicopter surveillance for unauthorized burning of the forest. Not used to outside control of any kind, the larger *fazendeiros* were quick to react by shooting at helicopters and torching at weekends, at dusk or on Independence Day when the helicopters were less likely to be around. An IBAMA inspector was killed in Marabá by two timber dealers, and there has been a growing number of attacks on and threats to IBAMA workers.

Still, there is a growing coalition of environmentalists and forest people uniting against the destruction of the forest (and in the case of the forest people, their own destruction). Indians, rubber tappers and recent settlers have identified a common enemy in the state-backed mega-company. Together the forest people are a growing political force both within Brazil and, since the death of Chico Mendes, on the international scene. In February 1989, the first meeting of Brazil's indigenous peoples was held in Marabá to protest about the Xingu Dam scheme. In March 1989, the **Forest People's Alliance** was formed in Rio Branco to lobby for the creation of "extractive forest reserves" as the first step towards an official policy for the exploitation of Amazon rainforest which might actually be sustainable into the twenty-first century.

One basic problem with many "**sustainable**" **forest products** is the danger for anyone, let alone tribal groups or subsistence extractors, of relying on what are essentially ephemeral markets in Western luxury products. Brazil-nut oil, for example, is a luxury rather than a basic product for the West. In fact, sustainably managed timber, which represents a more vital and basic, even long-lasting, product for foreign and domestic markets, is probably more likely to provide significant economic security in the long run. But even this depends on the sincerity of the "sustainable" foresters, their ability to reach their markets, and, of course, the attitude and perspective of the consumers in the world market.

THE EARTH SUMMIT

The United Nations Conference on Environment and Development (UNCED), more commonly known as the **Earth Summit**, took place, perhaps symbolically, in Rio de Janeiro in June 1992. Over 114 heads of government and thousands of lesser global officials and representatives gathered to discuss global environmental issues. At the same time, also in Rio, a parallel event, the **Global Forum**, brought together thousands more NGOs and interested organizations and individuals. Over a period of just two weeks, five major agreements were negotiated. Two of these were framework treaties setting out the principles for the Climate Change Convention and the Biodiversity Convention. The three further agreements were non-binding proposals constituting a moral rather than legal commitment: the Rio Declaration, containing 27 principles aiming for sustainable development; Forest Principles, aiming at sustainable management of the world's forests; and Agenda 21, a detailed attempt to deal with the fundamental problems of environmental and global development.

The summit raised awareness of international environmental problems rather than establishing paths to solutions, and some of the larger world nations, such as the USA, demonstrated disappointing levels of real commitment. Nevertheless, even in Brazil, the average person on the street knows that there are global environmental problems and that Brazil is under an international spotlight. However, this has had little or no effect on the majority of *fazendeiros*, loggers and prospectors who are still controlling the rape of Amazonia.

TRIBAL RESISTANCE: THE AMAZON INDIAN

The **Tupi** tribe was the first Brazilian "Indian nation" to come into serious conflict with the outside world. Twelve colonies had been established in Brazil by the Portuguese king, João III, to exploit trade in wood and sugar, but slavery and death were the only things that the Tupi got out of the exchange – a pattern which was to continue for the next five hundred years in Brazil. Perhaps even more devastating than murder or slavery was the spread of white man's **disease**: dysentery and influenza hit within the first two years; smallpox and the plague followed. When the Jesuit missionaries attempted to gather the natives into "reduction" missions, epidemics killed hundreds of thousands of Indians in just a few decades.

The first century and a half of contact was funded by the need for cheap labour and new resources. Spreading steadily into the savannas of the Ge-speaking peoples, and the forests of Pará and the Amazon, the colonists established cattle ranches, plantations, lumber extraction regions and mining settlements – all of which were met by considerable native resistance. Later, the development of vulcanization in the 1870s led to an international demand for **rubber**. Prices rose rapidly and, while there was a boom which lasted for almost fifty years, Indians were killed, moved around and enslaved by the rubber barons.

Even though it had always been going on, it wasn't until 1968 that the first reports accusing the **Indian Protection Service** (the forerunner of FUNAI) of "corruption, torture and murder" appeared in the world press. An example is the experience of the Nambikwara tribe, who have two main areas reserved for them. One zone of semi-arid scrubland lies to the east of the Cuiabá–Porto Velho highway (BR-364), an indigenous reservation since 1968; the other area is in the fertile Guaporé river valley, where most of the zone is taken over by cattle ranchers – the Indians complain of dung-polluted river waters. The progressive extermination of the tribe has been going on for years, initially with machine guns, then with FUNAI issuing certificates to allow cattle-ranching concessions to set up operations in Indian lands. In their attempt to save the Nambikwara from certain death, FUNAI tried to transfer the Indians south from the Guaporé valley to empty, arid scrubland. Many Indians became sick during and after the move – measles killed all the children of one group – and bedraggled, starving Indians could be seen walking back along the highways in 1976.

The government's **Programme of National Integration** (PIN) began in 1970. Aiming to colonize Amazonia by the construction of two highways – *Transamazônica* and Cuiabá–Santarém – the intention was to relocate some half a million families from the overpopulated and poor Northeast. Only some ten thousand have actually moved, but these alone have caused enormous devastation (mainly through unchecked diseases) to several tribes – Araba, Parkana, Kreen Akarore and Txukarramae. Other roads and further problems have followed. The Northern Perimeter highway (BR-210) affected the Yanomami. A road from Manaus to Caracarai (BR-17) hurt the Waimiri-Atroari people. And the Cuiabá–Porto Velho road (BR-364) – known as the *Polonoroeste* resettlement project – not only seriously disrupted the Nambikwara Indian tribe but also severely disappointed many thousands of peasants who found the soil lasted three or four years at most and that malaria was a common problem. The latest plan is to link up the north and south Amazon roads by cutting a highway through Acre and around the borders with Peru, Ecuador and Columbia, thereby endangering more Amazonian groups at the same time as putting them under border security control.

It was not until the **1980s** that the Indians started to display their political strength and will. In 1984, a group of Txukarramae Indians from the Xingu river held the director of the Xingu park and five other FUNAI employees hostage to demand demarcation of their lands, which had been cut off from the rest of the park by the BR-080 highway. The Indian leader, Raoni, had inspired prolonged resistance to the road since its construction in 1971. About thirteen employees from invading agricultural companies were killed and the Txukarramae even blockaded the BR-080 and took hostages for a period. After long negotiations, and with much support from Indian figures like Mario Juruna, they eventually received their land demarcation.

Mario Juruna – a Xavante Indian chief – didn't even see a white man until 1958, when he was seventeen. Yet in 1983, he became an overnight TV celebrity by being the first Indian elected to the Brazilian Congress. A controversial figure among Indians and non-Indians alike, he lost his seat in November 1986, along with another nine unsuccessful Indian candidates. But this emergence of **self-determined Indian**

organizations has been a significant feature over the last decade.

In 1986, 537 mining claims had been conceded for research in indigenous areas, and 1732 other claims were being processed, altogether affecting 77 of the 302 indigenous land areas of Brazil. Uncontacted Indians live on the lands of some ten percent of the claims.

SELF-DETERMINATION?

If Brazilian Indians were actually granted the minimal **rights** which they have under Brazilian law – that is, the right to their own land, and the right to protection against violence and exploitation – there would be no Indian problem. Daniel, a Pareci Indian from Rio Verde in the Mato Grosso, said, "We were born on the land, and we are children of the land. So our rights are greater than theirs (the cattle ranchers). Just as they are human beings, we too are human beings. In fact I have found that we are even more human because we place human dignity first, rather than economic interests and concern for profit-making which can lead to human destruction." He continued: "FUNAI (the government agency specializing in Indian affairs) plays a policing role, preventing us from holding meetings and discussing our own problems, even though we are the only ones who have a deep understanding of those problems."

The Brazilian anthropologist Professor Roberto Oliveira believes that the "most notable thing that the government could do would be to allow the Indians the freedom to decide on their own destiny. If the relations between the state and the Indian communities were conducted as a form of diplomatic exchange rather than by administrative fiat, then we could view **FUNAI** not as the National Indian Foundation but as the Foundation of Indian Nationalities, and the internal colonialism would at last give way to internal diplomacy." And another Brazilian anthropologist, Darcy Ribeiro, has said that "many Brazilians will blush with shame tomorrow for having yesterday – today, I mean – had such brutal ancestors as we. I also fear that many humane people throughout the world are already looking at us, appalled at what they see. Why so much violence against the defenceless Indians? What is the source of so much loathing for fellow men? What will become of the Yanomami?"

In February 1989, Indian tribal leaders and environmentalists from all over the world gathered in the Amazon town of **Altamira**. Co-ordinated by Friends of the Earth, the Altamira meeting brought together over five hundred Indians from various Amazon tribes. Although much publicity was gained for their cause, however, the promising reports that giant projects – like Brazilian Eletronorte's Xingu HEP Dam scheme – may be stopped or scaled down should be taken with a pinch of salt. At the end of the day, the decisions rest with the world's banking institutions, who are not noted for their sentimentality.

Only six months earlier, back in 1988, Eletronorte and the Brazilian government were doing their best to discredit two Indian tribal leaders who were on trial for supposedly "denigrating the image of Brazil abroad". What actually happened was that, on returning from a visit to the USA, they were blamed for influencing the World Bank in its decision to withold a US$500,000,000 loan to the Xingu project. On October 14, 1988, around four hundred Kayapo Indians arrived at the courthouse in Belém to see their two leaders on trial. They were prevented from entering the court by military police, and the defendants were not allowed into the court until they dressed in a shirt and trousers – the Indians' traditional garb evidently being judged a "sign of disrespect" to the judiciary.

CASE STUDIES

Straddling the hilly area of rainforest on the border between Brazil and Venezuela live the **Yanomami** tribe. One of the largest Amazon Indian groups still surviving today, there are around ten thousand of the tribe living on the Brazilian side of the frontier. Traditionally inhabiting circular, walled villages of up to two hundred people, the Yanomami led a way of life which was very much in balance with the natural environment, depending on a combination of hunting, gathering and gardening. Until recently, the tribe led simple, but reasonably content lives for the most part.

However, in 1987, coming in the wake of local military-built airstrips and the announcement that the Yanomami were soon to be given "official" rights to their traditional land, a trickle of **gold-miners** began to invade their territory. Sufficient gold was found in the Indians' hills to bring more and more miners, or *garimpeiros*, into the Yanomami Reserve, and by 1990 there were some 45,000 *garimpeiros* in the region – far outnumbering the Yanomami. The Indians began to suffer from newly introduced strains of malaria and mercury-poisoned rivers and are, consequently, rapidly declining in numbers, health and morale.

After much campaigning pressure from groups like Survival International, President Sarney drew up emergency measures in 1989 to deal with the worsening plight of the Yanomami. His plan was for the police and army to move the *garimpeiros* out, by force if necessary, within a sixty-day period. The plan, however, was never executed as the army refused to comply. One thing was certain: if there had been a move to evict the *garimpeiros* (all of whom are armed), it would have resulted in a bloodbath of historic proportions. Indeed, few ever believed it would happen, so there was little surprise when, in January 1990, Justice Minister Saulo Ramos capitulated to the *garimpeiros'* demands, rather than press ahead with the eviction operation.

Demarcation of the Yanomami reserves finally happened in 1992 when they were registered as Federal Territory. Nevertheless, around eleven thousand *garimpeiros* reinvaded Yanomami land in 1993, encouraged to do so by local politicians and miners' unions in the state of Roraima. Malaria, TB and other diseases tightened their grip on the tribe once again and the inevitable friction between *garimpeiros* and Indian communities exploded into violence. In August 1993, sixteen Yanomami of the Hashimu community were shot and then sliced into pieces by machete-wielding Brazilian gold-miners. Most of the dead were women and children since the attack happened while the men were visiting a neighbouring settlement.

Underlying the entire process, causing irreversible harm to the Yanomami people and the forests they have been guardians of for millennia, is the long-term strategic **military plan** known as *Calha Norte*. The main aim of this strategy is to populate relatively "uninhabited" and remote international border zones to ensure Brazilian territorial and national security, and the army's favoured method is to build airstrips, establish settlements, and then fill them with patriotic Brazilian frontierspeople.

Although gold-mining – initially at least – does much less environmental damage than

logging or ranching, the long-term effects of putting mercury in the rivers are frightening. And, with the airstrips, settlements and new tracks that are being opened into the Yanomami's once peaceful forests, come an increasing number of non-Indians; after the miners will come the settlers, the ranchers and an overland transport network – all of which spell doom for the Yanomami. Once the Yanomami have disappeared, there really won't be any large tribal groups left in the Brazilian Amazon.

The battle for and against fundamental rights for Indian people continues in **Roraima**, where other tribes too have taken defensive action to protect themselves against illegal prospecting on their land. In March 1994, the **Makuxi**, **Ingariko**, **Wapixana** and **Taurepang** Indian groups set up roadblocks to prevent supplies getting through to the mines. Delays in the proper demarcation of their reserves worsened the situation. Although up to five hundred Indians operated the blockades, they were violently attacked and literally bulldozed by armed police wearing black masks. But, as they were crushed, new blockades appeared.

In 1992, Roraima's state electricity company obtained permission to study the Raposa/Serra do Sol region with a view to building a dam. This is in the traditional territory of the Makuxi Indians, of whom nearly fifteen thousand live in Brazil and some seven thousand over the border in Guyana. The proposed illegal dam threatens to flood around four thousand hectares of the indigenous Makuxi land. In January 1995, fifty military police and seven soldiers invaded a camp set up by the Makuxi to prevent the dam's construction. Over four hundred Makuxi have since been expelled from the site of the dam.

In January 1996, President Fernando Henrique Cardoso severely damaged Indian land rights by signing **Decree 1775**, a "modification" of decree 22/91, the law which sets out the process of demarcation of Indian land. This destructive measure introduces the right of *contraditorio* which will make it easier for miners, loggers and settlers already occupying Indian land to challenge existing demarcations of indigenous areas which have not been ratified. The ratification process can take some time, during which the invaders will be able to continue occupying, and in most cases polluting, Indian land. According to Survival International,

For **action on the side of the forest** contact:

WWF Rain Forest Appeal
Panda House
Weyside Park
Godalming
Surrey
GU7 1BP

The Rainforest Action Network
301 Broadway, Suite A
San Francisco CA 94133
☎415/398-4404

Rainforest Alliance
270 Lafayette St, Suite 512
New York, NY 10012

For **action to protect the basic rights of Brazil's indigenous people**, contact:

Survival International,
11-15 Emerald St,
London,
WC1N 3QL
☎0171/242 1441
Fax 0171/242 1771
Email: survival@gn.apc.org

Survival International (Italy)
Casella Postal 1194
20101 Milan
Italy
☎0289-00671

Survival International (France)
45 Rue du Faubourg du Temple
Paris 75016
France
☎01.42.41.47.62

Cultural Survival
11 Divinity Ave
Cambridge MA 03128

In Brazil, contacts are:

Fundação Nacional do Indio (FUNAI),
    Ministerio do Interior
SAS Quadra 1, Bloco 1,
70070 Brasília

NGO's Comisão pela Ciacão do Parque
    Yanomami
Rua Sao Carlos do Pinhal 345
01333 São Paulo

Comisão Pro-Indio SP (CPI)
Rue Caiubi 126
São Paulo

Conselho Indígenista Missionário
Edifício Venâncio III, Sala 310
Caixa Postal 11.1159
70084 Brasília DF

this will open up large tracts of Indian territory to logging and mining companies: an estimated 3.7 million hectares (about half the size of Scotland) of indigenous land is threatened. A spokesperson for the Brazilian NGO COIAB (Co-ordinating Body of Indigenous Peoples of the Brazilian Amazon) claimed that the new law "endangered the lives of indigenous peoples".

The suspicion, almost certainly justified, is that Decree 1775 is designed to reduce the size of many of Brazil's 554 indigenous territories. At least thirteen indigenous areas have been invaded since Decree 1775, many of these in Yanomami territory which has already undergone the whole process of legal demarcation. Indigenous organizations say this massive rein-vasion proves that Decree 1775 is being seen as a "green light" for the colonization and exploitation of Indian land. On the political level there are fears that the US$22 million pledged by the German government could be used to fund the reduction in size of indigenous territories. The present brief for the German monies appears to involve demarcating a number of Indian lands as part of the pilot plan for the Amazon funded by the G7 nations.

RACE IN BRAZILIAN SOCIETY

The significance of race in Brazilian society has long been a controversial topic in Brazil. Until recently, despite the country's ethnic and racial diversity, official thinking refused to acknowledge the existence of minority groups, promoting the concept of the Brazilian "racial democracy" and denying absolutely the existence of racism or racial discrimination. If, in a country where blacks and mulattos form 65 percent of the population, there are few dark-skinned people at the upper levels of society – so the theory runs – this simply reflects past disadvantages, in particular poverty and lack of education.

MYTH . . .

No one contributed more to the consolidation of this myth of racial brotherhood than the anthropologist **Gilberto Freyre**. In the early 1930s he advanced the view that somehow the Portuguese colonizers were immune to racial prejudice, that they intermingled freely with Indians and blacks. If **Brazilian slavery** was a not entirely benevolent patriarchy, as some people liked to believe, the mulatto offspring of the sexual contact between master and slave was the personification of this ideal. The **mulatto** was the archetypal social climber, transcending class boundaries, and was upheld as a symbol of Brazil and the integration of the nation's cultures and ethnic roots. "Every Brazilian, even the light-skinned and fair-haired one," wrote Freyre in his seminal work, *Casa Grande e Senzala*, "carries about him in his soul, when not in soul and body alike, the shadow or even birthmark, of the aborigine or negro. The influence of the African, either direct or remote, is everything that is a sincere reflection of our lives. We, almost all of us, bear the mark of that influence."

Accepted with, if anything, even less questioning outside Brazil than within, the concept of a racial paradise in South America was eagerly grasped. For those outside Brazil struggling against the Nazis or segregation and racial violence in the USA, it was a belief too good to pass up. Brazil was awarded an international stamp of approval – and its **international image** is still very much that of the happy, unprejudiced melting pot.

Anomalies were easily explained away. A romanticized image of the self-sufficient **Indian** could be incorporated into Brazilian nationalism as, deep in the forested interior and numbering only a quarter of a million, they posed no threat. Picturesque Indian names – Yara and Iraçema for girls, Tibiriça and Caramuru for boys – were given to children, their white parents seeing them as representing Brazil in its purest form. Afro-Brazilian religion, folklore and art became safe areas of interest. **Candomblé**, practised primarily in the northeastern state of Bahia and perhaps the purest of African rituals, could be seen as a quaint remnant from the past, while syncretist cults, most notably **umbanda**, combining elements of Indian, African and European religion and which have attracted mass followings in Rio, São Paulo and the South, have been taken to demonstrate the happy fusion of cultures.

. . . AND REALITY

Many visitors to Brazil still arrive believing in the melting pot, and for that matter many leave without questioning it. It *is* undeniable that Brazil has remarkably little in the way of obvious **racial tension**; that there are no institutional forms of racial discrimination; and that on the beach the races do seem to mix freely. But it is equally undeniable that race is a key factor in determining social position.

To say this in Brazil, even now, is to risk being attacked as "un-Brazilian". Nevertheless, the idea that race has had no significant effect on social mobility and that socio-economic differentials of a century ago explain current differences between races is increasingly discredited. It is true that Brazil is a rigidly stratified society within which upward mobility is difficult for anyone. But the lighter your skin, the easier it appears to be. Clear evidence has been produced that although in general blacks and mulattos (because of the continuing cycle of poverty) have lower education levels than whites, even when they do have equal levels of education and experience whites still enjoy substantial economic benefits. The **average income** for white Brazilians is twice that for black.

Perhaps the most surprising realization is that, except amongst politically developed intellectuals and progressive sectors of the Church, there seems little awareness or resentment of the link between colour and class. The black consciousness movement has made slow progress in Brazil, and most people continue to acquiesce before the national myth that this is the New World's fortunate land, where there's no need to organize for improved status.

MUSIC

Brazil's talent for music is so great it amounts to a national genius. Out of a rich stew of African, European and Indian influences it has produced one of the strongest and most diverse musical cultures in the world.

Most people have heard of samba and bossa nova, or of Heitor Vila Lobos, who introduced the rhythms of Brazilian popular music to a classical audience, but they are only the tip of a very large iceberg of genres, styles and individual talents. Music – heard in bars, on the streets, car radios, concert halls and clubs – is a constant backdrop to social life in Brazil, and Brazilians are a very musical people. Instruments help but they aren't essential: matchboxes shaken to a syncopated beat, forks tapped on glasses and hands slapped on tabletops are all that is required. And to go with the music is some of the most stunning dancing you are ever likely to see. In Brazil, no one looks twice at a couple who would clear any European and most American dance floors. You don't need to be an expert, or even understand the words, to enjoy Brazilian popular music, but you may appreciate it better – and find it easier to ask for the type of record you want – if you know a little about its history.

THE ROOTS: REGIONAL BRAZILIAN MUSIC

The bedrock of Brazilian music is the apparently inexhaustible fund of "traditional" **popular music**. There are dozens of genres, most of them associated with a specific region of the country, which you can find in raw uncut form played on local radio stations, at popular festivals – *Carnaval* is merely the best known – impromptu recitals in squares and on street corners, and in bars and *dancetarias*, the dance halls that Brazilians flock to at the weekend. The two main centres are Rio and Salvador. There's little argument that the best Brazilian music comes from Rio, the Northeast and parts of Amazonia, with São Paulo and southern Brazil lagging a little behind. Samba, and later bossa nova, became internationally famous, but only because they both happened to get off the ground in Rio, with its high international profile and exotic image. There are, though, less famous but equally vital musical styles elsewhere in Brazil, and it's difficult to see why they remain largely unknown to audiences outside the country – especially given Western music's current obsession with the Third World.

Each local musical genre is part of a **regional identity**, of which people are very proud, and there's a distinct link between geographical rivalry and the development of Brazilian music. *Nordestinos*, in particular, all seem to know their way around the scores of Northeastern musical genres and vigorously defend their musical integrity against the influences of Rio and São Paulo, which dominate TV and national radio. A lot of people regret *Carioca* and *Paulista* domination of the airwaves, fearing that it's making Brazilian music homogeneous, but if anything it has the opposite effect. People react against the southeast music by turning to their local brands – which often develop some new enriching influences, picked up along the way.

SAMBA

The best-known genre, samba, began in the early years of this century, in the poorer quarters of Rio, as *Carnaval* music, and over the decades it has developed several variations. The deafening **samba de enredo** is the set-piece of *Carnaval*, with one or two singers declaiming a verse joined by hundreds, even thousands of voices and drums for the chorus, as the *bloco*, the full samba school, backs up the lead singers. A *bloco* in action during *Carnaval* is the loudest music you're ever likely to come across, and it's all done without the aid of amplifiers: if you stand up close, the massed noise of the drums vibrates every part of your body. No recording technology yet devised comes close to conveying the sound, and on record the songs and music often seem repetitive. Still, every year the main Rio samba schools make a compilation record of the music selected for the parade, and any record with the words *Samba de Enredo* or *Escola de Samba* will contain this mass *Carnaval* music.

On a more intimate scale, and musically more inventive, is **samba-canção**, which is produced by one singer and a small back-up band, who play around with basic samba rhythms to produce anything from a (relatively) quiet love song to frenetic dance numbers. This makes the transition to record much more effectively than *samba de enredo*, and in Brazil it's especially popular with the middle-aged, who are not able to gyrate quite as energetically as they did in their youth. Reliable, high-quality records of *samba-canção* are anything by **Beth Carvalho**, acknowledged queen of the genre, **Alcione**, **Roberto Ribeiro** – with a strong African influence as well – **Agepê** and the great **Paulinho da Viola**, who always puts at least a couple of excellent sambas on every record he makes.

Since the early 1990s, a refreshing trend in samba has been the revival of **samba-pagode**, a back-to-the-roots reaction against the increasing commercialization of samba in the 1980s. *Pagode* means a simple dance hall, and *samba de pagode* is not a different style of samba so much as a good-time samba, played by a small group, for dancing and general enjoyment in a bar or *dancetaria*. This has always flourished year-round in Rio, but since the 1970s *Carnaval* and glitzy versions of *samba-canção* had increasingly become the public face of samba, dominating recording output and being heavily marketed to outsiders. Many of the musicians on whom samba depended for its continuing vitality were sidelined, reduced to making a precarious living doing live shows in the lower-income parts of Rio. Fortunately, people are now returning to *samba-pagode* in a big way, with established *sambistas* like Agepê and Martinho da Vila following their audience and switching to *pagode* on their records. A number of *pagode* groups have become major national stars, including **Raça Negra**, **Ginga Pura** and **Banda Brasil**.

CHORO

Much less known, **choro** (literally "crying") appeared in Rio around the time of World War I, and by the 1930s had evolved into one of the most intricate and enjoyable of all Brazilian forms of music. Unlike samba, which developed variations, *choro* has remained remarkably constant over the decades. It's one of the few Brazilian genres which owes anything to Spanish-speaking America, as it is clearly related to the Argentinian tango (the real River Plate versions, that is, rather than the sequined ballroom distortions that get passed off as tango outside South America). *Choro* is mainly instrumental, played by a small group: the backbone of the combo is a guitar, picked quickly and jazzily, with notes sliding all over the place, which is played off against a flute, or occasionally a clarinet or recorder, with drums and/or maracas as an optional extra. It is as quiet and intimate as samba is loud and public, and of all Brazilian popular music is probably the most delicate. You often find it being played as background music in bars and cafés; local papers advertise such places. The loveliest *choros* on record are by **Paulinho da Viola**, especially a self-explanatory record called *Chorando*. After years of neglect during the postwar decades *choro* is now undergoing something of a revival, and it shouldn't be too difficult to catch a *choro conjunto* in Rio or São Paulo.

LAMBADA

In recent years a dance craze based on **lambada** has swept nightclubs in Europe and North America. *Lambada* is in fact a dance rather than a type of music, and the term as now used is simply a new name for quite long-established musical styles in Brazil. There's some argument over who originated *lambada* and where: the first big international *lambada* hit was actually Bolivian, and *lambada*-like rhythms are also a feature of music from lowland Bolivia. Nonetheless, most *lambada* that you hear on international dance floors is Brazilian.

What often happens, and has happened in this case, is that regional styles like *carimbó* and *forró* (see below) are souped up and re-issued under a new name. This means it's impossible to determine exactly what *lambada* is, as it encompasses a number of different styles. The one thing you can say is that most – and the best – *lambada* comes from northern

Brazil and is a close relative of *carimbó*. You will actually find *lambada* records far easier to get hold of outside Brazil.

OTHER GENRES

A full list of other "traditional" musical genres would have hundreds of entries and could be elaborated on indefinitely. Some of the best known are **forró**, **maracatu**, **repentismo** and **frevo**, described at greater length in the Northeast chapter: you'll find them all over the Northeast but especially around Recife. **Baião** is a Bahian style that bears a striking resemblance to the hard acoustic blues of the American Deep South, with hoarse vocals over a guitar singing of things like drought and migration; **carimbó** is an enjoyable, lilting rhythm and dance found all over northern Brazil but especially around Belém; and **bumba-meu-boi** is one of the strangest and most powerful of all styles, the music of Maranhão state.

A good start, if you're interested, is one of the dozens of records by the late **Luiz Gonzaga**, also known as **Gonzagão**, which have extremely tacky covers but are musically very good. They have authentic renderings of at least two or three Northeastern genres per record. His version of a beautiful song called *Asa Branca* is one of the best-loved of all Brazilian tunes, a national standard, and was played at his funeral in 1989.

THE GOLDEN AGE: 1930–1960 AND THE RADIO STARS

It was the growth of radio during the 1930s that created the popular music industry in Brazil, with home-grown stars idolized by millions. The best known was **Carmen Miranda**, spotted by a Hollywood producer singing in the famous Urca casino in Rio and whisked off to film stardom in the 1940s. Although her hats made her immortal, she deserves to be remembered more as the fine singer she was. She was one of a number of singers and groups loved by older Brazilians, like **Francisco Alves**, **Ismael Silva**, **Mário Reis**, **Ataulfo Alves**, **Trio de Ouro** and **Joel e Gaúcho**. Two great songwriters, **Ary Barroso** and **Pixinguinha**, provided the raw material.

Brazilians call these early decades *a época de ouro*, and that it really was a golden age is proved by the surviving music on record. It is

slower and jazzier than modern Brazilian music, but with the same rhythms and beautiful, crooning vocals. Even in Brazil it used to be difficult to get hold of **records** of this era but after years of neglect there is now a widely available series of reissues called *Revivendo*. They send catalogues abroad, if you can't make it to Brazil to buy the records: write to *Revivendo Músicas Comércio de Discos Ltda*, Rua Barão do Rio Branco 28/36 – 1. andar, Caixa Postal 122, Curitiba, Paraná, Brazil.

INTERNATIONAL SUCCESS – THE BOSSA NOVA

With this wealth of music to work with, it was only a matter of time before Brazilian music burst its national boundaries, something that duly happened in the late 1950s with the phenomenon of **bossa nova**. Several factors led to its development. The classically trained **Tom Jobim**, equally in love with Brazilian popular music and American jazz, met up with fine Bahian guitarist **João Gilberto** and his wife **Astrud Gilberto**. The growth in the Brazilian record and communications industries allowed bossa nova to sweep Brazil and come to the attention of people like Stan Getz in the United States; and, above all, there developed a massive market for a sophisticated urban sound among the newly burgeoning middle class in Rio, who found Jobim and Gilberto's slowing down and breaking up of what was still basically a samba rhythm an exciting departure. It rapidly became an international craze, and Astrud Gilberto's quavering version of one of the earliest Jobim numbers, *A Garota de Ipanema*, became the most famous of all Brazilian songs, *The Girl from Ipanema* – although the English lyric is considerably less suggestive than the Brazilian original.

Over the next few years the craze eventually peaked and fell away, though not before leaving most people with the entirely wrong impression that bossa nova is a mediocre brand of muzak well suited to lifts and airports. In North America it eventually sank under the massed strings of studio producers, but in Brazil it never lost its much more delicate touch, usually with a single guitar and a crooner holding sway. Early bossa nova still stands as one of the crowning glories of Brazilian music, and all the classics – you may not know the names of tunes like *Corcovado*, *Isaura*, *Chega de Saudade* and

Desafinado but you'll recognize the melodies – are on the easily available double album compilations called *A Arte de Tom Jobim* and *A Arte de João Gilberto*; Jobim's is the better of the two.

MORE BOSSA NOVA ARTISTS

The great Brazilian guitarist **Luiz Bonfá** also made some fine bossa nova records: the ones where he accompanies Stan Getz are superb. The bossa nova records of **Stan Getz and Charlie Byrd** are one of the happiest examples of inter-American co-operation, and as they're easy to find in European and American shops they make a fine introduction to Brazilian music. They had the sense to surround themselves with Brazilian musicians, notably Jobim, the Gilbertos and Bonfá, and the interplay between their jazz and the equally skilful Brazilian response is often brilliant. **Live bossa nova** is rare these days, restricted to the odd bar or hotel lobby, unless you're lucky enough to catch one of the great names in concert – Tom Jobim is still a superlative musician. But then bossa nova always lent itself more to records than live performance.

TROPICALISMO

The military coup in 1964 was a crucial event in Brazil. Just as the shock-waves of the cultural upheavals of the 1960s were reaching Brazilian youth, the lid went on in a big way: censorship was introduced for all song lyrics; radio and television were put under military control; and some songwriters and musicians were tortured and imprisoned for speaking and singing out – although fame was at least some insurance against being killed. The result was the opposite of what the generals had intended. A movement known as **tropicalismo** developed, calling itself cultural but in fact almost exclusively a musical movement, led by a young and extravagantly talented group of musicians. Prominent amongst them were **Caetano Veloso** and **Gilberto Gil** from Bahia and **Chico Buarque** from Rio. They used traditional popular music as a base, picking and mixing genres in a way no one had thought of doing before – stirring in a few outside influences like the Beatles and occasional electric instruments, and topping it all off with lyrics that often stood alone as poetry – and delighted in teasing the censors. Oblique images and comments were ostensibly

about one thing, but everyone knew what they really meant. Chico Buarque's great song, *Tanto Mar*, for example, is apparently about the end of a party, but everyone except the censor recognized it was a salute to the Portuguese revolution, the "Revolution of the Carnations", as it's known.

> It was a fine party
> I had a great time
> I've kept an old carnation as a memento
> And even though the party's been shut down
> They're bound to have forgotten a few seeds in some corner of the garden

Caetano, Gil and Chico – all of Brazil is on first-name terms with them – spent a few years in exile in the late 1960s and early 1970s, Caetano and Gil in London (both still speak fluent English with immaculate BBC accents) and Chico in Rome, before returning in triumph as the military regime wound down. They have made dozens of records between them: the best way to get to grips with their work quickly is through the compilation albums, *A Arte de. . . , O Talento de. . . ,* or *A Personalidade de. . .* , collections of their back catalogues with all their most famous songs up to the mid-1970s. They are still the leading figures of Brazilian music, despite being in their early fifties. Gilberto Gil, after a long period in the doldrums where he experimented unsuccessfully with rock-based formats, has recently returned to form, apparently inspired by a new wave of Bahian musicians (see opposite), to whom he is a father figure. Chico Buarque's dense lyrics and hauntingly beautiful melodies are still flowing, although he produces recordings more rarely now, devoting more of his time to novel-writing and theatre. Pride of place, however, has to go to Caetano Veloso. Good though he was in the 1960s and 1970s, he is improving with age, and his records in the late 1980s and 1990s have been his best: mature, innovative, lyrical and original as ever. His triumphal tour of New York, London and Paris in 1993, recorded as *Circulado Vivo*, proved beyond doubt that he is the leading Brazilian musician of his time, and one of the greatest figures of world music.

WOMEN SINGERS

Brazilian music has a strong tradition of producing excellent women singers. The best of all time was undoubtedly the great **Elis Regina**, from Rio Grande do Sul, whose magnificent voice was tragically stilled in 1984, when she was at the peak of her career, by a drugs overdose. She interpreted everything, and whatever Brazilian genre she touched she invariably cut the definitive version. Two of her songs in particular became classics, *Aguas de Março* and *Carinhoso*, the latter being arguably the most beautiful Brazilian song of all. Again, the *A Arte de Elis Regina* double album is the best bet, although there is also a superb record of Elis with Tom Jobim, called *Elis e Tom*. After her death the mantle fell on **Gal Costa**, a very fine singer although without the extraordinary depth of emotion Elis could project, whose version of *Aquarela do Brasil* inspired Terry Gilliam to the idea for the film "Brazil", and whose LP, named after the song, is highly recommended, along with the *A Arte de Gal Costa* compilation.

THE BAHIAN SOUND

Although Rio is the traditional capital of Brazilian music, for some years now it has been overtaken, in vitality and originality, by **Salvador**, the capital of Bahia. Bahia in general, and Salvador in particular, have always produced a disproportionate number of Brazil's leading musicians including Caetano Veloso, Gilberto Gil, Gal Costa, the Caymmi family and João Gilberto, but in recent years their status has progressed from important to dominant. The main reason is the extraordinary musical stew provided by deep African roots, Caribbean and Hispanic influences coming in through the city's port, and a local record industry that quickly realized the money-making potential of Bahian music. They didn't invent *lambada*, for example, but it was Salvador record producers who transformed it into a global hit. Tellingly, all over Brazil (except in Rio, naturally), it is now more common to hear the Salvador *Carnaval* hits than samba during *Carnaval*.

The new Bahian sound, an exhilarating blend of Brazilian and Caribbean rhythms, is exemplified by groups like **Reflexus**, and singers like **Luis Caldas** and **Margareth Menezes**. By some way the best, though, is the brightest star to have emerged in Brazil over the last few years, **Daniela Mercury**. She has it all: a fabulous voice, she writes her own music, is stunningly beautiful and is an extraordinary dancer. Her first album, just called *Daniela*, is one of the best recent Brazilian records. If she ever learns English and heads for the American market she will blow Gloria Estefan out of the water. You should catch her while she's still singing in Portuguese.

CONTEMPORARY SINGERS AND MUSICIANS

The number of high-quality singers and musicians in Brazilian music besides these leading figures is enormous. **Milton Nascimento** has a talent that can only be compared with the founders of *tropicalismo*, a remarkable soaring voice, a genius for composing stirring anthems and a passion for charting and celebrating the experience of blacks in Brazil. He has become the most prominent spokesperson of black Brazilians. **Fagner** and **Alceu Valença** are modern interpreters of Northeastern music, and strikingly original singers. The latter is the creator of what has been termed "*forró rock*". **Elba Ramalho** is a Northeastern woman with an excellent voice, which she too often wastes on banal rock rather than the more traditional material she excels at. **Renato Borghetti**, from Rio Grande do Sul, has done much to popularize *gaúcho*-influenced music through his skill on the accordion and his adaptations of traditional tunes. **Ney Matogrosso** has a striking falsetto voice which sounds female, but he is a man — although sometimes self-indulgent, he can be very good. **Jorge Ben** is a fine Rio singer who wrote the definitive Rio verse in his classic *País Tropical*:

> I live in tropical country
> Blessed by God with natural beauty
> In February there's Carnaval
> I own a guitar and drive a Beetle
> I support Flamengo and have a black girlfriend
>   called Tereza.

Vinícius de Morães and Toquinho are (or were in the case of Vinícius) a good singer and guitarist team, and **Dorival Caymmi** at over seventy is the doyen of Bahian musicians.

Too many musicians these days, though, waste their time attempting to fuse Brazilian genres with rock-based formats. It's not that it can't be done — *tropicalismo* pulled it off several times in the 1960s — but the type of rock music currently most popular in Brazil, appalling heavy metal and stadium rock, is completely

A SELECTED DISCOGRAPHY

Apart from the *A Arte de. . .*, *O Talento de. . .*, *A Personalidade de. . .* and *Revivendo* series mentioned on the previous page, recommended recordings easily **available in Brazil** include the following (**artists** in bold):

Agepê
Mistura Brasileira (Sigia 1984)

Araketu
Ara Ketu (Continental 1987)

Jorge Ben
Ao Vivo (WEA 1993)

Maria Bethania
Ambar (EMI 1996)

Bezerra da Silva
Se não fosse o samba (RCA Victor 1989)

Renato Borghetti
Renato Borghetti (RCA Victor 1987)

Chico Buarque
Ópera do Malandro (Philips 1979)
Vida (Philips 1980)
Para Todos (Philips 1994)
Uma Palavra (Ariola 1995)

Dorival Caymmi
A música de Caymmi (Continental 1981)

Gal Costa
Aquarela do Brasil (Philips 1980)

Gilberto Gil
Parabolicamera (Philips 1991)

Daniela Mercury
Daniela (Polygram do Brasil 1992)
Canto da Cidade (Polygram do Brasil 1993)

Milton Nascimento
Ao vivo (Polygram do Brasil 1983)
Clube da esquina (Polygram do Brasil 1981)

Olodum
Egito-Madagáscar (Continental 1987)

Paulinho da Viola
Eu canto samba (RCA Victor 1989)
Cantando (RCA Victor 1982)
Chorando (RCA Victor 1982)

Reflexús
Reflexús da mãe Africa (EMI 1987)

Elis Regina and Tom Jobim
Elis e Tom (Philips 1974)

Roberto Ribeiro
De Palmares ao tamborim (EMI 1984)

Alceu Valença
Mágica (Barclay 1984)

Caetano Veloso
Velo (Philips 1984)
Estrangeiro (Philips 1991)
Circulado Vivo (Philips 1993)
Fina Estampa (Polygram do Brasil 1994)

Caetano Veloso and Gilberto Gil
Tropicalismo 2 (Philips 1994)

Vinícius de Moraes
with Marilia Medalha and Toquinho
Como dizia o poeta. . . – música nova (RGE 1971)

As for Brazilian records **available abroad**, only the jazz/bossa nova records of Getz and his Brazilian collaborators are easily available. However, recent interest in Brazilian music has spawned a few new compilation albums: notably *Brazil Classics: Volume 1* (a sort of Brazilian greatest hits) and *Volume 2* (a samba collection), both on EMI and collected and presented by David Byrne; and *Forró: Music for Maids and Taxi Drivers* (Globestyle Records), a self-explanatory and excellent introduction to the effervescent Northeastern music. There are also a number of *lambada* compilations jumping on the bandwagon. One of the best international mail order suppliers is Globestyle Records (48–50 Steele Road, London NW10 7AS) – send an SAE for their catalogue.

incompatible with the subtle, versatile musical imagination of Brazilians. National radio and the dominant São Paulo radio stations pump out the worst kind of British and US FM blandness, and this has spawned a host of Brazilian imitations, almost all of them embarrassingly bad. A few worth mentioning are **Titãs**, a São Paulo punk band with a genuinely magnetic lead singer in the Johnny Rotten mould; **Os Raimundos**, a Brasília-based band who started out by doing covers of the punk band, the Ramones, but have since developed their own style and a distinctive *forró* accent; and **Premeditando o Breque**, also shortened to **PMB**, whose originality defies categorization. Their first record was called *Tubarões Voadores* – "Flying Sharks" – and was very good indeed, managing to be ominous and very funny at the same time. **Chico Science** and his band, **Nação Zumbi**, from Pernambuco produced a promising first record in 1994, *Da Lama ao Caos*, an exciting blend of rock and Northeastern rhythms.

Another, quite unexpected attempt at fusion achieved global success in 1997. Conveyor-belt Euro-pop is not where you would normally find Amazonian musical influences, but behind the infuriatingly catchy disco hit "Tic, Tic Tac" of the German–US manufactured trio **Chilli** lie impeccable folk roots. On a visit to a *bumba-meu-boi* festival, a French record producer "discovered" – and signed – **O Carrapicho**, took the eleven-piece band to Paris and released the original "Tic, Tic Tac" single and an album, selling well over a million copies. Success in Brazil and the rest of Latin America soon followed and the Anglo-techno version was created for the rest of the unsuspecting world. In all likelihood, Chilli are a one-hit wonder, but O Carrapicho's place in contemporary Brazilian music is certain to endure.

The other possible criticism of Brazilian music is that while its popular roots are healthier than ever, nobody of similar stature has come up to succeed the towering figures of the 1960s and 1970s. Elis is dead, Gil is in decline (although he may yet reverse it), Caetano, Chico and Milton are still producing but are no longer young, and, while younger talent abounds, there's nothing at the moment which could be called genius – a lot to demand of anyone, but it's a tribute to Brazilian music that its pedigree allows us to judge it by the highest standards.

LIVE MUSIC AND RECORDINGS

If you want to see or hear **live music**, look for suggestions in this book, buy local papers with weekend listings headed *Lazer*, which should have a list of bars with music, concerts and *dancetarias*, or ask a tourist office for advice.

Local radio is often worth listening to – you won't regret taking a transistor along and whirling the dial – and there are also local TV stations that often have **MPB** (*Música Popular Brasileira*) programmes; the *TVE*, *Televisão Educativa* network, funded by the Catholic Church and the Ministry of Culture, is worth checking – if you see the initials *FUNARTE*, it might well be a music programme.

Finally, a word about **buying recordings**. The price varies according to how well known the recording artist is. Recordings by leading artists are the same price as in the USA, but records by more obscure artists and regional music are much cheaper, so there are still bargains to be had. CDs are widely available in the big cities, but much of the regional music, and that aimed at more popular audiences, is still only released on record and cassette. At the upper end of the scale, but dependably high quality, are the *A Arte de. . .* , *O Talento de. . .* or *A Personalidade de. . .* series, often double albums, which are basically "Greatest Hits" compilations of the best-known singers and musicians. The best place to buy any music, no matter how regional, is São Paulo, then Rio, with cities like Recife, Salvador, Belo Horizonte and Porto Alegre a long way behind. Outside Rio and São Paulo there are good music shops, but they're few and far between: look in local papers to see if there are adverts for *Loja de Disco* (record shop), with *MPB* or *discos nacionais* mentioned in the advert.

BOOKS

The recent flood of books on the Amazon masks the fact that Brazil is not well covered by books in English. With some exceptions, good books on Brazil tend to be either fairly expensive or are out of print. Easily available paperbacks are given here, together with a selection of others that a good bookshop or library will have in stock or will be able to order. Even so, important areas are sparsely covered. Apart from the novels of Jorge Amado, for example, the riches of Brazilian literature lie largely untranslated. There is still no widely available translation of Machado's *Posthumous Memoirs of Brás Cubas*, the finest classic Brazilian novel, or of Graciliano's *Barren Lives*, the best modern Brazilian novel. Where separate editions exist in the UK and US, publishers are separated by a semicolon in the listings below, with the UK company given first. University Press is abbreviated to UP, out-of-print to o/p.

THE BEST INTRODUCTIONS

Annette Haddad & Scott Doggett (eds), *Travelers' Tales: Brazil* (Travelers' Tales). A superb anthology of extracts from books and magazine articles by journalists, anthropologists, historians and other travellers to Brazil, which will make you want to search out the publications they're drawn from. Although a great read, it's a pity that more wasn't done to include the work of Brazilian authors.

Claude Lévi-Strauss, *Tristes Tropiques* (Picador o/p; Random House). The great French anthropologist describes his four years spent in 1930s Brazil – the best book ever written about the country by a foreigner. There are famous descriptions of sojourns with Nambikwara and Tupi-Kawahib Indians, epic journeys and a remarkable eyewitness account of São Paulo exploding into a metropolis. Essential reading. *Saudades do Brasil: A Photographic Memoir* (Univ. of Washington Press) is a new and beautifully produced collection that makes a wonderful companion to *Tristes Tropiques*, featuring some of the thousands of photographs Lévi-Strauss took, few of which were ever published.

Jan Rocha, *Brazil in Focus* (Latin America Bureau). A brief guide to Brazil's history, society and arts. Written by a journalist long resident in the country, the book is especially strong on the politics and social movements of the post-military era.

Charles Wagley, *An Introduction to Brazil* (Columbia UP). Three decades old but still the best introduction to Brazil and the Brazilians. Lucidly written, with the authority of a lifetime involved with the country behind it. Available in many public libraries.

THE AMAZON

Catherine Caulfield, *In the Rainforest* (Pan o/p). Sharp-eyed journalist travels around the Brazilian Amazon, amongst other rainforests. Low on context but good on atmosphere: one of the best of the recent Amazon books.

J.M. Cohen, *Journeys Down the Amazon* (o/p). Published in 1975, but easy to find in libraries or second hand, this is a fascinating account of the first European journeys along the Amazon by religious fanatics and psychos known to history as the *conquistadores*. If you think that's putting it a bit strongly, read the chapter on Aguirre – Klaus Kinske's portrayal of him in the film *Aguirre, Wrath of God*, was nothing compared to the real thing.

Colonel P.H. Fawcett, *Exploration Fawcett* (o/p). Fawcett carries his stiff upper lip in and out of some of the most disease-infested, dangerous and downright frightening parts of interior Brazil. It's a rattling good read, compiled by his son from Fawcett's diaries and letters after his disappearance. Readily available in secondhand bookshops. For more on Fawcett, see p.433.

Peter Fleming, *Brazilian Adventure* (Penguin o/p; JP Tarcher o/p). Relentlessly cheery explorer makes light of appalling dangers in his travels in search of Colonel Fawcett. Funny despite – or perhaps because of – the *Ripping Yarns* feel to the book.

Stephen Nugent, *Big Mouth: The Amazon Speaks* (Fourth Estate o/p; Brown Trout Publications). Essential and hilarious reading, not least as an antidote to the gooey rainforest literature. Jaundiced anthropologist returns to old haunts in Belém and Santarém, debunking as he goes. There is no better guide to the complexities of modern Amazonia; convincing and depressing at the same time.

MATO GROSSO AND BRASÍLIA

Richard Gott, *Land Without Evil: Utopian Journeys Across the South American Watershed* (Verso). Although the subject matter is centred on eastern Bolivia, this is an important look at the swampland between the River Plate and the River Amazon, exploring the

region through the adventures of missionaries and explorers and through the travels of the author himself.

Alex Shoumatoff, *The Capital of Hope: Brasília and its People* (New Mexico UP, US, o/p). The author talked with government officials and settlers – rich and poor – to weave a very readable account of the first 25 years of the Brazilian capital.

THE SOUTH

Alexander Leonard, *The Valley of the Latin Bear* (o/p). A delightful account of everyday life in an isolated German village in Santa Catarina. Although written thirty years ago, the account remains very recognizable and it's still well worth seeking out.

Guy Walmisley-Dresser, *Brazilian Paradise* (o/p). Romantic reminiscences of growing up on a cattle ranch in Rio Grande do Sul in the late nineteenth century. The anecdotes are both amusing and full of insight and tell of a part of Brazil which, although distinctive in character, is all but ignored by travel writers.

HISTORY

Leslie Bethell (ed), *Colonial Brazil* (Cambridge UP); *Brazilian Empire and Republic 1818–1930* (Cambridge UP). The former is the best available introduction to Brazil's colonial period, scholarly but also easily accessible to the general reader. The latter, a collection of essays by leading historians, is essential reading for anyone interested in Brazilian history since independence.

Euclides da Cunha, *Rebellion in the Backlands* (Picador; Chicago UP). Also known by its Portuguese title *Os Seroes*, this remains perhaps Brazil's greatest historical documentary. An epic tale of Antônio Conselheiro's short-lived holy city, the Canudos Rebellion and its brutal suppression which left some 15,000 dead (see p.263), the book is also a powerful meditation on Brazilian civilization.

R. B. Cunningham Graham, *A Vanished Arcadia* (Century o/p). Cunningham Graham's passionate and rather romanticized account of the rise and fall of the Jesuit missions in South America was first published in 1901 and has become a classic on the subject.

Cyrus and James Dawsey (eds), *The Confederados: Old South Immigrants in Brazil* (Alabama UP). An extremely readable collection of essays by US and Brazilian scholars looking at different aspects of the experience of immigrants from the former Confederacy and their descendants. Contributions discuss the history of the agricultural settlements as well as the cultural (in particular religious) influence of the immigrants on the wider society and linguistic change.

Warren Dean, *With Brandaxe and Firestorm* (Columbia UP). Brilliant and very readable environmental history which tells the story of the almost complete destruction of the Mata Atlântica, the coastal rainforest of southern Brazil, from colonial times to the twentieth century.

Todd Diacon, *Millennarian Vision, Capitalist Reality: Brazil's Contestado Rebellion 1912–1916* (Duke UP). An analysis of the motivation behind the men and women caught up in the Contestado Rebellion, exploring both the millennarian aspects and the response to the seizure of territory by European immigrants. The rebels attacked train stations, sawmills and immigrant colonies in Santa Catarina and Paraná but were ultimately outnumbered and outgunned. An important ground-up look at the last dramatic attempts at survival on the part of a subsistence-based economy.

John Hemming, *Red Gold: The Conquest of the Brazilian Indians* (Papermac; Harvard UP). The definitive history of the topic, well-written and thoroughly researched. Both passionate and scholarly, it's a basic book for anyone interested in the Indian question in Brazil. A companion volume, *Amazon Frontier* (Harvard UP, US), brings the depressing story up to date.

Thomas H. Holloway, *Coffee and Society in São Paulo, 1886–1934* (North Carolina UP, US, o/p). A detailed look at the labour system that evolved on the coffee plantations of São Paulo, and the experiences of two million immigrants who worked them.

Billy Jaynes Chandler, *The Bandit King: Lampião of Brazil* (Texas UP, US). Compulsive reading that seems like fiction but is well-documented fact. Based on original sources and interviews with participants and witnesses, an American historian with a talent for snappy writing reconstructs the action-packed (and myth-encrusted) life of the famous social bandit, complete with fascinating photographs.

Robert M. Levine, *Vale of Tears: Revisiting the Canudos Massacre in Northeastern Brazil 1893–1897* (California UP). A vivid portrait of backland life and a detailed examination of the myths behind the community, arguing that the Canudos threatened the labour supply of local landowners, causing the state government to begin its campaign against the settlement by portraying the inhabitants as degenerate fanatics. Shocking but utterly compelling reading.

Frederick C. Luebke, *Germans in Brazil: A Comparative History of Cultural Conflict During World War I* (Louisiana State UP). One of the very few studies in English on Germans in Brazil. Despite the title, this social history covers the period 1818–1918, though the focus is World War I, when Brazilians of German origin began to accept that they could not remain foreigners in their own country.

Katia M. de Queiros Mattoso, *To be a Slave in Brazil, 1550–1888* (Rutgers UP, US). A history of slavery in Brazil, unusually written from the perspective of the slave. Intended for the general reader, the author divides her excellent study into three themes: the process of enslavement, life in slavery and the escape from slavery.

João José Reis, *Slave Rebellion in Brazil: The Muslim Uprising of 1835 in Bahia* (Johns Hopkins UP). The last major slave rebellion in Brazil began on January 24, 1835, confronting soldiers and civilians. This is a unique portrait of urban slavery and an absorbing account of the most important urban slave rebellion in the Americas and the only one where Islam played a major role, detailing the background of the conspiracy and the brutal repression and punishment of Africans that followed.

Eduardo Silva, *Prince of the People: The Life and Times of a Brazilian Free Man of Colour* (Verso; Norton). Was Dom Obá II d'Africa a genuine prince, or was he merely an unbalanced son of slaves with delusions? Whatever the truth, Dom Obá was revered by the poor around him, and his story also sheds light on the life of slaves and people of colour in Rio, and on popular thought during the final decades of slavery.

POLITICS AND SOCIETY

Gilberto Dimenstein, *Brazil: War on Children* (Latin American Bureau; Monthly Review). A grim but compelling picture of life for the street children of São Paulo, but true also for most Brazilian cities. The children, living in constant fear of death squads made up of off-duty police and other vigilantes, survive as best they can as petty criminals, beggars and prostitutes, supporting one another in small gangs.

Peter Flynn, *Brazil: A Political Analysis* (Westview Press, US, o/p). Massively detailed and authoritative political history of Brazil from the birth of the Republic to the beginning of the *abertura*. Best bet if you really want to get to grips with Brazilian politics; you should find it in public libraries.

Maxine L. Margolis, *Little Brazil: An Ethnography of Brazilian Immigrants in New York City* (Princeton UP). Since the early 1980s, there's been considerable migration from Brazil, especially to Europe and the US. The greatest concentration of expatriate Brazilians – especially educated middle classes from Minas Gerais – is in the New York City area, with most living in Long Island City and Astoria. The community's heart is Little Brazil, a one-block stretch of Manhattan's West 46th Street, and this is a thoroughly readable exploration into community life.

Roberto da Matta, *Carnival, Rogues and Heroes* (Notre Dame UP) A collection of essays by one of Brazil's leading anthropologists, who also teaches in the US. They include some very stimulating – and entertaining – dissections of *Carnaval*.

Ruben Oliven, *Tradition Matters: Modern Gaúcho Identity* (Columbia UP). This is not about the life of "cowboys" in southern Brazil, but rather an examination of the predominantly urban, middle-class social movement and their attachment to an idealized rural lifestyle of which they have no real experience. Oliven points up the apparent paradox in Brazil (as elsewhere) of ever-increasing cultural globalization and the strengthening of regional identity. An important study set against a background of a part of Brazil largely ignored by outsiders – Brazilian as well as foreign.

Emir Sader and Ken Silverstein, *Without Fear of Being Happy: Lula, the Workers Party and Brazil* (Verso; Norton). Focusing on the life of Lulu, this is the story of the rise of the PT, the most powerful and most representative socialist party in the Americas, charting its development out of trade union resistance to the military regime in São Paulo.

Thomas Skidmore, *Politics in Brazil 1930–1964*; *The Politics of Military Rule in Brazil 1964–85* (Oxford UP). The former is the standard work on Brazilian politics from the rise of Vargas until the 1964 military takeover. The latter continues the story to the resumption of Brazil's shaky democracy.

GENDER ISSUES

Caipora Women's Group, *Women in Brazil* (Latin America Bureau). Articles, poems and interviews explaining life for women on farms, in fishing communities and in *favelas*. The issues repeat themselves: racism, machismo, legal rights, religious and feminist beliefs. A welcome relief from published doctoral dissertations, this is both important and highly readable, both depressing and uplifting.

Herbert Daniel and Richard Parker, *Sexuality, Politics and AIDS in Brazil* (Falmer Press). Excellent, clearly written history of AIDS in Brazil, covering the way the epidemic has developed in relation to popular culture at one end, and government policy at the other. There are bright spots – Brazilian TV health education slots on AIDS may be the best in the world, completely frank, and often screamingly funny, but this book will help you understand how this can coexist with a scandalous lack of supervision of bloodbanks.

Richard Parker, *Bodies, Pleasures and Passions* (Beacon Press). A provocative analysis of the erotic in Brazilian history and popular culture, written by an American anthropologist resident in Brazil. Tremendous subject matter and some fascinating insights into sexual behaviour, combining insider and outsider perspectives.

Daphne Patai, *Brazilian Women Speak: Contemporary Life Stories* (Rutgers UP, US). Oral testimony forms the core of this very readable work that lets ordinary women from the Northeast and Rio speak for themselves to describe the struggles, constraints and hopes of their lives.

Nancy Scheper Hughes, *Death Without Weeping: The Violence of Everyday Life in Brazil* (California UP). An often shocking, ultimately depressing anthropological study of *favela* women, and in particular of childbirth, motherhood and infant death. Although over-long – judicious skipping in order – it is very accessible to the general reader, interesting, and often moving.

João Trevisan, *Perverts in Paradise* (GMP). This is a fascinating survey of Brazilian gay life ranging from the papal inquisition to pop idols, transvestite *macumba* priests and guerrilla idols.

RACE

Gilberto Freyre, *The Masters and the Slaves* (California UP). Classic history of plantation life in the Northeast, with a wealth of detail (includes index headings like "Smutty Stories and Expressions" and "Priests, Bastards of"). Very readable, even if Freyre's somewhat simplistic theories are now out of fashion or discredited (see p.623). His *The Mansion and the Shanties* deals with the early growth of urban Brazil.

Michael G. Hanchard, *Orpheus and Power: The Movimento Negro of Rio de Janeiro and São Paulo, Brazil 1945–1988* (Princeton UP). A look at the patterns of racial inequality in Brazil's two largest cities and the efforts of white elites to neutralize struggles for civil rights by promoting racial discrimination and the false premise of racial democracy.

George Reid Andrews, *Blacks and Whites in São Paulo 1888–1988* (Wisconsin UP). Why is the notion of a racial democracy still so widely accepted while at the same time people are fully aware that for all practical purposes it's a complete myth? For large proportions of Brazilians, racism is a fact of life and this is an interesting examination of how the state has long encouraged myths of black inferiority and perpetuates racial stereotypes.

Thomas E. Skidmore, *Black into White: Race and Nationality in Brazilian Thought* (Duke UP). First published in 1974, this 1993 edition has a new preface to bring the book up to date. A landmark in the intellectual history of Brazilian racial ideology examining scientific racism and the Brazilian intellectual elite's supposed belief in assimilation and the ideal of whitening.

THE AMAZON

David Cleary, *Anatomy of the Amazon Gold Rush* (Macmillan o/p; Iowa UP). Clearly written introduction to an important topic, with some spectacular photographs.

Shelton Davis, *Victims of the Miracle* (Cambridge UP). Important book looking at the implications of the construction of the Amazon highways for the Indians who were in its way. Good maps.

Warren Dean, *Brazil and the Struggle for Rubber* (Cambridge UP). Decent environmental history of the Amazon.

Peter A. Furley (ed), *The Forest Frontier: Settlement and Change in Brazilian Roraima* (Routledge, UK). An interesting and rare look at the state of Roraima, one of Brazil's last regions to be settled by outsiders. Dry academic geography in style but a wealth of up-to-date detail on Indian life and the history of colonization, land use, environmental change and the effects of deforestation.

Susanna Hecht and Alexander Cockburn, *The Fate of the Forest* (Penguin; HarperCollins). Head and shoulders above other studies of the crisis in the Amazon. Excellently written and researched – check out the footnotes – this is as good an introduction to the problem as you will find. Very strong on Amazonian history, too – essential to understanding what's going on, but often ignored by Amazon commentators.

Gordon Macmillan, *At the End of the Rainbow* (Earthscan; Columbia UP). Very interesting dissection of the issues behind the headlines about the Yanomami Indians and the invasion of their reserves by gold-miners.

Chico Mendes and Tony Gross, *Fight for the Forest: Chico Mendes in His Own Words* (Latin American Bureau; Monthly Review). Long, moving passages from a series of interviews the rubber tappers' union leader gave shortly before his assassination in 1988. Well translated and with useful notes giving background to the issues raised. Direct from the sharp end of the Amazon land crisis.

Marianne Schmink and Charles Wood, *Contested Frontiers in Amazonia* (Columbia UP). The best of the more recent academic books on modern Amazonia. This examines a town and region in southern Pará before, during and after the construction of the highway network. Clearly written and very interesting, especially in its description of how the Kayapo Indians adapted to a gold rush.

Candace Slater, *Dance of the Dolphins* (Chicago UP). Interesting compendium of the many legends and folktales centring around river dolphins, beautifully translated. There is a clumsy academic subtext linking the stories with environmental destruction in the Amazon, but you can skip those bits. There is no better book for giving you a feel for the popular imagination in the small towns you pass through on a river trip.

Charles Wagley, *Amazon Town* (o/p). Classic anthropological study of an interior Amazon town during the 1940s which inspired generations of students. Written with incisive style and complete command of the material.

FLORA AND FAUNA

Henry Bates, *The Naturalist on the River Amazon* (o/p in the UK; White Rose Press). A Victorian botanist describes his years spent collecting in the Amazon, in an unknown but wonderful book. Bates's boyish scientific excitement illuminates every page – a fascinated, and very English, eye cast over the Amazon and its people.

Balthasar Dubs, *Birds of Southwestern Brazil* (Beltrona, Switzerland). Essential reading if you're heading for the Pantanal. The main body of the book is a comprehensive annotated and illustrated list of species in the region.

Bruce Forrester, *Birding Brazil: A Check-list and Site Guide*. Top of anyone's reading list, the book contains general advice, habitat descriptions and write-ups on sites, including maps, a bibliography and useful addresses. Available from the author at Knockshinnoch Bungalow, Rankinston, Ayrshire KA6 7HL, Scotland.

Margaret Mee, *In Search of the Flowers of the Amazon Forest* (Nonesuch, UK). The best of the natural history books by some way. Mee was a British botanist who dedicated her life to travelling the Amazon and painting its plant life. She died in a car crash in 1988, and this beautiful book is a fitting tribute to her. It includes descriptions of her many journeys, good photographs, and lavish reproductions of her wonderful drawings and paintings.

Helmut Sick, *Birds in Brazil* (Princeton UP). An English translation of an encyclopedic Brazilian work. The illustrations are superb, but it's too hefty to travel with. More portable guides include **Hilty and Brown** *A Guide to the Birds of Colombia* (Princeton UP), and **Schaunsee** *Birds of Venezuela* (Princeton UP) which both have considerable overlap with Brazil's western and northern Amazonia, while **Narosky and Yzuriea**'s *Birds of Argentina and Uruguay: A Field Guide* (Vazques Mazzini) is valuable for southern Brazil.

THE ARTS

ARCHITECTURE

William Howard Adams, *Roberto Burle Marx: The Unnatural Art of the Garden* (The Museum of Modern Art, New York). A beautifully illustrated appreciation of perhaps the twentieth century's foremost landscape architect, who designed many of Brazil's most prominent parks, gardens and other urban spaces (perhaps the most famous being the flowing mosaics alongside Copacabana beach) and inspired generations of architects and gardeners.

Fernando Tasso Fracaso Pires, *Fazenda: The Great Houses and Plantations of Brazil* (Abbeville Press). A lavish coffee-table book, richly illustrated with photographs of coffee, sugar and cattle *fazenda* houses. There's a useful historical introduction discussing the importance of the *casa grande* in Brazilian society, followed by a look at individual houses, mainly in rural Rio de Janeiro and São Paulo, but also Minas Gerais, Pernambuco, Bahia and Rio Grande do Sul.

FINE ART AND PHOTOGRAPHY

Gilberto Ferraz, *Photography in Brazil 1840–1900* (New Mexico UP, US, o/p). One of the little-known facts about Brazil is that the first ever non-portrait photograph was taken of the Paco da Cidade in Rio in 1840, by a Frenchman hot off a ship with the new-fangled Daguerrotype. This is a fascinating compendium of the pioneering work of early photographers in Brazil, including material from all over the country, although the stunning panoramas of Rio from the 1860s onward are arguably the highlight.

Edward Lucie-Smith, *Latin American Art of the Twentieth Century* (Thames & Hudson). It's a pity there aren't volumes on other periods in Latin American art in this excellent and easy to obtain series. Still, this is valuable as a look at the Brazilian scene in the context of Latin American art in general.

The South Bank Centre, *Art in Latin America* (Yale UP). Lavishly illustrated catalogue to the 1989 exhibition, which includes thorough coverage of all periods of Brazilian art.

MUSIC, DANCE AND CAPOEIRA

Bira Almeida, *Capoeira – a Brazilian Art Form* (North Atlantic Books). A *capoeira mestre* (master) explains the history and philosophy behind this African–Brazilian martial art/dance form. The book offers valuable background information for those who practise *capoeira* and for those who are merely interested.

Alma Guillermoprieto, *Samba* (Bloomsbury o/p; Random House). The author, a trained dancer and a well-known journalist, describes a year that she spent with Rio's Mangueira samba school, introducing us to other participants who dedicate their lives to preparing for the four days of *Carnaval*.

Chris McGowan and Ricardo Pessanha, *The Brazilian Sound: Samba, Bossa Nova and the Popular Music of Brazil* (Temple UP). An easy to flick through and well-written basic manual on modern Brazilian music and musicians. Good to carry with you if you're planning on doing some serious music buying. There's a useful bibliography and a good discography.

Claus Schreiner, *Musica Brasileira* (Marion Boyars). Detailed coverage of all aspects of Brazilian music from colonial times through to the present within the broader context of the country's culture and history. One for the specialist.

COOKING

Jessica Harris, *Tasting Brazil* (o/p). Good illustrations and interesting background information on Brazilian food.

Christopher Idone, *Brazil: A Cook's Tour* (Pavilion; Crown). A region-by-region look at Brazilian cooking, its origins and influences, with a few recipes thrown in as well. The colour photos of ingredients, markets and dishes are mouthwatering and the text lively and informative. It's good to see São Paulo and the Amazon being discussed separately and at length (when it comes to cookbooks usually only Rio and Bahia get a look in), but why is the South completely ignored?

Elizabeth Lambert-Ortiz, *A Little Brazilian Cookbook* (Appletree Press; Chronicle o/p). A stocking-filler book which still manages to include all the basics.

Joan and David Peterson, *Eat Smart in Brazil: How to Decipher the Menu, Know the Market foods & Embark on a Tasting Adventure* (Ginkgo Press). The title says it all: a guide for selecting food, both in shops and markets and off a menu, in Brazil. The book is divided into three main sections: a region-by-region account of food ingredients and cooking styles, some recipes and listings of Brazilian ingredients and dishes. A must for any foodie who needs to know the difference between *pimenta malgueta*, *pimenta-do-cheiro* and *pimenta-do-reino*.

FICTION

There's an extremely useful listing of **translations** published since 1945, *The Babel Guide to the Fiction of Portugal, Brazil & Africa in English Translation* (Boulevard), which also includes lengthy book reviews, including the work of twenty Brazilian writers.

Jorge Amado, *Gabriela, Clove and Cinnamon*; *Tereza Batista* (both Abacus o/p; Avon); *Dona Flor and Her Two Husbands* (Serpent's Tail; Avon); *The Violent Lands* (Collins; Avon). Amado is the proverbial rollicking good read, a fine choice for the beach or on long bus journeys. He's by far the best-known Brazilian writer abroad – there is even a French wine named after him. Purists might quibble that the local colour is laid on with a trowel, but Amado's formula of vividly tropical settings and steamy eroticism has him laughing all the way to the bank.

Mário de Andrade, *Macunaíma* (Quartet Books, UK). First published in 1928, *Macunaíma* is considered one of the greatest works of Brazilian literature. In this comic tale of the adventures of a popular hero, Macunaíma, a figure from the jungle interior, Andrade presents his typical wealth of exotic images, myths and legends.

Machado de Assis, *The Devil's Church and Other Stories* (Texas UP, US, o/p); *Helena* (California UP). These are worth going to some trouble to get hold of: good translations of Machado's great short stories. His cool, ferociously ironic style veers between black comedy and sardonic analysis of the human condition. The finest novelist Brazil has yet produced.

Patrícia Galvão (Pagu), *Industrial Park, a Proletarian Novel* (Nebraska UP). An avant-garde novel first published in 1933. Set in the rapidly changing industrial inner-city São Paulo factory district of Brás, this remarkable novel captures the sense of time and place, reproducing the voice of a city in the midst of rapid change.

Clarice Lispector, *The Hour of the Star* (Carcanet, o/p in the US). The most instantly approachable translation of this work by the important Ukrainian-born writer. Her short stories are carefully constructed, but as an author to whom the existence of plot doesn't seem to matter, her books can be difficult. Other translated titles include *Family Ties* (Carcanet o/p; Texas UP) and *The Foreign Legion* (New Direction, US).

Antônio Olinto, *The Water House* (Carroll & Graf, US). A wonderful story about an African matriarch and her progeny over a seventy-year period and the story of her return to West Africa from Bahia after the abolition of slavery. The family saga continues in the *King of Ketu*.

Horacio Quiroga, *The Decapitated Chicken and Other Stories* (Texas UP, US). Anyone visiting the Jesuit ruins by the Argentine town of San Ignacio should read these sometimes creepy, sometimes funny, gothic horror stories set in Misiones. Also available in English is *The Exiles and Other Stories* (Texas UP, US), a more recent but not as enjoyable collection.

Graciliano Ramos, *Childhood* (o/p); *São Bernado* (o/p). Works by the Northeastern novelist who introduced social realism into modern Brazilian fiction. Neither are as good as his masterpiece *Barren Lives* (Texas UP, US), or his prison memoir, *Memories of Jail* (*Memórias do Cárcere*); a translation of the latter is apparently in the pipeline.

Darlene J. Sadlier (ed) , *One Hundred Years After Tomorrow* (Indiana UP). An excellent anthology of short stories introducing the work of twenty twentieth-century Brazilian women, some famous and others less well known.

Márcio Souza, *Mad Maria* (Avon, US). A comic drama set against the background of the absurdity of rail construction in nineteenth-century Amazonia. Souza's excellent *The Emperor of the Amazon* (Abacus o/p; Avon) is another humorous and powerful description of the decadence that characterized late nineteenth-century Amazonian society.

Antônio Torres, *The Land* (Readers International). Set in a decaying town in the parched interior of the Northeast, this is a grim tale of people trapped and people trying to get away. In *Blues for a Lost Childhood* (Readers International), Torres continues with the same theme, but this time focusing on a journalist who makes it to Rio but finds life there to be a living nightmare.

João Ubaldo Ribeiro, *An Invincible Memory* (Faber; HarperCollins o/p). A family saga spanning a 400-year period from the arrival of the Portuguese in Brazil to the present day, featuring anecdotes, history and myths narrated through the experiences of two Bahian families, one aristocratic, the other slaves. The book was wildly popular when published in Brazil and is considered a national epic.

Mario Vargas Llosa, *The War of the End of the World* (Faber; Penguin). Goes well with da Cunha (see p.633). The Peruvian writer produced this haunting novel based on the events of Canudos in the 1970s. The translation is good and the book's easy to get hold of.

LANGUAGE

Learning some Portuguese before you go to Brazil is an extremely good idea. Although many well-educated Brazilians speak English, and it's now the main second language taught in schools, this hasn't filtered through to most of the population. If you know Spanish you're halfway there: there are obvious similarities in the grammar and vocabulary, so you should be able to make yourself understood if you speak slowly, and reading won't present you with too many problems. However, Portuguese pronunciation is utterly different and much less straightforward than Spanish, so unless you take the trouble to learn a bit about it you won't have a clue what Brazilians are talking about.

Unfortunately, far too many people – especially Spanish-speakers – are put off going to Brazil precisely by the language, but in reality this should be one of your main reasons for going. Learning Brazilian Portuguese is a joy which only the most hardened linguistic Puritans would deny themselves. It's a colourful, sensual language full of wonderfully rude and exotic vowel sounds, swooping intonation and hilarious idiomatic expressions. You'll also find that Brazilians will greatly appreciate even your most rudimentary efforts, and every small improvement in your Portuguese will make your stay in Brazil ten times more enjoyable.

People who have learned their Portuguese **in Portugal or in Lusophone Africa** won't have any real problems with the language in Brazil, but there are some quite big differences. There are many variations in vocabulary and Brazilians

take more liberties with the language, but the most notable differences are in pronunciation: Brazilian Portuguese is spoken more slowly and clearly; the neutral vowels so characteristic of European Portuguese tend to be sounded in full; in much of Brazil outside Rio the slushy "sh" sound doesn't exist; and the "de" and "te" endings of words like *cidade* and *diferente* are palatalized so they end up sounding like "sidadgee" and "djiferentchee".

The best **dictionary** currently available is the *Collins Portuguese Dictionary*. There is a pocket edition, but you might consider taking the fuller, larger version which concentrates on the way the language is spoken today and gives plenty of specifically Brazilian vocabulary. For a **phrasebook**, look no further than *Portuguese: A Rough Guide Phrasebook*, with useful two-way glossaries and a brief and simple grammar section.

PRONUNCIATION

The rules of **pronunciation** are complicated, but the secret is to throw yourself wholeheartedly into this explosive linguistic jacuzzi.

NON-NASAL VOWELS

A shouldn't present you with too many problems. It's usually somewhere between the "a" sound of "bat" and that of "father".

E has three possible pronunciations. When it occurs at the beginning or in the middle of a word, it will usually sound either a bit like the "e" in "bet"– eg *ferro* (iron) and *miséria* (poverty) – or like the "ay" in "hay"– eg *mesa* (table) and *pêlo* (hair). However, the difference can be quite subtle and it's not something you should worry about too much at the start. The third pronunciation is radically different from the other two: at the end of a word, "e" sounds like "y" in "happy", eg *fome* ("fommy"; hunger) and *se* (if), which actually sounds like the Spanish "si".

I is straightforward. It's always an "ee" sound like the "i" in "police", eg *isto* (this).

O is another letter with three possible pronunciations. At the beginning or in the middle of a word, it normally sounds either the way it does in "dog" – eg *loja* (shop) and *pó* (powder) – or the way it does in "go"– eg *homem* (man) and *pôquer* (poker). At the end of a word "o" sounds like the "oo" in "boot", so *obrigado* (thank you) is pronounced "obri-GA-doo". And the definite article "o" as in *o homem* (the man) is pronounced "oo".

U is always pronounced like "oo" in "boot", eg *cruz* (cross).

There are also a variety of vowel combinations or diphthongs which sound pretty much the way you would expect them to. They are **ai** (pronounced like "i" in "ride"); **au** (pronounced as in "shout"); **ei** (pronounced as in "hay"); and **oi** (pronounced as in "boy"). The only one which has an unexpected pronunciation is **ou**, which sounds like "o" in "rose".

NASAL VOWELS

The fun really starts when you get into the **nasal vowel sounds**. Generally speaking, each "normal" vowel has its nasal equivalent. The trick in pronouncing these is to be completely uninhibited. To take one example, the word **pão** (bread). First of all, just say "pow" to yourself. Then say it again, but this time half close your mouth and shove the vowel really hard through your nose. Try it again, even more vigorously. It should sound something like "powng", but much more nasal and without really sounding the final "g".

There are two main ways in which Portuguese indicates a nasal vowel. One is through the use of the **tilde**, as in *pão*. The other is the use of the letters **m** or **n** after the vowel. As a general rule, whenever you see a vowel followed by "m" or "n" and then another consonant, the vowel will be nasal – eg *gente*. The same thing applies when the vowel is followed by "m" at the end of a word, eg *tem*, *bom* – in these cases, the "m" is not pronounced, it just nasalizes the vowel.

Below are some of the main nasal vowels and examples of words which use them. However, it must be emphasized that the phonetic versions of the nasal sounds we've given are only approximate.

Ã, and **-am** or **-an followed by a consonant** indicate nasal "a" – eg *macã* (apple), *campo* (field), *samba*.

-ão or **-am at the end of a word** indicate the "owng" sound, as explained above in *pão*. Other examples are in *estação* (station), *mão* (hand), *falam* ("FA-lowng"; they talk).

-em or **-en followed by a consonant** indicate a nasalized "e" sound – eg *tempo* (weather), *entre* (between), *gente* (people).

-em or **-ens at the end of a word** indicate an "eyng" sound – eg *tem* ("teyng"; you have or there is), *viagens* ("vee-A-zheyngs"; journeys).

-im or **-in** at the end of a word or followed by a consonant are simply a nasal "ee" sound, so *capim* (grass) sounds a bit like "ca-PEENG".

-om or **-on** at the end of a word or followed by a consonant indicate nasal "o". An obvious example is *bom* (good) which sounds pretty similar to "bon" in French.

-um or **-un** at the end of a word or followed by a consonant indicate nasal "u" – eg *um* (one).

-ãe sounds a bit like "eyeing" said quickly and explosively – eg *mãe* (mother).

-õe sounds like "oing". Most words ending in "-ão" make their plural like this, with an "s" (which is pronounced) at the end – eg *estação* (station) becomes *estações* (stations).

CONSONANTS

Brazilian **consonants** are more straightforward than the vowels, but there are a few little oddities you'll need to learn. We've only listed the consonants where they differ from their English counterparts.

C is generally pronounced hard, as in "cat" (eg *campo*). However, when followed by "i" or "e", it's pronounced softly, as in "ceiling"(eg *cidade*, city) . It's also pronounced softly whenever it's written with a cedilla (eg *estação*).

CH is pronounced like English "sh", so *chá* (tea) is said "sha".

D is generally pronounced as in English. However, in most parts of Brazil it's palatalized to sound like "dj"whenever it comes before an "i" or final "e". So *difícil* (difficult) is pronounced "djee-FEE-siw", and the ubiquitous preposition *de* (of) sounds like "djee".

G is generally pronounced hard as in English "god" (eg *gosto*, I like). But before "e" or "i" it's pronounced like the "s" in English "vision" or "measure" – eg *geral* (general) and *gíria* (slang).

H is always silent (eg *hora*, hour).

J is pronounced like the "s" in English "vision" or "measure"– eg *jogo* (game) and *janeiro* (January).

A GUIDE TO BRAZILIAN PORTUGUESE

The Basics

Yes, No	*sim, não*	Good, Bad	*bom, ruim*
Please, Thank You	*por favor, obrigado* (men)/*obrigada* (women)	Big, Small	*grande, pequeno*
		A little, A lot	*um pouco, muito*
Where, When	*onde, quando*	More, Less	*mais, menos*
What, How Much	*que, quanto*	Another	*outro/a*
This, That	*este, esse, aquele*	Today, Tomorrow	*hoje, amanhã*
Now, Later	*agora, mais tarde*	Yesterday	*ontem*
Open, Closed	*aberto/a, fechado/a*	But	*mas* (pronounced like "mice")
Entrance, Exit	*entrada, saída*		
Pull, Push	*puxe, empurre*	And	*e* (pronounced like "ee" in "seek")
With, Without	*com, sem*	Something, Nothing	*alguma coisa, nada*
For	*para*	Sometimes	*ás vezes*

Greetings and Responses

Hello, Goodbye	*oi, tchau* (like the Italian "ciao")	Excuse me	*com licença*
		How are you?	*como vai?*
Good Morning	*bom dia*	Fine	*bem*
Good Afternoon/Night	*boa tarde/boa noite*	Congratulations	*parabéns*
Sorry	*desculpa*	Cheers	*saúde*

Useful Phrases and Colloquial Expressions

I don't understand	*não entendo*	What's the matter?	*qual é o problema?*
Do you speak English?	*você fala inglês?*	I'll phone you	*vou ligar para você*
I don't speak Portuguese	*não falo português*	I can...	*posso...*
What's the Portuguese for this?	*como se diz em português?*	I can't...	*não posso...*
		I don't know...	*... não sei*
What did you say?	*o que você disse?*	It's hot	*está quente*
My name is...	*meu nome é'...*	It's cold	*está frio*
What's your name?	*como se chama?*	It's great	*está legal*
I am English/American	*sou inglês/americano*	It's boring	*é chato*
Everything's fine	*tudo bem*	I'm bored, annoyed	*estou chateado*
OK	*tá bom*	I've had it up to here	*estou de saco cheio*
I'm hungry	*estou com fome*	There's no way	*não tem jeito*
I'm thirsty	*estou com sede*	Crazy	*louco/a, maluco/a*
I feel ill	*me sinto mal*	Tired	*cansado/a*
I want to see a doctor	*quero ver um medico*		

L is usually pronounced as in English. But at the end of a word, it takes on a peculiar, almost Cockney pronunciation, becoming a bit like a "w". So **Brasil** is pronounced "bra-ZEEW". When followed by "h", it's pronounced "ly" as in "million"; so *ilha* (island) comes out as "EE-lya".

N is normally pronounced as in English, but when it's followed by "h" it becomes "ny". So *sonho* (dream) sounds like "SON-yoo".

Q always comes before "u" and is pronounced either "k-" or, more usually, "kw-". So *cinquen-ta* (fifty) is pronounced "sin-KWEN-ta", but *quero* (I want) is pronounced "KE-roo".

R is usually as in English. However, at the beginning of a word it's pronounced like an English "h". So "Rio" is actually pronounced "HEE-oo", and *rádio* (radio) is pronounced "HA-djee-oo".

RR is always pronounced like an English "h". So *ferro* is pronounced "FE-hoo".

S is normally pronounced like an English "s", and in São Paulo and the south this never changes. But in Rio and many places to the north, "s" sounds like English "sh" when it

Hotels and Transport

I want, I'd like...	*quero...*	the bus stop	*a parada de ônibus*
There is (is there?)	*há...(?)*	the nearest hotel	*o hotel mais próximo*
Do you have...?	*você tem...?*	the toilet	*o banheiro/sanitário*
...a room?	*...um quarto?*	Left, right,	*esquerda, direita,*
...the time?	*...as horas?*	straight on	*direto*
with two beds/	*om duas*	Go straight on	*vai direto e*
double beds	*camas/cama de*	and turn left	*dobra à esquerda*
casal		Where does the	*de onde sai o*
It's for one person/	*é para uma*	bus to...leave?	*ônibus para...?*
two people	*pessoa/duas pessoas*	Is this the bus to Rio?	*é esse o ônibus*
It's fine, how much is it?	*Está bom, quanto é?*		*para Rio?*
It's too expensive	*é caro demais*	Do you go to...?	*você vai para...?*
Do you have anything	*tem algo*	I'd like a (return)	*quero uma passagem*
cheaper?	*mais barato?*	ticket to...	*(ida e volta) para...*
Is there a hotel/	*Tem um hotel/*	What time does it	*Que horas sai/chega?*
campsite nearby?	*camping por aqui?*	leave/arrive?	
Where is...?	*Onde fica...?*	Far, Near	*longe, perto*
the bus station	*a rodoviária*	Slowly, Quickly	*devagar, rápido*

Numbers, Days and Months

1	*um, uma*	8	*oito*	15	*quinze*	50	*cinquenta*	300	*trezentos*
2	*dois, duas*	9	*nove*	16	*dezesseis*	60	*sesenta*	500	*quinhen-*
3	*tres*	10	*dez*	17	*dezesete*	70	*setenta*		*tos*
4	*quatro*	11	*onze*	20	*vinte*	80	*oitenta*	1000	*mil*
5	*cinco*	12	*doze*	21	*vinte e um*	90	*noventa*	2000	*dois mil*
6	*seis*	13	*treze*	30	*trinta*	100	*cem*	5000	*cinco mil*
7	*sete*	14	*quatorze*	40	*quarenta*	200	*duzentos*		

Monday	*segunda-feira* (or *segunda*)	March	*março*
Tuesday	*terça-feira* (or *terça*)	April	*abril*
Wednesday	*quarta-feira* (or *quarta*)	May	*mayo*
Thursday	*quinta-feira* (or *quinta*)	June	*junho*
Friday	*sexta-feira* (or *sexta*)	July	*julho*
Saturday	*sábado*	August	*agosto*
Sunday	*domingo*	September	*setembro*
		October	*outubro*
January	*janeiro*	November	*novembro*
February	*fevereiro*	December	*dezembro*

comes before a consonant and at the end of a word (*estação*, "esh-ta-SOWNG").

T is normally pronounced as in English but, like "d", it changes before "i" and final "e". So *sorte* (luck) is pronounced "SOR-chee", and the great hero of Brazilian history, Tiradentes, is pronounced "chee-ra-DEN-chees".

X is pronounced like an English "sh" at the beginning of a word, and elsewhere like an English "x" or "z". So *xadrez* (chess) is pronounced "sha-DREYZ", while *exército* (army) is pronounced "e-ZER-si-too".

STRESS

Any word which has an accent of any kind, including a tilde, is stressed on that syllable, so *miséria* (poverty) is pronounced "mi-ZE-ree-a". If there is no accent, the following rules generally apply (the syllables to be stressed are in capitals):

• Words which end with the vowels a, e and o are stressed on the penultimate syllable. So *entre* (between) sounds like "EN-tree", and compro (I buy) "KOM-proo". This also applies when these vowels are followed by -m, -s or -ns: *falam* is stressed "FA-lowng".

• Words which end with the vowels i and u are stressed on the final syllable: *abacaxi* (pineapple) is pronounced "a-ba-ka-SHEE". This also applies when i and u are followed by -m, -s or -ns, so *capim* is pronounced "ka-PEENG".

• Words ending in consonants are usually stressed on the final syllable, eg *rapaz* (boy), stressed "ha-PAZ".

SOME USEFUL EXAMPLES

Rio de Janeiro HEE-oo djee zha-NEY-roo
Belo Horizonte BE-loo o-ri-ZON-chee

Rio Grande do Sul HEE-oo GRAN-djee doo Soow
Recife he-SEE-fee
Rodoviária ho-do-vee-A-ree-a
onde (where) ON-djee
não entende (he doesn't understand) now en-TEN-djee
sim (yes) SEENG (but hardly sound the final "g")
ruim (bad) hoo-WEENG (again hardly sound the "g")
vinte (twenty) VEEN-chee
correio (post office) co-HAY-oo

A GLOSSARY OF BRAZILIAN TERMS AND ACRONYMS

AGRESTE In the Northeast, the intermediate zone between the coast and the *sertão*

ALDEIA Originally a mission where Indians were converted, now any isolated hamlet

ALFÂNDEGA Customs

AMAZÔNIA The Amazon region

ARTESANATO Craft goods

AZULEJO Decorative glazed tiling

BAIRRO Neighbourhood within town or city

BANDEIRANTE Member of a group that marched under a *bandeira* (banner or flag) in early missions to open up the interior; Brazilian *conquistador*

BATUCADA Literally, a drumming session – music-making in general, especially impromptu

BLOCO Large *Carnaval* group

BOSQUE Wood

CAATINGA Scrub vegetation of the interior of the Northeast

CABOCLO Native of river town or rural area of Amazônia

CANDOMBLÉ African–Brazilian religion

CANGACEIRO Outlaws from the interior of the Northeast who flourished in the early twentieth century; the most famous was Lampião

CAPOEIRA African–Brazilian martial art/dance form

CARIMBÓ Music and dance style from the north

CARIOCA Someone or something from Rio de Janeiro

CARNAVAL Carnival

CERRADO Scrubland

CHORO Musical style, largely instrumental

CONVENTO Convent

CORREIO Postal service/post office

CUT/CGT Brazilian trades union organizations

DANCETARIA Nightspot where the emphasis is on dancing

ENGENHO Sugar mill or plantation

ESTADO NOVO The period when Getúlio Vargas was effectively dictator, from the mid-1930s to 1945

EUA USA

EX VOTO Thank-offering to saint for intercession

FAVELA Shanty town, slum

FAZENDA Country estate, ranch house

FEIRA Country market

FERROVIÁRIA Train station

FORRÓ Dance and type of music from Northeast

FREVO Frenetic musical style and dance from Recife

FUNAI Government organization meant to protect the interests of Brazilian Indians; notoriously corrupt and underfunded

GARIMPEIRO Prospector or miner

GAÚCHO Person or thing from Rio Grande do Sul; also southern cowboy

GRINGO/A Foreigner, Westerner (not derogatory)

IBAMA Government organization for preservation of the environment; runs national parks and nature reserves

IEMANJÁ Goddess of the sea in *candomblé*

IGREJA Church

LARGO Small square

LATIFÚNDIOS Large agricultural estates

LEITO Luxury express bus

LITERATURA DE CORDEL Literally "string literature" – printed ballads, most common in Northeast but also found elsewhere, named after the string they are suspended from in country markets

LITORAL Coast, coastal zone

LOURO/A Fair-haired/blonde – Westerners in general

MACONHA Marijuana

MACUMBA African–Brazilian religion, usually thought of as more authentically "African" than *candomblé*; most common in the north

MARGINAL Petty thief, outlaw

MATA Jungle, remote interior

MERCADO Market

MINEIRO Person or thing from Minas Gerais

MIRANTE Viewing point

MOSTEIRO Monastery

MOVIMENTADO Lively, where the action is

MPB Música Popular Brasileira, common shorthand for Brazilian music

NORDESTE Northeastern Brazil

NORDESTINO/A Inhabitant thereof

NOVA REPUBLICA The New Republic – the period since the return to civilian democracy in 1985

PAULISTA Person or thing from São Paulo state

PAULISTANO Inhabitant of the city of São Paulo

PELOURINHO Pillory or whipping-post, common in colonial town squares

PLANALTO CENTRAL Vast interior tablelands of central Brazil

POSTO Highway service station, often with basic accommodation popular with truckers

PRAÇA Square

PRAIA Beach

PREFEITURA Town hall, and by extension city governments in general

PT Partido dos Trabalhadores or Workers' Party, the largest left-wing party in Brazil, led by Lula

QUEBRADO Out of order

RODOVIA Highway

RODOVIÁRIA Bus station

SAMBA Type of music most associated with *Carnaval* in Rio

SELVA Jungle

SERTANEJO Inhabitant of *sertão*

SERTÃO Arid, drought-ridden interior of Northeast

SESMARIA Royal Portuguese land grant to early settlers

SOBRADO Two-storey colonial mansion

TERREIRO House where *candomblé* or *umbanda* rituals and ceremonies take place

VAQUEIRO Cowboy in the north

VISTO Visa

INDEX